Y0-EHZ-643

Contemporary Authors®

NEW REVISION SERIES

ISSN 0275-7176

Contemporary

Authors®

A Bio-Bibliographical Guide to
Current Writers in Fiction, General Nonfiction,
Poetry, Journalism, Drama, Motion Pictures,
Television, and Other Fields

NEW REVISION SERIES
volume 137

Detroit • New York • San Francisco • San Diego • New Haven, Conn. • Waterville, Maine • London • Munich

Contemporary Authors, New Revision Series, Vol. 137

Project Editor
Tracey L. Matthews

Editorial
Katy Balcer, Sara Constantakis, Michelle Kazensky, Julie Keppen, Joshua Kondek, Lisa Kumar, Mary Ruby, Lemma Shomali, Maikue Vang

Permissions
Emma Hull, Jacqueline Key, Sue Rudolph

Imaging and Multimedia
Lezlie Light, Michael Logusz

Composition and Electronic Capture
Carolyn Roney

Manufacturing
Drew Kalasky

For more information, contact
Thomson Gale
27500 Drake Rd.
Farmington Hills, MI 48331-3535
Or you can visit our internet site at
http://www.gale.com

LIBRARY OF CONGRESS CATALOG CARD NUMBER 81-640179

ISBN 0-7876-7891-0
ISSN 0275-7176

Printed in the United States of America
10 9 8 7 6 5 4 3 2 1

Contents

Indexing note: All *Contemporary Authors* entries are indexed in the *Contemporary Authors* cumulative index, which is published separately and distributed twice a year.

As always, the most recent Contemporary Authors cumulative index continues to be the user's guide to the location of an individual author's listing.

Preface

Contemporary Authors (*CA*) provides information on approximately 115,000 writers in a wide range of media, including:

- Current writers of fiction, nonfiction, poetry, and drama whose works have been issued by commercial publishers, risk publishers, or university presses (authors whose books have been published only by known vanity or author-subsidized firms are ordinarily not included)
- Prominent print and broadcast journalists, editors, photojournalists, syndicated cartoonists, graphic novelists, screenwriters, television scriptwriters, and other media people
- Notable international authors
- Literary greats of the early twentieth century whose works are popular in today's high school and college curriculums and continue to elicit critical attention

A *CA* listing entails no charge or obligation. Authors are included on the basis of the above criteria and their interest to *CA* users. Sources of potential listees include trade periodicals, publishers' catalogs, librarians, and other users.

How to Get the Most out of *CA*: Use the Index

The key to locating an author's most recent entry is the *CA* cumulative index, which is published separately and distributed twice a year. It provides access to *all* entries in *CA* and *Contemporary Authors New Revision Series* (*CANR*). Always consult the latest index to find an author's most recent entry.

For the convenience of users, the *CA* cumulative index also includes references to all entries in these Thomson Gale literary series: *Authors and Artists for Young Adults, Authors in the News, Bestsellers, Black Literature Criticism, Black Literature Criticism Supplement, Black Writers, Children's Literature Review, Concise Dictionary of American Literary Biography, Concise Dictionary of British Literary Biography, Contemporary Authors Autobiography Series, Contemporary Authors Bibliographical Series, Contemporary Dramatists, Contemporary Literary Criticism, Contemporary Novelists, Contemporary Poets, Contemporary Popular Writers, Contemporary Southern Writers, Contemporary Women Poets, Dictionary of Literary Biography, Dictionary of Literary Biography Documentary Series, Dictionary of Literary Biography Yearbook, DISCovering Authors, DISCovering Authors: British, DISCovering Authors: Canadian, DISCovering Authors: Modules* (including modules for Dramatists, Most-Studied Authors, Multicultural Authors, Novelists, Poets, and Popular/Genre Authors), DISCovering Authors 3.0, *Drama Criticism, Drama for Students, Feminist Writers, Hispanic Literature Criticism, Hispanic Writers, Junior DISCovering Authors, Major Authors and Illustrators for Children and Young Adults, Major 20th-Century Writers, Native North American Literature, Novels for Students, Poetry Criticism, Poetry for Students, Short Stories for Students, Short Story Criticism, Something about the Author, Something about the Author Autobiography Series, St. James Guide to Children's Writers, St. James Guide to Crime & Mystery Writers, St. James Guide to Fantasy Writers, St. James Guide to Horror, Ghost & Gothic Writers, St. James Guide to Science Fiction Writers, St. James Guide to Young Adult Writers, Twentieth-Century Literary Criticism, 20th Century Romance and Historical Writers, World Literature Criticism,* and *Yesterday's Authors of Books for Children.*

A Sample Index Entry:

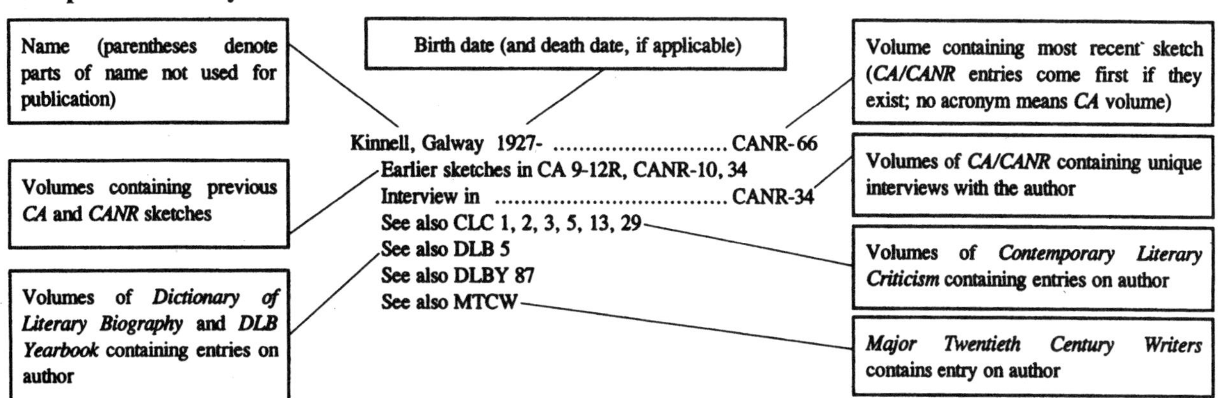

How Are Entries Compiled?

The editors make every effort to secure new information directly from the authors; listees' responses to our questionnaires and query letters provide most of the information featured in *CA*. For deceased writers, or those who fail to reply to requests for data, we consult other reliable biographical sources, such as those indexed in Thomson Gale's *Biography and Genealogy Master Index,* and bibliographical sources, including *National Union Catalog, LC MARC,* and *British National Bibliography.* Further details come from published interviews, feature stories, and book reviews, as well as information supplied by the authors' publishers and agents.

An asterisk (*) at the end of a sketch indicates that the listing has been compiled from secondary sources believed to be reliable but has not been personally verified for this edition by the author sketched.

What Kinds of Information Does An Entry Provide?

Sketches in *CA* contain the following biographical and bibliographical information:

- **Entry heading:** the most complete form of author's name, plus any pseudonyms or name variations used for writing

- **Personal information:** author's date and place of birth, family data, ethnicity, educational background, political and religious affiliations, and hobbies and leisure interests

- **Addresses:** author's home, office, or agent's addresses, plus e-mail and fax numbers, as available

- **Career summary:** name of employer, position, and dates held for each career post; resume of other vocational achievements; military service

- **Membership information:** professional, civic, and other association memberships and any official posts held

- **Awards and honors:** military and civic citations, major prizes and nominations, fellowships, grants, and honorary degrees

- **Writings:** a comprehensive, chronological list of titles, publishers, dates of original publication and revised editions, and production information for plays, television scripts, and screenplays

- **Adaptations:** a list of films, plays, and other media which have been adapted from the author's work

- **Work in progress:** current or planned projects, with dates of completion and/or publication, and expected publisher, when known

- **Sidelights:** a biographical portrait of the author's development; information about the critical reception of the author's works; revealing comments, often by the author, on personal interests, aspirations, motivations, and thoughts on writing

- **Interview:** a one-on-one discussion with authors conducted especially for *CA*, offering insight into authors' thoughts about their craft

- **Autobiographical essay:** an original essay written by noted authors for *CA*, a forum in which writers may present themselves, on their own terms, to their audience

- **Photographs:** portraits and personal photographs of notable authors

- **Biographical and critical sources:** a list of books and periodicals in which additional information on an author's life and/or writings appears

- **Obituary Notices** in *CA* provide date and place of birth as well as death information about authors whose full-length sketches appeared in the series before their deaths. The entries also summarize the authors' careers and writings and list other sources of biographical and death information.

Related Titles in the *CA* Series

Contemporary Authors Autobiography Series complements *CA* original and revised volumes with specially commissioned autobiographical essays by important current authors, illustrated with personal photographs they provide. Common topics include their motivations for writing, the people and experiences that shaped their careers, the rewards they derive from their work, and their impressions of the current literary scene.

Contemporary Authors Bibliographical Series surveys writings by and about important American authors since World War II. Each volume concentrates on a specific genre and features approximately ten writers; entries list works written by and about the author and contain a bibliographical essay discussing the merits and deficiencies of major critical and scholarly studies in detail.

Available in Electronic Formats

GaleNet. *CA* is available on a subscription basis through GaleNet, an online information resource that features an easy-to-use end-user interface, powerful search capabilities, and ease of access through the World-Wide Web. For more information, call 1-800-877-GALE.

Licensing. *CA* is available for licensing. The complete database is provided in a fielded format and is deliverable on such media as disk, CD-ROM, or tape. For more information, contact Thomson Gale's Business Development Group at 1-800-877-GALE, or visit us on our website at www.galegroup.com/bizdev.

Suggestions Are Welcome

The editors welcome comments and suggestions from users on any aspect of the *CA* series. If readers would like to recommend authors for inclusion in future volumes of the series, they are cordially invited to write the Editors at *Contemporary Authors*, Thomson Gale, 27500 Drake Rd., Farmington Hills, MI 48331-3535; or call at 1-248-699-4253; or fax at 1-248-699-8054.

Contemporary Authors Product Advisory Board

The editors of *Contemporary Authors* are dedicated to maintaining a high standard of excellence by publishing comprehensive, accurate, and highly readable entries on a wide array of writers. In addition to the quality of the content, the editors take pride in the graphic design of the series, which is intended to be orderly yet inviting, allowing readers to utilize the pages of *CA* easily and with efficiency. Despite the longevity of the *CA* print series, and the success of its format, we are mindful that the vitality of a literary reference product is dependent on its ability to serve its users over time. As literature, and attitudes about literature, constantly evolve, so do the reference needs of students, teachers, scholars, journalists, researchers, and book club members. To be certain that we continue to keep pace with the expectations of our customers, the editors of *CA* listen carefully to their comments regarding the value, utility, and quality of the series. Librarians, who have firsthand knowledge of the needs of library users, are a valuable resource for us. The *Contemporary Authors* Product Advisory Board, made up of school, public, and academic librarians, is a forum to promote focused feedback about *CA* on a regular basis. The seven-member advisory board includes the following individuals, whom the editors wish to thank for sharing their expertise:

- **Anne M. Christensen,** Librarian II, Phoenix Public Library, Phoenix, Arizona.

- **Barbara C. Chumard,** Reference/Adult Services Librarian, Middletown Thrall Library, Middletown, New York.

- **Eva M. Davis,** Youth Department Manager, Ann Arbor District Library, Ann Arbor, Michigan.

- **Adam Janowski, Jr.,** Library Media Specialist, Naples High School Library Media Center, Naples, Florida.

- **Robert Reginald,** Head of Technical Services and Collection Development, California State University, San Bernadino, California.

- **Stephen Weiner,** Director, Maynard Public Library, Maynard, Massachusetts.

International Advisory Board

Well-represented among the 115,000 author entries published in *Contemporary Authors* are sketches on notable writers from many non-English-speaking countries. The primary criteria for inclusion of such authors has traditionally been the publication of at least one title in English, either as an original work or as a translation. However, the editors of *Contemporary Authors* came to observe that many important international writers were being overlooked due to a strict adherence to our inclusion criteria. In addition, writers who were publishing in languages other than English were not being covered in the traditional sources we used for identifying new listees. Intent on increasing our coverage of international authors, including those who write only in their native language and have not been translated into English, the editors enlisted the aid of a board of advisors, each of whom is an expert on the literature of a particular country or region. Among the countries we focused attention on are Mexico, Puerto Rico, Spain, Italy, France, Germany, Luxembourg, Belgium, the Netherlands, Norway, Sweden, Denmark, Finland, Taiwan, Singapore, Malaysia, Thailand, South Africa, Israel, and Japan, as well as England, Scotland, Wales, Ireland, Australia, and New Zealand. The sixteen-member advisory board includes the following individuals, whom the editors wish to thank for sharing their expertise:

- **Lowell A. Bangerter,** Professor of German, University of Wyoming, Laramie, Wyoming.
- **Nancy E. Berg,** Associate Professor of Hebrew and Comparative Literature, Washington University, St. Louis, Missouri.
- **Frances Devlin-Glass,** Associate Professor, School of Literary and Communication Studies, Deakin University, Burwood, Victoria, Australia.
- **David William Foster,** Regent's Professor of Spanish, Interdisciplinary Humanities, and Women's Studies, Arizona State University, Tempe, Arizona.
- **Hosea Hirata,** Director of the Japanese Program, Associate Professor of Japanese, Tufts University, Medford, Massachusetts.
- **Jack Kolbert,** Professor Emeritus of French Literature, Susquehanna University, Selinsgrove, Pennsylvania.
- **Mark Libin,** Professor, University of Manitoba, Winnipeg, Manitoba, Canada.
- **C. S. Lim,** Professor, University of Malaya, Kuala Lumpur, Malaysia.
- **Eloy E. Merino,** Assistant Professor of Spanish, Northern Illinois University, DeKalb, Illinois.
- **Linda M. Rodríguez Guglielmoni,** Associate Professor, University of Puerto Rico—Mayagüez, Puerto Rico.
- **Sven Hakon Rossel,** Professor and Chair of Scandinavian Studies, University of Vienna, Vienna, Austria.
- **Steven R. Serafin,** Director, Writing Center, Hunter College of the City University of New York, New York City.
- **David Smyth,** Lecturer in Thai, School of Oriental and African Studies, University of London, England.
- **Ismail S. Talib,** Senior Lecturer, Department of English Language and Literature, National University of Singapore, Singapore.
- **Dionisio Viscarri,** Assistant Professor, Ohio State University, Columbus, Ohio.
- **Mark Williams,** Associate Professor, English Department, University of Canterbury, Christchurch, New Zealand.

CA Numbering System and Volume Update Chart

Occasionally questions arise about the *CA* numbering system and which volumes, if any, can be discarded. Despite numbers like "29-32R," "97-100" and "230," the entire *CA* print series consists of only 296 physical volumes with the publication of *CA* Volume 232. The following charts note changes in the numbering system and cover design, and indicate which volumes are essential for the most complete, up-to-date coverage.

***CA* First Revision**

- 1-4R through 41-44R (11 books)
  Cover: Brown with black and gold trim.
  There will be no further First Revision volumes because revised entries are now being handled exclusively through the more efficient *New Revision Series* mentioned below.

***CA* Original Volumes**

- 45-48 through 97-100 (14 books)
  Cover: Brown with black and gold trim.
  101 through 232 (132 books)
  Cover: Blue and black with orange bands.
  The same as previous *CA* original volumes but with a new, simplified numbering system and new cover design.

***CA* Permanent Series**

- *CAP*-1 and *CAP*-2 (2 books)
  Cover: Brown with red and gold trim.
  There will be no further Permanent Series volumes because revised entries are now being handled exclusively through the more efficient *New Revision Series* mentioned below.

***CA* New Revision Series**

- CANR-1 through CANR-137 (137 books)
  Cover: Blue and black with green bands.
  Includes only sketches requiring significant changes; **sketches are taken from any previously published CA, CAP, or CANR volume.**

If You Have:	You May Discard:
CA First Revision Volumes 1-4R through 41-44R and *CA Permanent Series* Volumes 1 and 2	*CA* Original Volumes 1, 2, 3, 4 and Volumes 5-6 through 41-44
CA Original Volumes 45-48 through 97-100 and 101 through 231	**NONE:** These volumes will not be superseded by corresponding revised volumes. Individual entries from these and all other volumes appearing in the left column of this chart may be revised and included in the various volumes of the *New Revision Series.*
CA New Revision Series Volumes *CANR*-1 through *CANR*-136	**NONE:** The *New Revision Series* does not replace any single volume of *CA*. Instead, volumes of *CANR* include entries from many previous *CA* series volumes. All *New Revision Series* volumes must be retained for full coverage.

A Sampling of Authors and Media People Featured in This Volume

Russell Baker
Baker, a Pulitzer-Prize-winning journalist and humorist, is well known for his "Observer" column in the *New York Times* and as host of PBS- TV's "Masterpiece Theater" series. Noted for charming readers with his witty and literate commentary on the follies and foibles of contemporary life, Baker is credited with turning newspaper humor into literature. Baker began his memoirs with *Growing Up* and *The Good Times,* and continued his personal story in *Looking Back,* published in 2002.

Julian Barnes
Barnes is an internationally acclaimed and best-selling author, recognized as one of the most celebrated British novelists of his generation. Critics admire his ability to infuse a complex, intellectual work with comic sensibility and witty language in *Flaubert's Parrot* as well as the dark satire of his more recent *England, England.* As David Kavanaugh, he has also written a succesful series of crime novels. Barnes's most recent novel is *The Lemon Table,* published in 2004.

Frederick Forsyth
Forsyth, credited with defining the international conspiracy thriller, is the British author of such blockbuster novels-turned-movies as *The Day of the Jackal, The Odessa File,* and *The Dogs of War.* Known for injecting his fast-paced plots with all the realistic detail of a documentary novel, Forsyth specializes in presenting an insider's view of world affairs alongside a view of flawed world figures. Forsyth's 2003 novel, *Avenger,* is his most recent effort.

Hazel Holt
Holt, author of the popular "Sheila Malory" mystery series, is well known to readers in her native Britain as well as the United States. Holt was also a longtime associate of the late novelist Barbara Pym, whom she served as biographer and literary executor. Holt's most recent excursion of the sleuthing widow Malory in the English village of Taviscombe is *Mrs. Malory and the Silent Killer,* published in 2004.

Nancy Price
Price, an award-winning American novelist, is best known for works like *An Accomplished Woman* and *Sleeping with the Enemy,* the last adapted as a 1991 film starring Julia Roberts. Although her novels focus on women and their personal relationships, critics note that Price avoids the introspective probings of her heroine's fears and desires in favor of a more distanced observation of her development in the novel. Price's most recent novel is *Two Liars and a Bride,* published in 2004.

Scott Turow
Turow, Chicago attorney-turned-novelist, has parlayed his insider knowledge of the law to produce gripping legal thrillers of unusual depth and complexity. In novels like *Presumed Innocent,* adapted as a 1990 film starring Harrison Ford, and which became a 1992 TV-movie, Turow depicts characters facing moral, ethical, and emotional challenges painted in shades of gray rather than black and white. In 2002, Turow published his most recent novel, *Reversible Errors,* followed in 2003 with *Ultimate Punishment: A Lawyer's Reflections on Dealing with the Death Penalty.*

Fay Weldon
Weldon, who was born in England and raised in New Zealand, is an award-winning author of novels and plays that chronicle the many facets of women's lives. Deemed a feminist by many, Weldon nevertheless speaks her own mind. With their rich imagery, vivid settings, and telling detail, novels like *Down among the Women* and *Praxis* have been praised for both their artistry and their social concerns. Weldon's most recent novel is 2005's *Mantrapped.*

Donald Westlake
Westlake, a Edgar Allan Poe Grand Master of the Mystery Writers of America, is the versatile and prolific author of such popular novels as *The Hot Rock, Bank Shot,* and *Two Much,* cops-and-robbers stories that combine comedy and crime. At the other end of the spectrum, Westlake wrote *The Ax* and *The Hook,* more dark and suspenseful views of modern society. His most recent novels, published in 2004, are *Thieves' Dozen* and *Nobody Runs Forever.*

Acknowledgments

Grateful acknowledgment is made to those publishers, photographers, and artists whose work appear with these authors' essays. Following is a list of the copyright holders who have granted us permission to reproduce material in this volume of *CA*. Every effort has been made to trace copyright, but if omissions have been made, please let us know.

Photographs/Art

Caroline Arnold: Arnold, photograph by Arthur Arnold. Reproduced by permission of Caroline Arnold.

Marc Aronson: Aronson, photograph. From a jacket of his Sir Walter Raleigh and the Quest for El Dorado. Clarion Books, a Houghton Mifflin Company imprint, 2000. Reproduced by permission of Marc Aronson.

Russell Baker: Baker, photograph by Sarah Hood. Archive Photos, Inc./Sara Agency Inc. Reproduced by permission.

Julian Barnes: Barnes, photograph. © Jerry Bauer. Reproduced by permission.

Malcolm Bradbury: Bradbury, photograph. © Jerry Bauer. Reproduced by permission.

Rick Bragg: Bragg, photograph. © Reuters/Corbis.

Susan Brownmiller: Brownmiller, photograph. AP/Wide World Photos. Reproduced by permission.

Joseph Bruchac III: Bruchac, photograph by Carol Bruchac. Reproduced by permission.

Peter A. Campbell: Campbell, photograph. Reproduced by permission.

Denise Chavez: Chavez, photograph. Getty Images. Reproduced by permission.

Tracy Chevalier: Chevalier, photograph. Jim Watson/AFP/Getty Images.

Susan Cooper: Cooper, photograph by Jeffrey Hornstein. Courtesy of Susan Cooper.

Marian Wright Edelman: Edelman, photograph. AP/Wide World Photos. Reproduced by permission.

Frederick Forsyth: Forsyth, photograph by Michael Probst. AP/Wide World Photos. Reproduced by permission.

Charles Ghigna: Ghigna, photograph. Reproduced by permission.

Ellen Howard: Howard, photograph. © Rices Photography. Reproduced by permission.

Frances Mayes: Mayes, photograph. AP/Wide World Photos. Reproduced by permission.

Anchee Min: Min, photograph. © by Jerry Bauer. Reproduced by permission.

Anne Nelson: Nelson, photograph by Richard Drew. AP/Wide World Photos. Reproduced by permission.

Nancy Price: Price, photograph by John Thompson. Reproduced by permission of Nancy Price.

Ian Rankin: Rankin, photograph. ©Jerry Bauer. Reproduced by permission.

Alberto (Alvaro) Rios: Rios, photograph. Reproduced by permission of Alvaro Rios.

Elaine Scott: Scott, photograph by Andrew L. Phares. Reproduced by permission of Elaine Scott.

Floyd Skloot: Skloot, photograph by Beverly Hallberg. Reproduced by permission of Floyd Skloot.

Hudson Talbott: Talbott, photograph by Rudie Berkhart. Courtesy of Hudson Talbott.

Gay Talese: Talese, photograph by Paul Hawthorne. Getty Images.

Michael O. Tunnell: Tunnell, photograph. Reproduced by permission.

Scott Turow: Turow, photograph. © Jerry Bauer. Reproduced by permission.

Fay Weldon: Weldon, photograph. © Jerry Bauer. Reproduced by permission.

Donald E. Westlake: Westlake, photograph. © Robert Eric/Corbis Sygma.

Joan Leslie Woodruff: Woodruff, photograph by Laura L. Klure. Reproduced by permission.

A

** Indicates that a listing has been compiled from secondary sources believed to be reliable, but has not been personally verified for this edition by the author sketched.*

ADAMS, Nicholas
See MACDONALD, James D.

* * *

AHEARN, (Edward) Allen 1937-

PERSONAL: Born May 29, 1937, in Washington, DC; son of Edward Michael and Esthere (Allen) Ahearn; married Patricia Webb (an antiquarian bookseller and writer), March 17, 1959; children: Elizabeth Ahearn Jones, Suzanne Ahearn Kalk, Edward Allen, Jr., Dyanne Ahearn Ryan. *Ethnicity:*"White." *Education:* University of Maryland—College Park, B.A., 1960; George Washington University, M.B.A., 1971. *Politics:* Democrat *Religion:* Roman Catholic

ADDRESSES: Office—Quill and Brush, 1137 Sugarloaf Mountain Rd., Dickerson, MD 20842. *E-mail*—firsts@qb.com.

CAREER: U.S. Department of the Navy, Washington, DC, contracting officer, 1960-73; Office of the U.S. Secretary of Defense, Arlington, VA, advisor on major systems acquisitions, 1973-80; Quill and Brush (antiquarian book store), Dickerson, MD, partner, 1976—. Worked as defense procurement consultant in Rockville, MD, 1980-84. Active in local Catholic Youth Organization and Boys' Club.

MEMBER: Antiquarian Booksellers Association of America (member of board of governors), Bibliographical Society of America.

WRITINGS:

The Book of First Books, privately printed, 1975, 4th edition, 1986.
(With wife, Patricia Ahearn) *Book Collecting: A Comprehensive Guide,* G. P. Putnam's Sons (New York, NY), 1989, 3rd edition published as *Book Collecting 2000: A Comprehensive Guide,* 2000.
(With Patricia Ahearn) *Collected Books: The Guide to Values,* G. P. Putnam's Sons (New York, NY), 1991, 1998 edition, 1997, 2002 edition, 2001.

Coauthor of more than 200 privately printed price guides to the works of individual authors.

SIDELIGHTS: Allen Ahearn once told *CA:* "The books we compile are intended to attract interest in book collecting and to provide detailed guidance on identifying edition and ascertaining condition. They also include price ranges."

BIOGRAPHICAL AND CRITICAL SOURCES:

PERIODICALS

Book World, December 2, 2001, review of *Collected Books: The Guide to Values,* 2001 edition, p. 15.
Library Journal, July, 1997, Eric Bryant, review of *Collected Books,* 1998 edition, p. 74.
Library Quarterly, January, 2001, Sidney E. Berger, review of *Book Collecting 2000: A Comprehensive Guide,* p. 78.*

ALLAN, John B.
See WESTLAKE, Donald E(dwin)

* * *

ANDERSON, Louie 1953(?)-

PERSONAL: Born March 24, c. 1953, in St. Paul, MN; son of Louie Anderson (a trumpet player); married, 1985 (divorced).

ADDRESSES: *Agent*—c/o International Creative Management, 8942 Wilshire Blvd., Beverly Hills, CA 90211.

CAREER: Worked as a children's counselor; comedian, beginning 1976, including appearances at the Comedy Store and on tour; writer, beginning 1989. Appeared in more than thirty television specials, including "Just for Laughs" and "Louie Anderson at the Guthrie," both presented by *Showtime Comedy Spotlight,* Showtime Network, 1987, "The Louie Anderson Show," presented by *On Location,* Home Box Office, 1988, and host of *The Funny Things Kids Do,* broadcast by Fox Network, 1997; narrator and voice performer for the animated television series *Life with Louie,* broadcast by Fox Network, 1995; guest on other television programs, including the *Late Show.* Creator of the television series *Life with Louie* (animated), broadcast by Fox Network, 1995, and *The Louie Show,* broadcast by Columbia Broadcasting System in 1996; also executive producer for television. Appeared in films, such as *Ferris Bueller's Day Off,* released by Paramount in 1986; *Coming to America,* released by Paramount in 1988; and *Mr. Wrong,* released by Buena Vista in 1996. HERO (mentoring program for the homeless), spokesperson, 1994.

AWARDS, HONORS: Shared Humanitas Prize, Human Family Educational and Cultural Institute, 1995; Daytime Emmy Award, Academy of Television Arts and Sciences, 1996.

WRITINGS:

Dear Dad: Letters from an Adult Child (memoir), Viking (New York, NY), 1989.

Goodbye Jumbo, Hello Cruel World, illustrated by Robert de Michiell, Viking (New York, NY), 1993.

(With Carl Kurlander) *The F Word: How to Survive Your Family,* Warner Books (New York, NY), 2002.

TELEVISION WRITING:

The Johnsons Are Home (pilot), Columbia Broadcasting System, 1988.

"Louie Anderson: Comedy on Canvas" (special), presented on *HBO Comedy Hour,* Home Box Office, 1990.

Louie Anderson: Louie in St. Louie (television special), Showtime Network, 1993.

ADAPTATIONS: Narrator of the audio-book adaptation of his memoir, *Dear Dad: Letters from an Adult Child,* released by Harper Audio in 1990. Episodes of the animated television series *Life with Louie* were adapted by Katy Hall as the books *A Christmas Surprise for Mrs. Stillman* and *Life with Louie: A Bully, a Bodyguard, and a Fish Called Pepper,* both published by HarperActive (New York, NY) in 1998.

SIDELIGHTS: Louie Anderson is a popular comedian who is known for his autobiographical material. He began his show-business career in St. Paul-Minneapolis at age twenty-six when he accepted a challenge to perform and promptly won a booking. For the next four years he continued performing regularly in the Twin Cities, where he developed a largely anecdotal act that also derived humor from life's more mundane aspects. Holiday gatherings, for instance, are among the domestic rituals that Anderson exploits for comedic effect. Personal well-being is another of Anderson's favorite subjects. The noticeably overweight comic—who, according to *People,* once weighed 300 pounds—regularly calls attention to his excessive eating, which he relates, in turn, to his father's alcoholism. "My weight thing is directly tied to my father and his drinking," he commented to *People.*

In 1989 Anderson released *Dear Dad: Letters from an Adult Child,* an occasionally funny, but more often unsettling, account of his childhood with an alcoholic father. Laurie Stone, writing in the *New York Times Book Review,* reported that in *Dear Dad* Anderson "reveals his pain without overdramatizing his plight," and she concluded that the book is "moving."

Anderson has won widespread praise for his television performances. His foremost appearances came with *Louie Anderson at the Guthrie* and *The Louie Anderson Show,* two presentations which originated on cable networks. Anderson has also toured the United States, notably with fellow comic Roseanne Barr. And in both television and stage performances Anderson continues to prove himself a master of what John J. O'Connor described in the *New York Times* as "old-fashioned, heart-warming humor."

BIOGRAPHICAL AND CRITICAL SOURCES:

BOOKS

Anderson, Louie, *Dear Dad: Letters from an Adult Child,* Viking (New York, NY), 1989.

Contemporary Theatre, Film, and Television, Volume 21, Thomson Gale (Detroit, MI), 1999.

PERIODICALS

Booklist, September 15, 2002, Brad Hooper, review of *The F Word: How to Survive Your Family,* p. 178.

New York Times, August 17, 1987, article by John J. O'Connor, p. C16.

New York Times Book Review, December 24, 1989, Laurie Stone, review of *Dear Dad,* p. 17; June 27, 1993, Andrea Cooper, review of *Goodbye Jumbo, Hello Cruel World,* p. 18.

People, September 7, 1987; April 18, 1988, pp. 105-106.

Publishers Weekly, March 1, 1993, review of *Goodbye Jumbo, Hello Cruel World,* p. 45.

St. Louis Post-Dispatch, February 14, 2003, Doug Kaufman, "Funnyman Louie Anderson Travels Forward into the Past," p. 3.

TV Guide, July 27, 1996, Craig Modderno, "Louie, Louie" (interview), p. 49.

Washington Post, October 25, 1990.

ONLINE

Welcome to the Official Louie Anderson Web Site, http://www.louieanderson.com/ (May 10, 2004).

ANDERS, Isabel 1946-

PERSONAL: Born December 16, 1946, in Gulfport, MS; children: Sarah Alison. *Education:* Wheaton College, Wheaton, IL, B.A., 1969; Loyola University, M.A., 1980; Mundelein College, M.R.S. *Religion:* Episcopalian.

ADDRESSES: Home—Winchester, TN. *Office*—P.O. Box 277, Winchester, TN 37398. *Agent*—Jane Jordan Browne, Multimedia Product Development, Inc., 410 South Michigan Ave., Suite 724, Chicago, IL 60605-1465.

CAREER: David C. Cook Publishing Co., Elgin, IL, religion editor, 1969-76; Tyndale House Publishers, Wheaton, IL, book editor, 1976-83; Synthesis Publications, Chattanooga, TN, managing editor of *Synthesis: Weekly Resource for Preaching and Worship in the Episcopal Tradition,* 1990—. Consultant to Eggman Publishing, 1995—.

AWARDS, HONORS: Ohio Arts Council Award for Creative Writing, 1988-89, for *Awaiting the Child: An Advent Journal.*

WRITINGS:

RELIGIOUS NONFICTION

Awaiting the Child: An Advent Journal, Cowley Publications (Cambridge, MA), 1987.

(With Ruth Harms Calkin) *Letters to Kristi* (juvenile) Tyndale House (Wheaton, IL), 1990.

The Faces of Friendship, Cowley Publications (Cambridge, MA), 1992.

The Lord's Prayer: Peace and Self-Acceptance for Those in Recovery, Oliver-Nelson Books (Nashville, TN), 1992.

The Lord's Blessings: Hope and Peace for Those in Recovery, Oliver-Nelson Books (Nashville, TN), 1992.

Walking with the Shepherd (devotional), Thomas Nelson Publishers (Nashville, TN), 1994.

Standing on High Places: The Story of Hannah Hurnard and "Hinds' Feet on High Places," (biography), Tyndale House (Wheaton, IL), 1994.

A Book of Blessings for Working Mothers, Liguori (Liguori, MO), 1994.

(Compiler) *The Wisdom of Little Women,* Eggman Publishing (Nashville, TN), 1995.

Sand and Shells, Carousels, Silver Bells: A Child's Seasons of Prayer, illustrated by Rick Incrocci, Concordia Publishing House (St. Louis, MO), 1996.

(Compiler) *Simple Blessings for Sacred Moments,* Liguori (Liguori, MO), 1998.

The Real Night before Christmas: Luke 2:8-20 (juvenile), illustrated by Shelly Rasche, Concordia Publishing House (St. Louis, MO), 1999.

Easter ABCs: Matthew 28:1-28; Mark 16:1-8; Luke 24:1-12; John 20:1-18 (juvenile), illustrated by Shelly Rasche, Concordia Publishing House (St. Louis, MO), 1999.

Soul Moments: Times When Heaven Touches Earth, Thomas More (Allen, TX), 2000.

Jesus' Spiritual Laws (e-book), iUniverse.com, 2000.

The Lord's Prayer for a New Millennium, Magnus Press (Carlsbad, CA) 2001.

Also contributor to *Understanding the Sunday Scriptures,* Synthesis Publications (Chattanooga, TN); contributor of articles and reviews to periodicals, including *Living Church, Christian Century, Christianity Today,* and *Partnership.* Book review editor, *New Oxford Review,* 1980-83.

SIDELIGHTS: Author and editor Isabel Anders has had a successful career in religious publishing for nearly three decades. In addition to her editorial projects, she has also penned or co-written several books in the religious field. The first was *Awaiting the Child: An Advent Journal;* three years later she teamed with Ruth Harms Calkin to write a book of advice for adolescents called *Letters to Kristi.* In 1992 three of Anders's books were published; two of them, *The Lord's Prayer: Peace and Self-Acceptance for Those in Recovery* and *The Lord's Blessings: Hope and Peace for Those in Recovery,* were aimed at readers recovering from addiction.

One of Anders's most notable volumes is her 1994 biography of religious writer Hannah Hurnard, titled *Standing on High Places: The Story of Hannah Hurnard and "Hinds' Feet on High Places."* Anders met Hurnard while working for Tyndale House, a publishing company. That same year Anders wrote a gift book titled *A Book of Blessings for Working Mothers.* The following year Anders penned *The Wisdom of Little Women,* a book of quotations from the beloved Louisa May Alcott classic *Little Women,* arranged by topics such as "work," "friendship," and "femininity."

BIOGRAPHICAL AND CRITICAL SOURCES:

BOOKS

Anders, Isabel, *Standing on High Places: The Story of Hannah Hurnard and "Hinds' Feet on High Places,"* Tyndale House (Wheaton, IL), 1994.

PERIODICALS

Publishers Weekly, September 27, 1999, review of *The Real Night before Christmas: Luke 2:8-20,* p. 63.*

* * *

APPLETON, Victor
See MACDONALD, James D.

* * *

ARNOLD, Caroline 1944-

PERSONAL: Born May 16, 1944, in Pittsburgh, PA; daughter of Lester L. (a social worker) and Catherine (a social worker) Scheaffer; married Arthur Arnold (a neuroscientist), June 24, 1967; children: Jennifer Elizabeth, Matthew William. *Education:* Grinnell College, B.A., 1966; University of Iowa, M.A., 1968.

ADDRESSES: *Home and office*—10353 Rossbury Pl., Los Angeles, CA 90064. *Agent*—1076 Eagle Dr., Salinas, CA 93905. *E-mail*—csarnoldbooks@yahoo.com.

CAREER: Freelance writer and artist. Art teacher and substitute teacher in Yellow Springs and Xenia, OH, both 1968-69; New York Hospital, New York, NY, secretary, 1969-70; Rockefeller University, New York, NY, laboratory assistant, 1971-72, 1972-76; University

Caroline Arnold

of California—Los Angeles, laboratory assistant, 1976-79; University of California—Los Angeles Extension, instructor in Writers' Program, 1982—.

MEMBER: Society of Children's Book Writers and Illustrators, Southern California Council on Literature for Children and Young People.

AWARDS, HONORS: Outstanding Science Trade Book citations, National Science Teachers Association-Children's Book Council Joint Committee, 1980, for *Five Nests* and *Electric Fish,* 1982, for *Animals That Migrate,* 1983, for *The Biggest Living Thing* and *Pets without Homes,* 1985, for *Saving the Peregrine Falcon,* 1987, for *Genetics: From Mendel to Gene Splicing, Trapped in Tar, Koala, Kangaroo, Giraffe,* and *Zebra,* 1988, for *Llama, Penguin,* and *A Walk of the Great Barrier Reef,* 1989, for *Tule Elk, Hippo,* and *Cheetah,* 1991, for *Flamingo* and *Snake,* 1992, for *House Sparrows Everywhere,* 1995, for *Rhino* and *Lion,* 1997, for *Bat* and *Fox,* and 1998, for *Hawk Highway in the Sky: Watching the Raptor Migration;* Children's Science Book Award honorable mention, 1983, for *Animals That Migrate;* Golden Kite Honor Book, Society of Children's Book Writers, 1984, for *Pets without Homes;* nonfiction award, Southern California Council on Literature for Children and Young People, 1985, for *Too Fat? Too Thin?: Do You Have a Choice?; Saving the Peregrine Falcon* was selected Children's Editors' Choice by *Booklist,* 1985, best book by *School Library Journal,* 1985, notable book by American Library Association, 1985, and received a special achievement award, PEN Los Angeles Center, 1986; Best Children's Books and Films selection, American Association for the Advancement of Science, 1987, for *Trapped in Tar* and *Koala,* 1988, for *A Walk on the Great Barrier Reef,* 1990, for *Orangutan* and *Wild Goat,* and 1999, for *Bobcats;* John Burroughs Nature Award, 1988, for *A Walk on the Great Barrier Reef;* Orbus Pictus Award for Outstanding Nonfiction, National Council of Teachers of English, 1989, for *Cheetah* and *Hippo;School Library Journal* Best Books selection, 1992, for *The Ancient Cliff Dwellers of Mesa Verde,* and 2001, for *Easter Island: Giant Stone Statues Tell of a Rich and Tragic Past.*

WRITINGS:

NONFICTION CHILDREN'S BOOKS

Five Nests, illustrated by Ruth Sanderson, Dutton (New York, NY), 1980.

Electric Fish, illustrated by George Gershinowitz, Morrow (New York, NY), 1980.

(And illustrator) *Sun Fun,* F. Watts (New York, NY), 1981.

Sex Hormones: Why Males and Females Are Different, illustrated by Jean Zallinger, Morrow (New York, NY), 1981.

Animals That Migrate, illustrated by Michele Zylman, Carolrhoda (Minneapolis, MN), 1982.

What Is a Community?, illustrated by Carole Bertol, F. Watts (New York, NY), 1982.

Where Do You Go to School?, illustrated by Carole Bertol, F. Watts (New York, NY), 1982.

Who Works Here?, illustrated by Carole Bertol, F. Watts (New York, NY), 1982.

Who Keeps Us Healthy?, illustrated by Carole Bertol, F. Watts (New York, NY), 1982.

Who Keeps Us Safe?, illustrated by Carole Bertol, F. Watts (New York, NY), 1982.

Why Do We Have Rules?, illustrated by Ginger Giles, F. Watts (New York, NY), 1983.

What Will We Buy?, illustrated by Ginger Giles, F. Watts (New York, NY), 1983.
How Do We Have Fun?, illustrated by Ginger Giles, F. Watts (New York, NY), 1983.
How Do We Travel?, illustrated by Ginger Giles, F. Watts (New York, NY), 1983.
How Do We Communicate?, illustrated by Ginger Giles, F. Watts (New York, NY), 1983.
(And illustrator) *The Biggest Living Thing,* Carolrhoda (Minneapolis, MN), 1983.
Pets without Homes, illustrated by Richard Hewett, Houghton Mifflin (Boston, MA), 1983.
Summer Olympics, F. Watts (New York, NY), 1983, 2nd updated edition, 1988.
Winter Olympics, F. Watts (New York, NY), 1983.
Measurements: Fun, Facts, and Activities, F. Watts (New York, NY), 1984.
Maps and Globes, F. Watts (New York, NY), 1984.
Charts and Graphs, F. Watts (New York, NY), 1984.
Too Fat? Too Thin?: Do You Have a Choice?, Morrow (New York, NY), 1984.
Land Masses, F. Watts (New York, NY), 1985.
Bodies of Water, F. Watts (New York, NY), 1985.
Natural Resources: Fun, Facts, and Activities, F. Watts (New York, NY), 1985.
Saving the Peregrine Falcon, Carolrhoda (Minneapolis, MN), 1985.
Music Lessons for Alex, photographs by Richard Hewitt, Houghton Mifflin (Boston, MA), 1985.
(With Herma Silverstein) *Anti-Semitism: A Modern Perspective,* Messner (New York, NY), 1985.
(With Herma Silverstein) *Hoaxes That Made Headlines,* Messner (New York, NY), 1985.
Bodies of Water: Fun, Facts, and Activities, illustrated by Lynn Sweat, F. Watts (New York, NY), 1985.
Pain: What Is It? How Do We Deal with It?, illustrated by Frank Schwarz, Morrow (New York, NY), 1986.
Genetics: From Mendel to Gene Splicing, F. Watts (New York, NY), 1986.
The Golden Gate Bridge, F. Watts (New York, NY), 1986.
Everybody Has a Birthday, F. Watts (New York, NY), 1987.
How People Get Married, F. Watts (New York, NY), 1987.
What We Do When Someone Dies, F. Watts (New York, NY), 1987.
Australia Today, F. Watts (New York, NY), 1987.
Coping with Natural Disasters, Walker, 1987.
Kangaroo, Morrow (New York, NY), 1987.
Giraffe, Morrow (New York, NY), 1987.
Zebra, Morrow (New York, NY), 1987.
A Walk on the Great Barrier Reef, Carolrhoda (Minneapolis, MN), 1987.
Trapped in Tar: Fossils from the Ice Age (Junior Literary Guild selection), Houghton Mifflin (Boston, MA), 1987.
Koala, photographs by Richard Hewett, Morrow (New York, NY), 1987.
Llama, Morrow (New York, NY), 1988.
Penguin, Morrow (New York, NY), 1988.
Saving the Tule Elk, Carolrhoda (Minneapolis, MN), 1988.
Juggler, Houghton Mifflin (Boston, MA), 1988.
Ole Swenson and the Hodag, Harcourt (New York, NY), 1988.
Dinosaur Mountain: Graveyard of the Past, Clarion (New York, NY), 1989.
Hippo, photographs by Richard Hewett, Morrow (New York, NY), 1989.
Cheetah, photographs by Richard Hewett, Morrow (New York, NY), 1989.
The Terrible Hodag, illustrated by Lambert Davis, Harcourt (New York, NY), 1989.
Dinosaurs Down Under: And Other Fossils from Australia, photographs by Richard Hewett, Clarion (New York, NY), 1990.
Ostriches and Other Flightless Birds, photographs by Richard Hewett, Carolrhoda (Minneapolis, MN), 1990.
A Walk in the Woods, illustrated by Freya Tanz, Silver Press (Parsippany, NJ), 1990.
Orangutan, photographs by Richard Hewett, Morrow (New York, NY),1990.
Wild Goat, photographs by Richard Hewett, Morrow (New York, NY), 1990.
A Walk up the Mountain, illustrated by Freya Tanz, Silver Press (Parsippany, NJ), 1990.
A Walk by the Seashore, illustrated by Freya Tanz, Silver Press (Parsippany, NJ), 1990.
Heart Disease, F. Watts (New York, NY), 1990.
A Walk in the Desert, illustrated by Freya Tanz, Silver Press (Parsippany, NJ), 1990.
Watch Out for Sharks!, photographs by Richard Hewett, Clarion (New York, NY), 1991.
A Guide Dog Puppy Grows Up, photographs by Richard Hewett, Harcourt (New York, NY), 1991.
Flamingo, photographs by Richard Hewett, Morrow (New York, NY),1991.
Snake, photographs by Richard Hewett, Morrow (New York, NY), 1991.
The Olympic Summer Games, F. Watts (New York, NY), 1991.

The Olympic Winter Games, F. Watts (New York, NY),1991.

Soccer: From Neighborhood Play to the World Cup, F. Watts (New York, NY), 1991.

The Ancient Cliff Dwellers of Mesa Verde, photographs by Richard Hewett, Clarion (New York, NY), 1992.

Camel, photographs by Richard Hewett, Morrow (New York, NY), 1992.

Panda, photographs by Richard Hewett, Morrow (New York, NY), 1992.

House Sparrows Everywhere, photographs by Richard Hewett, Carolrhoda (Minneapolis, MN), 1992.

Pele: The King of Soccer, F. Watts (New York, NY), 1992.

On the Brink of Extinction: The California Condor, photographs by Michael Wallace, Harcourt (San Diego, CA), 1993.

Dinosaurs All Around: An Artist's View of the Prehistoric World, photographs by Richard Hewett, Clarion (New York, NY), 1993.

Elephant, photographs by Richard Hewett, Morrow (New York, NY), 1993.

Monkey, photographs by Richard Hewett, Morrow (New York, NY), 1993.

Prairie dogs, illustrations by Jean Cassels, Scholastic, 1993.

Reindeer, illustrated by Pamela Johnson, Scholastic, 1993.

Cats: In from the Wild, photographs by Richard R. Hewett, Carolrhoda (Minneapolis, MN), 1993.

Sea Turtles, illustrated by Marshall Peck III, Scholastic (New York, NY), 1994.

Fireflies, illustrated by Pamela Johnson, Scholastic (New York, NY), 1994.

Killer Whale, photographs by Richard Hewett, Morrow (New York, NY), 1994.

Sea Lion, photographs by Richard Hewett, Morrow (New York, NY), 1994.

Watching Desert Wildlife, photographs by Arthur Arnold, Carolrhoda (Minneapolis, MN), 1994.

City of the Gods: Mexico's Ancient City of Teotihuacan, photographs by Richard Hewett, Clarion (New York, NY), 1994.

Rhino, photographs by Richard Hewett, additional photographs by Arthur P. Arnold, Morrow (New York, NY), 1995.

Lion, photographs by Richard Hewett, Morrow (New York, NY), 1995.

Bat, photographs by Richard Hewett, Morrow (New York, NY),1996.

Fox, photographs by Richard Hewett, Morrow (New York, NY), 1996.

Stories in Stone: Rock Art Pictures by Early Americans, photographs by Richard Hewett, Clarion (New York, NY), 1996.

African Animals, Morrow (New York, NY), 1997.

Stone Age Farmers beside the Sea: Scotland's Prehistoric Village of Skara Brae, photographs by Arthur P. Arnold, Clarion (New York, NY), 1997.

Hawk Highway in the Sky: Watching Raptor Migration, photographs by Robert Kruidenier, Harcourt (San Diego, CA), 1997.

Bobcats, photographs by Richard R. Hewett, Lerner (Minneapolis, MN), 1997.

Children of the Settlement Houses, Carolrhoda (Minneapolis, MN), 1998.

El Nino: Stormy Weather for People and Wildlife, Clarion (New York, NY), 1998.

(With Richard Hewett) *Baby Whale Rescue: The True Story of J.J.,* Bridgewater, 1999.

Cats, Lerner Publications (Minneapolis, MN), 1999.

Splashtime for Zoo Animals, photographs by Richard Hewett, Carolrhoda (Minneapolis, MN), 1999.

Sleepytime for Zoo Animals, photographs by Richard Hewett, Carolrhoda (Minneapolis, MN), 1999.

Noisytime for Zoo Animals, photographs by Richard Hewett, Carolrhoda (Minneapolis, MN), 1999.

Playtime for Zoo Animals, photographs by Richard Hewett, Carolrhoda (Minneapolis, MN), 1999.

Mother and Baby Zoo Animals, photographs by Richard Hewett, Carolrhoda (Minneapolis, MN), 1999.

Mealtime for Zoo Animals, photographs by Richard Hewett, Carolrhoda (Minneapolis, MN), 1999.

South American Animals, Morrow (New York, NY), 1999.

Shockers of the Sea: And Other Electric Animals, illustrated by Crista Forest, Charlesbridge (Watertown, MA), 1999.

Easter Island: Giant Stone Statues Tell of a Rich and Tragic Past, Clarion (New York, NY), 2000.

Australian Animals, Morrow (New York, NY), 2000.

Giant Shark: Megalodon, Prehistoric Super Predator, illustrated by Laurie Caple, Clarion (New York, NY), 2000.

Ostriches, photographs by Richard Hewett, Lerner (Minneapolis, MN), 2000.

Did You Hear That?: Animals with Super Hearing, illustrations by Cathy Trachok, Charlesbridge (Watertown, MA), 2001.

Dinosaurs with Feathers: The Ancestors of Modern Birds, Clarion Books (New York, NY), 2001.

Ostriches, Lerner Publications (Minneapolis, MN), 2001.

The Geography Book: Activities for Exploring, Mapping, and Enjoying Your World, Wiley (New York, NY), 2002.

When Mammoths Walked the Earth, Clarion Books (New York, NY), 2002.

Birds: Nature's Magnificent Flying Machines, Charlesbridge (Watertown, MA), 2003.

Uluru, Australia's Aboriginal Heart, Clarion Books (New York, NY), 2003.

Who Has More? Who Has Fewer?, Charlesbridge (Watertown, MA), 2004.

Who Is Bigger? Who Is Smaller?, Charlesbridge (Watertown, MA), 2004.

Pterosaurs: Rulers of the Skies in the Dinosaur Age, illustrated by Laurie Caple, Clarion Books (New York, NY), 2004.

The Skeletal System, Lerner Publications (Minneapolis, MN), 2005.

OTHER

My Friend from Outer Space (picture book), illustrated by Carol Nicklaus, F. Watts (New York, NY), 1981.

(Illustrator) Elizabeth Bremner and John Pusey, *Children's Gardens: A Field Guide for Teachers, Parents, and Volunteers,* Cooperative Extension, University of California, Los Angeles (Los Angeles, CA), 1982.

Also author of the television episode "Fire for Hire" for K-I-D-S series, KCET, Los Angeles, 1984. Contributor of articles and stories to magazines, including *Highlights for Children, Friend, Humpty Dumpty,* and *Cricket.*

ADAPTATIONS: My Friend from Outer Space has been made into a filmstrip, Westport Community Group, 1981.

WORK IN PROGRESS: (With Madeleine Comora) *Taj Mahal,* for Millbrook Press (Brookfield, CT).

SIDELIGHTS: Caroline Arnold told *CA:* "I grew up in Minneapolis, Minnesota, and when I was in elementary school I had many favorite authors, including Beverly Cleary, Laura Ingalls Wilder, and Maude Hart Lovelace. The books I loved the most were usually set in other times or far off places. One of my favorites was *Family Sabbatical* by Carol Ryie Brink. Like the children in that story, I dreamed that one day I might travel to Paris, learn to speak French, and climb the Eiffel Tower. Although I've never been to France, I do often travel to do research for my books, and that's one of the things I like best about being a writer.

"My love of reading came from my mother, who read to me from the time I was very small. But even though I loved books, I never imagined that I would be a writer when I grew up. I studied art in school and planned to be an artist and art teacher. After I got married and had my own children, I read stories to them. I realized that perhaps I could use my training in art to be a children's book illustrator. I started to write stories so that I could illustrate them and soon discovered that I liked writing very much. After illustrating three books, I stopped drawing and I've been writing ever since.

"I've always loved animals. I got my first kitten when I was three—I named her Snoozy after a character in one of my books—and have always had pets. During the summers our family spent in northern Wisconsin, I learned the thrill of spotting birds, deer, porcupines, and other wild animals in the forest. In 1971, I spent four months in East Africa with my husband and young daughter. We lived in a national park, side by side with lions, giraffes, zebras, and all sorts of other animals whose home is the African plain. A few of the photos we took on that trip are in my book *African Animals.*

"Birds have always been a favorite topic in my books. When I was a child, I went on early morning bird walks with my father, who was an amateur birdwatcher, and now my husband, Art, studies birds in his research at the University of California—Los Angeles. For my book *Hawk Highway in the Sky: Watching Raptor Migration,* I spent a week in the Goshutes watching and helping HawkWatch volunteers trap and band migrating hawks, eagles, and falcons. Nothing is more exciting than getting close to these magnificent birds, and my close involvement with the process helped me learn the details that I needed to write my book. My . . . book *Birds: Nature's Magnificent Flying Machines* also focuses on birds and their amazing ability to fly.

"There are so many different kinds of animals in the world that I could spend the rest of my life writing about animals and never run out of ideas. When I choose an animal for a book, I often pick endangered species such as pandas or cheetahs. The more we all know about these animals, the more we will care about saving them from extinction. Sometimes, as in my book about snakes, I pick an idea suggested to me by kids. I usually spend up to a year doing background reading on the subject of a book. Then I make trips to the zoo to make my own observations of animals and also to help the photographer decide what pictures to take. After I have all the information I need, I sit down to write the book. It takes me about two months to finish the manuscript for one of my animal books.

"Truth is often stranger than fiction and certainly just as much fun to write. With every book I've written, I have learned something that I never knew before. If the children who read my books are as excited about reading them as I am about writing them, then I feel that I have accomplished a great deal.

"In my future work, I hope to continue writing about animals and the places they live as well as other topics. And even though I have become well known mostly for my nonfiction writing, I also like to write fiction and perhaps I will try more of that in the future as well. In two . . . books for very young children, *Who's Bigger?* and *Who Has More?,* I have used my art training to illustrate them with bright, cutout paper animals.

"Children often ask me advice about becoming a writer. I tell them that the best writers, whether they write fiction or nonfiction, are those who have developed a keen sense of observation. They notice details about they way things look, feel, sound, and smell. They learn how to use words to paint a picture of a scene or action. You can develop your powers of observation by pretending you are a spy and making notes about what you see around you. Your 'spy reports' might make the beginning of a great story.

"The other secret of becoming a good writer is practice. Writing letters or keeping a journal are two ways of practicing writing. Writing is something like baseball—you are not likely to hit a home run the first time you step up to the plate. Your first stories will not be perfect either, but they will get better and better and soon you will be hitting the ball out of the park."

Arnold is the author of more than one hundred nonfiction books for children, on subjects ranging from monkeys, bats, and foxes to prehistoric natural history, the giant statues of Easter Island, and weather patterns. The author once commented to *CA:* "Like many writers of children's books, I began when my children were small. I thought I would write lovely stories for children and that because I was trained as a fine artist I would illustrate them myself. However, nearly all my books have been nonfiction, usually about scientific subjects, and most of them have been illustrated by other people. I have found that I enjoy the challenge of writing about complicated subjects in language that even a very young child can understand. My fascination with scientific subjects is reinforced by my own and other children's eagerness to know more about the world around them."

Bat is typical of Arnold's books on animals. Reviewing it and *Fox* in *Booklist,* Carolyn Phelan called them "succinct" and "readable." Although the books are short, they cover a great deal of material, including the animals' anatomy, habitat, behavior; their food and animals that may prey on them; myths and history of the animal; and threats to the continued survival of the species. Discussing the author's books *Lion* and *Rhino* in another review, Phelan noted that Arnold offers interesting comment on the differences in the animals' behavior based on whether they were living in the wild or in captivity. In similar style, Arnold has discussed many other species and types of animals.

In another realm of interest, Arnold illustrated Aztec culture and its remaining artifacts in *City of the Gods: Mexico's Ancient City of Teotihuacan.* Aerial photographs give excellent insight into the site that was one of the most important in the Aztec world, while the book's text explains the city's importance to Aztec culture. Another ancient, mysterious site is explored in Arnold's book *Easter Island: Giant Stone Statues Tell of a Rich and Tragic Past.* The island in the South Pacific is home to huge stone icons, and for decades no one has been able to definitely answer the many questions surrounding the figures, such as how the primitive inhabitants of the island ever managed to carve and erect them. A reviewer for *Horn Book* noted: "Arnold avoids theatrical speculation in this straightforward account." She also gives a great deal of information about the Rapanui people and their modern descendants, and the way the island suffered from the effects of overpopulation and disregard for its fragile environment.

BIOGRAPHICAL AND CRITICAL SOURCES:

BOOKS

Roginski, Jim, *Behind the Covers: Interviews with Authors and Illustrators of Children's Books,* Libraries Unlimited, 1989, pp. 28-40.

Something about the Author Autobiography Series, Volume 23, Gale (Detroit, MI), 1996.

PERIODICALS

Booklist, October 15, 1992, Stephanie Zvirin, review of *Camel,* p. 419; April 15, 1993, Stephanie Zvirin, review of *Dinosaurs All Around: An Artist's View of the Prehistoric World,* p. 1507; Chris Sherman, review of *On the Brink of Extinction: The California Condor,* p. 1512; August, 1993, Stephanie Zvirin, review of *Cats: In from the Wild,* p. 2051; November 1, 1993, Kay Weisman, review of *Elephant* and *Monkey,* p. 516; September 15, 1994, Carolyn Phelan, review of *Sea Lion* and *Killer Whale,* p. 128; December 1, 1994, Mary Harris Veeder, review of *Watching Desert Wildlife,* p. 670; December 15, 1994, Ilene Cooper, review of *City of the Gods: Mexico's Ancient City of Teotihuacan,* p. 747; September 15, 1995, Carolyn Phelan, review of *Rhino* and *Lion,* p. 154; December 15, 1996, Sally Estes, review of *Stories in Stone: Rock Art Pictures by Early Americans,* p. 722; October 15, 1999, Shelley Townsend-Hudson, review of *Shockers of the Sea: And Other Electrical Animals,* p. 448; August, 1996, Carolyn Phelan, review of *Fox* and *Bat,* p. 1897; March 15, 1997, Julie Corsaro, review of *African Animals,* p. 1236; April 15, 1997, Ilene Cooper, review of *Stone Age Farmers beside the Sea: Scotland's Prehistoric Village of Skara Brae,* p. 1424; June 1, 1997, Candace Smith, review of *Hawk Highway in the Sky: Watching Raptor Migration,* p. 1687; September 15, 1998, Shelle Rosenfeld, review of *Children of the Settlement Houses,* p. 221; October 1, 1998, Chris Sherman, review of *El Nino: Stormy Weather for People and Wildlife,* p. 326; March 1, 1999, Lauren Peterson, review of *Baby Whale Rescue: The True Story of J. J.,* p. 1204; June 1, 1999, Susan Dove Lempke, review of *Noisytime for Zoo Animals* and *Mealtime for Zoo Animals,* p. 1832; July, 1999, Lauren Peterson, review of *South American Animals,* p. 1939; March 15, 2000, Ilene Cooper, review of *Easter Island: Giant Stone Statues Tell of a Rich and Tragic Past,* p. 1371; November 1, 2000, Tod Morning, review of *Giant Shark: Megalodon, Prehistoric Super Predator,* p. 528; December 1, 2001, Carolyn Phelan, review of *Did You Hear That? Animals with Super Hearing,* p. 654; February 15, 2002, Carolyn Phelan, review of *The Geography Book: Activities for Exploring, Mapping, and Enjoying Your World,* p. 1001; August, 2002, Julie Cummins, review of *When Mammoths Walked the Earth,* p. 1952; June 1, 2003, John Peters, review of *Birds: Nature's Magnificent Flying Machines,* p. 1762; December 15, 2003, Carolyn Phelan, review of *Uluru: Australia's Aboriginal Heart,* p. 1220.

Horn Book, November-December, 1992, Margaret A. Bush, review of *Camel* and *Panda,* p. 735; June-May, 1993, Margaret A. Bush, review of *On the Brink of Extinction: The California Condor,* p. 343; July-August, 1993, Elizabeth S. Watson, review of *Dinosaurs All Around,* p. 474; November-December, 1994, Margaret A. Bush, review of *Sea Lion* and *Killer Whale,* p. 742; March-April, 1995, Elizabeth S. Watson, review of *City of the Gods,* p. 218; May, 2000, review of *Easter Island,* p. 329; October 1, 2001, John Peters, review of *Dinosaurs with Feathers: The Ancestors of the Modern Birds,* p. 313; November-December, 2002, Danielle J. Ford, review of *When Mammoths Walked the Earth,* p. 772; November-December, 2003, Barbara Bader, review of *Uluru,* p. 760.

Kirkus Reviews, June 15, 2003, review of *Birds,* p. 855; October 1, 2003, review of *Uluru,* p. 1220.

Los Angeles Times, November 8, 1996, "Author Gets a Read on What Students Want," p. 2.

Reading Teacher, September, 1998, review of *African Animals,* p. 58.

*School Library Journal,*November, 1992, Myra R. Oleynik, review of *Camel,* p. 100; January, 1993, Barbara B. Murphy, review of *Panda,* p. 106; May, 1993, Cathryn A. Campter, review of *Dinosaurs All Around,* p. 112; June, 1993, Amy Nunley, review of *On the Brink of Extinction,* p. 113; December, 1993, Barbara B. Murphy, review of *Monkey* and *Elephant,* p. 118; October, 1994, Frances E. Millhouser, review of *Killer Whale,* p. 130; December, 1994, Cynthia M. Sturgis, review of *City of the Gods,* p. 117; January, 1995, George Gleason, review of *Watching Desert Wild-*

life, p. 110; December, 1995, Barbara B. Murphy, review of *Lion* and *Rhino,* p. 111; September, 1996, Lisa Wu Stowe, review of *Fox* and *Bat,* p. 210; December, 1996, Pam Gosner, review of *Stories in Stone,* p. 126; March, 1997, Susan Oliver, review of *African Animals,* p. 170; June, 1997, Susan Scheps, review of *Hawk Highway in the Sky,* p. 130; July, 1997, Pam Gosner, review of *Stone Age Farmers beside the Sea,* p. 99; March, 1998, Susan Oliver, review of *Bobcats,* p. 191; December, 1998, Patricia Manning, review of *El Nino,* p. 132; January, 1999, Anne Chapman Callaghan, review of *Children of the Settlement Houses,* p. 109; March, 1999, Patricia Manning, review of *Baby Whale Rescue,* p. 216; August, 1999, Dawn Amsberry, review of *Splashtime for Zoo Animals* and *Sleepytime for Zoo Animals,* p. 143; September, 1999, Frances E. Millhouser, review of *South American Animals,* p. 210; January, 2000, Patricia Manning, review of *Shockers of the Sea: And Other Electric Animals,* p. 115; April, 2000, Jeanette Larson, review of *Easter Island,* p. 144; October, 2000, Krista Grosick, review of *Australian Animals,* p. 144; November, 2000, Patricia Manning, review of *Giant Shark,* p. 167; August, 2001, Margaret Bush, review of *Did You Hear That?,* p. 166; November, 2001, Steven Engelfried, review of *Dinosaurs with Feathers,* p. 140; March, 2002, Robyn Ryan Vandenbroek, review of *The Geography Book,* p. 206; October, 2002, Ellen Heath, review of *When Mammoths Walked the Earth,* p. 136.

Wilson Library Bulletin, February, 1994, Frances Bradburn, review of *Elephant,* p. 89A.

* * *

ARONSON, Marc 1948-

Marc Aronson

PERSONAL: Born 1948; married Marina Budhos (an author); children: two sons. *Education:* Earned a Ph.D. in American history.

ADDRESSES: Home—New York, NY. *Agent*—c/o Author Mail, Clarion Books, 215 Park Avenue, New York, NY 10020. *E-mail*—marc@marcaronson.com.

CAREER: Writer and editor. Editor of books for children and young adults; Harper & Row, New York, NY, and later, Henry Holt Books for Young Readers, New York, NY, became senior editor; Carus Publishing, Chicago, IL, editorial director and vice president of nonfiction development, 2000-04; *Zooba.com,* managing editor, 2001-02; acquisition editor for Candlewick Press and for other publishing houses; writer. Instructor in publishing courses at New York University, Simmons College, and Radcliffe Publishing program.

AWARDS, HONORS: Publishers Weekly Best Book of the Year and *New York Times* Notable Book citations, both 1998, both for *Art Attack: A Short Cultural History of the Avant-Garde; Boston Globe-Horn Book* Award for nonfiction, 2000, Blue Ribbon Award, *Bulletin of the Center for Children's Books,* 2000, and Robert F. Sibert Award for "most distinguished informational book for children," American Library Association, 2001, all for *Sir Walter Ralegh and the Quest for El Dorado.*

WRITINGS:

NONFICTION

(With Thomas Leonard and Cynthia Crippen) *Day by Day: The Seventies,* two volumes, Facts on File (New York, NY), 1988.

(With Ellen Meltzer) *Day by Day: The Eighties,* two volumes, Facts on File (New York, NY), 1995.

Art Attack: A Short Cultural History of the Avant-Garde, Clarion Books (New York, NY), 1998.

Exploding the Myths: The Truth about Teenagers and Reading, Scarecrow Press (Lanham, MD), 2000.

Sir Walter Ralegh and the Quest for El Dorado, Clarion Books (New York, NY), 2000.

(Editor, with Michael Cart and Marianne Carus) *911: The Book of Help,* Cricket Books (Chicago, IL), 2002.

Beyond the Pale: New Essays for a New Era, Scarecrow Press (Lanham, MD), 2003.

Witch-Hunt: Mysteries of the Salem Witch Trials, Atheneum (New York, NY), 2003.

John Winthrop, Oliver Cromwell, and the Land of Promise, Clarion Books (New York, NY), 2004.

The Real Revolution: The Global Story of American Independence, Clarion Books (New York, NY), 2005.

Contributor to *The Holocaust in Literature for Youth,* edited by Edward T. Sullivan, Scarecrow Press (Lanham, MD), 1999. Contributor to periodicals, including *New York Times Book Review* and *Los Angeles Times Book Review.*

WORK IN PROGRESS: Prejudice: A History, for Atheneum, publication expected in 2006.

SIDELIGHTS: Marc Aronson writes nonfiction titles for young adults that have been praised for the author's engrossing prose style and unique approach to source materials. For example, in *Art Attack: A Short Cultural History of the Avant-Garde,* Aronson explains that throughout history avant-garde artists have challenged the world with their personal visions, and that young artists, even adolescents, have often taken the greatest risks to bring their art to the public. "What an exciting invitation to a brisk but rigorous survey that connects Marcel Duchamp, the Russian avant-garde and Mondrian to Charles Ives and the Sex Pistols!" observed a reviewer in the *New York Times Book Review.* Indeed, it is through such cross-cultural and cross-generic connections that *Art Attack* manages to offer fresh insights into the history of twentieth-century art despite its brevity, according to reviewers. Throughout the volume, art movements and the work of individual artists are explored in conjunction with the evolution of twentieth-century music. "In fact, what is unique and appealing in Aronson's cultural history is his placing of experimental and popular music within the art world," remarked Shirley Wilton in *School Library Journal.* Thus, Aronson juxtaposes the artwork of the Dadaists and rap music, Jean-Michel Basquiat's expressive scribbles and the jazz innovations of Philip Glass. The result is "an exceptional resource," Wilton concluded.

Aronson turned to the more distant past in *Sir Walter Ralegh and the Quest for El Dorado,* a work for which he was named the first winner of the Robert F. Sibert Award for the "most distinguished informational book for children published in 2000." Ralegh (as the man himself rendered his name) was both an exceptional figure, in his talents, ambition, and willingness to take large risks, and representative of his times, in that his talents, ambition, and willingness to take risks were all pointed towards exploring and conquering the New World. Ralegh's intelligence and drive took him from rural obscurity to courtier in Queen Elizabeth's court to fame and fortune through his journeys to South America. The resulting story of his life is an exciting tale. "Aronson not only details Ralegh's career as soldier, sailor, explorer, writer, and schemer but consistently discusses causes, effects, and the broader significance of events large and small," commented a reviewer for *Kirkus Reviews.* Aronson's skills as a writer of histories for young people were extolled by reviewers. Ilene Cooper, writing in *Booklist,* noted that at just over 200 pages, there is not space enough to discuss every topic presented by the multifaceted life of Sir Walter Ralegh, but added that "the book is beautifully researched, and it is written with wit and passion." A reviewer for the *Los Angeles Times* praised Aronson's portrait of Ralegh as "both provocative and tantalizing, revealing his subject as a person of canny wit and magnetism with all-too-human shortcomings." In conclusion, Cooper dubbed *Sir Walter Ralegh and the Quest for El Dorado* "sweeping, multilayered nonfiction."

Aronson's experience as a publisher, editor, and critic comes to the fore in *Exploding the Myths: The Truth about Teens and Reading,* a collection of his speeches and articles that touches on the development of young adult literature as well as its major controversies. In a review for *Booklist,* Hazel Rochman found the author's style "clear, chatty, and tough" while pointing out that Aronson "shows that teenagers today are often more open to challenge and diversity in narrative and format than their adult guardians are." *School Library Journal* contributor Vicki Reutter called *Exploding the Myths* a "thought-provoking collection [that] should be not missed." A related work, *Beyond the Pale: New Essays for a New Era,* "reveals the wider context of Aronson's particular concerns as a publisher, writer, and reader of young adult literature," wrote Cathryn M. Mercier in *Horn Book. Beyond the Pale* contains fourteen essays covering such topics as multicultural book prizes and the challenges of reaching teenage male readers. "This excellent book should be required reading for anyone who cares about young adults and their literature," stated Ellen A. Greever in *School Library Journal.*

In 2002 Aronson coedited *911: The Book of Help,* a "highly personal, often affecting roundup of essays, short stories, and poems inspired by the events of September 11th," according to a reviewer in *Publishers Weekly.* The contributors to *911* include award-winning children's and young adult authors such as Katherine Paterson, Walter Dean Myers, Sharon Creech, Naomi Shihab Nye, Margaret Mahy, Russell Freedman, and Marion Dane Bauer. "Some of the best essays put the attacks in historical or autobiographical perspective," Roger Sutton noted in *Horn Book.* Claire Rosser, reviewing the work in *Kliatt,* felt that *911* "would be an excellent resource for teachers of writing, helping students realize the power of words to educate, inspire, to express deepest feelings."

In *Witch-Hunt: Mysteries of the Salem Witch Trials,* Aronson examines the events surrounding the infamous series of trials in Massachusetts in 1692. In *Witch-Hunt,* Aronson dispels misinformation about the trials, and he looks at the contentious social, economic, and religious issues facing the Salem community. According to Andrew Medlar in *School Library Journal,* the author "actively encourages the rethinking of past notions of the events leading up to the accusations and hearings." A *Publishers Weekly* contributor stated that Aronson "uses primary source documents and trial records to help tease out the facts of the highly charged court atmosphere," and *Booklist* critic Stephanie Zvirin remarked that the author produces "a dense, wide-angle view of the tragedy that evaluates causative theories ranging from deceit and outright fraud to spoiled food that caused hallucinations." Aronson also draws parallels to the "counterculture of the 1960s, modern terrorism, and current tensions between western countries and Islamic fundamentalists," a *Kirkus Reviews* critic noted.

The 2004 work *John Winthrop, Oliver Cromwell, and the Land of Promise* "charts a parallel history between seventeenth-century Great Britain and colonial New England, as represented by emblematic figures Oliver Cromwell and John Winthrop," wrote *Horn Book* reviewer Peter D. Sieruta. Both Cromwell and Winthrop were influential Puritan leaders: Cromwell deposed King Charles I of England, and Winthrop served as the first governor of the Massachusetts Bay Colony. In the work, "Aronson shows how events of the 1630s and '40s have affected political thought ever since," noted a *Kirkus Reviews* critic. According to *Booklist* contributor GraceAnne A. DeCandido, Aronson illuminates "the reality of religious faith and the cataclysmic clash of beliefs that created fertile ground for ideas about democracy and equality."

BIOGRAPHICAL AND CRITICAL SOURCES:

PERIODICALS

Booklist, July, 1998, Stephanie Zvirin, review of *Art Attack: A Short Cultural History of the Avant-Garde;* August, 2000, Ilene Cooper, review of *Sir Walter Ralegh and the Quest for El Dorado,* p. 2130; March 15, 2001, Hazel Rochman, review of *Exploding the Myths: The Truth about Teenagers and Reading,* p. 1406; November 1, 2003, Stephanie Zvirin, review of *Witch-Hunt: Mysteries of the Salem Witch Trials,* p. 488; June 1, 2004, GraceAnne A. DeCandido, review of *John Winthrop, Oliver Cromwell, and the Land of Promise,* p. 1751.

Horn Book, September-October, 2000, Peter D. Sieruta, review of *Sir Walter Ralegh and the Quest for El Dorado,* p. 593; September-October, 2002, Roger Sutton, review of *911: The Book of Help,* pp. 593-594; January-February, 2004, Cathryn M. Mercier, review of *Beyond the Pale: New Essays for a New Era,* pp. 107-108; July-August, 2004, Peter D. Sieruta, review of *John Winthrop, Oliver Cromwell, and the Land of Promise,* p. 465.

Kirkus Reviews, May 15, 2000, review of *Sir Walter Ralegh and the Quest for El Dorado,* p. 710; July 1, 2002, review of *911,* p. 950; October 15, 2003, review of *Witch-Hunt,* p. 1268; May 1, 2004, review of *John Winthrop, Oliver Cromwell, and the Land of Promise,* p. 437.

Kliatt, November, 2002, Claire Rosser, review of *911,* p. 29.

Los Angeles Times, October 22, 2000, review of *Sir Walter Ralegh and the Quest for El Dorado,* p. 6.

New York Times Book Review, February 14, 1999, review of *Art Attack,* p. 26.

Publishers Weekly, August 27, 2001, Jason Britton, "Marcato/Cricket Books," p. 23; July 29, 2002, review of *911,* p. 74; December 1, 2003, review of *Witch-Hunt,* p. 58; May 24, 2004, "Understanding History," p. 64.

Reading Teacher, March, 2003, review of *911,* p. 589.

School Library Journal, June, 1995, Linda Diane Townsend, review of *Day by Day: The Eighties,* pp. 144-145; July, 1998, Shirley Wilton, review of *Art Attack,* p. 102; December, 2000, review of *Sir Walter Ralegh and the Quest for El Dorado,* p. 52; May, 2001, Vicki Reutter, review of *Exploding the Myths,* p. 179; September, 2002, Wendy Lukehart, "One Year Later," pp. 44-46, and Joanne K. Cecere, review of *911,* pp. 241-242; November, 2003, Ellen A. Greever, review of *Beyond the Pale,* p. 175; December, 2003, Andrew Medlar, review of *Witch-Hunt,* pp. 163; April, 2004, Wendy Lukehart, review of *Art Attack,* p. 64.

ONLINE

Marc Aronson Web site, http://www.marcaronson.com/ (August 19, 2004).

* * *

ASPRIN, Robert L(ynn) 1946-

PERSONAL: Born June 28, 1946, in St. John's, MI; son of Daniel D. (a machinist) and Lorraine (an elementary school teacher; maiden name, Coon) Asprin; married Anne Brett (a bookkeeper), December 28, 1968 (marriage ended); married Lynn Abbey (an editor); children: (first marriage) Annette Maria, Daniel Mather. *Education:* Attended University of Michigan, 1964-65.

ADDRESSES: Home—New Orleans, LA. *Agent*—c/o Author Mail, Ace Books, 200 Madison Ave., New York, NY 10016.

CAREER: University Microfilm, Ann Arbor, MI, accounts payable clerk, 1966-69, accounts receivable correspondent, 1969-70, payroll-labor analyst, 1970-74; junior cost accountant, 1974-76, cost accountant, 1976-78; freelance writer, 1978—. *Military service:* U.S. Army, 1965-66.

MEMBER: Science Fiction Writers of America.

AWARDS, HONORS: Hugo Award nomination, World Science Fiction Convention, 1976, for *The Capture; Locus* Award for editing, 1982.

WRITINGS:

SCIENCE FICTION NOVELS

The Cold Cash War, St. Martin's Press (New York, NY), 1977.

The Bug Wars, St. Martin's Press (New York, NY), 1979.

The Star Stalkers, Playboy Press (New York, NY), 1979.

(With George Takei) *Mirror Friend, Mirror Foe,* Playboy Press (New York, NY), 1979.

Tambu, Ace Books (New York, NY), 1979.

(With Lynn Abbey) *Act of God,* Ace Books (New York, NY), 1980.

(With Bill Fawcett) *Cold Cash Warrior: Combat Command in the World of Robert Asprin's Cold Cash War,* Ace Books (New York, NY), 1989.

Phule's Company, Ace Books (New York, NY), 1990.

Phule's Paradise, Ace Books (New York, NY), 1992.

(With Lynn Abbey) *Catwoman,* Warner (New York, NY), 1992, published as *Catwoman: Tiger Hunt,* Millennium (London, England), 1992.

(With Linda Evans) *Time Scout,* Baen Books (New York, NY), 1995.

Wagers of Sin, Baen Books (New York, NY), 1996.

(With Peter J. Heck) *A Phule and His Money,* Ace Books (New York, NY), 1999.

(With Linda Evans) *The House That Jack Built,* Baen Books (Riverdale, NY), 2001.

(With Peter J. Heck) *Phule Me Twice,* Ace Books (New York, NY), 2001.

(With Peter J. Heck) *No Phule Like an Old Phule,* Berkley Publishing (New York, NY), 2004.

FANTASY NOVELS

Another Fine Myth, Donning (Norfolk, VA), 1978, revised edition, illustrated by Phil Foglio, 1985.

Myth Conceptions, illustrated by Polly Freas and Kelly Freas, Donning (Norfolk, VA), 1980.

The Demon Blade, St. Martin's Press (New York, NY), 1980.

Myth Directions, illustrated by Phil Foglio, Donning (Norfolk, VA), 1982.

Hit or Myth, illustrated by Phil Foglio, Donning (Norfolk, VA), 1983.

Myth Adventures (includes *Another Fine Myth, Myth Directions,* and *Hit or Myth*), Doubleday (Garden City, NY), 1984.

Myth-ing Persons, illustrated by Phil Foglio, Donning (Norfolk, VA), 1984.

Little Myth Marker, illustrated by Phil Foglio, Donning (Norfolk, VA), 1985.

(With Kay Reynolds) *M.Y.T.H. Inc. Link,* illustrated by Phil Foglio, Donning (Norfolk, VA), 1986.

Myth Alliances (includes *Myth-ing Persons, Little Myth Marker,* and *M.Y.T.H. Inc. Link*), Doubleday (Garden City, NY), 1987.

Myth-Nomers and Im-Pervections, illustrated by Phil Foglio, Donning (Norfolk, VA), 1987.

M.Y.T.H. Inc. in Action, illustrated by Phil Foglio, Donning (Norfolk, VA), 1990.

The Myth-ing Omnibus (includes *Another Fine Myth, Myth Conceptions,* and *Myth Directions*), Legend (London, England), 1992.

The Second Myth-ing Omnibus (includes *Hit or Myth, Myth-ing Persons,* and *Little Myth Marker*), Legend (London, England), 1992.

Sweet Myth-tery of Life, illustrated by Phil Foglio, Donning (Norfolk, VA), 1994.

(With Linda Evans) *Ripping Time,* Baen Books (New York, NY), 2000.

(With Jody Lynn Nye) *License Invoked,* Baen Books (Riverdale, NY), 2001.

Myth-ion Improbable, Meisha Merlin Publishing (Atlanta, GA), 2001.

(With Linda Evans) *For King and Country,* Baen Books (Riverdale, NY), 2002.

Something M.Y.T.H. Inc., Ace Books (New York, NY), 2003.

GRAPHIC NOVELS

Myth Adventures One (previously published in magazine form), illustrated by Phil Foglio, Starblaze Graphics (Norfolk, VA), 1985.

Myth Adventures Two (previously published in magazine form), illustrated by Phil Foglio, Starblaze Graphics (Norfolk, VA), 1985.

(With Lynn Abbey) *Thieves' World Graphics,* six volumes, illustrated by Tim Sales, Starblaze Graphics (Norfolk, VA), 1985–87.

(With Mel White) *Duncan and Mallory,* Starblaze Graphics (Norfolk, VA), 1986.

(With Mel White) *Duncan and Mallory: The Bar-None Ranch,* Starblaze Graphics (Norfolk, VA), 1987.

(With Mel White) *Duncan and Mallory: The Raiders,* Starblaze Graphics (Norfolk, VA), 1988.

EDITOR

Thieves' World, Ace Books (New York, NY), 1979.

Tales from the Vulgar Unicorn, Ace Books (New York, NY), 1980.

Shadows of Sanctuary, Ace Books (New York, NY), 1981.

Sanctuary (includes *Thieves' World, Tales from the Vulgar Unicorn,* and *Shadows of Sanctuary*), Doubleday (Garden City, NY), 1982.

Storm Season, Ace Books (New York, NY), 1982.

(With Lynn Abbey) *The Face of Chaos,* Ace Books (New York, NY), 1983.

(With Lynn Abbey) *Wings of Omen,* Ace Books (New York, NY), 1984.

(With Lynn Abbey) *Birds of Prey,* Ace Books (New York, NY), 1984.

(With Lynn Abbey) *Cross-Currents* (includes *Storm Season, The Face of Chaos,* and *Wings of Omen*), Doubleday (Garden City, NY), 1984.

(With Lynn Abbey) *The Dead of Winter,* Ace Books (New York, NY), 1985.

(With Lynn Abbey) *Soul of the City,* Ace Books (New York, NY), 1986.

(With Lynn Abbey) *Blood Ties,* Ace Books (New York, NY), 1986.

(With Lynn Abbey) *The Shattered Sphere* (includes *The Dead of Winter, Soul of the City,* and *Blood Ties*), Doubleday (Garden City, NY), 1986.

(With Lynn Abbey and Richard Pini) *The Blood of Ten Chiefs,* Tor (New York, NY), 1986.

(With Lynn Abbey) *Aftermath,* Ace Books (New York, NY), 1987.

(With Lynn Abbey) *Uneasy Alliances,* Ace Books (New York, NY), 1988.

(With Lynn Abbey and Richard Pini) *Wolfsong: The Blood of Ten Chiefs,* Tor (New York, NY), 1988.

(With Lynn Abbey) *Stealers' Sky,* Ace Books (New York, NY), 1989.

(With Lynn Abbey) *The Price of Victory* (includes *Aftermath, Uneasy Alliances,* and *Stealers' Sky*), Doubleday (Garden City, NY), 1990.

(With Lynn Abbey) *Thieves' World: First Blood,* Tor (New York, NY), 2003.

OTHER

The Capture (script for comedy slide show), Boojums Press, 1975.

Tambu Anthology (science fiction short stories), Ace Books (New York, NY), 1980.

(With Esther Friesner) *E. Godz,* Baen Books (Riverdale, NY), 2003.

Myth Adventures Three, Meisha Merlin Publishing (Atlanta, GA), 2003.

Myth Adventures Four, Meisha Merlin Publishing (Atlanta, GA), 2003.

Asprin Wars, Meisha Merlin Publishing (Atlanta, GA), 2004.

Work represented in anthologies, including *Forever After,* Baen Books (New York, NY), 1995.

ADAPTATIONS: Several of Asprin's novels have been recorded on cassette tape.

SIDELIGHTS: Robert L. Asprin is known in the science fiction and fantasy genres for his humorous novels which parody genre conventions and for his editorship, with wife Lynn Abbey, of the "Thieves' World" anthologies. Writing in the *St. James Guide to Fantasy Writers,* Stan Nicholls explained that "Asprin can take some credit for helping to move humorous fantasy away from the short form in which it was more usually found and making it acceptable at novel length. Sales as large as his suggest a readership extending far beyond fantasy enthusiasts, so it would be fair to assume he has contributed to the process of bringing the [fantasy] sub-genre to general attention." Comparing his work to that of author L. Sprague de Camp, Richard A. Lupoff commented in the *St. James Guide to Science Fiction Writers* on the "typical Asprin characteristics of rapid pace, slapstick action, and broad humor."

The Cold Cash War was Asprin's first published novel. Drawing from his personal experience as a financial analyst, Asprin wove a futuristic tale about mega-corporations that wage bloodless "warfare" on each other using war-game simulations. Ignoring the efforts of actual governments to stop them, these moneyed superpowers eventually lose control of the game when real weapons enter the picture and the hits become lethal. Calling it a "very good treatment of a SF concept popular in the 50s," a *Publishers Weekly* reviewer praised *The Cold Cash War* for its "satire, action, and character."

Asprin's second novel, the fantasy *Another Fine Myth,* was inspired by such heroic characters as Kane and Conan the Barbarian. Basing his two main characters—an apprentice wizard named Skeeve (who also serves as narrator) and his shifty-eyed cohort, Aahz—on the relationship between Bob Hope and Bing Crosby in their classic screwball "Road" films of the 1940s, Asprin developed a winning duo whose antics have fueled an entire series of humorous "Myth" books. Dragons, demons, and an amazing assortment of fantastic ne'er-do-wells keep Asprin's fumbling heroes on their toes throughout the series. The lighthearted tone and steady barrage of puns, jokes, and bumbling antics have made the series a popular and entertaining read. "Asprin isn't trying to be profound," Tom Easton noted in a review of *Hit or Myth* in *Analog Science Fiction/Science Fact.* "He's having fun."

In his continuing effort to keep the job of writing fun, Asprin has strived to keep his subject matter from becoming stale. As he once noted, "My first three books are intentionally dissimilar. *The Cold Cash War* is speculative near-future fiction involving corporate takeover of world government. *Another Fine Myth* is a sword-and-sorcery farce full of dragons, stranded demons, and very bad puns. *The Bug Wars* does not have a human in the entire book. It was written 'first-person alien, reptile to be specific' and has been one of my greatest writing challenges to date."

In 1990 Asprin added a new hero to his catalogue of space adventurers in *Phule's Company.* Willard Phule is a captain in the Space Legion, but his devil-may-care attitude soon finds him exiled to a remote command, where he is put in charge of a rag-tag band of fellow miscreants. Undaunted, the savvy Phule eventually shapes his troops into a highly effective—and profitable—military outfit. "This lighthearted tale is part science fiction, part spoof, part heart-warmer," noted a *Publishers Weekly* critic.

Another novel leaning more toward science fiction than fantasy is Asprin's *Time Scout,* which he wrote with Linda Evans. Taking place in the near future, the novel features a world where time travel has become a common vacation pastime. Kit Carson, a retired "time scout"—one of the daring explorers who enter new passages through time in advance of the common folk—must train his headstrong granddaughter to survive as the first female time scout. Calling the novel "engaging, fast moving, historically literate," and reflective of Asprin's broad knowledge of the martial arts, *Booklist* reviewer Roland Green dubbed *Time Scout* "first-class action sf."

In addition to writing novels, Asprin has also collaborated with Lynn Abbey to edit the popular "Thieves' World" series. Called "the toughest, seamiest backwater in the realm of fantasy" by Carolyn Caywood in a review of *Soul of the City* in *Voice of Youth Advocates,* "Thieves' World" brings together a collection of original short fiction written by a host of predominantly women writers, including Abbey, Janet Morris, and C. J. Cherryh. Each book in the series centers around the ongoing struggle between the evil Queen Roxanne and her nemesis, a blood-sucking enchantress named Ischade. The continuing battle between these two powerful witches continues through such collections as *Soul of the City* and *Blood Ties,* each of which takes place in a mythic city called Sanctuary.

Asprin has characterized the overall message behind his writing as "the case for Everyman. Like all science fiction writers, I promote space travel and development. I feel, however, that we will never see it until the average guy on the street can see a place for himself in space. We will have to have the support of the common man, not just the scientists and test pilots. . .. We are going to need grease monkeys as well as computer programmers. Few people see themselves as Superman, and as long as science fiction writers portray space travelers in that light, the taxpayers and voters could not care less about getting off the planet."

BIOGRAPHICAL AND CRITICAL SOURCES:

BOOKS

St. James Guide to Fantasy Writers, St. James Press (Detroit, MI), 1996.

St. James Guide to Science Fiction Writers, 4th edition, St. James Press (Detroit, MI), 1996.

PERIODICALS

Analog Science Fiction-Science Fact, October, 1984, Tom Easton, review of *Hit or Myth,* p. 147; September, 1987, p. 163; February, 1991, p. 181.

Booklist, December 1, 1977, p. 598; January 15, 1984, p. 715; April 1, 1986, p. 1120; March 15, 1987, p. 1097; June 15, 1990, p. 1960; January 15, 1992, pp. 915, 921; January 15, 1995, p. 689; December 15, 1995, Roland Green, review of *Time Scout,* p. 689; October 22, 2001, review of *Myth-ion Improbable,* p. 54.

Library Journal, November 1, 1977, p. 2279; January 15, 1980, p. 228.

Locus, March, 2001, review of *License Invoked,* p. 33.

Publishers Weekly, July 11, 1977, review of *The Cold Cash War,* p. 75; June 8, 1990, review of *Phule's Company,* p. 50; January 20, 1992, p. 60; August 5, 2002, review of *For King and Country,* p. 57.

School Library Journal, March, 1980, Claudia Morner, review of *Tambu,* p. 146.

Science Fiction Chronicle, April, 2001, review of *License Invoked,* p. 38; April, 2001, review of *The House That Jack Built,* p. 39.

Voice of Youth Advocates, April, 1981, p. 52; June, 1986, Carolyn Caywood, review of *Soul of the City,* p. 84; February, 1987, p. 290; December, 1987, p. 241.*

* * *

AYMÉ, Marcel (Andre) 1902-1967

PERSONAL: Born March 28 (some sources cite March 29), 1902, in Joigny, France; died of pneumonia, October 14, 1967, in Paris, France; son of a blacksmith; married Marie-Antoinette Arnaud, 1932; children: one daughter. *Education:* Studied medicine for one year.

CAREER: Novelist; author of short stories; playwright. Worked as bank clerk, insurance broker, movie extra, bricklayer, crime reporter, sales representative, export firm employee, and accountant in the Paris bourse. *Military service:* French Army, 1922-23.

AWARDS, HONORS: Théophraste Renaudot prize, 1929, for *La table-aux-crevés.*

WRITINGS:

NOVELS

Brulebôis, Poitiers, 1926.

Aller retour, Gallimard (Paris, France), 1927.

Les jumeaux du diable, 1928.

La table-aux-crevés, Gallimard (Paris, France), 1929, translation by Helen Waddell published as *The Hollow Field,* Dodd, Mead (New York, NY), 1933.

La rue sans nom, Gallimard (Paris, France), 1930.

Le vaurien, Gallimard (Paris, France), 1931.

La jument verte, Gallimard (Paris, France), 1933, translation by Norman Denny published as *The Green Mare,* Harper (New York, NY), 1955.

Le mauvais jars, Gallimard (Paris, France), 1935.

L'elephant, Gallimard (Paris, France), 1935.

Maison basse, Gallimard (Paris, France), 1935, translation published as *The House of Men,* 1952.

Lee moulin de la Sourdine, Gallimard (Paris, France), 1936, translation by Norman Denny published as *The Secret Stream,* Harper (New York, NY), 1953.

Gustalin, Gallimard (Paris, France), 1937.

Silhouette du scandale, Editions du Sagittaire (Marseilles, France), 1938.

Le boeuf clandestin, Gallimard (Paris, France), 1939.

La belle image, Gallimard (Paris, France), 1941, translation by Norman Denny published as *The Second Face,* Bodley Head (London, England), 1951, Harper (New York, NY), 1952, published as *The Grand Seduction,* 1958.

La vouivre, 1943, translation by Eric Sutton published as *The Fable and the Flesh,* Mayflower (Washington, DC), 1965.

Travelingue, Gallimard (Paris, France), 1943, translation by Eric Sutton published as *The Miraculous Barber,* Bodley Head (London, England), 1950, Harper (New York, NY), 1951.

Le chemin des écoliers, Gallimard (Paris, France), 1946, translation by Eric Sutton published as *The Transient Hour,* A. A. Wyn (New York, NY), 1948.

Uranus, Gallimard (Paris, France), 1948, translation by Norman Denny published as *The Barkeep of Blémont,* Harper (New York, NY), 1950, also published as *Fanfare in Blémont,* 1950.

L'hopital, illustrated by Rio, Amio-Dumont, Gallimard (Paris, France), 1951.

Romans de la province, illustrated by Pierre Berger, Gallimard (Paris, France), 1956.

Romans Parisiens, suivi d'Uranus (also see *Uranus* above), watercolors by Gen Paul, Gallimard (Paris, France), 1959.

Lucienne et le boucher, Le Club francais du livre, 1959.

Les tiroirs de l'inconnu, [France], 1960, translation by Norman Denny published as *The Conscience of Love,* Atheneum (New York, NY), 1962.

Oscar et Erik, illustrated by Jacques Carelman, Gautier-Languereau (Paris, France), 1961.

Enjambées, illustrated by Giani Esposito, Gallimard (Paris, France), 1967.

Istres historique dans son cadre provencal, Istres touristique, son folklore, illustrated by P. Fievet and E. Aquaron, Imprimerie Mistral, 1968.

SHORT STORY COLLECTIONS

Le puits aux images (title means "Pictures in the Well"), Gallimard (Paris, France), 1932.

Le nain, Gallimard (Paris, France), 1934.

Derrière chez Martin, Livre de poche (Paris, France), 1938.

Le passe-muraille, Gallimard (Paris, France), 1943, translation by Norman Denny published as *The Walker through Walls, and Other Stories* (contains "The Walker through Walls," "The Retreat from Moscow," "A Roll of Daughters," "Rue dell'Evangele" [also published in *Derrière Chez Martin*; see below], "The State of Grace," "The Proverb," "Legend of Poldevia," "The Walking Stick," "Couldn't Care Less," "The Wine of Paris," "Martin the Novelist," "The Seven League Books," "Josse" [also published in *Enamere: nouvelles*; see below], "The Life-Ration," and "The Last"), Bodley Head (London, England), 1972.

Le vin de Paris, Gallimard (Paris, France), 1947.

Les chiens, illustrated by Nathalie Parain, Gallimard (Paris, France), 1948.

En arrière; nouvelles, 1950.

Soties de la ville et des champs, Club des libraires de France (Paris, France), 1958.

Contes choisis, original copper plates by Gaston Barret, Cercle Grolier (Paris, France), 1961.

The Proverb and Other Stories, 1961.

Les meilleures nouvelles de Marcel Aymé, edited by James H. Baltzell, Scribner (New York, NY), 1964.

La fille du shérif; nouvelles, edited by Michel Lécureur, 1987.

Oeuvres romanesques complètes, Volume 3 (contains *La belle image, Travelingue, Le passe-muraille, Le chemin des écoliers, Le vin de Paris, Uranus, En arrière, Les tiroirs de l'inconnu,* and other selections), edited by Michel Lécureur, Gallimard (Paris, France), 2001.

Nouvelles complètes: Nouvelles et contes (includes *Le puits aux images, Le nain, Derrière chez Martin, Le passe-muraille, Le vin de Paris, En arrière, Les contes du chat perché,* and other works), illustrated by Nathan Altman, Madeleine Parry, and Nathalie Parain, Gallimard (Paris, France), 2002.

PLAYS

Vogue la galère (title means "Here Goes"), B. Grasset (Paris, France), 1944.

Lucienne et le boucher, 1947.

Clérambard (four-act), B. Grasset (Paris, France), 1950, translated by Norman Denny (produced in Paris, France, 1950; produced off-Broadway, 1957), prepared for stage by Leo Kerz and Alvin Sapinskley, Samuel French (New York, NY), 1958.

La tête des autres, produced in 1952.

Les quatres vérités (title means "Home Truths"), B. Grasset (Paris, France), 1954.

Les sorcières de Salem (adapted from *The Crucible* by Arthur Miller), [Paris, France], 1955.

Les oiseaux de la lune (four-act), Gallimard (Paris, France), 1956, translation by John Parker published as *Moonbirds,* Hart Stenographic Bureau (New York, NY), 1959.

La mouche bleue (four-act; title means "The Blue Fly"), 1957.

Desert vivant (screenplay; adaptation of *Living Desert*), Walt Disney Productions, 1957.

Vu du pont (adaptation of play by Arthur Miller), 1958.

Louisiane (four-act), Gallimard (Paris, France), 1961.

Les maxibules, Gallimard (Paris, France), 1962.

La nuit de l'iguane (adaptation of play by Tennessee Williams), 1962.

Le minotaure, La convention belzébir [and] Consommation (three plays; *La convention belzébir* produced in Paris, France, 1966; *Le minotaure* produced in 1966), Gallimard (Paris, France), 1967.

Also author of the screenplays *Papa, Mama, the Maid and Me* and *La jument verte* (adaptation of his original novel).

FOR CHILDREN

Les contes du chat perché (short stories), illustrated by N. Altman, 1934, translation by Norman Denny published as *The Wonderful Farm,* illustrated by Maurice Sendak, Harper (New York, NY), 1951.

Autres contes du chat perché, illustrated by Nathalie Parain, 1950, translation by Norman Denny published as *The Magic Pictures: More about the Wonderful Farm,* illustrated by Maurice Sendak, Harper (New York, NY), 1954.

(With Antoine Blondin and Jean-Paul Clébert) *Paris que j'aime,* 1956, translation (with Patrice Moulard) published as *The Paris I Love,* Tudor, 1956.

Derniers contes du chat perché, illustrated by Lesly Queneau, 1958.

Across Paris, and Other Stories, translated by Norman Denny, 1961.

Les contes bleus du chat perché, 1975.

OTHER

Silhouette du scandale (essays), Editions du Sagittaire (Marseilles, France), 1938.

Le trou de la serrure (essays), 1946.

Images de l'amour (essays), 1946, G. Guillot, 1957.

Le confort intellectuel (essays), Flammarion (Paris, France), 1949.

Marcel Leprin . . . Exhibition, Vestart, 1970.

Lettres d'une vie (correspondence), edited by Michel Lécureur and Christiane Lécureur, Archimbaud (Paris, France), 2001.

Author of the booklet "L'epuration et le delit d'opinion," preface by Lucien Rebalet, Editions dynamo (Liege, Belgium), 1968.

ADAPTATIONS: Le passe-muraille was translated by Jeremy Sams and adapted for the stage in a musical written by Michel Legrand, called *Amour.* The play opened at the Music Box Theater in New York, NY, in the fall of 2002.

SIDELIGHTS: Marcel Aymé was a prolific and respected French novelist, but as a man who sincerely enjoyed his vocation and life in general, the unpretentious Aymé shunned public recognition for his writings, deeming such accolades unnecessary. Members of the prestigious Academie Française sought to rank Aymé among them, but he refused even that highly coveted honor.

As he was growing up Aymé detested formal education. "I had a horror of school," he once admitted, "and even today in my most horrible nightmares, I dream that I am in the classroom." As a result, Aymé learned much on his own. At sixteen he discovered the earthy poetry of François Villon and the realistic novels of Honoré de Balzac, both of which later influenced his own writing. He eventually enrolled in medical school, but, after a year, dropped out.

Subsequently Aymé worked at a variety of jobs in Paris before finding his metier as an author. His colorful early stories take place in the country, reflecting his own provincial Franche-Comte background. Later Aymé wrote more acerbic satires of the Parisian bourgeoisie.

An astute observer of human foibles, Aymé often spoke through the mouths of children or animals, as in his novels *La jument verte* and *Gustalin.* Siding with the peasantry in *Gustalin,* Aymé illustrates how the malignant values of city mice disrupt a quiet community of country mice. However, while Aymé introduced supernatural elements in his work, he did so in a realistic manner. As Germaine Bree and Margaret Guiton noted in *An Age of Fiction,* "the supernatural" in Aymé's work "has none of the dreamlike, otherworldly qualities of the surrealists but is firmly planted in the terrestrial logic of everyday events."

Published in 1933, *La jument verte* is among Aymé's most important and popular works; after he received an international audience for this novel, he devoted himself to full-time writing. The story satirizes the hypocrisy, corruption, and mock heroism of two feuding families in the small town of Claquebue. Their interactions are observed by a green horse figure whose presence in a wall painting offers privy access to all perspectives of local events. Dorothy Brodin wrote in the *Dictionary of Literary Biography,* "This bawdy Rabelaisian tale pictures the life and politics of a village where personal, social, and partisan conflicts take on epic proportions." The mare's asides, or "propos de la jument," complement the action as a sort of Greek chorus.

Compared to *La jument verte, La vouivre* also describes divisive village politics and competing clans. In this novel, the title character is a beautiful forest divinity who wanders about the region accompanied by her snakes and seduces a young peasant who denies the supernatural. David O'Connell noted in the *Reference Guide to World Literature* that Aymé's novels "use local linguistic terms and exploit regional folklore, including the marvelous and fantastic, to put across Aymé's essentially moderate conservative, commonsense view of life. *La vouivre* is perhaps the best novel in this mode."

While his popularity flourished, Aymé's indiscriminate and thinly veiled attacks on both the political left and right caused him trouble during the turbulent 1930s and 1940s. *Travelingue* is set against the background of the Popular Front era in France. Revealing Aymé's interest in motion pictures, the original title refers to the cinematic technique in which a camera moves along with the action on a track or dolly during filming. In this novel, Aymé satirizes the mesmerizing influence of film on young people and the ridiculous philosophical pronouncements of the ill-informed, particularly those of a barber whose empty declamations win him undue honor and deference as a local dignitary.

Aymé's mordant wit is also in evidence in *Uranus,* which describes French society shortly after the German Occupation. Hailed as "a mirror of modern hypocrisy," according to Brodin in *Marcel Aymé, Uranus* reveals ubiquitous vice among the political and social leaders who succeeded the Nazis in France, including Communists and former Resistance members. According to O'Connell, the novel "lays bare the hypocrisy of successive governments of both Left and Right for the first forty years of the century and is a masterpiece of understatement."

Because of his affection for life as it really is, Aymé applauded those who follow their natural inclinations. He deplored hypocrisy and any form of escapism using these and other human vices as targets for his satire. It was in his allegorical short stories, written for children as well as adults, that Aymé lampooned social "stratification, preconceived ideas, cliches, and pomposity of men engaged in the posture of social relations," wrote Brodin in *Marcel Aymé.*

Aymé's best-known short stories are contained in *Les contes du chat perché* and *Autres contes du chat perché,* a sequel. Written for Aymé's granddaughter,

Françoise, the stories in these volumes display the author's ability to merge fantasy with straightforward observation to produce incisive commentary on human affairs. Though regarded as fiction for children and compared to the work of La Fontaine and Lewis Carroll, these works may also be read as deadly serious moral and sociopolitical allegories for adults. The stories recount the adventures of two French sisters, Marinette and Delphine, and their interactions with various barnyard and forest animals who speak with the girls and act out the vices and virtues of humans.

Mark J. Temmer wrote in the *French Review,* "Invested with a goodness and mischievousness abstracted from real life, these little girls have no personal history and yet they live, representative of girlhood in particular and mankind in general. . . . There is a breath of fresh air in these stories which relate the girl's adventures with fox and hens in the timeless setting of a French farm. Our fantasy is freed, and our belief and trust in the pleasures of childhood are once more justified." As Brodin concluded in the *Dictionary of Literary Biography,* "These tales are an excellent example of Aymé's humor as well as a summary of his tolerant and compassionate attitude toward people."

For the latter part of his career, Aymé focused most of his creative energies on writing plays. He became recognized as a playwright in 1950 when *Clérambard* became the biggest success of the year in Paris. The play is about a worldly aristocrat, Clérambard, who is suffering from financial problems. To help defray his family's living expenses, the protagonist forces each member to make and peddle woven goods. When St. Francis appears to Clérambard, the latter forgets such secular pursuits as money making and soon after devotes himself to converting the villagers to Christianity. He has just managed to convert some stubborn neighbors when St. Francis again appears, this time to everyone in the village except the local priest. Clérambard and his family then take to the road as evangelists.

Two years later Aymé produced *La tête des autres,* viewed as among his most caustic works. This play depicts the trial of an accused murderer as a sporting event in which competing lawyers vie for the life of the defendant as if it were a personal trophy. *La tête des autres* "provoked violent reactions," according to Brodin in the *Dictionary of Literary Biography.* "It is one of the most vitriolic of his works, a satire of the legal profession and of what passes for justice in a society motivated by greed, ruthless struggles for power, and insensitivity to the rights and feelings of individuals." Aymé followed with *La mouche bleue,* a biting commentary on the banality and humorlessness of American life.

For the humor and irony displayed in his novels, plays, and short stories alike, Aymé has been compared to Voltaire, Anatole France, and Molière. But he was an individualist who did not really fall into any particular school of writing. Aymé "wrote in absolute freedom exactly what he wished to write," remarked Brodin. He "appeals to readers of all kinds because of his vivid and unusual style, his extraordinary ability to put words through their paces, and especially because of the fresh and unexpected quality of his vision."

BIOGRAPHICAL AND CRITICAL SOURCES:

BOOKS

Bree, Germaine, and Margaret Guiton, *An Age of Fiction: The French Novel from Gide to Camus,* Rutgers University Press (New Brunswick, NJ), 1957.

Brodin, Dorothy R., *The Comic World of Marcel Aymé,* Debresse, 1964.

Brodin, Dorothy R., *Marcel Aymé,* Columbia University Press (New York, NY), 1968.

Children's Literature Review, Volume 25, Thomson Gale (Detroit, MI), 1991.

Contemporary Literary Criticism, Volume 11, Thomson Gale (Detroit, MI), 1979.

Dictionary of Literary Biography, Volume 72: *French Novelists, 1930-1960,* Thomson Gale (Detroit, MI), 1988.

Lécureur, Michel, *Album Marcel Aymé,* Gallimard (Paris, France), 2002.

Lord, Graham, *Marcel Aymé,* Peter Lang (New York, NY), 1987.

Reference Guide to Short Fiction, St. James Press (Detroit, MI), 1994.

Reference Guide to World Literature, 2nd edition, Volume 1, St. James Press (Detroit, MI), 1995.

Something about the Author, Volume 91, Thomson Gale (Detroit, MI), 1997.

PERIODICALS

Atlantic, April 23, 1951; April 14, 1952; February 8, 1954; February 2, 1959; April 21, 1961; May 4, 1962.

Books, April 9, 1933.

Commonweal, May 11, 1956.

French Review, April, 1962, review by Mark J. Temmer, pp. 453-462.

Modern Language Review, July, 2000, Christopher Lloyd, review of *Oeuvres romanesques complètes,* p. 845.

Nation, April 28, 1956.

New Republic, June 26, 1950; August 20, 1951.

New Statesman & Society, February 18, 1933; June 4, 1955.

Newsweek, October 30, 1967.

New Yorker, April 3, 1948; June 17, 1950; December 1, 1951; January 30, 1954; March 31, 1956; April 29, 1961.

New York Herald Book Review, May 6, 1951; February 7, 1954; July 8, 1955; April 1, 1956; January 25, 1959.

New York Times, April 9, 1933; March 28, 1948; May 15, 1950; April 22, 1951; November 11, 1951; April 13, 1952; February 7, 1954; April 1, 1956; January 25, 1959; April 30, 1961; October 15, 1967.

New York Times Book Review, April 30, 1961; March 25, 1962.

Saturday Review of Literature, April 17, 1948; May 15, 1950; April 21, 1951; April 19, 1952; February 6, 1954; January 24, 1959; July 22, 1961; April 7, 1962.

Time, April 23, 1951; April 14, 1952; February 8, 1954; February 2, 1959; April 21, 1961; May 4, 1962.

Times Literary Supplement, February 16, 1933; December 18, 1948; October 26, 1951; March 6, 1953; June 10, 1988, p. 642; October 15, 1999, Nicholas Hewitt and Michel Lécureur, review of *Oeuvres romanesques complètes,* Volume 2, p. 6; February 8, 2002, David Coward, review of *Oeuvres romanesques complètes,* Volume 3, p. 3.

World Literature Today, autumn, 1988, p. 621.*

B

BACON, Mark S. 1948-

PERSONAL: Born June 1, 1948, in Germany; son of Cole (an electrical engineer) and Jeanne (a homemaker) Bacon; married first wife, 1971; wife's name Elizabeth (marriage ended, 1980); married Anne Clark (a bank executive), May 29, 1982. *Ethnicity:* "English and Norwegian heritage." *Education:* Fresno State College (now California State University—Fresno), B.A., 1970; attended University of California—Irvine; University of Nevada—Las Vegas, M.A., 1993. *Hobbies and other interests:* Hiking, cycling, reading, travel.

ADDRESSES: Office—Department of Communication, California Polytechnic University, Pomona, CA 91768. *Agent*—David Fugate, Waterside Productions, Cardiff, CA.

CAREER: Ledger Newspapers, Montrose, CA, staff writer and reporter, 1971-73; Knott's Berry Farm, Buena Park, CA, copywriter, 1973-74; Jack Lawlor Advertising, Los Angeles, CA, copywriter, 1974-75; California Credit Union League, Pomona, public relations manager, 1975-81; Orange County Federal, Santa Ana, CA, director of marketing, 1981-83; Bacon and Co. Corporate Communications, Yucaipa, CA, writer, seminar leader, and communications consultant, 1983—. Fullerton College, instructor, 1987-91; University of Nevada—Las Vegas, instructor, 1993-95; Community College of Southern Nevada, instructor, 1995; California Polytechnic University, instructor and adviser, 1995—. Tuson Trails Homeowners Association, member of board of directors, 1993-95; American Cancer Society of Southern Nevada, volunteer trainer, 1993-95.

MEMBER: International Association of Business Communicators (past vice president of Las Vegas chapter; past president of Orange County chapter), Direct Marketing Club of Southern California.

AWARDS, HONORS: Do-It-Yourself Direct Marketing: Secrets for Small Business was named a "best business book of the year" by *Library Journal.*

WRITINGS:

Write Like the Pros: Using the Secrets of Ad Writers and Journalists in Business (Book-of-the-Month Club selection), Wiley (New York, NY), 1987.

Do-It-Yourself Direct Marketing: Secrets for Small Business (Book-of-the-Month Club selection), Wiley (New York, NY), 1992, 2nd edition, 1994.

The California Escape Manual: Your Guide to Finding A New Hometown, Archer & Clark Publishing (Redlands, CA) 1998.

Contributor of several hundred articles to magazines and newspapers, including *Newspaper Research Journal, USAir, Working Woman, Orange Coast,* and *Seventeen.*

WORK IN PROGRESS: Revising *Do-It-Yourself Direct Marketing;* a book on escaping city life for the country; a mystery novel.

SIDELIGHTS: Mark S. Bacon once told *CA:* "I was a journalism major in the 1960s. As I had always been interested in all forms of writing, I took a class in fiction writing. The instructor was novelist Nathan Heard, author of *Howard Street.* In one of the first classes, he went around the room and asked students why they wrote. When he heard my answer, which differed from the others, he said, 'You will be a writer.' My reason for writing then is the same as it is now: I write because I have to.

"In general, my book ideas come from questions for which I cannot find the answers. My book on business writing grew out of the notion that business people should be taught the shortcuts of journalists and copywriters. No one had done a book on that subject. When I looked for a book on direct marketing for small business, I found none and wrote one. My present projects come from similar sources. I have little interest in writing books similar to those written by others.

"I am hoping to publish a mystery novel. My detectives are different from any others—I am not sure yet if this will be a strength or weakness—and the setting and plot create a story I would like to read.

"When I am doing a book, I concentrate on it almost to the exclusion of everything else. I drive myself, finding satisfaction in a good paragraph, page, and chapter. I revise constantly as I write, then print it out and edit in pencil. I repeat the last two steps as many times as necessary."

BIOGRAPHICAL AND CRITICAL SOURCES:

PERIODICALS

Library Journal, December, 1997, Joseph L. Carlson, review of *The California Escape Manual: Your Guide to Finding a New Hometown,* p. 130.*

* * *

BAKER, Russell (Wayne) 1925-

PERSONAL: Born August 14, 1925, in Loudoun County, VA; son of Benjamin Rex (a stonemason) and Lucy Elizabeth (a schoolteacher; maiden name, Robinson) Baker; married Miriam Emily Nash, March 11, 1950; children: Kathleen Leland, Allen Nash, Michael Lee. *Education:* Johns Hopkins University, B.A., 1947.

Russell Baker

ADDRESSES: Office—c/o New York Times, 229 W. 43rd St., New York, NY 10036.

CAREER: Sun, Baltimore, MD, member of staff, 1947-53, London bureau chief, 1953-54; *New York Times,* member of Washington, DC, bureau, 1954-62, author of nationally syndicated "Observer" column for the *New York Times,* 1962—. Host of PBS television series "Masterpiece Theatre," 1993—. *Military service:* U.S. Naval Reserve, 1943-45.

MEMBER: American Academy and Institute of Arts and Letters (elected, 1984); American Academy of Arts and Sciences (fellow).

AWARDS, HONORS: Frank Sullivan Memorial Award, 1976; George Polk Award, 1979, for commentary; Pulitzer Prize, 1979, for distinguished commentary (in "Observer" column), and 1983, for *Growing Up;* Elmer Holmes Bobst prize, 1983, for nonfiction; American Academy and Institute of Arts and Letters,

1984; Howland Memorial Prize, Yale University, and Fourth Estate Award, National Press Club, all 1989; H.L.D., Hamilton College, Princeton University, Johns Hopkins University, Franklin Pierce College, Yale University, Long Island University, and Connecticut College; LL.D., Union College; D.Litt, Wake Forest University, University of Miami, Rutgers University, Columbia University; H.H.D., Hood College.

WRITINGS:

COLLECTIONS

No Cause for Panic, Lippincott (Philadelphia, PA), 1964.

Baker's Dozen, New York Times (New York, NY), 1964.

All Things Considered, Lippincott (Philadelphia, PA), 1965.

Poor Russell's Almanac, Doubleday (New York, NY), 1972.

So This Is Depravity, Congdon & Lattes (New York, NY), 1980.

The Rescue of Miss Yaskell and Other Pipe Dreams, Congdon & Weed (New York, NY), 1983.

AUTOBIOGRAPHY

Growing Up, Congdon & Weed (New York, NY), 1982.

The Good Times, Morrow (New York, NY), 1989.

Looking Back, New York Review of Books (New York, NY), 2002.

OTHER

(Author of text) *Washington: City on the Potomac,* Arts, 1958.

An American in Washington, Knopf (New York, NY), 1961.

Our Next President: The Incredible Story of What Happened in the 1968 Elections (fiction), Atheneum (New York, NY), 1968.

The Upside-Down Man (children's book), McGraw-Hill (New York, NY), 1977.

(Editor) *The Norton Book of Light Verse,* Norton (New York, NY), 1986.

There's a Country in My Cellar, Morrow, 1990.

(Editor) *Russell Baker's Book of American Humor,* Norton (New York, NY), 1993.

(With William Knowlton Zinsser) *Inventing the Truth: The Art and Craft of Memoir,* Houghton Mifflin (Boston, MA), 1995.

Also coauthor of musical play *Home Again,* 1979. Contributor to books, including John Brannon Albright, *Better Times,* Dolphin Books, 1975. Contributor to periodicals, including *Saturday Evening Post, New York Times Magazine, Sports Illustrated, Ladie's Home Journal, Holiday, Theatre Arts, Mademoiselle, Life, Look,* and *McCall's.*

ADAPTATIONS: One of Baker's columns, "How to Hypnotize Yourself into Forgetting the Vietnam War," was dramatized and filmed by Eli Wallach for *The Great American Dream Machine,* PBS, 1971.

SIDELIGHTS: Noted humorist Russell Baker has charmed readers for years with his witty, literate observations of the foibles and follies of contemporary life. Baker began his career as a journalist for the Baltimore *Sun* and the *New York Times,* where he enjoyed a reputation as a skilled reporter and astute political commentator. The author is perhaps best known for his "Observer" column, which has appeared in the *New York Times* since 1962 and in syndication in hundreds of other papers across the country. Regarded by *Washington Post Book World* critic Robert Sherrill as "the supreme satirist" of the late twentieth century, Baker has been credited with taking newspaper humor and turning it into "literature—funny, but full of the pain and absurdity of the age," according to *Time*'s John Skow.

Armed with a sense of humor described by *Washington Post* writer Jim Naughton as "quick, dry, and accessibly cerebral," Baker has taken aim at a wide range of targets, including the presidency, the national economy, and the military. In one "Observer" column, Baker spoofed the government's MX-missile plan, a proposal to transport nuclear weapons around the country using the nation's railroads. Baker took the idea even further by proposing the MX-Pentagon plan, a system of mobile Pentagon replicas, complete with a phony president and secretary of defense, that would criss-cross the United States and confuse the nation's enemies. In another essay, Baker suggested that the reason Congress voted against a bill requiring truth-in-advertising labels on defective used cars was the politicians' fear that the same fate would someday befall them: "Put yourself in your Congressman's shoes. One of these days he is going to be put out of office. Defeated, old, tired, 120,000 miles on his smile and two pistons cracked in his best joke. They're going to put him out on the used-Congressman lot. Does he want to have a sticker on him stating that he gets only eight miles on a gallon of bourbon? That his rip-roaring anti-Communist speech hasn't had an overhaul since 1969? That his generator is so decomposed it hasn't sparked a fresh thought in fifteen years?"

Though many of Baker's columns concern themselves with the dealings of pompous politicians and the muddled antics of government bureaucrats, not all of the author's essays are political in nature. All manner of human excesses, fads, and trendy behavior have come under Baker's scrutiny; among the topics he has satirized are Super Bowl Sunday, the Miss America pageant, and television commercials. Other selections have touched on the author's anger over the physical and moral decay of urban America. In "Such Nice People," Baker examines fellow New Yorkers' reactions to the deterioration of their city, finding a thin veneer of civility masking a barely suppressed rage. "In a city like this," he wrote, "our self-control must be tight. Very tight. So we are gentle. Civilized. Quivering with self-control. So often so close to murder, but always so self-controlled. And gentle." *Spectator* critic Joe Mysak applauded this type of essay, judging its significance to be "closer to the grain of American life" than Baker's politically tinged writings, and columns of this sort moved Sherrill to write that, "when it comes to satire of a controlled but effervescent ferocity, nobody can touch Baker." In addition to having his column appear in newspapers, Baker has published several compilations of selected "Observer" columns.

Baker has also written a fictional story of the 1968 presidential election, *Our Next President,* as well as a children's book, *The Upside-Down Man.* In *Russell Baker's Book of American Humor,* published in 1993, Baker presents a collection of humorous literary pieces, both fiction and nonfiction, from the past 200 years. The book includes one-line snippets as well as poems, short stories, and excerpts from longer essays from the likes of Mark Twain, Garrison Keillor, Mae West, Tom Wolfe, Fran Lebowitz, Abraham Lincoln, Annie Szymanski, and P. J. O'Rourke, among others. Christopher Buckley, writing in the *New York Times Book Review,* called the collection "mostly funny . . . generous and big-hearted," while *Washington Post Book World* contributor Burling Lowrey remarked that the pieces in the book "prove the validity of two familiar axioms: (1) We should always treat light things seriously and serious things lightly; and (2) All first-rate humor is subversive." Baker has also edited *The Norton Book of Light Verse* and coauthored *Inventing the Truth: The Art and Craft of Memoir.*

Along with his writings in the "Observer" and his other humorous literary endeavors, Baker is known for his memoirs, *Growing Up* and *The Good Times.* The former chronicles Baker's adventures as a youngster in Depression-era Virginia, New Jersey, and Baltimore, while the latter recounts his career as a journalist, from his early work on the crime beat at the Baltimore *Sun* to his days as a Washington correspondent with the *New York Times.* Both books earned critical and popular acclaim for their gentle humor and warm, retrospective narratives.

Described by Mary Lee Settle in the *Los Angeles Times Book Review* as "a wondrous book, funny, sad, and strong," *Growing Up* explores the often difficult circumstances of Baker's childhood with a mix of humor and sadness. His father, a gentle, blue-collar laborer fond of alcohol, died in an "acute diabetic coma" when Baker was five. Baker's mother, Lucy Elizabeth, suddenly widowed and impoverished, accepted her brother's offer to live with his family in New Jersey. Before moving, Lucy left her youngest daughter, Audrey, in the care of wealthier relatives who could provide the infant with a more comfortable existence than she. In *Growing Up,* Baker bore witness to his mother's pain and ambivalence over the decision: "It was the only deed of her entire life for which I ever heard her express guilt. Years later, in her old age, she was still saying, 'Maybe I made a terrible mistake when I gave up Audrey.'"

The family lived off the kindness of relatives for years, finally settling in Baltimore, where Lucy eventually remarried. Baker got his first taste of journalistic life at a young age when, at his mother's insistence, he began selling copies of the *Saturday Evening Post.* Lucy exerted a strong influence over Baker's life, serving as "goad, critic, and inspiration to her son," in the words of *New York Times Book Review* critic Ward Just. The loving but tempestuous relationship that existed between mother and son threaded its way through the work, so that *Growing Up* becomes as much the mother's story as the son's. Baker portrays Lucy as a driven woman, haunted by her life of poverty and obsessed with the idea that her son would achieve success. "I would make something of myself," Baker wrote in *Growing Up,* "and if I lacked the grit to do it, well then she would make me make something of myself." *Spectator* critic Peter Paterson saw the work as "a tribute" to the women in Baker's life, first and foremost to Lucy, "who dominates the book as she dominated her son's existence."

Baker's fully drawn portraits of his mother and other relatives were a result of his extensive research efforts. To gather information for his book, Baker interviewed dozens of family members, collecting a trove of facts about historical America in the process. In a *Washington Post* interview, the writer once said, "I was writing about a world that seemed to have existed 200 years ago. I had one foot back there in this primitive countrylife where women did the laundry running their knuckles on scrub boards and heated irons on coal stoves. That was an America that was completely dead." In a review of *Growing Up, Washington Post Book World* reviewer Jonathan Yardley wrote that Baker "passed through rites that for our culture are now only memories, though cherished ones, from first exposure to the miracle of indoor plumbing to trying on his first pair of long pants," and Settle found Baker's descriptions of such scenes "as funny and as touching as Mark Twain's."

Many critics also lauded Baker's ability to translate his personal memories into a work of universal experience. *New Statesman* critic Brian Martin admired the author's "sharp eye for the details of ordinary life," while Yardley offered even stronger praise, affirming that Baker "has accomplished the memorialist's task: to find shape and meaning in his own life, and to make it interesting and pertinent to the reader. In lovely, haunting prose, he has told a story that is deeply in the American grain, one in which countless readers will find echoes of their own, yet in the end is very much his own."

The Good Times continues Baker's story, recounting the author's coming of age as a journalist during the 1950s and 1960s. Hired in 1947 as a writer for the Baltimore *Sun,* Baker developed a reputation as a fast, accurate reporter and eventually earned a promotion to the post of London bureau chief. In the opinion of *New York Times* reviewer Frank Conroy, the time spent in London made Baker a better reporter and a better writer. Conroy determined that Baker's "ability to take the best from the Brits—who in general write better than we do . . . was perhaps the key event in his growth as a writer." Though Baker enjoyed London, he moved on to become the *Sun*'s White House correspondent, a decision he soon regretted. Once in Washington, Baker found the work boring, the atmosphere stifling, and his writing style unappreciated. Writing in *The Good Times,* Baker acknowledged: "I had swapped the freedom to roam one of the world's great cities and report whatever struck my fancy. And what had I got in return? A glamorous job which entitled me to sit in a confined space, listening to my colleagues breathe."

Frustrated at the *Sun,* Baker jumped at an offer to write for the *New York Times* Washington bureau, although he insisted on covering the Senate, hoping to capture the human side of the country's leaders. But in time even Congress, with its fawning politicians and controlled press briefings, proved disappointing. Recalling his dissatisfaction with the work, Baker told *Time,* "I began to wonder why, at the age of thirty-seven, I was wearing out my hams waiting for somebody to come out and lie to me." When the *Sun* attempted to regain Baker's services with the promise of a column, the *Times* promptly countered the offer with its own column, a proposal which convinced Baker to stay.

The Good Times is filled with Baker's portrayals of political heavyweights like John Kennedy, Lyndon Johnson, and Richard Nixon. Baker also profiled some of his fellow journalists, saving his harshest criticisms for those reporters who compromised their professional integrity by letting themselves become seduced by savvy politicians. Complimenting Baker on his balanced characterizations, Just reported that the author's "level gaze is on full display here in the deft, edged portraits" of his Congressional contacts, while William French of the Toronto *Globe and Mail* stated that "Baker's thumbnail sketches of the Washington movers and shakers of his time are vivid."

Many critics viewed *The Good Times* favorably, including Just who called the book "a superb autobiography, wonderfully told, often hilarious, always intelligent and unsparing." Some reviewers, however, felt that Baker's trademark sense of modesty is used to excess in the book. In Conroy's opinion, Baker takes too little credit for his early success, "ascribing much to luck and his ability to touch-type." Naughton was more critical of Baker's style, asserting that "his humility weakens the book." Other reviewers observed that, because of its subject matter, *The Good Times* necessarily evokes different feelings from its predecessor, *Growing Up*. "Some readers may find that this sequel lacks the emotional tug of the original," Robert Shogan stated in the *Los Angeles Times Book Review*, "what *The Good Times* offers instead is an insider's view of modern American journalism that illuminates both the author and his trade." Along those lines, Yardley added that "Baker seems to understand that it is one thing to write for public consumption about the distant years of childhood, and quite another to write about the unfinished stories of marriage and parenthood." He concluded, "In the end, though, *The Good Times* is every bit as much a personal document as was *Growing Up*."

Looking Back is a collection of essays, each of which originally appeared in the *New Yorker.* They are reflections on American public figures, among them Lyndon Johnson, William Randolph Hearst, Joe DiMaggio, Barry Goldwater, and Martin Luther King. Reviewing the book for the *New York Review of Books,* a contributor noted that, "With an elegiac yet shrewd sense of their accomplishments both enduring and ephemeral, he traces the impressions they left on twentieth-century America—and on him."

Describing his writing career to Naughton, Baker downplayed his talents, stating, "I've just had the good luck to escape the meaner reviewers." Readers of his work attribute Baker's success to things altogether different. Skow noted that while Baker most often uses humor to make his point, he "can also write with a haunting strain of melancholy, with delight, or . . . with shame and outrage." In addition, Baker's consistency and clarity are mentioned as strengths. "There is just a lucidity and a sanity about him that is so distinctive," U.S. Senator Daniel Patrick Moynihan told *Time.* "He writes clearly because he thinks clearly." Finally, summarizing the opinions of many critics, Mysak declared: "For a look at how we live now . . . Baker has no superiors, and few peers."

BIOGRAPHICAL AND CRITICAL SOURCES:

BOOKS

Baker, Russell, *So This Is Depravity,* Congdon & Lattes, 1980.

Baker, Russell, *Growing Up,* Congdon & Weed (New York, NY), 1982.

Baker, Russell, *The Rescue of Miss Yaskell and Other Pipe Dreams,* Congdon & Weed (New York, NY), 1983.

Baker, Russell, *The Good Times,* Morrow (New York, NY), 1989.

Contemporary Literary Criticism, Volume 31, Thomson Gale (Detroit, MI), 1985.

PERIODICALS

Chicago Tribune, January 16, 1987.

Detroit Free Press, June 27, 1989.

Detroit News, November 7, 1982; July 9, 1989.

Economist, January 22, 1994, p. 97.

Entertainment Weekly, December 31, 1993, p. 62.

Globe and Mail (Toronto, Ontario, Canada), January 19, 1985; June 24, 1989.

Library Journal, May 1, 1989.

Los Angeles Times, December 7, 1980; January 22, 1984; March 17, 1988.

Los Angeles Times Book Review, October 10, 1982; November 30, 1986; June 11, 1989.

New Statesman, March 16, 1984.

Newsweek, September 29, 1980; November 8, 1982.

New Yorker, March 8, 1993, p. 33.

New York Review of Books, August 6, 2004.

New York Times, January 30, 1972; October 6, 1982; May 23, 1989.

New York Times Book Review, January 30, 1972; October 18, 1982; May 28, 1989; July 8, 1990; February 20, 1994, p. 22.

New York Times Magazine, September 12, 1982.

People, December 20, 1982; October 4, 1993, p. 12.

Publishers Weekly, January 24, 1972; April 28, 1989.

Spectator, February, 1984; March, 1984.

Time, January 19, 1968; January 17, 1972; June 4, 1979; November 1, 1982; October 4, 1993, p. 81.

Times Literary Supplement, April 6, 1984.

Tribune Books (Chicago, IL), January 16, 1987; May 21, 1989.

Washington Post, July 25, 1989.

Washington Post Book World, October 5, 1980; October 3, 1982; October 9, 1983; January 18, 1987; May 28, 1989; December 5, 1993, p. 3.*

BALLARD, Michael B. 1946-

PERSONAL: Born November 24, 1946 in Louisville, MS; son of Ottis B. and Jessie Dola (a homemaker; maiden name, Stephenson) Ballard; married December 2, 2001; wife's name Jan; children: two stepchildren. *Education:* Mississippi State University, B.A., 1975, M.A., 1976, Ph.D, 1983. *Politics:* "Moderate Independent." *Religion:* Presbyterian *Hobbies and other interests:* Civil War re-enactment, writing gospel songs, writing Civil War history, spectator sports, gospel music.

ADDRESSES: Home—484 East Sides Ave., Ackerman, MS 39735. *Office*—Box 9570, University Library, Mississippi State University, Starkville, MS 39762; fax: 601-325-3560. *E-mail*—mballard@library.msstate.edu.

CAREER: Mississippi State University, Starkville, university archivist, 1983—.

MEMBER: Organization of American Historians, Society of American Archivists, Society of Civil War Historians, Southern Historical Association, Society of Mississippi Archivists, Mississippi Historical Society.

AWARDS, HONORS: Nonfiction Award, Mississippi Institute of Arts and Letters, 1991, for *Pemberton: A Biography.*

WRITINGS:

A Long Shadow: Jefferson Davis and the Final Days of the Confederacy, University Press of Mississippi (Jackson, MS), 1986.

Landscapes of Battle: The Civil War, University Press of Mississippi (Jackson, MS), 1988.

Pemberton: A Biography, University Press of Mississippi (Jackson, MS), 1991, published as *Pemberton: The General Who Lost Vicksburg,* 1999.

(Coeditor) *A Mississippi Rebel in the Army of Northern Virginia: The Civil War Memoirs of Private David Holt,* Louisiana State University Press (Baton Rouge, LA), 1996.

Campaign for Vicksburg, Eastern National Park and Monument Association (Fort Washington, PA), 1996.

The Battle of Tupelo, Blue and Gray Education Society (Danville, VA), 1996.

Civil War Mississippi: A Guide, University Press of Mississippi (Jackson, MS), 2000.

(With G. V. Montgomery and Craig S. Piper) *Sonny Montgomery: The Veteran's Champion,* Libraries, Mississippi State University (Jackson, MS), 2003.

Newsletter editor, Golden Triangle Civil War Roundtable.

WORK IN PROGRESS: A memoir of growing up in the South in the 1950s-60s; *The Vicksburg Campaign,* to be published by University of North Carolina Press.

SIDELIGHTS: Michael B. Ballard once told *CA:* "My motivation for writing is my strong desire to understand the past and how it affects the present. I try to explain not only what happened, but why it happened and why it is important to understand. I believe we can learn much from the past, but only if we have an in-depth understanding of people and events.

"Bruce Catton and Samuel Clemens are both literary inspirations for me. Several historians, including John Marszelak, Richard McMurray, and Herman Hattaway, have influenced me in the area of proper scholarship.

"When I write, I generally start with an outline and organize my research notes accordingly. I then plug in, and write the first draft following the outline. From then on, it is a matter of rewrites, refinements, and trying to get the narrative as tight as possible.

"Growing up in a Southern state, I have always had an interest in the Civil War. I found later that researching and writing about the war was the only way I could really understand its impact on both the South and American history in general. I also grew up during a time of racial turmoil in the South, and I am just now beginning to look back at that time. I hope, through fiction with an autobiographical flavor, to examine that period."

BIOGRAPHICAL AND CRITICAL SOURCES:

PERIODICALS

History: Review of New Books, winter, 1997, Lowell H. Harrison, review of *A Mississippi Rebel in the Army of Northern Virginia: The Civil War Memoirs of Private David Holt,* p. 91.

Journal of Southern History, May, 1997, Otho C. Campbell, review of *A Mississippi Rebel in the Army of Northern Virginia,* p. 421.

Mississippi Quarterly, spring, 1998, Earl J. Hess, review of *A Mississippi Rebel in the Army of Northern Virginia,* p. 373.

ONLINE

Mississippi Writers and Musicians Project at Starkville High School: Michael Ballard, http://shs.starkville.k12.ms.us/mswm/MSWritersAndMusicians/writers/BallardMichael/ (March, 2002).

* * *

BARKLEM, Jill 1951-
(Gillian Gaze)

PERSONAL: Maiden name, Gillian Gaze; born in 1951; married; children: Elizabeth, Peter.

ADDRESSES: *Home*—Epping Forest, England. *Agent*—c/o Author Mail, Atheneum Publishers, 597 5th Ave., New York, NY 1017.

CAREER: Writer and illustrator.

WRITINGS:

AUTHOR AND ILLUSTRATOR

Spring Story, Philomel (New York, NY), 1980, new edition, HarperCollins (London, England), 1995.

Summer Story, Philomel (New York, NY), 1980.

Autumn Story, Philomel (New York, NY), 1980, published as *Autumn Story: Primrose Meets the Harvest Mice,* Picture Lions (London, England), 1995.

Winter Story, Philomel (New York, NY), 1980, published as *Winter Story: A Party in the Ice Palace,* Picture Lions (London, England), 1995.

The Big Book of Brambly Hedge, Philomel (New York, NY), 1981.

The Secret Staircase, Philomel (New York, NY), 1983, new edition, HarperCollins (London, England), 1996.

The High Hills, Philomel (New York, NY), 1986, new edition, HarperCollins (London, England), 1996.

The Four Seasons of Brambly Hedge (contains *Spring Story, Summer Story, Autumn Story,* and *Winter Story*), Collins (London, England), 1988, Philomel (New York, NY), 1990.

Sea Story, Collins (London, England), 1990, Philomel (New York, NY), 1991, published as *Sea Story: Primrose and Wilfred Sail to Sandy Bay,* Picture Lions (London, England), 1996.

The Brambly Hedge Treasury (contains *The Secret Staircase* and *The High Hills*), Collins (London, England), 1991.

The Brambly Hedge Poster Book, Collins (London, England), 1991.

Through the Hedgerow: A Three-Dimensional Pop-up Book, Collins (London, England), 1993, published as *The World of Brambly Hedge,* Philomel (New York, NY), 1993.

Poppy's Babies, Collins (London, England), 1994, Philomel (New York, NY), 1995, published as *Poppy's Babies: Poppy and Dusty's New Family,* Picture Lions (London, England), 1996.

The Brambly Hedge Birthday Book, Philomel (New York, NY), 1994.

Poppy's Wedding, HarperCollins (London, England), 1995.

Primrose's Adventure: A Sliding Picture Book, HarperCollins (London, England), 1995.

The Snow Ball: A Sliding Picture Book, HarperCollins (London, England), 1995.

Wilfred's Birthday: A Sliding Picture Book, Collins (London, England), 1995.

Winter Story Sticker Book, Collins (London, England), 1996.

Brambly Hedge: Collectors Book, R. Dennis, 1999.

The Complete Brambly Hedge, 1999.

Also author and illustrator of picture books under the name Gillian Gaze. Illustrator of the "Haffertee Hamster" books by Janet and John Perkins.

ADAPTATIONS: Some of Barklem's "Brambly Hedge" books have been recorded on audiocassette.

SIDELIGHTS: Jill Barklem is the author and illustrator of the "Brambly Hedge" stories, a popular series of picture books that features a society of humanized mice living in tree homes in rural England. Evoking the Victorian and Edwardian eras in her texts and pictures, Barklem presents her audience with a nostalgic and idyllic picture of country life. She also imbues her works with rural English tradition and family warmth and security, as each of her characters maintains an important role in the daily functionings and social well-being of the community. Barklem's series has sold millions of copies in England, and her creations have been marketed on china, greeting cards, and other products both there and in the United States.

Barklem began her career in 1974 by writing and illustrating books under her maiden name, Gillian Gaze; she also provided pictures for the "Haffertee Hamster" books by Janet and John Perkins and a series of collections of prayers and graces. During this period, Barklem also researched English customs, flora, and other geographical and cultural details for her "Brambly Hedge" stories. Her first four books, *Spring Story, Summer Story, Autumn Story,* and *Winter Story,* were published simultaneously in 1980 as individual volumes in a "miniature" format.

Spring Story introduces the field mice who comprise the community of Brambly Hedge, centering on the picnic celebration of young mouse Wilfred Toadflax's birthday. *Summer Story* features a wedding; *Autumn Story,* the search for young Primrose Woodmouse, who is lost and frightened; and *Winter Story* the festivities surrounding the Snow Ball at the Ice Hall. These four works were collected in the omnibus volume *The Four Seasons of Brambly Hedge. School Library Journal* contributor Anita C. Wilson noted that these stories of normal childhood adventures "should provide both entertainment and reassurance" to youngsters, while "the exceptional illustrations should give many hours of pleasure."

Barklem is also the creator of other "Brambly Hedge" stories, *The Secret Staircase* and *The High Hills,* which were published as full-sized volumes. The former involves the intrigue and excitement of a secret staircase and a hidden treasure discovered during preparations for the annual mid-winter celebration, while the latter is an exploration adventure in which Wilfred, in hopes of finding gold, accompanies elderly Mr. Apple on a mission of charity to deliver blankets to the voles in the High Hills of Brambly Hedge. These two works have also been published together as *The Brambly Hedge Treasury.* In a *Growing Point* review of the treasury, Margery Fisher explained that "the plots are staples of junior adventures, used with a light tone, and the packed scenes have the perennial charm of the miniature."

Many critics have noted the resemblance between Barklem's stories and those of Beatrix Potter; most of these commentators observed, however, that while Potter remained true to animal nature when humanizing the actions of her characters, Barklem has created a world of children masquerading as mice. Further comparison between the two authors has prompted criticism for what has been described as the excessive wordiness of Barklem's text and the cluttered detail of her illustrations. Despite these comments, Barklem has garnered praise from reviewers who approve of the careful detail of her pictures. Crafting her illustrations with sepia ink and watercolor, Barklem is commended for offering much for young readers to discover through the patterned china, wallpaper, and fabrics, as well as the floral arrangements and other such features, with which she invests her work. Similarly, Barklem is noted for her realistic sense of scale—for example, small blossoms make large floral arrangements for the mice—and for the authenticity of her settings. Representative of these more positive responses to Barklem's "Brambly Hedge" series is Margaret Adamson's comment in *Reading Time* that the author has created a "delightfully intricate little world" with "charming" stories and illustrations that are "perfectly detailed representations of community living at its best, filled with colour, warmth and busyness."

BIOGRAPHICAL AND CRITICAL SOURCES:

BOOKS

Children's Literature Review, Volume 31, Thomson Gale (Detroit, MI), 1994.

PERIODICALS

Booklist, January 15, 1981, p. 695; February 1, 1984, p. 812; March 1, 1987, p. 1011; June 1, 1991, p. 1878; January 1, 1994, p. 837.

Books for Keeps, November, 1999, review of *The Complete Brambly Hedge,* p. 6.

Books for Your Children, autumn-winter, 1983, p. 3.

Bulletin of the Center for Children's Books, March, 1984, p. 122.
Christian Science Monitor, April 17, 1987, p. 26.
Growing Point, January, 1981, pp. 3803-3806; November, 1981, pp. 3960-3961; January, 1992, Margery Fisher, review of *The Brambly Hedge Treasury,* pp. 5632-5633.
Horn Book Guide, fall, 1995, p. 363.
Junior Bookshelf, February, 1981, pp. 9-10; October, 1983, p. 204; August, 1993, p. 131.
Publishers Weekly, August 29, 1980, p. 365; January 29, 1982, p. 67; January 13, 1984, p. 68.
Reading Time, Volume 34, number 2, 1990, Margaret Adamson, review of *The Secret Staircase* and *The High Hills,* pp. 8, 14.
School Librarian, December, 1983, p. 348.
School Library Journal, March, 1981, Anita C. Wilson, review of *Spring Story, Summer Story, Autumn Story,* and *Winter Story,* p. 128; March, 1982, p. 128; March, 1984, p. 138; March, 1987, p. 140.
Times Educational Supplement, November 14, 1980, p. 25.
Times Literary Supplement, September 19, 1980, p. 1029.

ONLINE

Brambly Hedge Web Site, http://www.bramblyhedge.co.uk/ (May 9, 2004).*

* * *

BARNES, Julian (Patrick) 1946-
(Dan Kavanagh, Edward Pygge)

PERSONAL: Born January 19, 1946, in Leicester, England; son of Albert Leonard (a French teacher) and Kaye (a French teacher) Barnes; married Pat Kavanagh (a literary agent), 1979. *Education:* Magdalen College, Oxford, B.A. (with honors), 1968.

ADDRESSES: *Agent*—Peters, Fraser, and Dunlop Ltd., Drury House, 34-43 Russell St., London WC2B 5HA, England.

CAREER: Freelance writer, 1972—. Lexicographer for *Oxford English Dictionary Supplement,* Oxford, England, 1969-72; *New Statesman,* London, England, as-

Julian Barnes

sistant literary editor, 1977-78, television critic, 1977-81; *Sunday Times,* London, deputy literary editor, 1979-81; *Observer,* London, television critic, 1982-86; London correspondent for *New Yorker* magazine, 1990-94.

AWARDS, HONORS: Somerset Maugham Prize, 1980, for *Metroland;* Booker Prize nomination, 1984, Geoffrey Faber Memorial Prize, and Prix Medicis, all for *Flaubert's Parrot;* American Academy and Institute of Arts and Letters award, 1986, for work of distinction; Prix Gutembourg, 1987; Premio Grinzane Carour, 1988; Prix Femina for *Talking It Over,* 1992; Shakespeare Prize (Hamburg), 1993; Officier de l'Ordre des Arts et des Lettres; shortlisted for Booker Prize, 1998, for *England, England.*

WRITINGS:

NOVELS

Metroland, St. Martin's Press (New York, NY), 1980.
Before She Met Me, Jonathan Cape (London, England), 1982, McGraw-Hill (New York, NY), 1986.
Flaubert's Parrot, Jonathan Cape (London, England), 1984, Knopf (New York, NY), 1985.
Staring at the Sun, Jonathan Cape (London, England), 1986, Knopf (New York, NY), 1987.

A History of the World in Ten and One-Half Chapters, Knopf (New York, NY), 1989.
Talking It Over, Knopf (New York, NY), 1991.
The Porcupine, Knopf (New York, NY), 1992.
Letters from London, Vintage (New York, NY), 1995.
England, England, Knopf (New York, NY), 1999.
Love, etc., Knopf (New York, NY), 2001.
In the Land of Pain, Jonathan Cape (London, England), 2002, Knopf (New York, NY), 2003.
The Lemon Table, Jonathan Cape (London, England), 2004.

UNDER PSEUDONYM DAN KAVANAGH; CRIME NOVELS

Duffy, Jonathan Cape (London, England), 1980, Pantheon (New York, NY), 1986.
Fiddle City, Jonathan Cape (London, England), 1981, Pantheon (New York, NY), 1986.
Putting the Boot In, Jonathan Cape (London, England), 1985.
Going to the Dogs, Pantheon (New York, NY), 1987.

OTHER

(Contributor) Charles Hobson, *Flaubert & Louise: Letters and Impressions,* Limestone (San Francisco, CA), 1988.
Cross Channel (short stories), Knopf (New York, NY), 1996.
Something to Declare (essays), Picador (London, England), 2002.
The Pedant in the Kitchen (nonfiction), Atlantic Books, 2003.

Contributing editor, under pseudonym Edward Pygge, to *New Review,* c. 1970s. Regular contributor to *Times Literary Supplement* and *New York Review of Books.*

ADAPTATIONS: Talking It Over was adapted for film in 1996; *Metroland* was adapted for film in 1999.

SIDELIGHTS: "Julian Barnes," wrote *Dictionary of Literary Biography* contributor Merritt Moseley, "is one of the most celebrated, and one of the most variously rewarding, of Britain's younger novelists." His work, the critic continued, "has been acclaimed by readers as different as Carlos Fuentes and Philip Larkin; reviewers and interviewers sum him up with praise such as Mark Lawson's claim that he 'writes like the teacher of your dreams: jokey, metaphorical across both popular and unpopular culture, epigrammatic.'" In addition to novels such as *Flaubert's Parrot, A History of the World in Ten and One-Half Chapters,* and *The Porcupine,* Barnes has also won a reputation as a writer of innovative detective fiction and an essayist. "Since 1990," Moseley concluded, "he has been the London correspondent of the *New Yorker* magazine, contributing 'Letters from London' every few months on subjects such as the royal family and the quirkier side of British politics." Barnes was also one of many writers—among them Stephen King and Annie Proulx—invited to read from their works at the first-ever New Yorker Festival in 2000.

Barnes published four novels, *Metroland, Before She Met Me,* and the detective novels *Duffy* and *Fiddle City*—both written under the pseudonym Dan Kavanagh—before he completed *Flaubert's Parrot,* his first great success. Critics have acclaimed these early books for their comic sensibility and witty language. *Metroland* tells the story of two young men who "adopt the motto *epater la bourgeoisie,*" explained *New Statesman* contributor Nicholas Shrimpton. "But this grandiose ambition is promptly reduced to the level of 'epats,' a thoroughly English field-sport in which the competitors attempt to shock respectable citizens for bets of sixpence a time." "After this vision of the Decadence in short trousers," the reviewer concluded, "it is hard to take the idea of outrage too solemnly." *Before She Met Me* is the tale of an older man who falls into an obsession about his actress wife's former screen lovers. The book, stated Anthony Thwaite in the *Observer,* presents an "elegantly hard-boiled treatment of the nastier levels of obsession, full of controlled jokes when almost everything else has got out of control."

Barnes's detective fiction also looks at times and characters for whom life has gotten out of control. The title character of *Duffy* is a bisexual former policeman who was blackmailed out of his job. "The thrillers are active, louche, violent, thoroughly plotted," stated Moseley. "*Duffy* shows the result of serious research into the seamy world of London's sex industry; in *Duffy,* as in its successors, the crime tends to be theft or fraud rather than murder, though Barnes successfully imbues the book with a feeling of menace." *Fiddle City,* for instance, takes place at London's

Heathrow airport and looks at the smuggling of drugs and other illegal items.

It was with the publication of *Flaubert's Parrot,* though, that Barnes scored his greatest success to date. The novel tells of Geoffrey Braithwaite, a retired English doctor, and his obsession with the great French novelist Gustave Flaubert. After his wife's somewhat mysterious death, Braithwaite travels to France in search of trivia concerning Flaubert; his chief aim is to find the stuffed parrot that the writer kept on his desk for inspiration while writing *Un coeur simple,* the story of a peasant woman's devotion to her pet. Barnes "uses Braithwaite's investigations to reflect on the ambiguous truths of biography, the relationship of art and life, the impact of death, the consolations of literature," explained Michael Dirda in the *Washington Post Book World.*

Far from a straightforward narrative, *Flaubert's Parrot* blends fiction, literary criticism, and biography in a manner strongly reminiscent of Vladimir Nabokov's *Pale Fire,* according to many critics. *Newsweek* reviewer Gene Lyons called it "too involuted by half for readers accustomed to grazing contentedly in the best-seller list," but recommended it to readers "of immoderate literary passions." Other reviewers stressed that, while a complex and intellectual work, *Flaubert's Parrot* is also "endlessly fascinating and very funny," in the words of London *Times* contributor Annabel Edwards. Dirda concluded that this "delicious potpourri of quotations, legends, facts, fantasies, and interpretations of Flaubert and his work . . . might seem dry, but Barnes' style and Braithwaite's autumnal wisdom make the novel into a kind of Stoic comedy. . . . Anyone who reads *Flaubert's Parrot* will learn a good deal about Flaubert, the making of fiction, and the complex tangle of art and life. And—not least important—have a lot of rather peculiar fun too."

Of Barnes's more recent works, *A History of the World in Ten and One-Half Chapters* and *The Porcupine* are probably best known to U.S. readers. *A History of the World in Ten and One-Half Chapters* "builds on Barnes' reputation as one of Britain's premier postmodernists," stated *Village Voice Literary Supplement* contributor Rob Nixon. "The anti-novel that emerges attempts to double as a novel of ideas—never Brit lit's forté. . . . The principal concern of the novel, which begins with corruption on the Ark and ends in the tedium of heaven (pretty much like life with lots of shopping), is to debunk religion and that most seductive of theologies, History." Barnes conceives of history in the book as a series of different, mostly unrelated events, and the connections individuals invent to link them together. "One of Barnes's characters rather improbably describes her supposed mental condition—imagining that she has survived a nuclear disaster, which, as it turns out, she has—as 'Fabulation. You keep a few true facts and spin a new story about them,'" declared Frank Kermode in the *London Review of Books.* "This is what Barnes himself, in this book, attempts. He fabulates this and that, stitches the fabulations together, and then he and we quite properly call the product a novel." "As a 'historian,'" stated Anthony Quinn in the *New Statesman and Society,* "he is unlikely to dislodge Gibbon or Macaulay; but as satirist and story-teller he has few equals at present."

The Porcupine is a short novel set in a fictional Eastern European country in the post-Communist era. "Stoyo Petkanov, the former president, a cross between [former Rumanian premier] Nicolae Ceaucescu and Bulgaria's Georgi Dimitrov," explained *New York Times Book Review* contributor Robert Stone, "is on trial in the courts of the shakily democratic successor government." His prosecutor is Peter Solinsky, born into a family prominent under the Communists. Solinsky is shaken by Petkanov's sincere belief in the principles of Communism. Contrasting them with the poverty and lack of respect that the reforms have brought, Solinsky begins to turn away from his new democratic ideals. "In the end," Mary Warner Marien declared in the *Christian Science Monitor,* "nothing is resolved except a clearer vision of the stupendous obstacles facing the former communist country." "Admirers of the earlier, Francophile Julian Barnes may regret that in his latest work . . . the author of *Flaubert's Parrot* and *Talking It Over* has shed his brilliance and dandyism to become a rather somber recorder of his times," stated *London Review of Books* contributor Patrick Parrinder. "The grayness seems inherent in his subject-matter, but it has not infected his acute and spiny prose."

England, England, a darkly satiric novel set in the twenty-first century, incorporates conflicting world situations and their connectedness to greed for power and money. Protagonist and businessman Sir Jack Pitman plots to replace England with a replica island—a Disneyland-type fantasy world—intending to reap huge financial rewards. John Kennedy, writing for the *Antioch Review,* concluded that the book falls short because the characters are underdeveloped. Even so, he commended Barnes's writing style, adding that he "cleverly puts his finger upon a central issue: how do we find our personal uniqueness and salvation when 'memory is identity' and everywhere history and heritage are being manipulated for profit." Philip Landon, in the *Review of Contemporary Fiction,* dubbed *England, England* "a novel of downright Swiftian darkness and ferocity." Comparing the fantasy island to Lilliput, Landon called the work a "stinging caricature" that "chills with the bleakness of its cultural panorama."

Commenting on *Love, etc.* for *Yomiuri Shimbun/Daily Yomiuri,* a reviewer called Barnes a "sensitive writer, whose specialty is a down-to-earth lucidity about the sad paradoxes of love and marriage." *Love, etc.* is a ten-years-later look into the lives of the characters of *Talking It Over,* although reading the latter is not a prerequisite to enjoying the former. Steven Rea, reviewing the book for *Knight-Ridder/Tribune News Service,* noted that *Love, etc.* "is penned in confession mode—in the voices of its protagonists, a knotty triangle of love, loathing, trust and betrayal known as Stuart, Gillian and Oliver." He called Barnes's prose "lively, lucid, ricocheting with wryly observed commentary on the human condition," adding that Barnes "pokes and prods into the dark corners of contemporary relationships." Dale Peck in the *New Republic,* however, found the writing clever but the story ultimately "soulless." As Peck explained, "Barnes is a terribly smart man, a terribly skilled writer . . . [but] intelligence and talent in the service of a discompassionate temperament are precisely the opposite of what one seeks from a novelist, or a novel."

In a departure from his longer fictional works, Barnes experimented with the short-story form in 1996's *Cross Channel.* A collection of ten short stories that span centuries, each tale is also linked by its depiction of a Brit heading for the far bank of the Channel, lured by the pleasures of neighboring France. Drawing on the similarities between the British and their Gallic cousins, Barnes's "imagination seems to work comfortably in a historical context, building fiction on bits of fact," according to Chicago's *Tribune Books* reviewer Bruce Cook. Among the stories—each set on French soil—are "Junction," which revolves around the perception of the French-born Channel-spanning railroad's builders' perception of their British coworkers during the railroad's 1840s construction. "Melon" finds a cross-cultural cricket match interrupted by the French Revolution, much to the dismay of the story's high-born protagonist who had hoped to sideline the populace's rush to rebel by sparking a far more healthy interest in sport. And in "Inferences," an older-than-middle-aged English musical composer now living in France awaits the performance of his latest composition on the radio, hoping to surprise his young mistress with its magnificence.

Slipping back and forth between the centuries, Barnes's "prose slips quietly back from its modern cadences into those of the early nineteenth century, into the cherished foreignness of the past," noted Michael Wood in a *New York Times Book Review* critique of *Cross Channel.* The author also slips back and forth between outlook, between the way the British view the French and vice versa, understanding the French perspective yet clearly aligned with the British. "*Cross Channel* reconfirms Barnes' sympathy for those characters whose Englishness accompanies them, like a sensible mackintosh, into the unpredictable depths of France," quipped critic Gerald Mangan in his review of the collection for the *Times Literary Supplement.* Praising the volume for its sensitive portrayal of a myriad of cultural subtleties, Cook had particular praise for the dry wit that imbues the collection. Barnes "may indeed be a comic writer at heart—and that may be why he appeals to French readers," surmised the critic. "His humor is the sort that translates well. It travels."

Returning again to the short-fiction format in *The Lemon Table,* Barnes combines eleven unique short stories that focus on individuals whose lives are connected through the unnerving themes of death and aging. As readers plunge into the lives of the characters, dark secrets are revealed, along with chilling answers to much-feared questions. Barbara Love in *Library Journal* called *The Lemon Table* a "superb collection" and added: "This is Barnes at his best." A reviewer for *Publishers Weekly* commented that the short tales "are as stylish as any of Barnes's creations, while also possessed of a pleasing heft. . . . the reader is taken for a delightful ride."

BIOGRAPHICAL AND CRITICAL SOURCES:

BOOKS

Contemporary Literary Criticism, Volume 42, Thomson Gale (Detroit, MI), 1987.

Contemporary Novelists, 6th edition, St. James Press (Detroit, MI), 1996.

Dictionary of Literary Biography Yearbook, Thomson Gale (Detroit, MI), 1994.

Moseley, Merritt, *Understanding Julian Barnes,* University of South Carolina Press (Columbia, SC), 1997.

Sesto, Bruce, *Language, History, and Metanarrative in the Fiction of Julian Barnes,* Peter Lang Publishing (New York, NY), 2001.

PERIODICALS

Antioch Review, winter, 2000, John Kennedy, review of *England, England,* p. 117.

Booklist, July, 1995, p. 1856; June 1, 2004, p. 1697.

Chicago Tribune, January 3, 1993, p. 3.

Christian Science Monitor, January 20, 1993, p. 13.

Commonweal, May 8, 1992, pp. 22-24.

Financial Times, September 16, 2002, James Haldane, "Reversibility, etc.," review of *Love, etc.,* p. 4.

Independent, July 13, 1991, pp. 34-36.

Journal of Literature and Theology, June, 1991, pp. 220-232.

Kirkus Reviews, November 1, 2002, p. 1585.

Knight-Ridder/Tribune News Service, March 28, 2001, Steven Rea, review of *Love, etc.,* p. K6406.

Library Journal, March 15, 1996, p. 98; June 1, 2004, p. 128.

London Review of Books, June 22, 1989, p. 20; February 11, 1993, pp. 18-19.

Los Angeles Time Book Review, March 17, 1985; November 8, 1992, p. 3.

National Review, August 30, 1999, Roger Kimball, "Faux Britannia," p. 48.

New Republic, April 2, 2001, Dale Peck, "Literature's Cuckold," review of *Love, etc.,* p. 32.

New Statesman, March 28, 1980, p. 483.

New Statesman and Society, June 23, 1989, p. 38; November 13, 1992, pp. 34-35; January 16, 1996, pp. 39-40; June 4, 2001, Jason Cowley, "Blame It on Amis, Barnes and McEwan," p. 36.

Newsweek, April 29, 1985.

New York Review of Books, March 21, 1996, p. 22.

New York Times, February 28, 1985; March 30, 1987, p. C16; July 5, 1990, pp. C11, C15; April 16, 1996, p. B2; May 11, 1999, Michiko Kakutani, "England As Theme Park, with Doubled Everything," p. E7.

New York Times Book Review, March 10, 1985; December 13, 1992, p. 3; April 21, 1996, p. 12.

New York Times Magazine, November 22, 1992, pp. 29, 68-72, 80.

Observer (London, England), April 18, 1982, p. 31; July 7, 1991, pp. 25-26.

Publishers Weekly, November 3, 1989, pp. 73-74; February 19, 1996, p. 204; April 12, 1999, review of *England, England,* p. 54, December 23, 2002, review of *In the Land of Pain,* p. 60; May 10, 2004, review of *The Lemon Table,* p. 33; August 9, 2004, review of *The Lemon Table,* p. 47.

Review of Contemporary Fiction, fall, 1999, Philip Landon, review of *England, England,* p. 174; summer, 2001, Philip Landon, review of *Love, etc.,* p. 167.

Spectator, January 26, 2002, Alberto Manguel, review of *Something to Declare,* p. 46.

Sunday Times (London, England), June 18, 1989, p. G9.

Time, April 8, 1985.

Times (London, England), March 21, 1980; October 4, 1984; November 7, 1985.

Times Literary Supplement, March 28, 1980; April 23, 1982; January 6, 1984, pp. 4214-4215; October 5, 1984, p. 1117; January 19, 1996, p. 24.

Tribune Books (Chicago, IL), April 21, 1996, p. 3.

Village Voice Literary Supplement, November, 1989, p. 5.

Wall Street Journal, December 11, 1992, p. A10.

Washington Post Book World, March 3, 1985; November 15, 1992.

Yale Review, summer, 1988, pp. 478-491.

Yomiuri Shimbun/Daily Yomiuri, April 2, 2001.

ONLINE

Julian Barnes Home Page, http://www.julianbarnes.com/ (August 4, 2004).

Salon.com, http://www.salon.com/ (May 13-17, 1996).*

* * *

BARROW, Andrew 1945-

PERSONAL: Born May 11, 1945, in Lancaster, England; son of George Erskine (a solicitor) and Margaret (a painter; maiden name, MacInnes) Barrow. *Education:* Attended private secondary school in Harrow, England.

ADDRESSES: Home—18 Eldon Rd., Kensington, London W8 and Brook Farmhouse, Brokenborough, Wiltshire. *Agent*—Gillon Aitken, 18-21 Cavaye Place, London SW10, England.

CAREER: Author of nonfiction works and novels. Professional comedian, 1963-66; advertising copywriter in London, England, 1967-68; freelance writer, 1968—.

AWARDS, HONORS: The Tap Dancer won the Hawthornden and McKitterick prizes.

WRITINGS:

Gossip: A History of High Society, 1920 to 1970, Hamish Hamilton (London, England), 1978, Coward, McCann & Geoghegan (New York, NY), 1979.

The Flesh Is Weak: An Intimate History of the Church of England, Hamish Hamilton (London, England), 1980.

International Gossip: A History of High Society, 1970-1980, Hamish Hamilton (London, England), 1983.

The Gossip Family Handbook, Hamish Hamilton (London, England), 1983.

The Great Book of Small Talk, Fourth Estate (London, England), 1987.

The Tap Dancer (novel), Duckworth (London, England), 1992.

The Man in the Moon (novel), Macmillan (London, England), 1996.

Quentin and Philip: A Double Portrait, Macmillan (London, England), 2002.

Contributor to newspapers and magazines, including *Harper's, Queen, Transatlantic Review, Vogue, Punch, Independent, Daily Telegraph, World of Interiors* and *Observer.*

SIDELIGHTS: Andrew Barrow once told *CA* that he had an "obsession with trivia, such as details of food, drink, dress, transport, and homes. I have no interest in politics, but am very interested in what politicians have for breakfast." This fascination with trivia is evident in Barrow's early writings, including *Gossip: A History of High Society, 1920 to 1970* and *The Flesh Is Weak: An Intimate History of the Church of England.* These works look at history from an unusual angle. In *Gossip,* Barrow invents the structure he would return to in other nonfiction works and in his novels, juxtaposing sequences of apparently unrelated paragraphs with little or no authorial commentary or narration. According to Anthony Quinton, a reviewer for the *Times Literary Supplement,* this style emphasizes the triviality of Barrow's subjects, whether they be members of high society, as in *Gossip,* or church officials, as in *The Flesh Is Weak.* This arrangement is perhaps fitting for Barrow's subject in the first book, "but it is distinctly saucy to set about the dear old C of E in this way," Quinton contended. In *The Flesh Is Weak,* Barrow offers a history of the misbehavior of Church of England officials from the sixteenth century to the present. In the *Spectator,* Benny Green noted that *The Flesh Is Weak* features a "succession of drunkards, lustpots, lechers, gourmands and drug addicts who parade through the pages of Mr. Barrow's book without so much as a reprimand." The author "is wisely content to let the facts speak for themselves." Quinton noted that only a small part of the narrative centers on the scandalous side of the church and more intriguing are glimpses of the church in the Empire. Both Quinton and Green concluded that although Barrow has not written an intellectual account, his work is entertaining. "For believers and infidels alike, Mr. Barrow has compiled a work of such surpassing triviality as to be quite irresistible," noted Green.

Barrow also infuses his novels with his fascination for human trivia. *The Tap Dancer* is a portrait of a middle-class English family of five sons dominated by an eccentric father. Cressida Connolly observed in the *Spectator* that "[Barrow's] insight into the minutiae of English family life is absolutely brilliant." The author, she stated, captures the gossip, wordless communication between married people, and banal chat of acquaintances with remarkable precision. "The people in this book seldom say anything important, much less profound, but the accumulation of their, mostly trivial, remarks provides the reader with a deep and satisfying knowledge of each personality," wrote Connolly. Barrow also adapted the narrative structure of his nonfiction to his fiction, slicing each chapter into brief vignettes separated by asterisks. "Had I the good fortune to be Andrew Barrow's editor," commented Connolly, "I should have tried to let the narrative flow with rather less resistance from the punctuation." Similarly, Tim Gooderham, writing for the *Times Literary Supplement,* noted the lack of plot in *The Tap Dancer,* and attributed Barrow's success in the novel to "the credibility and interest of its characters," each of whom is "perfectly realized, thanks largely to Barrow's remarkable skill at pinpointing the social and psychological undercurrents of casual conversation."

Like *The Tap Dancer,* Barrow's second novel, *The Man in the Moon,* is divided into vignettes, and, as in his earlier works, critics highlighted the author's facility for capturing personality through dialogue and his penchant for offering reams of it without commentary. Unlike *The Tap Dancer,* however, "the story [of *The Man in the Moon*] seems almost to tell itself," remarked Hal Jensen in the *Times Literary Supplement.* The novel is narrated by William, a young man who thinks he is very funny until he encounters abject failure at his first gig as a comedian, telling jokes at a pub called the Man in the Moon. The story proceeds through a series of interwoven remembrances of incidents covering the ensuing four years as William gets a job at an advertising agency, seeks out a psychiatrist, finds a new apartment, and so forth. Alan Coren, a contributor to the *Spectator,* saw the overarching theme of *The Man in the Moon* as the hilarity and tragedy of the failure to communicate, the thread that connects the disparate memories that populate this book. "That this highly comical book should also be a deeply sad one, is both deeply sad and highly comical," observed Coren, who described the novel as a "brilliant, hilarious and highly disturbing testament to what careless talk reveals."

In his biography *Quentin and Philip: A Double Portrait,* Barrow examines the intertwined lives of Quentin Crisp, an icon of the gay world, and Philip O'Connor, a writer who, like Crisp, was friends with Barrow. In alternating chapters, Barrow tells the story of the two men, both of them alienated from mainstream society. Crisp was born Dennis Pratt in 1908. Even as a teen he considered himself very different from those around him, and at a young age he left his home in Sutton to go to London. There he made a good living as a model, and he further made a name for himself by his generosity toward his friends. O'Connor was born some eight years after Crisp, and spent part of his boyhood in France. The two met in London's Soho district. O'Connor was a poet of some talent, but eventually, his sponsorship by a wealthy patron "sapped his will to write, and fuelled his will to drink," commented Philip Hoare in the *Guardian.* In August, 1963, O'Connor conducted a radio interview with Crisp which brought him to the attention of a wider audience. In addition to his modeling, Crisp also wrote, being best known for his memoir *The Naked Civil Servant,* which when adapted for television became "a piece of television history which coincided with a burgeoning gay liberation to reinvent the way 'we' thought about homosexuality." Hoare praised Barrow's depiction of the two men's lives, stating that in the author's "deft and cleverly constructed text, the two dance in and out of each other's lives and his own imagination." Reviewing the book for the *Daily Telegraph,* Will Cohu noted that the author's personal connection to the two men was perhaps a weakness as well as a strength, because "as a biographer, Barrow cannot bear to part with any of the material he's gleaned over the years. His own beautifully tuned writing undervalues itself in homage to the words of his subjects, and there are pages of non-essential gossip and marginal observations. . . . If *Quentin and Philip* were less of a work of love, it might be a better book." Roger Lewis, a reviewer for the London *Times,* was of a different opinion. Though he found little to admire about Crisp or O'Connor, he described Barrow's biography as "an eerie prose-poem—an evocation of a pair of creepy waxworks whom, in the end, I found it impossible to laugh off. This is a spellbinding, twisted book—a horrible masterpiece."

BIOGRAPHICAL AND CRITICAL SOURCES:

PERIODICALS

Daily Telegraph, December 7, 2002, Will Cohu, review of *Quentin and Philip: A Double Portrait,* p. 10.

Guardian, December 21, 2002, Philip Hoare, review of *Quentin and Philip,* p. 16.

Mankind, February, 1982, Douglas Hilt, review of *The Flesh Is Weak: An Intimate History of the Church of England,* p. 48.

Observer, December 1, 2002, Peter Conrad, review of *Quentin and Philip,* p. 16.

Spectator, February 28, 1981, pp. 23-24; June 13, 1992, p. 29; March 30, 1996, pp. 32-33.

Times (London, England), February 12, 2003, Roger Lewis, review of *Quentin and Philip,* p. 20.

Times Literary Supplement, November 14, 1980, p. 1278; December 18, 1987, pp. 1399-1400; June 19, 1992, p. 21; March 22, 1996, p. 24.*

BARSKY, Robert F. 1961-

PERSONAL: Born May 18, 1961, in Montreal, Quebec, Canada; son of Sydney (a merchant) and Patricia (a merchant) Barsky; married Yzabelle Martineau, 1990 (marriage ended); married Patricia Fozen, 2002; children: (first marriage) Tristan Victor, Benjamin Auguste. *Education:* Attended Vanier College, 1978-80; Brandeis University, B.A., 1984; McGill University, M.A., 1987, Ph.D., 1992; postdoctoral study at European Center for the Study of Argumentation, Free University (Brussels, Belgium). *Politics:* "Anarchist." *Religion:* "Atheist." *Hobbies and other interests:* Working with refugees, skiing.

ADDRESSES: Home—470 Prospect St., Unit 50, New Haven, CT 06511. *Office*—Department of Comparative Literature, Yale University, New Haven, CT 06520; fax: 519-661-3776. *E-mail*—robert.barsky@yale.edu.

CAREER: Trans-Canada Social Policy Research Centre, Montreal, Quebec, Canada, content analysis researcher, 1985-91; Institut québécois de recherche sur la culture, Montreal, ethnic studies and refugee studies researcher, 1991-93; Institut national de la recherche scientifique, Montreal, refugee studies researcher, 1993-95; University of Western Ontario, London, Ontario, Canada, assistant professor, 1995-98, associate professor of English, beginning 1998; Yale University, New Haven, CT, visiting fellow, 2000, Canadian Bicentennial Visiting Professor, beginning 2002. Inter-University Centre for Discourse Analysis and Text Sociocriticism, member; Immigration and Refugee Board, expert witness.

MEMBER: Phi Beta Kappa, Scarlet Key.

WRITINGS:

Constructing a Productive Other: Discourse Theory and the Convention Refugee Hearing, John Benjamins (Philadelphia, PA), 1994.

(Editor, with Michael Holquist) *Bakhtin and Otherness,* Discours Social Press (Montreal, Quebec, Canada), 1991.

Introduction a la theorie litteraire, Presses de l'Université du Québec (Quebec City, Quebec, Canada), 1997.

Noam Chomsky: A Life of Dissent, MIT Press (Cambridge, MA), 1997.

Arguing and Justifying: Assessing the Convention Refugees' Choice of Moment, Motive and Host Country, Ashgate Publishing (Burlington, VT), 2000.

(Translator and author of introduction) Michel Meyer, *Philosophy and the Passions,* Pennsylvania State University Press (University Park, PA), 2000.

Zellig Harris: Linguistics, Zionism, Radical Politics, MIT Press (Cambridge, MA), 2002.

Contributor to periodicals. Founder and past coeditor, *Discours social/Social Discourse: Discourse Analysis and Text Sociocriticism;* founder and past editor, *415 South Street;* associate editor, *SubStance.*

WORK IN PROGRESS: The Noam Chomsky Approach, for MIT Press (Cambridge, MA).

SIDELIGHTS: Robert F. Barsky once told *CA:* "My earliest published writings were poems that were accepted for publication in *415 South Street,* the literary journal of the Brandeis Literary Club, which I founded in 1981 as an alternative to the stodgy and apparently impenetrable literary organization that was active on campus at that time. This early experience in publishing was a positive and enlightening experience, probably one of the reasons why I pursued graduate studies in the field. When McGill University solicited candidates for a position as founding editor of a working paper series in 1987, I responded enthusiastically. Montreal was home to a community of gifted scholars working from various standpoints of discourse theory, so the working papers series quickly took on a life of its own. After a few issues it became a full-fledged journal called *Discours social/Social Discourse: Research Papers in Comparative Literature.* When McGill decided to close its comparative literature program, we decided to move the journal to the Inter-University Centre for the Study of Discourse Analysis and Text Sociocriticism, to be under the editorship of Marc Angenot, whose theory of social discourse had been the basis for the name of the journal and became the *raison d'être* for its continued existence.

"Working as an editor for a journal helped demystify the process of writing and publishing. Even though we were a small enterprise, we were solicited, sometimes very strongly, to publish works for no other reason than to further someone's career. Small journals also can easily become the tools for justifying research grants, the fruits of which were on occasion offered to us to offset publishing costs. The flip side of this coin was the realization of the power of the written word and the extreme seriousness with which some people approached the process of writing scholarly articles. I think we were lucky to have so many incredible people associated with the journal, because, at its best, it became an outlet for discussing issues which, strangely enough, were unknown to the vast majority of those working in the field of language studies at that time.

"My own writing and research was focused upon language studies as they pertain to legal hearings. My original intention was to pursue a purely academic career in literary studies, but I heard about a job opening in a new company that was bidding to transcribe the huge backlog of Convention refugee hearings that had piled up in Canada in the late 1980s. This company was, I discovered, treating these hearings like any other commodity in need of transformation from a primary (oral) state to a secondary (written) state. There were no precautions taken to protect this very sensitive material, which included details of torture, insurrection, resistance, and suffering, told by people from countries all around the world—even the United States. In the summer of 1987 I learned of imminent changes to the refugee determination system in Canada (which included a bill for boarding ships in international waters to turn back 'human cargo') and, using the materials that I was transcribing as evidence, I wrote a long exposé describing the lies upon which those laws and others like them were based. I wanted this to be a document that could be used to fight these laws and to attack the shoddy transcription system, so I offered it anonymously to the Canadian Broadcasting Corporation. They subsequently did a series of reports about it, keeping my name out of it, but one day the minister of immigration declared that the perpetrator of this 'crime' (telling the truth about the system) would be arrested and charged. I was subsequently questioned; I refused to hand over all of my documents and was threatened with a long jail term. In the end, I was never formally charged. In the course of the investigation, it was apparently learned that the private transcription was selling transcriptions to banks and embassies, and that the whole idea of privatizing the process was a political plum.

"I was later hired to pursue my refugee work and other immigration and ethnic studies research at the Institut quebecois de recherche sur la culture. While I was in Brussels, Belgium, doing postdoctoral research at the European Center for the Study of Argumentation, at the Free University of Brussels, I wrote what would become my biography of Noam Chomsky.

"Noam Chomsky had been an important influence upon my work since my first years in graduate school. I was fascinated by Chomsky and the whole milieu that surrounds him, including left-Zionism, anti-Bolshevik Communism, anarchism, and Jewish intellectual life. My first direct contact with him led to a wide-ranging field of discussions on a variety of subjects. The field of refugee studies is quite rigid, dominated by concerns relating to the movement of peoples, and Chomsky's work became important to me in rethinking the whole problem of refugee studies from a more radical perspective—the reason why borders and those trying to penetrate them exist in the first place.

"When I was asked to write a brief biography of his life, I was doubtful that Chomsky would participate but excited about the idea of writing about him. In the end, the book opened a whole new level of correspondence between us and broadened my understanding of the range of his work. It also reinforced my belief that much remained to be done about researching the early milieus, notably the work of Zellig Harris, Chomsky's teacher at the University of Pennsylvania. When I returned to Montreal in 1995, I had the opportunity to take up another challenge posed by Chomsky: to write a coherent and rigorous history of literary theory for a lay audience. There is nothing of this sort in French. Chomsky was the one who suggested I write a biography of Zellig Harris.

"I rely, for my understanding of critical issues, upon a constant dialogic exchange with figures of great inspiration. Marc Angenot, Noam Chomsky, Denise Helly, Patricia Foxen, Michael Holquist, and others have played this role for me. What I find exciting in this kind of exchange is to develop ideas and then measure them up to the response of people for whom I have great respect. With the passage of time, there are inevitable disagreements, which I now invent in my own mind based upon my knowledge of their views, between different figures who serve as influences. It is in this space that an 'authentic' voice of my own can at times surface, although (and this is probably especially the case with Chomsky) it is sometimes hard to distinguish one's own voice when in the company of such influences. Whatever the implications, this type of process is an inspiring and motivating one that keeps my research alive."

* * *

BARTOLOMEO, Joseph F(rancis) 1958-

PERSONAL: Born July 9, 1958, in Philadelphia, PA; son of Joseph F. (a carpenter) and Nina M. (a receptionist; maiden name, Pantaleo) Bartolomeo; married Lydia J. Sarro (a pediatrician), June 28, 1986; children: Julia A., Cara R. *Ethnicity:* "Italian-American." *Education:* Georgetown University, A.B., 1980; Harvard University, A.M., 1982, Ph.D., 1986. *Politics:* Democrat. *Religion:* Roman Catholic. *Hobbies and other interests:* Music (guitar, piano, voice).

ADDRESSES: Office—Department of English, Bartlett Hall, University of Massachusetts—Amherst, Amherst, MA 01003-0515; fax: 413-545-3880. *E-mail*—bartolomeo@english.umass.edu.

CAREER: University of Massachusetts—Amherst, Amherst, assistant professor, 1986-92, associate professor of English, beginning 1992. Twayne Publishers, eighteenth-century field editor for "Twayne English Authors Series."

MEMBER: Modern Language Association of America, American Society for Eighteenth-Century Studies, Northeast American Society for Eighteenth-Century Studies.

WRITINGS:

A New Species of Criticism, University of Delaware Press (Newark, DE), 1994.

Matched Pairs: Gender and Intertextual Dialogue in Eighteenth-Century Fiction, University of Delaware Press (Newark, DE), 2002.

Contributor to academic journals.*

* * *

BASTEN, Fred E(rnest)

PERSONAL: Born in Chicago, IL; son of Alfred H. (a salesman) and Jeanne (Bryan) Basten. *Education:* University of California—Los Angeles, B.A.

ADDRESSES: Office—3017 Santa Monica Blvd., Ste. 406, Santa Monica, CA 90404. *Agent*—Heacock Literary Agency, 1523 6th St., Ste. 14, Santa Monica, CA 90401.

CAREER: Foote, Cone & Belding (advertising), Los Angeles, CA, copywriter, 1955-57; Lennen & Newell (advertising), Los Angeles, CA, senior copywriter, 1958-59; A & W International, Inc., Santa Monica, CA, director of art and publications, 1960-74; full-time writer, 1974—.

WRITINGS:

Santa Monica Bay: The First One Hundred Years, Douglas-West (Los Angeles, CA), 1974.

Beverly Hills: Portrait of a Fabled City, Douglas-West (Los Angeles, CA), 1975.

Gringo: A Young American's Flight from Hell, Noble House, 1978.

Glorious Technicolor: The Movies' Magic Rainbow, A. S. Barnes (Cranbury, NJ), 1980.

Bruin Country: A Pictorial Grand Tour of the UCLA Campus, Graphics Press (Santa Monica, CA), 1980.

An Illustrated Guide to the Trees of Santa Monica Bay, Graphics Press (Santa Monica, CA), 1980.

Main Street to Malibu: Yesterday and Today, Graphics Press (Santa Monica, CA), 1980.

Steve McQueen: The Final Chapter, Vision House, 1983.

Life at the Marmont, Roundtable (Santa Monica, CA), 1987.

American Soviet Walk: Taking Steps to End the Nuclear Arms Race, United World of the Universe, 1988.

(With Robert A. Salvatore and Paul A. Kaufman) *Max Factor's Hollywood: Glamour, Movies and Make-Up,* General (Los Angeles, CA), 1995.

The Lost Artwork of Hollywood: Classic Images from Cinema's Golden Age, foreword by Ted Sennett, Watson-Guptill (New York, NY), 1996.

Santa Monica Bay: Paradise by the Sea: A Pictorial History of Santa Monica, Venice, Marina del Rey, Ocean Park, Pacific Palisades, Topanga & Malibu, introduction by Carolyn See, General (Los Angeles, CA), 1997.

The Way We Were: 20th Century Life As Reflected in Advertising, General (Los Angeles, CA), 1998.

(With Charles Phoenix) *Fabulous Las Vegas in the '50s: Glitz, Glamour & Games,* foreword by Keely Smith, Angel City Press (Los Angeles, CA), 1999.

Leis, Luaus and Alohas: The Lure of Hawaii in the Fifties, Island Heritage Publishing, 1999.

(With Frankie Gaye) *Marvin Gaye, My Brother,* Island Heritage Publishing, 1999.

(With Paddy Calistro) *Hollywood Archive: The Hidden History of Hollywood in the Golden Age,* Universe (New York, NY), 2000.

Santa Monica Bay: Paradise by the Sea, Hennessey & Ingalls (Santa Monica, CA), 2001.

Contributor to books, including *Fifty Golden Years with Oscar,* ESE California, 1979, *The Hollywood Reporter: The Golden Years,* Coward-McCann, 1984, and *The Beach Towns: A Walker's Guide to L.A.'s Beach Communities,* Chronicle, 1985. Contributor to journals.

WORK IN PROGRESS: The Art of the Movies: Sixty Years of Motion Picture Graphic Design and Illustration; a contemporary suspense novel, *Strangler!;* an autobiography of adult-film star John Holmes, *The Monkey Tree;* an autobiography of Ron "Zulu" Pope, *Blood Match: My Life As a Professional Wrestler;* a self-help guide for poor and troubled voices (with Dr. Morton Cooper), *Winning with Your Voice;* a pictorial history of Santa Monica's famed Palisades Park, *Palisades Park Panorama;* a biography of the infamous Lee Frances, *Hollywood Madam;* a biography of Father Damien, *The Flowers of Paradise.*

SIDELIGHTS: Fred E. Basten told *CA:* "I've always been a collector of vintage photographs, everything from local landmarks to movie stills. When I became disenchanted with the corporate world after years of writing, editing, and designing promotional pamphlets and house organs, I turned to books. My initial effort was a regional history, *Santa Monica Bay: The First One Hundred Years,* which was lavishly illustrated with photos from my collections. It became a runaway bestseller. Although I've since gone on to write books with broader appeal, it is still important for me to write for the regional market every few years. It helps keep my roots in the community."

Basten's interest in old photographs was an asset to his book *Hollywood Archive: The Hidden History of Hollywood in the Golden Age,* which evokes the American film capital's glory years from the silent film days until the 1960s through a collection of photographs and essays. Some of the writing is vintage, including Bette Davis's advice to lovelorn people, Shirley Temple's Christmas letter, and comments from Clayton Moore, who played the Lone Ranger, on western movies. Contemporary essays include one on animals in film by Jon Provost, who as a child starred in a television series with the famous collie dog, Lassie; remarks from producer/director Roger Corman on horror films; and a list of favorite films by Robert Osborne, who hosts the American Movie Classics television program. The sexual permissiveness of early Hollywood films is brought to light, and there is a section on the screen's most famous sex symbol, Marilyn Monroe. "There is always something surprising" in this book, noted Rob Lowman in the Los Angeles *Daily News.* K. D. Shirkani, reviewing the book for *Variety,* reported that the book reveals not so much a hidden history of Hollywood but "rather one that's simply slipped our minds." Shirkani described the more than seventy sections that make up the book as frequently "fun to peruse for their odd angles and imaginative ruminations." Basten examined another unique facet of Hollywood history in his collaborative work *Max Factor's Hollywood: Glamour, Movies and Make-Up.* This book, written with Robert A. Salvatore and Paul A. Kaufman, tells the story of Max Factor, the immigrant who transformed Hollywood with his specialized make-up techniques that led to stunning photographic effects.

BIOGRAPHICAL AND CRITICAL SOURCES:

PERIODICALS

Daily News (Los Angeles, CA), December 24, 2000, Rob Lowman, review of *Hollywood Archive: The Hidden History of Hollywood in the Golden Age,* p. L17.

Film Quarterly, summer, 1980, Ernest Callenbach, review of *Glorious Technicolor: The Movies' Magic Rainbow,* p. 58.

Publishers Weekly, August 28, 1987, Genevieve Stuttaford, review of *Life at the Marmont,* p. 60.

Star-Ledger, July 7, 1996, Harry Haun, review of *Max Factor's Hollywood: Glamour, Movies and Make-Up,* p. 6.

Variety, May 28, 1980, review of *Glorious Technicolor,* p. 20; February 12, 2001, K. D. Shirkani, review of *Hollywood Archive,* p. 45.*

BERNARD, Kenneth 1930-

PERSONAL: Born May 7, 1930, in Brooklyn, NY; son of Otis and Mary (Travaglini) Bernard; married Elaine Reiss (a teacher), September 2, 1952; children: Lucas, Judd, Kate. *Ethnicity:* "French, German, Italian, American Indian." *Education:* City College (now City College of the City University of New York), B.A., 1953; Columbia University, M.A., 1956, Ph.D., 1962.

ADDRESSES: *Home*—800 Riverside Dr., New York, NY 10032. *E-mail*—k.bernard@verizon.net.

CAREER: Long Island University, Brooklyn, NY, instructor, 1959-62, assistant professor, 1962-66, associate professor, 1967-70, professor of English, 1971-2003. New York Theater Strategy, vice president, 1974—. Consultant to state arts granting agencies in New York, 1974-75, Massachusetts, 1975, Wisconsin, 1975, and Maryland, 1978. *Military service:* U.S. Army, 1953-55.

AWARDS, HONORS: Grant from Office for Advanced Drama Research, 1971; Guggenheim play writing fellowship, 1972-73; New York Creative Artist Public Service grants, 1973, 1976; Rockefeller Foundation play writing grant, 1975; fiction grant, National Endowment for the Arts, 1978.

WRITINGS:

PLAYS

The Moke-Eater, produced in New York, NY, 1968.

Night Club, produced in New York, NY, 1970.

The Monkeys of the Organ Grinder, produced in New York, NY, 1970.

Night Club and Other Plays (contains *Night Club, The Lovers, The Monkeys of the Organ Grinder, The Moke-Eater, Mary Jane,* and *The Giants in the Earth*), Winter House (New York, NY), 1971.

Mary Jane, produced in New York, NY, 1973.

How We Danced while We Burned, produced in Yellow Springs, OH, 1974.

King Humpy, produced in New York, NY, 1975.

The Sixty Minute Queer Show, with music by John Braden, produced in New York, NY, 1977.

La Justice; or, The Cock That Crew, with music by John Braden, produced in New York, NY, 1979.

La Fin du Cirque, produced in New York, NY, 1984.

The Panel, produced in New York, NY, 1984.

Play with an Ending; or, Columbus Discovers the World, produced in New York, NY, 1984.

How We Danced while We Burned [and] *La Justice; or, The Cock That Crew,* Asylum Arts (Santa Maria, CA), 1990.

We Should. . . (A Lie), produced in New York, NY, 1992.

Curse of Fool: Three Plays, Asylum Arts (Santa Monica, CA), 1992.

(Final scene) *Why She Would Not* (unfinished play by George Bernard Shaw), produced in New York, NY, 2001.

OTHER

Two Stories, Perishable Press (Mount Horeb, WI), 1973.

The Maldive Chronicles, Performing Arts Journal Publications (New York, NY), 1987.

From the District File, Fiction Collective 2 (Boulder, CO), 1992.

The Baboon in the Nightclub: A Poem, Asylum Arts (Santa Monica, CA), 1994.

Clown at Wall: A Kenneth Bernard Reader, Confrontation Press (New York, NY), 1996.

The War of the Footnotists and Endnotists, Perishable Press (Mount Horeb, WI), 1996.

The Qui Parle Play and Poems, Asylum Arts (Paradise, CA), 1999.

Work appears in anthologies, including *Playwrights for Tomorrow 10,* University of Minnesota Press (Minneapolis, MN), 1973; and *Theatre of the Ridiculous,* Performing Arts Journal Publications (New York, NY), 1979, revised and expanded edition, Johns Hopkins University Press (Baltimore, MD), 1998. Contributor of fiction, poetry, and drama to *New American Review, Paris Review, Poetry New York, Harper's, Massachusetts Review, Minnesota Review,Penthouse, Grand Street,Salmagundi,* and *Fiction International.* Fiction editor, *Confrontation,* 1977—.

Collections of Bernard's manuscripts are housed at the Lincoln Center Library of the Performing Arts, New York, NY, and at the University of Minnesota, Minneapolis.

SIDELIGHTS: Michael Feingold, writing in *Contemporary Dramatists,* found that "the world-picture contained in [Kenneth Bernard's] plays is essentially that of a continuous nightmare . . . the emotional thrust of the material is constantly the same: towards revealing the sheer ludicrous horror of existence. . . . Bernard has carried the Artaudian project of raising and exorcizing the audience's demons about as far as it is likely to get through the theatrical metaphor."

Bernard told *Contemporary Dramatists:* "I like to think of my plays as metaphors, closer to poetic technique (the coherence of dream) than to rational discourse. I am not interested in traditional plot or character development. My plays build a metaphor; when the metaphor is complete, the play is complete."

BIOGRAPHICAL AND CRITICAL SOURCES:

BOOKS

Brecht, Stefan, *The Original Theatre of New York,* Suhrkamp (Frankfurt am Main, Germany), 1978.

Contemporary Dramatists, 5th edition, St. James Press (Detroit, MI), 1993.

Skloot, Robert, *The Darkness We Carry: The Drama of the Holocaust,* University of Wisconsin Press (Madison, WI), 1988.

PERIODICALS

Performing Arts Journal, spring-summer, 1978.

Witz: Journal of Contemporary Poetics, spring, 1997.

* * *

BOURGEOIS, Paulette 1951-

PERSONAL: Born July 20, 1951, in Winnipeg, Manitoba, Canada; daughter of Mathias (a chartered accountant) and Freda (a small business owner) Bourgeois; married Ian Urquhart (a journalist), May 3, 1980 (separated); children: Natalie, Gordon. *Education:* University of Western Ontario, B.Sc., 1974; attended Carleton University.

ADDRESSES: *Home*—Toronto, Ontario, Canada. *Agent*—c/o Author Mail, Kids Can Press, 29 Birch Ave., Toronto, Ontario M4V 1E2, Canada.

CAREER: Royal Ottawa Hospital, Ottawa, Ontario, Canada, staff occupational therapist, 1975-76; Canadian Broadcasting Corp., reporter, 1977-78, 1980-81; freelance writer, 1981—.

MEMBER: Writers Union of Canada, Canadian Society of Children's Authors, Illustrators, and Performers.

AWARDS, HONORS: Recipient of several Canada Council grants and numerous Children's Choice Awards from the Canadian Children's Book Centre.

WRITINGS:

FOR CHILDREN

Big Sarah's Little Boots, illustrated by Brenda Clark, Kids Can Press (Toronto, Ontario, Canada), 1987.

On Your Mark, Get Set: All about the Olympic Games, Then and Now, illustrated by Tina Holdcroft, Kids Can Press (Toronto, Ontario, Canada), 1987.

The Amazing Apple Book, illustrated by Linda Hendry, Kids Can Press (Toronto, Ontario, Canada), 1987, Addison-Wesley (Reading, MA), 1990.

The Amazing Paper Book, illustrated by Linda Hendry, Kids Can Press (Toronto, Ontario, Canada), 1989, Addison-Wesley (Reading, MA), 1990.

Grandma's Secret (also see below), illustrated by Maryann Kovalski, Kids Can Press (Toronto, Ontario, Canada), 1989, Joy Street Books (Boston, MA), 1990.

The Amazing Dirt Book, illustrated by Craig Terlson, Addison-Wesley (Reading, MA), 1990.

Too Many Chickens!, illustrated by Bill Slavin, Kids Can Press (Toronto, Ontario, Canada), 1990.

The Amazing Potato Book, Addison-Wesley (Reading, MA), 1991.

Canadian Fire Fighters ("My Neighborhood" series), illustrated by Kim LaFave, Kids Can Press (Toronto, Ontario, Canada), 1991, published as *Fire Fighters,* 1998.

Canadian Garbage Collectors ("My Neighborhood" series), illustrated by Kim LaFave, Kids Can Press (Toronto, Ontario, Canada), 1991, published as *Garbage Collectors,* 1998.

Canadian Police Officers ("My Neighborhood" series), illustrated by Kim LaFave, Kids Can Press (Toronto, Ontario, Canada), 1991, published as *Police Officers,* 1998.

Canadian Postal Workers ("My Neighborhood" series), illustrated by Kim LaFave, Kids Can Press (Toronto, Ontario, Canada), 1992, published as *Postal Workers,* 1998.

(With Martin Wolfish) *Changes in You and Me: A Book about Puberty, Mostly for Boys,* Andrews & McMeel (Kansas City, KS), 1994.

Changes in You and Me: A Book about Puberty, Mostly for Girls, Andrews & McMeel (Kansas City, KS), 1994.

Too Many Hats of Mr. Minches, illustrated by Kathryn Naylor, Stoddart (Toronto, Ontario, Canada), 1994.

The Sun ("Starting with Space" series), Kids Can Press (Toronto, Ontario, Canada), 1995.

The Moon ("Starting with Space" series), Kids Can Press (Toronto, Ontario, Canada), 1995.

Oma's Quilt, illustrated by Stephane Jorisch, Kids Can Press (Toronto, Ontario, Canada), 2001.

"FRANKLIN" SERIES

Franklin in the Dark (also see below; Book-of-the-Month Club selection), illustrated by Brenda Clark, Kids Can Press (Toronto, Ontario, Canada), 1986.

Hurry Up, Franklin (also see below), illustrated by Brenda Clark, Kids Can Press (Toronto, Ontario, Canada), 1989, Scholastic (New York, NY), 1990.

Franklin Fibs (also see below), illustrated by Brenda Clark, Scholastic (New York, NY), 1991.

Franklin Is Lost (also see below), illustrated by Brenda Clark, Scholastic (New York, NY), 1992.

Franklin Is Bossy (also see below), illustrated by Brenda Clark, Scholastic (New York, NY), 1993.

Franklin Is Messy, illustrated by Brenda Clark, Scholastic (New York, NY), 1994.

Franklin and Me: A Book about Me, Written and Drawn by Me (with a Little Help from Franklin), illustrated by Brenda Clark, Kids Can Press (Toronto, Ontario, Canada), 1994, published as *Franklin and Me: My First Record of Favourite Things, Personal Facts, and Special Memories,* 1997.

Franklin Goes to School (also see below), illustrated by Brenda Clark, Scholastic (New York, NY), 1995.

Franklin Plays the Game, illustrated by Brenda Clark, Scholastic (New York, NY), 1995.

Franklin's Blanket (also see below), illustrated by Brenda Clark, Scholastic (New York, NY), 1995.

Franklin Wants a Pet (also see below), illustrated by Brenda Clark, Scholastic (New York, NY), 1995.

Franklin and the Tooth Fairy (also see below), illustrated by Brenda Clark, Kids Can Press (Toronto, Ontario, Canada), 1995, Scholastic (New York, NY), 1996.

Franklin Has a Sleepover (also see below), illustrated by Brenda Clark, Kids Can Press (Toronto, Ontario, Canada), 1995, Scholastic (New York, NY), 1996.

Franklin's Halloween (also see below), illustrated by Brenda Clark, Scholastic (New York, NY), 1996.

Franklin's School Play (also see below), illustrated by Brenda Clark, Scholastic (New York, NY), 1996.

Franklin's Bad Day (also see below), illustrated by Brenda Clark, Kids Can Press (Toronto, Ontario, Canada), 1996, Scholastic (New York, NY), 1997.

Franklin Rides a Bike, illustrated by Brenda Clark, Scholastic (New York, NY), 1997.

Franklin's New Friend (also see below), illustrated by Brenda Clark, Scholastic (New York, NY), 1997.

Franklin's Valentines (also see below), illustrated by Brenda Clark, Scholastic (New York, NY), 1998.

Finders Keepers for Franklin, illustrated by Brenda Clark, Scholastic (New York, NY), 1998.

Franklin and the Thunderstorm, illustrated by Brenda Clark, Scholastic (New York, NY), 1998.

Franklin's Christmas Gift (also see below), illustrated by Brenda Clark, Scholastic (New York, NY), 1998.

Franklin's Secret Club (also see below), illustrated by Brenda Clark, Scholastic (New York, NY), 1998.

(With Sharon Jennings) *Franklin's Class Trip* (also see below), illustrated by Brenda Clark, Scholastic (New York, NY), 1999.

Franklin's Classic Treasury (contains *Franklin in the Dark, Franklin Fibs, Franklin Is Bossy,* and *Hurry Up, Franklin*), illustrated by Brenda Clark, Scholastic (New York, NY), 1999.

Franklin's Classic Treasury, Volume II (contains *Franklin Is Lost, Franklin Wants a Pet, Franklin's Blanket,* and *Franklin and the Tooth Fairy*), illustrated by Brenda Clark, Kids Can Press (Toronto, Ontario, Canada), 2000.

Franklin's Baby Sister (also see below), illustrated by Brenda Clark, Scholastic (New York, NY), 2000.

Franklin's Friendship Treasury (contains *Franklin Has a Sleepover, Franklin's Bad Day, Franklin's New Friend,* and *Franklin's Secret Club*), illustrated by

Brenda Clark, Kids Can Press (Toronto, Ontario, Canada), 2000.

Franklin and Harriet (also see below), illustrated by Brenda Clark, Scholastic (New York, NY), 2001.

Franklin's School Treasury (contains *Franklin Goes to School, Franklin's School Play, Franklin's Class Trip,* and *Franklin's Neighborhood*), illustrated by Brenda Clark, Kids Can Press (Toronto, Ontario, Canada), 2001.

Franklin Says I Love You (also see below), illustrated by Brenda Clark, Scholastic (New York, NY), 2002.

Franklin's Holiday Treasury (contains *Franklin's Halloween, Franklin's Valentines, Franklin's Christmas Gift,* and *Franklin's Thanksgiving*), illustrated by Brenda Clark, Kids Can Press (Toronto, Ontario, Canada), 2002.

Franklin's Family Treasury (contains *Franklin Goes to the Hospital, Franklin's Baby Sister, Franklin and Harriet* and *Franklin Says I Love You*), illustrated by Brenda Clark, Kids Can Press (Toronto, Ontario, Canada), 2003.

Many of Bourgeois's books have been translated into French; several have also been translated into Spanish.

ADAPTATIONS: A television series based on the "Franklin" books was created, airing on Canada's Family Channel, the Canadian Broadcasting Corporation (CBC), and Nickelodeon. An animated movie, *Franklin and the Green Knight,* was produced by Nelvana and Hong Guang Animation in 2000. Other authors have written books in the "Franklin" series which were based on Bourgeois's characters, including *Franklin's Neighborhood, Franklin Goes to the Hospital,* and *Franklin's Thanksgiving.*

SIDELIGHTS: Paulette Bourgeois is known across the United States and her native Canada as the creator of the classic, beloved children's book character Franklin. Franklin is a tiny turtle who suffers from all of the fears and trials of childhood. As he overcomes them, Franklin teaches preschool children lessons about trust, friendship, bravery, family, and many other topics, but he accomplishes this in a different way than most children's book characters do, note critics. As Valerie Hussey, co-owner of the "Franklin" series publisher Kids Can Press, explained to *Maclean's* interviewer Diane Turbide, "Very often, there's a kind of pedantry in children's books, with adults pointing out the lesson to be learned. . . . We try hard to avoid that. Franklin's parents are there to support him, but he usually resolves it himself. That's a large part of the appeal."

Around the time that her daughter, Natalie, was born, Bourgeois thought that she might like to write children's books, but she could not think of an original idea for one. She finally came up with the idea for Franklin while sitting up late one night with her infant daughter. She was watching an episode of the television series *M*A*S*H* in which the star, Hawkeye Pierce, declared that he was so claustrophobic that if he were a turtle, he would be afraid to go inside his shell. Bourgeois sat down and in less than a week wrote a story about just such a turtle. This story eventually became her first children's book, *Franklin in the Dark.*

The "Franklin" series has grown to encompass scores of books, a television series, and a movie, but the theme of facing one's fears remains common. In *Franklin and the Thunderstorm,* the little turtle wants to stay home with his mother instead of going to visit his friend Fox on a day when there might be a thunderstorm. His mother convinces him to go, and with his friends to support him, he learns that thunderstorms are not so bad after all. "Children will relate to the situation and the gentle humor of the solution," thought a *Resource Links* contributor. In *Franklin Is Lost,* Franklin and his friends have fun playing hide-and-seek. The little turtle forgets that he is not allowed to go in the woods, tries to hide there, and cannot find his way back out. "Bourgeois captures . . . well the surprise and fear that accompanies being lost," commented another *Resource Links* reviewer.

In *Franklin's Class Trip,* both Franklin and his friend Snail are afraid. Their classmate Beaver tells them that there are real dinosaurs at the museum the class is visiting. Franklin and Snail (who rides around the museum on Franklin's shell) spend the whole morning getting more and more worried about the dinosaurs, but finally, when they make it to the dinosaur room in the afternoon, the two critters realize that the dinosaurs are not alive and stop worrying.

The "Franklin" books also teach social skills like sharing, not being bossy, and cooperating. In *Franklin's Secret Club,* the turtle creates a club that excludes one of his classmates. The girl, offended, forms her own club that excludes Franklin. Franklin comes to realize that, rather than excluding others, it is better to be friends with everyone. It's another "wonderful, lesson story," from Bourgeois, a reviewer wrote in *Resource Links.*

Franklin learns another important insight about friendship in *Franklin's Valentines.* On his way to school on Valentine's Day, he accidentally drops all of his cards for his classmates in a mud puddle. Franklin is worried that his friends will be angry that he does not have valentines for them, and that they will not give him any valentines if they do not receive one in return. However, Franklin's friends are understanding and give him their cards, and the next day, Franklin brings "Friendship Day" cards for everyone.

Another holiday tale, *Franklin's Christmas Gift* finds the little turtle trying to make a very difficult decision. His class is collecting toys to give to poor children for the holidays. Franklin likes all of his toys and does not want to give any of them up. He finally discovers a broken toy that he would be willing to give away, but then his teacher, Mr. Owl, tells the class that the children who will be receiving these toys might not get any other presents this Christmas. Franklin realizes that his broken truck is not such a good present after all and donates one of his favorite toys instead.

Although she is best known for creating the Franklin character, Bourgeois has also written other books for children. *Oma's Quilt* offers "a gentle and subtle story about how the love and support of family members can make difficult transitions in life less painful," explained *Resource Links* reviewer Zoe Johnstone Guha. The beginning of the story finds Emily's grandmother, Oma, moving from her beloved house into a retirement home. At first, Oma hates the change. She wants to be able to cook her own meals, she misses her things, and she thinks that the other residents of the nursing home are "nincompoops." When Emily and her mother go to Oma's house to sort through her things, they realize that the old woman kept many items of clothing with sentimental value over the years. Together, Emily and her mother create a quilt for Oma out of those clothes, and being able to snuggle up with the quilt makes the move easier for Oma. The story is "told in simple, appealing language," thought *Booklist*'s Gillian Engberg, and *School Library Journal* contributor Sheilah Kosco dubbed the book "reassuring."

Bourgeois once commented: "I believe that children's books can give children a key to the world as it is, and as it can be. I try to give my characters—the children—a sense of power in a world where they are so often powerless."

BIOGRAPHICAL AND CRITICAL SOURCES:

BOOKS

Behind the Story: The People Who Create Our Best Children's Books . . . and How They Do It!, Pembroke (Markham, Canada), 1995.

PERIODICALS

Booklist, February 1, 1995, Stephanie Zvirin, review of *Changes in You and Me: A Book about Puberty, Mostly for Boys,* p. 1000A; September 1, 1997, Carolyn Phelan, review of *The Sun,* p. 108; April 15, 1998, Lauren Peterson, review of *Fire Fighters* and *Garbage Collectors,* p. 1447; March 1, 1999, Shelley Townsend-Hudson, review of *Franklin's Class Trip,* p. 1218; July, 1999, Carolyn Phelan, review of *Postal Workers* and *Police Officers,* p. 1948; June 1, 2000, Kathy Broderick, review of *Franklin Goes to the Hospital,* p. 1904; December 15, 2001, Gillian Engberg, review of *Oma's Quilt,* p. 738.

Canadian Children's Literature, spring, 2000, review of *Franklin's Secret Club, Franklin's New Friend, Finders Keepers for Franklin,* and *Franklin's Class Trip,* pp. 32-38; spring-summer, 2002, review of *Oma's Quilt,* p. 185.

Canadian Living, May, 2001, Paulette Bourgeois, "Franklin's Two Moms," pp. 121-122.

Canadian Materials, January, 1988, review of *The Amazing Apple Book,* p. 22; March, 1988, review of *Big Sarah's Little Boots,* p. 56; May, 1988, review of *On Your Mark, Get Set: All about the Olympics Then and Now,* pp. 107-108; September, 1989, review of *Hurry Up, Franklin,* p. 216; March, 1990, review of *Grandma's Secret,* p. 62; November, 1990, review of *Too Many Chickens!,* pp. 264-265; May, 1991, review of *Franklin Fibs,* p. 170; September, 1991, review of *Fire Fighters* and *Garbage Collectors,* pp. 226-227; September, 1992, review of *Franklin Is Lost,* p. 207; November, 1992, review of *Police Officers,* p. 308; January, 1993, review of *Postal Workers,* p. 20; March-April, 1994, review of *Franklin Is Bossy,* p. 56.

Horn Book, May-June, 1990, Hanna B. Zeiger, review of *Grandma's Secret,* p. 318.

Language Arts, September, 1992, Miriam Martinez and Marcia F. Nash, review of *Too Many Chickens!,* p. 372.

Maclean's, December 11, 1995, Diane Turbide, "A Million Dollar Turtle," pp. 50-51.

New York Times Book Review, March 12, 1995, Betsy Hearne, review of *Changes in You and Me: A Book about Puberty, Mostly for Girls,* p. 20.

Publishers Weekly, April 5, 1991, review of *Too Many Chickens!,* p. 144; June 5, 2000, review of *Franklin's Pet Problem,* p. 96; April 2, 2001, review of *Franklin's School Treasury,* p. 66; April 28, 2003, review of *Franklin's Family Treasury,* p. 73.

Quill & Quire, May, 1991, Peter Carver, "Paulette Bourgeois Branches Out," pp. 21, 24; June, 1991, review of *Fire Fighters* and *Garbage Collectors,* p. 24; July, 1991, review of *The Amazing Potato Book,* pp. 52-53; February, 1992, review of *Franklin Is Lost,* p. 32; August, 1992, review of *Postal Workers,* p. 28; July, 1993, review of *Franklin Is Bossy,* p. 56; December, 1994, review of *Changes in You and Me: A Book about Puberty, Mostly for Boys,* p. 34; September, 2001, review of *Oma's Quilt,* p. 52.

Resource Links, June, 1996, review of *Franklin Has a Sleepover,* p. 208; February, 1997, review of *Franklin's School Play,* p. 109; June, 1997, review of *Franklin Rides a Bike,* pp. 204-205; December, 1998, review of *Franklin's Secret Club,* p. 2; June, 1999, review of *Franklin's Class Trip,* p. 2; October, 1999, review of *Franklin Is Lost,* p. 2; February, 2000, review of *Franklin's Classic Treasury,* p. 2; April, 2000, review of *Franklin Goes to the Hospital* and *Franklin and the Thunderstorm,* p. 2; December, 2000, review of *Franklin's Baby Sister,* p. 2; April, 2001, Judy Cottrell, review of *Franklin's Pet Problem,* p. 3; December, 2001, Zoe Johnstone Guha, review of *Oma's Quilt,* pp. 4-5; April, 2002, Elaine Rospad, review of *Franklin Says I Love You,* pp. 2-3.

School Library Journal, November, 1989, Gail C. Ross, review of *Big Sarah's Little Boots,* p. 74; July, 1990, Jane Gardner Connor, review of *Grandma's Secret,* p. 56, and Barbara B. Murphy, review of *The Amazing Apple Book,* pp. 81-82; March, 1991, Susan L. Rogers, review of *The Amazing Dirt Book* and *The Amazing Paper Book,* pp. 198-199; June, 1991, Lee Bock, review of *Too Many Chickens!,* p. 72; February, 1992, Carolyn Kenks, review of *The Amazing Potato Book,* p. 92; March, 1995, Virginia E. Jeschelnig, review of *Changes in You and Me: A Book about Puberty, Mostly for Boys* and *Changes in You and Me: A Book about Puberty, Mostly for Girls,* p. 208; May, 1997, Elisabeth Palmer Abarbanel, review of *Franklin's Bad Day,* p. 93, and John Peters, review of *The Moon,* p. 200; December, 1997, Martha Topol, review of *Franklin's New Friend* and *Franklin Rides a Bike,* p. 87; June, 1998, Stephani Hutchinson, review of *Garbage Collectors* and *Firefighters,* pp. 127-128; July, 1998, Sally R. Dow, review of *Franklin and the Thunderstorm,* pp. 64-65; May, 1999, Dina Sherman, review of *Franklin's Class Trip,* p. 86; July, 1999, Paul Kelsey, review of *Postal Workers,* p. 84; November, 2001, Sheilah Kosco, review of *Oma's Quilt,* pp. 111-112.*

* * *

BRADBURY, Malcolm (Stanley) 1932-2000

PERSONAL: Born September 7, 1932, in Sheffield, England; died following a long illness and heart problems, November 27, 2000, in Norwich, England; son of Arthur and Doris Ethel (Marshall) Bradbury; married Elizabeth Salt, October, 1959; children: Matthew, Dominic. *Education:* University College, University of Leicester, B.A. (first-class honors), 1953; Queen Mary College, University of London, M.A., 1955; attended Indiana University, 1955-56, University of Manchester, 1956-58, Yale University, 1958-59; University of Manchester, Ph.D., 1962.

CAREER: University of Hull, Hull, England, staff tutor in literature and drama in department of adult education, 1959-61; University of Birmingham, Birmingham, England, lecturer in English language and literature, 1961-65; University of East Anglia, Norwich, England, lecturer, 1965-67, senior lecturer, 1967-69, reader in English, 1969-70, professor of American studies, 1970-95, professor emeritus, 1995-2000. Teaching fellow, Indiana University, 1955-56; junior fellow, Yale University, 1958-59; fellow, Harvard University, 1965-66; visiting professor, University of California—Davis, 1966; visiting fellow, All Souls

Malcolm Bradbury

College, Oxford University, 1969; visiting professor, University of Zurich, 1972; Fanny Hurst Professor of Writing, Washington University, 1982; Davis Professor, University of Queensland, and visiting professor, Griffith University, 1983; Senior Visiting Research Fellow, St. John's College, Oxford, 1994; Wells Professor, Indiana University, 1997. Chair of British Council English Studies Seminar, 1976-84; Booker-McConnell Prize for Fiction, chair of judges, 1981, member of management committee, 1984-91; member of management committee, Book Trust, 1987-89; judge of Royal Television Society Drama Awards, 1993; judge for British Academy of Film and Television Arts, 1995, 1998; chair of judges, Whitbread Prize, 1997. Founding director of Radio Broadland (independent radio station), 1984-96; director, East Anglian Radio, 1990-96.

MEMBER: British Association of American Studies, Society of Authors, PEN (executive committee, 1973-75), Royal Society of Literature (fellow).

AWARDS, HONORS: British Association of American Studies junior fellow in United States, 1958-59; American Council of Learned Societies fellow, 1965-66; Heinemann Prize, Royal Society of Literature, 1975, for *The History Man;* named among twenty best British writers by Book Marketing Council, 1982; shortlisted for Booker-McConnell Prize for Fiction, 1983, for *Rates of Exchange;* International Emmy Award, 1987, for *Porterhouse Blue;* Decorated Commander of the Order of the British Empire, 1991; Silver Nymph award for best screenplay for a series, Monte Carlo Television Festival, 1991, for *The Gravy Train;* Writers' Guild Macallan Award nomination, best drama serial for television, 1993, for *The Gravy Train Goes East;* best film made for television award, Banff Film Festival, 1995, for *Cold Comfort Farm;* Edgar Award nomination for best television feature, Mystery Writers of America, 1997, for "An Autumn Shroud," episode of television series *Dalziel and Pascoe*. D. Litt., University of Leicester, 1987, Birmingham University, 1989, University of Hull, 1994, and Nottingham University, 1996.

WRITINGS:

Eating People Is Wrong (novel), Secker & Warburg (London, England), 1959, Knopf (New York, NY), 1960.

Phogey!; or, How to Have Class in a Classless Society (also see below), Parrish, 1960.

All Dressed Up and Nowhere to Go: The Poor Man's Guide to the Affluent Society (also see below), Parrish, 1962.

Evelyn Waugh (critical study), Oliver & Boyd (London, England), 1962.

Stepping Westward (novel), Secker & Warburg (London, England), 1965, Houghton Mifflin (Boston, MA), 1966; reprinted, Penguin (New York, NY), 1995.

(With Allan Rodway) *Two Poets* (verse), Byron Press, 1966.

What Is a Novel?, Edward Arnold (London, England), 1969.

The Social Context of Modern English Literature (criticism), Schocken (New York, NY), 1971.

Possibilities: Essays on the State of the Novel, Oxford University Press (New York, NY), 1972.

The History Man (novel), Secker & Warburg (London, England), 1975, Houghton Mifflin (Boston, MA), 1976.

Who Do You Think You Are?: Stories and Parodies, Secker & Warburg (London, England), 1976.

The Outland Dart: American Writers and European Modernism, Oxford University Press (New York, NY), 1978.

Saul Bellow (critical study), Methuen (London, England), 1982.

All Dressed Up and Nowhere to Go (contains revised versions of *Phogey!* and *All Dressed Up and Nowhere to Go*), Pavilion (London, England), 1982, reprinted, Picador (London, England), 2000.

Rates of Exchange (novel), Knopf (New York, NY), 1983.

The Modern American Novel (criticism), Oxford University Press (New York, NY), 1983, revised edition, Viking (New York, NY), 1993.

Why Come to Slaka?, Secker & Warburg (London, England), 1986.

Cuts: A Very Short Novel (novella), Harper (New York, NY), 1987.

My Strange Quest for Mensonge, Penguin (New York, NY), 1988, also published as *Mensonge: Structuralism's Hidden Hero,* n.d.

No, Not Bloomsbury (collected essays), Columbia University Press (New York, NY), 1988.

Unsent Letters: Irreverent Notes from a Literary Life, Penguin (Harmondsworth, England), 1988.

The Modern World: Ten Great Writers (criticism), Penguin (New York, NY), 1989.

(With Richard Ruland) *From Puritanism to Postmodernism: A History of American Literature* (criticism), Viking (New York, NY), 1991.

Doctor Criminale (novel), Viking (New York, NY), 1992.

The Modern British Novel (criticism), Penguin (New York, NY), 1994.

Dangerous Pilgrimages: Trans-Atlantic Mythologies and the Novel (criticism), Secker & Warburg (London, England), 1995, Viking (New York, NY), 1996.

To the Hermitage (novel), Picador (London, England), 2000, Overlook Press (Woodstock, NY), 2001.

Contributor of more than 1,500 articles and reviews to periodicals, including *Punch, New Yorker, New York Times,* London *Times, Times Literary Supplement, New York Review of Books, Spectator,* and *New Republic.*

DRAMA:

(With David Lodge and James Duckett) *Between These Four Walls* (stage revue), first produced in Birmingham, England, 1963.

(With David Lodge, James Duckett, and David Turner) *Slap in the Middle* (stage revue), first produced in Birmingham, England, 1965.

(With Chris Bigsby) *The After-Dinner Game* (television play), British Broadcasting Corporation (BBC), 1975.

(With Chris Bigsby) *Stones* (television play), BBC, 1976.

Love on a Gunboat (television play), BBC, 1977.

The Enigma (television play; based on a story by John Fowles), BBC, 1980.

Standing in for Henry (television play), BBC, 1980.

Congress (radio play), BBC, 1981.

The After-Dinner Game: Three Plays for Television, Arrow Books, 1982, revised edition, 1989.

Rates of Exchange (television series; based on Bradbury's novel of the same title), BBC, 1985.

Blott on the Landscape (television series; adapted from the novel by Tom Sharpe), BBC, 1985.

Porterhouse Blue (television series; adapted from the novel by Tom Sharpe), Channel 4, 1987.

Imaginary Friends (television series; adapted from the novel by Alison Lurie), Thames, 1987.

The Green Man (television series; adapted from the novel by Kingsley Amis), BBC, 1990.

Cold Comfort Farm (television series; adapted from the novel by Stella Gibbons), BBC, 1996.

Inside Trading: A Comedy in Three Acts (drama; produced at the Norwich Playhouse, November-December, 1996), Methuen Drama (London, England), 1996, Heinemann (Portsmouth, NH), 1997.

In the Red (television series; adapted from the novel by Mark Tavener), BBC-2, 1998.

Author of plays *Scenes from Provincial Life,* based on the novel by William Cooper, and *Pemberton Billing and the Little Black Book.* Author, with wife, Elizabeth Bradbury, of radio play *This Sporting Life,* 1974-75. Author of six episodes of series *Anything More Would Be Greedy,* Anglia, 1989; four episodes of *The Gravy Train,* Channel 4, 1991; and four episodes of *The Gravy Train Goes West,* Channel 4, 1992. Adaptor of works by Reginald Hill, including "An Autumn Shroud," BBC-1, 1996, for the series *Dalziel and Pascoe.* Also author or adaptor of episodes of television series *A Touch of Frost, Kavanagh QC, Dalziel and Pascoe,* and *Inspector Morse.* Literary advisor for South Bank Show television series *The Modern World: Ten Great Writers,* LWT, 1988.

EDITOR:

E. M. Forster: A Collection of Critical Essays, Prentice-Hall (Englewood Cliffs, NJ), 1965.

Mark Twain, *"Pudd'nhead Wilson" and "Those Extraordinary Twins,"* Penguin (Harmondsworth, England), 1969.

E. M. Forster, *A Passage to India: A Casebook,* Macmillan (London, England), 1970.

(With David Palmer) *Contemporary Criticism,* Edward Arnold (London, England), 1970, St. Martin's Press (New York, NY), 1971.

(With Eric Mottram and Jean Franco) *The Penguin Companion to American Literature,* McGraw-Hill (New York, NY), 1971, published as *The Penguin Companion to Literature, Volume III: U.S.A.,* Allen Lane (London, England), 1971, published as *The Avenal Companion to English and American Literature,* Avenal, 1981.

(With David Palmer) *Metaphysical Poetry,* Indiana University Press (Bloomington, IN), 1971.

(With David Palmer) *The American Novel and the Nineteen Twenties,* Edward Arnold (London, England), 1971.

(With David Palmer) *Shakespearean Comedy,* Edward Arnold (London, England), 1972.

(With James McFarlane) *Modernism: A Guide to European Literature, 1890-1930,* Penguin (Harmondsworth, England), 1976, revised edition, 1990.

The Novel Today: Contemporary Writers on Modern Fiction, Rowman & Littlefield, 1977, revised edition, 1991.

(With David Palmer) *Decadence and the 1890s,* Edward Arnold (London, England), 1979.

(With David Palmer) *The Contemporary English Novel,* Edward Arnold (London, England), 1979.

(With David Palmer) *Contemporary Theatre,* Holmes & Meier (London, England), 1979.

(With Howard Temperley) *An Introduction to American Studies,* Longman (London, England), 1980, revised edition, 1997.

Stephen Crane, *The Red Badge of Courage* (critical edition), Dent (London, England), 1983.

(With David Palmer) *Shakespearean Tragedy,* Holmes & Meier (London, England), 1984.

(With Sigmund Ro) *Contemporary American Fiction,* Edward Arnold (London, England), 1987.

The Penguin Book of Modern British Short Stories, Penguin (Harmondsworth, England), 1988.

(With Judy Cooke) *New Writing,* Heinemann (London, England), 1992.

(With Andrew Motion) *New Writing 2,* Heinemann (London, England), 1993.

Washington Irving, *The Sketch Book of Geoffrey Crayon, Gent.,* J. M. Dent (London, England), 1993.

Present Laughter: An Anthology of Modern Comic Fiction, Weidenfeld & Nicolson (London, England), 1994.

Class Work: An Anthology of University of East Anglia Stories (anthology), Sceptre (London, England), 1995.

The Atlas of Literature, D'Agostini (New York, NY), 1996.

Henry James, *The American,* Everyman, 1997.

(And author of introduction and notes) E. M. Forster, *A Room with a View,* Penguin (New York, NY), 2000.

General editor, "Stratford-upon-Avon Studies" series, Edward Arnold, 1970-81, and "Contemporary Writers" series, Methuen. Associate editor, Leicester University literary magazine, *Luciad,* 1952-53, Indiana University literary magazine, *Folio,* 1955-56; joint editor of *Yale Penny Poems,* Yale University, 1958-59; advisory and guest editor to several literary magazines.

ADAPTATIONS: *The History Man* was adapted as a four-part television series by Christopher Hampton, BBC, 1979.

SIDELIGHTS: Malcolm Bradbury was a highly regarded English novelist and critic. Considered among England's preeminent scholars, Bradbury was also esteemed for his critically lauded satirical novels, including *Eating People Is Wrong, The History Man, Doctor Criminale,* and *To the Hermitage.* In addition to novels and literary criticism, Bradbury also authored short stories, stage revues, teleplays and dramas, and worked on many well-known television series in Great Britain, including *A Touch of Frost* and *Inspector Morse.* Bradbury was professor emeritus at the University of East Anglia, where he taught from 1965 until his death in 2000.

Herbert Burke in *Library Journal* called Malcolm Bradbury's first novel, *Eating People Is Wrong,* "a novel . . . about how weary academic life is in the English Midlands of the '50s—but this is not a weary novel. Often truly comic, its satire has many barbs and they often draw blood. . . . If seriousness of intent—a sociology of the British establishment of the times as seen through the microcosm of the academy—gets in the way of hearty satire, bawdiness is not lacking." According to Martin Tucker in the *New Republic,* the author wrote "a first novel that is sloppy, structurally flabby, occasionally inane, frequently magnificent and ultimately successful. It is as if [Charles] Dickens and Evelyn Waugh sat down together and said 'Let's write a comic novel in the manner of Kingsley Amis about a man in search of his lost innocence who finds it.' The result is one of the most substantial and dazzling literary feasts this year." Not all reviewers were so generous in their appraisal of the book, however. In the *New York Herald Tribune Book Review,* Patrick Dennis wrote: "While Malcolm Bradbury's first novel is brilliant, witty, sensitive, adult, funny and a lot of other pleasant and desirable things, it is not a good novel. And I know why: Mr. Bradbury has been so busy entertaining himself with his brilliance, wit, etc., that he has quite forgotten about those less gifted people who are expected to buy, read and enjoy his book. . . . While his knaves and fools are elegantly written, his 'sympathetic' characters are so feckless or so grotesque that one has almost no feeling for them." And a *New Yorker* critic found that "there are no funny situations, and the few comic episodes that occur are much too light, and perhaps also too tired, to stand up against the predominant, tragic predicament that is [the main character's] life . . . and even if this spectacle were more richly decorated than it is with jokes and puns and so on, it would not be good enough. Mr. Bradbury has created a serious and very human character, and has obscured him with jugglers."

Stepping Westward, Bradbury's second novel, also about university life, was hailed by a *Times Literary Supplement* reviewer as "a *vade mecum* for every youthful or aspiring first visitor to the United States. Every situational joke, every classic encounter is exactly and wittily exploited. The dialogue is often marvellously acute, the tricks of American speech expertly 'bugged.'" On the other hand, however, Rita Estok in *Library Journal* wrote that "the school, faculty and students do not ring true; in fact, it is almost a travesty on university life. James Walker, the principal character, never becomes believable and remains unsympathetic throughout the story. *Stepping Westward,* be it a travesty or satire on university life, fails to hit the mark as either." And Bernard McCabe in the *Saturday Review* wrote: "Within this very funny book Mr. Bradbury proposes a serious novel about freedom and community and friendship's inevitable failures. The result is interesting, but too schematic and analytical to be really successful. The comedy works, though, thanks to Bradbury's artful writing. I leave to some future scholar the precise significance of the recurrent buttocks-motif and ear-motif. . . . [The author's] exaggerated versions of [university life] work by lending a British ear and eye to the oddities of the American scene."

Robert Nye commented in the *Christian Science Monitor* that Bradbury, in his third novel, *The History Man,* achieved "some charming comic efforts—and not a few cruel ones. Bradbury has a baleful eye for human weakness. He describes with skill and obvious relish. The result is a clever, queer, witty, uncomfortable sort of book—a book whose prose possesses considerable surface brilliance but with a cutting edge concealed beneath." Margaret Drabble, in the *New York Times Book Review,* called the book "a small narrative masterpiece," and felt that "one of the reasons why this novel is so immensely readable is its evocation of physical reality; it may be a book about ideas, but the ideas are embodied in closely observed details. . . . A thoroughly civilized writer, [Bradbury] has written a novel that raises some very serious questions about the nature of civilization without for a moment appearing pretentious or didactic—a fine achievement."

Bradbury's fourth novel, *Rates of Exchange,* was published in 1983 to praise from critics such as *New York Times Book Review* contributor Rachel Billington, who labeled it "an astonishing tour de force." The tale of a linguist traveling to a fictive Eastern bloc country, *Rates of Exchange* takes on the subject of language itself and "manages to be funny, gloomy, shrewd and silly all at once," according to Joel Conarroe in the *Washington Post Book World.* Bradbury's inventive use of language—both the locals' fractured English and their native Slakan, a hybrid of several European languages—is a highlight for many reviewers. Noted Anatole Broyard in the *New York Times:* "Bradbury is in such virtuoso form that he can even make you enjoy an entire book in which the majority of the characters speak various degrees of broken English." Although some critics took issue with the book's pacing, characterization, and sometimes uneasy mixture of humor and seriousness, many valued its wit and pungent observations on travel. Wrote *Los Angeles Times* reviewer Elaine Kendall, "Hilarious and accurate, deepened by the author's concern for subtle political and social factors, *Rates of Exchange* turns tour de force into an unequivocal compliment, elevating the genre to a major literary category."

In the 1992 novel *Doctor Criminale,* Bradbury returns to the intellectual circuit for a satirical look at the charming and worldly Dr. Criminale, a fictional "superpower of contemporary thought." The doctor's shadowy past contributes to his mysterious appeal; students, scholars, and virtually all available members of the female gender are dazzled by his social, political, economic, philosophical, and literary wisdom. When a young journalist lands the job of researching the doctor's life for a TV documentary, the hunt for the *real* Criminale begins. This is, according to Michiko Kakutani of the *New York Times,* "an ambitious novel about large, unwieldly ideas. Mr. Bradbury raises questions about Criminale's past to examine the meaning of political commitment, the relationship between moral responsibility and esthetic principles, and the consequences of ethical pragmatism in an individual's public and private lives. . . . The . . . novel," she concluded, "is provocative and smart but also somehow bloodless." Other reviewers also felt that the character of Dr. Criminale needed fleshing out. "The eponymous subject is meant to be absolutely intriguing, but he is so 'elusive' that we have to attend instead to a thwarted narrator, in whom we're allowed no interest at all," asserted Mick Imlah in the *Times Literary Supplement.*

"In alternating chapters, our narrator, an unnamed British novelist, describes two journeys to St. Petersburg," wrote Hugo Barnacle in the *New Statesman* about Bradbury's 2000 novel, *To the Hermitage.* "One is his own, made as part of a slightly mysterious international junket in October 1993. The other is a visit paid by the French encyclopedist and philosopher [Denis] Diderot to the court of Catherine the Great in the 1770s." The novel, inspired in part by Laurence Stern's *Tristram Shandy,* is the story of the narrator's trip to a conference called the Diderot Project, the goal of which is to track down Diderot's papers after "his library had been bought by the Empress Catherine the Great, who also bought the philosopher himself as librarian," noted Brian Martin in the *Financial Times.* "In counterpoint to the shenanigans of the Project taking place in 1993," summarized Martin, "Bradbury tells the 1773 story of Diderot journeying to St. Petersburg and passing endless afternoons in philosophical and political discussions with the legendary tsarina."

"The book has its faults," found David Horspool in the London *Daily Telegraph,* "which are less to do with the intended lack of focus than the occasional relaxation of control. . . . But these are stray brushstrokes on a very broad canvas. The novel is a sweeping, engrossing and overwhelmingly impressive piece of work." Other critics had a similar reaction. "*To the Hermitage* is delightfully stimulating," argued Martin. "As readers, we watch and admire Bradbury's intellectual fireworks display." Barnacle, however, felt that if "the novel were roughly a third shorter, the amount of wit and ideas on display would fill it nicely. As it is, it feels rather padded." David Coward in the *Times Literary Supplement* cautioned that there is "no drama, no urgency, no characters to love or hate," but nonetheless concluded, "Ultimately it is his [Bradbury's] teasing, winking Shandyism which gives a centre to what may not be a story but is a wise and engaging entertainment."

In 1994, Bradbury's sweeping literary survey, *The Modern British Novel,* was published to mixed reviews. *Times Literary Supplement* critic Peter Kemp listed several instances in which the names of characters and the titles of books under discussion are cited incorrectly; furthermore, he called the author's accounts of various literary movements "little more than reaccumulations of the hackneyed. . . . As original critical analysis, [this book] is virtually nonexistent." But, Kemp conceded, "where it does briefly spark into life is as polemic. . . . Bradbury stirs into energetic and eloquent defence of the twentieth-century British novel's variety, versatility, and vitality. With comic regularity, he demonstrates, jeremiahs throughout the century have been announcing the death of the novel, only to be elbowed aside by the emergence of vigorous new practitioners of the genre."

Dangerous Pilgrimages: Trans-Atlantic Mythologies and the Novel, Bradbury's 1996 look at the reciprocal influence of British and American literary content and style, is generally regarded as an impressive and much-needed addition to the study of literary history. The book focuses largely on about a dozen American novelists and a half dozen Europeans (a couple of French writers along with British heavyweights of the last three centuries) and concludes that myths, rather than mimicry, have fueled the rich flow of ideas that make up "trans-Atlantic fiction." John Sutherland proclaimed in the *Times Literary Supplement:* "Academic criticism of American literature is currently densely theorized, introverted and, for anyone not professionally obliged to work with it, repugnant. This book is clearly a tool for the scholar but is generously accessible to any generally literate reader."

Bradbury also wrote numerous stage revues and television mini-series and teleplays, including the original television series *Anything More Would Be Greedy, The Gravy Train,* and *The Gravy Train Goes East.* In addition to writing original episodes for well-known television series, including *A Touch of Frost, Kavanagh QC, Dalziel and Pascoe,* and *Inspector Morse,* Bradbury adapted numerous works as teleplays. Bradbury's adaptation of Tom Sharpe's *Porterhouse Blue* garnered an International Emmy award; his adaptation of Stella Gibbons's *Cold Comfort Farm,* later released as a full-length motion picture directed by John Schlesinger that was based on the screenplay by Bradbury, received the best film-made-for-television award at the Banff Film Festival.

Bradbury once commented: "As a novelist, I achieved four novels (and a volume of short stories) in twenty-five years. It may seem a slow record, but then I have been a critic, reviewer, and professor of American studies too, as well as a regular writer for television. I believe the writer has a responsibility for literary study, and this belief has gone into my teaching of creative writing and my editorship of series like Methuen's "Contemporary Writers," where I and my fellow editor Chris Bigsby have sought to show that we live in a major period of literary creation very different from that of the earlier part of the century. I believe in fact we live in a remarkable international age of fiction, and this has affected my own writing. Though I started with provincial themes and in a relatively realistic mode I have grown vastly more international in preoccupation and far more experimental in method. Looking back over my books, they now seem to me to follow the curve of the development of British fiction from the 1950s: from the comic social realism of the postwar period through to a much harsher, more ironic vision which involves the use of fictiveness and fantasy—though always, in my case, with an edge of tragic commentary on the world we live in as this dark century moves to its end. I think I have grown far more exact as a writer, more concerned to deal with major themes, to escape provincial limitations, and to follow the fate of liberal hopes through the many intellectual, moral, and historical challenges it has now to face. As I said earlier: 'Serious writing is not an innocent act; it is an act of connection with the major acts of writing achieved by others. It is also . . . a new set of grammars, forms, and styles for the age we live in.'

"My books have been widely translated and are set-texts in schools and universities, and two—*The History Man* and *Rates of Exchange*—have been made into British Broadcasting Corporation television series. This has done a good deal to free me of the unfortunate label of being a 'university novelist,' since my aims are wider. I have myself been considerably influenced by writing for television, and I think the imagery and grammar of film and television has brought home new concepts of presentation and perception to the novel. I have also been influenced by (and perhaps also have influenced) younger writers like Ian McEwan and Clive Sinclair who have been in my creative writing classes at the University of East Anglia. I have fought for a view of the novel in Britain as a serious and experimental form, and I believe it has increasingly become so. I believe in our great need for fiction; in *Rates of Exchange,* set in Eastern Europe, I have tried to relate our awareness of an oppressive modern reality forged by the fictions of politicians and the structures of ideology to our need for true fictions that can challenge them. My basic themes, though, remain the same: the conflict between liberal humanism and the harsh systems and behaviorisms of the modern world, and the tragic implications, which, however, I believe must be expressed in comic form. In an age when the big ideologies grow tired, I think we need the abrasive vision of the writer, and in some of our great contemporaries of the novel, from Saul Bellow to Milan Kundera, I think we find that. So the novel is what gives me hope, and lasting pleasure."

BIOGRAPHICAL AND CRITICAL SOURCES:

BOOKS

Bigsby, Christopher, and Heide Ziegler, editors, *The Radical Imagination and the Liberal Tradition: Interviews with English and American Novelists,* Junction Books, 1982.

Contemporary Literary Criticism, Volume 32, Thomson Gale (Detroit, MI), 1985.

Dictionary of Literary Biography, Volume 14: *British Novelists since 1960,* Thomson Gale (Detroit, MI), 1983.

Morace, Robert A., *The Dialogic Novels of Malcolm Bradbury and David Lodge,* Southern Illinois University Press (Carbondale, IL), 1989.

PERIODICALS

Atlantic, November, 1992, p. 162; April, 2001, p. 107.

Booklist, April 15, 1960; July, 1996, p. 1796; December 15, 1996, review of *The Atlas of Literature,* p. 745; March 15, 2001, p. 1353.

Books and Bookmen, April, 1983.

California, October, 1988.

Christian Science Monitor, February 18, 1976.

Commentary, September, 1989.

Commonweal, April 22, 1960.

Contemporary Review, March, 2001, p. 159.

Daily Telegraph (London, England), May 20, 2000, David Horspool, review of *To the Hermitage.*

Economist (U.S.), July 15, 2000, review of *To the Hermitage,* p. 13.

Financial Times, June 10, 2000, Brian Martin, review of *To the Hermitage,* p. 4.

Globe and Mail (Toronto, Ontario, Canada), September 12, 1987; August 20, 1988.

Journal of European Studies March, 2003, p. 41.

Library Journal, March 1, 1960; June 1, 1966; May 15, 1988; June 15, 1988; January, 1989; November 15, 1991; April 1, 2001, p. 131.

Literary Review, October, 1983.

London Review of Books, September 24, 1992, p. 18; November 18, 1993, p. 23.

Los Angeles Times, October 21, 1983; December 9, 1988.

Los Angeles Times Book Review, October 18, 1987; September 25, 1988.

Mother Jones, October, 1987.

National Review, May 2, 1960; June 17, 1996, p. 57.

New Leader, January 11, 1988, pp. 20-21.

New Republic, December 14, 1987; May 27, 1996, pp. 28-29.

New Statesman, October 31, 1959; April 17, 1987; August 28, 1987; May 29, 2000, Hugo Barnacle, review of *To the Hermitage,* p. 54.

New Statesman and Society, October 12, 1990.

Newsweek, October 24, 1983.

New Yorker, July 16, 1960; May 3, 1976.

New York Herald Tribune Book Review, May 22, 1960.

New York Times, April 10, 1960; October 1, 1983; November 7, 1987; January 30, 1989.

New York Times Book Review, February 8, 1976; November 20, 1983; October 18, 1987; September 25, 1988; December 16, 1991; October 6, 1992, Michiko Kakutani, review of *Doctor Criminale,* p. C15; October 25, 1992, Joel Conarroe, review of *Doctor Criminale;* August 9, 1996, Michiko Kakutani, review of *Dangerous Pilgrimages;* September 22, 1996, Robert M. Adams, review of *Dangerous Pilgrimages.*

People, May 27, 1996, p. 19; March 26, 2001, p. 60.

Publishers Weekly, September 11, 1987; May 27, 1988; November 18, 1988; July 20, 1992, p. 220; June 10, 1996, p. 80; February 26, 2001, p. 60.

San Francisco Chronicle, April 26, 1960.

Saturday Review, April 9, 1960; May 21, 1966.

Spectator, September 12, 1992, p. 37; October 30, 1993, p. 29; April 15, 1995, p. 35.

Time, June 3, 1966; November 14, 1983; July 18, 1988, p. 70.

Times (London, England), April 7, 1983; January 14, 1988; May 12, 1988; June 4, 1988.

Times Literary Supplement, November 13, 1959; August 5, 1965; November 7, 1975; September 3, 1982; April 8, 1983, February 22, 1985; October 24, 1986; June 12, 1987; November 12, 1987; May 13, 1988; September 11, 1992, p. 23; November 12, 1993, p. 24; April 28, 1995, p. 21; May 19, 2000, David Coward, review of *To the Hermitage,* p. 22.

Tribune Books (Chicago, IL), August 28, 1988.

Washington Post, October 14, 1987.

Washington Post Book World, November 20, 1983; July 3, 1988; October 25, 1992, p. 5.

OBITUARIES:

PERIODICALS

Economist (U.S.), December 2, 2000, p. 4.

Independent (London, England), November 29, 2000, p. 6.

Newsweek International, December 11, 2000, p. 3.

New York Times, November 29, 2000, p. C25.

Time, December 11, 2000, p. 41.

Time International, December 11, 2000, p. 16.

Washington Post, December 2, 2000, p. B5.*

BRAGG, Rick 1959(?)-

PERSONAL: Born c. 1959, in Possum Trot, AL; son of Margaret Marie Bragg. *Education:* Attended Harvard University.

ADDRESSES: *Home*—347 Joseph St., New Orleans, LA 70115. *Agent*—c/o Pantheon Books, 201 E. 50th St., New York, NY 10022.

CAREER: Journalist and memoirist. Worked as reporter for various Alabama newspapers; worked as a reporter for *St. Petersburg Times,* St. Petersburg, FL, and *New York Times,* New York, NY.

AWARDS, HONORS: Nieman fellowship, Harvard University; Pulitzer Prize for feature writing, 1996, for coverage of Oklahoma City bombing; American Society of Newspaper Editors Distinguished Writing Award (twice); University of Alabama Clarence Cason Award for Nonfiction Writing, 2004.

WRITINGS:

All Over but the Shoutin', Pantheon (New York, NY), 1997, published as *Redbirds: Memories from the South,* Harville Press (London, England), 1999.

(With Walker Evans) *Wooden Churches: A Celebration,* Algonquin Books (Chapel Hill, NC), 1999.

Somebody Told Me: The Newspaper Stories of Rick Bragg, University of Alabama Press (Tuscaloosa, AL), 2000.

Ava's Man, Knopf (New York, NY), 2001.

(Author of foreword) *Best of the Oxford American: Ten Years from the Southern Magazine of Good Writing,* Hill Street Press (Athens, GA), 2002.

I Am a Soldier Too: The Jessica Lynch Story, Knopf (New York, NY), 2003.

ADAPTATIONS: *Ava's Man* was recorded on compact disc and released by Random Audio, 2001. *All Over but the Shoutin'* was narrated by Bragg and released as an audiobook produced by Random Audio, 1997.

SIDELIGHTS: In his acclaimed memoir, *All Over but the Shoutin',* Rick Bragg describes his personal journey from harsh childhood to national renown as a prize-winning journalist. A reporter who won a Pulitzer Prize for his coverage of the Oklahoma City bombing, Bragg pays special homage in his memoir to his mother, Margaret, for her heroic efforts to provide her children a good home despite nearly insurmountable hardships.

Rick Bragg

Bragg grew up in Possum Trot, Alabama, located in the Appalachian foothills on the border between Alabama and Georgia. He was the second of three sons, a fourth having died in infancy. The family was very poor, surviving on a fifty-dollar-per-month Social Security check in addition to what Margaret Bragg made as a field hand. Bragg's father, a Korean War veteran who became a physically abusive alcoholic and died at age forty, was rarely present; when he was, he often beat Margaret. She withstood mistreatment stoically and bestowed a compensating love on her children, which enabled Bragg to find eventual success as a writer. All in all, his childhood, Bragg wrote in *All Over but the Shoutin',* was "full, rich, original and real," as well as "harsh, hard, mean as a damn snake." "I am not a romantic figure," he added, ". . . but I have not led a humdrum life."

After graduating from high school, Bragg spent six months in college, then landed a job at a local newspaper after the paper's first choice for the job opening decided to remain in a fast-food restaurant position instead. After moving on to the *St. Petersburg Times,* Bragg covered Hurricane Andrew, problems in Haiti, and riots in Miami before spending a year at Harvard University on a Nieman fellowship. Subsequently, he joined the *New York Times,* covering the Susan Smith child murders and the U.S. intervention in Haiti.

In 1996 Bragg's coverage of the Oklahoma City bombing earned him the Pulitzer Prize. He brought his mother to New York City by plane for the awards ceremony; she had not only never been on a plane, or on an escalator, or in New York, but she had not bought a new dress in eighteen years. Bragg describes the prize ceremony in *All Over but the Shoutin'* and the scene is, according to Diane Hartman in the *Denver Post,* "the best in the book." Bragg also memorably recounts his cash purchase, with his prize money and book profits, of a new house for his mother. *Seattle Times* contributor Chris Solomon concluded that *All Over but the Shoutin'* is a "well-received effort to enshrine a saint (his mother), exorcise a demon (his father) and tell his own Horatio Alger story."

Many reviewers have praised Bragg's gripping real-life story, though the enthusiasm has been tempered by some of the story's psychological residue. For Hartman a maudlin tone, born of "survivor's guilt," enters the writing at points—"but Bragg is good and there's no denying it," she concluded. A writer for *Library Journal* recommended *All Over but the Shoutin'* highly for its "honest but unsentimental" style, its "plainspoken and lyrical" effects, and its "telling" details. A *Publishers Weekly* contributor, however, called the book "uneven" and "jolting," referring to it as "a mixture of moving anecdotes and almost masochistic self-analysis" but nonetheless praising Bragg's "gift for language." Similar admiration was expressed by *Times Literary Supplement* reviewer Charles McNair, who considered the memoir a "heartbreaking, inspiring account" that "is no sentimental, soft-lens nostalgic piece, but an uncomfortably honest portrait of growing up with less than nothing, a memoir fraught with sharp edges and hard truths."

Bragg's prequel to *All Over but the Shoutin',* titled *Ava's Man,* is, as he told *Book* writer Anthony DeCurtis, a "necessary response to his readers' righteous demands" after reading *All Over but the Shoutin'.* In this book he tells the story of his maternal grandparents, Ava and Charlie Bundrum. Because he knew few details about the lives of his grandparents, he had to reconstruct the story from an oral history he collected from his mother, aunts and uncles, and other family members and friends. These friends and relatives had rich tales to tell about Charlie Bundrum, a man who was much loved and admired. Bragg had never met his grandfather, as he died the year before Bragg's birth, but he did rely on his own recollections of his grandmother Ava, who lived on thirty-six years after her husband's death.

Charlie Bundrum raised his family in the Deep South during the heart of the economic depression of the 1930s, and moved his wife and eight children twenty-one times, determined to do whatever it took to keep his family fed and safe. Bundrum worked as a roofer and general laborer, as well as a bootlegger, for most of his life. While he developed a taste for the illegal corn liquor, which eventually killed him at a young age, he never let alcohol run his life. Bragg depicts his grandfather, in DeCurtis's words, as "a moonshine maker who worked hard and fiercely protected his family; loved to fight, fish, and tell stories, and cared little for any law but the unspoken, unquestioned code of his community."

At one point in Bragg's story, Bundrum gets arrested for vagrancy, based on his appearance, while trying to get home from a fishing trip. This was not an uncommon experience for poor white men living in Appalachia during the 1940s. Anthony Day in the *Los Angeles Times* pointed out that Bragg is one of the first authors to tell the story of poor whites in the south from an insider's perspective, and noted that Bragg writes "honestly and affectionately" regarding this topic. Robert Morgan, in the *New York Times Book Review,* acknowledged that "relatively few authors have truly caught the voice of the Southern working class," and in *Ava's Man* the characters and setting "grab you from the first sentence." Morgan went on to call *Ava's Man* "a kind of sublime testimonial" and added: "Bragg gets the combination of sentiment and independence and fear in this culture just right."

For Bragg, writing *Ava's Man* was an opportunity to acquaint himself with the grandfather he never knew and to build a monument to this beloved man. Though *Orlando Sentinel* writer John Harper found the book "structurally weak," a reviewer for *Publishers Weekly* reported that "Bragg delivers, with deep affection, fierce familial pride, and keen, vivid prose."

In 2003 Bragg was selected by Knopf to write the story of one of the first women to be injured in active duty while serving in the U.S. military. Discussing *I Am a Soldier, Too: The Jessica Lynch Story* with *Publishers Weekly* interviewer Charlotte Abbot, Bragg noted that the appeal of writing the book lay primarily in the "wonderful story" Lynch, a soldier fighting in the War on Terror in Iraq, has to tell. "What happened was unexpected: a nineteen-year-old supply clerk was pressed into driving a truck into a war. It was an unscripted drama. Some people died, others got broken. But at least where Jessie is concerned there's a win. I've written so many stories where there wasn't a win. . . . Jessie wanted to see what was 'on the other side of the holler.' These are people who fight and die and serve their country, and they deserve some good attention, something beyond the sneers of intellectuals."

BIOGRAPHICAL AND CRITICAL SOURCES:

BOOKS

Bragg, Rick, *All Over but the Shoutin'*, Pantheon (New York, NY), 1997.

PERIODICALS

Book, September, 2001, Anthony DeCurtis, "Southern Grit," p. 53.

Booklist, September 15, 1997, p. 182; June 1, 2001, Joanne Wilkinson, review of *Ava's Man,* p. 1795.

Denver Post, October 5, 1997, Diane Hartman, review of *All Over but the Shoutin'*.

Entertainment Weekly, November 21, 2003, Tina Jordan, review of *I Am a Soldier, Too: The Jessica Lynch Story,* p 88.

Geographical, September, 1999, Chris Martin, review of *Redbirds: Memories from the South,* p. 71.

Kliatt, January, 1999, review of *All Over but the Shoutin',* p. 23.

Library Journal, September 15, 1997, p. 81; January 5, 1998; September 1, 1999, Russell T. Clement, review of *Wooden Churches: A Celebration,* p. 186; November 15, 1999, review of *All Over but the Shoutin',* p. 115; May 1, 2000, Pam Kingsbury, review of *Somebody Told Me: The Newspaper Stories of Rick Bragg,* p. 128; June 15, 2001, Pam Kingsbury, review of *Ava's Man,* p. 81; September 1, 2001, Pam Kingsbury, "Building Himself a Grandfather," p. 194.

Los Angeles Times, October 12, 2001, Anthony Day, "An Affectionate Portrait of the South's Poor, Hard-Living Whites," p. E3.

Mississippi Quarterly, winter, 1999, Amy E. Weldon, "When Fantasy Meant Survival," p. 89.

New York Times, September 10, 2001, Theodore Rosengarten, "Hammer-Swinging Roofer, Not a Hillbilly, in Appalachia," p. E6.

New York Times Book Review, June 25, 2000, Ruth Bayard Smith, review of *Somebody Told Me;* September 2, 2001, Robert Morgan, review of *Ava's Man,* p. 9.

Orlando Sentinel, September 19, 2001, John Harper, review of *Ava's Man.*

Publishers Weekly, July 14, 1997, p. 73; August 6, 2001, review of *Ava's Man,* p. 74; September 8, 2003, Charlotte Abbot, "Bragg: Lynch Has a 'Wonderful Story to Tell,'" p. 16.

Rapport, May, 1999, review of *All Over but the Shoutin',* p. 39.

San Francisco Chronicle, September 16, 2001, review of *Ava's Man,* p. 68.

Sarasota Herald Tribune, November 5, 2000, Thomas Becnel, "Bragg Shares What *Somebody Told Me,*" p. E5; November 4, 2001, Susan L. Rife, "Bragg's Portrait of Grandfather Is Revealing and Very Human," p. E5.

Seattle Times, October 30, 1997, Chris Solomon, review of *All Over but the Shoutin'.*

Times Literary Supplement, October 16, 1998, Charles McNair, "The Struggle So Far," p. 34.

Washington Post, August 19, 2001, Fred Chappell, "Hardscrabble," p. T4.*

* * *

BRANT, Marley 1950-

PERSONAL: Born July 26, 1950 in Syracuse, NY; daughter of Herbert and Gladys Olmstead; married David Bruegger; children: Tim Bruegger. *Education:* Attended Lee Strasberg Theater Institute; California State University—Northridge, B.A. (political science). *Religion:* Christian. *Hobbies and other interests:* History, travel, music, film, and people.

ADDRESSES: Agent—c/o Author Mail, Billboard Books, 770 Broadway, New York, NY 10003.

CAREER: Chrysalis Records, Beverly Hills, CA, assistant national director of artist development, 1976-78; Paramount Television, Hollywood, CA, publicist, 1980-81; ICPR Public Relations, Los Angeles, CA, publicist, 1981-83; record producer, 1983-91; author, 1992—.

MEMBER: National Academy of Recording Arts and Sciences, Publicists Guild of America.

AWARDS, HONORS: Grammy Award nominee; Georgia Author of the Year nominee.

WRITINGS:

The Outlaw Youngers: A Confederate Brotherhood, Madison Books (Lanham, MD), 1992.
Outlaws: The Illustrated History of the James-Younger Gang, Elliott & Clark (Montgomery, AL), 1997.
Jesse James: The Man and the Myth, Berkley Books (New York, NY), 1998.
Southern Rockers: The Roots and Legacy of Southern Rock, Billboard Books (New York, NY), 1999.
Freebirds: The Lynyrd Skynyrd Story, Billboard Books (New York, NY), 2002.
Tales from the Rock and Roll Highway, Billboard Books (New York, NY), 2003.

SIDELIGHTS: Marley Brant told *CA:* "Very unique and special circumstances experienced while on a vacation trip to Missouri led me into the field of outlaws. I had worked in the entertainment field for many years and only after the publication of my first book did I realize that my affinity for outlaws continued to be a driving factor in my career as an author. What are music personalities, if not the outlaws of the here and now? I continue to meet these captivating personalities through my work and, as I did with Jessie James and the Younger Brothers, experience entertaining challenges as I attempt to tell of their lives and times."

Brant parlayed her interest into such books as *The Outlaw Youngers: A Confederate Brotherhood* and *Jesse James: The Man and the Myth.* In the latter work, Brant shows that while the legendary outlaw indeed earned some of his reputation as a train robber, bank robber and occasional gunslinger, "folklore, distortions and outright lies have shrouded the facts of Jesse's life," according to *Wild West* contributor Sierre Adare. As Adare related, Brant delves into James's early years in Missouri, uncovering a pattern of misfortune (a father who deserted; a mother with a "preference for Jesse's older brother, Frank") that led the younger brother to join a band of Confederate-supporting guerillas during the Civil War years. James felt he had made the right decision; "he was striking out at the Union Army's barbarity in dealing with Missouri's innocent women and children," wrote Adare. "Brant reveals the politics behind the Union government's continued terrorization of the James family after the war and the psychological profile of the guerilla turned avenging angel."

Brant told Adare that the information about James's home state helped inspire her book; "I hadn't realized just how strongly Missouri was involved in the War between the States," she said. As for the outlaw life of Jesse James, the author concluded that it "was not glamorous." Brant acknowledges that James was involved in some of the major crimes he was accused of, "but not in the beginning." Then there were what she calls the "copycats," feeding off James's reputation. They were easily identified: "Robbing stagecoaches and a gambling boat just wasn't Jesse's style." Nor was James the "Robin Hood" archetype later credited to him; according to Brant, he never doled out his ill-gotten money to the ravaged people of postwar Missouri, but "what he did was return their self-esteem."

Southern topics also enter into Brant's writing about music, her first career. A former music executive, Brant is the author of *Southern Rockers: The Roots and Legacy of Southern Rock* and *Freebirds: The Lynyrd Skynyrd Story.* In a review for *Popular Music and Society,* S. Renee Dechert deemed *Southern Rockers* "the first comprehensive history" of a genre "whose artists have, on occasion, been labeled 'redneck bands.'" Such stereotyping often led to a diminished reputation for the musicians.. Brant, noted Dechert, "attempts to correct these oversights." The author profiles such stadium-packing groups as the Allman Brothers, Marshall Tucker, and .38 Special, as well as lesser-known artists like the Atlanta Rhythm Section. Dechert found a "few problems" in Brant's cataloging, noting that she "omits Black Oak Arkansas, the Dixie

Dregs, and Elvin Bishop, questioning that any of these bands represent 'southern rock.'" Still, the critic concluded that in this volume the author "has done a good job . . . showing the relationships between bands emerging from a culture that has always valued community."

One southern-rock group in particular caught Brant's attention. She produced a separate book, *Freebirds,* about Lynyrd Skynyrd, mainly because "she feels the band is barely covered by the media and yet has some of the best guitar players and songwriters in the business," according to *Atlanta Journal-Constitution* reporter Kaye Cagle. The journalist added that Brant's "behind the scenes account of the group's climb to fame, band relationships, broken contracts, drugs, criminal charges and legal entanglements make for an in-depth report." *Booklist*'s Mike Tribby praised the author's "conversational, even chummy prose befitting a band that enjoys a community of fans and friends."

Brant continued her work in the field of music with *Tales from the Rock and Roll Highway.* Published in 2003 by Billboard Books, *Tales from the Rock and Roll Highway* features first-person stories collected from rock and roll artists from the 1950s to the present.

BIOGRAPHICAL AND CRITICAL SOURCES:

PERIODICALS

Atlanta Journal-Constitution, May 9, 2002, Kaye Cagle, "Southern Rock Gets Crusader," p. JF3.

Biography, spring, 2003, David M. Halbfinger, review of *Freebirds: The Lynyrd Skynyrd Story,* p. 392.

Booklist, June 1, 1999, Mike Tribby, review of *Southern Rockers: The Roots and Legacy of Southern Rock,* p. 1765; January 1, 2002, Tribby, review of *Freebirds,* p 788.

Los Angeles Times Book Review, June 6, 1993, review of *The Outlaw Youngers: A Confederate Brotherhood,* p. 6.

New York Times Book Review, October 20, 2002, David M. Halbfinger, review of *Freebirds,* p. 16.

Popular Music and Society, fall, 2000, S. Renee Dechert, review of *Southern Rockers,* p. 138.

Roundup, February, 1998, review of *Outlaws: The Illustrated History of the James-Younger Gang,* p. 23; August, 1998, *Jesse James: The Man and the Myth,* p. 22.

Wild West, April, 1998, review of *Outlaws,* p. 64; August, 1998, Sierre Adare, "Marley Brant Sets the Record Straight on Outlaw Jesse James" (interview), p. 62.

* * *

BROWNMILLER, Susan 1935-

PERSONAL: Born February 15, 1935, in Brooklyn, NY. *Education:* Attended Cornell University, 1952-55, and Jefferson School of Social Sciences. *Hobbies and other interests:* Travel.

ADDRESSES: Home—61 Jane St., New York, NY 10014. *Office*—Grove Weidenfeld, 841 Broadway, New York, NY 10003.

CAREER: Actress in New York, NY, 1955-59; *Coronet,* New York, NY, assistant to managing editor, 1959-60; *Albany Report,* Albany, NY, editor, 1961-62; *Newsweek,* New York, NY, national affairs researcher, 1963-64; *Village Voice,* New York, NY, staff writer, 1965; National Broadcasting Company, Inc. (NBC), New York, NY, reporter, 1965; American Broadcasting Companies, Inc. (ABC), New York, NY, network newswriter, 1966-68; freelance journalist, 1968-70; writer. Lecturer. Organizer of Women against Pornography.

MEMBER: New York Radical Feminists (cofounder).

AWARDS, HONORS: Grants from Alicia Patterson Foundation and Louis M. Rabinowitz Foundation; *Against Our Will: Men, Women, and Rape* was listed among the outstanding books of the year by *New York Times Book Review,* 1975; named among *Time*'s twelve Women of the Year, 1975.

WRITINGS:

Shirley Chisholm: A Biography (for children), Doubleday (New York, NY), 1970.

Against Our Will: Men, Women, and Rape, Simon & Schuster (New York, NY), 1975.

Femininity, Simon & Schuster (New York, NY), 1984.

Waverly Place (novel), Grove (New York, NY), 1989.

Susan Brownmiller

Seeing Vietnam: Encounters of the Road and Heart, HarperCollins (New York, NY), 1994.

In Our Time: Memoir of a Revolution, Dial Press (New York, NY), 1999.

Contributor of articles to magazines, including *Newsweek, Esquire,* and *New York Times Magazine.*

SIDELIGHTS: Susan Brownmiller was among the first of the politically active feminists in New York City during the 1960s. In 1968 she helped found the New York Radical Feminists, and as a member of that group, she took part in a number of protest demonstrations, including a sit-in at the offices of the *Ladies' Home Journal* opposing the magazine's "demeaning" attitude toward women. Her interest in women's rights surfaced in much of her work as a freelance journalist, and one article she wrote, about Shirley Chisholm, the first black U.S. congresswoman, developed into a biography for young readers. In 1971 Brownmiller helped to organize a "Speak-out on Rape," and in the process, she realized that once again she had the material for a book. She submitted an outline of her idea to Simon & Schuster, they contracted for the book, and Brownmiller began researching the subject of rape. After four years of research and writing, she published *Against Our Will: Men, Women, and Rape.*

Against Our Will explores the history of rape, exploding the myths that, as the author says, influence one's modern perspective. She traces the political use of rape in war from biblical times through Vietnam, explains the origins of American rape laws, and examines the subjects of interracial rape, homosexual rape, and child molestation. Brownmiller asserts that rape "is nothing more or less than a conscious process of intimidation by which *all men* keep *all women* in a state of fear." Supporting her thesis with facts taken from her extensive research in history, literature, sociology, law, psychoanalysis, mythology, and criminology, Brownmiller argues that rape is not a sexual act but an act of power based on an "anatomical fiat"; it is the result of early man's realization that women could be subjected to "a thoroughly detestable physical conquest from which there could be no retaliation in kind."

Against Our Will was serialized in four magazines and became a best-seller and Book-of-the-Month Club selection, and its nationwide tour made Brownmiller a celebrity. Her appearance on the cover of *Time* as one of the twelve Women of the Year and on television talk shows as a frequent guest confirmed the timeliness of her book. Brownmiller herself remarked, "I saw it as a once-in-a-lifetime subject that had somehow crossed my path," and she expressed gratitude to the women's movement for having given her "a constructive way" to use her rage.

In researching and writing *Against Our Will,* Brownmiller was motivated by "a dual sense of purpose," theorized Carol Eisen Rinzler in the *Village Voice,* "a political desire that the book be of value to feminism, and a personal desire to make a lasting contribution to the body of thought." Brownmiller mentions yet another goal in her conclusion to *Against Our Will:* "Fighting back. On a multiplicity of levels, that is the activity we must engage in, together, if we–women–are to redress the imbalance and rid ourselves and men of the ideology of rape. . . . My purpose in this book has been to give rape its history. Now we must deny it a future."

Brownmiller's next book, *Femininity,* is less confrontational in tone than *Against Our Will* but has still provoked mixed reactions. *Femininity* examines the ideal qualities—both physical and emotional—that are generally considered feminine and the lengths women go to conform to those ideals. The controversy arises, Brownmiller told *Detroit News* writer Barbara Hoover, when readers and reviewers "want to know where the blame is—is she blaming men or is she blaming us women? Well," the author explained, "I'm blaming neither. I don't criticize; I just explore the subject."

Brownmiller addresses the subject of child abuse in *Waverly Place,* her first novel. The book is a fictionalized account of the lives of Hedda Nussbaum and her abusive lover, Joel Steinberg, a New York attorney who was accused during the late 1980s of beating to death their illegally adopted daughter. Explaining why she chose to present the story as fiction instead of nonfiction, Brownmiller wrote in her introduction to *Waverly Place:* "I wanted the freedom to invent dialogue, motivations, events, and characters based on my own understanding of battery and abuse, a perspective frequently at variance with the scenarios created by the prosecution or the defense in courts of law." "Brownmiller's effort serves a potentially constructive purpose," assessed reviewer Christopher Lehmann-Haupt in the *New York Times.* "It tries to fill the emotional void created by any incomprehensible human act. It proposes how such a thing could have happened and allows us to participate in the drama of its answer. It offers us an experience of mourning, as well as some reassurance that we ourselves are safe from such disasters. . . . In all these respects," Lehmann-Haupt concluded, "Ms. Brownmiller's novel succeeds very well."

When reviewing *In Our Time: Memoir of a Revolution* for London's *Feminist Review,* Bryony Hoskins commented that—among many other important feminist issues—the book "brings alive" feminist activism in the United States during the late 1960s and 1970s. Hoskins pointed out that this historical and at times autobiographical account of women's second-wave revolution—in which Brownmiller played a pivotal role—"places into overall context the writing of second wave feminist texts. . . . *In Our Time* describes how the women's movement influenced the writing of these texts and the influence that these texts had on the movement." Brownmiller here depicts the "large scale collective action and demonstration, women being angry and standing up to patriarchy at every level of society: from the bedrooms, the law courts and working environments to the government," wrote Hoskins. Brownmiller recounts the rise and fall of many women's organizations, including the birth of the National Organization for Women (NOW) in 1966 and the influence certain agendas—including the New York Radical Feminist consciousness raising session—had on her conversion to feminist action. She also traces how key feminist issues arose during the era: "how to discuss sex and sexuality; women's right to abortion; new ways to understand rape; the acknowledgment and naming of the battery of women, sexual abuse of children and sexual harassment; and finally the divisive understandings of pornography as crime against women," wrote Hoskins, and Brownmiller then discusses "how these notions were used to change the many masculine-dominated cultures in the United States law and society."

In creating *In Our Time,* Brownmiller used what Sara M. Evans, in her review of the book for *Feminist Studies,* called "a wealth of interviews" while also being perfectly clear about her own judgments and points of view. "She endeavors to be fair to those with whom she disagrees," commented Evans, "although she pulls no punches when it comes to some of the most wretched conflicts." In Kathleen Endres's review of the book for *Journalism History,* she noted that *In Our Time* "is not the first book that tells an insider's story of the Women's Liberation Movement of the second half of the twentieth century. However, from the perspective of the journalism historian, it may be one of the best. She provides an insider's perspective of the role journalism played in this extraordinarily important radical reform movement."

BIOGRAPHICAL AND CRITICAL SOURCES:

BOOKS

Brownmiller, Susan, *Against Our Will: Men, Women, and Rape,* Simon & Schuster (New York, NY), 1975.

Brownmiller, Susan, *Waverly Place* (novel), Grove (New York, NY), 1989.

Edwards, Alison, *Rape, Racism, and the White Women's Movement: An Answer to Susan Brownmiller,* Sojourner Truth Organization (Chicago, IL), 1980.

PERIODICALS

Business Review Weekly, October 3, 1994, p. 107.

Commentary, February, 1976.

Commonweal, December 5, 1975.
Detroit News, February 1, 1984.
Far Eastern Economics Review, July 14, 1994, p. 52.
Feminist Review (London, England), 2003, Bryony Hoskins, review of *In Our Time: Memoir of a Revolution,* p. 179.
Feminist Studies, summer, 2002, Sara M. Evans, review of *In Our Time,* p. 258.
Journalism History, spring, 2001, Kathleen Endres, review of *In Our Time,* p. 44.
Nation, November 29, 1975.
National Review, March 5, 1976.
New Leader, January 5, 1976.
New Statesman, December 12, 1975.
New York Review of Books, December 11, 1975.
New York Times, February 2, 1989, Christopher Lehmann-Haupt, review of *Waverly Place,* p. B2.
New York Times Book Review, October, 1975; December 28, 1975; May 15, 1994, Arnold R. Isaacs, review of *Seeing Vietnam: Encounters of the Road and Heart,* p. 11.
Time, October 13, 1975; January 5, 1976.
Village Voice, October 6, 1975.

ONLINE

Susan Brownmiller Web site, http://www.susanbrownmiller.com/ (July 24, 2004).

*   *   *

BRUCHAC, Joseph, III 1942-

Joseph Bruchac III

PERSONAL: Surname is pronounced "*brew*-shack"; born October 16, 1942, in Saratoga Springs, NY; son of Joseph E., Jr. (a taxidermist and publisher) and Marion (a homemaker and publisher; maiden name, Bowman) Bruchac; married Carol Worthen (a director of a nonprofit organization), June 13, 1964; children: James Edward, Jesse Bowman. *Ethnicity:* "Native American (Abenaki)/Slovak/English." *Education:* Cornell University, A.B., 1965; Syracuse University, M.A., 1966; graduate study at State University of New York—Albany, 1971-73; Union Institute of Ohio Graduate School, Ph.D., 1975. *Politics:* Liberal Democrat. *Religion:* "Methodist and Native-American spiritual traditions." *Hobbies and other interests:* Gardening, music, martial arts.

ADDRESSES: Home and office—Greenfield Review Press, P.O. Box 308, Greenfield Center, NY 12833; fax: 518-583-9741. *Agent*—Barbara Kouts Agency, P.O. Box 560, Bellport, NY 11713. *E-mail*—nudatlog@earthlink.net.

CAREER: Keta Secondary School, Ghana, West Africa, teacher of English and literature, 1966-69; Skidmore College, Saratoga Springs, NY, instructor in creative writing and African and black literatures, 1969-73; University without Walls, coordinator of college program at Great Meadow Correctional Facility, 1974-81; writer and storyteller, 1981—. Greenfield Review Press, Greenfield Center, NY, publisher and editor of *Greenfield Review,* 1969—; director, Greenfield Review Literary Center, 1981—; musician with Dawn Land Singers, recording stories and music on *Abenaki Cultural Heritage* and *Alnobak,* Good Mind Records. Member of adjunct faculty at Hamilton College, 1983, 1985, and 1987, and State University of New York—Albany, 1987 and 1988; storyteller-in-residence at CRC Institute for Arts in Education, 1989-90, and at other institutions, including Oklahoma Summer Arts Institute, St. Regis Mohawk Indian School,

Seneca Nation School, Onondaga Indian School, Institute of Alaska Native Arts, and Annsville Youth Facility; featured storyteller at festivals and conferences; presents workshops, poetry readings, and storytelling programs. Print Center, member of board of directors, 1975-78; Returning the Gift, national chairperson, 1992; judge of competitions, including PEN Prison Writing Awards, 1977, National Book Award for Translation, 1983, and National Book Award for Poetry, 1995; past member of literature panels, Massachusetts Arts Council, Vermont State Arts Council, Illinois Arts Council, and Ohio Arts Council.

MEMBER: Poetry Society of America, PEN, National Storytelling Association (member of board of directors, 1992-94), Native Writers Circle of the Americas (chairperson, 1992-95), Wordcraft Circle of Native Writers and Storytellers, Hudson Valley Writers Guild, Black Crow Network.

AWARDS, HONORS: Poetry fellow, Creative Artists Public Service, 1973 and 1982; fellow, National Endowment for the Arts, 1974; editors' fellow, Coordinating Council of Literary Magazines, 1980; Rockefeller fellow, 1982; PEN Syndicated Fiction Award, 1983; American Book Award, 1984, for *Breaking Silence;* Yaddo resident, 1984 and 1985; Cherokee Nation Prose Award, 1986; fellow, New York State Council on the Arts, 1986; Publishers Marketing Association, Benjamin Franklin Audio Award, 1992, for *The Boy Who Lived with the Bears,* and Person of the Year Award, 1993; Hope S. Dean Memorial Award for Notable Achievement in Children's Literature, 1993; Mountains and Plains Award, 1995, for *A Boy Called Slow;* Knickerbocker Award, 1995; Paterson Children's Book Award, 1996, for *Dog People; Boston Globe-Horn Book* Honor Award, 1996, for *The Boy Who Lived with the Bears;* Writer of the Year Award, Wordcraft Circle of Native Writers and Storytellers, 1998; Storyteller of the Year Award, Wordcraft Circle of Native Writers and Storytellers, 1998; Lifetime Achievement Award, Native Writers Circle of the Americas, 1999.

WRITINGS:

Indian Mountain (poems), Ithaca House (Ithaca, NY), 1971.

The Buffalo in the Syracuse Zoo (poems), Greenfield Review Press (Greenfield Center, NY), 1972.

The Poetry of Pop (nonfiction), Dustbooks (Paradise, CA), 1973.

Great Meadow Poems, Dustbooks (Paradise, CA), 1973.

The Manabozho Poems, Blue Cloud Quarterly, 1973.

Turkey Brother and Other Iroquois Folk Tales, Crossing Press (Trumansburg, NY), 1975.

Flow (poems), Cold Mountain Press, 1975.

The Road to Black Mountain (fiction), Thorp Springs Press (Austin, TX), 1976.

This Earth Is a Drum (poems), Cold Mountain Press, 1976.

The Dreams of Jesse Brown (fiction), Cold Mountain Press, 1978.

Stone Giants and Flying Heads: Adventure Stories of the Iroquois, Crossing Press (Trumansburg, NY), 1978.

There Are No Trees inside the Prison (poems), Blackberry Press, 1978.

Mu'ndu Wi Go (poems), Blue Cloud Quarterly, 1978.

Entering Onondaga (poems), Cold Mountain Press, 1978.

The Good Message of Handsome Lake (poems), Unicorn Press (Greensboro, NC), 1979.

Translators' Son (poems), Cross-Cultural Communications (Merrick, NY), 1980.

How to Start and Sustain a Literary Magazine, Provision (Austin, TX), 1980.

Ancestry (poems), Great Raven (Fort Kent, ME), 1981.

Remembering the Dawn (poems), Blue Cloud Quarterly, 1983.

Iroquois Stories: Heroes and Heroines, Monsters and Magic, Crossing Press (Trumansburg, NY), 1985.

The Wind Eagle (traditional stories), Bowman Books, 1985.

Walking with My Sons (poems), Landlocked Press, 1985.

Tracking (poems), Ion Books, 1985.

Near the Mountains (poems), White Pine (Buffalo, NY), 1986.

Survival This Way: Interviews with American Indian Poets, University of Arizona (Tucson, AZ), 1987.

The Faithful Hunter and Other Abenaki Stories, Bowman Books, 1988.

The White Moose (fiction), Blue Cloud Quarterly, 1988.

Langes Gedachtnis/Long Memory (poems), OBEMA (Osnabruck, Germany), 1988.

(With Michael Caduto) *Keepers of the Earth,* Fulcrum Press (Golden, CO), 1989.

(With Michael Caduto) *Keepers of the Animals,* Fulcrum Press (Golden, CO), 1990.

Return of the Sun: Native American Tales from the Eastern Woodlands, Crossing Press (Trumansburg, NY), 1990.

Native American Stories, Fulcrum Press (Golden, CO), 1991.

Hoop Snakes, Hide-Behinds, and Sidehill Winders (folk stories), Crossing Press (Trumansburg, NY), 1991.

(With Jonathan London) *Thirteen Moons on Turtle's Back,* Philomel (New York, NY), 1992.

Turtle Meat and Other Stories, Holy Cow! Press (Minneapolis, MN), 1992.

The First Strawberries, Dial (New York, NY), 1993.

Fox Song, Philomel (New York, NY), 1993.

Dawn Land (novel), Fulcrum Press (Golden, CO), 1993.

Flying with the Eagle, Racing the Great Bear (traditional stories), Bridgewater (New York, NY), 1993.

Native American Animal Stories, Fulcrum Press (Golden, CO), 1993.

The Native American Sweat Lodge (traditional stories), Crossing Press (Trumansburg, NY), 1993.

The Great Ball Game, Dial (New York, NY), 1994.

(With Michael Caduto) *Keepers of the Night,* Fulcrum Press (Golden, CO), 1994.

(With Michael Caduto) *Keepers of Life,* Fulcrum Press (Golden, CO), 1994.

(With Gayle Ross) *The Girl Who Married the Moon* (traditional stories), Bridgewater (New York, NY), 1994.

A Boy Called Slow, Philomel (New York, NY), 1995.

The Earth under Sky Bear's Feet, Philomel (New York, NY), 1995.

Gluskabe and the Four Wishes, Cobblehill Books (Boston, MA), 1995.

(With Gayle Ross) *The Story of the Milky Way,* Dial (New York, NY), 1995.

Dog People: Native Dog Stories, Fulcrum Press (Golden, CO), 1995.

Long River (novel), Fulcrum Press (Golden, CO), 1995.

Native Wisdom, HarperSanFrancisco (San Francisco, CA), 1995.

Native Plant Stories, Fulcrum Press (Golden, CO), 1995.

The Boy Who Lived with the Bears: And Other Iroquois Stories, HarperCollins (New York, NY), 1995.

Between Earth and Sky: Legends of Native American Sacred Places, illustrated by Thomas Locker, Harcourt (San Diego, CA), 1996.

The Maple Thanksgiving, Celebration (Nobleboro, ME), 1996.

Children of the Longhouse (novel), Dial (New York, NY), 1996.

Roots of Survival: Native American Storytelling and the Sacred, Fulcrum Press (Golden, CO), 1996.

The Circle of Thanks (traditional stories), Bridgewater (New York, NY), 1996.

Four Ancestors: Stories, Songs, and Poems, Bridgewater (New York, NY), 1996.

(With Michael Caduto) *Native American Gardening,* Fulcrum Press (Golden, CO), 1996.

(With Melissa Fawcett) *Makiawisug: Gift of the Little People,* Little People (Warsaw, IN), 1997.

Many Nations: An Alphabet of Native America, Troll Publications (Mahwah, NJ), 1997.

Bowman's Store (autobiography), Dial (New York, NY), 1997.

Eagle Song (novel), Dial (New York, NY), 1997.

Lasting Echoes: An Oral History of Native American People, Harcourt (New York, NY), 1997.

Tell Me a Tale: A Book about Storytelling, Harcourt (New York, NY), 1997.

The Arrow over the Door (fiction; for children), illustrated by James Watling, Dial (New York, NY), 1998.

Buffalo Boy (biography), illustrated by Baviera, Silver Whistle Books (San Diego, CA), 1998.

The Heart of a Chief: A Novel (for children), Dial (New York, NY), 1998.

The Waters Between: A Novel of the Dawn Land, University Press of New England (Hanover, NH), 1998.

(With James Bruchac) *When the Chenoo Howls: Native-American Tales of Terror* (traditional stories), illustrated by William Sauts Netamu'xwe Bock, Walker (New York, NY), 1998.

No Borders (poems), Holy Cow! Press (Duluth, MN), 1999.

Seeing the Circle (autobiography), photographs by John Christian Fine, R. C. Owen (Katonah, NY), 1999.

The Trail of Tears, illustrated by Diana Magnuson, Random House (New York, NY), 1999.

Trails of Tears, Paths of Beauty, National Geographic Society (Washington, DC), 2000.

(With James Bruchac) *Native American Games and Stories,* illustrated by Kayeri Akwek, Fulcrum Press (Golden, CO), 2000.

Crazy Horse's Vision, illustrated by S. D. Nelson, Lee & Low Books (New York, NY), 2000.

Pushing Up the Sky: Seven Native American Plays for Children, illustrated by Teresa Flavin, Dial (New York, NY), 2000.

Sacajawea: The Story of Bird Woman and the Lewis and Clark Expedition, Silver Whistle (San Diego, CA), 2000.

Squanto's Journey: The Story of the First Thanksgiving, illustrated by Greg Shed, Silver Whistle (San Diego, CA), 2000.

(With James Bruchac) *How Chipmunk Got His Stripes,* illustrated by Jose Aruego and Ariane Dewey, Dial (New York, NY), 2001.

Skeleton Man, HarperCollins (New York, NY), 2001.

The Journal of Jesse Smoke: A Cherokee Boy, Scholastic (New York, NY), 2001.

Seasons of the Circle: A Native American Year, illustrated by Robert F. Goetzel, Bridgewater (New York, NY), 2002.

Navajo Long Walk: The Tragic Story of a Proud People's Forced March from Their Homeland, illustrated by Shonto Begay, National Geographic Society (Washington, DC), 2002.

Foot of the Mountain, Holy Cow! Press (Duluth, MN), 2002.

The Winter People, Dial (New York, NY), 2002.

Our Stories Remember: American Indian History, Culture, and Values through Storytelling, Fulcrum Press (Golden, CO), 2003.

Pocahontas (novel), Silver Whistle (Orlando, FL), 2003.

(With James Bruchac) *Turtle's Race with Beaver: A Traditional Seneca Story,* pictures by Jose Aruego and Ariane Dewey, Dial Books for Young Readers (New York, NY), 2003.

Above the Line (poetry), West End Press (Albuquerque, NM), 2003.

Hidden Roots (novel), Scholastic (New York, NY), 2004.

Jim Thorpe's Bright Path (biography), illustrated by S. D. Nelson, Lee & Low Books (New York, NY), 2004.

(With Thomas Locker) *Raccoon's Last Race: A Traditional Abenaki Story,* pictures by Jose Aruego and Ariane Dewey, Dial Books for Young Readers (New York, NY), 2004.

(With James Bruchac) *Rachel Carson: Preserving a Sense of Wonder,* Fulcrum Press (Golden, CO), 2004.

A Code Talker's Story, Dial Books (New York, NY), 2004.

Dark Pond, illustrated by Sally Wern Comport, HarperCollins (New York, NY), 2004.

Also editor of anthologies, including *The Last Stop: Prison Writings from Comstock Prison,* 1973; *Words from the House of the Dead: Prison Writing from Soledad,* 1974; *Aftermath: Poetry in English from Africa, Asia, and the Caribbean,* 1977; *The Next World: Thirty-two Third World American Poets,* 1978; *Songs from Turtle Island: Thirty-two American Indian Poets,* [Yugoslavia], 1982; *Songs from This Earth on Turtle's Back: Contemporary American Indian Poetry,* 1983; *Breaking Silence: Contemporary Asian-American Poets,* 1983; *The Light from Another Country: Poetry from American Prisons,* 1984; *North Country: An Anthology of Contemporary Writing from the Adirondacks and the Upper Hudson Valley,* 1986; *New Voices from the Longhouse: Contemporary Iroquois Writing,* 1989; *Raven Tells Stories: Contemporary Alaskan Native Writing,* 1990; *Singing of Earth,* 1993; *Returning the Gift,* 1994; *Smoke Rising,* 1995; and *Native Wisdom,* 1995. Audiotapes include *Iroquois Stories, Alnobak,Adirondack Tall Tales,* and *Abenaki Cultural Heritage,* all Good Mind Records; and *Gluskabe Stories,* Yellow Moon Press. Work represented in more than a hundred anthologies, including *Carriers of the Dream Wheel; Come to Power; For Neruda, for Chile; New Worlds of Literature;* and *Paris Review Anthology.* Contributor of more than three hundred stories, poems, articles, and reviews to magazines, including *American Poetry Review, Akwesasne Notes, Beloit Poetry Journal, Chariton Review, Kalliope, Mid-American Review, Nation, Poetry Northwest, River Styx,* and *Virginia Quarterly Review.* Editor, *Trojan Horse,* 1964, *Greenfield Review,* 1969-87, *Prison Writing Review,* 1976-85, and *Studies in American Indian Literature,* 1989—; student editor, *Epoch,* 1964-65; member of editorial board, *Parabola, Storytelling Journal, MELUS,* and *Obsidian.* Translator from Abenaki, Ewe, Iroquois, and Spanish. Cross-Cultural Communications, member of editorial board.

ADAPTATIONS: Several of Bruchac's books have been recorded on audio tapes, including *Keepers of the Earth, Keepers of the Animals, Keepers of Life,* and *Dawn Land,* all released by Fulcrum; and *The Boy Who Lived with the Bears,* Caedmon/Parabola.

SIDELIGHTS: Joseph Bruchac III, according to *Publishers Weekly* contributor Sybil Steinberg, ranks as "perhaps the best-known contemporary Native American storyteller." Bruchac draws on his heritage for his critically acclaimed collections, including *Flying with the Eagle, Racing the Great Bear: Stories from Native*

North America and *The Girl Who Married the Moon: Stories from Native North America.* These stories also influence Bruchac's novel *Dawn Land,* about the Abenaki living in the American northeast before the arrival of Columbus. "His stories," Steinberg concluded, "are often poignant, funny, ironic—and sometimes all three at once."

Dawn Land introduced readers to the character of Young Hunter. In a sequel to this novel, 1995's *Long River,* Bruchac again features Young Hunter in a series of adventures, as he battles a wooly mammoth and an evil giant. As with the earlier work, *Long River* incorporates actual myths from the author's Abenaki heritage. Bruchac's children's stories, like his novels, entertain and educate young readers by interweaving Native American history and myth. The biography *A Boy Called Slow* recounts the story of a Lakota boy named Slow, who would later be known as Sitting Bull. Bruchac's ability to "gently correct" stereotypes of Native-American culture was noted by Carolyn Polese in the *School Library Journal.* In *The Great Ball Game* he relates the importance of ball games in Native-American tradition as a substitute for war, tying neatly together history and ethics lessons in "an entertaining tale," commented Polese. He combines several versions of a Native-American tale in *Gluskabe and the Four Wishes.*

"I was born in 1942, in Saratoga Springs, New York, during October, that month the Iroquois call the Moon of Falling Leaves," Bruchac once explained. "My writing and my interests reflect my mixed ancestry, Slovak on one side and Native American (Abenaki) and English on the other. Aside from attending Cornell University and Syracuse and three years of teaching in West Africa, I've lived all of my life in the small Adirondack foothills town of Greenfield Center in a house built by my grandfather.

"Much of my writing and my life relates to the problem of being an American. While in college I was active in civil rights work and in the anti-war movement. . . . I went to Africa to teach—but more than that, to be taught. It showed me many things. How much we have as Americans and take for granted. How much our eyes refuse to see because they are blinded to everything in a man's face except his color. And, most importantly, how human people are everywhere—which may be the one grace that can save us all.

"I write poetry, fiction, and some literary criticism and have been fortunate enough to receive recognition in all three areas. After returning from Ghana in 1969, my wife, Carol, and I started the *Greenfield Review* and the Greenfield Review Press. Since 1975, I've been actively involved in storytelling, focusing on northeastern Native-American tales and the songs and traditions of the Adirondack Mountains of upstate New York, and I am frequently a featured performer at storytelling gatherings. I've also done a great deal of work in teaching and helping start writing workshops in American prisons. I believe that poetry is as much a part of human beings as is breath—and that, like breath, poetry links us to all other living things and is meant to be shared.

"My writing is informed by several key sources. One of these is nature, another is the Native-American experience (I'm part Indian). . . . I like to work outside, in the earthmother's soil, with my hands . . . but maintain my life as an academic for a couple of reasons: it gives me time to write (sometimes) and it gives me a chance to share my insights into the beautiful and all-too-fragile world of human life and living things we have been granted. Which is one of the reasons I write—not to be a man apart, but to share."

Bruchac has continued to write prolifically. In his 2003 book *Our Stories Remember: American Indian History, Culture, and Values through Storytelling,* he relates stories from many different Indian nations to illustrated their core values and culture. Writing in the *School Library Journal,* S. K. Joiner noted that, "Part cultural lesson, part history, and part autobiography, the book contains a wealth of information," while *Booklist* contributor Deborah Donovan dubbed it a "thought-provoking work, enriched with valuable annotated reading lists." Bruchac has also continued his work in picture books for children, including several biographies of Native Americans and others. In *Rachel Carson: Preserving a Sense of Wonder,* he presents a biography of the author of *Silent Spring* and one of the people credited with inspiring the environmental movement in the 1960s. Writing in *Booklist,* Carolyn Phelan noted that "Bruchac writes lyrically about [Carson's] . . . love of nature, particularly the ocean, and concludes with an appreciation of her impact on the environment." Another 2004 picture-book publication, *Jim Thorpe's Bright Path,* tells of the famed Native-American athlete. *School Library Journal* contributor Liza Graybill noted, "The theme of overcoming personal and societal obstacles to reach success is strongly expressed."

In an interview with Eliza T. Dresang on the Cooperative Children's Book Center Web site, Bruchac noted that he does not expect to run out of things to write about. He told Dresang: "The last thirty years of my life in particular have been blessed with so many . . . experiences and by the generosity of so many Native people who have shared their stories and their understanding of their land with me that I know I can never live long enough to share everything I've learned. But I'll try."

BIOGRAPHICAL AND CRITICAL SOURCES:

PERIODICALS

Alaska, December, 1992, p. 74.

Albany Times Union, June 1, 1980.

Booklist, February 15, 1993, p. 1075; July, 1993, p. 1969; October 15, 1993, p. 397; November 15, 1993, p. 632; December 15, 1993, p. 749; August, 1994, p. 2017; September, 1994, p. 55; October 15, 1994, p. 377; December 15, 1994, p. 756; September 1, 1997, p. 69; September 15, 1997, pp. 234, 237; December 5, 1997, p. 688; February 15, 1998; October 1, 2002, Heather Hepler, review of *Seasons of the Circle: A Native American Year,* p. 316, GraceAnne A. DeCandido, review of *The Winter People,* p. 322; April 15, 2003, Deborah Donovan, review of *Our Stories Remember: American Indian History, Culture, and Values through Storytelling,* p. 1444; September 15, 2003, John Peters, review of *Turtle's Race with Beaver,* p. 244, Ed Sullivan, review of *Pocahontas,* p. 229; July, 2004, Carolyn Phelan, review of *Rachel Carson: Preserving a Sense of Wonder,* p. 1838.

Bulletin, April, 1995, p. 265.

English Journal, January, 1996, p. 87.

Horn Book, January-February, 1994, p. 60; March-April, 1994, p. 209; November-December, 1994, p. 738; March-April, 1995, p. 203; September-October, 1995, p. 617.

Kirkus Reviews, March 15, 1996, p. 445; May 1, 1996, p. 685; December 1, 1996, p. 1734.

Publishers Weekly, March 15, 1993, p. 68; June 28, 1993, p. 76; July 19, 1993, pp. 254, 255; August 29, 1994, p. 79; January 9, 1995, p. 64; July 31, 1995, p. 68; July 14, 1997, p. 83; September 8, 1997, p. 78; November 24, 1997, p. 75; May 31, 2004, review of *Jim Thorpe's Bright Path,* p. 76.

School Library Journal, March, 1993, p. 161; August, 1993, p. 205; September, 1993, pp. 222, 238; February, 1994, p. 78; November, 1994, p. 112; December, 1994, p. 96; February, 1995, p. 104; October, 1995, Carolyn Polese, review of *A Boy Called Slow,* p. 145; July, 2002, Anne Chapman Callaghan, review of *Navajo Long Walk: The Tragic Story of a Proud People's Forced March from Their Homeland,* p. 131; November, 2002, Rita Soltan, review of *The Winter People,* p. 154; July, 2003, S. K. Joiner, review of *Our Stories Remember,* p. 155; May, 2004, Sean George, review of *Pocahontas,* p. 140; June, 2004, Liza Graybill, review of *Jim Thorpe's Bright Path,* p. 124.

Silver Whistle, spring-summer, 2000, p. 67.

Voice Literary Supplement, November, 1991, p. 27.

Wilson Library Bulletin, June, 1993, p. 103; September, 1993, p. 87; April, 1995, p. 110.

ONLINE

Cooperative Children's Book Center Web site, http://www.soemadison.wisc.edu/ccbc/ (October 22, 1999), Eliza T. Dresang, "An Interview with Joseph Bruchac."

Joseph Bruchac Storyteller and Writer, http://www.josephbruchac.com/ (September 16, 2003).*

C

CAMPBELL, Peter A. 1948-

PERSONAL: Born January 14, 1948, in Providence, RI; son of Roland (a grocer) and Irene (Laliberte) Campbell; married, April 22, 1978; wife's name Karen (a director of office operations); children: Seth, Jeremy, Brendan. *Education:* Vesper George School of Art, graduated, 1970. *Religion:* Roman Catholic.

ADDRESSES: *Home*—42 Holiday Dr., Lincoln, RI 02865. *Agent*—Stauch-Vetromile & Mitchell, 55 S. Brow St., East Providence, RI 02914. *E-mail*—peterc@svmmarcom.com.

CAREER: Artist. Also worked as an art director and creative director for several Rhode Island advertising agencies. Attleboro Museum, Attleboro, MA, member of board of directors.

MEMBER: National Society of Painters in Casein and Acrylic, Society of Children's Book Writers and Illustrators.

Peter A. Campbell

WRITINGS:

CHILDREN'S BOOKS; AUTHOR AND ILLUSTRATOR

Launch Day (juvenile), Millbrook Press (Brookfield, CT), 1995.

Alien Encounters (juvenile), Millbrook Press (Brookfield, CT), 2000.

Old-Time Baseball and the First Modern World Series, Millbrook Press (Brookfield, CT), 2002, published as *Boston Pilgrims vs. Pittsburgh Pirates: The First Modern World Series,* 2003.

SIDELIGHTS: Peter A. Campbell once commented to *CA:* "The completion of my first children's book, *Launch Day,* was the culmination of a wonderful journey. It began in 1989 when I was accepted as a member of the National Aeronautics and Space Administration (NASA) Space Art Program. Through this program I saw firsthand all the preparations and excitement that surround a space shuttle launch at the Cape Kennedy Space Center in Florida. I also witnessed a day launch and a spectacular night launch of the space shuttle Atlantis.

"How fortunate I was to be able to record with pencil, paper, and paint space history in the making. Very much in the spirit of artists like George Catlin, Winslow Homer, and Frederic Remington, who documented important events in their lifetimes.

"From these experiences came the idea for a book, *Launch Day,* a book that would show young children this great adventure through the words and paintings of a NASA space artist."

According to *Booklist* reviewer Carolyn Phelan, Campbell's paintings distinguish *Launch Day* from other books taking a close look at a space shuttle as it prepares for take-off. "Unusual, given the almost universal use of NASA photos (often the same ones) in books on the space program, are the attractive paintings that illustrate this volume," Phelan wrote.

Campbell said, "I owe much to Millbrook Press in Connecticut who shared my vision and gave an unpublished author the opportunity to design, write, and illustrate his first book. *Launch Day* was released to bookstores, libraries, and schools in September of 1995. The book has also given me the opportunity to speak to school children about the importance of NASA, space exploration, and what writing and illustrating a children's book is all about.

"In my lifetime, I have witnessed one of the greatest adventures in the history of mankind: man's first steps into space. I believe through my words and paintings I can help keep the dream of space exploration alive for future generations. So onward to the red sands of Mars and the moons of Jupiter, where wonder and mysteries await!"

More recently, Campbell commented: "As a boy I fell in love with illustrators and nonfiction picture books. I collected books and magazines that featured artwork by such popular illustrators as Isa Barnett, Robert Fawcett, Lynd Ward, Tom Lovell, Rockwell Kent, Robert Weaver, and Nick Eggenhofer. They were a big influence on my decision to write and illustrate nonfiction books for children and young adults.

"I am very fortunate to be able to design, write, and illustrate my children's books. Since I tend to be more of a visual person, I usually start a book idea by sketching and illustrating some of the scenes that might make up the book. Once I have a visual road map of how the book will lay out and have gotten a 'go' from the publisher, I start thinking about words. Before I can start to write and create the final illustrations for the book, though, I must do extensive research on the subject I have chosen. For me, researching a subject for a nonfiction book is very exciting. Discovering little-known information about people, places, and events and presenting it to young readers in a well designed and written book form is very rewarding for me."

BIOGRAPHICAL AND CRITICAL SOURCES:

PERIODICALS

Booklist, December 1, 1995, Carolyn Phelan, review of *Launch Day,* p. 630.

School Library Journal, March, 1996, p. 202; April, 2000, Ann G. Brouse, review of *Alien Encounters,* p. 146.

Science Books and Films, April, 1996, pp. 86-87.

* * *

CARNOY, Martin 1938-

PERSONAL: Born 1938 in Warsaw, Poland; brought to the United States, 1940; naturalized U.S. citizen, 1945; son of Alan L. and Teresa Carnoy; married Judith Merle Milgrom (an actress), August 6, 1961 (divorced, 1980); married Jean MacDonell, March 6, 1987; children: (first marriage) David, Jonathan; (second marriage) Juliet. *Education:* California Institute of Technology, B.S., 1960; University of Chicago, M.A., 1961, Ph.D., 1964.

ADDRESSES: Home—2378 Branner Dr., Menlo Park, CA 94025. *Office*—School of Education, Stanford University, Stanford, CA 94305.

CAREER: Brookings Institution, Washington, DC, research associate in economics, 1964-68; Stanford University, Stanford, CA, assistant professor, 1968-71, associate professor, 1971-77, professor of education and economics, 1977—, director of Latin American fellowship program, chairman of International Development Education Committee, 1971-72, 1975-77, 1980—. Cofounder and director of Center for Economic Studies, Palo Alto, CA. Coordinator for Robert Kennedy's presidential primary campaign, Washington, DC, 1968; cochairperson of Stanford Moratorium, 1969-70; chair of Social Studies and Educational Practice Committee, Stanford School of Education, 1995—. Consultant to Organization for Economic Cooperation and Development, World Bank, Venezuelan Ministry of Education, and Organization of American States.

MEMBER: American Educational Research Association, Latin American Studies Association, Negative Population Growth (member of national advisory board), Comparative and International Education Society (member of board of directors, 1998—), Union of Radical Political Economics, Concerned Citizens for Peace (founder; cochairperson, 1966-68).

AWARDS, HONORS: Ford Foundation fellowship, 1961-64; Fulbright fellowship, 1985; Center for Advanced Study in Behavioral Sciences fellowship, 1994-95; honorary doctorate, University of Stockholm, 1994.

WRITINGS:

(With Donald W. Baerrensen and Joseph Grunwald) *Latin American Trade Patterns,* Brookings Institution (Washington, DC), 1965.

Industrialization in a Latin American Common Market, Brookings Institution (Washington, DC), 1971.

(With Joseph Grunwald and Miguel Wionczek) *The United States and a Latin American Common Market,* Brookings Institution (Washington, DC), 1971.

The Economics of Schooling and International Development, Centro Intercultural de Documentation (Cuernavaca, Mexico), 1971.

(With Hans Thias) *Cost-Benefit Analysis in Education: A Case Study of Kenya,* Johns Hopkins Press (Baltimore, MD), 1972.

(Editor and contributor) *Schooling in a Corporate Society,* McKay (New York, NY), 1972, 2nd edition, 1975.

(With Joseph Grunwald) *Latin American Economic Integration and U.S. Policy,* Brookings Institution (Washington, DC), 1972.

The Social Benefits of Better Schooling, School of Education, Stanford University (Stanford, CA), 1972.

Education As Cultural Imperialism, McKay (New York, NY), 1974.

(With Michael Carter) *Theories of Labor Markets and Worker Productivity,* Center for Economic Studies (Palo Alto, CA), 1974.

(With Henry Levin) *The Limits of Educational Reform,* McKay (New York, NY), 1975.

(With Robert Girling and Russell Rumberger) *Education and Public Sector Employment,* Center for Economic Studies, 1976.

(With Hans Thias and Richard Sack) *The Payoff to "Better" Schooling: A Case Study of Tunisian Secondary Schools,* World Bank (Washington, DC), 1977.

Estudio de la education secundaria y superior en El Salvador: Las tendencias en los requerimentos de mano de obra con educacion secundaria y superior, y las implicaciones par la politica de educredito, Center for Economic Studies, 1977.

Education and Employment: A Critical Appraisal, UNESCO International Institute for Education Planning (Paris, France), 1977.

(With Jose Lobo, Alejandro Toledo, and Jacques Velloso) *Can Educational Policy Equalise Income Distribution in Latin America?,* Saxon House (Westmead, England), 1979.

(With Michael Levin and Kenneth King) *Education, Work and Employment-II,* UNESCO International Institute for Educational Planning (Paris, France), 1980.

(With Derek Shearer) *Economic Democracy: The Challenge of the 1980s,* M. E. Sharpe (Armonk, NY), 1980.

(With Jorge Werthein) *Cuba: Cambio Economico y Reforma Educativa, 1955-1978,* Editorial Nueva Imagen, 1980.

(With Michael Levin) *The Dialectic of Education and Work,* Stanford University Press (Stanford, CA), 1982.

(With Derek Shearer and Russell Rumberger) *A New Social Contract: The Economy and Government after Reagan,* Harper & Row (New York, NY), 1983.

The State and Political Theory, Princeton University Press (Princeton, NJ), 1984.

Expressions of Power in Education: Studies of Class, Gender, and Race, edited by Edgar B. Gumbert, Center for Cross-cultural Education, College of Education, Georgia State University (Atlanta, GA), 1984.

(With Henry M. Levin) *Schooling and Work in the Democratic State,* Stanford University Press (Stanford, CA), 1985.

Higher Education and Graduate Employment in India: A Summary of Three Case Studies, Indian Institute of Education (Pune, India), 1987.

(With Jeff Faux and Miles Kahler) *The U.S. Economy after Reagan,* Friedrich Ebert Stiftung (Bonn, Germany), 1989.

(With Joel Samoff) *Education and Social Transition in the Third World,* Princeton University Press (Princeton, NJ), 1990.

(Editor, with Jane Hannaway) *Decentralization and School Improvement: Can We Fulfill the Promise?,* Jossey-Bass (San Francisco, CA), 1993.

(With Seth Pollack and Pia Lindquist Wong) *Labour Institutions and Technological Change: A Framework for Analysis and a Review of the Literature,* International Institute for Labour Studies (Geneva, Switzerland), 1993.

(With others) *The New Global Economy in the Information Age: Reflections on Our Changing World,* Pennsylvania State University Press (University Park, PA), 1993.

Faded Dreams: The Politics and Economics of Race in America, Cambridge University Press (Cambridge, England, and New York, NY), 1994.

(Editor) *International Encyclopedia of Economics of Education,* Pergamon (Tarrytown, NY), 1995.

(With son, David Carnoy) *Fathers of a Certain Age: The Joys and Problems of Middle-aged Fatherhood,* Faber & Faber (Boston, MA), 1995.

Sustainable Flexibility: A Prospective Study on Work, Family, and Society in the Information Age, OECD (Paris, France), 1997.

Sustaining the New Economy: Work, Family, and Community in the Information Age, Russell Sage Foundation (New York, NY)/Harvard University Press (Cambridge, MA), 2000.

(Editor, with Richard Elmore and Leslie Santee Siskin) *The New Accountability: High Schools and High Stakes Testing,* Routledge (New York, NY), 2003.

(With Luis Benveniste and Richard Rothstein) *All Else Equal: Are Public and Private Schools Different?,* RoutledgeFalmer (New York, NY), 2003.

Contributor to books, including *Viewpoints on Education and Social Change in Latin America,* Center of Latin American Studies, University of Kansas, 1965; *The Movement for Latin Unity,* edited by Ronald Hilton, Praeger, 1970; *National Priorities,* edited by Kan Chen, San Francisco Press, 1970; *Latin American Scholarship since World War II,* edited by Roberto Esgaenazi-Mayo and Michael Meyer, University of Nebraska Press, 1971; *Education and Development in Latin America and the Caribbean,* edited by Thomas LaBelle and Leopoldo Solis, Latin American Center, University of California, Los Angeles, 1972; *La Economia Mexicana II: Politica y Desarrollo* (title means "The Mexican Economy II: Policy and Development"), edited by Leopoldo Solis, Fondo de Cultura Economia, 1973; *Structures of Dependency,* edited by Frank Bonilla and Robert Girling, Institute of Policy Studies, Stanford University, 1973; *Analytical Models in Educational Planning and Administration,* edited by Hector Correa, McKay, 1975; *The Problem of the Federal Budget,* Institute for Policy Studies Transnational, 1975; *Change in Tunisia: Studies in the Social Sciences,* edited by Russell Stone and John Simmons, State University of New York Press, 1976; *Power and Ideology in Education,* edited by A. H. Halsey and Jerome Karabel, Oxford University Press, 1977; *El Problema del Financiamiento de la Educacion,* Banco Interamericano de Desarrollo y el Gobierno de Mexico, 1978; *The Education Dilemma: Policy Issues for Developing Countries in the 1980s,* edited by John Simmons, Pergamon, 1980; *Cultural and Economic Reproduction in Education: Essays on Class, Ideology and the State,* edited by Michael W. Apple, Routledge & Kegan Paul, 1981; and *Hispanics in the Labor Force: Issues and Policies,* Bureau of Labor Statistics, 1993.

Also author of numerous Stanford IFG program reports. Contributor to journals, including *New Republic, Educational Review, Journal of Human Resources, Economic Review,* and *Comparative Education Review.*

WORK IN PROGRESS: Writing a book on globalization and educational reform for the International Institute of Educational Planning.

SIDELIGHTS: Martin Carnoy is a professor of education and economics at Stanford University who is interested in international education systems and, in his writings, often expresses his concern that government is not doing enough to support education, something that is becoming increasingly important in a global market in which advanced skills among labor are essential for economic success. Contrary to the viewpoint of some politicians and economists, Carnoy still believes that national policies should take a leading role in guiding the economy, a theme he expresses, for example, in his contribution to *The New Global Economy in the Information Age: Reflections on Our Changing World.* Here, Carnoy admits that multinational corporations indeed have a major impact on economies, but he insists that "nation-states can also be key actors in shaping what multinationals do." Government, he says, should be a major player in financing research and education in order to remain competitive in world markets.

But government can also be important in assuaging social ills, which can also make an economic impact. He explains this, for instance, in his *Faded Dreams: The Politics and Economics of Race in America,* in which he offers "a thoughtful and empirically based analysis of the factors responsible and the role of government in reducing [racial] inequities," according to Paula D. McClain in the *American Political Science Review.* In this book, Carnoy argues against simplistic explanations for why African Americans are still struggling in the American economy. It is not simply a matter of racism, nor a changing economy that is becoming more technological, nor is it, as some claim, that blacks have not shown enough initiative in seizing opportunities once they are made available; rather, says Carnoy, one must consider aspects of all of these arguments while tying them into the role government plays. "He concludes that economic inequality in the United States still has an important racial component," explained McClain, "and that a government with the will to reduce racial inequality can and should do so. Government has the capacity to invest in public education in ways that are favorable to low-income Americans and even more so to low-income minorities."

By encouraging private investment and leveling the playing field of the job market through such actions as setting wage guidelines, government can do much to improve minorities' lives, insists the author. "For Carnoy," concluded McClain, "market forces are inseparable from political ones." Although Carnoy notes a lack of political will to resolve this problem, *Nation* contributor David L. Kirp said that "Carnoy optimistically believes that improvement is possible," with the solution lying mainly in the redistribution of wealth. "If real progress is to be made on race," as Kirp summarized, "it's probably necessary to integrate our communities and also to redistribute the resources that affect success." While McClain concluded that many will disagree with Carnoy's position, "his work is balanced and empirically grounded. *Faded Dreams* has much to say to political science, and it contributes to our knowledge of the politics of economic inequality."

Sustaining the New Economy: Work, Family, and Community in the Information Age examines the ways in which globalization effects social changes. In *Journal of Sociology and Social Welfare,* the book was praised for its wealth of data, particularly concerning developing countries; its demonstration that social changes resulting from globalization are complex; and its helpful policy recommendations. Carnoy, according to the reviewer, argues that "a strong state is essential to guide nations through the current economic transformations" but that such governments must remain "flexible." Carnoy's thinking, according to Michael P. Todaro in the *Population and Development Review,* is "provocative and certainly not representative of mainstream thinking about the new economy." This perspective, the reviewer concluded, "is certainly to be welcomed."

In *All Else Equal: Are Public and Private Schools Different?,* Carnoy and coauthors Luis Benveniste and Richard Rothstein challenge conventional wisdom about vouchers to enable low-income public school students to attend private schools. As *New York Times Book Review* contributor Timothy A. Hacsi explained, the authors found that "what shapes a school's environment most powerfully is the community around it," not its public or private status. Often, private schools prove to be more rigid than their public counterparts, while public schools—accused of inflexibility—"-regularly respond to public pressure." Though Hacsi criticized *All Else Equal* for stylistic flaws and repetitive writing, he concluded that "Anyone who cares about public education should read [it]."

BIOGRAPHICAL AND CRITICAL SOURCES:

PERIODICALS

American Journal of Sociology, March, 1996, Chris Tilly, review of *Faded Dreams: The Politics and Economics of Race in America,* p. 1482.

American Political Science Review, June, 1994, Henry R. Nau, review of *The New Global Economy in the Information Age: Reflections on Our Changing World,* p. 511; December, 1996, Paula D. McClain, review of *Faded Dreams,* p. 867.

Journal of Economic Literature, June, 1996, Anne Beeson Royalty, review of *Faded Dreams,* p. 787.

Journal of Sociology and Social Welfare, March, 2002, review of *Sustaining the New Economy: Work, Family, and Community in the Information Age,* p. 199.

Monthly Labor Review, February, 1993, Peter Caltan, review of *Hispanics in the Labor Force: Issues and Policies,* p. 66.

Nation, April 24, 1995, David L. Kirp, review of *Faded Dreams,* p. 567.

New York Times Book Review, March 2, 2003, Timothy A. Hacsi, "Private Lessons," p. 16.

Population and Development Review, March, 2001, Michael P. Todaro, review of *Sustaining the New Economy,* p. 194.

Regional Studies, July, 2001, Diane Perrons, review of *Sustaining the New Economy,* p. 493.

ONLINE

Martin Carnoy Faculty Web site, http://www.stanford.edu/ (October 27, 2003).*

* * *

CHÁVEZ, Denise (Elia) 1948-

PERSONAL: Born August 15, 1948, in Las Cruces, NM; daughter of Ernesto E. (an attorney) and Delfina (a teacher; maiden name, Rede) Chávez; married Daniel Zolinsky (a photographer and sculptor), December 29, 1984. *Education:* New Mexico State University, B.A., 1971; Trinity University (San Antonio, TX), M.F.A., 1974; University of New Mexico, M.A., 1982. *Politics:* Democrat. *Religion:* Roman Catholic. *Hobbies and other interests:* Swimming, bowling, movies.

ADDRESSES: Home—80 La Colonia, Las Cruces, NM 88005.

CAREER: Northern New Mexico Community College, Espanola, instructor in English, 1975-77, professor of English and theatre, 1977-80; playwright, 1977—;

Denise Chavez

New Mexico Arts Division, Santa Fe, artist in the schools, 1977-83; University of Houston, Houston, TX, visiting scholar, 1988, assistant professor of drama, 1988-91; New Mexico State University, Las Cruces, assistant professor of creative writing, playwrighting, and Chicano literature, 1996—. Instructor at American School of Paris, 1975-77; visiting professor of creative writing at New Mexico State University, 1992-93 and 1995-96; artistic director of the Border Book Festival, 1994—; past member of faculty at College of Santa Fe; teacher at Radium Springs Center for Women (medium-security prison); gives lectures, readings, and workshops throughout the United States and Europe; has given performances of the one-woman show *Women in the State of Grace* throughout the United States. Writer in residence at La Compania de Teatro, Albuquerque, NM, and Theatre-in-the-Red, Santa Fe, NM; artist-in-residence at Arts with Elders Program, Santa Fe and Las Cruces; codirector of senior citizen workshop in creative writing and puppetry at Community Action Agency, Las Cruces, 1986-89.

MEMBER: National Institute of Chicana Writers (founding member), PEN USA, PEN USA West, Authors Guild, Western Writers of America, Women Writing the West, Santa Fe Writers Cooperative.

AWARDS, HONORS: Best Play Award, New Mexico State University, 1970, for *The Wait;* grants from New Mexico Arts Division, 1979-80, 1981, and 1988; award for citizen advocacy, Dona Ana County Human Services Consortium, 1981; grants from National Endowment for the Arts, 1981 and 1982, Rockefeller Foundation, 1984, and University of Houston, 1989; creative writing fellowship, University of New Mexico, 1982; Steele Jones Fiction Award, New Mexico State University, 1986, for short story "The Last of the Menu Girls"; Puerto del Sol Fiction award, 1986, for *The Last of the Menu Girls;* creative artist fellowship, Cultural Arts Council of Houston, 1990; Favorite Teacher Award, University of Houston, 1991; Premio Aztlan Award, American Book Award, and Mesilla Valley Writer of the Year Award, all 1995, all for *Face of an Angel;* New Mexico Governor's Award in literature and *El Paso Herald Post* Writers of the Pass distinction, both 1995; Luminaria Award for Community Service, New Mexico Community Foundation, 1996.

WRITINGS:

PLAYS

The Wait (one-act), 1970, also produced as *Novitiates,* Dallas Theater Center, Dallas, TX, 1971.

Elevators (one-act), produced in Santa Fe, NM, 1972.

The Flying Tortilla Man (one-act), produced in Espanola, NM, 1975.

The Mask of November (one-act), produced in Espanola, NM, 1977.

Nacimiento (one-act; title means "Birth"), produced in Albuquerque, NM, 1979.

The Adobe Rabbit (one-act), produced in Taos, NM, 1979.

Santa Fe Charm (one-act), produced in Santa Fe, NM, 1980.

Si, hay posada (one-act; title means "Yes, There Is Shelter"), produced in Albuquerque, NM, 1980.

El santero de Cordova (one-act; title means "The Woodcarver of Cordova"), produced in Albuquerque, NM, 1981.

How Junior Got Throwed in the Joint (one-act), produced in Santa Fe at Penitentiary of New Mexico, 1981.

(With Nita Luna) *Hecho en Mexico* (one-act; title means "Made in Mexico"), produced in Santa Fe, NM, 1982.

The Green Madonna (one-act), produced in Santa Fe, NM, 1982.

La morenita (one-act; title means "The Dark Virgin"), produced in Las Cruces, NM, 1983.

Francis! (one-act), produced in Las Cruces, NM, 1983.

El mas pequeno de mis hijos (one-act; title means "The Smallest of My Children"), produced in Albuquerque, NM, 1983.

Plaza (one-act), produced in Albuquerque, NM, 1984, also produced in Edinburgh, Scotland, and at the Festival Latino, New York, NY.

Novena narrativas (one-woman show; title means "The Novena Narratives"), produced in Taos, NM, 1986.

The Step (one-act), produced in Houston, TX, at Museum of Fine Arts, 1987.

Language of Vision (one-act), produced in Albuquerque, NM, 1987.

Women in the State of Grace (one-woman show), produced in Grinnell, IA, 1989; produced nationally since 1993.

The Last of the Menu Girls (one-act; adapted from Chávez's short story of the same title), produced in Houston, TX, 1990.

Author of unproduced plays *Mario and the Room Maria,* 1974, *Rainy Day Waterloo,* 1976, *The Third Door* (trilogy), 1979, *Plague-Time,* 1985, and *Cruz Blanca, Story of a Town.*

OTHER

(Editor) *Life Is a Two-Way Street* (poetry anthology), Rosetta Press (Las Cruces, NM), 1980.

The Last of the Menu Girls (stories), Arte Publico (Houston, TX), 1986, reprinted, Vintage Contemporaries (New York, NY), 2004.

The Woman Who Knew the Language of Animals (juvenile), Houghton Mifflin (Boston, MA), 1992.

(Selector) *Shattering the Myth: Plays by Hispanic Women,* edited by Linda Feyder, Arte Publico (Houston, TX), 1992.

Face of an Angel (novel), Farrar, Straus (New York, NY), 1994.

(Author of essays) *Writing down the River: Into the Heart of the Grand Canyon,* photographed and produced by Kathleen Jo Ryan, foreword by Gretel Ehrlich, Northland (Flagstaff, AZ), 1998.

Loving Pedro Infante, Farrar, Straus & Giroux (New York, NY), 2001.

Work represented in numerous anthologies, including *An Anthology of Southwestern Literature,* University of New Mexico Press, 1977; *An Anthology: The Indian Rio Grande,* San Marcos Press, 1977; *Voces: An Anthology of Nuevo Mexicano Writers,* El Norte Publications, 1987; *Iguana Dreams: New Latino Fiction,* HarperCollins, 1992; *Mirrors beneath the Earth,* Curbstone Press, 1992; *Growing Up Latino: Memories and Stories,* Houghton Mifflin, 1993; *New Mexico Poetry Renaissance,* Red Crane Books, 1994; *Modern Fiction about Schoolteaching,* Allyn & Bacon, 1996; *Mother of the America,* Riverhead Books, 1996; *Chicana Creativity and Criticism: New Frontiers in American Literature,* edited by Maraia Herrera-Sobek and Helena Maraia Viramontes, University of New Mexico Press, 1996; and *Walking the Twilight II: Women Writers of the Southwest,* edited by Kathryn Wilder, Northland, 1996. Contributor to periodicals, including *Americas Review, New Mexico, Journal of Ethnic Studies,* and *Revista Chicano-Riquena.*

SIDELIGHTS: Denise Chávez is widely regarded as one of the leading Chicana playwrights and novelists of the U.S. Southwest. She has written and produced numerous one-act plays since the 1970s; however, she is best known for her fiction, including *The Last of the Menu Girls,* a poignant and sensitive short-story collection about an adolescent girl's passage into womanhood, and *Face of an Angel,* an exploration of a woman's life in a small New Mexico town. With the publication of *Face of an Angel*—and its selection as a Book-of-the-Month Club title in 1994—Chávez gained a national readership for her portraits of Chicanos living in the Mexican-American borderlands.

Born in Las Cruces, New Mexico, Chávez was reared in a family that particularly valued education and self-improvement. The divorce of her father, an attorney, and her mother, a teacher, when Chávez was ten was a painful experience. She spent the rest of her childhood in a household of women that included her mother, a sister, and a half-sister, and has acknowledged that the dominant influences in her life—as well as in her work—have been female. From an early age Chávez was an avid reader and writer. She kept a diary in which she recorded her observations on life and the personal fluctuations in her own life. During high school she became interested in drama and performed in productions. Chávez recalled her discovery of the theater to *Journal North* interviewer Jim Sagel as a revelation: "I can extend myself, be more than myself." She wrote her first play while a senior in college at New Mexico State University. Originally titled *The Wait,* the play was renamed *Novitiates* when it was produced in 1971. A story about several persons in transitional periods in their lives, her play won a prize in a New Mexico literary contest.

Critics have noted that Chávez's plays typically focus on the characters' self-revelation and developing sense of their personal place within their community. *Mario and the Room Maria,* for example, is a play about personal growth: its protagonist, Mundo Reyes, is unable to develop emotionally due to his refusal to confront painful experiences from his past. Likewise, *Si, hay posada* depicts the agony of Johnny Briones, whose rejection of love during the Christmas season is the result of emotional difficulties experienced as a child. While Chávez's plays often concentrate on her characters' inner lives, some deal with external and cultural elements that impede social interaction. Set in Santa Fe, New Mexico, her well-known 1984 play *Plaza* contrasts characters who have different impressions of life in the town square. According to *Dictionary of Literary Biography* contributor Rowena A. Rivera, the theme of *Plaza* "emphasizes the importance of family and friendship bonds as a means by which individuals can recover their personal and cultural heritage."

Many of the themes pervading Chávez's plays are echoed and drawn together in her short-story collection *The Last of the Menu Girls.* Composed of seven related stories, the work explores the coming of age of Rocio Esquibel through high school and college. In the opening story, Rocio goes to work handing out menus in a hospital, where she is exposed to many different people and experiences. Her impressions are shaped, in large part, by the ordinary individuals whom she daily encounters: the local repairman, the grandmother, and the hospital staff, among others.

Reviewers have commented that Chávez interweaves the seven stories that comprise *The Last of the Menu Girls* in order to emphasize the human need for *comunidad,* or community. Although some scholars find her style to be disjointed and flawed, many laud her lively dialogue, revealing characterization, and ability to write with insight. Chávez does not look upon *The Last of the Menu Girls* as a novel, but as a series of dramatic vignettes that explore the mysteries of womanhood. In fact, she envisions all her work as a chronicle of the changing relationships between men and women as women continue to avow their independence. This assertion has led to the creation of non-stereotypical Chicana heroines like Rocio, who *Women's Studies Review* contributor Maria C. Gonzalez described as "an individual who fights the traditional boundaries of identity that society has set up and expects her to follow."

Chávez's ambitious first novel, *Face of an Angel,* centers on the life of Soveida Dosamantes and her relations with her family, coworkers, former husbands, and lovers in the small New Mexico town of Agua Oscura. Soveida has worked as a waitress for more than thirty years and is deeply involved in preparing a handbook, *The Book of Service,* that she hopes will aid other would-be waitresses. *Face of an Angel* received wide attention for a first novel. Groundbreaking in the Chicana fiction genre due to its nontraditional heroines and frank discussion of sexual matters, the book was generally hailed as the debut of an important new voice in Hispanic American letters. *Belles Lettres* correspondent Irene Campos Carr called *Face of an Angel* "engrossing, amusing, and definitely one to be savored," adding: "The author's mordant wit is pervasive, the language is pithy, blunt, and explicit." Campos Carr concluded: "Chávez has become a fine writer and a great storyteller. With *Face of an Angel,* her second book, her name can be added to the growing list of Chicana authors making their mark in contemporary American fiction."

Chávez once remarked, "I consider myself a performance writer. My training in theater has helped me to write roles that I myself would enjoy acting. My characters are survivors, and many of them are women. I feel, as a Chicana writer, that I am capturing the voice of so many who have been voiceless for years. I write about the neighborhood handymen, the waitresses, the bag ladies, the elevator operators. They all have something in common: they know what it is to love and to be merciful. My work as a playwright is to capture as best as I can the small gestures of the forgotten people, the old men sitting on park benches, the lonely spinsters inside their corner store. My work is rooted in the Southwest, in heat and dust, and reflects a world where love is as real as the land. In this dry and seemingly harsh and empty world there is much beauty to be found. That hope of the heart is what feeds me, my characters."

In her 2001 novel, *Loving Pedro Infante,* Chávez tells the story of a thirty-something teacher's aide named Teresina "Tere" Avila who is divorced and obsessed with a macho Mexican film star named Pedro Infante, despite the fact that he died in 1957. Tere has a married lover who, true to form, makes promises that he never intends to keep. Tere's deep emotional life, however, revolves around the Pedro Infante fan club and her friend Irma, who espouses the movies as one of the best ways to learn about Mexican culture and life in general. In reality, Tere's ability to function in the real world is being compromised by her obsession with the screen icon. *Library Journal* contributor Lee McQueen commented, "Through Tere, Chávez explores femininity and cultural identity." Bill Ott, writing in *Booklist,* noted, "This thoroughly engaging novel walks the delicate line between comedy and pathos perfectly, using laughter to pull us back from pain but never letting us forget that the laughs come with a price."

In an interview with William Clark of *Publishers Weekly,* Chávez commented on what writing means to her, noting, "Writing for me is a healing, therapeutic, invigorating, sensuous manifestation of the energy that comes to you from the world, from everything that's alive. Everything has a voice and you just have to listen as closely as you can. That's what's so exciting—a character comes to you and you can't write fast enough because the character is speaking through you. It's a divine moment."

BIOGRAPHICAL AND CRITICAL SOURCES:

BOOKS

Balassi, William, John Crawford, and Annie Eysturoy, editors, *This Is about Vision: Interviews with Southwestern Writers,* University of New Mexico Press (Albuquerque, NM), 1990.

Dictionary of Literary Biography, Volume 122: *Chicano Writers, Second Series,* Thomson Gale (Detroit, MI), 1992, pp. 70-76.

Kester-Shelton, Pamela, editor, *Feminist Writers,* St. James Press (Detroit, MI), 1996, pp. 94-96.

Saldivar, Jose-David, and Rolando Hinojosa, editors, *Criticism in the Borderlands: Studies in Chicano Literature, Culture, and Ideology,* Duke University Press (Durham, NC), 1991.

PERIODICALS

American Studies International, April, 1990, p. 48.

Americas Review, Volume 16, number 2, 1988.

Belles Lettres, spring, 1995, Irene Campos Carr, review of *Face of an Angel,* p. 35.
Bloomsbury Review, September-October 1993; May-June 1995.
Booklist, April 15, 2001, Bill Ott, review of *Loving Pedro Infante,* p. 1532.
Boston Globe, September 30, 1994, p. 61.
Journal North, August 14, 1982, Jim Sagel, interview with author, p. E4.
Journal of Semiotic and Cultural Studies, 1991, pp. 29-43.
Library Journal, April 1, 2001, Lee McQueen, review of *Loving Pedro Infante,* p. 132.
Los Angeles Times, November 9, 1994, pp. E1, E4.
New York Times Book Review, October 12, 1986, p. 28; September 25, 1994, p. 20.
Performance, April 8, 1983, p. 6.
Publishers Weekly, August 15, 1994, William Clark, "It's All One Language Here" (interview), pp. 77-78.
School Library Journal, September, 2001, Adriana Lopez, "Chávez Hunts for Translator," p. S7.
Village Voice, November 8, 1994, p. 18.
Women's Studies Review, September-October, 1986, Maria C. Gonzalez, review of *The Last of the Menu Girls.*
World Literature Today, autumn, 1995, p. 792.

ONLINE

Desert Exposure, http://www.zianet.com/desertx/ (March, 1998), "An Interview with Denise Chavez."*

* * *

CHEVALIER, Tracy 1962-

PERSONAL: Born October, 1962, in Washington, DC; married; children: one son. *Education:* Oberlin College, B.A., 1984; University of East Anglia, M.A., 1994.

ADDRESSES: Home—London, England. *Agent*—Jonny Geller, Curtis Brown, Haymarket House, 28/29 Haymarket, London SWIY 4SP, England. *E-mail*—hello@tchevalier.com.

Tracy Chevalier

CAREER: Writer.

WRITINGS:

NOVELS

The Virgin Blue, Penguin (London, England), 1997, Dutton (New York, NY), 2003.
Girl with a Pearl Earring, Dutton (New York, NY), 2000.
Falling Angels, Dutton (New York, NY), 2001.
The Lady and the Unicorn, Dutton (New York, NY), 2003.

Contributor of short stories to *Fiction* and various magazines.

EDITOR

Twentieth-Century Children's Writers, preface by Naomi Lewis, St. James Press (Chicago, IL), 1989.

Contemporary Poets, prefaces by C. Day Lewis and Diane Wakoski, 5th edition, St. James Press (Chicago, IL), 1991.

Contemporary World Writers, preface by Susan Bassnett, St. James Press (Detroit, MI), 1993.

Encyclopedia of the Essay, Fitzroy Dearborn (Chicago, IL), 1997.

ADAPTATIONS: *Girl with a Pearl Earring* was released as a film in 2003. All of Chevalier's novels have been adapted as audiobooks.

SIDELIGHTS: Beginning her career as an editor, Tracy Chevalier has gained a growing following as the author of historical fiction. Her novels include *Girl with a Pearl Earring,* an imagined account of the model who appears in Dutch master Johannes Vermeer's painting of the same title, as well as *The Lady and the Unicorn* and *The Virgin Blue.* Discussing *Girl with a Pearl Earring* in a *Fire and Water* interview, Chevalier noted that the girl in Vermeer's painting is "both universal and specific" and added that "you never really know what she's thinking." In Chevalier's story, the painting depicts an illiterate teenager, Griet, who works as a servant in Vermeer's household. Griet is responsible for maintaining Vermeer's studio, and thus she becomes familiar with the painter's interests and technical concerns. "By the time she sits for her portrait," wrote R. Z. Sheppard in *Time,* "Griet is a budding connoisseur."

Vermeer's wife, who recognizes her own earring as the one worn by Griet in the painting, soon grows to resent the bond that has developed between her husband and the servant. Likewise, Vermeer's mother-in-law suspects that an inappropriate relationship has developed between artist and model. "But the truth is loftier than a studio tryst," noted Sheppard, who described Chevalier's account as "an exquisitely controlled exercise that illustrates how temptation is restrained for the sake of art." Another critic, Ruth Coughlin, summarized *Girl with a Pearl Earring* in the *New York Times Book Review* as "marvelously evocative," and a *Publishers Weekly* reviewer called the novel "a completely absorbing story."

While *Girl with a Pearl Earring* is Chevalier's best-known novel, it was not her first; she began her fiction-writing career with *The Virgin Blue,* a story about an American midwife who moves to France and finds her life circumstances reflected in those of a sixteenth-century ancestor. In *Library Journal,* Jo Manning praised the debut novel as a "marvelous piece of writing" that possesses "fluid language, strong characters, and imaginative plotting." Ted Hipple offered a similar opinion in a *Booklist* interview, noting that Chevalier "demonstrates . . . admirable gifts with language."

The Lady and the Unicorn was inspired by a series of six tapestries that hang in the Cluny museum in Paris, their origins mysterious. In Chevalier's novel, the works are commissioned by a powerful and manipulative French nobleman whose female household ultimately becomes involved with the worldly and opportunistic artisan commissioned to do the work. Over time, the lives of these women become entwined—romantically and otherwise—in that of the artist and the work he creates, which was originally meant to be the battle of Nancy but comes to be something far different.

Praising *The Lady and the Unicorn* as a "luminous tale," *Booklist* contributor Kristine Huntley commended Chevalier for the insight she brings to the historical epoch she describes, as well as for "colorful characters" who "leap off the page." Such praise was echoed by other reviewers, with a *Kirkus Reviews* contributor noting that the book is "marvelously imagined and sharply constructed, with a good feel for the people and the era." "What makes the tale enthralling are the details Chevalier offers," added a *Publishers Weekly* contributor, as well as "the deft way she herself weaves together each separate story strand" to create "a work of genuine power and beauty." In *The Lady and the Unicorn,* Rochelle Ratner added in *Library Journal,* Chevalier continues to develop the theme begun in *Girl with a Pearl Earring:* taking "artworks beautiful beyond words" and creating from them "an enchanting novel."

Chevalier's shift from reference-book editor to novelist came in 1993, when she quit her editorial job and earned her M.A. in creative writing at the University of East Anglia. "I try to put the success of my previous books out of my head when I write," she explained on her Web site. "If I thought about it much I'd be paralyzed with the fear of everyone's expectations of me." However, she has been able to sustain the critical success of *Girl with a Pearl Earring,* as well as juggle motherhood and a host of other responsibilities. "It's kind of like running," the author added: "you feel terrible for those first ten minutes but then it gets better and afterwards you feel great."

BIOGRAPHICAL AND CRITICAL SOURCES:

BOOKS

American Reference Books Annual, Libraries Unlimited, 1998, Bernice Bergup, review of *Encyclopedia of the Essay,* p. 478.

PERIODICALS

Booklist, April 15, 1998, review of *Encyclopedia of the Essay,* p. 1462; September 15, 2003, Ted Hipple, review of *The Virgin Blue,* p. 252; November 1, 2003, Kristine Huntley, review of *The Lady and the Unicorn,* p. 458; April 15, 2004, Joyce Saricks, review of *The Lady and the Unicorn,* p. 1460.

Choice, April, 1998, A. C. Labriola, review of *Encyclopedia of the Essay,* p. 1347.

Cleveland Plain-Dealer, October 24, 2001, Donna Marchetti, "Fed-up Editor Starts Writing Her Own Books," p. E1.

Kirkus Reviews, November 15, 2003, review of *The Lady and the Unicorn,* p. 1325.

Library Journal, October 15, 1999, Barbara Hoffert, review of *Girl with a Pearl Earring,* p. 103; August, 2003, Jo Manning, review of *The Virgin Blue,* p. 127; January, 2004, Kellie Gillespie, review of *The Lady and the Unicron,* p. 152; June 15, 2004, Rochelle Ratner, review of *The Lady and the Unicorn,* p. 108.

New York Times Book Review, January 23, 2000, Ruth Coughlin, review of *Girl with a Pearl Earring,* p. 20.

People, January 12, 2004, Lee Aitken, review of *The Lady and the Unicorn,* p. 47.

Publishers Weekly, October 11, 1999, review of *Girl with a Pearl Earring;* December 8, 2003, review of *The Lady and the Unicorn,* p. 45.

Reference and User Services Quarterly, fall, 1998, Andrew B. Wertheimer, review of *Encyclopedia of the Essay,* p. 93.

RQ, spring, 1992, Anna M. Donnelly, review of *Contemporary Poets,* p. 435.

St. Louis Post-Dispatch, January 23, 2002, Gail Pennington, review of *Girl with a Pearl Earring,* p. E1.

School Library Journal, April, 2004, Molly Connally, review of *The Lady and the Unicorn,* p. 182.

Time, January 17, 2000, R. Z. Sheppard, "A Portrait of Radiance: Tracy Chevalier Brings the Real Artist Vermeer and a Fictional Muse to Life in a Jewel of a Novel," p. 94.

ONLINE

Fire and Water, http://www.fireandwater.com/ (February 2, 2000).

Tracy Chevalier Web site, http://www.tchevalier.com/ (August 5, 2004).

* * *

CHU, Petra ten-Doesschate 1942-

PERSONAL: Born October 15, 1942, in Greenville, SC; daughter of Jurriaan (an ophthalmologist) and Lidy (a pediatrician; maiden name, Ameling) ten-Doesschate; married Fen-Dow Chu (a naval architect), 1971; children: May-Ying, Lidy, Hsiao-Yun, Wei. *Education:* Sorbonne, University of Paris, Diplome Superieur Cours de Civilization Francaise, 1961; University of Utrecht, Doctoraal, 1967; Columbia University, Ph.D., 1972.

ADDRESSES: *Home*—22 Park Pl., South Orange, NJ 07079. *Office*—Department of Art and Music, Seton Hall University, South Orange, NJ 07079. *E-mail*—Chupetra@shu.edu.

CAREER: Educator, writer, and editor. Seton Hall University, South Orange, NJ, assistant professor, 1972-77, associate professor, 1977-80, chairperson of department of art and music, 1977-98; professor of art, 1980—. Princeton University, Princeton, NJ, visiting professor, 1990-92. Series editor, with Jacques de Caso, of "Princeton Series in Nineteenth-Century Art, Culture, and Society," 1991-97; managing editor of *Nineteenth-Century Art Worldwide,* 1999—.

MEMBER: College Art Association of America, Society for French Nineteenth-Century Studies, Historians of Netherlandish Art, Dutch Society of Art History, Association of Historians of Nineteenth-Century Art (president, 1999—).

AWARDS, HONORS: Guggenheim fellow, 1986-87, 1991; grant from National Endowment for the Humanities, 1986-88, 1994; Wheatland Foundation, research grant, 1990; Jane and Morgan Whitney Art History fellow, Metropolitan Museum of Art, 1994-95; Humanities Research Centre award, Australian National University, 2003; Netherlands Institute of Advanced Research grant, 2004.

WRITINGS:

French Realism and the Dutch Masters, Haentjens Dekker & Gumbert (Utrecht, Netherlands), 1974.
Courbet in Perspective, Prentice-Hall (Englewood Cliffs, NJ), 1977.
Dominique Vivant Denon (Volume 121 of *The Illustrated Bartsch),* Abaris (New York, NY), part one, 1985, part two, 1988.
(Editor and translator) *The Letters of Gustave Courbet,* University of Chicago Press (Chicago, IL), 1992.
(Contributor and coeditor, with Gabriel Weisberg) *The Popularization of Images: Visual Culture under the July Monarchy,* Princeton University Press (Princeton, NJ), 1994.
(Contributor) *Redefining Genre: French and American Painting, 1850-1900,* Trust for Museum Exhibitions (Washington, DC), 1995.
(With Joerg Zutter) *Courbet: Artiste et promoteur de son oeuvre* (exhibition catalogue), Flammarion (Paris, France), 1998.
Nineteenth-Century European Art, H. Abrams (New York, NY), 2002.

Work represented in anthologies, including *The European Realist Tradition in the Nineteenth Century,* edited by Gabriel Weisberg, Indiana University Press, 1982; *The Documented Image: Festschrift for Elizabeth Holt,* Syracuse University Press, 1987; and *The Macmillan Dictionary of Art.* Contributor of essays to art exhibition catalogues, including *Francisco Oller: A Realist-Impressionist, Im Lichte Hollands: Hollaendische Malerie des 17. Jahrhunderts aus dem Sammlungen des Fuersten von Liechtenstein und aus Schweizer Besitz,* Kunstmuseum (Basel, Switzerland), 1987, and *Art of the July Monarchy.* Contributor to art journals, including *Arts Magazine* and *Apollo.*

SIDELIGHTS: Petra ten-Doesschate Chu is a professor of art at Seton Hall University and author and editor of numerous articles and several books on nineteenth-century art, focusing largely on the French and European tradition. Working as both translator and editor, Chu collected more than 600 of the letters of the French impressionist painter Gustave Courbet in the *Letters of Gustave Courbet.* This correspondence chronicles Courbet's life from the time of his spoiled teenage years through his entry into the art world, his growing disgust with imperialism, his part in the Paris Commune, and finally his exile in Switzerland, where he died. In correspondence with writers and artists such as Charles Baudelaire, Claude Monet, and Victor Hugo, these letters confirm, according to *Journal of European Studies* reviewer Robert Lethbridge, "that behind the peasant buffoon there lay a deeply serious artist." Lethbridge further noted that "this volume will become the standard work of reference," and that it is "the measure of Professor Chu's achievement" that she was able to impose chronology on the correspondence despite the fact that Courbet famously neglected to date his letters. Writing in the *Wall Street Journal,* Jack Flam felt that the "chronicle of Courbet's embattled career is vividly evoked" in Chu's work. Flam added that Chu did an "exemplary job of editing, annotating and translating."

Working with Gabriel Weisberg, Chu also edited the 1994 study *The Popularization of Images: Visual Culture under the July Monarchy.* A collection of nine essays, including one from Chu, this collection provides a "new and noteworthy attempt to sidestep the shoals of both modernism and revisionism by looking at the art of the period from the point of view of popular culture," according to Patricia Mainardi, writing in the *Journal of Modern History.* The July Monarchy in France lasted from 1831 to 1848 and is one of the least studied periods of French art, usually regarded, as Mainardi further explained, as "a kind of art historical stepchild." Coming at the end of Classicism and Romanticism, and before the advent of Realism, the period is marked by the increase in landscape art and by the utilization of new techniques of visual representation, such as the lithograph; it thus helped to break down the strict bounds between high and low art. Chu's contribution to the collection, "Pop Culture in the Making: The Romantic Craze for History," articulates, according to Mainardi, "some of the most salient aspects" of the book's argument for a revised view of that epoch and its art. Similarly, Lethbridge, writing in the *Journal of European Studies,* felt that the "most far-reaching" essay in the volume is Chu's, "which is a supplementary overview beyond the editorial formalities of her Introduction." In a review for

History, Pamela Pilbeam called Chu's contribution a "wide-ranging chapter on the 'pop' craze for history." Lethbridge added, "This collection offers specialists of the July Monarchy intersecting scholarship at its best." Mainardi went on to note that the book "will provide enough fertile material for future investigations" and will also supply "valuable reading for a wide audience." And Pilbeam also had praise for the volume as a whole, noting that it was "handsomely produced" and that it "merits, and should attract, a wide readership."

In 2002 Chu published her overview of European art, *Nineteenth-Century European Art,* a book that "superbly conveys the interconnectedness of art, history, culture, society, and politics," according to Edward K. Owusu-Ansah, writing in *Library Journal.* Chu approaches her subject chronologically, in a series of twenty chapters with more than 500 illustrations, documenting the work of painters from Francisco Goya to John Ruskin. Owusu-Ansah further praised the book as both "eloquently written" and "deeply engaging," additionally calling it the "best single-volume" approach to the subject.

BIOGRAPHICAL AND CRITICAL SOURCES:

PERIODICALS

English Historical Review, February, 1997, Linda Whiteley, review of *The Popularization of Images: Visual Culture under the July Monarchy,* pp. 229-230.

History, July, 1996, Pamela Pilbeam, review of *The Popularization of Images,* pp. 480-481.

Journal of European Studies, March, 1994, Robert Lethbridge, review of *Letters of Gustave Courbet,* pp. 65-66; September, 1997, Robert Lethbridge, review of *The Popularization of Images,* pp. 378-379.

Journal of Modern History, September, 1997, Patricia Mainardi, review of *The Popularization of Images,* pp. 605-608.

Library Journal, February 15, 2003, Edward K. Owusu-Ansah, review of *Nineteenth-Century European Art,* pp. 131-132.

Publishers weekly, January 27, 1992, review of *Letters of Gustave Courbet,* p. 82.

Wall Street Journal, May 29, 1992, Jack Flam, review of *Letters of Gustave Courbet,* p. A9.

ONLINE

Seton Hall Web site, http://pirate.shu.edu/~chupetra/ (October 27, 2003), "Petra ten-Doesschate Chu."*

* * *

CLARK, Curt
See WESTLAKE, Donald E(dwin)

* * *

COE, Tucker
See WESTLAKE, Donald E(dwin)

* * *

COHN, Samuel K(line), Jr. 1949-

PERSONAL: Born April 13, 1949, in Birmingham, AL; son of Samuel Kline (a physician) and Mildred (an artist; maiden name, Hiller) Cohn. *Education:* Attended University of London, 1969-70; Union College, B.A., 1971; University of Wisconsin—Madison, M.A., 1972; Harvard University, Ph.D., 1978. *Politics:* Socialist

ADDRESSES: *Office*—Department of Medieval History, University of Glasgow, 10 University Gardens, Scotland G12 8QQ. *E-mail*—s.cohn@history.arts.gla.ac.uk.

CAREER: Wesleyan University, Middletown, CT, assistant professor of history, 1978-79; Brandeis University, Waltham, MA, assistant professor, 1979-85, associate professor, 1985-86, professor of history, 1986-95; University of Glasgow (Scotland), professor of medieval history, 1995—. Visiting professor, Brown University, 1991.

WRITINGS:

The Laboring Classes in Renaissance Florence, Academic Press (New York, NY), 1980.

Death and Property in Siena, 1205-1799: Strategies for the Afterlife, Johns Hopkins University Press (Baltimore, MD), 1988.

The Cult of Remembrance and the Black Death: Six Renaissance Cities in Central Italy, Johns Hopkins University Press (Baltimore, MD), 1992, revised, 1997.

Women in the Streets: Essays on Sex and Power in Renaissance Italy, Johns Hopkins University Press (Baltimore, MD), 1996.

(Editor, with Steven A. Epstein) *Portraits of Medieval and Renaissance Living: Essays in Memory of David Herlihy,* University of Michigan Press (Ann Arbor, MI), 1996.

(Editor and contributor of introduction) David Herlihy, *The Black Death and the Transformation of the West,* Harvard University Press (Cambridge, MA), 1997.

Creating the Florentine State: Peasants and Rebellion, 1348-1434, Cambridge University Press (New York, NY), 1999.

The Black Death Transformed: Disease and Culture in Early Renaissance Europe, Oxford University Press (New York, NY), 2002.

Contributor of "The Place of the Dead in Flanders and Tuscany: Towards a Comparative History of the Black Death" to *The Place of the Dead: Death and Remembrance in Late Medieval and Early Modern Europe,* edited by Bruce Gordon and Peter Marshall, Cambridge University Press (Cambridge, MA), 2000.

SIDELIGHTS: During a scholarly career that has spanned more than two decades, historian Samuel K. Cohn, Jr., has interpreted such facets of Italian Renaissance history as the role of women in Florence, testamentary giving patterns, and the effect of the bubonic plague on the rate of societal changes. On these and other topics he has published a more than a dozen books and journal articles.

The effects on Europe of the Black Death, commonly thought to be bubonic plague, has been one of Cohn's longtime interests. In *The Cult of Remembrance and the Black Death: Six Renaissance Cities in Central Italy,* he studied 3,389 testaments and 21,351 pious bequests to discern changes in charitable giving patterns after the outbreak of plague in 1362 and 1363. He found that prior to this period, benefactors gave smaller amounts to a wider variety of charities, while after this outbreak of plague benefactors gave larger sums to fewer charities and focused on creating monuments to themselves whether through a large donation to a monastery, friary, parish, civic hospital, or civic organization. The work caught the attention of scholars, among them Daniel Bornstein, who reviewed it for *Historian.* "Bold interpretations such as this have the signal merit of stirring fruitful debate," Bornstein wrote, "but a number of questions about Cohn's evidence and interpretation might give one pause," such as occasionally but possibly important mistranslations of Latin text in the documents studied. As D. R. Skopp explained in *Choice,* these questions revolve around Cohn's statistical analysis using multiple regression models, the unevenness of his database, and in his attention to "sheer numbers of bequests . . . [rather than] the actual proportion of the estate."

Cohn edited and wrote the introduction to *The Black Death and the Transformation of the West* by David Herlihy, founding associate editor of the *Journal of Interdisciplinary History.* And after Herlihy's death, Cohn edited *Portraits of Medieval and Renaissance Living: Essays in Memory of David Herlihy.* In 2002 Cohn served up another study of the disease and its effects: *The Black Death Transformed: Disease and Culture in Early Renaissance Europe.* In it he argues that the Black Death was not the bubonic plague and attempts to explain why the Renaissance arose from the most significant mortality event in the West's history.

In his 1996 publication *Women in the Streets: Essays on Sex and Power in Renaissance Italy,* a collection of essays on several topics, Cohn "adduces a mass of new evidence and rich argumentation in considering the important question of how women experienced the changes associated with the Renaissance in Italy," to quote Catherine King of the *English Historical Review.* Cohn presents a new interpretation of the condition of women in Italy, stating that Florence was the worst place in central Italy to have been born a woman during the fourteenth and fifteenth centuries. Basing his assertion on court records, Cohn argues that the Florentine criminal courts stopped prosecuting the perpetrators of rapes and assaults against women. He also notes that the rates of infanticide of female children rose, restrictions on female occupations increased (causing forced female migration), and women's control over property declined. A woman's treatment by others depended on several factors: her social class, whether she was secular or a member of a religious order, and her geographical location.

Another subject of this work is the economic conditions of the Florentine hill people, who were believed to live in poverty compared with the townspeople. However, Cohn makes a case for the hill dwellers' greater prosperity due to the increasing role of animal husbandry over grain farming. In addition to discussions of the treatment of women and the affluence and influence of the Florentine peasantry, Cohn formulates a new methodology. Rather than use a single or several well-documented and celebrated court cases to make a particular point, Cohn maintains that "a quantitative reckoning of court cases can provide clues to the past that no individual case history, no matter how 'thickly' described . . . can possibly reveal." Thus in his research Cohn uses a large number of primary sources in his research. Reviewing the work for the *Journal of the Historical Association* was Trevor Dean, who commented, "The challenging nature of these arguments will be evident, and these lucidly written essays (though sometimes clogged with archive Latin) will certainly provide stimulus for debate among Renaissance historians."

Some twenty years after Cohn published *The Laboring Classes in Renaissance Florence,* his *Creating the Florentine State: Peasants and Rebellion, 1348-1434* appeared. In this "bold new interpretation of the transition from the late medieval to the Renaissance state in Florence," to quote *Journal of Social History* contributor Sharon T. Strocchia, Cohn argues that a number of successful peasant uprisings from 1401 to 1405 prompted the Florentine government to tend more kindly to its peasant subjects, particularly in lightening their tax burden. Cohn compares the relationship of the mountain dwellers and lowland dwellers, proposing that they were not backward and pagan, but intelligent, religious, and sociable. He also maintains that the high tax burden forced many mountain dwellers to move outside of Florentine jurisdiction to survive, causing the remaining peasants to revolt. Finally, as far as the historical record is concerned, Cohn asserts that the urban historians in Florence attempted to cover up the existence and nature of the uprisings in writing the region's history.

Creating the Florentine State elicited discussion among scholars. Among them was Trevor Dean, who, in an article for the *English Historical Review* expressed reservations. "The argument [about the influence of the peasant rebellions] is conducted with force and pugnacity, and the book makes a most valuable addition to the historiography of European rebellions. But there are moments when Cohn might be suspected of overdoing it." Similarly, while Strocchia found that "Cohn effectively debunks the image of mountain peasants constructed by Braudel and others," she found his case to be "not completely convincing." In her opinion this is particularly the case for a "conspiracy of silence" about the peasant revolts by Florentine chroniclers, for which she believes Cohn "overplays the evidence." Despite these alleged flaws, Strocchia concluded: "This study provides an important reconsideration of the relationships binding peasants and elites, as well as those distinguishing peasants themselves." *Choice*'s P. Grendler also praised the study, calling it "clearly written" and "strongly argued," and *Renaissance Quarterly* reviewer Louis Haas found much to like about this "significant, well-researched, and well-argued book." Noting that Cohn's "spadework in the archives—especially his ability to link persons in various archival collections—evinces considerable doggedness on his part," Haas praised Cohn's use of statistical methods and his discussions of the results. "His quantitative discussion and its attendant tables and appendixes are clear and convincing enough for the average scholarly reader."

BIOGRAPHICAL AND CRITICAL SOURCES:

BOOKS

Cohn, Samuel K., Jr., *Women in the Streets: Essays on Sex and Power in Renaissance Italy,* Johns Hopkins University Press (Baltimore, MD), 1996.

PERIODICALS

American Historical Review, February, 1982, review of *Laboring Classes in Renaissance Florence,* p. 211; June, 1990, review of *Death and Property in Siena, 1205-1799: Strategies for the Afterlife,* p. 860; October, 1993, review of *The Cult of Remembrance and the Black Death: Six Renaissance Cities in Central Italy,* pp. 1283+; December, 1998, review of *Women in the Streets,* p. 1641; April, 2001, review of *Creating the Florentine State: Peasants and Rebellion, 1348-1434,* pp. 673+.

Catholic Historical Review, January, 1990, review of *Death and Property in Siena,* p. 95; October, 1993, review of *The Cult of Remembrance and the Black Death,* pp. 740+.

Choice, April, 1993, D. R. Skopp, review of *The Cult of Remembrance and the Black Death,* p. 1367; September, 2000, P. Grendler, review of *Creating the Florentine State,* p. 209.

English Historical Review, October, 1982, review of *Laboring Classes in Renaissance Florence,* p. 843; November, 1995, review of *The Cult of Remembrance and the Black Death,* pp. 1247+; February, 1999, Catherine King, review of *Women in the Streets,* p. 164; February, 2001, Trevor Dean, review of *Creating the Florentine State,* p. 198.

Historian, spring, 1994, review of *The Cult of Remembrance and the Black Death,* pp. 583+; summer, 1995, Daniel Bornstein, review of *The Cult of Remembrance and the Black Death,* pp. 583-584.

History, January, 1999, Trevor Dean, review of *Women in the Streets,* p. 144.

History: Reviews of New Books, spring, 1998, review of *Women in the Streets,* p. 140.

History Today, January, 1994, review of *The Cult of Remembrance and the Black Death,* pp. 55+.

Journal of Economic History, September, 1998, review of *Women in the Streets,* pp. 876+.

Journal of Interdisciplinary History, spring, 1982, review of *Laboring Classes in Renaissance Florence,* p. 690; spring, 1990, review of *Death and Property in Siena,* p. 672; fall, 1994, review of *The Cult of Remembrance and the Black Death,* pp. 308+; winter, 1998, Martha C. Howell, review of *Portraits of Medieval and Renaissance Living: Essays in Memory of David Herlihy,* pp. 417-425, review of *Women in the Streets,* pp. 460+.

Journal of Modern History, September, 1982, review of *Laboring Classes in Renaissance Florence,* p. 591; September, 1990, review of *Death and Property in Siena,* p. 624; June, 1995, review of *The Cult of Remembrance and the Black Death,* pp. 358+.

Journal of Social History, fall, 1990, review of *Death and Property in Siena,* p. 161; fall, 2001, Sharon T. Strocchia, review of *Creating the Florentine State,* p. 242.

New York Review of Books, January 21, 1982, Felix Gilbert, review of *The Laboring Classes in Renaissance Florence,* pp. 64-65.

Reference and Research Book News, August, 1997, review of *Women in the Streets,* p. 94.

Religious Studies Review, April, 1991, review of *Death and Property in Siena,* p. 170.

Renaissance Quarterly, fall, 1982, review of *Laboring Classes in Renaissance Florence,* p. 472; winter, 1989, review of *Death and Property in Siena,* p. 833; winter, 1994, review of *The Cult of Remembrance and the Black Death,* pp. 942+; winter, 1998, review of *Women in the Streets,* pp. 1341+; summer, 2001, Louis Haas, review of *Creating the Florentine State,* p. 593.

Sixteenth Century Journal, fall, 1994, review of *The Cult of Remembrance and the Black Death,* pp. 719+; summer, 1998, review of *Women in the Streets,* pp. 577+; spring, 2001, review of *Creating the Florentine State,* pp. 154+.

Speculum: A Journal of Medieval Studies, July, 1982, review of *Laboring Classes in Renaissance Florence,* p. 595; January, 1992, review of *Death and Property in Siena,* pp. 127+; October, 1994, review of *The Cult of Remembrance and the Black Death,* pp. 1140+; July, 1998, review of *Women in the Streets,* pp. 825+; January, 1999, Rosemary Horrox, review of *The Black Death and the Transformation of the West,* pp. 184-185.

Times Literary Supplement, January 15, 1982, review of *Laboring Classes in Renaissance Florence,* p. 61; September 1, 1989, review of *Death and Property in Siena,* p. 956.

University Press Book News, December, 1992, review of *The Cult of Remembrance and the Black Death,* p. 16.*

* * *

CONNIFF, Richard 1951-

PERSONAL: Born March 2, 1951, in Jersey City, NJ; son of James C. G. (a writer) and Dorothy (a homemaker; maiden name, Donnelly) Conniff; married Karen Braeder (a homemaker), May 23, 1981; children: James, Benjamin. *Education:* Yale University, B.A., 1973. *Religion:* Roman Catholic. *Hobbies and other interests:* Ireland, architectural restoration, Americana, travel.

ADDRESSES: Home—P.O. Box 64, Deep River, CT 06417. *Agent*—Robert Lescher, 155 E. 71st St., New York, NY 10021.

CAREER: Newark Star-Ledger, Newark, NJ, reporter, 1973-75; freelance writer, 1975-79; *Next,* New York, NY, senior writer, 1979-81; freelance writer, 1981-83; *Geo,* New York, NY, managing editor, 1983-85; freelance writer, 1985—. Deep River Book Co., founder.

WRITINGS:

The Devil's Book of Verse: Masters of the Poison Pen from Ancient Times to the Present Day, Dodd, Mead (New York, NY), 1983.

Irish Walls, photographs by Alen MacWeeney, Stewart, Tabori & Chang (New York, NY), 1986.

The Natural History of the Rich: A Field Guide, W. W. Norton (New York, NY), 2002.

Contributor to magazines and newspapers, including *National Geographic, Architectural Digest, Audubon, Smithsonian,* and *Time.*

SIDELIGHTS: Richard Conniff once told *CA:* "I'm interested in propagating audacious speech that is often satirical and usually humorous. I'm also interested in exploring the connections between human beings and the natural world."

Conniff's first book, *The Devil's Book of Verse: Masters of the Poison Pen from Ancient Times to the Present Day,* is a collection of nearly 400 poems of rude invective and wit, which have delighted critics since the volume appeared in 1983. The contributors are as ancient as Catullus and as contemporary as Dorothy Parker, Ogden Nash, and John Updike. The subjects of the poison pen are as varied as their authors: sex, the family, politics, religion, lawyers, and children are just a few.

Though *The Devil's Book of Verse* was acclaimed by its reviewers, it was not so well received by the publisher's parent company, a publisher of Bibles. When the author was asked to remove two poems containing an offensive word, Conniff refused, and it appeared that the book might not be distributed at all. The author filed a lawsuit and enlisted the support of such groups as the International PEN and the American Society of Authors and Journalists to fight what they described as an act of censorship. Finally the suit was settled and Conniff received the unsold copies of his book. He established the Deep River Book Company to distribute them and continued his career as a freelance writer.

In 1986 *Irish Walls* was published. This book, illustrated by the photographs of Alen MacWeeney, developed from Conniff's belief that the thousands of miles of walls dividing Ireland reveal the underlying nature of the Irish landscape and the people who live in it. The volume was described by Harriet Choice in the *Chicago Tribune* as "a charming and unique travel book."

BIOGRAPHICAL AND CRITICAL SOURCES:

PERIODICALS

Books in Canada, summer, 2003, Michael Hanlon, review of *The Natural History of the Rich: A Field Guide,* p. 3.

Chicago Tribune, October 5, 1986, Harriet Choice, review of *Irish Walls.*

Newsday, September 21, 1983.*

* * *

CONN, Nicole 1959-

PERSONAL: Born October 29, 1959, in Mesa, AZ; daughter of Frank, Jr. (an engineer) and Christa (a domestic engineer; maiden name, Rominger) Hoven. *Education:* Received degree from Elliott Business College, 1986.

ADDRESSES: *Office*—Demi-Monde Productions, 4515 St. Clair, Studio City, CA 91604.

CAREER: Videospectrum (video company), founder, 1985; Demi-Monde Productions (film development and production company), founder, president, and chief executive officer, 1985—.

AWARDS, HONORS: Nicholl Screenwriting Fellowship finalist, 1987, for *Aunnie Cole.*

WRITINGS:

(And director and executive producer) *Claire of the Moon* (screenplay), Demi-Monde Productions, 1993, published as *Claire of the Moon: One Woman's Journey into Her Sexual Identity: A Novel,* Naiad Press (Tallahassee, FL), 1993.

Passion's Shadow: A Novel, Simon & Schuster (New York, NY), 1995.
The Bottom Line (novel), Naiad Press (Tallahassee, FL), 1994.
Angel Wings: A Love Story, Simon & Schuster (New York, NY), 1997.
She Walks in Beauty, Naiad Press (Tallahassee, FL), 2001.

Writer of screenplays, including *Aunnie Cole* and *Cynara.*

SIDELIGHTS: Film writer and director Nicole Conn's first full-length feature, *Claire of the Moon,* received critical attention upon its release in 1993, the same year the screenplay was published as a novel. Following her success with *Claire,* Conn went on to write a number of novels and plays.

After receiving a degree in business, Conn began a filmmaking career, founding her own production company in order to bring out-of-the-mainstream screenplays to movie audiences. As writer, executive producer, and director of *Claire of the Moon,* Conn oversaw all aspects of the story, in which a heterosexual woman discovers another side of herself at an Oregon writers' colony for women. Noel Benedict, a therapist and writer, and Claire Jabrowski, author of a satirical volume titled *Life Can Ruin Your Hair,* are assigned to share living quarters, and Claire's attraction to openly gay Noel becomes the focal point of the film. Other women who have signed up for the retreat include a romance writer named Tara O'Hara, and a homemaker and mother of twins who is writing a work of fiction in which men experience childbirth. The workshops are run by Maggie, who has purposely placed Claire and Noel together. The film's plot is fueled by the workshop sessions, where the issues of gender politics and sexuality are explored through dialogues among the characters.

Several reviewers commended Conn's portrayal of lesbianism. Jay Carr in the *Boston Globe* found the work to be "a brave, often ungainly, but always heartfelt lesbian love story." *Los Angeles Reader*'s Paul Birchall called it "intelligent and beautifully atmospheric," and "a deep, philosophical analysis of the very definition of love and intimacy." *Chicago Tribune* contributor Johanna Steinmetz praised the serious tone of *Claire of the Moon,* but remarked that the characters "bog the film down with overheated and under-reasoned discussions of sexual identity." Janet Maslin, writing in the *New York Times* of the same discussions, stated that "the dialogue is ponderous at such times, undercutting what might seem a more daring drama." *Los Angeles Times,* critic Kevin Thomas noted in particular Conn's directorial skill, pointing out that she "is able to create a series of poetic images that continually subvert the film's torrent of words. Like a good semanticist, Conn knows the crucial difference between the map and territory."

Passion's Shadow is Conn's novel about a lesbian triangle in which a mother, workaholic architect Lindsay Brennan, and her daughter, married interior designer Samantha, unknowingly fall in love with the same woman. The object of their affections, alcoholic Sondra Pinchot, is also a designer, and, until meeting Lindsay, had been heterosexual. A *Publishers Weekly* contributor noted that "despite the 'incestuous' overtones to the love triangle, this tale is really just a routine, if chic, romantic potboiler."

Conn followed with *The Bottom Line* and then *Angel Wings: A Love Story.* The latter is a New Age romance about an angel named Carlita, who is put in charge of the fate of two people. When Matthew's parents die in a car crash, he is sent from England to live with his eccentric aunt in Los Angeles. There he meets Clancy, a young girl whose life is made difficult by her alcoholic mother. They are to meet several years later, when they are eighteen, but the event does not occur, putting Carlita's future as an angel in danger.

Lambda Book Report's Joy Parks called Conn's next book, *She Walks in Beauty,* "something fine and rare, a book of substance, a meaningful story that will linger with readers long after the last page is turned." The book is two stories in one. Spencer Atwood is a successful filmmaker who escapes the pain of childhood abuse by chasing fame and female companions. When her own ambition causes her to lose everyone and everything that matters to her, she retreats to a cabin on the Oregon coast, where she throws herself into the job of clearing a path to the beach. The solitude and physical labor rekindle her longing to write, and she does, a novel titled *Cynara.*

Lilian Harrington, the protagonist and the creator of poetry considered too raw to be written by a woman, changes her name to Byron Harrington, a pseudonym under which she is able to be published. She meets Dorothy Parker and becomes part of the Algonquin Hotel crowd, then moves to Paris with her mentor, gay Parnell "Rabbit" Walbrook. Sylvia Beach publishes her poetry, and through Sylvia and Rabbit, she meets the famous lesbian writers of the time, including Gertrude Stein. In order to pay for her high-rolling lifestyle, Lilian, now Byron, writes pulp detective stories that become very popular in the United States, and also discovers her own lesbianism. She returns to the States when her father is close to death and where she must confront the brother who was responsible for her leaving. She then meets Cynara, the woman who gives her love and the courage to face the future.

Parks commented on the parallels in the lives of Spencer and Lilian/Byron, both of whom were abused as children, and both of whom have a need to excel in order to overcome their guilt. Parks called *She Walks in Beauty* "a richly layered, genuinely stirring novel that doesn't shy away from difficult themes. It combines one of the most fascinating and elegant periods in lesbian history with the money and power-driven crassness of current-day Hollywood. And best of all, it tells a tremendously sensual, magnificently human story that lets readers come away believing in the healing power of love and creative expression."

Conn once told *CA:* "Film is not about technical wizardry for me. It's about the ride you take in the dark. It isn't about larger-than-life action heroes who violently live through the impossible; it's about the incredible impact of the simplest moment. It's about the human condition with all its exquisite flaws. It's about raw, real, and uncensored emotion."

BIOGRAPHICAL AND CRITICAL SOURCES:

PERIODICALS

Advocate, July 27, 1993; November 28, 1995, Chastity Bono, review of *Passion's Shadow,* p. 76.

Austin American-Statesman, July 24, 1992, p. 6.

Booklist, September 1, 1997, Whitney Scott, review of *Angel Wings,* p. 56.

Boston Globe, September 23, 1992, Jay Carr, review of *Claire of the Moon,* p. 46.

Chicago Tribune, June 11, 1993, Johanna Steinmetz, review of *Claire of the Moon,* p. 3.

Lambda Book Report, November, 1997, Julia Willis, review of *Angel Wings,* p. 12; October, 2001, Joy Parks, review of *She Walks in Beauty,* p. 15.

Library Journal, October 15, 1995, Rebecca S. Kelm, review of *Passion's Shadow,* p. 86.

Los Angeles Reader, January 29, 1993, Paul Birchall, review of *Claire of the Moon.*

Los Angeles Times, January 29, 1993, Kevin Thomas, review of *Claire of the Moon,* p. F8.

New York Times, April 16, 1993, Janet Maslin, review of *Claire of the Moon,* p. C11.

Out Front, September 30, 1992, p. 27.

Publishers Weekly, September 18, 1995, review of *Passion's Shadow,* p. 114; July 28, 1997, review of *Angel Wings,* p. 54.*

* * *

COOPER, Susan (Mary) 1935-

PERSONAL: Born May 23, 1935, in Burnham, Buckinghamshire, England; immigrated to the United States, 1963; daughter of John Richard (an employee of the Great Western Railway) and Ethel May (a teacher; maiden name, Field) Cooper; married Nicholas J. Grant (a scientist and college professor), August 3, 1963 (divorced, 1983); married Hume Cronyn (an actor and playwright), 1996; children: (first marriage) Jonathan, Katharine; Anne, Bill, Peter (stepchildren); (second marriage) Tandy (stepchild). *Education:* Somerville College, Oxford, M.A., 1956. *Hobbies and other interests:* Music, islands.

ADDRESSES: Home—CT and New York, NY. *Agent*—c/o Author Mail, Margaret K. McElderry, Simon & Schuster, 1230 Ave. of the Americas, New York, NY 10020.

CAREER: Author, playwright, screenwriter, and journalist. *Sunday Times,* London, England, reporter and feature writer, 1956-63. Narrator, with others, of *George Balanchine's Nutcracker,* Warner Bros., 1993.

MEMBER: Society of Authors (United Kingdom), Authors League of America, Authors Guild, Writers Guild of America.

AWARDS, HONORS: Horn Book Honor List citation for *Over Sea, under Stone; Horn Book* Honor List and American Library Association (ALA) Notable Book citations, both 1970, both for *Dawn of Fear; Boston Globe-Horn Book* Award, Carnegie Medal runner-up, and ALA Notable Book citation, all 1973, and New-

Susan Cooper

bery Award Honor Book, 1974, all for *The Dark Is Rising;* ALA Notable Book citation, for *Greenwitch;* Newbery Medal, Tir na N'og Award (Wales), Carnegie Medal commendation, *Horn Book* Honor List, and ALA Notable Book citation, all 1976, all for *The Grey King;* Tir na N'og Award, 1978, for *Silver on the Tree;* Parents' Choice Award, 1983, for *The Silver Cow;* Janusz Korczak Award, B'nai B'rith, and Universe Award runner-up, both 1984, both for *Seaward;* (with Hume Cronyn) Christopher Award, Humanitas Prize, Writers Guild of America Award, and Emmy Award nomination from Academy of Television Arts and Sciences, all 1984, all for *The Dollmaker;* Emmy Award nomination, 1987, and Writers Guild of America Award, 1988, for teleplay *Foxfire; Horn Book* Honor List citation, 1987, for *The Selkie Girl.*

WRITINGS:

FOR CHILDREN; FICTION

Dawn of Fear (historical fiction), illustrated by Margery Gill, Harcourt (New York, NY), 1970.

Jethro and the Jumbie (fantasy), illustrated by Ashley Bryan, Atheneum (New York, NY), 1979.

Seaward (fantasy), Atheneum (New York, NY), 1983.

(Reteller) *The Silver Cow: A Welsh Tale,* illustrated by Warwick Hutton, Atheneum (New York, NY), 1983.

(Reteller) *The Selkie Girl,* illustrated by Warwick Hutton, Margaret K. McElderry (New York, NY), 1986.

(Reteller) *Tam Lin,* illustrated by Warwick Hutton, Margaret K. McElderry (New York, NY), 1991.

Matthew's Dragon, illustrated by Joseph A. Smith, Margaret K. McElderry (New York, NY), 1991.

The Boggart (fantasy), Margaret K. McElderry (New York, NY), 1992.

Danny and the Kings, illustrated by Joseph A. Smith, Margaret K. McElderry (New York, NY), 1993.

The Boggart and the Monster (fantasy), Margaret K. McElderry (New York, NY), 1997.

(With Margaret Mahy, Uri Orlev, and Tjomg Khing) *Don't Read This! and Other Tales of the Unnatural* (short stories), Front Street, 1998.

King of Shadows (historical fiction), Margaret K. McElderry (New York, NY), 1999.

Frog, illustrated by Jane Browne, Margaret K. McElderry (New York, NY), 2002.

Green Boy, Margaret K. McElderry (New York, NY), 2002.

The Magician's Boy, Margaret K. McElderry Books (New York, NY), 2005.

Contributor to books, including *When I Was Your Age,* edited by Amy Ehrlich, Candlewick Press (New York, NY), 1996.

"DARK IS RISING" SERIES; FANTASY

Over Sea, under Stone, illustrated by Margery Gill, J. Cape (London, England), 1965, Harcourt (New York, NY), 1966.

The Dark Is Rising, illustrated by Alan E. Cober, Atheneum (New York, NY), 1973, illustrated by Lianne Payne, Puffin (London, England), 1994.

Greenwitch, Atheneum (New York, NY), 1974.

The Grey King, illustrated by Michael Heslop, Atheneum (New York, NY), 1975.

Silver on the Tree, Atheneum (New York, NY), 1977.

FOR ADULTS; NONFICTION, EXCEPT AS NOTED

Mandrake (science fiction), J. Cape (London, England), 1964.

Behind the Golden Curtain: A View of the U.S.A., Hodder & Stoughton (London, England), 1965, Scribner (New York, NY), 1966.

(Editor and author of preface) J. B. Priestley, *Essays of Five Decades,* Little, Brown (Boston, MA), 1968.

J. B. Priestley: Portrait of an Author, Heinemann (London, England), 1970, Harper (New York, NY), 1971.

Dreams and Wishes: Essays on Writing for Children, Margaret K. McElderry (New York, NY), 1996.

Contributor to books, including Michael Sissons and Philip French, editors, *The Age of Austerity: 1945-51,* Hodder & Stoughton (London, England), 1963, Scribner (New York, NY), 1966. Author of introductions to *The Christmas Revels Songbook: In Celebration of the Winter Solstice,* edited by John and Nancy Langstaff, David R. Godine, 1985, published as *The Christmas Revels Songbook: Carols, Processions, Rounds, Ritual, and Children's Songs in Celebration of the Winter Solstice,* 1995, and *A Revels Garland of Song: In Celebration of Spring, Summer, and Autumn,* edited by John Langstaff, Revels, Inc., 1996. Contributor of essays to *The Phoenix and the Carpet* by E. Nesbit, Dell, 1987, and to anthologies of children's literature criticism. Contributor to periodicals, including *Horn Book, New York Times Book Review, Magpies,* and *Welsh Review.*

PLAYS

(With Hume Cronyn) *Foxfire* (first produced in Stratford, Ontario, 1980; produced on Broadway at Ethel Barrymore Theatre, 1982; teleplay adaptation produced by Columbia Broadcasting System, Inc. [CBS], 1987), S. French (New York, NY), 1983.

(With Hume Cronyn) *The Dollmaker* (teleplay; adapted from the novel by Harriette Arnow), American Broadcasting Companies, Inc. (ABC), 1984.

To Dance with the White Dog (teleplay), CBS, 1993.

Also author of the teleplay *Dark Encounter,* 1976.

Cooper's papers are housed in the Lillian H. Smith collection, Toronto Public Library, Toronto, Ontario, Canada.

ADAPTATIONS: Cooper's Newbery Medal acceptance speech for *The Grey King* was released as a sound recording, Weston Woods, 1976; *The Dark Is Rising* was released on audio cassette, Miller-Brody, 1979; *The Silver Cow* was released as a filmstrip in 1985 and as a sound recording in 1986, both Weston Woods; *The Selkie Girl* was released as a filmstrip and on audio cassette, Weston Woods, 1988; *The Boggart* was released on audio cassette, Listening Library, 1994; *The Boggart and the Monster* was released on audio cassette, Listening Library, 1997.

SIDELIGHTS: Called "one of the most versatile, popular, and critically acclaimed children's writers of the twentieth century" by Joel D. Chaston in the *Dictionary of Literary Biography,* Susan Cooper is considered an exceptional author for the young whose works–fantasy novels and realistic fiction for young adults and stories and picture books for children–reflect her keen insight into human nature, her knowledge of folklore, history, and archaeology, and her ability to evoke place with authenticity. Credited with a rich, poetic literary style, Cooper is also well regarded as a writer of fiction, nonfiction, and plays for adult readers.

Characteristically, Cooper draws on the myths and legends of the British Isles as the basis for her works, and she is often praised for her ability to mesh the real and the fantastic, the ancient and the contemporary. She is best known as the creator of "The Dark Is Rising" series, a quintet of epic fantasies for young adults that depicts how a group of modern-day English children become involved in a cosmic battle between good and evil, which Cooper calls the Light and the Dark. As in several of her other books, volumes in the series feature magical experiences designed to prepare Cooper's young protagonists for conflicts which will occur throughout their lives. Favorably compared to the fantasies of J. R. R. Tolkien, C. S. Lewis, Ursula K. Le Guin, and Alan Garner, these works are rooted in the mythology of Britain and feature characters from and inspired by Arthurian legend, such as Merlin the great magician and Bran, the son of King Arthur and Guinevere. Cooper is often acknowledged for weaving social concerns within the supernatural events she depicts. In addition to her pervasive theme of the struggle between good and evil—a theme the author uses to explore the human potential for both qualities—Cooper addresses such issues as displacement, responsibility and choice, self-awareness, and the coexistence of magic and technology. Although her books include danger, violence, death, and a variety of manifestations of evil, Cooper is credited with presenting her readers with a positive view of human nature as well as with conclusions that demonstrate the ultimate triumph of good.

Critics have lauded Cooper as a gifted storyteller and superior craftsman whose works succeed in bringing together the ordinary and the extraordinary while capturing the thoughts and emotions of the young. Writing in *Children's Books and Their Creators,* Anne E. Deifendeifer noted that the "power of her fantasy for children places Cooper firmly among the best of children's authors. . . . The tremendous scope and intensity of Cooper's work marks her as a modern master of the high-fantasy genre." Commenting on what she called Cooper's "extraordinary prowess as an author of fantasy," *Twentieth Century Young-Adult Writers* contributor Karen Patricia Smith claimed that throughout her books "major themes resurface, allowing the reader to experience and internalize the depth of her commitment to her social ideals as well as to her art."

While often praised, Cooper has also been criticized by some reviewers for predictability and use of cliché in some of her books and for unevenness in "The Dark Is Rising" series; writing in *School Librarian,* David Rees claimed: "The whole quintet is shallow, relying on a box of magic tricks to disguise the poverty of the author's thinking and imagination." However, most observers view Cooper as the creator of rewarding, fascinating works with great relevance to their audience. Margaret K. McElderry wrote in *Horn Book* that Cooper is "one of the small and very select company of writers who—somehow, somewhere—have been touched by magic; the gift of creation is theirs, the power to bring to life, for ordinary mortals, 'the very best of symbolic high fantasy.' . . . Music and song, old tales and legends, prose and poetry, theater and reality, imagination and intellect, power and control, a strong sense of place and people both past and present—all are part of the magic that has touched Susan Cooper. . . . Her journeys add great luster to the world of literature."

When Cooper was four years old, World War II broke out in Great Britain, and would last until she was ten. By the time she was ten, Cooper had written original plays for a friend's puppet theater, a small illustrated book, and a weekly newspaper. She enjoyed reading, especially the books of Edith Nesbit, Arthur Ransome, Rudyard Kipling, John Masefield, and Jack London, and was entranced by poetry and by the rich tradition of mythology of Great Britain. In addition, she listened faithfully to the British Broadcasting Corporation (BBC) radio program *The Children's Hour,* which dramatized some of her favorite stories. Like her grandfather, Cooper was also enthralled by the theater, recalling, for example, the awe she felt when she saw her first pantomime at the age of three. At Slough High School, a school for girls, she was encouraged to develop her writing talent.

When she graduated, Cooper won a scholarship to Oxford, where she studied English literature and enjoyed what she later described as "a calm stretch of such good fortune that I can hardly describe it." While at Oxford, Cooper discovered and devoured the works of Shakespeare, Milton, and the English Metaphysical poets, heard lectures by J. R. R. Tolkien and C. S. Lewis, and worked for the university newspaper, becoming its first female editor. She also published her first short story and, on her last day at Oxford, submitted a long essay describing her feelings about the end of university life to the editors of the London *Times,* who published it in its entirety.

After her graduation, Cooper worked as a temporary reporter at the London *Sunday Express* before being hired by the *Sunday Times,* where she worked as a news reporter and feature writer for seven years, one of which she spent working for Ian Fleming, the author of the "James Bond" novels. Cooper wrote articles for the *Sunday Times* column "Mainly for Children"; later, she would use some of her subjects—King Arthur, medieval castles, Roman Britain, and brass rubbings—in her books for young people. While at the *Sunday Times,* Cooper began writing novels for adults. Her second attempt, the science-fiction novel *Mandrake,* was published in 1964. A dystopian novel in the manner of *Brave New World* and *1984,* the book addresses the concept of evil residing in ordinary people, a theme the author would later explore in her books for the young.

After completing *Mandrake,* Cooper began writing a children's story for a contest offered by publisher, Ernest Benn. The contest offered a prize in Victorian children's author Edith Nesbit's name for a family adventure story in the tradition of Nesbit's works. This project, Cooper once wrote, "offered the irresistible combination of a challenge, a deadline, and money, and I dived at it in delight." Cooper's story began, she noted, with the invention of "three rather Nesbitish children named Simon, Jane, and Barney Drew, and I sent them on a train journey from London to Cornwall." However, with the introduction of the children's great-uncle Merriman Lyon—actually Merlin the magician—the book transformed into something quite different than its author originally intended. "Merry took over," Cooper once wrote. "He led the book out of realism, to myth-haunted layers of story that took me way past a 'family adventure' and way past my deadline. Now I was no longer writing for a deadline or for money. I was writing for me, or perhaps for the child I once was and in part still am." When the book was finished, Cooper cut the first chapter about the railway journey; the result was *Over Sea, under Stone,* the first volume of "The Dark Is Rising."

Rejected by more than twenty publishers before its acceptance by Jonathan Cape, *Over Sea, under Stone* describes how the Drew children, who have traveled to Trewissick, Cornwall, for a holiday with their scholarly, white-haired great-uncle, use an ancient map they find in an attic to recover the Holy Grail. Plunged into the battle between good and evil, the children become misled by members of the Dark posing as the local vicar and a pair of tourists and encounter dangerous situations such as the kidnapping of Barney Drew. However, the powers of Great-Uncle Merry and the initiative of the children win a victory for the Light. At the end of the story, the Grail is placed in the British Museum and an ancient magical manuscript—which interprets the writing on the Grail, gives the outcome of the battle between the Light and the Dark, and promises that King Arthur will come again—is sent to the bottom of the sea. Writing in *Growing Point,* Margery Fisher commented that "perhaps this is a book with a theme too big for itself, but it is a fascinating book to read and it has considerable literary quality." *School Librarian* contributor C. E. J. Smith added: "The children are credible and their adventures shift so cunningly from the plausible to the legendary as to be totally absorbing. . . . The final scene on the jagged rocks amid an incoming tide is a feast for any imaginative twelve-or thirteen-year-old."

The London *Sunday Times* hired Cooper to cover U.S.-based stories, including the trial of Jack Ruby in Dallas. She also began to contribute a weekly column to the *Western Mail,* the national morning newspaper of Wales. Her column led to a nonfiction book for adults, *Behind the Golden Curtain: A View of the U.S. A.,* in which she explains the differences between the cultures of the United States and England. She also edited a collection of essays by friend J. B. Priestley, a notable English novelist, dramatist, and essayist, and later published a biography of Priestley. She also penned an autobiographical novel for adults about her childhood that was published in 1970 as *Dawn of Fear.*

Describing how a young boy is made aware of the horrors of World War II, *Dawn of Fear* outlines how Derek Brand—a middle grader who lives in a housing estate in the Thames Valley—learns the meaning of sadness, suffering, and fear when his best friend Peter and his family are killed by German bombs. Drawing parallels between Derek's private war—a rivalry between two gangs of local boys—and the larger one, Cooper is credited with evoking the pain of war while movingly describing the death of a child. A reviewer in *Publishers Weekly* commented that Cooper "has brought her insight and writing skills to creating another remarkable story." The critic concluded by calling *Dawn of Fear* a "moving chronicle of despair and of courage." Ethel L. Heins in *Horn Book* praised *Dawn of Fear* as "an uncommon kind of war story," and a reviewer in *Junior Bookshelf* claimed, "To date I have not come across a book which makes anything like the same impression."

In *The Dark Is Rising* Cooper continues the story she began in *Over Sea, under Stone.* In this work, Will Stanton, the seventh son of a seventh son, learns on his eleventh birthday that he is the last of the Old Ones, immortal beings who serve the Light and who are committed to keeping the world safe from the Dark. Will undertakes a journey to find and join together the Six Signs of the Light—wood, bronze, iron, fire, water, and stone—to be used in a final battle against the Dark. In his quest, in which he is guided by the first of the Old Ones, Merriman Lyon, Will encounters evil forces who appear in different forms as he moves back and forth in time. Finally, the Dark rises during a winter filled with violent blizzards and floods, but Will, using both his intuition and the knowledge given him by Merry, successfully joins the Signs of the Light. A reviewer in the *Times Literary Supplement* noted, "With a cosmic struggle between good and evil as her subject, Susan Cooper invites comparison with Tolkien, and survives the comparison remarkably well." Writing in the *Washington Post Book World,* Virginia Haviland noted that the book "is exceptional by any standard," while S. William Alderson of the *Children's Book Review* commented that *The Dark Is Rising* "captures and holds one's imagination, almost as if the magic forces within the story were themselves reaching out to spellbind the reader." Ethel L. Heins in *Horn Book* noted the strength of Cooper's writing, which she described as "as rich and as eloquent as a Beethoven symphony," while Sally Emerson of *Books and Bookmen* concluded that anyone "who fears that they or their children are becoming rigidly sensible should buy this book to enrich imagination and recover wonderment."

The sequel to *The Dark Is Rising, Greenwitch,* again features the three Drew children, the protagonists of *Over Sea, under Stone.* The siblings work with their great-uncle Merry and Will Stanton, the main character from *The Dark Is Rising,* to recover the Holy Grail—which has been stolen from the British Museum by a painter who is an emissary of the Dark—as well as the ancient manuscript that accompanies it. As the children engage in their pursuit, the forces of Wild Magic embodied by the Greenwitch, a tree woman woven by Cornish villagers that is given life by an ocean goddess, come to their defense through the sympathies of middle child Jane Drew. Through her compassion, Jane obtains the manuscript from the Greenwitch, thus allowing the Old Ones to learn about the next part of their quest. Writing in *Growing Point,* Margery Fisher claimed, "Fantasies like this depend most of all on the sheer power of the writing, on the literary synthesis between the sunlit world of here and now and the dark, misty otherwhere from which evil comes. The synthesis is less strong in this new book and the effect less consistent than in the other two books. . . . Nonetheless, it is a compelling story." A reviewer in the *Times Literary Supplement* predicted, "When Miss Cooper manages to knit her material into a single organic whole her achievement will be great."

The Grey King is often considered the most successful of the "Dark Is Rising" novels. In this book, Will Stanton has become ill with hepatitis and is sent to the seaside town of Tywyn, Wales, to recuperate. While in Wales, Will learns that he must undertake two quests: the recovery of a golden harp hidden in the nearby hills and the awakening of six ancient sleepers who are to be roused by the sound of the harp for the final battle between the Light and the Dark. Will is joined by Bran Davies, an albino boy who is revealed as the son of King Arthur, and Bran's white sheepdog Cafall. Bound by a preordained fate, the three retrieve the harp, but Will is thrust into a confrontation with the Grey King, an evil Lord of the High Magic who uses ghostly gray foxes and a crazed Welshman named Caradog Pritchard to carry out his wishes, which include the killing of Cafall. At the conclusion of the novel, the sleepers are raised and preparations begin for the final showdown between the opposing forces. Writing in *Horn Book,* Mary M. Burns called *The Grey King* a "spellbinding tour de force," while Zena Sutherland described it in her *Bulletin of the Center for Children's Books* review as a "compelling fantasy that is traditional in theme and components yet original in conception."

Two major fantasists, Natalie Babbitt and Jill Paton Walsh, also commented on *The Grey King.* Writing in the *New York Times Book Review,* Babbitt noted, "It is useless to try to recreate the subtleties of Susan Cooper's plotting and language. Enough to say that this volume, like those preceding it, is brimful of mythic elements and is beautifully told." Paton Walsh, reviewing *The Grey King* in the *Times Literary Supplement,* noted the book's "authentic evocative power" and the fact that Cooper "commands, to a rare degree, the power to thrill the reader, to produce a particular tremor of excitement and fear, in response not only to Arthurian magic . . . but rather to haunted places, to landscape deeply embedded in ancient fable, to a sense of secret forces breaking through." In 1976 *The Grey King* was awarded the Newbery Medal and the Tir na N'og Award; it also received a commendation for the Carnegie Medal.

The final volume of the "Dark Is Rising" sequence, *Silver on the Tree,* brings together the protagonists from the preceding books. In this story, which is again set in Wales, Will Stanton summons the Old Ones for a final battle with the forces of the Dark. Will, Bran, Merriman, and the Drew children travel through time to acquire the weapons needed for combat. At the end of their adventures, which range from incredibly dangerous to extremely beautiful, the children and the Old Ones find the legendary Midsummer Tree, the silver fruit of which determines the victor of the battle. At the end of the novel, the Six Sleepers finally defeat the Lords of the Dark, Will completes his tasks as the last of the Old Ones, and Bran, who is offered immortality, bids a final farewell to his father King Arthur by choosing to remain human. Writing in *Horn Book,* Ann A. Flowers called *Silver on the Tree* a "triumphant conclusion," while a reviewer for *Junior Bookshelf* commented that here, "crafted by the hand of a master, is a story of the ageless battle of good and evil, a book in one of the great traditions of children's literature and destined, perhaps, to become one of the high peaks of that tradition." Writing in *Growing Point,* Margery Fisher commented that the series "has given readers many moments of startled awareness and now that it is complete it deserves more deliberate consideration as a whole." Shirley Wilton of *School Library Journal* noted that Cooper "maintains a masterly control over the complex strands of her story sweeping readers along on a fantastic journey. It is an experience not to be missed and, for Cooper fans, a fitting wrap-up to the unfolding saga."

Following the completion of her fantasy quintet, Cooper began writing stories and picture books for younger children, an audience to whom most of her subsequent books have been directed. She returned to the genre of young-adult fantasy with her novel *Seaward.* Written during a particularly difficult period in her life—the author was dealing with a divorce from Nicholas Grant and the death of both her parents—*Seaward* describes how two teenagers, the girl Cally and the boy West, cross the borders of time as they try to reach the sea. Each involved with personal quests prompted by the deaths of their respective parents, Cally and West enter the world of Lady Taramis, who is actually Death, and her twin brother Lugan—Life—and encounter many dangers before they reach their destination. At the sea, the teens, who have fallen in love, learn the identity of Taramis and Lugan as well as the fact that Cally is the descendant of a selkie, a seal who can turn into a human. At the end of the novel Cally decides not to become a selkie and West decides to return to his own world; as a result, the friends are promised that, although they live in different countries, they will meet again and will spend their lives together. Writing in *Horn Book,* Paul Heins called *Seaward* an "uncanny, unconventional fantasy" and concluded that, like Scottish novelist and poet George MacDonald, Cooper "has endowed the concept of human responsibility—of human choice—with the face of fantasy." M. Hobbs noted in *Junior Bookshelf* that it "is a rare treat to have another novel from Susan Cooper" and concluded that *Seaward* is a "deeply moving, splendid novel, of unearthly beauty, and worthy of its predecessors."

The myths and legends of the British Isles have always been an important part of Cooper's novels. In 1983 she published *The Silver Cow: A Welsh Tale,* the first of several volumes of retellings illustrated by English artist Warwick Hutton. Another of Cooper's retellings, *The Selkie Girl,* is a story taken from the folk tales of Ireland and the Scottish Isles that, like *Seaward,* draws on the legends of seal maidens. The tale outlines how the lonely fisherman Donallan catches a beautiful selkie with whom he has fallen in love by stealing her seal skin so that she cannot go back to the sea. The couple has five children; when the youngest child finds the seal skin and tells his mother where it is hidden, she returns to her home in the water, where she also has five seal children. Before she goes, the selkie promises to meet with her land family once a year and blesses them with fine catches from their fishing. Writing in the *Junior Bookshelf,* Marcus Crouch noted that "Here, even in this small exercise, a master storyteller is at work, covering the bare bones of the story with living flesh." Ethel R. Twitchell concurred in her review for *Horn Book,* adding that Cooper "remains faithful to the spirit and magic of the story but gives it a fullness and inevitability that only a true storyteller can evoke."

Based on a Scottish ballad, *Tam Lin* is the third collaboration between Cooper and illustrator Hutton. The story outlines how Margaret, the spirited daughter of a king, runs away to a forbidden wood where she meets an enchanted knight, Tam Lin. Learning that Tam Lin is under a spell that can only be broken by the love of a mortal, Margaret holds on to Tam Lin on Midsummer's Eve as the fairy queen who cast the spell on him transforms him into a wolf, a snake, a deer, and a red-hot bar of iron; through Margaret's love, the enchantment of Tam Lin is broken. Writing in *Horn Book,* Heins called *Tam Lin* "a beautifully paced literary fairy tale, told and pictured with precision and restraint." Helen Gregory of *School Library Journal* noted that Cooper's version of the tale "is alive with dialogue." Critics also acknowledged the feminist slant brought by Cooper to her retelling.

With *The Boggart,* a humorous fantasy for middle graders, Cooper created one of her most popular books. The title character, a Scottish trickster spirit, has lived in Castle Keep as a companion of the MacDevon clan, who are the recipients of its lighthearted practical jokes. When the last MacDevon passes away, the Boggart is griefstricken until the Volnik family of Toronto—distant relatives of the MacDevons—come to the castle they have inherited.

After arrangements are made for the castle's sale, the boggart is accidentally shipped back to Canada in an old desk. Emily Volnik and her younger brother Jessup, a computer whiz, recognize the spirit's presence when it starts playing practical jokes on the family, tricks that become dangerous when they begin to involve electricity. Although the children have become fond of the mischievous sprite, they realize it needs to return home to Scotland, so, in conjunction with their Scottish friend Tommy, they ship the spirit back to its castle on diskette via a computer game created by Jessup. Writing in the *New York Times Book Review,* Rafael Yglesias commented that while the "plot of a mysterious and possibly ancient being befriending modern kids and making trouble in their world will be familiar to any reader" familiar with modern movies, "that doesn't make its working out in *The Boggart* any less suspenseful or . . . surprising and moving." "The inevitable failure of a spirit to coexist with our dreary practical world isn't a new theme," Yglesias added, "although in *The Boggart* it seems fresher than ever." Calling the title creature "fascinating . . . , sly, ingenious, and endearing—as long as he belongs to someone else," Ann A. Flowers of *Horn Book* added that what "is most admirable is Susan Cooper's seamless fusion of the newest technology and one of the oldest forms of wild magic." Writing in *Five Owls,* Gary D. Schmidt noted that Cooper makes "rich distinctions between the bustle of Toronto and the quiet of Scotland, between the new technology and the Old Magic, between imagination and pseudo-scientific pretension." Schmidt concluded, "The result is a delightful and quick read, with a conclusion perhaps not as high and noble and cosmic as that of *Silver on the Tree* but in its own way just as satisfying and just as complete."

In addition to penning novels and picture books, Cooper has often written about her craft in books and magazines and has spoken to groups about both the genre of fantasy and her own literary career. In 1996 she published *Dreams and Wishes: Essays on Writing for Children,* a collection of fourteen essays drawn from various speeches in which she explores the craft of writing, outlines the nature of fantasy, and recalls her experiences as an author and reporter. Writing in *Voice of Youth Advocates,* Mary Ann Capan commented that, "Through these major speeches, the reader gains insight into the author's personal life as well as her creative process." A critic in *Publishers Weekly* called *Dreams and Wishes* "essential reading not just for fans of Cooper or of fantasy novels, but for devotees of children's literature." Citing one of Cooper's anecdotes, the reviewer wrote that when a hurricane destroyed the author's family vacation home, her college-age son Jonathan nervously asked his mother if his favorite books from childhood, stories by the English writer Richmal Crompton, were unharmed. "I suspect," the critic concluded, "that under similar circumstances many other children might inquire worriedly about the safety of their Susan Cooper titles."

BIOGRAPHICAL AND CRITICAL SOURCES:

BOOKS

Celebrating Children's Books: Essays on Children's Literature in Honor of Zena Sutherland, edited by Betsy Hearne and Marilyn Kaye, Lothrop (New York, NY), 1981.

Children's Books and Their Creators, edited by Anita Silvey, Houghton Mifflin (Boston, MA), 1995.

Child ren's Literature Review, Volume 4, Thomson Gale (Detroit, MI), 1982.

Dictionary of Literary Biography, Volume 161: *British Children's Writers since 1960,* Thomson Gale (Detroit, MI), 1996.

Something about the Author Autobiography Series, Volume 6, Thomson Gale (Detroit, MI), 1989.

Speaking for Ourselves: Autobiographical Sketches by Notable Authors of Books for Young Adults, Volume 1, edited by Donald Gallo, National Council of Teachers of English, 1990.

Twentieth-Century Young-Adult Writers, St. James Press (Detroit, MI), 1994.

PERIODICALS

Booklist, October 15, 1993, Deborah Abbott, review of *Danny and the Kings,* p. 451; March 1, 1997, Stephanie Zvirin, review of *The Boggart and the Monster,* p. 1162; September 15, 1997, p. 226; October 15, 1999, Carolyn Phelan, review of *King of Shadows,* p. 442.

Books and Bookmen, October, 1973, Sally Emerson, review of *The Dark Is Rising,* pp. 130-131.

Bulletin of the Center for Children's Books, November, 1975, Zena Sutherland, review of *The Grey King,* p. 41; January, 1980, Zena Sutherland, review of *Jethro and the Jumbie,* p. 91; March, 1983, Zena Sutherland, review of *The Silver Cow,* p. 124;

February, 1994, Betsy Hearne, review of *Danny and the Kings,* p. 184; December, 1999, Janice M. Del Negro, review of *King of Shadows,* p. 126.

Children's Book Review, September, 1973, S. William Alderson, review of *The Dark Is Rising,* p. 112.

Five Owls, May-June, 1993, Gary D. Schmidt, review of *The Boggart,* p. 117.

Growing Point, September, 1965, Margery Fisher, "Arthurian Echoes," pp. 545-555; January, 1975, Margery Fisher, review of *Greenwitch,* pp. 2555-2556; March, 1978, Margery Fisher, "Dual Worlds," p. 3277.

Horn Book, October, 1970, Ethel L. Heins, review of *Dawn of Fear,* p. 477; June, 1973, Ethel L. Heins, review of *The Dark Is Rising,* p. 286; October, 1975, Mary M. Burns, review of *The Grey King,* p. 461; August, 1976, Margaret K. McElderry, "Susan Cooper," pp. 367-372; December, 1977, Ann A. Flower, review of *Silver on the Tree,* pp. 660-661; June, 1983, Mary M. Burns, review of *The Silver Cow,* pp. 287-288; February, 1984, Paul Heins, review of *Seaward,* pp. 59-60; November-December, 1986, Ethel R. Twitchell, review of *The Selkie Girl,* pp. 731-732; May-June, 1991, Ethel L. Heins, review of *Tam Lin,* pp. 340-341; May-June, 199 3, Ann A. Flowers, review of *The Boggart,* p. 330; JanuaryFebruary, 1997, p. 83; November-December, 1999, Jennifer M. Brabander, review of *King of Shadows,* p. 735.

Journal of Youth Services, spring, 1997, p. 305.

Junior Bookshelf, August, 1972, review of *Dawn of Fear,* p. 241; April, 1978, review of *Silver on the Tree,* pp. 99-100; April, 1984, M. Hobbs, review of *Seaward,* p. 80; April, 1988, Marcus Crouch, review of *The Selkie Girl,* pp. 77-78.

Kirkus Reviews, February 1, 1980, review of *Jethro and the Jumbie,* p. 120.

New York Times Book Review, November 28, 1975, Natalie Babbitt, review of *The Grey King,* pp. 10, 12; May 18, 1997, Jim Gladstone, "Magical Mysteries," p. 29; November 10, 1991, Susan Fromberg Schaeffer, "There's No Escaping Them," p. 53; May 16, 1993, Rafael Yglesias, "The Gremlin on the Floppy Disk," p. 23; January 16, 2000, David Paterson, review of *King of Shadows,* p. 27.

Publishers Weekly, August 31, 1970, Review of *Dawn of Fear,* p. 279; July 12, 1991, review of *Matthew's Dragon,* p. 65; May 27, 1996, review of *Dreams and Wishes,* p. 81.

School Librarian, December, 1965, C. E. J. Smith, review of *Over Sea, under Stone,* p. 358; September, 1984, David Rees, "Susan Cooper," pp. 197-205.

School Library Journal, December, 1977, Shirley Wilton, review of *Silver on the Tree,* p. 48; May, 1991, Helen Gregory, review of *Tam Lin,* p. 88; May June, 1997, p. 315; November, 1999, Sally Margolis, review of *King of Shadows,* p. 156.

Times Educational Supplement, June 20, 1980, Virginia Makins, "Blithe Spirits," p. 44.

Times Literary Supplement, July 5, 1974, review of *Greenwitch,* p. 721; June 15, 1975, review of *The Grey King,* p. 685; December 5, 1975, Jill Paton Walsh, "Evoking Dark Powers," p. 1457.

Voice of Youth Advocates, August, 1996, Mary Ann Capan, review of *Dreams and Wishes,* p. 187.

Washington Post Book World, July 8, 1973, Virginia Haviland, "A Child's Garden of Ghosts, Poltergeists, and Werewolves," p. 13; July 7, 1996, p. 15.*

* * *

CREELEY, Robert (White) 1926-2005

PERSONAL: Born May 21, 1926, in Arlington, MA; died, March 30, 2005, in Odessa, TX; son of Oscar Slade (a physician) and Genevieve (Jules) Creeley; married Ann MacKinnon, 1946 (divorced, c. 1955); married Bobbie Louise Hall, January 27, 1957 (divorced, 1976); married Penelope Highton, 1977; children: (first marriage) David, Thomas, Charlotte; (second marriage) Kirsten (stepdaughter), Leslie (stepdaughter; deceased), Sarah, Katherine; (third marriage) William, Hannah. *Education:* Attended Harvard University, 1943-44 and 1945-46; Black Mountain College, B.A., c. 1955; University of New Mexico, M.A., 1960.

CAREER: Poet, novelist, short story writer, essayist, and editor. Divers Press, Palma, Mallorca, Spain, founder and publisher, 1950-54; Black Mountain College, Black Mountain, NC, instructor in English, 1954-55; instructor at school for young boys, Albuquerque, NM, beginning 1956; University of New Mexico, Albuquerque, instructor in English, 1961-62, lecturer, 1963-66, visiting professor, 1968-69 and 1978-80; University of British Columbia, Vancouver, instructor in English, 1962-63; University of New Mexico, visiting lecturer, 1961-62, lecturer in English, 1963-66, visiting professor, 1968-69, 1979, 1980-81; State University of New York at Buffalo, visiting professor,

1966-67, professor of English, 1967-78, David Gray Professor of Poetry and Letters, 1978-89, University of New York at Buffalo, Samuel P. Capen Professor of Poetry and Humanities, 1989-2003, director of poetics program, 1991-92; distinguished professor of English for the Graduate Program in Creative Writing at Brown University, 2003—. San Francisco State College, visiting lecturer in creative writing, 1970-71; State University of New York at Binghamton, visiting professor, 1985 and 1986. Bicentennial chair of American studies at University of Helsinki, Finland, 1988. New York State Poet, 1989. Participated in numerous poetry readings and writers' conferences. *Wartime service:* American Field Service, India and Burma, 1944-45.

MEMBER: American Academy of Arts and Letters.

AWARDS, HONORS: Levinson Prize, 1960, for group of ten poems published in *Poetry* magazine; D. H. Lawrence fellowship (for summer writing), University of New Mexico, 1960; National Book Award nomination, 1962, for *For Love;* Leviton-Blumenthal Prize, 1964, for group of thirteen poems published in *Poetry;* Guggenheim fellowship in poetry, 1964-65 and 1971; Rockefeller Foundation grant, 1966; Union League Civic and Arts Foundation Prize, 1967; Shelley Award, 1981, and Frost Medal, 1987, both from Poetry Society of America; National Endowment for the Arts grant, 1982; Deutsche Austauschdienst Programme residency in Berlin, 1983 and 1987; Leone d'Oro Premio Speziale, Venice, 1984; Frost Medal, Poetry Society of America, 1987; Fulbright Award, 1988, 1995; Walt Whitman citation of merit, 1989; named New York State Poet, 1989-91; named distinguished professor, State University of New York at Buffalo, 1989; D.Litt., University of New Mexico, 1993; Horst Bienek Lyrikpreis, Bavarian Academy of Fine Arts, Munich, 1993; America Award for Poetry, 1995; Lila Wallace/*Reader's Digest* Writers Award, 1996; Bollingen Prize, 1999; Chancellor Norton Medal, 1999; Before Columbus Lifetime Achievement Award, 1999; Lannan Lifetime Achievement Award (with Edward Said), Lannan Literary Foundation, 2001.

WRITINGS:

POETRY

Le Fou, Golden Goose Press, 1952.
The Kind of Act Of, Divers Press (Mallorca, Spain), 1953.
The Immoral Proposition, Jonathan Williams, 1953.
A Snarling Garland of Xmas Verse (published anonymously), Divers Press (Mallorca, Spain), 1954.
All That Is Lovely in Men, Jonathan Williams (Asheville, NC), 1955.
(With others) *Ferrin and Others,* Gerhardt (Germany), 1955.
If You, Porpoise Bookshop (San Francisco, CA), 1956.
The Whip, Migrant Books, 1957.
A Form of Women, Jargon Books (New York, NY), 1959.
For Love: Poems, 1950-1960, Scribner (New York, NY), 1962.
Distance, Terrence Williams, 1964.
Mister Blue, Insel-Verlag, 1964.
Two Poems, Oyez, 1964.
Hi There!, Finial Press, 1965.
Words (eight poems), Perishable Press, 1965.
Poems, 1950-1965, Calder & Boyars (London, England), 1966.
About Women, Gemini, 1966.
For Joel, Perishable Press, 1966.
A Sight, Cape Coliard Press, 1967.
Words (eighty-four poems), Scribner (New York, NY), 1967.
Robert Creeley Reads (with recording), Turret Books, 1967.
The Finger, Black Sparrow Press (Santa Rosa, CA), 1968, enlarged edition published as *The Finger Poems, 1966-1969,* Calder & Boyars (London, England), 1970.
5 Numbers (five poems), Poets Press (New York, NY), 1968, published as *Numbers* (text in English and German), translation by Klaus Reichert, Galerie Schmela (Dusseldorf, Germany), 1968.
The Charm: Early and Collected Poems, Perishable Press, 1968, expanded edition published as *The Charm,* Four Seasons Foundation (San Francisco, CA), 1969.
Divisions and Other Early Poems, Perishable Press, 1968.
Pieces (fourteen poems), Black Sparrow Press (Santa Rosa, CA), 1968.
The Boy (poem poster), Gallery Upstairs Press, 1968.
Mazatlan: Sea, Poets Press (New York, NY), 1969.
Pieces (seventy-two poems), Scribner (New York, NY), 1969.
Hero, Indianakatz (New York, NY), 1969.
A Wall, Bouwerie Editions (New York, NY), 1969.
For Betsy and Tom, Alternative Press, 1970.
For Benny and Sabrina, Samuel Charters, 1970.
America, Press of the Black Flag, 1970.

In London, Angel Hair Books, 1970.

Christmas: May 10, 1970, Lockwood Memorial Library, State University of New York at Buffalo (Buffalo, NY), 1970.

St. Martin's, Black Sparrow Press (Santa Rosa, CA), 1971.

1-2-3-4-5-6-7-8-9-0, drawings by Arthur Okamura, Shambhala (New York, NY), 1971.

Sea, Cranium Press, 1971.

For the Graduation, Cranium Press, 1971.

Change, Hermes Free Press, 1972.

One Day after Another, Alternative Press, 1972.

For My Mother: Genevieve Jules Creeley, 8 April 1887-7 October 1972 (limited edition), Sceptre Press (London, England), 1973.

His Idea, Coach House Press (Toronto, Ontario, Canada), 1973.

The Class of '47, Bouwerie Editions (New York, NY), 1973.

Kitchen, Wine Press, 1973.

Sitting Here, University of Connecticut Library, 1974.

Thirty Things, Black Sparrow Press (Santa Rosa, CA), 1974.

Backwards, Sceptre Press (London, England), 1975.

Hello, Hawk Press (Christchurch, New Zealand), 1976, expanded edition published as *Hello: A Journal, February 29-May 3, 1976,* New Directions (New York, NY), 1978.

Away, Black Sparrow Press (Santa Rosa, CA), 1976.

Presences (also see below), Scribner (New York, NY), 1976.

Selected Poems, Scribner (New York, NY), 1976, revised edition, University of California Press (Berkeley, CA), 1991.

Myself, Sceptre Press (London, England), 1977.

Later, Toothpaste (West Branch, IA), 1978, expanded edition, New Directions (New York, NY), 1979.

Desultory Days, Sceptre Press (London, England), 1979.

Corn Close, Sceptre Press (London, England), 1980.

Mother As Voice, Am Here Books/Immediate Editions, 1981.

The Collected Poems of Robert Creeley, 1945-1975, University of California Press (Berkeley, CA), 1982.

Echoes, Toothpaste (West Branch, IA), 1982, New Directions (New York, NY), 1994.

Going On: Selected Poems, 1958-1980, Dutton (New York, NY), 1983.

Mirrors, New Directions (New York, NY), 1983.

A Calendar: Twelve Poems, Coffee House Press (West Branch, IA), 1984.

The Collected Prose of Robert Creeley, Scribner (New York, NY), 1984.

Memories, Pig Press, 1984.

Memory Gardens, New Directions (New York, NY), 1986.

The Company, Burning Deck, 1988.

Window, edited by Richard Blevins, State University of New York at Buffalo (Buffalo, NY), 1988.

(With Libby Larsen) *A Creeley Collection: For Mixed Voices, Solo Tenor, Flute, Percussion, and Piano,* E. C. Schirmer, 1989.

(With Francesco Clemente) *64 Pastels,* Bruno Bischofberger, 1989.

Places, Shuffaloff Press, 1990.

Windows, New Directions (New York, NY), 1990.

Have a Heart, Limberlost Press, 1990.

Selected Poems, University of California Press (Berkeley, CA), 1991.

The Old Days, Ambrosia Press, 1991.

Gnomic Verses, Zasterle Press, 1991.

A Poetry Anthology, Edmundson Art Foundation, 1992.

Life and Death, Grenfell Press, 1993, New Directions (New York, NY), 1998.

Loops: Ten Poems, Nadja, 1995.

Ligeia: A Libretto, Granary Books, 1996.

So There: Poems 1976-83, New Directions (New York, NY), 1998.

En Famille: A Poem by Robert Creeley, Granary Books, 1999.

(With Alex Katz) *Edges,* Peter Blum, 1999.

(With Max Gimblett and Alan Loney) *The Dogs of Auckland,* Holloway Press, 1998.

(With John Millei) *Personal: Poems,* Peter Koch, 1998.

(With Daisy DeCapite) *Cambridge, Mass 1944,* Boog Literature, 2000.

Thinking, Z Press, 2000.

Clemente's Images, Backwoods Broadsides, 2000.

For Friends, Drive He Sd Books, 2000.

(With Archie Rand, illustrations) *Drawn and Quartered,* Distributed Art Publishers, 2001.

Just In Time: Poems, 1984-1994, New Directions (New York, NY), 2001.

If I Were Writing This, New Directions (New York, NY), 2003.

EDITOR

Charles Olson, *Mayan Letters,* Divers Press (Mallorca, Spain), 1953.

(With Donald M. Allen, and contributor) *New American Story,* Grove (New York, NY), 1965.

(And author of introduction) Charles Olson, *Selected Writings,* New Directions (New York, NY), 1966.

(With Donald Allen, and contributor) *The New Writing in the U.S.A.,* Penguin (New York, NY), 1967.

Whitman: Selected Poems, Penguin (New York, NY), 1973.

(And contributor) *The Essential Burns,* Ecco Press (New York, NY), 1989.

Tim Prythero, Peters Corporation, 1990.

Olson, Selected Poems, University of California Press (Berkeley, CA), 1993.

(With David Lehman) *The Best American Poetry 2002,* Scribner (New York, NY), 2002.

PROSE

The Gold Diggers (short stories), Divers Press (Mallorca, Spain), 1954, expanded edition published as *The Gold Diggers and Other Stories,* J. Calder, 1965.

The Island (novel), Scribner (New York, NY), 1963.

A Day Book (poems and prose), Scribner (New York, NY), 1972.

Mabel: A Story, and Other Prose (includes *A Day Book* and *Presences*), Calder & Boyars (London, England), 1976.

Collected Prose, Marion Boyars (New York, NY), 1984, corrected edition, University of California Press (Berkeley, CA), 1988, Dalkey Archive Press (Chicago, IL), 2001.

NONFICTION

An American Sense (essay), Sigma Press, 1965.

A Quick Graph: Collected Notes and Essays, edited by Donald M. Allen, Four Seasons Foundation (San Francisco, CA), 1970.

Notebook, Bouwerie Editions (New York, NY), 1972.

A Sense of Measure (essays), Calder & Boyars (London, England), 1972.

Inside Out (lecture), Black Sparrow Press (Santa Rosa, CA), 1973.

The Creative (lecture), Black Sparrow Press (Santa Rosa, CA), 1973.

Was That a Real Poem and Other Essays, Four Seasons Foundation (San Francisco, CA), 1979.

Collected Essays, University of California Press (Berkeley, CA), 1989.

Autobiography, Hanuman Books, 1990.

Day Book of a Virtual Poet (essays), Spuyten Duyvil (New York, NY), 1998.

OTHER

Listen (play; produced in London, 1972), Black Sparrow Press (Santa Rosa, CA), 1972.

Contexts of Poetry: Interviews, 1961-1971, Four Seasons Foundation (San Francisco, CA), 1973.

Charles Olson and Robert Creeley: The Complete Correspondence, ten volumes, edited by George F. Butterick, Black Sparrow Press (Santa Rosa, CA), 1980–96.

Jane Hammond, Exit Art, 1989.

Irving Layton and Robert Creeley: The Complete Correspondence, edited by Ekbert Faas and Sabrina Reed, University of Toronto Press (Toronto, Ontario, Canada), 1990.

Tales out of School: Selected Interviews, University of Michigan Press (Ann Arbor, MI), 1993.

Robert Creeley, reading with jazz musicians David Cast, Chris Massey, Steve Swallow, and David Torn accompanying, Cuneiform Records, 1998.

(Author of foreword) *The Turning,* Hilda Morley, Asphodel Press, 1998.

(With Elizabeth Licata and Amy Cappellazzo) *In Company: Robert Creeley's Collaborations* (from a traveling art show), University of North Carolina Press (Chapel Hill, NC), 1999.

(Contributor; with others) *Susan Rothenberg: Paintings from the Nineties,* Rizzoli International (New York, NY), 2000.

Work represented in numerous anthologies, including *The New American Poetry: 1945-1960,* edited by Donald Allen, Grove (New York, NY), 1960; *A Controversy of Poets,* edited by Paris Leary and Robert Kelly, Doubleday (New York, NY), 1965; *Norton Anthology of Modern Poetry,* edited by Richard Ellmann and Robert O'Clair, Norton (New York, NY), 1973; *The New Oxford Book of American Verse,* edited by Richard Ellmann, Oxford University Press (New York, NY), 1976; and *Poets' Encyclopedia,* edited by Michael Andre, Unmuzzled Ox Press, 1980. Contributor to literary periodicals, including *Paris Review, Nation, Black Mountain Review, Origin, Yugen,* and *Big Table.* Founder and editor, *Black Mountain Review,* 1954-57; advisory editor, *Sagetrieb,* 1983—; advisory editor, *American Book Review,* 1983—; contributing editor, *Formations,* 1984—; and advisory editor, *New York Quarterly,* 1984—.

The major collection of Creeley's manuscripts and correspondence is housed in Special Collections, Stanford University, Stanford, CA. Other collections include the Beinecke Rare Book and Manuscript Library of the Yale University Library, New Haven, CT (correspondence with William Carlos Williams), Humanities Research Center, University of Texas Libraries, Austin (correspondence with Ezra Pound), John M. Olin Library, Washington University, St. Louis, MO (manuscripts and correspondence predating 1965), Lilly Library, Indiana University, Bloomington (manuscripts and correspondence with Cid Corman), Simon Fraser University Library, Burnaby, British Columbia, Canada (correspondence with Richard Emerson), and University of Connecticut Library, Storrs (correspondence with Charles Olson).

SIDELIGHTS: Once known primarily for his association with the group called the "Black Mountain Poets," Robert Creeley has become an important and influential literary figure in his own right. His poetry is noted as much for its concision as its emotional power. Albert Mobilio, writing in the *Voice Literary Supplement,* observed: "Creeley has shaped his own audience. The much imitated, often diluted minimalism, the compression of emotion into verse in which scarcely a syllable is wasted, has decisively marked a generation of poets."

Creeley first began to develop his writing talents while attending Holderness School in Plymouth, New Hampshire, on a scholarship. His articles and stories appeared regularly in the school's literary magazine, and in his senior year he became its editor in chief. Creeley was admitted to Harvard in 1943, but his academic life was disrupted while he served as an ambulance driver for the American Field Service in 1944 and 1945.

Creeley returned to Harvard after the war and became associated with such writers as John Hawkes, Mitchell Goodman, and Kenneth Koch. He began corresponding with Cid Corman and Charles Olson, two poets who were to have a substantial influence on the direction of his future work. Excited especially by Olson's ideas about literature, Creeley began to develop a distinctive and unique poetic style.

Throughout the 1950s, Creeley was associated with the "Black Mountain Poets," a group of writers including Denise Levertov, Ed Dorn, Fielding Dawson, and others who had some connection with Black Mountain College, an experimental, communal college in North Carolina that was a haven for many innovative writers and artists of the period. Creeley edited the *Black Mountain Review* and developed a close and lasting relationship with Olson, who was the rector of the college. The two engaged in a lengthy, intensive correspondence about literary matters that has been collected and published as *Charles Olson and Robert Creeley: The Complete Correspondence.* Olson and Creeley together developed the concept of "projective verse," a kind of poetry that abandoned traditional forms in favor of a freely constructed verse that took shape as the process of composing it was underway. Olson called this process "composition by field," and his famous essay on the subject, "Projective Verse," was as important for the poets of the emerging generation as T. S. Eliot's "Tradition and the Individual Talent" was to the poets of the previous generation. Olson credited Creeley with formulating one of the basic principles of this new poetry: the idea that "form is never more than an extension of content."

Creeley was a leader in the generational shift that veered away from history and tradition as primary poetic sources and gave new prominence to the ongoing experiences of an individual's life. Because of this emphasis, the major events of his life loom large in his literary work. Creeley's marriage to Ann MacKinnon ended in divorce in 1955. The breakup of that relationship is chronicled in fictional form in his only novel, *The Island,* which drew upon his experiences on the island of Mallorca, off the coast of Spain, where he lived with MacKinnon and their three children in 1953 and 1954. After the divorce Creeley returned to Black Mountain College for a brief time before moving west to make a new life. He was in San Francisco during the flowering of the "San Francisco Poetry Renaissance" and became associated for a time with the writers of the Beat Generation: Allen Ginsberg, Jack Kerouac, Michael McClure, and others. His work appeared in the influential "beat" anthology *The New American Poetry: 1945-1960,* edited by Donald Allen.

In 1956 Creeley accepted a teaching position at a boys' school in Albuquerque, New Mexico, where he met his second wife, Bobbie Louise Hall. Though Creeley published poetry and fiction throughout the 1950s and

1960s and had even established his own imprint, the Divers Press, in 1952, his work did not receive important national recognition until Scribner published his first major collection, *For Love: Poems 1950-1960,* in 1962. This book collected work that he had been issuing in small editions and magazines during the previous decade. When *For Love* debuted, Mobilio wrote, "it was recognized at once as a pivotal contribution to the alternative poetics reshaping the American tradition. . . . The muted, delicately contrived lyrics . . . were personal and self-contained; while they drew their life from the everyday, their techniques of dislocation sprang from the mind's naturally stumbled syntax."

The very first poem in *For Love,* "Hart Crane," with its unorthodox, Williams-like line breaks, its nearly hidden internal rhymes, and its subtle assonance and sibilance, announces the Creeley style—a style defined by an intense concentration on the sounds and rhythms of language as well as the placement of the words on the page. This intensity produces a kind of minimal poetry, which seeks to extract the bare linguistic bones from ongoing life experiences. In his introduction to *The New Writing in the U.S.A.,* Creeley cites approvingly Herman Melville's definition of "visible truth"—"the apprehension of the absolute condition of present things"—and supplements it with William Burroughs's famous statement from *Naked Lunch* about the writer's task: "There is only one thing a writer can write about: what is in front of his senses at the moment of writing. . . . I am a recording instrument . . . I do not presume to impose 'story' 'plot' 'continuity.'"

In *Pieces, A Day Book, Thirty Things,* and *Hello: A Journal, February 29-May 3, 1976,* all published between 1968 and 1978, Creeley attempts to break down the concept of a "single poem" by offering his readers sequential, associated fragments of poems with indeterminate beginnings and endings. All of these works are energized by the same heightened attention to the present that characterizes Creeley's earlier work, but in *Hello,* a book written as journal entries over a five-week period while Creeley traveled in the Orient and South Pacific, he speculates on the possibility of using memory rather than the present as a poetic source. The poetry remains stubbornly rooted in the present despite the insistent intrusion of memories, both recent and long past.

Many of the poems in *Hello* refer to the last days of Creeley's relationship with his second wife, Bobbie. That marriage ended in divorce in 1976, the same year he met Penelope Highton, his third wife, while traveling in New Zealand. In this sense, the book may be described in much the same terms as Sherman Paul, in his book *The Lost America of Love,* describes *For Love,* "Poems of two marriages, the breakup of one, the beginning of another." For all of Creeley's experimentation, he has always been in some ways an exceedingly domestic poet; his mother, children, wives, and close friends are the subjects of his best work. Because Creeley's second marriage lasted nearly twenty years, the sense of a major chunk of his life drifting away from him is very strong in *Hello.* Creeley here conveys the traumatic emotional state that almost always accompanies the breakup of long-term relationships. En route to Perth, he writes: "Sitting here in limbo, there are / people walking through my head." In Singapore he remarks on his tenuous hold on things: "Getting fainter, in the world, / fearing something's fading. . . ." Although *Hello* is superficially a record of Creeley's travels, the poems are not really about the countries he has visited, but rather about the landscape of mind he has brought with him.

It was not until Creeley's next major collection, 1979's *Later,* that the poetry seemed to shift into a new phase characterized by a greater emphasis on memory, a new sense of life's discrete phases, and an intense preoccupation with aging. In "Myself," the first poem in *Later,* he writes: "I want, if older, / still to know / why, human, men / and women are / so torn, so lost / why hopes cannot / find a better world / than this." This futile but deeply human quest captures the spirit of Creeley's later work. It embodies a commonly shared realization: one becomes older but still knows very little about essential aspects of life, particularly the mysteries of human relationships. And as Alan Williamson observed in his *New York Times Book Review* assessment of *Later,* "In general, the stronger the note of elegiac bafflement and rage (the past utterly gone, the compensating wisdom not forthcoming), the better the writing."

The ten-part title poem, "Later," was written over a period of ten days in September of 1977. The poem presents a kaleidoscopic view of various times and events important to Creeley's life, beginning with an evocation of lost youth. Youth, in later life, can only become a palpable part of the present through the evocative power of memory. Another section of the poem comments on how certain empirical sensations are repositories of memory. A taste, a smell, a touch, can evoke a lost world. "Later" continues to present a flood of childhood memories: a lost childhood dog that Creeley fantasizes running into again after all these years; memories of his mother and friends and neighbors; sights and sounds of his early days all evoked and made a part of the poetry he is composing in an attic room in Buffalo, September, 1977.

In the work produced after the material included in *The Collected Poems of Robert Creeley, 1945-1975* there is an increasing tendency to derive poetry from what the English Romantic poet William Wordsworth called "emotion recollected in tranquility." It is a poetry that remembers and reflects and seems much less tied to the exigencies of the present than the earlier work.

Mirrors reveals how much a part of our characters memories become with each passing year, so that as we age we accumulate the mannerisms of our parents and reexperience past situations. This theme of the present incorporating the past is most literal in "Prospect," one of the most memorable poems in *Mirrors.* It is an atypical Creeley poem because it utilizes conventional elements of poetry—symbolism, metaphor, and imagery—in a surprisingly traditional manner. In fact, the poem has a remarkably unique resonance because Creeley's physical description of nature conveys both present and past psychological states. It takes no deep looking into the poem to see the landscape as emblematic of the state of Creeley's later life, invigorated by a new marriage and the birth of a new child, his son William. The poem concludes with the reflections awakened by a contemplation of the landscape, which is described as peaceful and beautiful, yet in the end "faintly painful." The final phrase surprises, coming at the end of an otherwise tranquil and nearly celebratory poem. It reminds the reader that although embarking on a new life can create the illusion that it is possible to exist in an Edenic landscape apart from time, in reality the past remains an integral part of the present. "Faintly painful," with its echoing first syllable rhyme, is exactly right to convey the contrary feelings of both relief and regret that the poem ultimately leaves the reader with—relief that the thoughtfulness the landscape provokes is not more painful, regret that there is any pain at all.

Another of Creeley's collections, *Life and Death,* examines the poet's increasing age and mortality. A *Publishers Weekly* reviewer wrote: "For all of his complexity, [Creeley's] responses to his own sense of aging are surprisingly witty, lyrical, and grounded." Speaking of two specific poems in the collection, *Yale Review* contributor Stephen Burt offered the following praise for Creeley's work: "The best poems in *Life and Death* do touch on subjects other than isolation and dying—subjects that triangulate, that help Creeley place his obsessions. One such poem is 'Old Poems'; another is 'Given,' whose unfinished sentences, loping through their subdued quatrains, depict childhood as old age remembers it. It seems to me an extraordinary success, in part a triumph of prosody, and in part a triumph of a few details—never has one doughnut done more verbal work."

But pain has been one of the most constant elements in Creeley's work, and his later poetry continues to search for words to express it with sensitivity and exactness and without the sometimes maudlin excesses of "confessional" verse. Though these poems are more rooted in memory than the earlier work, Creeley remains committed to the poetic task of getting things exactly right. This has been the task of his writing throughout his career, and as readers look into the "mirror" of Creeley's work, they can see not only his aging, but their own.

After *Life and Death,* other volumes of poetry followed in regular succession. Some of them are *Loops: Ten Poems,* in 1995; *Ligeia: A Libretto,* in 1996; *So There: Poems 1976-83,* in 1998; *En Famille: A Poem by Robert Creeley,* in 1999; *Cambridge, Mass 1944,* with Daisy DeCapite in 2000; *Thinking,* in 2000; *For Friends,* in 2000; *Drawn and Quartered,* with Archie Rand's illustrations in 2001; *Just In Time: Poems, 1984-1994,* in 2001; and *If I Were Writing This,* in 2003. R. D. Pohl in the *Buffalo News,* praised *If I Were Writing This* highly, declaring that it "contains some of the starkest and most memorable poems Creeley has written." For instance, "'Conversion to Her' is a dense and emotionally charged meditation on sexual identity that appears to suggest that the male ego succumbs to the feminine order of the universe only in death." Pohl and a *Publishers Weekly* reviewer both saw *If I Were Writing This* as a companion volume to *Life and Death,* each of them "composed primarily of poems dedicated to family and friends (dead and living), collaborative verses, and such poems as 'For You' in which intimacy of tone coincides with cryptic, lyrical abstraction." Pohl noted that *If I Were Writing This* is the first major volume to appear since Creeley joined the ranks of such poetic giants as Ezra Pound, William Carlos Williams, Wallace Stevens and John Ashbery by winning the prestigious Yale University Bollingen Prize in 1999 and regretted that the publisher placed the fifty-four quatrains from Creeley's collaboration with artist Archie Rand early in the book without any explanation. "A casual or browsing reader might easily come to the mistaken conclusion that Creeley in his dotage had now turned to writing light verse," Pohl complained. However, Pohl delighted in the rest of the volume, in which, he said, Creeley "has no intention of presiding over his own canonization." He continued: "The fragility of our common experience in language and the world resonates through every line of Creeley's recent work" as in, "Somewhere in all the time that's passed / was a thing in mind became the evidence, / the pleasure even in fact of being lost / so quickly, simply that what it was could never last." To a question from J. M. Spalding of the 2003 *Cortland Review*—"What has changed in your work between *Echoes* and *Life and Death*?"—Creeley answered "Not a great deal. Perhaps a continuing relaxation, call it, an increased belief that says only being in the world matters at all and that it means, literally, finding one's way to others. I realized that just as childhood is lonely without other children to be with, old age is awful in isolation. One doesn't want to be stacked like planes waiting to take off, only with one's 'peer' group."

Creeley has also written a considerable amount of prose and been editor of a number of volumes, including *Best American Poetry 2002,* of which a *Publishers Weekly* writer remarked that it "is refreshing for what it isn't: a compendium of September 11 poems." Creeley, he said, has made a choice of poems that is "balanced and satisfying, providing space for contemplation, while opening a rare window on dissent." Among the poets included are John Ashbery, Frank Bidart, Anne Carson, W. S. Merwin, Sharon Olds, Carl Phillips, Charles Wright, Amiri Baraka, Alice Notley, Benjamin Friedlander, Steve Malmude, and Mong-Lan. The *Seattle Times*'s Richard Wakefield, however, asserted, "Most of the poems selected by Robert Creeley for inclusion in *The Best American Poetry 2002* are so awful that the reader is hard put to explain how five or ten good ones sneaked in." He found poems by W. S. Merwin, Donald Hall, and T. Alan Broughton among the few he would recommend. Amy Bracken Sparks in the *Plain Dealer,* on the other hand, enjoyed the "sea change" in poetry she recognized as "the avant-garde, going on fifty or so funneled from the margins by longtime progressive poet Robert Creeley." "It's thick," she wrote, "with lists, prose poems, fragments, foreign tongues and chunks of text dueling on the page." Even though she acknowledged that for "the legion of those who love Poet Laureate Billy Collins' poems," the poetry in this volume is not "accessible to all; they are innovative in both concept and structure, and therefore risk losing the reader," she added, "They are refreshingly unapologetic about being book-smart in an era when poetry has been dumbed-down at the microphone across America. Some have footnotes; one poem is entirely composed of them. Others juxtapose words in tight formation, or swing them across free-ranging lines that look like paint flung onto a canvas. Yes, it's a bit of work when not everything is explained. Pretension lurks about, but there's always Diane Di Prima keeping everything earthbound and Sharon Olds writing yet again about her father." As Eric McHenry of the Westchester *Journal News,* pointed out, "In the words of series editor David Lehman, *The Best American Poetry* is more properly viewed as a chronicle of 'the taste of our leading poets.' The best predictor of whether or not you'll like the poems in a given volume is whether or not you like the poetry of the person who chose them."

Creeley's prose includes a novel, essays, and short stories, as well as a play, collected letters, and an autobiography, published in 1990. But primarily a poet, he rejoices, as he says, in words, their immediacy, their availability to everyone, their insistence, in poems, that we just be with them. Don Byrd quoted him in *Contemporary Poets:* "I write to realize the world as one has come to live in it, thus to give testament. I write to move in *words,* a human delight. I write when no other act is possible." Asked by Spalding about "good" poems, Creeley, who had written in the introduction to *Best American Poetry 2002,* the poem is "that place we are finally safe in" where "understanding is not a requirement. You don't have to know why. Being there is the one requirement," responded, "If one only wrote 'good' poems, what a dreary world it would be. 'Writing writing' is the point. It's a process, like they say, not a production line. I love the story of Neal Cassidy writing on the bus with Ken Kesey, simply tossing the pages out the window as he finished each one. 'I wonder if it was any good,' I can hear someone saying. Did you ever go swimming without a place you were necessarily swimming to—the dock, say, or the lighthouse, the moored boat, the drowning woman? Did you always swim well, enter the water cleanly, proceed with efficient strokes and a steady flutter kick? I wonder if this 'good' poem business is finally some echo of trying to get mother to pay attention." Poets, he says, do not need encouragement. They live to write.

BIOGRAPHICAL AND CRITICAL SOURCES:

BOOKS

Allen, Donald M., editor, *Robert Creeley, Contexts of Poetry: Interviews, 1961-1971,* Four Seasons Foundation (San Francisco, CA), 1973.

Altieri, Charles, *Self and Sensibility in Contemporary American Poetry,* Cambridge University Press (New York, NY), 1984.

Butterick, George F., editor, *Charles Olson and Robert Creeley: The Complete Correspondence,* Black Sparrow Press (Santa Rosa, CA), 1980.

Clark, Tom, *Robert Creeley and the Genius of the American Common Place: Together with the Poet's Own Autobiography,* New Directions (New York, NY), 1993.

Conniff, Brian, *The Lyric and Modern Poetry: Olson, Creeley, Bunting,* Peter Lang (New York, NY), 1988.

Contemporary Authors Autobiography Series, Volume 10, Thomson Gale (Detroit, MI), 1989.

Contemporary Literary Criticism, Thomson Gale (Detroit, MI), Volume 1, 1973, Volume 2, 1974, Volume 4, 1975, Volume 8, 1978, Volume 11, 1979, Volume 15, 1980, Volume 36, 1986.

Contemporary Poets, 5th edition, edited by Tracy Chevalier, St. James Press (Detroit, MI), 1991.

Corman, Cid, editor, *The Gist of Origin,* Viking (New York, NY), 1975.

Creeley, Robert, *Hello,* Hawk Press (Christchurch, New Zealand), 1978.

Creeley, Robert, *Later,* Toothpaste (West Branch, IA), 1978.

Creeley, Robert, *If I Were Writing This,* New Directions (New York, NY), 2003.

Edelberg, Cynthia Dubin, *Robert Creeley's Poetry: A Critical Introduction,* University of New Mexico Press (Albuquerque, NM), 1978.

Faas, Ekbert, and Sabrina Reed, editors, *Irving Layton and Robert Creeley: The Complete Correspondence, 1953-1978,* McGill-Queen's University Press (Toronto, Ontario, Canada), 1990.

Faas, Ekbert, and Maria Trombaco, *Robert Creeley: A Biography,* University Press of New England (Hanover, NH), 2001.

Ford, Arthur L., *Robert Creeley,* Twayne (Boston, MA), 1978.

Foster, Edward Halsey, *Understanding the Black Mountain Poets,* University of South Carolina Press (Columbia, SC), 1995.

Fox, Willard, *Robert Creeley, Edward Dorn, and Robert Duncan: A Reference Guide.* G. K. Hall (Boston, MA), 1989.

Fredman, Stephen, *Poet's Prose: The Crisis in American Verse,* Cambridge University Press (New York, NY), 1983.

Giger, Esther, and Agnieszka Salska, editors, *Freedom and Form: Essays in Contemporary American Poetry.* Wydawnictwo Uniwersytetu Lódzkiego (Lódz, Poland), 1998.

Gwynn, R. S., editor, *New Expansive Poetry: Theory, Criticism, History,* Story Line (Ashland, OR), 1999.

Novik, Mary, *Robert Creeley: An Inventory, 1945-1970,* Kent State University Press (Kent, OH), 1973.

Oberg, Arthur, *Modern American Lyric: Lowell, Berryman, Creeley, and Plath,* Rutgers University Press (New Brunswick, NJ), 1977.

Paul, Sherman, *The Lost America of Love: Rereading Robert Creeley, Edward Dorn, and Robert Duncan,* Louisiana State University Press (Baton Rouge, LA), 1981.

Rifkin, Libbie, *Career Moves: Olson, Creeley, Zukofsky, Berrigan, and the American Avant-Garde,* University of Wisconsin Press (Madison, WI), 2000.

Roberts, Neil, editor, *A Companion to Twentieth-Century Poetry,* Blackwell (Oxford, England), 2001.

Sheffler, Ronald Anthony, *The Development of Robert Creeley's Poetry,* University of Massachusetts (Amherst, MA), 1971.

Tallman, Allen and Warren, editors, *The Poetics of the New American Poetry,* Grove (New York, NY), 1973.

Tallman, Warren, *Three Essays on Creeley,* Coach House Press (Toronto, Ontario, Canada), 1973.

Terrell, Carroll F., *Robert Creeley: The Poet's Workshop,* University of Maine Press (Orono, ME), 1984.

Von Hallberg, Robert, *American Poetry and Culture, 1945-80,* Harvard University Press (Cambridge, MA), 1985.

Wilson, John, editor, *Robert Creeley's Life and Work: A Sense of Increment,* University of Michigan Press (Ann Arbor, MI), 1987.

PERIODICALS

American Book Review, May-June, 1984.

American Poetry Review, November-December, 1976; May-June, 1997, p. 9; September-October, 1999, p. 17.

Atlantic Monthly, November, 1962; February, 1968; October, 1977.

Books Abroad, autumn, 1967.

Boundary 2, spring, 1975; spring and fall (special two-volume issue on Creeley), 1978.

Buffalo News, February 25, 1996, p. E1; February 7, 1999, p. E6; March 24, 2000, p. G18; September 7, 2003, p. G5.

Cambridge Quarterly, 1998, p. 87.

Christian Science Monitor, October 9, 1969.

Chronicle of Higher Education, November 1, 1996, p. B10.

Contemporary Literature, spring, 1972; fall, 1995, p. 79.

Cortland Review, April, 1998.

Critique, spring, 1964.

Denver Quarterly, winter 1997, p. 82.

ebr: The Alt-X Web Review, spring, 1999.

Encounter, February, 1969.

English: The Journal of the English Association, summer, 2001, p. 127.

Gentleman's Quarterly, June, 1996, p. 74.

Harper's, August, 1967; September, 1983.

Hudson Review, summer, 1963; summer, 1967; spring, 1970; summer, 1977.

Iowa Review, spring, 1982.

Journal News (Westchester, NY), August 31, 2003, p. 4E.

Journal of American Studies, August 1998, p. 263.

Kenyon Review, spring, 1970.

Library Journal, September 1, 1979; April 15, 1994, p. 81; April 1, 1997, p. 94; April 1, 1999, p, 95.

Listener, March 23, 1967.

London Magazine, June-July, 1973.

Los Angeles Times Book Review, April 17, 1983; October 30, 1983; March 4, 1984; June 24, 1984; June 23, 1991, p. 8.

Modern Language Quarterly, December, 1982, p. 369.

Modern Poetry Studies, winter, 1977.

Nation, August 25, 1962.

National Observer, October 30, 1967.

National Review, November 19, 1960.

New Leader, October 27, 1969.

New Orleans Review, spring, 1992, p. 14.

New Republic, October 11, 1969; December 18, 1976.

New Statesman, August 6, 1965; March 10, 1987.

New York Review of Books, January 20, 1966; August 1, 1968.

New York Times, June 27, 1967.

New York Times Book Review, November 4, 1962; September 22, 1963; November 19, 1967; October 27, 1968; January 7, 1973; May 1, 1977; March 9, 1980; August 7, 1983; June 24, 1984; September 23, 1984; November 3, 1991, p. 14.

North Dakota Quarterly, fall, 1987, p. 89.

Northwest Review, 2000, p. 102.

Observer (London, England), September 6, 1970.

Paris Review, fall, 1968.

Parnassus, fall-winter, 1984.

Partisan Review, summer, 1968.

Plain Dealer, September 29, 2002, p. J9.

Poetry, March, 1954; May, 1958; September, 1958; March, 1963; April, 1964; August, 1966; January, 1968; March, 1968; August, 1968; May, 1970; December, 1970; September, 1984.

Publishers Weekly, March 18, 1968; March 28, 1994; March 30, 1998, p. 77; September 24, 2001, p. 91; July 22, 2002, p. 170; September 1, 2003.

Review of Contemporary Fiction, fall, 1995, pp. 79, 82, 97, 107, 110, 116, 120, 127, 137, 141.

Sagetrieb: A Journal Devoted to Poets in the Imagist/ Objectivist Tradition, winter, 1982 (special issue); fall, 1988, p. 53; spring-fall, 1991, p. 209 (bibliog.); spring, 1999, pp. 131, 149.

San Francisco Chronicle, April 12, 1998, p. 12.

Saturday Review, August 4, 1962; December 11, 1965; June 3, 1967.

Seattle Times, October 6, 2002, p. L9.

Sewanee Review, winter, 1961.

Southwest Review, winter, 1964.

Talisman: A Journal of Contemporary Poetry and Poetics, 2001-2002, p. 49.

Time, July 12, 1971.

Times Literary Supplement, March 16, 1967; August 7, 1970; November 12, 1970; December 11, 1970; May 20, 1977; May 30, 1980; February 20, 1981; November 4, 1983; May 10, 1991, p. 22.

Village Voice, October 22, 1958; December 10, 1979; November 25, 1981.

Virginia Quarterly Review, summer, 1968; winter, 1972; spring, 1973.

Voice Literary Supplement, September, 1991, p. 14.

Washington Post Book World, August 11, 1991, p. 13.

Western Humanities Review, spring, 1970.

Winston-Salem Journal, March 5, 2000, p. E1.

World Literature Today, autumn, 1984; summer, 1992; spring, 1995.

Yale Review, October, 1962; December, 1969; spring, 1970; April, 1999, p. 175.

ONLINE

Academy of American Poets: Poetry Exhibit, http://www.poets.org/ (March 8, 2004).

Cortland Review, http://www.cortlandreview.com/ (April, 1998), interview with Creeley.

Levity, http://www.levity.com/ (March 8, 2004).

Providence Phoenix Book Reviews, http://www.providencephoenix.com/ (March 26-April 2, 1998), interview with Creeley.

Robert Creeley Home Page, http://wings.buffalo.edu/epc/authors/creeley/ (April 26, 2000).

University of Illinois, Department of English, http://www.english.uiuc.edu/ (March 8, 2004).*

* * *

CROSBY, Donald A(llen) 1932-

PERSONAL: Born April 7, 1932, in Mansfield, OH; son of Edmund Bevington (an accountant) and Mary Lou (Bogan) Crosby; married Charlotte Mae Robinson (a visiting nurse), September 15, 1956 (marriage ended); married second wife, 1999; children: (first marriage) Colleen Judith, Kathleen Bridgett. *Education:* Davidson College, A.B., 1953; Princeton Theological Seminary, B.D., 1956, Th.M., 1959; Columbia University, Ph.D., 1963.

ADDRESSES: *Home*—5151 Boardwalk Dr., Unit K2, Fort Collins, CO 80525. *Office*—Department of Philosophy, Colorado State University, Fort Collins, CO 80521. *E-mail*—donaldcrosby@compuserve.com.

CAREER: Ordained Presbyterian minister, 1956-67; minister in Christiana, DE, 1956-59, and Norwalk, CT, 1959-61; Centre College of Kentucky, Danville, assistant professor of philosophy and religion, 1962-65; Colorado State University, Fort Collins, assistant professor, 1965-69, associate professor, 1969-73, professor of philosophy, 1973—, honors professor, 1981.

MEMBER: American Philosophical Association, American Academy of Religion, Society for the Advancement of American Philosophy, Society for the Study of Process Philosophy, Highlands Institute for American Religious and Philosophical Thought.

AWARDS, HONORS: Burlington Northern Award, 1989; John N. Stern Distinguished Faculty Award, 1994.

WRITINGS:

Horace Bushnell's Theory of Language, Mouton (New York, NY), 1974.

Interpretive Theories of Religion, Mouton (New York, NY), 1981.

The Specter of the Absurd: Sources and Criticisms of Modern Nihilism, State University of New York Press (Albany, NY), 1988.

(Editor, with Charley D. Hardwick) *Religious Experience and Ecological Responsibility,* Peter Lang (New York, NY), 1996.

(Editor, with Charley D. Hardwick) *Pragmatism, Neo-Pragmatism, and Religion: Conversations with Richard Rorty,* Peter Lang (New York, NY), 1997.

(Editor, with Charley D. Hardwick) *Religion in a Pluralistic Age,* Peter Lang (New York, NY), 2001.

A Religion of Nature, State University of New York Press (Albany, NY), 2002.

Contributor to *Christian Scholar, Process Studies,* and *Journal of the American Academy of Religion.*

BIOGRAPHICAL AND CRITICAL SOURCES:

PERIODICALS

Choice, September, 1976, review of *Horace Bushnell's Theory of Language,* p. 840; January, 1989, review of *The Specter of the Absurd: Sources and Criticisms of Modern Nihilism,* p. 818.

International Journal for Philosophy of Religion, August, 1999, Kevin Schilbrack, review of *Pragmatism, Neo-Pragmatism, and Religion: Conversations with Richard Rorty,* p. 49.

Journal of the American Academy of Religion, fall, 1993, Karen L. Carr, review of *The Specter of the Absurd,* p. 591.

Journal of Religion, October, 1977, review of *Horace Bushnell's Theory of Language,* p. 433.
Journal of the History of Philosophy, October, 1990, George J. Stack, review of *The Specter of the Absurd,* p. 627.
Library Journal, August, 2002, Sandra Collins, review of *A Religion of Nature,* p. 103.
Reference and Research Book News, September, 1996, review of *Religious Experience and Ecological Responsibility,* p. 6; May, 2001, review of *Religion in a Pluralistic Age,* p. 13.
Religious Studies, December, 1983, review of *Interpretive Theories of Religion,* p. 525.
University Press Book News, March, 1989, review of *The Specter of the Absurd,* p. 3.
Zygon: Journal of Religion and Science, March, 1983, review of *Interpretive Theories of Religion,* p. 108.*

* * *

CUDJOE, Selwyn Reginald 1943-

PERSONAL: Born December 1, 1943, in Tacarigua, Trinidad; immigrated to the United States, 1964; son of Lionel R. (a signal operator) and Carmen Rose (a homemaker) Cudjoe; married Gwendolyn M. Long, December 21, 1968 (marriage ended); children: Frances Louise, Kwamena. *Education:* Fordham University, B.A., 1969, M.A., 1972; attended Columbia University, 1971-72; Cornell University, Ph.D., 1976; postdoctoral study at University of Strasbourg, 1978.

ADDRESSES: *Office*—Department of Africana Studies, Wellesley College, Wellesley, MA 02181. *E-mail*—scudjoe@wellesley.edu.

CAREER: Fordham University, Bronx, NY, instructor in Afro-American studies, 1970-72; Ithaca College, Ithaca, NY, assistant professor of Afro-American studies, 1973-74; Ohio University, Athens, associate professor of Afro-American studies, 1975-76; Harvard University, Cambridge, MA, assistant professor of Afro-American studies, 1976-81; Cornell University, Ithaca, senior lecturer, 1980, associate professor of Africana studies, 1981-82; Wellesley College, Wellesley, MA, professor of Africana studies, 1986—, Marion Butler McLean Professor of the History of Ideas, 1995-99. Harvard University, visiting fellow at W. E. B. DuBois Institute for African-American Research, 1991, visiting scholar in African-American studies, 1992-94; also taught at Brandeis University; speaker at Auburn State Prison, Auburn, NY, and teacher for Bedford-Stuyvesant Youth-in-Action. Calaloux Research Associates, president; interviewer for Trinidad and Tobago Television.

AWARDS, HONORS: Fellow, National Endowment for the Humanities, 1991-92, 1994-98, 1996-97; senior fellow, Society for the Humanities, Cornell University, 1992.

WRITINGS:

Resistance and Caribbean Literature, Ohio University Press (Athens, OH), 1981.
Grenada: Two Essays, Calaloux Publications (Wellesley, MA), 1983.
Movement of the People: Essays on Independence, Calaloux Publications (Wellesley, MA), 1983.
A Just and Moral Society, Calaloux Publications (Wellesley, MA), 1984.
V. S. Naipaul: A Materialist Reading, University of Massachusetts Press (Amherst, MA), 1988.
(Editor and author of introduction) *Caribbean Women Writers: Essays from the First International Conference,* University of Massachusetts Press (Amherst, MA), 1990.
(Editor) *Eric E. Williams Speaks: Essays on Colonialism and Independence,* Calaloux Publications (Wellesley, MA), 1993.
(Editor, with William E. Cain) *C. L. R. James: His Intellectual Legacies,* University of Massachusetts Press (Amherst, MA), 1995.
Tacarigua: A Village in Trinidad (documentary film), Calaloux Publications (Wellesley, MA), 1995.
(Editor and author of afterword) Maxwell Philip, *Emmanuel Appadocca, or, Blighted Life: A Tale of the Boucaneers,* University of Massachusetts Press (Amherst, MA), 1997.
Beyond Boundaries: The Intellectual Tradition of Trinidad and Tobago in the Nineteenth Century, Calaloux Publications (Wellesley, MA), 2002.

Contributor to books; author of foreword or introduction to *The Still Cry: Personal Accounts of East Indians in Trinidad and Tobago during Indentureship, 1845-1917,* Calaloux Publications (Wellesley, MA),

1985; *Those That Be in Bondage: A Tale of Indian Indentures and Sunlit Western Waters,* Calaloux Publications (Wellesley, MA), 1988; *History, Fable, and Myth in the Caribbean and Guianas,* by Wilson Harris, Calaloux Publications (Wellesley, MA), 1995; and *Free Mulatto,* by John Baptista Philip, Calaloux Publications (Wellesley, MA), 1996. Contributing editor, *Freedomways;* member of editorial board, *Encarta Africana.*

SIDELIGHTS: Selwyn Reginald Cudjoe once told *CA:* "I have always felt the need to articulate and to interpret the world from the point of view of a person who has always been considered as an 'object' in the world's historical process. At the moment, I am committed to writing for and about the liberation of my people. In this sense, my work is highly partisan and eschews all attempts at objectivity.

"I believe that a person, particularly a writer, must be a highly committed individual. One must believe in something, see the world from a particular vantage point, and hope—through publication—to give some sort of clarity to that point of view. To respond to one's material from a specific standpoint (bereft of the absent sense of 'objectivity') is not to be interpreted as a disregard for the integrity of the evidences that one encounters. One must always pay strict regard to the evidences and draw a conclusion from them. It is, however, to affirm that one interprets social (and even scientific) phenomena from a particular perspective—from a specific orientation to the world—and it is from that strictly partisan vantage point that I respond to my world.

"I am not, at this stage of my career, interested in responding to my world purely from an abstract or scholastic position. I believe that in order to understand the social phenomenon at its most revealing (and one might say, most 'truthful') one needs to be involved actively in the processes of practical life. Thus, I try to merge my theory of social development with the practical aspects of my everyday life, and that is the locus which directs the approach to my present set of writings. As such, *V. S. Naipaul: A Materialist Reading*—the product of about six years of arduous work—signifies the end of a particular aspect of my intellectual career. Highly theoretical and in response, in the main, to bourgeois critics from the First World, this text represents what I consider a work of my more mature period of writing."

BIOGRAPHICAL AND CRITICAL SOURCES:

PERIODICALS

American Literature, June, 1996, review of *C. L. R. James: His Intellectual Legacies,* p. 500.

Black Scholar, spring, 1995, review of *C. L. R. James,* p. 68.

Choice, February, 1989, review of *V. S. Naipaul: A Materialist Reading,* p. 938; July, 1991, review of *Caribbean Women Writers: Essays from the First International Conference,* p. 1778; April, 1994, B. B. Solnick, review of *Eric E. Williams Speaks: Essays on Colonialism and Independence,* p. 1349.

College English, January, 1994, Danny J. Anderson, review of *Caribbean Women Writers,* p. 82.

Contemporary Sociology, May, 1997, Obika Gray, review of *C. L. R. James,* p. 39.

English Journal, April, 1992, review of *Caribbean Women Writers,* p. 37.

English Language Notes, September, 1992, Roberta L. Salper, review of *Caribbean Women Writers,* p. 69.

Feminist Studies, spring, 1995, Maria Helena Lima, review of *Caribbean Women Writers,* p. 115.

Feminist Teacher, spring, 1993, Shirley P. Brown, review of *Caribbean Women Writers,* p. 62.

Journal of Modern Literature, fall-winter, 1989, Eric Sellin, review of *V. S. Naipaul,* p. 392.

Modern Fiction Studies, summer, 1989, Harveen Sachdeva Mann, review of *V. S. Naipaul,* p. 398.

New Directions for Women, May, 1991, review of *Caribbean Women Writers,* p. 17.

Reference and Research Book News, September, 1995, review of *C. L. R. James,* p. 55.

Religious Studies Review, July, 1989, review of *V. S. Naipaul,* p. 253.

University Press Book News, March, 1991, review of *Caribbean Women Writers,* p. 38.

Women's Review of Books, September, 1991, review of *Caribbean Women Writers,* p. 21.

World Literature Today, spring, 1989, Harold A. Waters, review of *V. S. Naipaul,* p. 356; winter, 1992, Charlotte H. Bruner, review of *Caribbean Women Writers,* p. 186.*

* * *

CULVER, Timothy J.

See WESTLAKE, Donald E(dwin)

CUNNINGHAM, J. Morgan
See WESTLAKE, Donald E(dwin)

* * *

CURRIE, Robert 1937-

PERSONAL: Born September, 1937, in Lloydminster, Saskatchewan, Canada; son of Duncan L. (an accountant) and Jean M. (a teacher) Currie; married Gwendolyn Emma May Gricvc, August 18, 1962; children: Bronwen, Ryan. *Education:* University of Saskatchewan, B.S.P., 1961, B.A., 1964, B.Ed., 1966.

ADDRESSES: Home—Moose Jaw, Saskatchewan, Canada. *Office*—Central Collegiate, Ross St., Moose Jaw, Saskatchewan, Canada.

CAREER: University of Saskatchewan, Saskatoon, Saskatchewan, Canada, lecturer in pharmacy, 1961-62, pharmacist at university hospital, 1962-63; Central Collegiate, Moose Jaw, Saskatchewan, teacher of English, 1966—. Thunder Creek Publishing Cooperative, founding coeditor.

MEMBER: League of Canadian Poets, Saskatchewan Writers Guild (chair, 1973-74).

AWARDS, HONORS: Ohio State Award for Radio Drama, Ohio State University, 1977, for "What about What I Want?" from the radio play "Whatcha Gonna Do, Whatcha Gonna Be?"; first prize for poetry, Saskatchewan Writers Guild contest, 1978, for "And Mother Called Him the Stallion Groom," and 1981, for "CPR Ice Gang—1959"; first prize for children's literature, 1979, for "What's Smooth and Brown and on the Bathroom Plug?"; Founders Award, 1984, for "contributions to the literature and the literary community of Saskatchewan"; third prize for poetry from national literary competition, Canadian Broadcasting Corp., 1980, for *Brother* (suite of related poems).

WRITINGS:

Quarterback (poetry), Delta, 1970.
Sawdust and Dirt (poetry), Fiddlehead Poetry Books (Fredericton, New Brunswick, Canada), 1973.
The Halls of Elsinore (poetry), Sesame Press (Windsor, Ontario, Canada), 1973.
Moving Out (poetry), Coteau Books (Regina, Saskatchewan, Canada), 1975.
Diving into Fire (poetry), Oberon Press (Ottawa, Ontario, Canada), 1977.
(Editor, with Gary Hyland, Barbara Sapergia, and Geoffrey Ursell) *Number One Northern* (poetry), Coteau Books (Regina, Saskatchewan, Canada), 1977.
Yarrow (poetry), Oberon Press (Ottawa, Ontario, Canada), 1980.
Night Games, Coteau Books (Regina, Saskatchewan, Canada), 1983.
(Editor, with Gary Hyland and Jim McLean) *One Hundred Per Cent Cracked Wheat,* Cotcau Books (Regina, Saskatchewan, Canada), 1983.
Learning on the Job (short stories), Oberon Press (Ottawa, Ontario, Canada), 1986.
Klondike Fever, Coteau Books (Regina, Saskatchewan, Canada), 1992.
Things You Don't Forget, Coteau Books (Regina, Saskatchewan, Canada), 1999.
Teaching Mr. Cutler (novel), Coteau Books (Regina, Saskatchewan, Canada), 2002.

Work represented in anthologies, including *Going for Coffee,* edited by Wayman, Harbour Publishing (Madeira Park, British Columbia, Canada), 1981; *The Spice Box,* edited by Sinclair and Wolfe, Lester & Orpen Dennys (Toronto, Ontario, Canada), 1981; *Saskatchewan Gold,* edited by Ursell, 1982; *Tributaries;* and *Poetspeak.* Contributor to magazines, including *Canadian Forum, Wascana Review,Grain, Nebula,* and *Fiddlehead.* Founder and editor of *Salt,* 1969-77.

RADIO PLAYS:

Whatcha Gonna Do, Whatcha Gonna Be?, CBC-Radio, 1976.
Pitch, Patch, Pepper, CBC-Radio, 1977.
Moose Jaw: The Struggle and the Sioux, CBC-Radio, 1979.
North of Moose Jaw, CBC-Radio, May,

SIDELIGHTS: Robert Currie once told *CA:* "I believe that poetry represents a heightened response to life, experience closely observed, highly imagined, then touched somehow by an indefinable magic as it is preserved on paper.

"In this unpoetic age, the poet must find a way to flourish in harsh climate and barren soil, working with detail and image, with memory, metaphor, language, kicking all the while against the odds. He must write poems because that is what he does best, and poems—even in the worst of times (perhaps especially in the worst of times)—have the power to touch others.

"My most satisfying experience as a writer came while working on *Yarrow.* It came with the discovery that through poetry I could achieve the qualities of a solid, well-built piece of fiction, the richness, depth, and sense of development of a novel. I knew that each part must stand on its own, but my novel could be many poems.

"It was like shucking off a straitjacket. I was no longer limited to what could be done in a single poem. Instead, poems could build on one another, play off one another, contradict one another, the tensions growing from poem to poem, themes resonating back and forth, truths emerging even in the silences between the poems. Here was a new freedom to create. Narratives, lyrics, dramatic monologues, portrait poems came spinning out until I'd created a whole family—a family that demanded its own life, arguing, loving, aging, torn by conflicts that I'd never even planned."

BIOGRAPHICAL AND CRITICAL SOURCES:

BOOKS

Cooley, Dennis, editor, *Replacing,* ECW Press (Toronto, Ontario, Canada), 1980.

PERIODICALS

Booklist, June 15, 1990, review of *Yarrow,* p. 1968.

Books in Canada, May, 1992, review of *Klondike Fever,* p. 60.

Canadian Book Review Annual, 2000, review of *Things You Don't Forget,* p. 172.

Canadian Literature, winter, 2000, review of *Things You Don't Forget,* p. 177; autumn, 2001, review of *Things You Don't Forget,* p. 236.

CM: Reviewing Journal of Canadian Materials for Young People, November, 1992, review of *Klondike Fever,* p. 301.

Queen's Quarterly, winter, 1987, review of *Learning on the Job,* p. 1042.

Quill & Quire, October, 2002, Steven Manners, review of *Teaching Mr. Cutler,* p. 32.*

D

D'ALFONSO, Antonio 1953-

PERSONAL: Born August 6, 1953, in Montreal, Quebec, Canada; son of Carlo (a welder) and Emilia (Salvatore) D'Alfonso; married second wife, Emilia Chiocca (a teacher), October 11, 1995; children: Elisa. *Education:* Loyola College, Montreal, Quebec, Canada, B.A., 1975; University of Montreal, M.Sc., 1979.

ADDRESSES: *Office*—Guernica Editions, Box 117, Station P, Toronto, Ontario M5S 2S6, Canada. *E-mail*—guernicaeditions@cs.com or 102036.1331@compuserve.com.

CAREER: Filmmaker and writer, 1974—; Guernica Editions, Toronto, Ontario, Canada, founder and editor, beginning 1978. *Vice Versa* magazine, cofounder, c. 1982. Presenter of conferences on literature, film, and multiculturalism.

MEMBER: Association of Canadian Publishers, Writers Union of Canada, League of Canadian Poets, Association of Italian-Canadian Writers (cofounder, 1986), Syndicat National du Cinema, Association des Editeurs, Union des écrivains québécois.

WRITINGS:

La chanson du shaman à Sedna (poetry; title means "Shaman's Song to Sedna"), privately printed, 1973.

L'ampoule brulee (screenplay), 1973

La coupe de Circe (screenplay), 1974.

Queror (poetry; title means "To Sing, to Cry, to Lament"), Guernica Editions (Toronto, Ontario, Canada), 1979.

Pour t'aimer (screenplay), 1982.

Black Tongue (poetry), Guernica Editions (Toronto, Ontario, Canada), 1983.

(Editor, with Fulvio Caccia, and contributor) *Quêtes: Textes d'auteurs italo-québécois,* Guernica Editions (Toronto, Ontario, Canada), 1983.

(Editor) *Voix-off: dix poètes Anglophones du Québec,* Guernica Editions (Toronto, Ontario, Canada), 1985.

(Translator) Philippe Haeck, *The Clarity of Voices* (prose poetry), Guernica Editions (Toronto, Ontario, Canada), 1985.

The Other Shore (prose and poetry), Guernica Editions (Toronto, Ontario, Canada), 1986.

L'Autre Rivage, VLB Éditeur (Montreal, Quebec, Canada), 1987.

L'amour panique (prose poetry), Levres Urbaines, 1988, published as *Panick Love,* Guernica Editions (Toronto, Ontario, Canada), 1992.

Avril ou L'anti-passion (novel), VLB Éditeur (Montreal, Quebec, Canada), 1990.

Lettre à Julia (long prose poem), L'Éditions du Silence, 1992.

Fabrizio's Passion (novel), Guernica Editions (Toronto, Ontario, Canada), 1995.

In Italics: A Defense of Ethnicity (essays), Guernica Editions (Toronto, Ontario, Canada), 1996.

L'apostrophe qui me scinde, Editions du Noroît (Montreal, Quebec, Canada), 1998.

(With Pasquale Verdicchio) *Duologue: On Culture and Identity,* Guernica Editions (Toronto, Ontario, Canada), 1998.

(Translator) Pasquale Verdicchio, *La paysage qui bouge,* Le Norôit (Quebec, Canada), 2000.

Comment ça se passe, Editions du Noroît (Montreal, Quebec, Canada), 2001.

Other screenplays include "The Minotaur" and "Antigone." Work represented in anthologies, including *Cross/Cut,* Véhicule Press (Montreal, Quebec, Canada), 1982; *Italian Canadian Voices,* edited by Caroline Morgan Di Giovanni, Mosaic Press (Oakville, Ontario, Canada), 1984; *Quebec Kaleidoscope,* Paje editeur, 1991; *The Oxford Companion to Canadian Literature,* 2nd edition, edited by Eugene Benson and William Toye, Oxford University Press (Oxford, England), 1997; and *Identity Lessons: Contemporary Writing about Learning to Be American,* edited by Maria Mazziotti Gillan and Jennifer Gillan, Penguin (New York, NY), 1999. Contributor to magazines, including *Canadian Forum, Nos Livres,* and *Poetry Canada Review.*

Some of D'Alfonso's works have been translated to other languages.

SIDELIGHTS: Antonio D'Alfonso once told *CA:* "Writing is my way of remembering what is come of me—be it in the form of a poem, a prose poem, an essay, an interview, a letter, or a film. Language is important, yet today I have come to believe that it is itself the worst of prisons. To be able to free myself I have to write in another language. I have written mostly in Italian, French, and English. Film, however, is what enables me to capture at once the social and private aspects of me. Writing is a selfish act of socialization: I have to express my being and fit this being into the historical patchwork of which I am temporarily part. But it is film—whenever I can make one—that allows me to immediately speak to the illiterate people I have grown up with. I speak of illiteracy in a symbolic manner: few are those who read and write around me, no matter from which class they come or belong to. Our world is one of images and we must try to use these to fit our needs and desires."

BIOGRAPHICAL AND CRITICAL SOURCES:

PERIODICALS

Books in Canada, November, 1979, review of *Queror,* p. 28; December, 1986, review of *The Other Shore,* p. 22; summer, 1993, review of *Panick Love,* p. 38; November, 1995, review of *Fabrizio's Passion,* p. 36.

Canadian Book Review Annual, 1996, review of *Fabrizio's Passion,* p. 158; 1997, review of *In Italics: A Defense of Ethnicity,* p. 368; 1998, review of *Duologue: On Culture and Identity,* p. 264.

Canadian Literature, summer, 1991, Andre Lamontagne, review of *L'Autre Rivage,* p. 230.

Translation Review Supplement, December, 2000, review of *Fabrizio's Passion,* p. 7.

University of Toronto Quarterly, winter, 1997, Joseph Pivato, review of *In Italics,* p. 154; winter, 1999, Anthony Julian Tamburri, review of *Duologue,* p. 305.

ONLINE

Antonio D'Alfonso Home Page, http://www.writersunion.ca/d/dalfonso/ (August 5, 2002).

* * *

DELRIO, Martin
See MACDONALD, James D.

* * *

Di CICCO, Pier Giorgio 1949-

PERSONAL: Born July 5, 1949, in Arezzo, Italy; immigrated to Canada, 1952; son of Giuseppe and Primetta (Liberatore) Di Cicco. *Education:* University of Toronto, B.A., 1972, B.Ed., 1976, M.Div., 1990; St. Paul's University, B.S.T., 1990. *Religion:* Roman Catholic.

ADDRESSES: Home—P.O. Box 839, Station P, Toronto, Ontario M5S 2Z1, Canada. *Office*—St. Anne's Church, Brampton, Ontario, Canada.

CAREER: Bartender in Toronto, Ontario, Canada, 1972-75; freelance writer, beginning 1979; Order of St. Augustine, member; ordained Roman Catholic priest, 1993; St. Anne's Church, Brampton, Ontario, Canada, associate pastor, 1993—. Instructor at educational institutions, including Three Schools of Art, Toronto, 1977-78, Humber College, Toronto, 1981-82, 1984, and Columbus Centre, Toronto, 1985.

Worked as chemist, detective, and teacher. Gives readings in the United States and Canada, including television and radio broadcasts. Consultant to Ontario Arts Council.

MEMBER: League of Canadian Poets.

AWARDS, HONORS: Canada Council awards for poetry, 1974, 1976, and 1980; Italo-Canadian Literary Award, Carleton University, 1979.

WRITINGS:

POETRY

We Are the Light Turning, Missing Link Press (Scarborough, Ontario, Canada), 1975, revised edition, Thunder City Press (Birmingham, AL), 1976.

The Virgin-Maker, McClelland & Stewart (Toronto, Ontario, Canada), 1976.

The Sad Facts, Fiddlehead Books (Vancouver, British Columbia, Canada), 1977.

The Circular Dark, Borealis Press (Ottawa, Ontario, Canada), 1977.

Dancing in the House of Cards, Three Trees Press (Toronto, Ontario, Canada), 1978.

A Burning Patience, Borealis Press (Ottawa, Ontario, Canada), 1978.

Dolce-Amaro, Papavero Press (Tuscaloosa, AL), 1979.

The Tough Romance, McClelland & Stewart (Toronto, Ontario, Canada), 1979.

A Straw Hat for Everything, Angelstone Press (Birmingham, AL), 1981.

Flying Deeper into the Century, McClelland & Stewart (Toronto, Ontario, Canada), 1982.

Dark to Light: Reasons for Humanness: Poems 1976-1979, Intermedia Press (Vancouver, British Columbia, Canada), 1983.

Women We Never See Again, Borealis Press (Ottawa, Ontario, Canada), 1984.

Post-Sixties Nocturne, Fiddlehead Books (Vancouver, British Columbia, Canada), 1985.

Twenty Poems, University of Guadalajara Press (Guadalajara, Mexico), 1985.

Virgin Science: Hunting Holistic Paradigms, McClelland & Stewart (Toronto, Ontario, Canada), 1986.

The City of Unhurried Dreams: Poems, 1977-1983, Guernica Editions (Montreal, Quebec, Canada), 1993.

Living in Paradise: New and Selected Poems, Mansfield Press (Toronto, Ontario, Canada), 2001.

Work represented in anthologies, including *This Is My Best: Poems Selected by Ninety-one Poets,* edited by Kenneth Peregrine Grist, Coach House Press (Toronto, Ontario, Canada), 1976; *Whale Sound,* edited by Greg Gatenby, J. J. Douglas (North Vancouver, British Columbia, Canada), 1977; *The New Oxford Book of Canadian Verse,* edited by Margaret Atwood, Oxford University Press (New York, NY), 1982; *Canadian Poetry Now: Twenty Poets of the Eighties,* edited by Ken Norris, House of Anansi (Toronto, Ontario, Canada), 1984; and *The New Canadian Poets, 1970-1985,* edited by Dennis Lee, McClelland & Stewart (Toronto, Ontario, Canada), 1985. Contributor of more than 200 poems to magazines, including *Poetry Canada Review, Canadian Literature,Canadian Forum, Fiddlehead,Quarry, Tamarack Review,Critical Quarterly, Kayak,Miss Chatelaine,* and *Denver Quarterly.*

OTHER

(Editor and contributor) *Roman Candles: An Anthology of Seventeen Italo-Canadian Poets,* Hounslow Press (Toronto, Ontario, Canada), 1978.

Founder and poetry editor, *Poetry Toronto Newsletter,* 1976-77; associate editor, *Books in Canada,* 1976-79; *Waves,* coeditor, 1976-79, poetry editor, 1980-82; contributing editor,*Argomenti Canadensi* and *Italia-America;* past editor, *Poetry View,Descant,* and *Grad Poet.*

BIOGRAPHICAL AND CRITICAL SOURCES:

BOOKS

Contemporary Poets, 7th edition, St. James Press (Detroit, MI), 2001.

Dictionary of Literary Biography, Volume 60: *Canadian Writers since 1960, Second Series,* Thomson Gale (Detroit, MI), 1987.

PERIODICALS

Canadian Literature, fall, 1985, Antonio D'Alfonso, "Per Pier Giorgio Di Cicco," p. 41.

Dalhousie Review, autumn, 1978, Douglas Barbour, "Canadian Poetry Chronicle: VI," pp. 555-578; winter, 1979-80, Douglas Barbour, "Canadian Poetry Chronicle: VII," pp. 154-175.

Poetry Canada Review, autumn, 1986, Robert Billings, "*Virgin Science:* The Hunt for Holistic Paradigms; An Interview with Pier Giorgio Di Cicco," pp. 3-4, 8-9.

Queen's Quarterly, autumn, 1988, review of *Virgin Science: Hunting Holistic Paradigms,* p. 726;

Tamarack Review, summer, 1979, Greg Gatenby, "Poetry Chronicle," pp. 77-94.

ONLINE

Athabasca University: Canadian Writers, http://www.athabascau.ca/cll/writers/didicco/ (June 19, 2002), "Pier Giorgio Di Cicco: Brief Biography."

* * *

DOVER, K(enneth) J(ames) 1920-

PERSONAL: Born March 11, 1920, in Croydon, England; son of Percy Henry James (a civil servant) and Dorothy (Healey) Dover; married Audrey Latimer, March 17, 1947; children: Alan Hugh, Catherine Ruth. *Ethnicity:* "White." *Education:* Balliol College, Oxford, M.A., 1947; attended Merton College, Oxford, 1948. *Politics:* "Left of center." *Religion:* Agnostic. *Hobbies and other interests:* "Unspoiled natural scenery, fauna and flora, comparative and historical linguistics, the processes of change in ethics, religion and society."

ADDRESSES: Home—49 Hepburn Gardens, St. Andrews, Fife KY16 9LS, Scotland.

CAREER: Oxford University, Balliol College, Oxford, England, fellow and tutor in classics, 1948-55; University of St. Andrews, St. Andrews, Scotland, professor of Greek, 1955-76, dean of faculty of arts, 1960-63, 1973-75; Oxford University, Corpus Christi College, president, 1976-86; University of St. Andrews, chancellor, 1986—. Harvard University, visiting lecturer, 1960; University of California—Berkeley, Sather Visiting Professor of Classics, 1967; Stanford University, professor, between 1988 and 1992. *Military service:* British Army, 1940-45; served in Africa and Italy; became lieutenant; mentioned in dispatches.

MEMBER: British Academy (fellow; president, 1978-81), Society for the Promotion of Hellenic Studies (president, 1971-74), Society for the Promotion of Roman Studies, Classical Association (president, 1976), Linguistics Association of Great Britain, Royal Society of Edinburgh (fellow).

AWARDS, HONORS: Knighted, 1977.

WRITINGS:

Greek Word Order, Cambridge University Press (Cambridge, England), 1960.

(Author of commentary) Thucydides, *History of the Peloponnesian War,* Books 6 and 7, Clarendon Press (Oxford, England), 1965.

Lysias and the Corpus Lysiacum, University of California Press (Berkeley, CA), 1968.

Aristophanic Comedy, University of California Press (Berkeley, CA), 1972.

Thucydides, Clarendon Press (Oxford, England), 1973.

Greek Popular Morality in the Time of Plato and Aristotle, Blackwell (London, England), 1974.

Greek Homosexuality, Duckworth (London, England), 1978.

The Greeks, BBC Publications (London, England), 1980.

(With A. W. Gomme and A. Andrewes) *Historical Commentary on Thucydides,* Clarendon Press (Oxford, England), Volume 4, 1970, Volume 5, 1981.

Greek and the Greeks: Collected Papers, Volume 1: *Language, Poetry, Drama,* Blackwell (London, England), 1987.

The Greeks and Their Legacy: Collected Papers, Volume 2: *Prose, Literature, History, Society, Transmission, Influence,* Blackwell (London, England), 1988.

Marginal Comment: A Memoir, Duckworth (London, England), 1994.

The Evolution of Greek Prose Style, Oxford University Press (Oxford, England), 1997.

EDITOR:

(And author of introduction and commentary) Aristophanes, *Clouds,* Clarendon Press (Oxford, England), 1968.

(And author of introduction and commentary) Theocritus, *Selected Poems,* Macmillan (New York, NY), 1971.

Plato, *Symposium,* Cambridge University Press (Cambridge, England), 1980.

(And contributor) *Ancient Greek Literature,* Oxford University Press (Oxford, England), 1980, 2nd edition, 1997.

Perceptions of the Ancient Greeks, Blackwell (London, England), 1992.

(And author of introduction and commentary) Aristophanes, *Frogs,* Clarendon Press (Oxford, England), 1993, student edition, 1997.

J. D. Denniston, *The Greek Particles,* 2d edition, Hackett Publishing (Indianapolis, IN), 1996.

Coeditor, *Classical Quarterly,* 1962-68.

SIDELIGHTS: K. J. Dover once told *CA:* "My main motivation for writing is love of my subject. When I have resolved a problem in ancient Greek literature or history, I want to communicate my findings to others, so that understanding of the subject, and interest in it, may be increased.

"In the case of my autobiography, *Marginal Comment: A Memoir,* my purpose was different: to try to influence the genre of autobiography by producing a specimen of what I thought it ought to be like.

"The main influences on my work have been (1) the work of certain scholars of my parents' generation, (2) any work on any subject which has attracted me, as its reader, by its method and style.

"Writing process: I always write first those portions of a work which come most easily, putting the most difficult off until the end. My main problem is always to find the right sequence and connection of thought in an exposition. I rewrite constantly, sometimes going through six or more versions until a feeling of 'That's it!' stops me.

"What determined my choice of subjects was a combination of my own deep-seated inclination (language and history) with the opportunities available to me as a school pupil and student, and thereafter the gaps in our understanding which became apparent to me as a teacher."

In addition to Greek, Dover is competent in Latin, Italian, Spanish, German, Dutch, French, and modern Greek.

BIOGRAPHICAL AND CRITICAL SOURCES:

PERIODICALS

American Journal of Philology, fall, 1995, Kenneth Reckford, review of *Frogs,* p. 488.

Antiquity, March, 1993, Timothy Taylor and Cyprian Broodbank, review of *Perceptions of the Ancient Greeks,* p. 160.

Christian Century, July 16, 1980.

Classical Philology, January, 1995, Simon Goldhill, review of *Frogs,* p. 86.

Greece & Rome, April, 1991, N. Hopkinson, "Aristophanes: Clouds, Acharnians, Lysistrata," p. 83.

National Review, December 19, 1994, John O'Sullivan, review of *Marginal Comment: A Memoir,* p. 8.

New Statesman, September 26, 1980, Julian Barnes, "Not the Nine O'Clock News . . . The Greeks," p. 34.

New Statesman & Society, December 9, 1994, Paul Cartledge, review of *Marginal Comment,* p. 39.

New York Times, November 28, 1994, John Darnton, review of *Marginal Comment,* p. A1.

New York Times Book Review, April 8, 1979.

Notes and Queries, March, 1989, M. L. West, review of *Greek and the Greeks: Collected Papers,* Volume 1: *Language, Poetry, Drama,* p. 88; March, 1990, Colin Leach, review of *The Greeks and Their Legacy: Collected Papers,* Volume 2: *Prose, Literature, History, Society, Transmission, Influence,* p. 69.

Past & Present, February, 2001, James Davidson, "Dover, Foucault, and Greek Homosexuality: Penetration and the Truth of Sex," p. 3.

Spectator, January 28, 1995, Hugh Lloyd-Jones, review of *Marginal Comment,* p. 30.

Times Higher Education Supplement, December 9, 1994, Valentine Cunningham, "Contract Terminated," p. 15; December 23, 1994, Max Beloff, review of *Marginal Comment,* p. 21.

Times Literary Supplement, April 3, 1981; January 13, 1995, Bernard Knox, review of *Marginal Comment,* p. 22; April 14, 1995, Erich Segal, review of *Frogs,* p. 3.

DOYLE, Debra 1952-
(Nicholas Adams, a joint pseudonym, Victor Appleton, a joint pseudonym, Martin Delrio, a joint pseudonym, Robyn Tallis, a joint pseudonym)

PERSONAL: Born 1952, in FL; married James D. Macdonald (Doyle's writing collaborator and a former navy officer), August 5, 1978; children: Katherine, Brendan, Peregrine, Alexander. *Education:* University of Pennsylvania, Ph.D.; also educated in Florida, Texas, and Arkansas.

ADDRESSES: *Home*—127 Main St., Colebrook, NH 03576. *Agent*—Russ Galen, Scovil Chichak Galen Literary Agency, 381 Park Avenue S., New York, NY 10016. *E-mail*—doylemacdonald@sff.net.

CAREER: Science-fiction and fantasy novelist. Computer Assisted Learning Center, teacher of fiction writing.

AWARDS, HONORS: Aslan Award for young adult literature, Mythopoeic Society, 1992, and Books for the Teen Age selection, New York Public Library, 1993, both for *Knight's Wyrd.*

WRITINGS:

"CIRCLE OF MAGIC" SERIES; WITH HUSBAND, JAMES D. MACDONALD

School of Wizardry, Troll (Mahwah, NJ), 1990.
Tournament and Tower, Troll (Mahwah, NJ), 1990.
City by the Sea, Troll (Mahwah, NJ), 1990.
The Prince's Players, Troll (Mahwah, NJ), 1990.
The Prisoners of Bell Castle, Troll (Mahwah, NJ), 1990.
The High King's Daughter, Troll (Mahwah, NJ), 1990.

"MAGEWORLDS" SERIES; WITH JAMES D. MACDONALD

The Price of the Stars, Tor (New York, NY), 1992.
Starpilot's Grave, Tor (New York, NY), 1993.
By Honor Betray'd, Tor (New York, NY), 1994.
The Gathering Flame, Tor (New York, NY), 1995.
The Long Hunt, Tor (New York, NY), 1996.
The Stars Asunder, Tor (New York, NY), 1999.
A Working of Stars, Tor (New York, NY), 2002.

"BAD BLOOD" SERIES; WITH JAMES D. MACDONALD

Bad Blood, Berkley (New York, NY), 1993.
Hunters' Moon, Berkley (New York, NY), 1994.
Judgment Night, Berkley (New York, NY), 1995.

OTHER NOVELS; WITH JAMES D. MACDONALD

Timecrime, Inc. (Robert Silverberg's "Time Tours" #3), Harper (New York, NY), 1991.
Night of the Living Rat (Daniel Pinkwater's "Melvinge of the Megaverse" #2), Ace (New York, NY), 1992.
Knight's Wyrd, Harcourt (New York, NY), 1992.
Groogleman, Harcourt (New York, NY), 1996.
Requiem for Boone (Gene Roddenberry's "Earth—Final Conflict" #3), Tor (New York, NY), 2000.

AS ROBYN TALLIS; WITH JAMES D. MACDONALD

Night of Ghosts and Lightning (Planet Builders #2), Ivy (New York, NY), 1989.
Zero-Sum Games (Planet Builders #5), Ivy (New York, NY), 1989.

AS NICHOLAS ADAMS; WITH JAMES D. MACDONALD

Pep Rally (Horror High #7), Harper (New York, NY), 1991.

AS VICTOR APPLETON; WITH JAMES D. MACDONALD

Monster Machine (Tom Swift #5), Archway Paperback, Pocket Books (New York, NY), 1991.
Aquatech Warriors (Tom Swift #6), Archway Paperback, Pocket Books (New York, NY), 1991.

AS MARTIN DELRIO; WITH JAMES D. MACDONALD

Mortal Kombat (movie novelizations: adult and young adult versions), Tor (New York, NY), 1995.
Spider-Man Super-Thriller: Midnight Justice, Byron Preiss Multimedia/Pocket Books (New York, NY), 1996.

Spider-Man Super-Thriller: Global War, Byron Press Multimedia/Pocket Books (New York, NY), 1996.

Prince Valiant (movie novelization), Avon (New York, NY), 1997.

Contributor, with James D. Macdonald, of short stories to anthologies, including "Bad Blood" in *Werewolves,* edited by Yolen & Greenberg, Harper Junior Books (New York, NY), 1988; "Nobody Has to Know" in *Vampires,* edited by Yolen & Greenberg, HarperCollins (New York, NY), 1991; "The Last Real New Yorker in the World" in *Newer York,* edited by Lawrence Watt-Evans, Roc (New York, NY), 1991; "Now and in the Hour of Our Death" in *Alternate Kennedys,* edited by Mike Resnick and Martin Greenberg, editors, Tor (New York, NY), 1992; "Uncle Joshua and the Grooglemen" in *Bruce Coville's Book of Monsters,* edited by Bruce Coville, Scholastic (New York, NY), 1993; "Why They Call It That" in *Swashbuckling Editor Stories,* edited by John Betancourt, Wildside Press, 1993; "The Queen's Mirror" in *A Wizard's Dozen,* edited by Michael Stearns, Harcourt (San Diego, CA), 1995; "Crossover" in *A Starfarer's Dozen,* edited by Michael Stearns, Harcourt (San Diego, CA), 1995; "Witch Garden" in *Witch Fantastic,* edited by Mike Resnick and Martin Greenberg, DAW (New York, NY), 1995; "Holly and Ivy" in *Camelot,* edited by Jane Yolen, Philomel (New York, NY), 1995; "Please to See the King" in *The Book of Kings,* edited by Richard Gilliam and Martin Greenberg, Roc (New York, NY), 1995; "Stealing God" in *Tales of the Knights Templar,* edited by Katherine Kurtz, Warner (New York, NY), 1995; "Ecdysis" in *Otherwere,* edited by Laura Anne Gilman and Keith R. A. DeCandido, Berkley/Ace (New York, NY), 1996; "Up the Airy Mountain" in *A Nightmare's Dozen,* edited by Michael Stearns, Harcourt (San Diego, CA), 1996; "Jenny Nettles" in *Bruce Coville's Book of Spine Tinglers,* edited by Bruce Coville, Scholastic (New York, NY), 1996; "Block G-18" in *High-Tech Wars #2,* edited by Jerry Pournelle and John F. Carr.

Contributor of "The Last God of Dura Europus," parts I and II, to the comic book *Timewalker #10,* Valiant Comics, April, 1995, and of "We Who Are about to Die" to the comic book *Timewalker #15,* Valiant Comics, June, 1995.

WORK IN PROGRESS: The novel *City of Dreadful Night,* Tor (New York, NY); untitled "Mageworlds" novel number 8.

SIDELIGHTS: Debra Doyle, along with her husband and coauthor James D. Macdonald, issued six fantasy novels in one series in one year's time. In 1990 their "Circle of Magic" series, about a young boy wizard, predated J. K. Rowling's "Harry Potter" books by nearly a decade. (The series was reissued in 2000, likely to capitalize on the "Potter" craze.) "Circle of Magic" were the first novels the duo published under their own names; previously, they had published a pair under the pseudonym Robyn Tallis for Ivy's "Planet Builders" series.

Doyle grew up in Florida, then studied in other locales, eventually receiving a doctorate in Old English literature from the University of Pennsylvania. While living and studying in Philadelphia, she met Macdonald, who was then serving with the Navy. (Over fifteen years MacDonald was promoted from enlisted man to officer.) In the intervening years, the pair traveled to Virginia, California, and Panama, acquiring "various children, cats and computers" along the way, Doyle once commented. The couple and their four children eventually settled in a rambling nineteenth-century Victorian house in northern New Hampshire, where the authors also collaborate equally in the chopping of firewood.

According to an interview with *Amazon.com,* Macdonald writes the first drafts, then gives them to Doyle for revising and stylistic improving. "I have final say on the plot and characters, she has final say on the words and descriptions," Macdonald elaborated. This working arrangement has produced dozens of stories and novels for adults, young adults, and children, under their authors' own and pen names. Some works have been entries in fantasy or science-fiction series; others have been novelizations of the computer game-based movie *Mortal Kombat* and the comic-book-based movie *Prince Valiant,* as well as "Spiderman" comic book stories; there have even been a couple of "Tom Swift" adventure novels. The pair have also written novels within series created by other writers, namely Robert Silverberg and Daniel Pinkwater.

The duo's "Mageworlds" series, begun in 1992, combines "magic, space opera and time travel," according to a *Publishers Weekly* critic who reviewed the 1999 entry, *The Stars Asunder.* The worlds of the Mage are star systems linked by magic. Those Mage who have trained in the Way are allowed access to the colonization of new worlds; along the way, brutal Magewars ensue. In *The Stars Asunder,* the authors go back in Mage history to explain "the origins of the Magewars and the apprenticeship and growth" of series hero 'Rehke, noted the *Publishers Weekly* contributor. A *Working of Stars* covers "a rousing attempt to reunite an entire galaxy" that's been held hostage by sinister forces. Leading the charge is Arekhon, "exiled from his native Eraasian system to the far side of the Gap Between," as *Booklist*'s Roland Green described it. A *Publishers Weekly* reviewer noted that for readers uninitiated in the ways of the Mage, "arriving in the middle of this complicated series can be daunting." However, added the reviewer, Doyle and Macdonald offer "plenty of action in this rapid-fire blend of sorcery and [science fiction]."

In 2000 Doyle and Macdonald contributed a book to the *Star Trek*-inspired "Earth—The Final Conflict" series. *A Requiem for Boone* centers on Major Will Boone, who finds himself caught up in the imminent arrival on Earth of the alien Taelons. Boone and his wife, computer wizard Kate, use strategy and technology to deal with the greater threat, an alien-resistance organization hoping to capitalize on alien-induced panic to take over the globe. "There are wheels within wheels and conspiracies within conspiracies" in this novel, remarked a *Publishers Weekly* writer. Green, in another *Booklist* piece, praised *A Requiem for Boone* as a "sound technothriller that rises above being just that, thanks to skillful characterization."

The duo wrote two notable novels unconnected to any series. *Knight's Wyrd,* published in 1992, is a knights-in-armor fantasy involving magic. In it, young Will Odosson must find his wyrd—his destiny. When he finds out that his destiny is doom, he travels bravely to meet it, with complex and adventurous results. The New York Public Library put this novel on its 1993 Books for the Teen Age list, and the novel won the Mythopoeic Fantasy Award for children's literature in 1992; the book also received enthusiastic praise from *Horn Book* and *School Library Journal* reviewers.

The team's other important solo novel was the 1996 production *Googleman,* which takes place in a quasi-medieval culture that has developed after an unspecified technological collapse of contemporary civilization. Young hero Dan Henchard possesses weller's blood, a kind of inherited immunity and healing ability. After Dan heals a stranger named Joshua, the two, along with local healer Leezie, travel to a nearby village to do more healing and find the environment terrorized by grooglemen. The nature of the mysterious grooglemen, and of the culture's past, is hinted at in interchapters. Reviewing the novel for *School Library Journal,* Susan L. Rogers called it a "successful" example of its genre: "Dan and Joshua quickly become sympathetic and interesting characters on a desperate journey through a foreboding landscape." Janice M. Del Negro, a reviewer for the *Bulletin of the Center for Children's Books,* admired the writing for conveying the sensory qualities of the setting and felt that Dan was "a believable adolescent in a grimly dangerous situation." Commending the way in which the authors created a vivid, convincing alternate culture in a few pages, Del Negro stated, "This intriguing novel suggests more than it reveals and could provoke some thoughtful group discussion."

BIOGRAPHICAL AND CRITICAL SOURCES:

PERIODICALS

Analog Science Fiction & Fact, February, 1999, Tom Easton, review of *The Stars Asunder,* p. 132; October, 2002, Tom Easton, review of *A Working of Stars,* p. 131.

Booklist, August, 2000, Roland Green, review of *Requiem for Boone,* p. 2124; April 15, 2002, Roland Green, review of *A Working of Stars,* p. 1387.

Bulletin of the Center for Children's Books, December, 1996, Janice M. Del Negro, review of *Googleman,* p. 132.

Kirkus Reviews, April 1, 1999, review of *The Stars Asunder,* p. 493; March 1, 2002, review of *A Working of Stars,* p. 297.

Library Journal, June 15, 1999, Jackie Cassada, review of *The Stars Asunder,* p. 112; April 15, 2002, Jackie Cassada, review of *A Working of Stars,* p. 127.

Publishers Weekly, May 31, 1999, review of *The Stars Asunder,* p. 72; August 7, 2000, review of *Requiem for Boone,* p. 80; March 11, 2002, review of *A Working of Stars,* p. 56.

Quill & Quire, April, 1999, review of *Googleman,* p. 39.

School Library Journal, December, 1996, Susan L. Rogers, review of *Googleman,* pp. 120-121.

ONLINE

Amazon.com, http://www.amazon.com/ (November 20, 1997), interview with James D. Macdonald.

SFF Net, http://www.sff.net/ (November 20, 1997), review of *Knight's Wyrd.*

DUBERMAN, Martin (Bauml) 1930-

PERSONAL: Born August 6, 1930, in New York, NY; son of Joseph M. (a dress manufacturer) and Josephine (Bauml) Duberman. *Education:* Yale University, B.A., 1952; Harvard University, M.A., 1953, Ph.D., 1957.

ADDRESSES: Home—475 W. 22nd St., New York, NY 10011. *Office*—Department of History, Herbert H. Lehman College of the City University of New York, Bronx, NY 10468-1589.

CAREER: Harvard University, Cambridge, MA, tutor, 1955-57; Yale University, New Haven, CT, instructor, 1957-61, assistant professor, 1961-62; Princeton University, Princeton, NJ, Bicentennial Preceptor, 1962-65, McCosh faculty fellow, 1963-64, associate professor, beginning 1965, became professor of history; Herbert H. Lehman College of the City University of New York, Bronx, distinguished professor of history, beginning 1971, and founder of Center for Lesbian and Gay Studies. Member of board of directors of Lambda Foundation, National Gay Task Force, Lion Theater Group, and Glines Theater; Actors' Studio, member. Historical advisor, *Utopian Communities in America* film project, *Sesame Street* television series on late nineteenth-century New York, and Labor History Series for the National Endowment for the Humanities. Organizer of Redress Conference on Amnesty, 1975.

MEMBER: Organization of American Historians, American Historical Association, Gay Academic Union, New Dramatists, Southern Historical Association.

AWARDS, HONORS: Morse fellow, Yale University, 1961-62; American Council of Learned Societies grant, 1963; Bancroft Prize, Columbia University, 1963, for *Charles Francis Adams, 1807-1886;* Vernon Rice Drama Desk Award, 1963-64, for *In White America;* National Book Award nomination, 1966, for *James Russell Lowell;* Rockefeller Foundation, grant, 1967-68, fellowship, 1976; National Academy of Arts and Letters Award for contributions to literature, 1971; American Academy Award, 1971; Manhattan Borough Presidents' gold medal, 1988; George Freedley Prize, 1990; Lambda Book Award, 1990; Myer Award, 1990.

WRITINGS:

NONFICTION

Charles Francis Adams, 1807-1886, Houghton Mifflin (Boston, MA), 1961.

(Editor and contributor) *The Antislavery Vanguard: New Essays on the Abolitionists,* Princeton University Press (Princeton, NJ), 1965.

James Russell Lowell, Houghton Mifflin (Boston, MA), 1966.

About Time: Exploring the Gay Past, Sea Horse Press (New York, NY), 1968, revised edition, Dutton (New York, NY), 1992.

The Uncompleted Past: Collected Essays, 1961-1969, Random House (New York, NY), 1969.

Black Mountain: An Exploration in Community, Dutton (New York, NY), 1972.

Black Power and American Radical Tradition (sound recording), W. W. Norton (New York, NY), 1974.

(Coauthor) *Sociology: Focus on Society,* Scott, Foresman (Glenview, IL), 1979.

Paul Robeson, Knopf (New York, NY), 1989.

(Editor, with Martha Vicinus and George Chauncey, Jr.) *Hidden from History: Reclaiming the Gay and Lesbian Past,* New American Library (New York, NY), 1989.

Cures: A Gay Man's Odyssey, Dutton (New York, NY), 1991.

Stonewall, Dutton (New York, NY), 1993.

Midlife Queer: Autobiography of a Decade, 1971-1981, Scribner (New York, NY), 1996.

(Editor) *Queer Representations: Reading Lives, Reading Cultures; A Center for Lesbian and Gay Studies Book,* New York University Press (New York, NY), 1997.

(Editor) *A Queer World: The Center for Lesbian and Gay Studies Reader,* New York University Press (New York, NY), 1997.

(Editor) *Beyond Gay or Straight: Understanding Sexual Orientation by Jan Clausen,* Chelsea House Publishers (New York, NY), 1997.

Left Out: The Politics of Exclusion; Essays, 1964-1999, Basic Books (New York, NY), 1999, expanded edition published as *Left Out: The Politics of Exclusion; Essays, 1964-2002,* South End Press (Boston, MA), 2002.

Author of introduction to *The Civil Rights Reader,* edited by Leon Friedman, Walker (New York, NY), 1967. General editor of "Issues in Lesbian and Gay

Life" and "Lives of Notable Gay Men and Lesbians" series for Chelsea House Publishers (New York, NY). Also author of television scripts *The Deed,* 1969; *Mother Earth: The Life of Emma Goldman,* 1971; and (with Ossie Davis) *Twelve Angry Men.* Contributor to books, including *Democracy and the Student Left,* Little, Brown (Boston, MA), 1968; *A Radical Reader,* Harper (New York, NY), 1970; and *Readings in Human Sexuality,* Harper (New York, NY), 1976. Drama critic, *Show* and *Partisan Review.* Contributor of articles and essays to *Win, New York Times, Village Voice, New Republic, Harper's,* and other publications. Member of editorial board, *Signs.*

PLAYS

In White America (first produced off-Broadway, 1963), Houghton Mifflin (Boston, MA), 1964.
Metaphors, first produced off-Broadway, at Cafe Au Go Go, 1968.
Groups, first produced in New York, NY, 1968.
The Colonial Dudes, first produced in New York, NY, at Actors Studio, 1969.
The Memory Bank (contains one-act plays *The Recorder* and *The Electric Map;* first produced in New York, NY, at Gate Theater, 1970), Dial (New York, NY), 1970.
Payments, first produced in New York, NY, 1971.
(Adaptor) Joseph Martinez Kookoolis and Scott Fagan, *Soon,* first produced in New York, NY, at Ritz Hotel, 1971.
Dudes, first produced in New York, NY, 1972.
Inner Limits, first produced in New York, NY, at Manhattan Theater Club, 1972.
Elagabalus, first produced in New York, NY, 1973.
Male Armor: Selected Plays, 1968-1974 (contains *Metaphors, The Colonial Dudes, The Recorder, The Guttman Ordinary Scale, Payments, The Electric Map,* and *Elagabalus*), Dutton (New York, NY), 1975.
Visions of Kerouac (first produced in New York, NY, at New Dramatists Theater, 1976), Little, Brown (Boston, MA), 1977.
Mother Earth: An Epic Drama of Emma Goldman's Life, St. Martin's Press (New York, NY), 1991.

Work appears in anthologies, including *The Best Short Plays of 1970,* Chilton Book Co. (Radnor, PA), 1970; and *The Best Short Plays of 1972,* Chilton Book Co. (Radnor, PA), 1972

ADAPTATIONS: In White America was filmed for television in 1970.

SIDELIGHTS: In a career spanning more than thirty years, Martin Duberman has produced influential, thought-provoking plays, essays, biographies, memoirs, and works of social history. In the 1970s, Duberman concentrated his writing talents primarily on plays, but over the next two decades he turned his attention to matters of concern to the gay community and became an eminent chronicler of the gay experience and movement in America.

"There are times," Duberman has stated, "when I have trouble deciding which I am, historian or playwright." An example of Duberman's merging of interests is found in his play *In White America,* which depicts historical events in dramatic form. It is based upon letters, diaries, court records, and other historical documents dealing with black slavery in America. Thomas B. Markus in *Contemporary Dramatists* believed that *In White America* "will prove more significant as an event of cultural history than as either an innovation in theatrical form or the first work in the career of a significant playwright." *In White America* was a success with contemporary audiences, enjoying a long run off-Broadway.

In his play *The Recorder,* Duberman again merges his two interests, exploring the relationship between history and the historian. The play concerns a young historian interviewing an old man for a book he is writing. During the course of the interview, the historian's own ideas and opinions, as well as those of the man he interviews, distort historical truth until the line between history and fiction becomes blurred and the writing of history seems a kind of literature.

This idea is again explored by Duberman in his book *Black Mountain,* a history of the experimental Black Mountain College. Duberman wrote the book in a subjective manner, allowing his own emotions and opinions to be expressed.

In 1993, Duberman published *Stonewall,* a groundbreaking work exploring the rise of the gay rights movement of the late 1960s. Duberman tells of the events preceding and following the night in June of 1969 when patrons at the Stonewall Inn, a drag queen bar in Manhattan, finally rebelled against continual police harassment. The ensuing riots touched off what Duberman calls a "seismic shift" in the consciousness of gays and lesbians. But Duberman sees the Stonewall riots as the natural culmination of two decades of social change, and he places the chapter containing the Stonewall riot toward the end of the book. Instead, he chooses to tell about the moment in history that he believes to be "*the* emblematic event in modern gay and lesbian history" through the life histories of six gay men and women whose collective experiences illuminate what it was like to be gay in America. Duberman explains that he chose this narrative strategy to "embrace precisely what most contemporary historians have discarded: the ancient, essential enterprise of *telling human stories.*" Wrote Alice Echolls in the *Nation,* "This Duberman does masterfully." Only one of the six narrators of *Stonewall* was present in the bar that evening, but all of them figure in the beginnings of the gay liberation movement. Echolls pointed out that this "powerful and compelling book" has an important function: it is one of the few to demand a place for the lesbian and gay movement in social and political histories of the 1960s.

Duberman's first memoir, *Cures: A Gay Man's Odyssey,* traces his life from childhood to the early 1970s. He followed up this effort with *Midlife Queer: Autobiography of a Decade, 1971-1981,* a memoir that chronicles his experiences through the 1970s, including his involvement with gay rights groups and his work as a writer. A *Publishers Weekly* reviewer found *Midlife Queer* a "searching, refreshingly optimistic memoir," but other reviewers criticized the book for providing endless detail of the New York gay activist scene and for a detached writing style and stance. However, a *Library Journal* critic pointed out that "this poignant memoir's lapses into self-indulgence are offset by the author's sincere attempts to understand his place in a pivotal history period of queer history." The *Publishers Weekly* reviewer also noted that this "relentless self-scrutiny reflects a continual search for ways to link the personal with the political."

BIOGRAPHICAL AND CRITICAL SOURCES:

BOOKS

Contemporary Dramatists, 5th edition, St. James Press (Detroit, MI), 1993.

Contemporary Literary Criticism, Volume 8, Thomson Gale (Detroit, MI), 1978.

Duberman, Martin, *Cures: A Gay Man's Odyssey,* Dutton (New York, NY), 1991.

Duberman, Martin, *Midlife Queer: Autobiography of a Decade, 1971-1981,* Scribner (New York, NY), 1996.

Simon, John, *Uneasy Stages: A Chronicle of the New York Theater, 1963-1973,* Random House (New York, NY), 1975.

PERIODICALS

Advocate, July 2, 1991, p. 76; May 4, 1993, p. 73; May 14, 1996, p. 70.

America, December 18, 1971.

American Historical Review, January, 1966; April, 1975.

Antioch Review, winter, 1970.

Booklist, May 1, 1993, p. 1552.

Books and Bookmen, June, 1974.

Book Week, August 22, 1965.

Christian Century, April 28, 1965.

Christian Science Monitor, February 2, 1967.

Commentary, May, 1989, p. 70.

Economist, March 11, 1989, p. 92.

Journal of American History, December, 1965; December, 1993, p. 1158.

Lambda Book Report, May, 1993, p. 16; July, 1994, p. 41.

Library Journal, February 15, 1991, p. 202; December, 1986, p. 126; February 15, 1991, p. 202; June 15, 1991, p. 76; March 15, 1993, p. 78; March 15, 1996, review of *Midlife Queer,* p. 76.

Los Angeles Times Book Review, January 27, 1991, p. 10; April 28, 1991, p. 6; June 27, 1993, pp. 2, 8.

Multicultural Review, April, 1992, p. 83; September, 1993, p. 50.

Nation, April 3, 1967; December 11, 1972; March 20, 1989, p. 383; June 10, 1991, p. 775; July 15, 1991, p. 85; August 23, 1993, Alice Echolls, review of *Stonewall,* p. 22; July 15, 1996, p. 33.

National Review, May 19, 1989, p. 55.

New England Quarterly, June, 1967.

New Leader, February 12, 1970; February 20, 1989, p. 17.

New Republic, November 4, 1972; December 20, 1993, pp. 17-35.

New Statesman, April 26, 1974.

Newsweek, January 2, 1967; November 27, 1972.

New York, February 2, 1970.

New York Review, March 27, 2003, Andrew Hacker, review of *Left Out: The Politics of Exclusion; Essays, 1964-2002,* pp. 14-16.
New York Review of Books, November 16, 1972; April 27, 1989, p. 3.
New York Times, June 1, 1969; October 28, 1969; December 15, 1969; November 7, 1972.
New York Times Book Review, December 25, 1966; April 21, 1991, p. 9; June 27, 1993, p. 15; May 19, 1996, p. 15.
Observer, March 3, 1991, p. 58.
Partisan Review, summer, 1967.
Progressive, May, 1970.
Publishers Weekly, October 31, 1986, p. 53; February 15, 1991, p. 79; March 15, 1993, p. 78; February 19, 1996, review of *Midlife Queer,* p. 193.
Quill & Quire, April, 1989, p. 23.
Saturday Review, May 22, 1965; January 3, 1970.
Science and Society, fall, 1965.
Show Business, January 17, 1970.
Smith, October, 1989, p. 221.
South Atlantic Quarterly, autumn, 1966.
Spectator, April 22, 1989, p. 30.
Time, March 13, 1989, p. 79.
Times Literary Supplement, November 25, 1965; May 12, 1989, p. 507.
Tribune Books (Chicago, IL), February 12, 1989, p. 1.
USA Today, February 17, 1989, p. D7; March 14, 1989, p. D6.
Variety, January 21, 1970; September 13, 1989, p. 95.
Village Voice, December 14, 1972; December 20, 1976; January 25, 1994, p. 81.
Wall Street Journal, April 6, 1989, p. A16.
Washington Post Book World, November 19, 1972; December 10, 1989, p. 5; June 5, 1994, p. 16.
World and I, July, 1989, p. 409.
World Journal Tribune, December 5, 1966.*

* * *

DUNBAR, Joyce 1944-

PERSONAL: Born January 6, 1944, in Scunthorpe, England; daughter of Russell (a steel worker) and Marjorie (a homemaker; maiden name, Reed) Miles; married James Dunbar-Brunton (an illustrator), January 27, 1972 (divorced, 2004); children: Ben, Polly. *Education:* Goldsmiths College, London University, B.A. (with honors). *Politics:* Labour. *Hobbies and other interests:* Walking, theatre, art, traveling, people.

ADDRESSES: Agent—Hilary Delamere, The Agency, 24 Pottery Lane, Holland Park, London WII 4LZ, England.

CAREER: Writer. English teacher, 1968-89, the last ten years in the drama department at the college at Stratford-on-Avon; teacher of creative writing, visitor to schools and literature festivals; member of judging panel for Mother Goose Award, 1996-1999; facilitator in creative writing on Greek Island of Skyros, 1998, 2000-2004.

MEMBER: Society of Authors, Norfolk Contemporary Art Society, East Anglian Society of Authors, International Board on Books for Young People.

AWARDS, HONORS: Guardian Children's Fiction Award runner-up, 1985, for *Mundo and the Weather-Child; A Bun for Barney* was shortlisted for *Parents'* Best Books for Babies Award, 1987; *This Is the Star* was named a *Publishers Weekly* Best Book, 1996, and a Pick of the Lists by the American Booksellers Association; *Before I Go to Sleep* was named an Editor's Choice by *Bookseller,* 1998, and *Child Education* Best Book, 1999.

WRITINGS:

Jugg, illustrated by James Dunbar, Scolar Press (England), 1980.
The Magic Rose Bough, illustrated by James Dunbar, Hodder & Stoughton (London, England), 1984.
Mundo and the Weather-Child, Heinemann (London, England), 1985, Dell (New York, NY), 1993.
A Bun for Barney, illustrated by Emilie Boon, Orchard Books (New York), 1987.
Software Superslug, illustrated by James Dunbar, Macdonald (London, England), 1987.
The Raggy Taggy Toys, illustrated by P. J. Lynch, Barron's (New York, NY), 1988.
Tomatoes and Potatoes, illustrated by Lynn Breeze, Ginn (London, England), 1988.
Billy and the Brolly Boy, illustrated by Nick Ward, Ginn (London, England), 1988.
Mouse Mad Madeline, illustrated by James Dunbar, Hamish Hamilton (London England), 1988.
One Frosty Friday Morning, illustrated by John Dyke, Ginn (London, England), 1989.

Joanna and the Bean-Bag Beastie, illustrated by Francis Blake, Ginn (London, England), 1989.

Software Superslug and the Great Computer Stupor, illustrated by James Dunbar, Simon & Schuster (New York, NY), 1989.

Ollie Oddbin's Skylark, illustrated by James Dunbar, Heinemann (London, England), 1989.

I Wish I Liked Rice Pudding, illustrated by Carol Thompson, Simon & Schuster (New York, NY), 1989.

Software Superslug and the Nutty Novelty Knitting, illustrated by James Dunbar, Simon & Schuster (New York, NY), 1990.

Ten Little Mice, illustrated by Maria Majewska, Harcourt Brace (San Diego, CA), 1990, 1999.

Five Mice and the Moon, illustrated by James Mayhew, Orchard Books (New York, NY), 1990.

The Scarecrow, illustrated by James Dunbar, Collins Educational (London, England), 1991.

Giant Jim and Tiny Tim, illustrated by James Dunbar, Collins Educational (London, England), 1991.

I Want a Blue Banana, illustrated by James Dunbar, Houghton Mifflin (Boston, MA), 1991.

Why Is the Sky Up?, illustrated by James Dunbar, Houghton Mifflin (Boston, MA), 1991.

Lollopy, illustrated by Susan Varley, Macmillan (New York, NY), 1991.

Four Fierce Kittens, illustrated by Jakki Wood, Orchard Books (New York, NY), 1991.

Can Do, illustrated by Carol Thompson, Simon & Schuster (New York, NY), 1992.

Mouse and Mole, illustrated by James Mayhew, Doubleday (London, England), 1993.

Mouse and Mole Have a Party, illustrated by James Mayhew, Doubleday (London, England), 1993.

Seven Sillies, illustrated by Chris Downing, Anderson Press (London, England), 1993.

The Read-Aloud Story Book, illustrated by Colin and Moira Maclean, Kingfisher (New York, NY), 1993.

The Spring Rabbit, illustrated by Susan Varley, Anderson Press (London, England), 1993, Artists and Writers Guild Books (New York, NY), 1994.

The Wishing Fish Tree, Ginn (London, England), 1994.

Brown Bear, Snow Bear, Candlewick Press (Cambridge, MA), 1994.

Little Eight John, illustrated by Rhian Nest-James, Ginn (London, England), 1994.

Doodlecloud, illustrated by James Dunbar, Longman (London, England), 1994, Sundance (Littleton, MA), 1997.

Doodledragon, illustrated by James Dunbar, Longman (London, England), 1994, Sundance (Littleton, MA), 1997.

Doodlemaze, illustrated by James Dunbar, Longman (London, England), 1994, Sundance (Littleton, MA), 1997.

Doodling Daniel, illustrated by James Dunbar, Longman (London, England), 1994, Sundance (Littleton, MA), 1997.

Oops-a-Daisy: And Other Tales for Toddlers, Candlewick Press (Cambridge, MA), 1995.

Happy Days for Mouse and Mole, illustrated by James Mayhew, Picture Corgi (London, England), 1996.

A Very Special Mouse and Mole, illustrated by James Mayhew, Picture Corgi (London, England), 1996.

Indigo and the Whale, illustrated by Geoffrey Patterson, BridgeWater Books (Mahwah, NJ), 1996.

This Is the Star, illustrated by Gary Blythe, Harcourt Brace (San Diego, CA), 1996.

Hansel and Gretel, illustrated by Ian Penney, Hove (England), 1997.

The Selfish Snail, illustrated by Hannah Giffard, Hamish Hamilton (London, England), 1997.

If You Want to Be a Cat, illustrated by Allan Curless, Hove (England), 1997.

Tell Me Something Happy before I Go to Sleep, illustrated by Debi Gliori, Harcourt Brace (San Diego, CA), 1998.

Baby Bird, illustrated by Russell Ayto, Candlewick Press (Cambridge, MA), 1998.

Pomegranate Seeds, Candlewick Press (Cambridge, MA), 1998.

The Secret Friend, illustrated by Helen Craig, Candlewick Press (Cambridge, MA), 1998.

Gander's Pond, illustrated by Helen Craig, Candlewick Press (Cambridge, MA), 1999.

Tutti Fruitti, illustrated by Helen Craig, Candlewick Press (Cambridge, MA), 1999.

Panda's New Toy, illustrated by Helen Craig, Candlewick Press (Cambridge, MA), 1999.

The Bowl of Fruit, illustrated by Helen Craig, Candlewick Press (Cambridge, MA), 1999.

The Pig Who Wished, illustrated by Selina Young, DK Publishers (New York, NY), 1999.

Eggday, illustrated by Jane Cabrera, Holiday House (New York, NY), 1999.

The Sand Children, illustrated by Mark Edwards, Crocodile Books (New York, NY), 1999.

The Glass Garden, illustrated by Fiona French, F. Lincoln (London, England), 1999.

The Very Small, illustrated by Debi Gliori, Harcourt Brace (San Diego, CA), 2000.

The Ups and Downs of Mouse and Mole, Corgi Pups (London, England), 2000.

Hip-Dip-Dip with Mouse and Mole, Corgi Pups (London, England), 2000.

(Editor) *The Kingfisher Read-Aloud Storybook,* illustrated by Colin and Moira MacLean, Kingfisher (New York, NY), 2000.

Tell Me What It's Like to Be Big, illustrated by Debi Gliori, Harcourt Brace (San Diego, CA), 2001.

Magic Lemonade, illustrated by Jan McCafferty, Crabtree Publishing (New York, NY), 2002.

A Chick Called Saturday, illustrated by Brita Granstrom, Eerdmans Books for Young Readers (Grand Rapids, MI), 2003.

The Railway Angel, Corgi Pups (London, England), 2003.

The Love-Me Bird, illustrated by Sophie Fatus, Orchard Books (New York, NY), 2004.

Boo to the Who in the Dark, illustrated by Sarah Massini, Scholastic, (New York, NY), 2004.

Shoe Baby, illustrated by Polly Dunbar, Candlewick Press (Cambridge, MA), 2005.

Also author of many stories for children's educational series; contributor of stories to anthologies, including *Tobie and the Face Merchant,* edited by Julia Eccleshare, Collins, 1991; *The Trick of the Tale,* edited by Eccleshare, Viking, 1991; *Bedtime Stories for the Very Young,* edited by Sally Grindley, Kingfisher, 1991; and *Fairy Tales,* edited by Sally Grindley, Little, Brown, 1993. Stories have been broadcast on the BBC Radio show *Listening Corner,* including "Jim Sparrow," 1982, "Sally and the Magic Rattle," 1983, "Doomuch and Doolittle," 1983, and "Shapes and Sounds," 1983 and 1984.

ADAPTATIONS: A Bun for Barney was adapted as an interactive video game by the Multi-Media Corporation of the BBC, 1990, and as a musical play performed by the Royal Shakespeare Company for their children's Christmas Pantomime, 1988 and 1989; *Software Superslug* was adapted into a musical play performed at the Angel Road School, Norwich, England, 1990.

SIDELIGHTS: Children's author Joyce Dunbar's impressive output has pleased children on both sides of the Atlantic for many years, beginning in the early 1980s. Dunbar's books are written for children as young as toddler age to those in the early grades, and her understanding of this age group has been praised by reviewers, including the *Guardian*'s Lillian French, who wrote of the pink-paged *Tutti Fruitti* that everything about it "is a total delight."

French also reviewed *Tell Me Something Happy before I Go to Sleep,* about a small rabbit named Willa, who wears chicken slippers, and her loving big brother, Willoughby. French noted that this book is special because big brothers often get a bad rap. She praised Dunbar for being one of the best children's writers and added that this book "is a wonderful example of her sensitivity, lyrical style, and gentle humour."

School Library Journal's Alison Kastner, who evaluated *Tell Me What It's Like to Be Big,* said that Dunbar "has captured exactly how children think in this loving dialogue between two siblings." In this story, Willa is frustrated by her inability to perform tasks for which she is too small, like reach the breakfast table. She wakes Willoughby, and what follows is his explanation to her of what it is like to be big. The story is filled with colorful patterns on the tablecloth, wallpaper, and the quilt that covers their mother's bed, and under which all three snuggle by the end of the story.

A Chick Called Saturday is about the seventh chick that hatches from a clutch of eggs, and who seems to possess enough inquisitiveness for all of them. He bothers his mother with questions about the other barnyard birds and tries to emulate them, soon learning that he can't swim like a duck or honk like a goose. His problem is solved when he learns that he will grow to become like the beautiful, crowing rooster. A *Kirkus Reviews* contributor noted that hens don't lay multi-colored eggs and that young cockerels are not born with combs, but added that "this gentle life lesson of pursuing one's potential without wishing for what cannot be is well-organized." A *Publishers Weekly* contributor called the story a "sunny-hued picture book about self-discovery and acceptance," but felt that "Mother Hen's admonitions to conform seem overdone."

A narcissistic bird dressed in pink is looking for love in *The Love-Me Bird,* and follows a series of suggestions from Shut-Eye, the owl she is keeping awake with her pleadings. After telling her to act helpless, then play hard-to-get, he finally tells her to change her call from "love me" to "love you," which brings an immediate response from a possible suitor. *Booklist*'s Connie Fletcher wrote that the colorful illustrations "perfectly match this whimsical tale with wisdom at its heart." A *Publishers Weekly* writer felt that children "may well absorb this worthwhile message about the pitfalls of self-absorption and the rewards of focusing on the needs of others."

Joyce Dunbar once commented: "I'd been writing for some time before a strange combination of circumstances turned me into a writer for children: First, I found myself married to an illustrator. A barrister by training, he used to draw a character called Jugg who was his alter ego. I liked this character so much that I thought he should have a story. *Jugg* became our first book. Secondly, my children. Writing children's stories was a way of entering into and sharing their world. Third, desperation. The house was falling down round my ears and I needed to do something to cheer myself up.

"The great thing about writing is that it makes almost every experience worthwhile because you can make a story out of it. The other great thing is that you can live two lives at once: one in the so-called 'real' world (which is never quite what we ordered), and one inside your head, which you can order in whatever way you like. This inner world is as full of possibilities as your imagination can make it, and gives one a wonderful excuse for daydreaming.

"I like to write in the mornings, and do something physical in the afternoons, like gardening. Even then I'm working, revising and developing in my head. A lot of a writer's work goes on in the subconscious, even while they are sleeping and dreaming. When it is 'real' writing and not what I call 'made-up,' it seems a very mysterious process. Like lots of things in life, it is sometimes painful, sometimes exhilarating.

"My favourite contemporary children's authors are Maurice Sendak, Arnold Lobel, and Russell Hoban. Two of them are also illustrators. They all write books that are just as interesting to adults as to children, and they all ask the same fundamental questions that children, relative newcomers in the world, also ask themselves: Goodness! The world! How did it get here and how did I come to be in it?

"I used to be a teacher and loved it, but deafness put an end to that career. I'm glad in a way, because it gave me a very strong motive to survive the early difficult stages of writing, when you are very unsure of yourself, and can't believe that anyone will want to read what you write, never mind publish it!"

BIOGRAPHICAL AND CRITICAL SOURCES:

PERIODICALS

Booklist, February 15, 2004, Connie Fletcher, review of *The Love-Me Bird,* p. 1062.

Guardian (London, England), September 29, 1998, Vivian French, review of *Tell Me Something Happy before I Go to Sleep,* p. 3; February 23, 1999, Vivian French, review of *Tutti Fruitti,* p. 4.

Kirkus Reviews, July 1, 2003, review of *A Chick Called Saturday,* p. 909.

Publishers Weekly, June 2, 2003, review of *A Chick Called Saturday,* p. 50; December 15, 2003, review of *The Love-Me Bird,* p. 46.

School Library Journal, September 2001, Alison Kastner, review of *Tell Me What It's Like to Be Big,* p. 188; August, 2003, Bina Williams, review of *A Chick Called Saturday,* p. 126; January, 2004, Sally R. Dow, review of *The Love-Me Bird,* p. 97.

ONLINE

Joyce Dunbar Web site, http://www.joycedunbar.com/ (March 11, 2005).

E

EDELMAN, Marian Wright 1939-

PERSONAL: Born June 6, 1939, in Bennettsville, SC; daughter of Arthur J. and Maggie (Bowen) Wright; married Peter Benjamin Edelman, July 14, 1968; children: Joshua Robert, Jonah Martin, Ezra Benjamin. *Education:* Attended University of Paris and University of Geneva, 1958-59; Spelman College, B.A., 1960; Yale University, LL.B., 1963.

ADDRESSES: *Office*—Children's Defense Fund, 122 C St. N.W., Washington, DC 20001.

CAREER: National Association for the Advancement of Colored People (NAACP), Legal Defense and Education Fund, Inc., New York, NY, staff attorney, 1963-64, director of office in Jackson, MS, 1964-68; partner of Washington Research Project of Southern Center for Public Policy, 1968-73; Children's Defense Fund, Washington, DC, founder and president, 1973—. W. E. B. Du Bois Lecturer at Harvard University, 1986. Member of Lisle Fellowship's U.S.-USSR Student Exchange, 1959; member of executive committee of Student Non-Violent Coordinating Committee (SNCC), 1961-63; member of Operation Crossroads Africa Project in Ivory Coast, 1962; congressional and federal agency liaison for Poor People's Campaign, summer, 1968; director of Harvard University's Center for Law and Education, 1971-73. Member of Presidential Commission on Americans Missing and Unaccounted for in Southeast Asia (Woodcock Commission), 1977, United States-South Africa leadership Exchange Program, 1977, National Commission on the International Year of the Child, 1979, and President's Commission for a National Agenda for the Eighties, 1979; member of board of directors of Carnegie Council on Children, 1972-77, Aetna Life and Casualty Foundation, Citizens for Constitutional Concerns, U.S. Committee for UNICEF, and Legal Defense and Education Fund of the NAACP; member of board of trustees of Martin Luther King, Jr., Memorial Center, and Joint Center for Political Studies.

Marian Wright Edelman

MEMBER: Council on Foreign Relations, Delta Sigma Theta (honorary member).

AWARDS, HONORS: Merrill scholar in Paris and Geneva, 1958-59; honorary fellow of Law School at University of Pennsylvania, 1969; Louise Waterman Wise Award, 1970; Presidential Citation, American Public Health Association, 1979; Outstanding Leadership Award, National Alliance of Black School Educators, 1979; Distinguished Service Award, National Association of Black Women Attorneys, 1979; National Award of Merit, National Council on Crime and Delinquency, 1979; named Washingtonian of the Year, 1979; Whitney M. Young Memorial Award, Washington Urban League, 1980; Professional Achievement Award, Black Enterprise magazine, 1980; Outstanding Leadership Achievement Award, National Women's Political Caucus and Black Caucus, 1980; Outstanding Community Service Award, National Hookup of Black Women, 1980; Woman of the Year Award, Big Sisters of America, 1980; Award of Recognition, American Academy of Pedodontics, 1981; Rockefeller Public Service Award, 1981; Gertrude Zimand Award, National Child Labor Committee, 1982; Florina Lasker Award, New York Civil Liberties Union, 1982; Anne Roe Award, Graduate School of Education at Harvard University, 1984; Roy Wilkins Civil Rights Award, National Association for the Advancement of Colored People (NAACP), 1984; award from Women's Legal Defense Fund, 1985; Hubert H. Humphrey Award, Leadership Conference on Civil Rights, 1985; fellow of MacArthur Foundation, 1985; Grenville Clark Prize from Dartmouth College, 1986; Compostela Award of St. James Cathedral, 1987; Gandhi Peace Award, 1989; Fordham Stein Prize, 1989; Murray-Green-Meany Award, AFL-CIO, 1989; Frontrunner Award, Sara Lee Corporation, 1990; Jefferson Award, American Institute for Public Service, 1991; recipient of more than thirty honorary degrees.

WRITINGS:

Families in Peril: An Agenda for Social Change, Harvard University Press (Cambridge, MA), 1987.

The Measure of Our Success: A Letter to My Children and Yours, Beacon Press (Boston, MA), 1992, with a new preface, 1994.

Guide My Feet: Prayers and Meditations on Loving and Working for Children, Beacon Press (Boston, MA), 1995.

Stand for Children, Hyperion Books for Children (New York, NY), 1998.

Lanterns: A Memoir of Mentors, HarperPerennial (New York, NY)), 1999.

I'm Your Child, God: Prayers for Children and Teenagers, Hyperion Books for Children (New York, NY), 2002.

Also author of *School Suspensions: Are They Helping Children?,* 1975, and *Portrait of Inequality: Black and White Children in America,* 1980. Contributor to books, including *Raising Children in Modern America: Problems and Prospective Solutions,* edited by Nathan B. Talbot, Little, Brown, 1975; and *Toward New Human Rights: The Social Policies of the Kennedy and Johnson Administrations,* edited by David C. Warner, Lyndon B. Johnson School of Public Affairs, University of Texas at Austin, 1977.

SIDELIGHTS: Dubbed "the 101st Senator on children's issues" by U.S. Senator Edward Kennedy, Marian Wright Edelman left her law practice in 1968, just after the assassination of civil rights leader Martin Luther King, Jr., to work toward a better future for American children. She was the first black woman to join the Mississippi Bar and had been a civil rights lawyer with the National Association for the Advancement of Colored People (NAACP). "Convinced she could achieve more as an advocate than as a litigant for the poor," wrote Nancy Traver in *Time,* Edelman moved to Washington, D.C., and began to apply her researching and rhetorical skills in Congress. She promotes her cause with facts about teen pregnancies, poverty, and infant mortality and—with her Children's Defense Fund—has managed to obtain budget increases for family and child health care and education programs. In *Ms.* magazine Katherine Bouton described Edelman as "the nation's most effective lobbyist on behalf of children . . . an unparalleled strategist and pragmatist."

Edelman's book *Families in Peril: An Agenda for Social Change* was judged "a powerful and necessary document" of the circumstances of children by *Washington Post* reviewer Jonathan Yardley, and it urges support for poor mothers and children of all races. The book is based on the 1986 W. E. B. Du Bois Lectures that Edelman gave at Harvard University. In making her case for increased support for America's children, Edelman offers numerous statistics that paint a grim portrait of life for the country's poor. Don Wycliff, reviewing the book for the *New York Times Book Review,* questioned Edelman's solutions as overly dependent on government support and neglectful of parental responsibility for children: "Governmental exertions . . . are indispensable. But . . . Edelman doesn't satisfactorily address how [parents] can be induced to behave wisely and responsibly *for their child's benefit.*" A *Kirkus Review* contributor, however, termed the book "graphic and eloquent."

In *Measure of Our Success: A Letter to My Children and Yours,* Edelman again deals with the problems and possible solutions of poverty and the neglect of children, in part by discussing her own experience as a parent. The book is divided into five sections: "A Family Legacy"; "Passing on the Legacy of Service"; "A Letter to My Sons"; "Twenty-five Lessons for Life"; and "Is the Child Safe?" Writing in the *New York Times Book Review* about the chapter "Twenty-five Lessons for Life," Clifton L. Taulbert commented, "In the twenty-five lessons for life that she presents here, she issues a call for parental involvement, a commitment of personal time on behalf of others, the primacy of service over self, and the assumption of individual responsibility for our nation's character."

Edelman's *I'm Your Child, God: Prayers for Our Children* follows in the footsteps of her previous collections of prayers, *Guide My Feet: Prayers and Meditations on Loving and Working for Children.* Divided into specific segments for younger children, young adults, and special occasions, the work features language that *Booklist* contributor Gillian Engberg described as at times "clunky and even banal." Nonetheless, the critic added, among the works Edelman assembles are some deeply "heartfelt selections." "She offers kids support, peace and empowerment in prayers," added a *Publishers Weekly* reviewer, the critic going on to state that *I'm Your Child, God* is "a book many will welcome."

Edelman once commented: "I have been an advocate for disadvantaged Americans throughout my professional career. The Children's Defense Fund, which I have been privileged to direct, has become one of the nation's most active organizations concerned with a wide range of children's and family issues, especially those which most affect America's children: our poorest Americans.

"Founded in 1968 as the Washington Research Project, the Children's Defense Fund monitors and proposes improvements in federal, state, and local budgets, legislative and administrative policies in the areas of child and maternal health, education, child care, child welfare, adolescent pregnancy prevention, youth employment, and family support systems. In 1983 the Children's Defense Fund initiated a major long-term national campaign to prevent teenage pregnancy and provide positive life options for youth. Since then, we have launched a multimedia campaign that includes transit advertisements, posters, and television and radio public service announcements, a national prenatal care campaign, and Child Watch coalitions in more than seventy local communities in thirty states to combat teen pregnancy.

"The Children's Defense Fund also has been a leading advocate in Congress, state legislatures, and courts for children's rights. For example, our legal actions blocked out-of-state placement of hundreds of Louisiana children in Texas institutions, guaranteed access to special education programs for tens of thousands of Mississippi's children, and represented the interests of children and their families before numerous federal administrative agencies."

BIOGRAPHICAL AND CRITICAL SOURCES:

PERIODICALS

Black Issues Book Review, January-February 2003, review of *I'm Your Child, God: Prayers for Our Children,* p. 71.

Booklist, October 1, 2002, Gillian Engberg, review of *I'm Your Child, God,* p. 340.

Ebony, July, 1987.

Harper's, February, 1993, p. 154.

Kirkus Reviews, February 1, 1987, p. 189; October 1, 2002, review of *I'm Your Child, God,* p. 1467.

Library Journal, March 1, 1987, p. 66.

Ms., July-August, 1987.

New Republic, March 4, 1996, p. 33.

Newsweek, June 10, 1996, p. 32.

New York Times Book Review, June 7, 1987, p. 12; August 23, 1992, p. 13.

Psychology Today, July-August, 1993, p. 26.

Publishers Weekly, October 28, 2002, review of *I'm Your Child, God,* p. 69.

School Library Journal, September, 1992, p. 290; December, 1992, p. 29; December 2002, Marge Louch-Wouters, review of *I'm Your Child, God,* p. 158.

Time, March 23, 1987.
Washington Post, March 4, 1987.
Washington Post Book World, April 19, 1992, p. 13.*

* * *

ELLISON, Katherine W.
See ELLISON, Katherine (Esther)

* * *

ELLISON, Katherine (Esther) 1957-
(Katherine W. Ellison)

PERSONAL: Born August 19, 1957, in Minneapolis, MN; daughter of Ellis (a physician) and Bernice Ellison. *Education:* Stanford University, B.A., 1979.

ADDRESSES: Office—Mercury News, Knight-Ridder Newspapers, 750 Ridder Park Dr., San Jose, CA 95190. *Agent*—Elise and Arnold Goodman, Goodman Associates, 500 West End Ave., New York, NY 10024.

CAREER: Intern at *Foreign Policy,* Center for Investigative Reporting, and *Los Angeles Times; Washington Post,* Washington, DC, intern, 1979; *Newsweek,* London, England, intern, 1979-80; *Mercury News,* San Jose, CA, staff member, 1980—, reporter from San Jose, 1983—, bureau chief in Mexico City, Mexico, 1987-92. *Miami Herald,* Latin American correspondent from Rio de Janeiro, Brazil, beginning 1992. Media Alliance, San Francisco, CA, member of board of directors, 1986—.

AWARDS, HONORS: Award for outstanding print reporting, Media Alliance of San Francisco, 1985; (with others) Pulitzer Prize for international reporting, 1986, George Polk Memorial Award, Long Island University, and Investigative Reporters and Editors Award, all 1986, for "Hidden Billions," a series of articles on Ferdinand Marcos; award from Inter American Press Association, 1994-95; Media Award, Latin American Studies Association, 1994; award, National Association of Hispanic Journalists, 1997.

WRITINGS:

Imelda: Steel Butterfly of the Philippines, McGraw-Hill (New York, NY), 1988.

(Under name Katherine W. Ellison; with Gretchen C. Daily) *The New Economy of Nature: The Quest to Make Conservation Profitable,* Shearwater Books (Washington, DC), 2002.

Contributor to periodicals.

BIOGRAPHICAL AND CRITICAL SOURCES:

PERIODICALS

Issues in Science and Technology, summer, 2002, David Simpson, review of *The New Economy of Nature: The Quest to Make Conservation Profitable,* p. 84.
Nature, April 25, 2002, Norman Myers, review of *The New Economy of Nature,* p. 788.
New York Times Book Review, January 8, 1989, review of *Imelda: Steel Butterfly of the Philippines,* p. 23.
San Francisco Chronicle, May 12, 2002, Alex Barnum, review of *The New Economy of Nature,* p. 3.*

* * *

ESTERHAZY, Peter 1950-

PERSONAL: Born April 1, 1950, in Budapest, Hungary; son of Matyas E. (a translator) and Lili (Manyoky) Esterhazy; married Gitti Reen (an artist), January 8, 1973; children: Dora, Marcell, Zsofia, Miklos. *Education:* University of Budapest, B.S. *Religion:* Roman Catholic.

ADDRESSES: Home—Emod 20, H-1031 Budapest, Hungary.

CAREER: Writer, 1978. Ministry of Metallurgy and Machine Industry, consultant, 1974-78; freelance writer, 1978—.

AWARDS, HONORS: Frankfurt Book Fair Peace Prize, 2004.

WRITINGS:

IN ENGLISH TRANSLATION

Kis Magyar pornográfia, Magveto (Budapest, Hungary), 1984, translation by Judith Sollosy published as *A Little Hungarian Pornography,* Hydra Books (Evanston, IL), 1995.

A sziv segédigéi, Magveto (Budapest, Hungary), 1985, translation by Michael Henry Heim published as *Helping Verbs of the Heart,* Grove Weidenfeld (London, England), 1991.

Hrabel könyve, Magveto (Budapest, Hungary), 1990, translation by Judith Sollosy published as *The Book of Hrabal,* Northwestern University Press (Evanston, IL), 1994.

Hahn-Hahn grófno pillantása, Magveto (Budapest, Hungary), 1991, translation by Richard Aczel published as *The Glance of Countess Hahn-Hahn: Down the Danube,* Weidenfeld & Nicholson (London, England), 1994.

(With Ferenc Banga) *Egy no,* Magveto (Budapest, Hungary), 1993, (without Banga's drawings) 1995, translation by Judith Sollosy published as *She Loves Me,* Northwestern University Press (Evanston, IL), 1997.

Harmonia Cælestis, Magveto (Budapest, Hungary), 2000, translation by Judith Sollosy published as *Celestial Harmonies,* Ecco (New York, NY), 2003.

Also author of Hungarian-language untranslated novels, stories, and screenplays.

SIDELIGHTS: Peter Esterhazy, one of Hungary's best-known contemporary writers, is the descendant of Esterhazys that go back to the early seventeenth century. There have been Esterhazys famous for their public service, and others who have ignited rebellion and dissent. Esterhazy's father was a count who was regarded as dangerous by the Communists. When his son was born, the family was relocated to a rural village where they worked in the fields until they were later allowed to return to Budapest. Esterhazy graduated from college to work in a government ministry, a job that lasted four years before he quit to become a full-time writer.

A number of Esterhazy's books have been translated into English, including *A Little Hungarian Pornography,* in which the author says that "pornography should be understood as meaning lies, the lies of the body, the lies of the soul." The novel reads more like a series of journal entries, political commentaries, and recollections. "But," noted a *Publishers Weekly* contributor, "the fragments are linked by the use of pornography as a metaphor for yielding disgracefully to—and becoming complicit in—oppression." "Portions of the book are titillatingly sexy and funny, others almost tragic," wrote Clara Gyorgyey in *World Literature Today.* "The texts interrelate but never cohere. Hungary's literary prodigy has done it again: with his imagination running wild, he has produced an audacious treatment of every taboo subject—and got away with it."

Helping Verbs of the Heart is perhaps Esterhazy's most popular translated work, an account of the illness and death of his mother in which each page is framed with a black border, like a death notice. Esterhazy writes of the process and difficulty of writing about life, and death.

The Book of Hrabal is the story of an unnamed writer, his wife, Anna, who talks to Hrabal, their unborn child, their live children, and two angels disguised as policeman who have been sent by God (who takes saxophone lessons from Charlie Parker) to save the unborn child. A *Publishers Weekly* reviewer felt that "though this discursive yarn will not strike all readers' fancies, those with a fondness for mittel-european whimsy may well be charmed." *Booklist*'s Aaron Cohen wrote that "its plot is not always comprehensible, yet *The Book of Hrabal* is filled with enough stunning imagery to reward patient readers."

The Glance of Countess Hahn-Hahn: Down the Danube is a satire, a postmodern history of Central Europe, and a travelogue contained in a series of telegrams. Esterhazy makes references to individuals unfamiliar to most American readers, as well as to Hegel and Wittgenstein, and bemoans the effects of communism and the degradation of the human spirit. A *Publishers Weekly* critic who described the writing as "wry, obscure," concluded by saying that "this ultimately chilling work will stay with the brave reader for days."

She Loves Me is a book of nearly 100 chapters, each of which begins with "There's this woman. She loves me," or "There's this woman. She hates me," or some variation thereof, "but nothing necessarily follows from this fact," noted Adam Phillips in the *New York Times Book Review.* "Each time, the simple, not-so-innocent phrase is the prelude to an always bizarre and often erotic love story. In that twilight zone between existential parable and political and domestic realism that has been the great territory of the eastern European writers—and Esterhazy, a Hungarian, is clearly in the tradition of Kafka, Hrabal, and Kundera—each of these tales is exemplary, but each is lacking a moral. . . . There are just stories about the wayward things couples do together in the name of love." *Library Journal*'s M. Anna Falbo noted that although some of Esterhazy's work is challenging, this book "is delightfully accessible, commendably translated, and graced with an earthy humor."

A *Kirkus Reviews* contributor called *Celestial Harmonies* "daunting at first, then richly rewarding. A major achievement." Esterhazy writes of his family history and all of his notable ancestors in the first part of the book then turns to his father, whose story he tells in great detail, from his life as a count who owned castles and great riches, to the laborer he became when the Communists came to power after World War II. He writes of their frugal life, but how, in many respects, it was also a happy life. He is clear on their suffering, how his father was arrested and beaten in 1956, and how Esterhazy himself was the target of his cruel Communist teacher. A *Publishers Weekly* writer called *Celestial Harmonies* a "masterpiece."

BIOGRAPHICAL AND CRITICAL SOURCES:

BOOKS

Dictionary of Literary Biography, Volume 232: *Twentieth Century Eastern European Writers, Third Series,* Thomson Gale (Detroit, MI), 2001, pp. 89-98.

PERIODICALS

Booklist, October 15, 1994, Aaron Cohen, review of *The Book of Hrabal,* p. 400.

Chicago Review, summer, 2001, Gabor Tamas Molnar, review of *The Glance of Countess Hahn-Hahn: Down the Danube,* p. 79.

Kirkus Reviews, December 15, 2003, review of *Celestial Ceremonies,* p. 1412.

Library Journal, October 15, 1997, M. Anna Falbo, review of *She Loves Me,* p. 91; March 15, 2004, Barbara Hoffert, review of *Celestial Harmonies,* p. 104.

New Statesman and Society, August 11, 1995, Peter Whittaker, review of *A Little Hungarian Pornography,* p. 37.

New Yorker, May 25, 1998, John Updike, review of *She Loves Me,* p. 120.

New York Times Book Review, November 13, 1994, Susan Miron, review of *The Book of Hrabal,* p. 59; November 19, 1995, James Polk, review of *A Little Hungarian Pornography,* p. 26; December 21, 1997, Adam Phillips, review of *She Loves Me,* p. 8.

Publishers Weekly, September 12, 1994, review of *The Book of Hrabal,* p. 81; September 11, 1995, review of *A Little Hungarian Pornography,* p. 76; September 15, 1997, review of *She Loves Me,* p. 52; February 2, 2004, review of *Celestial Harmonies,* p. 58.

Review of Contemporary Fiction, summer, 1996, Brooke Horvath, review of *A Little Hungarian Pornography,* p. 156.

Spectator, May 8, 2004, Adam Zamoyski, review of *Celestial Harmonies,* p. 45.

Times Literary Supplement, December 31, 1993, George Szirtes, review of *The Book of Hrabal,* p. 17; April 15, 1994, Philip Marsden, review of *The Glance of Countess Hahn-Hahn,* p. 24; July 18, 1997, Peter Sherwood, review of *She Loves Me,* p 23.

World Literature Today, spring, 1996, Clara Gyorgyey, review of *A Little Hungarian Pornography,* p. 438; summer, 2000, Marianna D. Birnbaum, review of *Celestial Harmonies,* p. 611.*

F

FALK, Gerhard 1924-

PERSONAL: Born August 22, 1924, in Hamburg, Germany; son of Leonhard and Hedwig (Cibulski) Falk; married Ursula Adler, January 8, 1950; children: Cynthia, Daniel, Clifford. *Education:* Western Reserve University (now Case Western Reserve University), B.A., 1953, M.A., 1955; State University of New York—Buffalo, Ed.D., 1969.

ADDRESSES: *Home*—109 Louvaine, Buffalo, NY 14223. *Office*—Department of Sociology, State University of New York College at Buffalo, 1300 Elmwood Ave., Buffalo, NY 14222. *E-mail*—falkgerhard@yahoo.com.

CAREER: South Dakota State College, Brookings, instructor in sociology, 1955-56; University of Pennsylvania, Philadelphia, instructor in sociology, 1956-57; State University of New York College at Buffalo, Buffalo, assistant professor, 1957-62, associate professor, 1962-70, professor of sociology, 1970—.

MEMBER: Western New York Sociological Association (past president), Western New York Group Psychotherapy Association (past president), Alpha Tau Kappa.

WRITINGS:

(With wife, Ursula Falk) *The Nursing Home Dilemma,* R & E Research Associates (Palo Alto, CA), 1976.

(With Ursula Falk and George Tomashevich) *Aging in America and Other Cultures,* R & E Research Associates (Palo Alto, CA), 1981.

Murder: An Analysis of Its Forms, Conditions and Causes, McFarland (Jefferson, NC), 1990.

The Life of the Academic Professional in America, Edwin Mellen (Lewiston, NY), 1990.

The Jew in Christian Theology, McFarland (Jefferson, NC), 1992.

A Study of Social Change in Six American Institutions, Edwin Mellen (Lewiston, NY), 1993.

American Judaism in Transition: The Secularization of a Religious Community, University Press of America (Lanham, MD), 1995.

(Coauthor) *Ageism, the Aged, and Aging in America: On Being Old in an Alienated Society,* C. C. Thomas (Springfield, IL), 1997.

Sex, Gender, and Social Change: The Great Revolution, University Press of America (Lanham, MD), 1998.

Hippocrates Assailed: The American Health Delivery System, University Press of America (Lanham, MD), 1999.

Stigma: How We Treat Outsiders, Prometheus Books (Buffalo, NY), 2001.

(With Ursula Falk) *Grandparents: A New Look at the Supporting Generation,* Prometheus Books (Buffalo, NY), 2002.

Man's Ascent to Reason: The Secularization of Western Culture, Edwin Mellen (Lewiston, NE), 2002.

Contributor to numerous books, including *Interdisciplinary Problems in Criminology,* edited by Walter Reckless, Ohio State University (Columbus, OH), 1966; *Marital Counseling,* edited by Hirsch L. Silverman, C.

C. Thomas (Springfield, IL), 1967; *An American Historian,* edited by Milton Plesur, State University of New York College at Buffalo (Buffalo, NY), 1980; and *S & M: Studies in Sado-Masochism,* edited by Thomas S. Weinberg and G. W. Levi Kamel, Prometheus Books (Buffalo, NY), 1983. Contributor to a wide variety of scholarly journals, including *Marital Counseling,Mental Hygiene, Criminology and Police Science, Criminologica, International Behavioral Scientist, Journal of Reform Judaism, Deviant Behavior, Nursing Outlook, Journal of Pastoral Counseling,* and *Improving College and University Teaching.*

WORK IN PROGRESS: The American Identity: What Football Means to U.S.; research for *Christian Zionism: A History.*

SIDELIGHTS: Gerhard Falk once told *CA:* "On becoming an assistant professor I recognized that progress in achieving promotion and salary increases depends on publication of scholarly articles and monographs. Therefore, I worked on such publications diligently and succeeded in producing forty-five journal articles and chapters in books. Then, in 1988 I happened to see the archives of a defunct newspaper in the library. This led me to look for material on murder because I teach a course in criminology. I found news clippings going back over forty years concerning murder. This led me to write a whole book on that subject including such matters as the place of the murder, whether inside or outside, the room in the house where the murder took place, the weapon used, the day of the week, the hour of the day, the relationship of the killer to the victim and many other details.

"Having published that book I recognized that writing books is much more enjoyable than writing articles, not only because books are more visible, but also because books permit the author much more leeway in expressing his views and intentions. In short, books are not as confining as articles. Thereupon I decided to write on anything that interested me. Hence I next wrote a book concerning my profession called *The Life of the Academic Professional in America.* Then I wrote *The Jew in Christian Theology* because I had come across the Holocaust murders while writing the previous book. Now I am working on *An American Century* because I seek to show how we lived these one hundred years. The book deals with daily life. It is not a history book but a sociology of the century.

"My principal purpose in writing these books is to bring these topics to the attention of readers and to 'put my two cents in.' I write on topics not well exposed and sometimes not researched at all. I want these topics to be available in libraries. Until I did so, there was no book on how to become and be a professor. While the relationship of Christianity to the Holocaust is mentioned in various publications, it was never before fully exposed, particularly since I translated, as part of my book, an 85-page work by Martin Luther which has never been translated before."

BIOGRAPHICAL AND CRITICAL SOURCES:

PERIODICALS

Ageing and Society, May, 1998, Neil Thompson, review of *Ageism, the Aged, and Aging in America: On Being Old in an Alienated Society,* p. 379.

Choice, March, 2000, J. P. Brickman, review of *Hippocrates Assailed: The American Health Delivery System,* p. 1327.

Contemporary Sociology, March, 1998, Robin D. Moremen, review of *Ageism, the Aged, and Aging in America,* p. 154; March, 2001, review of *Sex, Gender, and Social Change: The Great Revolution,* p. 181; July, 2002, Carol Brooks Gardner, review of *Stigma: How We Treat Outsiders,* p. 299.

Judaism: Quarterly Journal of Jewish Life and Thought, winter, 1997, Lawrence W. Raphael, review of *American Judaism in Transition: The Secularization of a Religious Community,* p. 122.

Library Journal, October 1, 2002, Ellen D. Gilbert, review of *Grandparents: A New Look at the Supporting Generation,* p. 118.

Publishers Weekly, May 28, 2001, review of *Stigma,* p. 78.

* * *

FATHER GOOSE
See GHIGNA, Charles

* * *

FEINSTEIN, Sascha 1963-

PERSONAL: Born March 13, 1963, in New York, NY; son of Sam and Anita (Askild) Feinstein; married Marleni Rajakrishnan, June 3, 1989; children: Kiran, Divia. *Ethnicity:* "Caucasian." *Education:* University of

Rochester, B.A. (magna cum laude), 1985; Indiana University, M.F.A., 1990, Ph.D., 1993.

ADDRESSES: Office—Department of English, Lycoming College, Williamsport, PA 17701; fax: 570-321-4090. *E-mail*—feinstei@lycoming.edu.

CAREER: Poet, educator, and essayist. Indiana University, Bloomington, assistant instructor, 1986-91, associate instructor, 1991-94, part-time instructor, 1994-95; Indiana University/Purdue University—Indianapolis, associate instructor, 1991-94; Lycoming College, Williamsport, PA, assistant professor, 1995-99, associate professor of English, 1999—, codirector of creative writing program, 1996—. Guest on media programs, including National Public Radio.

AWARDS, HONORS: Writer's Exchange Program award, 1995; Hayden Carruth Emerging Poets Award, 1999; Pennsylvania Council on the Arts fellowship, 2002.

WRITINGS:

Summerhouse Piano (poetry chapbook), Matchbooks Press (Unionville, IN), 1989.

(Editor, with Yusef Komunyakaa) *The Jazz Poetry Anthology*, Indiana University Press (Bloomington, IN), 1991.

Christmas Eve (poetry chapbook), Bookcellar (Bloomington, IN), 1994.

(Editor, with Yusef Komunyakaa) *The Second Set: The Jazz Poetry Anthology, Volume 2,* Indiana University Press (Bloomington, IN), 1996.

Blues Knowledge of Departure (poetry, chapbook), Bookcellar (Bloomington, IN), 1997.

Jazz Poetry: From the 1920s to the Present, Greenwood Press (Westport, CT), 1997.

A Bibliographic Guide to Jazz Poetry, Greenwood Press (Westport, CT), 1998.

Misterioso (poetry), Copper Canyon Press (Port Townsend, WA), 2000.

Contributor to books, including *The New Grove Dictionary of Jazz* and *The Penguin Book of the Sonnet,* Penguin (New York, NY). Contributor to literary journals, including *American Poetry Review, Ploughshares, Southern Review, Missouri Review, North American Review,* and *New England Review.* Founding editor, *Brilliant Corners,* 1996—.

SIDELIGHTS: Poet and professor Sascha Feinstein, author of the collection *Misterioso,* attained prominence in the 1990s as the coeditor of anthologies and critical scholar of jazz-inspired verse. With poet Yusef Komunyakaa, he edited *The Jazz Poetry Anthology,* which contains 132 poems arranged in alphabetical order by poet's name. Some of the works included were inspired directly by specific jazz performances; in others poets adapt jazz techniques to language. The poets represented include Langston Hughes, Melvin Tolson, Jack Kerouac, Bob Kaufman, Amiri Baraka, Jayne Cortez, and many others. According to Michael Collins in *Parnassus,* the anthology offers "an array of writers—well-known and obscure—who delight and enchant, infuriate and appall," a fitting representation of "a music that sparks reevaluation of one's place in the world" and therefore a rich subject for a collection of diverse writings.

About half of the poets in *The Jazz Poetry Anthology* provide autobiographical statements, often including their theories concerning the link between jazz and poetry. *MultiCultural Review* contributor Richard N. Albert noted that the contributors' theories "make for interesting and engaging reading beyond the poems themselves," and added of *The Jazz Poetry Anthology:* "What makes this work most enjoyable [for readers] is knowing the music and musicians and using that knowledge to understand and judge the poets' reactions to elements in the music that please and inspire." While commenting that the Beat poems included "suffer from a 'hipper-than-thou' attitude and the pseudo-profundity that attitude inspires," *Crazyhorse* reviewer David Jauss concluded that *The Jazz Poetry Anthology* assembles "many poems as extraordinary as the music and musicians that inspired them. . . . And for that . . . this fine book deserves not only applause but a standing ovation."

Feinstein and Komunyakaa have also teamed up for a sequel, *The Second Set: The Jazz Poetry Anthology, Volume 2,* which a Choice contributor praised as a valuable extension of the first volume compiled with "remarkably little overlap." Including works by Ntozake Shange, Hart Crane, Thulani Davis, Haki Madhubuti, and Paul Beatty, the volume is "as impetuous and bent as a Thelonious Monk song."

Feinstein has also produced the critical study *Jazz Poetry: From the 1920s to the Present.* In *JazzTimes* contributor Marcela Breton called the book "a definitive work," praising Feinstein's "penetrating criticism" and "fine ear, for verse and jazz alike." Noting that the author's overview of jazz poetry is "overdue," *American Book Review* contributor Jamie Hutchinson praised *Jazz Poetry* as "impressive," noting in particular the "poet's sensitivity" Feinstein brings to his "scholarly discussion" of the issues surrounding this poetic form.

In 1999 Feinstein's poetry collection *Misterioso* won the innaugural Hayden Carruth Emerging Poets Award from Copper Canyon Press. A *Booklist* contributor reported that the volume appropriately earned this award "because the poems in it are good, sturdy work" that focus on "one of Carruth's passions, jazz." Noting that Feinstein's poems range across areas as varied as the death of his mother and his love for his wife and children, his "jazz poems uniquely communicate what it is like to live with music one adores." A *Kirkus* contributor noted that Feinstein also "calls forth the music from everyday life" with a sensitivity that is "both vital and deft." *Misterioso* contains poems that resonate like the "everlasting moment of a sax solo," added a contributor to *Bloomsbury Review* in praise of the collection.

Feinstein once told *CA:* "I write about topics other than jazz, but I discovered jazz as a boy on the Upper West Side at the same time that I discovered poetry, and so the two have been quite naturally married in my work. I'm interested in capturing the musicality of jazz, with its thrilling promises of unexpected transitions, and celebrating the mythological history of its musicians—such as Thelonious Monk, Miles Davis, and John Coltrane—whose music has been central to my life. At the same time, I long ago rejected what has sadly become the stereotypical view of jazz poetry: hipster jargon and dated Daddy-O vernacular. Like the best jazz improvisations, poems written both in form and free verse should be firmly grounded in structure. I want my poems to unite passion with craft.

"Yusef Komunyakaa and I have tried to offer a wide range of responses to jazz in the two anthologies, and I hope the two critical books will help scholars explore the genre with still more depth. As the editor of *Brilliant Corners,* I plan to keep publishing the most engaging jazz-related poetry and prose from around the world."

BIOGRAPHICAL AND CRITICAL SOURCES:

PERIODICALS

American Book Review, July-August, 1998, Jamie Hutchinson, review of *Jazz Poetry: From the 1920s to the Present.*

Booklist, February 1, 2000, Ray Olson, review of *Misterioso,* p. 1002.

Choice, June, 1997, L. J. Parascandola, review of *The Second Set: The Jazz Poetry Anthology, Volume 2,* p. 1666; October 1997.

Crazyhorse, spring, 1992, David Jauss, review of *The Jazz Poetry Anthology,* pp. 125-140.

Jazziz, October-November 1991, p. 65.

JazzTimes, December, 1997, Marcela Breton, review of *Jazz Poetry,* p. 60.

Kirkus Reviews, February 1, 2000, review of *Misterioso,* p. 148.

Library Journal, May 15, 2000, Judy Clarence, review of *Misterioso,* p. 989.

MultiCultural Review, Volume 1, number 2, 1992, Richard N. Albert, review of *The Jazz Poetry Anthology,* p. 65; December, 1997, p. 68.

Parnassus, Volume 19, number 2, 1994, Michael Collins, review of *The Jazz Poetry Anthology,* p. 49.

Publishers Weekly, September 30, 1996, review of *The Second Set,* p. 83.

* * *

FIELDS, Jennie 1953-

PERSONAL: Born July 25, 1953, in Chicago, IL; daughter of Ira Samuel (a certified public accountant) and Belle Harriet (a homemaker; maiden name, Springer) Fields; married Steven W. Kroeter (marriage ended); children: Chloe Melinda. *Education:* University of Illinois, Urbana-Champaign, B.F.A., 1974; University of Iowa, M.F.A., 1976. *Hobbies and other interests:* Painting, writing, music.

ADDRESSES: *Home*—452 8th St., Brooklyn, NY 11215. *Agent*—Lisa Bankoff, International Creative Management, 40 W. 57th St., New York, NY 10019. *E-mail*—LilyBeach@aol.com.

CAREER: Affiliated with Foote, Cone, and Belding (advertising agency), Chicago, IL, 1977-79; affiliated with Needham, Harper, and Steers, Chicago, 1979-82;

Young and Rubicam (advertising agency), New York, NY, senior vice president, 1982-85; Leo Burnett, Chicago, senior vice president, 1985-89; Young and Rubicam, senior vice president and creative director, 1989-93; Lowe and Partners, senior vice president and creative director, 1993-95; Bozell, senior vice president and creative director, 1995-98; Robert A. Bicher Inc., 1999—.

AWARDS, HONORS: Clio award; National Addy award; Effie award; Chicago Addy Gold award; two Lions Cannes International festival awards.

WRITINGS:

Lily Beach, Atheneum (New York, NY), 1993.
Crossing Brooklyn Ferry: A Novel, Morrow (New York, NY), 1997.
The Middle Ages, Morrow (New York, NY), 2002.

Contributor of short stories to periodicals, including *Story Quarterly, Mississippi Review, Ball State Forum,* and *Chicago.*

SIDELIGHTS: Since the early 1990s, Jennie Fields has published a trio of novels that focuses on the intricacies of relationships. Her *Crossing Brooklyn Ferry,* whose title alludes to a poem by Walt Whitman, portrays the struggles of the Finney family as they try to recover from the accidental death of their eldest daughter. Hoping to snap her husband, Jamie, out of depression, Zoe decides to move their well-to-do family from Manhattan to Park Slope in Brooklyn. Zoe falls for her new neighbor, the high school English teacher Keeven, all the while hoping that her husband will recover. Several reviewers considered Park Slope to be a character in its own right, including a *Publishers Weekly* critic, who called the novel "an extended love letter" to the gentrified, old immigrant part of Brooklyn where Fields lives, and *Booklist* contributor Brian McCombie, who praised the author's "expertly evoked . . . almost tactile sense of time, place, and people." Michael Harris of the *Los Angeles Times* also called her writing "vivid" for its many sensory details, adding that "Fields is good at rendering the stop-and-start rhythm of relationships."

Despite the strengths of *Crossing Brooklyn Ferry,* a *Publishers Weekly* contributor found the denouement "pat" and female characters "unsympathetic," while *Entertainment Weekly* writer Vanessa V. Friedman thought characterizations marred the "already affecting love story." In *Library Journal,* Jan Blodgett approved of Fields's expressive language, summing up the novel as a "modern folktale about the redemptive powers of love and sacrifice."

If the power of love and sacrifice are the themes of *Crossing Brooklyn Ferry,* the need to change in order to avoid regrets is the theme of Fields's subsequent novel *The Middle Ages,* whose title refers to both midlife and a time prior to enlightenment, in this case personal enlightenment. The latter novel recounts the story of architect Jane Larsen, a divorced mother of teenaged twin daughters, who takes stock of her life after she is downsized. Fulfilling unfulfilled dreams or renewing a long-past love loom large on Jane's horizon in this "warm-hearted if wandering" novel, to quote a *Publishers Weekly* reviewer, who predicted the tale might "resonate" with middle-aged readers. Remarking on the "complexities [that] make for very enjoyable reading" in her *Library Journal* review, Sheila Riley also suggested that *The Middle Ages* would appeal to women in midlife.

BIOGRAPHICAL AND CRITICAL SOURCES:

PERIODICALS

Booklist, May 15, 1997, Brian McCombie, review of *Crossing Brooklyn Ferry,* p. 1561.
Entertainment Weekly, May 30, 1997, Vanessa V. Friedman, review of *Crossing Brooklyn Ferry,* pp. 66-67.
Kirkus Reviews, April 1, 1997, review of *Crossing Brooklyn Ferry,* pp. 485-486.
Library Journal, June 1, 1997, Jan Blodgett, review of *Crossing Brooklyn Ferry,* p. 146; July, 2002, Sheila Riley, review of *The Middle Ages,* p. 118.
Los Angeles Times, May 26, 1997, Michael Harris, review of *Crossing Brooklyn Ferry,* p. 5.
New York Times Book Review, July 13, 1997, Betsy Groban, review of *Crossing Brooklyn Ferry,* p. 18.
Publishers Weekly, February 22, 1993, review of *Lily Beach,* p. 83; April 28, 1997, review of *Crossing Brooklyn Ferry,* p. 48; June 24, 2002, review of *The Middle Ages,* p. 35.
Tribune Books (Chicago, IL), June 29, 1997, review of *Crossing Brooklyn Ferry,* p. 11.*

FLORA, Joseph M(artin) 1934-

PERSONAL: Born February 9, 1934, in Toledo, OH; son of Raymond Dwight (a factory worker) and Frances (Ricica) Flora; married Glenda Christine Lape (a correspondence instructor), January 30, 1959; children: Ronald James, Stephan Ray, Peter Joseph, David Benjamin. *Education:* University of Michigan, B.A., 1956, M.A., 1957, Ph.D., 1962; University of California, Berkeley, summer study, 1957.

ADDRESSES: Home—505 Caswell Rd., Chapel Hill, NC 27514. *Office*—Department of English, University of North Carolina, Chapel Hill, NC 27599-0001. *E-mail*—jflora@email.unc.edu.

CAREER: University of Michigan, Ann Arbor, instructor in English, 1961-62; University of North Carolina, Chapel Hill, instructor, 1962-64, assistant professor, 1964-67, associate professor, 1967-77, professor of English, 1977—; acting department chair, 1980-81, department chair, 1980-91; assistant dean of graduate school, 1967-72, associate dean, 1977-1978; assistant to chair, Duke University, University of North Carolina Cooperative Program in Humanities, 1963-67. Visiting professor at University of New Mexico, summer, 1976, 1996.

MEMBER: Modern Language Association of America, Western Literature Association (board of directors, 1978-81, 1983-86; vice president, 1990; president, 1992), South Atlantic Modern Language Association, Hemingway Society, Thomas Wolfe Society (vice president 1993-95; president, 1995-97), Society for the Study of Southern Literature, Phi Beta Kappa, Phi Eta Sigma.

AWARDS, HONORS: Mayflower Award, 1982, for *Hemingway's Nick Adams.*

WRITINGS:

Vardis Fisher, Twayne (New York, NY), 1965.

William Ernest Henley, Twayne (New York, NY), 1970.

Frederick Manfred, Boise State University (Boise, ID), 1974.

(Editor) James Branch Cabell, *The Cream of the Jest,* College and University Press (New Haven, CT), 1975.

(Editor, with Robert Bain and Louis D. Rubin, Jr.) *Southern Writers: A Biographical Dictionary,* Louisiana State University Press (Baton Rouge, LA), 1979.

Hemingway's Nick Adams, Louisiana State University Press (Baton Rouge, LA), 1982.

(Editor) *The English Short Story, 1880-1945: A Critical History,* Twayne (Boston, MA), 1985.

(Editor, with Robert Bain) *Fifty Southern Writers before 1900: A Bio-Biographical Sourcebook,* Greenwood Press (Westport, CT), 1987.

(Editor, with Robert Bain) *Fifty Southern Writers after 1900,* Greenwood Press (Westport, CT), 1987.

Ernest Hemingway: A Study of the Short Fiction, Twayne (Boston, MA), 1989.

(Editor, with Robert Bain) *Contemporary Fiction Writers of the South: A Bio-Bibliographical Source Book,* Greenwood Press (Westport, CT), 1993.

(Editor, with Robert Bain) *Contemporary Poets, Dramatists, Essayists, and Novelists of the South: A Bio-Bibliographical Sourcebook,* Greenwood Press (Westport, CT), 1994.

(Editor) *Rediscovering Vardis Fisher: Centennial Essays,* University of Idaho Press (Moscow, ID), 2000.

(Editor, with Lucinda H. MacKethan) *The Companion to Southern Literature: Themes, Genres, Places, People, Movements, and Motifs,* Louisiana State University Press (Baton Rouge, LA), 2002.

Contributor of articles to journals.

SIDELIGHTS: A professor of English at the University of North Carolina, Joseph M. Flora has specialized in literature of the American South, editing with Robert Bain four reference books on the topic for Greenwood Press. After publishing the biographical titles *Fifty Southern Writers before 1900* and *Fifty Southern Writers after 1900,* they devoted their attention to more contemporary American writers of the South in the critically acclaimed reference works *Contemporary Fiction Writers of the South: A Bio-Bibliographical Source Book* and *Contemporary Poets, Dramatists, Essayists, and Novelists of the South: A Bio-Bibliographical Sourcebook. Contemporary Fiction Writers of the South* contains forty-nine essays on individual writers, written by that many different scholars, as well as bibliographic updates on nine novelists from *Fifty Southern Writers after 1900.* As Thomas Bonner noted in the *Mississippi Quarterly,* this volume "provides a helpful resource" in which the editors do a "heroic" job of holding the individual contributors to the same standard of scholarship.

Nearly a decade later, Flora and coeditor Lucinda H. MacKethan published *The Companion to Southern Literature: Themes, Genres, Places, People, Movements, and Motifs,* a massive and far-ranging encyclopedia with over 500 entries on many topics related to southern literature. Because biographies of southern literary figures are available elsewhere, the editors limited the number of biographies included in this volume to about a dozen, plus a few nonliterary Southern figures of importance. Flora and MacKethan supervised the contributions of many scholars from a variety of universities. Like Flora's earlier reference works, *The Companion to Southern Literature* received praise from critics. In the *Bloomsbury Review,* Richard Lynch called the work "important," as did a *Booklist* reviewer, who called the work an "excellent resource" because it is "well-written, meticulously edited, and thoughtfully organized."

BIOGRAPHICAL AND CRITICAL SOURCES:

PERIODICALS

American Literature, June, 1994, review of *Contemporary Fiction Writers of the South: A Bio-Bibliographical Source Book,* p. 423.

American Reference Books Annual, Volume 25, 1994, review of *Contemporary Fiction Writers of the South,* p. 500.

Bloomsbury Review, July-August, 2002, Richard Lynch, review of *The Companion to Southern Literature: Themes, Genres, Places, People, Movements, and Motifs.*

Booklist, April 1, 2002, p. review of *The Companion to Southern Literature,* p. 1351.

Choice, January, 1994, A. J. Adam, review of *Contemporary Fiction Writers of the South,* pp. 748-749; April, 1995, S. R. Moore, review of *Contemporary Poets, Dramatists, Essayists, and Novelists of the South: A Bio-Bibliographical Source Book,* p. 1270; April, 2002, A. E. Bonnette, review of *The Companion to Southern Literature,* p. 1392.

Library Journal, November 15, 2001, Peter Dollard, review of *The Companion to Southern Literature,* p. 60; April 15, 2003, review of *The Companion to Southern Literature,* p. 41.

Mississippi Quarterly, fall, 1994, Thomas Bonner, Jr., review of *Contemporary Fiction Writers of the South,* pp. 673-674.

Reference & Research Book News, March, 1994, review of *Contemporary Fiction Writers of the South,* p. 48.

Southern Library Journal, fall, 1996, Robert J. Phillips, Jr., review of *Contemporary Poets, Dramatists, Essayists, and Novelists of the South,* pp. 93-96.*

* * *

FLUEHR-LOBBAN, Carolyn 1945-

PERSONAL: Born January 6, 1945, in Philadelphia, PA; daughter of Christopher and Anne (Wolsonovich) Fluehr; married Richard A. Lobban, Jr. (a college professor), August 31, 1968; children: Josina Parks, Nichola Felicia. *Education:* Temple University, B.A., 1967, M.A., 1968; Northwestern University, Ph.D., 1973.

ADDRESSES: *Home*—23 Fort Ave., Cranston, RI 02905. *Office*—Department of Anthropology, Rhode Island College, Providence, RI 02908.

CAREER: Anthropologist. Rhode Island College, Providence, assistant professor, 1972-78, associate professor, 1978-84, professor of anthropology, 1984—. Conducted field research in the Sudan, Egypt, and Tunisia.

MEMBER: Sudan Studies Association (founder; president, 1984-85), American Anthropological Association, Middle East Studies Association, African Studies Association.

AWARDS, HONORS: Distinguished Teacher Award, Rhode Island College, 1989-90; fellow of Rockefeller Foundation (at Institute for the Study of Applied and Professional Ethics, Dartmouth College), 1990, Mellon Foundation (at University of Pennsylvania), National Endowment for the Humanities, and American Research Center in Egypt.

WRITINGS:

Islamic Law and Society in the Sudan, Frank Cass (Totowa, NJ), 1986.

(Editor) *International Perspectives on Marxist Anthropology,* MEP Publications (Minneapolis, MN), 1989.

(Editor) *Ethics and the Profession of Anthropology: Dialogue for a New Era,* University of Pennsylvania Press (Philadelphia, PA), 1991, AltaMira Press (Walnut Creek, CA), 2002.

(With husband, Richard A. Lobban, Jr., and John Obert Voll) *Historical Dictionary of the Sudan,* 2nd edition, Scarecrow Press (Metuchen, NJ), 1992, 3rd edition (with Richard A. Lobban, Jr. and Robert S. Kramer, Scarecrow Press (Lanham, MD), 2000.

(Editor) *Islamic Society in Practice,* University of Florida Press (Gainesville, FL), 1994, published as *Islamic Societies in Practice,* 2004.

(Editor) Muhammad Said Ashmawi, *Against Islamic Extremism: The Writings of Muhammad Said al-Ashmawy,* University Press of Florida (Gainesville, FL), 1998.

(Editor, with Kharyssa Rhodes) *Race and Identity in the Nile Valley: Ancient and Modern Perspectives,* Red Sea Press (Trenton, NJ), 2003.

Contributor to numerous journals and series, including *Modern Egypt and Its Heritage* to the "Carnegie Series on Egypt," Carnegie Museum of Natural History, 1990.

SIDELIGHTS: Anthropologist Carolyn Fluehr-Lobban is the author of a number of volumes, including the *Historical Dictionary of the Sudan,* which has been regularly revised and reprinted. Peter Woodward reviewed the second edition in the *Journal of African History,* noting that it includes new entries on women, Islamic law, literature, slavery, the Sudan Peoples Liberation Army, demography, ethnography, and urbanization. He felt that the volume's "breadth will be welcomed by those making initial explorations into Sudanese studies."

Fluehr-Lobban is the editor of *Islamic Society in Practice,* called "a must for the diplomat, the journalist, or anyone with an interest in the Islamic world" by a *Publishers Weekly* contributor. It is an historical overview of how Islam is practiced in Tunisia, Egypt, and Sudan, and benefits from Fluehr-Lobban's five years of research and her own experiences in these countries. She addresses many of the fundamental values of Muslim society, including honor, generosity, sharing, hospitality, association, and the appreciation of knowledge. She says that family "is everything." She notes that the Arabic culture and language have greatly influenced Islam and then goes on to address Arab and Islamic tolerance of Judaism and Christianity.

Arab Studies Quarterly reviewer Ali Al-Taie noted that anthropologists adhere to a sociopolitical definition. "Following others, Fluehr-Lobban simply associates the Arab in modern time 'with the political movement of Arab nationalism, articulated by many nationalist leaders in anticolonial . . . [activism] throughout the Middle East and given international recognition and regional meaning by Gamal Abdel Nasser.'" Fluehr-Lobban feels an Arab is someone who thinks of himself or herself as such, a person who speaks Arabic as a first language, but who may be Muslim or Christian. She also states that Muslims are not prejudiced against Christians and Jews, who may be marginalized given their smaller numbers. Al-Taie wrote that "not even the Crusaders' sacking of Jerusalem in 1099 and the Christian and European colonialism of many Arab-Muslim lands have provoked Muslims against their fellow Christian citizens. Further, many Christian Arabs, one may add, have not only pioneered in raising the banner of Arab nationalism but through scholarly work have helped to unveil Islam and to uncover anti-Muslim Orientalist expressions."

A reviewer for the *Middle East Women's Studies Review* called *Islamic Society in Practice* "an excellent introductory text, for students and nonacademics alike, as it presents the diversity of the Muslim world in a clear, information-rich text." The reviewer commented that Fluehr-Lobban "conscientiously points to instances in which Western stereotypes about differences between Western and Islamic cultures are based upon false information about the Muslim world, and instances where other stereotypes are based upon incorrect assumptions about our differences. She corrects these misconceptions with charm and forbearance." The reviewer wrote further that Fluehr-Lobban "conducts several full and well-reasoned discussions concerning women's roles in the Middle East, placing these discussions in various chapters having to do with Islamic family law, culture change, gender relationships within the family and the community, debates concerning women's personal freedom, and women's roles in Islamic revival movements." The reviewer concluded by saying that the volume "is an eloquent, thought-provoking antidote to the American media's attempts to reduce the complexity of the Muslim world to thirty-second sound bites."

Fluehr-Lobban is the editor of *Against Islamic Extremism: The Writings of Muhammad Said al-Ashmawy.* Her subject was trained in law at Cairo University, and has served in many positions, including as a judge, chief prosecutor, and chief justice. The critic of Islamic extremism who opposes the idea of an Islamic state on both religious and historical grounds is the author of more than a dozen volumes on Islam and the law. Fluehr-Lobban's volume contains his reformist message and opinions on the place of Islamic law in contemporary politics.

Carolyn Fluehr-Lobban once told *CA:* "My writing has been an extension of my teaching, as each has sought clarity of thought and presentation. The scholar-educator has the special task of combining objectivity and balance in presenting facts with a passion for the subject matter. The author must love the subject and always keep the reader in mind."

BIOGRAPHICAL AND CRITICAL SOURCES:

PERIODICALS

Africa, winter, 1997, C. H. R. Tripp, review of *Historical Dictionary of the Sudan,* 2nd edition, p. 159.

American Ethnologist, August, 1994, Keith T. Kernan, review of *Ethics and the Profession of Anthropology: Dialogue for a New Era,* p. 633.

Arab Studies Quarterly, spring, 1996, Ali Al-Taie, review of *Islamic Society in Practice,* p. 95.

Choice, April, 1995, L. Beck, review of *Islamic Society in Practice,* p. 1344; November, 1998, B. B. Lawrence, review of *Against Islamic Extremism: The Writings of Muhammad Said al-Ashmawy,* p. 535.

International Journal of African Historical Studies, spring, 1997, Ousmane Kane, review of *Islamic Society in Practice,* p. 367.

International Journal of Middle East Studies, August, 1996, Arlene Elowe MacLeod, review of *Islamic Society in Practice,* p. 95.

Journal of African History, January, 1994, Peter Woodward, review of *Historical Dictionary of the Sudan,* p. 171.

Middle East Women's Studies Review, September 1, 1996, review of *Islamic Society in Practice.*

Publishers Weekly, November 7, 1994, review of *Islamic Society in Practice,* p. 71.

Reviews in Anthropology, Volume 27, 1998, review of *Islamic Society in Practice,* p. 57.*

FORSYTH, Frederick 1938-

PERSONAL: Born in 1938, in Ashford, Kent, England; son of a furrier, shopkeeper, and rubber tree planter; married Carole Cunningham (a model), September, 1973 (marriage ended); married Sandy Molloy, 1994; children: (first marriage) Frederick Stuart, Shane Richard. *Education:* Attended University of Granada. *Hobbies and other interests:* Sea fishing, snooker.

ADDRESSES: Home—St. John's Wood, London, England. *Agent*—c/o Author Mail, Bantam Books, 62/63 Uxbridge Rd., London W5 5SA, England.

CAREER: Author. *Eastern Daily Press,* Norwich, England, and King's Lynn, Norfolk, reporter, 1958-61; Reuters News Agency, reporter in London, England, and Paris, France, 1961-63, bureau chief in East Berlin, East Germany, 1963-64; British Broadcasting Corporation (BBC), London, reporter, 1965-66, assistant diplomatic correspondent, 1967-68; freelance journalist in Nigeria, 1968-69. *Military service:* Royal Air Force, 1956-58; pilot.

AWARDS, HONORS: Edgar Allan Poe Award, Mystery Writers of America, 1971, for *The Day of the Jackal.*

WRITINGS:

NOVELS

The Day of the Jackal, Viking (New York, NY), 1971.

The Odessa File, Viking (New York, NY), 1972.

The Dogs of War, Viking (New York, NY), 1974.

The Shepherd, Hutchinson (London, England), 1975, Viking (New York, NY), 1976.

The Novels of Frederick Forsyth (contains *The Day of the Jackal, The Odessa File,* and *The Dogs of War*), Hutchinson (London, England), 1978, published as *Forsyth's Three,* Viking (New York, NY), 1980, published as *Three Complete Novels,* Avenel Books (New York, NY), 1980.

The Devil's Alternative, Hutchinson (London, England), 1979, Viking (New York, NY), 1980.

The Four Novels (contains *The Day of the Jackal, The Odessa File, The Dogs of War,* and *The Devil's Alternative*), Hutchinson (London, England), 1982.

Frederick Forsyth

The Fourth Protocol, Viking (New York, NY), 1984.

The Negotiator, Bantam (New York, NY), 1989.

The Deceiver, Bantam (New York, NY), 1991.

The Shepherd, Bantam (New York, NY), 1992.

The Fist of God, Bantam (New York, NY), 1994.

Icon, Bantam (New York, NY), 1996.

The Phantom of Manhattan, St. Martin's Press (New York, NY), 1999.

Avenger, St. Martin's Press (New York, NY), 2003.

OTHER

The Biafra Story (nonfiction), Penguin (London, England), 1969, revised edition published as *The Making of an African Legend: The Biafra Story,* 1977.

Emeka (biography), Spectrum Books (Ibadan, Nigeria), 1982, 2nd edition, 1993.

No Comebacks: Collected Short Stories, Viking (New York, NY), 1982.

(And executive producer) *The Fourth Protocol* (screenplay; based on his novel of the same title), Lorimar, 1987.

Chacal, French and European Publications, 1990.

(Editor) *Great Flying Stories,* Norton (New York, NY), 1991.

I Remember: Reflections on Fishing in Childhood, Summersdale (London, England), 1995.

The Veteran and Other Stories, Bantam (London, England), 2001.

Also author of *The Soldiers,* a documentary for BBC. Contributor to *Visitor's Book: Short Stories of Their New Homeland by Famous Authors Now Living in Ireland,* Arrow Books, 1982. Contributor of articles to newspapers and magazines, including *Playboy.*

ADAPTATIONS: The Day of the Jackal was filmed by Universal in 1973; *The Odessa File* was filmed by Columbia in 1974; *The Dogs of War* was filmed by United Artists in 1981. The Mobil Showcase Network filmed two of Forsyth's short stories ("A Careful Man" and "Privilege") under the title *Two by Forsyth* in 1984; *The Fourth Protocol* was filmed by Lorimar in 1987; "A Careful Man" was also videotaped and broadcast on Irish television.

SIDELIGHTS: British writer Frederick Forsyth "helped define the international conspiracy thriller," according to *Booklist*'s Connie Fletcher. Further, he established, as a critic for *Publishers Weekly* noted, the "traditional formula of thrillers that educate as well as entertain." Realism is the key word behind Forsyth's novels, which originated a new genre, the "documentary thriller." Forsyth found sudden fame with the publication of his smash best-seller, *The Day of the Jackal,* a book that combines the suspense of an espionage novel with the detailed realism of the documentary novel, first made popular by Truman Capote's *In Cold Blood.* The detail in Forsyth's novels depends not only on the months of research he spends on each book, but also on his own varied personal experiences, which lend even greater authenticity to his writing. As *Dictionary of Literary Biography* contributor Andrew F. Macdonald explained, "The sense of immediacy, of an insider's view of world affairs, of all-too-human world figures," as well as quick-paced plots, are the keys to the author's popularity.

Critics, however, have sometimes faulted the novelist for shallow characterization and a simplistic writing style. Forsyth does not deny his emphasis on plotting over other considerations. In a *Los Angeles Times* interview he remarked, "My books are eighty percent plot and structure. The remaining twenty percent is for characters and descriptions. I try to keep emotions out. Occasionally a personal opinion will appear in the mouth of one of my characters, but only occasionally. The plot's the thing. This is how it works best for me." These plots find their resolution in Forsyth's painstaking attention to detail. "Forsyth's forte, with the added bonus of precise technical description worthy of a science writer," Macdonald explained, is "how things work, ranging from the construction of a special rifle (*The Day of the Jackal*) and improvised car bombs (*The Odessa File*), to gunrunning (*The Dogs of War*) and the innards of oil tankers (*The Devil's Alternative*), to the assembly of miniature nuclear bombs (*The Fourth Protocol*)."

For Forsyth the road to becoming a best-selling novelist was a long, circuitous route filled with adventurous detours that would later work their way into his writing. Early in his life, Forsyth became interested in becoming a foreign correspondent when his father introduced him to the world news as reported in the London *Daily Express*. In a London *Times* interview with John Mortimer, Forsyth related how his father "would get out the atlas and show me where the trouble spots were. And, of course, father had been to the Orient, he told me about tiger shoots and the headhunters in Borneo." Impatient to experience life for himself, Forsyth left school at the age of seventeen and went to Spain, where he briefly attended the University of Granada while toying with the idea of becoming a matador. However, having previously trained as a Tiger Moth biplane pilot, Forsyth decided to join the Royal Air Force in 1956. He learned to fly a Vampire jet airplane, and—at the age of nineteen—he was the youngest man in England at the time to earn his wings.

But Forsyth still dreamed of becoming a foreign correspondent, and toward that end he left the service to join the staff of the *Eastern Daily Press*. His talent for languages (Forsyth is fluent in French, German, Spanish, and Russian) later landed him his dream job as a correspondent for the Reuters News Agency and then for the British Broadcasting Corporation (BBC). It was during an assignment for the BBC that Forsyth's career took a sudden turn. Assigned to cover an uprising in the Nigerian region of Biafra, Forsyth began his mission believing he was going to meet an upstart rebellious colonel who was misleading his followers. He soon realized, though, that this leader, Colonel Ojukwu, was actually an intelligent man committed to saving his people from an English-supported government whose corrupt leaders were allowing millions to die of starvation in order to obtain their oil-rich lands. When Forsyth reported his findings, he was accused of being unprofessional, and his superiors reassigned him to covering politics at home. Outraged, Forsyth resigned, and he told Henry Allen in a *Washington Post* article that this experience destroyed his belief "that the people who ran the world were men of good will." This disillusionment is reflected in his writing. Forsyth revealed to Mortimer that he prefers "to write about immoral people doing immoral things. I want to show that the establishment's as immoral as the criminals."

Going back to Africa, Forsyth did freelance reporting in Biafra and wrote an account of the war, *The Biafra Story,* which *Spectator* critic Auberon Waugh asserted "is by far the most complete account, from the Biafran side [of the conflict], that I have yet read." In 1970, when the rebels were finally defeated and Ojukwu went into exile, Forsyth returned to England to find that his position on the war had effectively eliminated any chances he had of resuming a reporting career. He decided, however, that he could still put his journalism experience to use by writing fiction. Recalling his days in Paris during the early 1960s, when rumors were spreading that the Secret Organization Army had hired an assassin to shoot President Charles de Gaulle, Forsyth sat down and in just over a month wrote *The Day of the Jackal* based on this premise.

Forsyth had problems selling the manuscript at first because publishers could not understand how there could be any suspense in a plot about a presidential assassination that had obviously never come to pass. As the author explained to Allen, however, "The point was not whodunit, but how, and how close would he get?" The fascinating part of *The Day of the Jackal* lies in Forsyth's portrayal of the amoral, ultra-professional killer known only by his code name, "Jackal," and detective Claude Lebel's efforts to stop him. Despite what *New York Times Book Review* critic Stanley Elkin called Forsyth's "graceless prose style," and characterization that, according to J. R. Frakes in a *Book World* review, uses "every stereotype in the filing system," the author's portrayal of his nemesis weaving through a non-stop narrative has garnered acclaim from many critics and millions of readers. By boldly switching his emphasis from the side of the law to the side of the assassin, Forsyth adds a unique twist that gives his novel its appeal. "So plausible has Mr. Forsyth made his implausible villain . . . and so exciting does he lead him on his murderous mission against impossible odds," said Elkin, "that even saintly readers will be hard put not to cheer this particular villain along his devious way." The author, however, noted that he considered the positive response to his villain a distinctly American response. "There is this American trait of admiring efficiency," he explained to a *Washington Post* interviewer, "and the Jackal is efficient in his job."

"*The Day of the Jackal* established a highly successful formula," wrote Macdonald, "one repeated by Forsyth and a host of other writers." Using a tight, journalistic style, Forsyth creates an illusion of reality in his writing by intermixing real-life people and historical events with his fictional characters and plots; "the ultimate effect is less that of fiction than of a fictional projection into the lives of the real makers of history," Macdonald attested. The author also fills his pages with factual information about anything from how to assemble a small nuclear device to shipping schedules and restaurant menus. But the main theme behind the author's novels is the power of the individual to make a difference in the world, and even change the course of history. Macdonald described the Forsyth protagonist as "a maverick who succeeds by cutting through standard procedure and who as a result often has difficulty in fitting in, [yet he] lives up to his own high professional standards. Forsyth suggests that it is the lone professionals, whether opposed to the organization or part of it, who truly create history, but a history represented only palely on the front pages of newspapers."

Since Forsyth had a three-book contract with Viking, he quickly researched and wrote his next two novels, *The Odessa File,* about a German reporter's hunt for a Nazi war criminal, and *The Dogs of War,* which concerns a mercenary who orchestrates a military coup in West Africa. Forsyth drew on his experience as a reporter in East Berlin for *The Odessa File,* as well as interviewing experts such as Nazi hunter Simon Wiesenthal, to give the novel authenticity. Background to *The Dogs of War* also came from the author's personal experiences—in this case, his time spent in Biafra. When it comes to details about criminal doings, however, Forsyth goes right to the source. In a Toronto *Globe and Mail* interview with Rick Groen, Forsyth said, "There are only two kinds of people who really know the ins and outs of illegal activities: those who practice them and those who seek to prevent them from being practiced. So you talk to cops or criminals. Not academics or criminologists or any of those sorts." This tactic has gotten Forsyth into some dangerous situations. In a *Chicago Tribune* interview the author regaled Michael Kilian with one instance when he was researching *The Dogs of War.* Trying to learn more about gun trafficking in the black market, Forsyth posed as a South African interested in buying arms. The ploy worked until one day when the men he was dealing with noticed a copy of *The Day of the Jackal* in a bookstore window. It was "probably the nearest I got to being put in a box," said the author.

The Dogs of War became a highly controversial book when a London *Times* writer accused Forsyth of paying $200,000 to mercenaries attempting a coup against the President of Equatorial Guinea, Francisco Marcias Nguema. At first, the novelist denied any involvement. Later, however, David Butler and Anthony Collins reported in *Newsweek* that Forsyth admitted to having "organized a coup attempt for research purposes, but that he had never intended to go through with it." The controversy did not hurt book sales, though, and *The Dogs of War* became Forsyth's third best-seller in a row.

After *The Dogs of War* Forsyth did not attempt another thriller for several years. He credits exhaustion to this lengthy hiatus. "Those first three novels had involved a lot of research, a lot of traveling, a half-million words of writing, a lot of promotion," the novelist told *New York Times Book Review* contributor Tony Chiu. "I was fed up with the razzmatazz. I said I would write no more." To avoid heavy English taxes, Forsyth moved to Ireland, where tax laws are lenient on writers. One explanation as to why he returned to writing has been offered by *New York Times Book Review* critic Peter Maas, who recorded that when a tax man came to Forsyth's door one day and explained that only actively writing authors were eligible for tax breaks, Forsyth quickly told him that he was working on a novel at that moment. "I hasten to say," Maas wrote, "that all this may be apocryphal, but in the interests of providing us a greater truth, I like to think it happened. It's a wonderful thought, the idea of a tax person forcing a writer into more millions."

Forsyth made his comeback with *The Devil's Alternative,* an intricately plotted, ambitious novel about an American president who must choose between giving in to the demands of a group of terrorists and possibly causing a nuclear war in the process, or refusing their demands and allowing them to release the biggest oil spill in history from the tanker they have hijacked. "The vision is somewhat darker than in Forsyth's earlier works, in which a moral choice was possible," noted Macdonald. "Here . . . somebody must get hurt, no matter which alternative is chosen." The usual complaints against Forsyth's writing have been trained against *The Devil's Alternative.* Peter Gorner, for one, argued in the *Chicago Tribune Book World* that "his characters are paper-thin, the pages are studded with cliches, and the plot is greased by coincidence." But Gorner added that "things move along so briskly you haven't much time to notice." *Los Angeles Times* critic Robert Kirsch similarly noted that "Forsyth's banal writing, his endless thesaurus of cliches, his Hollywood characters do not interfere with page turning." Nevertheless, *New York Times Book Review* contributor Irma Pascal Heldman expressed admiration for Forsyth's ability to accurately predict some of the political crises that came to pass not long after the book was published. She also praised the "double-whammy ending that will take even the most wary reader by surprise. *The Devil's Alternative* is a many-layered thriller."

As with *The Devil's Alternative,* Forsyth's *The Fourth Protocol* and *The Negotiator* offer intrigue on a superpower scale. *The Fourth Protocol* is the story of a Soviet plot to detonate a small atomic device in a U.S. airbase in England. The explosion is meant to be seen as an American error and help put the leftist, antinuclear Labour Party into power. Reviews on the novel were mixed. *Time* magazine reviewer John Skow faulted the author for being too didactic: "[Forsyth's] first intention is not to write an entertainment but to preach a political sermon. Its burden is that leftists and peaceniks really are fools whose habitual prating endangers civilization." Michiko Kakutani of the *New York Times* also felt that, compared to Forsyth's other novels, *The Fourth Protocol* "becomes predictable, and so lacking in suspense." But other critics, including *Washington Post Book World* reviewer Roderick MacLeish, maintained a contrary view. MacLeish asserted that it is Forsyth's "best book so far" because the author's characters are so much better developed. "Four books and a few million pounds after *Jackal* Frederick Forsyth has become a well-rounded novelist."

Of *The Negotiator,* Forsyth's tale of the kidnapping of an American president's son, *Globe and Mail* critic Margaret Cannon declared that "while nowhere nearly as good as *The Day of the Jackal* or *The Odessa File,* it's [Forsyth's] best work in recent years." Harry Anderson, writing in *Newsweek,* also called the novel "a comparative rarity; a completely satisfying thriller." Critics such as *Washington Post* reviewer John Katzenbach have resurrected the old complaints that Forsyth "relies on shallow characters and stilted dialogue," and that while "the dimensions of his knowledge are impressive, rarely does the information imparted serve any greater purpose." Acknowledging that *The Negotiator* has "too many characters and a plot with enough twists to fill a pretzel factory," Cannon nevertheless added that "the endless and irrelevant descriptive passages are gone and someone has averted Forsyth's tendency to go off on tiresome tangents."

"Perhaps recognizing the need for sharply defined heroes and villains," stated Andrew Macdonald in the *St. James Guide to Crime and Mystery Writers,* "Forsyth's next book, *The Deceiver,* is a nostalgic look back to the good old days (at least for field agents and writers) of the Cold War, when political positions seemed eternally frozen and villainy could be motivated simply by nationality." For British agent Sam McCready, those days were a series of successes. With the collapse of the Soviet Union, however, the government is poised to eliminate his position. As part of his protest against the retirement forced on him, McCready recounts four of his most successful exploits. McCready loses the protest and is sent into retirement. Forsyth nonetheless ends the novel on an uncertain note, with Saddam Hussein's invasion of Kuwait. "The notion that international crises are over, that a new and peaceful world order will prevail, is immediately proved wrong," Macdonald noted. "All that has changed is the names, cultures, and ideologies of the players, and there will always be a need for new versions of Sam McCready, Forsyth suggests."

The author revisits this changing world order in *The Fist of God,* which tells of a secret mission to Iraq in an attempt to prevent the use of a catastrophic doomsday weapon. The intelligence situation in Iraq's closed society has become critical, and the western allies recruit a young version of Sam McCready—Major Mike Martin—to obtain the information they need. Martin's mission is to contact an Israeli "mole," a secret agent planted in Iraq by the Mossad, Israel's secret service, years before. In the process he also encounters rumors of Saddam's ultimate weapon—a weapon he must destroy in order to ensure a western victory. "As with his best works," wrote Macdonald in the *St. James Guide to Crime and Mystery Writers,* "Forsyth gives a sense of peering behind the curtains created by governments and media, allowing a vision of how the real battles, mostly invisible, were carried out."

In *Icon,* Forsyth turns to contemporary Russian politics for a thriller about a presidential candidate with ties to the Russian mafia and plans for wholesale ethnic cleansing at home and renewed Russian aggression abroad. Jason Monk, ex-CIA agent, is hired by an unlikely group of Russian and American global players to get rid of candidate Igor Komarov before the election. "As usual," wrote a reviewer for *Publishers Weekly,* "Forsyth interweaves speculation with historical fact, stitching his plot pieces with a cogent analysis of both Russian politics and the world of espionage." Although Anthony Lejeune, writing in the *National Review,* believed that "the scale is too large, the mood too chilly, for much personal involvement" with the novel's characters, J. D. Reed claimed in *People* that "*Icon* finds the master in world-class form."

Forsyth experimented with untypical projects in 1999 with his sequel to *Phantom of the Opera,* and in 2000 with a group of five short stories and a novella originally published online and then in book form. With *The Phantom of Manhattan,* Forsyth posits a new life for the Phantom, Erik Muhlheim, subject of the gothic classic and the fabulously popular musical. In Forsyth's take, Muhlheim makes it to New York where he makes millions on Wall Street, opens his own opera house, and hires his long-desired love interest, Christine de Chagney, to sing for him. A critic for *Publishers Weekly* found that Forsyth "brings the Phantom to life in a new way, in an invigorating parable about loneliness, greed, and love." With *The Veteran and Other Stories,* Forsyth presents a mixture of tales, from a police procedural, to a high-class art scam to Custer's Last Stand. Ronnie H. Terpening, writing in *Library Journal,* felt that the usual Forsyth trademarks, or "revenge, mystery, murder, [and] deception," are all present in these stories "that showcase the author's ability to capture character and generate suspense in remarkably few words." D. J. Taylor, reviewing the collection in the *Spectator,* also had praise for these five "'tall stories': brisk little conceits or incidents that in lesser hands would dry up in a dozen pages or so but which Forsyth's narrative guile has no trouble in fleshing out to, in some cases, novella length." However, for Taylor the downside to Forsyth's usual compilation of detail is that "it is clearly now an authorial fixation, a pageant of rococo embellishments that frequently elbows aside the narrative it adorns."

Forsyth has more scope for such accumulation of detail in his 2003 thriller *Avenger,* a "story of revenge and loyalty," according to Nola Theiss writing in *Kliatt.* This "taut suspense thriller . . . brings current world events and personal relationships into play," Theiss further commented. Calvin Dexter was a special operations man in Vietnam who worked in the tunnels stalking his Vietcong victims. Now a lawyer by day, he is the Avenger at other times, tracking down and bringing to justice those who try to escape the law. Hired by a mining tycoon to find the Serbian killer of his grandson in Bosnia, Dexter takes on the mission of his life, tracking the killer to South America and battling both the Serbian killer's impeccable security apparatus as well as an FBI man trying to use the killer as bait to capture the terrorist Usama bin Laden.

Critics spoke of this novel being on a par with the author's first three books. For example, a critic for *Publishers Weekly* felt that this "strong and memorable novel is [Forsyth's] best in decades," and that the machinations of the Avenger in getting his man are "pure gold." *Booklist*'s Connie Fletcher commended Forsyth's "crisp narration" as well as his "extraordinary care with detail, his solid voice, and his exquisite pacing." All these factors combined to make *Avenger* a "totally engrossing thriller," according to Fletcher. Similarly, *Library Journal*'s Robert Conroy dubbed the novel "gripping, complex, and exciting." Conroy concluded that this "well-written tale of evil and retribution" compares "favorably" to Forsyth's classic *The Day of the Jackal.*

It has always been the plots and technical details in his novels that have most fascinated Forsyth. "Invention of the story is the most fun," the author told Peter Gorner in the *Chicago Tribune.*"It's satisfying, like doing a jigsaw or a crossword." He admitted to Groen that he loves the research: "I quite enjoy going after the facts. I put into my books a pretty heavy diet of factuality." Recognizing that Forsyth is aiming to entertain his audience with these techniques, Macdonald wrote that a "common element in all the criticism [against the author] is a refusal to accept Forsyth's docudrama formula for what it is, but rather to assume it should be more conventionally 'fictional.'" Forsyth has sold over thirty million books to readers who know, as *Detroit News* contributor Jay Carr put it, that the thrill of the author's books lies not in finding out how "Forsyth is going to defuse the bomb whose wick he ignites, but rather to see how he works out the details."

BIOGRAPHICAL AND CRITICAL SOURCES:

BOOKS

Bestsellers 89, Issue 4, Thomson Gale (Detroit, MI), 1990.

Contemporary Literary Criticism, Volume 36, Thomson Gale (Detroit, MI), 1986.

Contemporary Novelists, 7th edition, St. James Press (Detroit, MI), 2001.

Critical Survey of Mystery and Detective Fiction, Salem Press (Pasadena, CA), 1988.

Dictionary of Literary Biography, Volume 87: *British Mystery and Thriller Writers since 1940, First Series,* Thomson Gale (Detroit, MI), 1989.

St. James Guide to Crime and Mystery Writers, 4th edition, St. James (Detroit, MI), 1996.

PERIODICALS

American Theatre, April, 2000, Celia Wren, "Money Sings," p. 49.

Armchair Detective, May, 1974; winter, 1985.

Atlantic, December, 1972; August, 1974.

Book, November-December, 2001, Helen M. Jerome, "Return to Formula: Frederick Forsyth Is Back in Business," p. 24.

Book and Magazine Collector, June, 1989.

Booklist, March 1, 1994, p. 1139; October 15, 1999, Ray Olson, review of *The Phantom of Manhattan,* p. 417; August, 2001, David Pitt, review of *The Veteran and Other Stories,* p. 2096; July, 2003, Connie Fletcher, review of *Avenger,* p. 1845.

Book World, September 5, 1971, J. R. Frakes, review of *The Day of the Jackal.*

Boston Herald, November 22, 1999, Terry Byrne Mug, "Frederick Forsyth's Uninspired Sequel Skimps on Story: *Phantom* Sequel Is Unmasked," p. 37.

Chicago Tribune, October 16, 1984; April 16, 1989; June 14, 1989.

Chicago Tribune Book World, March 2, 1980, Peter Gorner, review of *The Devil's Alternative.*

Christian Science Monitor, September 7, 1984.

Daily News, September 30, 1984.

Daily Telegraph, December 18, 1999, Hugh Massingberd, "After the Phantom Vanished into Thin Air Hugh Massingberd Is Hooked by the Sequel to a Tale of Obsessive and Unrequited Passion"; October 6, 2001, Will Cohu, "Let's Twist Again."

Detroit News, February 10, 1980; August 15, 1982; April 30, 1989.

Economist, December 7, 1996, p. S3; October 18, 2003, review of *Avenger,* p. 84.

Entertainment Weekly, May 20, 1994, p. 55; October 3, 2003, Marc Bernardin, review of *Avenger,* p. 78.

Globe and Mail (Toronto, Ontario, Canada), September 8, 1984; August 29, 1987; April 29, 1989, Margaret Cannon, review of *The Negotiator;* November 27, 1999, p. D38.

Guardian (London, England), August 16, 1994, p. 3.

Independent (London, England), December 12, 2001, p. S8.

Insight on the News, July 11, 1994, p. 28.

Kirkus Reviews, October 1, 1999, p. 1517.

Kliatt, March, 1998, p. 48; March 2001, p. 18; January, 2004, Nola Theiss, review of *Avenger* (audiobook), 40-41.

Library Journal, September 1, 2001, Ronnie H. Terpening, review of *The Veteran and Other Stories,* p. 237.

Life, October 22, 1971.

Listener, June 17, 1971; September 28, 1972; January 10, 1980.

Los Angeles Times, March 19, 1980; March 28, 1980; May 7, 1982; August 28, 1987; January 27, 2002, Eugene Weber, review of *The Veteran and Other Stories,* p. R8.

Los Angeles Times Book Review, April 16, 1989.

National Observer, October 30, 1971.

National Review, August 2, 1974; December 23, 1996, Anthony Lejeune, review of *Icon,* p. 56.

New Leader, April 7, 1980.

New Statesman, September 20, 1974; January 15, 1988.

New Statesman & Society, September 6, 1991, pp. 35-36.

Newsweek, July 22, 1974, Anthony Collins, review of *The Dogs of War;* May 1, 1978; April 24, 1989, Harry Anderson, review of *The Negotiator.*

New York Post, September 21, 1974.

New York Times, October 24, 1972; April 18, 1978; January 17, 1980; August 30, 1984, Michiko Kakutani, review of *The Fourth Protocol;* August 28, 1987; November 16, 1999, Alan Cowell, "Jackal's Day Has Passed: Forsyth Tails the Phantom," p. E1.

New York Times Book Review, August 15, 1971; December 5, 1971; November 5, 1972; July 14, 1974; October 16, 1977; February 24, 1980; March 2, 1980; May 9, 1982; September 2, 1984; April 16, 1989.

Observer (London, England), June 13, 1971; September 24, 1972; September 22, 1974.

People, October 22, 1984; July 18, 1994, p. 24; October 21, 1996, J. D. Reed, review of *Icon,* p. 40.

Playboy, July, 1989, p. 26; November, 1991, p. 34.

Publishers Weekly, August 9, 1971; September 30, 1974 March 17, 1989; August 9, 1991, p. 43; March 7, 1994, p. 51; August 12, 1996, review of *Icon,* p. 61; May 18, 1998, Jean Richardson, "Forsyth's *Phantom* Sequel," p. 22; September 6, 1999, review of *The Phantom of Manhattan,* p. 77; November 20, 2000, review of *The Veteran and Other Stories,* p. 37; July 28, 2003, review of *Avenger,* p. 77.

Saturday Review, September 4, 1971; September 9, 1972.

Spectator, August 2, 1969, Auberon Waugh, review of *The Biafra Story;* December 11, 1999, p. 62; September 8, 2001, D. J. Taylor, review of *The Veteran and Other Stories,* p. 41.

Time, September 3, 1984, John Skow, review of *The Fourth Protocol.*

Times (London, England), August 22, 1982; March 17, 1987; May 13, 1989; November 17, 2001, p. W1.

Times Educational Supplement, December 17, 1999, p. 19.

Times Literary Supplement, July 2, 1971; October 25, 1974; December 19, 1975; November 19, 1999, p. 24.

Wall Street Journal, April 12, 1989; April 18, 1989.

Washington Post, August 19, 1971; September 26, 1971; December 12, 1978; February 13, 1981; March 28, 1984; August 29, 1987; April 21, 1989, John Katzenbach, review of *The Negotiator.*

Washington Post Book World, February 3, 1980; August 26, 1984, Roderick MacLeish, review of *The Fourth Protocol.*

World Press Review, March, 1980; May, 1987.

ONLINE

Unofficial Frederick Forsyth Homepage, http://www.whirlnet.co.uk/forsyth/ (July 25, 2004).*

* * *

FRANCE, R(ichard) T(homas) 1938-

PERSONAL: Born April 2, 1938, in Derry, Northern Ireland; son of Edgar and Doris Woosnam (Morgan) France; married Barbara Wilding (a teacher of learning disabled children), July 30, 1965; children: David Martyn, Susan Janet. *Ethnicity:* "Welsh, English, Belgian." *Education:* Balliol College, Oxford, B.A. (with second-class honors), 1960, M.A., 1963; University of London, B.D. (with first-class honors), 1962; University of Bristol, Ph.D., 1967. *Politics:* Liberal Democrat. *Hobbies and other interests:* Mountains, wildlife, travel, music, theater.

ADDRESSES: *Home*—Ty'n-y'Twill, Llangelynin, Llwyngwril, Gwynedd LL37 2QL, Wales.

CAREER: Tyndale Hall, Bristol, England, lecturer in biblical theology, 1963-65; assistant curate of Church of England, Cambridge, England, 1966-69; University of Ife, Ife, Nigeria, lecturer in biblical studies, 1969-73; Tyndale House, librarian, 1973-76; Ahmadu Bello University, Zaria, Nigeria, senior lecturer in religious studies, 1976-77; Tyndale House, Cambridge, research fellow, 1977-78, warden, 1978-81; London Bible College, London, England, senior lecturer in New Testament, 1981-88, head of Department of Biblical Studies, 1982-88, vice principal, 1983-88; Wycliffe Hall, Oxford, England, principal, 1989-95; rector of Church of England parishes in Shropshire, England, including parish of Wentnor, 1995-99; retired, 1999. Trinity Evangelical Divinity School, Deerfield, IL, visiting professor, 1975; Cambridge University, member of faculty of divinity, 1979-81; Gordon-Conwell Theological Seminary, South Hamilton, MA, visiting professor, 1986; Oxford University, chair of faculty of theology, 1994-95. St. James' Cathedral, Ibadan, Nigeria, canon, 1994—. British New Testament Conference, leader of Jesus Seminar, 1985-92.

MEMBER: Studiorum Novi Testamenti Societas, Tyndale Fellowship for Biblical Research.

WRITINGS:

The Living God, Inter-Varsity Press (Chicago, IL), 1970.

Jesus and the Old Testament, Inter-Varsity Press (Chicago, IL), 1971.

The Man They Crucified: A Portrait of Jesus, Inter-Varsity Press (London, England), 1975, Inter-Varsity Press (Chicago, IL), 1976, revised edition published as *Jesus the Radical,* 1989.

(With A. R. Millard and G. N. Stanton) *A Bibliographical Guide to New Testament Research,* JSOT Press (Sheffield, England), 1979.

(Editor, with D. Wenham, and contributor) *Gospel Perspectives,* JSOT Press (Sheffield, England), Volume 1, 1980, Volume 2, 1981, Volume 3, 1983.

Matthew: An Introduction and Commentary, Eerdmans (Grand Rapids, MI), 1985.

The Evidence for Jesus, Inter-Varsity Press (Chicago, IL), 1986.

Matthew: Evangelist and Teacher, Zondervan (Grand Rapids, MI), 1989.

Divine Government: God's Kingship in the Gospel of Mark, Society for the Promotion of Christian Knowledge (London, England), 1990.

Jesus in a Divided Society: Bible Studies from St. Matthew's Gospel, British Church Growth Association (Bedford, England), 1993.

(Editor, with A. E. McGrath) *Evangelical Anglicans: Their Role and Influence in the Church Today,* Society for the Promotion of Christian Knowledge (London, England), 1993.

Women in the Church's Ministry: A Test-Case for Biblical Hermeneutics, Paternoster (Exeter, England), 1995, Eerdmans (Grand Rapids, MI), 1997.

Mark, Bible Reading Fellowship (Oxford, England), 1996.

(With Philip Jenson) *Translating the Bible,* Grove Books (Cambridge, England), 1997.

The Gospel of Mark, Doubleday (New York, NY), 1998.

A Slippery Slope? The Ordination of Women and Homosexual Practice—A Case Study in Biblical Interpretation, Grove Books (Cambridge, England), 2000.

Timothy, Titus, and Hebrews: The People's Bible Commentary, Bible Reading Fellowship (Oxford, England), 2001.

The Gospel of Mark: A Commentary on the Greek Text, Eerdmans (Grand Rapids, MI), 2002.

Contributor to books, including *Biblical Interpretation and the Church: Text and Context,* edited by D. A. Carson, Paternoster (Exeter, England), 1984; *Chosen by God: Mary in Evangelical Perspective,* edited by D. F. Wright, Marshall Pickering (London, England), 1989; *Jesus of Nazareth, Lord and Christ: Essays on the Historical Jesus and New Testament Christology,* edited by J. B. Green and M. M. B. Turner, Eerdmans (Grand Rapids, MI), 1994; *To Proclaim Afresh,* edited by S. Kuhrt, Society for the Promotion of Christian Knowledge (London, England), 1995; and *Romans and the People of God,* edited by S. K. Soderlund and N. T. Wright, Eerdmans (Grand Rapids, MI), 1999. Editor of "Commentary," a regular feature in *Third Way,* 1984-93. Contributor to periodicals, including *New Testament Studies, Evangelical Quarterly,Anvil, Reformed Theological Review, Churchman, Novum Testamentum,* and *Theology.* Editor, *Themelios,* 1975-78, and *Tyndale Bulletin,* 1978-81.

WORK IN PROGRESS: "Hebrews," to be included in *Expositor's Bible Commentary,* revised edition, for Zondervan (Grand Rapids, MI); "Matthew," to be included in *New International Commentary on the New Testament,* Eerdmans (Grand Rapids, MI).

SIDELIGHTS: R. T. France once told *CA:* "Most of what I have published has been commissioned by publishers or editors, or has been the expected publication of lectures given by invitation (where the choice of subject has usually been my own). Most has been derived from my teaching areas and known areas of research. I have very seldom had the experience of delivering manuscripts to publishers who had not already commissioned the work."

BIOGRAPHICAL AND CRITICAL SOURCES:

PERIODICALS

Interpretation, January, 2003, Michael E. Vines, review of *The Gospel of Mark: A Commentary on the Greek Text,* p. 74.

* * *

FRANKEL, Valerie 1965-

PERSONAL: Born January 15, 1965, in Newark, NJ; daughter of Howard (a physician) and Judy Frankel. *Education:* Dartmouth College, B.A., 1987. *Politics:* Democrat. *Religion:* Jewish.

ADDRESSES: Office—11 Garden Place, Brooklyn, NY 11201. *Agent*—Nancy Yost, Lowenstein-Yost, 121 W. 27th St., New York, NY 10001. *E-mail*—valerie@valeriefrankel.com.

CAREER: Editor and author. *New York Woman,* New York, NY, researcher, 1987-89; *Mademoiselle,* New York, NY, associate editor, 1990-95, articles editor, 1993-99.

MEMBER: Authors Guild.

WRITINGS:

"WANDA MALLORY" MYSTERY SERIES

A Deadline for Murder, Pocket Books (New York, NY), 1991.

Murder on Wheels, Pocket Books (New York, NY), 1992.

Prime Time for Murder, Pocket Books (New York, NY), 1994.

A Body to Die For, Pocket Books (New York, NY), 1995.

OTHER

(With Ellen Tien) *The Heartbreak Handbook: How to Survive the Worst 24 Hours of Your Life and Move On,* Fawcett/Columbine (New York, NY), 1994.

(With Ellen Tien) *The I Hate My Job Handbook: How to Deal with Hell at Work,* Fawcett/Columbine (New York, NY), 1995.

(With Ellen Tien) *Prime-Time Style: The Ultimate TV Guide to Fashion Hits and Misses,* Berkley (New York, NY), 1996.

Smart vs. Pretty, Avon Books (New York, NY), 2000.

The Accidental Virgin, Avon Books (New York, NY), 2003.

The Not-So-Perfect Man, Avon Books (New York, NY), 2004.

(With Shannon Mullen) *The Best You'll Ever Have: What Every Woman Should Know about Getting and Giving Knock-Your-Socks-Off Sex,* Crown (New York, NY), 2005.

The Girlfriend Curse, Avon Books (New York, NY), 2005.

Work represented in anthologies, including *Malice Domestic 1,* 1992.

SIDELIGHTS: Valerie Frankel is the author of humorous self-help books, novels, and the "Wanda Mallory" mystery series. Frankel actually began her writing career as a fact-checker at *New York Woman.* She later left that post for a position at *Mademoiselle* where, among other endeavors, she wrote a column about sex. The experience helped prepare Frankel for writing her collection of entertaining self-help titles.

Frankel's book-length publications began with her mystery *A Deadline for Murder,* which introduced readers to tough-talkin' female private investigator, Wanda Mallory. Frankel continued the series with the publication of *Murder on Wheels, Prime Time for Murder* and *A Body to Die For.* In *Murder on Wheels* Wanda helps the leader of a biker gang locate money stolen from his social club. Wanda investigates the shooting death of a guest on a dating game show in *Prime Time for Murder,* and becomes a member at a posh health club in order to investigate a series of crimes in *A Body to Die For.*

With Ellen Tien, Frankel penned several self-help books on a variety of topics, including *The Heartbreak Handbook: How to Survive the Worst 24 Hours of Your Life and Move On,* which provides readers with helpful and humorous advice on coping with a breakup. The book includes tips from the authors, true stories from their friends, and advice from therapists. The authors also include quizzes, surveys, and other fun tidbits to keep readers' minds focused on anything but what's-his-name.

The I Hate My Job Handbook: How to Deal with Hell at Work is a guide to surviving a less-than-desirable job. Frankel and Tien give readers advice on coping with bad bosses and exhausting job searches. According to Megan Harlan of *Entertainment Weekly,* "Anyone who has ever hated a job should love this book." *Booklist*'s Barbara Jacobs observed that while the book "provides quite a few solutions to laugh about," it also gives readers some "commonsense advice."

Prime Time Style: The Ultimate Guide to Fashion Hits and Misses critiques the fashions of stars on thirty-five of Hollywood's hit television shows. With the help of wardrobe experts and hairstylists, the authors reveal style secrets and offer helpful advice on fashion do's and don'ts.

In addition to her mystery novels, Frankel's solo projects include the novels *Smart vs. Pretty, The Accidental Virgin,* and *The Not-So-Perfect Man.* In *Smart vs. Pretty,* Greenfield sisters Francesca and Amanda must devise a way to save their family-owned coffee shop from being overtaken by the large chain next door. With the help of a college student named Clarissa MacFlanahagan, the sisters find their way out of their business troubles. Elizabeth Mary Mellett of *Library Journal* termed the book "light, amusing, and generally entertaining."

The Accidental Virgin, originally appeared on *USAToday.com* as a seven-week series comprising an online novel in which Stacy Temple, a single thirty-something working as a marketer at *Thong.com,* lives a rather uneventful life. Stacy, who has been sex-free since she broke up with her boyfriend, Brian, almost a year ago, is informed by a magazine article that going without sex for a year constitutes becoming a "born-again virgin." Stacy, determined not to revert to virgin status, begins searching for a man to help her break her sexual stalemate. *Booklist*'s Kristine Huntley dubbed the book "laugh-out-loud funny." A *Publishers Weekly* reviewer noted, "Frankel's wit and playfulness make the tale scroll right along."

In *The Not-So-Perfect Man,* Frankel once again puts a humorous slant on troubled relationships. The novel's main character, Frieda Schast, gets ready to hit the dating scene after the death of her husband, Gregg. Set on making sure their sister finds the perfect man, Ilene and Betty offer advice and matchmaking services to Frieda. The three sisters anchor a story full of twists and relationship quandaries.

BIOGRAPHICAL AND CRITICAL SOURCES:

BOOKS

Heising, Willetta L., *Detecting Women 2: A Reader's Guide and Checklist for Mystery Series Written by Women,* Purple Moon Press, 1996-97.

PERIODICALS

Booklist, December 1, 1995, Barbara Jacobs, review of *The I Hate My Job Handbook: How to Deal with Hell at Work,* p. 593; February 15, 2003, Kristine Huntley, review of *The Accidental Virgin,* p. 1057.

Entertainment Weekly, February 23, 1996, Megan Harlan, review of *The I Hate My Job Handbook,* p. 118.

Kirkus Reviews, December 15, 2002, review of *The Accidental Virgin,* p. 1788.

Library Journal, December, 1995, Joshua Cohen, review of *The I Hate My Job Handbook,* p. 124; February 1, 2000, Elizabeth Mary Mellett, review of *Smart vs. Pretty,* p. 116.

Publishers Weekly, July 24, 2000, review of *The Accidental Virgin,* p. 34; January 12, 2004, review of *The Not-So-Perfect Man,* p. 35.

San Francisco Review, March, 1997, review of *Prime-Time Style,* p. 8.

ONLINE

USA Today Web site, http://www.usatoday.com/ (March 14, 2003), "Talk Today (Community chat): *The Accidental Virgin: Valerie Frankel.*"*

* * *

FRAWLEY, William John 1953-

PERSONAL: Born September 17, 1953, in Newark, NJ. *Education:* Glassboro State College, B.A. (magna cum laude), 1975; Louisiana State University, M.A., 1977; Northwestern University, Ph.D., 1979. *Religion:* "Atheist." *Hobbies and other interests:* Motorcycles, three-cushion billiards.

ADDRESSES: Office—Faculties of Anthropology and Psychology, George Washington University, Washington, DC 20052.

CAREER: University of Delaware, Newark, assistant professor, 1979-82, associate professor of English, beginning 1982, assistant director of doctoral program in linguistics, beginning 1980; George Washington University, Washington, DC, member of anthropology and psychology faculties. Lecturer at linguistics institutes in Poznan, Poland, 1981, 1983, Szolnuk, Hungary, 1981, Pecs, Hungary, 1982, and Rabat, Morocco, 1982. Heartatech, vice president.

MEMBER: Dictionary Society of North America, Linguistic Society of America, Modern Language Association of America.

WRITINGS:

(Translator) *Instead of Music: Poems by Alain Bosquet,* Louisiana State University Press (Baton Rouge, LA), 1980.
(Editor, with Robert J. Di Pietro and Alfred Wedel) *The First Delaware Symposium on Language Studies: Selected Papers,* University of Delaware Press (Newark, DE), 1982.
(Editor) *Linguistics and Literacy,* Plenum (New York, NY), 1982.
(Editor) *Translation: Literary, Linguistic, and Philosophical Perspectives,* University of Delaware Press (Newark, DE), 1984.
(Editor, with Roger Steiner) *Advances in Lexicography,* Boreal Scholarly Publishers, 1986.
Text and Epistemology, Ablex Publishing (Norwood, NJ), 1987.
Linguistic Semantics, Lawrence Erlbaum Associates (Hillsdale, NJ), 1992.
Vygotsky and Cognitive Silence: Language and the Unification of the Social and Computational Mind, Harvard University Press (Cambridge, MA), 1997.
(Editor of revision) *International Encyclopedia of Linguistics,* four volumes, 2nd edition, Oxford University Press (New York, NY), 2003.

Contributor to *Studies in Science and Culture,* edited by M. Amsler. Contributor to language and linguistic journals.

SIDELIGHTS: William John Frawley once commented: "I write to wage a constant attack on boredom (my own); I write about language because I think that language makes humans human: I'm constantly surrounded by data."

BIOGRAPHICAL AND CRITICAL SOURCES:

PERIODICALS

Library Journal, July, 2003, Rosanne M. Cordell, review of *International Encyclopedia of Linguistics,* p. 73.*

* * *

FREDA, Joseph 1951-

PERSONAL: Born December 3, 1951, in Mobile, AL; son of Matthew J. (an Air Force pilot) and Betty (a homemaker; maiden name, Robbins) Freda; married Elise Andkjar (an artist and writer), June 9, 1974. *Education:* State University of New York, B.A., 1974; University of New Hampshire, M.A., 1978. *Hobbies and other interests:* Fine letterpress printing.

ADDRESSES: Home—P.O. Box 99, Kenoza Lake, NY 12750. *Agent*—Gail Hochman, Brandt & Hochman Literary Agents, 1501 Broadway, New York, NY 10036. *E-mail*—jfreda@joefreda.com.

CAREER: Writer. University of New Hampshire, Durham, instructor, 1977-81; Digital Equipment Corporation, Merrimack, NH, senior software writer, editor, and systems manager, 1981-84; Tegra, Inc., Billerica, MA, communications manager, 1984-88, product manager, 1988-92, manager of creative services, 1992-94; Prepress Solutions, East Hanover, NJ, creative director, beginning 1994; Freda + Flaherty Creative, Kenoza Lake, NY, co-owner. Freelance writer, 1995—.

AWARDS, HONORS: Individual Artists Fellowship, New Hampshire State Arts Council, 1993, for *Suburban Guerrillas;* 2003 Heritage Award, Upper Delaware Heritage Alliance, for *The Patience of Rivers.*

WRITINGS:

Suburban Guerrillas (novel), W. W. Norton (New York, NY), 1995.
The Patience of Rivers (novel), W. W. Norton (New York, NY), 2003.

Contributor of short stories to *Coffee Journal, New Writers, Kenyon Review, StoryQuarterly,* and *The Literary Gazette.*

SIDELIGHTS: Joseph Freda explained in *Publishers Weekly* that his debut novel, *Suburban Guerrillas,* did not begin as a novel, but rather as several short stories and a novella about the same characters in the same location. "Everyone who read it said it was a novel," he reported, "so I went back and pulled it together that way."

The resulting book is the story of a group of suburban neighbors in Hurley, New Hampshire, who discover a developer's intent to turn woodlands adjoining their properties into a site for cheap-looking condominiums.

The cast includes Ed Jacques, who is a pillar of the community with the best-kept lawn in the neighborhood, but who also secretly lusts after Susie Stevens, a flight attendant with a neglectful husband. Susie is having an affair with Leonard Walker, whose wife is also cheating on him. Also central to the novel are the Walkers' long-time friends, Ray and Marisse Vann. Despite all of the sexual intrigue between these people, they manage to band together to sabotage the developer. Their tactics include changing signs advertising ranch houses so that they read "raunchy houses," as well as using radio-controlled airplanes to distribute leaflets printed with the structural problems inherent in the condos. According to Gary Krist in the *New York Times Book Review,* the situation escalates until Ray Vann "oversteps the bounds of legitimate protest with a single tasteless act." After this, the Vanns feel that they must leave the suburbs and return to Boston, hoping to achieve a fresh start. The author himself summed up the novel's theme in *Publishers Weekly:* "The book deals with the realities of contemporary life." Referring to the new condo development central to the plot, he added that "the characters react against that and try to take control of the environment. They're not always effective. The story moves forward on plot, but the impetus to read is also the development of the main characters—people in their late thirties and early forties—and their concerns."

Including *Suburban Guerrillas* on a recommended summer reading list, Merle Rubin in the *Christian Science Monitor* called the novel "beguiling." The reviewer went on to describe it as "a very believable portrait of ordinary, real, everyday people." Krist credited Freda with helping to revive the reputation of the suburban novel, and, like Rubin, offered a tribute to the author's characterizations: "His suburbanites may not be the most flamboyant characters in our literature, but they are decent, passionate, and reflective people, full of submerged yearnings that they attempt to accommodate in as ethical a manner as their natures will permit."

Freda published his second novel, *The Patience of Rivers,* in 2003. The plot centers around Nick Lauria, who is spending his last summer before college hanging out with his best friend Charlie Miles and working at his family's campground in Delaware Ford, New York, just up the road from where Woodstock is about to be held. Personal problems weigh heavily on Nick's mind. He is worried about being drafted and sent to Vietnam, and his family is in financial trouble because of poor judgment on the part of his father's business partner, who is also Charlie's father. The family's financial situation may force them to sell their campground and is putting a strain on his parents' already troubled marriage. In *Publishers Weekly,* contributor Gail Hochman wrote, "Freda is an engaging storyteller, and the likeable Nick anchors this well-paced tale." Hochman went on to suggest, "Some readers may be put off by the remoteness of the scene-setting (a long passage has Nick watching the moon landing, for instance), but Freda's well-observed family dynamics make this a solid if unspectacular effort." A *Kirkus Reviews* contributor also deemed *The Patience of Rivers* "somewhat slow-paced" but concluded that it is a "well-crafted and leisurely account of public strifes intersecting with private griefs."

BIOGRAPHICAL AND CRITICAL SOURCES:

PERIODICALS

Booklist, January 1, 2003, Whitney Scott, review of *The Patience of Rivers,* p. 846.

Christian Science Monitor, June 29, 1995, pp. B1, B4.

Kirkus Reviews, November 1, 2002, review of *The Patience of Rivers,* pp. 1551-1553.

Library Journal, November 1, 2002, Lawrence Rungren, review of *The Patience of Rivers,* p. 128.

New York Times Book Review, May 7, 1995, p. 23.

Publishers Weekly, January 23, 1995, p. 44; November 11, 2002, Gail Hochman, review of *The Patience of Rivers,* p. 39.

ONLINE

Freda + Flaherty Creative, http://www.ffcreative.com/ (March 23, 2004).

Joseph Freda Home Page, http://www.joefreda.com/ (March 23, 2004).*

* * *

FRIEDMAN, Mickey
See FRIEDMAN, Michaele Thompson

* * *

FRIEDMAN, Michaele Thompson 1944-
(Mickey Friedman)

PERSONAL: Born August 30, 1944, in Dothan, AL; daughter of Carl Clinton (a railroad ticket agent) and Laura Lee (a teacher and librarian; maiden name, Allen; later surname, Geddie) Thompson; married Alan Jacob Friedman (director, New York Hall of Science), December 26, 1966. *Education:* Florida State University, B.A., 1966, M.A., 1968. *Politics:* Democrat. *Religion:* Methodist.

ADDRESSES: Home—276 W. 11th St., New York, NY 10014. *Agent*—Virginia Barber, 101 5th Ave., New York, NY 10003.

CAREER: Florida State University, Tallahassee, editorial assistant, 1968-69; Hiram College, Hiram, OH, staff editor, 1970-72; *San Francisco Examiner,* San Francisco, CA, reporter, 1977-83; mystery writer, 1984—.

MEMBER: International Association of Crime Writers, PEN, Authors Guild, Authors League of America, Mystery Writers of America (member of board of directors, 1989-93; publications chair), Sisters in Crime, Phi Beta Kappa.

WRITINGS:

MYSTERY NOVELS; UNDER NAME MICKEY FRIEDMAN

Hurricane Season, Dutton (New York, NY), 1983.
The Fault Tree, Dutton (New York, NY), 1984.
Paper Phoenix, Dutton (New York, NY), 1986.
Venetian Mask, Scribner (New York, NY), 1987.
Magic Mirror, Viking (New York, NY), 1988.
A Temporary Ghost, Viking (New York, NY), 1989.
Riptide, St. Martin's Press (New York, NY), 1994.

OTHER

A Booklover's Guide to San Francisco, Examiner Special Projects (San Francisco, CA), 1977.

(Compiler) *The Crown Crime Companion: The Top 100 Mystery Novels of All Time,* annotations by Otto Penzler, Crown Trade Paperbacks (New York, NY), 1995.

Short stories anthologized in *Sisters in Crime,* Berkley Publishing (New York, NY), 1989; *Christmas Stalkings,* Mysterious Press (New York, NY), 1991; *The New Mystery,* Dutton (New York, NY), 1992; *Missing in Manhattan,* Longmeadow Press (Stamford, CT), 1992; and *Justice in Manhattan,* Longmeadow Press (Stamford, CT), 1994. Author of "Book Scene," a column in *San Francisco Examiner,* 1978-82.

SIDELIGHTS: Before becoming a novelist under the name Mickey Friedman, Michaele Thompson Friedman was a reporter for the *San Francisco Examiner.* She once told *CA* how she fit fiction writing into her busy schedule: "I sat down after dinner with a notebook and wrote for about an hour—from eight to nine. In a year and a half I had finished [my first book]. If a person really wants to write a book, there are ways to do it; you don't, contrary to popular belief, have to have great blocks of time, or quiet, or even privacy." This first attempt produced *Hurricane Season,* a mystery about moonshine and murder in a small 1950s Florida town which was described in *Library Journal* as "a world of wide white sand beaches, juke joints, illicit passion, rusting ferries, greed, a derelict hotel, betrayal, pine woods and damp, oppressive heat."

Critics received *Hurricane Season* warmly and dubbed Friedman a writer to watch. Newgate Callendar in the *New York Times Book Review* remarked that Friedman's characters are portrayed with "the kind of realism that stems from William Faulkner." "*Hurricane Season* leaves the reader with a kind of itch," commented Carolyn See in the *Los Angeles Times,* "a yearning to go into every little ratty dime store with fly-specked windows in every little forgotten town across the country and see what's really going on." "A remarkable, compelling first novel," wrote Jean M. White in the *Washington Post Book World.* "What makes *Hurricane Season* special is its extraordinary sense of place," White continued; "the backwater land of Florida pervades the story. These are people and a way of life that few of us have met before."

Friedman's next novel, *The Fault Tree,* begins with a fatal amusement park mishap in San Francisco; the ensuing investigation ultimately leads "disaster analyst" Marina Robinson to the village in India where her sister supposedly died in a fire years ago. The lonely and neurotic Marina, though suffering guilt over her role in her sister's death, "functions expertly from a plucky, competent exterior," according to Carolyn See in the *Los Angeles Times.* Philip Galanes praised Friedman's "dramatic technique of timing her heroine's discovery of clues" in the *New York Times Book Review.* See, recognizing the fluidity of the plot, equated reading Friedman's story to "dancing . . . with a skill you never knew you possessed."

Paper Phoenix tells the story of the recently divorced San Francisco socialite Maggie Longstreet, who overcomes her depression only after learning of the "suicide" of a tabloid magazine editor. Based on a passing comment from her ex-husband, Maggie suspects murder and commences her own investigation. An *Armchair Detective* reviewer characterized the story as "conventional . . . but a pleasant diversion nonetheless," and Callendar commented in the *New York Times Book Review* that Friedman "has set out to entertain, and she has succeeded in doing so in a bright and sensitive manner."

The exotic festivities of the annual Winter Carnival in Venice provide the setting for *Venetian Mask.* Five friends plan to meet in costume in the Piazza San Marco where they will attempt to uncover one another's identity. Their plan goes awry when one of them, a young bisexual American, turns up dead in a canal, and his wife disappears into the reveling crowd to escape a similar fate. *People*'s John Stark praised the mystery for its "kaleidoscopic" setting, commenting that *Venetian Mask* is "a brainy, psychologically astute cut above most mysteries." *Chicago Tribune* contributor Alice Cromie described the plot as "twisted and [as] easy to get lost in as a back street in the city itself."

Georgia Lee Maxwell, a disillusioned American journalist-turned-Paris-magazine columnist, solves murders in Friedman's next two novels. In *Magic Mirror,* Maxwell becomes embroiled in an art museum heist involving a mirror that belonged to the Renaissance astrologer Nostradamus. Psychics, kidnappers, and a cat named Twinkle are woven into a narrative that "offers suspense with a light touch and bizarre, unexpected twists," observed Sean White of the *Washington Post Book World,* although a *Times Literary Supplement* reviewer lamented the absence of a romantic interlude for Maxwell, who "after all, . . . is in Paris." In *A Temporary Ghost,* Maxwell receives death threats when she agrees to ghostwrite the biography of the wealthy and widowed Vivien Howard—a biography that will proclaim Howard's innocence in her husband's murder. Vivien's French villa houses a tidy cast of suspicious characters, including Vivien's lover, Ross Santee, and her shady motorcycle-riding son.

Friedman once told *CA:* "I have chosen to write in the mystery-suspense genre because, first, it provides a form for a writer to play with. Limitations can be liberating. Also, it's an opportunity to look at the idea of death and what it means, but look at it in a way that isn't too disturbing and threatening. Mainly I want to engross and entertain, but I don't mind nibbling away at issues significant to our emotional lives, too.

"My advice is, if you aren't compelled to write a book, don't torture yourself. If you are, find the best way to fit it into your life and then do it."

BIOGRAPHICAL AND CRITICAL SOURCES:

PERIODICALS

Armchair Detective, spring, 1987, review of *Paper Phoenix.*

Booklist, February 15, 1994, Emily Melton, review of *Riptide,* p. 1063.

Chicago Tribune, August 2, 1987, Alice Cromie, review of *Venetian Mask.*

Library Journal, July, 1983, review of *Hurricane Season;* May 1, 1995, Rex E. Klett, review of *The Crown Crime Companion: The Top 100 Mystery Novels of All Time,* p. 136.

Los Angeles Times, June 20, 1983, Carolyn See, review of *Hurricane Season;* December 6, 1984, Carolyn See, review of *The Fault Tree.*

New York Times Book Review, November 27, 1983, Newgate Callendar, review of *Hurricane Season;* February 24, 1985, Philip Galanes, review of *The Fault Tree;* June 1, 1986, Newgate Callendar, review of *Paper Phoenix.*

People, September 21, 1987, John Stark, review of *Venetian Mask.*

Publishers Weekly, January 10, 1994, review of *Riptide,* p. 48; September 19, 1994, review of *Justice in Manhattan,* p. 54.

Times Literary Supplement, November 3, 1989, review of *Magic Mirror.*

Wall Street Journal, December 11, 1995, Tom Nolan, review of *The Crown Crime Companion,* p. A11.

Washington Post Book World, August 21, 1982, Jean M. White, review of *Hurricane Season;* September 18, 1988, Sean White, review of *Magic Mirror.**

* * *

FROHNEN, Bruce (P.) 1962-

PERSONAL: Born December 18, 1962, in Salt Lake City, UT; son of William Roger (in business) and Mary Grace (a homemaker; maiden name, Larsen) Frohnen. *Education:* California State University—Sacramento, B.A., 1984; University of California—Davis, M.A. (political science), 1985; Cornell University, M.A. (government), 1985, Ph.D., 1988; Emory University, J.D., 1993. *Religion:* Roman Catholic.

ADDRESSES: Home—3546 Fieldcrest Lane, Ypsilanti, MI 48197-6820. *Office*—Russell Kirk Center for Cultural Renewal, P.O. Box 4, Mecosta, MI 49332.

CAREER: National Federation of Independent Business, Sacramento, CA, legislative assistant, 1983-85; Reed College, Portland, OR, visiting assistant professor of political studies, 1988-89; Cornell College, Mount Vernon, IA, visiting assistant professor of political studies, 1989-90; Oglethorpe University, Atlanta, GA, instructor in political science, 1992-93; Ave Maria School of Law, Ann Arbor, MI, assistant professor of law. Cornell University, guest lecturer, 1987; also taught at Emory University and Catholic University of America. Heritage Foundation, adjunct fellow of Henry Salvatori Center, 1991-93, and Bradley Resident Scholar; Liberty Fund, senior research fellow; Johns Hopkins School of Advanced International Studies, Washington, DC, visiting scholar in Program on Social Change; Russell Kirk Center for Cultural Renewal, senior fellow. U.S. Department of Justice, summer law clerk in Office of Policy Development, 1992; speech writer for U.S. Senator Spencer Abraham. Guest on media programs, including *Encounter,* Voice of America, 1991.

WRITINGS:

Virtue and the Promise of Conservatism: The Legacy of Burke and Tocqueville University Press of Kansas (Lawrence, KS), 1993.

The New Communitarians and the Crisis of Modern Liberalism, University Press of Kansas (Lawrence, KS), 1996.

(Editor, with George W. Carey) *Community and Tradition: Conservative Perspectives on the American Experience,* Rowman & Littlefield (Lanham, MD), 1998.

(Editor and contributor) *The Anti-Federalists: Selected Writings and Speeches,* Regnery (Washington, DC), 1999.

(Editor) *The American Republic: Primary Sources,* Liberty Fund (Indianapolis, IN), 2002.

Work represented in anthologies, including *Tocqueville's Liberty: Defending Human Greatness in Democratic Times,* edited by Peter Lawler, Garland Publishing (New York, NY), 1992. Contributor of articles and reviews to political science journals, including *Annals of the American Academy of Political and Social Science* and *World and I,* and newspapers. Associate editor, *Bankruptcy Development Journal,* 1992-93.

WORK IN PROGRESS: The Age of Recovery: Public Meaning in American Life.

BIOGRAPHICAL AND CRITICAL SOURCES:

PERIODICALS

American Political Science Review, March, 2000, Steven Kautz, review of *Community and Tradition: Conservative Perspectives on the American Experience,* p. 164.

Choice, June, 1993, D. J. Maletz, review of *Virtue and the Promise of Conservatism: The Legacy of Burke and Tocqueville,* p. 1703; December, 1996, review of *The New Communitarians and the Crisis of Modern Liberalism,* p. 688.

Christian Century, October 27, 1993, review of *Virtue and the Promise of Conservatism,* p. 1066.

History: Review of New Books, summer, 1997, Keith Ian Polakoff, review of *The New Communitarians and the Crisis of Modern Liberalism,* p. 148.

Journal of American History, June, 1994, Matthew Mancini, review of *Virtue and the Promise of Conservatism,* p. 272.

Journal of Politics, August, 1995, Peter J. Diamond, review of *Virtue and the Promise of Conservatism,* p. 87; November, 1997, Charles Lockhart, review of *The New Communitarians and the Crisis of Modern Liberalism,* p. 1309.

Journal of Religion, October, 2000, Ted V. McAllister, review of *Community and Tradition,* p. 700.

Journal of Socio-Economics, May-June, 1997, Charles Lockhart, review of *The New Communitarians and the Crisis of Modern Liberalism,* p. 327.

Modern Age, summer, 1994, James E. Person, Jr., review of *Virtue and the Promise of Conservatism,* p. 373; spring, 1999, Bradley C. S. Watson, review of *The New Communitarians and the Crisis of Modern Liberalism* and *Community and Tradition,* p. 160.

National Review, February 1, 1993, Forrest McDonald, review of *Virtue and the Promise of Conservatism,* p. 54.

Review of Politics, spring, 1997, Kenneth R. Craycraft, Jr., review of *The New Communitarians and the Crisis of Modern Liberalism,* p. 398.

Social Science Quarterly, December, 1994, James W. Muller, review of *Virtue and the Promise of Conservatism,* p. 898.

Times Literary Supplement, June 18, 1993, John Gray, review of *Virtue and the Promise of Conservatism,* p. 4; January 17, 1997, Roger Kimball, review of *The New Communitarians and the Crisis of Modern Liberalism,* p. 24.

University Bookman, April, 1993, review of *Virtue and the Promise of Conservatism,* p. 4; fall, 1997, review of *The New Communitarians and the Crisis of Modern Liberalism,* p. 30.

Wall Street Journal, Midwest Edition, September 26, 1996, review of *The New Communitarians and the Crisis of Modern Liberalism,* p. A10.

ONLINE

Conservative Book Service, http://www.conservativebookservice.com/ (October 1, 2002), review of *The Anti-Federalists.*

Russell Kirk Center for Cultural Renewal, http://www.kirkcenter.org/ (May 12, 2004).

University Press of Kansas Web Site, http://www.kansaspress.ku.edu/ (October 1, 2002), publisher's description of *The New Communitarians and the Crisis of Modern Liberalism.**

* * *

FROMMER, Harvey 1937-

PERSONAL: Born October 10, 1937, in Brooklyn, NY; son of Max and Fannie (Wechsler) Frommer; married Myrna Katz (a writer, teacher, and freelance editor), January 23, 1960; children: Jennifer, Frederic, Jan. *Education:* New York University, B.S., 1957, M.A., 1961, Ph.D., 1974. *Religion:* Jewish. *Hobbies and other interests:* Gardening.

ADDRESSES: *Office*—MALS Program, Dartmouth College, 116 Wentworth, HB 6092, Hanover, NH 03755. *E-mail*—harvey.frommer@Dartmouth.edu.

CAREER: Professor, writer. United Press International (UPI), Chicago, IL, sportswriter, 1957-58; New York public schools, New York, NY, high school English teacher, 1960-70; City University of New York, New York City Technical College, professor of writing and speech, 1970—. Adjunct professor of journalism, Adelphi University, 1982-84; adjunct professor of history, New York University, 1984; Dartmouth College, Hanover, NH, professor of liberal studies. Has appeared on television and radio talk shows as a sports nostalgia and trivia expert. Historical consultant to Broadway play *The First,* 1983. Guest curator and executive producer of "Stars of David: Jews in Sports" exhibit at B'nai B'rith Klutznik Museum, Washington, DC, 1991. *Military service:* U.S. Army, 1958-59.

MEMBER: Association of American University Professors.

AWARDS, HONORS: City University of New York, Salute to Scholars Award, 1984; United States Olympic Committee, Olympic Book of the Year, 1984, for *Olympic Controversies;* Autobiography of the Year nomination, *Spitball* (magazine), 1988, for *Throwing Heat: The Autobiography of Nolan Ryan.*

WRITINGS:

A Baseball Century: The First 100 Years of the National League, Macmillan (New York, NY), 1976.

(With Ron Weinmann) *A Sailing Primer,* Atheneum (New York, NY), 1978.

The Martial Arts: Judo and Karate, Atheneum (New York, NY), 1978.

Sports Lingo: A Dictionary of the Language of Sports, Atheneum (New York, NY), 1979.

Sports Roots: How Nicknames, Namesakes, Trophies, Competitions, and Expressions in the World of Sports Came to Be, Atheneum (New York, NY), 1979.

The Great American Soccer Book, Atheneum (New York, NY), 1980.

New York City Baseball: The Last Golden Age, 1947-1957, Macmillan (New York, NY), 1980, with new preface by the author and new foreword by Monte Irvin, University of Wisconsin Press (Madison, WI), 2004.

The Sports Dates Book, Ace (New York, NY), 1981.

Rickey and Robinson: The Men Who Broke Baseball's Color Barrier, Macmillan (New York, NY), 1982, Taylor (New York, NY), 2003.

Baseball's Greatest Rivalry: The New York Yankees and the Boston Red Sox, Atheneum (New York, NY), 1982.

Baseball's Greatest Records: Streaks, and Feats, Atheneum (New York, NY), 1983.

Jackie Robinson, F. Watts (New York, NY), 1984.

Baseball's Hall of Fame, F. Watts (New York, NY), 1985.

Baseball's Greatest Managers, F. Watts (New York, NY), 1985.

City Tech: The First Forty Years, Technical College Press (Brooklyn, NY), 1986.

Olympic Controversies, F. Watts (New York, NY), 1987.

(With Red Holzman) *Red on Red,* Bantam Books (New York, NY), 1987.

Primitive Baseball: The First Quarter-Century of the National Pastime, Atheneum (New York, NY), 1988.

(With Nolan Ryan) *Throwing Heat: The Autobiography of Nolan Ryan,* Doubleday (New York, NY), 1988.

A Hundred and Fiftieth Anniversary Album of Baseball, F. Watts (New York, NY), 1988.

Growing Up at Bat: Fifty Years of Little League Baseball, Pharos Books (New York, NY), 1989.

(With Tony Dorsett) *Running Tough: Memoirs of a Football Maverick,* Doubleday (New York, NY), 1989.

(With Don Strock) *Behind the Lines: A Veteran Quarterback's Look inside the NFL,* introduction by Dan Mariano, Pharos Books (New York, NY), 1991.

(With Red Holzman) *Holzman on Hoops: The Man Who Led the Knicks through Two World Championships Tells It Like It Was,* Taylor (Dallas, TX), 1991.

Shoeless Joe and Ragtime Baseball, Taylor (Dallas, TX), 1992.

Big Apple Baseball: An Illustrated History from the Boroughs to the Ballparks, Taylor (Dallas, TX), 1995.

The New York Yankee Encyclopedia, Macmillan (New York, NY), 1997.

(Compiler, with son, Frederick J. Frommer) *Growing Up Baseball: An Oral History,* Taylor (Dallas, TX), 2001.

A Yankee Century: A Celebration of the First Hundred Years of Baseball's Greatest Team, introduction by Paul O'Neill, Berkley Books (New York, NY), 2002.

WITH WIFE, MYRNA KATZ FROMMER:

(With Nancy Lieberman-Cline) *Basketball My Way,* Scribner (New York, NY), 1982.

Sports Genes, Ace (New York, NY), 1982.

(Editor) *The Games of the Twenty-third Olympiad: Los Angeles 1984 Commemorative Book,* International Sport Publications, 1984.

(Compiler) *It Happened in the Catskills: An Oral History in the Words of Busboys, Bellhops, Guests, Proprietors, Comedians, Agents, and Others Who Lived It,* Harcourt Brace (San Diego, CA), 1991.

(Compiler) *It Happened in Brooklyn,* Harcourt Brace (New York, NY), 1993.

(Compiler)*Growing Up Jewish in America: An Oral History,* Harcourt Brace (New York, NY), 1995.

(Compiler) *It Happened on Broadway: An Oral History of the Great White Way,* Harcourt Brace (New York, NY), 1998, with new preface, University of Wisconsin Press (Madison, WI), 2004.

(Compiler) *It Happened in Manhattan: An Oral History of Life in the City during the Mid-Twentieth Century,* Berkley Books (New York, NY), 2001.

Contributor of articles and reviews to professional journals and periodicals, including *New York Times, New York Daily News, Los Angeles Times, Yankees* (magazine), *Library Journal,Golf Digest, St. Louis Post-Dispatch, Queens* (magazine), *Newsday* and United Features.

SIDELIGHTS: In 1974, Harvey Frommer wrote his doctoral dissertation on the influence of sports on television and of television on sports. His efforts to have the work published resulted in the opportunity to write *A Baseball Century: The First 100 Years of the National League.* He continued writing about sports throughout his academic career, turning out dozens of volumes of sports history, biography, and facts. He writes about several sports, but baseball is Frommer's specialty, understandable given that he was born in Brooklyn and spent most of his life in New York.

Frommer is editor of *The New York Yankee Encyclopedia,* which is a history of the team from its beginnings in 1903 through the 1996 World Series championship. *Growing Up Baseball: An Oral History,* which Frommer wrote with his son, draws on interviews with famous and not-so-famous ballplayers who share their memories of striving for the big leagues. They talk of playing with their fathers and friends, in inner-city neighborhoods and on rural farms, and of Little League games where their mothers sat in the bleachers cheering them on. Tidbits include the fact that Dom DiMaggio learned his fielding skills playing catch with his brother, Joe, in hilly San Francisco. Frommer includes an interview with Elden Auker, who at age ninety-one, was the oldest living player. *A Yankee Century: A Celebration of the First Hundred Years of Baseball's Greatest Team,* called a "gem" by *Booklist*'s GraceAnne A. DeCandido, takes Yankee history into the twenty-first century.

Black Issues Book Review contributor Art Rust, Jr. reviewed the reprinted *Rickey and Robinson: The Men Who Broke Baseball's Color Barrier* twenty years after its original publication. It is the story of how Branch Rickey, general manager of the Brooklyn Dodgers, chose Jackie Robinson to be the first black major league player, easier to accomplish after the death of baseball commissioner Kennesaw Mountain Landis, who had been firm in keeping it an all-white sport. Rickey first gained the support of club owners, then selected the talented Robinson, whom he instructed on how he could and could not respond to the slurs and obstacles that were sure to come. Another hurdle was gaining acceptance of Robinson by his teammates and of the idea within the black community. The barrier was broken in 1945. Landis had died the previous year. Rust wrote, "I've read more than a dozen books on the Rickey/Robinson tandem, and I must say that Frommer's is the best structured. He brings Robinson's persona alive, proving why he was the first black man selected to break the racial barrier."

Frommer and his wife, Myrna Katz Frommer, team teach oral history courses at Dartmouth College. They have created a number of books together, including several oral histories, such as their second, *It Happened in Brooklyn.* The 100 contributors range from celebrities like Jerry Stiller and Marvin Kaplan to ordinary people who relive three decades, from World War II to Vietnam, including their recollections of growing up in the multiethnic community and enjoying the experiences it had to offer, like trips to Coney Island.

The Frommers next compiled the essays for *Growing Up Jewish in America: An Oral History* and *It Happened on Broadway: An Oral History of the Great White Way,* which opens with a contribution from Carol Channing. *Booklist*'s Jack Helbig wrote, "There are plenty of diamonds in this loosely ordered heap of interviews." For this volume, the Frommers talked with actors, producers, directors, playwrights, composers, lyricists, stage managers, set designers, critics, and the children of now-gone Broadway greats. A *Publishers Weekly* contributor wrote that the "never-boring stories the Frommers have gathered demonstrate what it took to fill those seats." *Nation* reviewer Rachel Shteir remarked that the Frommers "cast the discussion of Broadway in the fabulous past. Broadway is over but let's celebrate it, thcy sccm to be saying."

It Happened in Manhattan: An Oral History of Life in the City during the Mid-Twentieth Century recalls the people, places, food, music, and cultural icons of the period, as well as memories of days past in Harlem and Greenwich Village, changing cultures, landmarks now gone (the famous Automats), and those that have survived and been restored. A *Kirkus Reviews* contributor called the volume a "self-congratulatory oral history, garrulous nostalgia, and great fun for those who recall the days of Tin Pan Alley and three baseball teams in one small, favored place."

Kendal Dodge Butler reviewed *It Happened in Manhattan* for *CultureVulture.net,* calling it "an irresistible collection of interviews with Manhattanites rich and poor, talented and ordinary, famous and unknown, clearly united in their unanimous conviction that Manhattan was, is, and always will be the most exciting place on earth."

Frommer told *CA:* "Sports and work and writing fascinate me; gardening acts as a release. I am involved all the time with one of these or another. I have written almost thirty books on sports and look forward to doing many more. I also have hopes of expanding my writing into other fields—gardening, travel, and institutional history. In 1986 *City Tech: The First Forty Years* was published. I spent three years on the project—the story of New York City Technical College of the City University of New York, an educational, cultural history.

"I enjoy my dual careers—as professor of writing and speech and as sports author and lecturer. My family functions as support and critic. My wife, Myrna, is at times my coauthor and always my editor. My daughter and two sons are involved in the world of sports, and we have been able to share anecdotes and good times playing and viewing games—especially baseball. I still find myself anchored in my own childhood world of games and fanhood. Perhaps that is what inspired *New York City Baseball* and *Rickey and Robinson*—both books deal with the golden heroes of my growing up years, when the world we all knew was very different.

"I received the 'Salute to Scholars Award' from the Chancellor of the City University of New York in 1984 and was invited by the government of Mexico in 1983 to tour that nation and write about its sports. Together with Myrna, I have expanded my publications to include travel writing. We have been guests of the governments of England (1986), Jamaica (1987), Finland (1987), Scotland (1988), Greece (1988), Barbados (1990), Dominican Republic (1990), Curacao (1990-91), and Spain (1993-95), invited to research and write about those nations' histories and cultures.

"It was my *Contemporary Authors* listing that was of critical help in my being selected in a national search of 500 sports authors to be the editor and major author of the Official Olympic Book in 1984. So far, that has been the crown jewel of my career. I take great satisfaction when I realize how far a poor kid from a seedy neighborhood in Brooklyn came in the United States of America. I dream now of other journeys, other accomplishments, other big and significant books for the future—in sports, in oral cultural history, in other areas."

BIOGRAPHICAL AND CRITICAL SOURCES:

PERIODICALS

Antioch Review, summer, 1996, Melinda Kanner, review of *It Happened in Brooklyn,* p. 372.

Black Issues Book Review, September-October, 2003, Art Rust, Jr., review of *Rickey and Robinson: The Men Who Broke Baseball's Color Barrier,* p. 64.

Booklist, October 15, 1998, Jack Helbig, review of *It Happened on Broadway: An Oral History of the Great White Way,* p. 385; October 1, 2002, GraceAnne A. DeCandido, review of *A Yankee Century: A Celebration of the First Hundred Years of Baseball's Greatest Team,* p. 295.

Boston Herald, November 6, 1998, Terry Byrne, review of *It Happened on Broadway,* p. 5.

Kirkus Reviews, August 15, 2001, review of *It Happened in Manhattan: An Oral History of Life in the City during the Mid-Twentieth Century,* p. 1187.

Library Journal, November 1, 1998, J. Sara Paulk, review of *It Happened on Broadway,* p. 83.

Nation, March 1, 1999, Rachel Shteir, review of *It Happened on Broadway,* p. 31.

Publishers Weekly, August 31, 1998, review of *It Happened on Broadway,* p. 54.

ONLINE

CultureVulture.net, http://culturevulture.net/ (May 1, 2004), Kendal Dodge Butler, review of *It Happened in Manhattan.**

* * *

FUREY, Maggie

PERSONAL: Born in England; married.

ADDRESSES: *Home*—Dublin, Ireland. *Agent*—c/o Author Mail, Bantam Books, 1540 Broadway, New York, NY 10036-4094.

CAREER: Novelist and teacher. Durham Reading Resources Center, advisor; British Broadcasting Corp., book reviewer for Radio Newcastle; organizer of children's book fairs.

WRITINGS:

"ARTEFACTS OF POWER" SERIES; FANTASY NOVELS

Aurian, Bantam Spectra (New York, NY), 1994.

Harp of Winds, Bantam Spectra (New York, NY), 1994.

The Sword of Flame, Bantam Spectra (New York, NY), 1995.
Dhiammara, Bantam Books (New York, NY), 1997.

"SHADOWLEAGUE" SERIES; FANTASY NOVELS

The Heart of Myrial, Bantam Books (New York, NY), 2000.
Spirit of the Stone, Bantam Books (New York, NY), 2001.
The Eye of Eternity, Bantam Books (New York, NY), 2003.

Work represented in anthologies, including *The Web: 2027,* Orion Publishing Group (London, England), 1999.

SIDELIGHTS: The first three volumes of Maggie Furey's fantasy series "Artefacts of Power" were published between 1994 and 1995. Their setting is a world composed of two continents and populated by decadent Mages and other exotic species. Aurian, the heroine of the series, is the daughter of two Mages: her father was killed in an accident, and her mother is a demented recluse. Aurian travels to the city where most of the remaining Mages live, in order to develop her powers. In the first volume, *Aurian,* she finds love with a mortal swordsman, but she is also the object of the lust of the ruling Mage, Miathan, who possesses a magic artifact he uses to kill his rival. Fleeing, Aurian organizes a resistance movement to find the remaining three magic artifacts but learns she is pregnant—a condition that can cause a female Mage to lose her powers.

In the second installment, *Harp of Winds,* Aurian has a new love interest named Anvar. Aurian, Anvar, and their friends are betrayed and subsequently captured by Miathan, who intends to kill Aurian's expected child and possess Aurian for himself. However, the recovery of a second magic artifact enables Aurian and company to escape. *Kliatt* reviewer Deirdre B. Root commented that *Harp of Winds* contained "few of the usual defects" that are found in the middle installments of a series. Root believed that its various species and cultures, which included winged people and shape-changing centaurs, were well described. "This is an extremely well-developed world for such a new author," Root observed, adding, "I enjoyed this even more than the first book."

The third novel in the series is *The Sword of Flame,* and the final chapter is *Dhiammara.* In *Dhiammara,* the various plot lines of the series diverge, the minor characters featured throughout the series make brief appearances, and the story of Aurian is resolved.

BIOGRAPHICAL AND CRITICAL SOURCES:

PERIODICALS

Kliatt, November, 1994, p. 20; May, 1995, Deirdre B. Root, review of *Harp of Winds,* pp. 12, 14.
Locus, April, 1994, p. 29; September, 1994, pp. 33, 70; October, 1994, p. 68; January, 1995, p. 35; February, 1995, pp. 35, 39, 76; October, 1999, review of *The Heart of Myrial,* p. 27.

ONLINE

BookBrowser.com, http://www.bookbrowser.com/ (April 28, 2002), Harriet Klausner, review of *Spirit of the Stone.*
Stormpages.com, http://www.stormpages.com/ (September 8, 2002), review of *The Heart of Myrial.*
TWBooks.com, http://www.twbooks.co/uk/ (September 8, 2002), review of *Spirit of the Stone.**

G

GABBARD, Glen O(wens) 1949-

PERSONAL: Born August 8, 1949, in Charleston, IL; son of Earnest Glendon (an actor) and Lucina Mildred (an actress; maiden name, Paquet) Gabbard; married Joyce Eileen Davidson (a psychiatrist), June 14, 1985; children: Matthew, Abigail, Amanda, Allison. *Education:* Eastern Illinois University, B.S., 1972; Rush Medical College, M.D., 1975; postdoctoral study at Karl Menninger School of Psychiatry, 1975-78, and Topeka Institute of Psychoanalysis, 1977-84.

ADDRESSES: *Home*—1290 Jimmy Phillips Blvd., Angleton, TX 77515. *Office*—Department of Psychiatry, Baylor College of Medicine, MS 350, One Baylor Plaza, Houston, TX 77030.

CAREER: Psychiatrist, writer. Kansas Correctional Vocational Training Center, Topeka, penal physician and psychiatric consultant, 1976-82; C. F. Menninger Memorial Hospital, Topeka, staff psychiatrist, 1978-83, section chief, 1984-89, director, 1989-94, vice president for adult services at the Menninger Clinic, 1991-94; Topeka Institute for Psychoanalysis, instructor, 1981-89, training and supervising analyst, 1989-2001; Karl Menninger School of Psychiatry, J. Cotter Hirschberg Professorship in Clinical Psychology, 1986-87, Karl and Mona Malden Professorship, 1993-94, Bessie Walker Callaway Distinguished Professor of Psychoanalysis and Education, 1994-2001; Baylor College of Medicine, Houston, TX, professor of psychiatry, 2001—. University of Kansas School of Medicine, professor of clinical psychiatry, 1991-2001; Distinguished visiting professor, Wilford Hall Air Force Hospital, San Antonio, TX, 1991, University of Hawaii, 1993; Hall Mercer visiting scholar, Pennsylvania Hospital, 1992; William Orr lecturer, Vanderbilt University School of Medicine, 1992; Distinguished visiting scholar, Beth Israel Medical Center, 1993; visiting professor, Hershey Medical Center, Penn State College of Medicine, 1993; Ben Weisel lecturer, Hartford Hospital, 1994; G. Henry Katz visiting professor, Institute of the Pennsylvania, 1994; Serota lecturer, San Diego Psychoanalytic Institute, 1994; visiting scholar, Southern California Psychoanalytic Institute, 1994; Jacob E. Finesinger visiting professor, University of Maryland, 1995; Prager visiting professor and lecturer in psychoanalytic psychiatry, George Washington University, 1995; Windholz lecturer, San Francisco Psychoanalytic Institute, 1995. Affiliated with organizations that include the Committee on the Practice of Psychotherapy and Forum for the Psychoanalytic Study of Film.

MEMBER: International Association for Near-Death Studies, International Psycho-Analytic Association, Academia, Medicina and Psychiatria Foundation, American Association for the Advancement of Science, American College of Psychiatrists, American College of Psychoanalysts, American Medical Association, American Psychiatric Association; American Psychoanalytic Association, American Society of Psychoanalytic Physicians, Benjamin Rush Society, Group for the Advancement of Psychiatry, Society for Psychotherapy Research, Central Neuropsychiatric Hospital Association (president, 1992), Kansas Medical Society, Shawnee County Medical Society, Topeka Psychoanalytic Society (president, 1991-93), Sigma Xi, Alpha Omega Alpha.

AWARDS, HONORS: Falk fellow, American Psychiatric Association, 1976; Topeka Institute for Psychoanalysis Publications award, 1978, 1982, 1986; Wood-Prince Award, 1980, 1983, 1984, 1985; named one of the Outstanding Young Men in America, U.S. Jaycees, 1984; Edward Hoedemaker award, Seattle Psychoanalytic Society, 1986, for article "The Treatment of the 'Special' Patient in a Psychoanalytic Hospital"; named Menninger Foundation Distinguished Clinical Researcher, 1987; Alumni award for scientific writing, Karl Menninger School of Psychiatry and Mental Health Sciences, 1989; William C. Menninger Teacher of the Year award, 1989 and 1990; Wolfe Adler award, Sheppard and Pratt Hospital, 1991; I. Arthur Marshall Distinguished Alumnus award, 1992; Teacher of the Year award, *Psychiatric Times,* 1992; Sigmund Freud award, American Society of Psychoanalytic Physicians, 1992; Edward A. Strecker award, American Psychiatric Association, 1994; Menninger professional writing award, Menninger Alumni Association, 1994; distinguished alumnus award, Eastern Illinois University, 1994; C. Charles Burlingame award, 1997; Mary S. Sigourney award, 2000.

WRITINGS:

(With Stuart W. Twemlow) *With the Eyes of the Mind: An Empirical Analysis of Out-of-Body States,* Praeger (New York, NY), 1984.

(With brother, Krin Gabbard) *Psychiatry and the Cinema,* University of Chicago Press (Chicago, IL), 1987, 2nd revised edition, 1999.

Psychodynamic Psychiatry in Clinical Practice: The DSM-IV Edition, American Psychiatric Press (Washington, DC), 1990, 3rd revised edition, 2000.

(With Sallye M. Wilkinson) *Management of Countertransference with Borderline Patients,* American Psychiatric Press (Washington, DC), 1994.

(With Eva P. Lester) *Boundaries and Boundary Violations in Psychoanalysis,* Basic Books (New York, NY), 1995.

Love and Hate in the Analytic Setting, Jason Aronson (Northvale, NJ), 1996.

Countertransference Issues in Psychiatric Treatment, American Psychiatric Press (New York, NY), 1999.

The Psychology of the Sopranos: Love, Death, Desire, and Betrayal in America's Favorite Gangster Family, Basic Books (New York, NY), 2002.

Long-Term Psychodynamic Psychotherapy: A Basic Text, American Psychiatric Press (Washington, DC), 2004.

EDITOR:

(With Roy W. Menninger, and contributor) *Medical Marriages,* American Psychiatric Press (Washington, DC), 1988.

Sexual Exploitation in Professional Relationships, American Psychiatric Press (Washington, DC), 1989.

(Contributing editor) Harold Kaplan and Benjamin Sadock, *Synopsis of Psychiatry,* 7th revised edition, William & Wilkins (Baltimore, MD), 1994.

(Editor in chief) *Treatments of Psychiatric Disorders,* 2nd edition, American Psychiatric Press (Washington, DC), 1995, 3rd revised edition, 2001.

(With Sarah D. Atkinson) *Synopsis of Treatments of Psychiatric Disorders,* 2nd edition, American Psychiatric Press (Washington, DC), 1996.

Also author and director of videotape, *The Royal Road: Psychoanalytic Approaches to the Dream,* Menninger Video Productions, 1988; author of audiotapes, *Management of Countertransference in the Psychotherapy of Borderline Patients,* 1992, and *Professional Boundaries in Psychiatric Practice,* 1995, both for American College of Psychiatrists "Update" series; *International Journal of Psychoanalysis,* joint editor-in-chief; member of editorial boards for various journals, including *American Journal of Psychiatry, American Journal of Psychotherapy, American Psychoanalyst, Ethics and Behavior, Journal of the American Psychoanalytic Association, Journal of Near-Death Studies, Journal of Psychotherapy Practice and Research, Journal of Sex and Marital Therapy,* and *Psychoanalytic Quarterly.* Editor of *The Menninger Letter,* 1992-96, and associate editor of *Journal of the American Psychoanalytic Association,* 1994—.

SIDELIGHTS: Glen O. Gabbard once told *CA:* "I grew up in a theatrical family and majored in drama as an undergraduate. At some ill-defined point in my college career, I became more interested in analyzing the psychology of the characters I was playing than in performing on stage. I switched to a premedical emphasis, but I was rejected by a registration computer because premedical studies and a drama major were deemed incompatible. I persevered nonetheless and eventually combined my interests in my writings on stage fright and the interface between psychiatry and movies. My interest in film culminated in *Psychiatry and the Cinema,* which I wrote in collaboration with my brother and fellow film buff, Krin Gabbard. This book will require frequent updates to keep abreast of current developments in film, so I anticipate work on future editions for the rest of my professional career."

The second edition of *Psychiatry and the Cinema* was reviewed in the *Journal of the American Medical Association* (*JAMA*) by Julia Frank, who began by saying that in the thirteen years since the book was first published, "psychiatry, especially psychoanalytic psychiatry, has taken its lumps . . . but its screen image is as vivid, and as ambiguous, as ever." The first half of this edition reviews the portrayal of psychiatry and psychotherapy in films from the industry's beginnings until present day and contains resources, including an extensive filmography, for physician educators who use films in their courses. Frank called the discussion in this first half "both comprehensive and deep" and noted that although the authors feel that the portrayal of psychiatry in film has changed little since the first edition, their inclusion of recent films that are familiar to students will be helpful. "More important," wrote Frank, "the Gabbards place the films they discuss in historical and literary context, simultaneously relating them to clinical experience. This approach fosters a sophisticated understanding of how films mirror clinical reality—and how they don't." The authors study how the business side of Hollywood and storytelling requirements (happy endings), influence how the medical aspects of the film are portrayed, and they provide psychoanalytic readings of several films in the second half of the book.

More than 400 films were discussed in *Psychiatry and the Cinema,* and Gabbard told *Los Angeles Times* writer Richard Natale that of all of them, "fewer than five had some semblance of real psychotherapy. . . . In movies, psychotherapy is generally used only as a plot device." But there is a dramatic portrayal of a psychiatrist that has received Gabbard's stamp of approval, and that is the character of Jennifer Melfi (Lorraine Bracco), the psychiatrist of the lead character, Tony Soprano (James Gandolfini) of the Home Box Office (HBO) hit *The Sopranos.* Gabbard told Natale the show "is by far the most accurate portrayal of psychiatry ever to appear in any electronic media."

Gabbard liked the show enough that he wrote an entire book about it. *The Psychology of the Sopranos: Love, Death, Desire, and Betrayal in America's Favorite Gangster Family,* in which he says that the show gets other things right, as well, including the geographical setting of northern New Jersey, and the Roman Catholicism of the Italian community. Gabbard comments on advances in mental health as he writes of the relationships on the show, between Tony and his psychiatrist and Tony and his wife, Carmela (Edie Falco), and considers whether Tony the gangster can be successfully treated. Psychiatrists who have experienced an increase in male patients attribute the trend to the popularity of the show, with its macho main character.

BIOGRAPHICAL AND CRITICAL SOURCES:

PERIODICALS

Houston Chronicle, August 12, 2002, Barbara Karkabi, "Mob Psychology: Houston Doctor Fascinated by Tenor of *The Sopranos,*" p. 1; December 15, 2002, Barbara Karkabi, "Psychiatrist Sings Praises of *The Sopranos,*" p. 3.

JAMA: Journal of the American Medical Association, February 9, 2000, Julia Frank, review of *Psychiatry and the Cinema,* 2nd edition, p. 810.

Los Angeles Times, October 24, 2001, Richard Natale, "Analyze This: What's behind These Psychodramas?," p. F1.

New York Times, February 5, 2002, Erica Goode, "A Rare Day: The Movies Get Mental Illness Right" (interview), p. D6.

New York Times Book Review, September 15, 2002, David Kelly, review of *The Psychology of the Sopranos: Love, Death, Desire, and Betrayal in America's Favorite Gangster Family,* p. 8.*

* * *

GAZE, Gillian
See BARKLEM, Jill

* * *

GENTLE, Mary 1956-
(Roxanne Morgan)

PERSONAL: Born March 29, 1956, in Eastbourne, East Sussex, England; daughter of George William (a cinema manager) and Amy Mary (Champion) Gentle. *Education:* University of Bournemouth, B.A.; Goldsmiths' College, London, M.A.; King's College, London, M.A. *Politics:* "Feminist." *Hobbies and other interests:* Sewing historical costumes, sword fighting, live role-playing games.

ADDRESSES: Home—29 Sish Lane, Stevenage, Hertfordshire, England.

CAREER: Writer. Worked as assistant movie projectionist, clerk for a wholesale bookseller, and civil servant. Voice director for the computer game *Zombieville,* 1996.

MEMBER: Society for Creative Anachronism, Bournemouth Writers Circle (secretary, 1979-80).

AWARDS, HONORS: The Architecture of Desire was nominated for the James Tiptree, Jr. Award, 1992.

WRITINGS:

NOVELS

A Hawk in Silver (young adult), Gollancz (London, England), 1977, Lothrop, Lee & Shepard Books (New York, NY), 1985.
Golden Witchbreed, Gollancz (London, England), 1983, Morrow (New York, NY), 1984.
Ancient Light, Gollancz (London, England), 1987, Signet (New York, NY), 1989.
Rats and Gargoyles, Bantam (London, England), 1990, ROC (New York, NY), 1991.
The Architecture of Desire, Bantam (London, England), 1991, ROC (New York, NY), 1993.
Grunts! A Fantasy with Attitude, Bantam (London, England), 1992, ROC (New York, NY), 1995.
Wild Machines, EOS (New York, NY), 2000.
A Sundial in a Grave—1610, Perennial (New York, NY), 2005.

SHORT STORY COLLECTIONS; "BOOK OF ASH" SERIES

A Secret History, EOS (New York, NY), 1999, published in *Ash: A Secret History,* 2001.
Carthage Ascendant, EOS (New York, NY), 2000, published in *Ash: A Secret History,* 2001.
The Wild Machines, EOS (New York, NY), 2000, published in *Ash: A Secret History,* 2001.
Lost Burgundy, Avon Books (New York, NY), 2000, published in *Ash: A Secret History,* 2001.

UNDER PSEUDONYM ROXANNE MORGAN

Who Dares Sins, Little Brown (London, England) 1995.
Dares, X Libris (Philadelphia, PA) 1995.
Sinner Takes All, X Libris (Philadelphia, PA) 1997.
*Bets,*Warner Furtura (London, England) 1997.
A Game of Masks, X Libris (Philadelphia, PA) 1999.
Degrees of Desire, Little Brown (London, England) 2001.

OTHER

Scholars and Soldiers (short stories), Macdonald (London, England), 1989.
(Editor, with Roz Kaveney) *Villains!,* ROC (New York, NY), 1992.
(Editor, with Roz Kaveney and Neil Gaiman) *The Weerde,* two volumes, ROC (New York, NY), 1992.
Left to His Own Devices (short stories), Orbit (London, England), 1994.

Author of a script for the computer game *Zombieville,* 1996. Work represented in anthologies, including *Worlds That Weren't,* ROC (New York, NY), c. 2002. Contributor of short stories, reviews and articles to *Vector, Interzone, Isaac Asimov's Science Fiction,* and other publications.

SIDELIGHTS: Mary Gentle's science fiction novels are marked by a leisurely narrative pace, lush description of landscapes and architecture, occult philosophy, and witty language. Her first two novels for adults—*Golden Witchbreed* and *Ancient Light*—follow Lynne de Lisle Christie as she travels on a diplomatic mission to the distant planet of Orthe. Seemingly primitive compared to Earth, the planet of Orthe is in fact quite developed, but not in a technological sense. The eventual conflicts between Earthlings and the natives of Orthe resemble "a gathering storm: decent people on both sides see the danger coming and take steps to avert it, but they are enmeshed in obligations that defeat their purpose," as Gerald Jonas explained in the *New York Times Book Review.*

In *Rats and Gargoyles* Gentle envisions a nameless city where despotic god-demons rule and a few brave humans struggle to free themselves from their oppressive masters. The magic they turn to for power combines Rosicrucian and Masonic elements. A *Publishers Weekly* critic called the world of *Rats and Gargoyles* "a dark, vivid and complex alternative medieval world." "Gentle's feel for language and character," wrote Jackie Cassada in the *Library Journal,* "provide both immediacy and a sense of timelessness to a complex and evocative tale."

Gentle returns to the same scenario in *The Architecture of Desire,* this time extending the action to an alternate historical city of London where a magical temple must be constructed to insure the victory of the rebellious humans. "There is an intricate and subtle imagination at work here," admitted Tom Easton in *Analog,* "expressed in a story rich with sex and intrigue, adventure and color galore. Yet it did not succeed in persuading me to suspend my disbelief." Reviewing *The Architecture of Desire* for the *Washington Post Book World,* Paul Di Filippo explained that Gentle has relied "solely on the strength of her vivid and gorgeous descriptions of light, weather, clothing, buildings and faces" to tell her story. "Her subtlety in depicting the supernatural events of her world," Di Filippo believed, "is well nigh miraculous." Although the reviewer for *Publishers Weekly* judged *The Architecture of Desire* to be too "compressed, its turns of plots underrationalized," he nonetheless concluded that "Gentle's witty prose and the unusual and intriguing atmosphere of her world more than compensate."

Gentle once told *CA:* "I was writing for a good long while before I realized it was a serious occupation. Since then it has taken up progressively larger amounts of my time, though I am a lazy writer and should be chained forcibly to a typewriter. In short, I hate writing, but love having written."

BIOGRAPHICAL AND CRITICAL SOURCES:

PERIODICALS

Analog, August, 1993, Tom Easton, review of *The Architecture of Desire,* p. 161.

Booklist, June 15, 1984, p. 1437; March 1, 1993, p. 1160.

Books and Bookmen, November, 1983, p. 30.

British Book News, March, 1984, p. 136.

Fantasy Review, August, 1985, p. 20.

Library Journal, March 15, 1989, p. 88; March 15, 1991, Jackie Cassada, review of *Rats and Gargoyles,* p. 119; February 15, 1993, p. 195; February 15, 1994, p. 216.

Locus, May, 1989, p. 46; September, 1990, p. 23; June, 1992, p. 15; September, 1992, p. 17.

Magazine of Fantasy and Science Fiction, January, 2001, Robert K. J. Killheffer, review of *Lost Burgundy* and *Wild Machines,* p. 29.

New Scientist, April 7, 2001, review of *Ash: A Secret History,* p. 48.

New York Times Book Review, July 2, 1989, review by Gerald Jonas, p. 15.

Publishers Weekly, January 13, 1989, p. 78; March 1, 1991, review of *Rats and Gargoyles,* p. 62; March 1, 1993, review of *The Architecture of Desire,* p. 44.

Science Fiction Chronicle, June, 1991, p. 5; November, 1991, p. 35; July, 1992, p. 33; March, 1993, p. 30.

Science Fiction Review, February, 1985, p. 44.

Times Literary Supplement, April 7, 1978, p. 376.

Washington Post Book World, August 26, 1984, p. 6; May 26, 1991, p. 6; January 26, 1992, p. 6; March 28, 1993, Paul Di Filippo, review of *The Architecture of Desire,* p. 9.*

* * *

GERSHATOR, Phillis 1942-

PERSONAL: Born July 8, 1942, in New York, NY; daughter of Morton Dimondstein (an artist) and Miriam Honixfeld Green (an artist); married David Gershator (an author, translator, and songwriter), October 19, 1962; children: Yonah, Daniel. *Education:* Attended University of California—Berkeley, 1959-63; Rutgers University, B.A., 1966; Pratt Institute, M.L.S., 1975. *Hobbies and other interests:* Reading, gardening, cooking.

ADDRESSES: *Home*—P.O. Box 303353, St. Thomas, U.S. Virgin Islands 00803-3353. *E-mail*—gershator@islands.vi.

CAREER: St. Thomas Public Library, St. Thomas, U.S. Virgin Islands, librarian, 1974-75; Enid M. Baa and Leonard Dober Elementary School libraries,

Brooklyn, NY, children's librarian, 1977-84; Department of Education, St. Thomas, children's librarian, 1984-86; St. Thomas Public Library, librarian, 1988-89; writer, 1989—. Also worked as a secretary and in library promotion for various New York City publishers. Reading Is Fundamental, volunteer in St. Thomas, 1984—.

MEMBER: Society of Children's Book Writers and Illustrators, Virgin Islands Library Association, Friends of the St. Thomas Library.

AWARDS, HONORS: "Choice book" selection, Cooperative Children's Book Center, University of Wisconsin, 1994, for *Tukama Tootles the Flute: A Tale from the Antilles,* and 1999, for *When It Starts to Snow;* "children's book of the year" selection, Bank Street's Child Study Children's Book Committee, 1994, for *Tukama Tootles the Flute,* and 1994, for *The Iroko-man: A Yoruba Folktale;* commended title, American Children's and Young Adult Literature Award, Consortium of Latin American Studies Programs, and Blue Ribbon Book, *Bulletin of the Center for Children's Books,* all 1994, for *Tukama Tootles the Flute;* Junior Library Guild selection, National Council of Teachers of English Notable Trade Book in the Language Arts, 1995, for *Rata-pata-scata-fata: A Caribbean Story,* and 2000, for *Only One Cowry: A Dahomean Tale;* "best black history for young people" selection, *Booklist,* 1995, for *Rata-pata-scata-fata;* featured selection, Reading Rainbow, c. 1995, for *Bread Is for Eating;* "best of '98" selection, *Working Mother,* 1998, for *When It Starts to Snow;* Anne Izard Storytellers' Choice Award, 2000, for *Zzzng! Zzzng! Zzzng!: A Yoruba Tale.*

WRITINGS:

FOR CHILDREN

Honi and His Magic Circle, illustrated by Shay Rieger, Jewish Publications Society of America (Philadelphia, PA), 1979, revised edition published as *Honi's Circle of Trees,* illustrated by Mim Green, 1994.

Rata-pata-scata-fata: A Caribbean Story, illustrated by Holly Meade, Little, Brown (Boston, MA), 1993.

(Reteller) *Tukama Tootles the Flute: A Tale from the Antilles,* illustrated by Synthia St. James, Orchard Books (New York, NY), 1994.

(Reteller) *The Iroko-man: A Yoruba Folktale,* illustrated by Holly Kim, Orchard Books (New York, NY), 1994.

Sambalena Show-off, illustrated by Leonard Jenkins, Macmillan (New York, NY), 1995.

(With husband, David Gershator) *Bread Is for Eating,* illustrated by Emma Shaw-Smith, Holt (New York, NY), 1995.

Sweet, Sweet Fig Banana, illustrated by Fritz Millevoix, Albert Whitman (Morton Grove, IL), 1996.

Sugar Cakes Cyril, illustrated by Cedric Lucas, Mondo (Greenvale, NY), 1997.

Palampam Day, illustrated by Enrique O. Sánchez, Marshall Cavendish (Freeport, NY), 1997.

When It Starts to Snow, illustrated by Martin Matje, Holt (New York, NY), 1998.

(Reteller) *Zzzng! Zzzng! Zzzng!: A Yoruba Tale,* illustrated by Theresa Smith, Orchard Books (New York, NY), 1998.

(With David Gershator) *Greetings, Sun,* illustrated by Synthia St. James, DK Ink (New York, NY), 1998.

Tiny and Bigman, illustrated by Lynne Cravath, Marshall Cavendish (Freeport, NY), 1999.

Someday Cyril, illustrated by Cedric Lucas, Mondo (Greenvale, NY), 2000.

(Reteller) *Only One Cowry: A Dahomean Tale,* illustrated by David Soman, Orchard Books (New York, NY), 2000.

(With David Gershator) *Moon Rooster,* illustrated by Megan Halsey, Marshall Cavendish (Freeport, NY), 2001.

(Reteller) *Wise and Not So Wise: Ten Tales from the Rabbis,* illustrated by Alexa Ginsburg, Jewish Publication Society (Philadelphia, PA), 2004.

The Babysitter Sings, illustrated by Mélisande Potter, Henry Holt (New York, NY), 2004.

(Reteller, with David Gershator) *Kallaloo: A Caribbean Tale,* illustrated by Diane Greenseid, Marshall Cavendish (New York, NY), in press.

Gershator's books have been published in French and Japanese.

OTHER

A Bibliographic Guide to the Literature of Contemporary American Poetry, 1970-1975, Scarecrow Press (Metuchen, NJ), 1976.

(Translator, with Robin Blum) Lucia Scuderi, *To Fly,* Kane Miller Book Publishers (Brooklyn, NY), 1998,

Contributor of short stories, poetry, and book reviews to periodicals, including *Cricket.*

WORK IN PROGRESS: Who's Awake?, a picture book, with Mim Green, illustrated by Martin Matji, for Henry Holt (New York, NY); *Summer Is Summer Is Summer,* a picture book, with David Gershator, Henry Holt (New York, NY).

SIDELIGHTS: Phillis Gershator is the author of award-winning picture books based on the black folklore of such places as the Caribbean and Africa. Her stories include both original works, like *Rata-pata-scata-fata: A Caribbean Story,* and retellings, such as *Tukama Tootles the Flute: A Tale from the Antilles.*

Gershator's career as an author began with an early love of books. "[My] family was in the book business in New York," she explained in a *Junior Library Guild* interview, and she often received books as gifts. She read so much that her mother often had to force her to go outside to play and get some exercise. As a graduate student, Gershator majored in library science. Her first job as a librarian was on the island of St. Thomas, where her family had moved from New York City in 1969. The Caribbean eventually became the setting for *Rata-pata-scata-fata* and *Tukama Tootles the Flute.*

After working for several years at libraries and publishing companies in New York City, Gershator returned to St. Thomas in 1984. Gleaning much satisfaction through her library work and as a Reading Is Fundamental volunteer, Gershator wanted to contribute even more to children by writing her own stories. Career and family kept her from spending much time on her writing, though she published her first book, *Honi and His Magic Circle,* in 1979 and has been composing poetry and short stories since the early 1970s. It was not until the mid-1990s that her career would really attract notice, however. In 1993 and 1994 she published three very successful books: *Rata-pata-scata-fata, Tukama Tootles the Flute,* and *The Iroko-Man: A Yoruba Tale,* all of which have won awards.

Rata-pata-scata-fata is about a young St. Thomas boy named Junjun who tries to avoid household chores by chanting "Caribbean gobbledygook" in the hope that his tasks will be completed by magic. Although luck, not magic, smiles on him to grant him all his wishes, Junjun attributes everything to his gobbledygook. A *Kirkus Reviews* critic called the tale "an engagingly cadenced story that will be just right for sharing aloud." "Gershator has a light and lively sense of language," commented Betsy Hearne in the *Bulletin of the Center for Children's Books,* "along with a storytelling rhythm that shows experience with keeping young listeners involved."

In a similar vein to *Rata-pata-scata-fata, Tukama Tootles the Flute* is about another St. Thomas boy who is unreliable in his chores. In this yarn, young Tukama loves to play his flute so much that he does not help his grandmother like he should, although she warns him that his disobedient ways might one day cause him to wind up in the stomach of the local two-headed giant. Tukama's grandmother's words prove unsurprisingly prophetic when the boy is captured by the giant, but he manages to escape by playing his flute for the giant's wife. The frightening experience teaches Tukama a lesson, and thereafter he restricts his playing until after his chores are done. Pointing out the similarities between this story and "Jack and the Beanstalk," *School Library Journal* reviewer Lyn Miller-Lachman commented that *Tukama Tootles the Flute* "offers an opportunity to observe similarities and differences in folklore around the world." A *Publishers Weekly* critic favorably remarked that the "text pulses with the rhythms of island dialect and is laced with the casual asides of an oral storyteller."

Like the Caribbean children in these stories, Gershator considers herself to be very lucky. "Wishes do, once in a while, [come true]," she noted in *Junior Library Guild,* "so I don't consider *Rata-pata-scata-fata* a fairy tale, and oddly enough, that little boy seems very familiar."

BIOGRAPHICAL AND CRITICAL SOURCES:

PERIODICALS

Appraisal: Science Books for Young People, winter, 1999, review of *When It Starts to Snow,* p. 20.

Booklist, April 15, 1994, p. 1541; May 1, 1994, p. 1603; May 15, 1994, p. 1676; February 15, 1995, p. 1094; August, 1997, Susan Dove Lempke, review of *Palampam Day,* p. 1905; March 15, 1998, Susan Dove Lempke, review of *Greetings, Sun,* p. 1247; August, 1998, review of *Zzzng! Zzzng! Zzzng!: A Yoruba Tale,* p. 2010; November 15, 1998, review of *When It Starts to Snow,* p. 595; October 15, 1999, review of *Tiny and Bigman,* p. 452.

Bulletin of the Center for Children's Books, April, 1994, Betsy Hearne, review of *Rata-pata-scata-fata: A Caribbean Story,* p. 257; April, 1998, review of *Greetings, Sun,* p. 279; October, 1998, review of *Zzzng! Zzzng! Zzzng!,* p. 60; December, 1998, review of *When It Starts to Snow,* p. 130; December, 1999, review of *Tiny and Bigman,* p. 129.

Caribbean Writer, 1997, review of *Sweet, Sweet Fig Banana* and *Sambalena Show-off,* p. 252; 1999, review of *Zzzng! Zzzng! Zzzng!* and *Greetings, Sun,* p. 227.

Horn Book Guide, fall, 1994, p. 340; fall, 1998, review of *Greetings, Sun,* p. 272; spring, 1999, review of *When It Starts to Snow,* p. 30; spring, 1999, review of *Zzzng! Zzzng! Zzzng!,* p. 94; spring, 2001, review of *Only One Cowry: A Dahomean Tale,* p. 100.

Horn Book Magazine, May-June, 2004, Lauren Adams, review of *The Babysitter Sings,* p. 313.

Junior Library Guild, April-September, 1994, interview, p. 14.

Kirkus Reviews, February 1, 1994, p. 142; May 1, 1994, review of *Rata-pata-scata-fata,* p. 629; February 1, 1998, review of *Greetings, Sun,* p. 196; August 15, 1998, review of *Zzzng! Zzzng! Zzzng!,* p. 1188; October 1, 1998, review of *When It Starts to Snow,* p. 1457; April 15, 2004, review of *The Babysitter Sings,* p. 393.

Publishers Weekly, January 10, 1994, review of *Tukama Tootles the Flute,* p. 60; April 4, 1994, p. 79; November 9, 1998, review of *When It Starts to Snow,* p. 75; October 11, 1999, review of *Tiny and Bigman,* p. 75.

School Librarian, November, 1994, p. 145.

School Library Journal, April, 1994, Lyn Miller-Lachman, review of *Tukama Tootles the Flute: A Tale from the Antilles,* p. 118; July, 1995, p. 27; September, 1995, p. 194; September, 1997, Nina Lindsay, review of *Palampam Day,* p. 182; May, 1998, Tana Elias, review of *Greetings, Sun,* p. 116; October, 1998, review of *Zzzng! Zzzng! Zzzng!,* p. 122; November, 1998, review of *When It Starts to Snow,* p. 85; November, 1999, review of *Tiny and Bigman,* p. 116; December, 2001, Susan Heppler, review of *Moon Rooster,* p. 102; July, 2004, Ajoke' T. I. Kokodoko, review of *The Babysitter Sings,* p. 75.

* * *

GHIGNA, Charles 1946-
(Father Goose)

PERSONAL: Surname is pronounced "*geen*-ya"; born August 25, 1946, in Bayside, NY; son of Charles Vincent and Patricia Ghigna; married Nancy Minnicks, June 24, 1967 (divorced, June 5, 1973); married Debra Holmes (a writer), August 2, 1975; children: (first marriage) Julie Ann; (second marriage) Chip. *Education:* Florida Atlantic University, B.A., 1968, M.Ed., 1969; also attended Edison Community College, 1964-66, University of South Florida, 1968-69, and Florida State University, 1973.

ADDRESSES: Agent—c/o Author Mail, Random House Children's Books, 1745 Broadway, New York, NY 10019. *E-mail*—PaGoose@aol.com.

CAREER: High school English teacher in Fort Myers, FL, 1967-73; Edison Community College, Fort Myers, instructor in creative writing, 1973; National Council of Teachers of English, Urbana, IL, poetry editor of *English Journal,* 1974; Alabama School of Fine Arts, Birmingham, poet-in-residence, 1974-93; Samford University, instructor in creative writing, 1979. Creator, director, performer on *Cabbages and Kings* (children's television series), Alabama Education Television, 1976. Correspondent for *Writer's Digest* magazine, 1989—. Author of nationally syndicated light verse feature "Snickers" for Tribune Media Services, 1993-98. Has given hundreds of readings at colleges and secondary schools and has made hundreds of visits to elementary and middle schools.

AWARDS, HONORS: Fellowship grants from the National Endowment for the Arts, the Library of Congress, the Mary Roberts Rinehart Foundation, and the Rockefeller Brothers Fund; First Place, *Writer's Digest* National Poetry Writing Competition, 1977, for "Divers"; Pulitzer Prize nomination, 1990, for *Returning to Earth;* Helen Keller Literary Award, 1993; First Place, International Sakura Haiku Writing Competi-

Charles Ghigna

tion, 1993, for "October"; Pick of the Lists, American Booksellers Association, 1994, for *Tickle Day: Poems from Father Goose,* and 1995, for *Riddle Rhymes.* Ghigna performed his poetry at the Library of Congress in 1978 and at the Kennedy Center for the Performing Arts in 1984; his poetry was featured on the American Broadcasting Corporation (ABC-TV) program *Good Morning America* in 1991.

WRITINGS:

FOR CHILDREN

Good Dogs, Bad Dogs, illustrated by David Catrow, Hyperion (New York, NY), 1992.

Good Cats, Bad Cats, illustrated by David Catrow, Hyperion (New York, NY), 1992.

The Day I Spent the Night in the Shelby County Jail, Best of Times (New York, NY), 1994.

Tickle Day: Poems from Father Goose, illustrated by Cyd Moore, Hyperion (New York, NY), 1994.

Riddle Rhymes, illustrated by Julia Gorton, Hyperion (New York, NY), 1995.

Animal Trunk: Silly Poems to Read Aloud, illustrated by Gabriel, Harry N. Abrams (New York, NY), 1999.

Mice Are Nice, illustrated by Jon Goodell, Random House (New York, NY), 1999.

See the Yak Yak, illustrated by Brian Lies, Random House (New York, NY), 1999.

(With wife, Debra Ghigna) *Christmas Is Coming,* illustrated by Mary O'Keefe Young, Talewinds (Watertown, MA), 2000.

The Alphabet Parade, illustrated by Patti Woods, River City Publishing (Montgomery, AL), 2002.

Halloween Night: Twenty-one Spooktacular Poems, illustrated by Adam McCauley, Running Press Kids (Philadelphia, PA), 2003.

One Hundred Shoes: A Math Reader, illustrated by Bob Staake, Random House (New York, NY), 2003.

My Country: Children Talk about America, Crane Hill Publishers (Birmingham, AL), 2003.

A Fury of Motion: Poems for Boys, Boyds Mills Press (Honesdale, PA), 2003.

Animal Tracks: Wild Poems to Read Aloud, illustrated by John Speirs, Harry N. Abrams (New York, NY), 2004.

If You Were My Valentine, Simon & Schuster (New York, NY), 2004.

Dylan the Smokey Dragon, Maris, West & Baker (Jackson, MS), 2004.

Oh My, Pumpkin Pie!, Simon & Schuster (New York, NY), 2005.

FOR ADULTS; POETRY, EXCEPT AS NOTED

Plastic Tears, Dorrance (Philadelphia, PA), 1973.

Stables: The Story of Christmas (chapbook), Creekwood Press (Birmingham, AL), 1976.

Cockroach (one-act play), Contemporary Drama Service (New York, NY), 1977.

Divers and Other Poems, Creekwood Press (Birmingham, AL), 1978.

Circus Poems, Creekwood Press (Birmingham, AL), 1979.

Father Songs, Creekwood Press (Birmingham, AL), 1989.

Returning to Earth, Livingston University Press (Livingston, AL), 1989.

Wings of Fire, illustrated by Patricia See Hooten, Druid (Birmingham, AL), 1992.

The Best of "Snickers," Best of Times (New York, NY), 1994.

Speaking in Tongues: New and Selected Poems, 1974-1994, Livingston University Press (Livingston, AL), 1994.

Plastic Soup: Dream Poems, Black Belt (Montgomery, AL), 1999.

Love Poems, Crane Hill Publishers (Birmingham, AL), 1999.

Haiku: The Travelers of Eternity, River City Publishers (Montgomery, AL), 2001.

Works represented in anthologies, including *Confront, Construct, Complete,* Hayden Book Co. (Rochelle, NJ), 1979; *Contemporary Literature in Birmingham,* Thunder City Press (Birmingham, AL), 1983; *Anthology of Magazine Verse,* Monitor Book Co. (Beverly Hills, CA), 1985; *Italian-American Poets,* Fordham University (Bronx, NY), 1985; *This Sporting Life,* Milkweed Editions (Minneapolis, MN), 1987; *American Sports Poems,* Orchard Books (New York, NY), 1988; *Light Year,* 1985, 1986, 1987, 1988, 1989, Bits Press (Cleveland, OH), 1989; *North of Wakulla: Poets of Florida State,* Anhinga Press (Tallahassee, FL), 1989; *Alabama Poets: A Contemporary Anthology,* Livingston University Press (Livingston, AL), 1990; *Creative Writer's Handbook,* Prentice Hall (Englewood Cliffs, NJ), 1990; *Mixed Voices: Poems about Music,* Milkweed Editions (Minneapolis, MN), 1991; *A New Geography of Poets,* University of Arkansas Press (Fayetteville, AR), 1992; (With X. J. Kennedy and Richard Kostelanetz) *Sticks,* Sticks Press, 1992; *Poetry Works!: The First Verse Idea Book,* Simon & Schuster (New York, NY), 1992; *If We'd Wanted Quiet,* Meadowbrook Press (Deephaven, MN), 1994; *The Funny Side of Parenthood,* Meadowbrook Press (Deephaven, MN), 1994; *Familiarity Breeds Children,* Meadowbrook Press (Deephaven, MN), 1994; *The Runner's Literary Companion,* Breakaway Books (Halcottsville, NY), 1994; *For Better or Worse,* Meadowbrook Press (Deephaven, MN), 1995; *Fighting Words,* Black Belt Press, 1995; *Age Happens,* Meadowbook Press (Deephaven, MN), 1996; *Holidays and Seasonal Celebrations,* Teaching & Learning Co. (New York, NY), 1996; *Enjoy!: Invitations to Literacy,* Houghton Mifflin (Boston, MA), 1996; *My Buddy,* Houghton Mifflin (Boston, MA), 1996; *Leading Kids to Books through Puppets,* American Library Association (Chicago, IL), 1997; *Work and Other Occupational Hazards,* Meadowbrook Press (Deephaven, MN), 1998; *Advent Cookbook,* Advent Episcopal School, 1997; *McDonald's Cookbook,* Ronald McDonald House (New York, NY), 1998; *Lighten Up!,* Meadowbook Press (Deephaven, MN), 1998; *Creative Writer's Handbook,* 3rd edition, Prentice Hall (Englewood Cliffs, NJ), 1999; *A Twentieth Century Treasury of Poetry for Children,* Alfred A. Knopf (New York, NY), 1999; *Leading Kids to Books through Crafts,* American Library Association (Chicago, IL), 1999; *Laugh Twice and Call Me in the Morning,* Meadowbrook Press (Deephaven, MN), 1999; *Knock at a Star: A Child's Introduction to Poetry,* Alfred A. Knopf (New York, NY), 1999; *Harcourt Brace Reading Program,* Harcourt Brace (New York, NY), 2000; *Urban Nature,* Milkweed Editions (Minneapolis, MN), 2000; *Hidden Surprises, Grade 3,* Harcourt Brace (New York, NY), 2000; *Becoming One with the Lights,* National Council of Teachers of English (Urbana, IL), 2001; *Books Day by Day: Anniversaries and Anecdotes,* Heinemann (New York, NY), 2001; *Our Bundle of Joy,* Meadowbrook (Deephaven, MN), 2001; *Eat Their Words: Southern Writers and Recipes,* Fairhope Literary Council, 2001; *Rolling in the Aisles: Kids Pick the Funniest Poems,* Meadowbrook Press (Deephaven, MN), 2002; *Language Arts Program, Grade 1,* Harcourt Brace (New York, NY), 2002; *Stories from the Blue Moon Café II,* MacAdam/Cage (San Francisco, CA), 2003; and *Read a Rhyme, Write a Rhyme,* Alfred A. Knopf (New York, NY), 2005.

Contributor of hundreds of adult and children's poems to magazines and newspapers, including *Harper's, McCall's, Good Housekeeping, Ladies' Home Journal, Kansas Quarterly, Texas Quarterly, Christian Science Monitor, Highlights for Children, Cricket, Ranger Rick, Jack and Jill, Children's Digest, Hopscotch, Children's Playmate, Crayola Kids, Guideposts for Kids, Humpty Dumpty, Ladybug, Lollipops, New York Times, Pockets, Poem Train, Pre-K Today, Turtle,* and *Child Life.* Some of Ghigna's poems have been translated into Italian, German, French, and Russian.

SIDELIGHTS: Charles Ghigna, sometimes known as Father Goose, is a popular poet for children and adults. Ghigna divides his time between writing poetry and making personal appearances at schools from the elementary level through college. He is equally adept at entertaining the youngest listeners and enlightening adult would-be writers who solicit his advice on creating and publishing books. In the realm of juvenile literature, he is best known for his rhyming books that offer amusing portraits of animals and holidays. In an interview published on his Web site, he said: "Writing, especially for children, is one of the most honorable professions in the world. It is one of the few professions that allows you to dream, that encourages you to dream, and to capture those dreams on paper and to make them come alive in the minds and hearts of others."

Ghigna was born on Long Island but moved to Fort Myers, Florida, as a five-year-old and has lived in the South ever since. In his interviews he describes himself as a happy child who earned notice for his writing skills as early as third grade, when he wrote an essay about a talking freckle on a boy's face. He began keeping a journal as a teen but told no one, so that when he began publishing poetry many years later he seemed like an overnight success. In fact he wrote obsessively for years before seeing any of his work in print, and his first sales were of adult poetry to magazines such as *Harper's.* Between 1967 and 1993 he worked as a school teacher. Since 1993, "Father Goose" has primarily been a full-time writer.

Ghigna's verse for adults is free-form, but when he writes for children he employs rhyme. His first two books, *Good Dogs, Bad Dogs* and *Good Cats, Bad Cats,* are upside-down books. If a reader chooses to read about the good dogs first, the good dogs and their behavior comprise the first half of the book. At the center the reader must turn the book upside down to continue with the other half, depicting the bad dogs. The same form animates the volume about cats. Ghigna's rhymes work in concert with illustrations by David Catrow that literalize the humorous absurdity of such commonplace notions as the ideas that dogs defend those they love and cats always land on their feet. A *Publishers Weekly* reviewer found both volumes "witty," adding: "By turns slapstick and sophisticated, the humor here will snare adults as well as children."

Tickle Day: Poems from Father Goose collects some of the many poems Ghigna has contributed to children's magazines. The collection reveals its author's interests that will find further coverage in future books: animal behavior, holidays, weather, and childhood antics. A *Publishers Weekly* critic liked the book's "flashes of personality." *Riddle Rhymes* combines two popular genres of children's literature to "appealing" effect, according to Julie Corsaro in *Booklist.* By joining the fun of riddles to the playfulness of rhymes, Ghigna has produced "a lighthearted guessing game about everyday objects in a young child's life," noted Pamela K. Bomboy in *School Library Journal.* The topics covered by Ghigna's riddles include shadows, mirrors, leaves, rainbows, and kites. "And because they are in verse, the riddles are especially fun to read out loud," remarked Campbell Geeslin in the *New York Times Book Review.*

The holidays offer children's writers ample ideas for picture books, and Ghigna has written two rhyming texts on the subject. *Halloween Night: Twenty-one Spooktacular Poems* takes a holiday that frightens some youngsters and makes it silly, reassuring children that the goblins and ghosts are made larger by the imagination. *Christmas Is Coming!,* written with wife Debra Ghigna, describes how a family prepares for the favorite holiday, from readying decorations and buying gifts to packing all away again at the season's end. Shelley Townsend-Hudson in *Booklist* concluded that the verses and illustrations by Mary O'Keefe Young "reflect the holiday excitement."

Ghigna has also written *A Fury of Motion: Poems for Boys,* recognizing that boys sometimes have a difficult time enjoying verse. The spare rhymes in this volume aim at a young adult audience, covering such topics as sports, feelings, vacation activities, and even haircuts. In her *School Library Journal* review of the work, Donna Cardon noted that the poems would be appropriate for the intended age group as well as younger boys. Cardon praised *A Fury of Motion* as "the perfect book for boys who might not want to advertise the fact that they are reading poetry."

Animal Tracks: Wild Poems to Read Aloud searches through the animal kingdom for silly behavior and word-games that relate to familiar creatures. Some of the poems rely upon puns for their humor, while others describe the animals in question with light verse, easily read or memorized. Carolyn Phelan in *Booklist* liked the way Ghigna's poems "draw connections between animals and people or things," and Susan Scheps in *School Library Journal* called the title "charming," with "significant appeal."

In an interview with Tracy Hoffman in *Word Museum* online, Ghigna commented: "My ideas [for poems] come from everywhere! They pop into my head when

I least expect them. Many poem and story ideas come to me while I am driving or mowing or taking a shower! I also do thirty to forty school visits each year. Sometimes ideas come to me while I'm around children, especially while I'm playing with my son and his friends. Ideas also come to me while looking out the window of my upstairs office. My son and I often spend time after school jumping on his trampoline. Sometimes after jumping we collapse on the trampoline and lie still looking up at the clouds and watching Mother Nature's movie screen. We always find something new to think about while looking toward the sky. Other ideas for poems and stories also come from memories of my childhood—which still hasn't ended!"

Ghigna once commented: "I hope my poems offer children the opportunity to explore and celebrate the joys of childhood and nature, and to see some of the wondrous ironies all around them. I also hope my humorous poems tickle the funny bone of their imaginations. I usually do not sit down to write a poem with a preconceived 'goal.' I like to enter each poem with a sense of wonderment and discovery. My favorite poems are those that contain little surprises that I did not know were there until I wrote them."

In his spare time, Ghigna enjoys collecting things. In addition to baseball cards, letter openers, and kaleidoscopes, he has a growing collection of geese that fans have sent him over the years in honor of "Father Goose." In an interview published on his Web site, he said of his geese miniatures: "At night when I turn out the lights and go downstairs they sneak around the room and visit each other. . . . Most of the time they are well-behaved."

BIOGRAPHICAL AND CRITICAL SOURCES:

PERIODICALS

Booklist, November 15, 1995, Julie Corsaro, review of *Riddle Rhymes,* p. 562; October 1, 1999, Hazel Rochman, review of *Mice Are Nice,* p. 364; September 1, 2000, Shelley Townsend-Hudson, review of *Christmas Is Coming!,* p. 132; May 1, 2004, Carolyn Phelan, review of *Animal Tracks: Wild Poems to Read Aloud,* p. 1560.

New York Times Book Review, April 7, 1996, Campbell Geeslin, review of *Riddle Rhymes,* p. 21.

Publishers Weekly, August 24, 1992, review of *Good Cats, Bad Cats* and *Good Dogs, Bad Dogs,* p. 78; September 12, 1994, review of *Tickle Day: Poems from Father Goose,* p. 91; September 27, 1999, review of *Animal Trunk: Silly Poems to Read Aloud,* p. 103; August 4, 2003, review of *Halloween Nights: Twenty-one Spooktacular Poems,* p. 78; March 29, 2004, "Earth Day," p. 65.

School Library Journal, September, 1994, Kathleen Whalin, review of *Tickle Day,* p. 208; November, 1995, Pamela K. Bomboy, review of *Riddle Rhymes,* p. 89; October, 2000, review of *Christmas Is Coming!,* p. 59; October, 2003, Donna Cardon, review of *A Fury of Motion: Poems for Boys,* p. 192; April, 2004, Susan Scheps, review of *Animal Tracks,* p. 132.

Writer's Digest, August, 1999, Brad Crawford, "Charles Ghigna: Our Baseball Coach Made Us Take Ballet," p. 6.

ONLINE

Charles Ghigna Home Page, http://charlesghigna.com/ (June 2, 2004), includes interviews, bibliography, and book reviews.

Ink Spot, http://www.inkspot.com/ (June 2, 2004), interview with Ghigna.

Word Museum, http://www.wordmuseum.com/ (June 2, 2004), Tracy Hoffman, "An Exclusive Interview with Father Goose, Charles Ghigna."

* * *

GILBERT, Elizabeth 1969-

PERSONAL: Born 1969 in Waterbury, CT; daughter of a chemical engineer and a nurse; married. *Education:* Attended New York University.

ADDRESSES: *Home*—Hudson Valley, NY. *Agent*—c/o Author Mail, Viking Publicity, 375 Hudson St., New York, NY 10014.

CAREER: Writer. Former staff writer for *Spin* magazine; writer-at-large, *GQ* magazine.

AWARDS, HONORS: John C. Zacharis First Book Award, *Ploughshares*/Emerson College, 1999, for *Pilgrims;* National Book Award nomination in nonfiction, and National Book Critics Circle Award nomination in biography/autobiography, both 2002, both for *The Last American Man;* nominated for National Magazine Award; Pushcart Prize winner.

WRITINGS:

Pilgrims, Houghton Mifflin (Boston, MA), 1997.
Stern Men, Houghton Mifflin (Boston, MA), 2000.
The Last American Man, Viking (New York, NY), 2002.

Contributor to magazines, including *Harper's Bazaar* and *Esquire.*

ADAPTATIONS: Three of Gilbert's stories were adapted by Shira Piven as the play *Pilgrims* and produced in 2001. Gilbert's *GQ* article on working in a Manhattan bar was optioned and loosely adapted into the film *Coyote Ugly; The Last American Man* has been optioned by Warner Brothers.

SIDELIGHTS: The twelve short stories in Elizabeth Gilbert's debut collection, *Pilgrims,* range in locale from New York City to the ranchlands of the American West. Gilbert's tales do not always end predictably, giving readers the sense that they have been allowed a glimpse into the life of a character that will continue learning and growing even after the window opened by the story is closed. According to *Times Literary Supplement* reviewer Wendy Brandmark, personal epiphany links each story in the collection. In the title story, a city girl longs to run off with a Wyoming ranch hand even though each realizes that the psychologically inhospitable landscape would become a trap. Another story, "Elks," plays on the irony of a city woman who, having moved to the West, now resents the urban ways of her city family when they come to visit. According to Brandmark, "Elks" effectively illustrates parallels in isolation: the family visitors are just as "self-contained" as the woman has come to be in her rural lifestyle. The reviewer claimed that Gilbert subtly illustrates how "no one can be truly isolated." In another tale of introspective epiphany, "Alice from the East," an older woman who helps the inhabitants of a broken-down car shows one of them the depth of his own desires and losses.

Sometimes Gilbert's characters search for their own personal revelations, as in "The Names of Flowers and Girls," which features an artist who makes experience-seeking trips to the seedy side of town but fails to capture a new female friend in his artwork. In a New York City-based story, "Tall Folks," a female bar owner senses the end of her business when a strip bar opens across the street. A contributor to *Publishers Weekly* commented on the author's skills with detail, illustrated in "Tall Folks" when Gilbert describes her protagonist's habit of hiring female bartenders, by writing: "She had done very well this way, brokering these particular and necessary loves." While the *Publishers Weekly* reviewer opined that Gilbert's endings sometimes lacked closure, the reviewer liked the premise and the ending of "The Finest Wife," a story about an aged school bus driver who enters a fantasy realm and picks up all her lovers for a final bus ride. The critic concluded that "The Finest Wife" was a good portent for the "full length, warm blooded, compelling work to come" from Gilbert. Several reviewers remarked on the author's talent for making much of the silence between the lines, for showing the reader the subtleties of her characters. According to Brandmark, Gilbert's effort is a "rare mixture of compassion and keen observation."

Gilbert followed up *Pilgrims* with her first novel, *Stern Men.* Writing it was a struggle, she told *Beatrice* interviewer Ron Hogan. "It's difficult to go from a short story, which is just such a lovely moment—not even a chapter, just a glimpse. You don't have to provide more than a glimpse, and you can't get away with that in a novel, though people try to." The author uses another unique setting, two lobstering towns on neighboring Maine islands, to tell the coming-of-age story of Ruth Ellis, who has returned home after four years at boarding school. She doesn't fit in with her mother's wealthy family, and considers becoming a "stern man" on a lobster boat rather than go to college. When Ruth falls in love with a lobsterman from a competing island, it complicates matters even further. "In this breezily appealing first novel, Elizabeth Gilbert presents us a heroine as smart, sly, plucky and altogether winning as her own prose; it's difficult, in fact, not to develop a knee-weakening crush on both," *Salon* contributor Jonathan Miles observed. Gilbert's "gift for lively, authentic dialogue and atmospheric settings continually lights up this entertaining, and surprisingly thought-provoking, romp," a *Publishers Weekly* critic noted. *Library Journal* contributor Debbie Bogenschutz similarly hailed Gilbert's "beautiful novel," concluding that *Stern Men* is "funny and moving at the same time and populated by some quite memorable characters."

Although Gilbert has written many nonfiction profiles for magazines such as *GQ* and *Esquire,* it wasn't until 2002's *The Last American Man* that she produced an entire nonfiction volume on one subject. Eustace Conway is a modern woodsman whose determination to promote a more natural lifestyle has led him to build a 1,000-acre camp in the Appalachians, cross America by horseback, and lecture on environmental topics. "I've met some extraordinary people, fascinating characters, but I've never met anyone who thought of himself as being a *man of destiny*—and lived every moment as though he were that," Gilbert told the *Powell's Books* Web site. "That makes for an enormous amount of material, just in terms of the strict biography." Gilbert traces Conway's troubled childhood, recalls how he left home at seventeen to live on his own in the mountains, and details his life's mission—not only to live in harmony with nature, but to teach others how to do the same.

Critics found much to praise in *The Last American Man,* which earned nominations for both the National Book Award and the National Book Critics Circle Award. "In the end, her view of him is as balanced as it is entertaining," Janet Maslin wrote in the *New York Times.* "Without compromising her obvious admiration, Ms. Gilbert presents a warts-and-all portrait of Mr. Conway and a sophisticated understanding of why those warts are only natural." *New York Times Book Review* contributor James Gorman similarly called *The Last American Man* a "wickedly well-written and finally pain-filled biography," particularly in its exploration of how young Conway's emotional abuse by a cruelly demanding father is reflected in his own perfectionist personality. "It is hard to imagine a deeper, more insightful portrait," Anthony Brandt stated in *National Geographic Adventure.* The critic called *The Last American Man* "an important book" for its exploration of Conway's efforts to bring people back to nature, and concluded: "If the message of Conway's life is inherently sad, not just for him but for all of us, Gilbert's book is wise and knowing. She understands the dimensions of the loss we must all suffer through his failure."

BIOGRAPHICAL AND CRITICAL SOURCES:

PERIODICALS

Booklist, April 1, 2000, Carolyn Kubisz, review of *Stern Men,* p. 1434; April 1, 2002, Donna Seaman, review of *The Last American Man,* p. 1297.

Entertainment Weekly, May 31, 2002, Karen Valby, "The *Man* Show: Journalist Elizabeth Gilbert Tracks Down a Recluse Lured by the Call of the Wild," p. 99.

Kirkus Reviews, March 1, 2002, review of *The Last American Man,* p. 307.

Library Journal, April 1, 2000, Debbie Bogenschutz, review of *The Last American Man,* p. 129.

National Geographic Adventure, June-July, 2002, Anthony Brandt, "The No-Comfort Zone: Eustace Conway Is Modern America's Daniel Boone," p. 48.

New Yorker, May 20, 2002, Dana Goodyear, "Solitary Man," p. 25.

New York Times, June 3, 2002, Janet Maslin, "How a Woodsman Found High-Profile Solitude," p. B6.

New York Times Book Review, June 2, 2002, James Gorman, "Endangered Species," p. 16.

Publishers Weekly, July 7, 1997, review of *Pilgrims,* p. 47; March 20, 2000, review of *Stern Men,* p. 71; April 22, 2002, review of *The Last American Man,* p. 63.

Times Literary Supplement, May 29, 1998, Wendy Brandmark, review of *Pilgrims,* p. 27.

ONLINE

Beatrice Author Interviews, http://www.beatrice.com/interviews/ (November 13, 2003), Ron Hogan, "Elizabeth Gilbert."

Penguin Putnam Online, http://www.penguinputnam.com/Author/ (November 6, 2003).

Powell's Books: Author Interviews, http://www.powells.com/authors/ (October 31, 2003).

Salon.com, http://dir.salon.com/books/ (November 13, 2003), Jonathan Miles, review of *Stern Men.**

* * *

GOLD, Joseph 1933-

PERSONAL: Born June 30, 1933, in London, England; son of Maurice and Kitty (Goldberg) Gold; married Sandra Abramson, December 23, 1955; children: Deborah, Anna Michelle, Joel Martin Kit. *Education:* University of Birmingham, B.A. (with honors), 1955; University of Wisconsin, Ph.D., 1959. *Politics:* Socialist. *Religion:* Jewish. *Hobbies and other interests:* Reading, cooking, fishing, archery, canoeing.

ADDRESSES: Home—P.O. Box 1332, Haileybury, Ontario P0J 1K0, Canada. *E-mail*—jgold@sympatico.ca.

CAREER: Whitewater State College (now University of Wisconsin—Whitewater), Whitewater, WI, member of English faculty, 1959-60; University of Manitoba, Winnipeg, Manitoba, Canada, began as associate professor, became professor of English, 1960-70; University of Waterloo, Waterloo, Ontario, Canada, professor of English, 1970-94, professor emeritus, 1994—, department chair, 1970-73. Therapy North, Inc., president; marriage and family therapist. Manitoba Theater Centre, member of board of governors, 1969; Haileybury Public Library, board chair, 1996-99; Classic Theater, Cobalt, Ontario, Canada, board member, 1996-98. Canadian Broadcasting Corp., presenter of talks and literary criticism.

MEMBER: Alliance of Canadian Cinema, Television, and Radio Artists, Association for Bibliotherapy in Canada (founder; president, 1992-93, 1997—), American Association of Marriage and Family Therapists (clinical member).

WRITINGS:

William Faulkner: A Study in Humanism from Metaphor to Discourse, University of Oklahoma Press (Norman, OK), 1966.

(Editor) Charles G. D. Roberts, *King of Beasts, and Other Stories,* Ryerson (Toronto, Ontario, Canada), 1967.

(Compiler) *The Stature of Dickens: A Centenary Bibliography,* University of Toronto Press (Toronto, Ontario, Canada), 1971.

Charles Dickens: Radical Moralist, Copp Clark Publishing (Toronto, Ontario, Canada), 1972.

(Editor) Charles G. D. Roberts, *The Heart of the Ancient Wood,* McClelland & Stewart (Toronto, Ontario, Canada), 1973.

(Editor) *In the Name of Language,* Macmillan (New York, NY), 1975.

Read for Your Life: Literature As a Life Support System, Fitzhenry & Whiteside (Markham, Ontario, Canada), 2001.

The Story Species: Our Life-Literature Connection, Fitzhenry & Whiteside (Markham, Ontario, Canada), 2002.

Contributor to *Canadian Literature, Dalhousie Review, Mississippi Quarterly,* and other journals.

BIOGRAPHICAL AND CRITICAL SOURCES:

PERIODICALS

Emergency Librarian, March, 1991, review of *Read for Your Life: Literature As a Life Support System,* p. 45.

Globe and Mail (Toronto, Ontario, Canada), July 13, 2002, review of *The Story Species: Our Life-Literature Connection,* p. 1.

Library Journal, June 1, 2002, Nancy P. Shires, review of *The Story Species,* p. 147.*

* * *

GOM, Leona 1946-

PERSONAL: Born August 29, 1946, in Fairview, Alberta, Canada; daughter of Tony (a farmer) and Mary (a farmer; maiden name, Baron) Gom. *Education:* University of Alberta, B.Ed. (with honors), 1968, M.A. (with honors), 1971.

ADDRESSES: Home—British Columbia, Canada. *Agent*—c/o Author Mail, Sumach Press, 1415 Bathurst St., Ste. 202, Toronto, Ontario M5R 3H8, Canada.

CAREER: University of Alberta, Edmonton, Alberta, Canada, instructor in English, c. 1970-73; Kwantlen College, Surrey, British Columbia, Canada, instructor in English, 1975-92; University of British Columbia, Vancouver, teacher of creative writing, 1993-95; writer, 1995—. University of Alberta, writer in residence, 1987-88; University of Lethbridge, writer in residence, 1989; University of Winnipeg, writer in residence, 1990; also taught English at secondary schools in British Columbia.

MEMBER: League of Canadian Poets (regional representative of British Columbia, 1974-76), Federation of British Columbia Writers.

AWARDS, HONORS: Award from Canadian Authors Association, 1980, for *Land of the Peace;* Ethel Wilson Award for Fiction, 1986; British Columbia Book Prize, 1987.

WRITINGS:

POETRY

Kindling, Fiddlehead Poetry Books (Fredericton, New Brunswick, Canada), 1972.

The Singletree, Sono Nis Press (Vancouver, British Columbia, Canada), 1975.

Land of the Peace, Thistledown Press (Saskatoon, Saskatchewan, Canada), 1980.

North Bound: Poems Selected and New, Thistledown Press (Saskatoon, Saskatchewan, Canada), 1984.

Private Properties, 1986.

The Collected Poems, 1991.

NOVELS

Housebroken, NeWest Press (Edmonton, Alberta, Canada), 1986.

Zero Avenue, Douglas & McIntyre (Vancouver, British Columbia, Canada), 1989.

The Y Chromosome, Second Story Press (Toronto, Ontario, Canada), 1990.

After-Image: A Vicky Bauer Mystery, St. Martin's Press (New York, NY), 1996.

Double Negative: A Vicky Bauer Mystery, Second Story Press (Toronto, Ontario, Canada), 1998.

Freeze Frame: A Vicky Bauer Mystery, Second Story Press (Toronto, Ontario, Canada), 1999.

Hating Gladys, Sumach Press (Toronto, Ontario, Canada), 2002.

OTHER

The Inheritance (radio play), Canadian Broadcasting Corp., 1973.

Sour Air (radio play), Canadian Broadcasting Corp., 1974.

Author of a pamphlet, "North," League of Canadian Poets (Toronto, Ontario, Canada), 1980. Work represented in anthologies, including *Canadian Humour and Satire; Going for Coffee;* and *Forty Women Poets of Canada.* Contributor to magazines, including *Dalhousie Review, Malahat Review, Queen's Quarterly, West Coast Review, Canadian Forum,* and *Fiddlehead. Event,* began as poetry editor, became editor, beginning 1979.

SIDELIGHTS: Leona Gom once told *CA* that much of her writing describes the Peace River country of northern Alberta.

BIOGRAPHICAL AND CRITICAL SOURCES:

PERIODICALS

Books in Canada, November, 1986, review of *Housebroken,* p. 37; March, 1987, review of *Private Properties,* p. 31; January, 1991, review of *The Y Chromosome,* p. 42; May, 1992, review of *The Collected Poems,* p. 60.

Canadian Book Review Annual, 1996, review of *After-Image: A Vicky Bauer Mystery,* p. 162; 1999, review of *Double Negative: A Vicky Bauer Mystery,* p. 168.

Canadian Literature, winter, 1997, Ian Dennis, "Thru the Smoky End Boards: Canadian Poetry about Sports and Games," p. 181.

Essays on Canadian Writing, spring, 1988, review of *Housebroken,* p. 81; spring, 1991, Paul Denham, "'My Modern Life:' The Poetry of Leona Gom," p. 144; spring, 1991, review of *Land of the Peace, The Singletree, Northbound: Poems Selected and New,* and *Private Properties,* p. 152.

Kirkus Reviews, August 15, 1996, review of *After-Image,* p. 1189.

Queen's Quarterly, autumn, 1988, review of *Housebroken,* p. 568.

Quill & Quire, October, 1986, review of *Housebroken,* p. 44; November, 1989, review of *Zero Avenue,* p. 23; October, 1998, review of *Double Negative,* p. 28.*

* * *

GOOR, Ron(ald Stephen) 1940-

PERSONAL: Born May 31, 1940, in Washington, DC; son of Charles G. (a statistician) and Jeanette (a statistician; maiden name, Mindel) Goor; married Nancy Ruth Miller (an author and illustrator), March 12, 1967; children: Alexander, Daniel. *Education:* Swarthmore College, B.A. (magna cum laude), 1962; graduate study at University of Chicago, 1962-63; Harvard University, Ph.D., 1967, M.P.H., 1977.

ADDRESSES: Office—Choice Diets, Inc., P.O. Box 2053, Rockville, MD 20847-2053. *E-mail*—goor@choicediets.

CAREER: National Institutes of Health, Bethesda, MD, laboratory assistant, 1967-70; Smithsonian Institution, Natural History Museum, Washington, DC, special assistant to director, 1970-72; National Science Foundation, Washington, DC, program manager, 1972-76; National Institutes of Health, National Heart, Lung, and Blood Institute, Bethesda, clinical trial coordinator, 1976-84, national coordinator of Cholesterol Education Program, beginning 1984; creator of Eater's Choice dietary programs.

MEMBER: American Chemical Society, American Association for the Advancement of Science, Children's Book Guild, Phi Beta Kappa.

AWARDS, HONORS: Shadows: Here, There, and Everywhere was chosen as outstanding children's science book by National Science Teacher's Association/Children's Book Council Joint Committee, as notable book by American Library Association, and as one of Library of Congress's best books of the year, all 1981; *In the Driver's Seat* was chosen as one of the best children's books of the year by *New York Times* and *School Library Journal,* both 1982; *Signs* was named one of the Notable Children's Books for the Language Arts, 1983; *All Kinds of Feet* was named an Outstanding Science Trade Book for Children, 1984; Best Books of 1986 citation, *School Library Journal,* 1986, for *Pompeii,* which was also named on the American Library Association *Booklist*'s Children's Editor's Choices list, the Notable Children's Trade Books in the Field of Social Studies list, and the Notable Children's Trade Books for the Language Arts list, all 1986; *Heads* was named an Oustanding Trade Book for Children, 1988.

WRITINGS:

NONFICTION; WITH WIFE, NANCY GOOR

Eater's Choice: A Food Lover's Guide to Lower Cholesterol, Houghton Mifflin (Boston, MA), 1987, 5th edition, 1999.

(With Katherine Boyd) *The Choose to Lose Diet: A Food Lover's Guide to Permanent Weight Loss,* Houghton Mifflin (Boston, MA), 1990, revised edition published as *Choose to Lose: A Food Lover's Guide to Permanent Weight Loss,* 1995.

Eater's Choice Low-Fat Cookbook: Eat Your Way to Thinness and Good Health, Houghton Mifflin (Boston, MA), 1999.

Choose to Lose Weight-Loss Plan for Men: A Take-Control Program for Men with the Guts to Lose, Houghton Mifflin (Boston, MA), 2000.

NONFICTION FOR CHILDREN; SELF ILLUSTRATED WITH PHOTOGRAPHS

(With Millicent Selsam) *Backyard Insects,* Scholastic (New York, NY), 1981.

(With Nancy Goor) *Shadows: Here, There, and Everywhere,* Crowell (New York, NY), 1981.

(With Nancy Goor) *Williamsburg: Cradle of the Revolution,* Atheneum (New York, NY), 1994.

ILLUSTRATOR WITH PHOTOGRAPHS; WRITTEN BY NANCY GOOR

In the Driver's Seat (Junior Literary Guild Selection), Crowell (New York, NY), 1982.

Signs, Crowell (New York, NY), 1983.

All Kinds of Feet, Crowell (New York, NY), 1984.

Pompeii: Exploring a Roman Ghost Town, Crowell (New York, NY), 1984.

Heads, Atheneum (New York, NY), 1988.

Insect Metamorphosis: From Egg to Adult, Atheneum (New York, NY), 1990.

SIDELIGHTS: Ron Goor has achieved success as a health care worker, a photographer, and an author. When Goor was thirty-one years old, he learned that he had dangerously high cholesterol levels in his blood. His wife, Nancy, began creating and adapting recipes that would be tasty as well as low in saturated fat, the substance that raises blood cholesterol levels. Goor soon became the National Coordinator of the Coronary Primary Prevention Trial sponsored by the National Institutes of Health (NIH). This trial determined that lower cholesterol levels mean a lowered risk of heart disease. Goor also noted that the factors that lowered cholesterol almost inevitably led to weight loss as well. Later, Goor left the NIH to develop health programs on his own. Together with Nancy Goor, he created some books based on his small-group weight-loss counseling program, which has been offered in many hospital and workplace wellness programs and cardiac rehabilitation programs across the United States.

Their first offering on the subject was *Eater's Choice: A Food Lover's Guide to Lower Cholesterol.* That was followed by *The Choose to Lose Diet: A Food Lover's Guide to Permanent Weight Loss,* which guides the reader to determine his own fat budget. Then, by becoming aware of the fat contents of foods, the dieter can choose whatever he or she wants to eat as long as it fits into the daily fat budget. A light, humorous tone to the text helps to encourage readers and dieters, as do the 320 recipes created for the books and program. The authors contend that if one keeps an eye on fat calories and restricts them, it will be very difficult to consume too many calories in the total diet, no matter what else is eaten. Reviewing *Eater's Choice,* a writer for *Environmental Nutrition* credited the Goors with doing a "first-rate job" in explaining how fat leads to heart disease and why everyone should eat a heart-healthy diet. In an *Environmental Nutrition* review of *The Choose to Lose Diet,* another writer remarked: "While the concept of reducing total fat in the diet for weight loss is not new, the Goors' approach of counting fat calories simplifies the process."

Goor once told *CA* that he has been interested in biology for as long as he can remember. It wasn't until he had a Ph.D. in biochemistry and was doing lab research, however, that he decided he needed to express himself through teaching. He began to take photographs while at the Smithsonian Institution developing biological exhibits for the lay public. He discovered that "photography opened up new avenues of self-expression as well as exploring and documenting the world."

Goor believes that writing books for children was a natural outgrowth of his interest in photography. As he stated: "Good photography helps us see the world through fresh eyes. In my books I share with the reader a heightened awareness and appreciation of the beautiful and intricate natural world and new ways to see the complex man-made world."

Backyard Insects, Goor's first book, explores the many ways that the shapes and colors of insects protect them from their enemies. He recalled, "Ever since my wife, Nancy, and I started the nation's first live insect zoo at the Smithsonian's Natural History Museum in 1971, I became aware of the natural interest most children have in insects. These tiny, ubiquitous creatures illustrate many of the most important biological principles and are so easily found, observed, and raised that they make ideal teaching tools for understanding biology."

The enlarged photographs of the insects in the book help the reader see the insects in more detail than is possible with the naked eye. The text describes the variety of ways that color and shape protect the insects. Goor explained: "The lessons learned in the book provide a basis for seeing the animal world with fresh eyes. The use of domestic insects, easily found in both city and countryside, as examples in the book encourages readers to go outside to observe firsthand the phenomena described. Armed with this knowledge, the readers can go beyond the examples to understand and appreciate new observations in the field."

In *Shadows: Here, There, and Everywhere,* Ron and Nancy Goor explore the world of shadows, using carefully conceived black-and-white photographs. Set-ups consisting of a child's blocks and hand-held flashlight accompany each environmental scene and show how shadows are formed. As Goor observed: "Shadows are all around us—on the floor, the ground, the walls. They are long, short, bent, folded. They are beautiful, useful, scary. Yet how often do we notice them? The book is designed not only to heighten awareness of shadows but to increase understanding of the interactions of light, objects, and surfaces in the making of shadows."

With *In the Driver's Seat,* the Goors explore what it is like to drive a variety of vehicles—a blimp, a tank, an engine, the Concorde supersonic jet, a race car, a combine, a wrecking crane, a front-end loader, and an eighteen-wheel truck. Wide-angle lens photographs put the reader into the driver's seat of these nine vehicles. The text, by Nancy Goor, explains how to drive each vehicle and what each is like to operate. Additional pictures show the vehicles in action.

Prior to producing their third book, *Signs,* the Goors questioned a number of children and discovered that all either learned to read or practiced their reading on signs. As a result, *Signs* is aimed at reading-ready children or children who are just learning to read. Photographs on every page show signs in settings that help to convey their meanings and reinforce the beginning reader's sense of accomplishment in word-recognition.

Of another collaboration, Ron Goor said: "In *All Kinds of Feet* we focus on how animals' feet have adapted to moving in different environments, getting food, defending themselves, or escaping from enemies, and, in the case of man, making and using tools. The book is designed to make children look at animals analytically and see differences in animal structure as solutions to problems."

The husband-and-wife team have developed a compatible working method when producing their books. Goor told *CA:* "Nancy and I are often asked how we work together on a book. Generally, I begin by exploring the topic photographically. At the same time, Nancy and I begin to develop conceptual approaches to the subject matter. As Nancy develops the text, she suggests specific pictures that I have not yet taken during the early photographic exploration. Likewise, the photographs sometimes suggest changes in the text. Obviously, it is most helpful to have the writer and photographer working so closely together. Also, it is more fun that way!"

BIOGRAPHICAL AND CRITICAL SOURCES:

PERIODICALS

Booklist, January 15, 1995, Carolyn Phelan, review of *Williamsburg: Cradle of the Revolution,* p. 916.

Environmental Nutrition, December, 1988, "New Cholesterol Treatment Program," p. 2; September, 1990, review of *The Choose to Lose Diet: A Food Lover's Guide to Permanent Weight Loss,* p. 8; December, 1995, review of *Eater's Choice: A Food Lover's Guide to Lower Cholesterol* and *Choose to Lose: A Food Lover's Guide to Permanent Weight Loss,* p. 8.

Horn Book, February, 1982, Nancy Sheridan, review of *Shadows: Here, There, and Everywhere,* p. 63; December, 1983, Ann A. Flowers, review of *Signs,* p. 700; August, 1984, Nancy C. Hammond, review of *All Kinds of Feet,* p. 484; January-February, 1987, Margaret A. Bush, review of *Pompeii: Exploring a Roman Ghost Town,* p. 72; September-October, 1990, Elizabeth S. Watson, review of *Insect Metamorphosis: From Egg to Adult,* p. 619.

Instructor and Teacher, November-December, 1982, Allan Yeager, review of *In the Driver's Seat,* p. 151; May, 1984, Allan Yeager, review of *All Kinds of Feet,* p. 102.

Library Journal, April 15, 1987, Allayne C. Heyduk, review of *Eater's Choice: A Food Lover's Guide to Lower Cholesterol,* p. 92; February 1, 1990, Linda S. Karch, review of *The Choose to Lose Diet,* p. 100.

New York Times, November 14, 1982, Sherwin D. Smith, review of *In the Driver's Seat,* p. 60; November 30, 1982, George A. Woods, review of *In the Driver's Seat,* p. 23; July 26, 1989, Marian Burros, review of *Eater's Choice,* p. B6.

Popular Photography, February, 1982.

Publishers Weekly, December 12, 1986, Diane Roback, review of *Pompeii,* p. 58; December 19, 1986, Penny Kaganoff, review of *Eater's Choice,* p. 41; January 26, 1990, Molly McQuade, review of *The Choose to Lose Diet,* p. 416.

School Library Journal, September, 1981, Ann G. Brouse, review of *Shadows,* p. 107; November, 1982, review of *In the Driver's Seat,* p. 68; September, 1984, Carolyn Vang, review of *All Kinds of Feet,* p. 102; December, 1986, Marguerite F. Raybould, review of *Pompeii,* p. 103; December, 1988, Leda Schubert, review of *Heads,* p. 98; June, 1990, Diane Nunn, review of *Insect Metamorphosis: From Egg to Adult,* p. 112; December, 1990, review of *Insect Metamorphosis,* p. 22; June, 1995, Margaret C. Howell, review of *Williamsburg,* p. 120.

Scientific American, December, 1981, Philip Morrison, review of *Shadows,* p. 38.

Washington Post, June 16, 1987, Carole Sugarman, review of *Eater's Choice,* p. WH14; July 20, 1993, Jay Siwek, review of *Eater's Choice,* p. WN15.*

* * *

GOTLIEB, Sondra 1936-

PERSONAL: Born December 30, 1936, in Winnipeg, Manitoba, Canada; daughter of David Samson (an agricultural chemist) and Fanny Clare (Rossen) Kaufman; married Allan Gotlieb (a lawyer and diplomat), 1955; children: Rebecca, Marc, Rachel. *Education:* Attended University of Manitoba and Carleton University.

ADDRESSES: Home—Toronto, Ontario, Canada. *Agent*—c/o Author Mail, McArthur and Co., 322 King St. W., Ste. 402, Toronto, Ontario M5V 1J2, Canada.

CAREER: Author, journalist, and former columnist for the *Washington Post.* Also an artist.

MEMBER: Writers' Union of Canada.

AWARDS, HONORS: Leacock Medal for Humour, 1978, for *True Confections, or How My Family Arranged My Marriage.*

WRITINGS:

The Gourmet's Canada (cookbook), New Press (Toronto, Ontario, Canada), 1972.
Cross-Country Cooking: Favorite Ethnic Recipes from across the Continent, Hancock House Publishers (Seattle, WA), 1976.
True Confections, or How My Family Arranged My Marriage (novel), Musson Book Co. (Toronto, Ontario, Canada), 1978.
First Lady, Last Lady (novel), McClelland & Stewart (Toronto, Ontario, Canada), 1981, published as *A Woman of Consequence,* St. Martin's Press (New York, NY), 1983.
Wife of . . . An Irreverent Account of Life in Powertown (collected columns), Macmillan (Toronto, Ontario, Canada), 1985, Oxford University Press (New York, NY), 1987.
Washington Rollercoaster (memoir), Doubleday (New York, NY), 1990.
Dogs, Houses, Gardens, Food, and Other Addictions (memoir), McArthur (Toronto, Ontario, Canada), 2003.

Also editor, with Anne Hardy, of *Where to Eat in Canada* (restaurant guide), 1971-72, 1972-73. Author of "Dear Beverly," a twice-monthly humor column, *Washington Post.* Contributor of articles and sketches to periodicals, including *Maclean's, Chatelaine, Homemakers,* and *Saturday Night.*

SIDELIGHTS: In addition to other writings, Sondra Gotlieb's life as wife of the Canadian ambassador to the United States has inspired a novel, a collection of humorous columns, and a memoir. Critics have generally praised Gotlieb's "frothy satire," in the words of Christopher Schmering in the *Washington Post Book World,* and her "deliciously witty, snippy, tongue-in-chic account of official cocktail parties and dinners," according to Magda Krance in the *Chicago Tribune.*

Gotlieb's success as a writer may seem ironic since, as she once told *CA,* she "failed two universities," the University of Manitoba as a teenager and, years later, after her marriage to Oxford don and Canadian diplomat Allan Gotlieb, Carleton University. Then, an offer from a neighbor who was a publisher opened the door to Gotlieb's writing career. She was made coeditor of *Where to Eat in Canada,* a restaurant guidebook that, as Gotlieb told Krance, "paid me absolutely nothing. . . . I ate my way through Canada at my husband's expense."

Gotlieb continued to write about food, producing two acclaimed cookbooks. Anthony Appenzell, writing in *Canadian Literature,* called *The Gourmet's Canada* "a great food-searching journey across Canada . . . in which the author seeks out regional foods and dishes, talks of their natural and social history, [and] relates them to local lifestyles." *Cross-Country Cooking: Favorite Ethnic Recipes from across the Continent* is likewise a compendium of Canada's ethnic specialties. While breaking away from cookbook writing, a food theme pervades Gotlieb's first novel, *True Confections, or How My Family Arranged My Marriage*—which, as she told Krance, received a glowing review from a professor who had failed her in her college days.

After Allan Gotlieb became Canada's ambassador to the United States, the couple moved to Washington, DC, where Gotlieb began to write "Dear Beverly," a twice-monthly column in the *Washington Post* about the life (somewhat fictionalized) of an ambassador's wife. Addressed to a fictional friend named Beverly, the column appeared as letters from an ambassador's wife living in Washington. Each entry of "Dear Beverly" detailed life in the United States capital, including a host of characters based on real-life Washingtonians. There were, among others, the crusty diplomat Baron Spitte, professional socialite Popsie Tribble, and high-powered lobbyist Joe Promisall.

Apparently, some members of Washington's elite—as well as fellow Canadians—were offended by Gotlieb's column. "At first some Canadians thought an ambassador's wife should not do this sort of thing," Gotlieb told a chapter of the Canadian Club in 1984, quoted in the *Chicago Tribune* by Krance. Nevertheless, Gotlieb continued to defend her right to publish a humorous look at diplomatic life, claiming that most Americans like to laugh at themselves. Gotlieb also speculated to Krance that people may have taken exception to her column because it appeared in the *Post*'s op-ed section, alongside more serious material, rather than the feature page. In 1985, Macmillan published a collection of "Dear Beverly" columns as

Wife of . . . An Irreverent Account of Life in Powertown. Eve Drobot, writing in the Toronto *Globe and Mail,* found the collection "charming and frequently . . . hilarious," although somewhat repetitive: "what may be necessary in newspaper pieces that run with a two-week grace between them . . . clog up a book that's read all of a piece."

Gotlieb again drew on her past as a diplomat's wife for her second novel, *First Lady, Last Lady,* a story of ambition and intrigue set in the world of politics. The novel's protagonist is Nini Pike, the wife of a Canadian prime minister. While Nini's current situation is one of comic chaos, it is the events of twenty years ago that she is relating to an old friend. Prior to his ascension to prime minister, Nini's husband had served as a junior foreign service officer to the Canadian ambassador to Geneva, Switzerland, a particularly offensive man known as Sir Hillary-Moulds. It was during this time that Nini grew from a naive, complacent wife to a woman well-versed in the true machinations of power politics. Along her path to enlightenment, she discovers various pearls of wisdom, including the realizations that boredom is her greatest adversary and that the proper selection of a new chef for the ambassador may do more to advance her husband's career than any brilliant political maneuver. She also, along with everyone in his service, grows to despise Hillary-Moulds. The reminiscence is tied to the novel's present by a blackmail threat to Nini. It seems that twenty years earlier, Ambassador Hillary-Moulds was found dead in his bedroom. A mysterious person claims to have proof that Nini committed the crime and is threatening to tell all if she does not meet certain demands. *New York Times Book Review* writer Elisabeth Jakab commented that "Mrs. Gotlieb is very skillful at blending her characters' personal histories with the larger issues that eventually come to light. Her basic gift, however, appears to be for exploring the vagaries of human nature; it's this talent that makes [the novel] such entertaining, and occasionally hilarious, reading."

While Gotlieb's husband was still an ambassador, she had him review every "Dear Beverly" column that she wrote to make sure her work would not in any way interfere with his career. To protect her husband's position, she often disguised real people by blending elements of their personality into fictional beings such as Baron Spitte and Popsie Tribble. After Allan Gotlieb left his position, however, Gotlieb named the subjects of her commentaries, according to *Maclean's* reviewer E. Kaye Fulton. Gotlieb's memoir, *Washington Rollercoaster,* tells the story of Gotlieb's walks through the corridors of power, including juicy tidbits about numerous politicians and their spouses. Most critics concur, however, that the standout anecdote in the book revolves around Gotlieb's own impropriety: at a March, 1986, party to honor Canadian Prime Minister Brian Mulroney, Gotlieb publicly slapped the face of her social secretary, Connie Connor. As Gotlieb explains in the book, she was in a terrible, harried state-of-mind, owing in part to a period of self-imposed starvation so she could fit into a new dress, and momentarily lost control—in front of numerous luminaries. The Connie Connor incident may serve as a metaphor for the overall tone of the book; as Fulton wrote, "Slaps resound throughout *Washington Rollercoaster.*" Fulton went on to praise the book, saying that its barbs "may delight readers but will no doubt leave Gotlieb's targets as red-faced and embarrassed as the hapless Connie Connor."

BIOGRAPHICAL AND CRITICAL SOURCES:

BOOKS

Gotlieb, Sondra, *Washington Rollercoaster,* Doubleday (New York, NY), 1990.

Gotlieb, Sondra, *Dogs, Houses, Gardens, Food, and Other Addictions,* McArthur (Toronto, Ontario, Canada), 2003.

PERIODICALS

Books in Canada, March, 2003, Sharon Abron Drache, review of *Dogs, Houses, Gardens, Food, and Other Addictions.*

Chicago Tribune, October 25, 1984, article by Magda Krance, pp. 1, 5.

Globe and Mail (Toronto, Ontario, Canada), November 16, 1985, Eve Drobot, review of *Wife of . . . An Irreverent Account of Life in Powertown.*

Maclean's, May 14, 1990, E. Kaye Fulton, review of *Washington Rollercoaster,* p. 67.

New York Times Biographical Service, July 8, 1982, pp. 850-851.

New York Times Book Review, June 19, 1983, Elisabeth Jakab, review of *First Lady, Last Lady,* pp. 12, 21.

Washington Post Book World, June 5, 1983, article by Christopher Schmering, p. 11.*

GOTTWALD, Norman K(arol) 1926-

PERSONAL: Born October 27, 1926, in Chicago, IL; son of Norman Karl (in automotive sales) and Carol (Copeland) Gottwald; divorced; children: Lise, Sharon. *Education:* Eastern Baptist Theological Seminary, A.B. and Th.B., both 1949; Union Theological Seminary, M.Div., 1951; Columbia University, Ph.D., 1953.

ADDRESSES: *Home*—99 Claremont Ave., New York, NY 10027.

CAREER: Ordained minister of American Baptist Convention, 1949; Columbia University, New York, NY, lecturer, 1953-54, assistant professor of religion, 1954-55; Andover Newton Theological School, Newton Centre, MA, professor of Old Testament, 1955-62, Lowry Professor, 1962-65; Graduate Theological Union, Berkeley, CA, professor of Old Testament, 1965-82; New York Theological Seminary, New York, NY, professor of biblical studies, beginning 1980. Visiting assistant professor at Princeton University, 1955; visiting lecturer at Brown University, 1962-63, and Brandeis University, 1963-65; professor at American Baptist Seminary of the West, 1965-73; visiting professor at University of California, Santa Cruz, 1967, University of California, Berkeley, 1974-75, University of the Pacific, 1975-76, and Bryn Mawr College, 1977-78; lecturer at Ecumenical Institute for Advanced Theological Studies, Jerusalem, Israel, 1973-74. Research fellow at Hebrew Union College, Jerusalem, 1968-69.

MEMBER: American Academy of Religion, Society of Biblical Literature.

AWARDS, HONORS: Fulbright scholar in Jerusalem, Israel, 1960-61.

WRITINGS:

Studies in the Book of Lamentations, A. R. Allenson (Chicago, IL), 1954, revised edition, 1962.

A Light to the Nations: An Introduction to the Old Testament, Harper (New York, NY), 1959, revised edition published as *A Light to the Nations: A Socio-Literary Introduction to the Hebrew Bible,* Fortress (Philadelphia, PA), 1983.

All the Kingdoms of the Earth: Israelite Prophecy and International Relations in the Ancient Near East, Harper (New York, NY), 1964.

The Church Unbound: A Human Church in a Human World, Lippincott (Philadelphia, PA), 1967.

The Tribes of Yahweh: A Sociology of the Religion of Liberated Israel, 1250-1050 B.C.E., Orbis (Maryknoll, NY), 1979.

The Bible and Liberation: Political and Social Hermeneutics, Orbis (Maryknoll, NY), 1983.

(Editor) *Social Scientific Criticism of the Hebrew Bible and Its Social World: The Israelite Monarchy,* Scholars Press (Atlanta, GA), 1986.

(With Daniel L. Smith) *The Religion of the Landless,* HarperCollins (New York, NY), 1989.

God and Capitalism: A Prophetic Critique of Market Economy, edited by J. Mark Thomas and Vernon Visick, A-R Editions (Madison, WI), 1991.

The Hebrew Bible in Its Social World and in Ours, Scholars Press (Atlanta, GA), 1993.

Proclamation 4: Aids for Interpreting the Lessons of Church Year, Fortress Press (Philadelphia, PA), 1999.

The Politics of Ancient Israel, Westminster John Knox Press (Louisville, KY), 2001.

Contributor to *Interpreter's Dictionary of the Bible.* Contributor to theology journals.

SIDELIGHTS: As John Barton noted in the *Times Literary Supplement,* Norman K. Gottwald "made his name with *The Tribes of Yahweh: A Sociology of the Religion of Liberated Israel, 1250-1050 B.C.E.*" Gottwald, an Old Testament scholar who for many years taught at the New York Theological Seminary as well as at numerous other colleges and universities around the country, is a "pioneer in the social-scientific study of the Hebrew Bible," as Barton further pointed out. In *The Tribes of Yahweh* he puts forth the argument that, contrary to the Old Testament claims that Israel came into Palestine from Egypt, it was instead created out of the groups of lower-class refugees who fled the oppression of the city states of Canaan. Coalescing into the polity of Israel, these tribes then created a national tale of liberation from Egypt. That 1979 publication caused a stir in biblical studies. J. Andrew Dearman, writing in *Interpretation,* called the book a "massive, ground-breaking work, combining sociological analysis and Marxist theory in an investigation of Israel's origins."

Gottwald continued to ask and investigate new questions in biblical studies in other works. With *The Hebrew Bible in Its Social World and in Ours,* he collects twenty-nine essays, reviews, lectures, and other previously published and unpublished material with the shared theme of "the social history of ancient Israel as articulated in the Hebrew Bible, and as relevant to contemporary Christian theology and ethics," as Chris Seeman described the work in the *Catholic Biblical Quarterly.* These essays are organized by subject matter, including topics such as the origins of Israel, an examination of canon and more contemporary theology, and political and social ethics, among others. The contents are further organized chronologically, thus providing a look at the development of Gottwald's thoughts. "Taken together," wrote Seeman, "these essays are particularly valuable for clarifying the key features of [Gottwald's] 'Marxist' perspective." Dearman came up with a different interpretation of the same work, finding in the gathered essays the reason "why some scholars did not previously, and do not now, assess the relevant evidence the way Gottwald does; in large part, they believe his methodological presuppositions drive his historical analysis and dictate many of his conclusions."

In his 2001 work, *The Politics of Ancient Israel,* Gottwald "ventures beyond the authoritative perspective of the Bible's final editors to catch a glimpse of the diverse players constituting that society," wrote Paul D. Hanson in *Interpretation.* Employing an "interdisciplinary approach," as Hanson typified it, Gottwald views biblical text through the lens of modern critical disciplines such as historiography, literary analysis, and social theory. In so doing, he places "Israel within the matrix of ancient Near Eastern politics," according to Hanson. That same critic went on to call the book a "pioneering work that promises to contribute to a fresh approach to the politics of ancient Israel." For John Van Seters, however, writing in *Shofar,* "Gottwald's method of 'critically imagining' Israel's politics is a case of too little criticism and too much imagination." More positive was James M. Kennedy's assessment of the work in his *Catholic Biblical Quarterly* review. Kennedy found *The Politics of Ancient Israel* to be a "prime example of creative scholarship." According to Kennedy, Gottwald "assumes that a critical questioning of the biblical writers' own ideological assumptions is procedurally valid. The result is a depiction of Israel's politics that blends critical reconstructions with the Bible's own reporting of events." Kennedy went on to conclude that "this book is a major contribution and offers a component of the scholarly dialogue concerning ancient Israel that is worthy of an equally serious response."

BIOGRAPHICAL AND CRITICAL SOURCES:

PERIODICALS

Catholic Biblical Quarterly, April, 1995, Chris Seeman, review of *The Hebrew Bible in Its Social World and in Ours,* pp. 427-428; July, 2003, James M. Kennedy, review of *The Politics of Ancient Israel,* pp. 428-429.

Interpretation, July, 1995, J. Andrew Dearman, review of *The Hebrew Bible in Its Social World and in Ours,* pp. 302-304; July, 2003, Paul D. Hanson, review of *The Politics of Ancient Israel,* pp. 306-308.

Shofar, summer, 2003, John Van Seters, review of *The Politics of Ancient Israel,* pp. 130-132.

Times Literary Supplement, May 3, 2002, John Barton, review of *The Politics of Ancient Israel,* p. 32.

ONLINE

Pacific School of Religion Web site, http://www.psr.edu/ (February 9, 2004).

Westminster John Knox Press Web site, http://www.wjkbooks.com/ (February 9, 2004).*

* * *

GROSS, Jonathan David 1962-

PERSONAL: Born November 26, 1962, in New York; son of Theodore L. Gross (a university president); married Jacqueline Russell, March, 1993; children: Sheri Nicole. *Ethnicity:* "Jewish." *Education:* Haverford College, B.A., 1985; Columbia University, M.A., 1986, Ph.D., 1992. *Politics:* Democrat.

ADDRESSES: *Home*—3812 N. Whipple, Chicago, IL 60618. *Office*—Department of English, DePaul University, 802 W. Belden Ave., Chicago, IL 60614-3214; fax: 773-267-8502. *E-mail*—jgross@depaul.edu.

CAREER: DePaul University, Chicago, IL, assistant professor, 1992-98, associate professor of English, 1998—. University of Santa Clara, guest lecturer, 1995.

AWARDS, HONORS: Grant from National Endowment for the Humanities, 1992; grant for England, DePaul University, 1993; Mayer Fund fellow, Huntington Library, 1994; Gladys Krieble Delmas travel grant, American Council of Learned Societies, 1994; fellow, International Center for Jefferson Studies, 2002; Spirit of Inquiry Award, De Paul University, 2002.

WRITINGS:

(Editor and author of introduction) *Byron's "Corbeau Blanc": The Life and Letters of Elizabeth Milbanke, Lady Melbourne (1751-1818),* Rice University Press (Houston, TX), 1997.

Byron: The Erotic Liberal, Rowman & Littlefield (Lanham, MD), 2001.

Contributor to books, including *Byronic Negotiations,* Peter Lang (New York, NY), 2002; *Freemasonry on Both Sides of the Atlantic,* edited by Bill Weisberger, Columbia University Press (New York, NY), 2002; *Mapping Male Sexualities,* Fairleigh Dickinson University Press (Madison, NJ); and *Byron East and West.* Contributor of articles and reviews to scholarly journals, including *European Romantic Review, European Legacy, Studies in English Literature,* and *Philological Quarterly.* Bibliographer, *Keats-Shelley Journal,* 1995-99.

BIOGRAPHICAL AND CRITICAL SOURCES:

PERIODICALS

Choice, June, 2001, N. Fruman, review of *Byron: The Erotic Liberal,* p. 1793.

Keats-Shelley Journal (annual), 2002, Peter W. Graham, review of *Byron,* pp. 216-219.

* * *

GRYNBERG, Henryk 1936-

PERSONAL: Born July 4, 1936, in Warsaw, Poland; immigrated to the United States, 1967; son of Abraham (a dairy merchant) and Sofia (some sources say Sura; maiden name, Stolik) Grynberg; married Ruth Maria Meyers, January 24, 1964 (divorced, 1966); married Krystyna Walczak (an actress), July 30, 1967 (divorced, 1981); children: (second marriage) Deborah Maria, Adam. *Ethnicity:* "Polish-Jewish-American" *Education:* University of Warsaw, M.A. (journalism), 1959; University of California, Los Angeles, M.A. (Russian literature), 1971. *Religion:* Jewish

ADDRESSES: *Home*—6251 N. Kensington St., McLean, VA 22101. *Agent*—Alan Adelson, Jewish Heritage Project, 150 Franklin St., #1W, New York, NY 10013. *E-mail*—grynbe@aol.com.

CAREER: Jewish State Theatre, Warsaw, Poland, actor and translator, 1959-67; Union of Workers of Culture and Art, secretary, 1966-67; U.S. Information Agency, journalist, editor, and translator working primarily for Voice of America, 1971-1991; freelance writer.

MEMBER: Union of Polish Writers Abroad, Polish Film and Theater Artists Association, Polish Authors Union, PEN (American Center), Polish Authors Association.

AWARDS, HONORS: Annual literary prize of Koscielski Foundation, Switzerland, 1966, for *Zydowska wojna;* Tadeusz Borowski fellowship, Polish Authors Union, Poland, 1966; Wiadomości award, London, England, 1975; A. Jurzykowski Award, 1990; S. Vincenz Award, Krakow, Poland, 1991; Koret Jewish Book Award, fiction, 2002, for *Drohobycz, Drohobycz and Other Stories: True Tales from the Holocaust and Life After;* recipient of other major Polish literary prizes, including the Kultura, and the Karski and Nireńska; Nike prize nomination, for *Drohobycz, Drohobycz and Other Stories* and *Memorbuch.*

WRITINGS:

Ekipa "Antygona" (short stories), Państwowy Instytut Wydawniczy (Warsaw, Poland) 1963.

Swieto kamieni (poems), Instytut Wydawniczy "Pax" (Warsaw, Poland), 1964.

Antynostalgia (poems; title means "Anti-Nostalgia"), Oficyna Poetów i Malarzy (London, England), 1971.

Zycie ideologiczne (title means "Ideological Life"; also see below), Polska Fundacja Kulturalna (London, England), 1975.

Zycie osobiste (sequel to *Zycie ideologiczne;* title means "Personal Life"; also see below), Polska Fundacja Kulturalna (London, England), 1979.

Zycie codzienne i artystyczne (title means "Everyday and Artistic Life"; also see below), Instytut Literacki (Paris, France), 1980.

Wiersze z Ameryki (poems; title means "Poems from America"), Oficyna Poetów i Malarzy (London, England), 1980.

Wśród nieobecnych, Oficyna Poetów i Malarzy (London, England), 1983.

Prawda nieartystyczna (title means "The Non-Artistic Truth"), Archipelag (West Berlin, Germany), 1984, 4th edition, Wydawnictwo "Czarne" (Wolowiec, Poland), 2002.

Kadisz (title means "Kaddish"), Wydawnicto Znak (Krakow, Poland), 1987.

Pomnik nad Potomakiem, Oficyna Poetów i Malarzy (London, England), 1989.

Szkice rodzinne (title means "Family Sketches"), Czytelnik (Warsaw, Poland), 1989.

Wrocilem: wiersze wybrane z lat 1964-1989 (title means "I Have Returned") Państwowy Instytut Wydawniczy (Warsaw, Poland), 1991.

Zycie ideologiczne; Zycie osobiste, Państwowy Instytut Wydawniczy (Warsaw, Poland), 1992.

Pamietnik Marii Koper, Wydawnicto Znak (Krakow, Poland), 1993.

Dziedzictwo (title means "Heritage") Aneks (London, England), 1993.

Kronika, 86 Press (Lodz, Poland), 1994.

Rysuje w pamieci (title means "Sketching in Memory"), Wydawnictwo a5 (Poznań, Poland), 1995.

Zycie ideologiczne, osobiste, codzienne i artystyczne, Świat Ksiazki (Warsaw, Poland), 1998.

Ojczyzna (title means "Fatherland"), Wydawnicto W.A.B. (Warsaw, Poland), 1999.

Memorbuch, Wydawnicto W.A.B. (Warsaw, Poland), 2000.

(With Jan Kostanski) *Szmuglerzy* (title means "Smugglers"), Twój Styl (Warsaw, Poland), 2001.

Monolog polsko-zydowski, Wydawnictwo "Czarne" (Wolowiec, Poland), 2003.

Uchodźcy (title means "Refugees"), Świat Ksiazki (Warsaw, Poland), 2004.

Also contributor and translator from English to Polish for *Kultura* Paris, France), *Wiadomosci* (London, England), *Commentary, Midstream, Soviet-Jewish Affairs* (London, England), and *America Illustrated.* Works have been translated into English, German, Italian, French, Dutch, Hebrew, Czech, and Hungarian.

IN ENGLISH TRANSLATION:

Zydowska wojna (novella; title means "The Jewish War"; also see below), Czytelnik (Warsaw, Poland), 1965, 2nd edition, 1989, translation by C. Wieniewska published as *Child of the Shadows, including The Grave,* Vallentine, Mitchell (London, England), 1969.

Zwyciestwo (novel), Institut Litteraire (Paris, France), 1969, translation by Richard Lourie published as *The Victory* (also see below), Northwestern University Press (Evanston, IL), 1993.

Dzieci Syjonu, Wydawnicto Karta (Warsaw, Poland), 1994, translation by Jacqueline Mitchell published as *Children of Zion,* afterword by Israel Gutman, Northwestern University Press (Evanston, IL), 1997.

Drohobycz, Drohobycz, Wydawnicto W.A.B. (Warsaw, Poland), 1997, translation by Alicia Nitecki published as *Drohobycz, Drohobycz and Other Stories: True Tales from the Holocaust and Life After,* edited by Theodosia Robertson, Penguin (New York, NY), 2002.

The Jewish War [and] *The Victory,* Northwestern University Press (Evanston, IL), 2001.

WORK IN PROGRESS: Poems.

SIDELIGHTS: Fiction writer, poet, actor, and biographer Henryk Grynberg survived the Nazi occupation of Poland in hiding; forged Aryan identification papers saved his and his mother's lives. Grynberg's father was killed, "not by the Nazis but by villagers who took his money," related Michael Elkin in the *Jewish Exponent.* He was a victim of rampant distrust and anti-Semitism in Poland, "where hate was very much a part of the soil," Elkin remarked. After graduating from Warsaw University in 1959 with a master's in journalism, Grynberg joined the Jewish State Theater as an actor, subsequently defecting to the United States during the acting company's tour there. After earning a master's in Russian literature from UCLA, Grynberg moved to Washington, D.C., and went to work for the U.S. Information Agency, where he stayed for twenty years.

Much of Grynberg's fiction and poetry addresses issues related to the Holocaust and the traumatic aftereffects of the Holocaust. "Each new book is a further record of the fates of people who have been saved from oblivion by the writer in the conviction that doing so is not only the duty of literature towards the victims of the Holocaust, but also a confirmation of the sanctity of human life itself," stated a biographer on the *Polska 2000* Web site.

In *Drohobycz, Drohobycz* (translated as *Drohobycz, Drohobycz and Other Stories: True Tales from the Holocaust and Life After*), "the ordeal of Europe's Jews during and following WWII is anatomized in this chilling collection of thirteen richly developed stories" by Grynberg, wrote a *Kirkus Reviews* critic. Each story is dedicated to a particular man or woman whose life story served as background or inspiration for Grynberg's fictional work, noted Ruth Franklin in the *Los Angeles Times.* "More monologues than narratives, the extraordinary pieces in Grynberg's book are told in a rambling, conversational style that is astonishingly similar to the way many Holocaust survivors actually speak," Franklin further wrote, adding that the book's title story "appears simply to recount the family saga of one Dr. Leopold Lustig, but Grynberg has subtly shaped it into a group portrait of the Jews of the Galician town of Drohobycz." A detailed description of the occupants of a two-story house in the town mentions individual families, relatives, aunts and uncles and grandparents in an "almost Biblical catalog of ancestors and descendants," Franklin observed. But then Grynberg begins an involved description of where the residents of this building went when the Nazis arrived, concluding that "Slowacki Street 17 was a two-story house like most buildings in Drohobycz." Grynberg's "concluding sentence, an apparent non sequitur, serves as a jarring reminder that of an entire apartment building full of people, only the narrator and his Aunt Tonia have survived the war," Franklin observed. Readers of the book are "more than rewarded by the brilliance of the narrator in portraying life as it was and is," commented Jerzy J. Maciuszko in *World Literature Today.* "The ugly side of the human soul is shown to us by a master."

Grynberg's novel *Zwyciestwo* (translated as *The Victory*) contains some autobiographical elements at its base. The book tells the story of the young male narrator and his mother, who survived the war thanks to Aryan identification papers and carefully constructed denials of their Jewish heritage. The boy's father is thought to have been killed by Polish peasants, and the rest of the family sent to Treblinka. In the time between the end of the war and the Communist takeover of Poland, the narrator and his mother deal with the profoundly disturbing aftermath of the horror and brutality from the war years. The boy decides that he does not want to be Jewish anymore, and his mother copes through relationships with a Russian officer who returns to combat and a man who is ultimately sentenced to a labor camp. "Grynberg's deadpan, uninflected prose becomes wearing after a while, but the book has moments of appalling power, particularly in its scenes of violence," remarked a *Publishers Weekly* reviewer. Molly Abramowitz, writing in *Library Journal,* commented, "How people cope in the face of such tragedy and how they try to maintain a shred of dignity in their lives while grappling with difficult choices gives this book its power."

Originally published as *Dzieci Syjonu, Children of Zion* offers the nonfiction account of seventy-three Jewish children from Poland who lived through both the German and Soviet occupations of their country. Originally recorded in 1943 by members of the Polish government, the recollections present "the unvarnished, artless, and naive story of children who, to put it mildly, had no theory to defend," wrote Daniel Jonah Goldhagen in the *New Republic.* "Most of these children survived because they were in the part of Poland that the Germans first occupied and then, as border issues were ironed out to settle the Hitler-Stalin pact, they ended up under Soviet control," Goldhagen related. But no matter where they went, the children were constant witness to hatred, violence, and brutality against Jews, including such humiliating acts as beard-cutting and forcing Jews to dance in the streets while their synagogues burned. The stories form "a powerful, relentless document that bears grim testimony to the suffering endured by the children and their families as they journeyed from horror to horror," stated M. Anna Flabo in *Library Journal.* The children, persecuted as both Poles and as Jews, "suffered the worst imaginable fate of all Holocaust victims," remarked Alice-Catherine Carls in *World Literature Today.* "Their story illuminates the multifaceted nature of an evil which occurred during a time that we perhaps are in danger of stereotyping."

Henryk Grynberg once told *CA:* "My original writing is inspired by my being one of the very few child-survivors of the Jewish holocaust in Eastern Europe and recently by the revival of Jewish prosecution in my homeland which forced me to self-exile. My writing is concerned with ethics, including its religious and ideological aspects, problems of identity. My stories are realistic and so are my poems."

BIOGRAPHICAL AND CRITICAL SOURCES:

BOOKS

Contemporary Jewish Writing in Poland, University of Nebraska Press, 2001.

Wieniewska, W., editor, *Polish Writing Today,* Penguin, 1967.

PERIODICALS

Booklist, November 1, 1991, review of *Szkice Rodzinne,* p. 497.

Forward, January 8, 1968.

Hadassah, March, 1968.

Jewish Exponent, April 21, 1995, Michael Elkin, "Poland's Killing Fields: Documentary Focuses on a Writer's Return to the Land Where His Father Died during the Holocaust," p. 8X.

Kirkus Reviews, December 15, 1997, review of *Children of Zion,* p. 1827; November 1, 2002, review of *Drohobycz, Drohobycz and Other Stories: True Tales from the Holocaust and Life After,* p. 1567.

Kliatt Young Adult Paperback Book Guide, May, 1999, review of *Children of Zion,* p. 5.

L'Arche (Paris, France), June-July, 1970.

Library Journal, May 1, 1994, Molly Abramowitz, review of *The Victory,* pp. 136-137; February 15, 1998, M. Anna Flabo, review of *Children of Zion,* pp. 155-156.

Los Angeles Times, December 31, 1967; January 12, 2003, Ruth Franklin, "A Testimony to Survival," p. R4.

New Republic, March 29, 1999, Daniel Jonah Goldhagen, "Pride and Prejudice," p. 37.

New York Times, December 31, 1967.

Publishers Weekly, November 15, 1993, review of *The Victory,* p. 74.

Slavic Review, spring, 1986, Madeline G. Levine, review of *Prawda nieartystyczna,* p. 172.

Translation Review Supplement, July, 1998, review of *Children of Zion,* p. 7.

Tribune Books (Chicago, IL), October 21, 2001, review of *The Jewish War* [and] *The Victory,* p. 6.

Variety, October 25, 1993, Greg Evans, review of *Birthplace* (documentary), p. 81.

Volksbote (Munich, Germany), May 17, 1969.

World Literature Today, autumn, 1994, Jerzy J. Maciuszko, review of *The Victory,* pp. 849-850; spring, 1998, Jerzy J. Maciuszko, review of *Drohobycz, Drohobycz,* pp. 412-413; summer, 1998, Alice-Catherine Carls, review of *Children of Zion,* p. 651; spring, 2001, Jerzy R. Krzyzanowski, review of *Memorbuch,* p. 388.

Yiddisher Kemfer, December 15, 1967.

ONLINE

Polish Culture, http://www.culture.pl/ (February 2, 2003), review of *Memorbuch.*

Polish Writing, http://www.polishwriting.net/ (February 24, 2004), biography of Henryk Grynberg.

Polska 2000, http://www.polska2000.pl/ (February 24, 2004), biography and bibliography of Henryk Grynberg.

Public Broadcasting Service, http://www.pbs.org/ (February 24, 2004), biography of Henryk Grynberg.

H

HARLEY, Bill
See HARLEY, Willard F., Jr.

* * *

HARLEY, Willard F., Jr. 1941-
(Bill Harley)

PERSONAL: Born September 6, 1941, in Philadelphia, PA; son of Willard F. (a psychologist and professor) and Rita (a social worker and elementary schoolteacher; maiden name, Fels) Harley; married Joyce Shander (a radio talk show producer and hostess), December 15, 1962; children: Jennifer Harley Chalmers, Steven Willard. *Ethnicity:* "White." *Education:* University of California—Santa Barbara, Ph.D. *Religion:* Protestant. *Hobbies and other interests:* Genealogical research, history, science.

ADDRESSES: Home—12568 Ethan Ave. N., White Bear Lake, MN 55110; fax: 612-429-0253. *E-mail*—bharley@marriagebuilders.com.

CAREER: Westmont College, Santa Barbara, CA, chair of psychology department, 1968-71; Bethel College and Seminary, St. Paul, MN, professor of psychology, 1972-77; Harley Clinics of Minnesota, president, 1976-93; Marriage Builders, St. Paul, president, 1993—. Producer of self-help recordings, including the albums *Learning to Meet the Marital Needs of Men,* 1989, and (under name Bill Harley) *Big, Big World* 1993.

MEMBER: American Psychological Association.

WRITINGS:

Get Growing, Christian!, D. C. Cook Publishing (Elgin, IL), 1975.

His Needs, Her Needs, Fleming H. Revell (Old Tappan, NJ), 1986, 15th anniversary edition published as *His Needs, Her Needs: Building an Affair-Proof Marriage,* Fleming H. Revell (Grand Rapids, MI), 2001.

Marriage Insurance, Fleming H. Revell (Grand Rapids, MI), 1988.

Love Busters, Fleming H. Revell (Grand Rapids, MI), 1992, 2nd edition published as *Love Busters: Overcoming Habits That Destroy Romantic Love,* 1997, revised edition, 2002.

Five Steps to Romantic Love: A Workbook for Readers of "Love Busters" and "His Needs, Her Needs," Fleming H. Revell (Grand Rapids, MI), 1994, revised edition, 2002.

Give and Take: The Secret to Marital Compatibility, Fleming H. Revell (Grand Rapids, MI), 1996.

Your Love and Marriage: Dr. Harley Answers Your Most Personal Questions, Fleming H. Revell (Grand Rapids, MI), 1997.

Four Gifts of Love: Preparing for Marriage That Will Last a Lifetime, Fleming H. Revell (Grand Rapids, MI), 1998.

(With daughter, Jennifer Harley Chalmers) *Surviving an Affair,* Fleming H. Revell (Grand Rapids, MI), 1998.

Fall in Love, Stay in Love, Fleming H. Revell (Grand Rapids, MI), 2001.

I Cherish You: Words of Wisdom from "His Needs, Her Needs," Fleming H. Revell (Grand Rapids, MI), 2002.

Buyers, Renters, and Freeloaders: Turning Revolving-Door Romance into Lasting Love, Fleming H. Revell (Grand Rapids, MI), 2002.

His Needs, Her Needs for Parents: Keeping Romance Alive, Fleming H. Revell (Grand Rapids, MI), 2003.

Harley's books have been published in eighteen foreign languages.

SIDELIGHTS: Willard F. Harley, Jr. once told *CA:* "I have spent most of my professional life saving marriages. At first it was an avocation, while I was teaching psychology, but eventually it took enough of my time to turn into a full-time career. Each book I write is an outgrowth of my experience solving a particular marital problem.

"My counseling experience involves direct contact with more than 10,000 couples. Even now I have an opportunity to interact with thousands more over the Internet through my Web site, marriagebuilders.com. It is one of the most popular sites on marriage on the Internet.

"Both of my children are professional marriage counselors who work with me full time."

BIOGRAPHICAL AND CRITICAL SOURCES:

PERIODICALS

Library Journal, August, 2002, Douglas C. Lord, review of *Buyers, Renters, and Freeloaders: Turning a Revolving-Door Romance into Lasting Love,* p. 122.

ONLINE

Marriage Builders: Building Marriages to Last a Lifetime, http://www.marriagebuilders.com/ (May 16, 2004).

* * *

HARRIS, Dorothy Joan 1931-

PERSONAL: Born February 14, 1931, in Kobe, Japan; immigrated to Canada, 1938; daughter of Hubert and Alice Langley; married Alan Harris (a company secretary-treasurer), October 8, 1955; children: Kim, Douglas. *Education:* University of Toronto, B.A. (with honors), 1952. *Religion:* Anglican.

ADDRESSES: Home—159 Brentwood Rd. N., Toronto, Ontario M8X 2C8, Canada. *Agent*—Dorothy Markinko, McIntosh & Otis, 475 5th Ave., New York, NY 10017.

CAREER: Elementary school teacher in Kobe, Japan, 1954-55; editor for Copp Clark Publishing Company, 1955-60; writer.

WRITINGS:

The House Mouse, illustrated by Barbara Cooney, Frederick Warne (New York, NY), 1973.

The School Mouse, illustrated by Chris Conover, Frederick Warne (New York, NY), 1977.

The School Mouse and the Hamster, illustrated by Judy Clifford, Frederick Warne (New York, NY), 1979.

Don't Call Me Sugarbaby!, Scholastic Canada (Richmond Hill, Ontario, Canada), 1983.

Goodnight, Jeffrey, illustrated by Nancy Hannans, Frederick Warne (New York, NY), 1983.

Four Seasons for Toby, Scholastic Canada (Richmond Hill, Ontario, Canada), 1987.

Even If It Kills Me, Scholastic Canada (Richmond Hill, Ontario, Canada), 1987.

Speedy Sam, Scholastic Canada (Richmond Hill, Ontario, Canada), 1989.

No Dinosaurs in the Park, Scholastic Canada (Richmond Hill, Ontario, Canada), 1990.

Annabel the Detective, HarperCollins Canada (Scarborough, Ontario, Canada), 1991.

SIDELIGHTS: Dorothy Joan Harris once commented: "*The House Mouse* sprang from the doings of my own children, for Kim had a doll's house which she never played with (just as Elizabeth had in the book) and Douglas at the age of three liked it (just as Jonathan did in the book). The mouse, though, was purely imaginary, because our house was ruled by a very bossy Siamese cat called Samitu—and Sam would never tolerate any other animal on his property.

"*The School Mouse,* too, came from my children's experience, arising from the various fears and worries they had about school. Adults tend to forget how real and overpowering fears are to them, even when they seem trivial to grown-ups.

"But though much of my writing springs from actual children, editors do not always believe it. In *The House Mouse* I originally made Jonathan three years old, and one of the first criticisms I received from editors was that Jonathan did not talk like a three-year-old and should be a six-year-old. I felt like replying that my own three-year-old talked in *exactly* that way—but instead I compromised and made Jonathan four years old.

Now that my own children are growing up I try to strike up friendships with the children of neighbours and friends, so as to keep in touch with the world of childhood. And I never lose any chance to strike up a friendship with animals, wild or tame—especially with any cat. It takes me a long time to walk along our street because I have to stop and have a word with each cat I meet.

"My own cat, Sam, absolutely hates the sight of me sitting at my typewriter. Even if he is sound asleep under his chair he wakes at the first tap and goes into his act: First he jumps up on the mantelpiece or buffet (so that I have to get up and lift him down), then he jumps up on the typewriter table, drapes his tail over the keyboard, and finally settles on my lap, with both paws firmly clamped on my wrist—which make typing extremely difficult. Someday I'm going to dedicate a book 'To Sam, without whose help I could have finished this darned book in half the time!'"

Jonathan's mouse is special. In all three of his titles, *The House Mouse, The School Mouse,* and *The School Mouse and the Hamster,* the little rodent talks to Jonathan and helps the youngster through trying situations. In *The School Mouse and the Hamster,* for instance, the mouse persuades Jonathan that the other class pet, a hamster, needs goodies and visits. Jonathan and his mouse feed the hamster, and the mouse exercises with the hamster. Confusion develops when the hamster has no appetite or energy during the day. In *Goodnight, Jeffrey,* a little boy fights going to sleep by playing with his daytime toys, until he finds a trusty stuffed animal that lulls him into inactivity. Harris's *Don't Call Me Sugarbaby!* is based on the true-life story of a friend's daughter who developed childhood onset diabetes. The book explores the life-altering changes for the girl and her family as she copes with a chronic condition. A *Maclean's* reviewer felt that the story "rings true in its detailing of the disease."

BIOGRAPHICAL AND CRITICAL SOURCES:

PERIODICALS

Maclean's, July 4, 1983, review of *Don't Call Me Sugarbaby!,* p. 50.

*Publishers Weekly,*September 9, 1983, review of *Goodnight, Jeffrey,* p. 65.

School Library Journal, March, 1980, Patricia Smith Butcher, review of *The School Mouse and the Hamster,* p. 121; December, 1983, Margaret C. Howell, review of *Goodnight, Jeffrey,* p. 56.*

* * *

HARVEY, Jack
See RANKIN, Ian (James)

* * *

HAYGOOD, Wil 1954-

PERSONAL: Born September 19, 1954, in Columbus, OH; son of Ralph (an automotive mechanic) and Elvira (a cook; maiden name, Burke) Haygood. *Education:* Miami University of Ohio, B.A., 1976. *Religion:* Baptist.

ADDRESSES: Home—26 Suffolk St., Cambridge, MA 02139. *Office*—Boston Globe, 135 Morrissey Blvd., Boston, MA 02107. *Agent*—Esther Newberg, International Creative Management, 40 W. 57th St., New York, NY 10019.

CAREER: Call and Post, Columbus, OH, reporter, 1977-78; Community Information and Referral, hotline operator, 1978-79; R. H. Macy's, New York, NY, retail manager, 1980-82; *Charleston Gazette,* Charleston, WV, copy editor, 1982-84; *Pittsburgh Post-Gazette,* Pittsburgh, PA, reporter, 1984-85; *Boston Globe,* Boston, MA, writer, beginning 1985.

AWARDS, HONORS: National Headliner Award, National Headliners Club, 1986, for outstanding feature writing; fellow of Alicia Patterson Foundation, 1988; New England Associated Press Award, 1990;

International Reporting Award, National Association of Black Journalists, 1990; Sunday Magazine Editors Association Award for profile writing, 1993; D.H.L. from Ohio Dominican College, 1993.

WRITINGS:

Two on the River, photographs by Stand Grossfield, Atlantic Monthly Press, 1986.

King of the Cats: The Life and Times of Adam Clayton Powell, Jr., Houghton Mifflin (Boston, MA), 1993.

The Haygoods of Columbus: A Love Story, Houghton Mifflin (Boston, MA), 1997.

In Black and White: The Life of Sammy Davis, Jr., Knopf (New York, NY), 2003.

Contributor of articles to periodicals.

SIDELIGHTS: Wil Haygood once told *CA:* "I'm lucky in a way, inasmuch as I came to writing and journalism with experience of life itself, grit and woe: I had worked as a dishwasher in Brooklyn, a hotline telephone operator in Columbus, Ohio, a retail manager at Macy's department store, and a university typist. I didn't know I wanted to write until I decided I cared to do nothing else except write. I am a trained journalist, lucky enough to have reported for the *Boston Globe* from across most of America and many foreign countries.

"If there is a weed that grows through and underneath my work, I like to think it is a concern for the unknown stories, the lost stories, the stories in the back country. In my first book, I explored forgotten towns along the Mississippi River; in my second book, a forgotten New York politician. My third book is about the Midwest and a family farm in Georgia, about the history of the two places and the hidden and obvious growth of a family."*

* * *

HECK, Peter J(ewell)

PERSONAL: Born in Chestertown, MD; son of Preston Patterson (a lawyer) and Ermyn (a teacher; maiden name, Jewell) Heck; married Flora Metrick, 1966 (divorced, 1988); married Jane Jewell, December 29, 1989; children: (first marriage) Daniel P. *Education:* Harvard University, B.A. (magna cum laude); Johns Hopkins University, M.A.; Indiana University—Bloomington, doctoral study. *Hobbies and other interests:* Guitar, chess, travel.

ADDRESSES: Home and office—Chestertown, MD. *Agent*—c/o Author Mail, 345 Hudson St., New York, NY 10014. *E-mail*—peteheck@dmv.com.

CAREER: Ace Books, New York, NY, editor, 1990-92; freelance writer and editor; author and editor of science fiction and mystery marketing newsletters. Temple University, Philadelphia, PA, instructor in English. Sam Ash Music, worked as sales manager; manager of an air freight company, Astoria, NY.

MEMBER: Science Fiction Writers of America, Mystery Writers of America, Sisters in Crime, U.S. Chess Federation.

AWARDS, HONORS: Silver Noose Award, New York chapter, Mystery Writers of America.

WRITINGS:

MYSTERY NOVELS

Death on the Mississippi, Berkley Publishing (New York, NY), 1995.

A Connecticut Yankee in Criminal Court, Berkley Publishing (New York, NY), 1996.

The Prince and the Prosecutor, Berkley Publishing (New York, NY), 1997.

The Guilty Abroad, Berkley Publishing (New York, NY), 1999.

The Mysterious Strangler, Berkley Publishing (New York, NY), 2000.

Tom's Lawyer, Berkley Publishing (New York, NY), 2001.

OTHER

(With Robert Asprin) *A Phule and His Money* (science fiction novel), Ace Books (New York, NY), 1999.

(With Robert Asprin) *Phule Me Twice* (science fiction novel), Ace Books (New York, NY), 2000.

(With wife, Jane Jewell) *The Great War and the Lost Generation: A Musical/Historical Review* (theater piece), produced by Kent County Arts Council, 2002.

(With Robert Asprin) *No Phule Like an Old Phule* (science fiction novel), Ace Books (New York, NY), 2004.

Contributor to magazines, including *Isaac Asimov's Science Fiction, Kirkus Reviews,* and *Newsday.* Past editor, *Xignals* (science fiction/fantasy newsletter) and a mystery newsletter, both for Waldenbooks.

WORK IN PROGRESS: A fourth "Phule's Company" novel, with Robert Asprin; research for a science fiction series involving a group of teenagers; research on time travel to the Mesozoic era.

SIDELIGHTS: Novelist Peter J. Heck's lifelong interest in writer Samuel Clemens (Mark Twain) led him to produce a successful series of mystery novels that feature the great American author as their protagonist. The titles all "play off" the titles of Twain books, such as *Life on the Mississippi, A Connecticut Yankee in King Arthur's Court,* and *The Prince and the Pauper.* The narrator of all the novels is William Wentworth Cabot, Clemens's traveling secretary, who serves as a Watson to Twain's Sherlock Holmes in the series.

In *Death on the Mississippi,* Clemens, about to set off on a lecture tour, is confronted by a self-proclaimed New York City police detective who says that a murdered man has been found with Clemens's address in his pocket. Clemens suspects that the detective is a fake and sets out to solve the mystery, largely because he wishes to conceal the fact that his lecture tour is a cover for a buried-treasure dig. Clemens and Cabot find the "detective" traveling to the Mississippi River on their train; so are a group of thugs from Clemens's past. Clemens and Cabot unravel the knots and stop the villains in what *Library Journal* contributor Rex E. Klett termed a "catchy adventure" and "a well-done historical." *Booklist* reviewer Wes Lukowsky called the novel "a thoroughly enjoyable period mystery. . . . A very pleasant debut that will have readers eagerly awaiting the next entry."

The second volume in the trilogy, *A Connecticut Yankee in Criminal Court,* finds Clemens on an 1894 lecture tour to New Orleans, where fellow humorist George Washington Cable involves him in attempting to clear African-American cook Leonard Galloway of the murder of a mayoral candidate. Suspects turn up among the dead man's relatives and associates; New Orleans characters such as trumpeter Buddy Bolden and voodoo priestess Eulalie Echo show up; and Clemens, although initially reluctant, eventually attacks the mystery with what a *Kirkus* reviewer admiringly termed "all the aplomb of Perry Mason." For the *Kirkus Reviews* critic, the novel's characters provide "exactly the sort of colorful cast that brings its satiric hero's famous talent for unmasking pretension into brilliant relief." *Booklist* contributor Jennifer Henderson warned amiably, "Try not to start this novel on an empty stomach. It will have you craving gumbo, finely seasoned pompano, and pecan pie as this Crescent City mystery simmers." A critic for *Publishers Weekly* called *A Connecticut Yankee in Criminal Court* "an entertaining sequel" and commended it for providing "an enjoyable tour of 1890s New Orleans." Added the reviewer, "Twain can take a bow for his performance here, with readers assured that Heck will give him a chance for an encore."

The encore came the following year in *The Prince and the Prosecutor.* The scene this time is a trans-Atlantic steamer on which Twain's and Cabot's fellow passengers include Rudyard Kipling and his wife, a German prince, and a boorish Philadelphia scion and his fiancee. The young Philadelphia snob disappears during a storm, and his father, a prosecutor, accuses the prince of murder. Kipling joins the Twain-Cabot team to solve this mystery, and both authors flash their wit and their anecdotal prowess. For a *Publishers Weekly* critic, this was apparently the most satisfying of Heck's three Clemens novels to date: "Mark Twain's abilities as a detective seem to have grown substantially in this third adventure. . . . Heck's Twain proves to be an entertaining replica of the original and a clever detective to boot."

Heck once told *CA:* "I wanted to be a writer at an early age, but (like most others, I think) had no idea how to become one. My parents encouraged me to read, and I did: Poe, Twain, science fiction, Hemingway, and the Beats—who gave me an image of the writer pouring out his soul onto paper, like a jazz musician inventing a solo. It wasn't until much later that I learned I couldn't work that way.

"I was an English major at Harvard, where I learned a great deal about how to read but very little about how to write anything but academic papers. Inertia took me to graduate school, where I taught the usual graduate assistant courses. I went on to teach at Temple University, until I realized I couldn't finish my dissertation on Keats and dropped out. To pay the bills, I ran an air freight office, then worked at a music store, selling sheet music and instruments. My only contact with literature was as a book reviewer.

"By 1983 I was dead-ended and dissatisfied. Waldenbooks was looking for a freelancer to edit *Xignals,* a newsletter for science fiction/fantasy readers, and I got the job. They later added a mystery newsletter, which I also did. Editing a regular newsletter (interviewing more than a hundred authors in the process) gave me the tools and discipline to become a professional writer. Doing *Xignals* also led to a job offer as an editor at Ace Books.

"The Ace job was the equivalent of a doctoral degree in the theory and practice of genre fiction. I learned a lot about how a novel is put together from working with Spider Robinson, Lynn S. Hightower, Robert Sawyer, Shariann Lewitt, Esther Friesner, and many others. Maybe even more usefully, I learned the publishing business from the inside—a perspective from which I think many other writers could benefit.

"In 1993, after leaving Ace, I wrote a proposal for a series of historical mysteries with Mark Twain as the detective. It sold almost immediately. That began what I hope will be a permanent career as a novelist, although I continue to do freelance editing and copywriting. I have sold several books in the 'Mark Twain Mystery' series and have recently agreed to continue the 'Phule's Company' series of science fiction novels begun by Robert L. Asprin. Like the Twain mysteries, these will be essentially light comedy with serious underpinnings.

"The freelance life is inherently unstable, but I remain optimistic that I've finally figured out a way to earn a living by my wits."

BIOGRAPHICAL AND CRITICAL SOURCES:

PERIODICALS

Booklist, December 15, 1995, Wes Lukowsky, review of *Death on the Mississippi,* p. 688; November 15, 1996, Jennifer Henderson, review of *A Connecticut Yankee in Criminal Court,* p. 574.

Bookwatch, February, 1996, p. 9; February, 1997, p. 7.

Kirkus Reviews, September 15, 1995, p. 1312; October 1, 1996, review of *A Connecticut Yankee in Criminal Court,* p. 1428.

Kliatt, January, 1997, p. 8.

Library Journal, November 1, 1995, p. 109, Rex E. Klett, review of *Death on the Mississippi.*

Publishers Weekly, October 9, 1995, p. 80; September 23, 1996, review of *A Connecticut Yankee in Criminal Court,* p. 59; October 20, 1997, review of *The Prince and the Prosecutor,* p. 58.

Science Fiction Chronicle, May, 1996, p. 58.

* * *

HERBERT, Thomas Walter, Jr. 1938-

PERSONAL: Born September 7, 1938, in Rome, GA; son of Thomas Walter (a professor) and Jean Elizabeth (Linton) Herbert; married Marjorie Millard (an attorney), July 13, 1963; children: Thomas Walter III, Elizabeth Crate. *Education:* Harvard University, B.A., 1960; Union Theological Seminary, New York, NY, M.Div., 1963; Princeton University, Ph.D., 1969.

ADDRESSES: Office—Department of English, Southwestern University, Georgetown, TX 78626.

CAREER: University of California—Berkeley, Berkeley, director of experimental program in ministry, 1963-66; University of Kentucky, Lexington, assistant professor of English, 1969-75; Southwestern University, Georgetown, TX, Herman Brown Professor of English and department chair, 1975—, university scholar, 1981—.

MEMBER: Modern Language Association of America, Society for Religion in Higher Education, South Atlantic Modern Language Association.

AWARDS, HONORS: Younger humanist fellow, National Endowment for the Humanities, 1973-74; Guggenheim fellow, 1981-82.

WRITINGS:

Moby Dick and Calvinism: A World Dismantled, Rutgers University Press (New Brunswick, NJ), 1977.

Marquesan Encounters, Harvard University Press (Cambridge, MA), 1980.
Dearest Beloved: The Hawthornes and the Making of the Middle-Class Family, University of California Press (Berkeley, CA), 1993.
Sexual Violence and American Manhood, Harvard University Press (Cambridge, MA), 2002.

Contributor to theology and language journals.

BIOGRAPHICAL AND CRITICAL SOURCES:

PERIODICALS

American Anthropologist, March, 1983, review of *Marquesan Encounters,* p. 220.
Journal of American Studies, April, 1983, review of *Marquesan Encounters,* p. 114.
Library Journal, October 15, 2002, Andrew Brodie Smith, review of *Sexual Violence and American Manhood,* p. 87.
Religious Studies Review, January, 1984, review of *Marquesan Encounters,* p. 61.*

* * *

HEYMANN, C. David
See HEYMANN, Clemens Claude

* * *

HEYMANN, Clemens Claude 1945-
(C. David Heymann)

PERSONAL: Born January 14, 1945, in New York, NY; son of Ernest Frederick (a writer) and Renee Kitty (in real estate; maiden name, Vago) Heymann; married Jeanne Ann Lunin (a private school administrator), November 10, 1974 (divorced, 1995); married Rebecca Coughlan, 1995 (divorced, 1996); children: Chloe Colette, Paris Kent Fineberg-Heymann. *Ethnicity:* "Caucasian." *Education:* Cornell University, B.S., 1966; University of Massachusetts, M.F.A., 1969; doctoral study at state University of New York—Stony Brook, 1976. *Politics:* Independent.

ADDRESSES: Home and office—360 Central Park W., No. 12-F, New York, NY 10025. *E-mail*—gwvi@columbia.edu.

CAREER: State University of New York—Stony Brook, Stony Brook, lecturer in English, 1969-74; Antioch College—New York Campus, New York, NY, lecturer in English, 1975; writer. American Book Awards, member of panel of judges, 1979-80.

MEMBER: International PEN, Authors Guild, Authors League of America, National Book Critics Circle.

AWARDS, HONORS: Borestone Mountain Poetry Award, 1969; *Ezra Pound: The Last Rower* and *American Aristocracy: The Lives and Times of James Russell, Amy, and Robert Lowell* were listed among the most notable books of the year for 1976 and 1980, respectively, by *New York Times Book Review;* writer's grant from Israeli Government, 1984-85.

WRITINGS:

UNDER NAME C. DAVID HEYMANN

The Quiet Hours (poetry), Poets' Press, 1968.
Ezra Pound: The Last Rower, Viking (New York, NY), 1976.
American Aristocracy: The Lives and Times of James Russell, Amy, and Robert Lowell, Dodd, Mead (New York, NY), 1980.
Poor Little Rich Girl: The Life and Legend of Barbara Hutton, Random House (New York, NY), 1983.
A Woman Named Jackie, Lyle Stuart (Secaucus, NJ), 1989.
Liz: An Intimate Biography of Elizabeth Taylor, Carol Publishing Group (New York, NY), 1995.
RFK: A Candid Biography of Robert F. Kennedy, Dutton (New York, NY), 1998.
The Georgetown Ladies' Social Club: Power, Passion, and Politics in the Nation's Capital, Atria Books (New York, NY), 2003.

Fishing columnist, *Diversion.* Contributor of articles and reviews to numerous periodicals, including *Chicago Tribune,Commentary, Cosmopolitan,Encounter, New Republic,Paris Match, Partisan Review,Redbook, Saturday Review,* and *Vanity Fair.*

ADAPTATIONS: Poor Little Rich Girl: The Life and Legend of Barbara Hutton was adapted for a Golden Globe and Emmy award-winning television miniseries, produced by Lester Persky, broadcast on NBC-TV, 1987; *A Woman Named Jackie* was adapted for a six-hour television miniseries, produced by Lester Persky and broadcast by NBC-TV; *Liz: An Intimate Biography of Elizabeth Taylor* was adapted for a five-hour television miniseries, produced by Lester Persky and broadcast by NBC-TV.

SIDELIGHTS: Clemens Claude Heymann's many works of biography include *RFK: A Candid Biography of Robert F. Kennedy,* which chronicles the life of a man who, had he lived, would probably have become president, and at the very least would have united the Democratic Party. In writing the book, Heymann used more than thirty researchers and interviewers, who delved into Kennedy archives and library collections and gleaned information from Kennedy friends and acquaintances.

Richard Young reviewed *RFK* in *America,* noting that the first half of the book is "a carefully researched political biography," while the second "seems to report every bit of sexual gossip about Kennedy, his parents, wife, siblings, and children that has some credibility or a source willing to be quoted."

In *The Georgetown Ladies' Social Club: Power, Passion, and Politics in the Nation's Capital,* Heymann's subjects are Katharine Graham, Lorraine Cooper, Evangeline Bruce, Sally Quinn, and Pamela Harriman, supported by a cast of others, including John F. Kennedy, Warren Buffett, Ben Bradlee, and Liz Taylor. The five women influenced politics in the latter half of the twentieth century, notably by throwing the parties where their husbands influenced major policy decisions. Heymann interviewed the friends and foes, families, and admirers of the women in writing this anecdotal history that a *Publishers Weekly* reviewer described as "a winning combination of sex, scandal, and political escapade."

Booklist's Ilene Cooper wrote that Heymann "pulls out all the stops here, and the result is a well-researched, fast-paced, and fascinating look at dinner-party power-broking."

Heymann once told *CA:* "I detest literary cliques and professional a**-kissing. There are too many writers and too many books and not enough people who read. There are also too many newspapers and magazines—too many words in the world, floating about on meaningless sheets of paper."

More recently Heymann added: "I fully subscribe to my original contention that there are too many writers and too many words in the universe and too few readers. This contention has been reinforced during the late nineties and early twenty-first century by the overgrowth of cable television networks, radio talk shows, Internet geometrics, million-dollar special cinema-graphic effects, aspiring neighborhood newspapers, and other forms of media confabulations. The nation has been dumbed down to the point where Big Brother's axiom 'War is peace' has not only become the common parlance of the day, but America's guiding principle.

"One of the influencing sources in my ongoing literary career is the political situation that entrenches all of us. Being 'policeman for the world' is indeed a daunting responsibility. This said, I find deplorable the fact that every other book on the *New York Times* best-seller's list is somehow related to the current political situation. My recent work, *The Georgetown Ladies' Social Club: Power, Passion, and Politics in the Nation's Capital,* is a chronicle of the women that ran and run Washington, a one-industry town that for all intents and purposes has been historically male-oriented since the birth of Adam. It is a political book, but only tangentially. My true desire in the future would be to write something of a highly personal nature. I would hope that my own experiences would be universal enough so that even a reader living in Kyoto, Japan, could derive some beneficial and vicarious identification. As Ezra Pound once said, 'All ages are contemporaneous,' by which I assume he meant that the very problems that beset the ancient Greeks and Romans—housing, love, government, health, wealth, sustenance, et cetera—are the very problems which dog us today.

"The writers that have influenced my own work include Homer, Pound, Eliot, Hemingway, Conrad, Dickens, Thoreau, Mailer, Capote, Dante, Ovid, Kafka, Rilke, Beckett, Nabokov, Borges, Ginsburg, and Bob Dylan.

"My primary motivation for writing is to have something to do, as I am constitutionally and psychologically unable to do anything else.

"My writing process can be related to Henry Miller's infamous saw: 'A good meal, a good talk, a good f**k, what better way is there to spend a day?' To this I would add 'a good hour at the computer.' I am certain old Henry would wholeheartedly agree. I am the village idiot, the man on the street corner with a basket of pain, dropping tidbits into other people's pockets. The hole in our lives and all the garbage: if only we could fill the holes.

"The mechanics of my writing are unchanged. I sleep, I wake, I write again. Every four years or so, a book gets done."

BIOGRAPHICAL AND CRITICAL SOURCES:

PERIODICALS

America, June 5, 1999, Richard Young, review of *RFK: A Candid Biography of Robert F. Kennedy,* p. 16.
Booklist, October 15, 2003, Ilene Cooper, review of *The Georgetown Ladies' Social Club: Power, Passion, and Politics in the Nation's Capital,* p. 385.
Chicago Tribune, May 10, 1989.
Chicago Tribune Book World, September 7, 1980.
Detroit Free Press, May 5, 1989.
Detroit News, May 4, 1989.
Esquire, October, 1984.
Globe and Mail (Toronto, Ontario, Canada), June 24, 1989.
Kirkus Reviews, October 1, 2003, review of *The Georgetown Ladies' Social Club,* p. 1209.
Library Journal, October 15, 2003, Cynthia Harrison, review of *The Georgetown Ladies' Social Club,* p. 83.
Los Angeles Times, December 9, 1984; May 12, 1989.
New York Review of Books, April 1, 1976.
New York Times Book Review, April 4, 1976; August 3, 1980; May 28, 1989.
Publishers Weekly, November 19, 1979; September 1, 2003, review of *The Georgetown Ladies' Social Club,* p. 73.
Saturday Review, August 8, 1980.
Time, March 8, 1976.
Washington Post, December 14, 1983; December 20, 1983; December 21, 1983; February 8, 1984; May 31, 1989.
Washington Post Book World, August 10, 1980; December 18, 1983.

HILFIKER, David 1945-

PERSONAL: Surname is pronounced "*hil*-fick-er"; born February 12, 1945, in Buffalo, NY; son of Warren T. (a clergyman) and Carol (Koepf) Hilfiker; married Marja Kaikkonen (a teacher), June 21, 1969; children: Laurel, Karen, Kai. *Education:* Yale College (now University), B.A., 1967; University of Minnesota—Twin Cities, M.D., 1974. *Politics:* "Independent/Socialist." *Religion:* Ecumenical Christian. *Hobbies and other interests:* "Individual spiritual journey as it relates to health, politics, and community"; running; cross-country skiing.

ADDRESSES: Home—1538 Monroe St. N.W. #2, Washington, DC 20010-3148. *Office*—Joseph's House, 1750 Columbia Rd. N.W., Washington, DC 20009. *Agent*—c/o Author Mail, Seven Stories Press, 140 Watts St., New York, NY 10013. *E-mail*—hilfiker@pol.net.

CAREER: Physician, medical director, and author. Cook County Community Clinic, Grand Marais, MN, family practitioner, 1975-82; on sabbatical in Finland, 1982-83; Community of Hope Health Services, Washington, DC, physician to the indigent, 1983-92; cofounder of Christ House (a medical recovery shelter for the homeless), 1985; founder, financial director, and past medical director of Joseph's House (a community for homeless men with AIDS), 1990—; on sabbatical, 1993-94.

AWARDS, HONORS: First place award in trade category, American Medical Writers Association, 1986; Christopher Award, 1994, for *Not All of Us Are Saints: A Doctor's Journey with the Poor;* Virtual Mentor Award, American Medical Association.

WRITINGS:

Healing the Wounds: A Physician Looks at His Work, Pantheon (New York, NY), 1985; with a new introduction, Creighton University Press (Omaha, NE), 1998.
Not All of Us Are Saints: A Doctor's Journey with the Poor, Hill & Wang (New York, NY), 1994.
Urban Injustice: How Ghettos Happen, foreword by Marian Wright Edelman, Seven Stories Press (New York, NY), 2002.

Also contributor to *New England Journal of Medicine, Journal of the American Medical Association,* and *Other Side.*

SIDELIGHTS: David Hilfiker began practicing medicine in a rural clinic in northern Minnesota after graduating from medical school in 1974 and completing his internship in 1975. Admittedly at odds with the demands for increased productivity in his work as well as the "unrealistic expectations" of his patients, wrote John G. Deaton in the *New York Times Book Review,* Hilfiker withdrew from his profession after seven years and went on retreat. He resumed doctoring one year later in Washington, DC, administering health care to the indigent at a local clinic, at a recovery shelter for homeless men and women, and later, for homeless men with AIDS.

Healing the Wounds: A Physician Looks at His Work is an autobiographical account of Hilfiker's early experiences in medicine, which he wrote during a one-year sabbatical. Reviewing the book, Deaton observed that Hilfiker "is brutally honest" in revealing his personal anguish, conflicts, and mistakes. We "witness the pain that accompanies the discovery" of errors, continued Deaton, as well as the anguish of a failed attempt to save a life, or of telling a patient that he or she has cancer. In these instances "the book explores the stress and frustrations . . . of a sensitive physician," determined the reviewer, but *Healing the Wounds* is also "a medical odyssey from idealism to disenchantment and back."

Expressing a similar opinion in the *Washington Post,* Jonathan Yardley remarked that it is Hilfiker's purpose "to describe 'the conflicting pressures [doctors] face, which often seem to defy solution.'" From the standpoint of the lay person, assessed Yardley, "what is most useful about *Healing the Wounds* is its depiction, from the inside, of the stresses that make doctors behave the way they too often do." As Hilfiker points out, noted Yardley, physicians resort to "elaborate defense mechanisms in order to cope" with their patients' "utterly unrealistic" expectations of them as "ultimate healers, technological wizards, total authorities." The reviewer noted that Hilfiker has "by his own confession . . . fallen into some of the very traps he deplores," which range from clinical detachment and callousness to condescension. Nonetheless, Yardley added, "he has earned our esteem" for both his convictions and this "thoughtful" book. Deaton also judged *Healing the Wounds* "triumphant," while a critique in *Newsweek* deemed it an "exceptionally interesting memoir . . . extraordinary."

Hilfiker once again uses his own life experiences as the basis for his *Not All of Us Are Saints: A Doctor's Journey with the Poor.* In this book, Hilfiker examines "poverty medicine," the treatment of individuals too poor and too broken to afford traditional health care in the United States. Hilfiker, who has worked to provide health care to poor communities in Washington, DC, presents readers with a glimpse into a world which is, as Philip Berryman mentioned in the *Christian Century,* "closer to health care in Third World countries than to the kind of medicine most of his readers encounter at their HMOs." Berryman continued, "Ordinary medical problems like high blood pressure or substance abuse become more complicated among poor people, who may not be able to afford medicine, pursue follow-up care, or escape the effects of chaotic neighborhoods and homes." Hilfiker willingly and ably demonstrates the hardships faced by doctors practicing poverty medicine. He relates the physical, mental, and emotional struggles he faces in his personal and professional life. *Lancet*'s Reed Tuckson noted, "In *Not All of Us Are Saints,* David Hilfiker raises uncomfortable, provocative, maddeningly frustrating, and important questions for human beings in general and physicians in particular."

Hilfiker's next book, *Urban Injustice: How Ghettos Happen,* attempts to explain the many reasons why people continue to live in poverty, outlines reasons why current programs to help the poor do not necessarily work, and offers suggestions for remedying the poverty problem in the United States. He explains that there are certain forces and policies that make it impossible for people living in poor communities to escape. "For Hilfiker," wrote John A. Coleman in *America,* "the essential causes of American poverty are primarily structural: the paucity of jobs on which one can support a family; inadequate access to health care and child care; meager educational resources in inner cities; the workings of the criminal justice system; and, for African Americans, a painful history of slavery, segregation, and discrimination." After years of working in poor communities, Hilfiker discusses the problems afflicting these communities. Rather than just pontificating about the many injustices, however, Hilfiker offers suggestions and solutions to end poverty and give the poor a second chance. Coleman praised, "Hilfiker culls the best of studies on urban poverty and carefully weighs data," all while writing "in a lively prose, juxtaposing personal experience with social science studies of poverty." Janice Dunham wrote in *Library Journal,* "The last chapter suggests very practical public policies and budgets that could win a real war on poverty." A *Publishers Weekly* contributor concluded, "This accessible, clearly written book . . . may inspire ordinary people to work toward full desegregation of our society."

Hilfiker once told *CA:* "My motivation has been to find in my work and in my writings the source of our fullest life."

BIOGRAPHICAL AND CRITICAL SOURCES:

PERIODICALS

America, December 9, 2002, John A. Coleman, "Look and See!," review of *Urban Injustice: How Ghettos Happen,* p. 20.

Christian Century, February 15, 1995, Phillip Berryman, review of *Not All of Us Are Saints: A Doctor's Journey with the Poor,* p. 182.

Hastings Center Report, July, 1996, review of *Not All of Us Are Saints,* p. 39.

Lancet, April 1, 1995, Reed V. Tuckson, review of *Not All of Us Are Saints,* p. 845.

Library Journal, October 1, 2002, Janice Dunham, review of *Urban Injustice,* p. 118.

Los Angeles Times Book Review, May 19, 1996, review of *Not All of Us Are Saints,* p. 11.

National Catholic Reporter, February 6, 2004, Denny Kinderman, "Poverty As We Know It: Lutheran Pastor's Journey, Study of Ghettos Uncover Inner-city Life," review of *Urban Injustice,* p. 12A.

Newsweek, December 30, 1985.

New York Times Book Review, November 3, 1985, John G. Deaton, *Healing the Wounds: A Physician Looks at His Work.*

Other Side, March-April, 2003, Kevin Thrun, review of *Urban Injustice,* p. 41.

Publishers Weekly, September 2, 2002, review of *Urban Injustice,* pp. 72-74.

Readings, March, 1995, review of *Not All of Us Are Saints,* p. 20.

SciTech Book News, December, 1998, review of *Healing the Wounds,* p. 56.

Second Opinion, Arthur W. Frank, review of *Not All of Us Are Saints,* p. 53.

Washington Post, September 18, 1985, Jonathan Yardley, review of *Healing the Wounds.**

* * *

HILLIER, Bevis 1940-

PERSONAL: Born March 28, 1940, in Redhill, Surrey, England; immigrated to the United States, 1984; son of Jack Ronald (an author) and Mary Louise (an author; maiden name, Palmer) Hillier. *Education:* Attended Magdalen College, Oxford, 1959-62. *Hobbies and other interests:* Piano, collecting antiques.

ADDRESSES: Home—Goldbeaters House, Manette St., London W1, England. *Office*—Los Angeles Times, Times Mirror Sq., Los Angeles, CA 90012. *Agent*—The Maggie Noach Literary Agency, 21 Redan St., London W14 0AB, England.

CAREER: Times, London, England, home news reporter, 1963-65, sale room correspondent, 1965-69, antiques correspondent, 1970-84, deputy literary editor, 1981-84; British Museum, London, editor of *Museum Society Bulletin,* 1968-70, public relations director, 1969-71; full-time writer, 1971-73; *Connoisseur* (magazine), London, editor, 1973-76; freelance editor, 1976-80; *Telegraph Sunday* (magazine), London, features editor, 1980-82; *Los Angeles Times,* Los Angeles, CA, associate editor, 1984—. Guest curator and organizer of Art Deco exhibition, Minneapolis Institute of Arts, 1971; visiting fellow, Huntington Library, 1983.

MEMBER: Society of Authors, Royal Society of Arts (fellow), English Ceramic Circle, Beefsteak Club (London, England), Garrick Club (London, England).

AWARDS, HONORS: Gladstone Memorial prize, 1961.

WRITINGS:

Master Potters of the Industrial Revolution, Cory, Adams & Mackay (London, England), 1965.

Pottery and Porcelain, 1700-1914, Meredith (New York, NY), 1968.

Art Deco of the Twenties and Thirties, Dutton (New York, NY), 1968, revised edition, Schocken Books, 1985.
Posters, Stein & Day (New York, NY), 1969.
Cartoons and Caricatures, Dutton (New York, NY), 1970.
The World of Art Deco, Dutton (New York, NY), 1971.
(Compiler) *100 Years of Posters,* Harper (New York, NY), 1972.
(Compiler and author of introduction) *Punorama; or, The Best of the Worst: Victorian Puns,* illustrated by Peter Mackarell, Whittington Press (Andoversford, England), 1974.
The Decorative Arts of the Forties and Fifties: Austerity Binge, C. N. Potter (New York, NY), 1975, published as *Austerity Binge: The Decorative Arts of the Forties and Fifties,* Studio Vista (London, England), 1975.
(With Brian Coe, Russell Ash, Helen Varley) *Victorian Studio Photographs from the Collections of Studio Bassano and Elliott & Fry,* Ash & Grant (London, England), 1975.
(Editor, with Mary Banham) *A Tonic to the Nation: The Festival of Britain 1951,* prologue by Roy Strong, Thames & Hudson (London, England), 1976.
Travel Posters, Dutton (New York, NY), 1976.
Victorian Studio Photographs, David R. Godine (Boston, MA), 1976.
(Editor) *Dead Funny,* Ash & Grant (London, England), 1976.
The New Antiques, Times Books (London, England), 1977.
Asprey of Bond Street, 1781-1981, Quartet Books (New York, NY), 1981.
The Simon and Schuster Pocket Guide to Antiques, Simon & Schuster (New York, NY), 1981.
The Style of the Century, 1900-1980, Dutton (New York, NY), 1983, 2nd edition with new chapter by Kate McIntyre published as *The Style of the Century,* Watson-Guptill Publications (New York, NY), 1998.
(Compiler and author of introduction) *John Betjeman: A Life in Pictures,* J. Murray/Herbert Press (London, England), 1984.
Young Betjeman, J. Murray (London, England), 1988.
John Betjeman: New Fame, New Love, J. Murray (London, England), 2002.

Also author of introduction to *Walt Disney's Mickey Mouse Memorabilia: The Vintage Years, 1928-1938,* Abrams (New York, NY). Regular reviewer for *Sunday Times;* contributor to *Connoisseur, Apollo, Cornhill, Daily Telegraph,* and *Guardian.* Editor, *British Museum Society Bulletin,* 1968-70.

WORK IN PROGRESS: A third volume on John Betjeman.

SIDELIGHTS: Bevis Hillier is a journalist and antiques expert who is especially knowledgeable about styles of the early twentieth century, such as Art Deco and the art forms of posters, cartoons, and photography of that period. One of his more recent books on Art Deco, 1998's *Art Deco Style,* was praised by *Library Journal* critic P. Steven Thomas for its "crisply written" style and "lively discussion" of the 1920s and 1930s.

An authority on the poet and critic John Betjeman, Hillier has written two volumes of a projected trilogy on the poet, including *Young Betjeman* and *John Betjeman: New Fame, New Love.* The first book, according to *Times Literary Supplement* contributor Samuel Hynes, "lingers in the mind as a meticulously detailed catalogue of the slights, humiliations and failures suffered by a shy outsider with a foreign name who desperately wants to be inside." The second volume details the period in which Betjeman achieved recognition; Hynes praised its comprehensiveness, concluding that readers "can sink back in a state of pleasant biographical fatigue, satisfied, after 600 pages, that we must know all there is to know about Betjeman's middle period."

BIOGRAPHICAL AND CRITICAL SOURCES:

PERIODICALS

Biography, spring, 2003, Samuel Hynes, review of *John Betjeman: New Fame, New Love,* p. 348.
Hobbies, February, 1982, review of *The Simon and Schuster Pocket Guide to Antiques,* p. 77.
Library Journal, May 1, 1998, P. Steven Thomas, review of *Art Deco Style,* p. 97.
New Yorker, June 24, 1985, V. S. Pritchett, review of *John Betjeman: A Life in Pictures,* p. 94.
Publishers Weekly, September 30, 1983, review of *The Style of the Century, 1900-1980,* p. 101; May 3, 1985, review of *John Betjeman,* p. 57.
Times Higher Education Supplement, April 11, 2003, Timothy Mowl, review of *John Betjeman,* p. 24.

Times Literary Supplement, January 17, 2003, Samuel Hynes, review of *John Betjeman,* p. 5.

Yankee, December, 1981, Geoffrey Elan, review of *The Simon and Schuster Pocket Guide to Antiques,* p. 184.*

* * *

HOLM, Bill
See HOLM, Oscar William

* * *

HOLM, Oscar William 1925-
(Bill Holm)

PERSONAL: Born March 24, 1925, in Roundup, MT; married; wife's name Marty; children: Carla, Karen. *Education:* University of Washington, B.A. and M.F.A.

ADDRESSES: Home—1027 Northwest 190th St., Shoreline, WA 98177. *Office*—Burke Museum, University of Washington, Seattle, WA 98195.

CAREER: Seattle Public Schools, teacher of art, c. 1952-1967; University of Washington, Seattle, professor of art history and curator of Northwest Coast Indian Art at the Thomas Burke Memorial Museum, 1968-85. Consultant on Northwest Coast art for museums. *Military service:* U. S. Army, during World War II.

WRITINGS:

UNDER NAME BILL HOLM

Northwest Coast Indian Art: An Analysis of Form, Douglas & McIntyre (Vancouver, British Columbia, Canada), 1965.

Indian Art of the Northwest Coast: A Dialogue on Craftsmanship and Aesthetics, Institute for the Arts, Rice University (Houston, TX), 1976.

Edward S. Curtis in the Land of the War Canoes: A Pioneer Cinematographer in the Pacific Northwest, University of Washington Press (Seattle, WA), 1980.

Smoky-Top: The Art and Times of Willie Seaweed, University of Washington Press (Seattle, WA), 1983.

The Box of Daylight: Northwest Coast Indian Art, University of Washington Press (Seattle, WA), 1983.

(Author of annotations) *Soft Gold: The Fur Trade and Cultural Exchange on the Northwest Coast of America,* 1983, 2nd edition, University of Nebraska Press, 1993.

Spirit and Ancestor: A Century of Northwest Coast Indian Art at the Burke Museum, University of Washington Press (Seattle, WA), 1988.

(Illustrator) Gary Snyder, *North Pacific Lands and Waters: A Further Six Sections,* Brooding Heron Press (Waldron Island, WA), 1993.

Sun Dogs and Eagle Down: The Indian Paintings of Bill Holm, compiled by Steven C. Brown and Lloyd J. Averill, University of Washington Press (Seattle, WA), 2000.

SIDELIGHTS: Oscar William Holm has written prolifically to increase the general reader's understanding of and appreciation for Northwest Indian art and culture. He worked for seventeen years as the curator of Northwest Coast Indian Art at the University of Washington's Thomas Burke Memorial Museum. In a biography posted at the Canadian Museum of Civilization Web site, Holm is stated to have taught himself how to make many Indian artifacts, "from full size plank houses, canoes, and totem poles to bead-and-porcupine-quill-decorated clothing of the Plains and Plateau." An artist as well as writer, Holm has also illustrated a collection by noted poet Gary Snyder and published a collection of his own paintings depicting American Indian subjects. Among his books are *Soft Gold: The Fur Trade and Cultural Exchange on the Northwest Coast of America, Spirit and Ancestor: A Century of Northwest Coast Indian Art at the Burke Museum,* and *Sun Dogs and Eagle Down: The Indian Paintings of Bill Holm.*

Soft Gold is a history of the fur trade in the American Northwest and includes hundreds of illustrations of Native art and handicrafts for which Holm provides the annotations. According to Robert Coutts in the *American Indian Quarterly,* "*Soft Gold* is a handsome catalogue of ethnographic materials from the north Pacific Coast."

To celebrate its one hundredth anniversary, the Thomas Burke Memorial Museum gathered photographs of one hundred of its Northwest Indian artifacts and published them as *Spirit and Ancestor.* The objects depicted range over a wide spectrum of Indian daily life, from fishing and hunting items to religious artifacts. Holm wrote the text accompanying the photographs. As Phoebe-Lou Adams wrote in the *Atlantic,* Holm's text "adroitly extended the pedigrees of the individual pieces to encompass history, ethnography, and the principles underlying Indian design."

After retiring from his position as a museum curator, Holm devoted himself to a long-standing interest in art. The book *Sun Dogs and Eagle Down* is a collection of nearly fifty of his paintings, as well as drawings and water colors, depicting Native American peoples. Drawing on his extensive knowledge of Indian folkways and traditional artifacts, Holm presents not only accurate scenes of daily life, but mythological scenes as well. As the University of Washington Press Web site explained it, "In addition to being visually compelling, the pictures provide a wealth of ethnographic detail, from the eagle down scattered by the Kwakiutl to welcome important guests, to the sun dogs—bright spots near the horizon that mimic the sun—featured in myths from many northern tribes." Patricia Monaghan in *Booklist* noted that Holm has created "meticulously detailed, historically precise paintings of American Indian life" and called *Sun Dogs and Eagle Down* "a fascinating look at the life and work of an unusual and gifted artist."

BIOGRAPHICAL AND CRITICAL SOURCES:

PERIODICALS

Americana, September-October, 1984, review of *Smoky-Top: The Art and Times of Willie Seaweed,* p. 108.

American Indian Quarterly, spring, 1990, Aldona Jonaitis, review of *Spirit and Ancestor: A Century of Northwest Coast Indian Art at the Burke Museum,* p. 224; winter, 1993, Robert Coutts, review of *Soft Gold: The Fur Trade and Cultural Exchange on the Northwest Coast of America,* p. 125.

American West, May-June, 1983, review of *Soft Gold,* p. 60; March-April, 1984, review of *Smoky-Top,* p. 67.

Atlantic, July, 1988, Phoebe-Lou Adams, review of *Spirit and Ancestor,* p. 88.

Booklist, October 15, 2000, Patricia Monaghan, review of *Sun Dog and Eagle Down: The Indian Paintings of Bill Holm,* p. 403.

Library Journal, October 15, 1980, Marshall Deutelbaum, review of *Edward S. Curtis in the Land of the War Canoes: A Pioneer Cinematographer in the Pacific Northwest,* p. 2225; May 1, 1988, David Byrant, review of *Spirit and Ancestor,* p. 72.

Popular Photography, August, 1981, Natalie Canavor, review of *Edward S. Curtis in the Land of the War Canoes,* p. 34.

Publishers Weekly, August 29, 1980, Genevieve Stuttaford, review of *Edward S. Curtis in the Land of the War Canoes,* p. 360; March 11, 1988, Penny Kaganoff, review of *Spirit and Ancestor,* p. 98.

Scientific American, December, 1980, review of *Edward S. Curtis in the Land of the War Canoes,* p. 56.

ONLINE

Canadian Museum of Civilization Web site, http://www.civilization.ca/ (November 15, 2002), "Biography: Bill Holm."

University of Washington Press Web site, http://www.washington.edu/uwpress/ (November 15, 2002), description of *Sun Dogs and Eagle Down.*

* * *

HOLT, Hazel 1928-

PERSONAL: Born September 3, 1928, in Birmingham, England; daughter of Charles Douglas (an advertising manager) and Roma (Simpson) Young; married Geoffrey Louis Holt (a company director), 1951; children: Tom. *Education:* Newnham College, Cambridge, B.A. (with honors), 1950. *Politics:* "None." *Religion:* Church of England.

ADDRESSES: *Home*—Tivington Knowle, Nr. Minehead, Somerset TA24 85X, England. *Agent*—James Hale, 47 Peckham Rye, London SE15 3NX, England.

CAREER: International African Institute, London, England, editor, 1950-74; *Stage and Television Today,* London, reviewer and feature writer, 1975-80; writer, 1989—.

WRITINGS:

"SHEILA MALORY MYSTERY" SERIES

Mrs. Malory Investigates, St. Martin's Press (New York, NY), 1989.

The Cruellest Month, St. Martin's Press (New York, NY), 1991.

Mrs. Malory and the Festival Murders, St. Martin's Press (New York, NY), 1993.

Mrs. Malory: Detective in Residence, Dutton (New York, NY), 1994.

Mrs. Malory's Shortest Journey, St. Martin's Press (New York, NY), 1994.

Mrs. Malory Wonders Why, Dutton (New York, NY), 1995.

Mrs. Malory: Death of a Dean, Dutton (New York, NY), 1996.

Mrs. Malory and the Only Good Lawyer, Dutton (New York, NY), 1997.

Mrs. Malory and the Lilies That Fester, Signet (New York, NY), 2001.

Mrs. Malory and the Fatal Legacy, Macmillan (London, England), 2001.

Mrs. Malory and the Delay of Execution, Signet (New York, NY), 2002.

Leonora, Macmillan (London, England), 2002.

Mrs. Malory and Death in Practice, Signet (New York, NY), 2003.

Mrs. Malory and Death by Water, Signet (New York, NY), 2003.

Mrs. Malory and the Silent Killer, Signet (New York, NY), 2004.

OTHER

(Editor and annotator, with Hilary Pym) Barbara Pym, *A Very Private Eye: An Autobiography in Diaries and Letters,* Dutton (New York, NY), 1984.

(Editor) Barbara Pym, *Civil to Strangers and Other Writings,* Dutton (New York, NY), 1988.

Gone Away, Macmillan (London, England), 1989.

A Lot to Ask: A Life of Barbara Pym, Dutton (New York, NY), 1991.

Superfluous Death, Macmillan (London, England), 1995.

SIDELIGHTS: Hazel Holt earned a degree from Cambridge University in 1950 and went to work for the International African Institute in London the same year. She would spend the next two and a half decades there, making the acquaintance of another young Englishwoman, Barbara Pym, an aspiring novelist. The two became friends, and Holt would often conspire with Pym on their lunch-hour jaunts around London, during which the imaginative Pym would devise "biographies" of strangers. Holt was witness to her friend's initial literary successes during the 1950s; but, when public reading tastes shifted, Pym's manuscripts met with rejection for much of the next two decades. It was only a "rediscovery" of Pym's earlier novels in a 1977 *Times Literary Supplement* article that resurrected her career and brought her enormous success late in life. When she died in 1980, Pym's will named Hazel Holt as her estate's literary executor.

In this role, Holt came to serve as coeditor of *A Very Private Eye: An Autobiography in Diaries and Letters.* The book was a project undertaken with Pym's sister, Hilary, and revealed much about the genteel, introspective woman to whom the term "spinster" was commonly applied. Seven years later, Holt revisited the same topic—now as an author herself—in *A Lot to Ask: A Life of Barbara Pym.* The biography won praise from the critical world and lovers of Pym's fiction alike for the insider's glimpse it provided into the novelist's life through her own words, interviews with friends, and Holt's recollections.

Writing in the *Washington Post Book World,* Anne Tyler praised *A Lot to Ask* primarily because "it somewhat eases the suspicion aroused by the earlier book, which was that Barbara Pym in person was a very silly woman." For example, Tyler addressed the matter of Pym's "schoolgirl crushes" recorded in the journal entries from her days at Oxford and reproduced in both biographies. In *A Lot to Ask,* Holt's commentary shows them to have enriched Pym's talents as a writer, her powers of observation, "as well as confirming her preference for recording life as opposed to taking part in it," Tyler noted.

Some critics cited *A Lot to Ask* for what they considered a lack of critical insight. Penelope Lively wrote in the *Listener,* "There is no attempt to discuss Pym's work, or to place it within a literary context." But Caroline Moore, writing in the *Spectator,* noted that "Holt's discussion of her friend is workmanlike and perceptive, without being offensively speculative. . . . Her knowledge and love of Pym's novels shines through." Linsay Duguid noted in the *Times Literary Supplement* that Holt "marshals all the personal material deftly to give a narrative of a circumscribed life."

Holt is also the author of several works of fiction in the mystery genre. The first in her "Sheila Malory" series appeared under the title *Mrs. Malory Investigates.* The novel introduces both the sleuthing English widow and her rural milieu of Taviscombe. The next offering in the series, *The Cruellest Month,* transplants the unassuming armchair detective to the college town of Oxford, where she investigates the murder of a librarian. In *Mrs. Malory and the Festival Murders,* Holt weaves a whodunit tale around the murder of a literary executor of a famous aged writer; the deceased had taken over a local historic festival, and his body is discovered as the fair opens. Holt's next novel, *Mrs. Malory: Detective in Residence,* transports Sheila Malory to America to take a guest lecturer post at a Pennsylvania college rife with faculty tension, where the murder of one of her new colleagues sets Malory's sleuthing abilities into motion. *The Shortest Journey* finds Malory investigating the nursing-home disappearance of an elderly friend. In *Mrs. Malory Wonders Why,* Holt has her protagonist looking into the poisoning of an elderly Taviscombe resident.

BIOGRAPHICAL AND CRITICAL SOURCES:

PERIODICALS

Booklist, December 1, 1994, p. 656; December 15, 1996, p. 712; April 15, 1999, GraceAnne A. DeCandido, review of *Mrs. Malory and the Only Good Lawyer,* p. 1461; March 15, 2000, GraceAnne A. DeCandido, review of *Mrs. Malory and the Fatal Legacy,* p. 1333.

Christian Science Monitor, June 7, 1991, p. 12.

Kirkus Reviews, December 15, 1989, p. 1786; April 15, 1991, p. 507; March 15, 1993, p. 334; November 1, 1994, p. 1447.

Library Journal, February 1, 1991, Bryan Aubrey, review of *A Lot to Ask: A Life of Barbara Pym,* December, 1994, p. 138; October 1, 1996, p. 131.

Listener, November 1, 1990, Penelope Lively, review of *A Lot to Ask,* pp. 30-31.

London Review of Books, November 22, 1990, p. 23.

Los Angles Times Book Review, April 7, 1991.

New York Times, June 14, 1984.

New York Times Book Review, April 14, 1991.

Publishers Weekly, December 12, 1989, p. 47; February 1, 1991, Genevieve Stuttaford, review of *A Lot to Ask,* March 29, 1993, p. 38; June 13, 1994, p. 54; October 2, 1995, p. 58; September 16, 1996, p. 72; March 6, 2000, review of *Mrs. Malory and the Fatal Legacy,* p. 89.

Spectator, November 17, 1990, Caroline Moore, review of *A Lot to Ask,* pp. 45-46.

Times (London, England), February 4, 1989; February 28, 1991.

Times Literary Supplement, November 16, 1990, Linsay Duguid, review of *A Lot to Ask,* p. 1228.

Tribune Books, January 6, 1991, p. 4.

Washington Post Book World, March 17, 1991, Anne Tyler, review of *A Lot to Ask,* pp. 1, 10.

ONLINE

BookBrowser, http://www.bookbrowser.com/ (April 17, 2002), Harriet Klausner, review of *Mrs. Malory and the Delay of Execution.*

Mystery Reader, http://www.themysteryreader.com/ (September 13, 2002), Andy Plonka, review of *Mrs. Malory and the Only Good Lawyer.**

* * *

HOWARD, Ellen 1943-

PERSONAL: Born May 8, 1943, in New Bern, NC; daughter of Gerald Willis (in sales) and Betty Jeane (a banker; maiden name, Slate; present surname, Chord) Phillips; married Kermit W. Jensen, June 15, 1963 (divorced, June 15, 1969); married Charles Howard, Jr. (a scientist), June 29, 1975; children: (first marriage) Anna Elizabeth Jensen; stepchildren: (second marriage) Cynthia, Laurie Howard Wilson, Shaley Franc. *Education:* Attended University of Oregon, 1961-63; Portland State University, B.A. (with honors), 1979. *Politics:* Liberal Democrat. *Religion:* Unitarian-Universalist. *Hobbies and other interests:* Reading, travel.

ADDRESSES: *Home*—980 Holiday Ct. S., Salem, OR 97302. *E-mail*—cfhjreh@comcast.net.

CAREER: Office and library worker, 1963-77; Collins Foundation, Portland, OR, secretary, 1980-88; writer,

Ellen Howard

1983—. Vermont College, Montpelier, VT, MFA program in Writing for Children and Young Adults, faculty member, 1998—.

MEMBER: Authors Guild, Society of Children's Book Writers (regional adviser, 1985-88, 1993-96; board member, 2000—).

AWARDS, HONORS: Golden Kite Honor Book Award from Society of Children's Book Writers, 1984, for *Circle of Giving;* National Council for the Social Studies and Children's Book Council Joint Committee listed *When Daylight Comes* in 1985, *Gillyflower* in 1986, and *Edith Herself* in 1988 as Notable Trade Books for Children in the Field of Social Sciences; *School Library Journal* included *Edith Herself* on its list of Best Books of 1987; Children's Middle-Grade Award from International PEN, U.S. Center West, 1989, for *Her Own Song;* Oregon Book Award and Judy Lopez Memorial Award, for *The Gate in the Wall;* Christopher Award for *The Log Cabin Quilt.*

WRITINGS:

FOR CHILDREN

Circle of Giving, Atheneum (New York, NY), 1984.
When Daylight Comes, Atheneum (New York, NY), 1985.
Gillyflower, Atheneum (New York, NY), 1986.
Edith Herself, Atheneum (New York, NY), 1987.
Her Own Song (Junior Literary Guild selection), Atheneum (New York, NY), 1988.
Sister, Atheneum (New York, NY), 1990.
The Chickenhouse House, Atheneum (New York, NY), 1991.
The Cellar, Atheneum (New York, NY), 1992.
The Big Seed, Simon & Schuster (New York, NY), 1993.
The Tower Room, Atheneum (New York, NY), 1993.
Murphy and Kate, Simon & Schuster (New York, NY), 1995.
The Log Cabin Quilt, Holiday House (New York, NY), 1996.
A Different Kind of Courage, Atheneum (New York, NY), 1996.
The Gate in the Wall, Atheneum (New York, NY), 1999.
The Log Cabin Christmas, Holiday House (New York, NY), 2000.
The Log Cabin Church, Holiday House (New York, NY), 2002.

Contributor to *Lion and the Unicorn.*

ADAPTATIONS: The Gate in the Wall has been recorded as an audiobook, read by Jenny Sterlin.

SIDELIGHTS: Ellen Howard has written a number of historical novels for young readers, including *The Tower Room, A Different Kind of Courage,* and *The Gate in the Wall.*

In *The Tower Room* Howard tells of ten-year-old orphan Mary Brooke, who is sent to live with her aunt in a small Michigan town during the 1950s. The aunt's rambling old house includes a tower which has been sealed off, but Mary finds a way into the room and uses it as a secret hideaway when her life gets too much to bear. The story has "good style and flow," according to Julie Corsaro in *Booklist,* while a critic for *Publishers Weekly* praised the book's "fresh and honest moments."

A Different Kind of Courage concerns two French refugee children during World War II who are rescued by the Unitarian Service Committee, a charity group. Their dangerous journey across France to the safety of Portugal is set against the children's trauma at being sent away by their parents. Hazel Rochman in *Booklist* believed that "what Howard captures with extraordinary power is the children's sense of abandonment at being sent away by their parents, even to safety." "The narrative style, punctuated with French phrases readily understood in context, evokes time and place," wrote Mary M. Burns in *Horn Book,* "and the unusual subject is treated with the sensitivity and insight characteristic of Howard's writing."

The Gate in the Wall is set in Victorian England and concerns young Emma, who escapes the grueling poverty of work in a factory mill to a job on a canal boat delivering goods in rural England. While the boat job is hard work, Emma finds a degree of independence she has never known before. Rochman concluded that "readers will be gripped by the social history, the setting, and the personal struggle of one brave child." The critic for *Horn Book* found that "Howard has created a cast of characters who are fully dimensional and engaging."

Howard once told *CA:* "Sometimes I am asked why I write for young people. When I meet young people, I know the answer to that question: I write for them because I want to tell them something they may not know yet. Many know that life is hard and that they are in pain. But they may not know how strong they can be, how beautiful, how good. I write for them, and I write for myself, the way I used to as a child tell myself stories in bed at night—to lighten the darkness, to help dispel the loneliness and the sorrow and the fear.

"Writers are lucky people. We are the people who can express how we think and feel so others understand what we mean. We can make other people laugh and cry. We can learn to understand ourselves through our writing. We can make something important—a poem, a story, an essay, a book. And we can find joy doing it. The joy goes on and on, and so does the doubt that I have done as well as I could, the pride when—sometimes—I know I have, and the sense of accomplishment. That is the thing about writing—it is an important thing to do and an awesome responsibility. Words have impact—for good and for ill. Minds and hearts can be molded by words. Young lives can be changed. I dare not think about this too much, or my courage would fail.

"It is a privilege to have come, in the middle of my life, to writing. It is a special privilege to be writing for the young."

BIOGRAPHICAL AND CRITICAL SOURCES:

PERIODICALS

Booklist, December 15, 1993, Julie Corsaro, review of *The Tower Room,* p. 754; May 1, 1995, Ellen Mandel, review of *Murphy and Kate,* p. 1580; September 15, 1996, Hazel Rochman, review of *A Different Kind of Courage,* p. 230; December 15, 1996, Carolyn Phelan, review of *The Log Cabin Quilt,* p. 731; February 15, 1999, Hazel Rochman, review of *The Gate in the Wall,* p. 1070; April 15, 2000, Barbara Baskin, review of *The Gate in the Wall,* p. 1561; November 15, 2000, Shelley Townsend-Hudson, review of *The Log Cabin Christmas,* p. 648; October 1, 2002, Kay Weisman, review of *The Log Cabin Church,* p. 345.

Horn Book, November-December, 1996, Mary M. Burns, review of *A Different Kind of Courage,* p. 736; March, 1999, review of *The Gate in the Wall,* p. 208; May, 2000, Kristi Beavin, review of *The Gate in the Wall,* p. 341.

Publishers Weekly, September 28, 1990, review of *Sister,* p. 103; April 6, 1992, review of *The Cellar,* p. 65; August 30, 1993, review of *The Tower Room,* p. 97; March 15, 1999, review of *The Gate in the Wall,* p. 59.

School Library Journal, December, 1993, Marilyn Long Graham, review of *The Tower Room,* p. 112; June, 1995, Marianne Saccardi, review of *Murphy and Kate,* p. 87; October, 1996, Jane Claes, review of *The Log Cabin Quilt,* p. 122; November, 1996, Ann W. Moore, review of *A Different Kind of Courage,* p. 106; March, 1999, Carol Fazioli, review of *The Gate in the Wall,* p. 210; October, 2000, review of *The Log Cabin Christmas,* p. 59; October, 2002, Margaret Bush, review of *The Log Cabin Church,* p. 112.

ONLINE

Ellen Howard's Home Page, http://usawrites4kids.drury.edu/authors/howard/ (December 10, 2002).

* * *

HUDSON, Miles (Matthew Lee) 1925-

PERSONAL: Born August 17, 1925, in Belfast, Northern Ireland; son of Charles Edward (a soldier) and Gladys (Lee) Hudson; married Mercedes Shaw, May 19, 1956; children: Mark, Veronica, Peter, Richard. *Education:* Trinity College, Oxford, M.A., 1949.

ADDRESSES: *Home*—Priors Farm, Reading Road, Mattingley, Hook, Hampshire RG27 8JU, England.

CAREER: British Army, career officer, 1943-64, retiring as lieutenant colonel; in charge of Rhodesian affairs for the Conservative Research Department, England, 1964-67, Lead of overseas department, 1967-70; political secretary to the British Foreign secretary, Sir Alec Douglas, 1970-74; farmer in Basingstoke, England, 1974—. Secretary of Hansard Commission for Electoral Reform, 1976; director of Conservative Group for Europe, 1977; member of Boyd Commission, 1979.

AWARDS, HONORS: Officer of Order of the British Empire.

WRITINGS:

Triumph or Tragedy: Rhodesia to Zimbabwe, Hamish Hamilton (London, England), 1981.

(With John Stanier) *War and the Media: A Random Searchlight,* New York University Press (New York, NY), 1998.

Assassination, Sutton, 2000.

Intervention in Russia, 1918-1920: A Cautionary Tale, Leo Cooper, 2004.

ADAPTATIONS: *Assassination* has been translated into Spanish, Portuguese, and Korean.

SIDELIGHTS: Miles Hudson brings his experience as a soldier in the British army and as a diplomat to bear in his writings about military affairs. In *War and the Media: A Random Searchlight,* written with John Stanier, Hudson examines both the positive and negative roles played by the media in times of war. He believes the media should be a kind of watchdog to the military. In the Crimean War, Hudson explains in his study, reports in the London *Times* documenting shortcomings in how the military was handling medical and management problems led to a major reorganization of the army for the better. But modern-day media tend to be run by commercial interests who put the size of their audience above all other considerations, including the safety or effectiveness of the nation's troops. Eliot A. Cohen, reviewing *War and the Media* in *Foreign Affairs,* found that "the treatment of the press is often patronizing. Still, those in the world of journalism may find this a useful view from the other side of the hill." John J. Smee in the *Political Science Quarterly* thought that the book "offers media practitioners, politicians, and the military a sober, balanced view of how all three groups act and interact in war situations."

In *Assassination* Hudson looks at the most infamous political assassinations of the past two thousand years and wonders what effect they had, if any, on the course of history. Focusing on those assassinations done purely for political reasons and where the motives of the killers are known, Hudson chronicles a wide range of effects. He concludes that assassination cannot actually change history, but it can speed up or slow down inherent tendencies already at work in a society. "Hudson," wrote Jay Freeman in *Booklist,* "has provided a thoughtful and stimulating look at an old question."

BIOGRAPHICAL AND CRITICAL SOURCES:

PERIODICALS

Booklist, July, 2000, Jay Freeman, review of *Assassination,* p. 1980.

Economist, July 25, 1981, review of *Triumph or Tragedy: Rhodesia to Zimbabwe,* p. 85.

Foreign Affairs, September-October, 1998, Eliot A. Cohen, review of *War and the Media: A Random Searchlight,* p. 151.

New Statesman, July 3, 1981, David Caute, review of *Triumph or Tragedy,* p. 17.

Political Science Quarterly, spring, 1999, John J. Smee, review of *War and the Media,* p. 157.

Spectator, August 15, 1981, review of *Triumph or Tragedy.*

Times (London, England), July 23, 1981, review of *Triumph or Tragedy.**

* * *

HUMPHREY, Sandra McLeod 1936-

PERSONAL: Born August 6, 1936, in Salt Lake City, UT; daughter of Murdoch John (in military public relations) and Virginia (a social worker; maiden name, Matthews; later surname, Sveeggen) McLeod; married Brian Neil Humphrey (a merchandiser), September 16, 1961; children: Jade Humphrey Sholty, Brandon McLeod, Patricia Humphrey Warren. *Ethnicity:* "Caucasian." *Education:* University of Minnesota, B.A. (cum laude), 1958, M.A., 1963. *Politics:* Independent. *Religion:* Protestant. *Hobbies and other interests:* Tennis, swimming, horseback riding, canine obedience classes, reading.

ADDRESSES: Home—19 Westwood Rd., Minnetonka, MN 55305. *E-mail*—Sandra305@aol.com.

CAREER: Minneapolis Veterans Administration Hospital, Minneapolis, MN, counseling psychologist, 1960; Anoka Metro Regional Treatment Center, Anoka, MN, clinical psychologist, 1961-62; writer of children's books, 1992—. Heroes and Dreams Foundation, writer and consultant; public speaker; guest on media programs. Volunteer with a local death-row ministry and a local youth ministry team; former volunteer with Hennepin County Foster Care Review Board, Western Hennepin County Literacy Action Committee, numerous church-related committees, and animal rights groups, including People for the Ethical Treatment of Animals, Hennepin County Humane Society, and National Humane Education Society.

MEMBER: Society of Children's Book Writers and Illustrators, Children's Literature Network.

AWARDS, HONORS: Certificates of commendation from National Police Officers Association of America, 1973, State of Minnesota, 1979, 1992, and United Federation of Teachers, 2002; award from Character Education Center, 2000, for "exemplary leadership in ethics education."

WRITINGS:

FOR CHILDREN

A Dog Named Sleet, May Davenport Publishers (Los Altos Hills, CA), 1984.

If You Had to Choose, What Would You Do?, illustrated by Brian Strassburg, Prometheus Books (Amherst, NY), 1995.

It's Up to You . . . What Do You Do?, illustrated by Brian Strassburg, Prometheus Books (Amherst, NY), 1999.

Keepin' It Real: A Young Teen Talks with God, CSS Publishing (Lima, OH), 2003.

More If You Had to Choose, What Would You Do?, illustrated by Brian Strassburg, Prometheus Books (Amherst, NY), 2003.

Contributor of short stories to magazines, including *Once upon a Time, Highlights for Children, Listen, Touch, Pockets,* and *My Friend.*

WORK IN PROGRESS: In the Beginning, for Pink Tree Press; *When Bad Things Happen,* Heroes and Dreams Foundation; *Dare to Succeed; A Family Affair—One Family's Experience with Cancer; Letters from Camp;The Case of the Counterfeit Teacher.*

SIDELIGHTS: Sandra McLeod Humphrey once told *CA:* "After working more than thirty-one years as a clinical psychologist, I retired to write books and stories for children.

"My purpose in writing my books and stories is to help our young people develop a strong sense of who they are, where they want to go in this life, and how they intend to get there. And hopefully, my books will make the trip easier (and more fulfilling) for them by helping them to make good choices along the way.

"Every book and every story I write is written to, in some way, help our young people develop strong character and a strong sense of who they are, so that they will not be unduly influenced by peer pressures later on in life and so that they will be able to stand up for what they believe—even when sometimes it may mean standing alone.

"Both of my books about moral choices have received very positive reviews and have also been well received by teachers, parents, and the kids themselves. This is why my publisher asked me to write a third book about moral choices. Teachers tell me that reading and talking about the stories in my books in class make their students much more sensitive to each other's feelings, and some teachers report that their students enjoy role-playing the stories.

"As I continue to visit schools and confirmation groups to talk about my books and about moral choices in general, it never ceases to amaze me how willing our young people are to share their personal, and sometimes painful, experiences. When I see how very wise and empathic these young people are, I must confess that I feel very reassured about the future of our country."

BIOGRAPHICAL AND CRITICAL SOURCES:

PERIODICALS

Bay Area Parent, September, 1999, review of *It's Up to You . . . What Do You Do?*

Bloomsbury Review, July-August, 1999, review of *It's Up to You . . . What Do You Do?*

Bookviews, March, 1999, Alan Caruba, review of *It's Up to You . . . What Do You Do?*

Children's House, October, 1995, pp. 17-18.

Christian Science Monitor, February 10, 1999, review of *It's Up to You . . . What Do You Do?*

Family Times, February, 1996; March, 1999, review of *It's Up to You . . . What Do You Do?*

L.A. Parent, June, 1999, Susan K. Perry, review of *It's Up to You . . . What Do You Do?*

Metro Lutheran, March, 1996; May, 1999, Michael L. Sherer, review of *It's Up to You . . . What Do You Do?*

Minnetonka SunSailor, January 3, 1996, p. 1B.

Napra Review, May-June, 1999, review of *It's Up to You . . . What Do You Do?*

ONLINE

Kids Can Do It, http://www.kidscandoit.com/ (August 14, 2002).

HUTCHINS, Hazel J. 1952-

PERSONAL: Born August 9, 1952, in Calgary, Alberta, Canada; daughter of Bill (a cowboy and farmer) and Peggy (a farmer; maiden name, McKinnon) Sadler; married James Edward Hutchins, January 13, 1973; children: Wil, Leanna, Ben Brodie. *Education:* Attended University of Calgary. *Hobbies and other interests:* Travel, skiing, hiking, visiting high alpine lakes.

ADDRESSES: *Home*—Box 185, 521 4th St., Canmore, Alberta T1W 2G6, Canada. *Agent*—c/o Author Mail, Annick Press, 15 Patricia Ave, Willowdale, Ontario M2M 1H9, Canada. *E-mail*—hjhutch@telusplanet.net.

CAREER: Writer. Visiting author and speaker in schools.

MEMBER: Writers' Union of Canada, Writers Guild of Alberta, Young Alberta Book Society, Canadian Society of Children's Authors, Illustrators and Performers.

AWARDS, HONORS: Selection for the Read Magic Awards List, *Parenting* magazine, for *The Three and Many Wishes of Jason Reid;* Award for Children's Literature, Alberta Writer's Guild, for *A Cat of Artimus Pride;* Mr. Christie's Book Award Silver for *Two So Small* and *Tess;* Governor-General's Short List for *Tess;* Silver Birch Award Honour Book for *T. C. and the Cats;* White Raven International Youth Library selection for *Leanna Builds a Genie Trap.*

WRITINGS:

FOR CHILDREN; PICTURE BOOKS EXCEPT AS NOTED

The Three and Many Wishes of Jason Reid (novel), illustrated by John Richmond, Annick (Willowdale, Ontario, Canada), 1983, reissued, 2000.

Anastasia Morningstar and the Crystal Butterfly (novel), illustrated by Barry Trower, Annick (Willowdale, Ontario, Canada), 1984.

Leanna Builds a Genie Trap, illustrated by Catherine O'Neill, Annick (Willowdale, Ontario, Canada), 1986.

Ben's Snow Song, illustrated by Lisa Smith, Annick (Willowdale, Ontario, Canada), 1987.

Casey Webber, the Great (novel), illustrated by John Richmond, Annick (Willowdale, Ontario, Canada), 1988.

Norman's Snowball, illustrated by Ruth Ohi, Annick (Willowdale, Ontario, Canada), 1989.

Nicholas at the Library, illustrated by Ruth Ohi, Annick (Willowdale, Ontario, Canada), 1990.

A Cat of Artimus Pride (novel), illustrated by Ruth Ohi, Annick (Willowdale, Ontario, Canada), 1991.

Katie's Babbling Brother, illustrated by Ruth Ohi, Annick (Willowdale, Ontario, Canada), 1991.

And You Can Be the Cat, illustrated by Ruth Ohi, Annick (Willowdale, Ontario, Canada), 1992.

The Best of Arlie Zack (novel), illustrated by Ruth Ohi, Annick (Willowdale, Ontario, Canada), 1993.

The Catfish Palace, illustrated by Ruth Ohi, Annick (Willowdale, Ontario, Canada), 1993.

Within a Painted Past (novel), illustrated by Ruth Ohi, Annick (Willowdale, Ontario, Canada), 1994.

Tess, Annick (Willowdale, Ontario, Canada), 1995.

Believing Sophie, Albert Whitman (Niles, IL), 1995.

Tess, Annick (Willowdale, Ontario, Canada), 1996.

Yancy and Bear, Annick (Willowdale, Ontario, Canada), 1996.

The Prince of Tarn (novel), Annick (Willowdale, Ontario, Canada), 1997.

Shoot for the Moon, Robyn (novel), Formac (Halifax, Nova Scotia, Canada), 1997.

It's Raining, Yancy and Bear, illustrated by Ruth Ohi, Annick (Willowdale, Ontario, Canada), 1998.

One Duck, Annick (Willowdale, Ontario), 1999.

Robyn Looks for Bears (novel), Formac (Halifax, Nova Scotia, Canada), 2000.

Two So Small, illustrated by Ruth Ohi, Annick (Willowdale, Ontario, Canada), 2000.

The Wide World of Suzie Mallard, Ducks Unlimited (Memphis, TN), 2000.

One Dark Night, Viking (New York, NY), 2001.

Robyn's Art Attack, Formac (Halifax, Nova Scotia, Canada), 2002.

T. J. and the Cats (novel), Orca (Victoria, British Columbia, Canada), 2002.

I'd Know You Anywhere, Annick (Willowdale, Ontario, Canada), 2002.

The Sidewalk Rescue, illustrated by Ruth Ohi, Annick (Willowdale, Ontario, Canada), 2002.

T. J. and the Haunted House (novel), Orca (Victoria, British Columbia, Canada), 2003.

Robyn Makes the News (novel), Formac (Halifax, Nova Scotia, Canada), 2003.

WORK IN PROGRESS: Beneath the Bridge, a picture book for Annick Press, with illustrations by Ruth Ohi; *T. J. and the Rockets,* third in the "T. J." series, Orca Young Readers; *Skate Robyn, Skate!,* seventh in the Formac First Novel series about Robyn; *A Second Is a Hiccup,* picture book from Scholastic Canada; "various other picture books and children's novels in various stages of progress."

SIDELIGHTS: "At the beginning of a Hazel Hutchins novel," wrote an essayist for the *St. James Guide to Children's Writers,* "magical powers suddenly enter into the lives of ordinary children. . . . At the end of each novel, the magic has left their lives; however, because of its influence, the central characters have come to a better understanding of themselves and the people around them. For a boy granted a seemingly endless supply of wishes, another who finds a jacket that makes him invisible, or a girl who can enter the paintings hanging in her aunt's guest room, the magic is a catalyst for the inner changes of their lives." Hutchins has also written a number of picture books for young readers, including *Two So Small* and *One Dark Night.*

In *The Prince of Tarn* young Fred meets a prince from a story his mother once told him who has somehow stumbled into the everyday world and must be helped to return to his kingdom. There, Fred and the prince overcome an enchantment that threatens Tarn. Carolyn Phelan in *Booklist* found that "Hutchins creates some memorable scenes, including the poignant moment when the prince realizes he's not in Tarn anymore, and the eventful day when he attends school with Fred."

In *Two So Small* Hutchins tells the story of a young boy who is sent to deliver a quilt to his grandmother. Along the way, he picks up a number of castoff items and puts them in his goat-drawn cart. When he discovers a giant's baby deep in the forest, the odd items he has been collecting are suddenly useful: the baby uses them as a hat, a shoelace, and a button. Catherine Andronik in *Booklist* found that "this original story has the look and sound of a folktale." "The clever story is satisfying," according to Jean Gaffney in *School Library Journal.*

One Dark Night is the story of a storm in the country. Young Jonathan is snugly indoors with his grandparents when the storm is just beginning, but outside there is a stray cat with newborn kittens who must find shelter. When Jonathan notices the mother cat's plight, he runs to help her, and everybody is safely inside before the rain begins to fall. Shelle Rosenfeld of *Booklist* noted that the story "is about the welcome comfort of safe havens, for humans and animals alike." Shara Alpern, reviewing the book in *School Library Journal,* believed that "children will share Jonathan's concern for the cats and will take comfort in the story's resolution." The reviewer for *Horn Book* concluded that "*One Dark Night* is full of elemental power and high drama—unusual attributes in a book intended for quite young children. It succeeds because both power (an approaching thunderstorm) and drama (the rescue of newborn kittens) are child-sized, pitched perfectly to a child's scope and experience."

"Hutchins's stories are both light and serious, humorous and profound," the essayist for the *St. James Guide to Children's Writers* stated. "The magic in them relates to fantasies, such as unlimited wishes or invisibility, in which most children have indulged. However, it does not overwhelm the stories; it is an intriguing and entertaining plot device that enhance the events, but more important, provides a means of examining the personalities of the people it touches. The heroes, boys and girls around the ages of eleven or twelve (younger in the picture books), face problems not uncommon to children of their ages: insecurity, sense of peer group inadequacy, the difficulties of single parent families. . . . Hutchins treats her characters with seriousness and respect. They participate in adventures that are convincing to readers both as stories and as explorations of conflicts with which the readers can quickly identify."

Hutchins, who grew up on a farm in southern Alberta, Canada, told *CA:* "I like words—how they sound and feel. I love the way ideas in fiction open so many doors in my mind. The most rewarding part is making the words say exactly what I want. When that happens, it's wonderful." Hutchins credits her family with story inspiration and writes first drafts longhand, followed by editing and printing on a computer. She advises aspiring writers: "Always write about things you're intrigued by, not just about things you know. Don't talk about your stories, write about them. And don't be discouraged. It takes time to be a good writer."

On her Web site, Hutchins recounted how she first began writing when she was a girl: "I was about ten years old when I realized I wanted to be an author. After that, although I had many other hobbies and interests, I also spent a good deal of time writing stories. I wrote quietly and secretly, never telling anyone my plans. The first stories I tried to have published, sent out secretly when I was in high school, were promptly rejected. So were the next batch. And the next. I didn't give up, however. I went ahead with other things, further education and numerous jobs, but I continued to write. I finally learned to do two things—write with great care and write about what truly intrigued me. My stories began to sell!"

BIOGRAPHICAL AND CRITICAL SOURCES:

BOOKS

St. James Guide to Children's Writers, 5th edition, St. James Press (Detroit, MI), 1999.

PERIODICALS

Booklist, September 1, 1995, Julie Corsaro, review of *Believing Sophie,* p. 87; December 15, 1995, Kay Weisman, review of *Tess,* p. 704; February 15, 1998, Carolyn Phelan, review of *The Prince of Tarn,* p. 1011; November 15, 2000, Catherine Andronik, review of *Two So Small,* p. 648; May 15, 2001, Shelle Rosenfeld, review of *One Dark Night,* p. 1758.

Childhood Education, summer, 2002, Liane Ford, review of *One Dark Night,* p. 239.

Horn Book, July, 2001, review of *One Dark Night,* p. 440.

School Library Journal, October, 2000, Jean Gaffney, review of *Two So Small,* p. 127; June, 2001, Shara Alpern, review of *One Dark Night,* p. 118.

ONLINE

Annick Press Web site, http://www.annickpress.com/ai/hutchins.html/ (November 18, 2002).

Hazel J. Hutchins' Home Page, http://www.telusplanet.net/public/hjhutch/home.html/ (November 18, 2002).

* * *

HYDE, Margaret O(ldroyd) 1917-

PERSONAL: Born February 18, 1917, in Philadelphia, PA; daughter of Gerald James and Helen (Lerch) Oldroyd; married Edwin Y. Hyde, Jr., 1941; children: Lawrence Edwin, Bruce Geoffrey. *Education:* Arcadia

University, A.B., 1938; Columbia University, M.A., 1939; Temple University, additional studies, 1942-43. *Hobbies and other interests:* Travel, computers, health.

ADDRESSES: Home—336 Essex Meadows, Essex, CT 06426. *E-mail*—ehyde@snet.net.

CAREER: Columbia University, Teachers College, New York, NY, science consultant, 1941-42; Shipley School, Bryn Mawr, PA, teacher, 1942-48. Lecturer in elementary education, Temple University, Philadelphia, PA, part-time and summers, 1942-43; writer for young people, 1944—.

MEMBER: Authors League of America, Authors Guild.

AWARDS, HONORS: Thomas Alva Edison Foundation National Mass Media Award, 1961, for best children's science book, *Animal Clocks and Compasses;* honorary doctor of letters from Beaver College, 1971; VOYA nonfiction horror list, 2003, for *Depression.*

WRITINGS:

(With Gerald S. Craig) *New Ideas in Science,* Ginn, 1947.

Playtime for Nancy (fiction), Grosset (New York, NY), 1951.

(With Frances W. Keene) *Hobby Fun Book for Grade School Boys and Girls: A Collection of Carefully Chosen Creative To-Do Hobbies,* Seahorse Press, 1952.

Flight Today and Tomorrow, illustrated by Clifford N. Geary, McGraw-Hill (New York, NY), 1953, revised edition, 1962.

Driving Today and Tomorrow, illustrated by Clifford N. Geary, McGraw-Hill (New York, NY), 1954, revised edition, 1965.

Atoms Today and Tomorrow, illustrated by Clifford N. Geary, McGraw-Hill (New York, NY), 1955, 4th edition, 1970.

(With husband, E. Y. Hyde, Jr.) *Where Speed Is King,* illustrated by Clifford N. Geary, McGraw-Hill (New York, NY), 1955, revised edition, 1961.

Medicine in Action: Today and Tomorrow, McGraw-Hill (New York, NY), 1956, revised edition, 1964.

Exploring Earth and Space: The Story of the I.G.Y., McGraw-Hill (New York, NY), 1957, 5th edition, illustrated by E. Winson, 1970.

From Submarines to Satellites: Science in Our Armed Forces, McGraw-Hill (New York, NY), 1958.

Off into Space! Science for Young Space Travelers, McGraw-Hill (New York, NY), 1959, 3rd edition, illustrated by B. Myers, 1969.

Plants Today and Tomorrow, illustrated by P. A. Hutchison, McGraw-Hill (New York, NY), 1960.

Animal Clocks and Compasses, illustrated by P. A. Hutchison, McGraw-Hill (New York, NY), 1960.

This Crowded Planet, illustrated by Mildred Waltrip, McGraw-Hill (New York, NY), 1961.

Animals in Science: Saving Lives through Research, McGraw-Hill (New York, NY), 1962.

Molecules Today and Tomorrow, illustrated by Mildred Waltrip, McGraw-Hill (New York, NY), 1963.

Your Brain, Master Computer, illustrated by P. A. Hutchison, McGraw-Hill (New York, NY), 1964.

(With Edward S. Marks) *Psychology in Action,* illustrated by Carolyn Cather, McGraw-Hill (New York, NY), 1967, 2nd edition, 1976.

(And editor) *Mind Drugs,* McGraw-Hill (New York, NY), 1968, revised edition, Dodd (New York, NY), 1986.

The Earth in Action, McGraw-Hill (New York, NY), 1969.

The Great Deserts (adapted from the book by Folco Quilici), McGraw-Hill (New York, NY), 1969.

Your Skin, illustrated by Richard Jones, McGraw-Hill (New York, NY), 1970.

(With B. G. Hyde) *Know about Drugs,* illustrated by Bill Morrison, McGraw-Hill (New York, NY), 1971, 4th edition, Walker (New York, NY), 1996.

For Pollution Fighters Only, illustrated by Don Lynch, McGraw-Hill (New York, NY), 1971.

(With Edward S. Marks and James B. Wells) *Mysteries of the Mind,* McGraw-Hill (New York, NY), 1972.

VD: The Silent Epidemic, McGraw-Hill (New York, NY), 1972, 2nd edition published as *VD-STD: The Silent Epidemic,* 1983.

The New Genetics: Promises and Perils, F. Watts (New York, NY), 1974.

Alcohol: Drink or Drug?, McGraw-Hill (New York, NY), 1974.

Hotline!, McGraw-Hill (New York, NY), 1974, 2nd edition, 1976.

(With Elizabeth H. Forsyth) *What Have You Been Eating? Do You Really Know?,* McGraw-Hill (New York, NY), 1975.

(With E. H. Forsyth) *Know Your Feelings,* F. Watts (New York, NY), 1976.

Speak Out on Rape, McGraw-Hill (New York, NY), 1976.

Juvenile Justice and Injustice, F. Watts (New York, NY), 1977, 2nd edition, 1983.

Fears and Phobias, McGraw-Hill (New York, NY), 1977, revised edition (with E. H. Forsyth) published as *Horror, Fright and Panic,* Walker (New York, NY), 1987.

Brainwashing and Other Forms of Mind Control, McGraw-Hill (New York, NY), 1977.

Know about Alcohol, foreword by Morris E. Chafetz, illustrated by Bill Morrison, McGraw-Hill (New York, NY), 1978.

Addictions: Smoking, Gambling, Cocaine Use and Others, McGraw-Hill (New York, NY), 1978.

(With E. H. Forsyth) *Suicide: The Hidden Epidemic,* F. Watts (New York, NY), 1978, 3rd revised edition, 1991.

(With B. G. Hyde) *Everyone's Trash Problem: Nuclear Wastes,* McGraw-Hill (New York, NY), 1979.

My Friend Wants to Run Away, McGraw-Hill (New York, NY), 1979.

Crime and Justice in Our Time, F. Watts (New York, NY), 1980.

Cry Softly: The Story of Child Abuse, Westminster (Louisville, KY), 1980, revised and enlarged edition, 1986.

Is the Cat Dreaming Your Dream?, McGraw-Hill (New York, NY), 1980.

My Friend Has Four Parents, McGraw-Hill (New York, NY), 1981, revised edition (with E. H. Forsyth) published as *Parents Divided, Parents Multiplied,* Westminster (Louisville, KY), 1989.

Energy: The New Look, McGraw-Hill (New York, NY), 1981.

Foster Care and Adoption, F. Watts (New York, NY), 1982.

Computers That Think? The Search for Artificial Intelligence, Enslow (Springfield, NJ), 1982, revised edition published as *Artificial Intelligence,* 1986.

The Rights of the Victim, F. Watts (New York, NY), 1983.

Know about Smoking, illustrated by Dennis Kendrick, McGraw-Hill (New York, NY), 1983, 3rd edition, Walker (New York, NY), 1995.

(With son, Lawrence E. Hyde) *Is This Kid "Crazy"? Understanding Unusual Behavior,* Westminster (Louisville, KY), 1983.

Cloning and the New Genetics, Enslow (Springfield, NJ), 1984.

Sexual Abuse: Let's Talk about It, Westminster (Louisville, KY), 1984, revised and enlarged edition, 1987.

(With L. E. Hyde) *Cancer in the Young: A Sense of Hope,* Westminster (Louisville, KY), 1985.

(With L. E. Hyde) *Missing Children,* F. Watts (New York, NY), 1985.

(With E. H. Forsyth) *AIDS: What Does It Mean to You?,* Walker (New York, NY), 1986, revised edition, 1990.

(With E. H. Forsyth) *AIDS,* Walker (New York, NY), 1986.

(With E. H. Forsyth) *Terrorism: A Special Kind of Violence,* Putnam (New York, NY), 1987.

(With E. H. Forsyth) *Know about AIDS,* illustrated by Deborah Weber, Walker (New York, NY), 1987, 3rd edition, 1995.

Teen Sex, Westminster (Louisville, KY), 1988.

Alcohol: Uses and Abuses, Enslow (Springfield, NJ), 1988.

The Homeless: Profiling the Problem, Enslow (Springfield, NJ), 1989.

(With L. E. Hyde) *Meeting Death,* Walker (New York, NY), 1989.

(With E. H. Forsyth) *Medical Dilemmas,* Putnam (New York, NY), 1990.

Drug Wars, Walker (New York, NY), 1990.

(With E. H. Forsyth) *The Violent Mind,* F. Watts (New York, NY), 1991.

Peace and Friendship = Mir I Druzhba: Russian and American Teens Meet, 1992.

Know about Abuse, Walker (New York, NY), 1992.

Know about Tuberculosis, Walker (New York, NY), 1995.

Know about Gays and Lesbians, Walker (New York, NY), 1995.

Living with Asthma, Walker (New York, NY), 1995.

Kids in and out of Trouble: Juveniles and the Law, Dutton (New York, NY), 1995.

Know about Mental Illness, Walker (New York, NY), 1996.

Gambling: Winners and Losers, Millbrook (Brookfield, CT), 1996.

The Sexual Abuse of Children and Adolescents, 1997.

The Disease Book: A Kids' Guide, Walker (New York, NY), 1997.

Missing and Murdered Children, 1998.

(With John F. Setaro) *Alcohol 101: An Overview for Teens,* 21st Century Books, 1999.

(With E. H. Forsyth) *Vaccinations: From Smallpox to Cancer,* F. Watts (New York, NY), 2000.

(With John F. Setaro) *When the Brain Dies First,* F. Watts (New York, NY), 2000.

(With John F. Setaro) *Medicine's Brave New World: Bioengineering and the New Genetics,* Millbrook (Brookfield, CT), 2001.

(With E. H. Forsyth) *Depression: What You Need to Know,* F. Watts (New York, NY), 2002.

(With John F. Setaro) *Drugs 101: An Overview for Teens,* 21st Century Books, 2003.

(With E. H. Forsyth) *Diabetes,* F. Watts (New York, NY), 2003.

(With John F. Setaro) *Smoking 101: An Overview for Teens,* Millbrook (Brookfield, CT), 2004.

Also author of two television scripts, *How the Mind Begins* and *Can Human Nature Be Changed?,* for *Animal Secrets,* NBC-TV, 1967.

SIDELIGHTS: Margaret O. Hyde is one of the most prolific and respected of today's writers on science for young readers, though, as a young girl, Hyde's ambition was to become a doctor. She stated in her *Something about the Author Autobiography Series* (*SAAS*) entry that she was probably inspired by a distant relative, with whom she stayed during the summer, who practiced medicine in a rural Pennsylvania town. "In addition to the novelty of shopping at the country store and playing with friends who remained the same summer after summer, I enjoyed driving through country roads in the doctor's car when he took me on calls to see patients." Occasionally Hyde was allowed to witness simple operations, "a tonsillectomy, the removal of a small growth on an arm or leg, or some other procedure that was considered simple enough to perform in the office.

"Although I was not a tomboy," Hyde wrote, "I liked subjects that, in those days, appealed most to boys. Perhaps I liked math and science because they were the subjects that were easiest for me. My parents were very tolerant of my collections of insects, earthworms, and other animals, although I remember my mother sounding disgusted when she emptied some worms from my pockets." However, "when I was growing up," Hyde continued, "women became nurses, secretaries, teachers, librarians, or had other ladylike careers. Many of my friends were totally consumed with the idea of getting married and raising children. My mother, who had always wanted to be a teacher herself, decided I should teach. Although I had many ideas about what I wanted to be when I grew up, a teacher was not one of them."

In college, Hyde specialized in science, intending to enter medical school. However, "when it came near the time to apply for admission to medical school," she wrote, "my parents balked at the idea. According to them, medicine should be left to men; women should be teachers, etc. They were willing to pay for graduate school, providing I considered becoming a teacher. Research was an acceptable option, but they still hoped I would change my mind and enter the teaching profession." Hyde attended graduate school in zoology at Columbia University, and began looking for work as a researcher. "In those days, women were usually relegated to inferior jobs in the field of science, and even those jobs were scarce." She enrolled at Columbia University Teachers College to prepare for a career as a public school teacher.

It was while at Columbia University Teachers College that Hyde first met Dr. Gerald Craig. "Dr. Craig apparently liked my way of teaching, for when there was an opening at Lincoln School of Teachers College, he recommended me for that position," Hyde wrote. Some time later, Craig invited her to rewrite a science textbook he had originally written for sixth-graders. "My response to Dr. Craig's suggestion was a hasty no," Hyde recalled, "and I explained that I had no writing ability. He felt that I could do the job based on my science background and he finally persuaded me to accept the offer." The resulting book, *New Ideas in Science,* was published in 1947.

Among Hyde's books are those in the "Know About" series, including *Know about AIDS, Know About Gays and Lesbians, Know about Abuse,* and *Know about Mental Illness.* Speaking of *Know about Gays and Lesbians,* Stephanie Zvirin in *Booklist* called the book "an extremely useful overview that includes a little bit about a lot that's important to understand." Susan Dove Lempke in *Booklist* found that *Know about Mental Illness* successfully sorted "out the confusing messages and information about mental illness disseminated in our society [and described] the symptoms of some of the better-known illnesses, such as agoraphobia and anorexia."

Hyde has also written a number of titles aimed at helping young readers learn about societal problems. Her *Alcohol 101: An Overview for Teens,* for example, introduces readers to the problem of alcoholism. "The book," explained Joyce Adams Burner in *School Library Journal,* "is remarkably nonjudgmental, non-sensationalized, and compassionately objective in its presentation of information."

Scientific advances have also been the subject of several of Hyde's books, including *Medicine's Brave New World: Bioengineering and the New Genetics,* an overview of the breakthrough research going on in the field of bioengineering. Anne O'Malley, writing in *Booklist,* found that "the book's best features are its clear explanations of bioengineering processes." Mary R. Hofmann in the *School Library Journal* believed that "what makes this work stand out is the way that incredibly complex cellular processes are lucidly explained. . . . Students with any scientific bent will be enthralled."

Hyde once told *CA:* "Writing is a wonderful way to learn more about the exciting world of science, for today one must contact people who are active in research to find out what is happening. Such people are most cooperative in talking about their projects and in checking material for accuracy. I gather material for several years from many sources and sometimes work on as many as four books at once."

BIOGRAPHICAL AND CRITICAL SOURCES:

BOOKS

Contemporary Literary Criticism, Volume 21, Thomson Gale (Detroit, MI), 1982.

Something about the Author Autobiography Series, Volume 8, Thomson Gale (Detroit, MI), 1989.

PERIODICALS

Booklist, July, 1992, Hazel Rochman, review of *Peace and Friendship,* p. 1930; November 1, 1992, Gary Young, review of *Know about Abuse,* p. 499; March 1, 1994, Stephanie Zvirin, review of *Know about Gays and Lesbians,* p. 1248; May 15, 1995, Stephanie Zvirin, review of *Kids in and out of Trouble,* p. 1638; June 1, 1995, Stephanie Zvirin, review of *Living with Asthma,* p. 1766; December 15, 1995, Stephanie Zvirin, review of *Gambling: Winners and Losers,* p. 695; September 1, 1996, Susan Dove Lempke, review of *Know about Mental Illness,* p. 116; February 15, 1997, Sally Estes, review of *The Sexual Abuse of Children and Adolescents,* p. 1012; September 15, 1997, Randy Meyer, review of *The Disease Book: A Kids' Guide,* p. 228; March 1, 1998, Roger Leslie, review of *Missing and Murdered Children,* p. 1123; April 15, 2000, Mary Romano Marks, review of *When the Brain Dies First,* p. 1536; November 15, 2000, Roger Leslie, review of *Vaccinations: From Smallpox to Cancer,* p. 630; December 15, 2001, Anne O'Malley, review of *Medicine's Brave New World: Bioengineering and the New Genetics,* p. 718; October 15, 2002, Roger Leslie, review of *Depression: What You Need to Know,* p. 398; May 15, 2003, Ed Sullivan, review of *Depression,* p. 1654.

Book Report, September-October, 1990, Barbara Pollock, review of *AIDS: What Does It Mean to You?,* p. 59, Dianne Meyers, review of *Medical Dilemmas,* p. 68, and Patricia S. Brown, review of *Drug Wars,* p. 68; September-October, 1991, Becky Copeland, review of *Suicide,* p. 57; November-December, 1991, Rose M. Kent, review of *The Violent Mind,* p. 59; January-February, 1993, Rosemary Sackleh, review of *Peace and Friendship,* p. 61; May-June, 1994, Lee Diane Gordon, review of *Know about Gays and Lesbians,* p. 52; September-October, 1995, Diane C. Pozar, reviews of *Know about Smoking, Know about Tuberculosis, Know about AIDS,* and *Living with Asthma,* p. 51, and Susan Yallaly, review of *Kids in and out of Trouble,* p. 59; May-June, 1996, Sherry Hoy, review of *Gambling,* p. 58; November-December, 1998, Laura Moe, review of *Missing and Murdered Children,* p. 80.

Canadian Journal of Human Sexuality, fall, 1997, Ruth Miller, review of *Know about Gays and Lesbians,* p. 255.

School Library Journal, October, 1982, review of *Foster Care and Adoption,* p. 162; April, 1984, Nancy J. Horner, review of *Is This Kid Crazy?,* p. 124; April, 1990, Anne Osborn, review of *AIDS,* p. 148; June, 1990, Steve Matthews, review of *Drug Wars,* p. 141; July, 1990, Christine A. Moesch, reviews of *Know about AIDS, Know about Smoking,* and *Know about Drugs,* p. 85, and Martha Gordon, review of *Medical Dilemmas,* p. 92; April, 1991, Libby K. White, review of *Suicide,* p. 148; November, 1991, Kathleen L. Atwood, review of *The Violent Mind,* p. 139; September, 1992, Celia A. Huffman, review of *Know about Abuse,* p. 267; October, 1992, Ann Welton, review of *Peace and Friendship,* p. 129; November, 1992,

Sue A. Norkeliunas, review of *AIDS,* p. 129; April, 1994, Libby K. White, review of *Know about Gays and Lesbians,* p. 161; March, 1995, Martha Gordon, review of *Know about Tuberculosis,* p. 214; May, 1995, Jacqueline Rose, review of *Kids in and out of Trouble,* p. 126, and Martha Gordon, review of *Know about AIDS,* p. 127; July, 1995, Martha Gordon, review of *Living with Asthma,* p. 86; September, 1995, Martha Gordon, review of *Know about Smoking,* p. 209; March, 1996, Libby K. White, reviews of *Know about Drugs* and *AIDS,* p. 225, and Tim Wadham, review of *Gambling,* p. 225; July, 1996, Christine A. Moesch, review of *Know about Mental Illness,* p. 90; March, 1997, Melissa Gross, review of *The Sexual Abuse of Children and Adolescents,* p. 202; November, 1997, Sheila G. Shellabarger, review of *The Disease Book,* p. 128; March, 1998, Lois McCulley, review of *Missing and Murdered Children,* p. 234; March, 2000, Joyce Adams Burner, review of *Alcohol 101,* p. 254; July, 2000, Ann G. Brouse, review of *When the Brain Dies First,* p. 117; December, 2001, Mary R. Hofmann, review of *Medicine's Brave New World,* p. 163; December, 2002, Lynn Evarts, review of *Depression,* p. 162; May, 2003, Debbie Stewart, review of *Drugs 101: An Overview for Teens,* p. 172.

Science Teacher, May, 1992, Robert H. Davis, review of *Medical Dilemmas,* p. 74.

Voice of Youth Advocates, October, 2003, Heather Hepler, review of *Drugs 101.*

Wilson Library Bulletin, October, 1986, Patty Campbell, review of *AIDS,* p. 52; September, 1987, Patty Campbell, review of *AIDS,* p. 72; April, 1988, pp. 74-75; March, 1990, Frances Bradburn, review of *Meeting Death,* p. 105; May, 1995, Cathi Dunn MacRae, review of *Know about Gays and Lesbians,* p. 104.

I-J

IVES, Colta Feller 1943-

PERSONAL: Born April 5, 1943, in San Diego, CA; married E. Garrison Ives (a lawyer), June 14, 1966; children: Lucy Barrett. *Education:* Mills College, B.A., 1964; Columbia University, M.A., 1966.

ADDRESSES: *Office*—c/o Metropolitan Museum of Art, 5th Ave., New York, NY 10028-0198.

CAREER: Metropolitan Museum of Art, New York, NY, staff member, 1965-75, curator of prints and photographs, 1975-93, curator in charge of prints and photographs, 1975-93. Columbia University, adjunct professor, 1970-87. Bidwell House, member of board of directors.

MEMBER: Print Council of America (member of executive board, 1976-78, 1984-87; vice president, 1989-93), Grolier Club.

AWARDS, HONORS: First-place award for exhibition catalogs from Art Libraries Association of New York, 1975, for *The Great Wave;* "best of show" designation, New York City museums category, International Association of Art Critics, 1997-98, for *The Private Collection of Edgar Degas: A Summary Catalogue.*

WRITINGS:

The Flight into Egypt, Metropolitan Museum of Art (New York, NY), 1972.

The Great Wave: The Influence of Japanese Woodcuts on French Prints, Metropolitan Museum of Art (New York, NY), 1974.

(With David Kiehl, Barbara Shapiro, and Sue Welsh Reed) *The Painterly Print,* Metropolitan Museum of Art (New York, NY), 1980.

Introduction to Rauschenberg: Photographs in and out of the City Limits of New York, Universal Limited Art Editions (Bay Shore, NY), 1982.

French Prints in the Era of Impressionism and Symbolism, 1988.

(With Helen Giambruni and Sasha M. Newman) *Pierre Bonnard, the Graphic Art,* Metropolitan Museum of Art (New York, NY), 1989.

(With Margret Stuffmann and Martin Sonnabend) *Daumier Drawings,* Metropolitan Museum of Art (New York, NY), 1992.

(With Susan Alyson Stein) *Goya in the Metropolitan Museum of Art,* Metropolitan Museum of New York (New York, NY), 1995.

Toulouse-Lautrec in the Metropolitan Museum of Art, Metropolitan Museum of New York (New York, NY), 1996.

(Compiler, with others) *The Private Collection of Edgar Degas: A Summary Catalogue,* Metropolitan Museum of Art (New York, NY), 1997.

(With Elizabeth E. Barker) *Romanticism and the School of Nature: Nineteenth-Century Drawings and Paintings from the Karen B. Cohen Collection,* Yale University Press (New Haven, CT), 2000.

(With Susan Alyson Stein, Charlotte Hale, and Marjorie Shelley) *The Lure of the Exotic: Gauguin in New York Collections,* Yale University Press (New Haven, CT), 2002.

Contributor to *Artnews* and *Print Collector's Newsletter.*

BIOGRAPHICAL AND CRITICAL SOURCES:

PERIODICALS

Bloomsbury Review, November, 1999, review of *Toulouse-Lautrec in the Metropolitan Museum of Art,* p. 13.

Choice, September, 1993, review of *Daumier Drawings,* p. 100; December, 1996, review of *Toulouse-Lautrec in the Metropolitan Museum of Art,* p. 602.

Library Journal, November 1, 2002, Ellen Bates, review of *The Lure of the Exotic: Gauguin in New York Collections,* p. 85.

New York Review of Books, March 25, 1993, review of *Daumier Drawings,* p. 56.

Reference and Research Book News, August, 1993, review of *Daumier Drawings,* p. 33; February, 2001, review of *Romanticism and the School of Nature: Nineteenth-Century Drawings and Paintings from the Karen B. Cohen Collection,* p. 166.

Wilson Library Bulletin, June, 1993, review of *Daumier Drawings,* p. 111.*

* * *

JACKSON, Hialeah
See WHITNEY, Polly (Louise)

* * *

JAMISON, Kay Redfield

PERSONAL: Daughter of a meteorologist and a teacher; married second husband, Richard Wyatt (a medical researcher). *Education:* University of California—Los Angeles, Ph.D.

ADDRESSES: Agent—c/o Author Mail, Alfred A. Knopf, 299 Park Ave., New York, NY 10171.

CAREER: University of California—Los Angeles, Los Angeles, worked as associate professor of psychiatry; Johns Hopkins University, Baltimore, MD, began as associate professor, became professor of psychiatry.

WRITINGS:

(With Bruce L. Baker and Michael J. Goldstein) *Abnormal Psychology: Experiences, Origins, and Interventions,* Little, Brown (Boston, MA), 1980, 2nd edition, 1986.

(Compiler, with Frederick K. Goodwin) *Manic-Depressive Illness,* Oxford University Press (New York, NY), 1990.

Touched with Fire: Manic-Depressive Illness and the Creative Temperament, Free Press (New York, NY), 1993.

An Unquiet Mind (memoir), Knopf (New York, NY), 1995.

Night Falls Fast: Understanding Suicide, Knopf (New York, NY), 1999.

Exuberance: The Passion for Life, Knopf (New York, NY), 2004.

SIDELIGHTS: Kay Redfield Jamison is a psychologist and educator who is considered an authority on manic-depressive illness. Her volume *Manic-Depressive Illness,* compiled with Frederick K. Goodwin, is regarded as a key contribution to the study of manic-depressive illness, a biochemical disorder which results in periods of mania alternating with bouts of depression. The book encompasses a range of issues and subjects, including diagnosis, clinical studies, psychological ramifications, and patho-physiological elements. Larry S. Goldman, reviewing the work in the *New England Journal of Medicine,* acknowledged Jamison and Goodwin as "two highly regarded senior clinicians and researchers" and proclaimed their book "thorough and most readable." Goldman concluded, "It is hard to imagine a clinician working with patients with the illness . . . or a researcher in any part of the field of mood disorders who should not have this tour de force available."

Jamison followed *Manic-Depressive Illness* with *Touched with Fire: Manic-Depressive Illness and the Creative Temperament,* a detailed account of the ties between artistic sensibilities and manic-depressive illness. While conceding that not all artists are manic-depressive, Jamison argues that a significant association exists between the artistic and manic-depressive temperaments. There is, for example, a high rate of suicide among both types. In her analysis, Jamison incorporates scientific and medical data, including diagnostic methods and genetic information, and she applies this data to a host of creative individuals, including the composer Robert Schumann, the painter Vincent Van Gogh, and such American writers as Ernest Hemingway, John Berryman, and Hart Crane. Jamison notes that many of the creative individuals considered in *Touched with Fire* had little recourse to any suitable psycho-medical care.

Since its appearance in 1993, *Touched with Fire* has been praised as a detailed and compelling study. "This book," reported Myrna M. Weissman in *Contemporary Psychology,* "provides information about the experience of manic depressive illness from unique and creative individuals, factual information about our current scientific understanding, and a forum for some 'very careful thought.'" She called Jamison "a scientifically knowledgeable and remarkable author." Another reviewer, Hugh Freeman, wrote in *Nature* that *Touched with Fire* constitutes "an important work that should provoke some serious rethinking in several corners of academe," while Larry S. Goldman, in his *New England Journal of Medicine* appraisal, deemed Jamison's book "clear and enjoyable."

In 1995 Jamison published *An Unquiet Mind,* a memoir of her own experiences with manic depression. In this volume Jamison recounts her extreme moodiness as a child and relates her first, exhilarating experience of mania when she was in her mid-teens. She notes that mania and depression sometimes exist simultaneously. It is during these periods, when the depths of despair are coupled with the impulsiveness characteristic of mania, that sufferers, according to Jamison, are more likely to consider suicide. Jamison discloses in *An Unquiet Mind* that she attempted to take her own life, and she credits psychotherapy with helping her realize greater acceptance and stability. *Time* reviewer Anastasia Toufexis hailed *The Unquiet Mind* as "a rare and insightful view of mental illness from inside the mind of a trained specialist." Sharon O'Brien, writing in the *New York Times Book Review,* also responded favorably, lauding Jamison's book as "an invaluable memoir of manic depression, at once medically knowledgeable, deeply human and beautifully written."

BIOGRAPHICAL AND CRITICAL SOURCES:

PERIODICALS

Atlantic Monthly, April, 1993, p. 133.

Contemporary Psychology, May, 1994, Myrna M. Weissman, review of *Touched with Fire: Manic-Depressive Illness and the Creative Temperament,* pp. 469-470.

Los Angeles Times Book Review, August 1, 1993, p. 6.

Nature, April 15, 1993, Hugh Freeman, review of *Touched with Fire,* pp. 666-667.

New England Journal of Medicine, March 14, 1991, Larry S. Goldman, review of *Manic-Depressive Illness,* pp. 778-779; October 7, 1993, Larry S. Goldman, review of *Touched with Fire,* pp. 1133-1134.

New York Times Book Review, October 1, 1995, Sharon O'Brien, review of *An Unquiet Mind,* pp. 16-18.

Time, September 11, 1995, Anastasia Toufexis, review of *An Unquiet Mind,* p. 83.

Washington Post, May 6, 1993, p. D2.

* * *

JOHNS, Elizabeth 1937-

PERSONAL: Born October 28, 1937, in Dallas, TX; daughter of Samuel B. (a naval chaplain) and Gerta (a homemaker; maiden name, Gray) Bennett; married Lester H. Butsch, December 20, 1958 (divorced, 1970); married Max T. Johns (an economist), June 15, 1971; children: (first marriage) Alan L., Nancy E. *Education:* Birmingham Southern College, B.A., 1959; University of California—Berkeley, M.A., 1965; Emory University, Ph.D., 1974. *Politics:* Democrat. *Religion:* Lutheran.

ADDRESSES: *Office*—c/o Department of the History of Art, University of Pennsylvania, 3405 Woodland Walk, Philadelphia, PA 19104-3325.

CAREER: Albany State College, Albany, GA, instructor in English, 1968-71; Clayton Junior College, instructor in English, 1971-72; Savannah State College, Savannah, GA, assistant professor of English, 1972-75; University of Maryland—College Park, College Park, assistant professor, 1975-80, associate professor of art, 1980-84, associate professor of American studies, 1984-87; University of Pittsburgh, Pittsburgh, PA, Andrew Mellon Professor of Fine Arts, 1986-89; University of Pennsylvania, Philadelphia, Silfen Term Professor, beginning 1989, now professor emeritus. College of the Holy Cross, Lilly fellow at Center for Religion, Ethics, and Culture.

MEMBER: American Studies Association, Organization of American Historians, College Art Association of America, Association of Art Historians, Phi Beta Kappa.

AWARDS, HONORS: Mitchell Prize for the History of Art, 1984; Woodrow Wilson international fellow, 1985; Guggenheim fellow, 1985.

WRITINGS:

Thomas Eakins: The Heroism of Modern Life, Princeton University Press (Princeton, NJ), 1983.

American Genre Painting: The Politics of Everyday Life, Yale University Press (New Haven, CT), 1991.

(Illustrator) Ann Dixon, *The Sleeping Lady,* Alaska Northwest Books (Anchorage, AK), 1994.

(With Sylvia Yount) *To Be Modern: American Encounters with Cezanne and Company,* Museum of American Arts, Pennsylvania Academy of the Fine Arts (Philadelphia, PA), 1996.

(Illustrator) Janet Anderson, *Sunflower Sal,* Albert Whitman (Morton Grove, IL), 1997.

(With others) *New Worlds from Old: Nineteenth Century Australian and American Landscapes,* Wadsworth Atheneum (Hartford, CT), 1998.

Winslow Homer: The Nature of Observation, University of California Press (Berkeley, CA), 2002.

Contributor to books, including *George Caleb Bingham,* Abrams (New York, NY), 1990; *The West As America: Reinterpreting Images of the Frontier, 1820-1920,* Smithsonian Institution Press (Washington, DC), 1991; *The Still Life Paintings of William Michael Harnett,* Abrams (New York, NY), 1992; *William Sidney Mount: Painter of American Life,* by Deborah J. Johnson, American Federation of Arts (New York, NY), 1998; and *Philadelphia's Cultural Landscape: The Sartain Family Legacy,* edited by Katharine Martinez and Page Talbott, Temple University Press (Philadelphia, PA), 2000. Contributor to periodicals, including *Art Bulletin, Art Journal, Winterthur Portfolio: Journal of American Material Culture, American Quarterly, Journal of Interdisciplinary History,* and *Arts.*

SIDELIGHTS: With her book *Thomas Eakins: The Heroism of Modern Life,* Elizabeth Johns attracted the attention of such critics as Theodore Stebbins, Jr., who described it in the *New York Times Book Review* as "one of the best studies ever written about an American painter." Eakins, a master realist known primarily for his portraiture, is generally regarded as one of the greatest artists of the nineteenth century. But, as Johns's book points out, he sold few of his 250 portraits and did not achieve recognition as a major painter until the very end of his life. This was partly because art patrons of Eakins's time considered his remarkably honest approach to be moody, somber, and unflattering to his sitters, Johns explains, and they preferred the more pleasant styles of such painters as Eakins's contemporaries John Singer Sargent and William Merritt Chase.

Johns's premise, according to Suzanne Muchini in the *Los Angeles Times Book Review,* is that "Eakins's role as a portraitist has been neglected and his technique inadequately analyzed." She begins the biography with a discussion of Eakins's education and intellectual development and then examines five of his master pieces. Describing each portrait in detail, Johns places them in their sociological contexts and provides information regarding the lives and personalities of the sitters and the artistic conventions of the period.

Reviewers commended *Thomas Eakins* for its fresh approach to a much discussed subject. As Stebbins observed, Eakins is "the most thoroughly studied American painter," and therefore "Eakins scholarship has been even more subject to acrimonious nit-picking than most other art history." But despite all that has been previously written about Eakins's work, Stebbins said, Johns's book tells us more about his "subjects and his era than one would have thought necessary or possible."

Eakins chose his early subjects, Johns's book emphasizes, for the discipline and dedication demanded of them by their professions—medicine, athletics, the arts, religion. As Wanda M. Corn noted in the *Times Literary Supplement,* Eakins's sitters were more than friends and relatives; to him "they were modern egalitarian heroes." While Eakins's early portraits depicted active men and women in their professional settings, his later paintings focused on pensive figures, posed standing or sitting. According to Corn, Johns sees these later portraits as a progression of "Eakins's obsession with heroic behavior but argues that his definition of heroism has changed." In contrast with the early sitters, whose heroism derived from their professions, Eakins's later models were "heroes of endurance," whose "heroism consists in surviving the wear and tear of daily life." Corn further stated that she considered Johns's perspective "wholly original and unexpected."

Johns once told *CA:* "I believe that art history, at its best, is cultural history. For me, researching, thinking through, and writing history is the most exhilarating work imaginable."

BIOGRAPHICAL AND CRITICAL SOURCES:

PERIODICALS

AB Bookman's Weekly, March 25, 1991, review of *Thomas Eakins: The Heroism of Modern Life,* p. 1143.

American Historical Review, February, 1993, review of *American Genre Painting: The Politics of Everyday Life,* p. 241.

American Quarterly, March, 1993, review of *American Genre Painting,* p. 151.

Art Journal, winter, 1992, review of *American Genre Painting,* p. 95.

Burlington, February, 1994, review of *American Genre Painting,* p. 120.

Choice, April, 1992, review of *American Genre Painting,* p. 1217; May, 1999, review of *New Worlds from Old: Nineteenth Century Australian and American Landscapes,* p. 1604.

Journal of American History, September, 1993, review of *American Genre Painting,* p. 674.

Journal of Interdisciplinary History, summer, 1993, review of *American Genre Painting,* p. 170.

Library Journal, September 15, 1991, review of *American Genre Painting,* p. 52; April 15, 1992, review of *American Genre Painting,* p. 88; December, 2002, Kraig A. Binkowski, review of *Winslow Homer: The Nature of Observation,* p. 118.

Los Angeles Times Book Review, March 4, 1984, Suzanne Muchini, review of *Thomas Eakins.*

New York Review of Books, December 3, 1998, review of *New Worlds from Old,* p. 32.

New York Times Book Review, May 20, 1984, Theodore Stebbins, Jr., review of *Thomas Eakins,*

School Arts, January, 1993, review of *American Genre Painting,* p. 41.

Times Literary Supplement, May 28, 1984, Wanda M. Corn, review of *Thomas Eakins.*

Virginia Quarterly Review, summer, 1984.

Wilson Quarterly, February, 1992, review of *American Genre Painting,* p. 96.

ONLINE

Home Page of Professor Elizabeth Johns, http://www.arthistory.upenn.edu/faculty/ejohns.html/ (November 3, 1994).

University of California Press Web Site, http://www.ucpress.edu/ (April 16, 2003), publisher's description of *Winslow Homer.*

Yale University Press Web Site, http://www.yale.edu/yup/ (April 16, 2003), publisher's description of *American Genre Painting.**

* * *

(JONES), Owen Marshall
See MARSHALL, Owen

* * *

JOYCE, Michael 1945-

PERSONAL: Born November 9, 1945, in Lackawanna, NY; son of Thomas Robert (a steelmaker) and Joanne Hannah (Poth) Joyce; married Martha Jean Petry, October 12, 1975 (divorced, November, 1994); married Carolyn Jane Guyer, November 2, 1997; children: (first marriage) Eamon, Jeremiah. *Education:* Canisius College, B.A., 1972; University of Iowa, M.F.A., 1974. *Politics:* "Irish-American anarcho-leftist." *Religion:* "Quasi-Buddhist Roman Catholic." *Hobbies and other interests:* Exotic cooking, dance, Shakespearean acting.

ADDRESSES: Home—43 Point St., New Hamburg, NY 12590. *Office*—Department of English, 124 Raymond Ave., Box 360, Vassar College, Poughkeepsie, NY 12601. *Agent*—Young Agency, 156 5th Ave., New York, NY 10010.

CAREER: Jackson Community College, Jackson, MI, associate professor of language and literature and coordinator of Center for Narrative and Technology, 1975-95; Vassar College, Poughkeepsie, NY, visiting professor of hypertext media, technology, and culture,

1992-93, Randolph Visiting Distinguished Professor of English and the Library, 1993—. Consultant on computers and hypertext programs.

AWARDS, HONORS: Fellowship from Iowa Writers Workshop, 1973-74; Great Lakes New Writers Award, 1983, for *The War outside Ireland;* fellowship from Yale University, 1984-85; teaching fellowship from Apple Computers, 1991.

WRITINGS:

(Translator, with Mischa Cain) Anton Chekhov, *The Cherry Orchard* (play), produced in Jackson, MI, at Jackson Civic Theater, 1980.

The War outside Ireland (novel), Tinkers Dam Press (Jackson, MI), 1982.

afternoon, a story (interactive novel), Eastgate Systems (Watertown, MA), 1987, revised edition, 1993.

(Editor, with Larry McCaffery) *WAXWeb* (hypermedia fiction; adapted from David Blair's video *Wax; or, The Discovery of Television among Bees*), Eastgate Systems (Watertown, MA), 1994.

Of Two Minds: Hypertext, Pedagogy, and Poetics (essays), University of Michigan Press (Ann Arbor, MI), 1995.

(With Carolyn Guyer and Rosemary Joyce) *Sister Stories* (hypermedia fiction), Eastgate Systems (Watertown, MA), 1996.

Twelve Blue, 1997.

(Editor, with Ilana Snyder) *Page to Screen: Taking Literacy into the Electronic Era,* Routledge (New York, NY), 1998.

Othermindness: The Emergence of Network Culture, University of Michigan Press (Ann Arbor, MI), 2000.

Moral Tales and Meditations: Technological Parables and Refractions, State University of New York Press (Albany, NY), 2001.

Liam's Going (novel), McPherson (Kingston, NY), 2002.

Contributor to *Bioapparatus,* edited by Catherine Richards and Nel Tenhaaf, Banff Centre for the Arts (Banff, Alberta, Canada), 1991; *Works and Days,* edited by David B. Downing and James J. Sosnowski, 1994; *The Future of the Book,* edited by Geoffrey Nunberg, University of California Press (Berkeley, CA), 1996; and *In Memoriam to Postmodernism: Essays on the Avant-Pop,* edited by Mark Amerika and Lance Olsen, San Diego State University Press (San Diego, CA), 1996. Contributor to periodicals, including *Academic Computing, American Book Review, College English, Computers and Composition, Feed,Issues in Higher Education, North Dakota Quarterly, PostModern Culture,* and *Writing on the Edge.* Member of editorial board, *Prison Arts,* 1976, *WPA: Journal for Writing Program Administrators,* 1977-79, *Computers and Composition,* 1992—, *Electronic Journal of Virtual Culture,* 1993—, and *Works and Days,* 1995—.

SIDELIGHTS: Michael Joyce is a versatile writer who is best known for his hypertext fiction. Among his hypertext achievements is *afternoon, a story,* which is an interactive work of fiction centering on an insecure poet who fears that his wife and child may have perished in an automobile accident. Robert Coover, writing in the *New York Times Book Review,* described *afternoon, a story* as "a graceful and provocative work."

Joyce once told *CA:* "In 1982, I had published a prize-winning, small-press novel, *The War outside Ireland,* and, like any novelist, I knew that it was an awful thing to have to type successive drafts, and a worse thing to discover, midway in the last draft, that something on page 265 would work wonderfully on page seven. I believed that a word processor would allow me an option for making such changes.

"Immediately, I discovered that what I really wanted to do was not merely move a paragraph from page 265 to page seven but to do so almost endlessly. I wanted, quite simply, to write a novel that would change in successive readings, and to make those changing versions according to the connections which I had for some time naturally discovered in the process of writing, and which I wanted my readers to share. In my eyes paragraphs on many different pages could just as well go with paragraphs on many other pages, although with different effects and for different purposes. All that kept me from doing so was the fact that, in print at least, one paragraph inevitably follows another. It seemed to me that if I, as author, could use a computer to move paragraphs about, it wouldn't take much to let readers do so according to some scheme I had predetermined and which they could shape.

"By that time, I had begun to read numerous computer magazines, and sometimes even begun to understand an occasional word or sentence in at least the ads. At any rate, I found in some obscure computer magazine a thoroughly frightening article about a woman, Natalie Dehn, at the Yale Artificial Intelligence Lab who was trying to teach computers to write novels. Her face seemed kind so I wrote her a letter and asked her to tell me, please, where I could buy a computer program that would let me write novels that changed every time someone read them. She wrote me back an eight-page letter which explained how this was impossible and would be for twenty years, and argued—vociferously and much more ably than most literary critics I know—for the virtues of linearity in prose fiction, and for the aesthetic function of constrained choices in imagination. I began a long correspondence with Natalie, which resulted in my invitation to Yale and, more importantly, in her suggestion that I contact Jay Bolter, a curious combination of classicist and computerist, who she said had previously been a visiting fellow there, and who was 'also crazy,' and was interested in using computers to tell stories in the way Homer did. My correspondence with Jay led to foundation funding of my sabbatical and our initial work (with John B. Smith) on our hypertext program, *Storyspace,* while I was visiting at Yale.

"By the end of my Yale year Bolter and I had a (mostly) working version of *Storyspace* which, in January, 1986, I began to use with developmental writing (what used to be called remedial or college preparatory writing) students and soon after also began to use with my creative writing students. *Storyspace* enabled me to write a hyperfiction, *afternoon, a story,* which changes every time you read it and which in some sense defined the beginning of a new literature (albeit a transitory one in an uncertain medium)."

BIOGRAPHICAL AND CRITICAL SOURCES:

BOOKS

Bolter, Jay David, *Writing Space: The Computer, Hypertext, and the History of Writing,* Lawrence Erlbaum (Hillsdale, NJ), 1991.

Landow, George, *Hypertext: The Convergence of Contemporary Critical Theory and Technology,* Johns Hopkins University Press (Baltimore, MD), 1992.

Landow, George, editor, *Hyper/Text/Theory,* Johns Hopkins University Press (Baltimore, MD), 1994.

PERIODICALS

Choice, March, 2001, J. E. Gates, review of *Othermindedness: The Emergence of Network Culture,* p. 1264.

College English, February, 1998, Charles Moran, review of *Of Two Minds: Hypertext, Pedagogy, and Poetics,* p. 202.

Computers and the Humanities, August, 1996, Epen Aarseth, review of *Of Two Minds,* p. 343.

Details, October, 1994, pp. 162-65, 199.

Drama Review, spring, 1993.

Globe and Mail (Toronto, Ontario, Canada), September 5, 1993.

IEEE Transactions on Professional Communication, March, 2000, John Eldard, review of *Page to Screen: Taking Literacy into the Electronic Era,* p. 103.

MacWorld, January, 1991.

Modern Fiction Studies, winter, 1996, James J. Sosnoski, review of *Of Two Minds,* p. 938.

Newsweek, February 27, 1995, p. 71.

New York Times Book Review, June 21, 1992, pp. 1, 23-25; August 29, 1993, Robert Coover, review of *afternoon: a story,* pp. 1, 8-12.

Poets and Writers, March-April, 1994, pp. 20-27.

Publishers Weekly, August 5, 2002, review of *Liam's Going,* p. 52.

Scientific American, October, 1995; January, 1996, N. Katherine Hayles, review of *Of Two Minds,* p. 104.

Spin, July, 1994, p. 79.

Technical Communication, February, 2000, John Eldard, review of *Page to Screen,* p. 103.

Utne Reader, March-April, 1994, pp. 131-132.

Wall Street Journal, August 16, 1994, p. A8.

Washington Post Book World, July 11, 1993.

Whole Earth Review, spring, 1991.

ONLINE

McPherson and Company: Great Books for Great Readers, http://www.mcphersonco.com/ (November 4, 2002), publisher's description of *Liam's Going.*

State University of New York Press Web Site, http://www.sunypress.edu/ (November 4, 2002), interview with Michael Joyce.*

K

KAPLOW, Robert 1954-

PERSONAL: Born May 30, 1954, in NJ; son of Jerome and Doris (Hartman) Kaplow. *Education:* Rutgers University, B.A., 1976.

ADDRESSES: *Agent*—c/o Author Mail, MacAdam/Cage Publishing, 155 Sansome St., Ste. 550, San Francisco, CA 94104-3615.

CAREER: Journalist, educator, and writer.

WRITINGS:

Two in the City, Houghton Mifflin (Boston, MA), 1979.

Alex Icicle: A Romance in Ten Torrid Chapters, Houghton Mifflin (Boston, MA), 1984.

Alessandra in Love, Lippincott (New York, NY), 1989.

Alessandra in Between, HarperCollins (New York, NY), 1992.

Me and Orson Welles, MacAdam/Cage Publishing (San Francisco, CA), 2003.

The Cat Who Killed Lilian Jackson Braun: A Parody, New Millennium Press (Beverly Hills, CA), 2003.

Writer of satirical songs and sketches for National Public Radio's *Morning Edition* (sketches performed as "Moe Moskowitz and the Punsters") and *Fresh Air* (sketches performed as "Basil Starling"), beginning 1984.

SIDELIGHTS: Journalist, teacher, and author Robert Kaplow has distinguished himself with his novels for young adults. His books generally focus on the joy and hardship associated with love. In *Two in the City* a young couple decides to put off college and live together in New York City after they graduate from high school. *Alex Icicle: A Romance in Ten Torrid Chapters,* a story of unrequited love, features an anguished main character who introduces himself as "all the loathsomeness of the human condition distilled into one horrible, malignant growth and fashioned into the fourteen-year-old features of Alexander Preston Sturges Swinburne—boy monster." *Alessandra in Love* concerns a high school girl who, after falling for and dating a musician, finds herself happier when she is away from her ambivalent, aloof beau.

With the 2003 publication of *Me and Orson Welles,* Kaplow presented his first novel written for an adult audience. The story focuses on a New Jersey high school student named Richard Samuels who improbably lands a small role in the Orson Welles Mercury Theater production of *Julius Caesar.* In real life, the New York production propelled Welles to eventual Hollywood fame. In the novel, the young Richard learns a lot about the theater, love, life, and being a man.

Writing in *Publishers Weekly,* a contributor noted that the conceit of Richard's minor role as Lucius in the play "forms a nice counter-point to the coming-of-age material." The reviewer also noted that Kaplow "doesn't quite capture the dark side of the enigmatic Welles" but that the book is "an entertaining offering." A contributor to *Kirkus Reviews* also praised the book, noting, "It's a pity that Kaplow appears to be aiming for the grown-up market in this adult outing, because, as a young adult author, he has crafted one of the best depictions of male adolescent yearning ever to hit the page—though one that few adolescents are likely to read."

Kaplow remained focused on the adult market with his next book, 2003's *The Cat Who Killed Lilian Jackson Braun: A Parody.* The book tells the story of a noted children's book author who, along with his cats, investigates the ghastly murder of Ms. Braun. Her body is found in a bar in Lower Manhattan, but her head is missing. The resulting investigation gives Kaplow plenty of leeway to parody everything from the police who are too busy making reality TV shows to solve the crime to pop culture divas like Britney Spears and Oprah Winfrey.

BIOGRAPHICAL AND CRITICAL SOURCES:

BOOKS

Kaplow, Robert, *Alex Icicle: A Romance in Ten Torrid Chapters,* Houghton Mifflin, 1984.

PERIODICALS

Entertainment Weekly, October 24, 2003, Melissa Rose Bernardo, review of *Me and Orson Welles,* p. 112.

Kirkus Reviews, August 1, 2003, review of *Me and Orson Welles,* p. 980.

Publishers Weekly, September 1, 2003, review of *Me and Orson Welles,* p. 63.

School Library Journal, October 15, 2003, Judith Kicinski, review of *Me and Orson Welles,* p. 98.*

* * *

KAVANAGH, Dan

See BARNES, Julian (Patrick)

* * *

KEATING, Diane (Margaret) 1940-

PERSONAL: Born July 20, 1940 (some sources cite 1943), in Winnipeg, Manitoba, Canada; daughter of Ernest Sidney (a teacher) and Muriel Beatrice (a teacher; maiden name, Dudley) Heys; married Christopher Keating (in business), August 13, 1967; children: Stephanie, Justin. *Education:* University of Manitoba, B.A., c. 1962. *Politics:* None.

ADDRESSES: Home—55 Heath St. W., Toronto, Ontario M4V 1T2, Canada. *Office*—P.O. Box 630, Station Q, Toronto, Ontario, Canada.

CAREER: Freelance travel writer in Rome, Italy, 1962-64; Hudson Bay Co., Montreal, Quebec, Canada, fashion writer, 1965-67; Keating Educational Tours, Toronto, Ontario, Canada, director, 1968-78, and vice president. Poet; gives readings from her works.

MEMBER: League of Canadian Poets.

WRITINGS:

(With husband, Chris Keating) *Montreal,* McGraw/Ryerson (Toronto, Ontario, Canada), 1967.

In Dark Places (poetry), Black Moss Press (Toronto, Ontario, Canada), 1978.

No Birds or Flowers (poetry), Exile Editions (Scarborough, Ontario, Canada), 1982.

The Optic Heart (poetry), illustrated by Ingrid Style, Exile Editions (Scarborough, Ontario, Canada), 1984.

The Salem Diary (novel), c. 1989.

The Salem Letters (novel), Exile Editions (Scarborough, Ontario, Canada), 1992.

The Year One: New and Selected Poems, Exile Editions (Scarborough, Ontario, Canada), 2002.

Contributor to anthologies, including *Lords of Winter and of Love,* edited by Callaghan, Exile Editions (Scarborough, Ontario, Canada), 1983; *Full Moon: An Anthology of Canadian Women Poets,* edited by Cabalte and Luxton, Quadrant Editions (Dunvegan, Ontario, Canada), 1983; *Canadian Poetry Now: Twenty Poets of the Eighties,* edited by Ken Norris, House of Anansi Press (Toronto, Ontario, Canada), 1984; *Canadian Travellers in Italy,* 1989; and *Journey Prize Anthology,* 1989. Contributor of poetry to magazines, including *Antigonish Review, Malahat Review, Northern Lights, Quarry,* and *CV/II.* Founding editor of *Anthol.*

SIDELIGHTS: Diane Keating once commented to *CA:* "The underlying motivation of all my writing is to come to terms with the childhood loss of innocence and with the opposing forces of mind and feeling. I've always been intrigued with words. As a child, rather than count sheep on nights I couldn't sleep, I made up rhyming couplets. After years of producing the glossy language of fashion and travel, I woke up one morning and found myself on the bottom of a black hole—thankfully I hadn't been metamorphosed into Kafka's beetle. When I finally dug my way out, I had completed twelve poems (the spine of my first poetry volume, *In Dark Places*) and knew the truth of Tolkien's words, 'without darkness there can be no light.'"

BIOGRAPHICAL AND CRITICAL SOURCES:

PERIODICALS

Books in Canada, October, 1983; August, 2002, Harold Heft, review of *The Year One: New and Selected Poems,* pp. 29-30

Globe and Mail (Toronto, Ontario, Canada), August 17, 1985.

Quill & Quire, July, 1978.

Toronto Star, May, 1983.*

* * *

KEMPOWSKI, Walter 1929-

PERSONAL: Born April 29, 1929, in Rostock, Germany; son of Karl-Georg (in shipping) and Margarethe (a teacher and homemaker; maiden name, Collasius) Kempowski; married Hildegard Janssen (a teacher), April 20, 1960; children: Karl-Friedrich, Renate. *Ethnicity:* "Norddeutscher." *Education:* Graduated from Padagogische Hochschule (teaching college), Göttingen, West Germany (now Germany), 1960.

ADDRESSES: *Home*—Haus Kreienhoop, 27404 Nartum, Germany; fax: 04288-600. *Agent*—c/o Author Mail, Random House, Neumarkterstraße 17, 81673 Munich, Germany.

CAREER: Teacher and archivist in Nartum, Germany, 1960-80; freelance writer, 1969—. University of Oldenburg, professor of literature and pedagogy, 1980-90. *Military service:* German Army, Luftwaffe, 1945.

MEMBER: PEN International, Freie Akademie Hamburg.

AWARDS, HONORS: Prize for Developing Writers under auspices of Lessing Prize, City of Hamburg, 1971; Prize for Developing Writers under auspices of Gryphius Prize, 1972; Karl Szuka Prize, 1977; Lower Saxony Prize, 1979; Federal Service Cross, First Class, German government, 1979; Bambi Prize, 1980; Jakob Kaiser Prize (with Eberhard Fechner), 1980; Radio Play Prize of the War-Blinded, 1981, for *Moin Vaddr læbt;* Konrad Adenauer Prize, 1994, and Uwe-Johnson-Prize, 1995, both for *Das Echolot: ein kollektives Tagebuch, Januar und Februar 1943;* Großes Bundesverdienst-kreuz du Bundesrepublik Deutschland, 1996; Heimito-von-Dodever Preis, 2000.

WRITINGS:

NOVELS

Tadellöser & Wolff: ein bürgerlicher Roman, C. Hanser (Munich, Germany), 1971.

Uns geht's ja noch gold: Roman einer Familie (title means "We're Still Doing Well"), C. Hanser (Munich, Germany), 1972.

Ein Kapitel für Sich (title means "A Chapter in Itself"), C. Hanser (Munich, Germany), 1975.

Aus grosser Zeit A. Knaus (Munich, Germany), 1978, translation by Leila Vennewitz published as *Days of Greatness,* Knopf (New York, NY), 1981.

Schöne Aussicht (title means "Beautiful View"), A. Knaus (Hamburg, Germany), 1981.

Herzlich willkommen (title means "Hearty Welcome"), A. Knaus (Hamburg, Germany), 1984.

Hundstage, A. Knaus (Munich, Germany), 1988, translation by Norma S., Garold N. Davis, and Alan F. Keele published as *Dog Days,* Camden House (Columbia, SC), 1991.

Mark und Bein: eine Episode, A. Knaus (Munich, Germany), 1992.

Weltschmerz: kinderszenen fast zu ernst, A. Knaus (Munich, Germany), 1995.

Heile Welt, A. Knaus (Munich, Germany), 1998.

Letzte Grüsse, A. Knaus (Munich, Germany), 2003.

OTHER

Im Block: ein Haftbericht (autobiography; title means "In the Block"), Rowohlt (Reinbeck, Germany), 1969.

Der Hahn im Nacken: Mini-Geschichten, Rowohlt (Reinbeck, Germany), 1973.

(Compiler) *Haben Sie Hitler gesehen? Deutsche Antworten,* C. Hanser (Munich, Germany), 1973, translation by Michael Roloff published as *Did You Ever See Hitler? German Answers,* Avon (New York, NY), 1975.

(Compiler) *Immer so durchgemogelt: Erinnerungen an unsere Schulzeit* (nonfiction; title means "Always Tricked My Way Through"), C. Hanser (Munich, Germany), 1974.

Walter Kempowskis Harzreise erläutert (travel; title means "Walter Kempowski's Trip to the Harz Mountains"), C. Hanser (Munich, Germany), 1975.

Alle unter einem Hut: Über 179 Witzige und Amüsante Alltags-Minimini-Geshicten in Großdruckschrift, Loewe Verlag (Bayreuth, Germany), 1976.

Wer will unter die Soldaten?, photographs by Rolf Betyna and Jürgen Stahf, C. Hanser (Munich, Germany), 1976.

Schnoor: Bremen zwischen Stavendamm und Balge, photographs by Hansgerhard Westphal, Schmalfeldt (Bremen, Germany), 1978.

Unser Herr Böckelmann, illustrated by Roswitha Quadflieg, A. Knaus (Hamburg, Germany), 1979.

(Compiler) *Haben Sie davon gewusst? Deutsche Antworten* (nonfiction; title means "Did You Know about It? German Answers"), A. Knaus (Hamburg, Germany), 1979.

(Compiler) *Mein Lesebuch,* Fischer-Taschenbuch-Verlag (Frankfurt, Germany), 1979.

Kempowskis einfache Fibel, Westermann (Brunswick, Germany), 1980.

Beethovens Fünfte und Moin Vaddr læbt (manuscripts and notes for two radio plays), Knaus, 1982.

Herrn Böckelmanns Schoenste Tafelgeschichten nach dem ABC Geordnet, Knaus, 1983.

(With others) *105 Jahre Bertelsmann, 1835-1985: die Geschichte des Verlagsunternehmens in Texten, Bildern, und Dokumenten,* C. Bertelsmann Verlag (Munich, Germany), 1985.

Haumiblau: Kindergeschichten, Bertelsmann (Munich, Germany), 1986.

(Editor) Christian Morgenstern, *Ein Knie geht einsam durch die Welt: mein liebstes Morgenstern-Gedicht,* Piper (Munich, Germany), 1989.

Sirius: eine art Tagebuch, A. Knaus (Munich, Germany), 2nd edition, 1990.

(Compiler) *Das Echolot: ein kollektives Tagebuch, Januar und Februar 1943* (diaries; title means "The Echo-Sounder"), four volumes, A. Knaus (Munich, Germany), 2nd edition, 1993.

(Compiler) *Bloomsday '97,* A. Knaus (Munich, Germany), 1997.

(Compiler) *Das Echolot: fuga furiosa; ein kollektives Tagebuch, Winter 1945,* four volumes, A. Knaus (Munich, Germany), 1999.

(Compiler) *Alkor: Tagebuch 1989,* A. Knaus (Munich, Germany), 2001.

(Compiler) *Das Echolot: Barbarossa '41; ein kollektives Tagebuch,* A. Knaus (Munich, Germany), 2002.

ADAPTATIONS: Many of Kempowski's novels have been adapted for German television and radio.

SIDELIGHTS: German author, playwright, and teacher Walter Kempowski is perhaps best known for his semi-autobiographical novels about a family which bears the same name as his own. Through these novels, he not only discusses things which actually happened to himself and his parents and siblings, but provides a fictional portrait of Germany's history from the turn of the century through its division following World War II. Kempowski did not pen these stories in chronological order; the first in terms of chronological setting was translated as *Days of Greatness* for English-speaking readers in 1981. Kempowski is also notable in his own country for his radio plays. One, titled "Moin Vaddr läbt," uses a made-up language based on Yiddish and garnered him a Radio Play Prize of the War-Blinded. He has won several other German literary awards. One of the author's nonfiction works has also been translated into English; he compiled *Haben Sie Hitler gesehen? Deutsche Antworten,* which became available in the United States as *Did You Ever See Hitler? German Answers* in 1975.

Kempowski was born in the German city of Rostock in 1929, to a family of shipping merchants. He was the youngest child, and his early days were fairly untroubled, except for a struggle against scarlet fever during the year 1940. As Patricia H. Stanley reported in her entry on Kempowski for the *Dictionary of Literary Biography,* he "was not an athletic child" but instead "inherited the parents' artistic interests: he played the piano and the organ, went to concerts with his mother, and read voraciously."

Like many boys of his time and place, Kempowski was a member of the Hitler Youth organization, starting in 1939. In Stanley's words, this meant that "he wore a uniform on required occasions, learned to march, went on camping trips, and spent some vacation time working on a farm." Within the Hitler Youth, Kempowski was valued for his musical talent and often helped provide entertainment at the group's larger events. When Germany became actively engaged in World War II, however, both Kempowski's father and older brother Robert were sent to fight. In early 1945, as war fortunes grew increasingly worse for Germany, the Nazi army drafted Kempowski himself as a courier, though he was not yet sixteen years old. His father died in combat.

For the rest of the Kempowski family, the war ended when the forces of the Soviet Union took Rostock. Walter Kempowski temporarily relocated to the part of Germany occupied by the United States, but only three years later, he returned to Rostock because of homesickness. Not long afterwards, the Kempowski brothers were arrested by the Soviets as spies; not long after that, their mother was also arrested. She spent a little under six years in a women's work camp; Walter and Robert spent eight years in a similar facility for men.

Upon his release, Walter Kempowski determined he would become both a teacher and a writer, and enrolled in a teachers' college in Göttingen. By 1960 he had married a fellow student, Hildegard Janssen, and obtained his first school position. His first book, *Im Block: ein Haftbericht,* was a factual account of his years in the Soviet prison camp, published in 1969. The book did not do well commercially; Stanley explained this phenomenon thus: "That was not . . . a good time to bring out revelations of East German prison life; the public was more interested in the political consequences of the student movement of the past year."

Kempowski's next book, though based on factual events in his family's history, was fictionalized into novel form. *Tadellöser & Wolff: ein bürgerlicher Roman* takes its title from an untranslatable yet joyous exclamation habitual to Kempowski's father, and the story begins in 1939, when Kempowski was ten years old. For the most part, he gives the characters the real names of the family members who inspired them, including himself. The tale stems from the Kempowskis' celebratory move into a larger apartment to the end of World War II when Rostock is invaded by the Soviets. As Stanley explained, "The reader sees a mixture of trivial and significant moments so representative of life in that traumatic wartime period that Germans who read the book recaptured part of their own past." As a result, she continued, "the novel immediately became popular, and in the same year several passages were dramatized for radio."

The fictionalized Kempowski family chronicle continues with *Uns geht's ja noch gold: Roman einer Familie,* which comes from another family colloquialism meaning "we're still doing well." This title is somewhat ironic, because the novel deals with the time between the end of the war and Kempowski's imprisonment, a time in which the family learned of the father's death and in which the mother had to work very hard to ensure the family's survival. Following that was *Ein Kapitel für Sich,* which means "a chapter in itself," the novelization of the life events he had already chronicled in *Im Block.* Of this version, Stanley observed that "Walter's chapters occupy most of the novel and show his development to manhood in the unusual environment of prison. The book is thus a bildungsroman of sorts"; she added, "Even the negative impact of the delicately described homosexual episodes and the periods of solitary confinement contribute to Walter's education."

For the next book in his family saga, Kempowski goes back to what would prove the beginning. In *Aus grosser Zeit,* readers see the upbringing of the parental characters from the other books; the novel opens in the year 1900. "The reader, who has already met the family, will find here the origin of many sayings and incidents alluded to in the other novels," Stanley reported. "He knows already that the grandparents' coldness, rigidity, and even cruelty did not repeat themselves in Karl-Georg and Margarethe's parental roles but produced the opposite effect." Idris Parry, reviewing the English-language version, *Days of Greatness,* in the *Times Literary Supplement,* noted that the author "seems to have deliberately muted the plot in order to emphasize that human destiny is . . . only part of the total scene. His concern is not merely human character but the character of an age, and this he establishes forcefully and convincingly."

Kempowski's novel *Schöne Aussicht* bridges the gap between *Aus grosser Zeit* and *Tadellöser & Wolff.* The "beautiful view" of the title is that of the splendid apartment Karl-Georg decides to rent for his family at the end of the novel—the apartment in which *Tadellöser & Wolff* begins. One of *Schöne Aussicht*'s highlights, according to Stanley, is the section in which the mother and her siblings have a family reunion at the seashore. "Whether or not this episode actually happened, it is charmingly portrayed," she remarked. Kempowski ended his long family saga with *Herzlich willkommen,* which means "hearty welcome." In this volume, his semi-autobiographical protagonist returns to his family after being released from prison, goes to teaching college, and acquires a bride. Wes Blomster, reviewing the saga's end in *World Literature Today,* compared Kempowski to famed German novelist Thomas Mann, and concluded that "the superb quality of Kempowski's writing—and this is perhaps stronger and more touching here than in any of the earlier volumes—is the authenticity of sentiment encountered in it."

Another Kempowski novel, *Hundstage,* unrelated to his family saga, and published in his native land in 1988, was translated into English as *Dog Days* in 1991. In the novel, protagonist Alexander Sovtschick, in his late fifties, is trying to work on his next novel while his wife is away on vacation. The matter is complicated when a mentally retarded girl he has always been kind to is murdered, and he becomes the chief suspect. Critical opinion of the work was somewhat divided; a *Publishers Weekly* reviewer felt that the combination of serious literature with murder mystery did not mix well, and added that "Sovtschick's interminable musings make this lengthy novel . . . a slow read." R. Swenson in *Choice,* however, described it as "a lively, readable story with an unending variety of literary pleasures." Similarly, Wes Blomster in *World Literature Today* declared it an "exceedingly enjoyable and well-written novel. Kempowski's honesty about the nature of human sensuality makes the narrative especially compelling."

Kempowski's efforts in the capacity of editor or compiler are also worthy of attention. In *Haben Sie Hitler gesehen?,* Kempowski collected the anonymous answers and anecdotes of 230 people with whom he talked during his travels throughout Germany. In *Immer so durchgemogelt: Erinnerungen an unsere Schulzeit,* which means "Always Tricked My Way Through," Kempowski records similar recollections from anonymous German interviewees about their primary schooling. A later project, *Das Echolot: ein kollektives Tagebuch, Januar und Februar 1943,* provides readers with letters and diary entries about how the first two months of the year 1943 were perceived by various German participants in World War II. Kempowski's selected sources range from a female inmate of the concentration camp Auschwitz to Nazi leader Adolf Hitler's physician. Denis Stauton gave high praise to *Das Echolot* in the *Observer,* concluding that "in bringing together all these memories Kempowski has undoubtedly created an important work of art but, more significantly, he has produced a profound and moving monument to national shame, spoken by the individual, authentic voices of the German nation."

Kempowski has continued his work with additional publications related to *Das Echelot.*

BIOGRAPHICAL AND CRITICAL SOURCES:

BOOKS

Dictionary of Literary Biography, Volume 75: *Contemporary German Fiction Writers, Second Series,* Thomson Gale (Detroit, MI), 1988.

Hacken, Richard, and Bernd Hagenau, compilers, *Walter Kempowski zum sechzigsten Geburtstag,* A. Knaus (Munich, Germany), 1989.

PERIODICALS

Choice, March, 1992, R. Swenson, review of *Dog Days,* p. 1083.

Journal of European Studies, March, 2002, Richard Aston, "Amnesia and Anamnesis in the Works of Walter Kempowski: Language, History, and Evasion of Guilt," p. 27.

New York Times Book Review, August 25, 1991, p. 14.

Observer, January 16, 1994, Denis Stauton, review of *Das Echolot: ein kollektives Tagebuch, Januar und Februar 1943.*

Publishers Weekly, April 5, 1991, review of *Dog Days,* p. 136.

Times Literary Supplement, January 22, 1982, Idris Parry, review of *Days of Greatness,* p. 76.

World Literature Today, spring, 1985, Wes Blomster, review of *Herzlich willkommen,* p. 262; autumn, 1989, pp. 671-672; summer, 1991, Wes Blomster, review of *Dog Days,* p. 484; autumn, 1992, pp. 710-711.

KIPFER, Barbara Ann 1954-

PERSONAL: Born August 25, 1954, in La Porte, IN; daughter of Albert V. (a certified public accountant) and Dorothy Hinton; married Paul Magoulas (an editor); children: Kyle B. Kipfer. *Ethnicity:* "Caucasian." *Education:* Valparaiso University, B.S., 1978; University of Exeter, M.Phil., 1985, Ph.D. (linguistics) 1989; Greenwich University, Ph.D. (archaeology), 1998, M.A. (Buddhist studies), 2002. *Politics:* Democrat. *Religion:* Methodist.

ADDRESSES: *Home*—Milford, CT. *Agent*—c/o Author Mail, Workman Publishing Co., 708 Broadway, New York, NY 10003-9555. *E-mail*—bkipfer@earthlink.net.

CAREER: *Vidette-Messenger,* Valparaiso, IN, sports editor, 1976-79; *Gary Post-Tribune,* Gary, IN, news correspondent, 1979; *Chicago Tribune,* Chicago, IL, sports scoreboard editor, 1979; City of Valparaiso, assistant to the mayor, 1979-81; University of Houston, Houston, TX, director of word processing center, 1981-82; Laurence Urdang, Inc., assistant to the publisher, 1982; Yale University, New Haven, CT, editor of newsletter for school of organization and management, 1982-83; Wang Electronic Publishing, New York, NY, lexicographer, 1984-85; International Business Machines Corp., T. J. Watson Research Center, Yorktown Heights, NY, lexicographer for lexical systems group, 1984-85; Bellcore, Morristown, NJ, lexicographer in artificial intelligence and information science research, 1988; General Electric Corporate Research, Schenectady, NY, lexicographer for artificial intelligence program, 1988-90; Philip Lief Group, New York, NY, lexicographer and senior editor, beginning 1990; independent lexicographer and part-time archaeologist. Ameritech Publishing, lexicographer, 1989. Member of Connecticut State House of Representatives, 1988; candidate for Connecticut State Senate, 1990; member of Milford Democratic Town Committee; member of Milford Pension and Retirement Board, 1987—.

MEMBER: European Association for Lexicography, Dictionary Society of North America, Association of Computational Linguistics, Milford Tennis Association, Milford Tennis Club, Milford Yacht Club.

WRITINGS:

EDITOR

Workbook on Lexicography: A Course for Dictionary Users, University of Exeter Press (Exeter, England), 1984.

14,000 Things to Be Happy About, Workman Publishing (New York, NY), 1990.

Roget's Twenty-first Century Thesaurus in Dictionary Form: The Essential Reference for Home, School, or Office, Dell (New York, NY), 1992.

Random House Kid's Encyclopedia, Knowledge Adventure (La Crescenta, CA), 1993.

Twenty-first Manual of Style, Laurel (New York, NY), 1993.

Twenty-first Spelling Dictionary, Dell (New York, NY), 1993.

Twenty-first Synonym and Antonym Finder, Dell (New York, NY), 1993.

Sisson's Word and Expression Locater, Prentice-Hall (Tappan, NJ), 1994.

Bartlett's Book of Business Quotations, Little, Brown (Boston, MA), 1994.

Bartlett's Book of Love Quotations, Little, Brown (Boston, MA), 1994.

1,400 Things for Kids to Be Happy About: The Happy Book, Workman (New York, NY), 1994.

(With Robert L. Chapman) *Dictionary of American Slang,* HarperCollins (New York), 1995, 3rd edition, 1998.

(With Charles Preston and Paul Magoulas) *The USA Today Crossword Puzzle Dictionary,* Hyperion (New York, NY), 1995.

(With Ed Strnad) *The Optimist's/Pessimist's Guide to the Millennium,* Berkley Publishing (New York, NY), 1996.

Webster's Twenty-first Century Large Print Dictionary, Delta (New York, NY), 1996.

The Order of Things: How Everything in the World Is Organized into Hierarchies, Structures, and Pecking Orders, Random House (New York, NY), 1997.

The Wish List, Workman Publishing (New York, NY), 1997.

Encyclopedic Dictionary of Archaeology, Kluwer Academic (New York, NY), 2000.

5,001 Things for Kids to Do, Plume (New York, NY), 2000.

The World of Order and Organization: How Things Are Arranged into Hierarchies, Structures, and Pecking Orders, Gramercy Books (New York, NY), 2000.

The Writer's Digest Flip Dictionary, Writer's Digest (Cincinnati, OH), 2000.

Something to Talk About (e-book), iUniverse.com (Lincoln, NE), 2000.

8,789 Words of Wisdom, Workman Publishing (New York, NY), 2001.

Roget's Thesaurus of Phrases, Writer's Digest Books (Cincinnati, OH), 2001.

Roget's International Thesaurus, 6th edition, HarperCollins (New York, NY), 2001.

Roget's Descriptive Word Finder: A Dictionary/Thesaurus of Adjectives and Adverbs, Writer's Digest Books (Cincinnati, OH), 2003.

Karma, Dharma, Yoga, Tao, Workman Publishing (New York, NY), 2003.

Creator and editor of "The Best of 14,000 Things to Be Happy About Page-a-Day Calendars," Workman Publishing (New York, NY), beginning 1995.

Contributor to books, including *The Dictionary and the Language Learner,* edited by Anthony Cowie, Max Niemeyer Verlag (Tübingen, Germany), 1987. Contributor to periodicals, including *Dictionaries: Journal of the Dictionary Society of North America.*

Kipfer's book *14,000 Things to Be Happy About* was been published in Bulgarian, Danish, Dutch, Finnish, German, Hebrew, Japanese, Korean, Norwegian, and Swedish. *The Wish List* has been published in Japanese.

BIOGRAPHICAL AND CRITICAL SOURCES:

PERIODICALS

American Antiquity, April, 2001, Mark Blackham, review of *Encyclopedic Dictionary of Archaeology,* p. 378.

Antiquity, September, 2000, N. James and Simon Stoddart, review of *Encyclopedic Dictionary of Archaeology,* p. 772.

Booklist, June 1, 2001, Donald Altschiller, review of *The World of Order and Organization: How Things Are Arranged into Hierarchies, Structures, and Pecking Orders,* p. 1920.

Library Journal, April 1, 1997, Debra Moore, review of *The Order of Things: How Everything in the World Is Organized into Hierarchies, Structures, and Pecking Orders,* p. 84; June 1, 2003, Marianne Orme, review of *Roget's Descriptive Word Finder: A Dictionary/Thesaurus of Adjectives and Adverbs,* p. 106.*

KIVY, Peter Nathan 1934-

PERSONAL: Born October 22, 1934, in New York, NY. *Education:* University of Michigan, A.B., 1956, M.A., 1958; Yale University, M.A., 1960; Columbia University, Ph.D., 1966.

ADDRESSES: *Office*—Department of Philosophy, Rutgers University, New Brunswick, NJ 08903. *E-mail*—kivy@philosophy.rutgers.edu.

CAREER: Rutgers University, New Brunswick, NJ, assistant professor, 1967-70, associate professor, 1970-76, professor of philosophy, 1976—.

MEMBER: American Society of Aesthetics, American Musicological Society, American Philosophical Association.

AWARDS, HONORS: Deems Taylor Award, ASCAP, 1980.

WRITINGS:

Speaking of Art, Nijhoff (Zoetermeer, Netherlands), 1973.

(Editor and author of introduction and notes) *Thomas Reid's Lectures on the Fine Arts,* Nijhoff (Zoetermeer, Netherlands), 1973.

The Seventh Sense: A Study of Francis Hutchinson's Aesthetics and Its Influence in Eighteenth-Century Britain, B. Franklin (New York, NY), 1976.

The Corded Shell: Reflections on Musical Expression, Princeton University Press (Princeton, NJ), 1980.

Sound and Semblance: Reflections on Musical Representation, Princeton University Press (Princeton, NJ), 1984.

Osmin's Rage: Philosophical Reflections on Opera, Drama, and Text, Princeton University Press (Princeton, NJ), 1988.

Sound Sentiment: An Essay on the Musical Emotions, including the Complete Text of "The Corded Shell," Temple University Press (Philadelphia, PA), 1989.

Music Alone: Philosophical Reflections on the Purely Musical Experience, Cornell University Press (Ithaca, NY), 1990.

(Editor) *Essays on the History of Aesthetics,* University of Rochester Press (Rochester, NY), 1992.

The Fine Art of Repetition: Essays in the Philosophy of Music, Cambridge University Press (New York, NY), 1993.

Authenticities: Philosophical Reflections on Musical Performance, Cornell University Press (Ithaca, NY), 1995.

Philosophies of Arts: An Essay in Differences, Cambridge University Press (New York, NY), 1997.

The Possessor and the Possessed: Handel, Mozart, Beethoven, and the Idea of Musical Genius, Yale University Press (New Haven, CT), 2001.

New Essays on Musical Understanding, Oxford University Press (Clarendon, England), 2001.

Introduction to the Philosophy of Music, Oxford University Press (New York, NY), 2002.

The Blackwell Guide to Aesthetics, Blackwell (London, England), 2004.

Contributor to philosophy journals.

SIDELIGHTS: Peter Nathan Kivy has been praised by critics in the fields of music history and aesthetics for rejuvenating the discipline of music aesthetics. The philosophy of music has flourished in the last thirty years, with great advances made in the understanding of the nature of music and its aesthetics. Kivy's specialty is musical philosophy and eighteenth-century aesthetic theory.

Kivy has been at the center of this flourishing; his essays show how he sees the most important and interesting philosophical issues relating to music. Essentially Kivy addresses the question of what makes a musical work profound and what really makes music attractive and rewarding to the listener.

Kivy often writes on the place of music in a liberal education or arcane academic inquiries. According to the Cambridge University Press Web site, "His essay subjects range from the biological origin of music to the very nature of music itself. Kivy uses no musical notation, so no technical knowledge is required to appreciate his work."

On the Rutgers University Philosophy Department Web site Kivy said, "My field of specialization is aesthetics and the philosophy of art. My early work in this area was centered on eighteenth-century British aesthetics. . . . In the late seventies, I turned my hand, as a kind of interlude between projects, to the philosophical problem of the emotions in music. The philosophy of music became, from that time onwards, my principal interest, although I still work in the eighteenth century, and in contemporary Analytic Aesthetics as well.

"In my most recent book, *Philosophies of Arts,* I have departed somewhat from the musical problems, and tried to deal with issues centering on how the various arts differ. This has led me to become deeply interested in the philosophy of literature, which is currently occupying about half of my research time."

Douglas Dempster, writing on the Kivy essay collection *The Fine Art of Repetition: Essays in the Philosophy of Music,* summarized Kivy's understanding of the philosophical value of music. "The most vexing problem for Kivy, one which he addresses in both the opening and closing essays of *The Fine Art of Repetition,* and which absorbed his entire earlier book, *Music Alone*—is explaining the value, indeed, what is sometimes the 'exalted' and *profound* value, of an inherently meaningless decorative art form."

Kivy's 2001 book, *The Possessor and the Possessed: Handel, Mozart, Beethoven, and the Idea of Musical Genius,* explores the concept of musical genius; the idea that some artists have something that others don't. Kivy observes that two theories have emerged from antiquity to explain the concept of genius to us lesser mortals. The first, dating back to Plato, has it that the genius is possessed by some outside, godlike force that visits and flows through the artist at the moment called inspiration. The second, attributed to Longinus, a third-century critical theorist, sees the genius himself possessing a gift of godlike powers. Kivy takes for his examples the work of Handel, Mozart, and Beethoven. The Yale University Press Web site noted, "He explores why this pendulum swing from the concept of the possessor to the concept of the possessed has occurred and how the concepts were given philosophical reformulations as views toward Handel, Mozart, and Beethoven as geniuses changed in the eighteenth, nineteenth, and twentieth centuries."

The author commented in *Focus* magazine: "What separates the average music lover or amateur musician from Mozart or Beethoven is not the gulf between

God and Man, angel and ape. We are all of the same substance as they. And by small increments, you get from me to Mozart. We are separated by degree, not kind. But, of course, in practice, no person can become a Mozart: one can only be born one."

BIOGRAPHICAL AND CRITICAL SOURCES:

BOOKS

Directory of American Scholars, 10th edition, Thomson Gale (Detroit, MI), 2002.

Kivy, Peter, *The Possessor and the Possessed: Handel, Mozart, Beethoven, and the Idea of Musical Genius,* Yale University Press (New Haven, CT), 2001.

Kuhn, Laura, editor, *Baker's Biographical Dictionary of Musicians,* 9th edition, Schirmer Music (New York, NY), 2001.

Kuhn, Laura, editor, *Baker's Dictionary of Opera,* Schirmer Music (New York, NY), 2001.

PERIODICALS

Antioch Review, winter, 1991, review of *Music Alone: Philosophical Reflections on the Purely Musical Experience,* p. 152.

Booklist, April 1, 1990, review of *Music Alone,* p. 1517; October 1, 2001, Alan Hirsch, review of *The Possessor and the Possessed,* p. 291.

British Journal of Aesthetics, April, 1991, Malcolm Budd, review of *Sound Sentiment: An Essay on the Musical Emotions, including the Complete Text of "The Corded Shell,",* p. 190; July, 1991, R. A. Sharpe, review of *Music Alone,* p. 276; April, 1995, R. A. Sharpe, *The Fine Art of Repetition: Essays in the Philosophy of Music,* p. 194; July, 1996, Max Paddison, review of *Authenticities: Philosophical Reflections on Musical Performance,* p. 330.

Canadian Philosophical Review, January, 1990, review of *Osmin's Rage,* p. 31; September, 1990, review of *Music Alone,* p. 368; June, 1994, review of *The Fine Art of Repetition: Essays in the Philosophy of Music,* p. 175; spring, 1997, Paul Dumouchel, review of *The Fine Art of Repetition,* p. 416.

Choice, April, 1985, *Sound and Semblance: Reflections on Musical Representation,* p. 1174; September, 1989, review of *Osmin's Rage,* p. 141; October, 1990, review of *Music Alone,* p. 320; January, 1994, R. Stahura, review of *The Fine Art of Repetition,* p. 796; November, 1995, B. J. Murphy, review of *Authenticities,* 475; February, 1998, M. C. Rose, review of *Philosophies of Arts: An Essay in Differences,* p. 1002; September, 2002, R. Stahura, review of *New Essays on Musical Understanding,* p. 110.

Cresset, April 1989, review of *Osmin's Rage,* p. 22.

Journal of Aesthetic Education, winter, 1982, review of *Sound Sentiment,* p. 105.

Journal of Aesthetics and Art Criticism, summer, 1985, *Sound and Semblance,* p. 405; spring, 1987, review of *Sound and Semblance,* p. 113; spring, 1990, Robert Stecker and Gary Fuller, review of *Osmin's Rage,* p. 165; winter, 1991, Stephen Davies, review of *Sound Sentiment,* p. 48; spring, 1991, review of *Osmin's Rage,* p. 123; summer, 1991, Colin Radford, review of *Sound Sentiment,* p. 83; fall, 1991, Douglas Dempster, review of *Music Alone,* p. 381; summer, 1994, Mary Sirridge, *Essays on the History of Aesthetics,* p. 369; fall, 1994, Kathleen Marie Higgins, review of *The Fine Art of Repetition,* p. 472; spring, 1996, James O. Young, review of *Authenticities,* 198; fall, 1999, Robert Stecker, review of *Philosophies of Arts,* p. 476.

Journal of the American Musicological Society, summer, 2000, John Butt, *Authenticities,* p. 402.

Journal of the History of Ideas, summer, 2000, review of *The Fine Art of Repetition,* p. 702.

Journals of Aesthetics, winter, 1977; spring, 1991.

Mind, October, 2000, John E. Mackinnon, *Authenticities,* p. 949; April 1993, Christine Tappolet, review of *Music Alone,* p. 377.

Music & Letters, May, 1990, Tim Carter, review of *Osmin's Rage,* p. 246; May, 1991, J. O. Urmson, review of *Music Alone,* p. 273; August, 1994, Nicholas Cook, *The Fine Art of Repetition,* p. 453; February, 1997, Jonathan Dunsby, review of *Authenticities,* p. 132.

Musical Quarterly, April, 1982, review of *Sound Sentiment,* p. 287.

Musical Times, winter, 2001, Michael Fuller, review of *The Possessor and the Possessed,* p. 66.

Music Educators Journal, March, 1993, review of *Music Alone,* p. 12.

New York Times, January 5, 2002, Edward Rothstein, *The Possessor and the Possessed,* p. B11.

Nineteenth Century Music, summer, 1990, Ellen Rosand, review of *Osmin's Rage,* p. 75.

Notes, summer, 1988, *Sound and Semblance,* p. 65; December, 1989, Linda L. Tyler, review of *Osmin's*

Rage, p. 385; December, 1991, Naomi Cumming, review of *Music Alone,* p. 450; June, 1996, Rennee Cox Lorraine, review of *Authenticities,* 1151.

Opera Quarterly, summer, 1989, William R. Wians, review of *Osmin's Rage,* p. 95.

Philosophical Quarterly, October, 1994, Roger Scruton, *The Fine Art of Repetition,* p. 503; April, 1997, Stephen Davies, review of *Authenticities,* p. 238.

Philosophical Review, April, 1986, *Sound and Semblance,* p. 284; October, 1997, Gunter Zoller, review of *Authenticities,* p. 638; January, 2000, Jennifer Robinson, *Philosophies of Arts,* p. 138.

Philosophy in Review, June, 1998, review of *Philosophies of Arts,* p. 188.

Review of Metaphysics, December, 1998, Albert E. Gunn, review of *Philosophies of Arts,* p. 460.

San Francisco Review of Books, Volume 1, 1990, review of *Music Alone,* p. 35.

Sewanee Review, spring, 1992, Robert Miles, review of *Music Alone,* p. 43.

Times Literary Supplement, February 26, 1989, Roger Scruton, review of *Authenticities,* p. 20; June 16, 1989, Richard Osborne, review of *Osmin's Rage,* p. 667; December 24, 1990, review of *Music Alone,* p. 1403; December 28, 1990, Sebastian Gardner, review of *Sound Sentiment,* and *Music Alone,* p. 1103; May 8, 1998, Michael Tanner, review of *Philosophies of Arts,* p. 19; November 23, 2001, Malcolm Budd, review of *The Possessor and the Possessed,* p. 12.

University Press Book News, September, 1992, *Essays on the History of Aesthetics,* p. 4.

Wall Street Journal, January 17, 2002, Mitchell Cohen, review of *The Possessor and the Possessed,* p. A12.

ONLINE

Cambridge University Press, http://uk.cambridge.org/, (October 20, 2002), article on *The Fine Art of Repetition.*

Focus, http://ur.rutgers.edu/focus/ (October 20, 2001), Douglas Frank, article on Peter Kivy.

Music Theory Online, http://www.smt.ucsb.edu/ (May 10, 2002), Douglas Dempster, review of *The Fine Art of Repetition.*

Yale University Press, http://www.yale.edu/ (October 20, 2002), article on *The Possessor and the Possessed.**

KLINE, Peter 1936-

PERSONAL: Born February 7, 1936, in Madison, WI; son of O. L. (in nutritional research) and Susan (White) Kline; married Barbara Knopf (a church organist and choir director), August 30, 1958 (divorced); married Nancy Meadows (a teacher and author), June 27, 1972; children: (first marriage) Stephanie Lynn, Maureen Susan, Wendy Anne. *Education:* Amherst College, B.A., 1957; Catholic University of America, M.A., 1960.

ADDRESSES: Home—19109 Johnson Rd., South Bend, IN 46614.

CAREER: Maret School, Washington, DC, teacher and head of English department, 1958-65; Dunbarton College, Washington, DC, instructor in speech and drama, 1960-65; Valerie Warde Drama School, Washington, DC, director, 1963-65; Sandy Spring Friends School, Sandy Spring, MD, teacher and head of English department, 1965-70; Sidwell Friends School, Washington, DC, English teacher, 1970-72; Maret School, teacher and coordinator, 1972-73; Interlocking Curriculum School, cofounder, codirector, and teacher, 1973-83; public speaker and consultant, 1983-90; Integra Learning Systems, South Bend, IN, founder and board chair, 1990—. Lyric Theater Company, founder and director, 1951-65.

WRITINGS:

The Theatre Student: Scenes to Perform, Richards Rosen Press (New York, NY), 1969.

The Theatre Student: Playwriting, Richards Rosen Press (New York, NY), 1970.

(With Nancy Meadors) *The Theatre Student: Physical Movement for the Theatre,* Richards Rosen Press (New York, NY), 1971.

The Theatre Student: Gilbert and Sullivan Production, Richards Rosen Press (New York, NY), 1972.

The Theatre Student: The Actor's Voice, Richards Rosen Press (New York, NY), 1972.

Enjoying the Arts: Opera, Richards Rosen Press (New York, NY), 1977.

Diary of a Play Production: An Account of a High School Production of "Romeo and Juliet," Richards Rosen Press (New York, NY), 1980.

The Everyday Genius: Restoring Children's Natural Joy of Learning, and Yours Too, Great Ocean Publishers (Arlington, VA), 1988.

(With Laurence D. Martel) *School Success: The Inside Story,* Learning Matters (Arlington, VA), 1992.

(With Bernard Saunders) *Ten Steps to a Learning Organization,* Great Ocean Publishers (Arlington, VA), 1993, 2nd edition, 1998.

(With Syril Kline) *The Butterfly Dreams,* Great Ocean Publishers (Arlington, VA), 1998.

(With Hal Isen) *The Genesis Principle: A Journey into the Source of Creativity and Leadership,* Great Ocean Publishers (Arlington, VA), 1999.

Why America's Children Can't Think: Creating Independent Minds for the 21st Century, Inner Ocean (Makawao, Maui, HI), 2002.

SIDELIGHTS: Peter Kline once told *CA:* "I feel two basic needs as a writer. One is to educate: to provide new information about how to do something or how to enjoy something. I am deeply involved professionally in developing new teaching methods and approaches to education, and in the future my books will reflect more and more of these. I am also concerned more widely with our society's failure to make effective use of its human resources and its knowledge. For example, my wife's recovery from terminal cancer by unorthodox means will be the subject for a future book.

"The second is to explore: through fiction, drama, and philosophy to probe the nature and depths of the human spirit. . . . Since my early writing was simplistic and lacking in emotional depth I sought self exploration through optometric training, re-evaluation counseling and mind control."

BIOGRAPHICAL AND CRITICAL SOURCES:

PERIODICALS

Booklist, August, 2002, Vanessa Bush, review of *Why America's Children Can't Think: Creating Independent Minds for the 21st Century,* p. 1904.

Curriculum Review, October, 1978, review of *Enjoying the Arts: Opera,* p. 296.

Educational Leadership, October, 1989, review of *The Everyday Genius: Restoring Children's Natural Joy of Learning, and Yours Too,* p. 91.

ONLINE

Inner Ocean Publishing Web Site, http://www.innerocean.com/ (November 21, 2002), publisher's description of *Why America's Children Can't Think.**

* * *

KONDOLEON, Harry 1955-1994

PERSONAL: Born February 26, 1955, in New York, NY; died of AIDS, March 16, 1994, in New York, NY; son of Sophocles (a public accountant) and Athena (a secretary; maiden name, Cola) Kondoleon. *Education:* Hamilton College, B.A., 1977; Yale University, M.F.A., 1981.

CAREER: Actors Studio, New York, NY, member of playwrights and directors unit, 1978-80; Manhattan Theatre Club, New York, NY, member of playwrights unit, 1982—; New School for Social Research, New York, NY, playwriting instructor, 1983-84; Columbia University, New York, NY, playwriting instructor, 1985-87.

AWARDS, HONORS: Wallace Bradley Playwriting Prize, Hamilton College, 1974, 1975, 1976, 1977; International Institute of Education fellowship, 1977; Kazan Award from Yale Drama School, 1979 and 1980, for best original script; Oppenheimer Award for "best new American playwright" from *Newsday,* 1983; Obie Award for "most promising young playwright" from *Village Voice,* 1983; New York Foundation for the Arts grant, 1984; National Endowment for the Arts grant, 1985.

WRITINGS:

PLAYS

The Cote d'Azur Triangle (one-act), first produced in New York City at Actors Studio, May, 1980.

The Brides (one-act; first produced in Stockbridge, MA, at Lenox Arts Center, July, 1980; produced Off-Off Broadway at Cubiculo Theatre, May,

1981), published in *Wordplays 2,* edited by Bonnie Marranca and Gautam Dasgupta, Performing Arts Journal, 1982.

Rococo (two-act), first produced in New Haven, CT, at Yale Repertory Theatre, January, 1981.

Andrea Rescued (one-act), first produced in New York, NY, at Double Image Theatre, June, 1982.

The Fairy Garden (one-act), first produced in New York, NY, at Double Image Theatre, June, 1982.

Self-Torture and Strenuous Exercise (one-act), first produced in New York, NY, at Double Image Theatre, June, 1982.

Clara Toil (teleplay), first produced in Waterford, CT, at Eugene O'Neill Playwriting Conference, July, 1982.

Slacks and Tops (one-act; first produced in New York, NY, at Manhattan Theatre Club, March, 1983), Dramatists Play Service (New York, NY), 1983.

Christmas on Mars (two-act; first produced Off-Broadway at Playwrights Horizons, June, 1983), Dramatists Play Service (New York, NY), 1983.

The Vampires (two-act), first produced in Seattle, WA, at Empty Space Theatre, January, 1984, Dramatists Play Service (New York, NY), 1984.

Linda Her (one-act; first produced Off-Broadway at Second Stage, May, 1984), published as *Linda Her, and The Fairy Garden: Two Short Plays,* Dramatists Play Service (New York, NY), 1985.

Anteroom: A Play in Two Acts, Dramatists Play Service (New York, NY), 1986.

Andrea Rescued: An Act of Faith, Caliban Press (Montclair, NJ), 1987.

Zero Positive, Dramatists Play Service (New York, NY), 1989.

Love Diatribe, Dramatists Play Service (New York, NY), 1991.

Self Torture and Strenuous Exercise: Selected Plays, Theatre Communications Group (New York, NY), 1991.

The Houseguests, Dramatists Play Service (New York, NY), 1993.

The Little Book of Professor Enigma, first produced in New York, NY, at Theater for the New City, 1995.

Play Yourself, produced in New York, NY, at Century Center for the Performing Arts,2002.

*Saved or Destroyed,*Dramatists Play Service (New York, NY)2002

OTHER

The Death of Understanding: Love Poems, Caliban (Montclair, NJ), 1987.

The Whore of Tjampuan: A Novel, PAJ Publications (New York, NY), 1988.

Diary of a Lost Boy: A Novel, Knopf (New York, NY), 1994.

SIDELIGHTS: Harry Kondoleon's first plays were offbeat poetic comedies wrought with dark humor. A reviewer in the *Village Voice* said Kondoleon's writing "couldn't be less fashionable or commercial." Kondoleon thrust his flawed characters into desperate situations that made them grapple with intense emotions. *Library Journal* reviewer Rebecca S. Kelm observed that Kondoleon's "humor may be black and the situations often absurd, but the result is perceptive and poignant." Kondoleon's writing became even darker when he contracted AIDS. After this, he created characters who also suffered from the disease, which consumed them both physically and emotionally.

Kondoleon first gained recognition with the production of "Self-Torture and Strenuous Exercise," published in *Best Short Plays, 1984.* "Self-Torture" centers around two couples' struggles with infidelity, loneliness, and desire.

Writing in the *New York Times,* Frank Rich termed Harry Kondoleon's play *Slacks and Tops* "an absurdist nightmare" and declared that its "caustic, surreal humor and bizarre vision are original and special." The one-act comedy, set in a motel room near Kennedy International Airport, revolves around the insane antics of an "all-American family determined to uproot to Africa," according to Rich. The critic concluded that Kondoleon's "strong, fresh voice" is witnessed "to exceptional advantage" in the play.

In *The Houseguests,* relationships are defined as two couples swap mates and then must come to grips with financial devastation. *Back Stage* reviewer Martin Schaeffer described *The Houseguests* as "witty, crisp, and rich in a sort of black philosophical humor." Many of Kondoleon's other plays follow suit. In *Love Diatribe* a grown man and daughter return home to live with their parents after failed personal relationships. *Love Diatribe* is one of the first works in which Kondoleon brings AIDS into the picture. Eva Resnikova wrote in the *National Review:* "*Love Diatribe* ostensibly deals with heterosexual relationships, but homosexuality and AIDS are constant presences, both through a neighbor whose son was an early victim of the disease and who remains convinced that his son would not have died had the neighborhood children treated him more kindly, and metaphorically, through the 'diatribe' of the title, a heated call for love in the face of death."

From here on, most of Kondoleon's writing focuses on characters inflicted with the AIDS. In *Play Yourself* a character's friend dies of the disease. Some critics felt that the integration of AIDS into this play was awkward and contrived. The main characters Jean and Yvonne spend a great deal of time awaiting letters from their friend Bobby, who is on tour in Europe with his wealthy lover. *Variety* reviewer Charles Isherwood considered "the reading of these missives" to be "one of play's weaker dramatic devices and . . . an awkward way of drawing in the specter of AIDS." Isherwood concluded that *Play Yourself* "is a less cohesive piece of writing" than some of Kondoleon's other works.

The Little Book of Professor Enigma and *Saved or Destroyed* are Kondoleon's last plays. The characters in *The Little Book* take part in a game in which they fill in pages of an empty book with fantasies that they imagine heir friends have had. Instead of reading the fantasies aloud, however, the characters act them out. *Back Stage*'s Dan Isaac described the play as "haunting and bizarre," but remarked that it "serves to blur the difference between fantasy and reality for the audience." In "Saved or Destroyed" a group of actors rehearses a family play that focuses on an unborn child. *Back Stage*'s Karl Levitt considered the play a paradox, "entertaining yet intellectually challenging, wispily ethereal yet theatrically satisfying."

Kondoleon published his debut novel, *The Whore of Tjampuan,* in 1988, about a young man who leaves his job in an art gallery and flies to Tjampuan, Bali, where he meets and falls in love with an eccentric young woman. Kondoleon's second novel, *Diary of a Lost Boy,* garnered more critical acclaim. *Diary* tells the story of Hector Diaz, an AIDS victim obsessed with his approaching death. Hector's doctor tells him that he has, at best, two more years to live. To detach himself from his own crumbling world, Hector focuses his energy on his best friend Susan's failing marriage with her philandering husband and immerses himself in the works of medieval German Meister Eckhart. A *Publishers Weekly* reviewer concluded that Hector "faces his situation with a mixture of black humor, despair, and philosophical detachment." The same reviewer praised Kondoleon's characterization in *Diary* by adding that he "paints a wryly comic, if familiar, portrait of trendy Manhattan types, straight and gay, with the compulsive sex lives, therapists and self-important careerism." Remarked Kelm: "This is not a perfect novel, but its messages are served up with great wit and powerful observation, both of New York City and of the human condition."

BIOGRAPHICAL AND CRITICAL SOURCES:

BOOKS

Contemporary Dramatists, 5th edition, St. Martin's Press (New York, NY), 1973.

Osborn, Elizabeth, M., editor, *The Way We Love Now: American Plays and the AIDS Crisis,* Theatre Communications Group (New York, NY), 1990.

PERIODICALS

American Theater, July-August, 1994, Robert Brustein, "Harry Kondoleon: 1955-1994," p. 53.

Back Stage, June 4, 1993, Martin Schaeffer, review of *The Houseguests,* p. 44; January 6, 1995, Dan Isaac, review of *The Little Book of Professor Enigma,* p. 40; December 1, 2000, Karl Levett, review of *Saved or Destroyed,* p. 56.

Daily Variety, July 11, 2002, Charles Isherwood, review of *Play Yourself,* p. 8.

Drama-Logue, November 24-30, 1983.

Hollywood Reporter, November 17, 1983.

Kirkus Reviews, December 1, 1993, review of *Diary of a Lost Boy* p. 1481; April 15, 1988, review of *The Whore of Tjampuan,* p. 562.

Lambda Book Report, March, 1994, review of *Diary of a Lost Boy,* p. 162.

Library Journal, January, 1994, review of *Diary of a Lost Boy,* p. 15.

National Review, March 18, 1991, Eva Resnikova, review of *Love Diatribe,* pp. 65-66.

Newsday, October 12, 1983.

New York Times, January 12, 1994, review of *Diary of a Lost Boy,* January 12, 1994; March 30, 1983; October, 22, 1995, *Diary of a Lost Boy,* p. 44.

New York Times Book Review, November 6, 1988, review of *The Whore of Tjampuan,* p. 22.

Parnassus, January, 1995, review of *Diary of a Lost Boy,* p. 197.
Publishers Weekly, November 22, 1993, review of *Diary of a Lost Boy,* p. 50.
Variety, July 15, 2002, Charles Isherwood, review of *Play Yourself,* pp. 31-32.
Village Voice, June 8, 1982.
Wall Street Journal, March 7, 1994, review of *Diary of a Lost Boy,* p. 15.

ONLINE

Don Shewey Web site, http://www.donshewey.com/ (October 23, 2003,) Don Shewey, "Harry Kondoleon's Ferocious Fairy Tales."
NYTheatre.com, http://www.nytheatre.com/ (July 8, 2002), Martin Denton, review of *Play Yourself.*
Shotgun Players Web site, http://www.shotgunplayers.org/ (July 21, 1999).
Theatre Zone Web site, http://www.theatrezone.org/ (November 7, 2002), review of *Self-Torture and Strenuous Exercise.*

OBITUARIES:

PERIODICALS

Chicago Tribune, March 20, 1994, p. 6.
New York Times, March 17, 1994, p. D21.
Washington Post, March 21, 1994, p. D5.*

* * *

KORT, Carol 1945-

PERSONAL: Born July 25, 1945, in Jersey City, NJ; daughter of Jack and Florence (Tunkel) Chvat; married Michael Kort (a professor), August 30, 1968; children: Eleza Natasha. *Education:* Attended Washington University, St. Louis, 1963-65, and Sorbonne, University of Paris, 1965-66; New York University, B.A., 1968. *Politics:* Liberal. *Religion:* Jewish.

ADDRESSES: Home—20 Abbottsford Rd., Brookline, MA 02146. *Office*—Graduate School of Design, Harvard University, Cambridge, MA 02138. *Agent*—Stephen Axelrod, Curtis Brown Ltd., 575 Madison Ave., New York, NY 10022.

CAREER: Writer, editor, and advertising and public relations professional. Schenkman Publishing Co., Inc., Cambridge, MA, director of advertising, 1970-72; Harvard University, Cambridge, MA, editor of newsletter of Fogg Art Museum, 1972-73; Lesley College, Cambridge, MA, director of public relations, 1973-78; Harvard University, director of public relations of special programs at Graduate School of Design, 1978—. Member of board of directors of Wider Opportunities for Women.

MEMBER: Women in Communications, Authors Guild.

AWARDS, HONORS: Award from Council for Advancement and Support of Education, 1977, for article "Do One Thing and Do It Well."

WRITINGS:

(Editor, with Ronnie Friedlander) *The Mothers' Book: Shared Experiences,* Houghton Mifflin (Boston, MA), 1981.
(Editor, with Ronnie Friedlander) *The Fathers' Book: Shared Experiences,* G. K. Hall (Boston, MA), 1986.
A to Z of American Women Writers, Facts on File (New York, NY), 2000.
(With Liz Sonneborn) *A to Z of American Women in the Visual Arts,* Facts on File (New York, NY), 2002.

Contributor of articles and poems to magazines and newspapers, including *Sojourner, Genesis, Gnosis, Boston Sunday Globe Magazine, New York Times Education Life Magazine,* and *Tufts Literary Review.* Coeditor of local newsletter of Women in Communications. Contributor of weekly and monthly columns to the *Boston Herald American.*

SIDELIGHTS: In *A to Z of American Women Writers,* Carol Kort offers biographical profiles and critical summaries for more than 150 important women writers from the seventeenth century to modern times. The biographical sketches cover authors who have significantly influenced American writing and literature. Profiles contain biographical information on each listee, including personal details, information on literary influences, analysis of the importance of the listee's works, and more. Sketches include bibliographical citations for further readings on the author. About fifty sketches include photographs. A detailed index provides indexing by writer's birth year, literary genre, region where the writer lived, and the author's subject matter, personal background, and literary style. Included are profiles of major literary figures, genre writers, epistolarians, journalists, and other writers such as Maxine Hong Kingston, Ursula K. LeGuin, Sara Paretsky, Sue Grafton, Rita Dove, Doris Kearns Goodwin, Nellie Bly, Kate Chopin, and Willa Cather. A *Booklist* reviewer noted that "the writers profiled represent diversity of style, genre, ethnicity, and subject matter as well as time period and region in which they lived and worked." Neal Wyatt, writing in *Library Journal,* called the book "a solid compendium of biographical profiles." Kort "notes that she has chosen these writers because they have all created an impressive body of work and contributed to the usually male-dominated canon of American letters," the *Booklist* critic remarked.

Kort's *A to Z of American Women in the Visual Arts* is structured similarly to her volume on writers, providing biographical sketches of more than 130 important American women working in the visual arts from colonial-era America to the present day. Listees come from media such as photography, sculpture, painting, printmaking, performance art, architecture, and other areas of visual art. Sketches provide biographical information on each artist, plus dates of activity and details on media used. Brief bibliographies provide references to additional secondary sources for more information. Fifty-five entries include a portrait of the artist. The book includes a section entitled "Recommended Sources on American Women in the Visual Arts," which includes references to books, periodicals, and Web sites relevant to the subject matter. A detailed index rounds out the volume's contents. A *Booklist* reviewer called the book "a well-written reference tool that gives a good deal of information in a relatively short space." Cynthia A. Johnson, writing in *Library Journal,* noted that "the informal tone makes the text extremely readable." In a review in *Feminist Collections: A Quarterly of Women's Studies Resources,* critic Carrie Kruse commented, "The substantial length and readability of the profiles in A to Z, however, offer a nice introduction to each artist, and the bibliographies are thoughtfully selected and include information for finding some articles online." Both Kruse and the *Booklist* reviewer remarked on the lack of pictures of the artists' works in the book, but still awarded high praise for the work's conciseness and usefulness.

The Fathers' Book: Shared Experiences, edited by Kort and Ronnie Friedland and published in 1986, is a follow-up to the duo's 1981 volume *The Mothers' Book.* Roselle M. Lewis, writing in the *Los Angeles Times,* called *The Fathers' Book* a "fine anthology." The essays explore the profoundly transformative power of the birth of a child, and how fathers are deeply affected by the experience of becoming a parent. Fathers of varying types, including those awaiting planned and unplanned births, fathers of children with disabilities, older and younger fathers, and stepfathers all share their experiences. "With candor, force, and sometimes passionate intensity, seventy fathers express and describe widely varying viewpoints and experiences," Lewis noted.

Carol Kort told *CA:* "The combination of being a freelance writer and editor, mother, and author of freelance travel articles makes for an unstable but captivating life."

BIOGRAPHICAL AND CRITICAL SOURCES:

PERIODICALS

Booklist, June 1, 2000, review of *A to Z of American Writers,* p. 1942; July, 2002, review of *A to Z of American Women in the Visual Arts,* p. 1874.

Feminist Collections: A Quarterly of Women's Studies Resources, summer, 2002, Carrie Kruse, review of *A to Z of American Women in the Performing Arts* and *A to Z of American Women in the Visual Arts,* p. 23.

Library Journal, April 15, 1981, review of *The Mothers' Book: Shared Experiences,* p. 876; May 1, 1986, Susan A. McBride, review of *The Fathers' Book: Shared Experiences,* p. 127; October 15, 1999, Neal Wyatt, review of *A to Z of American Writers,* p. 64; May 1, 2002, Cynthia A. Johnson, review of *A to Z of American Women in the Visual Arts,* pp. 90-91.

Los Angeles Times, November 6, 1986, Roselle M. Lewis, review of *The Fathers' Book,* p. 12.

Ms., April, 1982, Lisa Cronin Wohl, review of *The Mothers' Book,* p. 77.

Publishers Weekly, March 13, 1981, Sally A. Lodge, review of *The Mothers' Book,* p. 85.

School Library Journal, June, 2000, Claudia Moore, review of *A to Z of American Women Writers,* p. 176.

ONLINE

Interfaith Family Web site, http://www.interfaithfamily.com/ (February 24, 2005), Carol Kort, "Passage to India."*

* * *

KOVEL, Joel S. 1936-

PERSONAL: Born August 27, 1936, in Brooklyn, NY; son of Louis and Rose (Farber) Kovel; married Dee Dee Halleck; children: Jonathan, Erin, Molly. *Ethnicity:* "Caucasian." *Education:* Yale University, B.S. (summa cum laude), 1957; Columbia University, M.D., 1961.

ADDRESSES: Home—P.O. Box 89, Willow, NY 12495. *Office*—Bard College, Annandale on Hudson, NY 12504; fax: 914-679-7535. *E-mail*—jkovel@prodigy.net.

CAREER: Bronx Municipal Hospital Center, Bronx, NY, intern in medical service, 1961-62; Yeshiva University, New York, NY, began as assistant resident, became resident in psychiatry at Albert Einstein College of Medicine and Bronx Municipal Hospital Center, 1962-64, chief resident in psychiatry, 1964-65, instructor at medical college, 1967-69, assistant professor, 1969-74, associate professor, 1974-79, professor of psychiatry, 1979-86; Bard College, Annandale on Hudson, NY, Alger Hiss Professor of Social Studies, 1988—. Psychoanalyst and psychiatrist in private practice, 1967-86. New School for Social Research, visiting professor of anthropology, 1980-85; University of California—San Diego, visiting professor of politics and communication, 1986-87.

AWARDS, HONORS: Nomination for National Book Award in philosophy and religion, 1972, for *White Racism: A Psychohistory;* Guggenheim fellowship, 1987.

WRITINGS:

White Racism: A Psychohistory, Pantheon (New York, NY), 1970, 2nd edition, Columbia University Press (New York, NY), 1984.

A Complete Guide to Therapy: From Psychoanalysis to Behavior Modification, Pantheon (New York, NY), 1976.

The Age of Desire: Case Histories of a Radical Psychoanalyst, Pantheon (New York, NY), 1981.

Against the State of Nuclear Terror, Pan Books (London, England), 1983, South End Press (Boston, MA), 1984.

In Nicaragua, Free Association Books (London, England), 1988.

The Radical Spirit: Essays in Psychoanalysis and Society, Free Association Books (London, England), 1988.

History and Spirit, Beacon Press (Boston, MA), 1990.

Red Hunting in the Promised Land, Basic Books (New York, NY), 1995.

The Enemy of Nature: The End of Capitalism or the End of the World?, Zed Books (New York, NY), 2002.

Contributor to books, including *Women in Analysis: Dialogues on Psychoanalytic Views of Femininity,* edited by Jean Strouse, David Grossman (New York, NY), 1974. Contributor of articles and reviews to periodicals, including *Telos, New York Times Book Review,Monthly Review, Capitalism,Nature, Socialism,* and *Psychoanalytic Review.*

WORK IN PROGRESS: Dialectical Meditations.

SIDELIGHTS: Joel S. Kovel once told *CA:* "Having begun with medicine, psychiatry, and psychoanalysis, and then increasingly shifted to critical social theory, my writings led me to consider, in turn, racism, schools of psychotherapy, the relations between Freud and Marx, the nuclear arms crisis, Sandinista Nicaragua, radical spirituality, and anticommunism. Now my efforts are directed toward an in-depth study of the ecological crisis—that disordered relation between humanity and nature which threatens to bring civilization to an end. The first volume, *The Enemy of Nature: The End of Capitalism or the End of the World?,* identifies the destructive forces within the prevailing system of social production, capitalism, and discusses ecological alternatives. The second volume, *Dialectical Meditations,* will undertake various speculative paths in order to fully grasp the true extent of the crisis and the possibilities of overcoming it."

BIOGRAPHICAL AND CRITICAL SOURCES:

BOOKS

Kovel, Joel S., *The Age of Desire: Case Histories of a Radical Psychoanalyst,* Pantheon (New York, NY), 1981.

PERIODICALS

Hungry Mind Review, spring, 1998, review of *White Racism: A Psychohistory,* p. 57.
Library Journal, May 15, 2002, Robert F. Nardini, review of *The Enemy of Nature: The End of Capitalism or the End of the World?,* p. 113.
Los Angeles Times, March 19, 1982.
Nation, January 30, 1982.
New Leader, October 25, 1976.
New York Times, June 24, 1976; January 14, 1982.
New York Times Book Review, July 18, 1976.
Psychology Today, January, 1982.
Reference and Research Book News, February, 1998, review of *Red Hunting in the Promised Land,* p. 36.
Synthesis/Regeneration, spring, 2000, Walt Contreras Sheasby, review of *The Enemy of Nature,* p. 28.
Times Literary Supplement, July 15, 1977.
Village Voice, January 20-26, 1982.

ONLINE

Joel Kovel Home Page, http://www.joelkovel.org/ (September 11, 2004).
Zed Books Web Site, http://zedweb.hypermart.net/ (August 16, 2002), description of *The Enemy of Nature.**

* * *

KUSPIT, Donald B(urton) 1935-

PERSONAL: Born March 26, 1935, in New York, NY; son of Morris (a manager) and Celia Kuspit; married Judith Price (a psychologist), 1962. *Education:* Columbia University, B.A., 1955; Yale University, M.A., 1958; University of Frankfurt, Ph.D., 1960; Pennsylvania State University, M.A., 1964; University of Michigan, Ph.D., 1971.

ADDRESSES: Office—Department of Art, State University of New York at Stony Brook, 4212 Staller Center for the Arts, Stony Brook, NY 11794. *E-mail*—Donald.Kuspit@stonybrook.edu.

CAREER: University of Frankfurt, Frankfurt, West Germany (now Germany), lecturer in English, 1957-59; Pennsylvania State University, University Park, assistant professor of philosophy, 1960-64; University of Saarland, Saarbruecken, Germany, Fulbright lecturer in philosophy and American studies, 1964-65; University of Windsor, Windsor, Ontario, associate professor of philosophy, 1966-70; University of North Carolina, Chapel Hill, professor of art history, 1970-78; State University of New York at Stony Brook, professor of art, 1978—, head of department, 1978-83. Guest lecturer at School for Visual Arts, 1976—; A. D. White Professor at Large, Cornell University, 1991—. Contributing editor to *Artforum, Sculpture,* and *New Art Examiner;* editor of *Art Criticism.*

MEMBER: American Society of Aesthetics, College Art Association of America.

AWARDS, HONORS: Canada Council fellowship, 1968-69; National Endowment for the Humanities younger humanist fellowship, 1973-74; Guggenheim fellowship, 1977-78; Frank Jewett Mather Award for Distinction in Art Criticism, College Art Association, 1983; Citation for Distinguished Service to the Visual Arts—Lifetime Achievement Award, National Association of the Schools of Art and Design, 1997. Honorary doctorates from Davidson College, 1993, San Francisco Institute of Art, 1996, and University of Illinois at Urbana-Champaign, 1998.

WRITINGS:

The Philosophical Life of the Senses, Philosophical Library (New York, NY), 1969.
Clement Greenberg, Art Critic, University of Wisconsin Press (Madison, WI), 1979.
Leon Golub: Existentialist Activist Painter, Rutgers University Press (New Brunswick, NJ), 1985, 2nd edition published as *The Existential Activist Painter: The Example of Leon Golub,* 1986.

(With Betty Collings) *Thomas Macaulay: Sculptural Views on Perceptual Ambiguity,* Dayton Art (Dayton, OH), 1986.

(With Stephen S. High) *Aggression, Subversion, Seduction: Young German Painters,* Portland School Baxter (Portland, ME), 1986.

Erich Fischl, Random House (New York, NY), 1987.

(With Bruce McWright) *Constitution: Group Material,* Temple University Gallery (Philadelphia, PA), 1987.

Louis Bourgeois, edited by Elisabeth Avedon, Random House (New York, NY), 1988.

The New Subjectivism: Art in the 1980s, UMI Research Press (Ann Arbor, MI), 1988.

Stephen de Staebler: The Figure, Chronicle Books (San Francisco, CA), 1988.

(Author of introduction) *Fables and Fantasies: From the Collection of Susan Kasen and Robert D. Summer,* Duke, 1988.

The Critic Is Artist: The Intentionality of Art, UMI Research Press (Ann Arbor, MI), 1988.

Alex Katz: Night Paintings, Abrams (New York, NY), 1991.

Arman: Monochrome Accumulations, Abbeville Press (New York, NY), 1991.

The Cult of the Avant-Garde Artist, Cambridge University Press (New York, NY), 1993.

The Dialect of Decadence, Stux Press (New York, NY), 1993.

Albert Renger-Patazch: Joy before the Object, Aperture (New York, NY), 1993.

Signs of Psyche in Modern and Postmodern Art, Cambridge University Press (New York, NY), 1993.

Primordial Presences: The Sculpture of Karel Appel, Abrams (New York, NY), 1994.

Szczesny, DuMont (Cologne, Germany), 1995.

George Chemeche: The Aya Series, Art Resources & Technologies (New York, NY), 1995.

(Contributor) *The Mountain Lake Workshop: Artists in Locale,* Virginia Commonwealth University (Richmond, VA), 1996.

Health and Happiness in Twentieth-Century Avant-Garde Art, Binghamton University Art Museum (Ithaca, NY), 1996.

Idiosyncratic Identities: Artists at the End of the Avant-Garde, Cambridge University Press (New York, NY), 1996.

Chihuly, Abrams (New York, NY), 1997.

Sam Francis: Elements and Archetypes, Fundacion Caja Madrid (Madrid, Spain), 1997.

(With others) *Daniel Brush: Gold without Boundaries,* Abrams (New York, NY), 1998.

Basil Alkazzi, New Horizons, Izumi Art Publications (St. Helier, Jersey, Channel Islands), 1998.

Reflections of Nature: Paintings by Joseph Raffael, Abbeville Press (New York, NY), 1998.

Apocalypse: With Jewels in the Distance (poetry), Allworth Press (New York, NY), 1999.

The Rebirth of Painting in the Late Twentieth Century, Cambridge University Press (New York, NY), 2000.

Redeeming Art: Critical Reveries, Allworth Press (New York, NY), 2000.

(With others) *Jimmy Ernst,* Hudson Hills (New York, NY), 2000.

Psychostrategies of Avant-Garde Art, Cambridge University Press (New York, NY), 2000.

(With Marjorie Strider) *Marjorie Strider,* Hard Press Editions (West Stockbridge, MA), 2001.

Shekhina, photographs by Leonard Nimoy, Umbrage Editions (New York, NY), 2001.

Don Eddy: The Art of Paradox, Hudson Hills Press (New York, NY), 2002.

Hunt Slonem: An Art Rich and Strange, Abrams (New York, NY), 2002.

Steve Tobin's Natural History, Hudson Hills Press (New York, NY), 2003.

The End of Art, Cambridge University Press (New York, NY), 2004.

(With Louis Meisel) *Mel Ramos Pop Art Fantasies: The Complete Paintings,* Watson-Guptill (New York, NY), 2004.

Dramatic Gestures: The Art of Marjorie Strider, Hard Press Editions (West Stockbridge, MA), 2004.

Also the author or contributor to numerous small gallery catalogues on a wide variety of artists, sculptors, and photographers.

EDITOR:

Sandra L. Underwood, *Charles H. Caffin: A Voice for Modernism,* UMI Research Press (Ann Arbor, MI), 1983.

Amy C. Simowitz, *Theory of Art in the "Encyclopedie,"* UMI Research Press (Ann Arbor, MI), 1983.

Misook Song, *Art Theories of Charles Blanc, 1813-1882,* UMI Research Press (Ann Arbor, MI), 1984.

Lawrence Alloway, *Network: Art and the Complete Present,* UMI Research Press (Ann Arbor, MI), 1984.

Joseph Masheck, *Historical Present: Essays of the 1970s,* UMI Research Press (Ann Arbor, MI), 1984.

Robert Pincus-Witten, *Eye to Eye: Twenty Years of Art Criticism,* UMI Research Press (Ann Arbor, MI), 1984.

Martin Pops, *Vermeer: Consciousness and the Chamber of Being,* UMI Research Press (Ann Arbor, MI), 1984.

Dennis Adrian, *Sight out of Mind: Essays and Criticism on Art,* UMI Research Press (Ann Arbor, MI), 1985.

Nicolas Calas, *Transfigurations: Art Critical Essays on the Modern Period,* UMI Research Press (Ann Arbor, MI), 1985.

Susan N. Platt, *Modernism in the 1920s: Interpretations of Modern Art in New York from Expressionism to Constructivism,* UMI Research Press (Ann Arbor, MI), 1985.

Patricia Mathews, *Aurier's Symbolist Art Criticism and Theory,* UMI Research Press (Ann Arbor, MI), 1986.

Beverly Twitchell, *Cezanne and Formalism in Bloomsbury,* UMI Research Press (Ann Arbor, MI), 1986.

Roger Benjamin, *Matisse's "Notes of a Painter": Criticism, Theory, and Context, 1891-1908,* UMI Research Press (Ann Arbor, MI), 1986.

Miriam K. Levin, *Republican Art and Ideology in Late Nineteenth-Century France,* UMI Research Press (Ann Arbor, MI), 1986.

Peter Plagens, *Moonlight Blues: An Artist's Art Criticism,* UMI Research Press (Ann Arbor, MI), 1986.

(And author of foreword) Dore Ashton, *Out of the Whirlwind: Three Decades of Arts Commentary,* UMI Research Press (Ann Arbor, MI), 1987.

Matthew L. Rohn, *Visual Dynamics in Jackson Pollock's Abstractions,* UMI Research Press (Ann Arbor, MI), 1987.

Kent Hooper, *Ernest Barlach's Literary and Visual Art: The Issue of Multiple Talent,* UMI Research Press (Ann Arbor, MI), 1987.

Annette Kahn, *J. K. Huysmans: Novelist, Poet and Art Critic,* UMI Research Press (Ann Arbor, MI), 1987.

Lawrence W. Markert, *Arthur Symons: Critic of the Seven Arts,* UMI Research Press (Ann Arbor, MI), 1987.

Stewart Buettner, *American Art Theory, 1945-70,* UMI Research Press (Ann Arbor, MI), 1988.

Bernard Schultz, *Art and Anatomy in Renaissance Italy,* UMI Research Press (Ann Arbor, MI), 1988.

Carol M. Zemel, *The Formation of a Legend: Van Gogh Criticism, 1890-1920,* UMI Research Press (Ann Arbor, MI), 1988.

Stephen C. Foster, *The Critics of Abstract Expressionism,* UMI Research Press (Ann Arbor, MI), 1988.

Peter Selz, *Art in a Turbulent Era,* UMI Research Press (Ann Arbor, MI), 1988.

Jeanne Siegel, *Artword 2: Discourse on the Early '80s,* UMI Research Press (Ann Arbor, MI), 1988.

Robert Pincus-Witten, *Postminimalism into Maximalism: American Art, 1966-1986,* UMI Research Press (Ann Arbor, MI), 1988.

Arlene Raven, *Feminist Art Criticism: An Anthology,* UMI Research Press (Ann Arbor, MI), 1988.

Arlene Raven and others, *Crossing Over: Feminism and Art of Social Concern,* UMI Research Press (Ann Arbor, MI), 1988.

Michael D. Hall, *Stereoscopic Perspective: Reflections on American Fine and Folk Art,* UMI Research Press (Ann Arbor, MI), 1988.

Jo Anna Isaak, *The Ruin of Representation in Modernist Art and Texts,* UMI Research Press (Ann Arbor, MI), 1988.

Carol A. Mahsun, *Pop Art Criticism: An Anthology,* UMI Research Press (Ann Arbor, MI), 1988.

(Coeditor) Katherine Hoffman, *Collage: Critical Views,* UMI Research Press (Ann Arbor, MI), 1989.

Barbara B. Lynes, *O'Keefe, Steiglitz, and the Critics, 1916-1929,* UMI Research Press (Ann Arbor, MI), 1989.

(With Arlene Raven) *Art in the Public Interest,* UMI Research Press (Ann Arbor, MI), 1989.

Editor of series "American Art and Art Criticism," Cambridge University Press.

WORK IN PROGRESS: On the Gathering Emptiness, a book of poems.

SIDELIGHTS: A professor of art at the State University of New York at Stony Brook, Donald B. Kuspit specializes in twentieth-century and northern Renaissance art. A contributing editor to several prominent journals, and holder of degrees in art history and philosophy with a background in psychoanalytic theory, Kuspit is the author and/or editor of scores of books on the arts and art criticism. One of his first titles, the 1979 *Clement Greenberg, Art Critic,* traces the professional life of the man who for decades charted the course of modernism and abstract expressionism in the visual arts. Kuspit's study was an attempt to discover the Formalist structures of this criticism through a rigorous examination of Greenberg's articles and reviews. For Joyce Brodsky, however, reviewing the book in the *Journal of Aesthetics and Art Criticism,* Kuspit "does an injustice to Greenberg's best critical insights by making them bear the burden of the philosophy of Kant, Marx, Hegel, and Dewey."

With *The New Subjectivism: Art in the 1980s,* Kuspit gathers much of his own criticism, influenced by his "reading in psychoanalysis and Frankfurt School of philosophy," as a contributor noted in the *Journal of Aesthetics and Art Criticism.* His reviews in the book deal mostly with European painters; in a second section of the book he compares these artists with their American contemporaries, and in a third section lays forth his theories of art criticism, acknowledging that such art "investigates the nature of self," as the same critic commented. This reviewer for the *Journal of Aesthetics and Art Criticism* went on to comment that because of Kuspit's influence in the art world, the "book deserves serious attention from aestheticians," but also complained of "murky writing." Reviewing the same work in *Choice,* P. Brauch also found that Kuspit's "style is dense" but further commented that the "best [essays] are toward the end, when [Kuspit] attempts to synthesize his ideas."

Kuspit examines the changing role of the artist and his or her "object" during the shift from modernism to postmodernism with his 1993 *The Cult of the Avant-Garde Artist.* For Kuspit, avant-garde art "has a therapeutic intention," as Will Wadlington noted in his *Creative Research Journal* review. However, with the shift to postmodernism or neo-avant-garde, this healing power was lost in the rush for fortune and fame. Examining artists from Pablo Picasso and Marcel Duchamp to Andy Warhol, Kuspit portrays "postmodernism as a narcissistic style," according to Wadlington, who further noted that "for Kuspit, Warhol is the beginning of the end of the belief in the healing power of art." Wadlington also praised Kuspit's "rich and expressive" writing, observing that he "has successfully integrated aesthetic and psychological perspectives" in a work that "brings together a cultural critique of capitalism and of postmodernism with a penetrating psychological analysis of the cult phenomena that pervade the contemporary art world." Bradley Collins, writing in *Art Journal* commented that Kuspit's purpose in the book was to "offer a sort of fantasy or meditation on an ideally sympathetic viewer's psychological response to various kinds of twentieth-century art." For Collins, the author's "strengths . . . are his combativeness, his ability to draw with authority on writers as divers as Adorno, Baudelaire, and Spinoza, and his penchant for dialectical excursions," while the book's "great weaknesses, which are endemic to theory-laden criticism, consist of a maddening lack of specificity and a refusal to flesh out abstractions." Reviewing the same title in *Choice,* S. L. Jenkins was more positive, calling the book a "profoundly intelligent and provocative psychological discussion" and "thought-provoking."

Kuspit gathers more of his criticism in *Idiosyncratic Identities,* essays on artists from the scrap-metal horse sculptures of Deborah Butterfield to the videos of Bill Viola, as well as an explication of his theory of the power of the idiosyncratic artist in contemporary art. Merlin James, reviewing the book in *Burlington Magazine,* felt that its "theoretical positions are clear and strong; and, as so often, they appear convincingly 'demonstrated' in compelling negative verdicts on some works." Two books from the year 2000 further investigate painting of the twentieth century from the avant-garde to postmodernist. With *Psychostrategies of Avant-Garde Art,* he sets out to show, as Keith Miller explained in the *Times Literary Supplement,* that modern art came about "because artists were repelled by the environment they were expected to document, and retreated into self-referential shadow-play, or 'pure' painting." Miller further observed that for Kuspit this resulted in a "fatal confusion of object and subject . . . a form of madness . . . which has left us all in a muddle." Here Kuspit investigates artists from Edouard Manet to Georges Seurat and Edvard Munch. Richard Kuhns, writing in the *Journal of Aesthetics and Art Criticism,* praised the author's "originality in interpretation of individual works." In Kuspit's *The Rebirth of Painting in the Late Twentieth Century,* the critic explores the work of twenty-six modern painters, including Picasso and Jackson Pollock, but also moving to more recent artists such as Nancy Spero, Lucien Freud, and Archie Rand. He also provides a profile of Jewish art historian Meyer Schapiro. Iain Biggs, writing in the *Journal of Visual Practice,* felt that "much of what is included here adds little to the position that Kuspit developed in previous collections."

Kuspit has also published numerous books on and with individual artists, adding cogent text to books illustrating their work. In *Chihuly,* for example, the work of glass sculptor Dave Chihuly is "rewardingly discussed by Mr. Kuspit," according to Phoebe-Lou Adams in the *Atlantic Monthly.* Reviewing the same work, *Booklist*'s Donna Seaman praised Kuspit's "agile and articulate commentary." In *Hunt Slonem: An Art Rich and Strange,* Kuspit examines the work of New York painter Slonem and "deftly provides . . . a stimulating discourse on artistic concerns that move beyond the decorative," according to Alice Joyce in a *Booklist* review. And M. Kren, reviewing the same title in *Choice,* commented that Kuspit "has prepared this beautifully designed book that well represents the work of artist Slonem."

BIOGRAPHICAL AND CRITICAL SOURCES:

PERIODICALS

Art Journal, winter, 1993, Bradley Collins, review of *The Cult of the Avant-Garde Artist,* pp. 91-93.

Booklist, April 15, 1998, Donna Seaman, review of *Chihuly,* pp. 1409-1410; June 1, 2002, Alice Joyce, review of *Hunt Slonem: An Art Rich and Strange,* pp. 1663-1664.

Burlington Magazine, June, 1998, Merlin James, review of *Idiosyncratic Identities,* pp. 402-403.

Choice, February, 1989, P. Brauch, review of *The New Subjectivism: Art in the 1980s;* July, 1993, S. L. Jenkins, review of *The Cult of the Avant-Garde Artist,* p. 1762; November, 2002, M. Kren, review of *Hunt Slonem.*

Creativity Research Journal, 1996, Will Wadlington, review of *The Cult of the Avant-Garde Artist,* pp. 291-294.

Journal of Aesthetics and Art Criticism, autumn, 1980, Joyce Brodsky, review of *Clement Greenberg, Art Critic,* pp. 107-108; autumn, 1989, review of *The New Subjectivism,* p. 400; June, 2002, Richard Kuhns, review of *Psychostrategies of Avant-Garde Art* and *The Rebirth of Painting in the Late Twentieth Century,* pp. 279-280.

Journal of Visual Art Practice, 2001, Iain Biggs, review of *The Rebirth of Painting in the Late Twentieth Century,* pp. 59-62.

Library Journal, July, 2002, Nadine Dalton Speidel, review of *Hunt Slonem,* pp. 75-76.

Los Angeles Times Book Review, May 26, 1985.

New York Times Book Review, February 17, 1980.

Times Literary Supplement, June 15, 2001, Keith Miller, review of *Psychostrategies of Avant-Garde Art.*

ONLINE

Allworth Press Web site, http://www.allworth.com/ (February 18, 2004).

Blackbird, http://www.blackbird.vcu.edu/ (February 17, 2004).

Cambridge University Press Web site, http://www.cup.org/ (February 18, 2004).

State University of New York Stony Brook Web site, http://naples.cc.sunysb.edu/ (August 16, 2002).*

L

LANG, Nancy M.
See MACE, Nancy L(awson)

*   *   *

LEVEY, Michael (Vincent) 1927-

PERSONAL: Born June 8, 1927, in London, England; son of O. L. H. and Gladys Mary (Milestone) Levey; married Brigid Brophy (a novelist and critic), June 12, 1954; children: Katharine Jane. *Education:* Exeter College, Oxford, B.A., 1950.

ADDRESSES: *Home*—Flat 3, 185 Old Brompton Rd., London SW5 0AN, England.

CAREER: National Gallery, London, England, assistant keeper, 1951-66, deputy keeper, 1966-68, keeper, 1968-73, director, 1973-86. Cambridge University, Cambridge, England, Slade Professor of Fine Art, 1963-64. *Military service:* British Army, King's Shropshire Light Infantry, 1945-48; became captain.

MEMBER: Royal Society of Literature (fellow).

AWARDS, HONORS: Member of Royal Victorian Order, 1965; Hawthornden Prize, 1968, for *Early Renaissance;* honorary fellow, Exeter College, Oxford, 1973; knighted by Queen Elizabeth, 1981; Banister Fletcher Prize, 1986, for *Giambattista Tiepolo: His Life and Art.*

WRITINGS:

Six Great Patiners, Hamish Hamilton (London, England), 1956.

The Eighteenth Century Italian Schools (catalogue), National Gallery (London, England), 1956.

A Brief History of the National Gallery, Pitkin Pictorials (London, England), 1957, 3rd edition published as *A Brief History of the National Gallery with a Representative Selection of Pictures,* 1960.

Painting in Eighteenth Century Venice, Phaidon (London, England), 1959, revised edition, Cornell University Press (Ithaca, NY), 1980.

The German School (catalogue), National Gallery (London, England), 1959.

A Concise History of Painting: From Giotto to Cezanne, Thames & Hudson (London, England), 1962, Praeger (New York, NY), 1964.

A Room-to-Room Guide to the National Gallery, National Gallery (London, England), 1964, 2nd revised edition, 1966.

Dürer, Weidenfeld & Nicolson (London, England), 1964.

Canaletto Paintings in the Collection of Her Majesty the Queen, Phaidon (London, England), 1964.

The Later Italian Pictures in the Collection of Her Majesty the Queen, Phaidon (London, England), 1964.

Rococo to Revolution: Major Trends in Eighteenth Century Painting, Praeger (New York, NY), 1966, reprinted, Thames & Hudson (London, England), 1985.

(With wife, Brigid Brophy, and Charles Osborne) *Fifty Works of English and American Literature We Could Do Without,* Rapp & Carroll (London, England), 1967, Stein & Day (New York, NY), 1968.

Early Renaissance, Penguin (New York, NY), 1967, reprinted, 1987.

A History of Western Art, Praeger (New York, NY), 1968.

The Seventeenth and Eighteenth Centuries, Thames & Hudson (London, England), 1969.

Painting at Court (Wrightsman Lectures), New York University Press (New York, NY), 1971.

The Life and Death of Mozart, Weidenfeld & Nicolson (London, England), 1971, Stein & Day (New York, NY), 1972.

The Seventeenth and Eighteenth Century Italian Schools, National Gallery (London, England), 1971.

(With Wendgraf Kalnein) *Art and Architecture of the Eighteenth Century in France,* Penguin (New York, NY), 1972.

The Nude, National Gallery (London, England), 1972.

The Venetian Scene, National Gallery (London, England), 1973.

Botticelli, National Gallery (London, England), 1974.

High Renaissance, Penguin (New York, NY), 1975.

The World of Ottoman Art, Scribner (New York, NY), 1975.

Ruisdael: Jacob van Ruisdael and Other Painters of His Family, National Gallery (London, England), 1977.

The Case of Walter Pater, Thames & Hudson (London, England), 1978.

Sir Thomas Lawrence, 1769-1830, National Portrait Gallery (London, England), 1979.

The Painter Depicted: Painters As a Subject in Painting, Thames & Hudson (London, England), 1982.

Tempting Fate (novel), Hamish Hamilton (London, England), 1982.

An Affair on the Appian Way (novel), Hamish Hamilton (London, England), 1984.

(Editor and author of introduction) Walter Pater, *Marius the Epicurean,* Penguin (New York, NY), 1985.

Kenneth Mackenzie Clark, 1903-1983, British Academy (London, England), 1985, Longwood Publishing Group (Dover, NH), 1986.

Giambattista Tiepolo: His Life and Art, Yale University Press (New Haven, CT), 1986.

(Editor, with G. M. S. Scimone) *London Museums and Collections,* Canal (London, England), 1986.

Complete Paintings of Botticelli, Penguin (New York, NY), 1986.

Director's Choice, National Gallery (London, England), 1986.

The National Gallery Collection, National Gallery (London, England), 1987.

The Later Italian Pictures in the Collection of Her Majesty the Queen, Cambridge University Press (New York, NY), 1991.

Painting and Sculpture in France, 1700-1789, Yale University Press (New Haven, CT), 1993.

Florence: A Portrait, Harvard University Press (Cambridge, MA), 1996.

(Editor) *The Burlington Magazine: A Centenary Anthology,* Yale University Press (New Haven, CT), 2003.

Also author of the novel *Men at Work,* Hamish Hamilton (London, England). Contributor to books, including *Essays on Dürer,* edited by C. R. Dodwell, Manchester University Press (Manchester, England), 1973. Contributor to *Burlington, London, New Statesman,* and other periodicals.

SIDELIGHTS: Art historian and author Michael Levey was affiliated with the prestigious National Gallery in London, England, for over three decades. His retirement came after thirteen years as director of the gallery. Levey's *Early Renaissance* was applauded by a *Times Literary Supplement* contributor for featuring the Renaissance as "the story of human actions and reactions, as the story of man and his world. Mercifully it is not treated as some vague conceptual movement taking place in the no-man's-land of historicism." In his biography *Giambattista Tiepolo: His Life and Art,* Levey turns his talents to what some would consider the Italian master painter of the eighteenth century. In a *Spectator* review of the Tiepolo biography, David Ekserdjian maintained that Levey "belongs to an increasingly endangered but happily not yet extinct species of art historian, whose scholarship is impeccable and who have the far rarer gift of being able to write like a dream. There will be more time for books now, but even Sir Michael Levey will not find it easy to rival this exceptionally articulate and elegant labour of love."

BIOGRAPHICAL AND CRITICAL SOURCES:

PERIODICALS

New York Review of Books, May 18, 1972.

New York Times Book Review, March 12, 1972.

Spectator, July 1, 1978; September 11, 1982; December 20-27, 1986, David Ekserdjian, review of *Giambattista Tiepolo: His Life and Art.*
Times Literary Supplement, February 1, 1968, review of *Early Renaissance;* January 14, 1972; April 30, 1976; September 22, 1978; September 3, 1982; March 27, 1987.
Washington Post Book World, December 19, 1971.*

* * *

LEVINE, Allan 1956-

PERSONAL: Born February 10, 1956, in Winnipeg, Manitoba, Canada; son of Marvin H. (an insurance agent) and Bernice (a homemaker; maiden name, Kliman) Levine; married Angela Tenenbein (a nurse), September 2, 1982; children: Alexander, Mia. *Education:* University of Manitoba, B.A., 1977; University of Toronto, M.A., 1979, Ph.D., 1985.

ADDRESSES: Home—Winnipeg, Manitoba, Canada. *Office*—St. John's-Ravenscourt School, 400 South Dr., Winnipeg, Manitoba R3T 3K5, Canada. *Agent*—Hilary Stanley, Westwood Creative Artists, 94 Harbord St., Toronto, Ontario M5S 1G6, Canada. *E-mail*—levina@sjr.mb.ca.

CAREER: University of Manitoba, Winnipeg, Manitoba, Canada, instructor in education, 1983-84; St. John's-Ravenscourt School, Winnipeg, teacher of history, beginning 1984. Camp Massad, member of board of directors, 1986-95; Winnipeg Board of Jewish Education, member, 1993-97.

MEMBER: Writers Union of Canada, Canadian Historical Association.

AWARDS, HONORS: Grants from Manitoba Arts Council, 1987-91, 1996, 2001, and Canada Council, 1989-90, 1996, 2000; Margaret McWilliams Medal for best historical fiction, Manitoba Historical Society, for *The Blood Libel;* Yad Vashem Prize in Holocaust History, for *Fugitives of the Forest.*

WRITINGS:

The Exchange: One Hundred Years of Trading Grain in Winnipeg, Peguis Publishers (Winnipeg, Manitoba, Canada), 1987.
(Editor and contributor) *Your Worship: The Lives of Eight of Canada's Most Unforgettable Mayors,* James Lorimer (Toronto, Ontario, Canada), 1989.
Scrum Wars: The Prime Ministers and the Media, Dundurn Press (Toronto, Ontario, Canada), 1993.
The Blood Libel: A Sam Klein Mystery, Great Plains (Winnipeg, Manitoba, Canada), 1997.
Fugitives of the Forest: The Heroic Story of Jewish Resistance and Survival during the Second World War, Stoddart (Toronto, Ontario, Canada), 1998.
Sins of the Suffragette: A Sam Klein Mystery, Great Plains (Winnipeg, Manitoba, Canada), 2000.
Scattered among the People: The Jewish Diaspora in Ten Portraits, McClelland & Stewart (Toronto, Ontario, Canada), 2003.

Contributor of articles and reviews to Canadian magazines and newspapers.

SIDELIGHTS: Allan Levine once told *CA:* "My main objective is to write well-researched popular history that is readable, entertaining, and informative. Unlike Americans, Canadians believe their history is dull. I aim to prove them wrong."

BIOGRAPHICAL AND CRITICAL SOURCES:

PERIODICALS

Books in Canada, summer, 2003, Sharon Abron Drache, review of *Scattered among the People: The Jewish Diaspora in Ten Portraits.*
Globe and Mail (Toronto, Ontario, Canada), September 9, 1989.*

* * *

LEVINSON, Jay Conrad

PERSONAL: Male; married; children: two.

ADDRESSES: Office—Guerrilla Marketing International, P.O. Box 1336, 260 Cascade Dr., Mill Valley, CA 94942. *Agent*—c/o Author Mail, Avon Books, 1350 Avenue of the Americas, New York, NY 10019. *E-mail*—GMINTL@aol.com.

CAREER: Played professional hockey in Europe until 1989; has taught marketing at University of California, Berkeley; former creative director and member of the board for Leo Burnett Advertising; former senior vice-president of J. Walter Thompson (advertising agency); Guerrilla Marketing, Inc., Mill Valley, CA, cofounder and chair; also founder of other businesses. Has served on the 3Com Small Business Advisory Board and Microsoft Small Business Council.

WRITINGS:

Earning Money without a Job: The Economics of Freedom, Holt (New York, NY), 1979, revised edition published as *Earning Money without a Job: Revised for the '90s,* 1991.

555 Ways to Earn Extra Money, Holt (New York, NY), 1982, revised edition published as *555 Ways to Earn Extra Money: Revised for the '90s,* 1991.

Guerrilla Marketing: Secrets for Making Big Profits from Your Small Business, Houghton Mifflin (Boston, MA), 1984, 3rd edition, 1998.

An Earthling's Guide to Satellite TV, illustrated by Jane Marriott, Quantum (Mendocino, CA), 1985.

Quit Your Job!: Making the Decision, Making the Break, Making It Work, Dodd (New York, NY), 1987.

Guerrilla Marketing Attack: New Strategies, Tactics, and Weapons for Winning Big Profits from Your Small Business, Houghton Mifflin (Boston, MA), 1989.

Guerrilla Marketing Weapons: One Hundred Affordable Marketing Methods for Maximizing Profits from Your Small Business, Plume (New York, NY), 1990.

The Ninety-Minute Hour, Dutton (New York, NY), 1990.

(With Bruce Jan Blechman) *Guerrilla Financing: Alternative Techniques to Finance Any Small Business,* Houghton Mifflin (Boston, MA), 1991.

(With Bill Gallagher and Orvel Ray Wilson) *Guerrilla Selling: Unconventional Weapons and Tactics for Increasing Your Sales,* Houghton Mifflin (Boston, MA), 1992.

Guerrilla Marketing Excellence: The Fifty Golden Rules for Small-Business Success, Houghton Mifflin (Boston, MA), 1993.

Guerrilla Marketing for the '90s: The Newest Secrets for Making Big Profits from Your Small Business, Houghton Mifflin (Boston, MA), 1993.

Guerrilla Advertising: Cost-Effective Techniques for Small-Business Success, Houghton Mifflin (Boston, MA), 1994.

(With Seth Godin) *The Guerrilla Marketing Handbook,* Houghton Mifflin (Boston, MA), 1994.

(With Charles Rubin) *Guerrilla Marketing Online: The Entrepreneur's Guide to Earning Profits on the Internet,* Houghton Mifflin (Boston, MA), 1995, 2nd edition, 1997.

(With Seth Godin) *Guerrilla Marketing for the Home-based Business,* Houghton Mifflin (Boston, MA), 1995.

(With Charles Rubin) *Guerrilla Marketing Online Weapons: One Hundred Low-Cost, High-Impact Weapons for Online Profits and Prosperity,* Houghton Mifflin (Boston, MA), 1996.

Jay Conrad Levinson's Guerilla Marketing (computer disk), HMI (Somerville, MA), 1996.

The Way of the Guerrilla: Achieving Success and Balance As an Entrepreneur in the 21st Century, Houghton Mifflin (Boston, MA), 1997.

(With Seth Godin) *Get What You Deserve!: How to Guerrilla Market Yourself,* Avon (New York, NY), 1997.

Guerrilla Marketing with Technology: Unleashing the Full Potential of Your Small Business, Addison-Wesley (Reading, MA), 1997.

(With Orvel R. Wilson and Mark S. A. Smith) *Guerrilla Trade Show Selling: New Unconventional Weapons and Tactics to Meet More People, Get More Leads, and Close More Sales,* John Wiley (New York, NY), 1997.

(With Orvel Wilson and Mark S. A. Smith) *Guerrilla Teleselling: New Unconventional Weapons and Tactics to Sell when You Can't Be There in Person,* John Wiley (New York, NY), 1998.

(With Mark S. A. Smith, Orvel Ray Wilson) *Guerrilla Negotiating: Unconventional Weapons and Tactics to Get What You Want,* John Wiley (New York, NY), 1999.

Mastering Guerrilla Marketing: 100 Profit-Producing Insights You Can Take to the Bank, Houghton Mifflin (Boston, MA), 1999.

(With Kathryn Tyler) *Guerrilla Saving: Secrets for Keeping Profits in Your Home-Based Business,* John Wiley, (New York, NY), 2000.

(With Rick Frishman and Michael Larsen) *Guerrilla Marketing for Writers,* Writer's Digest Books (Cincinnati, OH), 2001.

Guerrilla Marketing: The Best of Guerrilla Marketing, edited by Ginger Conlon, Aspatore Books (Boston, MA), 2001.

Guerrilla Creativity: Make Your Message Irresistible, Houghton Mifflin (Boston, MA), 2001.

Guerilla Marketing: Make Your Message Irresistible with the Power of Memes, Houghton Mifflin (Boston, MA), 2001.

Guerrilla Publicity: Hundreds of Sure-Fire Tactics to Maximum Sales for Minimum Dollars, Adams Media Corporation (Avon, MA), 2002.

Guerrilla Marketing for Financial Advisors, Trafford (Victoria, British Columbia, Canada), 2003.

Guerrilla Marketing for Free: One Hundred No-Cost Tactics to Promote Your Business and Energize Your Profits, Houghton Mifflin (Boston, MA), 2003.

(With Theo Brandt-Sarif) *Guerrilla Travel Tactics: Hundreds of Simple Strategies Guaranteed to Save Road Warriors Time and Money,* American Management Association (New York, NY), 2004.

(With David Perry) *Career Guide for the High-Tech Professional: Where the Jobs Are Now and How to Land Them,* Career Press (Franklin Lakes, NJ), 2004.

Columnist for *Entrepreneur, Inc.,* and *America's Network;* author of online columns for Microsoft and GTE. Contributor to periodicals, including the *San Francisco Examiner* and *Guerrilla Marketing Newsletter.* Levinson's books have been translated into thirty-seven languages.

ADAPTATIONS: The "Guerrilla Marketing" series of books has been adapted to audiotapes, videotapes, a CD-ROM, and a Web site.

SIDELIGHTS: The self-styled mahatma of management, Jay Conrad Levinson is a writer specializing in moneymaking tactics as well as unconventional business, advertising, public relations, and time-management strategies. Over a career that has spanned more than two decades, he has published more than thirty titles in his "Guerrilla" series, which is geared to the nonspecialist and has rivaled the "Dummies Guide" collection for giving novices the need-to-know information on the subject at hand. Levinson's widely read books have been translated into some thirty-five languages and are required reading in some master's in business programs. While some professionals have criticized various of the Guerrilla guides for trivializing what it takes to become a professional in such disciplines as public relations and advertising, the sales figures for the books prove their popularity among general readers.

Levinson published his first book, *Earning Money without a Job: The Economics of Freedom,* in 1979 after forsaking a career in advertising and finding success as the founder of various businesses. In *Earning Money without a Job,* Levinson recommends sales and mail-order ventures as certain moneymaking businesses for independent workers, and he urges readers to seize opportunities for realizing income independent of conventional employment.

Levinson followed *Earning Money without a Job* with many more titles, including several volumes on what he describes as "guerrilla" business, financing, and marketing practices. In 1984, for example, he produced *Guerrilla Marketing: Secrets for Making Big Profits from Your Small Business,* which concentrates on various advertising practices. Levinson's advice was deemed "practical guidance for the target, small-business audience" by a *Kirkus Reviews* writer. Levinson was prolific in the 1990s, publishing such titles as *Guerrilla Marketing Weapons: One Hundred Affordable Marketing Methods for Maximizing Profits from Your Small Business,* in which the "weapons" include pricing, brand-name awareness, and customer service, and *Guerrilla Financing: Alternative Techniques to Finance Any Small Business.*

In *The Way of the Guerrilla: Achieving Success and Balance As an Entrepreneur in the 21st Century,* Levinson makes the surprising assertion that "time is not money . . . [and] achieving balance in life is preferable to workaholism," according to a writer for *Library Journal.* A *Publishers Weekly* reviewer echoed this sentiment, stating that Levinson believes that "entrepreneurs of the future . . . will better blend work, health, family and fun." The critic concluded, "Those looking to gear down from the fast track will find Levinson's encouragement bracing." Similarly, another reviewer for *Publishers Weekly* said "there is a lot to like" in *Get What You Deserve: How to Guerrilla Market Yourself,* Levinson's book on how to use personal style to one's advantage. Realizing that many of the rules that govern the business world are senseless, Levinson and coauthor Seth Godin give tips on how to understand this concept and to dress and act accordingly.

As the 1990s wound down, Levinson did not. With coauthors Orvel Wilson and Mark S. A. Smith, he penned titles with specific focuses on using technology, trade shows, and telemarketing: *Guerrilla Marketing with Technology: Unleashing the Full Potential of*

Your Small Business, Guerrilla Trade Show Selling: New Unconventional Weapons and Tactics to Meet More People, Get More Leads, and Close More Sales, and *Guerrilla Teleselling: New Unconventional Weapons and Tactics to Sell When You Can't Be There in Person.* At his home office, from which he has worked exclusively since 1971, he also developed audio-and videotapes, CD-ROMs, and an Internet Web site. As he had before, Levinson promoted his message that by using unconventional techniques high on creativity and energy, small business owners could be successful in competing against larger companies. Levinson himself is proof that his techniques can work.

In 1999 Levinson changed publishers, yet he continued to put out his message. He wrote *Guerrilla Saving: Secrets for Keeping Profits in Your Home-Based Business* with Kathryn Tyler and published the solo work *Mastering Guerrilla Marketing: 100 Profit-Producing Insights You Can Take to the Bank,* which *Library Journal* critic Littleton M. Maxwell called his "most comprehensive guide yet," one that offers a "great deal of valuable information." After his compendium *Guerrilla Marketing: The Best of Guerrilla Marketing* and *Guerrilla Creativity: Make Your Message Irresistible* rolled off presses in 2001, Levinson wrote and repackaged his message for more specific users, such as financial advisors, writers, and travelers. In 2004 Levinson teamed up with David Perry to help job hunters with their *Career Guide for the High-Tech Professional: Where the Jobs Are Now and How to Land Them.*

BIOGRAPHICAL AND CRITICAL SOURCES:

PERIODICALS

Booklist, April 1, 1982, p. 993; February 1, 1984, p. 778; February 1, 1989, p. 903; March 15, 1990, p. 1403; June 1, 1994, pp. 1740-1742; February 1, 1995, p. 979; July, 1995, p. 1846; August, 1996, p. 1865; December 15, 1996, p. 699; October 1, 1999, review of *Mastering Guerrilla Marketing: 100 Profit-Producing Insights You Can Take to the Bank,* p. 327.

Business Press (Ontario, Canada), August 12, 2002, Robert Chacon, "Small Business; Guerrilla Tactics All Fair in Unconventional Marketing War," p. 10.

Choice, March, 2000, S. A. Schulman, review of *Mastering Guerrilla Marketing.*

Communication World (San Francisco, CA), April-May, 2003, "*Guerrilla Publicity* Trivializes the Strategic Role of Public Relations," p. 12.

Inc., August, 1991, p. 87; August, 1999, "Face to Face" (interview), p. 60.

Kirkus Reviews, January 1, 1984, p. 35.

Kliatt, fall, 1982, pp. 38-39.

Library Journal, April 1, 1982, p. 725; February 15, 1984, p. 371; February 15, 1989, p. 166; February 1, 1990, p. 103; November 15, 1990, p. 77; August, 1995, p. 88; January, 1997, p. 116; December, 1999, Littleton M. Maxwell, review of *Mastering Guerrilla Marketing,* p. 154; August, 2002, Littleton M. Maxwell, review of *Guerrilla Publicity: Hundreds of Sure-Fire Tactics to Maximum Sales for Minimum Dollars,* p. 112.

Long Island Business News, June 14, 2002, Jane Applegate, review of *Guerrilla Publicity,* p. 23A.

PC Magazine, April 8, 1997, p. 76.

Publishers Weekly, July 2, 1979, p. 103; January 12, 1990, p. 56; July 8, 1996, p. 80; December 30, 1996, p. 52; August 4, 1997, p. 57; October 1, 2001, review of *Guerrilla Creativity: Make Your Message Irresistible,* p. 51; May 20, 2002, review of *Guerrilla Publicity,* pp. 61-62.

Reference & User Services Quarterly, fall, 1999, review of *The Guerilla Marketing Handbook,* p. 12.

Washington Post Book World, April 25, 1982, p. 14.

ONLINE

Author Network, http://www.author-network.com/ (November 21, 2002), review of *Guerrilla Marketing for Writers.*

Writers Write, http://www.writerswrite.com/ (November 21, 2002), review of *Guerrilla Marketing for Writers.**

* * *

LEWIS-WILLIAMS, J(ames) David 1934-

PERSONAL: Born August 5, 1934, in Cape Town, South Africa. *Education:* University of Cape Town, B.A., 1955, S.T.D., 1956; University of South Africa, B.A. (with honors), 1964; University of Natal, Ph.D., 1978.

ADDRESSES: Home—P.O. Box 1892, Rivonia 2128, South Africa. *Office*—Department of Archaeology, University of the Witwatersrand, Johannesburg 2050, South Africa.

CAREER: Archeologist. Teacher of English at secondary school, East London, South Africa, 1958-63; head of English department at secondary school, Botha's Hill, South Africa, 1964-78; University of the Witwatersrand, Johannesburg, South Africa, lecturer, 1978-80, senior lecturer, 1981-84, reader in cognitive archaeology, 1984-87, professor of cognitive archaeology, 1987-c. 2000, director of the Rock Art Institute, professor emeritus.

MEMBER: South African Archaeological Society (president).

WRITINGS:

Believing and Seeing: Symbolic Meanings in Southern San Rock Paintings, Academic Press (New York, NY), 1981.

The Rock Art of Southern Africa, Cambridge University Press (New York, NY), 1983.

(Editor) *New Approaches to Southern African Rock Art,* South African Archaeological Society (Cape Town, South Africa), 1983.

(With Thomas A. Dowson) *Images of Power: Understanding Southern African Rock Art,* Southern Book Publishers (Johannesburg, South Africa), 1989.

Discovering Southern African Rock Art, David Philip (Cape Town, South Africa), 1990.

Bushmen: A Changing Way of Life, photographs by Anthony Bannister, Struik (Cape Town, South Africa), 1991.

(With Thomas A. Dowson) *Rock Paintings of the Natal Drakensberg,* University of Natal Press (Pietermaritzburg, South Africa), 1992.

(Editor, with Thomas A. Dowson) *Contested Images: Diversity in Southern African Rock Art Research,* Witwatersrand University Press, 1994.

(With Jean Clottes) *Les chamanes de la préhistoire: transe et magie dans les grottes ornées,* Seuil (Paris, France), 1996, translation by Sophie Hawkes published as *The Shamans of Prehistory: Trance and Magic in the Painted Caves,* Harry N. Abrams (New York, NY), 1998.

(With Geoffrey Blundell) *Fragile Heritage: A Rock Art Fieldguide,* Witwatersrand University Press (Johannesburg, South Africa), 1998.

(Editor and author of introduction) *Stories That Float from Afar: Ancestral Folklore of the San of Southern Africa,* Texas A&M University Press (College Station, TX), 2000.

The Mind in the Cave: Consciousness and the Origins of Art, Thames & Hudson (New York, NY), 2002.

A Cosmos in Stone: Interpreting Religion and Society through Rock Art, AltaMira Press (Walnut Creek, CA), 2002.

Images of Mystery: Rock Art of the Drakensberg, Double Storey (Cape Town, South Africa), 2003.

(With D. G. Pearce) *San Spirituality: Roots, Expression, and Social Consequences,* AltaMira Press (Walnut Creek, CA), 2004.

Contributor to professional publications, including *Current Anthropology, Proceedings of the Prehistoric Society,* and *L'Anthropologie.*

SIDELIGHTS: J. David Lewis-Williams is a retired professor of archeology who has had a lifelong interest in the rock drawings of the San people, or Bushmen, of southern Africa. He is also editor of *Stories That Float from Afar: Ancestral Folklore of the San of Southern Africa.* This volume collects stories that were discovered and interpreted through the ancestors of the artists by German linguist Wilhelm Heinrich Emmanuel Bleek. In 1870, he first turned to San Bushman Kabbo, who was incarcerated in Breakwater Prison, a shaman who then became Bleek's teacher. When Bleek died, his sister-in-law, Lucy Lloyd, continued his work of collecting oral histories and stories, myths and folklore, saving them from extinction in a collection that grew to twelve thousand pages, and which won the UNESCO Memory of the World Program award, the most prestigious honor any historical document or collection can receive.

Lewis-Williams began to study the collection at the University of Cape Town and found that nothing from it had been published in decades, nor had anyone continued the work. Consequently, *Stories That Float from Afar* respects Kabbo's wish that the record of his people be protected, and provides the details of life that might have otherwise been lost.

Lewis-Williams wrote *Shamans of Prehistory: Trance and Magic in the Painted Caves* with Jean Clottes, an expert on the prehistoric paintings in the caves of

France and Spain, to produce a study in which they conclude that the cave art of Europe is shamanistic. They explain shamanism and how rituals common to the neurological patterns of all animals can lead to hallucinations and out-of-body experiences. *Library Journal*'s Mary Morgan Smith said that "the bulk of the book is both fascinating and thought-provoking."

Lancet reviewer Kelly Morris wrote that "the result is not a scientific monograph, but a luxurious art book filled with fascinating and well-referenced narrative. . . . Coupled with striking color photographs and diagrams of prehistoric art, the authors' theory is wholly convincing. . . . Their theory appeals, not merely because of the evidence from the San but also because some aspects of the shamanic cosmos still persist in today's modern religions. And if true, these ideas have lasted for 10,000 years, perhaps since the people of that region became recognizably human."

The Mind in the Cave: Consciousness and the Origins of Art also studies the caves of Western Europe, but here Lewis-Williams uses more scholarly methodology and research in developing his premise that rock drawings created from 10,000 to 45,000 years ago were produced by hunter-gatherer shamans of the Upper Paleolithic period who wanted to document on the cave walls the states they had experienced. Lewis-Williams develops two hypotheses, that man had to have reached a state of "fully modern consciousness," or the ability to process mental images, in order to engage in image-making, and that cave painting was tied to religious beliefs and helped enforce class distinctions within society. In the first two-thirds of the book, he strengthens his case with recent findings in the physical and social sciences. In the final third, he interprets geometric and animal imagery found in a number of caves. A *Publishers Weekly* contributor noted that Lewis-Williams "is particularly winning as he subtly reveals his devotion to the art and people he attempts to explain" and sensitively writes of "those who 'saw real things, real spirit animals and beings, real transformations' on cave walls."

Antiquity's Robert Layton wrote that *The Mind in the Cave* "presents a readable account of arguments that Lewis-Williams has steadfastly advocated for some years, and adds a new theory about the origin of rock art in Western Europe. The book provides a clear discussion of method."

A Cosmos in Stone: Interpreting Religion and Society through Rock Art consists of one new chapter and previously published articles. Lewis-Williams first explains South African rock art of the San through documented sources, including the work of Bleek and Lloyd. "Subsequently," noted Lawrence H. Robbins in *American Antiquity,* "Lewis-Williams takes us from the ethnographic data on a substantial theoretical leap into neuropsychology where the stages of hallucination are described, beginning with 'entopic phenomena' (wavy lines, grids, etc.) and eventually reaching a deep state of trance where a vortex or tunnel and associated images are seen. . . . He also discusses the role of agency as well as vision quests in interpreting Upper Paleolithic cave art."

Lewis-Williams once told *CA:* "My interest in archaeology dates back to my undergraduate days, with rock art always being a special interest. Since then I have conducted intensive field research in a number of areas in southern Africa and have studied San beliefs and rituals. It now seems clear that rock art was closely associated with the symbols, power, and hallucinations of San medicine men, or shamans, who entered trances to control game, cure the sick, and make rain. I'm glad to say the work has been well received, though much remains to be done. We are only beginning to understand the complexities of this breathtaking art."

BIOGRAPHICAL AND CRITICAL SOURCES:

PERIODICALS

African Arts, January, 1991, Merrick Posnansky, review of *Images of Power: Understanding Southern African Rock Art,* p. 91; winter, 1996, Lawrence H. Robbins, review of *Contested Images: Diversity in Southern African Rock Art Research,* p. 98.

American Antiquity, April, 1992, Zenon Pohorecky, review of *Images of Power,* p. 380; June, 2003, Robert Layton, review of *The Mind in the Cave: Consciousness and the Origins of Art,* p. 422; January, 2004, Lawrence H. Robbins, review of *A Cosmos in Stone: Interpreting Religion and Society through Rock Art,* p. 157.

Booklist, January 1, 1999, Donna Seaman, review of *The Shamans of Prehistory: Trance and Magic in the Painted Caves,* p. 816; October 15, 2002, Donna Seaman, review of *The Mind in the Cave,* p. 375.

Lancet, January 30, 1999, Kelly Morris, review of *The Shamans of Prehistory,* p. 417.

Library Journal, February 1, 1999, Mary Morgan, review of *The Shamans of Prehistory,* p. 82; November 15, 2002, Anne Marie Lane, review of *The Mind in the Cave,* p. 68.

New Scientist, November 2, 2002, Mike Pitts, review of *The Mind in the Cave,* p. 57.

Publishers Weekly, November 18, 2002, review of *The Mind in the Cave,* p. 55.

Times Higher Education Supplement, April 11, 2003, Seven Mithen, review of *The Mind in the Cave,* p. 25.*

* * *

LHAMON, W(illiam) T(aylor), Jr. 1945-

PERSONAL: Born January 3, 1945, in Washington, DC; son of William Taylor (a physician and teacher) and Elizabeth (a psychologist; maiden name, Kearton) Lhamon; married Judith Clay; children: William Taylor III, Catherine Elizabeth. *Education:* Johns Hopkins University, B.A., 1966; Indiana University, Ph.D., 1973. *Politics:* "Homeless Left."

ADDRESSES: Home—2412 Willow Ave., Tallahassee, FL 32303. *Office*—Department of English, Florida State University, Tallahassee, FL 32306. *Agent*—Donald Cutler, Sterling Lord Agency, 660 Madison Ave., New York, NY 10021.

CAREER: Fresno State College (now California State University, Fresno), Fresno, CA, assistant professor of English, 1970-71; Florida State University, Tallahassee, assistant professor, 1971-75, associate professor of English, beginning 1975, now George Mills Harper Professor of English.

MEMBER: College English Association, Modern Language Association of America, Popular Culture Association.

AWARDS, HONORS: Amoco Foundation award, 1975.

WRITINGS:

(Editor, with Kenneth R. Johnston) *The Rhetoric of Conflict,* Bobbs-Merrill (New York, NY), 1969.

Deliberate Speed: The Origins of a Cultural Style in the American 1950s, Smithsonian Institution Press (Washington, DC), 1990.

Raising Cain: Blackface Performance from Jim Crow to Hip Hop, Harvard University Press (Cambridge, MA), 1998.

Jump Jim Crow: Lost Plays, Lyrics, and Street Prose of the First Atlantic Popular Culture, Harvard University Press (Cambridge, MA), 2003.

Contributor to books, including *Selected Essays on Thomas Pynchon,* edited by George L. Levine and David Leverenz, Little, Brown (Boston, MA), 1975; and *American Humor: A Study of the National Character,* University Presses of Florida (Tallahassee, FL), 1986. Author of "Record Review," a jazz and rock music column in *New Republic.* Contributor of articles and reviews to popular magazines and literary journals, including *Western Humanities Review, Studies in Black Literature,* and *American Studies.*

SIDELIGHTS: W. T. Lhamon, Jr. once told *CA:* "What this country needs along with justice and a modicum of dignity is a magazine that takes popular culture seriously, one that pays attention to the same things that *Rolling Stone* does, but at the level that *New York Review* attends to books."

BIOGRAPHICAL AND CRITICAL SOURCES:

PERIODICALS

Library Journal, July, 2003, Carol J. Binkowski, review of *Jump Jim Crow: Lost Plays, Lyrics, and Street Prose of the First Atlantic Popular Culture,* p. 85.*

* * *

LO-JOHANSSON, (Karl) Ivar 1901-1990

PERSONAL: Born February 23, 1901, in Oesmo, Stockholm, Sweden; died April 10, 1990 (some sources cite April 11), in Stockholm, Sweden; son of Gottfrid (a laborer) and Lovisa (a manual laborer; maiden name, Ersson) Lo-Johansson.

CAREER: Stonecutter, farmhand, journalist, and manual laborer in France, England, and Hungary, 1925-29; writer, beginning 1927.

AWARDS, HONORS: Prize from Nio Society, 1941, for *Bara en Mor;* award from Foundation for the Promotion of Literature, 1953; Dobloug Prize, 1953 and 1973; Ph.D., University of Uppsala, 1964; Nordic Council Prize, 1979, for *Pubertet;* officer of French Order of Arts and Letters, 1986.

WRITINGS:

IN ENGLISH TRANSLATION

Godnatt, Jord (novel; title means "Goodnight, Earth"), Bonnier (Stockholm, Sweden), 1933, translation, notes, and afterword by Rochelle Wright published as *Breaking Free,* University of Nebraska Press (Lincoln, NE), 1990.

Bara en Mor (novel), Bonnier (Stockholm, Sweden), 1939, translation, afterword, and notes by Robert E. Bjork published as *Only a Mother,* University of Nebraska Press (Lincoln, NE), 1991.

Lyckat (novel), Bonnier (Stockholm, Sweden), 1962, translation from the Swedish by Allan Tapsell published as *Bodies of Love,* Souvenir Press, 1971.

Peddling My Wares, translated, and with an introduction, by Rochelle Wright, Camden House (Columbia, SC), 1995.

FICTION

Måna är Död (novel; title means "Maana Is Dead"), Bonnier (Stockholm, Sweden), 1932.

Kungsgatan (novel; title means "The King's Street"), Bonnier (Stockholm, Sweden), 1935, reprinted with epilogue by Ragner Oldberg, 1966.

Statarna (short stories; title means "The Farm Workers"), two volumes, Bonnier (Stockholm, Sweden), 1936–37, reprinted, 1961.

Jordproletärerna (title means "Proletarians of the Soul"), Bonnier (Stockholm, Sweden), 1941, reprinted, Foerfattarförlaget, 1970.

Traktorn (novel; title means "The Tractor"), Bonnier (Stockholm, Sweden), 1943, reprinted, Trevi (Stockholm, Sweden), 1973.

Statarnoveller: Statarna och Jordproletärerna (title means "Stories of the Farm Workers"), two volumes, Bonnier (Stockholm, Sweden), 1945.

Geniet: En Roman om Pubertet (novel; title means "The Genius"), Bonnier (Stockholm, Sweden), 1947, reprinted, 1964.

Ungdoinsnoveller: Ett Lag Historier; Tidiga Noveller (title means "Stories of Youth"), Bonnier (Stockholm, Sweden), 1948.

Noveller (title means "Short Stories"), commentary by Arne Haeggqvist, Svenska Bokförlaget, 1960.

Astronomens Hus (title means "House of the Astronomer"), Bonnier (Stockholm, Sweden), 1966.

Elektra, Kvinna år 2070 (novel; title means "Electra, Woman of the Year 2070"), Bonnier (Stockholm, Sweden), 1967.

Martyrerna (title means "The Martyrs"), Bonnier (Stockholm, Sweden), 1968.

Passionerna: Älskog (short stories; title means "The Passions"), seven volumes, Bonnier (Stockholm, Sweden), 1968–72.

Girigbukarna (title means "The Misers"), Bonnier (Stockholm, Sweden), 1969.

Karriäristerna (title means "The Careerists"), Bonnier (Stockholm, Sweden), 1969.

Vällustingarna (title means "The Lechers"), Bonnier (Stockholm, Sweden), 1970.

Lögnhalsarna (title means "The Liars"), Bonnier (Stockholm, Sweden), 1971.

Vishetslärerna (title means "The Teachers of Wisdom"), Bonnier (Stockholm, Sweden), 1972.

Nunnan i Vadstena: Sedeskildringar (title means "The Nun of Vadstena: Moral Stories"), Bonnier (Stockholm, Sweden), 1973.

Ordets Makt: Historien om Spraket (title means "The Power of Words"), Bonnier (Stockholm, Sweden), 1973.

Folket och Herrarna (title means "The People and the Masters"), two volumes, Norstedt (Stockholm, Sweden), 1973.

Furstarna: en Krönika från Gustav Vasa till Karl XII (title means "The Rulers"), Bonnier (Stockholm, Sweden), 1974.

Lastbara Berättelser (title means "Stories of Vice"), Bonnier (Stockholm, Sweden), 1974.

Passionsnoveller (title means "Stories of Passion"), two volumes, Aldus (Stockholm, Sweden), 1974.

Statarnoveller: Jordproletärerna (sequel to *Statarnoveller: Statarna och Jordproletärerna;* title means "Stories of the Farm Workers: The Proletarian of the Earth"), Forum (Stockholm, Sweden), 1975.

Romanem om Måna (title means "A Novel about Måna"; contains *Måna är Död* and *Astronomens Hus;*), Trevi (Stockholm, Sweden), 1976.

En Arbetares Liv: Proletärnoveller (title means "A Worker's Life: Proletarian Stories"), Bonnier (Stockholm, Sweden), 1977.

AUTOBIOGRAPHICAL SERIES

Analfabetan: En Berätteise från Min Ungdom (title means "The Illiterate"), Bonnier (Stockholm, Sweden), 1951, reprinted, Aldus/Bonnier (Stockholm, Sweden), 1966.

Stockholmaren (title means "The Stockholmer"), Bonnier (Stockholm, Sweden), 1956, reprinted, Aldus/Bonnier, 1964.

Journalisten (title means "The Journalist"), Bonnier (Stockholm, Sweden), 1956.

Socialisten (title means "The Socialist"), Bonnier (Stockholm, Sweden), 1958.

Soldaten (title means "The Soldier"), Bonnier (Stockholm, Sweden), 1959.

Proletärförfattaren (title means "The Proletarian Writer"), Bonnier (Stockholm, Sweden), 1960.

Gårdfarihandlaren (title means "The Country Peddler"), Bonnier (Stockholm, Sweden), reprinted, 1963.

Also author of *Författaren* (title means "The Writer"), published by Bonnier (Stockholm, Sweden).

OTHER

Vagabondliv i Frankrike (title means "Vagabondage in France"), Wahlstroem & Widstrand (Stockholm, Sweden), 1927.

Kolet i Våld (title means "The Power of Coal"), Wahlstroem & Widstrand (Stockholm, Sweden), 1928.

Statarliv (title means "The Life of the Farm Worker"), Folket i Bild Förlag (Stockholm, Sweden), 1941.

Stridsskrifter (title means "Polemical Pamphlets"), Bonnier (Stockholm, Sweden), 1946.

Statarna i Bild (title means "Farm Workers in Pictures"), illustrated by Gunnar Lundh, KF's Bokförlag (Stockholm, Sweden), 1948.

Monism, Bonnier (Stockholm, Sweden), 1948.

Ålderdom (title means "Old Age"), illustrated by Sven Jaerlass, KF's Bokförlag (Stockholm, Sweden), 1949.

Vagabondliv (title means "Vagabondage"; contains *Vagabondliv i Frankrike, Kolet i Våld,* "Nederstigen i Dödsriket," *Zigenare,* and "Mina Staeders Ansikten"), Bonnier (Stockholm, Sweden), 1949.

Ålderdoms-Sverige (title means "Old Age in Sweden"), Bonnier (Stockholm, Sweden), 1952.

Okänt Paris (title means "Unknown Paris"), illustrated by Tore Johnson, Bonnier (Stockholm, Sweden), 1954.

Zigenarväg (title means "Gypsy Ways"), illustrated by Anna Riwkin-Brick, Bonnier (Stockholm, Sweden), 1955.

Att Skriva en Roman: Ett Självbiografisk Berättelse (autobiography; title means "Writing a Novel"), illustrated by Nisse Zetterberg, Bonnier (Stockholm, Swedcn), 1957.

Ur Klyvnadens Tid (poems; title means "The Splitting Time"), FIB's Lyrikklubb, 1958.

Zigenare (title means "Gypsies"), Bokförlaget Prisma, 1963.

Statarnas Liv och Död (title means "Farm Workers Alive and Dead"), Bonnier (Stockholm, Sweden), 1963.

(With Mats Janson and Ingemar Liman) *Statarlängan från Berga,* Stiftelsen Skensen (Stockholm, Sweden), 1968.

Stridsskrifter (title means "Polemical Pamphlets"), two volumes, Svensk Vidifon, 1971, reprinted, Fax, 1974.

Statarskolen i Litteraturen (title means "The Literary School of the Farm Workers"), Författarförlaget (Göeborg, Sweden), 1972.

Dagbok från Tjugo-Talet (title means "Diary from the Twenties"), two volumes, Corona, 1974.

Dagar och Dagsverken: Debatter och Memoarer (title means "Days and Day's Work"), Bonnier (Stockholm, Sweden), 1975.

Under de Gröna Ekarna i Sörmland (title means "Under the Green Oaks in Sörmland"), Forum (Stockholm, Sweden), 1976.

Passioner i Urval, Bra Böcker, 1976.

Den Sociala Fotobildboken (title means "The Social Photograph Book"), Raben & Sjögren, 1977.

Pubertet (memoirs; title means "Puberty"), Bonnier (Stockholm, Sweden), 1978.

Leidenschaften, Wilhelm Heyne, 1978.

Das Liebesgiück, Wilhelm Heyne, 1978.

Asfalt (memoirs; title means "Asphalt"), Bonnier (Stockholm, Sweden), 1979.

Tröskeln (memoirs; title means "The Threshold"), Bonnier (Stockholm, Sweden), 1982.

Trihet (memoirs; title means "Freedom"), [Sweden], 1985.

Author of *Till en Författare* (title means "To an Author"), 1988. Works by Lo-Johansson have been translated into twenty-five languages. Lo-Johansson's papers are archived at the University of Uppsala Library, Carolina Rediviva. Papers and memorabilia may also be found at Ivar Lo-muséet (The Ivar Lo Museum) in Stockholm. Additional correspondence is held by the Royal Library and in the private archives of Albert Bonniers Förlag, both in Stockholm.

ADAPTATIONS: The novel *Godnatt, Jord* was filmed in 1978.

SIDELIGHTS: "In the period between the world wars," Rochelle Wright explained in the *Dictionary of Literary Biography,* "many writers from impoverished rural backgrounds attained prominence in Sweden, their rise corresponding roughly to the establishment of a welfare state. Lacking formal academic training, they educated themselves however they could: through lending libraries, at folk high schools, and by writing for the radical press. Several of these writers drew attention to their class origins by creating fictional worlds that portrayed Swedish society, past and present, from the perspective of the disadvantaged. Ivar Lo-Johansson, whose career spanned seven decades, was the most prolific of these epic realists and an active participant in literary and cultural debates. Known familiarly as Ivar Lo, he was both critically acclaimed and popular with readers. His early works depicted oppressive social and economic conditions among agricultural laborers but resonate in equal measure from penetrating psychological insight. In his middle years Lo-Johansson turned to the autobiographical novel; employing humor and irony, he projected his fictional alter ego against a backdrop of nearly a half century of Swedish social history. His many short stories, particularly those written toward the end of his career, rejuvenated the genre in Sweden. Though a consummate stylist, Lo-Johansson was not an innovator of form. Rather, his contribution to Swedish literature results from his illumination of culturally specific subject matter in the context of universal themes."

Lo-Johansson wrote numerous books on a wide variety of subjects, including travel, sports, politics, and Swedish social life, as well as books for young people. His most important work is considered by some critics to be the body of material that contributed to the abolition of Sweden's *statare* system in 1935. Lo-Johansson was himself born to a family of *statare,* which Torborg Lundell described in the *Reference Guide to World Literature* as "the lowest class of agricultural workers, the estate workers . . . who were tied to the big estates, being paid in kind and enduring substandard living conditions, and for all practical purposes not 'free.'"

The best known example of this writing may be *Bara en Mor* (title means "Only a Mother"), whose character was modeled, some critics claim, after that of Lo-Johansson's mother and other *statare* women he had met. According to Lundell, the novel is "about a beautiful young woman, Rya-Rya, who swims nude in an isolated lake on a hot summer day and is branded by the conservative estate workers as a fallen woman. Defiantly, she marries [a man unworthy of her attention] . . . and produces one child after another, like the rest of the women. . . . She is . . . trapped in a life of repression while lacking the ability to change it. Only as a mother can she realize some of her strength." Lundell praised the author for "a keen eye for documentary details" and for his conviction "that literature should have a definite social function which is best met through realistic journalistic methods."

Another frequent theme of Lo-Johansson's writing is the argument that, as Lundell described it, "young men should have access to young women as a natural outlet for their sexuality." The eroticism and sexuality in his novels shocked the conservative Swedes of his day, beginning with Lo-Johansson's first novel, *Måna är Död* (title means "Maana Is Dead"). This was one of the earliest Swedish novels to deal openly and frankly with such issues as a young man's yearning for sex and related topics of prostitution and sexually transmitted disease.

Lo-Johansson also wrote a substantial number of autobiographical works. The first volume, *Analfabeten* (title means "The Illiterate") is "a touching and loving portrayal of his father," Lundell observed, "and a masterpiece in Swedish literature." Later volumes follow the author through stages of his own life, defined by simple, descriptive titles like "the country peddler," "the journalist," "the socialist," or later, "puberty," "the threshold," and finally "freedom."

Lundell attributed Lo-Johansson's success to a number of factors: "His characters are multidimensional and show a deep insight into what makes a human being human. He translated social consciousness and compassion into great literature and created many unforgettable characters. His language is rich and powerful, poetic and realistic, entertaining and captivating."

According to the obituary writer in the *Independent,* Lo-Johansson once explained: "'Roughly speaking, I consider a writer's tasks to be principally two. . . . One is taking care of the language. The other is to rebel against oppression.' Lo-Johansson remained, to the end, a writer and a very political person. As a member and representative of the lower, 'un-academic' classes he felt it to be his duty to keep the language from remaining an upper-class privilege and preserve." Wright concluded: "Ivar Lo-Johansson's literary career encompasses the better part of the twentieth century. Within his lifetime he saw Sweden change from a provincial rural society to a modern industrialized nation, and he wrote extensively about the transformation. By examining, in many earlier works, his class of origin, he helped bring new subject matters and a fresh perspective to Swedish literature. Yet, Lo-Johansson was, by no means, only a social realist. His predominant theme, the search for freedom, alludes not only to emancipation—from oppressive social systems—but also to psychological independence and existential autonomy, quests that have universal relevance."

BIOGRAPHICAL AND CRITICAL SOURCES:

BOOKS

Dictionary of Literary Biography, Volume 259: *Twentieth-Century Swedish Writers before World War II,* Thomson Gale (Detroit, MI), 2002.

Edstroem, Maurice, *Lo-Johansson,* Bonnier (Stockholm, Sweden), 1954, revised edition published as *Ävan, Käleken, Klassen: En Bok om Lo-Johanssonsförfattarskap,* Forum (Stockholm, Sweden), 1976.

Furuland, Lars, and Ragner Oldberg, *Lo-Johansson i Trycksvärtans Ijus,* Bonnier (Stockholm, Sweden), 1961.

Holmgren, Olga, *Kärlek och Ära,* Liber (Stockholm, Sweden), 1978.

Lo-Johansson, Ivar, *Analfabetan: En Berätteise från Min Ungdom,* Bonnier (Stockholm, Sweden), 1951, reprinted, Aldus/Bonnier (Stockholm, Sweden), 1966.

Lo-Johansson, Ivar, *Stockholmaren,* Bonnier (Stockholm, Sweden), 1956, reprinted, Aldus/Bonnier (Stockholm, Sweden), 1964.

Lo-Johansson, Ivar, *Journalisten,* Bonnier (Stockholm, Sweden), 1956.

Lo-Johansson, Ivar, *Att Skriva en Roman: Ett Sjaelvbiografiskberättelse,* Bonnier (Stockholm, Sweden), 1957.

Lo-Johansson, Ivar, *Socialisten,* Bonnier (Stockholm, Sweden), 1958.

Lo-Johansson, Ivar, *Soldaten,* Bonnier (Stockholm, Sweden), 1959.

Lo-Johansson, Ivar, *Proletärförfattaren,* Bonnier (Stockholm, Sweden), 1960.

Lo-Johansson, Ivar, *Gårdfarihandlaren,* Bonnier (Stockholm, Sweden), reprinted, 1963.

Lo-Johansson, Ivar, *Pubertet,* Bonnier (Stockholm, Sweden), 1978.

Lo-Johansson, Ivar, *Asfalt,* Bonnier (Stockholm, Sweden), 1979.

Lo-Johansson, Ivar, *Troeskeln,* Bonnier (Stockholm, Sweden), 1982.

Lo-Johansson, Ivar, *Trihet,* [Sweden], 1985.

Öhman, Nina, editor, *Ivar Lo-Johansson och konsten,* Moderna Museet (Stockholm, Sweden), 1990.

Oldberg, Ragner, *Lo-Johansson,* Bonnier (Stockholm, Sweden), 1957.

Palmqvist, Bertil, *Lo-Johansson,* Fax, 1974.

Reference Guide to World Literature, 2nd edition, St. James Press (Detroit, MI), 1995.

PERIODICALS

American Scandinavian Review, number 59, 1971, Jan-Ander Paulsson, "Ivar Lo-Johansson: Crusader for Social Justice," pp. 21-31.

Swedish Book Review, 1991, Rochelle Wright, "Meeting Ivar Lo," pp. 5-9.

World Literature Today, winter, 1990, Yvonne L. Sandstroem, review of *Till en forfattare,* p. 136.

ONLINE

Kuusankoski Public Library in Finland Books and Writers Web site, http://www.kirjasto.sci.fi/ivarlo.htm/ (December 16, 2002).

OBITUARIES:

PERIODICALS

Boston Globe, April 12, 1990, p. 59.

Chicago Tribune, April 18, 1990.

Independent (London, England), April 13, 1990, p. 28.
Newsday, April 13, 1990, p. 36.
Times (London, England), April 13, 1990.*

* * *

LONG, Cathryn J. 1946-

PERSONAL: Born January 12, 1946, in Oakland, CA; daughter of Thomas W. (an educational administrator) and Erna (a teacher; maiden name, Dixon) Long; married Don Bogen (a poet and professor), September 5, 1976; children: Anna, Theodore. *Ethnicity:* "Caucasian." *Education:* University of California—Berkeley, B.A., 1968, graduate study, 1968-76. *Hobbies and other interests:* Music (amateur chamber music performer), local history, travel.

ADDRESSES: Home—362 Terrace Ave., Cincinnati, OH 45220. *E-mail*—cjlong2@yahoo.com.

CAREER: Freelance writer, 1976—; University of Cincinnati, Cincinnati, OH, writer and educational consultant for Center for the Electronic Reconstruction of Historical and Archaeological Sites, 1996—. Curriculum Design for Tomorrow's World, Inc., associate, 1982—; creator of "The Riverboat Age" (billboard display for Tallstacks festivals), City of Cincinnati, 1988, 1991, and 1995. "U-Kids" (cooperative infant care center at University of Cincinnati), cofounder, 1981-82; volunteer tutor for local public school system.

WRITINGS:

(With Rudy Tretten) *The Future of American Government: What Will It Be?,* Allyn & Bacon (Boston, MA), 1978.
(With David C. King) *Themes for Teaching U.S. History: Conflict and Change,* Global Perspectives in Education (New York, NY), 1979.
(With Rudie W. Tretten and Margaret S. Branson) *Work in Tomorrow's World,* Global Perspectives in Education (New York, NY), 1979.
Out on the Town with Taft (children's play), performed in Cincinnati, OH, at Cincinnati Public Library, 1983.
(With Mary Jane Turner, John S. Bowes, and Elizabeth J. Lott) *Civics: Citizens in Action,* Merrill Publishing, 1986, revised edition, 1990.
The Middle East in Search of Peace, Millbrook Press (Brookfield, CT), 1994, revised edition, 1996.
Ohio: Past and Present, Graphic Learning/Abrams 1995.
Crossword America: American History 1776 to 1990, Lowell House Juvenile (Los Angeles, CA), 1998.
Crossword America: The Fifty States, illustrated by Larry Nolte, Lowell House Juvenile (Los Angeles, CA), 1999.
Crossword America: The Presidents, illustrated by Larry Nolte, Lowell House Juvenile (Los Angeles, CA), 1999.
The Cherokee, Lucent Books (San Diego, CA), 2000.
Ancient America, Lucent Books (San Diego, CA), 2002.
Westward Expansion, Kidhaven Press (San Diego, CA), 2003.
The Agricultural Revolution, Lucent Books (San Diego, CA), 2004.

Contributor to books, including *The World: Lands and Peoples,* by Lynn S. Parisi, Graphics Learning/Abrams, 1992; author of curriculum material on global affairs for Global Perspectives in Education, 1975-79. Author (with David C. King) of the booklets "A Teacher's Guide to Great Decisions, 1981" and "A Teacher's Guide to Great Decisions, 1982," for Foreign Policy Association (New York, NY).

SIDELIGHTS: Cathryn J. Long once commented: "I use my literary training to try to make nonfiction as exciting as fiction. It *is,* of course, but many historians and fact collectors tell only dull tales."

BIOGRAPHICAL AND CRITICAL SOURCES:

PERIODICALS

Booklist, October 15, 1994, p. 422.
Curriculum Review, March 1995, p. 12.
Horn Book Guide, spring 1995, p. 160; spring, 1997, review of *The Middle East in Search of Peace,* p. 167.
School Library Journal, August 1994, p. 164; January, 1997, review of *The Middle East in Search of Peace,* p. 130.
Voice of Youth Advocates, June, 2001, Kevin Beach, review of *The Cherokee.*

M

MACDONALD, James D. 1954-

(Nicholas Adams, a house pseudonym, Victor Appleton, a house pseudonym, Martin Delrio, Douglas Morgan, Robyn Tallis, a house pseudonym)

PERSONAL: Born 1954, in White Plains, NY; son of a chemical engineer and an artist; married Debra A. Doyle (a writer and teacher); children: four. *Education:* University of Rochester, received degree in medieval studies. *Hobbies and other interests:* Science fiction, cats, computers.

ADDRESSES: *Home*—Colebrook, NH. *Agent*—c/o Author Mail, Tor Books, 175 5th Ave., New York, NY 10010. *E-mail*—doylemacdonald@sff.net.

CAREER: Journalist and science fiction author. Volunteer with a local ambulance company. *Military service:* U.S. Navy, served fifteen-year tour of duty as both an enlisted man and an officer.

AWARDS, HONORS: Mythopoetic Fantasy Award for children's literature, 1992, and New York Public Library Books for the Teen Age citation, 1993, both for *Knight's Wyrd;* Best Young Adult Science Fiction Award, *Science Fiction Chronicle,* 1997, for *Groogleman.*

WRITINGS:

NOVELS; "CIRCLE OF MAGIC" SERIES; WITH WIFE, DEBRA A. DOYLE

School of Wizardry, Troll Books (Mahway, NJ), 1990.

Tournament and Tower, Troll Books (Mahway, NJ), 1990, reissued as *Secret of the Tower,* 2000.

City by the Sea, Troll Books (Mahway, NJ), 1990, reissued as *The Wizard's Statue,* 2000.

The Prince's Players, Troll Books (Mahway, NJ), 1990, reissued as *Danger in the Palace,* 2000.

The Prisoners of Bell Castle, Troll Books (Mahway, NJ), 1990.

The High King's Daughter, Troll Books (Mahway, NJ), 1990.

NOVELS; "MAGEWORLDS" SERIES; WITH DEBRA A. DOYLE

The Price of the Stars, Tor (New York, NY), 1992.

Starpilot's Grave, Tor (New York, NY), 1993.

By Honor Betray'd, Tor (New York, NY), 1994.

The Gathering Flame, Tor (New York, NY), 1995.

The Long Hunt, Tor (New York, NY), 1996.

The Stars Asunder, Tor (New York, NY), 1999.

A Working of Stars, Tor (New York, NY), 2002.

NOVELS; "BAD BLOOD" SERIES; WITH DEBRA A. DOYLE

Bad Blood, Berkley (New York, NY), 1993.

Hunter's Moon, Berkley (New York, NY), 1994.

Judgment Night, Berkley (New York, NY), 1995.

OTHER NOVELS; WITH DEBRA A. DOYLE

(Under house pseudonym Robyn Tallis) *Night of Ghosts and Lightning* ("Planet Builders" no. 2), Ivy, 1989.

(Under house pseudonym Robyn Tallis) *Zero-Sum Games* ("Planet Builders" no. 5), Ivy, 1989.

Timecrime, Inc. (Robert Silverberg's "Time Tours" no. 3), Harper (New York, NY), 1991.

(Under house pseudonym Nicholas Adams) *Pep Rally* ("Horror High" no. 7), Harper (New York, NY), 1991.

(Under house pseudonym Victor Appleton) *Monster Machine* ("Tom Swift" no. 5), Pocket Books (New York, NY), 1991.

(Under house pseudonym Victor Appleton) *Aquatech Warriors* ("Tom Swift" no. 6), Pocket Books (New York, NY), 1991.

Night of the Living Rat (Daniel Pinkwater's "Melvinge of the Megaverse" no. 2), Ace (New York, NY), 1992.

Knight's Wyrd, Harcourt (New York, NY), 1992.

Groogleman, Harcourt (New York, NY), 1996.

Requiem for Boone (based on television series "Gene Roddenberry's Earth—Final Conflict"), Tor (New York, NY), 2000.

NOVELS; UNDER PSEUDONYM MARTIN DELRIO

Mortal Kombat (movie novelization; adult and young adult versions), Tor (New York, NY), 1995.

Spider-Man Super-Thriller: Midnight Justice, Byron Preiss Multimedia/Pocket Books (New York, NY), 1996.

Spider-Man Super-Thriller: Global War, Byron Preiss Multimedia/Pocket Books (New York, NY), 1996.

Prince Valiant (movie novelization), Avon (New York, NY), 1997.

A Silence in the Heavens ("Mechwarrior Dark Age," no. 4), Roc (New York, NY), 2003.

Truth and Shadows ("Mechwarrior Dark Age," no. 5), Roc (New York, NY), 2003.

Service for the Dead ("Mechwarrior Dark Age," no. 6), Roc (New York, NY), 2003.

OTHER

(Under pseudonym Douglas Morgan) *Tiger Cruise* (novel), Forge (New York, NY), 2001.

(Under pseudonym Douglas Morgan; editor and annotator) *What Do You Do with a Drunken Sailor: Unexpurgated Sea Chanties* (nonfiction), Swordsmith (Pomfret, CT), 2002.

(Under pseudonym Martin Delrio) *The Loch Ness Monster* (juvenile nonfiction), Rosen (New York, NY), 2002.

The Apocalypse Door (novel), Tor (New York, NY), 2002.

Author and coauthor, with Debra A. Doyle, of short stories appearing in numerous anthologies, including *Werewolves,* edited by Jane Yolen and Martin Greenberg, Harper Junior Books, 1988; *Vampires,* edited by Jane Yolen and Martin Greenberg, HarperCollins, 1991; *Newer York,* edited by Lawrence Watt-Evans, Roc, 1991; *Alternate Kennedys,* edited by Mike Resnick and Martin Greenberg, Tor, 1992; *Bruce Coville's Book of Monsters,* edited by Bruce Coville, Scholastic, 1993; *Swashbuckling Editor Stories,* edited by John Betancourt, Wildside Press, 1993; *Bruce Coville's Book of Ghosts,* edited by Bruce Coville, Scholastic, 1994; *A Wizard's Dozen,* edited by Michael Stearns, Harcourt, 1995; *A Wayfarer's Dozen,* edited by Michael Stearns, Harcourt, 1995; *Witch Fantastic,* edited by Mike Resnick and Martin Greenberg, DAW, 1995; *Camelot,* edited by Jane Yolen, Philomel, 1995; *The Book of Kings,* edited by Richard Gilliam and Martin Greenberg, Roc, 1995; *Tales of the Knights Templar,* edited by Katherine Kurtz, Warner, 1995; *Otherwere,* edited by Laura Ann Gilman and Keith R. A. DeCandido, Berkley/Ace, 1996; *A Nightmare's Dozen,* edited by Michael Stearns, Harcourt, 1996; and *Bruce Coville's Book of Spine Tinglers,* edited by Coville, Scholastic, 1996.

WORK IN PROGRESS: *City of the Dreadful Night,* a fantasy novel; "Mageworlds" volume no. 8; *Mist and Snow,* a Civil War fantasy.

SIDELIGHTS: In close collaboration with his wife, Debra A. Doyle, James D. Macdonald writes science fiction and fantasy for children, young adults, and adults. In an interview with *Amazon.com,* Macdonald related that he writes the first drafts of the stories and novels and that his wife works on the revisions. Macdonald said, "I have final say on the plot and characters, she has final say on the words and descriptions." He commented that the books of J. R. R. Tolkien have had an impact on his writing and said that he also enjoys reading the work of Robert Heinlein and Alexandre Dumas. Together, Macdonald and Doyle have written over twenty novels and innumerable short stories, primarily fantasy and science fiction for young adults.

Doyle and Macdonald's first series, "Circle of Magic," intended for an elementary and junior high school audience, consists of six novels chronicling the story of Randal and his adventures in fulfilling his destiny to become a wizard. *School of Wizardry* introduces twelve-year-old Randal, who is determined to become a wizard after a wayfaring wizard visits his home. Initially delighted to be admitted as an apprentice into the famous Schola Sorceriae (School of Wizardry), he soon realizes that before becoming a master wizard he must conquer many enemies, among them Lord Fess, who plans to destroy the school and gain supreme power through his evil spells.

Tournament and Tower, later published as *Secret of the Tower,* is the second installment in the "Circle of Magic" series. The novel opens with Randal being granted permission to graduate from the School of Wizardry with the provision that he refrain from using his magic until Balpesh, the master wizard, exonerates him for breaking his pledge not to use a weapon. In the meantime, Randal becomes a squire to his cousin Walter. In a tournament, Walter sustains serious injuries, but Randal, lacking his magical powers, cannot rescue Walter. Balpesh, who could rescue him, is himself in great peril. It is up to Randal to free the wizard, who can then save Walter and restore Randal's magical powers.

In *City By the Sea* (later published as *The Wizard's Statue*) Randal, now a fifteen-year-old journeyman wizard, embarks on one of his most hazardous undertakings when he accepts a statue from a dying stranger and promises to fulfill the man's deathbed wish that the statue be brought to Dagon, a soldier of fortune. Randal soon learns that the statue has magical powers of its own, and that Dagon is not the only person seeking the statue.

The series continues with *The Prince's Players* (later published as *Danger in the Palace*), which places Randal and his friend Lys on their way to visit Prince Vespian's palace. Here, Randal learns tricks of illusion from the court's master wizard, Petrucio. He thinks his new talent is to be used in royal stage productions; instead, he discovers that Petrucio has more diabolical plans for his new skills. A dangerous adversary seeks to conquer Prince Vespian's kingdom, drawing Randal and Lys into political intrigue.

In *The Prisoners of Bell Castle,* Randal confronts Lord Fess, his old enemy, when he and his friends agree to guard a boatload of gold needed as wages for Baron Ector's armies, who have put Fess's ancestral home, Bell Castle, under siege. When the gold disappears, Randal is implicated in the theft and must triumph over Lord Fess in order to prove his innocence and recover the gold. The final novel in the "Circle of Magic," series, *The High King's Daughter* follows Randal, Walter, and Lys as they journey into Elfland to rescue Diamante, the High King's daughter, and restore her to her rightful throne. In order to do so, they must enter a magical realm and confront Lord Hugo de la Corre, who has proclaimed himself High King in Diamante's absence.

Doyle and Macdonald's fantasy novel *Knight's Wyrd* won the Mythopoetic Fantasy Award for Children's Literature in 1992 and was placed on the New York Public Library Books for the Teen Age list in 1993. *Knight's Wyrd* combines a realistic story of knighthood with the fantasy elements of magic, dragons, and wizards. Just as young Will Odosson is about to be knighted, the castle wizard predicts his wyrd (fate): Will is not destined to inherit his father's title and lands and will soon meet death. Although the wizard's prophecy comes to pass, it does not occur in the manner Will expects. A young man of strong character, Will becomes a knight despite his wyrd and leaves home seeking adventure. In the course of the novel, Will rescues Isobel, his betrothed, is double-crossed by his Duke, and becomes entangled in high magic. Indeed, he does meet death, but it is in the form of Lord Death, who observes Randal slay the ogre who cannot be killed. A *Kirkus Reviews* critic praised *Knight's Wyrd*'s "strong sense of time, place, and code of honor." *Horn Book* reviewer Ann A. Flowers called it "a lively story," and a *School Library Journal* critic recommended it as "suspenseful," with a lively tempo.

In the next series, the spine-tingling "Bad Blood" trilogy, Macdonald and Doyle explore the kind of horror stories told around campfires after dark. *Bad Blood,* which takes its name from the series, begins with hair-raising tales shared around a campfire in the woods. But Valerie Sherwood and her friends never expected any of the stories to come true. After all, Jay's strange tale of moonlight and werewolves was just make believe. That night, however, they hear the beast prowling around the camp and they remember Jay's words: "By morning, you'll all be dead."

In *Hunter's Moon,* the sequel to *Bad Blood,* Valerie, now a werewolf, uses her power to protect her community from a group of vampires while trying to live a "normal" suburban life. But soon she suspects that werewolves are powerless against vampires and she must find a way to save her loved ones. In *Judgment Night,* the final installment, Valerie is haunted by her own nightmares and by the Wendigo, an ancient force that calls to her from the mountains and thrives on her fear.

The popular "Mageworlds" series, begun in 1992, focuses on the centuries-long conflict between the human Republic and the mysterious Mageworlds. In *The Price of the Stars,* the first in the series, Beka Rosselin-Metadi is tired of consistently hearing about her parents' heroic roles in the human galaxy's history. When her mother is murdered on the Senate floor, however, she finds new pride in her heritage and vows to bring the assassin to justice. Her father offers her *Warhammer,* his cherished ship, for her use in capturing the murderer. As the plot develops, Beka plans her own demise so that she can, with a different identity, conquer the dangerous enemies of the galaxy.

In *Starpilot's Grave,* Beka continues the search for the man who arranged her mother's assassination, but soon it is revealed that the Magelords have breached the Republic's stronghold. Beka, in searching for her mother's killer, infiltrates the Magezone and learns that the Republic is far more vulnerable than she ever imagined. The Magelords have triumphed over the Republic in the third of the series, *By Honor Betray'd.* Confronted with betrayal and surrounded by enemies, Beka strives to reclaim what she can from the wreckage of the Republic.

The Gathering Flame, fourth in the "Mageworlds" series, describes Beka's parents' contributions to the Republic's struggle against the Magelords. The novel chronicles attempts by the Magelords to ravage the galaxy, planet by planet. However, the Magelords must take on three individuals to succeed in their plans: Perada Rosselin, Domina of Entibor, Jos Metadi (a notorious privateer who prefers to battle Mage ships one-on-one), and Errec Ransome, who is acquainted with the customs of the Magelords but has confidences he will not reveal. When the Magelords attack Entibor, the three must work together.

In *The Long Hunt,* set in the era following the Second Magewar, Entibor faces attack by the Magelords. Meanwhile, on the planet Khesat, a crisis unfolds and all depends on Jens Metadi-Jessan D'Rosselin, unwilling heir to the throne. Warring factions and criminal guilds know that control of the heir means control of Khesat and the galaxy. But young Jens, eager for adventure, sets off with his cousin Faral to see the galaxy. However, in their travels they encounter more action than anticipated. Writing in *Locus,* Carolyn Cushman called the "Mageworlds" series "a space opera with unusual depth, and some wonderful characters I'm eager to see in further adventures."

The sixth installment in the series, *The Stars Asunder,* is a prequel set some 500 years before previous volumes, examining the beginnings of the Magewars. The novel focuses on the Mageworlds rather than the Republic, and specifically on Arekhon, a young mage from a prominent family. When Arekhon is drawn into a Mage-Circle determined to breach the legendary Gap Between that separates the Galaxy, he finds romance, danger, and betrayal. A *Publishers Weekly* writer noted that readers didn't have to be familiar with the series to enjoy *The Stars Asunder,* and added that with its combination of "magic, space opera and time travel, the plot offers some surprises, though less suspense and action than expected."

The next novel in the series, 2002's *A Working of Stars,* continues Arekhon's story as he is compelled to return home to complete the work of his broken Mage-Circle and span the Gap Between. A *Publishers Weekly* critic observed that the changing locations and relationships were sometimes confusing, but added that Macdonald and Doyle "manage a bright note of genuine human warmth in the chilly reaches of outer space, as well as offering plenty of action in this rapid-fire blend of sorcery and SF." *Booklist* critic Roland Green similarly noted that the novel emphasizes action more than character, but stated that "this is imaginative, intelligent, fast-paced space opera, in the positive sense of the term."

Macdonald has also written or cowritten several stand-alone works, including *Groogleman,* which a critic for *Science Fiction Chronicle* declared "the best young adult science fiction" of 1996. In this fantasy novel, the plot centers around thirteen-year-old Dan Henchard, a student healer who must save his teacher Leezie, a natural healer, from her abductor. Dan, believing the kidnapper is the Groogleman, travels to the Dead Lands in his search for Leezie, knowing that failure means certain death for him. Along the way he receives help from a hunter named Joshua and in the process learns much about himself. Selections from "historical documents" introduce each chapter and provide clues to the secret purpose of the Grooglemen. A reviewer for *Realm of Fantasy* magazine wrote that *Groogleman* is "filled with adventure and action—a must read," and a *Science Fiction Chronicle* writer praised it as "an old fashioned post-collapse adventure."

Macdonald's 2002 novel *The Apocalypse Door* is based on a short story he and Doyle wrote for Katherine Kurtz's anthology *Tales of the Knights Templar.* Hero Peter Crossman is not a medieval knight, however, but a modern-day member of the religious fighting order that was supposedly disbanded over 600 years ago. Crossman is an agent for the secretive Knights Templar, assigned to investigate the disappearance of a United Nations peacekeeping team. The task leads him and his partner Maggie, a nun and trained assassin, to a supernatural plot to open a gate to Hell. A *Kirkus Reviews* writer enjoyed the humor of this "breezy spy spoof," describing it as "cloak-and-dagger meets robe-and-Psalter with jokes and swagger, all just for fun." Calling Crossman a "refreshingly original hero," a *Publishers Weekly* critic observed that "though other novels have blended mysticism, mystery and fantasy, few have done it as smartly or succinctly as this one."

In an interview with *Amazon.com,* Macdonald explained that he attempts to write every day but said that it "can be an hour or it can be ten hours, depending on how things are going." Reflecting that he served fifteen years in the U.S. Navy as both an enlisted man and an officer before becoming a full-time writer, he advised would-be writers to "go out and have a life to write about, then write and keep writing."

BIOGRAPHICAL AND CRITICAL SOURCES:

PERIODICALS

Booklist, April 15, 2002, Roland Green, review of *A Working of Stars,* p. 1387.

Horn Book, January-February, 1993, Ann A. Flowers, review of *Knight's Wyrd,* pp. 89-90; March-April, 1996, p. 202.

Kirkus Reviews, October 1, 1992, review of *Knight's Wyrd;* October 1, 2002, review of *The Apocalypse Door,* p. 1434.

Publishers Weekly, May 31, 1999, review of *The Stars Asunder,* p. 72; March 11, 2002, review of *A Working of Stars,* p. 56; October 14, 2002, review of *The Apocalypse Door,* p. 68.

Realms of Fantasy, April, 1997, review of *Groogleman.*

School Library Journal, December, 1996, Susan L. Rogers, review of *Groogleman,* pp. 120-121.

Science Fiction Chronicle, April-May, 1997, review of *Groogleman.*

ONLINE

Amazon.com, http://www.amazon.com/ (December 11, 1998), interview with Macdonald.

Doyle and Macdonald—About Our Books, http://www.sff.net/people/doylemacdonald/ (February 16, 2004).

Eternal Night, http://www.eternalnight.co.uk/chronicle/ (February 16, 2004), interview with Macdonald.*

* * *

MACE, Nancy L(awson) 1941-
(Nancy M. Lang)

PERSONAL: Born December 27, 1941, in Twin Falls, ID; daughter of Francis R. (an entomologist) and V. (Tremblay) Lawson; divorced; children: Charles Lang, Catherine Lang. *Education:* University of North Carolina at Chapel Hill, B.A., 1964; Antioch University Maryland, M.A., 1978.

ADDRESSES: *Home*—1215 Cowpens Ave., Baltimore, MD 21204. *Agent*—c/o Author Mail, Johns Hopkins University Press, Baltimore, MD 21211.

CAREER: Baltimore City Department of Social Services, Baltimore, MD, social worker, 1964-65; instructor in needlework and American handicrafts at Harford, Dundalk, and Essex community colleges, 1966-77; Harford Community College, Bel Air, MD, instructor in gerontology, 1977-79; Johns Hopkins University, Baltimore, assistant in psychiatry and coordinator of T. Rowe and Eleanor Price Teaching Service, 1979-84; Office of Technology Assessment,

U.S. Congress, consultant and writer, 1984—. Founder of Senior Citizens Resource Institute, Bel Air; member of Harford County Community Housing Resources Board, 1977-79; chairman of Family Life Education Study Group, Harford Council of Community Services, 1977-79; board member of Alzheimer's Disease and Related Disorders Association, 1982-86; member of Maryland State Governor's Task Force on Alzheimer's Disease, 1984-85; member of board of directors of Maryland Adult Day Care Association; consulting member of Dementia Panel of the American Medical Association, 1984, and of the Veterans Administration, 1985; member of ad hoc clinical advisory group of Long-Term Health Care Group of National Medical Enterprises, 1985; consultant to Congressional Office of Technology Assessment.

MEMBER: Gerontological Society, Maryland Gerontological Society, Alzheimer's Disease Association of Maryland (cofounder, 1978), Baltimore Washington Society for Psychogeriatrics.

WRITINGS:

(As Nancy M. Lang) *Getting Started in Egg Decorating,* Bruce (New York, NY), 1971.

(As Nancy M. Lang) *Getting Started in Plastics,* Collier Books (New York, NY), 1972.

(With Peter V. Rabins) *The Thirty-six-Hour Day: A Family Guide to Caring for Persons with Alzheimer's Disease, Related Dementing Illnesses, and Memory Losses in Later Life,* Johns Hopkins University Press (Baltimore, MD), 1981, 3rd edition, 1999.

(With Peter V. Rabins) *Survey of Day Care for the Demented Adult in the United States* (monograph), National Council on the Aging (Washington, DC), 1984.

(Designer) Jitka M. Zgola, *Doing Things: A Guide to Programming Activities for Persons with Alzheimer's Disease and Related Disorders,* Johns Hopkins University Press (Baltimore, MD), 1987.

(Editor) *Dementia Care: Patient, Family, and Community,* Johns Hopkins University Press (Baltimore, MD), 1990.

(With Dorothy H. Coons) *Quality of Life in Long-Term Care,* Haworth Press (New York, NY), 1996.

Contributor to books, including *Physical Therapy of the Geriatric Patient,* edited by Osa Jackson, Churchill Livingstone (New York, NY), 1983; and *Alzheimer's Disease and Related Disorders: Research and Management,* edited by William E. Kelly, C. C Thomas (Springfield, IL), 1984. Also author of "Facts of Dementia," a column in *Journal of Geriatric Nursing,* 1983—. Contributor to professional journals.

SIDELIGHTS: After a career as an instructor in handiworks, and a couple of how-to books on egg decorating and working with plastic, Nancy L. Mace turned to the study of gerontology and the complex issues surrounding long-term care for the elderly. Through her work with the Johns Hopkins Department of Psychiatry and Behavioral Sciences and numerous organizations devoted to treating geriatric diseases, Mace has emerged as a leading advocate for those suffering from Alzheimer's and other forms of dementia. In 1981, she collaborated with Johns Hopkins professor Peter V. Rabins to produce *The Thirty-six-Hour Day: A Family Guide to Caring for Persons with Alzheimer's Disease, Related Dementing Illnesses, and Memory Losses in Later Life.* The book covers the medical, emotional, financial, and legal challenges that face caregivers coping with a relative who may often act inappropriately, wander off, and may not even remember them. Its straightforward language and practical advice based on the authors' long experience with these diseases and numerous interviews with caregivers have made the book extremely popular, and with over one million copies sold, it is now in its third edition. As Simone DaSilva, a social worker with the Alzheimer's Association, told *South Florida Sun-Sentinel* reporter Diane Lade, "I would say, eventually, almost everyone who walks in our door buys it and uses it." Physicians and other professional caregivers have also found the book useful in understanding both their patients and the day-to-day hurdles that family members face. *Journal of Family Practice* contributor Kenneth Holtzapple wrote simply, "If you care for demented patients or simply have an interest in dementia, read this book, and recommend it to all families and nursing personnel caring for demented patients."

Mace next edited a collection of pieces by medical professionals, social workers, and lawyers dealing with Alzheimer's and other diseases which cause a loss of mental faculties. *Dementia Care: Patient, Family, and Community* begins with "an excellent overview of the multidisciplinary diagnostic assessment," according to *Annals of Internal Medicine* contributor Daniel Gianturco, and goes on to provide advice on devising care plans, implementing behavior modification strategies, and building volunteer programs. "Mace has done an exceptional service in synthesizing the many faces of dementia care seen by the patient, the family, the community, and the professional," noted *Health & Social Work* contributor Susan Mercer.

In her next book, *Quality of Life in Long-Term Care,* written with gerontologist Dorothy Coons, Mace combines photographs, case studies, and straightforward narrative to reveal innovative and hopeful solutions to caring for the institutionalized elderly. "I found it refreshing to read the effects of a therapeutic and wellness concept to care rather than 'aging in place,'" commented *Educational Gerontology* contributor J. Conrad Glass. The authors provide advice on including elderly residents in decision-making, offering age-appropriate activities, and respecting the dignity and privacy of patients. In addition, they offer suggestions on overcoming regulations and high costs that might stand in the way of better long-term care. If every caregiver and administrator "read *Quality of Life in Long-Term Care* and made genuine efforts to implement the suggested changes, long-term care facilities might not be as dreaded by our nation's elderly citizens as they are today," concluded *Health and Social Work* reviewer Dianne Garner.

BIOGRAPHICAL AND CRITICAL SOURCES:

PERIODICALS

Annals of Internal Medicine, July 15, 1990, Daniel Gianturco, review of *Dementia Care: Patient, Family, and Community,* p. 79.

Educational Gerontology, June, 1997, J. Conrad Glass, review of *Quality of Life in Long-Term Care,* p. 403.

Health & Social Work, February, 1991, Susan Mercer, review of *Dementia Care,* p. 79; February, 1998, Dianne Garner, review of *Quality of Life in Long-Term Care,* p. 78.

Jerusalem Post, March 24, 198, Leah Abramowitz, review of *The Thirty-six-Hour Day: A Family Guide to Caring for Persons with Alzheimer's Disease, Related Dementing Illnesses, and Memory Losses in Later Life,* p. 338.

Journal of Family Practice, September, 1992, Kenneth Holtzapple, review of *The Thirty-six-Hour Day,* p. 338.

Library Journal, July, 1999, Jodith Jones, review of *The Thirty-six-Hour Day,* p. 122.

South Florida Sun-Sentinel, November 30, 2000, Diane Lade, "Seeking Answers to Alzheimer's: Book Written 20 Years Ago by Neuropsychiatrist Continues to Offer Hope, Direction for Today's Caregivers," p. 3B.*

* * *

MALONE, Bill C(harles) 1934-

PERSONAL: Born August 25, 1934, in Smith County, TX; son of Cleburne and Maude (Owins) Malone. *Education:* University of Texas, B.A., 1956, M.A., 1958, Ph.D., 1965. *Politics:* Democrat. *Religion:* Unaffiliated.

ADDRESSES: Home—Madison, WI. *Agent*—c/o University Press of Kentucky, 663 South Limestone St., Lexington, KY 40508-4008.

CAREER: Southwest Texas State University, San Marcos, instructor, 1962-64, assistant professor of history, 1964-67; Murray State University, Murray, KS, associate professor of history, 1967-69; Wisconsin State University, Whitewater, WI, associate professor of history, 1969-71; Tulane University, New Orleans, LA, associate professor of history, beginning in 1971, became professor emeritus. Host, "Back to the Country," weekly radio show, WORT (Madison, WI), 2003—.

MEMBER: Organization of American Historians, American Folklore Society, Popular Culture Association, Country Music Association, Southern Historical Association, Louisiana Historical Association.

WRITINGS:

Country Music, USA: A Fifty-Year History, University of Texas Press (Austin, TX), 1968, revised, 2002.

(Editor, with Judith McCulloh) *Stars of Country Music: Uncle Dave Macon to Johnny Rodriguez,* University of Illinois Press (Urbana, IL), 1975, reprinted, 1991.

(With David Stricklin) *Southern Music, American Music,* University Press of Kentucky (Lexington, KY), 1979, revised, 2003.

Singing Cowboys and Musical Mountaineers: Southern Culture and the Roots of Country Music, University of Georgia Press (Athens, GA), 1993.

Don't Get above Your Raisin': Country Music and the Southern Working Class, University of Illinois Press (Urbana, IL), 2002.

Editor and annotator of recording *Classic Country Music: A Smithsonian Collection,* Smithsonian Collection of Recordings (Washington, DC), 1990. Contributor to *Encyclopedia of Southern History* and *Grove's Dictionary of Music and Musicians.* Contributor to folklore and country music magazines.

SIDELIGHTS: Country music aficionado and history professor Bill C. Malone has done ground-breaking work in making country music a legitimate subject of study by the academic community. Malone's doctoral dissertation on country music, which was first marketed to the public in 1968 as *Country Music, USA: A Fifty-Year History,* garnered favorable reviews and has since undergone two revisions. Since that time Malone has written about country music for both the popular press and scholarly publications. Yet Malone does not look at country music from an outsider's viewpoint. "I was a fan long before I ever became a writer," Malone told Laurie Joulie in a *Take Country Back* interview. Over the years, Malone has performed with various country music groups, including singing old-time duets with his wife, Bobbie, also a historian. In 2002 Malone's study *Don't Get above Your Raisin': Country Music and the Southern Working Class* was published to much acclaim, and the following year he began hosting "Back to the Country," a weekly radio show broadcast on WORT from Madison, Wisconsin.

Born in rural Texas in 1934, Malone grew up in what he called "a country music family. We got our first Philco battery radio when I was five years old. . . . From the very moment we got the radio we started listening to local shows out of Dallas/Fort Worth and Tulsa, and of course the Grand Ole Opry became a network show that same year," he remembered to Joulie. Their farming family also made its own music, singing old gospel songs and sentimental tunes, and as teenagers Malone's brothers started playing guitars. "I just grew up with it and all my life I've identified the music with good hard-working people. I think it's always told their stories." So Malone decided to tell country music's story in a number of publications, including the 1975 biographical dictionary *Stars of Country Music: Uncle Dave Macon to Johnny Rodriguez,* which was revised in 1991, and the 1979 study with David Stricklin, *Southern Music, American Music,* which was revised in 2003. In the latter book, the authors look at the changes made in southern music due to advances in technology.

The print version of three lectures given at Mercer University as part of its Lamar Memorial lecture, *Singing Cowboys and Musical Mountaineers: Southern Culture and the Roots of Country Music,* gave readers a hint as to the direction of Malone's ongoing research. In the first essay, he discusses the multi-ethnic origins of what had been largely thought to be the Celtic basis for country music. Instead, Malone proposes that "'British' styles met and meshed with German, Spanish, French, Caribbean, Mexican, and African-derived forms." In the second essay, Malone takes a look at the variety of nineteenth-century traveling shows—among them minstrel shows, circuses, showboats, theatrical troupes, medicine shows, and horse shows—that spread popular music throughout the rural South. The final essay treats the mountaineer and cowboy images that emerged during the 1920s and the reasons for their dominance in the perception of what was defined as country music after World War II. An addition to the essays forming the basis of *Singing Cowboys and Musical Mountaineers* are Malone's thoughts about the appeal of country music to blue-collar Americans. He stated that such music provides an "escape and catharsis from present realities" as well as "self-affirmation through such security-laden symbols as home, family, church, and the South."

For the next seven years, Malone continued his research about the cultural basis of country music. In 2002 he published his monumental study *Don't Get above Your Raisin',* "an insightful examination of the process by which a people, a place, and the past interacted to create an sustain a culture," to quote Michael T. Bertrand of the *Journal of Southern History.* "The result is a comprehensive portrait that underscores the complex and dynamic nature of southern culture." Using extensive primary and secondary sources, Malone traces the evolution of such themes as piety vs. hedonism, home vs. rambling, companionship vs. individualism, nostalgia vs. modernity, allotting a chapter to each theme. Because they are universal themes, they have long-lasting currency, even in the twenty-first century, which accounts in part for the broad appeal of country music. Yet the fate of country music as a genre remains uncertain, Malone acknowledges, as it is diluted into more mainstream and suburban middle-class popular culture.

With few exceptions, reviewers applauded the work. For example, *Progressive*'s Matthew Rothschild praised its analysis and depth and suggested it "ought to be required reading" for those interested in the topic, as did *Library Journal* reviewer James E. Perone, who dubbed it a "lucid study" and "thoughtful book." *Choice*'s R. D. Cohen, noting that *Don't Get above Your Raisin'* "supersedes any title . . . available to date," recommended it highly. Several reviewers expressed more qualified praise, however. Among them was Patrick Huber, who, reviewing the work for *Southern Cultures,* wished that Malone had better defined such terms as *rural, urban, South.* Malone's "reverence for his subjects sometimes leads him to overly romantic interpretations," noted Huber, who cited the example of Malone's use of the term *America's truest music* to describe country music. As Huber pointed out, in making such a statement Malone ignores the American-ness of such musical styles as blues and hip hop. In the same vein, Bertrand also mentioned the white-male emphasis of Malone's work, noting that "insights gained from recent scholarship on gender and race are conspicuously absent." "Despite these problems [lack of definitions and over-enthusiasm for his subject]," Huber continued, the work "is a welcome and important study that deepens our understanding of both country music and, to a lesser degree, southern white working people." Finally, Bertrand commented, "*Don't Get above Your Raisin'* is an instant classic, destined to become a standard in modern southern historiography."

BIOGRAPHICAL AND CRITICAL SOURCES:

BOOKS

Malone, Bill C., *Singing Cowboys and Musical Mountaineers: Southern Culture and the Roots of Country Music,* University of Georgia Press (Athens, GA), 1993.

PERIODICALS

AB Bookman's Weekly, December 9, 1985, review of *Country Music USA: A Fifty-Year History,* revised edition, p. 4333.

American Heritage, November, 1994, review of *Country Music USA,* p. 122.

Booklist, October 1, 1985, review of *Country Music USA,* p. 182.

BooksWest, March, 1978, review of *Stars of Country Music: Uncle Dave Macon to Johnny Rodriguez,* p. 29.

Choice, May, 1980, review of *Southern Music, American Music,* p. 398; December, 1985, review of *Country Music USA,* revised edition, p. 614; January, 1994, review of *Singing Cowboys and Musical Mountaineers,* p. 797; June, 2002, R. D. Cohen, review of *Don't Get above Your Raisin': Country Music and the Southern Working Class,* pp. 1779-1780.

Come-All-Ye, winter, 1993, review of *Singing Cowboys and Musical Mountaineers,* p. 7.

Herald (Glasgow, Scotland), July 6, 1998, Ann Donald, "Torn between Two Lovers," review of *Singing Cowboys and Musical Mountaineers,* p. 15.

Journal of American Folklore, April, 1982, review of *Southern Music, American Music* p. 251; July, 1986, review of *Country Music USA,* revised edition, p. 356.

Journal of American History June, 1977, review of *Stars of Country Music,* p. 206; September, 1994, review of *Singing Cowboys and Musical Mountaineers,* pp. 745+.

Journal of American Studies, August, 1982, review of *Southern Music, American Music,* p. 267.

Journal of Popular Culture, winter, 1982, review of *Country Music USA,* p. 91.

Journal of Southern History, August, 1980, review of *Southern Music, American Music,* p. 464; August, 1986, review of *Country Music USA,* revised edition, p. 483; November, 1994, review of *Singing Cowboys and Musical Mountaineers,* pp. 849+; November, 2003, Michael T. Bertrand, review of *Don't Get above Your Raisin',* pp. 996-997.

Kliatt, winter, 1977, review of *Stars of Country Music,* p. 32; winter, 1986, review of *Country Music USA,* revised edition, p. 65.

Library Journal, November 1, 1996, review of *Country Music USA,* p. 42; March 1, 2002, James E. Perone, review of *Don't Get above Your Raisin',* p. 104.

Music Educators Journal, December, 1979, review of *Country Music USA,* p. 91.

Notes (Music Library Association), September, 1980, review of *Southern Music, American Music,* p. 52;

March, 1995, Anthony Lis, review of *Singing Cowboys and Musical Mountaineers,* pp. 905-909.

Progressive, January, 2003, Matthew Rothschild, review of *Don't Get above Your Raisin',* pp. 35-39.

Sing Out!, fall, 2003, Ronald Lankford, Jr., review of *Southern Music, American Music,* p. 121.

Southern Cultures, summer, 2003, Patrick Huber, review of *Don't Get above Your Raisin',* pp. 102-105.

Southern Living, May, 1980, review of *Southern Music, American Music,* p. 102.

Southwest Review, fall, 1985, review of *Country Music USA,* revised edition, p. 547.

Virginia Quarterly Review, winter, 1981, review of *Southern Music, American Music,* p. 29.

Wilson Quarterly, Volume 12, number 3, 1988, review of *Country Music USA,* p. 89.

ONLINE

Take Country Back, http://www.takecountryback.com/ (February 6, 2004), Laurie Joulie, "The State of Country: A Conversation with Bill C. Malone."*

* * *

MARSHALL, Allen
See WESTLAKE, Donald E(dwin)

* * *

MARSHALL, Owen 1941-
(Owen Marshall Jones)

PERSONAL: Born August 17, 1941, in Te Kuiti, New Zealand; son of Alan and Jane (Marshall) Jones; married Jacqueline Hill, December, 1965; children: two daughters. *Ethnicity:* "European." *Education:* University of Canterbury, 1960-1963, M.A. (with honors), 1963; Christchurch Teachers College, teaching diploma, 1964.

ADDRESSES: Home—10 Morgan's Rd., Glenwood, Timaru, New Zealand. *E-mail*—owen-marshall@timaru.com.

CAREER: Short story writer, novelist, and educator. Began teaching career at a school in Timaru, New Zealand, mid-1960s; Waitaki Boys High School, Oamaru, New Zealand, deputy rector, 1983-85; Craighead Diocesan School, Timaru, deputy principal, 1986-91; Aoraki Polytechnic, Timaru, teacher of fiction writing, 1993—. Creative New Zealand, member of Arts Board, 1998-2001. *Military service:* Performed national service in the armed forces.

AWARDS, HONORS: Literary fellowship, University of Canterbury, 1981; Lillian Ida Smith Award, International PEN, 1986, 1988; Queen Elizabeth II Arts Council scholarship, 1987; *Evening Standard* Award for short story, 1987; American Express award for short story, 1987; New Zealand Literary Fund, scholarship in letters, 1988, Distinction Award, 1989; Robert Burns Fellowship, University of Otago, 1992; Katherine Mansfield Memorial Fellowship for Menton, France, 1996; decorated officer, New Zealand Order of Merit, 2000; Deutz Medal for fiction, Montana New Zealand Book Awards, Montana Wines Ltd., 2000, for *Harlequin Rex;* Litt.D., University of Canterbury, 2002.

WRITINGS:

Supper Waltz Wilson and Other New Zealand Stories, Pegasus Press (Christchurch, New Zealand), 1979.

The Master of Big Jingles and Other Stories, McIndoe (Dunedin, New Zealand), 1982.

The Day Hemingway Died and Other Stories, McIndoe (Dunedin, New Zealand), 1984.

The Lynx Hunter and Other Stories, McIndoe (Dunedin, New Zealand), 1987.

The Divided World: Selected Stories, McIndoe (Dunedin, New Zealand), 1989.

Tomorrow We Save the Orphans, McIndoe (Dunedin, New Zealand), 1992.

The Ace of Diamonds Gang, McIndoe (Dunedin, New Zealand), 1993.

Coming Home in the Dark, Vintage (Auckland, New Zealand), 1995.

The Best of Owen Marshall's Short Stories, Vintage (Auckland, New Zealand), 1997.

When Gravity Snaps: Short Stories, Vintage (Auckland, New Zealand), 2002.

EDITOR:

Burning Boats: Seventeen New Zealand Short Stories, Longman (Auckland, New Zealand), 1994.

Letter from Heaven: Sixteen New Zealand Poets, Longman (Auckland, New Zealand), 1995.
Beethoven's Ears: Eighteen New Zealand Short Stories, Longman (Auckland, New Zealand), 1996.
Spinning a Line: New Zealand Writing about Fishing, Vintage (Auckland, New Zealand), 2001.
Authors' Choice: Leading New Zealand Writers Choose Their Favourite Stories, Penguin Putnam (New York, NY), 2001.
Essential New Zealand Short Stories, Random House New Zealand (Auckland, New Zealand), 2002.

OTHER:

An Indirect Geography (radio play), 1989.
A Many Coated Man (novel), Longacre (Dunedin, New Zealand), 1995.
Harlequin Rex (novel), Vintage (Auckland, New Zealand), 1999.

Work represented in anthologies, including *I Have Seen the Future,* edited by Bernard Gadd, Penguin (Auckland, New Zealand), 1989. Contributor of short stories and articles to periodicals, including *Sport.*

SIDELIGHTS: Trained as a schoolteacher, Owen Marshall aspired from childhood to be a writer. His early attempts at novels went unpublished; turning to the short story form in the 1970s, he first achieved magazine publication with a story in the New Zealand *Listener* in 1977. Two years later, he was able to publish a volume of fourteen stories, *Supper Waltz Wilson and Other New Zealand Stories.* Although he subsidized publication with his own funds, the book was critically and commercially a success. In particular, according to W. S. Broughton in *Contemporary Novelists,* it brought influential words of praise from celebrated New Zealand short-story writer Frank Sargeson. Soon, using the name Owen Marshall for all his writings, the author was publishing regularly in notable New Zealand literary outlets; some of his stories were also aired on Radio New Zealand. A second collection, *The Master of Big Jingles and Other Stories,* was published in 1982. In the title stories of the first two collections, which Broughton singled out as among his best pieces, Marshall was establishing his voice as a traditional realist who wrote about lower-middle-class New Zealanders in small-town or rural settings that were so well-described as to become virtual characters in their own right. Many of his stories used the first-person narrative mode, and whether they did or not, they displayed a skill with dialogue that found favor with readers and critics alike. In Broughton's view, "Marshall is distinctive among New Zealand writers . . . for his quiet ironic detachment, and for the clear-eyed recognitions of inevitability and common culpability in his little scenes from the human comedy." He is also distinguished, said that critic, for treating his women characters "with more subtlety and sensitivity than has traditionally been associated with male New Zealand writers."

Other striking stories of Marshall's include the title piece from his third collection, *The Day Hemingway Died;* "Kenneth's Friend," "Valley Day," "The Paper Parcel," "A Poet's Dream of Amazons," and "The Seed Merchant," an examination of the relationship between a dying father and his son which Broughton called "superb." Marshall changed direction, at least temporarily, in his fourth volume, *The Lynx Hunter and Other Stories:* he experimented with postmodern metafictional forms, an approach that was popular with New Zealand short-story writers in the late 1980s. In some of the *Lynx* stories, according to Carolyn Bliss in *World Literature Today,* the narrator forgoes a conventional ending for direct commentary. In a piece on the nature of literature, Marshall, as quoted by Bliss, describes the writer as a "sacred cripple" lurching with "amazement" through an "opulent" world. However, the stories, Bliss wrote, still contain "social and natural settings which both refract and foster theme and character"; and the book, in the view of a *Canadian Literature* reviewer, "burns with quiet desperation."

A volume of selected stories, *The Divided World,* appeared in 1989. Though the title story was nonrealistic, the bulk of these pieces and of his later stories showed the author, in Broughton's phrase, as "still primarily a teller of tales." Stories written after that selected volume were published in *Tomorrow We Save the Orphans* and *The Ace of Diamonds Gang.* Additionally, in 1992, while on a Robert Burns Fellowship at the University of Otago, Marshall wrote a novel, *A Many Coated Man.* It was a view of a near-future New Zealand in which the national identity was in even greater flux than at the time of writing; though it displayed Marshall's considerable literary skill, it also seemed uneven, Broughton found, as if the author's true metier were in the short form. At either length, however, Broughton saw Marshall as one whose "writings seek to remind us of the known and the forgotten alike; their narrative vision suggests the wish to reveal sympathies that are never sentimental, seldom other than compassionate, and always couched in the language of one who is thoroughly sensitive to the power of words."

BIOGRAPHICAL AND CRITICAL SOURCES:

BOOKS

Contemporary Novelists, 7th edition, St. James Press (Detroit, MI), 2001.

Reference Guide to Short Fiction, 2nd edition, St. James Press (Detroit, MI), 1999.

Sewell, Bill, editor, *Sons of the Fathers,* Tandem Press (Auckland, New Zealand), 1997.

PERIODICALS

Canadian Literature, autumn, 1990, review of *The Lynx Hunter and Other Stories,* pp. 191-192.

New Zealand Books, December, 1995, review by Lydia Wevers.

New Zealand Herald, August 17, 2002, Gordon McLauchlan, review of *When Gravity Snaps: Short Stories.*

Sport (Wellington, New Zealand), spring, 1989, review by Vincent O'Sullivan.

World Literature Today, winter, 1989, Carolyn Bliss, review of *The Lynx Hunter and Other Stories,* pp. 166-167.*

* * *

MATTHEWS, Alex

PERSONAL: Married Allen Matthews (a therapist).

ADDRESSES: *Home and office*—P.O. Box 4021, Oak Park, IL 60303. *E-mail*—MsAlexM@aol.com.

CAREER: Writer. Clinical social worker.

AWARDS, HONORS: Wordweaving Award for Excellence, *Midwest Book Review,* for the "Cassidy McCabe" series; Readers Choice Award for Best Series Character, 1999; Cat Writers Association Certificate of Excellence.

WRITINGS:

"CASSIDY MCCABE" MYSTERY SERIES

Secret's Shadow, Intrigue Press (Angel Fire, NM), 1996.

Satan's Silence, Intrigue Press (Angel Fire, NM), 1997.

Vendetta's Victim, Intrigue Press (Angel Fire, NM), 1998.

Wanton's Web, Intrigue Press (Angel Fire, NM), 1999.

Cat's Claw, Intrigue Press (Angel Fire, NM), 2000.

Death's Domain, Intrigue Press (Philadelphia, PA), 2001.

Wedding's Widow, Intrigue Press (Denver, CO), 2003.

SIDELIGHTS: Alex Matthews has earned praise for her creation of Cassidy McCabe, the psychotherapist/sleuth heroine she introduced in *Secret's Shadow.* A flawed and realistic character, McCabe's anxieties are plentiful: the mob is chasing her ex-husband, her old, but architecturally unique house is falling apart, she pays her ex-husband's back taxes, and one of her clients in psychotherapy has committed suicide and the family is considering a law suit. Consumed with these worries, McCabe attempts to unravel the mystery of the suicide of her patient, Ryan, with the aid of his brother Zach, who believes Ryan was murdered. McCabe uncovers secrets about Ryan's past, which lead to a startling discovery.

Matthews's second mystery, *Satan's Silence,* continues the adventures of McCabe. When Dana, one of McCabe's patients, reveals a vision of satanic rituals in the woods, Zach, McCabe's friend and an investigative reporter, pushes McCabe to help him look into the matter. Shortly thereafter, Dana's child is kidnaped. After finding a skull in a well, McCabe begins to fear for her and Zach's lives. A reviewer for *Publishers Weekly* remarked that "Matthews goes out of her way to create flaws in her heroine, whose interior observations are revealed." Matthews's writing style combines a personal psychological process with the elements of mystery.

In *Vendetta's Victim,* McCabe finds herself caught up in the machinations of a malicious stranger who is purposely infecting women with AIDS and then referring them to her for therapy. Fearing that this psychopath is one of her own patients, Cassidy sets out to track him down, again with Zach's help. A *Publishers Weekly* reviewer found the book "an awkward affair that mixes genuine suspense with some grating storytelling affectations," particularly Matthews's use of italicized interjections from Cassidy's conscience. *Library Journal* reviewer Rex Klett was more impressed, commending its "easy-to-take prose." For Klett, this third McCabe novel was "a decided improvement over *Satan's Silence.*"

In *Wanton's Web,* it is Zach who must face a stranger when his ex-girlfriend Xandra, a high-priced escort, calls to tell him he has to take care of the son he never even knew existed. When Xandra is murdered, Zach finds himself the prime suspect, and Cassidy is soon involved in a frantic race to clear her boyfriend and save his son. Klett, writing in another *Library Journal* review, found this installment in the series to be a "successful mix of relationships, passions, and revenge." "Matthews's suspenseful writing will keep readers reading," commented *Booklist* reviewer John Rowen.

Engaged in *Wanton's Web,* Cassidy and Zach are newlyweds in *Cat's Claw,* but Zach's new assignment is already putting strains on their marriage. Zach has gone undercover, impersonating a drug dealer in order to expose police corruption, and he is having a hard time keeping his hard-edged dealer persona from spilling over into his home life. Meanwhile, Cassidy is growing increasingly worried about an eccentric, reclusive neighbor, Olivia, and goes to check up on her one night. Rebuffed by a visibly nervous Olivia, she returns the next day to find a drunken ex-con in Olivia's living room and Olivia's body in the basement. The ex-con is arrested, but Cassidy is not convinced of his guilt and begins to hunt through Olivia's private papers for clues. What she finds is a wealth of suspects, including loony relatives, a suspicious employer, and a number of victims of Olivia's spiteful and malicious actions. *Library Journal*'s Klett remarked that "Matthews hits her stride in this exciting addition to the "Cassidy McCabe" series."

Death's Domain opens with a bizarre incident, when McCabe comes across her own obituary, complete with photo, while flipping through the local paper. The accompanying article claims she was killed in a car accident, and gradually it dawns on McCabe that her obit appeared on the same date as a fatal car crash for which she holds herself partly responsible. She and Zach are soon uncovering clues to the culprit's identity, and uncovering a sad chapter in Cassidy's own life. "Matthews offers one of her best mysteries in this tale dealing with marital infidelity and disturbed psyches," wrote *Chicago Sun-Times* reviewer Edward Gilbreth.

There is no question of marital infidelity in Matthews's sixth novel, *Wedding's Widow,* because the victim, named Max, is shot at his own wedding before he can take the vows. Cassidy herself had talked the reluctant bride, Claire, into going ahead with the nuptials, and now she and Zach must help her find her would-be husband's killer. Naturally, things are not as they seem, and Max turns out to be quite different from his image as an upstanding citizen. Business partners, disgruntled employees, and Max's own sisters become suspects, along with Claire's vindictive ex-husband. "Some rather stilted dialogue gets in the way here, but series fans will find much to enjoy," commented *Booklist* reviewer Sue O'Brien.

BIOGRAPHICAL AND CRITICAL SOURCES:

PERIODICALS

Booklist, April 15, 1999, John Rowen, review of *Wanton's Web,* p. 1482; May 1, 2003, Sue O'Brien, review of *Wedding's Widow,* p. 1549.

Chicago Sun-Times, October 14, 2001, Edward Gilbreth, review of *Death's Domain,* p. 14.

Library Journal, March 1, 1997, Rex Klett, review of *Satan's Silence,* p. 107; April 1, 1998, Rex Klett, review of *Vendetta's Victim,* p. 129; April 1, 1999, Rex Klett, review of *Wanton's Web,* p. 132; March 1, 2000, Rex Klett, review of *Cat's Claw,* p. 127.

Publishers Weekly, March 11, 1996, review of *Secret's Shadow,* pp. 46-47; January 6, 1997, review of *Satan's Silence,* p. 68; March 9, 1998, review of *Vendetta's Victim,* p. 52; April 10, 2000, review of *Cat's Claw,* p. 79.

ONLINE

BookBrowser, http://www.bookbrowser.com/ (December 31, 1997), review of *Satan's Silence.*

Ed's Internet Book Review, http://www.clark.net/ (December 31, 1997), review of *Secret's Shadow.**

MAYES, Frances

PERSONAL: Born in Fitzgerald, GA; daughter of Garbert (a cotton mill manager) and Frankye (Davis) Mayes; married William Frank King (a computer research scientist); children: Ashley. *Education:* Attended Randolph-Macon Woman's College; University of Florida, B.A.; San Francisco State University, M.A., 1975.

ADDRESSES: *Home*—2022 Broderick St., San Francisco, CA 94115; and Cortona, Italy. *Office*—514 Bryant St., Palo Alto, CA 94301; Creative Writing Program, San Francisco State University, San Francisco, CA 94132.

CAREER: Educator, novelist, and poet. Former freelance copywriter for cookbook publishers and newspapers; currently member of department of English and chair of creative writing department, San Francisco State University, San Francisco, CA; teacher at writing workshops at Foothill College and Cañada College.

AWARDS, HONORS: Award from Academy of American Poets, 1975.

WRITINGS:

POETRY COLLECTIONS

Sunday in Another Country, Heyeck Press (Woodside, CA), 1977.
Climbing Aconcagua, Seven Woods Press (New York, NY), 1977.
After Such Pleasures, Seven Woods Press (New York, NY), 1979.
The Arts of Fire, Heyeck Press (Woodside, CA), 1982.
Hours, Lost Roads Publishers (Providence, RI), 1984.
Ex Voto, Lost Roads Publishers (Providence, RI), 1995.

NOVELS

Swan, Broadway Books (New York, NY), 2002.

OTHER

The Discovery of Poetry, Harcourt (San Diego, CA), 1987.
Under the Tuscan Sun: At Home in Italy, Chronicle Books (San Francisco, CA), 1996.

Frances Mayes

Bella Tuscany: The Sweet Life in Italy, Broadway Books (New York, NY), 1999.
(Coauthor) *In Tuscany,* Broadway Books (New York, NY), 2000.
(Editor) *The Best American Travel Writing 2002,* Houghton Mifflin (Boston, MA), 2002.

Contributor of poems to literary journals, including *Atlantic, Carolina Quarterly, Epoch, Gettysburg Review,* and *Southern Review.*

ADAPTATIONS: *Under the Tuscan Sun* was adapted for film and released by Touchstone Pictures, 2003.

SIDELIGHTS: Although Frances Mayes received critical praise for her six books of poetry—often limited editions with small presses—as early as 1977, it was not until the commercial success in 1996 of her memoir *Under the Tuscan Sun: At Home in Italy* that she came to the attention of the general reading public.

Mayes's first book of poems, *Sunday in Another Country,* shows how she "works in the manner of a fine photographer placing unlikely objects into surprising conjunctions," as a *Choice* critic explained. Celebrating the commonplace in simple, accessible language, Mayes describes motherhood in *After Such Pleasures,* for example, by noting that "You're the cheerleader with the megaphone / announcing that oleander is poison and / everyone will need a sweater." In *The Arts of Fire,* Mayes shifts to poems which are "feminist by virtue of their power of their female presences, rather than . . . for their thematic politics," observed Mark Livingston in *Fine Print.* The fire of the book's title is both hearth-fire and muse-fire, so that the women in these poems become like "votive priestesses" who "weave together, and at times try to unravel, their own hereditary identity," noted Livingston, as Mayes uses fire as a metaphor which binds all women, past and present: "you feel it catch / fire, spontaneous combustion. It didn't start there and it / won't end." Mayes "has an urgent interest in the way the past and present converge," Holly Prado observed in *Los Angeles Times Book Review.*

Hours is a collection of poems revolving around a central essay in which Mayes considers her growing up in Georgia and trying to understand what "to be, and in which order, writer, woman, Southern." Essentially, the reader comes to see Mayes as "raised by a network of women," so that the poems reflect this network, allowing her, like other women poets, noted Maxine Kumin in the *Georgia Review,* to put "custom, birth, food, nature back into the continuum." Thus, the feminist perspective of *The Arts of Fire* shifts to the regional as Mayes weaves together these diverse strands into the wholeness of her life.

It is Mayes's life and lifestyle that surface in her popular nonfiction work, *Under the Tuscan Sun: At Home in Italy.* Here, the two worlds she weaves together are of the hectic San Francisco lifestyle of a university professor with the idyllic, languid summers spent in enjoying the seventeen-room Italian villa with its extensive gardens Mayes and her companion, Ed, have restored. Stories of the complexity of international real estate transactions, of reclaiming gardens, of attending an olive harvest, of drinking local wine on the lawn, and of observations of the local landscape, architecture, neighbors and local villagers: all are topics for this book, written in a style which Alida Becker in the *New York Times Book Review* called "casual and conversational."

This book brings together Mayes's experiences as poet, teacher, food and travel writer; as such, readers are surprised and delighted to find recipes interspersed within the narratives and observations. Whether Mayes is walking with a book of poems, for, as she notes, "The rhythm of my walking matches the poet's cadence," or whether she is sharing her observations about the village of Cortona, Italy, her book is "so enchanting that an armchair traveler will find it hard to resist jumping out of the chair and following in her footsteps," commented a critic for *Publishers Weekly.*

The popularity of *Under the Tuscan Sun* may be rooted in its being more than merely a travel memoir, or an Italian version of Peter Mayle's books about the Provence region of France, however. As William R. Smith commented in *Library Journal,* the book speaks to a generation of women by its being "an unusual memoir of one woman's challenge to herself and the successful transformation into a satisfying opportunity to improve the quality of her life."

With *Bella Tuscany: The Sweet Life in Italy,* Mayes returns to the Italian milieu she described in *Under the Tuscan Sun.* The book relates Mayes and her husband Ed's immersion in their version of an extended-vacation paradise. She describes continued efforts to repair and renovate a two-hundred-year-old Tuscan farmhouse the couple uses as their home while in Italy. As Mayes and her husband repair recalcitrant bathrooms, choose decorations for their new home, and manicure the gardens, they bask in the culture and customs of their newly adopted second home. A *Publishers Weekly* critic found that the book served as little more than an extension of *Under the Tuscan Sun,* and Bill Ott, writing in *Booklist,* observed, "Here it's just one damn perfect thing after another." Other critics found more to admire, such as *BookPage* Web site reviewer Carolyn Porter, who commented that Mayes "writes about the Tuscan countryside with such powerful description and sensuality, the reader is transported to the slow pace of Cortona, Italy, where one simply breathes, notices, and appreciates life's small pleasures." Woodene Merriman, writing on the *Pittsburgh Post-Gazette* Web site, remarked that *Bella Tuscany* is "a beautifully written book about life in the Tuscan hills, where long siestas in the middle of the day are routine, where a first Communion calls for a six-hour feast, and where friends never say 'I'm so busy' when you ask 'How are you?'" Nancy R. Ives, reviewing the book in *Library Journal,* observed that "Mayes writes with a poet's attention to sensuous detail" throughout *Bella Tuscany.* Even the *Publishers Weekly* critic admitted, "Occasionally, Mayes hits a pretty note or includes a compelling detail" in the book.

Mayes takes a third trip to her beloved Italian countryside with *In Tuscany.* Her poetic contemplations of the entire Tuscan region come complete with sensual and epicurean descriptions of foods common to the area where Mayes and her husband maintain a second home. She includes recipes for those who want to try their hand at dishing up a taste of Tuscan fare. The volume includes more than 200 color photographs by Bob Krist, and "the text and the handsome pictures are well integrated," wrote Julie Gray in the *New York Times.* Olga B. Wise, writing in *Library Journal,* remarked on the book's combination of "beautiful images" and "vibrant text" that create "a fine introduction to the region's atmosphere."

Swan, Mayes's first novel, is set in the small Georgia town of Swan—familiar territory to Mayes, who spent her childhood in similar rural Georgia settings. Adult siblings J. J. and his sister, Ginger, are forced to reconsider the circumstances around their mother Catherine's suicide in the mid-1950s, when they were children. J. J. is a near-recluse who spends most of his time in the family's cabin, hunting and fishing. Ginger works as an archaeologist in Tuscany. When Catherine's grave is inexplicably desecrated and Ginger finds her mother's corpse dumped in the grass, evidence is uncovered that indicates Catherine might have been murdered. Eccentric characters interact with Ginger and J. J. as they spend an intense week searching for clues, looking for the party or parties responsible for desecration of the grave, and trying to solve their mother's murder. Stephen Whited, writing in *Book,* remarked that *Swan* "attempts to be all things to all readers: a romance, a murder mystery, a literary novel," and suffers for the mingling of genres. Nancy Pearl, reviewing the book in *Library Journal,* commented, "Mayes clearly never met a quirky character she didn't like, and she's seemingly put every one of them in this book, whether or not they move the plot forward (and most do not)." Other critics, such as Maggie Galehouse in the *New York Times,* found more to like about *Swan.* "Loaded with finely drawn minor characters and the alluring atmosphere of the American South, *Swan* is a well-paced if modest entertainment," Galehouse remarked. Michele Leber in *Booklist* concluded, "With a memorable, full-bodied cast and an evocative sense of place, this is a surefire best-seller."

BIOGRAPHICAL AND CRITICAL SOURCES:

PERIODICALS

Book, September-October, 2002, Stephen Whited, review of *Swan,* pp. 83-84.

Booklist, September 15, 1996, p. 217; February 1, 1999, Bill Ott, review of *Bella Tuscany: The Sweet Life in Italy,* p. 939; July, 1999, audio book review of *Under the Tuscan Sun: At Home in Italy,* p. 1965; November 15, 2000, Mark Knoblauch, review of *In Tuscany,* p. 594; March 1, 2001, Nancy Spillman, audio book review of *In Tuscany,* p. 1295; September 1, 2002, Michele Leber, review of *Swan,* pp. 6-7; September 15, 2002, Brad Hooper, review of *The Best American Travel Writing 2002,* p. 202.

Books, spring, 1999, review of *Bella Tuscany,* p. p. 20.

Choice, December, 1978, p. 1370.

Fine Print, July, 1984, p. 95.

Georgia Review, spring, 1985, p. 169.

Globe and Mail, April 24, 1999, review of *Bella Tuscany,* p. E11.

Harper's, December, 1980. p. 75.

House Beautiful, December, 1993, p. 16.

Kirkus Reviews, February 1, 1999, review of *Bella Tuscany,* p. 204; July 1, 2002, review of *Swan,* pp. 908-909; August 15, 2002, review of *The Best American Travel Writing 2002,* p. 1200.

Kliatt, May, 2001, audio book review of *In Tuscany,* p. 58.

Library Journal, January 1, 1980, p. 106; September 1, 1996, p. 201; April 1, 1998, p. 143; February 15, 1999, review of *Under the Tuscan Sun,* p. 127; April 15, 1999, Nancy R. Ives, review of *Bella Tuscany,* p. 133; February 1, 2001, Olga B. Wise, review of *In Tuscany,* p. 116; April 15, 2001, Gordon Blackwell, audio book review of *In Tuscany,* p. 155; November 1, 2001, Lisa J. Cihlar, review of *The Discovery of Poetry,* p. 106; September 15, 2002, Nancy Pearl, review of *Swan,* p. 93; October 1, 2002, John McCormick, review of *The Best American Travel Writing 2002.*

Los Angeles Times Book Review, August 12, 1984, p. 6; May 9, 1999, review of *Bella Tuscany,* p. 11.

Maclean's, June 21, 1999, review of *Bella Tuscany,* p. 53.

National Geographic Adventure, December, 2002, Kalee Thompson, review of *The Best American Travel Writing 2002,* p. 45.

New York Times, November 17, 1996, p. 10; January 7, 2001, Julie Gray, review of *In Tuscany,* section 7, p. 19; October 27, 2002, Maggie Galehouse, review of *Swan,* section 7, p. 29.
New York Times Book Review, July 11, 1999, review of *Bella Tuscany,* p. 23.
North American Review, March, 1985, p. 65.
Publishers Weekly, January 12, 1988, pp. 17-18; July 29, 1996, p. 75; February 22, 1999, review of *Bella Tuscany,* p. 72; October 22, 2001, review of *The Discovery of Poetry,* p. 73; July 22, 2002, review of *Swan,* p. 156; August 16, 2002, review of *The Best American Travel Writing 2002,* pp. 57-58.
Reference & Research Book News, review of *In Tuscany,* p. 38.
Washington Post Book World, June 6, 1999, review of *Bella Tuscany,* p. 5.

ONLINE

BookPage.com, http://www.bookpage.com/ (November 20, 2003), Carolyn Porter, review of *Bella Tuscany.*
Houghton Mifflin Web site, http://www.houghtonmifflinbooks.com/ (November 20, 2003).
Pittsburgh Post-Gazette Online, http//www.post-gazette.com/ (June 6, 1999), Woodene Merriman, review of *Bella Tuscany.*
Random House Web site, http://www.randomhouse.com/ (November 20, 2003).*

* * *

MEGARRY, Tim 1941-

PERSONAL: Born May 17, 1941, in London, England; son of Bill (a film editor) and Peggy (a secretary; maiden name, Harris) Megarry; married Lady Henrietta Paget (a teacher), February 16, 1980; children: Katy, Matty. *Education:* Attended West Ham College of Technology (now University of East London), 1966-69; University of London, B.Sc. (with honors), 1969; London School of Oriental and African Studies, London, M.A., 1970; University of Greenwich, Ph.D., 2000. *Politics:* "Left of center." *Hobbies and other interests:* Classical music, walking, travel in Greece, reading novels.

ADDRESSES: *Home*—43 Woodsome Rd., London NW5 1SA, England. *Office*—School of Social Science and Law, Old Royal Naval College, Maritime Greenwich University Campus, University of Greenwich, 30 Park Row, Greenwich, London SE10 9LS, England; fax: +44-0-20-8331-8905. *E-mail*—t.w.megarry@gre.ac.uk.

CAREER: University of Greenwich, London, England, senior lecturer in sociology and anthropology, 1972—.

MEMBER: Zoological Society of London (fellow).

WRITINGS:

Society in Prehistory, New York University Press (New York, NY), 1995.
(Editor and author of introduction) *From the Caves to Capital: Readings in Historical and Comparative Sociology,* University of Greenwich Press (London, England), 1995.
(Editor and author of introduction) *The Making of Modern Japan,* University of Greenwich Press (London, England), 1995.
The Changing Third World, University of Greenwich Press (London, England), 1997.

Contributor to periodicals, including *Psychology, Evolution, and Gender.*

WORK IN PROGRESS: *From the Caves to Capitalism,* for Palgrave Press (New York, NY).

SIDELIGHTS: Tim Megarry once told *CA:* "Writing is a part of my overall work as a university teacher. Teaching comparative sociology has given me the opportunity to investigate a fascinating variety of societies and behavior that I wish to explore in greater depth.

"A most basic motivation for writing is the desire to produce books in order to gain a more profound understanding of questions which have become long-term interests and to communicate their intrinsic excitement. Research and writing is a 'working-out' process, in which I attempt to integrate material and ideas that are presented in a range of academic domains. I am particularly concerned to work on interdisciplinary areas that unite historical, biological, and anthropological aspects of the social sciences and humanities. While I recognize the value of research produced in specialist fields, my desire is to produce work that overlaps current subject boundaries and attempts to provide a comprehensive theoretical overview of large-scale issues.

"A very early introduction to H. G. Wells's *Outline of World History* and Gordon Childe's *What Happened in History* generated an interest which later became enlarged through an education in general sociology, in which anthropology and Marxist social theory were prominent centers of my attention. The awareness that social change and cultural variation are revealed through the study of comparative history has always been a strong element of fascination and a driving force behind my work. My discovery of Darwin became joined to a lifelong interest in natural history, earth sciences, evolution, and human cultural origins.

"Only rarely have I ever been able to follow what I consider to be the ideal pattern of writing, which I conceive as complete and continuous commitment to reading, note-making, drafting, discussion, revision, and more reading. Usually this pattern has been interrupted by teaching and other institutional demands. This has meant that weeks of research are often followed by months of diverting demands before I can return to the writing project.

"Having taught an undergraduate course on the sociology of pre-industrial societies at the end of the 1970s, I began to work on a general book in this area. The book was to cover much the same material as my course, which specialized in complex historical societies in Europe and Asia. Since it seemed appropriate to include a chapter on human origins and the emergence of society if the book was to be comprehensive, I began to read material on physical anthropology and prehistory. In particular I was struck by the work of Sherwood Washburn, Glynn Isaac, Stephen Jay Gould, Richard Lee, Jared Diamond, and Charles Redman. Reading the work of these authors began a process in which I became captivated by the issues that are raised in the study of prehistory. The general book was abandoned accordingly, and *Society in Prehistory* resulted more than a decade later."

* * *

MEYERS, Carole Terwilliger 1945-

PERSONAL: Born June 30, 1945, in San Francisco, CA; daughter of Earl Walter (a civil servant) and Esther (Furst) Terwilliger; married Gene Howard Meyers (a computer programmer), May 2, 1971; children: David Charles, Suzanne Michelle. *Education:* Attended University of California—Los Angeles, 1962-64; San Francisco State College, B.A., 1967; Fresno State College, teaching credential, 1969; graduate study at University of California—Berkeley.

ADDRESSES: Home—Berkeley, CA. *Office*—Carousel Press, P.O. Box 6038, Albany, CA 94706-0038.

CAREER: Worked as secretary, 1962-68; elementary school teacher in Fresno, CA, 1968-69, East Palo Alto, CA, 1969-70, and Oakland, CA, 1970-72; American Society for Psychoprophylaxis in Obstetrics, San Francisco, CA, newsletter editor, beginning 1973; Carousel Press, Albany, CA, editor in chief, beginning 1976. San Francisco International Toy Center and Museum, member of board of advisors, 1986-91.

MEMBER: International Food, Wine, and Travel Writers Association, Committee of Small Magazine Editors and Publishers, California Teachers Association, Northern California Book Publicists Association, Bay Area Travel Writers, Writer's Connection.

AWARDS, HONORS: First-place award, self-published travel book category, Travel Publisher News Awards, 1990, for *Weekend Adventures for City-Weary People: Overnight Trips in Northern California.*

WRITINGS:

(With Gail Kramer) *Eating Out with the Kids in the East Bay,* Hunger Pang Press, 1974.

How to Organize a Babysitting Cooperative and Get Some Free Time Away from the Kids, Carousel Press (Albany, CA), 1976.

Eating Out with the Kids in San Francisco and the Bay Area, Carousel Press (Albany, CA), 1976, revised edition published as *San Francisco Family Fun: Eating Out with the Kids in San Francisco and the Bay Area,* 1990.

Weekend Adventures for City-Weary Families: A Guide to Overnight Trips in Northern California, Carousel Press (Albany, CA), 1977, 5th edition published as *Weekend Adventures for City-Weary People: Overnight Trips in Northern California,* 1980, 6th edition published as *Weekend Adventures in Northern California,* 1997, 7th edition, 2001.

Getting in the Spirit: Annual Bay Area Christmas Events, Carousel Press (Albany, CA), 1979.
San Francisco Family Fun, 1990.
Miles of Smiles: 101 Great Car Games and Activities, illustrated by Victoria Carlson, Carousel Press (Albany, CA), 1992.
(Editor and author of introduction) *The Family Travel Guide: An Inspiring Collection of Family-Friendly Vacations,* Carousel Press (Albany, CA), 1995.
Miles of Smiles: 101 Great Car Games for Kids and the Adults Who Travel wth Them, illustrated by Victoria Carlson, Gramercy Books (New York, NY), 2002.
FamilyFun Vacation Guide: California and Hawaii, Disney Editions (New York, NY), 2003.

Columnist for *San Jose Mercury News,* 1978-79, 1989-90, *Oakland,* 1980, *Parents' Press, 1980-90, California,* 1981-88, *California Travel Report,* 1982-83, *Goodlife,* 1983, *San Francisco Focus,* 1988-90, *San Francisco Examiner,* 1989-91, and *Adventure West,* 1994—. Contributor to magazines, including *Sesame Street Parents, Parenting, Family Circle, Family Fun, Travel Holiday, Self-Publishing Writer,* and *Mothering.* Editor and publisher, *Family Travel Guides Catalogue,* 1986—.

SIDELIGHTS: Carole Terwilliger Meyers once commented: "My writing is motivated by an interest in passing information I've collected on to other people. I write in an effort to help parents cope with child-rearing and to promote healthy, happy family life." Meyers has traveled throughout the United States and Canada, in Mexico, Europe, and the Middle East.

BIOGRAPHICAL AND CRITICAL SOURCES:

PERIODICALS

Berkeley Gazette, December 18, 1976.
Bloomsbury Review, May, 1989, review of *Weekend Adventures for City-Weary People: Overnight Trips in Northern California,* p. 22.
Booklist, September 1, 1984, review of *Weekend Adventures for City-Weary People,* p. 19.
Bookwatch, July, 1993, review of *Weekend Adventures for City-Weary People,* p. 10; July, 2001, review of *Weekend Adventures in Northern California,* p. 5.
Children's Bookwatch, October, 1992, review of *Miles of Smiles: 101 Great Car Games and Activities,* p. 8.
Library Journal, November 15, 1994, review of *The Family Travel Guide: An Inspiring Collection of Family-Friendly Vacations,* p. 82.
Oakland Tribune, December 23, 1974.
San Francisco Examiner, January 5, 1977.
Small Press, April, 1990, review of *Weekend Adventures for City-Weary People,* p. 42.
Wilson Library Bulletin, October, 1992, review of *Miles of Smiles,* p. 125.

ONLINE

Carousel Press Web Site, http://www.carousel-press.com/ (September 12, 2004).
TravelLady.com, http://www.travellady.com/ (September 6, 2001), Shel Horowitz, review of *Weekend Adventures in Northern California.**

* * *

MILLGATE, Michael (Henry) 1929-

PERSONAL: Born July 19, 1929, in Southampton, England; son of Stanley (a civil servant) and Marjorie Louisa (Norris) Millgate; married Eunice Jane Barr (a university teacher), February 27, 1960. *Education:* St. Catharine's College, Cambridge, B.A., 1952, M.A., 1956; University of Michigan, graduate study, 1956-57; University of Leeds, Ph.D., 1960.

ADDRESSES: *Home*—1 Balmoral Ave., Toronto, Ontario M4V 3B9, Canada.

CAREER: Workers' Educational Association, tutor and organizer in South Lindsey, England, 1953-56; University of Leeds, Leeds, England, lecturer in English literature, 1958-64; York University, Downsview, Ontario, Canada, professor of English and chair of the department, 1964-67; University of Toronto, Toronto, Ontario, professor of English, 1967-94, professor emeritus, 1994—; John Guggenheim Memorial Foundation, educational advisory board member, 1994-2004. Ohio Wesleyan University, Carpenter lecturer, 1978; Meiji University, visiting scholar, 1985. *Military service:* Royal Air Force, 1947-49.

MEMBER: Modern Language Association, Victorian Studies Association of Ontario (president, 1970-72), Thomas Hardy Society (vice president, 1973), Bibliographical Society of America, Society for Study of Southern Literature (executive council, 1972-76, 1981-83), Society for Textual Scholarship, Tennyson Society.

AWARDS, HONORS: Leave fellow, Canada Council, 1968-69, S. W. Brooks fellow, University of Queensland, 1971; grantee, Canada Council 1973-77; Killam Senior Research scholarship, 1974-76; John Simon Guggenheim Memorial fellow, 1977-78; grantee, Social Sciences and Humanities Research Council of Canada, 1977, leave fellow, 1981-82; Connaught senior fellow, 1979-80; fellow, Royal Society of Canada, 1981—, Pierre Chauveau Medal, 1999; fellow, Royal Society of Literature, 1983—; Killam Research fellowship, 1986-88.

WRITINGS:

William Faulkner, Grove (New York, NY), 1961.

American Social Fiction: James to Cozzens, Barnes & Noble (New York, NY), 1964.

The Achievement of William Faulkner, Random House (New York, NY), 1966, University of Georgia Press (Athens, GA), 1989.

(Author of introduction) Edith Wharton, *The House of Mirth,* Constable (London, England), 1966.

Thomas Hardy: His Career As a Novelist, Random House (New York, NY), 1971, St. Martin's Press (New York, NY), 1994.

Thomas Hardy: A Biography, Random House (New York, NY), 1982.

Testamentary Acts: Browning, Tennyson, James, Hardy, Oxford University Press (New York, NY), 1992.

Faulkner's Place, University of Georgia Press (Athens, GA), 1997.

Thomas Hardy: A Biography Revisited, Oxford University Press (New York, NY), 2004.

EDITOR, EXCEPT AS NOTED:

(And author of introduction) Alfred Tennyson, *Selected Poems,* Oxford University Press (New York, NY), 1963.

(And author of introduction) Theodore Dreiser, *Sister Carrie,* Oxford University Press (New York, NY), 1965.

(And author of introduction, with Paul F. Mattheisen) *Transatlantic Dialogue: Selected American Correspondence of Edmund Gosse,* University of Texas Press (Austin, TX), 1965, UMI Publications, 1988.

(With James B. Meriwether) *Lion in the Garden: Interviews with William Faulkner, 1926-1962,* Random House (New York, NY), 1968.

(With Richard Little Purdy) *The Collected Letters of Thomas Hardy,* Oxford University Press (New York, NY), Volume 1: *1840-92,* 1978, Volume 2: *1893-1901,* 1980, Volume 3: *1902-08,* 1982, Volume 4: *1909-13,* 1984, Volume 5: *1914-19,* 1985, Volume 6: *1920-25,* 1987, Volume 7: *1926-27,* 1988.

Thomas Hardy, *The Life and Work of Thomas Hardy,* Macmillan (London, England), 1984, University of Georgia Press (Athens, GA), 1985.

(Arranger and author of introduction) William Faulkner, *William Faulkner Manuscripts 20: A Fable,* Garland Publishing (New York, NY), 1986.

(Arranger and author of introduction) William Faulkner, *William Faulkner Manuscripts 21: The Town,* Garland Publishing (New York, NY), 1986.

(Arranger and author of introduction) *William Faulkner Manuscripts 22: The Mansion,* Garland Publishing (New York, NY), 1987.

(Arranger and author of introduction) *William Faulkner Manuscripts 23: The Reivers,* Garland Publishing (New York, NY), 1987.

(And author of introduction) *New Essays on "Light in August,"* Cambridge University Press, 1987 (Cambridge, England).

Thomas Hardy: Selected Letters, Oxford University Press (New York, NY), 1990.

(With Pamela Dalziel) *Thomas Hardy's Studies, Specimens and Notebook,* Oxford University Press (New York, NY), 1994.

Letters of Emma and Florence Hardy, Oxford University Press, 1996 (New York, NY).

Thomas Hardy's Public Voice: The Essays, Speeches, and Miscellaneous Prose, Oxford University Press (New York, NY), 2001.

Also contributor of articles on English and American literature and of reviews to journals.

SIDELIGHTS: A scholar of English and American literature, Michael Millgate is frequently noted for his extensively researched writing and editing concerning the life and works of William Faulkner and Thomas

Hardy. His book *Thomas Hardy: A Biography* has received praise from critics such as *New York Times* reviewer Anatole Broyard, who wrote: "Mr. Millgate is the kind of biographer writers dream of. He gives us all the necessary details; but none of the gratuitous ones." Robert E. Keuhn described the biography in a *Chicago Tribune Book Review* article as being "a magnificent biography—learned, thorough, judicious, sympathetic, in every sense definitive."

In an effort to shed more light into the very private man, Millgate edited *Thomas Hardy's Public Voice,* which includes numerous uncollected pieces. *Choice* reviewer R. D. Morrison praised the book for its contribution to Hardy studies, commenting that it "provides new insights into the opinions of a writer usually considered deeply private."

Review of English Studies critic J. R. Watson described Millgate's study of the self-fashioning behavior of authors in *Testamentary Acts: Browning, Tennyson, James, Hardy* by writing, "It is the combination of out-of-the-way facts, literary judgment, and human sympathy, which makes this a remarkable book." Millgate is also considered to be one of the foremost critics and interpreters of Faulkner's fiction, and the issue of Faulkner's standing in the ranks of the masters of fiction is the subject of *Faulkner's Place.* This work is a series of eight essays which had previously been delivered by Millgate on various occasions. *University of Toronto Quarterly* reviewer David Minter commented, "It is to the ongoing and even accelerating process of assessment and interpretation of Faulkner's fiction that *Faulkner's Place* makes its important contribution."

BIOGRAPHICAL AND CRITICAL SOURCES:

PERIODICALS

American Review, September, 1998, review of *Faulkner's Place,* p. 695.

Chicago Tribune Book World, May 23, 1982.

Choice, April, 2002, R. D. Morrison, review of *Thomas Hardy's Public Voice: The Essays, Speeches, and Miscellaneous Prose,* p. 1422.

Journal of English and Germanic Philology, William M. Morgan, review of *Thomas Hardy's Studies, Specimens and Notebook,* p. 581.

Los Angeles Times, June 4, 1982, October 13, 1985.

Mississippi Quarterly, summer, 1999, Christoph Irmscher and Roy R. Behrens, review of *Faulkner's Place,* p. 511.

Modern Language Review, April, 2000, Pamela Knights, review of *Faulkner's Place,* p. 493.

New Yorker, June 15, 1968.

New York Times, May 12, 1982.

New York Times Book Review, June 30, 1968; May 9, 1982.

Review of English Studies, May, 1995, J. R. Watson, review of *Testamentary Acts: Browning, Tennyson, James, Hardy,* p. 286; May, 1996, Catherine Maxwell, review of *Thomas Hardy's Studies, Specimens and Notebook,* p. 280.

Sewanee Review, April, 1995, review of *Testamentary Acts,* p. 309.

Times Literary Supplement, July 16, 1982; September 10, 1982; March 23, 1984; June 7, 1985; July 3, 1987; June 7, 2002, John Lucas, review of *Thomas Hardy's Public Voice,* p. 24.

University of Toronto Quarterly, winter, 1998, David Minter, review of *Faulkner's Place,* pp. 520-522.

* * *

MIN, Anchee 1957-

PERSONAL: Born January 14, 1957, in Shanghai, China; immigrated to the United States, 1984; daughter of Naishi (an astronomy instructor) and Dinyun (a teacher; maiden name, Dai) Min; married Qigu Jiang (a painter), 1991 (divorced, 1994); children: Lauryan (daughter). *Education:* Attended the School of the Art Institute of Chicago, 1985-91, received B.F.A., M.F.A. *Hobbies and other interests:* Promoting education in China.

ADDRESSES: Home—CA. *Agent*—Sandra Dijkstra Literary Agency, 1155 Camino del Mar, Ste. 515-C, Del Mar, CA 92014.

CAREER: Writer. Worked in China at Red Fire communal farm, near East China Sea, 1974-76; Shanghai Film Studio, Shanghai, actress, 1976-77, set clerk, 1977-84; worked in the United States as a waitress, messenger, gallery attendant, and babysitter.

AWARDS, HONORS: Carl Sandburg Literary Award, 1993, for *Red Azalea; Red Azalea* was named a Notable Book of the Year, 1994, by the *New York Times.*

Anchee Min

WRITINGS:

Red Azalea (memoir), Pantheon (New York, NY), 1994.

Katherine (novel), Riverhead/Putnam (New York, NY), 1995.

Becoming Madame Mao (novel), Houghton Mifflin (Boston, MA), 1999.

Wild Ginger, Houghton Mifflin (Boston, MA), 2002.

Empress Orchid, Houghton Mifflin (Boston, MA), 2004.

SIDELIGHTS: Anchee Min, who grew up in China during the Cultural Revolution, describes her personal experiences in the memoir *Red Azalea,* and also focuses on that period of history in several works of fiction, among them the novels *Becoming Madame Mao* and *Wild Ginger.* The Cultural Revolution, initiated by Chinese Communist Party Chairman Mao Tse-Tung and lasting from 1966 until Mao's death in 1976, was a radical movement intended to revitalize devotion to the original Chinese Revolution. During this time, China's urban youths were organized into cadres of Red Guards and empowered to attack citizens, including party officials, who did not uphold the strict tenets of the Revolution. Recounting her participation in the Little Red Guards, a group of students selected for their fidelity to the Communist Party, Min tells of an attempt to prove her own loyalty to the Party by denouncing Autumn Leaves, a favorite teacher, and accusing her of imperialist activities. Before an assembly of two thousand people, Autumn Leaves was beaten and humiliated and pressured to confess that she was "an American spy." Min then writes, "Autumn Leaves called my name and asked if I really believed that she was an enemy of the country. . . . She asked me with the same exact tone she used when she helped me with my homework. . . . I could not bear looking at her eyes. They had looked at me when the magic of mathematics was explained. . . . When I was ill, they had looked at me with sympathy and love. I had not realized the true value of what all this meant to me until I lost it forever that day at the meeting."

At age seventeen, Min was sent to Red Fire Farm, a collective of some 13,000 workers near the East China Sea. She lived there for three years, enduring hardship, laboring to grow cotton in unyielding soil. Seeking solace from the deprivations, Min engaged in a love affair with a female platoon leader, although both could have easily been betrayed and condemned by other workers. Min eventually escaped Red Fire Farm when picked as a finalist—from a pool of twenty thousand candidates—for a film version of a political opera by Madame Mao, *Red Azalea.* But Min's success was short-lived: in September, 1976, Mao died, Madame Mao fell into disfavor, the political system was thrown into chaos, and the film was abandoned in mid-production. Min worked at the film studio as a set clerk for six years.

With the assistance of actress Joan Chen, a friend from acting school, Min came to the United States in 1984 as a student at the School of the Art Institute of Chicago. She knew virtually no English when she arrived in the United States, and immersed herself in English studies. Min told Penelope Mesic of *Chicago* magazine that she forbade herself to speak any Chinese, "so I would learn the language." In a writing course at the institute, Min wrote about Red Fire Farm. She sent the story to the literary magazine *Granta,* where it was published in the spring of 1992. Based on this story, an agent sold Pantheon the rights to Min's autobiography for a large advance. Min finished writing *Red Azalea* on Christmas Day, 1992. "I was vomiting, my whole body was shaking after a year of living my past life and having to face myself," Min recounted to Mesic. "I was so driven and so glad to be given the opportunity." Min tells *Red Azalea* in uncomplicated declarative sentences, a style that reviewers noted for its effective rendering of the subject matter. According to a *New York* contributor, the writing "suits the brutality of Min's story as well as her own childlike frankness and ferocity." As Min once noted: "I write what I know. I write about what I can't escape from. I don't love writing, but I enjoy the mind battle. I fight with myself to be a winner."

Reviewers also appreciated Min's account of the Cultural Revolution, finding it a significant contribution to Chinese studies. In *Publishers Weekly,* a critic stated that *Red Azalea* "is earthy, frank, filled with stunning beauty and of enormous literary and historical interest." Describing the book as a "roller-coaster ride through Chinese art and politics," *New York Times Book Review* contributor Judith Shapiro remarked that *Red Azalea,* a "memoir of sexual freedom," exists as "a powerful political as well as literary statement."

Katherine, Min's "lyrical" debut novel, according to Bernadine Connelly of the *New York Times Book Review,* recounts the story of Katherine, an American teacher who travels to China to teach English. The novel, declared Connelly, is narrated by one of Katherine's students, who "uses the clash of their cultures to create a vivid portrait of life in contemporary China." *New Statesman and Society*'s Sarah A. Smith observed, "The romantic sway of Min's language and the perniciously hopeful influence of Katherine wreck the novel's finer points." Smith assessed: "This is a guileless book about a far from guileless time, and a difficult story, too simply told."

Min's 1999 novel *Becoming Madame Mao,* traces the rise to power of Madame Mao in the years 1919 through 1991. *Library Journal* reviewer Shirley N. Quan observed that Min's "characterization of Madame Mao is so strong that one may tend to forget that this work is a novel and not a true biography." A *Publishers Weekly* critic praised Min's "complex psychological portrait of a driven, passionate woman and a period in history which she would suffer, rise and prosper, and then fall victim to her own insatiable thirst for power." The critic commented that "striking metaphors and vivid Chinese proverbs enhance Min's tensile prose." Kristine Huntley, writing in *Booklist,* called the novel "nothing less than brilliant."

Wild Ginger focuses on the later years of the Cultural Revolution in its focus on Maple and Wild Ginger, two teen girls who manage to navigate the difficulties of Mao's regime in different ways. Described as "both a tragic love story and a parable that illustrates the corruption caused by political and moral fanaticism" by *Book* reviewer Susan Tekulve, *Wild Ginger* finds Wild Ginger at first defending her more gentle schoolmate Maple from the attacks of Maoist zealots when both girls are branded suspicious by Maoist officials. While Maple attempts to distance herself from the political fight, the strong-willed Wild Ginger is determined to find acceptance, and she gradually adopts the repressive party line that helps her move up in the ranks of Mao's Red Guard until a love affair causes her to question her priorities. A *Kirkus Reviews* contributor described *Wild Ginger* as "a striking story of love and betrayal [that] recreates the terror and animosities that informed the Cultural Revolution," while in *Library Journal* Edward Cone praised Min for her "lean, expressive prose" and her "talent for mixing irony with humor." "Min continues her extraordinarily acute inquiry into the wounded psyches of martyrs to and survivors of China's horrific Cultural Revolution in her shattering third novel," added Donna Seaman in *Booklist,* writing that the author's "taut and compassionate tale of oppressed teenagers kept in ignorance of the wider world" holds a special relevance for modern teens.

A more historical novel, Min's *Empress Orchid* returns readers to the China of the mid-nineteenth century, and the life of Tsu Hsi, or "Orchid," a seventeen-year-old woman of a poor, rural family who becomes the Chinese emperor's seventh wife, bears the son that will become the "Last Emperor," and, after the emperor's death, rules the country as regent for over four decades. Based on an actual story, the novel follows Orchid's efforts to survive court life and gain the influence needed to ensure that her child will become heir to the dynasty, painting the woman as "a smart politician and demanding mother," according to *People* contributor John Freeman. "Min . . . brilliantly lifts the public mask of a celebrated woman to reveal a contradictory character," noted a *Publishers Weekly* contributor, comparing *Empress Orchid* favorably with

Becoming Madame Mao. Booklist reviewer Donna Seaman noted that with the novel the author "continues to fulfill her mission to tell the truth about her homeland, particularly China's long tradition of demonizing women," and praised the resulting novel as "insightful, magnetic," and "bewitching."

BIOGRAPHICAL AND CRITICAL SOURCES:

BOOKS

Min, Anchee, *Red Azalea,* Pantheon (New York, NY), 1994.

PERIODICALS

Book, May-June, 2002, Susan Tekulve, review of *Wild Ginger,* p. 81.

Booklist, April 1, 1995, Donna Seaman, review of *Katherine,* p. 1378; March 15, 2000, Kristine Huntley, review of *Becoming Madame Mao,* p. 1293; February 15, 2002, Donna Seaman, review of *Wild Ginger,* p. 971; November 15, 2003, Donna Seaman, review of *Empress Orchid,* p. 548.

Chicago, January, 1994, pp. 55-57, 13-14.

Differences, summer, 2002, Shu-Mei Shih, "Toward and Ethics of Transnational Encounter," p. 90.

Entertainment Weekly, March 25, 1994, p. 50.

Kirkus Reviews, February 15, 2002, review of *Wild Ginger,* p. 214; December 1, 2003, review of *Empress Orchid,* p. 1376.

Kliatt, May, 2004, review of *Wild Ginger,* p. 21.

Library Journal, March 15, 2000, Shirley N. Quan, review of *Becoming Madame Mao,* p. 128; March 1, 2002, Edward Cone, review of *Wild Ginger,* p. 140; December, 2003, Edward Cone, review of *Empress Orchid,* p. 158.

New Statesman & Society, August 25, 1995, Sarah A. Smith, review of *Katherine,* p. 33.

New York, January 31, 1994, p. 63.

New Yorker, February 21, 1994, p. 119.

New York Times, January 26, 1994, p. C19.

New York Times Book Review, February 27, 1994, p. 11; September 10, 1995, Bernadine Connelly, review of *Katherine.*

People, February 16, 2004, review of *Empress Orchid,* p. 43.

Publishers Weekly, December 13, 1993, p. 21; December 20, 1993, p. 57; March 13, 1995, review of *Katherine,* p. 58; April 3, 2000, review of *Becoming Madame Mao,* p. 60; June 5, 2000, Roxane Farmanfarmaian, "After the Revolution," pp. 66-67; March 4, 2002, review of *Wild Ginger,* p. 56; January 19, 2004, review of *Empress Orchid,* p. 53.

ONLINE

Chinese Culture Web site, http://www.chineseculture.net/ (December 2, 1999), "Anchee Min."

USA Today Online, http://www.usatoday.com/ (December 2, 1999), "Anchee Min."*

* * *

MORE, Julian 1928-

PERSONAL: Born June 15, 1928, in Llanelli, Wales; son of Frank Hugh (a land agent) and Guinevere (a painter; maiden name, Lyne) More; married Sheila Christine Hull (an artist's agent), August 9, 1951; children: Camilla and Carey (twins). *Education:* Trinity College, Cambridge, B.A., 1951. *Hobbies and other interests:* Travel, walking, cooking, wine.

ADDRESSES: Home—Provence, France. *Agent*—(theater) Sebastian Born, Curtis Brown, Ltd., 162-168 Regent St., London W1R, England; (literary) Abner Stein, 10 Roland Gardens, London SW7 3PH, England.

CAREER: Playwright, lyricist, screenwriter, journalist, and author.

MEMBER: Writers Guild of Great Britain, Society of Authors, Performing Right Society, Songwriters' Guild (United States and England), Dramatists Guild (United States), Groucho Club.

AWARDS, HONORS: Evening Standard Award and Society of West End Theater Award, both best musical, 1979, for *Songbook;* Antoinette Perry Award nomination, best book to a musical, American Theater Wing, 1981, for *The Moony Shapiro Songbook;* Prix Litteraire Alexandre Dumaine, 1989, for *A Taste of Provence.*

WRITINGS:

Don't Go Away, I Might Fall Down, J. Cape (London, England), 1963.
Views from a French Farmhouse, Henry Holt (New York, NY), 1985.
Views from the Hollywood Hills, photographs by daughter, Carey More, Henry Holt (New York, NY), 1986.
Views from a Tuscan Vineyard, photographs by Carey More, Henry Holt (New York, NY), 1987.
A Taste of Provence: The Food and People of Southern France, with Forty Delicious Recipes, photographs by Carey More, Henry Holt (New York, NY), 1988.
Impressions of the Seine, photographs by Carey More, Rizzoli (New York, NY), 1991.
More about France: A Sentimental Journey, J. Cape (London, England), 1992.
A Taste of Burgundy, photographs by Carey More, Abbeville (New York, NY), 1993.
Pagnol's Provence, photographs by Carey More, Pavilion Books (London, England), 1996.
Impressionist Paris: The Essential Guide to the City of Light, Pavilion Books (London, England), 1998.
Tour de Provence, photographs by John Miller, Pavilion Books (London, England), 2001.

STAGE PLAYS:

(Contributor) *Airs on a Shoestring* (revue), produced in London, England, on West End, 1953.
(With James Gilbert) *The World's the Limit,* produced by Windsor Theater, 1955.
(Book, with James Gilbert) *Grab Me a Gondola* (musical), produced in London, England, at Lyric Theater, 1956.
(Book) *Expresso Bongo* (musical), produced in London, England, at Saville Theater, 1958.
(Book with Wolf Mankowitz; lyrics with David Heneker and Monty Norman) *Irma La Douce* (musical; based on a short story by Wolf Mankowitz), produced in London, England, at Lyric Theater, 1958, then in New York, NY, at Plymouth Theater, 1961.
(Book, with David Heneker and Monty Norman) *The Art of Living* (musical revue), produced in London, England, at Criterion Theater, 1960.
(Book, with David Heneker and Monty Norman) *Songbook* (musical), based on columns by Art Buchwald), produced in London, England, at Globe Theater, 1978, retitled *The Moony Shapiro Songbook,* produced in New York, NY, at Morosco Theater, 1981.
(Book, with Gilbert Becarol) *Roza* (musical; based on a novel by Romain Gary), produced in New York, NY, at Royale Theater, 1987.
(Adaptor of book) *Can-Can* (musical; based on original book by Abe Burrows), produced in London, England, 1988.

Other stage writings include (with composer James Gilbert) *The Golden Touch,* (with Monty Norman) *The Perils of Scobie Prilt,* (with David Russell) *The Man from the West,* (with Monty Norman) *Quick, Quick, Slow,* (with James Gilbert) *Good Time Johnny,* (with Alexander Ferris) *Bordello,* and (with Al Frisch and Bernard Spiro) *Bordello.* Also contributor to productions of Watergate Theater.

SCREENPLAYS:

Red and Blue, United Artists, 1966.
(With William E. Bast) *The Valley of Gwangi,* Warner Bros., 1969.
Incense for the Damned (also known as *Doctors Wear Scarlet* and *The Bloodsuckers*), Lucinda, 1970.
(With Sheila More) *The Catamount Killing,* Hallmark, 1975.
Chanel Solitaire, United Film Distribution, 1981.

Contributor of travel articles to various periodicals, including the *Daily Mail, New York Times,* London *Times, European Travel and Life,* and *Los Angeles Times.*

SIDELIGHTS: Julian More has penned the book and lyrics to a number of popular stage musicals, including *Irma La Douce, Songbook,* and *Roza.* Enid Nemy described the plot of *Roza* in the *New York Times* as "the story of an over-the-hill Jewish prostitute who makes her living raising her colleagues' children." More has also written screenplays, including director Tony Richardson's *Red and Blue* as well as collaborating with William E. Bast on *The Valley of Gwangi,* a science fiction film in which cowboys encounter dinosaurs and other prehistoric creatures in a hidden Mexican valley.

A native of Wales, More has since relocated to a farmhouse in the south of France. His experiences there have inspired a number of books, such as *Views from a French Farmhouse* and *A Taste of Provence: The Food and People of Southern France, with Forty Delicious Recipes.* In *Views from a French Farmhouse* More delivers the prose while his daughter, Carey, provides photographs of Provence. A critic in the *Washington Post Book World* noted that this partnership permitted Julian and Carey More "to share the insights they've gained into the rhythms of the people and the land." Their gastronomic book, *A Taste of Provence,* once again combines More's "warm, wry text" with Carey More's "charming, quirky" pictures, according to a reviewer in *Booklist.* Included in *A Taste of Provence* are forty recipes for Provencal dishes. More's memories of France, which extend back to his boyhood, are also the subject of *More about France: A Sentimental Journey.* "Each of his fourteen chapters gives us his first impressions of a particular part of France, gathered between 1937 and 1979, interwoven with experiences drawn from recent visits," pointed out Jacquey Visick in the *Times Literary Supplement.*

More once told *CA:* "My multifaceted writing is an escape from one self to another. And some of these selves—by no means all—have been among my best collaborators."

BIOGRAPHICAL AND CRITICAL SOURCES:

PERIODICALS

Booklist, November 15, 1988, review of *A Taste of Provence: The Food and People of Southern France, with Forty Delicious Recipes,* p. 527.

Library Journal, July, 1998, George M. Jenks, review of *Impressionist Paris: The Essential Guide to the City of Light,* p. 119; May 15, 2002, Olga B. Wise, review of *Tour de Provence,* p. 116.

New York Times, December 19, 1986; February 20, 1987; May 15, 1987; October 2, 1987, Enid Nemy, review of *Roza.*

Publishers Weekly, December 30, 1996, review of *Pagnol's Provence,* p. 51.

Times Literary Supplement, June 5, 1992, Jacquey Visick, review of *More about France: A Sentimental Journey,* p. 26.

Washington Post Book World, December 8, 1985, review of *Views from a French Farmhouse,* p. 11.

ONLINE

Bonjour Paris.com, http://www.bparis.com/ (January, 1999), Karen Fawcett, "Julian More—A Man of Many Talents Who Calls Provence Home."*

MORGAN, Douglas
See MACDONALD, James D.

* * *

MORGAN, Roxanne
See GENTLE, Mary

* * *

MULLER, Jerry Z(ucker) 1954-

PERSONAL: Born June 7, 1954, in Niagara Falls, Ontario, Canada; son of Henry (an entrepreneur) and Bella (a homemaker and bookkeeper; maiden name, Zucker) Muller; married Sharon Sachs (an archivist), August 8, 1976; children: Elisha, Sara, Joseph. *Education:* Brandeis University, B.A., 1977; Columbia University, M.A., 1978, Ph.D., 1984. *Religion:* Jewish. *Hobbies and other interests:* Listening to jazz piano music.

ADDRESSES: Home—11610 Yeatman Terr., Silver Spring, MD 20902. *Office*—Department of History, Catholic University of America, 620 Michigan Ave. NE, Washington, DC 20064-0001; fax: 202-319-5569. *E-mail*—mullerj@cua.edu.

CAREER: Catholic University of America, Washington, DC, assistant professor, 1984-90, associate professor of history, 1990-96, professor, 1996—. Harvard University, teaching fellow, 1983. Jerusalem Center for Public Affairs, Jerusalem, Israel, visiting scholar in residence, 1993-94.

MEMBER: American Historical Association, German Studies Association, Jewish Studies Association, Ramsey Colloquium of Institute on Religion and Public Life, International Society for Intellectual History, Phi Beta Kappa.

AWARDS, HONORS: Presidential fellow, Columbia University, 1978-80; Whiting fellow, Columbia University, 1981-82; International Doctoral Research fellow, Social Science Research Council, 1981-82; Doctoral fellow, Social Science and Humanities Research Council of Canada, 1978-81, 1982-83; Shepard B. Clough Dissertation Prize in European History, Columbia University, 1984; fellow, American Council of Learned Societies, 1985-86; Olin Foundation fellow, 1987-88, 1999; research grant, Catholic University, 1987-88, 1995; research grant, Bradley Foundation, 1990-91; fellow, Rockefeller Foundation Study Center, Bellagio, Italy, 2001; also a fellow of the ACLS.

WRITINGS:

The Other God That Failed: Hans Freyer and the Deradicalization of German Conservatism, Princeton University Press (Princeton, NJ), 1987.

Adam Smith in His Time and Ours: Designing the Decent Society, Free Press (New York, NY), 1993.

(Editor) *Conservatism: An Anthology of Social and Political Thought from David Hume to the Present,* Princeton University Press (Princeton, NJ), 1997.

(Editor, with Marion F. Deshmukh) *Fritz Stern at 70,* German Historical Institute (Washington, DC), 1997.

The Mind and the Market: Capitalism in Modern European Thought, Knopf (New York, NY), 2002.

Advisory editor of *Social Science and Modern Society,* 1997—. Serves on board of advisors of *Critical Review: An Interdisciplinary Journal of Politics and Society,* 2001—. Contributor to periodicals, including *Commentary, First Things, Public Interest,* and *Times Literary Supplement.*

SIDELIGHTS: Jerry Z. Muller, a professor of history at the Catholic University of America, once told *CA:* "I write books and articles that I would like to read but that are not already available. . . . I also publish essays on intellectuals and politics in modern Europe and on the politics of contemporary intellectual life. I hope to publish some of these essays as a book in the not too distant future."

Muller's first book, *The Other God That Failed: Hans Freyer and the Deradicalization of German Conservatism,* explores the political transformation of pro-totalitarian intellectuals during the National Socialist (Nazi) era. Muller focuses much of the book on Hans Freyer, a prominent German sociologist who advocated a right-wing revolution during the early 1930s. As the National Socialists rose to power, however, Freyer came to regret his political convictions. Muller commented on the book, saying, "*The Other God That Failed* explores three questions that interested me: Why were some of the best and brightest German intellectuals attracted to the idea of a total state before 1933? What happened to such intellectuals during the Nazi era? How did their experience of a totalitarian regime affect their thought after 1945? The phenomenon of intellectual disillusionment with totalitarianism had been explored on the political left, yet, as I tried to show, it played an important part on the political right as well, contributing to the development of a liberal democratic political culture after 1945." Richard John Neuhaus, writing in the *Los Angeles Times Book Review,* affirmed that *The Other God That Failed* is written with "engaging brilliance."

Muller is also the author of *Adam Smith in His Time and Ours: Designing the Decent Society,* in which he argues that eighteenth-century Scottish economist Smith's book *The Wealth of Nations,* best known for its examination of how markets work, was part of a political project of designing institutions that would make society more decent and self-controlled. Muller told *CA* that the idea for *Adam Smith in His Time and Ours* actually came to him while working on another project, *The Mind and the Market: Capitalism in Modern European Thought.* Muller said, "In the course of working on the chapter on Adam Smith, I came to believe that no existing volumes recaptured Smith's larger purposes and his characteristic mode of thought and social analysis. [The book] presents a rather new and, I think, more accurate portrait of Smith but places his writings on the market in the larger context of his work and in the relevant historical contexts." *National Review* critic John Gray called *Adam Smith in His Time and Ours* a "profoundly erudite and timely study," and *Commentary* reviewer George Russell found the book "thoughtful and accessible" and noted that it holds "plenty . . . for modern policy wonks to consider."

Muller's next work, *Conservatism: An Anthology of Social and Political Thought from David Hume to the Present,* is, according to the author, "a collection of writings on social and political policy by conservative analysts from the mid-eighteenth century to the present, which I hope conveys some of the recurrent characteristics of conservative thought." According to an *Ethics* contributor, "The editor makes it clear that the central aim of conservatism is to promote human well-being within particular societies; that doing so depends on conserving institutions and customs that have endured in a society; and that conservatism may take different forms in different contexts because the prevailing conditions, institutions, and customs are different." *Library Journal*'s Stephen Kent Shaw commented, "Muller argues persuasively that conservative social and political thought emerges essentially as a response to challenges to existing institutions and attempts, therefore, to refute such challenges." Daniel J. Mahoney of *First Things: A Monthly Journal of Religion and Public Life* explained, "Muller locates conservatism in an approach that he calls 'historical utilitarianism.' It emphasizes the wisdom of long-established historical practices, the latent function served by seemingly obsolete institutions and traditions, the indispensable role of custom and habit as 'second nature,' and the unintended consequences that stem from efforts to radically transform the social order." Mahoney dubbed *Conservatism* "a first-rate anthology of conservative thought," and Shaw felt the book was "impressive" and "long overdue." *Wilson Quarterly*'s Charles R. Kesler declared, "Muller's book is a bracing commentary on the present-day condition of American conservatism, and a welcome invitation to rethink what conservatives ought to be conserving."

Muller told *CA:* "A number of books and essays of the late 1970s and early 1980s led me to examine more carefully the history of the debate on the cultural ramifications of economic developments. The result of this work is *The Mind and the Market: Capitalism in Modern European Thought.*" The book, according to Muller, explores the ways in which a number of European intellectuals "thought of the cultural, moral, and political ramifications of the market economy. Each chapter puts the arguments of a prominent or representative thinker in the larger context of his thought and of the political, economic, and cultural contexts in which he was writing." Among the great thinkers Muller examines in *The Mind and the Market* are Voltaire, Adam Smith, Edmund Burke, G. W. F. Hegel, Max Weber, Joseph Schumpeter, Friedrich Hayek, Karl Marx, Matthew Arnold, Georg Lukacs, Hans Preyer, and Herbert Marcuse. *Booklist*'s David Siegfried noted, "This work is an in-depth study of the origins of thought about markets and their effects on people, when thinking men easily questioned whether capitalism is good for people. It is a wonderful contrast to today's blind worship of materialism and economic progress." As Fred Stahl explained in *Manufacturing and Technology News,* "Capitalism is a complex tapestry of economic arrangements, governmental obligations, cultural traditions, personal behavioral norms, concepts for production enterprises, methods of managements, public acceptance of the concept of return on investment, preservation of competition, religious and ethnic tolerance, and ideas of personal property." "There is no other work quite like it," remarked Alan Kahan of *History: Review of New Books.* "Its chief merit is in the ideas and authors it brings together for critical comparison and in the stimulation those ideas may provide for further reflection on what is perhaps the most important subject of our times."

Reviews of *The Mind and the Market* were generally positive. While a *Publishers Weekly* critic felt that some of Muller's conclusions were "too restrained," overall the reviewer noted, "This study illuminates the long lineage of engagement with social consequences of capitalism." David Harsanyi of the *World and I* said the book was "important and informative," and *National Review*'s Arthur Herman called it "brilliant and engaging." Sheri Berman of *Foreign Affairs* concluded, "Muller has written a lively and accessible survey of what dozens of major European thinkers have thought about capitalism." Brian J. Fox of the *Review of Metaphysics* felt that Muller "dedicates himself to the project of laying out the positives and negatives of the market as reflected upon by Europe's best minds over the last few centuries and allowing his audience to come to their own conclusions." Stahl surmised, "*The Mind and the Market* should be read by every world citizen to understand how we got the flow of wealth we enjoy."

BIOGRAPHICAL AND CRITICAL SOURCES:

PERIODICALS

American Historical Review, June, 1994, review of *Adam Smith in His Time and Ours: Designing the Decent Society,* p. 868.

Booklist, September 15, 2002, David Siegfried, review of *The Mind and the Market: Capitalism in Modern European Thought,* p. 186.

Books & Culture, January, 1998, review of *Conservatism: An Anthology of Social and Political Thought from David Hume to the Present,* p. 45.

Challenge, September-October, 1996, M. E. Sharpe, review of *Adam Smith in His Time and Ours,* p. 62.

Commentary, May, 1993, pp. 60, 62.

Ethics, April, 1994, review of *Adam Smith in His Time and Ours,* p. 669; April, 2000, review of *Conservatism,* p. 657.

First Things: A Monthly Journal of Religion and Public Life, February, 1998, Daniel J. Mahoney, review of *Conservatism,* p. 55.

Foreign Affairs, July-August, 2003, Sheri Berman, "We Didn't Start the Fire: Capitalism and Its Critics, Then and Now," review of *The Mind and the Market,* p. 176.

History: Review of New Books, winter, 2004, Alan Kahan, review of *The Mind and the Market,* p. 66.

Journal of Economic Literature, June, 1994, review of *Adam Smith in His Time and Ours,* p. 683.

Journal of Modern History, December, 1995, review of *Adam Smith in His Time and Ours,* p. 921.

Kirkus Reviews, September 1, 2002, review of *The Mind and the Market,* pp. 1286-87.

Library Journal, April 15, 1997, Stephen Kent Shaw, review of *Conservatism,* p. 100.

Los Angeles Times Book Review, December 18, 1988, pp. 3, 11.

Manufacturing and Technology News, August 4, 2003, Fred Stahl, "Why Are Some Cultures Wealthy and Others Not?," review of *The Mind and the Market,* p. 10.

Modern Age, fall, 1998, review of *Conservatism,* p. 410.

National Review, May 24, 1993, pp. 56-58; May 5, 2003, Arthur Herman, "Free Men, Free Markets," review of *The Mind and the Market,* p. NA.

New Republic, June 7, 1999, review of *Conservatism,* p. 34.

Philosophy in Review, December, 1997, review of *Conservatism,* p. 432.

Publishers Weekly, April 28, 1997, review of *Conservatism,* p. 67; September 30, 2002, review of *The Mind and the Market,* p. 58.

Quadrant, July-August, 2003, Andrew Norton, "Capitalism and Its Critics," review of *The Mind and the Market,* p. 114.

Review of Metaphysics, June, 1998, Mark Wegierski, review of *Conservatism,* p. 948; December, 2003, Brian J. Fox, review of *The Mind and the Market,* p. 425.

Review of Politics, winter, 1994, review of *Adam Smith in His Time and Ours,* p. 183.

Times Literary Supplement, March 27, 1998, review of *Conservatism,* p. 14.

University Bookman, summer, 1997, review of *Conservatism,* p. 10.

Virginia Quarterly Review, winter, 1998, review of *Conservatism,* p. 26.

Wilson Quarterly, spring, 1997, Charles R. Kesler, review of *Conservatism,* p. 103.

World and I, April, 2003, David Harsanyi, "The Idea of Capitalism: A Historian Helps Clarify the Great Historical European Debate on Market Capitalism," review of *The Mind and the Market,* p. 220.

ONLINE

Catholic University of America, Department of History Web site, http://www.history.cua.edu/faculty/Muller/ (June 28, 2004), "Jerry Z. Muller."

Princeton University Press Web site, http://pup.princeton.edu/ (January 15, 2003), descriptions of *Conservatism* and *Adam Smith in His Time and Ours.*

Random House of Canada Web site, http://www.randomhouse.ca/ (June 28, 2004), description of *The Mind and the Market.**

* * *

MURR, Naeem

PERSONAL: Born in London, England; son of Samir and Eileen (a teacher) Murr. *Education:* Attended Stanford University; Syracuse University, M.A.

ADDRESSES: Home—875 Clayton St., Lower Floor, San Francisco, CA 94117. *Agent*—c/o Louise Quayle-Ellen Levine Literary Agency, Inc., 15 E. 26th St., Ste. 1801, New York, NY 10010.

CAREER: Stanford University, Stanford, CA, teaching assistant, 1993; Pembroke College, Oxford, England, creative writing teacher, 1995; University of Houston, Houston, TX, fiction instructor, 1996-97; freelance writer, 1997—. Writer in residence, Lynchburg College, 1998; visiting professor of creative writing, Northwestern University.

AWARDS, HONORS: Award for Best Story, *Gettysburg Review,* 1993, for "Benjamin," and 1995, for "The Writer"; Margaret Bridgman Fellow in Fiction, 2003; Stegner fellowship and Scowcroft fellowship, both Stanford University; Raymond Carver prize for poetry; *New York Times* Notable Book, for *The Boy.*

WRITINGS:

The Boy (novel), Houghton Mifflin (Boston, MA), 1998.

The Genius of the Sea, Free Press (New York, NY), 2003.

Contributor of stories and novellas to literary journals. *The Boy* has been translated into six languages.

WORK IN PROGRESS: The King of Infinite Space.

SIDELIGHTS: Poet and fiction writer Naeem Murr achieved critical acclaim for his first novel, 1998's *The Boy.* The novel recounts social worker Sean Hennessey's search through the London underworld for his lost foster son, Durward, an orphan who Sean believes may be his natural son. The boy has proved to be emotionally disturbed, manifesting several different personalities during his stay with the Hennesseys. After wreaking havoc in Sean's family, Durward runs away, disappearing into London's mean streets. Parallel to the narrative of Sean's search is the story of Theresa, a former nun who runs the orphanage where Durward once lived and who sees the boy as a kind of Messiah figure. At the same time, however, other narrative strands show the demonic side of the boy, who destroys Sean's family and prompts the "fat man" who adores him toward evil actions.

Many reviewers praised Murr's ability to evoke a nightmarish world in which good and evil exist in constant conflict. For example, Reba Leiding, writing in *Library Journal,* praised Murr's "rich, literary style." Hans Johnson, in the *Washington Post Book World,* wrote that "Murr traffics in images so capably that the novel's space becomes a kind of magnetic field, alluring, almost confining." And in the *New York Times Book Review,* novelist Margot Livesey admired Murr's ability to make Durward a fully believable character: "Much of the impact of *The Boy* depends on Murr's ability to make this beautiful, bisexual, charismatic Messiah-Satan credible, and to a large extent [Murr] does." Though Livesey found some of Durward's extraordinary behavior difficult to accept, she considered the character richly drawn and emotionally believable, concluding with high praise for "Murr's dark energy, his sharply intelligent prose, his genius for the unexpected, his keen sense of atmosphere."

At the same time, however, some critics who admired Murr's descriptive abilities faulted *The Boy* for exaggerated prose and dependence on cliché. A *Publishers Weekly* reviewer, for one, deemed the novel "overwrought," noting that the characters "seduce each other and explain themselves with operatic gusto: they seem to communicate in arias." In the *Times Literary Supplement,* critic Lesley McDowell observed that "for many reasons, *The Boy* is a disturbing novel, although perhaps not as disturbing as it should be." McDowell likened Murr's central theme, the erotic attraction of an older man to an innocent youth, to Thomas Mann's *Death in Venice* and Vladimir Nabokov's *Lolita.* Admiring the ambiguity with which *The Boy* opens, McDowell noted that the reader does "not know whether the boy is a con artist . . . or whether Hennessey is guilty of abusing the child put into his care." Yet as the narrative becomes more simplistic, wrote McDowell, the complex themes break down. "Possibilities that the boy is a projection of Hennessey's, that Hennessey may be presenting us with an untruthful account, fail to engage here in the way the novel might have seemed to suggest." McDowell concluded that "the novel's suggestion that the irresistibility of the boy is one with the irresistibility of evil is unexamined. And for so disturbing a subject, perhaps examination is needed more."

The grandiloquent prose that seeps into *The Boy* at times can also be found in Murr's second novel, *The Genius of the Sea,* in which social worker Daniel Mulvaugh finds solace from his wrecked life in the sea tales of an old man who is fraudulently accepting government checks. Amos Radcliff is living in the same flat where Mulvaugh grew up, and when the social worker visits Amos in an effort to expose him for taking welfare checks when he is not eligible for them, the location brings back strong memories and guilt over the things he never said to his mother and a childhood friend before they died. Mulvaugh is also plagued by guilt over his wife's nervous breakdown, feeling that he in some way caused it. But Amos's riveting tales of his younger days in the merchant marine, intertwined with a tragic tale of love and murder, sweep Mulvaugh away and threaten to drag him from the more painful, but more relevant realities of his life. Critics of *The Genius of the Sea* were especially impressed with Murr's blending of the stylized tales of the old sailor with the modern drama of Mulvaugh's personal dilemmas. "Murr draws the reader in with natural storytelling ability and uses great literary style to perfect the atmosphere," wrote Jeanine K. Raghunathan in *Library Journal,* while a *Kirkus Reviews* contributor said the novel "is full to bursting with ripe, powerful imagery, and he has an almost uncanny sense for the mechanics of group conversation." Although a *Publishers Weekly* writer felt that the character of Daniel was not fully drawn, the reviewer concluded that the novel is "a queer, mesmerizing hybrid of a book . . . [and a] notable, highly original work."

BIOGRAPHICAL AND CRITICAL SOURCES:

PERIODICALS

Houston Chronicle, August 23, 1998, Fritz Lanham, "Fostering a Mystery," p. 10.

Kirkus Reviews, March 14, 1998, review of *The Boy,* p. 359; April 1, 2003, review of *The Genius of the Sea,* p. 500.

Library Journal, April 1, 1998, Reba Leiding, review of *The Boy,* p. 124; May 1, 2003, Jeanine K. Raghunathan, review of *The Genius of the Sea,* p. 156.

New York Times Book Review, July 19, 1998, Margot Livesey, review of *The Boy,* p. 13.

Publishers Weekly, April 6, 1998, review of *The Boy,* p. 58; April 28, 2003, review of *The Genius of the Sea,* p. 43.

Times Literary Supplement, April 17, 1998, Lesley McDowell, review of *The Boy.*

Washington Post Book World, June 7, 1998, Hans Johnson, review of *The Boy,* p. X5.*

N-O

NELSON, Anne 1954-

PERSONAL: Born November 26, 1954, in Fort Sill, OK; daughter of Ted R. (a professor) and Gerada Elydia (an academic adviser; maiden name, Leitner) Nelson; married George Henry Scott Black (an editor and writer), June 2, 1984; children: two. *Education:* Yale University, B.A., 1976. *Hobbies and other interests:* Classical music, literature.

ADDRESSES: *Home*—New York, NY. *Office*—Columbia University, School of Journalism, 604D Journalism, Mail Code 3800, New York, NY 10027; 202 Riverside Drive 5A, New York, NY 10025-7265; fax: 212-865-1213. *Agent*—Geri Thoma, Elaine Markson Literary Agency Inc., 44 Greenwich Ave., New York, NY 10011. *E-mail*—an115@columbia.edu; nelblack@aol.com.

CAREER: *New Yorker,* New York, NY, editorial assistant, 1976-77; free-lance writer specializing in Latin America and the Caribbean, based in New York, NY, and Washington, DC, 1977-80; *Maclean's,* Canada, reporter, 1980-83. On-camera news analyst for Public Broadcasting Service programs "Frontline," "Inside Story," and "MacNeil/Lehrer Report," 1981-83; associate producer for New York bureau of Canadian Broadcasting Corp., 1983-84; consultant to Americas Watch (human rights organization), 1985-86. Executive director, Committee to Protect Journalists, 1989—; director, international program, Columbia Graduate School of Journalism, 1995—. Lecturer at colleges and universities; director, Maria Moors Cabot Awards.

MEMBER: PEN, Council on Foreign Relations.

Anne Nelson

AWARDS, HONORS: Best Feature Article for 1983 and Honorable Mention for photography, both from Associated Church Press, 1983, both for "El Salvador's Struggle: The Revolution Has a History," published in *Christianity and Crisis;* Royal Television Society

Award for best documentary, Royal Television Society (United Kingdom), 1984, for *In Search of a Brother;* Thomas More Storke Award for best international reporting in a magazine, 1988, for article on the Philippines; Livingston Award for best international reporting by an American journalist under thirty-five, 1989, for article on the Philippines; Professional Excellence Award, American Educators in Journalism and Mass Communication, 1993.

WRITINGS:

Human Rights in Honduras after General Alvarez, Americas Watch Committee (New York, NY), 1986.

(Translator and editor, with Jorge Valls) *Twenty Years and Forty Days: Memoirs of a Cuban Political Prisoner,* Human Rights Watch (New York, NY), 1986.

Murder under Two Flags: The U.S., Puerto Rico, and the Cerro Maravilla Cover-Up, Ticknor & Fields (New York, NY), 1986.

The Guys (play; first produced in New York, NY, 2001), Random House (New York, NY), 2002.

(With Jim Simpson) *The Guys* (screenplay based on Nelson's play of the same title), Focus Features, 2002.

Contributor to publications such as *Maclean's, Los Angeles Times, Columbia Journalism Review, Mother Jones, New York Times,* and *Nation.* Author of articles on Latin America and the Caribbean for *Life, Rolling Stone, Harper's, Christianity and Crisis,* Baltimore *Sun,* and other periodicals. Photography published in *New York Times, Newsweek, Washington Post, Christian Science Monitor,* and other periodicals.

Contributor to volumes such as *El Salvador: Central America in the New Cold War,* edited by Marvin E. Gettleman and others, Grove Press (New York, NY), 1981; *Trouble in Our Backyard,* edited by Martin Diskin, Pantheon (New York, NY), 1983; *Encyclopedia of Political Systems and Parties,* edited by George Delury, Facts on File (New York, NY), 1983; and *Puerto Rico's Political Status,* edited by Pamela Falk, Lexington Books (Lanham, MD), 1985.

Producer of radio and television documentaries, news reports, and related material.

ADAPTATIONS: Murder under Two Flags: The U.S., Puerto Rico, and the Cerro Maravilla Cover-Up was produced as a Hollywood feature film entitled *Show of Force,* 1990.

SIDELIGHTS: Murder under Two Flags: The U.S., Puerto Rico, and the Cerro Maravilla Cover-Up is Anne Nelson's account of the Cerro Maravilla incident, a public scandal in Puerto Rico that some critics have likened to the White House cover-up attempt in the Watergate affair during the presidency of Richard M. Nixon in the United States. According to Nelson, a police informer lured two young dissidents named Carlos Soto and Arnaldo Rosado to Cerro Maravilla, a hill outside the Puerto Rican city of Ponce. There police shot and killed them. The local government's report of their deaths, echoed by U.S. Department of Justice officials, called the two men terrorists and claimed that the police acted in self-defense. But an investigation by civil rights workers and journalists—Nelson among them—held that Soto and Rosado were murdered for their involvement in the struggle for Puerto Rican independence from the United States.

Augusta Dwyer of the Toronto *Globe and Mail* called *Murder under Two Flags* "compelling reading," in part because Nelson places the incident in the context of Puerto Rico's history as an "adopted child" of the United States. First ceded to the United States by Spain in 1898, the island became a commonwealth under American jurisdiction in 1952. Since that time, Nelson reports, Puerto Ricans have been divided between those citizens who seek complete autonomy and those who favor continued ties to the United States. In the *Los Angeles Times Book Review,* Frank Del Olmo noted that the bitterness of the controversy in Puerto Rico contrasts sharply to the general indifference of Americans concerning the issue. Nelson's book, he concluded, "succeeds in raising the larger question of Puerto Rico's future, a long-range issue that has never received the attention it deserves from citizens and decision makers on the mainland."

Nelson turned her attention to playwriting with *The Guys,* a two-person, one-act play based on her experiences helping a New York fire captain compose eulogies for eight of his men who died in the September 11, 2001, World Trade Center attacks. In the play, Jane, an advertising writer, meets with Nick, a fire chief nearly immobilized by grief and remorse, to refine workaday stories and sketchy remembrances of the fallen firefighters into eulogies that Nick must deliver. "No special effects-laden blockbuster could be as heart-wrenching as this simple piece of theatre," wrote David Sheward in *Back Stage.*

First-time playwright Nelson composed *The Guys* in a marathon seven-night session after meeting Jim Simpson, owner of the Flea Theatre, at a dinner for a human rights organization in New York. The Flea was a small New York City theatrical venue near the World Trade Center site, in financial danger after attendance dropped following the attacks. Simpson encouraged Nelson to transform her experiences with the fire captain into dramatic form, and *The Guys* premiered at the Flea in December, 2001, starring well-known actors Sigourney Weaver (Simpson's wife) and Bill Murray.

Some reviewers saw *The Guys* as a form of necessary catharsis, a healing balm for a city and a nation still reeling from unprecedented attack and profound tragedy. "Through skillful dialogs and monologs, minimal props and setting, Nelson transcended time and space to create a moving, cathartic work," remarked Ming-ming Shen Kuo in *Library Journal.* Byron Woods, reviewing a Carolina Arts Festival production of *The Guys* on the *Independent Weekly* Web site, commented that Nelson's "spare and undeniably moving tribute to the atrocities of [September 11] was vital enough to remind us all of the necessary work the theater can do in the world when it's actually asked to."

With some remove from the immediate effects of the attacks, other critics noted flaws in the play. "Ms. Nelson's script shows all the earmarks of a talented writer who is lacking in experience who could certainly make use of time for a rewrite," noted Bruce Weber in the *New York Times.* In a review from late 2003, Damien Jacques observed that the play's "writing is pedestrian" and "the characters repeatedly state the obvious." However, Jaques continued, "those flaws hardly mattered to a city groping for understanding and healing two years ago. Then, it reflected New Yorkers' reality." Despite any problems, however, "As a time capsule of the strong, irreducible emotions of that moment, *The Guys* may be as worthy a document in its own was as any *NY Times* 'Portrait of Grief,' American flag pin, or celebrity benefit concert," observed Bob Kendt in *Back Stage West.* Weber concluded that the play, and particularly the character of Nick, "gives credible and powerful voice to a very specific kind of pain that we crave these days to understand but from the outside seems only blindingly enormous and beyond sharing." Nelson and Simpson adapted the play into a feature film that was directed by Simpson and released in 2002.

Nelson once told *CA:* "Although my educational background was in history and music, much of my writing has been shaped by my experience as a journalist working in Latin America and the Caribbean."

BIOGRAPHICAL AND CRITICAL SOURCES:

PERIODICALS

Back Stage, February 15, 2002, David Sheward, review of *The Guys,* p. 52.

Back Stage West, July 18, 2002, Rob Kendt, "The Guys at the Actors' Gang," review of *The Guys,* pp. 14-15.

Booklist, August, 2002, Ray Olson, review of *The Guys,* p. 1912.

Daily Variety, April 4, 2002, Charles Lyons, "Content to film 9/11 Play," pp. 3-4.

Library Journal, October 15, 2002, Ming-ming Shen Kuo, review of *The Guys,* pp. 72-73.

Milwaukee Journal Sentinel, November 30, 2003, Damien Jaques, "Grief No Longer Masks *Guys* Flaws," review of *The Guys,* p. 7B.

New York Times, January 28, 2002, Bruce Weber, "Standing In for New Yorkers; Expressions of Grief over Sept. 11," review of *The Guys,* p. E1.

Reference Services Review, February, 1996, review of *Murder under Two Flags: The U.S., Puerto Rico, and the Cerro Maravilla Cover-Up,* p. 65.

ONLINE

Columbia News Web site, http://www.columbia.edu/cu/news/ (December 13, 2001), Jo Kadlecek, "The WTC Tragedy Turned Journalism Professor Anne Nelson into a Playwright," profile of Anne Nelson.

Independent Weekly Web site, http://www.indyweek.com/ (September 18, 2002), Byron Woods, "The Working Stage: A Musical and a Drama Probe the Real Labor the Theater Can—and Should—Do," review of *The Guys.*

Telegraph Web site (London), http://www.telegraph.co.uk/ (December 8, 2002), Sam Leith, "The Fire Captain and Me," profile of Anne Nelson.*

* * *

NYENHUIS, Jacob E(ugene) 1935-

PERSONAL: Born March 25, 1935, in Mille Lacs County, MN.

ADDRESSES: Agent—c/o Author Mail, Wayne State University Press, 4809 Woodward Ave., Detroit, MI 48201-1309.

CAREER: Wayne State University, Detroit, MI, faculty member for nearly fifteen years; Hope College, Holland, MI, professor of classics, beginning 1975, dean of arts and humanities, beginning 1978, now professor emeritus. American School of Classical Studies in Athens, past member of managing committee; Michigan Council for the Humanities, past vice chair.

AWARDS, HONORS: Probus Award, 1966.

WRITINGS:

(Editor) *Plautus: Amphitruo,* Wayne State University Press (Detroit, MI), 1970.

(Editor) *Petronius: Cena Trimalchionis,* Wayne State University Press (Detroit, MI), 1970.

Latin via Ovid: A First Course, Wayne State University Press (Detroit, MI), 1977.

Journey through a Labyrinth: A Study of the Works of Michael Ayrton, Secker & Warburg (London, England), 1979.

Myth and the Creative Process: Michael Ayrton and the Myth of Daedalus, the Maze Maker, Wayne State University Press (Detroit, MI), 2003.

BIOGRAPHICAL AND CRITICAL SOURCES:

PERIODICALS

Library Journal, May 15, 2003, Nadine Dalton Speidel, review of *Myth and the Creative Process: Michael Ayrton and the Myth of Daedalus, the Maze Maker,* p. 86.*

* * *

OSBORNE, Richard (Ellerker) 1943-

PERSONAL: Born February 22, 1943, in Hessle, England; son of William Harold (a banker) and Georgina Mary (Farrow) Osborne; married Hailz-Emily Wrigley (a literature teacher), January 18, 1986. *Education:* University of Bristol, B.A., 1965, M.Litt., 1967.

ADDRESSES: Home—2 Vaughan Copse, Eton, Berkshire SL4 6HL, England. *E-mail*—h.Osborne@etoncollege.org.uk.

CAREER: Bradfield College, Berkshire, England, English teacher and head of department, 1967-88, head of sixth-form general studies, 1979-88. British Broadcasting Corporation (BBC), London, England, *Radio Three,* presenter; Critic's Circle, London, chairman of music section, 1984-87.

WRITINGS:

Rossini ("Master Musicians" series) Dent (London, England), 1986, revised edition, 1987, reprinted, Oxford University Press (New York, NY), 2001.

(Editor) *Conversations with von Karajan,* Harper & Row (New York, NY), 1989.

Herbert von Karajan: A Life in Music, Northeastern University Press (Boston, MA), 2000.

Till I End My Song: English Music and Musicians, 1440-1940: A Perspective from Eton, Cygnet Press (London, England), 2002.

Contributor to *Opera on Record* and *Dictionary of Composers,* and to periodicals, including *Gramophone, Times Literary Supplement,* and *Spectator;* the *Oldie,* music critic.

SIDELIGHTS: After reading a review by Richard Osborne of a production of Gioacchino Antonio Rossini's opera *Il turco in Italia,* British Broadcasting Corporation producer and Giuseppe Verdi scholar Julian Budden commissioned Osborne to conduct a series of radio talks on Rossini. In 1978 Dent publishers commissioned Osborne to write a volume on Rossini for their long-established "Master Musicians" series. The subsequent study of Rossini's life and works was the first to appear in English in fifty years (books in the intervening period had been biographical only). John Rosselli lauded Osborne's *Rossini* in the *Times Literary Supplement,* noting that "it deserves to become the standard account in English." The volume's popularity has ensured continued reprints.

Osborne is also editor of *Conversations with von Karajan* and author of *Herbert von Karajan: A Life in Music.* The latter was called "the most comprehensive biography yet published of the Austrian conductor, one of the most significant, yet controversial musical figures of the twentieth century" by *Notes* reviewer Gary A. Galo. Karajan joined the Nazi Party (a career move), but during the war was married to a Jewish woman, a fact that offset his membership, and he eventually went through a "de-Nazification" hearing in order to clear his name. This, however, worked against him, in that it called attention to his status within the Party. He married three times, each time to fill different needs in both his professional and personal lives. Osborne builds on previous research in producing this volume, large at 851 pages, in documenting the life of the opera builder and conductor, who, following the war, earned an international reputation. He recorded with British record producer Walter Legg's new Philharmonia Orchestra, then became leader of the Berlin Philharmonic. His recordings for Deutsche Grammophon sold in numbers that rivaled pop recordings.

Osborne studies Karajan's relationships with performers, producers, directors, and various orchestras. Galo noted that "Osborne's close relationship with Karajan may cause readers to question his objectivity, but such doubts are without foundation, since the author's findings are consistently supported by diligent research; he is exhaustive in his documentation, offering sixty-four pages of detailed notes and references, listed by chapter. Nor does he shy away from criticism when it is warranted. He frequently comments on Karajan's performances, both recorded and live, and his observations are invariably well-founded."

Patrick J. Smith wrote in *Opera News* that "whether Karajan is seen as the ultimate careerist or as the successor to Toscanini and Furtwangler, his story is worth the telling. Bravo to Osborne for telling it so well." A *Publishers Weekly* reviewer wrote that "beautifully written, eminently fair-minded and full of enthralling anecdotes, this book will be catnip to any serious music lover."

Osborne's *Till I End My Song: English Music and Musicians, 1440-1940: A Perspective from Eton* is a history of music at Eton College, beginning with the formation of its choir by decree of Henry VI. Osborne notes the many famous composers who studied at Eton, including Thomas Arne, who wrote the music for "God Save the King" and "Rule Britannia." He writes that all of England's national songs have been touched by writers of music and lyrics from Eton. Cecil Spring-Rice wrote the words to the hymn "I Vow to Thee, My Country," and set it to the music of Holst's "Jupiter." The choir school was closed in 1968, but music continues to be funded and remains an important component of an Eton education.

BIOGRAPHICAL AND CRITICAL SOURCES:

PERIODICALS

Economist, September 5, 1998, review of *Herbert von Karajan: A Life in Music,* p. 80.

Library Journal, May 1, 2000, Bonnie Jo Dopp, review of *Herbert von Karajan,* p. 116.

Notes, December, 2001, Gary A. Galo, review of *Herbert von Karajan,* p. 386.

Opera News, July, 2000, Patrick J. Smith, review of *Herbert von Karajan,* p. 73.

Publishers Weekly, April 24, 2000, review of *Herbert von Karajan,* p. 74.

Times Literary Supplement, September 26, 1986, John Rosselli, review of *Rossini.**

* * *

OSTROM, Hans 1954-

PERSONAL: Born January 29, 1954, in Grass Valley, CA; son of Alex (a carpenter, stone mason, and gold miner) and Alice (a teacher; maiden name, Brady) Ostrom; married Jacquelyn Bacon (a fundraising consultant), July 18, 1983; children: Spencer. *Education:* Attended Sierra College, 1971-73; University of California, Davis, B.A., 1975, M.A., 1978, Ph.D., 1982. *Politics:* "Swedish socialist." *Religion:* Buddhist.

ADDRESSES: Home—Lakewood, WA. *Office*—Department of English, University of Puget Sound, 1500 N. Warner, Wyatt 336, Tacoma, WA 98416. *E-mail*—ostrom@ups.edu.

CAREER: Johannes Gutenberg University, Mainz, Germany, visiting lecturer, 1980-81; University of California, Davis, assistant director of composition, 1981-82; University of Puget Sound, Tacoma, WA, associate professor, 1983-2000, distinguished professor of English, 2000—, director of Center for Writing across the Curriculum, 1984-88. Member of editorial board, *Writing on the Edge,* 1990—; manuscript reviewer for publications such as *Journal of Advanced Composition and College English, Publications of the Modern Language Association,* and *College English,* and for publishers such as Boynton/Cook-Heinemann.

MEMBER: National Book Critics Circle, Mystery Writers of America, National Council of Teachers of English, Academy of American Poets, Conference on College Composition and Communication, Modern Language Association of America, Fulbright Association.

AWARDS, HONORS: Regents Fellowship, University of California, Davis, 1977-78; Harvest Award for poetry, University of Houston, 1978, for "Spider Killing"; grand prize, Ina Coolbrith Memorial Awards, 1979, for "Elegy for a Distant Relative"; first prize, Warren Eyster Competition, *New Delta Review,* 1985, for "The Collector"; fiction prize from *Redbook,* 1985, for the story "Hostage in Residence;" teaching award for outstanding graduate students, University of California, Davis, 1982; Burlington Northern Faculty Achievement Award, University of Puget Sound, 1986, 1989; Martin Nelson Sabbatical Fellowship, 1987; Alumni Association's Citation for Excellence, University of California, Davis, 1989; J. William Fulbright Fellowship for Senior Lecturers, Uppsala University, Uppsala, Sweden, spring, 1994; John Lantz Fellowship, University of Puget Sound, 1996-97.

WRITINGS:

(Editor, with Linda A. Morris and Linda P. Young) *The Living Language: A Reader* (anthology), Harcourt Brace Jovanovich (San Diego, CA), 1984.

(With Timothy J. Lulofs) *Leigh Hunt: A Reference Guide,* G. K. Hall (Boston, MA), 1985.

(Editor, with Mary T. Turnbull and Robert F. Garratt) *Spectrum: A Reader,* Harcourt Brace Jovanovich (San Diego, CA), 1987.

(Compiler) *Lives and Moments: An Introduction to Short Fiction* (anthology), Holt, Rinehart & Winston (Fort Worth, TX) 1991.

Three to Get Ready (novel), Cliffhanger Press (Oakland, CA), 1991.

(With Wendy Bishop) *Water's Night: Poems* (chapbook), Mariposite Press (Grass Valley, CA), 1992.

Langston Hughes: A Study of the Short Fiction, Twayne Publishers (New York, NY), 1993.

(Editor, with Wendy Bishop) *Colors of a Different Horse: Rethinking Creative Writing Theory and Pedagogy,* National Council of Teachers of English (Urbana, IL), 1994.

(Editor, with Wendy Bishop) *Genres of Writing: Issues, Arguments, Alternatives,* Boynton/Cook-Heinemann (Portsmouth, NH), 1997.

(With Wendy Bishop and Katharine Haake) *Metro: A Sourcebook for Writing Creatively,* Addison Wesley Longman (New York, NY), 2000.

Subjects Apprehended: Poems, Pudding House Press (Johnstown, OH), 2000.

A Langston Hughes Encyclopedia, Greenwood Press (Westport, CT), 2002.

(Editor, with Wendy Bishop) *The Subject Is Story: Essays for Writers and Readers,* Boynton/Cook-Heinemann (Portsmouth, NH), 2003.

Contributor to *Dictionary of Literary Biography,* Volume 106: *British Literary Publishing Houses, 1820-1880,* edited by Jonathan Rose and Patricia J. Anderson, Thomson Gale (Detroit, MI), 1991; *From These Hills: An Anthology of California Writers,* edited by Judith Shears, Castle Peak Editions (Corvalis, OR), 1991; *Essays in Honor of William Everson,* edited by Bill Hotchkiss, Castle Peak Editions (Corvalis, OR), 1992; *A Reference Guide to American Literature,* edited by Thomas Riggs, St. James Press (Detroit, MI), 1999; and *Acts of Revision,* edited by Wendy Bishop, Boynton/Cook-Heinemann (Portsmouth, NH), 2004. Author of book column, *Morning News Tribune* (Tacoma, WA).

Contributor of articles, stories, poems, and reviews to magazines and newspapers, including *California Quarterly, Ploughshares, Poetry Northwest, American*

Poetry, Cream City Review, Morning News Tribune (Tacoma, WA), *Arches, Barbaric Yawp, Commonweal, Northern Review, Washington Post,* and *Willow Springs.*

WORK IN PROGRESS: Editor, with J. David Macey, *An Encyclopedia of African American Literature,* five volumes, for Greenwood Press.

SIDELIGHTS: California native Hans Ostrom grew up surrounded by nature in his Sierra City home in the Sierra Nevada. "Bears, deer, raccoons, and rattlesnakes were often in our neighborhood, or we were in theirs," Ostrom wrote in an autobiography on his Internet home page. In this remote location (his grade school was twelve miles away), Ostrom read widely in literature and genre fiction, "reading novels by candlelight when winter storms knocked out electrical service," he wrote on his home page. From this background, Ostrom pursued poetry, fiction writing, and academics in the field of English. His scholarly interests include "composition studies, creative writing pedagogy, rhetoric, and African American literature."

In keeping with his interests, Ostrom is the author of two books on African American author Langston Hughes. In *Langston Hughes: A Study of the Short Fiction,* Ostrom presents a chronological analysis of the development of Hughes's short fiction. Ostrom focuses primarily on themes and thematic issues in Hughes's short stories, "but he remains alert to Hughes's relationship to literary and political movements" such as literary modernism and the Harlem Renaissance, commented J. A. Miller in *Choice.* The book includes excerpts from Hughes's essays, speeches, and autobiographies, with an eye toward establishing a sense of what Hughes thought of his own work. Ostrom also offers detailed surveys of articles, reviews, and criticism of Hughes's short works.

A Langston Hughes Encyclopedia is a "fascinating and ambitious" project featuring detailed descriptive entries, bibliographic citations, chronologies, and overviews of multiple aspects of Hughes's life and work, observed S. A. Vega Garcia in *Choice.* The book includes entries on Hughes's best-known poetry and fiction, but it also covers his more obscure and lesser-known works, including journalistic pieces, essays, dramatic works, children's literature, translations, songs, and even liner notes written for musical recordings by activist and folk artist Joan Baez. Ostrom also covers relevant themes and topics important to Hughes's work, and includes biographical entries on Hughes's key contemporaries. Reviewer Donna Akiba Sullivan Harper, writing in the *African American Review,* noted that "Ostrom has undertaken a noble effort" but remarked on a number of inconsistencies and inaccuracies in the encyclopedia, including bibliographical errors, omissions of information on important works and characters, and some factual mistakes. However, Harper noted, "In a volume of nearly 500 pages, the nature and specifics of the inconsistencies, oversights, and errors documented here are certainly far outnumbered by the accurate entries, and the enormous scope of this venture represents an appreciable volume of work." Vega Garcia concluded that *A Langston Hughes Encyclopedia* is "a carefully prepared, invaluable aid" and "thoroughly enjoyable reading."

Hans Ostrom told *CA:* "I grew up in Sierra City, a town of two hundred people in California's High Sierra. At the University of California, Davis, I studied with Pulitzer Prize–winning poet Karl Shapiro. One of my interests is depicting the experience of rural, working-class Americans."

BIOGRAPHICAL AND CRITICAL SOURCES:

PERIODICALS

African American Review, spring, 2003, Donna Akiba Sullivan Harper, review of *A Langston Hughes Encyclopedia,* pp. 162-165.

Choice, December, 1993, review of *Langston Hughes: A Study of the Short Fiction,* p. 605; October, 2002, S. A. Vega Garcia, review of *A Langston Hughes Encyclopedia,* p. 257.

ONLINE

Hans Ostrom Home Page, http://www.ups/edu/faculty/ostrom/ (February 6, 2004).

Heinemann Web site, http://www.heinemann.com/ (February 17, 2004).

University of Puget Sound Web site, http://www.ups.edu/ (February 6, 2004), biography of Hans Ostrom.*

P

PAGE, Kathy 1958-

PERSONAL: Born April 8, 1958, in London, England; immigrated to Canada; daughter of Harold Stanley (a surveyor) and Madge (a homemaker; maiden name, Toby) Page; children: two. *Education:* University of York, B.A. (with first-class honors), 1980; University of East Anglia, M.A., 1988. *Politics:* "Feminist." *Religion:* None.

ADDRESSES: *Home*—British Columbia, Canada. *Agent*—c/o Author Mail, Weidenfeld & Nicolson, Orion House, 5 Upper St. Martin's Lane, London WC2H 9EA, England.

CAREER: Carpenter in Brixton and London, England, 1982-86; tutor and writer, 1986—. Has taught at universities in England, Finland, and Estonia; has served as writer in residence for schools and other organizations.

MEMBER: Writers' Union of Canada.

AWARDS, HONORS: Eastern Arts writer's bursary, 1989; Hawthornden International Writers' Retreat fellowship, 1992; Traveller Writing Award, 1992, for "Pike"; Arts Council major bursary, 1994; Bridport Short Story Prize, 1994, for "My Beautiful Wife."

WRITINGS:

Back in the First Person (novel), Virago (London, England), 1986.
The Unborn Dreams of Clara Riley (novel), Virago (London, England), 1987.
Island Paradise (novel), Methuen (London, England), 1989.
As in Music, and Other Stories, Methuen (London, England), 1989.
Frankie Styne and the Silver Man (novel), Weidenfeld & Nicolson (London, England), 1992.
The Story of My Face (novel), Weidenfeld & Nicolson (London, England), 2002.
Alphabet (novel), Weidenfeld & Nicolson (London, England), 2004.

Also author of pieces for television and radio. Contributor of short stories to numerous anthologies.

SIDELIGHTS: Kathy Page once told *CA:* "Most of my work . . . is preoccupied with the relationship between individuals and the Law—with a capital 'L': not just the judicial system but the bottom-line rules of the communities in which people live. This preoccupation is particularly relevant to women."

In her 2002 novel *The Story of My Face,* Page explores how outsiders can affect communities. As professor of religious studies Natalie Baron searches to uncover the history of Tuomas Envall, founder of a religious sect that forbids all forms of images. While Natalie visits Envall's native Finland, she must face her own childhood memories of a tragic encounter with the sect. The story of Envall's transformation from community outsider to religious leader is intercut with young Natalie's trip to an Envallist retreat with a neighboring family—a trip where she, also an outsider, ends up being disfigured. The two interwoven stories result in "a deeply layered mixture of psychological thriller and historical analysis," Aisling Foster observed in the *Times Literary Supplement.* While Foster found the ending somewhat "implausible," she added that Page's writing "is lit with an immediate sense of period, summoning images which are by turns softly painterly, sharply filmic or as murky as those first television images of the moon landing." A *Kirkus Reviews* critic enjoyed unraveling both strands of the story and concluded that *The Story of My Face* is "quietly powerful, with considerable emotional depth: an intriguing account of tortured faith and thwarted desire."

BIOGRAPHICAL AND CRITICAL SOURCES:

PERIODICALS

Kirkus Reviews, August 1, 2003, review of *The Story of My Face,* p. 986.

New Statesman, February 7, 1986, Sheila MacLeod, review of *Back in the First Person,* p. 29.

New Statesman & Society, December 14, 1990, Katie Campbell, review of *As in Music, and Other Stories,* p. 39.

Times Literary Supplement, July 7, 1989, Colin Greenland, review of *Island Paradise,* p. 738; April 26, 2002, Aisling Foster, "A Cuckoo in the Nest," p. 21.

ONLINE

Writers Union of Canada Web site, http://www.writersunion.ca/ (February 18, 2004).*

* * *

POPKIN, Jeremy D(avid) 1948-

PERSONAL: Born December 19, 1948, in Iowa City, IA; son of Richard and Juliet Popkin; married; wife's name Beate, 1980; children: two. *Education:* University of California, Berkeley, B.A., 1970, Ph.D., 1977; Harvard University, M.A., 1971.

ADDRESSES: *Office*—Department of History, University of Kentucky, Lexington, KY 40506. *E-mail*—popkin@pop.uky.edu.

CAREER: Professor and author. University of Pittsburgh, Pittsburgh, PA, visiting assistant professor, 1977-78; University of Kentucky, Lexington, assistant professor of history, 1978—.

MEMBER: American History Association, Society of French History Studies, ASECS.

AWARDS, HONORS: Newberry Library fellow, 1983; Max-Planck Institut fur Geschichte, 1985; National Endowment for the Humanities, Summer Seminar for College Teachers, 1987; National Endowment for the Humanities, resident fellow, 1988-89; Fulbright Resident fellow (France), 1991-92; visiting scholar at Maison des Sciences de l'Home-Rhone-Alpes, 1991-92; John Simon Guggenheim fellow, 1992-93; UK Arts and Sciences Distinguished Professor, 1995-96.

WRITINGS:

The Right-Wing Press in France, 1792-1800 (monograph), University of North Carolina Press (Chapel Hill, NC), 1980.

(Editor, with Jack R. Censer) *Press and Politics in Pre-Revolutionary France,* University of California Press (Berkeley, CA), 1987.

News and Politics in the Age of Revolution: Jean Luzac's "Gazette de Leyde," Cornell University Press (Ithaca, NY), 1989.

Revolutionary News: The Press in France, 1789-99, Duke University Press (Durham, NC), 1990.

A History of Modern France, Prentice Hall (Englewood Cliffs, NJ), 1994.

(Editor) *Media and Revolution: Comparative Perspectives,* University Press of Kentucky (Lexington, KY), 1995.

A Short History of the French Revolution, Prentice Hall (Englewood Cliffs, NJ), 1995.

(Editor, with Bernadette Fort) *The Memoirs, Secrets, and the Culture of Publicity in Eighteenth-Century France,* Voltaire Foundation (Paris, France), 1998.

(Editor, translator, and author of preface) Louis-Sebastien Mercier, *Panorama of Paris: Selections from "Tableau de Paris,"* Pennsylvania State University Park (University Park, PA), 1999.

(Editor, with Richard H. Popkin) *The Abbé Grégoire and His World,* Kluwer (Boston, MA), 2000.

A History of Modern France, Prentice Hall (Upper Saddle River, NJ), 2001.

Press, Revolution, and Social Identities in France, 1830-1835, Pennsylvania State University Press (University Park, PA), 2002.

History, Historians and Autobiography, University of Chicago Press (Chicago, IL), 2004.

Also contributor to journals including *American Historical Review, Journal of Modern History, Historical Journal, Revue d'histoire moderne et contemporaine, Journalism Quarterly,* and *Jewish Social Studies.*

SIDELIGHTS: Jeremy Popkin is an authority on French history and the history of the press in France. In an interview with *CA* Popkin explained, "My first book, *The Right-Wing Press in France, 1792-1800,* is a study of how communications media influence and are affected by political and social movements. I was interested to find that the conservative opponents of the French Revolution used the newspaper press extensively and effectively to combat the movement which had made a free press in France possible in the first place. I have been led to ask whether our traditional equation of freedom of the press with freedom and progress in general is correct."

Media and Revolution: Comparative Perspectives contains thirteen essays written mostly by historians, but also by literature professors and journalists. The essays explore the role of mass media in reporting revolutionary events in France spanning 350 years. Writing in the *American Political Science Review,* Doris A. Graber explained that the essay-writers do not reach a conclusion regarding mass media's role in revolution. "The assessments they make about media influence run the gamut from considering the media central to revolutionary processes to deeming them peripheral," remarked Graber. "The case studies assembled in *Media and Revolution* represent a motley array of news sources covering successful and failed revolutions in dissimilar countries during different historical periods," Graber explained.

Popkin coedited *The Abbé Grégoire and His World.* The book is an analysis of the ideas and influence of the Abbé Henri Grégoire, an important figure during the French Revolution. Grégoire was a social activist, who fought for the rights of blacks and Jews and reform in the Catholic church. In the *English Historical Review,* William Doyle described the book as "an important and useful collection which underlines how unjustly neglected this fascinating figure has been until recently."

Popkin's *Press, Revolution, and Social Identities in France, 1830-1839* examines the role of the press during the French Revolutionary crisis of the early 1830s, with particular emphasis on newspapers and publishers in the Early July Monarchy. In *Nineteenth-Century French Studies,* reviewer Janice Best explained that Popkin "argues that the press of the early 1830s and principally that of France's second largest city, Lyon, must be seen as a 'prime force in defining the conflicts that shaped the early years of nineteenth-century bourgeois society.'" Best went on to say, "Through a close—although perhaps too strictly monologic—reading of journalistic texts produced in Lyon in the 1830s, Popkin shows the emergence of new discourses aimed not entirely at the conquest of political legitimacy, but rather at a redefinition of the notion of the public, particularly the notion of a unified public opinion." *Library Cultures*' Thomas C. Sosnowski deemed the book "a significant contribution to the historical literature of the July Monarchy." Sosnowski observed that Popkin's "superior archival skills are apparent everywhere in this work." He also considered Popkin's argument on the development of social identities of the bourgeoisie to be "well crafted and supported." While most reviewers praised the book, they criticized the title. Sosnowski acknowledged that the title would have been better if it hinted at the book's "strong Lyonnais roots," but went on to explain that with such a title change "the academic public might have ignored its significance because of its provincial focus."

BIOGRAPHICAL AND CRITICAL SOURCES:

PERIODICALS

American Historical Review, October, 1991, review of *Revolutionary News: The Press in France, 1789-99,* p. 1205; review of *News and Politics in the Age of Revolution: Jean Luzac's "Gazette de Leyde,",* p. 1206.

American Political Science Review, December, 1995, Doris A. Graber, review of *Media and Revolution: Comparative Perspectives,* pp. 1058-1060.

Choice, April, 1990, review of *News and Politics in the Age of Revolution,* p. 1314; July, 1990, review of *Revolutionary News,* p. 1880; November, 1995, review of *Media and Revolution,* p. 456.

Eighteenth-Century Studies, fall, 1991, review of *Revolutionary News,* p. 85; fall, 2001, *Panorama of Paris: Selections from "Tableau de Paris,",* p. 153.

English Historical Review, January, 1983, review of *The Right Wing Press in France, 1792-1800,* p. 210; William Doyle, review of *The Abbé Grégoire and His World,* pp. 993-995.

Foreign Affairs, September, 1995, Francis Fukuyama, review of *Media and Revolution,* p. 160.

French Review, March, 1993, review of *Revolutionary News,* p. 707.

Journal of Interdisciplinary History, spring, 1991, review of *Revolutionary News,* p. 684.

Journal of Modern History, June, 1981, review of *The Right Wing Press in France, 1792-1800,* p. 339; December, 1991, review of *News and Politics in the Age of Revolution,* p. 762.

Journal of the History of Ideas, January, 1990, review of *News and Politics in the Age of Revolution,* p. 171; October, 1991, review of *Revolutionary News,* p. 685.

JQ: Journalism Quarterly, summer, 1990, review of *News and Politics in the Age of Revolution,* p. 442; autumn, 1990, review of *News and Politics in the Age of Revolution,* p. 608; winter, 1991, review of *Revolutionary News,* p. 860.

Libraries and Culture, fall, 1992, Thomas C. Sosnowski, review of *Press, Revolution, and Social Identities in France, 1830-1835,* pp. 392-394.

Library Journal, March 15, 1995, review of *Media and Revolution,* p. 86.

Nineteenth-Century French Studies, fall, 2002, Janice Best, review of *Press, Revolution, and Social Identities in France, 1830-1835,* pp. 155-157.

Reference and Research Book News, November, 1995, review of *Media and Revolution,* p. 64; May, 2001, review of *The Abbé Grégoire and His World,* p. 36.

Times Literary Supplement, December 14, 1990, review of *Revolutionary News,* p. 1355.

ONLINE

University of Kentucky Web site, http://www.rgs.uky.edu/vpresearch/popkin.html/ (January 23, 2004), "2003-2004 University Research Professors."

University of North Carolina Web site, http://www.nhc.rtp.nc.us/dupont/popkin.htm/ (January 23, 2004), "Jesse Ball duPont Summer Seminars: Seminar Leader."*

PRADO, Holly 1938-

PERSONAL: Born May 2, 1938, in Lincoln, NE; daughter of Philip (a newspaper circulation manager) and Gladys (a homemaker) Johnson; married Harry Northup (an actor and poet), May 12, 1990; stepchildren: Dylan Northup. *Ethnicity:* "Anglo." *Education:* Albion College, B.A., 1960. *Politics:* Democrat. *Religion:* "Southern California Jungian." *Hobbies and other interests:* Gardening, cooking.

ADDRESSES: *Home*—1256 N. Mariposa Ave., Los Angeles, CA 90029. *E-mail*—hollyprado@earthlink.net.

CAREER: Poet and author. Secretary, 1960-65; high school English teacher, 1965-73; writer and teacher of writing, 1973—. University of Southern California, teacher in writing program.

MEMBER: Analytical Psychology Club, Phi Beta Kappa.

AWARDS, HONORS: First prize, Fin de Millennium L.A. Poetry Award, Los Angeles Poetry Festival and Poets Anonymous, 1999; winner of Sense of Site poetry competition, Writers at Work, Los Angeles Cultural Affairs Department, and Durfee Foundation, 2002.

WRITINGS:

Feasts, Momentum Press (Los Angeles, CA), 1976.

Nothing Breaks Off at the Edge, photographs by Vicki Brager, New Rivers Press (New York, NY), 1976.

Losses, Laurel Press, 1977.

How the Creative Looks Today, Jesse Press, 1980.

Gardens (novel), Harcourt (San Diego, CA), 1985.

Specific Mysteries, Cahuenga Press (Los Angeles, CA), 1990.

Esperanza: Poems for Orpheus, Cahuenga Press (Los Angeles, CA), 1998.

Holly Prado: Greatest Hits, 1976-2000, Pudding House Press (Johnstown, OH), 2001.

Contributor to periodicals, including *Exquisite Corpse,Denver Quarterly, Kenyon Review,* and *Colorado Review.*

ADAPTATIONS: Prado's work has been recorded on the spoken-word album *Word Rituals,* New Alliance Records, 1993.

SIDELIGHTS: In her collection titled *Esperanza: Poems for Orpheus,* Holly Prado uses the metaphor of Orpheus to illustrate the nature of creative inspiration. Prado also, according to *Women's Review of Books* contributor Alison Townsend, shows how mythology is a part of our everyday life. She starts by describing the mythic character of Orpheus in her introduction. Orpheus's music enchanted people, animals, and gods alike. Even trees uprooted themselves in ecstasy. As Prado notes in her introduction to *Esperanza,* "Orpheus becomes the background for all inspiration and represents a personal union with the divine."

In Townsend's opinion, Prado has also become one with the divine or a spiritual force in the creation of these poems. The reviewer noted that Prado has the capacity in her writing to unite the tangible and the spiritual, using the backdrop of everyday life. For example, in Prado's poems angels experience creative blocks. In another poem Orpheus sits amongst cars in a traffic jam. Prado takes the Orpheus analogy one step further: Orpheus was torn apart at his death. The poet must give of herself/himself in a similar way during the act of creation. To illustrate this idea in a poem titled "We Move Our Food Outdoors," Prado says "this is what gods want; their / sparks on flesh. creation as unfinished product." According to Townsend, Prado recognizes that, since spirituality is such a part of creation, no poet or artist ever entirely owns his or her creation. In another poem Prado speaks of returning poetry to its source and acknowledges the "greater-than-ordinary energy" required to create original works.

Townsend called Prado a Los Angeles literary legend who deserves a wider readership. The collection, in Townsend's opinion, captures the everyday details and the mysteriousness and spirituality that are an inherent part of creativity. Reviewer Robert Peters, in the *Chicago Review,* also gave the volume a positive review, commenting, "Many of the poems in *Esperanza* rank with the most ambitious poems on personal visions published today. . . . Prado has fashioned a most memorable verse suite, an impressive advance over her earlier fine collections." That reviewer found Prado to be "primarily an elegiac poet whose flashes of humor palliate the dourness. She is also attentive to psychology, particularly to Jungian ideas, without ever turning slick or gimmicky."

Prado's debut novel *Gardens* is the intergenerational story of three women coping with age-related transitions. Kate is a middle-aged artist with a stop-and-start career. As the novel begins she is working through a creative rut which manifests itself in many red and orange paintings. Her husband is taking up his art again after a twenty-year vacation. Her daughter Sheila hopes to pursue a literary career and is as anxious to get out of the house and start college as Kate is to have her stay. Kate's mother is a poised, business-savvy woman who has just retired as the vice president of a retail clothing line. *Gardens* received mixed reviews—a *Publishers Weekly* reviewer found the plot weak, the dialog stunted, and the characters undeveloped. Anna Shapiro of the *New York Times Book Review* commented similarly and noted that the book and dialog read like a cast of characters that is stoned. However, in an article for the *Sewannee Review,* Gary Davenport praised the novel, commenting, "writing an unsentimental novel about lives in emotional crisis remains possible. . . . Prado's *Gardens* is an encouraging debut in this regard, managing a bracingly objective and yet poetic narrative about three Los Angeles women." The reviewer also commented favorably on the book's floral imagery as an embodiment of the passage of time and found that the present-tense narration preserved the novel's objective style. Davenport concluded: "The nature, human and otherwise, to which this prose holds up a mirror is often intensely moving, and it is to . . . Prado's credit that she sees no need to exhort her characters . . . to a degree or kind of feeling that is not inherent in the world she presents. Such a grasp of art and life is unusual in our age of exploitative and recreational emotionalism." Sharon Dirlam of the *Los Angeles Times Book Review* also praised the novel and wrote that the book is a "gently told story, with a strong sense of place and a respect for human yearnings."

BIOGRAPHICAL AND CRITICAL SOURCES:

BOOKS

Prado, Holly, *Esperanza: Poems for Orpheus,* Cahuenga Press (Los Angeles, CA), 1998.

PERIODICALS

Chicago Review, summer, 1998, Robert Peters, review of *Esperanza: Poems for Orpheus.*
Kirkus Reviews, September 15, 1985, p. 976.
Library Journal, November 1, 1985, p. 112.
Los Angeles, March, 1987, p. 84.
Los Angeles Times Book Review, November 24, 1985, Sharon Dirlam, review of *Gardens,* p. 12.
New York Times Book Review, November 17, 1985, Anna Shapiro, review of *Gardens,* p. 30.
Publishers Weekly, September 27, 1985, review of *Gardens,* p. 84.
Sewanee Review, fall, 1986, Gary Davenport, review of *Gardens.*
Women's Review of Books, July, 1998, Alison Townsend, review of *Esperanza,* pp. 34-35.

* * *

PRICE, Nancy 1925-

PERSONAL: Born 1925, in Sioux Falls, SD; married Howard J. Thompson (a university educator), 1945; children: Catherine, John, David. *Ethnicity:* "Scotch/Dutch/Norwegian." *Education:* Attended Tufts University; University of Northern Iowa, M.A., 1964; further graduate study at University of Iowa.

ADDRESSES: *Office*—Department of English Language and Literature, University of Northern Iowa, Cedar Falls, IA 50614.

CAREER: University of Northern Iowa, Cedar Falls, faculty member, 1964-68, professor of creative writing, beginning 1979. Karolyi Foundation, writer in residence, 1975; Rockefeller Foundation Study and Conference Center, Lake Como, Italy, resident scholar, 1982; Tyrone Guthrie Centre, Ireland, resident scholar, 1983.

AWARDS, HONORS: Writing fellow, National Endowment for the Arts, 1978; fiction selections, National Syndicated Fiction Project Competition, National Endowment for the Arts and PEN American Center, 1983, 1985.

WRITINGS:

A Natural Death (novel), Little, Brown (Boston, MA), 1973.

Nancy Price

An Accomplished Woman (novel), Coward, McCann & Geoghegan (New York, NY), 1979.
Sleeping with the Enemy (novel), Simon & Schuster (New York, NY), 1987.
Night Woman (novel; Literary Guild selection), Pocket Books (New York, NY), 1992.
Bonfire's Daughter (novel), Presses de la Cité (Paris, France), 1998.
Snake in the Blackberries (novel), Presses de la Cité (Paris, France), 2000.
Two Liars and a Bride (novel), Presses de la Cité (Paris, France), 2004.

Also contributor of poetry and short stories to periodicals, including *Atlantic Monthly, New York Times,Quarterly Review of Literature, Virginia Quarterly Review, Newsday, San Francisco Chronicle,* and *Oregonian Northwest.*

Price's novels have been published in Norway, France, Sweden, Brazil, Italy, Spain, the Netherlands, Germany, Israel, Poland, Denmark, Russia, Czechoslovakia, Korea, and Japan.

ADAPTATIONS: Sleeping with the Enemy was adapted for a film starring Julia Roberts in 1991.

SIDELIGHTS: Nancy Price was a published poet and a college educator when her first novel, *A Natural Death,* was published in 1973. Since then, she has penned several more well-received books, including the suspenseful thriller *Sleeping with the Enemy,* which was made into a successful film in 1991. As one *Publishers Weekly* reviewer noted, "Nancy Price is a very talented writer and her characters are unique."

The title and theme of *A Natural Death,* according to Jonathan Yardley of the *New York Times Book Review,* is taken from a quotation by civil rights figure Eldridge Cleaver: "No slave should die a natural death." The novel, set during the time of slavery in the United States, focuses on two black children, a girl and a boy, raised in freedom by an eccentric white man. At the death of their guardian, however, they are caught by slave traders and sold to work on two neighboring plantations. As Yardley explained further, "The mistress of one of the plantations is a white girl with her own qualms about slavery, and the point of the novel is that all three, in order to survive, have to make hard compromises with the system."

Six years passed before the publication of Price's next novel, *An Accomplished Woman.* The book portrays the life of Catherine, an intelligent girl who grows up helping her step-uncle with natural biology projects and as a result is more interested in things intellectual than the feminine accomplishments necessary for social ease in the 1920s and 1930s. To further complicate matters, both her step-uncle and another man she becomes involved with are past lovers of her beautiful mother, who is now deceased. "Ironic, humorous and understated, *An Accomplished Woman* avoids the agonized soul-searching that characterizes much of contemporary women's fiction," according to a *New Republic* critic. "The novel is not an introspective probing of Catherine's fears and desires, but a somewhat distanced observation of her development as a misfit in a stultifying social world." A *New Yorker* reviewer concluded that the novel would "keep most readers attentive to the end."

In *Sleeping with the Enemy* the heroine Sara Gray fakes her death in a boating accident in order to leave her abusive husband. She runs away to Iowa, where she assumes an alias and gets a job as a companion to an elderly female English professor. She begins a new life, including a new relationship with another professor, but her visits to her mother in a nursing home put her husband on her trail. *Publishers Weekly* commended the novel's "chilling scenes of observation and pursuit," and judged it to be "powerful, moving and well-controlled."

Price's fourth effort, *Night Woman,* concerns "a character who is her own worst enemy," in the words of Margaret Cannon in the Toronto *Globe and Mail.* Mary Eliot, the protagonist, is the real brains behind the work of her husband, acclaimed novelist Randal Eliot. She even has Randal convinced that he does his own work, dictated to her while he is in trance. In reality, however, Mary writes from his disjointed notes, and Randal is "both psychotic and manic-depressive," as reviewer Joyce Slater put it in the *Chicago Tribune.* When Randal is killed in a car accident, Mary is free to write for herself under her maiden name, but she then becomes involved with a man intent on writing Randal's biography. Slater called *Night Woman* "fine" and "moving"; Cannon labeled it "a terrific book . . . a timely and affecting novel about a woman who betrays herself in the name of love."

BIOGRAPHICAL AND CRITICAL SOURCES:

PERIODICALS

Chicago Tribune, July 26, 1992, Joyce Slater, review of *Night Woman,* p. 4.

Globe and Mail (Toronto, Ontario, Canada), June 20, 1992, Margaret Cannon, review of *Night Woman,* p. C7.

New Republic, January 6, 1979, review of *An Accomplished Woman,* pp. 39-40.

New Yorker, March 19, 1979, review of *An Accomplished Woman.*

New York Times Book Review, December 23, 1973, Jonathan Yardley, review of *A Natural Death,* p. 11.

Publishers Weekly, December 11, 1978, p. 56; February 20, 1987, review of *Sleeping with the Enemy,* p. 74.

* * *

PYGGE, Edward

See BARNES, Julian (Patrick)

R

RAKO, Susan (Mandell) 1939-

PERSONAL: Born September 4, 1939, in Springfield, MA; children: Jennifer. *Education:* Attended Wellesley College, 1957-60; University of Cincinnati, B.S., 1961; Albert Einstein College of Medicine, M.D., 1966; Boston University, M.S. (film), 1986 *Politics:* Independent.

ADDRESSES: *Office*—P.O. Box 600762, Newtonville, MA 02460. *E-mail*—susanrako@aol.com.

CAREER: Worcester Foundation for Experimental Biology, Shrewsbury, MA, medical research assistant, 1959; May Institute, Cincinnati, OH, medical research assistant, 1961-62; Mount Auburn Hospital, Cambridge, MA, intern, 1966-67; Massachusetts Mental Health Center, Boston, MA, resident, 1967-69; Harvard Medical School, Boston, teaching fellow in psychiatry, 1967-69, clinical fellow in psychiatry, 1969-70, clinical instructor in psychiatry, 1970-75; Beth Israel Hospital, Boston, resident, 1969-70; private practice of psychiatry, 1970—; Massachusetts Mental Health Center, Boston, staff psychiatrist, 1970-77; Newton-Wellesley Hospital, Newton, MA, staff psychiatrist, 1982; Cutler Counseling Center, Norwood, MA, consultant in child and adult psychiatry, 1983; Veterans Administration Hospital, San Juan, PR, consultant in psychiatry, 1990-94.

WRITINGS:

(Editor, with Harvey Mazer) *Semrad: The Heart of a Therapist,* Jason Aronson (New York, NY), 1980.

The Hormone of Desire: The Truth about Sexuality, Menopause, and Testosterone, Harmony Books (New York, NY), 1996, revised edition, Three Rivers Press/Random House (New York, NY), 1999.

No More Periods? The Risks of Menstrual Suppression and Other Cutting-Edge Issues about Hormones and Women's Health, Harmony Books (New York, NY), 2003.

Contributor to periodicals, including *Journal of Women's Health and Gender Based Medicine, Directions in Psychiatry, Psychiatric Annals. The Hormone of Desire: The Truth about Sexuality, Menopause, and Testosterone* has been translated into Spanish and Japanese.

SIDELIGHTS: Psychiatrist Susan Rako has written and lectured extensively on the issues of women's health, especially in the areas of menstrual pain and post-menopausal hormonal problems. She has published two books on the subject: *The Hormone of Desire: The Truth about Sexuality, Menopause, and Testosterone* and *No More Periods? The Risks of Menstrual Suppression and Other Cutting-Edge Issues about Hormones and Women's Health.* In the former, Rako advocates the careful use of testosterone to help alleviate post-menopausal symptoms, while in the latter she warns that use of the birth control pill can lead to undesirable, even dangerous side effects. In both books, she advocates better education in the area of hormonal therapy for women, both on the part of patients and for their physicians.

In *The Hormone of Desire,* Rako writes that the usual estrogen therapy many post-menopausal women receive is not enough; they also need some testosterone—specifically in the form of methytestosterone—in their systems to prevent such problems as hair loss, decreased libido, and decreased mental agility. However, the male-dominated field of medicine has been reticent to prescribe such therapy, largely because of "fear, ideological resistance and sexual politics," according to a *Publishers Weekly* reviewer. Overcoming this ignorance and reticence is the key in helping women with hormonal imbalances, believes Rako. "What is so astonishing about this book" commented Judith S. Askew in *Menopause News,* "is the thoroughness of the coverage of the subject of testosterone and how marvelous it is to find all this information in one place."

While *The Hormone of Desire* recommends hormonal therapy for post-menopausal women, Rako's *No More Periods?* opposes the growing movement of suppressing menstrual cycles in healthy, fertile women through the use of the birth-control pill and Depo-Provera. Such drugs can make women vulnerable to cervical cancer, for example; on the other hand, Rako notes that the blood loss caused by monthly periods can actually be beneficial to women by reducing the risk of heart attack and stroke. Martha E. Stone, writing in *Library Journal,* complained mainly that Rako's book, which is only 192 pages long, does not delve deeply enough into the issues despite its "impressive amount of research." Nevertheless, the critic concluded that libraries "will want to purchase Rako's book."

In addition to her medical background, Rako also has a degree in film communication. She once told *CA:* "While maintaining a primary interest in the practice of psychiatry, I completed a graduate degree in film production at Boston University's College of Communication. I have produced one documentary film on the subject of healing massage and one *cinema verite* film, 'Susan and Janni,' that was a finalist in the New England region of the Student Academy Award competition in 1984. I have a strong interest, as well, in directing theatre. The leading edge of my growth in film production and in theatre direction has as its main thrust communication that does not rely on dialogue but on design, movement, non-verbal sound, light, and color."

BIOGRAPHICAL AND CRITICAL SOURCES:

PERIODICALS

Booklist, February 15, 1996, William Beatty, review of *The Hormone of Desire: The Truth about Sexuality, Menopause, and Testosterone,* p. 975.

Boston Globe, July 4, 1994, Judy Foreman, "Testosterone's Use as a Love Potion—For Women," p. 25.

Chicago Sun-Times, December 2, 2003, Jennifer Fried, "Ending Your Monthly Cycle. Period," p. 44.

Library Journal, March 1, 2003, Martha E. Stone, "No More Periods?: The Risks of Menstrual Suppression and Other Cutting-Edge Issues in Women's Reproductive Health," p. 110.

Menopause News, March-April, 1996, Judith S. Askew, review of *The Hormone of Desire,* p. 6; January-February, 1998, "Expert on Testosterone Talks about Supplementation," p. 2.

New York Times, October 14, 2003, Tina Kelley, "New Pill Fuels Debate over Benefits of Fewer Periods," p. F5.

Publishers Weekly, January 8, 1996, review of *The Hormone of Desire,* p. 66.

ONLINE

Susan Rako Home Page, http://www.susanrako.com/ (May 3, 2004).*

* * *

RANKIN, Ian (James) 1960-
(Jack Harvey)

PERSONAL: Born April 28, 1960, in Cardenden, Fife, Scotland; married; two sons. *Education:* University of Edinburgh, M.A. (with honors), 1982.

ADDRESSES: *Agent*—Dominick Abel, 146 W. 82nd St., No. 1B, New York, NY 10024.

CAREER: Novelist and short-story and nonfiction writer. Worked variously as a swineherd, a taxman, viticulturist, hi-fi journalist, and folktale collector.

MEMBER: Crime Writers' Association (United Kingdom), International Association of Crime Writers.

AWARDS, HONORS: Elected a Hawthornden fellow in 1987; Chandler-Fulbright fellowship in detective fiction, 1991-92; Dagger Award for best short story, Crime Writers' Association, 1994; Edgar Allan Poe Award, 2004, for *Resurrection Men;* various short story prizes.

Ian Rankin

WRITINGS:

NOVELS

The Flood, Polygon (Edinburgh, Scotland), 1986.
Watchman, Bodley Head (London, England), 1988, Doubleday (New York, NY), 1991.
Westwind, Barrie & Jenkins (London, England), 1990.
Set in Darkness, Orion (London, England), 2000.
The Falls, Orion (London, England), 2001.

"INSPECTOR REBUS" SERIES; DETECTIVE NOVELS

Knots and Crosses, Doubleday (Garden City, NY), 1987.
Hide and Seek: A John Rebus Mystery, Barrie & Jenkins, 1991, Penzler Books (New York, NY), 1994.
Strip Jack, Orion (London, England), 1992, St. Martin's Press (New York, NY), 1994.
Wolfman, Century (London, England), 1992.
The Black Book: An Inspector Rebus Novel, Orion (London, England), 1993, Penzler Books (New York, NY), 1994.
Mortal Causes, Orion (London, England), 1994, Simon & Schuster (New York, NY), 1995.
Let it Bleed, Orion (London, England), 1995, Simon & Schuster (New York, NY), 1996.
Black and Blue, St. Martin's Press (New York, NY), 1997.
The Hanging Garden, St. Martin's Press (New York, NY), 1998.
Dead Souls, St. Martin's Minotaur (New York, NY), 1999.
Death Is Not the End, St. Martin's Minotaur (New York, NY), 2000.
Set in Darkness, Orion (London, England), 2000.
Resurrection Men, Little, Brown (Boston, MA), 2004.
A Question of Blood, Little, Brown (Boston, MA), 2004.
Fleshmarket Close, Orion (London, England), 2004.

NOVELS; AS JACK HARVEY

Witch Hunt, Headline (London, England), 1993.
Bleeding Hearts, Headline (London, England), 1994.
Blood Hunt, Headline (London, England), 1995.

OTHER

A Good Hanging and Other Stories (short stories), Little, Brown (Boston, MA), 1992.

Contributor of short stories to periodicals, including *Ellery Queen Mystery Magazine;* contributor of articles to periodicals.

SIDELIGHTS: Ian Rankin has "established himself as one of the most talented young British crime novelists," in the opinion of *Twentieth-Century Crime and Mystery Writers* essayist Ian A. Bell. Rankin is best known for his series of crime novels featuring Detective Inspector John Rebus. In these works, which are often referred to as "police procedurals" for their focus on solving a crime, Rankin combines the dialect and setting of his native Scotland with poetic prose and gritty realism.

The "Rebus" stories are set in Edinburgh, and Bell noted that they "often exploit the stark contrast between that city's genteel facade and some of its squalid realities." Rebus himself is a complex, well-drawn character, in the opinion of numerous reviewers. He is sensitive, brooding, and somewhat insecure, but he is also tough and relentless. He is aware that even when he solves a case, the triumph of justice is fleeting; there will always be more evil and corruption. *Booklist* contributor Emily Melton noted that "Rankin is a genius at finding the perfect blend of curmudgeonly guile, stubborn gruffness, and unsuspecting vulnerability for Rebus, who . . . is a refreshing if lonely champion of truth and justice." Melton also praised Rankin for delivering "sparkling wit, superb plotting, and a host of surprising twists."

Rankin introduced readers to Rebus with his second novel, *Knots and Crosses.* In this work, the detective attempts to find the murderer of several young girls with the help of his policewoman girlfriend and Jim Stevens, a reporter. A critic for *Books* dubbed *Knots and Crosses* a "well constructed, exciting" story, and a *Kirkus Reviews* contributor praised Rankin's "solidly drawn characters, [and] keen psychological insights." Reporter Stevens makes a brief appearance in Rankin's next effort, *Watchman,* in which British Secret Service agent Miles Flint struggles with IRA terrorists. Although a contributor for *Kirkus Reviews* found this work "slightly disappointing" in comparison with *Knots and Crosses,* the reviewer also highlighted the book's "tense, convincing finale."

In *Wolfman,* Rebus is temporarily reassigned to the London office to help in the investigation of a serial killer whose signature mark is the bite he takes out of his victims. A reviewer for *Books* remarked that "Rebus is a character drawn in the round, and realism is the hallmark of the book." In *Strip Jack,* Rankin's next mystery to feature Rebus, a popular member of the British Parliament is found in a brothel during a police raid, shortly after which his wife is beaten to death. Critical response was generally positive to what *New York Times Book Review* critic Marilyn Stasio dubbed an "intricately knotted murder plot"; in the *Chicago Tribune,* Dick Adler singled out Rankin's "crisp, refreshing prose," and a *Kirkus Reviews* contributor highlighted Rankin's "offbeat characters and . . . eccentric but appealing narrative style."

In *Hide and Seek,* Rebus investigates a modern-day Dr. Jekyll and Mr. Hyde case. Male prostitutes are the victims, and their killer appears to be a devil worshiper. "For all its modern grit, this multilayered story is as deeply moralistic as Stevenson's classic horror tale about the divided passions of the human soul," mused Marilyn Stasio in the *New York Times Book Review.* "In Mr. Rankin's subtle treatment of the theme, every character seems to have two faces—or a Cain-like brother—to reflect his corrupt dark side." *Black and Blue* finds Rebus looking into another serial killer case—this one involving a "copycat killer" who imitates the grisly crimes of another murderer Rebus was involved with thirty years earlier. A *Kirkus Reviews* writer called *Black and Blue* Rebus's "biggest and most grueling" case and added, "Rankin's dexterity in juggling plots and threats and motives lights up the darkness with a poet's grace. Reading him is like watching somebody juggle a dozen bottles of single malt without spilling a drop."

Rebus's adult daughter, Sammy, is depicted throughout the series as one of the few bright points in his personal life. In *The Hanging Garden,* Sammy is almost killed in a suspicious hit-and-run accident. Rebus believes the incident is related to some of his recent work. With his daughter threatened, Rebus's "ferocity is ratcheted up a notch," according to Bill Ott in *Booklist.* As Ott continued: "Nobody does grit like Rankin. The Rebus novels live on texture; the taste of cold coffee and the grinding edges of frayed nerves take on a visceral reality as the cops slog toward answers that only bring more questions. Against the unremitting grayness of this world, Rebus's beleaguered humanity shines in bold relief."

In *Fleshmarket Close,* the crusty policeman discovers that he has sympathy for the collectively oppressed. Senay Boztas wrote in the London *Sunday Times,* "The case forces [Rebus] . . . to confront the plight of refugees and the conditions in which they are held at a detention camp, based on the notorious Dungavel centre in Lanarkshire," and described *Fleshmarket Close* as Rankin's "most overtly political novel to date."

As Bell observed, although there is often extreme violence in the "Rebus" books, Rankin's "cool and laconic tone prevents the narratives from sensationalising the events they include, and perhaps the most impressive feature of his writing is the way it seems to meditate on the complexities of human motivation. . . . Earlier Rebus novels struggled to articulate these complex issues, but more recent efforts have been extremely successful."

Rankin once noted of his series: "My Inspector Rebus books are Scottish novels first, and mysteries second. I want to write about contemporary Scotland, and particularly contemporary Edinburgh, showing how the past infuses (and infects) the present. A novel like *The Black Book* depends more on the writings of Robert Louis Stevenson and James Hogg than it does on any whodunit forebear. Edinburgh is schizophrenic; it exhibits a definite dual personality. A look into history told me that this was nothing new, and hinted that in writing about my nation's twisted present, I might be saying something about its past psychoses too. A critic with an eye for an oxymoron once stated that I'd invented 'Tartan *Noir.*' Maybe that's not so far from the truth."

BIOGRAPHICAL AND CRITICAL SOURCES:

BOOKS

St. James Guide to Crime and Mystery Writers, 6th edition, St. James Press (Detroit, MI), 1996.

Spy Fiction: A Connoisseur's Guide, Facts on File (New York, NY), 1990.

PERIODICALS

Booklist, December 1, 1996, p. 643; October 1, 1997, p. 309; August 19, 1998.

Books, April, 1987, review of *Knots and Crosses,* p. 32; March, 1992, p. 12.

Chicago Tribune, March 6, 1994.

Entertainment Weekly, January 30, 1998, p. 61.

Kirkus Reviews, August 1, 1987, p. 1117; May 1, 1991, p. 568; January 1, 1994, p. 22; September 1, 1994, p. 1171; October 1, 1996, p. 1430; October 1, 1997, review of *Black and Blue.*

Library Journal, December, 1996, p. 151; August, 1997, p. 168.

Los Angeles Times Book Review, July 10, 1994, p. 8.

New Statesman and Society, November 13, 1992, p. 36.

New York Times Book Review, April 17, 1994, p. 19; July 3, 1994, p. 17; October 9, 1994, p. 34; January 21, 1996, p. 31; January 5, 1997, p. 20; December 14, 1997, p. 30.

Publishers Weekly, January 17, 1994, p. 410; September 12, 1994, p. 85; October 7, 1996, p. 64; August 25, 1997, review of *Black and Blue,* p. 48.

Sunday Times (London, England), March 28, 2004, Senay Boztas, "It's PC Rebus As Detective Finds His Conscience," p. 14.

Times Literary Supplement, May 2, 1986; September 23, 1994, review of *Mortal Causes,* p. 22; February 28, 1997, p. 22.

Tribune Books (Chicago, IL), March 6, 1994, p. 6; January 5, 1997, p. 4.

Wilson Library Bulletin, April, 1994, p. 98.

ONLINE

Ian Rankin Home Page, http://www.ianrankin.net/ (August 15, 2004).*

* * *

RICHARDSON, R. C. 1944-

PERSONAL: Born August 31, 1944, in Middleton, Lancashire, England; son of Clifford (a painting contractor) and Doris (a shop owner; maiden name, Taylor) Richardson. *Education:* University of Leicester, B.A. (with honors in history), 1965; University of Manchester, Ph.D., 1968. *Politics:* Labour *Religion:* "Evangelical." *Hobbies and other interests:* Theater, music, travel, reading.

ADDRESSES: Home—5 Partridge Down, Oliver's Battery, Winchester SO22 4HL, England. *Office*—Department of History, King Alfred's University College, Winchester SO22 4NR, England. *E-mail*—r.richardson@wkac.ac.uk.

CAREER: Thames Polytechnic, London, England, began as lecturer, became senior lecturer, 1968-77; King Alfred's University College, Winchester, England, head of history department, 1977-97, professor of history, beginning 1993, head of research and graduate center, 1997-2001, director of international relations, 2001. Visiting professor in the United States, 1982—.

MEMBER: Royal Historical Society (fellow).

WRITINGS:

Puritanism in North-west England: A Regional Study of the Diocese of Chester to 1642, Manchester University Press (Manchester, England), 1972.

(With W. H. Chaloner) *British Economic and Social History: A Bibliographical Guide,* Manchester University Press (Manchester, England), 1976, 3rd edition, 1996.

The Debate on the English Revolution, Methuen (London, England), 1977, 2nd edition published as *The Debate on the English Revolution Revisited,* Routledge (New York, NY), 1988, 3rd edition, Manchester University Press (Manchester, England), 1998.

(With T. B. James) *The Urban Experience: English, Scottish, and Welsh Towns, 1450-1700,* Manchester University Press (Manchester, England), 1983.

(With G. M. Ridden) *Freedom and the English Revolution,* Manchester University Press (Manchester, England), 1986.

The Study of History: A Bibliographical Guide, Manchester University Press (Manchester, England), 1988, 2nd edition, 2000.

Town and Countryside in the English Revolution, Manchester University Press (Manchester, England), 1992.

Images of Oliver Cromwell, Manchester University Press (Manchester, England), 1993.

The English Civil Wars: Local Aspects, Sutton (Herndon, VA), 1997.

(Editor) *The Changing Face of English Local History,* Ashgate Publishing (Burlington, VT), 2000.

General editor of two series of books for Manchester University Press (Manchester, England). Coeditor, *Literature and History.*

WORK IN PROGRESS: A book about domestic servants in the seventeenth century.

SIDELIGHTS: R. C. Richardson once told *CA:* "My publications record long-standing interests in seventeenth-century English historiography, historiography, and bibliography. The first preoccupation is with what I take to be the key century in English history—politically, economically, socially, and intellectually. The others stem from my conviction that so much of history as a discipline is to do with refractions and with the role of historians as mediators of the past. An extension of this is my concern with the interface between literature and history and with the benefits of bringing together the subject matter and methodologies of both disciplines."

RICHARDS, Eugene 1944-

PERSONAL: Born April 25, 1944, in Dorchester, MA; married Dorothea Lynch (a reporter; died, 1983); married Janine Altongy (a writer, video editor, and documentary film producer). *Education:* Northeastern University, B.A., 1967; graduate study at Massachusetts Institute of Technology.

ADDRESSES: Office—Many Voices, 472 13th Street, Brooklyn, NY 11215-5207. *Agent*—c/o Author Mail, Aperture, 20 E. 23rd St., New York, NY 10010.

CAREER: Photojournalist, director, and publisher. Art Institute of Boston, Boston, MA, instructor of photography, 1974-76; Union College, Schenectady, NY, instructor of photography, 1977; Maine Photo Workshop, Rockport, ME, artist in residence, 1977-78; International Center of Photography, New York, NY, artist in residence, 1978-79; Many Voices, Brooklyn, NY, codirector. Work exhibited in various galleries and museums, including Museum of Modern Art, International Center of Photography, San Francisco Museum of Modern Art, Addison Gallery of American Art, and J. B. Speed Art Museum. Work included in various exhibitions, including *We the People,* 1975, and *Fourteen New England Photographers,* 1978. Also VISTA volunteer, 1968, and cofounder of RESPECT, Inc., a private social agency providing food and clothing to the West Memphis black community.

AWARDS, HONORS: National Endowment for the Arts grants, 1974, 1980; Massachusetts Artists Foundation grant, 1978; Massachusetts Artists Foundation fellowship, 1979; Guggenheim fellowship in photography, 1980; Book of the Year Award, Nikon, 1986, for *Exploding into Life;* Infinity Award for outstanding accomplishment in photographic reporting, International Center of Photography, 1987, for *Below the Line: Living Poor in America;* Canon Photo Essay Award, National Press Photographers Association (NPPA), 1989; award of excellence, American College of Emergency Physicians, 1989, for *The Knife and Gun Club: Scenes from an Emergency Room;* Leica Medal of Excellence, 1990, for series of photographs on drug abuse in Philadelphia; Kraszna-Krausz Award for Photogenic Innovation, 1994, for *Cocaine True, Cocaine Blue;* Henry J. Kaiser Family Foundation fellowship, 1997; Best Short Film, DoubleTake Documentary Film Festival, Best Documentary Award,

Hope Film Festival, and Eastman Kodak Cinematographer Award, 2000, all for *but, the day came;* NPPA/Nikkon Documentary Sabbatical, 2002; Rosalynn Carter Fellowship for Mental Health Journalism, Carter Center, 2002-03.

WRITINGS:

AUTHOR AND PHOTOGRAPHER

Few Comforts or Surprises: The Arkansas Delta, MIT Press (Cambridge, MA), 1973.

Dorchester Days, Many Voices Press (Wollaston, MA), 1978, revised edition, Phaidon Press (New York, NY), 2001.

(With Dorothea Lynch) *Exploding into Life,* Aperture (New York, NY), 1986.

Below the Line: Living Poor in America, Consumer Reports Books (Mount Vernon, NY), 1988.

The Knife and Gun Club: Scenes from an Emergency Room, Atlantic Monthly Press (New York, NY), 1989.

(With Edward Barnes and Danny J.) *Cocaine True, Cocaine Blue,* Aperture (New York, NY), 1994.

Americans We: Photographs and Notes, Aperture (New York, NY), 1994.

The Fat Baby (collection of photographs and articles), Phaidon Press (Boston, MA), 2004.

OTHER

(Photographer) Janine Altongy, *Stepping through the Ashes,* Aperature (New York, NY), 2002.

Also author, director, and coproducer of the documentary film *but, the day came,* 2000. Contributor of photographs to periodicals, including *Geo, Life,* and *New York Times Magazine.* Contributor of photographs to books, including *Photographer's Choice,* Addison House (Reading, MA), 1976; *Family of Children,* Ridge Press, 1977; and *Family of Women,* Ridge Press, 1978.

SIDELIGHTS: Eugene Richards is a respected photographer who seems himself in the tradition of such esteemed photorealists as Robert Frank and Gene Smith. "Sometimes I look at their photographs and wonder why I even bother to try," Richards told Joe Novak in a 1980 *Photographic* profile. "At other times I feel them riding along with me."

Richards began his photography career in the early 1970s, after studying under photographer Minor White at the Massachusetts Institute of Technology (MIT). After leaving MIT, Richards worked as a VISTA volunteer in Arkansas, where he often ran afoul of his community's authorities. After having suffered beatings, Richards finally left the Arkansas Delta in 1973 and returned to his hometown of Dorchester, Massachusetts. There, he produced *Few Comforts or Surprises: The Arkansas Delta,* which garnered positive reviews from critics. Among the book's enthusiasts was *Commonweal* reviewer Todd Gitlin, who wrote, "Without political pointers to the future, we are left with the raw present, the terror and the pity of it. Richards's photographs have that eloquence which insists on the present."

Following the publication of *Few Comforts or Surprises,* he decided to photograph Dorchester, the city he grew up in, and its inhabitants. An influx of immigrants had altered the population since Richards's boyhood days, making him neither an insider nor an outsider to the working-class neighborhood. His efforts resulted in *Dorchester Days,* first published in 1978. The collection earned Richards further praise for his ability to capture the grim and disturbing aspects of everyday life. Julia Scully, writing in *Modern Photography,* noted that Richards employs some unlikely, idiosyncratic techniques—including blurred focus and awkward framing—to more graphically render his subjects. Through such devices, noted Scully, Richards "emphasizes the sense of craziness, of danger, of a world falling apart." *Dorchester Days* was republished in 2001 with additional images. "Artful touches, like text written in the photographer's own hand, have also been added," explained Rosemary Ranck in a review of the new edition for the *New York Times Book Review.* Ranck concluded, "The result is a book that is much more accessible to contemporary readers."

In the ensuing years, Richards continued to focus on life's tragic aspects. In 1986, he completed *Exploding into Life,* a collection of photos detailing the course of his wife Dorothea Lynch's ultimately fatal bout with breast cancer. Included in this volume are pictures of Lynch's disfigured torso, as well as a shot of Lynch vomiting from the effects of chemotherapy. Despite the grim and despairing nature of these photos, Richards described the project as a positive experience. "I had a great time making those photos," Richards related to *American Photographer* in 1989, "They're awful pictures, but it was a strangely joyous collaboration."

Richards's next volume is *Below the Line: Living Poor in America,* which appeared in 1988. In this stark photo-essay, Richards includes interviews with some of the poor that he photographed. The following year, Richards published *The Knife and Gun Club: Scenes from an Emergency Room.* "This," cautioned *People* reviewer Ralph Nowak, "is no book for the squeamish." Likewise, Sandra G. Boodman affirmed in the *Washington Post* that *The Knife and Gun Club* "is not a coffee-table book." Boodman described Richards's work as a "kaleidoscope of stark, sometimes brutally graphic, images."

Cocaine True, Cocaine Blue documents the catastrophic impact of this highly addictive narcotic in America's urban northeast. Brent Staples, writing in the *New York Times Book Review,* called Richards's book "a record of the carnage as it is carried out" in various urban areas, and deemed Richards "a master of the brutal image."

In 1994, Richards completed *Americans We: Photographs and Notes,* a photograph collection devoted to the more arduous aspects of life in the United States. The volume includes images of violence and suffering, and it details the hardships endured by the increasing numbers of Americans living in poverty. Accompanying Richards's photographs are his own comments and observations on the photographs.

Richards and second wife, Janine Altongy, published *Stepping through the Ashes* in time for the one-year anniversary of the September 11, 2001, terrorist attacks on the United States. The book is a collection of powerful images of the days following the destruction of the World Trade Center. Richards was visiting Budapest at the time of the attacks and could not get home for several days. In an article published on the National Press Photographers Association Web site, Richards explained how he felt once back in the United States: "I really just wanted to stay home. I was very troubled by what I saw coming, a war, more violence, a major change in the values of our country. I couldn't just look across the river and see what was once there."

To compose *Stepping through the Ashes,* Altongy interviewed survivors and relatives of victims while Richards snapped shots from nearby buildings and streets, since the husband and wife were only allowed into Ground Zero twice. "We saw the site not just as a place of horror, but as a tremendous cemetery," Richards explained. Critics praised Richards and Altongy for viewing the devastation in this way. "His photos from the scene, filtered through shafts of dust, are murky, hellish, disorienting," observed Michael More in a review of the book for the *Albuquerque Journal.* Vince Passaro, writing in *O, The Oprah Magazine,* expressed similar sentiments, observing, "The photos are a smoky black-and-white, composed with eerie stillness, perfectly reflecting the paralyzed grief of the city." Passaro concluded that *Stepping through the Ashes* "may be the best photo book of those hard days."

BIOGRAPHICAL AND CRITICAL SOURCES:

BOOKS

Bowden, Charles, *Eugene Richards,* Phaidon Press (New York, NY), 2001.

PERIODICALS

Albuquerque Journal, September 6, 2002, Michael More, "9-11 Book Steps Lightly," p. 5.

American Photographer, November, 1989, pp. 36-49, 71-72.

Commonweal, November 30, 1973, Todd Gitlin, review of *Few Comforts or Surprises: The Arkansas Delta,* pp. 242-244.

Modern Photography, June 9, 1979, Julia Scully, review of *Dorchester Days,* pp. 9, 15, 178, 196.

New York Times Book Review, February 6, 1994, Brent Staples, review of *Cocaine True, Cocaine Blue,* pp. 11-12; August 19, 2001, Rosemary Ranck, review of *Dorchester, Days,* p. 16.

O, The Oprah Magazine, September, 2002, Vince Passaro, review of *Stepping through the Ashes,* p. 102.

People, June 12, 1989, Ralph Nowak, review of *The Knife and Gun Club: Scenes from an Emergency Room,* p. 33.

Photographic, August, 1980, p. 19.

Publishers Weekly, August 26, 2002, review of *Stepping through the Ashes,* p. 53.

Washington Post, February 27, 1990, Sandra G. Boodman, review of *The Knife and Gun Club,* p. Z17; April 10, 1994, G4.

ONLINE

National Press Photographers Association Web site, http://www.nppa.org/ (January 16, 2003), Margot Carmichael Lester, "*Stepping through the Ashes:* A Profile of Eugene Richards, winner of the 2002 Nikon Documentary Sabbatical."*

* * *

RÍOS, Alberto (Alvaro) 1952-

Alberto Ríos

PERSONAL: Born September 18, 1952, in Nogales, AZ; son of Alberto Alvaro (a justice of the peace) and Agnes (a nurse; maiden name, Fogg) Ríos; married Maria Guadalupe Barron (a librarian), September 8, 1979; children: Joaquin. *Education:* University of Arizona, B.A. (English literature and creative writing), 1974, B.A. (psychology), 1975, M.F.A., 1979; attended law school at the University of Arizona, 1975-76. *Politics:* "Liberal/Democrat." *Religion:* "Cultural Catholic."

ADDRESSES: Home—3038 N. Pennington Dr., Chandler, AZ 85224. *Office*—Department of English, Arizona State University, Tempe, AZ 85287. *E-mail*—aarios@asu.edu.

CAREER: Arizona Commission on the Arts, Phoenix, artist in Artists-in-Education Program, 1978-83, consultant, 1983—; Arizona State University, Tempe, assistant professor, 1982-85, associate professor, 1985-89, professor, 1989-94, Regents' Professor of English, 1994—, cochair of Hispanic Research and Development Committee, 1983—, director, Creative Writing Program, 1986-89. Counselor and instructor in English and algebra in Med-Start Program at University of Arizona, summers, 1977-80. Writer-in-residence at Central Arizona College, Coolidge, 1980-82. Board of directors, Associated Writing Programs, 1988—, secretary, 1989—; board of directors, Arizona Center for the Book, 1988—, vice chairman, 1989—. Member of National Advisory Committee to the National Artists-in-Education Program, 1980; member of grants review panel, Arizona Commission on the Arts, 1983; member, National Endowment for the Arts Poetry Panel. Judge of New York City High School Poetry Contest. Gives poetry readings, lectures, and workshops.

AWARDS, HONORS: First place in Academy of American Arts poetry contest, 1977, for "A Man Then Suddenly Stops Moving"; writer's fellowship in poetry from the Arizona Commission on the Arts, 1979; fellowship grant in creative writing from National Endowment for the Arts, 1980; Walt Whitman Award from the National Academy of American Poets, 1981, for *Whispering to Fool the Wind;* second place in *New York Times* annual fiction award competition, 1983, for "The Way Spaghetti Feels"; Western States Book Award (fiction), 1984, for *The Iguana Killer;* New Times Fiction Award, 1983; Pushcart Prize for fiction, 1986, and poetry, 1988, 1989; Chicanos Por La Causa Community Appreciation Award, 1988; National Book Award nominee in poetry category, 2002, for *The Smallest Muscle in the Human Body;* Distinguished Achievement Award, Western Literature Association, 2002.

WRITINGS:

Elk Heads on the Wall (poetry chapbook), Mango Press (San Jose, CA), 1979.

Sleeping on Fists (poetry chapbook), Dooryard Press (Story, WY), 1981.

Whispering to Fool the Wind (poetry), Sheep Meadow (New York, NY), 1982.
The Iguana Killer: Twelve Stories of the Heart, Blue Moon/Confluence (Lewiston, ID), 1984.
Five Indiscretions (poetry), Sheep Meadow (New York, NY), 1985.
The Lime Orchard Woman: Poems, Sheep Meadow (New York, NY), 1988.
The Warrington Poems, Pyracantha Press (Tempe, AZ), 1989.
Teodoro Luna's Two Kisses, Norton (New York, NY), 1990.
Pig Cookies and Other Stories, Chronicle Books (San Francisco, CA), 1995.
The Curtain of Trees: Stories, University of New Mexico Press (Albuquerque, NM), 1999.
Capirotada: A Nogales Memoir, University of New Mexico Press (Albuquerque, NM), 1999.
The Smallest Muscle in the Human Body (poetry), Copper Canyon Press (Port Townsend, WA), 2002.

Contributor of poetry, fiction, and drama to anthologies, including *Southwest: A Contemporary Anthology,* edited by Karl Kopp and Jane Kopp, Red Earth Press, 1977; *Hispanics in the United States: An Anthology of Creative Literature,* edited by Gary D. Keller and Francisco Jimenez, Bilingual Review Press, 1980; *The Norton Anthology of Modern Poetry,* edited by Richard Ellmann, Robert O' Clair, and John Benedict, Norton, 1988; and *American Literature,* Prentice-Hall, 1990. Contributor to periodicals, including *American Poetry Review, Little Magazine, Bloomsbury Review,* and *Paris Review.* Also contributor of translations to *New Kauri* and *Poetry Pilot.* Corresponding editor, *Manoa,* 1989—; editorial board, *New Chicano Writing,* 1990—.

ADAPTATIONS: Ríos's poetry has been set to music in "Toto's Say," by James DeMars, and "Away from Home," EMI.

WORK IN PROGRESS: A novel "about a married couple who move to Arizona from Mexico."

SIDELIGHTS: Alberto Ríos has won acclaim as a writer who uses language in lyrical and unexpected ways in both his poems and short stories, which reflect his Chicano heritage and contain elements of magical realism. "Ríos's poetry is a kind of magical storytelling, and his stories are a kind of magical poetry," commented Jose David Saldivar in the *Dictionary of Literary Biography.* Ríos grew up in a Spanish-speaking family but was forced to speak English in school, leading him to develop a third language, "one that was all our own," as he described it. Ríos once commented, "I have been around other languages all my life, particularly Spanish, and have too often thought of the act of translation as simply giving something two names. But it is not so, not at all. Rather than filling out, a second name for something pushes it forward, forward and backward, and gives it another life."

Saldivar wrote of Ríos, "Many of his important early poems dramatize the essence of this uncanny third language." There are examples of these in the prize-winning collection *Whispering to Fool the Wind,* which contains poems that Mary Logue, writing in the *Voice Literary Supplement,* called "written miracles" that "carry the feel of another world." These poems, she noted, are informed by his upbringing in the border town of Nogales, Arizona, "where one is neither in this country nor the other."

Saldivar explained that Ríos tells stories in verse, something that many writers have been unable to do successfully. Ríos, however, is able to bring to life characters such as a man who dies of anger when a seamstress refuses to give him pins with which to display his butterfly collection. "Throughout *Whispering to Fool the Wind* magical-realist events are related with the greatest of accuracy without being forced on the reader," Saldivar wrote. "It is left up to readers to interpret things for themselves in a way that is most familiar to them."

Saldivar deemed "Nani," about Ríos's grandmother, the best poem in the collection "and one of the most remarkable poems in Chicano literature." It "captures the reality of the invented third language," he said, with lines such as "'To speak, now-foreign words I used to speak, too, dribble down her mouth. . . . By the stove she does something with words and looks at me only with her back.'" Logue also praised the poet's unusual use of language, observing that "Ríos's tongue is both foreign and familiar, but always enchanting."

In *Five Indiscretions,* "most of the poems achieve a level of excellence not far below the peak moments of [Ríos's] earlier poetry," Saldivar asserted. Almost all of these poems deal with romantic and sexual relationships between men and women, with the poet taking both male and female viewpoints. This collection has "regrettably . . . not received the acclaim and attention it deserves," Saldivar opined. "The few book reviews, however, praised his ability to represent gender issues and his use of the American language."

Ríos's award-winning book of short stories, *The Iguana Killer: Twelve Stories of the Heart,* contains tales "explor[ing] the luminous world of his childhood and border culture," Saldivar related. The title story centers on a young Mexican boy who uses a baseball bat to become his country's leading iguana killer. "The Birthday of Mrs. Pineda" is about an oppressed wife who finally gets a chance to speak for herself. This and "The Way Spaghetti Feels" are, in Saldivar's estimate, "the best stories in the book"; he commented that they "border on the metafictional and magical-realist impulse in postmodern fiction."

These characteristics also are evident in the 1995 work *Pig Cookies and Other Stories,* set in a small Mexican town where cookies exhibit supernatural powers and life takes other surprising twists and turns. "The tales in this collection glisten with a magical sheen, at once other-worldly and real," remarked Greg Sanchez in *World Literature Today.* "Ríos takes us from the realm of imagination to the concrete and back again with surprising fluidity." Ríos also creates winning characters, wrote a *Publishers Weekly* reviewer: "These poignant, funny tales of the rich, unsuspected lives of regular folks transcend time and place." In 1999 Ríos published a collection titled *The Curtain of Trees: Stories,* which focuses on residents of small towns along the border of Arizona and Mexico. A *Publishers Weekly* critic stated that the "characters are from another era (circa the 1950s), roaming the unpaved streets of small villages, their lives made vividly real through the author's powerful sensitivity and sharp eye for detail."

Capirotada: A Nogales Memoir, "a monologue that is funny, intimate, and as sweet as a candy placed in your palm by a friend," according to *Booklist* critic GraceAnne A. DeCandido, appeared in 1999. In *Capirotada,* Ríos describes his experiences growing up in Nogales, Arizona, which shared a border with its sister city of Nogales, Mexico. A *Publishers Weekly* reviewer called the work "an extremely personal family history filled with small anecdotes and finely drawn landscapes." In *Library Journal,* Gwen Gregory remarked, "This well-balanced narrative recalls the universal experiences of childhood and unique personal reminiscences of the author."

The Smallest Muscle in the Human Body, a 2002 collection of poems, "focuses squarely on childhood experiences and memories," noted a *Publishers Weekly* reviewer. Poems like "My Chili" and "Chinese Food in the Fifties" celebrate local dining customs, and "Gray Dogs" is one of several poems that contain animal imagery. According to Robert Murray Davis in *World Literature Today,* Ríos "is most successful . . . when, on the one hand, he does not strive too hard for paradox and, on the other, when he does not take refuge in mere nostalgia." The book's title, taken from the poem "Some Extensions on the Sovereignty of Science," refers to the stapedius muscle in the ear, which prevents humans from hearing their own heartbeat. "The muscle does important work I think, but at the same time, it keeps us from something that belongs to us," Ríos told Leslie A. Wootten in *World Literature Today.* "We are protected from particular sounds for our own good. There are many things in life we are protected from hearing, seeing, smelling, tasting, touching, and feeling. In large measure, the poems in this book—and all my books—struggle to bring into view what we've been protected from experiencing. But by this, I mean the small things as well as the large."

Indeed, while Ríos's Chicano heritage informs his writing and while he is one of that culture's important voices, his work "is anything but narrow and exclusive," contended Robert McDowell in an essay for *Contemporary Poets.* Ríos, McDowell said, is dedicated "to finding, declaring, and celebrating the diversity and power of community in the experience of those around him. Thus, his vision is more outward directed, less private than might at first glance be apparent." Saldivar added that "Ríos is surely one of the major vernacular voices in the postmodern age."

BIOGRAPHICAL AND CRITICAL SOURCES:

BOOKS

Contemporary Poets, 7th edition, St. James Press (Detroit, MI), 2001.

Dictionary of Literary Biography, Volume 122: *Chicano Writers, Second Series,* Thomson Gale (Detroit, MI), 1992.

Poetry for Students, Volume 11, Thomson Gale (Detroit, MI), 2001.

PERIODICALS

American Book Review, October, 1993, John Jacob, "Androgyny's Whisper."

Americas Review, fall-winter, 1996, William Barillas, "Words Like the Wind: An Interview with Alberto Ríos," pp. 116-129.

Bloombury Review, January-February, 1996, Leslie A. Wootten, "Writing on the Edge: An Interview with Alberto Alvaro Ríos."

Booklist, October 15, 1999, GraceAnne A. DeCandido, review of *Capirotada: A Nogales Memoir,* p. 411.

Confluencia, fall, 1990, Lupe Cárdenas and Justo Alarcón, "Entrevista: An Interview with Alberto Ríos," p. 119.

Glimmer Train, spring, 1998, Susan McInnis, "Interview with Alberto Ríos," pp. 105-121.

Hayden's Ferry Review, fall-winter, 1992, Deneen Jenks, "The Breathless Patience of Alberto Rios," pp. 115-123.

Library Journal, October 1, 1999, Gwen Gregory, review of *Capirotada,* p. 120.

New York Times Book Review, February 9, 1986; September 17, 1995, p. 25.

Publishers Weekly, March 20, 1995, review of *Pig Cookies and Other Stories,* p. 54; April 26, 1999, review of *The Curtain of Trees,* p. 55; August 30, 1999, review of *Capirotada,* p. 62; April 29, 2002, review of *The Smallest Muscle in the Human Body,* pp. 65-66.

Research, spring-summer, 1997, Sheilah Britton, "Discovering the Alphabet of Life: An Interview with Alberto Ríos," pp. 38-41.

South Carolina Review, fall, 2001, Timothy S. Sedore, "An American Borderer: An Interview with Alberto Ríos," pp. 7-17.

Voice Literary Supplement, October, 1982.

World Literature Today, spring, 1996, Greg Sanchez, review of *Pig Cookies and Other Stories,* p. 415; July-September, 2003, Leslie A. Wootten, "The Edge in the Middle: An Interview with Alberto Ríos," pp. 57-60, and Robert Murray Davis, review of *The Smallest Muscle in the Human Body,* p. 105.

ONLINE

Academy of American Poets Web site, http://www.poets.org/poets/ (July 9, 2004), "Alberto Ríos."

Arizona State University Web Site, http://www.public.asu.edu/˜aarios/index.html/ (August 10, 2004), "Alberto Ríos."*

* * *

ROBSON, Roy R(aymond) 1963-

PERSONAL: Born June 19, 1963, in Erie, PA; son of Joe B. and Anita (Evanoff) Robson; married Kim Elizabeth Pawlak, July 19, 1987. *Education:* Allegheny College, B.A. (cum laude), 1985; Pennsylvania State University, graduate study, 1985-86; University of Pittsburgh, M.A., 1987; Boston College, Ph.D., 1992. *Hobbies and other interests:* Rowing.

ADDRESSES: Home—223 Congress Ave., Lansdowne, PA 19050. *Office*—Department of Humanities, University of the Sciences in Philadelphia, 600 S. 43rd St., Philadelphia, PA 19104-4495. *E-mail*—r.robson@usip.edu.

CAREER: Boston College, Chestnut Hill, MA, adjunct assistant professor of history, 1992-94; Fayetteville State University, Fayetteville, NC, assistant professor of history, 1994-97; University of the Sciences in Philadelphia, Philadelphia, PA, began as assistant professor, became associate professor of humanities, 1997—. Harvard University, fellow of Russian Research Center, 1992-95; University of North Carolina/Duke University Joint Center for the Research of Russia, East Europe, and Central Asia, fellow, 1997.

MEMBER: American Historical Association, American Association for the Advancement of Slavic Studies, Southern Conference of Slavic Studies.

AWARDS, HONORS: Fulbright fellow in Helsinki, Finland, 1990; National Endowment for the Humanities, grant, 1993, fellowship, 1997; fellow of American Council of Learned Societies and Social Science Research Council, 1993-95; grants from International Research and Exchanges Board, 1996, 1997, and American Council of Learned Societies, 1996.

WRITINGS:

Old Believers in Modern Russia, Northern Illinois University Press (DeKalb, IL), 1995.

Solovki: The Story of Russia Told through Its Most Remarkable Islands, Yale University Press (New Haven, CT), 2004.

Contributor to books, including *Seeking God: The Recovery of Religious Identity in Russia, Georgia, and Ukraine; Essays on Confessionality and Religious Culture,* edited by Stephen K. Batalden, Northern Illinois University Press (DeKalb, IL), 1993. Contributor of articles and reviews to periodicals in the United States and abroad, including *Slavic Review.*

* * *

ROSENBERG, Joel 1954-

PERSONAL: Born May 1, 1954, in Winnipeg, Manitoba, Canada; immigrated to the United States, 1955; son of Mervin E. (a physician) and Irene (a housewife; maiden name, Yamron) Rosenberg; married Felicia Gail Herman, October 23, 1978; children: Judy, Rachel. *Education:* University of Connecticut, 1972-76. *Politics:* "Idiosyncratic." *Religion:* Jewish.

ADDRESSES: Office—3925 15th Ave. S., Minneapolis, MN 55407. *Agent*—Richard Curtis, Richard Curtis Associates, Inc., 164 E. 64th St., Ste. 1, New York, NY 10021. *E-mail*—joelr@bigfoot.com.

CAREER: Writer, certified firearms instructor. Worked variously as a short-order cook, truck driver, aide for the mentally retarded, gambler, bookkeeper, motel desk clerk, gas pumper, and door-to-door encyclopedia salesman.

MEMBER: Science Fiction Writers of America.

WRITINGS:

"THOUSAND WORLDS" SERIES

Ties of Blood and Silver, New American Library (New York, NY), 1984.

Emile and the Dutchman, New American Library (New York, NY), 1985.

Not for Glory, New American Library (New York, NY), 1988.

Hero, Roc (New York, NY), 1990.

"GUARDIANS OF THE FLAME" SERIES

The Sleeping Dragon, New American Library (New York, NY), 1983.

The Sword and the Chain, New American Library (New York, NY), 1984.

*The Silver,*New American Library (New York, NY), 1985.

The Heir Apparent, New American Library (New York, NY), 1987.

The Warrior Lives, New American Library (New York, NY), 1988.

The Road to Ehvenor, Roc (New York, NY), 1991.

The Road Home, Roc (New York, NY), 1995.

Not Exactly the Three Musketeers, Tor (New York, NY), 1999.

Not Quite Scaramouche, Tor (New York, NY), 2001.

Not Really the Prisoner of Zenda, Tor (New York, NY), 2003.

The Guardians of the Flame (contains *The Sleeping Dragon, The Sword and the Chain,* and *The Silver Crown*), Baen Books (Riverdale, NY), 2003.

Legacy, Baen Books (Riverdale, NY), 2004.

To Home and Ehvenor, 2004.

"KEEPERS OF THE HIDDEN WAYS" SERIES

The Fire Duke, Morrow (New York, NY), 1995.

The Silver Stone, Avon Books (New York, NY), 1996.

The Crimson Sky, Eos (New York, NY), 1998.

OTHER

(With Kevin O'Donnell, Jr., Mark J. McGarry, Mary Kittredge, and Ester Friesner-Stutzman) *The Electronic Money Machine* (nonfiction), Avon (New York, NY), 1984.

D'Shai ("D'Shai" series), Ace (New York, NY) 1991.

Hour of the Octopus ("D'Shai" series), Ace (New York, NY), 1994.

Home Front ("Ernest Hemingway" mystery series), Forge (New York, NY), 2003.

Family Matters ("Ernest Hemingway" mystery series), Forge (New York, NY), 2004.
Paladins, Baen Books (Riverdale, NY), 2004.

Author of *Everything You Need to Know about (Legally) Carrying a Handgun in Minnesota;* work represented in anthologies, including *Perpetual Light* and *Men of War;* contributor to magazines, including *Isaac Asimov's Science Fiction,Amazing Stories, Dragon,* and *Writer's Digest;* past contributing editor of *Gameplay.*

SIDELIGHTS: Joel Rosenberg is the author of a number of successful science fiction and fantasy series, including "Keepers of the Hidden Ways," based on Norse mythology. The first book, *The Fire Duke,* finds a group of college friends, Ian, Torrie, and Maggie, expert fencers, vacationing in North Dakota with Torrie's family. A wolf lures the males away from the house, enabling agents of the Fire Duke to kidnap the women, and the men use their talent to facilitate their rescue. In the sequel, *The Silver Stone,* Ian is drawn into a parallel world ruled by Odin, the trickster, who sends him on a mission. The other characters from the first installment attempt to find Ian after passing through a secret passageway in the basement of the North Dakota farmhouse.

Rosenberg's longest series is "Guardians of the Flame." *Not Exactly the Three Musketeers* is about a trio of characters that experience adventures similar to the original. They are Kethol, a dandy swashbuckler, the giant Durine, and the ugly Pirojil. Other characters from previous books in the series, including the dragon Ellegon, appear here, as well as new ones, like the wizard Erenor and Lady Leria, a noblewoman who needs rescuing. *Booklist*'s Roland Green wrote that "all the old virtues of Rosenberg's first and most enduring creation are here, along with the distinct promise of more to come. Good."

Green also reviewed the sequel, *Not Quite Scaramouche,* which he called "a treat," in which Erenor has joined the trio in protecting the House of Cullinane. A *Publishers Weekly* contributor wrote that the next book in the series, *Not Really the Prisoner of Zenda,* "darts between aggressive whimsy and deep introspection, sometimes within a single page." The trio has been reduced to one, Pirojil, after Durine is killed, and Kethol changes shape to simulate the exiled Baron Forinel to prevent the takeover of an inheritance by Forinel's half-brother, Miron. Although he has access to the palace and the lovely Lena, he longs to be back in the wood and soldiering. Green said to "expect a thoroughly intelligent piece of fantastic entertainment, and get it!"

Rosenberg tried something new with his "Ernest Hemingway" mystery series. In *Home Front,* we meet the protagonist, Ernest "Sparky" Hemingway, an aging copy editor who is contacted by Tenisha, the teen daughter of his Vietnam buddy, George "Prez" Washington, who has been killed by gangbangers. Prez left instructions that his daughter should go to Sparky for help in such an event. Sparky leaves his North Dakota town with his pal, Doc Holliday, for Minneapolis and returns with the girl, whose black urban looks make the folks of Homewood sit up and take notice. But the killing continues when four black males are found dead in a car near the town. *Booklist*'s David Pitt noted Rosenberg's use of famous names, which he found to be "tiresome," but felt that Rosenberg "has a sound premise . . . and readers looking for something offbeat may enjoy the story."

In the mid-1980s, Rosenberg commented on the circumstances that led to his writing career: "Part of it is straightforward: Like H. G. Wells, I became a writer out of necessity. Due to an injury, for a long time I was unable to do anything more strenuous than sit at a typewriter keyboard.

"I write because I like eating, having a roof over my head and clothes on my back. But . . . there's quite a bit more to it than that. The field of science fiction was, in more ways than one, my first love; it's always been a faithful one. For more than twenty years, it has been evident to me that the grandest thing one can be is a science fiction writer. Others might aspire to becoming president of the United States, a heart surgeon, Rogerian psychotherapist, oil billionaire, or whatever. That doesn't bother me; I'm perfectly willing to let them have the lesser professions. So, here I am, not only a published science fiction writer, but finding that I can support myself increasingly well by doing what I love best.

"There's an old saying: 'Be careful what you wish for—you may get it.' That's remarkably irrelevant to my life. Each year is better than the preceding. I'm enjoying both the practice and the rewards of my chosen profession more and more all the time. The only negative side to it all is that I've become almost intolerably smug. People who don't like that are invited to hold their hands over their ears so that my chuckling won't bother them.

"It's unlikely that I'm going to restrict myself as a writer, beyond the limitations of my abilities and interests. My primary orientation is toward science fiction. I have worked as a short-order cook, truck driver, mental retardation aide, gambler, bookkeeper, motel desk clerk, gas pumper, and door-to-door encyclopedia salesman. I like writing better. *Much* better."

BIOGRAPHICAL AND CRITICAL SOURCES:

PERIODICALS

Booklist, February 1, 1999, Roland Green, review of *Not Exactly the Three Musketeers,* p. 966; December 15, 2000, Roland Green, review of *Not Quite Scaramouche,* p. 794; January 1, 2003, David Pitt, review of *Home Front,* p. 856; May 15, 2003, Roland Green, review of *Not Really the Prisoner of Zenda,* p. 1652.

Kirkus Reviews, December 1, 2002, review of *Home Front,* p. 1738; April 15, 2003, review of *Not Really the Prisoner of Zenda,* p. 578.

Publishers Weekly, April 10, 1995, review of *The Fire Duke,* p. 58; August 26, 1996, review of *The Silver Stone,* p. 81; January 18, 1999, review of *Not Exactly the Three Musketeers,* p. 333; January 8, 2001, review of *Not Quite Scaramouche,* p. 52; December 16, 2002, review of *The Guardians of the Flame,* p. 50; February 10, 2003, review of *Home Front,* p. 165; May 5, 2003, review of *Not Really the Prisoner of Zenda,* p. 204.

ONLINE

Fantasy Reviews, http://www.fantasyreviews.com/ (May 24, 2004), Chris Hart, reviews of *The Fire Duke* and *The Silver Stone.*

Green Man Review, http://www.greenmanreview.com/ (May 24, 2004), Laurie Thayer, reviews of *Not Exactly the Three Musketeers* and *Not Quite Scaramouche.*

Joel Rosenberg Home Page, http://www.ellegon.com/ (May 24, 2004).

Slovotsky's Laws (unofficial fan site), http://www.slovotskys-laws.com/ (May 24, 2004).*

* * *

ROSENBLUM, Nancy L. 1947-

PERSONAL: Born November 11, 1947, in San Francisco, CA; married Richard Rosenblum (a sculptor), 1970; children: Anna. *Education:* Radcliffe College, B.A., 1969; Harvard University, Ph.D., 1973.

ADDRESSES: Home—63 Lake Ave., Newton Centre, MA 02459. *Office*—Harvard University, Littauer 318, North Yard, Cambridge, MA 02138. *E-mail*—nrosenblum@latte.harvard.edu.

CAREER: Educator and author. Harvard University, assistant professor, 1973-77, associate professor, 1977-80, visiting professor, 1985, Senator Joseph Clark Professor of Ethics in Politics and Government, 2001—; Brown University, Providence, RI, professor, 1980—, professor of political science, 1985-2001, chairperson of political science department, 1989-95, Henry Merritt Wriston Professor, 1997—, Steven Robert Initiative for the Study of Values, founder and director, 1998-2000.

MEMBER: Conference for the Study of Political Thought (executive committee, 1988—, planning board), American Political Science Association (council member, 1991-93), National Commission on Civic Values, 1996-98, Tocqueville Society (council member, 2001—).

AWARDS, HONORS: Harvard University, Graduate Prize Fellowship, 1969-72, Toppan Prize, best doctoral dissertation in political science, 1975; National Endowment of the Humanities, 1975, 1980; Bunting Institute fellow, Radcliffe College, 1988; Harvard Law School Liberal Arts fellowship, 1992-93; Kalamazoo College, honorary degree, 1993; David Easton Award, Foundations of Political Theory Group, 2002, for *Membership and Morals: The Personal Uses of Pluralism in America.*

WRITINGS:

Bentham's Theory of the Modern State, Harvard University Press (Cambridge, MA), 1978.
Another Liberalism: Romanticism and the Reconstruction of Liberal Thought, Harvard University Press (Cambridge, MA), 1988.
Liberalism and the Moral Life, Harvard University Press (Cambridge, MA), 1989.
(Editor) *Political Writings/Thoreau,* Cambridge University Press (New York, NY), 1996.
Membership and Morals: The Personal Uses of Pluralism in America, Princeton University Press (Princeton, NJ), 1998.
(Editor) *Obligations of Citizenship and Demands of Faith: Religious Accommodation in Pluralist Democracies,* Princeton University Press (Princeton, NJ), 2000.
(Editor) Martha Minow, *Breaking the Cycles of Hatred: Memory, Law and Repair,* Princeton University Press (Princeton, NJ), 2002.
(Editor, with Robert C. Post) *Civil Society and Government,* Princeton University Press (Princeton, NJ), 2002.

Review editor, 1989-93, and member of editorial board, 1993-97, *Political Theory;* member of editorial board, *Annual Review of Political Science,* 2002—.

WORK IN PROGRESS: Two books, *Primus Inter Pares: Political Parties and Civil Society,* and *American Romanticism.*

SIDELIGHTS: Nancy L. Rosenblum is an acclaimed political theorist, professor, and author. In her many works as both author and editor, Rosenblum explores the relationship between individuals, groups, and government, religion's place in society and government, liberalist thought, and a variety of other topics. Rosenblum's works provide insight into political conventions affecting contemporary American society.

Rosenblum's early works include *Bentham's Theory of the Modern State, Another Liberalism: Romanticism and Reconstruction of Liberal Thought,* and *Liberalism and Moral Life.* The latter was praised by *National Review* critic Joseph Sobran as "rich, original, and stimulating." Sobran claimed *Liberalism and Moral Life* made him "see familiar questions in a new light." The book examines liberalist thought in terms of an individual's moral convictions and differentiates between those moral convictions and their place in a political spectrum. Sobran explained, "To ask a judge to ignore a defendant's religion is in no way to disparage the importance of religion in the defendant's own life, merely to affirm its irrelevance to the cause at hand." The book provides "more than one insight that any political philosophy worthy of the name will have to reckon with," concluded Sobran.

In her *Membership and Morals: The Personal Uses of Pluralism in America,* Rosenblum examines individuals' associations with groups, and the relevance of these associations in politics. Rosenblum describes people's experiences with groups to which they do and do not belong. According to Jon Mandle of the *American Political Science Review,* "The importance of civil society in character formation has led social theorists to focus increasingly on associations." Rosenblum explains how individuals help shape a group and how groups shape individuals. Her argument is that associations and groups fill a person's psychological and moral needs. She contemplates democracy's role in creating and maintaining associations, as well as a person's freedoms to join or leave an association at any time. Critic H. Mark Roelofs of the *Review of Politics* noted that Rosenblum does not give readers a "sustaining definition of her central subject," but Mandle concluded that the book "is essential for anyone interested in the theory and practice of civil society in the United States."

In *Obligations of Citizenship and Demands of Faith: Religious Accommodation in Pluralist Democracies,* Rosenblum explains religion's role among the contemporary American public. Many authors contributed to the book, including Alan Wolfe, Ronald Thiemann, and Michael McConnell. The writers argue that more room should be made for religion in today's society. A critic for the *Law and Politics Book Review* Web site commented that the book "contains a diversity of voices and perspectives" and "gives a new and thoughtful voice to believers and to the significance or value of their beliefs for democratic politics and civic engagement."

Rosenblum edited Martha Minow's book, *Breaking the Cycles of Hatred: Memory, Law, and Repair. Breaking the Cycles of Hatred* is, according to a writer for *Law and Social Inquiry,* an examination of "the double-edged role of memory in fueling cycles of hatred and maintaining justice and personal integrity." The book's contributors include political theorists, psychologists, historians, and law experts. Among the many topics debated in the book are hate crimes, child sexual abuse, and the statute of limitations.

Rosenblum collaborated with Robert C. Post, a professor of law, on the book, *Civil Society and Government.* Together, Rosenblum and Post collected a number of essays and perspectives about the relationship between civil society and the government. The editors and contributing authors attempt to explain, among other topics, the line between civil society and the state, the duties of citizenship, and the role of civil society in creating good citizens. *Civil Society and Government,* commented *Foreign Affairs* reviewer John Ikenberry, summarizes that civil society is the realm in which individuals can decide for themselves their identity and purpose, while government is "the domain of common purpose and identity." Ikenberry recommended the book as "a cautionary tale for those in search of universal principles of freedom, pluralism, and social justice."

BIOGRAPHICAL AND CRITICAL SOURCES:

PERIODICALS

American Historical Review, October, 1989, Bruce Mazlish, review of *Another Liberalism: Romanticism and the Reconstruction of Liberal Thought,* p. 1059.

American Political Science Review, December, 1988, Susan Moller Okin, review of *Another Liberalism,* p. 1360; December, 1990, Steven Kelman, review of *Liberalism and the Moral Life,* p. 1362; June, 1999, Jon Mandle, review of *Membership and Morals: The Political Uses of Pluralism in America,* p. 439.

Choice: Current Reviews for Academic Libraries, October, 2002, P. Coby, review of *Civil Society and Government,* p. 356.

Church History, March, 2002, Nancy T. Ammerman, review of *Obligations of Citizenship and Demands of Faith: Religious Accommodation in Pluralist Democracies,* p. 224.

Harvard Law Review, May, 1999, review of *Membership and Morals,* p. 1798.

Journal of Politics, November, 1999, review of *Membership and Morals,* p. 1183.

Law and Social Inquiry, summer, 2003, review of *Breaking the Cycles of Hatred: Memory, Law, and Repair,* p. 881.

National Review, November 24, 1989, Joseph Sobran, review of *Liberalism and the Moral Life,* p. 48.

New Republic, June 1, 1998, Alan Wolfe, review of *Membership and Morals,* p. 36.

Political Studies, June, 1989, Richard Jay, review of *Another Liberalism,* p. 333.

Review of Politics, spring, 2000, H. Mark Roelofs, "Joining Up," review of *Membership and Morals,* p. 385.

Times Literary Supplement, May 4, 1990, George Crowder, review of *Liberalism and the Moral Life,* p. 476; September 25, 1998, review of *Membership and Morals,* p. 8.

Virginia Quarterly Review, winter, 1999, review of *Membership and Morals,* p. 26.

Yale Journal of International Law, summer, 2003, Steven Wu, review of *Breaking the Cycles of Hatred,* p. 593.

ONLINE

Foreign Affairs Web site, http://www.foreignaffairs.org/ (November 23, 2002), John Ikenberry, review of *Civil Society and Government.*

Law and Politics Book Review Web site, http://www.bsos.umd.edu/gvpt/lpbr/ (November 23, 2002), John Paul Ryan, review of *Obligations of Citizenship and Demands of Faith.*

Princeton University Press Web site, http://pup.princeton.edu/ (November 23, 2002), reviews and summaries of *Civil Society and Government, Obligations of Citizenship and Demands of Faith, Breaking the Cycles of Hatred,* and *Membership and Morals.**

S

SAGALYN, Lynne B. 1947-

PERSONAL: Born October 16, 1947, in Flushing, NY; daughter of Preston (a manufacturing executive) and Helen (a homemaker; maiden name, Geller) Beyer; married James Sagalyn, June 12, 1969 (divorced, 1985); married Gary Arthur Hack (a professor and university dean), January 1, 2002; children: (first marriage) Emily. *Education:* Cornell University, B.S. (with distinction), 1969; Rutgers University, M.C.R.P., 1971; Massachusetts Institute of Technology, Ph.D., 1980.

ADDRESSES: *Office*—Graduate School of Business, Columbia University, 708 Uris Hall, New York, NY 10027. *E-mail*—lbs4@columbia.edu.

CAREER: Rutgers University, New Brunswick, NJ, research associate at Center for Urban Policy Research, 1971-72; Massachusetts Institute of Technology, Cambridge, instructor, 1980, assistant professor, 1980-86, associate professor of planning and real estate development, 1987-91; Columbia University, New York, NY, visiting associate professor, 1990, visiting professor of business, 1991-92, professor and Earle W. Kazis and Benjamin Shore Director of the MBA Real Estate Program and the Paul Mistein Center for Real Estate, Columbia Graduate School of Business, 1992—; research associate, Lincoln Institute of Land Policy, 1988-89, faculty associate, 1994—; Homer Hoyt Institute for Advanced Studies in Real Estate and land Economics, faculty, 1993—; consultant. Scholar in residence, Taubman Center for State and Local Government, Kennedy School of Government, Harvard University, 1991; consultant to Kirkland Group, Massachusetts Industrial Finance Agency, and New York City Public Development Corp. Member of Northampton Planning Board, 1983; vice president of board of directors, Cambridge Young Women's Christian Association, beginning 1988. Director of the United Dominion Realty Trust, of the Retail Initiative, and of the New York School Chancellor's Commission on the Capital Plan.

MEMBER: Urban Land Institute (member of national policy council, 1988-90), American Real Estate and Urban Economics Association, American Society of Real Estate Counselors, National Association of State Universities and Land-Grant Colleges, Bunting Institute, Citizens Housing and Planning Association (member of board of directors, 1983-89), New England Women in Real Estate (charter member).

AWARDS, HONORS: Ballard Award, 1989, for "Measuring Financial Returns when the City Acts As an Investor: Boston and Faneuil Hall Marketplace"; Best Article Award, *Journal of the American Planning Association,* 1991, for "Explaining the Improbable: Local Redevelopment in the Wake of Federal Cutbacks"; grants from City Club of New York and J. M. Kaplan Fund.

WRITINGS:

(With G. Sternlieb and R. W. Burchell) *The Affluent Suburb: Princeton,* Transaction Books (New Brunswick, NJ), 1971.

(Editor, with G. Sternlieb) *Housing: An Annual Anthology, 1970-1971,* AMS Press (New York, NY), 1972.

Zoning and Housing Costs: The Impact of Land-Use Controls on Housing Price, Center for Urban Policy Research, Rutgers University (New Brunswick, NJ), 1973.

(With Bernard J. Frieden) *Downtown, Inc.: How America Rebuilds Cities,* MIT Press (Cambridge, MA), 1989.

Cases in Real Estate Finance and Investment Strategy, Urban Land Institute (Washington, DC), 1999.

Times Square Roulette: Remaking the City Icon, MIT Press (Cambridge, MA), 2001.

Contributor to professional journals. Member of editorial board, *Journal of the American Planning Association,* 1988—.

SIDELIGHTS: A professor and director of the real estate program at New York's Columbia University, Lynne B. Sagalyn is a specialist in real estate finance and development. With books such as *Times Square Roulette: Remaking the City Icon* and *Downtown, Inc.: How America Rebuilds Cities,* and in a number of award-winning articles, Sagalyn has presented cogent studies about public-private development and redevelopment finance and public policy.

Collaborating with Bernard J. Frieden, Sagalyn produced with *Downtown, Inc.* an "interesting but flawed book," according to Joe R. Feagin in *Contemporary Sociology.* The book explores the means by which many redevelopment projects in American cities were carried out after the 1970s. Written mostly from the point of view of developers, corporate executives, and government officials, the book examines the processes in Boston, San Diego, Seattle, St. Paul, and Pasadena, five studies of "development success stories," as Feagin noted. Suburban and urban failures were also tracked in the work. Funding for such projects was largely subsidized by taxes, yet Feagin argued that such "tax abatements for large-scale redevelopment have often come at the expense of services for central city residents." However, such considerations were outside of the scope of Sagalyn's study. Feagin therefore concluded, "A deeper analysis is clearly required." Writing in the *American Review of Public Administration,* however, DeLysa Burnier noted that Sagalyn's book attempts to "revise the popular view that downtown-rebuilding efforts have been dismal failures." Burnier went on to comment that the authors "succeeded in their mission." For the same critic, *Downtown, Inc.* "is a well-written and valuable guide to the changes in redevelopment policy that have occurred since the 1970s."

With *Times Square Roulette,* Sagalyn traces the story of the redevelopment of New York's Times Square in the 1990s, creating the "definitive study of its turbulent implementation and a rich resource for planners and redevelopment officials," as David Gordon observed in the *Journal of the American Planning Association.* According to Gordon, Sagalyn "explodes five myths" about the project, among which are that Disney led the way and that then-Mayor Rudolph Giuliani deserves the credit. Sagalyn goes on to show in her study that Governor Mario Cuomo and Mayor Edward Koch deserve much of the credit for this daring project, so long in the planning. Alexander J. Reichl, reviewing the same book in *Architecture,* called it "the real deal." Reichl further noted, "Sagalyn masterfully recounts the two decades of deal-making behind the latest 'rescripting' of Times Square." Similarly, a reviewer for the *Economist* commented that Sagalyn "gives us a scholarly yet gripping enough account of the boldest urban redevelopment programmes in midtown Manhattan since the Rockefeller Centre was built in the 1930s." A contributor for *Publishers Weekly* also had praise for the book, noting that the "jumble of symbolisms, politics, policies and business plans characterizing twentieth-century 42nd Street has never before been subject to such a thorough and perspicacious scrutiny." Dubbed a "massive chronicle" by *Planning*'s Harold Henderson, *Times Square Roulette* was also the subject of a lengthy article in the *New York Review of Books.* James Traub, author of that review, commented that Sagalyn "has much to say both about the character of the peculiar place and about the processes that created it." Traub concluded that Sagalyn is "upbeat both about the process and the place it produced."

BIOGRAPHICAL AND CRITICAL SOURCES:

PERIODICALS

American Review of Public Administration, June, 1990, DeLysa Burnier, review of *Downtown, Inc.: How America Rebuilds Cities,* pp. 130-132.

Architecture, December, 2001, Alexander J. Reichl, review of *Times Square Roulette: Remaking the City Icon,* p. 46.

Contemporary Sociology, November, 1990, Joe R. Feagin, review of *Downtown, Inc.,* pp. 960-861.

Economist, December 1, 2001, review of *Times Square Roulette.*

Journal of the American Planning Association, spring, 2003, David Gordon, review of *Times Square Roulette,* pp. 198-199.

New York Review of Books, February 14, 2002, James Traub, review of *Times Square Roulette,* pp. 29-31.

Planning, April, 2002, Harold Henderson, review of *Times Square Roulette,* pp. 39-40.

Publishers Weekly, October 8, 2001, "New York In Black and White," p. 60.

ONLINE

Columbia University Web site, http://www.columbia.edu/ (February 12, 2004).

Massachusetts Institute of Technology Press Web site, http://mitpress.mit.edu/ (February 12, 2004).*

* * *

SAKURAI, Gail 1952-

PERSONAL: Born February 9, 1952, in Detroit, MI; daughter of Peter Robert (an automotive parts inspector) and Virginia Evelyn (a homemaker) Kwentus; married Eric Sakurai (an executive), July 31, 1971; children: Nicholas, Cameron. *Education:* Oakland University, B.A., 1979. *Hobbies and other interests:* Spending time with family, listening to classical music, reading.

ADDRESSES: Office—P.O. Box 1532, West Chester, OH 45071.

CAREER: Writer.

MEMBER: Society of Children's Book Writers and Illustrators.

WRITINGS:

Peach Boy: A Japanese Legend, Troll Associates (Mahwah, NJ), 1994.

Mae Jemison: Space Scientist, Children's Press (Chicago, IL), 1995.

The Liberty Bell, Children's Press (Chicago, IL), 1996.

Stephen Hawking: Understanding the Universe, Children's Press (New York, NY), 1996.

The Jamestown Colony, Children's Press (New York, NY), 1997.

Paul Revere, Children's Press (New York, NY), 1997.

The Library of Congress, Children's Press (New York, NY), 1998.

The Louisiana Purchase, Children's Press (New York, NY), 1998.

Asian-Americans in the Old West, Children's Press (New York, NY), 2000.

The Thirteen Colonies, Children's Press (New York, NY), 2000.

Juan Ponce de León, Franklin Watts (New York, NY), 2001.

Japanese American Internment Camps, Children's Press (New York, NY), 2002.

Also author of "Why the Sea Is Salty" (a re-told Japanese folk tale), *Jack and Jill* magazine, 1995.

SIDELIGHTS: Gail Sakurai commented that she "always wanted to be a writer, ever since I learned to read as a child. I planned to have my first book published by the time I was thirteen! Things didn't quite work out that way, however. For many years, other interests and needs interfered with writing, but I never lost my love of books. After getting married, holding a variety of jobs, graduating from college, and having two children, I finally returned to writing. My childhood dream came true with the publication of my first book in 1994—only twenty-nine years later than originally planned."

Sakurai described her first book, *Peach Boy: A Japanese Legend,* as a retelling of a Japanese folktale. "I learned the tale years ago from my Japanese husband, who told it to our two sons as a bedtime story," she said. "When I decided to write for children, it just seemed natural to choose *Peach Boy* for my first story. I wanted American children to be able to enjoy it as much as Japanese children have for centuries.

"My second book, a biography of Dr. Mae Jemison, the first African-American woman astronaut, grew out of my lifelong interest in space exploration. I get the ideas from my books from everywhere—from things I read, from my children, and even from television. I have more ideas than I'll ever have time to use.

"I specialize in writing nonfiction and retelling folktales from many lands. Through reading I developed an interest in other countries and cultures at an early age. I have studied French, Spanish, Italian, and Japanese, and have traveled widely.

"The hardest parts of writing are finding the time to write in a busy schedule full of family obligations, and getting started. Once I start, the words usually come quickly, because I have planned them in my head before my fingers ever touch the keyboard.

"The best parts of writing are the sense of accomplishment I feel when I have finished a story to my satisfaction, and when I sell that story to a publisher. I also enjoy meeting my readers and giving presentations at schools and libraries. My advice to aspiring writers is to read. Read everything you can get your hands on!"

Most of Sakurai's books are nonfiction history and biography texts suitable for elementary-age students who want to research famous people or landmarks. Some of her work is part of the "Cornerstones of Freedom" series, published by Children's Press. Sakurai can cover broad topics, such as the founding of the nation in *The Thirteen Colonies,* or more specific subjects, as in *The Jamestown Colony, The Liberty Bell* and *The Library of Congress.* In her *School Library Journal* review of *The Liberty Bell,* Margaret C. Howell observed that Sakurai includes many facts about the national icon that might not be known even to adults. Howell praised the book as "useful."

Sakurai has profiled several notable Americans in easy-to-read biographies, from the explorer Ponce de León to Paul Revere and Stephen Hawking. These also fall into two series, "Cornerstones of Freedom" and "Picture-Story Biographies." She has also explored the history of Asian Americans in this nation in two books: *Asian-Americans in the Old West* and *Japanese American Internment Camps.* The latter title describes how Japanese Americans were rounded up during World War II and forced to live in camps far from home. Carolyn Angus in *School Library Journal* has found Sakurai's nonfiction work "appropriate for young readers," for its inclusion of photographs, drawings, and chronologies that help children fix events on a particular date.

BIOGRAPHICAL AND CRITICAL SOURCES:

PERIODICALS

Booklist, August, 1996, Ilene Cooper, review of *Stephen Hawking: Understanding the Universe,* p. 1897.

School Library Journal, August, 1996, Margaret C. Howell, review of *The Liberty Bell,* p. 150; September, 1996, Carolyn Angus, review of *Stephen Hawking,* p. 220.*

* * *

SALZMAN, Mark (Joseph) 1959-

PERSONAL: Born December 3, 1959, in Greenwich, CT; son of Joseph (an artist) and Martha (a musician; maiden name, Zepp) Salzman; married Jessica Yu (a documentary filmmaker). *Education:* Yale University, B.A. (summa cum laude), 1982. *Hobbies and other interests:* Playing the cello, martial arts.

ADDRESSES: *Agent*—Neil Olsen, Donadio and Olson, Inc., 121 W. 27th St. No. 704, New York, NY 10001.

CAREER: Hunan Medical College, Changsha, China, teacher of English, 1982-84; writer and actor. Once worked as a dishwasher in a Chinese restaurant.

MEMBER: Phi Beta Kappa.

AWARDS, HONORS: Literary Lions Award, New York Public Library, Christopher Award, and Pulitzer Prize nomination for nonfiction, all 1987, all for *Iron and Silk;* Alex Award, Young Adult Library Services Association, 2004, for *True Notebooks.*

WRITINGS:

Iron and Silk: A Young American Encounters Swordsmen, Bureaucrats, and Other Citizens of Contemporary China (memoir), Random House (New York, NY), 1987.

The Laughing Sutra (novel), Random House (New York, NY), 1991.

(With Shirley Sun) *Iron and Silk* (screenplay; adapted from Salzman's book), Prestige, 1991.

The Soloist (novel), Random House (New York, NY), 1994.

Lost in Place: Growing Up Absurd in Suburbia (memoir), Random House (New York, NY), 1995.

Lying Awake (novel), Knopf (New York, NY), 2000.

True Notebooks (nonfiction), Knopf (New York, NY), 2003.

SIDELIGHTS: Mark Salzman is a scholar of Chinese language and literature who has distinguished himself as an author of nonfiction and fiction books; he is also a screenwriter and actor. He is well known for his *Iron and Silk: A Young American Encounters Swordsmen, Bureaucrats, and Other Citizens of Contemporary China,* his memoir about his experiences in China. Salzman learned Chinese while working as a dishwasher in a Chinese restaurant and became interested in martial arts after watching action films. In 1982, after graduating with honors from Yale University, he went to China and began working at Hunan Medical College, where he taught English to doctors and medical students. He stayed in China for two years, and in that time he studied martial arts and calligraphy and practiced to maintain his skills as a cellist. More importantly, he managed to befriend a range of people and thus obtain keen, personal insights into Chinese life.

Iron and Silk is essentially a series of sketches and vignettes, some of which are particularly amusing. In one notable episode, Salzman attends a lecture and notes its dullness to a just-awakened audience member, who relates that one's appreciation of such a speech is directly related to one's ability to sleep through it. On another occasion, Salzman assigns his students the task of relating their happiest moments, whereupon one student fondly recalls eating duck in Beijing, then confesses that his wife had actually dined in Beijing, not him, and that she had related the tale on so many occasions that he felt as if he too had enjoyed it.

Salzman also writes in *Iron and Silk* of his efforts to master *wushu,* China's traditional martial art. Notable in these sketches is the portrait of his teacher, Pan Qinfu, one of the art's most accomplished exponents. Pan is a fearsome instructor who intimidates with his spellbinding gaze as well as with his actual physical prowess. Indeed, Salzman discovers that concentrated staring is actually an integral aspect of *wushu.* He also learns that mastery—whether of *wushu* or calligraphy—can be perceived as the easily realized result of focused attention and diligence. "All you have to do is be kind and work hard," his calligraphy instructor tells him in the book, as quoted by Jean Fritz in the *Washington Post Book World.* The instructor adds that the mastery of eating and sleeping are more difficult because they are less easy to actually control.

Upon publication in 1987, *Iron and Silk* received substantial praise. *New York Times* critic John Gross found Salzman's book "altogether admirable," and Carolyn Wakeman, writing in the *Los Angeles Times Book Review,* deemed the memoir "remarkable" and "utterly compelling." Another reviewer, J. D. Brown, wrote in Chicago's *Tribune Books* that with *Iron and Silk* Salzman had fashioned "a rich series of anecdotes." Richard Selzer, in his appraisal for the *New York Times Book Review,* found the book compelling and appealing. "If there were a prize for most winning writer," Selzer affirmed, "Mark Salzman would [win] it."

Iron and Silk intrigued filmmakers as a work of considerable potential for adaptation. Salzman, however, was determined to write the adaptation himself. In addition, he planned to play the lead role. Nicholas D. Kristof, in a *New York Times* article, reported that moguls "laughed" when Salzman revealed his film ambitions. But in 1989 he collaborated with filmmaker Shirley Sun on an adaptation, and by the end of that year they had actually completed filming. Much of the film is derived from the book's episodes. There are even martial-arts sequences, complete with Pan Qinfu playing himself. But in fashioning the film, Salzman and Sun, who directed the adaptation, also developed a romance story line in which Salzman—named Mark Franklin in the film—falls in love with a Chinese woman whose parents are aghast at her attraction to the foreigner. The love story does not end in a conventionally happy manner.

Iron and Silk was well received upon its release in 1991. *Los Angeles Times* reviewer Kevin Thomas found the film "unsophisticated and bittersweet," and noted Salzman's "impressive martial arts skills" and "pleasant screen presence." Likewise, Janet Maslin reported in the *New York Times* that the film "has an essential guilelessness." She also observed that it "includes a lot of interesting observations about

Chinese life," and she described Salzman's perspective as that of "an affectionate and sharp-eyed observer."

In 1991 Salzman also published a novel, *The Laughing Sutra,* about a Chinese man, Hsun-ching, who travels to the United States in search of a legendary Buddhist text. Accompanying Hsun-ching on his adventure is Colonel Sun, a two-thousand-year-old warrior of penetrating gaze. Together, the adventurers conduct an essentially comic journey. In San Francisco, for instance, they witness a dwarf-tossing exhibition, attend an art exhibit full of buffoonish patrons, and encounter profiteering Buddhists.

Writing about *The Laughing Sutra* in the *Chicago Tribune,* William H. Banks, Jr. deemed it a "fish-out-of-water adventure story." Among the novel's enthusiasts was Allan Appel, who declared in the *Washington Post Book World* that Salzman produced "a wonderful book." He concluded that "the fortunate reader will find himself entranced, entertained and very definitely enlightened."

For his next work, Salzman drew upon another passion in his life—the cello, which he began playing at the age of seven—to create a novel about thwarted artistic ambitions. He dedicated *The Soloist,* his 1994 novel, to his mother, who abandoned her career as harpsichordist to raise her family. Its hero is thirty-four-year-old Reinhart (Renne) Sundheimer, who was once a child virtuoso on the instrument, but who now teaches at a university. "I wanted to create a character who had a hard time with his dreams," the author told Suzanne Mantell in *Publishers Weekly.* Once a feted teenager, Renne became obsessed with the notion of perfect pitch at eighteen and felt his hearing was failing him. Now, he cannot bear to hear his own music and survives by teaching music at a Los Angeles university, though he fantasizes about returning to the concert stage.

Renne's life begins to change when he agrees to teach a nine-year-old Korean girl, an apparent prodigy herself. Then Renne is called for jury duty, and he is selected to decide the outcome of a trial for a gruesome urban slaying. A disturbed young man went on a Zen retreat, and his teacher gave him a koan, or spiritual riddle, to solve; the student's solution was to beat the master to death. "Just as you begin to suspect that the novel will end inconclusively, Salzman winds the story down subtly," stated a *Publishers Weekly* reviewer. Renne is the lone jury holdout on the case, and he solves the koan himself. He also awakens from a long period of romantic inactivity when he falls for another juror. The author, wrote Diane Cole in the *New York Times Book Review,* "finds engaging points of comparison between the disciplines of meditation and music."

The heroine of Salzman's 2000 novel *Lying Awake* is a Roman Catholic nun, Sister John of the Cross, whose all-night prayer vigils have brought her visions and even spiritual ecstasies. She then writes about them in verse form, and her published works have earned her and her Carmelite order a degree of international fame. But Sister John's visions begin to coincide with painful migraine headaches, and after she collapses from one, she consents to an appointment with a specialist. The doctor tells her that it is a form of epilepsy that is triggering the visions and it is treatable; in fact, it may endanger her life if she lets it go untreated. The news triggers a crisis of faith for the sister. A *Publishers Weekly* reviewer remarked that expressing such abstract concepts as spiritual ecstasy in fiction is difficult, but "what Salzman conveys with perfect clarity is that momentary, extraordinary mental state in which physical pain becomes pure, lucid grace poised between corporeal reality and eternity." *Entertainment Weekly* reviewer George Hodgman observed that *Lying Awake* "should be shortlisted for all the literary prizes, but it has the kind of grace that doesn't demand them."

In 1995 Salzman published a memoir of his eccentric but pleasant childhood under the title *Lost in Place: Growing Up Absurd in Suburbia.* Here he recounts his early years in Connecticut, living in an artistically gifted household; his father painted in the evenings as a salve against a day job he hated, while his mother gave music lessons. Salzman recounts his discovery of martial arts at the age of thirteen, and his interest in Buddhism, the Chinese language, and martial arts, which he studied until his early teens. Salzman's obsession then turned to the cello, and he studied music at Yale University until he burned out after a year and underwent an existential crisis for which his father provided pragmatic advice. In a review of *Lost in Place* by Sara Nelson for *People,* the critic praised Salzman as "a charming, self-effacing writer" who is still familiar "with the peculiar combination of arrogance and terror that comprises teenage angst." Blake Morrison, in a *New York Times Book Review* assessment, described the book as a "Bildungsroman," or coming-of-age story and added that several of the book's adult characters, including Salzman's parents, "are beautifully observed."

In his 2003 work *True Notebooks,* Salzman focuses on the lives and thoughts of a teen culture far different from that of his own past. The book was inspired by his experience teaching creative writing to a group of teenagers incarcerated in the Los Angeles Juvenile Hall. Most of these "high-risk" offenders had committed serious crimes and were destined to continue through the prison system, some of them for life. Salzman presents their writings, and "documents his insecurities, his frustrations, and his occasional inability to coax much work or interest . . . from the class," noted a *Kirkus Reviews* contributor. Salzman does not dwell on the negative, however, but instead finds humor, poignancy, and talent in these teens' writings. As a reviewer noted in *Publishers Weekly,* Salzman's book's "power comes from keeping its focus squarely on these boys, their writing, and their coming-to-terms with the mess their lives had become."

BIOGRAPHICAL AND CRITICAL SOURCES:

PERIODICALS

America, March 19, 2001, John B. Breslin, "Mad for God," p. 34.

Booklist, September 1, 1995, Joanne Wilkinson, review of *Lost in Place: Growing Up Absurd in Suburbia,* p. 37; September 15, 2000, Michael Spinella, review of *Lying Awake,* p. 219.

Chicago Tribune, February 18, 1991, section 2, p. 3, William H. Banks, Jr., review of *The Laughing Sutra.*

Christian Century, November 22, 2000, Gordon Houser, review of *Lying Awake,* p. 1227.

Detroit Free Press, January 6, 1991.

Entertainment Weekly, August 18, 1995, D. A. Ball, review of *Lost in Place,* p. 51; October 6, 2000, George Hodgman, review of *Lying Awake,* p. 80.

Globe and Mail (Toronto, Ontario, Canada), February 16, 1991, p. C8.

Kirkus Reviews, July 3, 2003, review of *True Notebooks,* p. 900.

Library Journal, October 15, 2000, Starr Smith, review of *Lying Awake,* p. 104.

Los Angeles Times, March 8, 1991, Kevin Thomas, review of film *Iron and Silk,* p. F8.

Los Angeles Times Book Review, May 24, 1987, Carolyn Wakeman, review of *Iron and Silk,* p. 2.

National Catholic Reporter, March 23, 2001, Judith Bromberg, review of *Lying Awake,* p. 12.

National Review, September 25, 1987, Katherine Dalton, review of *Iron and Silk,* p. 62.

New York Times, January 9, 1987, John Gross, review of *Iron and Silk;* January 22, 1989; February 15, 1991, Janet Maslin, review of film *Iron and Silk,* p. C12.

New York Times Book Review, February 1, 1987, Richard Selzer, review of *Iron and Silk,* p. 9; February 6, 1994, Diane Cole, review of *The Soloist,* p. 22; August 13, 1995, Blake Morrison, "Growing Up Somehow," p. 11.

People, October 2, 1995, Sara Nelson, review of *Lost in Place,* p. 30.

Publishers Weekly, October 12, 1990, Sybil Steinberg, review of *Laughing Sutra,* p. 47; October 11, 1993, review of *The Soloist,* p. 68; January 17, 1994, Suzanne Mantell, "Mark Salzman: He Uses Fiction to Question What Happens when Dreams Don't Come True," p. 357; June 26, 1995, review of *Lost in Place,* p. 101; July 17, 2000, review of *Lying Awake,* p. 171; June 16, 2003, review of *True Notebooks,* p. 57.

Smithsonian, July, 1987, William Dieter, review of *Iron and Silk,* p. 142.

Time, March 2, 1987, p. 76.

Tribune Books (Chicago, IL), January 25, 1987, J. D. Brown, review of *Iron and Silk,* p. 6.

Washington Post Book World, January 25, 1987, p. 8; March 3, 1991, Allan Appel, review of *The Laughing Sutra,* p. 9.*

* * *

SANDIN, Joan 1942-

PERSONAL: Born April 30, 1942, in Watertown, WI; daughter of Robert L. (a teacher) and Frances K. (an interviewer; maiden name, Somers) Sandin; married Sigfrid Leijonhufvud (a journalist), April 30, 1971 (divorced, 1986); remarried; husband's name Brian; children: Jonas, Jenny. *Education:* University of Arizona, B.F.A., 1964.

ADDRESSES: *Home*—Tucson, AZ. *Agent*—c/o Author Mail, Books for Young Readers, Henry Holt and Company, 115 W. 15th St., New York, NY 10011.

CAREER: Illustrator, author, and translator of children's books. *Exhibitions:* Solo shows in Sweden and the United States featuring illustrations from *The Long Way to a New Land.* Art represented in the Kerlan Collection.

MEMBER: FST, Swedish Society of Illustrators.

AWARDS, HONORS: Best Children's Books citation, American Institute of Graphic Artists, 1970, for *Crocodile and Hen;* travel and work grants from Forfattarfonden (Swedish Writers' Fund); exhibition grant from Bildkonstnarsfonden (Swedish Artists' Fund); Notable Children's Trade Book in the Field of Social Studies citations, National Council for the Social Studies/Children's Book Council, 1971, for *Hill of Fire,* 1975, for *The Lemming Condition,* 1981, for *The Long Way to a New Land,* and 1981, for *Time for Uncle Joe;* Georgia Children's Award, 1973, for *"Hey, What's Wrong with This One?";* Outstanding Science Trade Book for Children citation, National Science Teachers Association/Children's Book Council, 1974, for *Woodchuck;* Edgar Allan Poe Award nominee, Mystery Writers of America, 1975, for *The Mysterious Red Tape Gang;* Notable Book citations, American Library Association, 1981, for *The Long Way to a New Land,* and 1988, for translation of Christina Bjork's *Linnea's Windowsill Garden.*

WRITINGS:

SELF-ILLUSTRATED

The Long Way to a New Land, Harper & Row (New York, NY), 1981.

The Long Way Westward, Harper & Row (New York, NY), 1989.

Pioneer Bear: Based on a True Story, Random House (New York, NY), 1995.

Coyote School News, Holt (New York, NY), 2003.

ILLUSTRATOR

Carol Beach York, *The Blue Umbrella,* Watts (New York, NY), 1968.

Randolph Stow, *Midnite: The Story of a Wild Colonial Boy,* Prentice-Hall (Englewood Cliffs, NJ), 1968.

Harold Felton, *True Tall Tales of Stormalong: Sailor of the Seven Seas,* Prentice-Hall (Englewood Cliffs, NJ), 1968.

Edith Brecht, *The Little Fox,* Lippincott (Philadelphia, PA), 1968.

Eleanor Hull, *A Trainful of Strangers,* Atheneum (New York, NY), 1968.

Ellen Pugh, *Tales from the Welsh Hills,* Dodd (New York, NY), 1968.

Maia Wojciechowska, *"Hey, What's Wrong with This One?",* Harper (New York, NY), 1969.

Joan Lexau, *Crocodile and Hen,* Harper (New York, NY), 1969.

Jan M. Robinson, *The December Dog,* Lippincott (Philadelphia, PA), 1969.

Constantine Georgiou, *Rani, Queen of the Jungle,* Prentice-Hall (Englewood Cliffs, NJ), 1970.

Joan Lexau, *It All Began with a Drip, Drip, Drip,* McCall/Dutton (New York, NY), 1970.

Jean Little, *Look through My Window,* Harper (New York, NY), 1970.

Joanna Cole, *The Secret Box,* Morrow (New York, NY), 1971.

Thomas P. Lewis, *Hill of Fire,* Harper (New York, NY), 1971.

Barbara Brenner, *A Year in the Life of Rosie Bernard,* Harper (New York, NY), 1971.

Ellen Pugh, *More Tales from the Welsh Hills,* Dodd (New York, NY), 1971.

Jean Little, *From Anna,* Harper (New York, NY), 1972.

Nathaniel Benchley, *Small Wolf,* Harper (New York, NY), 1972.

Edna Mitchell Preston, *Ickle Bickle Robin,* Watts (New York, NY), 1973.

Alison Morgan, *A Boy Called Fish,* Harper (New York, NY), 1973.

Joan L. Nixon, *The Mysterious Red Tape Gang,* Putnam (New York, NY), 1974.

Hans Eric Hellberg, *Grandpa's Maria,* translated by Patricia Crampton, Morrow (New York, NY), 1974.

Faith McNulty, *Woodchuck,* Harper (New York, NY), 1974.

Kathryn Ewing, *A Private Matter,* Harcourt Brace Jovanovich (New York, NY), 1975.

Liesel Skorpen, *Michael,* Harper (New York, NY), 1975.

Liesel Skorpen, *Bird,* Harper (New York, NY), 1976.

Sandra Love, *But What about Me?,* Harcourt Brace Jovanovich (New York, NY), 1976.

Alan Arkin, *The Lemming Condition,* Harper (New York, NY), 1976.

Thomas P. Lewis, *Clipper Ship,* Harper & Row (New York, NY), 1978.

Clyde Robert Bulla, *Daniel's Duck,* Harper & Row (New York, NY), 1979.

Nancy Jewell, *Time for Uncle Joe,* Harper & Row (New York, NY), 1981.

Eleanor Coerr, *The Bell Ringer and the Pirates,* Harper & Row (New York, NY), 1983.

Doreen Rappaport, *Trouble at the Mines,* Crowell (New York, NY), 1987.

Aileen Fisher, *The House of a Mouse: Poems,* Harper & Row (New York, NY), 1988.

Aileen Fisher, *Always Wondering: Some Favorite Poems of Aileen Fisher,* HarperCollins (New York, NY), 1991.

Nancy Smiler Levinson, *Snowshoe Thompson,* HarperCollins (New York, NY), 1992.

Elaine Marie Alphin, *A Bear for Miguel,* HarperCollins (New York, NY), 1996.

Elizabeth Winthrop, *As the Crow Flies,* Clarion (New York, NY), 1998.

Illustrator of the serial story *Army of Two,* by Betty Miles, which ran in the *Boston Herald,* 2000.

TRANSLATOR

Gunilla Bergstrom, *Who's Scaring Alfie Atkins?,* Farrar, Straus & Giroux (New York, NY), 1987.

Christina Bjork and Lena Anderson, *Linnea's Windowsill Garden,* Farrar, Straus & Giroux (New York, NY), 1988.

Christina Bjork, *Elliot's Extraordinary Cookbook,* Farrar, Straus & Giroux (New York, NY), 1991.

Christina Bjork, *The Other Alice: The Story of Alice Liddell and Alice in Wonderland,* R & S Books (New York, NY), 1993.

Christina Bjork, *Big Bear's Book: By Himself,* Farrar, Straus & Giroux (New York, NY), 1994.

Olof and Lena Landström, *Boo and Baa in a Party Mood,* R & S Books (New York, NY), 1996.

Olof and Lena Landström, *Boo and Baa in Windy Weather,* R & S Books (New York, NY), 1996.

Olof and Lena Landström, *Boo and Baa at Sea,* R & S Books (New York, NY), 1997.

Olof and Lena Landström, *Boo and Baa on a Cleaning Spree,* R & S Books (New York, NY), 1997.

Lena Arro, *Good Night, Animals,* illustrated by Catarina Kruusval, R & S Books (New York, NY), 2002.

Lena Landström, *The Little Hippos' Adventure,* R & S Books (New York, NY), 2002.

Lena Landström, *The New Hippos,* R & S Books (New York, NY), 2003.

Peter Cohen, *Boris's Glasses,* illustrated by Olaf Landström, R & S Books (New York, NY), 2003.

Jeanette Milde, *Once upon a Wedding,* R & S Books (New York, NY), 2004.

SIDELIGHTS: A prolific illustrator, Joan Sandin is also a skilled translator and a storyteller in her own right. As Sandin once commented: "I most enjoy working with folktales and books demanding research and/or travel." Indeed, Sandin's self-illustrated works have all been well-researched historical tales, often based on her ancestors' experiences. Her extensive travels in Europe and Mexico as well as the United States have also inspired her work.

Among the many books Sandin has illustrated is *A Bear for Miguel,* written by Elaine Maria Alphin. It is an unusual story for early readers, according to reviewers, but one that is effectively done and sensitively rendered in pictures and words. When Maria brings her stuffed toy bear, Paco, along to the market with her father, she has no intention of trading him. Her feelings change, however, as she begins to understand how the war in her country of El Salvador has affected her father's ability to find work. Sensing that a little boy injured in the war would love to have Paco, Maria decides to trade the toy for food for her family. "Sandin's watercolors add to the emotional impact . . . and do an effective job of setting the scene," remarked Gale W. Sherman in *School Library Journal.*

Sandin lived in Sweden for more than a decade before returning to the United States in the mid-1980s. Since her return, she has translated several children's books from Swedish into English. Many of these translations have been of picture books by Olof and Lena Landström, including their series about Boo and Baa, two hapless little sheep who find themselves in humorous jams no matter what they try to do. In *Boo and Baa in a Party Mood,* the two prepare for a birthday party by practicing their dance steps, but things get sticky when they try to wrap the present. In *Boo and Baa in Windy Weather,* the two go to the grocery store, but dragging home a sled laden with their purchases through a snow storm presents a problem. Sandin also translated Lena Landström's books about a family of hippopotami, including *The Little Hippos' Adventure* and *The New Hippos.* In the first book, three baby hippos get bored with swimming in the safe river near their home. Instead, they want to go diving off of the forbidden Tall Cliff. But when they are finally allowed to go swimming there, catastrophe nearly strikes. In the latter book, the hippos must get used to a new family who moves into their part of the jungle, discovering that the new family does not do everything the same way they do.

Big Bear's Book: By Himself, according to *School Library Journal* contributor Marilyn Taniguchi, is not a picture book but "a whimsical reminiscence of childhood" best suited to sentimental adults. Written by Christina Bjork, *Big Bear's Book* tells the story of a toy bear's relationship to his owner, from childhood, through a sojourn in the attic, to a place in the child's adult life and a career in the movies. Sandin is also the translator of Bjork's tribute to the children's classic *Alice in Wonderland.* In *The Other Alice: The Story of Alice Liddell and Alice in Wonderland,* Bjork describes the model for Lewis Carroll's main character, Alice Liddell, and explains some of the games and other trivia associated with the book. The result is "a unique pleasure," Ann A. Flowers wrote in *Horn Book.*

Sandin's own background—her ancestors immigrated to the United States from Sweden in the nineteenth century—inspired the research that went into *The Long Way to a New Land* and *The Long Way Westward,* two self-illustrated early readers which tell the story of an immigrant family's journey from Sweden to the United States in the 1860s. Told from the perspective of Carl Erik, the family's elder son, *The Long Way to a New Land* describes a drought that forces Erik's family to sell their farm and try to make a fresh start in America. The story continues with an account of their trip by boat to the United States, where bad weather, bad smells, and crowding mean long days of discomfort before they reach their destination. Critics noted that Sandin uses her illustrations effectively to augment a necessarily spare text intended for beginning readers. "It isn't always easy to make history comprehensible to younger children," remarked Zena Sutherland of the *Bulletin of the Center for Children's Books,* but "Sandin does a nice job of it." Similarly praised as "an interesting, well-researched slice of history" by a critic for *Kirkus Reviews, The Long Way Westward* completes the story of the Erik family's journey as they travel from New York by railroad to Minnesota to live among their relatives.

Also set in the nineteenth century, *Pioneer Bear: Based on a True Story* tells the story of John Lacy, a photographer who learns that young Andrew Irwin taught a bear to dance. Lacy travels thirty miles to the Irwin farm to photograph the bear; but when he arrives, Bearly the Bear is nowhere to be found. Sandin provides a visual survey of pioneer life on a farm while the family goes from room to room, from barn to outhouse, in search of the cub. "Pioneer activities such as washing laundry in tubs . . . and smoking meats are realistically presented in warm watercolor illustrations," Mary Ann Bursk observed in *School Library Journal.* Reviewers also noted Sandin's sly infusion of humor into the story through her illustrations. "Primary schoolers will enjoy sighting Bearly . . . as he peeks from behind outbuildings and foliage," remarked Elizabeth Bush in the *Bulletin of the Center for Children's Books.*

Coyote School News was inspired by actual newspapers printed by five tiny rural schools in Depression-era Arizona. Sandin stumbled across the original newspapers, titled *The Little Cowpuncher,* while doing research for a book about her high school friend who went to one of the schools which contributed to the paper. As well as writing *Coyote School News,* Sandin also got involved in a project to digitally archive the crumbling originals of *The Little Cowpuncher* so that the materials would be available to researchers in future generations.

A *Kirkus Reviews* contributor praised the "delightful authenticity" of *Coyote School News,* which follows student Monchi Ramirez and his five siblings through the 1938-39 school year. The story is partially told from Monchi's point of view and partially conveyed through nine included issues of "Coyote School News," which are printed to look like they came from an old-fashioned, purple-inked mimeograph. "Sandin's love and knowledge of this land and its history are evident," the *Kirkus Reviews* critic concluded, as she sketches with pictures and words the lives of the twelve students of the Coyote School. Observing that the book offers young readers a look at "Mexican traditions [that] have been part of the American cultural landscape for generations," *School Library Journal* reviewer Eve Ortega found *Coyote School News* "an entertaining bit of historical fiction."

BIOGRAPHICAL AND CRITICAL SOURCES:

PERIODICALS

Arizona Daily Star (Tucson, AZ), September 17, 2002, Bonnie Henry, interview with Sandin, p. B1.

Booklist, December 1, 1993, Carolyn Phelan, review of *The Other Alice: The Story of Alice Liddell and Alice in Wonderland,* pp. 686-687; July, 1995, Stephanie Zvirin, review of *Pioneer Bear: Based on a True Story,* p. 1885; November 1, 1996, Carolyn Phelan, review of *Boo and Baa in Windy Weather* and *Boo and Baa in a Party Mood,* pp. 507-508; April, 1998, Hazel Rochman, review of *As the Crow Flies,* p. 1334.

Boston Herald, April 24, 2000, Kristen Bradley, review of *Army of Two,* p. 16.

Bulletin of the Center for Children's Books, March, 1982, Zena Sutherland, review of *The Long Way to a New Land,* p. 138; July, 1995, Elizabeth Bush, review of *Pioneer Bear,* p. 397.

Horn Book, February, 1982, Nancy Sheridan, review of *The Long Way to a New Land,* p. 39; March-April, 1987, Hanna B. Zeiger, review of *Trouble at the Mines,* p. 212; September-October, 1989, Mary M. Burns, review of *The Long Way Westward,* p. 618; January-February, 1992, Mary M. Burns, review of *Showshoe Thompson,* p. 66; March-April, 1994, Ann A. Flowers, review of *The Other Alice,* p. 215; May-June, 1996, Maeve Visser Knoth, review of *A Bear for Miguel,* pp. 331-332.

Kirkus Reviews, November 15, 1981, pp. 1406-1407; August 15, 1989, review of *The Long Way Westward,* p. 1250; August 1, 2002, review of *Good Night, Animals,* p. 1121; July 1, 2003, review of *Coyote School News,* p. 914.

Publishers Weekly, April 10, 1987, review of *Trouble at the Mines,* p. 96; September 30, 1988, review of *Linnea's Windowsill Garden,* p. 64; August 25, 1989, review of *The Long Way Westward,* p. 63; January 19, 1990, review of *Linnea's Almanac,* p. 106; August 5, 1996, review of *Boo and Baa in Windy Weather* and *Boo and Baa in a Party Mood,* p. 440; April 8, 2002, review of *The Little Hippos' Adventure,* p. 225; July 28, 2003, review of *Coyote School News,* pp. 94-95.

Reading Teacher, October, 1989, Lee Galda, review of *The House of a Mouse,* pp. 66-71.

School Library Journal, December, 1981, review of *The Long Way to a New Land,* p. 75; April, 1987, Mary Beth Burgoyne, review of *Trouble at the Mines,* p. 102; February, 1988, Shirley Wilton, review of *Linnea in Monet's Garden,* p. 72; November, 1988, Frances E. Millhouser, review of *Linnea's Windowsill Garden,* p. 100; January, 1989, Kathleen Whalin, review of *The House of a Mouse,* p. 70; September, 1989, Sharron McElmeel, review of *The Long Way Westward,* p. 234; April, 1990, Amy Adler, review of *Linnea's Almanac,* p. 102; May, 1991, Carolyn Jenks, review of *Elliot's Extraordinary Cookbook,* p. 100; December, 1991, Barbara Chatton, review of *Always Wondering: Some Favorite Poems of Aileen Fisher,* pp. 109-110; January, 1992, Gale W. Sherman, review of *Snowshoe Thompson,* p. 104; December, 1993, Patricia A. Dollisch, review of *The Other Alice,* pp. 140-141; April, 1995, Marilyn Taniguchi, review of *Big Bear's Book: By Himself,* p. 130; October, 1995, Mary Ann Bursk, review of *Pioneer Bear,* p. 117; June, 1996, Gale W. Sherman, review of *A Bear for Miguel,* p. 92; July, 1997, Darla Remple, review of *Boo and Baa at Sea* and *Boo and Baa on a Cleaning Spree,* p. 70; June, 1998, Faith Brautigan, review of *As the Crow Flies,* pp. 124-125; April, 2002, Be Astengo, review of *The Little Hippos' Adventure,* p. 114; February, 2003, Kathy Piehl, review of *Good Night, Animals,* p. 102; April, 2003, Bina Williams, review of *The New Hippos,* pp. 130-131; September, 2003, Edith Ching, review of *Boris's Glasses,* p. 176; October, 2003, Eve Ortega, review of *Coyote School News,* p. 138.

ONLINE

Joan Sandin Web Site, http://www.authorsguild.org/ (February 27, 2004).*

* * *

SCHOTTER, Roni 1946-

PERSONAL: Born May 9, 1946, in New York, NY; son of Alan (a merchandise manager) and Edna (an artist) Goldgerg; married Richard Schotter; children: Jesse. *Ethnicity:* "Russian/Austrian/Polish/Romanian/American." *Education:* New York University, B.A., 1968; attended Carnegie Mellon University. *Hobbies and other interests:* Drawing, tennis, cross-country skiing, gardening, speaking French.

ADDRESSES: *Agent*—Susan Cohen, Writers House, 21 W. 26th St. New York, NY 10010. *E-mail*—ronisch@aol.com.

CAREER: Former editor with publishing houses; has taught writing at Queens College, City University of New York, and at Manhattanville College. Speaker,

Vassar College's Summer Institute in Children's Publishing, and at annual conferences of the Society of Children's Book Writers and Illustrators.

AWARDS, HONORS: National Jewish Book Award for best children's picture book, 1991, for *Hanukkah!;* Parents' Choice Award for *Captain Snap and the Children of Vinegar Lane; Hungry Mind Review* Award for *A Fruit and Vegetable Man;* Washington Irving Children's Choice Award for *F Is for Freedom* and *Nothing Ever Happens on 90th Street; Dreamland* and *A Fruit and Vegetable Man* were cited as Washington Irving Honor Book Awards; *Passover Magic* and *Nothing Ever Happens on 90th Street* named notable children's books by National Council of Teachers of Social Studies; *Dreamland* named an Irma Simonton Black Award honor book, Bank Street College of Education.

WRITINGS:

FOR YOUNG ADULTS

A Matter of Time, Collins (New York, NY), 1979.
Northern Fried Chicken, Philomel (New York, NY), 1983.
Rhoda, Straight and True, Lothrop, Lee & Shepard (New York, NY), 1986.
(With husband, Richard Schotter) *There's a Dragon About: A Winter's Revel,* illustrated by R. W. Alley, Orchard Books (New York, NY), 1994.
Nothing Ever Happens on 90th Street, illustrated by Kyrsten Brooker, Orchard Books (New York, NY), 1996.
F Is for Freedom, illustrated by C. B. Mordan, DK Ink (New York, NY), 2000.

FOR CHILDREN

Efan the Great, illustrated by Rodney Pate, Lothrop, Lee & Shepard (New York, NY), 1986.
Bunny's Night Out, illustrated by Margot Apple, Joy Street Books (Boston, MA), 1989.
Captain Snap and the Children of Vinegar Lane, illustrated by Marcia Sewall, Orchard Books (New York, NY), 1989.
Hanukkah!, illustrated by Marilyn Hafner, Joy Street Books (New York, NY), 1990, Little, Brown (Boston, MA), 2003.
A Fruit and Vegetable Man, illustrated by Jeannette Winter, Joy Street Books (New York, NY), 1993.
Warm at Home, illustrated by Dara Goldman, Maxwell (New York, NY), 1993.
When Crocodiles Clean Up, illustrated by Thor Wickstrom, Macmillan (New York, NY), 1993.
That Extraordinary Pig of Paris, illustrated by Dominic Catalano, Philomel (New York, NY), 1994.
Passover Magic, illustrated by Marilyn Hafner, Little, Brown (Boston, MA), 1995.
Dreamland, illustrated by Kevin Hawkes, Orchard Books (New York, NY), 1996.
Purim Play, illustrated by Marilyn Hafner, Little, Brown (Boston, MA), 1997.
Captain Bob Sets Sail, illustrated by Joe Cepeda, Atheneum (New York, NY), 2000.
Missing Rabbit, Clarion (New York, NY), 2002.
In The Piney Woods, Farrar, Straus (New York, NY), 2003.
Captain Bob Takes Flight, Atheneum (New York, NY), 2003.
Room for Rabbit, Houghton Mifflin (Boston, MA), 2003.
The World, illustrated by Susan Gallagher, Atheneum (New York, NY), 2004.

ADAPTATIONS: A Matter of Time was made into a sixty-minute *ABC Afterschool Special,* written by Paul W. Cooper, directed by Arthur Allan Seidelman, and produced by Martin Tahse, Learning Corp. of America (New York, NY), 1981. The special was awarded an Emmy in 1981 for outstanding children's entertainment special; *Captain Snap and the Children of Vinegar Lane, Dreamland, F is for Freedom,* and *Captain Bob Sets Sail* were adapted for the stage by Stages Theatre Company, Hopkins, Minnesota.

WORK IN PROGRESS: When the Wizzy Foot Goes Walking, illustrated by Mike Wohnoutka, Dutton (New York, NY), 2006; *Passover,* illustrated by Erin Eitter Kono, Little, Brown (Boston, MA); *Doo-Wop Pop,* illustrated by Brian Collier, HarperCollins (New York, NY).

SIDELIGHTS: An award-winning writer of fiction and nonfiction for young people, Roni Schotter has written novels for teenagers and picture books for small children.

Schotter's first young adult novel, *A Matter of Time,* was published in 1979. The novel is a "moving" story, according to a *Booklist* reviewer, that has as its protagonist a high school senior, Lisl Gilbert, whose vivacious, artistic mother is dying of cancer. To complicate the emotional background, Lisl has always felt inferior to her mother; now she realizes that not only is her mother vulnerable, but that her mother has felt unloved and inferior at times. Lisl sorts out her tangled feelings with the help of sympathetic friends, relatives, and a social worker. The *Booklist* reviewer described Lisl as "believable and appealing" and asserted that the way in which she is depicted as maturing rapidly under tragic circumstances is "convincing." A *Horn Book* reviewer lauded Schotter's "honest" and "straightforward" handling of the broad and difficult themes of life and death in *A Matter of Time.* A dissenting opinion came from Cyrisse Jaffee, of *School Library Journal,* who argued that the resolution of conflicts was too pat and, for adult readers at least, obviously tied to current psychological theories. Nevertheless, Jaffee called the book "reassuring and positive." The book was ultimately adapted for television, being made into an *ABC Afterschool Special* and winning the Emmy Award for outstanding children's entertainment special.

Schotter's next venture into the young adult market was *Northern Fried Chicken,* whose heroine, Betsy Bergman, is a shy Jewish girl living in 1962 in Providence, Rhode Island. *Northern Fried Chicken* traces Betsy's involvement in civil rights protests, detailing the personal growth that results from her participation in the movement. A *Bulletin of the Center for Children's Books* reviewer, although assessing the pace of the novel as slow and uneven, applauded it for providing "a touching picture of the way in which devotion to a cause can bring a reclusive individual to active participation." The characters and their relationships, the *Bulletin of the Center for Children's Books* critic wrote, were skillfully portrayed. A *Booklist* reviewer was not enthusiastic about Schotter's characterizations, but praised *Northern Fried Chicken* as an "effective and true" portrayal of the time and place in which it was set; similarly, a contributor to *Horn Book* declared that the novel "evokes the era's feeling of hope and of change."

Three years later, in 1986, Schotter followed with another young adult novel, *Rhoda, Straight and True,* in which the title character, a twelve-year-old girl in Brooklyn in the summer of 1953, realizes that appearances—such as those of a huge family of scruffy-looking neighbors—are not reliable when assessing a person's character. A commentator for *Publishers Weekly* felt the moral was a bit "heavyhanded," but added, "the sense of locale is nicely drawn, with original characters and humor rounding out a pleasant story." A critic for *Booklist* praised the "strong, sure characterizations," "careful plotting," and vivid setting in *Rhoda, Straight and True.*

During the late 1980s and early 1990s the children's book market proved highly successful for Schotter. Her first children's book, *Efan the Great,* was "[a] touching and unusually substantial Christmas story," in the words of a *Bulletin of the Center for Children's Books* reviewer. Ten-year-old Efan, who lives in a poor neighborhood, wants to buy a Christmas tree with his life savings of six dollars and sixty-three cents. Finding the prices of trees too high, he agrees to work for a tree-seller, and to be paid with his pick of the trees at the end of the day. When the tree he picks is too big to fit into his apartment, Efan leaves it outside and decorates it for all to see. A *Publishers Weekly* reviewer called the tale "heartwarming" and "jubilantly told." A *Bulletin for the Center for Children's Books* reviewer asserted that "Efan's emotions are varied, genuine, and set into a context of vividly projected secondary characters." Schotter's 1989 book, *Captain Snap and the Children of Vinegar Lane,* tells the simple story of a group of children who are initially afraid of an old man, who, at first glance, appears odd and different from everyone else in the neighborhood, but who turns out to be an artist with recycled objects. The children show their courage and independent thinking by befriending him, depsite their narrow-thinking advice of their elders. A *New York Times Book Review* critic responded favorably to *Captain Snap,* and a *Kirkus Reviews* critic offered praise for the book's "engaging detail and the enthusiasm of a compelling storyteller." In 1989 Schotter turned to animals as characters in her work *Bunny's Night Out,* in which Bunny, who hates bedtime, leaves his room to explore the world. Although Bunny finds the night world busy and full of interesting creatures, he discovers that he prefers his warm, safe bed. A critic for *School Library Journal* termed *Bunny's Night Out* a "cheerful morality tale," while Ellen Mandel of *Booklist* applauded it as "perfect for settling restless youngsters into sweet dreams."

In Schotter's 1993 book, *Warm at Home,* Bunny has a cold and complains that there is nothing to do. By using his imagination, Bunny eventually creates a long list of things to do (mostly involving vegetables). A *Publishers Weekly* reviewer called *Warm at Home* "a total charmer," elaborating, "An especially endearing tone . . . permeates all of Schotter's tale, which along the way celebrates a particularly active imagination and a quietly accepting mother." Karen James of *School Library Journal* called Bunny "the embodiment of any young child looking for amusement." Schotter returned to human characters in *A Fruit and Vegetable Man* in which longtime grocer Ruby Rubinstein, who has been tending his stand for fifty years, falls ill, and is aided by young Asian immigrant Sun Ho and his family. Reviewing a *Fruit and Vegetable Man,* a *Publishers Weekly* reviewer responded favorably, praising the "sweet sense of continuity" in the story's portrayal of generational and cultural transition in immigrant businesses. The book was, she asserted, "[a]s irresistible as a ripe peach." *School Library Journal* reviewer Cynthia K. Richey also applauded this "satisfying story about taking pride in one's work and helping others," and Hazel Rochman of *Booklist* praised the "unaffected" writing.

The end of 1993 saw the publication of *When Crocodiles Clean Up.* The story is about a crocodile mother who gives her four little crocodile children thirty minutes to clean up their room. They begin playing instead and when they hear their mother returning, they frantically and successfully begin cleaning, which includes gobbling down their very last toy before their mother appears. A *School Library Journal* reviewer called *When Crocodiles Clean Up* "full of laughs" and theorized that "children will recognize their own behavior as they enjoy the antics of the crocodile kids."

That Extraordinary Pig of Paris features Monsieur Cochon, a vegetarian pig with a more-than-healthy appetite, especially for pastries. He loves to eat, and becomes so fat that he is slated for slaughter by the evil butchers. Fortunately, he is saved by a variety of animal friends. A *Publishers Weekly* reviewer called *That Extraordinary Pig* "a pleasing romp." The book contains a glossary of French words, which, in *Booklist* reviewer Rochman's view, helped create a sense of "world." Ann W. Moore for *School Library Journal* responded negatively to the book, faulting what she termed a "tedious, wordy," and humorless narrative. Moore also felt that Schotter's use of French words would be difficult for the intended audience.

Beginning with the 1990 *Hanukkah!,* Schotter wrote a series of books about Jewish holidays. *Hanukkah!* contains "free and occasionally rhyming verse," according to a reviewer in the *Bulletin of the Center for Children's Books,* and further described one family's celebration of the winter festival that commemorates the victory of the Maccabees against their Greek rulers. James Howe of the *New York Times Book Review* faulted the inconsistency of the verse form, assessing the text as "cheerful," but imperfectly crafted. The book received the National Jewish Book Award for best children's picture book on a Jewish theme. Schotter returned to the topic of Jewish holidays in 1995 with *Passover Magic,* a portrayal of one family's seder dinner. The emphasis of the story is on colorful characters, such as amateur magician Uncle Harry, as well as on holiday lore. The result, in the view of a *Publishers Weekly* reviewer, was a warm, original story filled with "intricate, often amusing details," and engagingly recounted by its narrator, daughter Molly. Stephanie Zvirin of *Booklist* held similar views, calling the book "very charming." Schotter's third book on Jewish holidays was the 1997 *Purim Play.* Like *Hanukkah!* and *Passover Magic,* it was illustrated by Marilyn Hafner, whose pictures for Schotter's stories have garnered considerable praise.

Schotter's 1996 book, titled *Dreamland,* was also well received. The tale revolves around a family of tailors, some of whom possess an abundance of common sense and some who do not. Among the latter group are young Theo, who sketches plans for fantastic machines, and his uncle Gurney, who moves out west to seek his fortune. At a time when the family business is failing, Gurney writes back to Theo, asking him for exact instructions on how to build his machines. Gurney turns the machines into an amusement park. A *Publishers Weekly* reviewer wrote that the story was "both fantastic and credible," and praised its "eloquent, image-studded prose." Carolyn Phelan for *Booklist* noted a lack of credibility in the narrative, but characterized the story as appealing to "dreamers who long for a brighter reality." A *New York Times Book Review* critic applauded *Dreamland* as a "splendid" book, asserting that "Schotter deftly builds suspense to a wondrous climactic scene in which Theo's family sees Uncle Gurney's project." Pointing out, as well, that Schotter is the granddaughter of a tailor, the reviewer observed that "her engaging phrases . . . spring from a tailor's world."

Another children's story, *Nothing Ever Happens on 90th Street,* focuses again on the importance of imagination, and encouraging children to write their own stories. Facing a writing assignment for school, Eva, the main character, sits outside her house in the city and watches the people on her street. She receives advice from several neighbors and witnesses some extraordinary events, including a bicycle accident, in which a ballerina falls in love with a pizza delivery man. A *New York Times Book Review* critic enjoyed the "clever sprinkles" of characters to create a "spicy ethnic stewpot." A critic for *Publishers Weekly* observed that Schotter has "a knack for creating dramatic situations filled with romantic characters."

With *Captain Bob Sets Sail* and *Captain Bob Takes Flight,* Schotter recounts the adventures of a young boy with a vivid imagination. In *Captain Bob Sets Sail,* he pictures himself as a pirate captain within the confines of his bubble-filled bathtub, while in *Captain Bob Takes Flight,* he is a pilot whose mission is to clean up his room. Bob's pirate adventures are "a series of vignettes energetically describing Bob's bath play from start to finish," Tim Arnold in *Booklist* explained. These adventures make for an "irresistible bathtime book," as a *Publishers Weekly* critic noted. In *Captain Bob Takes Flight,* Bob imagines himself as a pilot soaring around his room, cleaning up the mess along the way. Diane Foote of *Booklist* remarked that Schotter makes "cleaning one's room seem less of a chore in this colorfully illustrated story." A critic for *Kirkus Reviews* found *Captain Bob Takes Flight* to be "even more delightful than the first" book, as well as being "refreshingly clever."

Schotter's *Missing Rabbit* concerns a young girl whose parents have divorced. Young Kara is shuttled between the two parents, living with each of them for a time under a joint custody arrangement. When she decides to leave her toy rabbit at her father's house to ease the pain of goodbye, she finds that she begins to miss her rabbit once she is at her mother's house. Leaving the rabbit at her mother's house, she misses him once she is back at her father's. The rabbit begins to wonder: "Where do I live?" The book raises the disturbing question, as a critic for *Kirkus Reviews* put it, of "just where one does belong in a divorced family of two households." Susan Weitz in *School Library Journal* believed that, "for young children dealing with divorce—and their parents—this book is a winner." In *Room for Rabbit,* the sequel to *Missing Rabbit,* Kara's father has remarried and she and rabbit wonder if there will be room for them in Kara's father's home and heart. Kathleen Kelly Macmillan in *School Library Journal* wrote, "In this delightful follow-up, Schotter again explored issues related to divorce and remarriage. . . . Children will find this tale reassuring." Gillian Engberst in *Booklist* commented, "As in *Missing Rabbit* Schotter and Moore explore the complicated sadness of divorce within a story that's as reassuring and snug as a favorite blanket. . . . A good read aloud for children who are struggling with their own feelings of displacement."

Schotter's *F Is for Freedom,* for young children, recounts the story of ten-year-old Manda who upon investigating strange noises in her house at night, learns that her home is a stop on the underground railroad. Manda's precious time with Hannahm, the ten-year-old escaped slave who hides out in Manda's home, teaches her much about both friendship and the power and value of literacy.

Schotter told *CA:* "I've always felt filled with wonder at the world. Inside, I feel very much like a child. In fact, I often feel like I'm only pretending to be a grown up and that if I'm not careful, the real grown ups will find me out. So, it's less of a stretch for me to write about adults and how they feel. In addition, I've always been shy. My shyness, though at time exhausting, is helpful. It keeps me ever watchful, which helps my writing and often gives me ideas for my stories. Writers, after all, are spies—eavesdropping on conversations, carefully observing the details of what someone is wearing, or noticing how the wrinkles under that old woman's eyes look—like lace? Or maybe a spider's web? I love paying attention to the details of life—noticing how something smells or tastes or feels—and then just jotting it all down in my notebook. I also spend a lot of time daydreaming—using my imagination (like many of my characters do) wondering about people, life, the world, trying to make up answers to the many questions I have about everything. I'm always wondering how things would be if . . . and also, if only. . ."

"I love working with words. I love playing with them and making discoveries while I'm playing with them—like the delicious way certain words sound when they rub up against each other, and the particular, wonderful things they can mean. I love the power of words and how powerful I feel when I use them well. Often, I don't know exactly how I feel about something until after I've read what I've written. Like my character Eva in *Nothing Ever Happens on 90th Street,* I even get to change reality simply by asking 'what if?' and making up a story by way of explanation."

"When I speak to children about how I write, I show them my notebooks so they can see how much I struggle when I write. I start with a small notebook in which I take notes—my ideas, feelings, and observations. When I'm ready to begin a book, I buy a large notebook and begin writing by hand. I love to show children how messy my notebooks are—how much I change, delete, add. My first drafts are usually pretty bad, but once I have something down it gives me great pleasure to adjust, alter, tinker, add, and subtract. In other words, I love rewriting! That's where I start to feel proud of myself—as I polish and sharpen my words and improve the storytelling. When my handwritten manuscript becomes too difficult to read, I type it on the computer, then print up a hard copy, then continue the writing process. With a crisp sheet of freshly-typed words I can usually see what doesn't work even more clearly, and so I continue to rewrite. Then I retype and the process continues through many, many revisions. As my work improves, I feel prouder and prouder of myself."

"Most of my ideas come from events or occurrences that echo inside my heart. I have to feel something intensely in order to write. As I've said, I'm always paying attention to the world. When something resonates inside me in a particular way, I find I have an idea. The characters in my books and the situations they find themselves in could be me."

"I love writing for children. I love the fact that I'm forced to use my imagination on a daily basis. I treasure the various components of what I do—children, imagination, words, books. I am fortunate."

BIOGRAPHICAL AND CRITICAL SOURCES:

PERIODICALS

Booklist, November 15, 1979, review of *A Matter of Time,* p. 495; November 1, 1983, review of *Northern Fried Chicken,* p. 404; October 1, 1986, p. 275; October 15, 1986, pp. 356-357; April 15, 1989, p. 1471; September 1, 1993, p. 71; January 15, 1994, pp. 938-939; March 1, 1995, pp. 1249-1250; April 1, 1996, Carolyn Phelan, review of *Dreamland,* p. 1374; March 1, 1997, Ilene Cooper, review of *Nothing Ever Happens on 90th Street,* p. 1173; February 1, 1998, Ilene Cooper, review of *Purim Play,* p. 923; July, 2000, Tim Arnold, review of *Captain Bob Sets Sail,* p. 2043; March 1, 2003, Gillian Engberg, review of *Room for Rabbit,* p. 1204; March 15, 2003, Diane Foote, review of *Captain Bob Takes Flight,* p. 1334.

Bulletin of the Center for Children's Books, February, 1984, review of *Northern Fried Chicken,* p. 117; December, 1986, p. 75; November, 1990, review of *Hanukkah!,* pp. 69-70.

Horn Book, February, 1980, review of *A Matter of Time,* pp. 65-66; February, 1984, review of *Northern Fried Chicken,* p. 65; January, 1991, p. 95.

Kirkus Reviews, April 1, 1989, p. 554; February 15, 2002, review of *Missing Rabbit,* p. 265; February 1, 2003, review of *In the Piney Woods,* p. 238; March 15, 2003, review of *Captain Bob Takes Flight,* p. 478.

New York Times Book Review, September 17, 1989, p. 39; December 9, 1990, James Howe, review of *Hanukkah!,* p. 31; April 13, 1997; August 3, 1997.

Publishers Weekly, August 22, 1986, p. 99; September 26, 1986, pp. 75-76; March 8, 1993, p. 77; September 20, 1993, p. 71; April 11, 1994, p. 64; March 20, 1995, pp. 60-61; March 11, 1996, review of *Dreamland,* p. 64; February 3, 1997, review of *Nothing Ever Happens on 90th Street,* p. 106; February 23, 1998, review of *Purim Play,* p. 67; May 8, 2000, review of *Captain Bob Sets Sail,* p. 220; January 21, 2002, review of *Missing Rabbit,* p. 88; November 25, 2002, review of *In the Piney Woods,* p. 67; February 24, 2003, review of *Captain Bob Takes Flight,* p. 74.

School Library Journal, December, 1979, Cyrisse Jaffee, review of *A Matter of Time,* p. 92; July, 1989, p. 76; June, 1993, pp. 88-89; October, 1993, p. 112; December, 1993, p. 93; July, 1994, pp. 88-89; March, 1997, John Peters, review of *Nothing Ever Happens on 90th Street,* p. 166; April, 1998, Libby K. White, review of *Purim Play,* p. 110; December, 2000, William McLoughlin, review of *F Is for Freedom,* p. 125; April, 2002, Susan Weitz, review of *Missing Rabbit,* p. 122.

ONLINE

Roni Schotter's Home Page, http://members.aol.com/ronisch/ (April 14, 2003).

SCOTT, Beth (Bailey) 1922-1994

PERSONAL: Born February 6, 1922, in Bryn Mawr, PA; died 1994; daughter of Carl C. (a civil and mechanical engineer) and Ethel (a writer; maiden name, Colvin) Bailey; married Lawrence W. Scott (a university professor), March 19, 1949; children: Rosemary Scott Tyson, Jeffery, Jonathan. *Education:* Attended Guilford College, 1940-43; University of Pennsylvania, B.A., 1944; graduate study at Kansas State University, 1950-53, and Oregon State University, 1953-54.

CAREER: Editor, educator, lecturer, and freelance writer. American Society of Testing Materials, Philadelphia, PA, editor's assistant, 1944-46; Indianhead District of Adult, Vocational, and Technical Program of Western Wisconsin, New Richmond, part-time creative writing teacher, 1970-74; University of Wisconsin—River Falls, lecturer in journalism, 1983-85. Full-time freelance writer until 1994. President of St. Croix Valley chapter of American Civil Liberties Union of Wisconsin, 1983-86.

MEMBER: Authors Guild, Authors League of America.

AWARDS, HONORS: Haunted Heartland was included on the list of readers' favorite books in *English Journal*'s 1987 Books for Young Adults Poll.

WRITINGS:

(With Michael Norman) *Haunted Wisconsin,* Stanton & Lee (Sauk City, WI), 1980, revised and updated edition, Trails Books (Black Earth, WI), 2001.

(With Michael Norman) *Haunted Heartland,* Stanton & Lee (Madison, WI), 1985.

(With Michael Norman) *Haunted America,* Tor (New York, NY), 1994.

(With Michael Norman) *Historic Haunted America,* Tor (New York, NY), 1995.

(With Michael Norman) *Haunted Heritage: The Definitive Collection of North American Ghost Stories,* Forge (New York, NY), 2002.

Contributor of articles, fiction, and verse to American, Canadian, and Japanese periodicals.

SIDELIGHTS: Prior to her death in early 1994, Beth Scott entertained readers with hundreds of stories about haunted America. It would be impossible to mention Scott without also mentioning her longtime writing partner, Michael Norman. Together, the two labored to anthologize ghost stories and paranormal tales from all over the United States and Canada. Years of researching documents, conducting interviews, and traveling throughout North America introduced Scott and Norman to a plethora of ghost stories and legends. They have shared many of these spine-tingling tales in their series of "Haunted" books.

The chilling chapters of Scott and Norman's "Haunted" series began with *Haunted Wisconsin,* which serves up "true" stories from around the Badger State. The legends are recounted through interviews, newspaper articles, archives, and other sources. A review of the updated and revised edition of *Haunted Wisconsin* on the *Prairie Ghosts* Web site praised the "more than sixty stories of ghosts and hauntings" and called the book "a must-have for all ghost enthusiasts." The scarefest continues in Scott and Norman's *Haunted Heartland.* This collection focuses on terrifying tales from the American Midwest. The book includes more than 150 of what the Time Warner Books Web site called "true, flesh-tingling stories of supernatural America."

In *Haunted America,* Norman and Scott include at least one eerie legend from each of the fifty states and some of the Canadian provinces. Again the authors focus on "true" stories, weaving newspaper articles, interviews, and other sources into the narrative to lend authenticity to the tales. According to *Library Journal*'s Eloise R. Hitchcock, "The stories recount sightings of ghostly apparitions and mysterious happenings." Keith Dixon wrote in the *New York Times Book Review* that while there are "a few spots where the authors seem to be reaching to find a tale for each state, the stories are vibrant enough to hold the reader's attention."

Historic Haunted America ventures into the past to dig up some old-fashioned ghost stories. As with *Haunted America,* all fifty states and some Canadian provinces are represented in the anthology. This volume provides eye-witness accounts of ghost sightings in hotels, theaters, trains, and other common locations. Among the bone-chilling ghosts that appear in the collection are soldiers, lovers, and murder victims. The end result of eighteen years of research by the authors is, as Ann E. Cohen commented in *Library Journal,* "mesmerizing, spine-tingling—and not to be missed by any folklore collection."

Scott and Norman continued their writing partnership after the publication of *Historic Haunted America.* However, the next volume in the series, *Haunted Heritage: The Definitive Collection of North American Ghost Stories,* was published several years after Scott's death. *Haunted Heritage* maintains the tradition of the other "Haunted" volumes. The book recounts tales that have been passed on, generation to generation, by word of mouth and memory throughout all of North America. Again the authors lace the narrative with eyewitness accounts, newspaper articles, and other sources that lend the stories an air of truth and authenticity. This volume includes a section called "Haunts of Ivy," which explores ghostly sightings on college campuses.

Scott once told *CA:* "I write because it is the thing I do best. I love words. From the time that I learned my letters and could hold a pencil, I've written something (even one sentence) every day. When I'm writing, I am often miserable when the words don't flow, but when I'm not writing I am *more* miserable. Geoffrey Chaucer said it well: 'The life so short, the craft so long to learn.' I write to entertain, and if my work brings a smile, a tear, or a 'quiet remembrance of things past' to the reader, I feel richly rewarded."

BIOGRAPHICAL AND CRITICAL SOURCES:

PERIODICALS

Booklist, November 15, 1985, review of *Haunted Heartland,* p. 452; October 15, 1995, Joe Collins, review of *Historic Haunted America,* p. 365.

Chicago, December, 1985, Lesley Sussman, review of *Haunted Heartland,* p. 150.

Come-All-Ye, summer, 1990, review of *Haunted Wisconsin,* p. 13.

Detroit Free Press, October 11, 1985.

English Journal, January, 1988, John W. Conner and Kathleen M. Tessmer, review of *Haunted Heartland,* p. 101.

Fantasy Review, January, 1986, review of *Haunted Heartland,* p. 28.

Fate, October, 1981, Jerome Clark, review of *Haunted Wisconsin,* p. 140.

Journal of the West, April, 1987, Fred W. Viehe, review of *Haunted Heartland,* pp. 111-112.

Kirkus Reviews, September 15, 2002, review of *Haunted Heritage,* p. 1370.

Library Journal, November 1, 1994, Eloise R. Hitchcock, review of *Haunted America,* p. 82; November 1, 1995, Ann E. Cohen, review of *Historic Haunted America,* p. 72.

New York Times Book Review, November 20, 1994, Keith Dixon, review of *Haunted America,* p. 22.

Reference and Research Book News, September, 1995, review of *Haunted America,* p. 2.

School Library Journal, March, 1986, review of *Haunted Heartland,* p. 180.

ONLINE

Prairie Ghosts Web site, http://www.prairieghosts.com/wi_books.html/ (April 2, 2004), review of *Haunted Wisconsin.*

RiverTowns.net Web site, http://www.rivertowns.net/ (October 15, 2002), "UW-RF Professor Relates Campus Ghost Stories," discussion of *Haunted Heritage.*

Time Warner Books Web site, http://www.twbookmark.com/ (April 2, 2004), review of *Haunted Heartland.**

* * *

SCOTT, Elaine 1940-

PERSONAL: Born June 20, 1940, in Philadelphia, PA; daughter of George Jobling (a banker) and Ethel (Smith) Watts; married Parker Scott (a geophysical engineer), May 16, 1959; children: Cynthia Ellen, Susan Elizabeth. *Education:* Attended Southern Methodist University, 1957-59, and Southern Methodist University and University of Houston, 1979-81. *Politics:* Independent. *Religion:* Methodist. *Hobbies and other interests:* Sailing, travel, reading, teaching, learning new things.

ADDRESSES: Home—13042 Taylorcrest, Houston, TX 77079. *Agent*—Susan Cohen, Writer's House, 21 W. 26th St., New York, NY 10010. *E-mail*—Scottent@aol.com.

Elaine Scott

CAREER: Writer, 1975—. Teacher of leadership workshops for Texas Conference of the United Methodist Church, 1978; teacher of writing workshops at Southwest Writer's Conference, Houston, TX, 1979, and at Trinity University, San Antonio, TX, 1980. Volunteer teacher of leadership workshops at United Methodist Church, Houston, 1959-77; volunteer publicity director for Camp Fire Girls of America, 1973-74. Board member and chair of committee on international adoptions, Homes of St. Mark (a private nonprofit adoption agency), Houston, TX. Board member, teacher of adults, Chapelwood United Methodist Church, Houston, TX, 1975—.

MEMBER: Authors Guild, Authors League of America, Society of Children's Book Writers and Illustrators.

AWARDS, HONORS: Parenting Magazine Reading Magic Award and American Library Association Notable Book citation, both for *Ramona: Behind the Scenes of a Television Show; School Library Journal* Best Book of the Year, *Booklist* Editor's Choice, and *Voice of Youth Advocates* Nonfiction Honor List, all 1995, and *Choice* Children's Literature Choices List, 1996, all for *Adventure in Space: The Flight to Fix the Hubble;* American Institute of Physics Award and Outstanding Science Trade Book, National Science Teachers Association, both 1999, both for *Close Encounters: Exploring the Universe with the Hubble Space Telescope;* one of thirteen featured authors in "Laura Bush Celebrates America's Authors," part of the extended Inaugural Activities on January 19, 2001; featured author at the 2002 West Texas Book and Author Festival in Abilene, TX.

WRITINGS:

CHILDREN'S NONFICTION

Adoption, F. Watts (New York, NY), 1980.

The Banking Book, illustrated by Kathie Abrams, Warne (New York, NY), 1981.

Doodlebugging: The Treasure Hunt for Oil, Warne (New York, NY), 1982.

Oil!: Getting It, Shipping It, Selling It, Warne (New York, NY), 1984.

Stocks and Bonds, Profits and Losses, F. Watts (New York, NY), 1985.

Ramona: Behind the Scenes of a Television Show, Morrow (New York, NY), 1988.

Kidnapped: Could It Happen to You?, F. Watts (New York, NY), 1988.

Safe in the Spotlight: The Dawn Animal Agency and the Sanctuary for Animals, Morrow (New York, NY), 1991.

Look Alive: Behind the Scenes of an Animated Film, Morrow (New York, NY), 1992.

From Microchips to Movie Stars: The Making of Super Mario Brothers, Hyperion (New York, NY), 1993.

Funny Papers: Behind the Scenes of the Comics, Morrow (New York, NY), 1993.

Adventure in Space: The Flight to Fix the Hubble, Hyperion (New York, NY), 1995.

Movie Magic: Behind the Scenes with Special Effects (photo essay), Morrow (New York, NY), 1995.

Twins!, Atheneum (New York, NY), 1998.

Close Encounters: Exploring the Universe with the Hubble Space Telescope, Hyperion (New York, NY), 1998.

Friends!, Atheneum (New York, NY), 2000.

Penguins and Polar Bears: Why the Arctic and Antarctic Are Poles Apart, Viking, (New York, NY), 2004.

YOUNG ADULT FICTION

Choices, Morrow (New York, NY), 1988.

WORK IN PROGRESS: "An as-yet untitled YA novel based on Picasso's masterpiece of his Rose Period, *The Family Saltimbanque,* which hangs at the National Gallery in Washington, DC, to be published . . . by Watson-Guptill."

SIDELIGHTS: Award-winning author Elaine Scott writes nonfiction for young readers, particularly on outer space and other science topics. Among her most popular titles are *Adventure in Space: The Flight to Fix the Hubble* and *Close Encounters: Exploring the Universe with the Hubble Space Telescope.*

Adventure in Space recounts the 1993 NASA mission to repair the Hubble Space Telescope. The Hubble had been placed in orbit around the Earth so that it could see into the universe from a vantage point above the distortions of the Earth's atmosphere. But the space telescope had not been installed correctly before launch, limiting its use, and so the 1993 mission was sent up to set things right. Scott's book details the original launch of the Hubble, its subsequent problems, the backgrounds of the astronauts involved in the repair mission, and the challenges and achievements of the mission itself. Carolyn Phelan in *Booklist* explained that *Adventure in Space* offered "children a rare look behind the scenes at NASA" and was "an excellent presentation of the mission." The book has won several awards, including a place on the *Voice of Youth Advocates* Nonfiction Honor List.

Close Encounters is a companion volume to *Adventure in Space,* this time detailing the accomplishments of the repaired Hubble Space Telescope. With its powerful telescope and unobstructed view of space, the Hubble has been able to provide astronomers with the clearest photographs of distant stars and planets ever seen before. A *Horn Book* reviewer noted that Scott "explains what is being learned from the spectacular photographs." She particularly explains how the space telescope has enabled scientists to better examine such things as the birth of stars, black holes, and planet formation. "Scott's comparisons and examples make highly complex information easier to understand," according to Karen Hutt in *Booklist.*

In January of 2001, Scott participated in "Laura Bush Celebrates America's Authors," part of the inaugural festivities surrounding the new president, George W. Bush. As a participant, Scott met with the First Lady and the President, had a luncheon with the other invited authors, and spent time in a local Washington, D.C., elementary school reading from her books and talking with the children. Scott told Cynthia Leitich Smith in an interview posted at the Children's Literature Resources Web site: "I was deeply honored to be part of the Inaugural Activities that Mrs. Bush sponsored. In addition to enjoying a weekend full of heart-thumping patriotism, it was wonderful to know that our First Lady is a woman who is deeply committed to children, books, and literacy. The thirteen children's authors who were part of the program spent an afternoon visiting Washington, D.C., public schools, and I left with hope in my heart. Though poor, and with few resources, the teachers in those schools were full of determination that their children succeed, and the children were full of the belief that they could do so." In an article posted at her own Web site, Scott concluded that the inaugural event was "one of the most exciting experiences I have ever had."

Scott once told *CA* that she first considered a career as an author at the age of ten: "Our teacher decided on a dreary, early March afternoon that the entire class would write a poem during recess instead of sliding around the frozen turf of the school yard. Along with the rest of the class, I agonized as I stared at the blank piece of paper that lay in front of me on the desk. What to write about? What did I have to say about anything? Any writer, no matter how young, writes about what he knows, and I was no exception. That very morning as I left for school, I noticed the sorry state of the snowman I had built the week before. The thirty-two-degrees-plus temperature was playing havoc with his physique, pulling him steadily toward his demise, so I wrote my poem called 'A Tale of Woe' about three snowmen whose fate it was to melt with the coming of spring. I got an 'A' for my efforts and that grade thrilled me, but not nearly as much as the thrill I received when I heard that my teacher had entered my poem in a state-wide contest in Pennsylvania, and it won second prize." Her creative writing career was put on hold when her family moved to Texas a few months later, "and for the next twenty-five years I wrote nothing creative other than term papers and letters home," Scott related. "I never really thought about writing for children until I went to the Southwest Writer's Conference at the University of Houston. Because of a lull in my schedule, I dropped into a workshop on writing nonfiction for children. As I listened to an editor speak about the need for good philosophical books for children, the idea for my book

Adoption began to form in my subconscious. By the end of the day, the idea had forced itself into my conscious thought and was no longer merely an idea, but a tangible form—a rough outline of the book. It was published in 1980 by Franklin Watts, and I have continued to write for children ever since.

"As I think about the books I have written up to now, I realize I haven't traveled too far from the child of ten who wrote about her melting snowmen. I still write about subjects I know and care about. I believe that without caring (and caring can mean hating, as well as loving) about his subject, the writer is in real danger of becoming nothing but a flesh and blood word processor—spitting out facts and nothing more. I think a writer should share himself, as well as his information, with his reader. . . . For me that is the essence of writing—it's really a dialogue between me and my reader. I am grateful for the reader, and out of that gratitude comes a willingness to share myself and my experience of life with him."

More recently, Scott told *CA:* "I . . . remember the tremendous influence of my favorite teacher, who taught me for both fifth and sixth grade. His name is Paul Wilson, from Abington, PA. I was recently reunited with him, and I cannot describe the joy of being able to thank him in person for all he did for a nine-and ten-year-old girl so long ago.

"My writing process is somewhat prosaic. Ideas come first, followed by my research, followed by the process itself. I write, and rewrite, and rewrite! I often say that I love the time between sending a manuscript off to the editor and waiting for his or her notes to be returned, the best. It's a nice limbo period between the writing and the rewriting. Truthfully, I love rewriting and polishing.

"I'm tempted to use the old cliché about books being a writer's children, and that is true. However, some books demand more of your attention than others. The new YA novel about Picasso's painting of the Saltimbanques was a grand adventure to research, and I loved doing it. And I loved the research for *Penguins and Polar Bears* too. Doing research is like going on a treasure hunt. You never know what gems you will find.

"I hope my books will cause readers to pause and think, wonder, question. I frequently get responses like, 'I didn't know that!' Hooray! That's exactly what I wanted to hear."

BIOGRAPHICAL AND CRITICAL SOURCES:

PERIODICALS

Booklist, July, 1995, Carolyn Phelan, review of *Adventure in Space: The Flight to Fix the Hubble,* p. 1879; February 15, 1996, Stephanie Zvirin, review of *Movie Magic: Behind the Scenes with Special Effects,* p. 1018; October 15, 1996, Jeanette Larson, review of audiocassette edition of *Adventure in Space,* p. 445; August, 1997, Barbara Baskin, review of audiocassette edition of *Safe in the Spotlight: The Dawn Animal Agency and the Sanctuary for Animals,* p. 1920; May 15, 1998, Karen Hutt, review of *Close Encounters: Exploring the Universe with the Hubble Space Telescope,* p. 1625, and Carolyn Phelan, review of *Twins!,* p. 1628; May 15, 2000, Shelley Townsend-Hudson, review of *Friends!,* p. 1746.

Horn Book, July-August, 1998, Margaret A. Bush, review of *Close Encounters,* p. 516.

Houston Chronicle, November 30, 1980; January 8, 1981.

Profile, August, 1982.

Publishers Weekly, June 15, 1992, review of *Look Alive: Behind the Scenes of an Animated Film,* p. 105; May 22, 2000, review of *Friends!,* p. 92.

School Library Journal, May, 2000, Susan Hepler, review of *Friends!,* p. 164.

Texas Association for Childhood Education News, fall, 1981.

ONLINE

Elaine Scott's Home Page, http://www.elainescott.com/ (April 14, 2003).

* * *

SHARRATT, Nick 1962-

PERSONAL: Born August 9, 1962, in London, England; son of Michael John (a brewer) and Jill Alexandra (Davison) Sharratt. *Education:* Saint Martin's School of Art (London, England), B.A. (with honors), 1984.

ADDRESSES: *Home*—Gloucestershire, England. *Agent*—c/o Author Mail, Candlewick Press, 2067 Massachusetts Ave., Cambridge, MA 02140.

CAREER: Children's book illustrator and author.

AWARDS, HONORS: Under Fives Book Prize (3-5 nonfiction category), SHE/W. H. Smith Award, 1995, for *Ketchup on Your Cornflakes?;* Sheffield Children's Book Award, 1997, for *A Cheese and Tomato Spider;* Gold Winner, Best First Book, *Parents* magazine, for *Twinkle, Twinkle, Little Star;* Best Children's Book selection, *Independent,* 2001, for *Vicky Angel.*

WRITINGS:

FOR CHILDREN; SELF-ILLUSTRATED

Look What I Found!, Walker (London, England), 1991, Candlewick Press (Cambridge, MA), 1992.

Monday Run-Day, Candlewick Press (Cambridge, MA), 1992.

The Green Queen, Candlewick Press (Cambridge, MA), 1992.

I Look Like This, Candlewick Press (Cambridge, MA), 1992.

Snazzy Aunties, Walker (London, England), 1993, Candlewick Press (Cambridge, MA), 1994.

Don't Put Your Finger in the Jelly, Nelly!, Andre Deutsch (London, England), 1993, Scholastic (New York, NY), 1997.

Mrs. Pirate, Walker (London, England), Candlewick Press (Cambridge, MA), 1994.

My Mum and Dad Make Me Laugh, Walker (London, England), 1994, published as *My Mom and Dad Make Me Laugh,* Candlewick Press (Cambridge, MA), 1994.

Caveman Dave, Candlewick Press (Cambridge, MA), 1994.

The Pointy-Hatted Princesses, Walker (London, England), 1994, Candlewick Press (Cambridge, MA), 1996.

I Went to the Zoopermarket, Scholastic (London, England), 1995.

Rocket Countdown, Candlewick Press (Cambridge, MA), 1995.

Stack-a-Plane (board book), Levinson, 1996.

A Cheese and Tomato Spider, Scholastic (London, England), 1996, Barron's (Hauppauge, NY), 1998.

The Animal Orchestra, Candlewick Press (Cambridge, MA), 1997.

(With Stephen Tucker) *My Day,* Oxford University Press (Oxford, England), 1997.

(With Stephen Tucker) *My Games,* Oxford University Press (Oxford, England), 1997.

Come and Play!, Levinson, 1997.

Ketchup on Your Cornflakes?: A Wacky Mix-and-Match Book, Scholastic (New York, NY), 1997.

What Do I Look Like?, Walker (London, England), 1998.

(With Stephen Tucker) *The Time It Took Tom,* Scholastic (London, England), 1998.

The Best Pop-Up Magic Book . . . Ever!, Orchard Books (London, England), 1998.

Dinosaurs' Day Out, Candlewick Press (Cambridge, MA), 1998.

(With Stephen Tucker) *My Days Out,* Oxford University Press (Oxford, England), 1999.

Croc with a Clock, Campbell (London, England), 1999.

Bear with a Pear, Campbell (London, England), 1999.

A Giraffe in a Scarf, Campbell (London, England), 1999.

Kangaroo in a Canoe, Campbell (London, England), 1999.

Turning Points, Hodder (London, England), 1999.

(With Stephen Tucker) *My Friends,* Oxford University Press (Oxford, England), 1999.

(With Stephen Tucker) *My Colours,* Oxford University Press (Oxford, England), 2000.

Buzz Buzz, Bumble Kitty, Barron's (Hauppauge, NY), 2000.

Split Ends, Phyllis Fogelman Books (New York, NY), 2000.

Mouse Moves House, Candlewick Press (Cambridge, MA), 2000.

(Reteller, with Stephen Tucker) *Cinderella,* Macmillan (London, England), 2001.

(Reteller, with Stephen Tucker) *Three Little Pigs,* Macmillan (London, England), 2001.

(Reteller, with Stephen Tucker) *Jack and the Beanstalk,* Macmillan (London, England), 2002.

(Reteller, with Stephen Tucker) *Little Red Riding Hood,* Macmillan (London, England), 2002.

Once upon a Time, Walker (London, England), Candlewick Press (Cambridge, MA), 2002.

Shark in the Park, David Fickling Books (New York, NY), 2002.

(With Sue Heap) *Red Rockets and Rainbow Jelly,* Puffin (London, England), 2003.

Pirate Pete, Walker (London, England), 2003, published as *Ahoy, Pirate Pete,* Candlewick Press (Cambridge, MA), 2003.

(Reteller, with Stephen Tucker) *The Three Billy Goats Gruff,* Macmillan (London, England), 2004.

(Reteller, with Stephen Tucker) *Goldilocks,* Macmillan (London, England), 2004.

CHILDREN'S BOOKS; ILLUSTRATOR

Louis Fidge, *Learning to Spell 4,* Parent and Child Programme, 1987.

Carol Watson, *If You Were a Hamster,* Dinosaur, 1988.

Jill Bennett, compiler, *Noisy Poems,* Oxford University Press (Oxford, England), 1989.

Jerome Fletcher, *A Gerbil in the Hoover,* Doubleday (London, England), 1989.

Rosemary Stones, *Where Babies Come From,* Dinosaur, 1989.

Ruth Merrtens, *Adding and Subtracting,* Parent and Child Programme, 1989.

Gina Fost, *Robots Go Shopping,* Ginn (Aylesbury, England), 1990.

Jill Bennett, compiler, *People Poems,* Oxford University Press (Oxford, England), 1990.

Jill Bennett, compiler, *Machine Poems,* Oxford University Press (Oxford, England), 1991.

Jacqueline Wilson, *The Story of Tracy Beaker,* Doubleday (London, England), 1991, Delacorte (New York, NY), 2001.

Jill Bennett, compiler, *Tasty Poems,* Oxford University Press (Oxford, England), 1992, Oxford University Press (New York, NY), 1998.

Jacqueline Wilson, *The Suitcase Kid,* Doubleday (London, England), 1992.

Tat Small, *My First Sticker Diary,* Scholastic (London, England), 1993.

Jacqueline Wilson, *The Mum-Minder,* Doubleday (London, England), 1993.

Elizabeth Hawkins, *The Lollipop Witch,* Orchard Books (London, England), 1994.

Valerie Bierman, editor, *Snake on the Bus and Other Pet Stories,* Methuen (London, England), 1994.

Judy Hindley, *Crazy ABC,* Walker (London, England), 1994, Candlewick Press (Cambridge, MA), 1996.

Judy Hindley, *Isn't It Time?,* Walker (London, England), 1994, Candlewick Press (Cambridge, MA), 1996.

Judy Hindley, *Little and Big,* Walker (London, England), 1994.

Judy Hindley, *One by One,* Walker (London, England), 1994, Candlewick Press (Cambridge, MA), 1996.

Vince Cross, compiler, *Sing a Song of Sixpence,* Oxford University Press (Oxford, England), 1994.

Roy Apps, *How to Handle Your Mum,* Hippo (London, England), 1994.

Jeremy Strong, *My Dad's Got an Alligator,* Viking (London, England), 1994.

Jacqueline Wilson, *The Bed and Breakfast Star,* Doubleday (London, England), 1994, published as *Elsa, Star of the Shelter,* A. Whitman (Morton Grove, IL), 1996.

Jacqueline Wilson, *Cliffhanger,* Doubleday (London, England), 1995.

Jacqueline Wilson, *The Dinosaur's Packed Lunch,* Doubleday (London, England), 1995.

(With Sue Heap) Jacqueline Wilson, *Double Act,* Doubleday (London, England), 1995.

Roy Apps, *How to Handle Your Gran,* Hippo (London, England), 1995.

Jill Bennett, compiler, *Playtime Poems,* Oxford University Press (Oxford, England), 1995.

Thomas Rockwell, *How to Eat Fried Worms,* Orchard Books (London, England), 1995.

Jeremy Strong, *The Indoor Pirates,* Dutton (London, England), 1995.

David Kitchen, *Never Play Leapfrog with a Unicorn,* Heinemann (London, England), 1995.

Gillian Cross, *The Crazy Shoe Shuffle,* Methuen Children's Books (London, England), 1995.

Jeremy Strong, *There's a Pharaoh in Our Bath!,* Dutton (London, England), 1995.

Jon Blake, *Danger Eyes,* Mammoth (London, England), 1995.

Roy Apps, *How to Handle Your Dad,* Hippo (London, England), 1996.

Jacqueline Wilson, *Bad Girls,* Doubleday (London, England), 1996, Delacorte (New York, NY), 2001.

Elizabeth Lindsay, *Hello Nellie and the Dragon,* Hippo (London, England), 1996.

Jeremy Strong, *The Hundred-Mile-an-Hour Dog,* Viking (London, England), 1996.

Thomas Rockwell, *How to Get Fabulously Rich,* Orchard Books (London, England), 1997.

Jacqueline Wilson, *Girls in Love,* Doubleday (London, England), 1997.

Jeremy Strong, *My Granny's Great Escape,* Viking (London, England), 1997.

Gina Willner-Pardo, *Spider Storch's Teacher Torture,* A. Whitman (Morton Grove, IL), 1997.

Gina Willner-Pardo, *Spider Storch's Carpool Catastrophe,* A. Whitman (Morton Grove, IL), 1997.

Emma Laybourn, *Robopop,* Yearling (London, England), 1997.

Gaby Goldsack, *Flower Power,* Hippo (London, England), 1997.

Jacqueline Wilson, *The Lottie Project,* Doubleday (London, England), 1997, Delacorte (New York, NY), 1999.

Jacqueline Wilson, *The Monster Story-Teller,* Doubleday (London, England), 1997.
Jeremy Strong, *Giant Jim and the Hurricane,* Viking (London, England), 1997.
Jeremy Strong, *The Indoor Pirates on Treasure Island,* Puffin (London, England), 1998.
Gillian Clements, *Calligraphy Frenzy,* Hippo (London, England), 1998.
Briane Morese, *Horse in the House,* Mammoth (London, England), 1998.
Anita Naik, *Is This Love,* Hodder (London, England), 1998.
Jill Bennett, compiler, *Seaside Poems,* Oxford University Press (New York, NY), 1998.
Jacqueline Wilson, *Girls under Pressure,* Doubleday (London, England), 1998.
Pat Moon, *Little Dad,* Mammoth (London, England), 1998.
Gina Willner-Pardo, *Spider Storch's Fumbled Field Trip,* A. Whitman (Morton Grove, IL), 1998.
Gina Willner-Pardo, *Spider Storch's Music Mess,* A. Whitman (Morton Grove, IL), 1998.
Tony Meeuwissen, *Remarkable Animals: 1000 Amazing Amalgamations,* Orchard Books (New York, NY), 1998.
(With Sue Heap) Jacqueline Wilson, *Buried Alive!,* Doubleday (London, England), 1998.
Roy Apps, *How to Handle Your Brother/Sister,* Hippo (London, England), 1998.
Geraldine Taylor and Gillian Harker, *Twinkle, Twinkle, Little Star,* Ladybird (London, England), 1998.
Jacqueline Wilson, reteller, *Rapunzel,* Scholastic (London, England), 1998.
Jill Bennett, compiler, *Christmas Poems,* Oxford University Press (New York, NY), 1999.
Jeremy Strong, *Dinosaur Pox,* Puffin (London, England), 1999.
Jacqueline Wilson, *The Illustrated Mum,* Doubleday (London, England), 1999.
Jacqueline Wilson, *Girls Out Late,* Doubleday (London, England), 1999.
Kaye Umansky, *Tickle My Nose and Other Action Rhymes,* Puffin (London, England), 1999.
Gina Willner-Pardo, *Spider Storch's Desperate Deal,* A. Whitman (Morton Grove, IL), 1999.
Chris d'Lacey, *Bubble and Float,* Hippo (London, England), 1999.
Roy Apps, *How to Handle Your Teacher,* Hippo (London, England), 1999.
Kes Gray, *Eat Your Peas,* Dorling Kindersley Publishing (New York, NY), 2000.
Kathy Tucker, *Do Knights Take Naps?,* A. Whitman (Morton Grove, IL), 2000.
Jacqueline Wilson, *The Dare Game,* Doubleday (London, England), 2000.
Roy Apps, *How to Handle Your Friends/Enemies,* Hippo (London, England), 2000.
Jeremy Strong, *I'm Telling You, They're Aliens!,* Puffin (London, England), 2000.
Jacqueline Wilson, *Vicky Angel,* Doubleday (London, England), 2000, Delacorte (New York, NY), 2001.
Irene Yates, *My First Picture Dictionary,* Collins (London, England), 2001.
Roy Apps, *How to Handle Your Cat/Dog,* Hippo (London, England), 2001.
Christine Mabileau and Irene Yates, *My First French Picture Dictionary,* Barron's (Hauppauge, NY), 2001.
Christine Mabileau and Irene Yates, *My First Spanish Picture Dictionary,* Barron's (Hauppauge, NY), 2001.
Gina Willner-Pardo, *Spider Storch, Rotten Runner,* A. Whitman (Morton Grove, IL), 2001.
Jacqueline Wilson, *The Cat Mummy,* Doubleday (London, England), 2001.
Jacqueline Wilson, *Sleepovers,* Doubleday (London, England), 2001.
Jacqueline Wilson, *Dustbin Baby,* Doubleday (London, England), 2001.
Jeremy Strong, *Krazy Kow Saves the World—Well, Almost,* Puffin (London, England), 2002.
Jeremy Strong, *The Monster Muggs,* Puffin (London, England), 2002.
Jeremy Strong, *The Shocking Adventures of Lightning Lucy,* Puffin (London, England), 2002.
Jacqueline Wilson, *The Worry Website,* Doubleday (London, England), 2002.
Kaye Umansky, *Wiggle My Toes,* Puffin (London, England), 2002.
Kes Gray, *Really, Really,* Bodley Head (London, England), 2002.
Jeremy Strong, *The Beak Speaks,* Puffin (London, England), 2003.
Giles Andreae, *Pants,* David Fickling Books (New York, NY), 2003.
Pippa Goodhart, *You Choose!,* Doubleday (London, England), 2003.
Julia Donaldson, *Conjurer Cow,* Puffin (London, England), 2003.
Thomas Rockwell, *How to Fight a Girl,* Orchard Books (New York, NY), 2003.
Kes Gray, *You Do!,* Bodley Head (London, England), 2003.

Jacqueline Wilson, *Lola Rose,* Doubleday (London, England), 2003.

Kes Gray, *Yuk!,* Bodley Head (London, England), 2004.

Julia Donaldson, *Wriggle and Roar!: Rhymes to Join in With,* Macmillan (London, England), 2004.

SIDELIGHTS: English author and illustrator Nick Sharratt is known for his child-appealing early-reader books. Sometimes his texts teach numbers, counting, or colors, but usually they are just plain fun for children who are learning to read, note critics. Sharratt generally illustrates his work in bold, bright colors to portray situations from the everyday to the adventurous. In *Look What I Found!,* for example, a little girl goes to the beach with her family and discovers fascinating objects along the shore, while in *Rocket Countdown,* readers learn about numbers while getting ready for a moon trip. Sharratt also uses humor in some of his books to keep young readers entertained. *Monday Run-Day* depicts funny scenes, such as dogs dressed in ties for Friday's tie day; and in *Snazzy Aunties,* a little boy's aunts wear or carry bizarre accessories.

My Mum and Dad Make Me Laugh, published in the United States as *My Mom and Dad Make Me Laugh,* is about a boy who has very odd parents. Father always wears clothes with stripes, while Mother always wears outfits with spots. Simon, however, prefers clothes that are gray. When the family goes on a safari, Father likes the animals that have stripes, such as the zebra, and Mother likes spotted creatures, including the leopards. Simon's favorite, though, is the elephant, and this explains why he always dresses in gray. *My Mom and Dad Make Me Laugh* drew praise from reviewers who enjoyed both Sharratt's narrative and illustrative techniques. *School Library Journal* contributor Marianne Saccardi lauded the "pleasant, rhythmic quality" of the author's writing, as well as the "cartoon-style crayon drawings perfectly suit[ed to] the child narrator's tone." Carolyn Phelan, writing in *Booklist,* especially liked the illustrations, calling them "bold and sassy and full of spotty-stripy detail."

Graphic design also comes into play in books such as *Ketchup on Your Cornflakes?* Here, Sharratt uses a Dutch-door technique that lets children combine pictures in funny ways. Sharratt's text can be split up as well, so that equally inappropriate combinations can created: "Do you like ice cream in your bathtub?" or "Do you like toothpaste on your head?" "Useful as toy, game, and concept book, this seems likely to provoke endless giggles and riffs on the theme," declared Deborah Stevenson in the *Bulletin of the Center for Children's Books.* Sharratt uses the same Dutch-door technique in *A Cheese and Tomato Spider* to combine people, animals, and various kinds of food.

Another book sure to provoke giggles from the preschool set is *Pants,* a book that is one long jingle about underpants. And not just any underpants, but underpants that are "bigger, bolder and more ridiculous than any in real life," Julia Eccleshare declared in the *Guardian.* There are "giant frilly pig pants," "cheeky little monkey pants," even pants meant to be donned by camel humps. Sharratt's illustrations of Giles Andreae's text "reinforce the sense of fun with a series of gleeful, boldly outlined images in an electric palette," noted a *Publishers Weekly* reviewer.

In *Shark in the Park,* Sharratt once again combines "bright, cheerful, clean-lined illustrations and bouncy, repetitive text" to create an "enjoyable" easy reader, in the words of *Booklist* contributor Todd Morning. A little boy named Timothy has just received a new telescope, and now he is testing it out in the park. He keeps thinking that he sees a shark in the duck pond, and indeed, through a hole cut in the page, the reader can see what appears to be a shark's fin. But upon turning the page, the object in view is always shown to be something else: a cat's ear, a crow's wing, his father's black hair. The final spread reveals the truth—there really is a shark in the duck pond—but Timothy does not see it. Sharratt's carefully engineered illustrations combine with his text to make the point that one should beware of drawing hasty conclusions. "This crafty interactive picture book is one hundred percent bliss and very toothsome indeed," Lyn Gardner declared in the *Guardian.*

Sharratt has also become known to older audiences as the illustrator of Jacqueline Wilson's massively popular books for middle-graders and young adults. Wilson's stories tackle challenging topics, including death, mental illness, abandonment by one's parents, and the formation of blended families, although often with a light tone. Sharratt's cartoon-like illustrations are a good compliment for Wilson's style, reviewers have generally remarked. For example, Sharratt's drawings for *The Lottie Project* and *The Story of Tracy Beaker,* both of which are told partially through journals kept by their pre-teen protagonists, "match the book's informal tone and help lighten some of the more serious moments," as Kitty Flynn wrote in a *Horn Book* review of the first title, while a *Publishers Weekly* critic said of *The Story of Tracy Beaker,* "Sharratt's drawings help to keep the mood light."

Sharratt once commented: "I've been making pictures for as long as I can remember, and I was nine when I decided I was going to be an illustrator by profession. As a child, I always wanted the same things for birthdays and Christmas: a bumper pack of felt-tip pens and lots of drawing paper, and I liked nothing better than to spend all day in my room, drawing, eating sweets, and listening to the radio. Nothing's changed—except that nowadays I use other media besides felt tips. A complete workaholic, I find it very hard to have weekends off, and I invariably sneak ongoing projects into my suitcase when I'm supposed to be taking a holiday. That's what happens when you really love your work!"

BIOGRAPHICAL AND CRITICAL SOURCES:

BOOKS

Andreae, Giles, *Pants,* David Fickling Books (New York, NY), 2003.

Sharratt, Nick, *Ketchup on Your Cornflakes?: A Wacky Mix-and-Match Book,* Scholastic (New York, NY), 1997.

PERIODICALS

Booklist, June 1, 1994, Carolyn Phelan, review of *My Mom and Dad Make Me Laugh,* p. 1845; September 1, 2002, Todd Morning, review of *Shark in the Park,* p. 137.

Bulletin of the Center for Children's Books, June, 1997, Deborah Stevenson, review of *Ketchup on Your Cornflakes?,* pp. 373-374.

Guardian (London, England), May 11, 1999, Philip Pullman, review of *The Illustrated Mum,* p. 4; October 31, 2000, Vivian French, review of *Eat Your Peas,* p. 59; December 11, 2001, Lindsey Fraser, review of *Remarkable Animals,* p. 49; March 12, 2002, Lindsey Fraser, review of *Secrets,* p. 63; May 29, 2002, Lyn Gardner, review of *Shark in the Park,* p. 11; November 16, 2002, Julia Eccleshare, review of *Pants,* p. 33; June 3, 2003, Lindsey Fraser, review of *Conjurer Cow,* p. 61; September 23, 2003, review of *The Beak Speaks,* p. 61; October 25, 2003, Julia Eccleshare, review of *You Choose,* p. 33.

Horn Book, November, 1999, Kitty Flynn, review of *The Lottie Project,* p. 746; September, 2001, review of *The Story of Tracy Beaker,* p. 598.

Independent (London, England), February 24, 2001, Nicholas Tucker, "The Fifty Best Books for Children," p. 4.

Kirkus Reviews, May 1, 1997, p. 727.

New York Times Book Review, July 19, 1998, review of *Seaside Poems,* p. 24.

Publishers Weekly, March 23, 1992, review of *I Look Like This* and *Look What I Found!,* p. 71; May 23, 1994, review of *My Mom and Dad Make Me Laugh,* p. 86; September 25, 1995, review of *Rocket Countdown,* p. 56; December 18, 1995, review of *Elsa, Star of the Shelter!,* p. 55; January 12, 1998, review of *Double Act,* p. 60; July 5, 1999, review of *Tickle My Nose and Other Action Rhymes,* p. 73; August 9, 1999, review of *Stack-a-Plane,* p. 355; November 29, 1999, review of *The Lottie Project,* p. 72; January 3, 2000, review of *The Time It Took Tom,* p. 74; January 8, 2001, review of *Bad Girls,* p. 68; July 23, 2001, review of *The Story of Tracy Beaker,* p. 77; August 13, 2001, review of *Vicky Angel,* p. 312; June 3, 2002, review of *Once upon a Time,* pp. 89-90; April 21, 2003, review of *Vicky Angel,* p. 65; June 2, 2003, review of *Pants,* pp. 50-51.

School Library Journal, February, 1992, Andrew W. Hunter, review of *Machine Poems,* p. 81; June, 1992, Linda Wicher, review of *I Look Like This* and *Look What I Found,* pp. 102-103; November, 1992, Linda Wicher, review of *The Green Queen,* p. 78; December, 1992, Linda Wicher, review of *Monday Run-Day,* p. 91; August, 1994, Marianne Saccardi, review of *My Mom and Dad Make Me Laugh,* pp. 145-146; February, 1996, Jane Gardner Connor, review of *Elsa, Star of the Shelter!,* p. 104; November, 1997, Maura Bresnahan, review of *Spider Storch's Teacher Torture,* and Carrie A. Guarria, review of *Spider Storch's Carpool Catastrophe,* p. 103; March, 1998, Miriam Lang Budin, review of *Double Act,* p. 266; January, 1999, Judith Constantinides, review of *Seaside Poems,* p. 110; March, 1999, Elaine E. Knight, review of *Spider Storch's Fumbled Field Trip* and *Spider*

Storch's Music Mess, p. 188; October, 1999, Maureen Wade, review of *Christmas Poems,* p. 65; January, 2000, Yapha Nussbaum Mason, review of *Spider Storch's Desperate Deal,* p. 114; March, 2000, Lisa Smith, review of *The Time It Took Tom,* p. 212; April, 2000, Ginny Gustin, review of *Do Knights Take Naps?,* p. 116; September, 2000, Lisa Dennis, review of *Eat Your Peas,* p. 198; March, 2001, Marilyn Ackerman, review of *Bad Girls,* p. 258; July, 2001, B. Allison Gray, review of *The Story of Tracy Beaker,* p. 116; October, 2001, Marlyn K. Roberts, review of *Vicky Angel,* p. 175; December, 2002, Kristin de Lacoste, review of *Shark in the Park,* p. 108.

Scotland on Sunday (Edinburgh, Scotland), June 3, 2001, review of *Eat Your Peas,* p. 15.

Sunday Times (London, England), October 29, 2000, Nicolette Jones, review of *Vicky Angel,* p. 46; August 11, 2002, Nicolette Jones, review of *Krazy Kow Saves the World—Well, Almost,* p. 47.

Times Educational Supplement, April 25, 2003, Geraldine Brenna, review of *Red Rockets and Rainbow Jelly,* p. 37.

ONLINE

Association of Illustrators Web Site, http://www.theaoi.com/ (February, 1999), interview with Sharratt.

British Broadcasting Company Web Site, http://www.bbc.co.uk/ (November 3, 2003), interview with Sharratt.*

* * *

SIMMIE, Lois (Ann) 1932-

PERSONAL: Born June 11, 1932, in Edam, Saskatchewan, Canada; daughter of Edwin Maurice (a pool elevator agent) and Bessie Margaret (a homemaker; maiden name, Thomson) Binns; divorced; children: Odell, Leona, Anne, Scott. *Education:* Attended Saskatchewan Business College, 1951-52, and University of Saskatchewan, 1973-77.

ADDRESSES: Home—1501 Cairns Ave., Saskatoon, Saskatchewan S7H 2H5, Canada.

CAREER: Novelist, short story writer, poet, and author of children's books. Saskatoon Public Library, writer-in-residence, 1987-88; University of Saskatchewan, Extension Department, fiction instructor at Saskatoon Summer School of the Arts; instructor at community colleges.

MEMBER: Canadian Children's Book Center, Writers Union of Canada, Association of Canadian Television and Radio Artists, Saskatchewan Writers' Guild.

AWARDS, HONORS: Award from Saskatchewan Department of Culture and Youth, 1976, for a short story collection; artist's grant, Saskatchewan Arts Board, 1983; award from Saskatchewan Writers' Guild, 1983, for a book-length story collection, 1983; Saskatchewan Book Award for Children's Literature, 1995, for *Mister Got to Go: The Cat That Wouldn't Leave;* Arthur Ellis Award for nonfiction, Crime Writers of Canada, for *The Secret Lives of Sgt. John Wilson;* other awards from Saskatchewan Writers' Guild.

WRITINGS:

ADULT FICTION

Ghost House (short stories), Coteau Books (Moose Jaw, Saskatchewan, Canada), 1976.

They Shouldn't Make You Promise That (novel), New American Library (Canada), 1981, reprinted, Coteau Books (Moose Jaw, Saskatchewan, Canada), 2002.

Pictures (short stories), Fifth House (Saskatoon, Saskatchewan, Canada), 1984.

Betty Lee Bonner Lives There (short stories) Greystone (Vancouver, British Columbia, Canada), 1993.

FOR CHILDREN

Auntie's Knitting a Baby (poetry), illustrated by daughter, Anne Simmie, Western Producer Prairie Books (Saskatoon, Saskatchewan, Canada), 1984, Orchard Books (New York, NY), 1988.

An Armadillo Is Not a Pillow (poetry), 1986.

What Holds Up the Moon?, 1987.

Who Greased the Shoelaces? (poetry), 1989.

Oliver's Chickens, 1992.

Mister Got to Go: The Cat That Wouldn't Leave, illustrated by Cynthia Nugent, Red Deer College Press (Red Deer, Alberta, Canada), 1995, published as *No Cats Allowed,* Chronicle Books (San Francisco, CA), 1996.

OTHER

(Editor) *Julie,* 1985.
(Editor) *The Doll,* 1987.
(Editor) *A Gift of Sky,* 1988.
The Secret Lives of Sgt. John Wilson: A True Story of Love and Murder (nonfiction), Greystone (Vancouver, British Columbia, Canada), 1995.

Contributor to numerous anthologies, including *Best of Grain, Sundogs, Saskatchewan Gold, Number One Northern,* and *Inquiry into Literature.* Contributor to periodicals, including *Saturday Night* and *McCall's.*

ADAPTATIONS: Simmie's short story "Red Shoes" was adapted as a efeature film, directed by Allan Kroeker, produced by Susan A'Court and William Weintraub, Atlantis Films and National Film Board of Canada, 1986.

SIDELIGHTS: Canadian fiction writer Lois Simmie has spun a career that includes novels, short story collections, an award-winning true-crime book, and several volumes of prose and verse for children. Her first novel, *They Shouldn't Make You Promise That,* is the story of an unhappy homemaker who gradually loses her emotional grip. In the book, Eleanor Smith goes to a psychiatrist with no success, then leaves her husband. Don Strachan, reviewing the work in the *Los Angeles Times Book Review,* observed that Eleanor's "charm and eloquence" are such that "her inner workings hold our attention" and "we never pooh-pooh her plight, even while she keeps us in stitches." *Quill & Quire* contributor Victoria Freeman remarked that the subject of unhappy housewives had been overdone in contemporary fiction, although Simmie's rendition is commendable for its "sardonic descriptions of married life" and vivid evocation of the sense of her protagonist's loneliness.

By the time of her first novel's publication, Simmie had already released a volume of short stories, *Ghost House;* her next book of stories, *Pictures,* won praise from Matthew Clark of *Quill & Quire,* who hailed the "intimate accuracy" of the author's narratives of ordinary domestic life, and her "clean, direct, and simple style that suits her subject." Clark commended the stories "Behind the Lines" and "In the Valley of the Kings"; an additional four stories about girls growing up in prairie towns in the 1940s were well crafted but lacking in urgency, the reviewer commented. "Simmie's work is uneven, but at her best she is very good," Clark concluded.

When Simmie's third collection of stories, *Betty Lee Bonner Lives There,* was published, Kathryn Woodward of *Books in Canada* was enthusiastic, saying that Simmie had created "characters one wants to trumpet, share, pass on." Delighting in the stories' wacky touches, Woodward singled out "Mrs. Bleasdale's Terrible Day," "Sunflowers," "I'll Take You Home Again, Kathleen," "Swinging," and "The Swing," all of which, for her, were "engrossing." Concluded Woodward, "*Betty Lee Bonner Lives There* offers us solid glimpses into the lives of people who are all too often and all too easily dismissed." Jill Robinson in the *Edmonton Journal* singled out the story "Sunflowers," stating, "this is as lovely a piece of writing as I've read anywhere." *Betty Lee Bonner Lives There* also drew praise from Louise E. Allin in the *Canadian Book Review Annual 1994,* who said that "Simmie is a marvelous storyteller. . . . There are no false moments. This collection is a passport to the best secrets of the human heart."

Simmie ventured into true crime with *The Secret Lives of Sgt. John Wilson.* Wilson was a Scot who stole money from his wife's family in order to help his brother's failing business. Fleeing to Canada in 1912, he became a Canadian Mountie and did not, as he had promised, return to his wife and child in Scotland. Instead, he took up with a teenage girl named Jessie Patterson. When Wilson's wife, Polly, traveled across the ocean in search of her errant husband, he tried to establish a bigamous arrangement for a while, but, finding it cumbersome, shot Polly to death. By putting off his Scottish in-laws with lies, Wilson might have gotten away with the crime, had his sister-in-law not pressed the Canadian authorities to investigate the case. The story of the unrepentant Wilson's crime made headlines at the time, and has since been resurrected by Simmie, who—in the opinion of Carolyn Purden in *Quill & Quire*—tells the story well, using "finely honed descriptive powers."

In a *Canadian Book Review Annual 1995* critique of *The Secret Lives of Sgt. John Wilson,* J. L. Granatstein commented, "Simmie has done her research, and she writes well." Robert Calder in *Saskatchewan History* stated that the volume "is a compelling murder story" and "a fascinating look at the loneliness of the immigrant experience for many people, the emergence of law enforcement in western Canada, and of a world before televised trials, DNA testing, and 'Dream Team' lawyers." *The Secret Lives* was nominated for a Saskatchewan Book Award for nonfiction and won the Crime Writers of Canada Arthur Ellis Award for Nonfiction.

Simmie over the years has also established herself as a respected writer for children. *Auntie's Knitting a Baby* presents fifty-two poems, mostly humorous and some of them gruesome as well, in the vein of Shel Silverstein and Jack Prelutsky. A *Publishers Weekly* reviewer and *School Library Journal* critic Barbara S. McGinn were among those who enjoyed the poems' energetic, dark humor. Praise was also bestowed upon the book's illustrations, which were done by Simmie's daughter, Anne Simmie, who had majored in painting at the Alberta College of Art.

Simmie issued the children's picture book *Mister Got to Go: The Cat That Wouldn't Leave* in 1995. Set in the grand old Sylvia Hotel in Vancouver, British Columbia, the story concerns a cat who enters the hotel to get out of the rain. The manager maintains that the cat must leave when the rain stops, but in Vancouver, the rain rarely stops. As the cat lingers, he gains the affection of staff and guests, including the manager himself. *School Library Journal* contributor Kathy Piehl predicted that "*Mister Got to Go* will win listeners and readers as surely as he convinced Mr. Foster to let him stay." Phil Hall of *Books in Canada* was grateful to Simmie's book for providing him an enjoyable evening with his own daughter. When the book was issued in the United States under the title *No Cats Allowed,* a *Kirkus Reviews* critic praised it as a "cozy tale of coming home, executed with an edge that makes it interesting." A *Children's Book Review Service* contributor simply called it "quietly delightful."

Simmie once told *CA:* "Although I always intended to write, I didn't actually get serious until I saw forty looming on the horizon. A late starter has some advantages—all that life experience and years of writing in your head plus all those good and bad books you've read. The good ones fill you with longing and the bad ones make you say I can write a better book than that! (You can only say this so often before you have to put up or shut up.) Your apprenticeship is shorter, and you don't struggle with developing a voice or style; your voice is simply who you have become.

"When I write for children I write with one aim in mind, to entertain the child. I hate message plays, books, songs, for children. What's wrong with just making them laugh? In a wonderful children's book, like *Charlotte's Web,* there is a message but never at the expense of the story. Though I write to entertain, I take writing for children very seriously. We must take it seriously. What we can't take too seriously is ourselves."

BIOGRAPHICAL AND CRITICAL SOURCES:

BOOKS

Wilson, Joyce R., editor, *Canadian Book Review Annual 1994,* CBRA (Toronto, Ontario, Canada), 1995, Louise E. Allin, review of *Betty Lee Bonner Lives There.*

Wilson, Joyce R., editor, *Canadian Book Review Annual 1995,* CBRA (Toronto, Ontario, Canada), 1996, J. L. Granatstein, review of *The Secret Lives of Sgt. John Wilson.*

PERIODICALS

Books in Canada, November, 1993, Kathryn Woodward, review of *Betty Lee Bonner Lives There,* p. 42; November, 1995, Phil Hall, review of *Mister Got to Go: The Cat That Wouldn't Leave,* p. 40.

Calgary Herald, July 8, 1995.

Children's Book Review Service, February, 1997, review of *Mister Got to Go,* pp. 78-79.

Daily Miner, November 13, 1989.

Edmonton Journal, March 21, 1987; May 29, 1994, Jill Robinson, review of *Betty Lee Bonner Lives There,* p. B5.

Globe and Mail (Toronto, Ontario, Canada), August 11, 1984.

Kirkus Reviews, November 15, 1996, review of *Mister Got to Go,* p. 1675.

Los Angeles Times Book Review, January 16, 1983, Don Strachan, review of *They Shouldn't Make You Promise That,* p. 5.

Publishers Weekly, September 9, 1988, review of *Auntie's Knitting a Baby,* p. 135.

Quill & Quire, July, 1981, Victoria Freeman, review of *They Shouldn't Make You Promise That,* p. 58; June, 1984, Matthew Clark, review of *Pictures,* p. 32; January, 1994, p. 27; August, 1995, Carolyn Purden, review of *The Secret Lives of Sgt. John Wilson,* p. 36; November, 1995, p. 30.

Saskatchewan History, spring, 1997, Robert Calder, review of *The Secret Lives of Sgt. John Wilson,* p. 39.

Saskatoon Star Phoenix, July, 1984.

School Library Journal, December, 1988, Barbara S. McGinn, review of *Auntie's Knitting a Baby,* p. 102; January, 1996, Kathy Piehl, review of *Mister Got to Go,* p. 96.

Theatrewest, April-May, 1992.

Vancouver Sun, November 20, 1993.*

* * *

SKLOOT, Floyd 1947-

PERSONAL: Born July 6, 1947, in Brooklyn, NY; son of Harry (a butcher) and Lillian Alfus (a homemaker; maiden name, Rosen) Skloot; married Betsy Lee, August 10, 1970 (divorced, September, 1992); married Beverly Hallberg, May 14, 1993; children (first marriage): Rebecca Lee; stepchildren: Matthew Coale. *Education:* Franklin and Marshall College, B.A., 1969; Southern Illinois University, M.A., 1971, doctoral studies, 1972. *Politics:* Democrat. *Religion:* Jewish. *Hobbies and other interests:* Reading, cinema, music, watching baseball, cooking.

ADDRESSES: Home and office—5680 Karla's Ln., Amity, OR 97101. *E-mail*—fskloot@viclink.com.

CAREER: Poet, essayist, and novelist. Worked in public policy, on the staffs of three Illinois governors, the Washington legislature, and a large energy corporation, 1972-88.

AWARDS, HONORS: McGinnis-Ritchie Award for best essay of the year, *Southwest Review,* 1997; Emily Clark Balch Prize in Poetry, *Virginia Quarterly Review,* 2000; Oregon Book Award in Poetry, 2001, for *The Evening Light;* best book of 2003, *Chicago Tribune,* for *In the Shadow of Memory;* Puschcart Prize, 2004, for "A Measure of Acceptance"; W. M. A. Stafford

Floyd Skloot

Fellowship in Poetry, Oregon Literary Arts Fellowship; annual prizes for the best essays from *Southwest Review* and *Creative Fiction.*

WRITINGS:

Kaleidoscope (poems), Silverfish Review (Eugene, OR), 1986.

Wild Light (poems), Silverfish Review (Eugene, OR), 1989.

Pilgrim's Harbor (novel), Story Line Press (Brownsville, OR), 1992.

Summer Blue (novel), Story Line Press (Brownsville, OR), 1994.

Music Appreciation (poems), University Press of Florida (Gainesville, FL), 1994.

Poppies (poems), Story Line Press (Brownsville, OR), 1994.

Lawrence B. Salander: Small Landscapes, Mark De Montebello Fine Art (New York, NY), 1995.

Jedd Novatt, Sculpture, Salander-O'Reilly Galleries (New York, NY), 1996.

The Night-Side: Chronic Fatigue Syndrome and the Illness Experience (essays), also published as *The Night-Side: Years in the Kingdom of the Sick,* Story Line Press (Brownsville, OR), 1996.

The Open Door (novel), Story Line Press (Brownsville, OR), 1997.

The Evening Light (poems), Story Line Press (Ashland, OR), 2001.

The Fiddler's Trance (poems), Bucknell University Press (Lewisburg, PA), 2001.

In the Shadow of Memory, University of Nebraska Press (Lincoln, NE), 2003.

Contributor of essays to *The Best American Essays,* 1993, *The Art of the Essay,* 1999, *The Best American Essays,* and *The Penguin Book of the Sonnet.* Contributor of essays and poems to periodicals, including *Atlantic Monthly, Harper's, Poetry, Antioch Review, Prairie Schooner, Three-Penny Review, Gettysburg Review,* and *Virginia Quarterly Review.*

WORK IN PROGRESS: Another essay collection; *Fragmentary Blue,* a sequel to *In the Shadow of Memory*

SIDELIGHTS: Award-winning poet, essayist, and novelist Floyd Skloot has turned personal adversity into a mine for his artistic endeavors. After graduating from college, he led a dream existence. He was a successful senior public policy analyst with a fast-track career, he won medals running in weekend road races, he was an accomplished gourmet cook, and he had written—but not published—two novels and one book of poetry. Everything changed for him on December 7, 1988, his personal "Day of Infamy." In Washington, D.C., for an energy conference, he woke up in his hotel room curiously lacking in personal energy. Disoriented, dizzy, and believing himself to be suffering from jet lag, he thought he might be able to overcome his lethargy with a little exercise. So he laced up his running shoes and set out for the Capital Mall. He soon exhausted himself; his usual powers had been "systematically stripped away," as he later recalled. Skloot would remain in this state for over a decade and, indeed, he still feels the effects of his debilitating illness, an illness he did not even have a name for during the first five months he suffered from it. When a doctor finally diagnosed him as suffering from Chronic Fatigue Syndrome (CFS), he could name his nemesis. Before the onset of his illness Skloot had written fiction and verse, but only after being knocked down by illness did he start to write essays, many about his experiences with disease. In 1996 *The Night-Side: Seven Years in the Kingdom of the Sick* rolled off the presses. Skloot had cribbed the book's title from a sentence in Susan Sontag's *Illness As Metaphor:* "Illness is the night-side of life. Everyone who is born holds dual citizenship, in the kingdom of the well and in the kingdom of the sick." As he detailed in these essays, even after a decade Skloot had not managed to get a passport back to the day-side. In an interview published on the *Amazon.com* Web site, Skloot admitted, "Now I am able to write for two hours on a good day, and good days might happen three times a week. Nevertheless, it is astonishing how much can get done under those circumstances." Time for writing is not all Skloot has lost. "I've had to small-down my life," Skloot told Cecelia Goodnow of the *Seattle Post-Intelligencer,* "I don't try to do more than what I'm capable of doing."

Because of his bout with CFS, Skloot's brain is not what it used to be either. In his book he describes asking a friend for a piece of "decaffeinated gum" and of floundering in his mind for "car antenna" and coming out with "umbrella" instead. It was as if "my brain had been rewired by Gracie Allen," he wrote. As Skloot explained to Goodnow, "I can't learn new tasks. I still can't figure out how to build a fire in our wood stove, although my wife has shown me repeatedly. And I was a very bright man."

Chronic Fatigue Syndrome or not, Skloot was able to complete a dozen essays in *The Night-Side* that range in topics from humor to baseball, music to poetry, and contain insights from the likes of Oliver Sacks and Norman Cousins. A number of reviewers applauded the collection, including the *Sewanee Review*'s Sanford Pinsker, who wrote: "That the essays of *The Night-Side* appeared originally in such quarterlies as the *American Scholar,* the *Antioch Review, Prairie Schooner, Three-Penny Review,* the *Gettysburg Review,* and the *Virginia Quarterly Review* reflects something of their merit; but, taken together, they have the cumulative effect that the individual pieces merely suggest."

Skloot's first published novel, *Pilgrim's Harbor,* which appeared in 1992—some sixteen years after he wrote the first pages—features Dewey Howser, a motel manager in an unidentified western state. Howser has no family or friends and his only contact with humanity is through the guests who stay at his motel. He starts a relationship with a woman he meets at a mall, but it ends disastrously when she leaves him for one of the motel's guests. While a *Kirkus Reviews* contributor dismissed the book as "this barely breathing first novel," *Prairie Schooner*'s Lee Lemon found *Pilgrim's Harbor* to be "one of those novels that delivers more than it promises. . . . The setting and Skloot's skill turn the novel into a small delight."

Two years later Skloot published *Summer Blue,* a coming-of-age novel about a father and daughter on a journey of self-discovery. As a reward for straightening out in school, fourteen-year-old Jill Packard earns a summer-long road trip with her father, Tim. One destination is her grandmother's home in Long Island, where Jill must come to terms with both her mother's abandonment and the woman's leukemia. Other stops include a lakeside cabin in Michigan and an aunt's home in Oregon. Along the way both father and daughter are altered by their experiences, and their relationship to each other is altered in turn. The novel caught the attention of reviewers. According to a *Publishers Weekly* reviewer, "Skloot blends well-limned personalities and neatly construed events with an evocative atmosphere," and Mary Carroll of *Booklist* dubbed *Summer Blue* "a caring and compassionate story."

A dysfunctional Jewish family's interactions from the 1930s to the 1970s make up the plot of the 1997 novel *The Open Door.* The novel opens in Brooklyn and describes Myron Adler's youth and his eventual courtship of Faye Raskin. Myron is the crude proprietor of a live poultry market and Faye is a would-be social climber, so it is not surprising that their marriage is doomed from the start. But instead of taking his frustrations out on Faye, Myron regularly beats his two boys, Richard and Danny. One such beating results in Richard's losing sight in one eye. Richard grows up to become an overweight, troubled salesman, but Danny's nature is near-angelic, and he finds happiness as a father and as a successful architect. How the boys cope with their shared legacy is the subject of the novel's second half. The novel earned qualified praise. While a *Kirkus Reviews* contributor noted it is "filled with sloppy writing and a transparently manipulated cast," *Booklist*'s Jim O'Laughlin found that "the book's modulations of tone are reassuring, effectively salvaging the humor of this world."

While working on his master's degree at Southern Illinois University, Skloot had the good fortune to study with Irish poet Thomas Kinsella. He has been writing poetry ever since, publishing individual poems in literary magazines and then a handful of poetry chapbooks and book collections, including *Wild Light, Music Appreciation, Poppies,* and *The Evening Light.* There exists an autobiographical thread to collections such as *Music Appreciation* and *The Evening Light.* The former work received favorable reviews from Pat Monaghan of *Booklist,* who hailed it as "a rare book that begins strong, moves strongly, and ends in strength." Monaghan noted the work's resemblance to an autobiography, with poems about a troubled childhood followed by poems about dealing with those problems while looking back from the safety of adulthood. These, in turn, are followed by poems about suffering from a debilitating illness. The verses that close out the book are devoted to memory and the sensory life. In the *Hudson Review,* John Greening, who also grasped the autobiographical nature of the collection, remarked: "This makes for a very satisfactory one-hundred-page book, yet there is no compromising of individual poems." Greening continued, "[Skloot] will no doubt be labeled a formalist, for he is highly sensitive to the shapes words make on the page and to the sculpting of his themes."

In Skloot's 2001 poetic offering, *The Evening Light,* he continues his autobiographical, poetical musings, which "at their best . . . glow with the lambent radiance of the poet's highly constrained world," to quote Richard Wakefield of the *Sewanee Review.* Monaghan pointed out that only a portion of the poems deal with the poet's illness; others, as Judy Clarence mentioned in *Library Journal,* provide readers with "wittily entertaining" looks at artistic figures. Among the book's enthusiasts is Vincente F. Gotera, who described Skloot's craft as "masterful" in the *North American Review,* and Monaghan, who cited a "strong, clean, and clear" poetic voice that shines through these largely celebratory poems.

In 2004 Skloot published a sequel to *The Night-Side. In the Shadow of Memory* is a "remarkably cohesive collection of essays [that] chronicles his attempts to reassemble himself," according to Kyle Minor in the *Antioch Review,* and in the view of *Washington Post* reviewer David Guy, Skloot has succeeded, for the evidence is clear in this work. "While the early descriptions of his condition are fascinating, by far the more vivid part of the book," Guy wrote, is "where he gives us distant and recent memories of his family," in chapters that are "tightly written and beautifully constructed." As with its subject matter, reviewers commented favorably on the work's poetic and lapidary style, which in its "glassy formal structure . . . strikes back at his [Skloot's] confusion," noted Steven L. Glazer in *Literature and Medicine.* In these essays, which are laced with a "vulnerable and gentle humor," as Glazer described them, Skloot discusses various aspects of the changes wrought by his illness. One such change is a greater understanding and compassion for his own mother, who was formerly abusive but now suffers from a dementia that has softened her personality. The third section, titled "A Measure of Acceptance," won the Puschart Prize. In Glazer's opinion, this final twenty-two-page section, which took Skloot eleven months to write, is the strongest: Skloot "writes with the power of a life well lived, uncontained by the change he has undergone."

Skloot once told *CA:* "My writing has always begun with poetry. It is the only genre I formally studied, having worked with the Irish poet Thomas Kinsella in 1969 and 1970, and my first publications were poems in literary magazines the next year. After leaving academia and beginning a career in public policy, I worked on my poems at night and then, in 1974, began to try short fiction, always returning to poetry as the core of my endeavors. By 1976 I was also writing book reviews and had begun the novel *Pilgrim's Harbor,* which was completed a full decade later.

"I wrote *Pilgrim's Harbor* three times, essentially teaching myself to write a novel in the process. The initial draft, told in the first person by the innkeeper protagonist, failed to develop a viable plot, moving along instead by an accumulation of character details. The second draft shifted to a third-person narrator, which granted me enough distance to see the story line clearly but, I realized, stripped the novel of its most essential quality, the narrator's warm and quirky voice. A final draft, back in the first person, allowed both the narrative and the character to cohere.

"My second novel, *Summer Blue,* took only ten months to write. A short, 217-page novel, it is composed of sixty-five brief chapters because I wrote the book during my lunch hours at work and had very little time to be expansive. Each chapter is a scene, something I could manage to hold in view during these bursts of composition. The first draft of my third novel, *The Open Door,* was written in ten weeks, largely during a residency at the Villa Montalvo in Saratoga, California. Though this trend is encouraging, I do not expect my next novel to be written in ten days. Each of my novels has gotten progressively more autobiographical, reversing the customary journey most novelists make. Each has gotten more intimate and, I think, dangerous in its materials.

"In 1988 I became totally disabled by a viral illness that targeted my brain. For a year I was unable to write at all. Brain damage dramatically affected my ability to work and, when I could work again, affected my writing itself. I began to write essays, using personal experience and the personal voice to explore the meaning of my experience. Throughout I have continued to write poetry. All genres seem to feed on one another, to bring out core images, emotions and narratives that move back and forth across the boundaries."

BIOGRAPHICAL AND CRITICAL SOURCES:

PERIODICALS

Antioch Review, winter, 2004, Kyle Minor, review of *In the Shadow of Memory,* pp. 173-174.

Book, March-April, 2003, Beth Kephart, review of *In the Shadow of Memory,* pp. 81-82.

Booklist, November 1, 1994, Pat Monaghan, review of *Music Appreciation,* p. 474; December 1, 1994, Mary Carroll, review of *Summer Blue,* p. 655; September 15, 1997, Jim O'Laughlin, review of *The Open Door,* p. 211; December 15, 2000, Patricia Monaghan, review of *The Evening Light,* p. 782; March 15, 2003, Bryce Christensen, review of *In the Shadow of Memory,* p. 1259.

Dallas Morning News, September 22, 2003, "Writer with MS Losing His Words and Finding His Way."

Hudson Review, autumn, 1995, John Greening, review of *Music Appreciation,* pp. 512-513; spring, 2002, Robert Phillips, "O Lost!," pp. 146-151.

Journal of the American Medical Association, November 26, 1997, Michael Loudon, review of *The Night-Side: Years in the Kingdom of the Sick,* p. 1709.

Kirkus Reviews, September 1, 1992, review of *Pilgrim's Harbor,* p. 1085; August 1, 1997, review of *The Open Door,* p. 1146.

Library Journal, November 15, 1994, Jane S. Bakerman, review of *Summer Blue,* p. 88; June 15, 1996, James Swanton, review of *The Night-Side,* p. 85; January 1, 2001, Judy Clarence, review of *The Evening Light,* p 112.

Literature and Medicine, fall, 2003, Steven L. Glazer, review of *In the Shadow of Memory,* p. 261.

Los Angeles Times Book Review, January 24, 1993, p. 9; April 8, 2003, Bernadette Murphy, "Memories of a Normal Life," p. E8.

New York Times Book Review, Stan Friedman, review of *Summer Blue,* p. 18.

North American Review, January-February, 2002, Vincente F. Gotera, review of *The Evening Light,* p. 44.

Prairie Schooner, summer, 1993, Lee Lemon, review of *Pilgrim's Harbor,* pp. 146-149.

Publishers Weekly, October 24, 1994, review of *Summer Blue,* pp. 52-53; June 17, 1996, review of *The Night-Side,* p. 61; August 11, 1997, review of *The Open Door,* p. 386; February 24, 2003, review of *In the Shadow of Memory,* p. 65.

San Francisco Chronicle, March 27, 2003, Adair Lara, "Poet Learns to Live—and Write—with Brain Damage," p. E2.

Seattle Post-Intelligencer, April 17, 1998, Cecelia Goodnow, review of *The Night-Side.*

Sewanee Review, fall, 1996, Sanford Pinsker, review of *The Night-Side,* pp. xc-xcii; summer, 2003, Richard Wakefield, "Light and More Light," pp. 348-351.

U.S. Catholic, August, 1994, Brian Doyle, "Graceful Falls: How Physical Injuries Can Lead to Spiritual Growth."

Virginia Quarterly Review, summer, 2001, review of *The Evening Light.*

Washington Post, May 4, 2003, David Guy, "Past Forgetting," T5.

ONLINE

Amazon.com, http://www.amazon.com/ (June 10, 2004), interview with Floyd Skloot.

Barnes & Noble, http://www.barnesandnoble.com/ (summer, 2003), "Good to Know."

Story Line Press, http://www.storylinepress.com/ (June 10, 2004), interview with Floyd Skloot.*

SLATER, Niall W. 1954-

PERSONAL: Born August 19, 1954, in Massillon, OH, USA; son of John Eick (a teacher) and Thelma (a teacher; maiden name, Tourney) Slater. *Education:* College of Wooster, B.A. (with honors), 1976; Princeton University, M.A., 1978, Ph.D., 1981; graduate study at American School of Classical Studies at Athens, Greece, 1979-80. *Religion:* Lutheran.

ADDRESSES: *Office*—Center for Language, Literature, and Culture, Emory University, 1380 S. Oxford Rd., Atlanta, GA 30322. *E-mail*—nslater@emory.edu.

CAREER: Concordia College, Moorhead, MN, assistant professor of classics, 1981-82; University of Southern California, Los Angeles, assistant professor, 1982-87, associate professor of classics, 1987-91; Emory University, Atlanta, GA, professor of classics, 1991—, chair of Department of Classics, 1991-94, director of Center for Language, Literature, and Culture, 1998—. National Endowment for the Humanities Comedy Institute, codirector, summer, 1987; Embassy Residential College, University of Southern California, faculty master, 1989-90; conference organizer for Performance Criticism of Greek Comedy, Emory University, 1991; visiting fellow at various universities.

MEMBER: Archaeological Institute of America, American Philological Association, Petronian Society, Women's Classical Caucus, Cambridge Philological Society, Classical Association of the Middle West and South, Georgia Classical Association, Pacific Ancient and Modern Language Association, Phi Beta Kappa (president, 2003—).

AWARDS, HONORS: Fellow of American Council of Learned Societies, 1984-85; junior fellow at Center for Hellenic Studies, 1987-88; Alexander von Humboldt fellow at University of Konstanz, 1988-89; *Plautus in Performance: The Theatre of the Mind* was named one of the outstanding academic books of 1985 by *Choice.* Recipient of many grants.

WRITINGS:

Plautus in Performance: The Theatre of the Mind, Princeton University Press (Princeton, NJ), 1985, 2nd edition, Harwood Academic (Amsterdam, Netherlands), 2000.

Reading Petronius, Johns Hopkins University Press (Baltimore, MD), 1990.

Spectator Politics: Metatheater and Performance in Aristophanes, University of Pennsylvania Press (Philadelphia, PA), 2002.

Contributor to journals of classical studies and philology.

SIDELIGHTS: Niall W. Slater, a professor of classical studies at Emory University, has long been interested in ancient drama. In addition to teaching about the works of classical Greek and Roman authors, he has helped to arrange conferences about and performances of ancient works, participated in archaeological excavations of ancient sites, and published several studies about Greek and Roman dramatists. In his first such study, *Plautus in Performance: The Theatre of the Mind,* Slater focuses on performance aspects of the dramas by Roman playwright Plautus, a topic that had been little explored at that time. As *Phoenix* reviewer Peter L. Smith noted, the work's "achievement is to bring into focus crucial aspects of Plautine technique that we have all probably sensed but not consciously articulated." Smith praised Slater's work of literary criticism for its originality and basis in "sound philological principles." "These are not routine textual analyses: time and again, Slater offers highly original theatrical suggestions and imaginative critical insight," lauded Smith, who added that in this "deceptively slim and elegantly written volume, Niall Slater has produced a work of literary criticism that is guaranteed to instruct, challenge, delight, and provoke every student of Roman drama."

In 1990 Slater published his next study, *Reading Petronius,* which, according to *Choice*'s C. J. Zabrowski, is a "sensitive narratological analysis" of the *Satyricon,* Petronius's fragmentary novel. Slater's study is made up of three different readings of the novel. In each reading he employs a different analytical format and method, and in the opinion of Graham Anderson, writing in the *Classical Review,* each subsequent reading is more difficult than the previous interpretation to understand, particularly as it pertains to methodology. One such analytical technique is the reader-response method, and *Phoenix*'s Roger Beck pondered if this method is the best technique to use in analyzing *Satyricon,* in part because it begs the question "Which audience—ancient or modern" is providing the response to the work? David Konstan also expressed reservations about this method in his *Classical Philology* review. Yet while Konstan did not agree with all of Slater's conclusions, he appreciated Slater's interpretations for enabling "a sensitive encounter with the text." For the contemporary reader, "the achievement of *Reading Petronius* is that it finally lets us put to rest our scruples about anachronism and read the *Satyricon* as a thing marvellously ahead of its time, a novel in the fullest sense," continued Beck, adding, "Slater is a perceptive reader of Petronius and will prove an informative, witty, and genial guide for other readers of the *Satyricon,* both new and old." In the *Virginia Quarterly Review* a critic judged this study to be "erudite, brilliant, and stylishly written."

In *Spectator Politics: Metatheater and Performance in Aristophanes,* Slater provides "compelling readings" of eight comedic plays by Greek dramatist Aristophanes, noted a *Virginia Quarterly Review* contributor. Metatheater, the method by which the playwright reveals in the work that the play in question is an artifice, is the primary topic of Slater's analysis. Amy R. Cohen, who noted that Slater "demonstrates considerable theatrical sensitivity," praised the title as well. In the *American Journal of Philology,* she remarked that "Slater finds a welcome alternative to thoroughly ironic readings of the plays and to readings that acknowledge no unity of thought behind the performances, only laugh-creating gimmicks." Although, Cohen added, "the book shows some signs of having been put together in part from previously published works," she found its faults to be minor. "Slater's partisanship on behalf of comedy and Aristophanes is well grounded and persuasive" and his "admiration for the comedian's genius is infectious, which is by no means the least of the virtues of his book," she added. Several scholars remarked on the currency of the plays' themes, including Emily Wilson of the *Times Literary Supplement,* who wrote, "Slater certainly makes Aristophanes seem like essential reading for anyone interested in contemporary American or British politics." Finally, a *Choice* reviewer summed up *Spectator Politics* as "a fine and learned addition to the field."

Slater told *CA:* "My principal interest is in performance criticism of ancient drama. I have also excavated at Pella, Jordan, with the Wooster/Sydney expedition."

BIOGRAPHICAL AND CRITICAL SOURCES:

PERIODICALS

American Journal of Philology, summer, 2003, Amy R. Cohen, review of *Spectator Politics: Metatheater and Performance in Aristophanes,* p. 309.

Choice, January, 1991, C. J. Zabrowski, review of *Reading Petronius;* February, 2003, D. Konstan, review of *Spectator Politics,* p. 979.

Classical Philology, January, 1992, David Konstan, review of *Reading Petronius,* pp. 85-90.

Classical Review, Volume 41, number 2, 1991, Graham Anderson, review of *Reading Petronius,* pp. 340-341.

Phoenix, summer, 1986, Peter L. Smith, review of *Plautus in Performance,* pp. 218-220; spring, 1992, Roger Beck, review of *Reading Petronius,* pp. 69-72.

Times Literary Supplement, January 17, 2003, Emily Wilson, "Cut the Orchestra," review of *Spectator Politics.*

Virginia Quarterly Review, spring, 1991, review of *Reading Petronius,* p. 48; summer, 2003, review of *Spectator Politics,* p. 84.

ONLINE

Emory University, http://www.emory.edu/ (September 29, 2003), Eric Rangus, "A Classical President."*

* * *

SPADA, James 1950-

PERSONAL: Born January 23, 1950, in Staten Island, NY; son of Joseph Vincent and Mary (Ruberto) Spada. *Education:* Attended Wagner College, 1968-71, Hunter College of the City University of New York, 1972-75, and California State University, 1979-80. *Politics:* Liberal Democrat. *Religion:* "Discarded." *Hobbies and other interests:* Physical education, sports, drawing, painting, music, photography, antiques, cooking, collecting (books, prints, records, magazines, photos, quilts).

ADDRESSES: *Home*—Brookline, MA. *Agent*—c/o Author Mail, St. Martin's Press, 175 5th Ave., New York, NY 10010. *E-mail*—jamesspada@attbi.com.

CAREER: Writer and publisher. New York State Council on the Arts, New York, NY, office assistant, 1966 and 1969; Wagner College Library, Staten Island, NY, assistant librarian in periodicals department, 1969-70; *EMK: The Edward M. Kennedy Quarterly,* editor and publisher, 1969-72; U.S. Senate, Washington, DC, intern to Senator Edward M. Kennedy, 1970; *In the Know,* New York, NY, managing editor, 1975, editor, 1975-76; *Barbra Quarterly,* Los Angeles, CA, editor and publisher, 1980-83.

MEMBER: Authors Guild, Authors League of America, American Civil Liberties Union.

WRITINGS:

Barbra: The First Decade—The Films and Career of Barbra Streisand, Citadel (Secaucus, NJ), 1974.

The Films of Robert Redford, Citadel (Secaucus, NJ), 1977.

The Spada Report: The Newest Survey of Gay Male Sexuality, New American Library (New York, NY), 1979.

(With Christopher Nickens) *Streisand: The Woman and the Legend,* Doubleday (New York, NY), 1981, updated paperback edition, 1983.

(With George Zeno) *Monroe: Her Life in Pictures,* Doubleday (New York, NY), 1982.

(With Karen Swenson) *Judy and Liza,* Doubleday (New York, NY), 1983.

Hepburn: Her Life in Pictures, Doubleday (New York, NY), 1984.

The Divine Bette Midler, Macmillan (New York, NY), 1984.

Fonda: Her Life in Pictures, Doubleday (New York, NY), 1985.

Shirley and Warren, Macmillan (New York, NY), 1985.

Grace: The Secret Lives of a Princess—An Intimate Biography of Grace Kelly, Doubleday (New York, NY), 1987.

Peter Lawford: The Man Who Kept the Secrets, Bantam (New York, NY), 1991.

More Than a Woman: An Intimate Biography of Bette Davis, Bantam (New York, NY), 1993.

Streisand: Her Life, Crown (New York, NY), 1995.

Jackie: Her Life in Pictures, St. Martin's Press (New York, NY), 2000.

Black and White Men: Images by James Spada (collection of photographs), Pond Street Press (Natick, MA), 2000.

Ronald Reagan: His Life in Pictures, St. Martin's Press (New York, NY), 2001.

John and Caroline: Their Lives in Pictures, St. Martin's Press (New York, NY), 2001.

Julia Roberts: An Intimate Biography, St. Martin's Press (New York, NY), 2004.

Grace: The Secret Lives of a Princess has been translated into twelve languages.

WORK IN PROGRESS: Legend, a novel.

SIDELIGHTS: Celebrity biographer James Spada has published a number pictorial profiles and full-length biographies of such Hollywood and political luminaries as Marilyn Monroe, Jackie Kennedy Onassis, Ronald Reagan, Katharine Hepburn, Bette Davis, Robert Redford, and Peter Lawford.

Spada was working on a biography of the late Grace Kelly, Princess of Monaco, when, as he once told *CA,* he stumbled upon "a remarkable story that hadn't been told before." Kelly, an Oscar-winning actress of the 1950s—cinema's "ice-princess"—became a top audience-draw with her stunning looks, subtle English accent, and controlled, mannered demeanor. In 1956, at the height of her career, the Philadelphia-born Kelly made world headlines when she abandoned Hollywood to become real-life royalty: the wife of Prince Rainier of Monaco, ruler of the tiny Mediterranean principality nestled on the coast of southeastern France. There she lived as Princess Grace of Monaco—raising three children—until her sudden death in 1982 from injuries received in an automobile accident.

While conducting interviews for his book on Grace Kelly, and in reviewing some of her early personal correspondence, Spada, however, discovered a woman much different than the one suggested by her public persona. As he candidly remarked to Michael Kilian of the *Chicago Tribune,* Spada came upon two important revelations about Grace Kelly: "The first . . . was how the most sexually active woman in Hollywood was able to come across as the most chaste. The second was that Prince Rainier actually believed that she was a virgin." Spada's original picture-book project expanded into a full-length narrative text, 1987's *Grace: The Secret Lives of a Princess—An Intimate Biography of Grace Kelly,* which, as Yvonne Cox noted in *Maclean's,* "portrays a beautiful young actress whose cool, white-gloved exterior concealed a smouldering sexuality and a compulsion to bed her leading men."

In the biography which, he explained to Kilian, is "not a hatchet job," Spada shows how in her early career, young Grace rebelled against the mores of both her wealthy authoritarian family and strict Catholic upbringing, and conducted sexual affairs with a number of Hollywood's leading men, including William Holden, Gary Cooper, Ray Milland, and Bing Crosby. Spada's account does much to describe Grace's actions in light of the influences of her family—the prominent Kellys of Philadelphia. In particular, Grace's father, Jack—Irish immigrant, ex-Olympic rowing champion, and self-made millionaire—emerges, according to Ellin Stein in the *New York Times Book Review,* "as a bigoted domestic tyrant" whose lack of faith in Grace was a large factor in the young actress's attraction to married older men. One account tells of how the elder Kelly, upon hearing of Grace's Best Actress Oscar for *The Country Girl,* expressed astonishment at such an accomplishment coming from his meekest daughter—and not from his favorite, Peggy. Other family insights surface in the story of how Grace's mother threatened to campaign against her own son, John—a promising mayoral candidate—because he once dated a transsexual. Some reviewers found the tales of the Kelly family one of the book's more intriguing features. "Although it can, and no doubt will, be read simply as a now-it-can-be-told report on the life and loves of America's favorite movie star-turned-princess," wrote Bruce Cook in the *Washington Post Book World,* "nevertheless, it is far more interesting considered as a history of the Kelly family of Philadelphia told from the point-of-view of its most prominent (though by no means most powerful) member."

Outside of her family woes, Grace's marriage to Prince Rainier was also less than ideal, according to Spada. "More of a business merger than a fairy-tale romance," remarked Piers Brendon in the *Observer,* the Kelly family paid a two-million-dollar dowry for their daughter's entrance into high society. Prince Rainier on the other hand, noted Cook, "thought that an American movie star on the throne would almost certainly increase tourism in the five-mile square principality (it did, tremendously); he needed an heir; and, when it came right down to it, he—and Monaco—

could use the money [Grace's] rich father could provide." Regarding Grace's motivations in the marriage, Cook agreed with Spada's contention that guilt played a major role. Grace's "Catholic upbringing left her guilty about her sexual dalliances," wrote Spada, "and angry at her family for continually objecting to her attempts to legitimize herself in their eyes through marriage."

Reception of *Grace: The Secret Lives of a Princess* included the claim that disclosures of Kelly's sexual exploits are not all that astonishing. "People who want to find out if Grace Kelly was a sensuous woman need only see *To Catch a Thief,*" wrote a critic for *Time,* while Cox commented that Spada's account "simply adds a light sexual frosting to her already well-documented life." Heather Neill in the *Listener,* acknowledging that "Spada presents us with a sympathetic portrait of his heroine," added that his "book hovers between voyeurism and hagiography." Other reviewers, however, have found the biography more than just an exposé of a revered screen idol. "Indeed, the truly interesting new light the book sheds on Grace Kelly is not that her love life was more active than previously suspected," commented Stein, "but that she suffered a very modern conflict over her real-life role." Spada himself remarked to Kilian that he wanted to "put aside [Kelly's] 'one-dimensional' image and reveal her as the vital human being she was. She was very complex, very troubled, very passionate and very intelligent." *Times Literary Supplement*'s Victoria Glendinning lauded the biographer's achievement: "In exposing for the first time Grace Kelly's promiscuity, James Spada claims justifiably to be revealing a more interesting person than the legend allows."

In addition to his books about Hollywood celebrities, Spada has also written several titles concerning the Kennedy family: *Peter Lawford: The Man Who Kept the Secrets, Jackie: Her Life in Pictures,* and *John and Caroline: Their Lives in Pictures. Peter Lawford: The Man Who Kept the Secrets* is the life story of the English-born actor who married into the Kennedy family. The "secrets" of the book's title refers to Lawford's unsavory role in keeping confidential the scandalous details of President John F. Kennedy's numerous sexual affairs so that the president could continue to play the public role of faithful husband and devout Catholic. Lawford was especially important in introducing Kennedy to Marilyn Monroe, in keeping that relationship private, and in assisting Kennedy after the president decided to end the affair. The critic for *Video Age International* called the biography "well researched and colorfully described. . . . Spada does a fine job."

Jackie: Her Life in Pictures and *John and Caroline: Their Lives in Pictures* are collections of photographs taken by a number of people chronicling the lives of the Kennedy clan members. *Jackie: Her Life in Pictures* contains 250 photographs, ranging from baby pictures of the famous First Lady to a final shot of her two children standing next to her open casket. As the heiress to a fortune, the wife of a president, then the wife of a shipping tycoon, Jackie Kennedy became one of the most widely-known women in the world. A critic for *Publishers Weekly* believed that the collection effectively captured "her well-lived, much-photographed life in adoring detail." Donna Seaman in *Booklist* called the book "a fascinating array of photographs." Speaking of why he had chosen to do a collection of photographs about Jackie Kennedy instead of an in-depth biography, Spada explained to Stephen MacMillan Moser in the *Austin Chronicle:* "There have been plenty of books purporting to reveal her innermost secrets; I wanted mine to be a celebration of her glamour, beauty, and style."

Jackie's two children are presented in Spada's book *John and Caroline: Their Lives in Pictures,* a collection of 255 photographs. Many of these photos are from private sources and never before published. As the youngest children to ever live in the White House, the two Kennedy children have always been members of the celebrity culture. When their father was assassinated in 1963, the nation's heart went out to them in a way no other celebrities have experienced. John Kennedy, Jr.'s own tragic death in an airplane crash brought further sympathetic attention to the pair.

Spada turned to another political figure in his book *Ronald Reagan: His Life in Pictures,* a collection of 350 photographs of the popular president. While Spada admits having political differences with Reagan, he told Moser that in the process of doing his book, "I have gained a measure of admiration for him as a man." Published to celebrate Reagan's ninetieth birthday in 2001, the book begins with childhood and school photos, covers his time as a college football hero, moves through his years as a Hollywood actor, and then documents his successful career in politics as governor of California and American president. While some of the photographs are familiar from news reports of the time, the collection includes many family photos not seen before. Carole L. Philipps in the *Cincinnati Post* described Spada's book as "the story of a man who dreamed and realized the American dream several times over as athlete, actor, governor and president." *Ronald Reagan: His Life in Pictures,* Ray Olson wrote in *Booklist,* "forcibly recalls his enormous popularity when in office."

While his previous books featured the works of many different photographers, *Black and White Men: Images by James Spada* contains only Spada's own photographic work. The book contains sixty black-and-white photographs of young men taken by Spada in his own home. He used real people in the photographs, including his own lover, instead of professional models. Moser found that "Spada's lens caresses his subjects. His work is a paean to male beauty, with the same appreciation seen in classical Greek art. But Spada's compositions have an intimacy and sexuality that is lacking in most classical art." According to Jesse Monteagudo in *Gay Today Magazine,* "*Black and White Men* is a wonderful book, and an essential text for anyone who appreciates the male art form."

Although primarily known for his celebrity biographies, Spada is branching out into other areas of writing. He once commented to *CA:* "I hope that my recent writings have greatly improved on my earlier efforts. Writing is a vocation I find rewarding, educational, rending, draining, fulfilling, frustrating, and lovely. My writings will continue to grow as I do. Although I have enjoyed much success with celebrity biographies, I hope to be as well known as a novelist. . . . My first novel, *Legend,* will be a fictional biography of a legendary female movie star."

BIOGRAPHICAL AND CRITICAL SOURCES:

BOOKS

Spada, James, *Grace: The Secret Lives of a Princess—An Intimate Biography of Grace Kelly,* Doubleday (New York, NY), 1987.

PERIODICALS

American Spectator, November, 1991, M. G. Lord, review of *Peter Lawford: The Man Who Kept the Secrets,* p. 45.

Atlanta Journal-Constitution, September 9, 2001, Teresa K. Weaver, "Staying True to Life, Fresh Approach Invigorates Some Familiar Subjects," p. D4.

Austin Chronicle, June 9, 2000, Stephen MacMillan Moser, "Spada Speaks"; December 22, 2000, Stephen MacMillan Moser, review of *Black and White Men: Images by James Spada.*

Booklist, August, 1993, Donna Seaman, review of *More Than a Woman: An Intimate Biography of Bette Davis,* p. 2011; October 1, 1995, Donna Seaman, review of *Streisand: Her Life,* p. 211; April 15, 2000, Donna Seaman, review of *Jackie: Her Life in Pictures,* p. 1521; January 1, 2001, Ray Olson, review of *Ronald Reagan: His Life in Pictures,* p. 909.

Chicago Tribune, May 3, 1987.

Cincinnati Post, February 3, 2001, Carole L. Philipps, "Reagan Book a Fine Tribute," p. 7C.

Cosmopolitan, July, 1991, Louise Bernikow, review of *Peter Lawford,* p. 28.

Entertainment Weekly, October 27, 1995, review of *Streisand: Her Life,* p. 85; September 13, 1996, review of *Streisand: Her Life,* paperback edition, p. 127.

Library Journal, August, 1991, Kim Holston, review of *Peter Lawford,* p. 104; September 1, 1993, Sherle Abramson, review of *More Than a Woman,* p. 187; November 15, 1995, Rosellen Brewer, review of *Streisand: Her Life,* p. 77.

Listener, July 16, 1987.

Maclean's, July 27, 1987.

Newsweek, April 27, 1987.

New York Times Book Review, November 4, 1984; July 19, 1987.

Observer, June 28, 1987.

People, July 6, 1987; May 29, 2000, David Cobb Craig, review of *Jackie,* p. 41.

Publishers Weekly, July 26, 1993, review of *More Than a Woman,* p. 49; October 2, 1995, review of *Streisand: Her Life,* p. 61; April 17, 2000, review of *Jackie,* p. 69; September 25, 2000, review of *Ronald Reagan,* p. 54.

Spectator, December 16, 1995, Mark Steyn, review of *Streisand: The Intimate Biography,* p. 63.

Time, April 27, 1987.

Times Literary Supplement, July 24, 1987, Victoria Glendinning, review of *Grace: The Secret Lives of a Princess—An Intimate Biography of Grace Kelly.*

US Weekly, July 23, 2001, Janet Steen, review of *John and Caroline: Their Lives in Pictures,* p. 68.

Variety, July 15, 1991, review of *Peter Lawford,* p. 56.

Video Age International, October-November, 1991, review of *Peter Lawford,* p. 14.

Washington Post Book World, June 21, 1987.

ONLINE

Gay Today Magazine Web site, http://gaytoday.badpuppy.com/garchive/reviews/ (May 1, 2003), Jesse Monteagudo, review of *Black and White Men: Images by James Spada.*

James Spada Home Page, http://www.jamesspada.com/ (May 1, 2003).*

* * *

SQUIRES, Michael (George) 1941-

PERSONAL: Born July 18, 1941, in Alexandria, VA; son of Fay Calvin (a statistician) and Arvilla (Windell) Squires; married Sylvia Nottingham (a learning disabilities teacher), August 15, 1964 (divorced, 1981); married Lynn K. Talbot (a Spanish professor), June 27, 1987; children: Kelly Michael, Cameron Windell, Andrew. *Education:* Bucknell University, B.A., 1963; University of Virginia, M.A., 1964; University of Maryland, Ph.D., 1969.

ADDRESSES: Home—1416 Palmer Drive, Blacksburg, VA 24060. *Office*—Department of English, Virginia Tech, Blacksburg, VA 24061-0112. *E-mail*—msquires@vt.edu.

CAREER: Virginia Commonwealth University, Richmond, instructor in English, 1964-65; University of Maryland, College Park, instructor in English, 1967-69; Virginia Tech, Blacksburg, assistant professor, 1969-75, associate professor of English, 1975-80; professor of English, 1980-2001; professor emeritus, 2001.

MEMBER: Modern Language Association of America, College English Association, Conference on College Composition and Communication.

AWARDS, HONORS: Harry T. Moore Award for Distinguished Scholarship on D. H. Lawernce, 1994.

WRITINGS:

The Pastoral Novel: Studies in George Eliot, Thomas Hardy, and D. H. Lawrence, University Press of Virginia (Charlottesville, VA), 1974.

The Creation of "Lady Chatterley's Lover," Johns Hopkins University Press (Baltimore, MD), 1983.

(With wife, Lynn K. Talbot) *Living at the Edge: A Biography of D. H. Lawrence and Frieda von Richthofen,* University of Wisconsin Press (Madison, WI), 2002.

EDITOR:

(With Dennis Jackson) *D. H. Lawrence's "Lady": A New Look at Lady Chatterley's Lover,* University of Georgia Press (Athens, GA), 1985.

(With Keith Cushman) *The Challenge of D. H. Lawrence,* University of Wisconsin Press (Madison, WI), 1990.

D. H. Lawrence's Manuscripts: The Correspondence of Frieda Lawrence, Jake Zeitlin, and Others, St. Martin's Press (New York, NY), 1991.

D. H. Lawrence, *Lady Chatterley's Lover; A Propos of "Lady Chatterley's Lover,"* Cambridge University Press (New York, NY), 1993.

SIDELIGHTS: A past president of the D. H. Lawrence Society of America, Michael Squires has parlayed his expertise into a number of books about the author of *Lady Chatterley's Lover, The Rainbow,* and other classic novels. As editor of *Lady Chatterley's Lover; A Propos of "Lady Chatterley's Lover,"* Squires presents some of the hundreds of letters written by Lawrence toward the end of his life. Though sick with tuberculosis, Lawrence still took an active part in the publishing of his controversial novel. "What comes across" in Squires's work, noted Karen McLeod Hewitt in the *Review of English Studies,* "is the quality of life still within the dying man. Through the 784 letters and cards written over this period we learn of his continuing activity in publishing and distributing *Lady Chatterley's Lover,* and of his schemes for outwitting the many perpetrators of pirated copies."

In 2002, Squires and his wife, Lynn K. Talbot, produced *Living at the Edge: A Biography of D. H. Lawrence and Frieda von Richthofen.* The married couple were celebrities of their day, publishing books and associating with the notable Bloomsbury Group. But the marriage was not without its obstacles. A *Publishers Weekly* contributor wrote that *Living at the Edge* "may offer the last word on the Lawrence's volatile partnership, which was famously beset by sexual identity crises (his) and infidelities (hers)." Indeed, Lawrence struggled with latent homosexual tendencies; at the same time, von Richthofen left her first husband and children behind to take up with Lawrence.

In her assessment for the *New Leader,* Carolyn Heilbrun noticed that Squires and Talbot seek to maintain separate identifies for their subjects, even to the extent of using "his last name and her first" in the book. "This 'double biography' is, moreover, written by a married couple who bring to their work the 'lens of our own marriage,'" Heilbrun continued. "Squires and Talbot, perhaps because of this dual viewpoint, are especially astute in reading much in Lawrence's novels as disguised but evident messages to Frieda that he could not deliver any other way." The critic did feel that von Richthofen's role in the book—and the marriage—may have been less significant; "doesn't her entire claim upon our interest abide in her husband?" she asked. Still, Heilbrun summarized *Living at the Edge* as "a biography for anyone coming to Lawrence anew, or anyone wishing to revive an acquaintance with him." In reading this volume, she said, "we understand his unique interpretation of life, and his endless pursuit of its ideal form, which he never found."

BIOGRAPHICAL AND CRITICAL SOURCES:

PERIODICALS

Antioch Review, winter, 1984, review of *D. H. Lawrence's "Lady": A New Look at "Lady Chatterley's Lover,"* p. 372.

British Book News, April, 1980, review of *The Pastoral Novel: Studies in George Eliot, Thomas Hardy, and D. H. Lawrence,* p. 20; July, 1984, review of *The Creation of "Lady Chatterley's Lover,"* p. 437.

Choice, May, 1984, review of *The Creation of "Lady Chatterley's Lover,"* p. 1310; November, 1990, review of *The Challenge of D. H. Lawrence,* p. 481.

Criticism, winter, 1985, review of *The Creation of "Lady Chatterley's Lover,"* p. 103.

English Literature in Transition, 1880-1920, Number 3, 1991, review of *D. H. Lawrence's Manuscripts,* p. 119.

Journal of English and Germanic Philology, April, 1992, review of *The Challenge of D. H. Lawrence,* p. 270.

Library Journal, September 15, 1990, review of *The Challenge of D. H. Lawrence,* p. 78; June 15, 1991, review of *D. H. Lawrence's Manuscripts,* p. 76; May 15, 2002, Morris Hounion, review of *Living at the Edge: A Biography of D. H. Lawrence and Frieda von Richthofen,* p. 98.

Los Angeles Times Book Review, March 4, 1984, review of *The Creation of "Lady Chatterley's Lover,"* p. 6.

Modern Fiction Studies, winter, 1984, review of *The Creation of "Lady Chatterley's Lover,"* p. 766; summer, 1985, review of *D. H. Lawrence's "Lady,"* p. 357; winter, 1990, review of *The Challenge of D. H. Lawrence,* p. 604.

Modern Language Review, January, 1989, review of *D. H. Lawrence's "Lady,"* p. 146.

New Leader, May-June, 2002, Carolyn Heilbrun, "A Search for Manhood," p. 38.

New York Times Book Review, September 22, 1991, review of *D. H. Lawrence's Manuscripts,* p. 26.

Publishers Weekly, May 20, 2002, review of *Living at the Edge,* p. 61.

Review of English Studies, November, 1976, review of *The Pastoral Novel,* p. 510; November, 1995, Karen McLeod Hewitt, review of *Lady Chatterley's Lover; A Propos of "Lady Chatterley's Lover"* p. 606.

Southern Humanities Review, fall, 1986, review of *D. H. Lawrence's "Lady",* p. 385.

Times Literary Supplement, September 7, 1990, review of *The Challenge of D. H. Lawrence,* p. 940.

University Press Book News, June, 1990, review of *The Challenge of D. H. Lawrence,* p. 32.

Western Humanities Review, autumn, 1985, review of *The Creation of "Lady Chatterley's Lover,"* p. 278.

* * *

STARK, Richard
See WESTLAKE, Donald E(dwin)

STONE, Katherine 1949-

PERSONAL: Born 1949 in Seattle, WA; married Jack Chase (a novelist). *Education:* Stanford University, B.A.; University of Washington, M.D.

ADDRESSES: *Home*—Pacific Northwest. *Agent*—c/o Author Mail, Warner Books, Time-Life Building, 1271 Avenue of the Americas, New York, NY 10020.

CAREER: Romance and mystery writer. Physician.

WRITINGS:

Roommates, 1987, reprinted, Wheeler (Rockland, MA), 1996.
Twins, Kensington (New York, NY), 1989.
Bel Air, Kensington (New York, NY), 1990.
Love Songs, Kensington (New York, NY), 1991.
Rainbows, Kensington (New York, NY) 1992.
Promises, Kensington (New York, NY), 1993.
Illusions, Kensington (New York, NY), 1994.
Happy Endings, Kensington (New York, NY), 1994.
Pearl Moon, Fawcett Columbine (New York, NY), 1995.
A New Collection of Three Complete Novels (contains *Promises, Rainbows,* and *Twins*), Wings Books (New York, NY), 1995.
Imagine Love, Fawcett Columbine (New York, NY), 1996.
The Carlton Club, Wheeler (Rockland, MD), 1997.
Bed of Roses, Warner (New York, NY), 1998.
(With Anne Stuart, Donna Julian, and Jodie Larsen; and editor) *Sisters & Secrets: A Novel in Four Parts,* Onyx Books, 1998.
Home at Last, Warner (New York, NY), 1999.
A Midnight Clear, Warner (New York, NY), 1999.
Thief of Hearts, Warner (New York, NY), 1999.
Island of Dreams, Warner (New York, NY), 2000.
Star Light, Star Bright, Mira (Don Mills, Ontario, Canada), 2002.
The Other Twin, Mira (Don Mills, Ontario, Canada), 2003.
Another Man's Son, Mira (Don Mills, Ontario, Canada), 2004.

SIDELIGHTS: A medical doctor by training, Katherine Stone has become a prolific writer of romances that often combine elements of the mystery novel. Her style has been compared to that of authors Danielle Steel, Nora Roberts, and Sandra Brown. Most of her novels take place in glamorous settings and are peopled with accomplished, beautiful characters. While critics cannot agree on whether Stone's lavish prose and intricate plots are commendable, her fans have made her a best-selling author.

Among her early novels are *Twins, Bel Air,* and *Love Songs.* The first title is about feuding twin sisters who are forced to mend their relationship in order to fix other problems in their lives. A *Publishers Weekly* critic deemed the book to be "absorbing" and concluded that if some plot elements were artificial, "for the most part, the twists and turns . . . are devilishly realistic and true to human nature." *Publishers Weekly* contributor Penny Kaganoff reviewed *Bel Air* less kindly, calling this story of six rich and talented characters who are drawn into a potential murder case "overstuffed" and "more atmospheric glitz than plot." Kaganoff also reviewed *Love Songs,* noting that the characters are "handsome or successful, but also confused." The article concluded that "realism is not a prime factor" in the novel.

Stone's hardcover debut came with *Rainbows,* the story of a pianist named Catherine Taylor and her movie-actress sister, Alexa. Their lives are turned upside down when Catherine learns she is adopted, having been given to her mother—along with a stunning sapphire necklace that ultimately links her to the royal family of a small island kingdom—by a mysterious woman. A *Publishers Weekly* reviewer remarked that "Stone keeps the reader pleasantly off guard, and her finale is a veritable torrent of cataclysms and revelations." A *Kirkus Reviews* contributor commented, "Fairy-tale elements mix with those of a present-day romance—for wholly improbable yet thoroughly enjoyable results."

Stone has also involved multiple central characters in several of her romances. Her novel *Promises* has three heroines: one a model, another a surgeon, and the third a dress designer. Each woman has a love life turned upside down by violence, distrust, or death. A critic for *Publishers Weekly* found the book entertaining and that it had a "slick tension that will please fans," but considered Stone's prose "pedestrian" and declared that her plots lean "heavily on misunderstandings and coincidences."

Booklist's Melanie Duncan responded favorably to Stone's *Happy Endings,* noting that it is "not without suspense"; this book ultimately lives up to its title after following the (separate) romantic ups and downs of Hollywood lawyer Raven Winter and writer Holly Elliot. Both women are fighting with demons from their pasts as they form promising but troubled romantic relationships. Similarly, a *Library Journal* critic recommended the book to "devotees" as "a delightful read."

In 1995's *Pearl Moon,* Stone departed from her typically ritzy American settings and placed her story in Hong Kong. In addition, she gave a twist to the sisters theme used earlier in a story of two women—one American, one Chinese—who find they have the same father, a deceased Vietnam War veteran. A critic for *Kirkus Reviews* cast a cynical eye on the novel, commenting that "the bang of romantic cymbals never drowns out the steady hum of predictable cliches." A reviewer for *Publishers Weekly,* however, maintained that "Stone's vivid narrative and glamorous settings energize this melodramatic tale," and a *Library Journal* contributor recommended the book for fans of Steel and Brown as "light and fluffy formula reading."

Stone more markedly changed her pace in 1996 with *Imagine Love,* a romance combined with mystery set in the Louisiana bayou. Famous singer Cole Taylor returns to his small hometown to discover that his childhood sweetheart, Claire, was blinded on her wedding day and abandoned before her marriage was ever consummated. When Cole takes Claire to London, they are caught up in a serial murderer's web. *Library Journal* reviewer Kristin Ramsdell described the novel as "lushly worded, somewhat reflective" and, as a mystery, "chillingly done." A contributor to *Publishers Weekly* characterized the book's writing and plot as "overheated," while a *Kirkus Reviews* critic called it "soap at its most operatic, though the playing on the heartstrings occasionally strikes an affecting emotional note."

Returning to the rich and famous of California in *Bed of Roses,* Stone crafts a crime story about a winemaker named Chase and his estranged wife, Cassandra, an actress who is nearly killed in a brutal attack. Chase is drawn to Cassandra's bedside and also assists in solving the crime. A *Publishers Weekly* contributor expressed disappointment in Stone's treatment of a promising premise, describing the novel as "a haphazard mishmash of abuse, murder, unrequited love, dead babies, pop psychology and mistaken identities." A *Booklist* reviewer judged that the mystery-romance was just the stuff to satisfy Stone's fans: "an easy read about an unrealistic, fantasy-based relationship."

With her 2002 title *Star Light, Star Bright,* Stone left Warner Books for Mira, a Canadian-based publisher. In her first romance for the new publisher, the author follows Rafe McClure, a Mexican immigrant who is the sole survivor when a mudslide destroys his village. After spending a stint at a Texas ranch, Rafe ends up at a horse farm in Virginia, where he befriends the teenage sisters Brooke and Lily. After their parents are murdered, Lily inherits the farm and Brooke leaves for the West Coast. Only when Brooke returns twelve years later will the mysteries surrounding the women's pasts be solved. *Star Light, Star Bright* caught the attention of several reviewers, including one for *Publishers Weekly,* who believed that Stone tried to pack too much into a single novel, making it a "confusing read." On the other hand, Maria Hatton of *Booklist* faulted what she considered underdeveloped characters, yet predicted that because of its "fast-paced" plot, the novel would be welcomed by Stone's fans.

In several novels, including her earliest, Stone has used the existence of twins as a plot device. Such is the case in *Thief of Hearts,* a novel about heart surgeon Caitlyn Taylor that Melanie Duncan dubbed a "high-quality romance" in her *Booklist* review. When Taylor tries to save her best friend, Patrick Falconer, from a fatal illness, the solution involves trying to reconcile Falconer with his estranged twin brother. As the title suggests, *The Other Twin,* Stone's 2003 novel, also features twins, this time women. In this "moving story of family love," to quote Maria Hatton of *Booklist,* Gwen St. James and Claire Forrester share a rare friendship, one that they discover means much more than they could imagine.

BIOGRAPHICAL AND CRITICAL SOURCES:

PERIODICALS

Booklist, January 1, 1992, Cynthia Ogorek, review of *Rainbows,* p. 812; August, 1994, Melanie Duncan, review of *Happy Endings,* pp. 2024-2025; February 1, 1995, Mary Carroll, review of *Pearl Moon,* p. 971; April 15, 1996, Melanie Duncan, review of *Imagine Love,* p. 1423; January 1, 1998, Kathleen Hughes, review of *Bed of Roses,* p. 744; February 1, 1999, Melanie Duncan, review of *Thief of Hearts,* p. 966; August, 2000, Patty Engelmann, review of *Island of Dreams,* p. 2124; December 15, 2001, Maria Hatton, review of *Star Light, Star Bright,* p. 709; January 1, 2003, Maria Hatton, review of *The Other Twin,* p. 852.

Kirkus Reviews, November 15, 1991, review of *Rainbows,* pp. 1432-1433; February 1, 1995, review of *Pearl Moon,* p. 101; February 1, 1996, review of *Imagine Love,* p. 170.

Library Journal, November 15, 1991, Marilyn Jordan, review of *Rainbows,* p. 108; August, 1994, Margaret Hanes, review of *Happy Endings,* p. 134; February 1, 1995, Dawn L. Anderson, review of *Pearl Moon,* p. 101; February 15, 1996, Kristin Ramsdell, review of *Imagine Love,* p. 139.

Publishers Weekly, March 24, 1989, review of *Twins,* p. 63; April 6, 1990, Penny Kaganoff, review of *Bel Air,* p. 112; March 22, 1991, Penny Kaganoff, review of *Love Songs,* p. 76; November 29, 1991, review of *Rainbows,* p. 44; January 18, 1993, review of *Promises,* p. 452; January 10, 1994, review of *Illusions,* p. 46; January 23, 1995, review of *Pearl Moon,* p. 58; January 29, 1996, review of *Imagine Love,* p. 83; January 26, 1998, review of *Bed of Roses,* p. 71; November 26, 2001, review of *Star Light, Star Bright,* p. 40.*

T-V

TALBOTT, Hudson 1949-

PERSONAL: Born July 11, 1949, in Louisville, KY; son of Peyton (a mortgage loan officer) and Mildred (a dress shop manager; maiden name, Pence) Talbott. *Education:* Attended University of Cincinnati; received B.F.A. from Temple University. *Politics:* "Registered Democrat." *Religion:* Siddha yoga.

ADDRESSES: *Home and office*—119 5th Ave., New York, NY 10003. *E-mail*—hudsontal@aol.com.

CAREER: Freelance illustrator, New York, NY, 1974—. Clients include Metropolitan Museum of Art, Museum of Modern Art, Metropolitan Opera Guild, Bloomingdale's Department Store, Harper & Row and Crown publishers, Paper Moon Graphics, and Ruby Street, Inc. Member of board of directors of Art Awareness (a nonprofit arts-presenting organization), Lexington, NY.

MEMBER: Society of Children's Book Writers.

AWARDS, HONORS: Kentucky Bluegrass Award nomination, 2002-03, Readers Choice Award nomination, Michigan Reading Association, 2003, William Allen White Award nomination, 2003, American Library Association's Book Picks, 2002, Notable Children's Books List, Association for Library Service to Children, and Honor List, *Voice of Youth Advocates* Nonfiction, all for *Leonardo's Horse.*

Hudson Talbott

WRITINGS:

How to Show Grown-Ups the Museum, Museum of Modern Art (New York, NY), 1986.

The Lady at Liberty: Memoirs of a Monument, Avon (New York, NY), 1986.

We're Back! A Dinosaur's Story, Crown (New York, NY), 1987.

(Illustrator) Stephen Sondheim and James Lapine, *Into the Woods,* Crown (New York, NY), 1988.

Going Hollywood: A Dinosaur's Dream, Crown (New York, NY), 1989.

King Arthur: The Sword in the Stone, Morrow (New York, NY), 1991.

Your Pet Dinosaur: An Owner's Manual, Morrow (New York, NY), 1992.

King Arthur and the Round Table, Morrow (New York, NY), 1995.

Excalibur, Morrow (New York, NY), 1996.

(With Mark Greenberg) *Amazon Diary: The Jungle Adventures of Alex Winters,* Putnam (New York, NY), 1996.

Lancelot, Morrow (New York, NY), 1999.

O'Sullivan Stew: A Tale Cooked Up in Ireland, Putnam (New York, NY), 1999.

Forging Freedom: A True Story of Heroism during the Holocaust, Putnam (New York, NY), 2000.

(Illustrator) Jan Fritz, *Leonardo's Horse,* Putnam (New York, NY), 2001.

Safari Journal: The Adventures in Africa of Carey Monroe, Harcourt (San Diego, CA), 2003.

(Illustrator) Jan Fritz, *The Lost Colony of Roanoke,* Putnam (New York, NY), 2004.

ADAPTATIONS: We're Back! A Dinosaur's Story was adapted as an animated film by Steven Spielberg in 1993.

SIDELIGHTS: Hudson Talbott's self-illustrated books for children range from adventures among the dinosaurs to recountings of the stories of King Arthur and the knights of the Round Table to a young man's exploits against the Nazis in occupied Holland.

In *We're Back! A Dinosaur's Story, Going Hollywood: A Dinosaur's Dream,* and *Your Pet Dinosaur: An Owner's Manual,* Talbott introduces Dr. Rex, a talking Tyrannosaurus, and his dinosaur friends whose adventures, according to Steve Daly in *Entertainment Weekly,* have "style, invention, and energized wit." In one adventure, for example, the dinosaurs disrupt the Macy's Thanksgiving Day parade and must hide away by disguising themselves as exhibits at the natural history museum. In *Your Pet Dinosaur,* Dr. Rex presents his advice for those wishing to buy and raise a dinosaur of their own. His often humorous advice—"-Housebreaking often lives up to its name"—is delivered in a serious tone. A critic for *Publishers Weekly* remarked that "this mock manual's corniness and deadpan delivery are frequently funny." In 1993, Steven Spielberg adapted Talbott's *We're Back!* as an animated film.

In a series of four books, Talbott has recounted the legendary adventures of King Arthur and the Knights of the Round Table. *King Arthur: The Sword in the Stone* retells the story of how Arthur became king of England by pulling a magical sword from its resting place within a stone. A *Publishers Weekly* reviewer believed that, in Talbott's version, "Arthur's feat of removing the famous sword from the stone on Christmas Day is not merely preserved but heightened." *King Arthur and the Round Table* finds the young king assembling his knights dedicated to the betterment of England, while in *Excalibur* Arthur battles King Pellinore and gains the magic sword Excalibur. A reviewer for *Publishers Weekly* especially praised Talbott's illustrations for his tale, noting that "the intriguingly misty landscapes lend the classic story an air of mystery." According to Karen Morgan in *Booklist,* many readers "will relish Talbott's abundant detailing of bloody battles or enjoy the story for its fantasy and drama." *Lancelot* traces the story of Arthur's most famous knight from his childhood as an orphan to his arrival at King Arthur's court.

Talbott turned to recent history to write his *Forging Freedom: A True Story of Heroism during the Holocaust,* a story based on the real-life adventures of a friend who lived through World War II. Jaap Penraat was a young man when the Nazis invaded Holland and began a persecution of the Jewish population in Amsterdam. Jaap, a trained artist, worked secretly forging identity documents for his Jewish friends so they could leave the country safely. Some 400 people were saved in this manner. A *Publishers Weekly* reviewer wrote that Talbott "overcomes a mildly strained narrative by virtue of his freshly conceived and powerfully rendered paintings." Kathleen Isaacs in *School Library Journal* called *Forging Freedom* a "compelling biography," while a reviewer for *Horn Book* claimed that "exciting graphics and adventurous doings make this Holocaust memoir (based on the story of a friend of the author) stand out in a genre that tends toward the sober and contemplative."

Talbott once told *CA:* "I came into book authorship through my artwork. David Allender, an editor at Crown Publishers, saw my art on a calendar and called to ask if I would be interested in writing and illustrating a book. Although I'm still principally a visually-oriented person, I am very excited by the new challenge of exploring the verbal portion of my creativity."

BIOGRAPHICAL AND CRITICAL SOURCES:

PERIODICALS

Booklist, November 15, 1996, Karen Morgan, review of *Excalibur,* p. 585; February 1, 1999, Kay Weisman, review of *O'Sullivan Stew: A Tale Cooked Up in Ireland,* p. 983; July, 2000, Hazel Rochman, review of *Forging Freedom: A True Story of Heroism during the Holocaust,* p. 2026; October 15, 2001, Carolyn Phelan, review of *Leonardo's Horse,* p. 394.

Entertainment Weekly, December 10, 1993, Steve Daly, "Going Hollywood: A Dinosaur's Dream," p. 86.

Horn Book, January, 2001, review of *Forging Freedom,* p. 119; September, 2001, review of *Leonardo's Horse,* p. 609.

Kirkus Reviews, September 15, 2001, review of *Leonardo's Horse,* p. 1357; April 1, 2003, review of *Safari Journal: The Adventures in Africa of Carey Monroe,* p. 541.

Publishers Weekly, October 18, 1991, review of *King Arthur: The Sword in the Stone,* p. 60; August 3, 1992, review of *Your Pet Dinosaur: An Owner's Manual,* p. 72; July 22, 1996, review of *Excalibur,* p. 240; August 12, 1996, review of *Amazon Diary: The Jungle Adventures of Alex Winters,* p. 83; January 11, 1999, review of *O'Sullivan Stew,* p. 72; September 13, 1999, review of *Lancelot,* p. 85; October 23, 2000, review of *Forging Freedom,* p. 77; January 1, 2001, review of *O'Sullivan Stew,* p. 94.

School Arts, February, 2002, Ken Marantz, review of *Leonardo's Horse,* p. 56.

School Library Journal, November, 2000, review of *Forging Freedom,* p. 176; April, 2003, Genevieve Gallagher, review of *Safari Journal,* p. 169.

ONLINE

Hudson Talbott's Home Page, http://www.hudsontalbott.com/ (October 28, 2002).*

TALESE, Gay 1932-

PERSONAL: Given name originally Gaetano; born February 7, 1932, in Ocean City, NJ; son of Joseph Francis and Catherine (DePaolo) Talese; married Nan Ahearn (a publishing executive), June 10, 1959; children: Pamela, Catherine. *Education:* University of Alabama, B.A., 1953.

ADDRESSES: *Home*—109 E. 61st St., New York, NY 10021-8101; and 154 E. Atlantic Blvd., Ocean City, NJ 08226-4511 (summer).

CAREER: *New York Times,* New York, NY, 1953-65, began as copy boy, became reporter; full-time writer, 1965—. *Military service:* U.S. Army, 1953-55; became first lieutenant.

MEMBER: PEN (vice president, 1984-87; member of board of directors, beginning 1980), Authors League of America, Sigma Delta Chi, Phi Sigma Kappa.

AWARDS, HONORS: Best Sports Stories Award for Magazine Story, E. P. Dutton, 1967, for "The Silent Season of a Hero"; Christopher Book Award, 1970, for *The Kingdom and the Power.*

WRITINGS:

NONFICTION

New York: A Serendipiter's Journey, Harper (New York, NY), 1961.

The Bridge, Harper (New York, NY), 1964; Walker (New York, NY), 2003.

The Overreachers, Harper (New York, NY), 1965.

The Kingdom and the Power, World Publishing (Cleveland, OH), 1969.

Fame and Obscurity, World Publishing (Cleveland, OH), 1970.

Honor Thy Father, World Publishing (Cleveland, OH), 1971.

Thy Neighbor's Wife, Doubleday (New York, NY), 1980.

(Editor, with Robert Atwan) *The Best American Essays 1987,* Ticknor & Fields (New York, NY), 1987.

Unto the Sons, Knopf (New York, NY), 1992.

Gay Talese

(With Barbara Lounsberry) *Writing Creative Nonfiction: The Literature of Reality,* HarperCollins (New York, NY), 1995.

The Gay Talese Reader: Portraits and Encounters, Walker (New York, NY), 2003.

Contributor of articles to magazines, including *Reader's Digest, New York Times Magazine,* and *Saturday Evening Post.* Contributing editor, *Esquire,* beginning 1966.

ADAPTATIONS: Honor Thy Father was filmed as a made-for-television movie by Columbia Broadcasting System, 1973.

SIDELIGHTS: As a pioneer of the new journalism, Gay Talese was one of the first writers to apply the techniques of fiction to nonfiction. In a *Writer's Digest* interview with Leonard Wallace Robinson, Talese described how and why he began writing in this style while reporting for the *New York Times:* "I found I was leaving the assignment each day, unable with the techniques available to me or permissible to the *New York Times,* to really tell, to report, all that I saw, to communicate through the techniques that were permitted by the archaic copy desk. . . . [So] I started . . . to use the techniques of the short story writer in some of the *Esquire* pieces I did in the early Sixties. . . . It may read like fiction, it may give the impression that it was made up, over-dramatizing incidents for the effect those incidents may cause in the writing, but without question . . . there is reporting. There is reporting that fortifies the whole structure. Fact reporting, leg work."

Now considered classics of the genre, Talese's *Esquire* articles probed the private lives of celebrities such as Frank Sinatra, Joe DiMaggio, and Floyd Patterson. The success of these stories prompted Talese to apply this new technique to larger subjects, and, in 1969, he produced his first best-seller, *The Kingdom and the Power,* a nonfiction work about the *New York Times* written in novelistic style. Since then Talese has explored such controversial topics as the Mafia in 1971's *Honor Thy Father* and sexuality in America in 1980's *Thy Neighbor's Wife.* Widely respected as a master of his craft, Talese thought of writing fiction, but, as he explained to the *Los Angeles Times*'s Wayne Warga, nonfiction has challenged him more: "I suggest there is art in journalism. I don't want to resort to changing names, to fictionalizing. The reality is more fascinating. My mission is to get deep into the heart and soul of the people in this country."

Talese grew up in Ocean City, a resort town in New Jersey that he describes as "festive and bright in the summertime" and "depressing" the rest of the year. As the son of an Italian immigrant, young Talese was "actually a minority within a minority," according to *Time* magazine's R. Z. Sheppard. He was Catholic in a Protestant community and Italian in a predominately Irish parish. A repressed, unhappy child, Talese remembers himself as a loner who failed most of the classes at his conservative parochial school. Then, when he was thirteen, he made a discovery. "I became involved with the school newspaper," he told Francis Coppola in an *Esquire Film Quarterly* interview, and realized that "you can be shy, as I was, but you can still approach strangers and ask them questions." Throughout high school and college, Talese continued his writing, majoring in journalism at the University of Alabama, contributing sports columns to the campus newspaper, and hoping to work someday for the *New York Herald Tribune,* where his literary idol, Red Smith, had a column of his own. After graduation,

Talese made the rounds of the major New York newspapers, applying for a job and finally being offered one by the paper where he thought his chances were least promising—the *New York Times.* Hired as a copy boy, he was promoted to reporter in just two years.

In 1961, Talese published his first book, *New York: A Serendipiter's Journey.* Composed largely of material from his *New York Times* articles, the book was a critical success and sold about 12,000 copies, mostly in New York. His next venture was *The Bridge,* a book in which, according to a *Playboy* magazine contributor, "he took the plunge into the book-length nonfiction novel style." To prepare for this story, Talese spent over a year observing the workers who built the Verrazano-Narrows Bridge connecting Brooklyn and Staten Island. In the *New York Times Book Review,* Herbert Mitgang called the book "a vivid document," noting that Talese "imparts drama and romance to this bridge-building story by concentrating on the boomers, the iron workers who stitch steel and live high in more ways than one." While the publication was not a best-seller, it was critically well received, and set the scene for the three larger works that would follow in the next sixteen years.

The first of these, *The Kingdom and the Power,* is an intimate portrait of the *New York Times* where Talese worked as a reporter for ten years. Published four years after he left the paper, the book is "rich in intimate detail, personal insights and characterizations," according to Ben H. Bagdikian in the *New York Times Book Review.* "In this book," Bagdikian continued, "the men of The Times emerge not as godlike models of intrepid journalism, but as unique individuals who, in addition to other human traits, have trouble with ambitions, alcohol, wives and analysts." In his author's note, Talese describes the book as "a human history of an institution in transition." Specifically, he relates the infighting between James "Scotty" Reston, a respected columnist and head of the *New York Times* Washington bureau, and E. Clifton Daniel, managing editor of the paper, for control of the Washington bureau, which had maintained independent status for years. In the end, Reston wins and is appointed executive editor. "That outcome, of great moment inside the *Times,* is of less than secondary interest to the rest of the world," explained a *Time* critic, who added that "to curry reader excitement, Talese has had to transform the newsroom on the third floor of the *Times* building into a fortress of Machiavellian maneuver. (One wonders, sometimes, how the paper ever got put out at all.)"

Talese's decision to dramatize the story and to relate the process of change at an American institution from the human perspective has been more praised than criticized. Detractors of *The Kingdom and the Power* argue that the *New York Times* owners and employees are ultimately unworthy of such elaborate attention, that their petty squabbling diminishes the institution they represent. Supporters argue that Talese's approach is the best way to reveal the inside story and is an example of new journalism at its best. Among critics, John Leo wrote in *Commonweal:* "The new journalist in Talese is forever trying to capture the real *Times* by a telling scene of explaining what everyone felt at a critical moment. But the effort doesn't amount to much. . . . It is often spectacularly effective in delineating a person, a small group of people or a social event. But for an institution, and a ponderous non-dramatic one at that, well, maybe only the boring old journalism will do." Because his focus is on personality rather than issues, some critics found the book's perspective skewed. As Harold E. Fey noted in the *Christian Century,* Talese "seems unable to understand or to formulate adequately the *Times*'s high purpose, its worthy conceptions of public responsibility, its firm identification of personal with journalistic integrity. These also have something to do with power. And they have much to do with the *New York Times.* They help to explain, as Talese does not, why the *Times,* in his own words, 'influences the world.'"

Fred Powledge, reviewing *The Kingdom and the Power* in the *Nation,* found merit in Talese's approach, noting that the journalist "does not attempt to resolve questions [about journalistic procedure and social responsibility,] and some may consider this a fault. I do not think so. If he had entered this vast and relatively unexplored territory the book would have lost some of its timeless, surgically clean quality." And, writing in *Life,* Murray Kempton noted that "by talking about their lives [Talese] has done something for his subjects which they could not do for themselves with their product, and done it superlatively well." "There are surely criticisms to be made [of the great power the *New York Times* wields over public opinion]," David Bernstein noted in the *New Leader,* "but they are meaningless without an understanding of the private worlds of individual reporters, editors, and publishers and of how these worlds interact. Gay Talese is quite right to place his emphasis upon all this when he describes the kingdom that is the *Times*. What might appear at first glance to be a frivolous book is in fact a serious and important account of one of the few genuinely powerful institutions in our society." Powledge remarked, "The inner conflicts and passions of these men are beautifully documented in *The Kingdom and the Power*. It is no less than a landmark in the field of writing about journalism."

In 1971, Talese produced what many consider to be another landmark—*Honor Thy Father*, an inside look at the life of mafioso Bill Bonanno and a book so popular that it sold more than 300,000 copies within four months of its publication. Like all of Talese's efforts, the story was extensively researched and written in the intimate style of the new journalism. Almost six years elapsed between the day in 1965 when Talese first met Bonanno outside a New York courtroom and the publication of the book. During that time Talese actually lived with the Bonanno family and persuaded them to talk about their business and personal lives, becoming, to use his words, "a source of communication within a family that had long been repressed by a tradition of silence."

While the tone of the book is nonjudgmental, Talese's compassionate portrayal of underworld figures—including Bill and his father, New York boss Joseph Bonanno—incited charges that Talese was giving gangsters moral sanction. Writing in the *New York Times Book Review*, Colin McInnes argued that "Talese has become so seduced by his subject and its 'hero,' that he conveys the impression that being a mobster is much the same as being a sportsman, film star or any other kind of public personality." But others, such as a *Times Literary Supplement* critic, defended Talese's treatment, noting that the author's "insight will do more to help us understand the criminal than any amount of moral recrimination." Writing in the *New York Review of Books*, Wilfrid Sheed expressed a similar view: "Talese has been criticized for writing what amounts to promotional material for the Bonanno family, but his book is an invaluable document and I don't know how such books can be obtained without some compromise. It is a lot to ask of an author that he betray the confidence of a Mafia family. As with a tapped phone call, one must interpret the message. . . . Talese signals occasionally to his educated audience—dull, aren't they? Almost pathetic. But that's all he can do." Furthermore, Sheed argued, the technique of new journalism, "an unfortunate strategy for most subjects, is weirdly right" here: "The prose matches the stiff watchful façade of the Mafia. One is reminded of a touched-up country wedding photo, with the cheeks identically rouged and the eyes glazed, of the kind the Bonanno family might have ordered for themselves back in Sicily."

After the success of *Honor Thy Father*, Doubleday offered Talese a $1.2 million contract for two books. "I was interested in sexual changes and how . . . morality was being defined," Talese told a *Media People* interviewer. To gather material for a chronicle of the American sexual revolution, he submerged himself in the subculture of massage parlors, pornographic publishing, blue movies, and, ultimately, Sandstone, a California sexual retreat. He also studied First Amendment decisions in the Supreme Court and law libraries, tracing the effect of Puritanism on Americans' rights. As his research stretched from months into years, however, Talese realized that what began as a professional exploration had become a personal odyssey. And because he was asking others to reveal their most intimate sexual proclivities, he felt it would be hypocritical not to reveal his own. Thus, before he had written a word of his book, Talese became the subject of two revealing profiles in *Esquire* and *New York* magazines, the latter titled "An Evening in the Nude with Gay Talese." The public was titillated, and the resulting publicity virtually guaranteed the book's financial success. In October of 1979, months before the publication reached bookstores, United Artists bid a record-breaking $2.5 million for film rights to the book Talese titled *Thy Neighbor's Wife*. Published in 1980, the book was number one on the *New York Times* best-seller list for three consecutive months.

Despite its popularity, *Thy Neighbor's Wife* received negative reviews from many literary critics. Virginia Johnson-Masters, a respected sex researcher, foresaw the ensuing controversy when she wrote an early *Vogue* review saying that Talese "shows us many things about ourselves and the social environment in which we live. Some of them we may not appreciate or want any part of. However, Talese, the author, is fair. Read carefully and perceive that he really does not proselytize, he informs." Johnson-Masters added: *Thy Neighbor's Wife* "is a scholarly, readable and thoroughly entertaining book. . . . It is a meticulously researched context of people, events, and circumstances through which a reader can identify the process of breakdown in repressive sexual myths dominating our society until quite recently."

Writing in the *New York Times Book Review,* psychiatrist Robert Coles noted that Talese "has a serious interest in watching his fellow human beings, in listening to them, and in presenting honestly what he has seen and heard. He writes clear unpretentious prose. He has a gift, through a phrase here, a sentence there, of making important narrative and historical connections. We are given, really, a number of well-told stories, their social message cumulative: A drastically transformed American sexuality has emerged during this past couple of decades." Despite such praise from sociologists and psychologists, many reviewers criticized the book. Objections ranged from Ernest van den Haag's charge in the *National Review* that *Thy Neighbor's Wife* is "remarkably shallow" to Robert Sherrill's allegation in the *Washington Post* that it is "constructed mostly of the sort of intellectual plywood you find in most neighborhood bars: part voyeurism, part amateur psychoanalysis, part sixpack philosophy." The most common objections included Talese's apparent lack of analysis, his omission of homosexuality, and his supposed anti-female attitude.

In his *Playboy* review of the book, critic John Leonard articulated each of these objections: "Since Talese parajournalizes so promiscuously—reaching into [his subjects'] minds, reading their thoughts, scratching their itches—one would expect at the very least to emerge from his book, as if from a novel, with some improved comprehension of what they stand for and a different angle on the culture that produced them. One emerges instead, as if from a soft-porn movie in the middle of the afternoon, reproached by sunlight and feeling peripheral to the main business of the universe. If Talese expects us to take his revolutionaries as seriously as he himself takes them, he has to put them in a social context and make them sound interesting. He doesn't." Furthermore, Leonard continued, "Talese almost totally ignores feminism. Gay liberation doesn't interest him. Children, conveniently, do not exist; if they did exist, they would make group sex—Tinkertoys! Erector Sets!—an unseemly hassle. . . . Missing from *Thy Neighbor's Wife* are history and stamina and celebration and mystery, along with birth, blood, death and beauty, not to mention earth, fire, water, politics, and everything else that isn't our urgent plumbing, that refuses to swim in our libidinal pool."

Returning to large-scale nonfiction after over a decade, in his 1992 work *Unto the Sons* Talese "recreates the transformation of hundreds of thousands of immigrants and their descendants from Italians into Americans by tracing his own family" history, explained Joseph A. Califano in the *Washington Post Book World.* The product of more than a decade of research in the small southern Italian town of Maida, the book, as Talese told Jerry Adler in *Newsweek,* was a conscious change from writing about other famous figures. "After a lot of writing about people I didn't know," the author added, "I wanted to write about my private province." Califano compared *Unto the Sons* to Alex Haley's *Roots,* and declared that the author "has constructed from fact, scraps of memories and perceptive fancy a yeasty blend of public and family history that will ring true to anyone whose parents or grandparents migrated from Italy around the turn of the century." In some ways, the story Talese presents is a metaphor for the American immigrant experience. "In accepting and coming to terms with his own father," stated reviewer William Broyles, Jr. in the *Los Angeles Times Book Review,* "Talese discovers how much of his father lives in him, and lets us see how much the Old World still lives in us."

In 2003 Talese published *The Gay Talese Reader: Portraits and Encounters,* which draws from his journalistic works published between 1961 and 1997. Terren Ilana Wein, in a review for *Library Journal,* considered the book a "beautifully written collection of essays" that "truly represents the best of this still highly prolific author's work." David Pitt, reviewing the collection in *Booklist,* called *The Gay Talese Reader* "a sterling introduction to the multitalented Talese."

BIOGRAPHICAL AND CRITICAL SOURCES:

BOOKS

Authors in the News, Volume 1, Thomson Gale (Detroit, MI), 1976.

Contemporary Issues Criticism, Volume 1, Thomson Gale (Detroit, MI), 1982.

Contemporary Literary Criticism, Volume 37, Thomson Gale (Detroit, MI), 1986.

PERIODICALS

Booklist, October 15, 2003, David Pitt, review of *The Gay Talese Reader: Portraits and Encounters,* p. 360.

Chicago Tribune, June 8, 1980, review of *Thy Neighbor's Wife;* October 2, 1987.
Christian Century, October 8, 1969.
Commonweal, October 17, 1969, review of *The Kingdom and the Power.*
Entertainment Weekly, February 21, 1992, p. 46; April 3, 1992, p. 26; March 26, 1993, p. 74; December 19, 2003, review of *The Gay Talese Reader,* p. 80.
Esquire Film Quarterly, July, 1981.
Library Journal, November 15, 2003, p. 68.
Life, June 27, 1969.
Los Angeles Times, May 23, 1980.
Los Angeles Times Book Review, April 27, 1980; February 23, 1992, William Broyles, Jr., review of *Unto the Sons,* pp. 2, 9.
Media People, May, 1980.
MELUS, fall, 2003, review of *The Gay Talese Reader,* p. 149.
Nation, September 15, 1969.
National Review, August 12, 1969; March 6, 1981.
New Leader, May 26, 1969.
Newsweek, July 21, 1969, review of *The Kingdom and the Power;* April 28, 1980, review of *Thy Neighbor's Wife;* February 10, 1992, review of *Unto the Sons,* p. 62.
New York Review of Books, July 20, 1972.
New York Times, May 21, 1969, review of *The Kingdom and the Power;* October 5, 1971, review of *Honor Thy Father;* April 30, 1980.
New York Times Book Review, January 17, 1965; June 8, 1969; August 2, 1970; October 31, 1971; May 4, 1980; February 9, 1992, p. 3; March 21, 1993, p. 32.
New York Times Magazine, April 20, 1980.
Nieman Reports, fall, 1999, p. 44.
People, April 14, 1980, review of *Thy Neighbor's Wife;* March 2, 1992, p. 25; March 9, 1992, review of *Unto the Sons,* p. 96.
Playboy, May, 1980.
PR Week (U.S.), September 15, 2003, p. 12.
Publishers Weekly, January 7, 1983; July 25, 1991, p. 16; January 1, 1992, p. 42; October 20, 2003, pp. 46-47.
San Francisco Review of Books, May-June, 1993, pp. 27-28.
Sports Illustrated, October 13, 1997, p. 20.
Time, July 4, 1969, review of *The Kingdom and the Power;* October 4, 1971, review of *Honor Thy Father;* February 10, 1992, p. 72.
Times Literary Supplement, May 14, 1971; April 4, 1972; July 4, 1980.
Vogue, June, 1980, Virginia Masters-Johnson, review of *Thy Neighbor's Wife;* February, 1992, review of *Unto the Sons,* p. 120.
Washington Post, October 18, 1979; April 27, 1980, review of *Thy Neighbor's Wife;* May 7, 1980; May 15, 1980.
Washington Post Book World, November 15, 1987; February 16, 1992, Joseph A. Califano, review of *Unto the Sons,* pp. 1-2.
Writer's Digest, January, 1970.*

ONLINE

Gay Talese Home Page, http://www.gaytalese.com/ (August 23, 2004).*

* * *

TALLIS, Robyn
See MACDONALD, James D.

* * *

TAYLOR, John 1955-

PERSONAL: Born April 20, 1955, in Yokosuka, Japan; son of Jay (an American diplomat) and Elizabeth (Rose) Taylor; married Maureen Sherwood (a journalist), December 19, 1982 (divorced, 1994); children: Jessica. *Education:* University of Chicago, B.A., 1977.

ADDRESSES: *Home*—East Moriches, NY. *Agent*—c/o Author Mail, Random House, 1745 Broadway, New York, NY 10009.

CAREER: Journalist and author. *Newsweek,* New York, NY, editorial assistant, 1980-83; *Business Week,* New York, NY, staff editor, 1984; *Manhattan, Inc.,* New York, NY, senior writer, 1984-87; *New York,* New York, NY, contributing editor, beginning in 1987.

AWARDS, HONORS: *Storming the Magic Kingdom* was named a Notable Book of the Year, *New York Times,* 1987; Edgar Allan Poe Award nomination for best fact crime, Mystery Writers of America, 2003, for *The Count and the Confession.*

WRITINGS:

Storming the Magic Kingdom: Wall Street, the Raiders, and the Battle for Disney, Knopf (New York, NY), 1987.

Circus of Ambition: The Culture of Wealth and Power in the Eighties, Warner Books (New York, NY), 1989.

Falling: The Story of One Marriage, Random House (New York, NY), 1999.

The Count and the Confession: A True Mystery, Random House (New York, NY), 2002.

Contributor to magazines and newspapers, including *Architectural Digest.*

SIDELIGHTS: In addition to writing for major magazines, journalist John Taylor has written a handful of nonfiction books. In them he has chronicled such events as changes in the Walt Disney company, changes in New York society during the 1980s, changes in his own marriage, and a major change in the life of Roger Burke—his murder—and the subsequent investigation and conviction of the supposed murderer, who was later acquitted.

Taylor's book *Storming the Magic Kingdom* details the changes that Walt Disney Productions underwent during the 1980s to become the more varied Walt Disney Company. As David McClintick reported in the *New York Times Book Review,* "Taylor portrays well the diverse cultures and styles of the people and institutions that govern contemporary show business and fight the eternal battle over who should run things." The book recounts how the unsuccessful takeover attempt by famed corporate raider Saul Steinberg weakened the company and allowed the subsequent takeover by Roy E. Disney (nephew of cartoonist and entrepreneur Walt Disney) and his corporate ally Sid Bass. According to Taylor, Roy Disney had reportedly become increasingly disturbed by the drop in Disney stock prices, which he blamed on mismanagement of the company's film studios by his uncle's hand-picked successors. Under the direction of Roy Disney's appointees, the new company has produced films, such as *Down and Out in Beverly Hills* and *Ruthless People,* of a type not associated with its previous orientation towards children. These diversification efforts have been largely successful, and Disney stock had risen to record prices by the book's publication.

Taylor "employs the fly-on-the-wall narrative that is now standard for such business tales," described Peter Behr in the *Washington Post Book World,* "recreating the flow of conversations, telephone calls, arguments, conferences and scheming by which the takeover fight progressed." McClintick lauded *Storming the Magic Kingdom* as having "told [its] story quite well overall, capturing the supreme importance of egos and personal relationships in the governance of business, particularly show business." "For those unfamiliar with the combination of ego and economics that drive takeovers," concluded Behr, "the Disney story is a good primer."

Taylor told *CA:* "Growing up abroad and moving every two years or so instilled a sort of restlessness in me that made me very suited for journalism. What interested me in business was the drama and the psychology of the deal. The business side of Hollywood is almost entirely deal-driven, and that is one of the reasons the entertainment industry is so intriguing to write about. The Walt Disney Company made a deal with the corporate raider Saul Steinberg to prevent him from acquiring the company in a hostile takeover and liquidating it. It was this deal that initially interested me. But as I pursued the story I became more interested in the corporate culture of Disney—the anthropological side of business. Disney is one of the strangest and most fascinating corporations in the country. To research the book, I interviewed virtually all of the participants and combed through the Disney archives."

In *Circus of Ambition: The Culture of Wealth and Power in the Eighties,* Taylor puts the era in historical perspective, "comparing it with the Gilded Age that followed the Civil War," to quote *People*'s Elizabeth Wurtzel. The eighties were infamous for the prevailing attitude that more was more and having wealth did not obligate one to contribute to the broader community. Taylor presents New York men who are members of this *nouveau* (and irresponsible) *riche.* Among the portraits in this "amusing book," as *Wall Street Journal* reviewer Amy Gamerman dubbed it, are investor Charlie Atkins, artist Mark Kostabi, and financier John Gutfreund. According to Wurtzel, the book's flaw is in Taylor's "treatment of women"; that is, he ignores them, except as the wives of powerful men.

Taylor's *Falling: The Story of a Marriage* is really the story of a divorce, the eventual end of his twelve-year marriage to writer Maureen Sherwood. A year after the couple married, Maureen learned that she had Parkinson's disease. The couple decided to have a child and that Maureen would be an at-home mother with their daughter, Jessica. Then the Taylors' marriage began to disintegrate. John had a series of affairs but could not call it quits, and finally Maureen ended their relationship. A first version of this story, one that was made up of side-by-side articles by both people, appeared in *Esquire,* and then John produced the book *Falling.* The work caught the attention of critics, who commented on Taylor's prose style and compared the subject matter to that of Hanif Kureishi's novel *Intimacy.* While Taylor's writing is "lucid and lovely," noted *Time*'s Elizabeth Gleick, "his best efforts to explain what brought him and his wife Maureen to the point of divorce . . . are not completely satisfactory." "Seemingly in an attempt to make sense of it all, Taylor continues to explore, with admirable seriousness, the concepts of love, duty, fidelity and commitment," wrote Joyce Maynard in the *Los Angeles Times.* She noted as well that his "story includes the element—rare in a memoir—of a certain scholarship and intellectual curiosity." While a *Publishers Weekly* contributor described the work as "eloquent and deeply felt," *Library Journal* reviewer Joyce Sparrow found this level of detail to be "excruciating." Looking from another perspective was Richard A. Shweder of the *New York Times Book Review,* who noted the work's satirical tone. In his opinion, Taylor "burlesques almost everything in sight: liberated women, marriage counselors, trial separations, mediated settlements, even the various women with whom he had extramarital affairs." This bitter tone wreaks havoc with the reader's perception of the author, as Shweder explained: "The more he intermingles mordacious taunts with apparently earnest reflections on the feelings and choices of a man suffocated by a less than satisfying matrimony, the harder it is to take him seriously or to distinguish what's satirical from what's sincere."

When Taylor read an article in the *New York Times* about Beverly Monroe appealing her conviction for the 1992 murder of Roger de la Burde, he became interested in the case. His interest led to the writing of *The Count and the Confession: A True Mystery.* In researching the trial, Taylor read the 300-page habeas corpus petition and 300 more pages of exhibits sent to him by Monroe's daughter. "By the time I finished reading all that, I realized that I'd stumbled on an incredibly fascinating story," Taylor later told Bella Stander at the *Bella Stander* Web site. Taylor felt compelled to write the book because he had come to believe that Beverly Monroe was innocent of the murder for which she was convicted through a series of personal and juridical mistakes. Ten days before the book was scheduled to debut, Taylor learned that Monroe had been acquitted on appeal and released. Taylor was happy to rewrite the ending of *The Count and the Confession* in a mere week and a half. Critical assessments of this true-crime story varied. "Taylor does a nuanced job on the elements of scandal and personal weakness, never allowing this true story to slip into titillating sensationalism," praised Kai Maristed in the *Los Angeles Times.* "But it is when he lays bare the legal, procedural and institutional scandal and weakness that his work really shines," Maristed added. James B. Stewart, writing in the *New York Times Book Review,* noted that the book "has all the elements of a compelling murder mystery," yet found it lacking in suspense. Nevertheless, Stewart commented that while "some readers may be left unsatisfied by so many unresolved mysteries, others will be fascinated by them." "In any event," he concluded, "*The Count and the Confession* is an important study in the legal principle of reasonable doubt, not to mention good reading."

BIOGRAPHICAL AND CRITICAL SOURCES:

PERIODICALS

Booklist, February 15, 1999, Danise Hoover, review of *Falling: The Story of a Marriage,* p. 1015; April 15, 2002, James Klise, review of *The Count and the Confession: A True Mystery,* pp. 1367-1368.

Detroit News, May 3, 1987, review of *Storming the Magic Kingdom: Wall Street, the Raiders, and the Battle for Disney.*

Guardian (Manchester, England), March 15, 1999, Markie Robson-Scott, "Women: Crying All the Way to the Bank," review of *Falling,* p. T.006.

Kirkus Reviews, March 1, 2002, review of *The Count and the Confession,* p. 321.

Knight Ridder/Tribune News Service, June 19, 2002, Doris Bloodsworth, review of *The Count and the Confession.*

Library Journal, February 15, 1999, Joyce Sparrow, review of *Falling,* p. 163; April 1, 2002, Deirdre Bray Root, review of *The Count and the Confession,* p. 126.

Los Angeles Times, June 28, 1987, review of *Storming the Magic Kingdom;* June 3, 1990, Charles Solomon, review of *Circus of Ambition: The Culture *of Wealth and Power in the Eighties,* p. 14; May 18, 1999, Joyce Maynard, "A Lopsided Account of One Couple's Split-Up," review of *Falling,* p. 1; May 31, 2002, Kai Maristed, "Case of the Cavalier 'Count' and the Scorned Woman," review of *The Count and the Confession,* p. E3.

New York Times, May 4, 1987, review of *Storming the Magic Kingdom.*

New York Times Book Review, May 10, 1987, David McClintick, review of *Storming the Magic Kingdom;* April 4, 1999, Richard A. Shweder, "Reader, I Divorced Her," review of *Falling;* May 26, 2002, James B. Stewart, review of *The Count and the Confession.*

People, March 5, 1990, Elizabeth Wurtzel, review of *Circus of Ambition,* pp. 30-31.

Publishers Weekly, January 18, 1999, review of *Falling,* p. 321; March 18, 2002, review of *The Count and the Confession,* pp. 85-86.

Time, February 19, 1990, John Greenwald, review of *Circus of Ambition,* p. 71; March 22, 1999, Elizabeth Gleick, "Bittersweet Sorrows," review of *Falling,* p. 102.

Toronto Star (Toronto, Ontario, Canada), July 28, 2002, "Dumb As a Post," review of *The Count and the Confession.*

Wall Street Journal, January 19, 1990, Amy Gamerman, "A Look Back at the Money-loving '80s," review of *Circus of Ambition,* p. A8; May 24, 2002, Melanie Thernstrom, "Fake Count, True Crime, Unlikely Suspect," review of *The Count and the Confession,* p. W.11.

Washington Post Book World, June 7, 1987, Peter Behr, review of *Storming the Magic Kingdom.*

ONLINE

Bella Stander Web site, http://www.bellastander.com/ (August-September, 2002), Bella Stander, "John Taylor."*

* * *

TOMPERT, Ann 1918-

PERSONAL: Born January 11, 1918, in Detroit, MI; daughter of Joseph (a farmer) and Florence (Pollitt) Bakeman; married Robert S. Tompert (a social service employee; deceased), March 31, 1951. *Education:* Siena Heights College, B.A. (summa cum laude), 1938; Wayne State University, graduate study, 1941-46. *Politics:* "Independent with Republican leanings." *Religion:* Christian. *Hobbies and other interests:* Reading and mentoring new writers, collecting paperweights and milkglass, gardening, caning chairs, refinishing furniture, sewing, needlework, dining with friends, "intense discussions about life, religion, politics, and literature."

ADDRESSES: Home—3900 Aspen Dr., Port Huron, MI 48060. *Agent*—Liza Voges, Kirchoff/Wohlberg Inc., 866 United Nations Plaza, New York, NY 10017.

CAREER: Teacher in elementary and junior and senior high schools in St. Clair Shores, East Detroit, Grosse Pointe, Marine City, and other cities in Michigan, 1938-59; writer, 1959—.

MEMBER: Society of Children's Book Writers and Illustrators, River District Hospital Auxiliary (life member; St. Clair, MI), Friends of the Port Huron Library, Port Huron Museum.

AWARDS, HONORS: Notable children's book citations, American Library Association and *School Library Journal,* 1976, Friend of American Writers citation, 1977, honors citation, Chicago Children's Reading Round Table, 1979, and "Best of the Best: 1966-1978," *School Library Journal,* 1979, all for *Little Fox Goes to the End of the World;* Irma Simonton Black award honor book, 1980, for *Charlotte and Charles;* Notable Children's Trade Book in the Field of Social Studies, Children's Book Council, 1988, for *The Silver Whistle,* 1990, for *Grandfather Tang's Story: A Tale Told with Tangrams;* "Pick of the List," American Booksellers Association (ABA), 1991, for *Savina, the Gypsy Dancer,* and 1993, for *Just a Little Bit;* Children's Reading Roundtable Service Award, 1994; Memorial Fund Award, Michigan branch of the Society for Children's Book Writers and Illustrators, 1994, for outstanding work in children's literature; *The Jade Horse, the Cricket and the Peach Stone* was named Bank Street College Book of the Year, 1996; *Saint Patrick* was selected by *Booklist* as one of the top ten religious books for children, 1998; honorary degree from Siena Heights University, 2003.

WRITINGS:

What Makes My Cat Purr?, Whitman Publishing (Racine, WI), 1965.

The Big Whistle, Whitman Publishing (Racine, WI), 1968.

When Rooster Crowed, Whitman Publishing (Racine, WI), 1968.

Maybe a Horse Will Come, illustrated by Frank Aloise, Follett (Chicago, IL), 1968.

A Horse for Charlie, Whitman Publishing (Racine, WI), 1969.

The Crow, the Kite, and the Golden Umbrella, illustrated by Franklin Luke, Abelard-Schulman (New York, NY), 1971.

Fun for Ozzie, illustrated by Elizabeth Rice, Steck (Austin, TX), 1971.

Hyacinth, the Reluctant Duck, illustrated by John Paul Richards, Steck (Austin, TX), 1972.

It May Come in Handy Someday, illustrated by Bruce Cayard, McGraw-Hill (New York, NY), 1975.

Little Fox Goes to the End of the World, illustrated by John Wallner, Crown (New York, NY), 1976.

Little Otter Remembers and Other Stories, illustrated by John Wallner, Crown (New York, NY), 1977.

The Clever Princess, illustrated by Patricia Riley, Lollipop Power, 1977.

Badger on His Own, illustrated by Diane de Groat, Crown (New York, NY), 1978.

Three Foolish Tales, illustrated by Diane Dawson, Crown (New York, NY), 1979.

Charlotte and Charles, illustrated by John Wallner, Crown (New York, NY), 1979.

Nothing Sticks Like a Shadow, illustrated by Lynn Munsinger, Houghton Mifflin (Boston, MA), 1983.

The Greatest Showman on Earth: A Biography of P. T. Barnum, Dillon (Minneapolis, MN), 1987.

Will You Come Back for Me?, illustrated by Robin Kramer, Whitman Publishing (Racine, WI), 1988.

The Silver Whistle, illustrated by Beth Park, Macmillan (New York, NY), 1988.

Sue Patch and the Crazy Clocks, illustrated by Rosekrans Hoffman, Dial (New York, NY), 1989.

The Tzar's Bird, illustrated by Robert Rayevsky, Macmillan (New York, NY), 1990.

Grandfather Tang's Story: A Tale Told with Tangrams, illustrated by Robert Andrew Parker, Crown (New York, NY), 1990.

Savina, the Gypsy Dancer, illustrated by Dennis Nolan, Macmillan (New York, NY), 1991.

Just a Little Bit, illustrated by Lynn Munsinger, Houghton Mifflin (Boston, MA), 1993.

Bamboo Hats and a Rice Cake: A Tale Adapted from Japanese Folklore, illustrated by Demi, Crown (New York, NY), 1993.

A Carol for Christmas, illustrated by Laura Kelly, Macmillan (New York, NY), 1994.

The Jade Horse, the Cricket and the Peach Stone, illustrated by Winson Trang, Boyds Mills Press (New York, NY), 1996.

How Rabbit Lost His Tail, illustrated by Jacqueline Chwast, Houghton Mifflin (Boston, MA), 1997.

Saint Patrick, illustrated by Michael Garland, Boyds Mills Press (New York, NY), 1998.

Hungry Black Bag, illustrated by Jacqueline Chwast, Houghton Mifflin (Boston, MA), 1999.

Saint Nicholas, illustrated by Michael Garland, Boyds Mills Press (New York, NY), 2000.

The Pied Piper of Peru, illustrated by Kestutis Kasparavicius, Boyds Mills Press (New York, NY), 2002.

Joan of Arc: Heroine of France, illustrated by Michael Garland, Boyds Mills Press (New York, NY), 2003.

The Errant Knight, illustrated by Doug Keith, Illumination Arts, 2003.

Harry's Hats, Children's Press (Danbury, CT), 2003.

Saint Valentine, illustrated by Kestutis Kasparavicius, Boyds Mills Press (New York, NY), 2004.

Contributor to children's magazines, including *Jack and Jill, Wee Wisdom,* and *Friend.* Contributor to *The Real Books of First Stories,* edited by Dorothy Haas, and *Sea Treasures,* edited by Ira E. Aaron. Author of column "Salmagundi," *Once upon a Time;* author of column "Addenda," *Newsletter* of the Michigan branch of the Society of Children's Book Writers and Illustrators. *Little Fox Goes to the End of the World* and *Little Otter Remembers and Other Stories* have been translated into Japanese. *Just a Little Bit* has been translated into French, German, and Japanese, *Nothing Sticks Like a Shadow* into French, and *Little Fox Goes to the End of the World* and *Sue Patch and the Crazy Clocks* into Spanish.

SIDELIGHTS: Ann Tompert is the author of more than three dozen children's picture books, stories for the beginning reader, and folktales, including the award-winning *Little Fox Goes to the End of the World* and *Charlotte and Charles.* Although almost fifty years of age when her first book was published, Tompert had dreamed of being a writer from age twelve, modeling herself on Jo from *Little Women.* The necessities of life, however, intervened.

When Tompert was twelve, her mother died, and her father, a small farmer on the outskirts of Detroit, was left to care for Tompert and her two sisters. "I am just now realizing what a profound influence my father has had on me," she once told *CA*. "He did not let the fact that his formal education was limited to attendance at a typical rural school of the time hinder him in any way. He . . . would tackle any job because he did not fear failure. There was a stubbornness about him that helped him get things done in spite of what must have seemed insurmountable obstacles." As a child, Tompert helped her father sell vegetables at the roadside stand in front of their farm, and her sisters and she went with him whenever they were not in school. "An especially fond memory is of playing in the fields while my father mowed hay for the horses," Tompert recalled. Unaware of the fact that they were what might be today called "underprivileged," Tompert and her sisters invented their own fun rather than relying on toys. It was an upbringing that gave her a strong creative core and an optimistic approach to life.

Tompert left home for college at sixteen, majoring in English and still dreaming of becoming a writer. Practical concerns dictated that she work toward becoming a teacher, however, as it was "one of the few professions opened to women at that time," Tompert noted in *CA*. She continued to write during college, and upon graduation began her teaching career in a two-room schoolhouse. In 1940 she won an honorable mention and five dollars for a play she submitted to a writing contest. "That small success kept the spark of my desire alive during the next twenty years while I taught school in various parts of Michigan." In 1951 Tompert married and began working toward her master's in English part time. Finally, in 1959, she decided to devote herself to her dream of writing. "I was teaching first grade at the time," Tompert told *CA*, "and after reading hundreds of books to my pupils, I was convinced that I could write stories that were just as good, if not better." So for the next three years she wrote and submitted stories and "built up one of the world's finest collections of rejection slips." Finally however, the stubbornness inherited from her father paid off. Her first story was accepted by *Jack and Jill*, and her writing career was underway.

Initially, Tompert wrote picture books for Whitman Publishing, a division of Western Publishing. "Many people do not consider this type of book worth mentioning," Tompert told *CA*, "although I do not understand why. Writing a manuscript for this type of book requires as much time, effort and talent as do manuscripts for hard-cover books." Many of these early books feature animal protagonists, a device she has continued to use throughout her career. *Fun for Ozzie*, one of her first publications, tells the tale of a playful otter who tries hobbies enjoyed by other animals until he finally hits on the right one for him. Tompert's 1971 *The Crow, the Kite, and the Golden Umbrella* was inspired by a newspaper account of how the people in a Malaysian town were trying to cure themselves of a plague of crows. In Tompert's story, the town of Kota Kobis offers a golden umbrella to whoever can rid the town of the crows. Young Muda, who has a pet crow, constructs a kite with which to lure the other crows away. How Muda attempts to win the prize while at the same time keeping his own pet crow forms the crux of the story.

Tompert's own farm background provided some of the inspiration for her next title, *It May Come in Handy Someday*, in which an old man collects all sorts of paraphernalia that he thinks may come in handy on his farm. The old man neglects his garden while he scavenges, and the farm risks becoming engulfed in the junk until a passerby offers to tell the townspeople to come and take what they want. Zena Sutherland in the *Bulletin of the Center for Children's Books* remarked that "the collected items get sillier as the pile grows and overflows."

With her next title, *Little Fox Goes to the End of the World*, Tompert began to hit her stride. Inspired by her own childhood dream to follow a rainbow to the pot of gold, she originally wrote a story featuring a little boy's journey. An editor, however, suggested that she use an animal protagonist and Tompert thought of a fox, an animal she felt was sadly misunderstood by humans. The little fox in question is a bushy-tailed kit who wears jeans and sandals and who tells her mother what she would do if she set off to the end of the world. She relates all the adventures she would have, which involve bears with honey, banana-wielding monkeys, and mountain snows. Virginia Haviland commented in *Horn Book* that "it's all a whimsical and childlike game of pretend," while Cynthia Percak Infantino in *School Library Journal* concluded that "story hour audiences will relish Little Fox's escapades."

Tompert's ideas come from a variety of sources: the newspapers, personal experience, and her years of teaching young children. "For me," she once told *CA*, "ideas are everywhere, just waiting to be picked up. . . . The idea for a story is just the beginning, of course. It is somewhat like the first piece of a jigsaw puzzle. The rest of the pieces must be found and fitted into the right places before the picture is completed. Sometimes, the process goes quickly, but more often, it is a long series of trials and errors. When the story is finished, I know it has been worth the effort. And I know, too, that I can hardly wait to start on a new puzzle." For her next "puzzle," Tompert teamed up again with John Wallner and employed an otter as the main character, as she had done with the earlier *Fun for Ozzie.* In *Little Otter Remembers and Other Stories,* the animal protagonist selects a gift for Mother Otter, searches for a lost pine cone, and goes to a sliding party with relatives. "The tone here is pleasantly warm," noted a reviewer for *Booklist,* and a contributor in *Publishers Weekly,* commenting on the success of the previous joint effort of Tompert and Wallner, remarked that "they now have another able contender for honors."

A cuddly animal also figures in *Badger on His Own,* in which Badger, tired of his father hounding him about turning cartwheels, sets up house in a new burrow. Befriended by Owl, Badger soon wonders if the bossy bird is any better than his parents. A *Booklist* reviewer concluded that the book's adult message "goes straight to the heart of most youngsters," while a critic in *Publishers Weekly* called it "a droll, original story." *Three Foolish Tales,* employing a story-within-the-story format, features Skunk, Raccoon, and Fox who vie for a purple umbrella, the prize for whomever can tell the most foolish tale. In the end it is Fox who makes the other two look foolish. A contributor in *School Library Journal* noted that the book had "a refreshing degree of wit," but a *Publishers Weekly* reviewer commented that Tompert often "expresses a grownup's hindsight," and that the book seemed geared more "to adults than to children."

With *Charlotte and Charles,* Tompert features human protagonists, though in this case they are two giants living on a lonely island. Normal-sized people come to settle the island, and at first Charlotte is happy about this, though Charles has his doubts. Such doubts are confirmed when the humans, out of a blind fear of difference, force the giants to flee to another island. "This is a highly readable story, almost an allegory of race relations and bigotry," noted Ruth K. MacDonald in *School Library Journal.* A nonsense tale is at the heart of Tompert's next title, *Nothing Sticks Like a Shadow,* in which Rabbit, egged on by Woodchuck, tries futilely to outrun his shadow. Judith Gloyer, reviewing the book in *School Library Journal,* noted that it was "a well-rounded tale that hangs together from start to finish," and Barbara Ellerman in *Booklist* concluded that "librarians looking for lively Groundhog Day stories, will latch on to this with pleasure."

Tompert took a break from children's picture books with 1987's *The Greatest Showman on Earth: A Biography of P. T. Barnum,* written for a juvenile audience. Relatively longer in format than the author's previous works and illustrated with photographs, this biography covers the career of the showman who created the three-ring circus, among other achievements. Barnum was also something of a hoaxer and a minor fraud, who, as Tompert shows in her biography, also helped to create modern advertising. Todd Morning, in *School Library Journal,* called the book an "effective biography," though noting that the author's tendency to skip back and forth in time might confuse some young readers. "Tompert has assembled the facts of [Barnum's] life competently," a reviewer in the *Bulletin of the Center for Children's Books* concluded.

Three books from 1988 deal with human protagonists and with themes ranging from the meaning of Christmas to the difficulties of adjusting to day care. In *The Silver Whistle,* set in Mexico, Miguel saves all year to buy a silver whistle to set on the altar as a gift to the Christ Child, but his savings go instead to save a burro being beaten by its master. In the end, it is the crude clay whistle that Miguel has fashioned that is the best altar gift of all. *Will You Come Back for Me?* examines four-year-old Suki's fear at being left for the first time at a day-care center. In the end the girl's fears are eased when her mother cuts out a red heart and gives Suki half of it: "When I leave you at Mrs. Clara's on Monday, I'll leave a part of my heart, too," the mother tells Suki. Both a multicultural story as well as a problem book, it is a tale "certain to calm the fears of little ones in the same situation as Suki," noted Ilene Cooper in *Booklist.* Tompert's *Sue Patch and the Crazy Clocks* tells the story of Sue who can fix anything until she is challenged by the king to set all the clocks in his huge palace to the same time. While she is first daunted by the challenge, in the end, logic prevails. "An entertaining story with whimsical logic to tickle minds and funny bones," stated a contributor in *Kirkus Reviews.*

A quartet of stories from the 1990s told in folktale and legend format are set from China to Russia to Japan.

Grandfather Tang's Story: A Tale Told with Tangrams is about shape-changing fox fairies who compete against each other until they are finally reminded of their friendship by the danger a hunter presents. Employing the Chinese tangram, an ancient seven-piece puzzle that can be put together to tell a story, Tompert's book also relates the loving bond between an old man and his granddaughter and "will be valued by storytellers and listeners alike," according to Carolyn Noah in *School Library Journal. The Tzar's Bird* tells the story of a Russian king who is afraid of going to the edge of the world, a fear only increased by the threats of the witch Baba Yaga, the well-known figure from folklore. Ultimately the tzar, Prince Yaroslav, learns to overcome his fear of the unknown in this "lively story," as Denise Anton Wright characterized the book in *School Library Journal.* "Striking just the right balance between traditional folktales and modern morality tales, the text is filled with rich imagery," Wright noted. Another legend-like tale is *Savina, the Gypsy Dancer,* in which a gypsy girl captivates people with her marvelous dancing and ultimately arouses the jealousy and hatred of King Walid, who is fearful that such dancing might threaten his own power. In *Bamboo Hats and a Rice Cake: A Tale Adapted from Japanese Folklore,* Tompert adapted a Japanese folktale about a poor old couple who, wishing to have good luck in the New Year, are forced to trade the wife's wedding kimono for rice cakes that insure such luck. Once at the market, however, the old man, out of the goodness of his heart, makes trades that leave him worse off than before. "Kindness and generosity are the virtues celebrated in this pleasant adaptation," commented Nancy Vasilakis in a *Horn Book* review.

Tompert returns to animal protagonists with *Just a Little Bit,* the story of Mouse and Elephant who decide to go on a seesaw together. Mouse ends up needing the help of many other animals before they are able to go up and down, reinforcing the idea that help, even in small packages, can be of benefit in the aggregate. Mary M. Burns in *Horn Book* called the work "a charming tale of collaborative effort," and Harriett Fargnoli in *School Library Journal* noted that "repetitive phrasing, the parade of animal types, and the variety of the verb actions make this a beginning language pleaser." A mouse also figures in Tompert's *A Carol for Christmas,* set in Austria in 1818. This retelling of the origins of "Silent Night" is narrated by Jeremy, one of seventeen mouse children, who is present at the creation of the famous Christmas carol—he has slipped into the Pastor's pocket in search of cheese just as the man decides to take a walk in the night air in search of inspiration. Deborah Abbott in *Booklist* thought that "the story's crisp descriptive details add a sense of holiday magic" and concluded that the book was "a solid addition for Christmas collections."

Tompert tells the stories of two famous saints in her books *Saint Patrick* and *Saint Nicholas.* In *Saint Patrick,* she recounts the life story of Ireland's patron saint, a man who survived slavery and kidnaping to become a missionary to his own people. "Tompert concentrates on facts rather than legend," noted Ilene Cooper in *Booklist,* adding that *Saint Patrick* is an "appealing look at the life of Ireland's patron saint." The critic for *Publishers Weekly* found Tompert's biography to be "a highly accessible look at one of history's best-known spiritual leaders."

In *Saint Nicholas,* Tompert presents the real-life story of the Catholic bishop whose career inspired the legend of Santa Claus. An orphan, Nicholas became a priest and then the bishop in the coastal town of Patara in present-day Turkey. Renowned for the miracles he worked in the lives of his people, he was eventually made the patron saint of children. Centuries later, his good deeds and his connection to doing good works for children led to his transformation into the Santa Claus of today. A *Publishers Weekly* reviewer noted that "Tompert employs a swift-moving chronology to emphasize Nicholas's purity, selflessness and faith." Gillian Engberg in *Booklist* described the text as "engaging and simple" and concluded that "children interested in the lives of saints will find a good introduction here."

In her many books, Tompert has managed to impart messages about kindness and cooperation, the evils of jealousy, and the power of friendship in a light manner. "I am very committed to the idea of fostering positive values in my books for children," she once explained. "We as a nation are so dedicated to preserving our physical environment and our quality of life (making ourselves safe from harm—auto safety, cancer research, pure food laws, etc.); yet, when it comes to dealing with our minds, anything and everything is permissible. I find this very disturbing, to say the least." In a letter to the editor of *Horn Book,* Tompert posited a question that sums up her efforts as a children's writer: "It seems to me that the media keep us well informed about 'how things are,'" she wrote.

"Should not we writers consider presenting our readers with the possibilities of how things can be or perhaps should be?"

BIOGRAPHICAL AND CRITICAL SOURCES:

PERIODICALS

Booklist, February 15, 1978, p. 1013; April 15, 1978, p. 1358; April 1, 1984, p. 1122; November 1, 1988, p. 488; October 15, 1994, Deborah Abbott, review of *A Carol for Christmas,* p. 440; February 1, 1998, Ilene Cooper, review of *Saint Patrick,* p. 916; October 1, 1998, Ilene Cooper, review of *Saint Patrick,* p. 343; May 15, 1999, Shelley Townsend-Hudson, review of *The Hungry Black Bag,* p. 1704; October 1, 2000, Gillian Engberg, review of *Saint Nicholas,* p. 360; March 1, 2003, Ilene Cooper, review of *Joan of Arc: Heroine of France,* p. 1208.

Bulletin of the Center for Children's Books, October, 1969, p. 32; March, 1976, pp. 119-120; January, 1978, p. 87; April, 1980, p. 161; April, 1988, p. 171; May, 1991, p. 229.

Horn Book, September, 1976, pp. 616-617; July, 1989, p. 64; September-October, 1989, p. 548; January, 1990, p. 226; fall, 1991, p. 260; September-October, 1993, pp. 592-593; February, 1994, p. 79; spring, 1994, pp. 57, 111; spring, 1995, p. 59.

Humpty Dumpty's Magazine, March, 1995, review of *Just a Little Bit,* p. 10.

Kirkus Reviews, October 1, 1975, p. 125; August 1, 1976, p. 843; March 1, 1978, p. 241; February 15, 1980, p. 213; March 1, 1984, p. 111; September 1, 1988, p. 1329; October 15, 1989, p. 1538; April 15, 1990, p. 586; August 1, 1990, p. 1092; September 1, 1993, p. 1153; November 15, 1994, p. 1549; March 1, 2002, review of *The Pied Piper of Peru,* p. 347; March 1, 2003, review of *Joan of Arc,* p. 399.

New York Times Book Review, November 14, 1976, p. 39; July 1, 1990, p. 19.

Publishers Weekly, November 14, 1977, p. 66; February 27, 1978, p. 158; February 5, 1979, p. 95; September 19, 1994, review of *A Carol for Christmas,* p. 31; September 23, 1996, review of *The Jade Horse, the Cricket, and the Peach Stone,* p. 76; March 24, 1997, review of *How Rabbit Lost His Tail,* p. 82; January 26, 1998, review of *Saint Patrick,* p. 86; May 3, 1999, review of *The Hungry Black Bag,* p. 75; September 25, 2000, review of *Saint Nicholas,* p. 113; February 10, 2003, review of *Joan of Arc,* p. 187.

School Library Journal, December, 1976, pp. 51-52; May, 1979, p. 80; January, 1980, p. 62; May, 1984, p. 75; March, 1988, p. 210; April, 1988, p. 171; May, 1990, p. 92; November, 1990, p. 99; December, 1993, p. 95; October, 1994, Jane Marino, review of *A Carol for Christmas,* p. 44; December, 1996, Margaret A. Chang, review of *The Jade Horse, the Cricket, and the Peach Stone,* p. 107; May, 1997, Judith Constantinides, review of *How Rabbit Lost His Tail,* p. 115; March, 1998, review of *Saint Patrick,* p. 207; May, 1999, review of *The Hungry Black Bag,* p. 99; October, 2000, review of *Saint Nicholas,* p. 63; March, 2003, Ann Welton, review of *Joan of Arc,* p. 225.

OTHER

Boyds Mills Press Web Site, http://www.boydsmillspress.com/ (December 16, 2002).

* * *

TUNNELL, Michael O('Grady) 1950-

PERSONAL: Born June 14, 1950, in Nocona, TX; son of Billie Bob Tunnell and Mauzi Chupp; legally adopted by Grady and Trudy Chupp (maternal grandparents); married Glenna Maurine Henry (a librarian); children: Heather Anne Wall, Holly Lyne Argyle, Nikki Leigh, Quincy Michael. *Ethnicity:* "White." *Education:* University of Utah, B.A., 1973; Utah State University, M.Ed., 1978; Brigham Young University, Ed.D., 1986. *Politics:* Democrat. *Religion:* Church of Jesus Christ of Latter-day Saints (Mormons). *Hobbies and other interests:* Reading, photography.

ADDRESSES: Office—210-K McKay Building, Brigham Young University, Provo, UT 84602; fax: 801-226-8514. *E-mail*—mike_tunnell@byu.edu.

CAREER: Uintah School District, Vernal, UT, sixth-grade teacher, 1973-75; Wasatch School District, Heber City, UT, teacher and library/media specialist, 1976-85; Arkansas State University, Jonesboro, assistant professor of elementary education, 1985-87;

Michael O. Tunnell

Northern Illinois University, DeKalb, assistant professor of language arts and children's literature, 1987-92; Brigham Young University, Provo, UT, began as associate professor, became professor of children's literature, 1992—.

MEMBER: International Reading Association, American Library Association (member of Newbery Award Committee, 1990), National Council of Teachers of English (board member of Children's Literature Assembly, 1992-94; member of board of directors, 1995-97; chair of Poetry Award Committee, 1995-97), Society of Children's Book Writers and Illustrators.

AWARDS, HONORS: American Booksellers Pick of the Lists, 1993, for both *Chinook!* and *Beauty and the Beastly Children;* three Awards in Children's Literature, Association of Mormon Letters, 1993, for *Chinook!, The Joke's on George,* and for *Beauty and the Beastly Children;* selection as "notable children's trade book in the field of social studies," Children's Book Council and National Council for the Social Studies, 1996, for *The Children of Topaz: The Story of a Japanese-American Internment Camp Based on a Classroom Diary,* and 1998, for *Mailing May;* Parents' Choice Award, 1996, for *The Children of Topaz;* Cooperative Children's Book Center Choices, 1996, for *The Children of Topaz,* and 1997, for *Mailing May;* included among "notable books in the language arts," National Council of Teachers of English, 1997, for *The Children of Topaz,* and 1998, for *Mailing May;* International Reading Association, included among "notable books for a global society," 1997, for *The Children of Topaz,* and 2002, for *Brothers in Valor: A Story of Resistance,* and "Teachers' Choices" selection, 1998, for *Mailing May;* selection for "Books for the Teen Age" list, New York Public Library, named "distinguished title," Public Library Association, cited in "Nonfiction Honor List," *Voice of Youth Advocates,* all 1997, Carter G. Woodson Honor Book Award, National Council for the Social Studies, and included in master lists for state awards in Utan and Maine, 1997-98, all for *The Children of Topaz;* included in "Best Books" list, *Crayola Kids* magazine and *Child* magazine, both 1997, selection as "notable children's book," American Library Association, *Storytelling World* Honor Award, both 1998, award for outstanding achievement in picture books, *Parent's Guide to Children's Media, 1998,* featured at National Postal Museum, Smithsonian Institution, 2002, and included in master lists for state awards in Utah, Virginia, Missouri, North Dakota, Nebraska, Arkansas, Delaware, Washington, Nevada, Indiana, California, Georgia, Colorado, and Ohio, all for *Mailing May;* Parents' Choice Story Book Recommendation, 1998, and included in master list for state award in Utah, both for *School Spirits.*

WRITINGS:

FOR CHILDREN

Chinook!, illustrated by Barry Boot, Tambourine Books (New York, NY), 1993.

The Joke's on George, illustrated by Kathy Osborn, Tambourine Books (New York, NY), 1993.

Beauty and the Beastly Children, illustrated by John Emil Cymerman, Tambourine Books (New York, NY), 1993.

(With George W. Chilcoat) *The Children of Topaz: The Story of a Japanese-American Internment Camp Based on a Classroom Diary,* Holiday House (New York, NY), 1996.

Mailing May, illustrated by Ted Rand, Greenwillow Books (New York, NY), 1997.

School Spirits, Holiday House (New York, NY), 1997.

Halloween Pie, illustrated by Kevin O'Malley, Lothrop, Lee & Shepard (New York, NY), 1999.

Brothers in Valor: A Story of Resistance (Junior Library Guild selection), Holiday House (New York, NY), 2001.

Contributor of articles and short stories to magazines, including *Cricket* and *Spider.*

OTHER

The Prydain Companion: A Reference Guide to Lloyd Alexander's "Prydain Chronicles," Greenwood Press (Westport, CT), 1989, Henry Holt (New York, NY), 2003.

(With James S. Jacobs) *Lloyd Alexander: A Bio-Bibliography,* Greenwood Press (Westport, CT), 1991.

(Editor, with Richard Ammon) *The Story of Ourselves: Teaching History through Children's Literature,* Heinemann (Portsmouth, NH), 1993.

(With James S. Jacobs) *Children's Literature, Briefly,* Merrill/Prentice Hall (Upper Saddle River, NJ), 1996.

(With James S. Jacobs and Daniel L. Darigan) *Children's Literature: Engaging Teachers and Children in Good Books,* Merrill-Prentice Hall (Upper Saddle River, NJ), 2002.

Contributor to books. Contributor of articles and reviews to periodicals, including *Reading Teacher, Language Arts,Horn Book, Children's Literature in Education, School Library Journal, Reading Improvement, Book Links,Social Education, New Advocate* and *Journal of Educational Research.*

WORK IN PROGRESS: Wishing Moon, a novel for young readers, for Dutton (New York, NY); revising *Children's Literature: Engaging Teachers and Children in Good Books,* with James S. Jacobs and Daniel L. Darigan.

SIDELIGHTS: Michael O. Tunnell is the author of several picture books, including the award-winning *Mailing May,* and of nonfiction works and novels for middle-grade readers. A professor of children's literature at Brigham Young University, Tunnell thoroughly knows the terrain of which he writes. Yet when he came to creating his own stories and novels, it was as if he were in uncharted territory. "I discovered critiquing someone else's work is an entirely different process than creating your own stories," Tunnell once told *CA.* "Perhaps I was simply too close to my own work, which made applying what I thought I knew about quality literature difficult. In any case, I had a lot to learn (and the learning has just begun!) about the creative process. I guess writers are born perhaps more than they are made. (I feel the same way about teachers.) So, part of the challenge has been to find and cultivate any spark of literary creativity with which I might have been blessed."

Born in Texas, Tunnell was raised in Canada by his grandparents. His love affair with books started at a young age. "My grandmother . . . would read to me every day," Tunnell commented, "fairy tales, comic books, and wonderful picture books like *Caps for Sale* and *Mike Mulligan and His Steam Shovel.* I soon discovered that books were the world's best teachers and entertainers. I grew up wanting to spend my life working with books." At university he was studying for a career in law when he rediscovered this early commitment. Working part-time for an automobile dealer in Salt Lake City, Utah, he was sent to deliver a car to a customer at a nearby elementary school. "The second I walked through the school doors, I was flooded with the strangest feelings. I remembered my favorite books and my magical childhood years. The next day I changed my major to education. Since then, I've completed several degrees, all relating to reading, children's literature, and teaching." A classroom teacher and media specialist for several years, Tunnell eventually wound up teaching children's literature at the university level.

Tunnell's love of books and language encouraged him to try writing short stories as a child, and in his twenties he wrote his first novel, one that was rejected by more than twenty publishers. "For a number of years, instead of creating stories I channeled my writing efforts into professional educational books and journal articles," Tunnell remarked. "All the while, my desire to write books for young readers stayed strong. In the early 1990s, I found my way back to writing stories. My first effort was the manuscript for the picture book *Chinook!,* which was accepted on my third submission attempt." For this book, Tunnell harkened back to some of his own childhood memories of growing up in Alberta, Canada, and the warm, dry wind—the chinook—that blows off the eastern slopes of the Rockies. The result is a book of original tales told by old-timer Andrew Delaney McFadden to two ice-skating children. While out ice-fishing, McFadden pulls the children into his boat that sits on top of the ice, warning them about the possible dangers of being stranded far from shore should the weather suddenly change because of a chinook. He relates the story of one such chinook which swept down in 1888 and quickly melted the ice, explaining why he prefers to sit in a boat while ice fishing on a frozen lake. Other tales follow as McFadden gives these newly arrived siblings a taste for Western weather: tomato seeds sprouting in February; apple blossoms and fruit in winter. "Few tall tales focus so intently on weather," Deborah Abbott commented in her *Booklist* review, "and this one, with its flamboyant shift from winter to summer, radiates a gentle warmth."

The Joke's on George, Tunnell's second picture book, again employs historical situations in an amusing manner. Taken from the eighteenth-century journals of Rembrandt Peale, the book deals with an incident involving Peale's father, painter and museum keeper Charles Willson Peale, and George Washington. Visiting Peale's Philadelphia museum, the president—renowned for his courtesy to all—is fooled by one of Peale's *trompe l'oeil* paintings. He politely bows to two children on a staircase, but oddly they make no reaction, no response. Only when the children in question turn out to be paintings on a wall does President Washington realize that he has been fooled. Deborah Stevenson, writing in the *Bulletin of the Center for Children's Books,* called *The Joke's on George* "an entertaining tale that shows Washington in a different light," and also commented that the book could lead to "some entertaining artistic discussions."

Tunnell turned a traditional fairy tale on its head with his what-if rendition of Beauty and the Beast. In his *Beauty and the Beastly Children,* Tunnell imagines what might have happened after Beauty married the Beast. Beast, also known as Auguste, regresses to ale drinking and darts while Beauty gives birth to rather horrid beast-like triplets. Auguste finally accepts his parental responsibilities, however, and helps to bring the unruly children around. When he does, the witch lifts the spell on the children, and finally there is a "happily ever after" ending. Tunnell relates his tale in "colloquial, sassy prose," according to Susan Hepler in *School Library Journal.*

Returning to history for inspiration, Tunnell told the actual story of a girl sent by parcel post to visit her grandmother in 1914. "I especially like to write about 'little people' in history rather than the famous ones," Tunnell commented, "for instance May Pierstorff in my picture book *Mailing May.* Parcel post was a brand new item in 1914, and May's financially strapped parents saw the new postal regulations as a way to afford sending their five-year-old daughter to visit her grandmother. For fifty-three cents they mailed her! (Her mother's cousin was the mail clerk in the railway postal car.) This may seem an insignificant bit of Americana to many people, but to me it is the marvelous story of ordinary people using creative means to solve a difficult problem. That's the stuff of history!" With a mailing label and fifty-three cents worth of stamps stuck to her coat—she is luckily under the fifty-pound parcel post limit—May sets off one morning for her visit. Her cousin Leonard is in charge of the mail, so he accompanies her on the train. Seventy-five miles later, having passed through the mountainous terrain of Idaho, she arrives safely at her grandmother's home.

An American Library Association "notable children's book," *Mailing May* also earned critical praise. Carolyn Phelan noted in *Booklist:* "Told in the first person from May's point of view, the story has a folksy quality and a ring of truth that will hold children's interest beyond the central anecdote." Applauding the "child-like understated quality" of the story, Betsy Groban observed in the *New York Times Book Review* that *Mailing May* "is a heartwarming period piece based on a true incident, lovingly told, beautifully illustrated and extremely well produced in an oversized format." Pat Mathews concluded in the *Bulletin of the Center for Children's Books* that "May tells the story of her bygone journey with homespun perfection, so stamp this one 'First Class' and make a special delivery to a storytime in your area."

Highly interested in historical accuracy when compiling *Mailing May,* Tunnell not only rode on the rail line which May followed, and but also found and interviewed May's son—May herself died in 1987. Additionally, he used a two-page account of the trip written by May's Cousin Leonard, the postal clerk in charge of May on her trip in February, 1914. However, for Tunnell's nonfiction book on Japanese-American internment during World War II, *The Children of Topaz: The Story of a Japanese-American Internment Camp Based on a Classroom Diary,* the research was much more extensive. There was library work and also the tracking down of primary sources. "I was privileged to run into the story of Lillian 'Anne' Yamauchi Hori and her third-grade class, who were interned during World War II in the Japanese-American relocation camp at Topaz, Utah. These children and their young teacher appear in no history textbooks, yet they are the ones who experienced firsthand the fallout of decisions made by well-known personalities such as Franklin Delano Roosevelt. Their illustrated class diary, an integral part of *The Children of Topaz,* helps us see and feel the effects of war hysteria and prejudice on a personal level." Tunnell and his coauthor, George W. Chilcoat, located the widower of the teacher as well as several of the men who, as boys, had been interned in the camp and interviewed them for the book. Female students were harder to track down because of name changes with marriage. After publication of the book however, several of the other former students contacted Tunnell and in 1996 a reunion of the class was held in Berkeley, California. "Fifteen of the twenty-three Japanese-American students, now in their sixties, attended," Tunnell related. "It was one of the most moving experiences of my life."

About a third of the class diary was used in *The Children of Topaz;* each entry is further annotated by "well-researched commentaries explaining the children's allusions, expanding upon the diary text, and placing events in socio-historical perspective," according to reviewer John Philbrook in *School Library Journal.* "Here readers are exposed to nine-year-olds writing as it happened," Philbrook reported. *Booklist* reviewer Hazel Rochman noted that "the primary sources have a stark authority; it's the very ordinariness of the children's concerns that grabs you as they talk about baseball, school, becoming Scouts and Brownies." A critic in *Kirkus Reviews* commented that "Tunnell and Chilcoat provide a valuable, incisive, comprehensive text," while Elizabeth Bush concluded in a review for the *Bulletin of the Center for Children's Books* that "the ingenuous testimony left by Yamauchi's third-graders may make the Topaz story accessible to an audience slightly younger" than those for whom other such internment books have been written.

Tunnell's first novel for young readers, *School Spirits,* likewise deals with history. Set in a small town in 1958, the book is a ghost story; its writing thus combined two of Tunnell's favorite themes. "I'd say history and fantasy, not as odd a combination as some might think, are my two favorite genres when it comes to writing," Tunnell remarked. "Both history and fantasy have the ability to reveal the ageless qualities of being human. In fairytales, for instance, universal truths about the hearts and souls of people are presented in 'primary colors,' the complexities stripped away to show the basic motivations for human behaviors. In historical literature, readers are allowed to experience those same motivations throughout the millennia. History has the power to connect us to the entire human family."

Though himself a child of the 1950s, Tunnell once again heavily researched the period. "What music was popular? What was playing at the movies? What were the current world events? I used the town where I grew up in Alberta, Canada, as the model for Waskasoo City in the book, so I read pictorial histories of the place in order to refresh my memory. At one point, I even had to learn some particulars about locks and keys, circa 1900. Eventually I had to find a locksmith, who explained at some length what I needed to know. And I had my characters eating Oreo cookies, but I couldn't remember eating them in the fifties. Just to be sure I contacted Nabisco. Oreos hit the scene in 1912!" But Tunnell is also careful not to overburden his readers with too much history. "Authors must repress the urge to tell all the historical facts that their research has revealed. To weave historical facts deftly into the narrative is a true art form; otherwise, the story is overpowered and becomes textbook-like. That knowledge helped me when I wrote *School Spirits.* I knew to deal carefully with all the facts about the wonderful fifties I wanted to share with my readers—still I found the job difficult, even exasperating."

School Spirits tells the story of Patrick, whose father has just become principal of Craven Hill School, a castle-like building and scene of the twentieth-century gothic tale Tunnell weaves. Though reluctant to move, Patrick quickly becomes involved in the new town, becoming friends with Nairen, the girl next door, and encountering the ghost of Barney Dawe, whose disappearance in 1920 has gone unexplained. Patrick and Nairen soon take up the investigation, which involves researching in the town library and time-traveling down a tube-like school fire escape. Molly S. Kinney observed in *School Library Journal* that "this fast-paced story" has "solid writing and doesn't rely on buckets of blood or hacked bodies to entice readers." Writing in *Booklist,* Susan Dove Lempke noted that the "very large type makes this novel a good choice for children who are outgrowing Goosebumps books, and the 1958 setting is a change of pace from contemporary horror tales."

While still writing picture books, Tunnell now concentrates on longer works. "I enjoy trying my hand at the various genres and formats of literature. The economy required by the picture book format makes that sort of writing a challenge. Naturally, nonfiction books demand careful attention to factual detail, but the biggest challenge is writing nonfiction with flair. . . . The novel, however, I find the most challenging. Writing novels requires sustained imaginative output unlike picture or informational books. Creating and developing believable characters who are doing things worth reading about for one hundred pages or more is difficult yet extremely fulfilling business."

Recently, Tunnell informed *CA:* "Fantasy surfaces again in my picture book *Halloween Pie* and in *Wishing Moon.* Like many kids, Halloween was my favorite holiday. I was determined some day to write a Halloween story, so it was great fun finally to send a ragtag group of graveyard creatures in search of a simple pleasure usually reserved for the living—a warm piece of pumpkin (Halloween) pie. *Wishing Moon* is set in the ninth-century Arab world and intersects with the magical world of *1001 Arabian Nights.*

"*Brothers in Valor: A Story of Resistance* is a historical novel based on the true story of the Helmuth Hübener Group, German boys who resisted Hitler by launching a propaganda campaign of their own against the Nazis. I've always been fascinated with acts of moral courage, and I've been fascinated by young people who perform amazing feats at an early age, such as the young operatic singer Charlotte Church or the Olympic champion gymnast Nadia Comaneci. When I ran on to the story of Helmuth Hübener, I discovered a young man who was a prodigy when it came to moral courage. As a sixteen-year-old, he saw clearly through the Nazi propaganda of his native Germany and dared to stand up for the right—even at the cost of his life. It was a story I had to tell.

"*The Prydain Companion: A Reference Guide to Lloyd Alexander's "Prydain Chronicles"* represents the fulfillment of a dream. It is an encyclopedic guide to the magical world of Prydain similar in form to other well-known works written about *The Narnia Chronicles* by C. S. Lewis or the *Lord of the Rings* by J. R. R. Tolkien. I wrote the companion some years ago, and at long last—hooray!—Henry Holt has produced a marvelous edition of my book, with a wonderful foreword by Lloyd Alexander himself. It is the same trim size as the hardcover Prydain novels and has a dust jacket that matches them, too! They all sit together quite nicely on one's bookshelf, and I couldn't be more pleased."

BIOGRAPHICAL AND CRITICAL SOURCES:

PERIODICALS

Booklist, August 15, 1993, Deborah Abbott, review of *Chinook!,* p. 1524; October 1, 1993, Carolyn Phelan, review of *The Joke's on George,* p. 349; December 15, 1993, Emily Melton, review of *Beauty and the Beastly Children,* p. 766; July, 1996, Hazel Rochman, review of *The Children of Topaz: The Story of a Japanese-American Internment Camp Based on a Classroom Diary,* p. 1818; August, 1997, Carolyn Phelan, review of *Mailing May,* p. 1908; February 15, 1998, Susan Dove Lempke, review of *School Spirits,* p. 1012; September 15, 1999, Kay Weisman, review of *Halloween Pie,* p. 270; May 1, 2001, Hazel Rochman, review of *Brothers in Valor: A Story of Resistance,* p. 1676.

Bulletin of the Center for Children's Books, October, 1993, p. 60; September, 1996, pp. 34-35; October, 1997, Elizabeth Bush, review of *The Children of Topaz,* p. 69.

Horn Book, July-August, 1993, Nancy Vasilakis, review of *Chinook!,* p. 451; September-October, 1997, Margaret A. Bush, review of *Mailing May,* p. 564.

Kirkus Reviews, February 15, 1993, p. 235; July 1, 1993, p. 867; December 15, 1995, p. 1777; June 15, 1997, review of *The Children of Topaz,* p. 958.

Language Arts, March, 1994, review of *The Story of Ourselves: Teaching History through Children's Literature,* p. 234; May, 2002, Mingshui Cai and Junko Yokata, review of *Brothers in Valor,* pp. 433-434.

New York Times Book Review, March 15, 1998, Betsy Groban, review of *Mailing May,* p. 24.

Publishers Weekly, March 15, 1993, review of *Chinook!,* p. 87; July 12, 1993, review of *The*

Joke's on George, p. 80; June 9, 1997, review of *Mailing May,* p. 45; December 8, 1997, review of *School Spirits,* p. 72; September 27, 1999, review of *Halloween Pie,* p. 47; July 31, 2000, review of *Mailing May,* p. 97; May 28, 2001, review of *Brothers in Valor,* p. 89; September 10, 2001, review of *The Joke's on George,* p. 95.

School Library Journal, June, 1993, Lisa Dennis, review of *Chinook!,* pp. 91-92; November, 1993, JoAnn Rees, review of *The Joke's on George,* p. 95; January, 1994, Susan Hepler, review of *Beauty and the Beastly Children,* p. 100; August, 1996, John Philbrook, review of *The Children of Topaz,* pp. 161-162; September, 1997, Lucinda Snyder, review of *Mailing May,* p. 197; March, 1998, Molly S. Kinney, review of *School Spirits,* p. 224; September, 1999, Wendy Lukehart, review of *Halloween Pie,* p. 208; June, 2001, Francisca Goldsmith, review of *Brothers in Valor,* p. 158.

Voice of Youth Advocates, December, 1996, p. 292; August, 1997, p. 167.

* * *

TUROW, Scott 1949-

PERSONAL: Born April 12, 1949, in Chicago, IL; son of David D. (a physician) and Rita (a writer; maiden name, Pastron) Turow; married Annette Weisberg (an artist), April 4, 1971; children: Rachel, Gabriel, Eve. *Education:* Amherst College, B.A., 1970; Stanford University, M.A., 1974; Harvard University, J.D., 1978. *Religion:* Jewish.

ADDRESSES: Office—Sonnenschein, Carlin, Nath & Rosenthal, Sears Tower, Suite 8000, Chicago, IL 60606. *E-mail*—SFT@Sonnenschein.com.

CAREER: Attorney and novelist. Stanford University, Stanford, CA, E. H. Jones Lecturer in Creative Writing, 1972-75; Suffolk County District Attorney's Office, Boston, MA, clerk, 1977-78; U.S. Court of Appeals for the Seventh District, Chicago, IL, assistant U.S. district attorney, 1978-86; Sonnenschein, Carlin, Nath, & Rosenthal (law firm), Chicago, partner, beginning 1986. Writer, 1972—.

AWARDS, HONORS: Writing award, College English Association/Book-of-the-Month Club, 1970; Edith Mirrielees fellow, 1972; Silver Dagger Award, Crime Writers Association, 1988, for *Presumed Innocent;* Writer for Writers award, 2001.

Scott Turow

WRITINGS:

One L: An Inside Account of Life in the First Year at Harvard Law School (nonfiction), Putnam (New York, NY), 1977.

Presumed Innocent (novel), Farrar, Straus (New York, NY), 1987.

The Burden of Proof (novel), Farrar, Straus (New York, NY), 1990.

Pleading Guilty (novel), Farrar, Straus (New York, NY), 1993.

The Laws of Our Fathers (novel), Farrar, Straus (New York, NY), 1996.

Personal Injuries (novel), Farrar, Straus (New York, NY), 1999.

(Editor) *Guilty As Charged: A Mystery Writers of America Anthology,* Compass Press (Thorndike, ME), 2001.

Reversible Errors, Farrar, Straus (New York, NY), 2002.

Ultimate Punishment: A Lawyer's Reflections on Dealing with the Death Penalty (nonfiction), Farrar, Straus (New York, NY), 2003.

Also author of unpublished novel *The Way Things Are.* Work anthologized in *Best American Short Stories,*

1971, 1972. Contributor of stories, articles, and reviews to literary journals, including *Transatlantic Review, Ploughshares, Harvard, New England,* and *Place,* and to newspapers.

ADAPTATIONS: Presumed Innocent, a film based on Turow's novel of the same title, was released by Warner Bros., written by Frank Pierson and Alan J. Pakula, directed by Pakula, starring Harrison Ford, Bonnie Bedelia, Brian Dennehy, and Raul Julia, 1990; *The Burden of Proof,* a two-part television film based on the novel, was adapted by John Gay and starred Hector Elizondo, Brian Dennehy, and Adrienne Barbeau, 1992; *Reversible Errors* was adapted as a television miniseries in 2004.

SIDELIGHTS: Scott Turow uses his insider's knowledge of the American legal system to form the basis for best-selling suspense novels. A practicing attorney who has also studied creative writing, Turow explores the murky terrain of urban justice through highly plotted fiction. "No one on the contemporary scene writes better mystery-suspense novels than Chicago attorney Scott Turow," noted Bill Blum in the *Los Angeles Times Book Review.* "In a genre overcrowded with transparent plots and one-dimensional super-sleuths, Turow's first novel, *Presumed Innocent,* was a work of serious fiction as well as a gripping tale of murder and courtroom drama." *New York Times Magazine* correspondent Jeff Shear praised Turow for the "brash, backroom sensibility that informs his work as a novelist." Noting the range of legal thrillers available to readers, *Trial* reviewer Rebecca Porter noted that Turrow's 2003 novel *Reversible Errors* is exceptional due to the author's "refusal to paint the issue in black and white." Turow's "characters are challenged morally, ethically, and emotionally," Porter added—"-and respond with a depth lacking in most legal potboilers. Add an intricate plot, in which Good and Evil are both clothed in gray, and the reader can't plow through without paying attention."

It is a rare writer indeed who collects millions of dollars from a first novel. Even more rare is the author who crafts a novel while holding a full-time, high-profile job. Turow did both, writing drafts of *Presumed Innocent* in his spare moments on the commuter train while working as an assistant U.S. district attorney in Chicago. *Washington Post* contributor Steve Coll wrote that through his determination to write fiction without sacrificing his profession, Turow "has fulfilled every literate working stiff's fantasy."

For his part, Turow maintains that his background in the legal system has provided him with subject matter for fiction as well as practical experience in crafting a narrative. He told a *Publishers Weekly* writer, "As a lawyer, I never decided I didn't want to be a writer. I decided it would have to be a private passion, rather than something I could use. . . . My idea was to stay *alive* as a writer, just to continue to nurture that part of my soul." Turow not only "stayed alive" as a writer, he prospered. His novels have topped the best-seller lists and have found favor with many of the nation's book critics. *Time* reviewer Paul Gray contended that the author's works "revolve around a nexus of old-fashioned values: honesty, loyalty, trust. When those values are violated—sometimes salaciously, always entertainingly—lawyers and the legal system rush in to try to set things right again. But the central quest in Turow's fiction is not for favorable verdicts but for the redemption of souls, the healing of society. Best-sellers seldom get more serious than that."

Turow was born and raised in the Chicago area, the son of an obstetrician. In his early years the family lived in the city. Later they moved to an affluent suburb, Winnetka, Illinois, where Turow attended New Trier High School. As the author told a *Washington Post* contributor, he inherited his own driving ambition from his father, who was "out delivering babies at all hours of the day and night and wasn't around very much." The author added, "I suppose that's the embedded mental image of the hard-working male that I have become." Both of Turow's parents helped to nurture that spirit of hard work, because they wanted their son to become a physician too. Turow had other ideas, however. Even though he flunked freshman English at New Trier High, he grew to love writing, eventually becoming the editor of the school newspaper. He decided he wanted to be a writer, so enrolled in Amherst College in Massachusetts as an English major.

At Amherst Turow began to write short stories and novels, and a few of his short pieces were printed in literary magazines such as the *Transatlantic Review,* a rare feat for an undergraduate. After earning his bachelor's degree in 1970, Turow won a fellowship to the Stanford University creative-writing program. There he taught while working on a novel about Chicago called *The Way Things Are.* He began to question the direction of his career when he received twenty-five rejections for his completed manuscript;

only one publisher, Farrar, Straus & Giroux, offered even the slightest encouragement. Turow told a *New York Times Magazine* writer that the cool reception his novel earned "made me realize that I wasn't one-tenth the writer I hoped to be. . . . I could not sustain the vision of myself as a writer only." In a *Los Angeles Times* interview he said, "I became convinced that one could not make a living in the U.S. writing serious fiction. I was never terribly bitter about that. I didn't see why the world had an obligation to support novelists."

Even while writing *The Way Things Are* Turow was becoming interested in the law, and in 1975, he entered Harvard Law School. Even then he put his writing talents to work. When his literary agent secured him a contract for a personal, nonfiction account of the first year in the law school, Turow took notes during his hectic class schedule and finished the book during summer recess. In 1977 Putnam published Turow's *One L: An Inside Account of Life in the First Year at Harvard Law School.* The work sold modestly at first, but it eventually became "required reading for anyone contemplating a career in law," noted Justin Blewitt in *Best Sellers. New York Times* critic P. M. Stern called *One L* "a compelling and important book. It is compelling in its vivid portrayal of the high-tension competitiveness of Harvard Law School and of the group madness it seems to induce in the student body. It is important because it offers an inside look at what law students do and don't learn and who they are and are not equipped to represent when they graduate."

After receiving his law degree in 1978, Turow returned to Chicago to work with the U.S. District Attorney's office there. As a prosecutor, he was assigned to the infamous "Operation Greylord," a series of trials that exposed judicial corruption in the city's courts. Little by little, the intrigues of corruption and legal wrangling began to work their way into the notebooks Turow kept for his fiction. He set aside a novel he was drafting and began to tinker with a story about an attorney. "I was learning a lot about bribery and I wanted to write about that," he told the *Washington Post.*

For several years Turow did his writing in the little spare time left him after meeting the demands of Operation Greylord and his growing family in the suburbs. He edited chapters of his new novel during his commute to and from work on the train and rose early in the morning to work on his fiction before he left for the office. Finally, his wife convinced him to quit his job and finish the novel. He accepted a partnership at the downtown Chicago firm of Sonnenschein, Carlin, Nath & Rosenthal and then took a three-month hiatus from the firm in order to write. His finished manuscript was mailed to a New York agent just two weeks before he was due to start his new job.

Turow was confident that his novel would be published, but he was astonished by the level of interest shown by New York's biggest publishing houses. A bidding war ensued over the rights to publish the work, and the sums soon exceeded $200,000. Ultimately, Turow did not choose the high bidder but instead took an offer from Farrar, Straus because of the firm's literary reputation—and because of the encouragement he had received from its editors during his student days. The $200,000 payment Farrar, Straus offered Turow was the largest sum that company had ever paid for a first novel.

Presumed Innocent tells the story of a troubled deputy prosecutor in a big city who is assigned to investigate the murder of a female colleague. As the nightmare case unfolds, the prosecutor, Rusty Sabich, finds himself on trial for murdering the woman with whom he once had an adulterous affair. Gray wrote that in *Presumed Innocent* Turow "uses [a] grotesque death as a means of exposing the trail of municipal corruption that has spread through [fictitious] Kindle County. The issue is not merely whether a murderer will be brought to justice but whether public institutions and their guardians are any longer capable of finding the truth." Turow told *Publishers Weekly* that his book is "a comment on the different kinds of truth we recognize. If the criminal-justice system is supposed to be a truth-finding device, it's an awkward one at best. There are all kinds of playing around in the book that illuminate that, and yet by the same token, the results in the end are just. And that's not accidental. . . . Absolutely everybody in the novel is guilty of something. That's a truth of life that I learned as a prosecutor. We all do things we wish we hadn't done and that we're not necessarily proud of."

Fellow attorney-turned-author George V. Higgins noted in the *Chicago Tribune* that *Presumed Innocent* is a "beautifully crafted tale. . . . Packed with data, rich in incident, painstakingly imagined, it snags both of your lapels and presses you down in your chair until you've finished it." Toronto *Globe & Mail* correspondent H. J. Kirchhoff called the novel "surprisingly assured," adding, "The prose is crisp and polished, every character is distinct and fully realized, and the dialogue is authentic. Turow has blended his experience in the rough-and-tumble of the criminal courts with a sympathetic eye for the vagaries of the human condition and an intimate understanding of the dark side of the human soul." Shear concluded that the criminal-justice system *Presumed Innocent* portrays, "without tears or pretense, has seldom appeared in literature quite like this."

"*Presumed Innocent* won the literary lottery," observed Mei-Mei Chan in *USA Weekend.* The novel spent more than forty-three weeks on the best-seller lists, went through sixteen hardcover printings, and sold four million paperback copies. Turow reaped three million dollars for the paperback rights and another one million dollars for the movie rights. A film adaptation of the work, released in 1990, was one of the ten top-grossing movies of that year. When Turow published his second novel—almost simultaneously with the debut of the movie version of *Presumed Innocent*—he joined the ranks of Ernest Hemingway, J. D. Salinger, and Alex Haley by becoming the ninety-second writer to appear on the cover of *Time* magazine.

By the time *The Burden of Proof* appeared in the summer of 1990, Turow had established a routine that included several hours a day for his writing. He still practiced law, but he spent his mornings at home, in contact with the downtown firm by telephone and fax machine. His schedule remained daunting, however, as his celebrity status made him a sought-after interview subject in the various media. But, as Turow told *New York Times Magazine,* he does his best work under such pressure. "I run on a combination of fear, anxiety, and compulsion," he said. "I have to control my habit to work all the time."

The Burden of Proof takes its hero from among the characters in *Presumed Innocent.* Sandy Stern is a middle-aged defense attorney who returns home from a business trip to find his wife dead in an apparent suicide. As he confronts the loss and the circumstances behind it, he becomes enmeshed in a web of family intrigues, insider stock trading schemes, and unanswered questions about his wife's private life. Toronto *Globe & Mail* reviewer Margaret Cannon wrote that in *The Burden of Proof* Turow "has let his imagination loose and, while courtroom derring-do is still a hefty part of the plot, it doesn't subsume the tragic story about some very damaged people." In the *Washington Post Book World,* Jonathan Yardley wrote that "Turow's second novel proves beyond any reasonable doubt that his hugely successful first was no fluke. . . . It's that rare book, a popular novel that is also serious, if not 'literary' fiction. *The Burden of Proof* means to entertain, and does so with immense skill, so if all you want is intelligent amusement it will serve you handily: but it is also a complex, multilayered meditation on 'the heartsore arithmetic of human events,' and as such rises far above the norm of what is generally categorized as 'commercial' fiction."

Turow's third novel, *Pleading Guilty,* broke new ground for the author. "Although fully peopled with lawyers," explained Charles Champlin in the *Los Angeles Times Book Review,* "the story hardly peeps into a courtroom." A high-placed partner in a prestigious Midwestern law firm has suddenly gone missing, along with about five and a half million dollars of the firm's funds. Instead of calling in the police (which would raise a scandal and cost the firm business), the partners turn to one of their employees, Mack Malloy, a former policeman, to find the missing partner and the missing money. In the process, Malloy encounters a body in a refrigerator, an old nemesis, and, eventually, the missing man and money. "*Pleading Guilty,* written as Mack's diary of the . . . events, demonstrates that Mr. Turow, at his best descriptive form, is worthy to be ranked with Dashiell Hammett or Raymond Chandler," said Champlin. "Scott Turow writes as well as ever," declared *Washington Post Book World* contributor Ross Thomas, "and is skilled enough not only to entertain his readers but also convince them they are acquiring vital inside stuff about the legal profession."

Although *The Laws of Our Fathers* reintroduces Turow's famous court scenes, it also moves in different directions compared to the author's previous work. The shooting death of the wife of a state senator reunites a group of 1960s radicals who had been friends but had gone their separate ways at the end of the decade. "The novel is less a legal thriller than a meditative examination of the hold that time past exerts over time present," said Michiko Kakutani in the *New York Times Book Review.* "Beneath the layers of a deep legal deviousness," stated a *Kirkus Reviews* contributor, "Turow never lets you forget that his characters lived and loved before they ever got dragged into court." "The resulting story is by turns moving and manipulative, compelling and contrived," Kakutani concluded. "Though deeply flawed, it stands as Mr. Turow's most ambitious novel yet."

Robbie Feaver is the failed actor and corrupt personal injury lawyer of *Personal Injuries,* a novel based on elements of Turow's experiences with Operation Greylord. "Without knowing anything about the Greylord case, I can attest that this novel has the ring of authenticity," wrote Dennis Drabelle in the *Washington Post Book World.* "It blends widespread graft, a spidery villain insulated at the heart of a complex web, suffering, murder, suicide, and also a measure of humor into a narrative that proceeds with the inevitability—and the surprises—of real life." The story is narrated by Feaver's lawyer, George Mason, called "a colorless fellow who readily admits that he did not witness most of the events he is describing," said Kakutani.

Feaver pays off judges from a secret bank account which is discovered by the F.B.I. while the agency is setting up a sting to nail those judges. Feaver is offered an ultimatum—wear a wire and turn informant or face prosecution. Feaver, a womanizer, but devoted to his wife dying of Lou Gehrig's disease, is assigned an F.B.I. agent, Evon Miller, who, because she is a lesbian, resists Feaver's charm. Gary Krist wrote in the *New York Times Book Review* that "to watch the two of them gradually probing the multiple veils, curtains, and trapdoors of each other's personalities, penetrating a little deeper each time, is to experience the kind of reading pleasure that only the best novelists—genre or otherwise—can provide. . . . And Robbie Feaver may be [Turow's] most inspired creation yet—a slick, mercurial, bighearted con artist, as flawed yet somehow as noble as those tragic figures he never got to play onstage."

In reviewing the novel for *Salon.com,* Jonathan Groner wrote that "the book doesn't pack much mystery. . . . Once the main action is under way and Feaver, wired for sight and sound, has set out among the judges and the courtroom lackeys, there are few surprises. But *Personal Injuries* succeeds as a long look at a world where greed, sloth, and lust holds sway despite the efforts of some good men and women." Drabelle concluded by saying that "lawyers like to differentiate between substance, the content of the law, and procedure, the steps by which you make the system work. In Turow's first novel, *Presumed Innocent,* substance dominated, in the form of a magnificently surprising answer to the whodunit question. *Personal Injuries* holds no similar shock, but the loving attentiveness to procedure—the nuts and bolts of that sting—makes it an absorbing crime novel, perhaps Turow's best."

In *Ultimate Punishment: A Lawyer's Reflections on Dealing with the Death Penalty,* Turow tackles the controversial issue of capital punishment. He first lays the groundwork by providing a history of the death penalty in America, along with overviews of the differing positions on its use. Laurie Selwyn of *Library Journal* praised the book for its even-handed approach to the issue, adding that it is "useful for law, debate, political science, and ethics students." A reviewer for *Publishers Weekly* found the book to be "a sober and elegantly concise examination" containing "useful insights into this fiercely debated subject." William Vance Trollinger, Jr. of the *Christian Century* found Turow's book compelling. In his review, he wrote, "Those who carefully follow his reasoning will not be surprised when, at the end, he declares that he is now opposed to capital punishment. But his compelling logic leaves us with a crucial question: Why do so many Americans and American politicians continue to support the death penalty?"

Turow has said repeatedly that he does not intend to retire from his law practice, even though the profits from his writing career give him that option. The author told the *Chicago Tribune* that he spent many years defining himself as a writer before he became a lawyer. "I really didn't have any sense of identity as a lawyer. I really felt I was faking it," he said. "Somewhere along the way that changed; somewhere along the line I went through this kind of shift of identity. People ask me what I do. I certainly answer I am a lawyer. I don't say I'm a writer. I find that kind of a grandiose claim for somebody who spends sixty hours a week doing something else." Turow told *Publishers Weekly* that he is grateful for the level of success he has achieved with his books but that his perspective on writing has not changed. "Making money was not my intention," he said. "I wrote out of the same impulse that everyone else writes out of—I wrote because there were parts of my experience that I could best deal with that way." He concluded, "Obviously it was enormously fulfilling."

BIOGRAPHICAL AND CRITICAL SOURCES:

BOOKS

Bestsellers 90, issue 3, Thomson Gale (Detroit, MI), 1991.

Contemporary Popular Writers, St. James Press (Detroit, MI), 1997.

Lundy, Derek, *Scott Turow: Meeting the Enemy,* ECW Press, 1995.

St. James Guide to Crime and Mystery Writers, 4th edition, St. James Press (Detroit, MI), 1996.

PERIODICALS

Best Sellers, November, 1977, Justin Blewitt, review of *One L: An Inside Account of Life in the First Year at Harvard Law School.*

Booklist, July, 1999, review of *Personal Injuries,* p. 1896; September 1, 2002, Kristine Huntley, review of *Reversible Errors,* p. 8.

Books, autumn, 1999, review of *Personal Injuries,* p. 19.

Chicago Tribune, June 7, 1987; June 10, 1987; February 16, 1990.

Christian Century, February 10, 2004, William Vance Trollinger, Jr., "No More Death Row," p. 24.

Christian Science Monitor, October 24, 2000, "*One L*—a Survivor's Tale," p. 13.

Esquire, October, 1999, review of *Personal Injuries,* p. 84.

Globe and Mail (Toronto, Ontario, Canada), July 11, 1987; August 8, 1987; June 16, 1990; October 9, 1999, review of *Personal Injuries,* p. D15; November 27, 1999, review of *Personal Injuries,* p. D50.

Harper's Bazaar, June, 1990.

Interview, June, 1990, p. 170.

Kirkus Reviews, August 1, 1996, review of *The Laws of Our Fathers,* p. 1090; July 1, 1999, review of *Personal Injuries,* p. 997.

Kliatt, November, 1998, review of *The Laws of Our Fathers,* p. 49; May, 2003, Sue Rosenzweig, review of *Reversible Errors,* p. 63.

Ladies' Home Journal, July, 1996, p. 124.

Library Journal, August, 1996, p. 115; August, 1999, review of *Personal Injuries,* p. 143; March 1, 2004, Laurie Selwyn, review of *Ultimate Punishment: A Lawyer's Reflections on Dealing with the Death Penalty,* p. 127.

Los Angeles Times, July 24, 1987; October 12, 1989; June 11, 1990; July 27, 1990; September 9, 1990.

Los Angeles Times Book Review, June 3, 1990; June 13, 1993, Charles Champlin, review of *Pleading Guilty,* p. 11; October 10, 1999, review of *Personal Injuries,* p. 10; September 15, 2003, Stephen L. Hupp, review of *Reversible Errors,* p. 106.

New Republic, March 14, 1994, pp. 32-38.

Newsweek, October 17, 1977; June 29, 1987; June 4, 1990; July 5, 1993; July 26, 1993; September 27, 1999, review of *Personal Injuries,* p. 66.

New York Times, September 15, 1977; February 8, 1987; June 15, 1987; August 6, 1987; December 1, 1987; April 19, 1988; May 31, 1990.

New York Times Book Review, September 25, 1977; June 28, 1987, pp. 1, 29; June 3, 1990; June 6, 1993, p. 7; October 8, 1996, Michiko Kakutani, review of *The Laws of Our Fathers,* p. 4; October 5, 1999, Michiko Kakutani, "The Case of a Lawyer and His Judicial Sting," p. 6; October 24, 1999, Gary Krist, "When in Doubt, Lie," p. 7.

New York Times Magazine, June 7, 1987, Jeff Shear, review of *Presumed Innocent.*

Publishers Weekly, July 10, 1987; September 15, 1989; April 1, 1996, p. 22; August 2, 1999, review of *Personal Injuries,* p. 69; November 1, 1999, review of *Personal Injuries,* p. 47; August 19, 2002, review of *Reversible Errors,* p. 64; August 25, 2003, review of *Ultimate Punishment,* p. 48.

Time, July 20, 1987, Paul Gray, review of *Presumed Innocent;* June 11, 1990; October 18, 1999, review of *Personal Injuries,* p. 114; September 6, 1999, review of *Personal Injuries,* p. 76; December 20, 1999, review of *Personal Injuries,* p. 104.

Times Literary Supplement, November 5, 1999, review of *Personal Injuries,* p. 24.

Trial, March, 2003, Rebecca Porter, review of *Reversible Errors,* p. 68.

USA Weekend, June 1, 1990, Mei-Mei Chan, review of *Presumed Innocent.*

Wall Street Journal, October 1, 1999, Nicholas Kulish, review of *Personal Injuries,* p. 6.

Washington Post, October 2, 1977; August 30, 1987; June 9, 1990; June 12, 1990; July 27, 1990.

Washington Post Book World, June 3, 1990; December 2, 1990; June 27, 1993, Ross Thomas, review of *Pleading Guilty,* pp. 1, 8; October 3, 1999, Dennis Drabelle, "Legal Lies," p. 5.

ONLINE

BookPage, http://www.bookpage.com/ (October 1, 2001), James Buckley, Jr., "Going Undercover in Life and Law: A Talk with Scott Turow."

January Magazine, http://www.januarymagazine.com/ (November, 1999), Shannon O'Leary, "Legal Letdown."

Salon.com, http://www.salon.com/ (October 5, 1999), Jonathan Groner, review of *Personal Injuries.*

Scott Turow Home Page, http://www.scottturow.com/ (September 10, 2004).*

* * *

TWOMBLY, Wells A. 1935-1977

PERSONAL: Born October 24, 1935, in St. Johnsbury, VT; died of liver disease, May 30, 1977, in San Francisco, CA; son of Albert F. and Dale (Wells) Twombly; married Margaret Zera, December 9, 1955; children: Wells, Jr., Scott, Jason, Dale Helen. *Education:* University of Connecticut, B.A., 1957; University of Houston, M.A., 1966. *Politics:* Democrat. *Religion:* Episcopalian.

CAREER: Willimantic Daily Chronicle, Willimantic, CT, columnist-editor, 1956-58; *Pasadena Star-News,* Pasadena, CA, columnist, 1958-59; *Hollywood Citizen-News,* Hollywood, CA, columnist, 1959-62; *San Fernando Valley Times,* Hollywood, columnist, 1959-62; *Houston Chronicle,* Houston, TX, columnist, 1962-68; *Detroit Free Press,* Detroit, MI, columnist, 1968-69; *San Francisco Examiner,* San Francisco, CA, columnist, 1969-72. Sports director for KXYZ, Houston, TX, 1964-66.

MEMBER: Baseball Writers of America, Football Writers of America, Delta Chi.

AWARDS, HONORS: Named Texas sports writer of the year, 1966-67; United Press International awards, 1966, 1967, 1968; best sports story of the year award from Newspaper Publishers Association, 1967; best sports story of the year award for E. P. Dutton series, 1970; best sports story of the year awards from San Francisco Press Club, 1970, 1971; named California sports writer of the year, 1971.

WRITINGS:

Blanda, Alive and Kicking: The Exclusive, Authorized Biography, Nash Publishing (Los Angeles, CA), 1972.

Oakland's Raiders: Fireworks and Fury, Prentice-Hall (Englewood Cliffs, NJ), 1973.

Shake Down the Thunder!: The Official Biography of Notre Dame's Frank Leahy, Chilton (Radnor, PA), 1974.

200 Years of Sports in America: A Pageant of a Nation at Play, McGraw-Hill (New York, NY), 1976.

Work anthologized in *Best Sports Stories, 1961, 1963, 1964, 1967, 1968, 1969, 1970, 1971, 1972, 1973, 1974, 1975,* and *1976.* Contributor of over one hundred magazine articles to *Sports, New York Times Sunday Magazine, Esquire, Playboy, Saturday Evening Post, Golf, Pro, West,* and other periodicals. Weekly columnist for *St. Louis Sporting News;* columnist for *Clear Creek* and *Rolling Stone.*

SIDELIGHTS: Wells A. Twombly, according to a writer at the Baseball Library Web site, "was on his way to becoming the most honored sportswriter in America when he died at forty-one." Ron Briley in the *Dictionary of Literary Biography* explained: "Rather than engaging in hero worship of athletes or extolling the virtues of the home team, the college-educated Twombly raised questions about the role of athletics in American society. While some readers found his consciously literary prose enigmatic and confusing, Twombly defended his style, asserting: 'I try to be as literate as I can be. Anybody who writes down to a reader in this age of higher education is living in the past.'"

After working as a sports columnist for several newspapers, including the *Detroit Free Press* and the *Houston Chronicle,* Twombly began working at the *San Francisco Examiner* in 1969. "Twombly's reputation as a sports journalist is based not on his books but on his columns for the *San Francisco Examiner,*" according to Briley. These columns—published six days a week—were idiosyncratic in subject matter and approach, ranging from Twombly extolling the virtues of the baseball park hot dog to a discussion of Casey Stengel's eccentric use of the English language. Speaking of Twombly's legacy, Briley concluded: "Wells Twombly left behind a body of writing that suggests the literary possibilities of sports reporting and the enigmatic quality of American sports, which is both a business and a game."

Twombly once tried to explain the critical acclaim he had received in this way: "Maybe it's because I write in essay-style, try to remember what I learned in

English classes, don't consider athletes anything more godly than the man who delivers the mail. I also try to be a newsman and a writer first, a sloppy, hero-worshipping sports writer way, way down the track. My motivation for getting into this business was twofold: (1) It was all I ever wanted to do from age four onward, and (2) It seemed like the most sensible way to live without working and see the world on somebody else's money."

BIOGRAPHICAL AND CRITICAL SOURCES:

BOOKS

Dictionary of Literary Biography, Volume 241: *American Sportswriters and Writers on Sport,* Thomson Gale (Detroit, MI), 2001.

PERIODICALS

Editor and Publisher, August 7, 1971.
Esquire, October, 1974, Randall Poe, "The Writing of Sports," pp. 173-176, 373-379.
Newsweek, July 1, 1968.
Sporting News, September 26, 1970, "The Eyes of Texas," p. 14; July 30, 1977, Art Spander, "What Drove Wells Twombly?," pp. 43-44; January 6, 1979, Bob Broeg, "Schumacher's Classic Tales: Great Writer, Story Teller," p. 38; October 13, 1979, Dave Klein, "For Some Stars, Mum's the Word," p. 26.

ONLINE

Baseball Library Web site, http://www.pubdim.net/baseballlibrary/ (December 11, 2002).

OBITUARIES:

PERIODICALS

New York Times, May 31, 1977.*

* * *

VOLSKY, Paula

PERSONAL: Female. *Education:* Attended Vassar College.

ADDRESSES: *Agent*—c/o Author Mail, Random House, 1745 Broadway, New York, NY 10019.

CAREER: Fantasy novelist.

WRITINGS:

FANTASY NOVELS

The Curse of the Witch-Queen, Ballantine (New York, NY), 1982.
The Sorcerer's Lady, Ace (New York, NY), 1986.
The Luck of Relian Kru, Ace (New York, NY), 1987.
The Sorcerer's Heir, Ace (New York, NY), 1988.
The Sorcerer's Curse, Ace (New York, NY), 1989.
Illusion, Gollancz (London, England), 1991, Bantam (New York, NY), 1992.
The Wolf of Winter, Bantam (New York, NY), 1993.
The Gates of Twilight, Bantam (New York, NY), 1996.
The White Tribunal, Bantam (New York, NY), 1997.
The Grand Ellipse, Bantam Doubleday Dell (New York, NY), 2000.

Contributor of short stories to anthologies, including *The Resurrected Holmes: New Cases from the Notes of John H. Watson, M.D.,* edited by Marvin Kaye, St. Martin's Press (New York, NY), 1996.

SIDELIGHTS: Fantasy novelist Paula Volsky is the author of several books in the "Sorcerer" series, as well as other popular works in the genre. Volsky began writing fantasies in the 1980s and has continued for more than two decades, and as James Seidman observed in an *SF Site* review, she is noted for "excellent character development and rich, detailed settings." Although her works make liberal use of magic, Volsky also presents political situations that remind readers of real historic movements and events. She is also an author with depth, avoiding facile happy endings and taking aim at twenty-first-century issues through her otherworldly adventurers.

Volsky's first "Sorcerer" novel, *The Sorcerer's Lady,* is the story of Lady Verran, who is forced to marry Lord Terra Fal Grizhni, the old and very powerful magician of Lanthi Ume, capital city of the island of Dalyon. Laurel Anderson Tryforos, in reviewing the novel for

Fantasy Review, praised Volsky's characterization skills and described the sorcerer's rival, Gless Vallage as "appropriately slimy." While recommending the novel, Tryforos did feel that Volsky might have shown more of the heroine's "growing love for and understanding of her husband, particularly in light of the truly effective ending." Reviewing *The Sorcerer's Lady* in *Voice of Youth Advocates,* Dorothy Solomon noted that Volsky's "blend of gothic romance, sorcery, and political intrigue . . . is a good read." The second and third books of the trilogy are *The Sorcerer's Heir* and *The Sorcerer's Curse.*

Volsky's 1987 novel *The Luck of Relian Kru* follows the adventures of protagonist Relian, an apprentice/ slave to the wizard Keprose. He falls in love with Mereth, a female apprentice, and does Keprose's bidding as the sorcerer attempts to clone himself. Tom Easton wrote in *Analog* that the humor of thc novcl lies in the wizard's pets, two metal snakes "that twine around Relian's and Mereth's throats and command them hither and thither at Keprose's behest."

In the critically acclaimed *Illusion,* Eliste vo Derrivalle is a lady-in-waiting to the wife of the king, the Exalted Class ruler of Nirienne. The Exalted Class, to which Eliste also belongs, is suffering from the loss of magical powers that had enforced their rule. The serfs and citizens rise against the Exalted, the monarchy falls, and Eliste fights for survival. A reviewer for *Publishers Weekly* commented that the book is "richer" than Volsky's first two novels, "a delicious fantasy that reads like a historical novel."

The setting of *The Wolf of Winter* is Rhazauelle, a land that resembles eighteenth-century Russia. Its inhabitants practice necromancy, or communication with the dead, through the use of drugs and potions. The villain Varis is the sickly youngest of three brothers in the royal family. Tired of being the brunt of family jokes and longing to be ruler, he kills his middle brother Breziot, then calls up Breziot's ghost to lure his eldest brother, the ruling Ulor, to a roof, where he falls to his death. Breziot's widow wisely hides her two children, Cerrov and his sister, Shalindra, from Varis, who has now become ruler. Twelve years pass and Cerrov and Shalindra have raised an army to battle their uncle and his supernatural fighters. *Locus* contributor Wendy Bradley wrote that the author "deftly juggles the complex plot and supernatural elements while preserving the humaneness of the characters." Bradley also noted that Volsky "manages to devise an ending which is both logically and emotionally consistent, a pleasing end to an eminently readable book." In *Booklist,* Candace Smith asserted: "From intriguing opening to satisfying conclusion, this is pure entertainment." Joyce Davidson pointed out in *Voice of Youth Advocates* that *The Wolf of Winter* is "long and complicated. . . . A novel with vivid scenes of murder and madness. Not for the casual fantasy reader, or the faint of heart. . . . I couldn't put it down."

A reviewer for *Publishers Weekly* called Volsky's 1996 work, *The Gates of Twilight,* "an uncommonly sophisticated fantasy." A revolution is planned by the residents of the Aveshquian city of ZuLaysa against the western Vonahrish occupiers. Critics commented that the setting suggests India during British rule. Renille vo Chaumelle, a westerner of local ancestry, and Ghochanna Jethondi, an Aveshquian princess, solicit help from the gods who walk the earth in rebellion against their foes. A *Publishers Weekly* reviewer cited as Volsky's greatest accomplishments "the depth of her characterizations and the subtlety of her portrait of the clash of dissimilar cultures." Roland Green wrote in *Booklist* that the author's "pacing and characterization . . . are thoroughly sound" and called *The Gates of Twilight* "her best book since *Illusion.*"

The White Tribunal begs comparison to *The Count of Monte Cristo* and other novels where a wronged hero seeks revenge. In a land where sorcery has been outlawed, a White Tribunal sits in judgment of those who try to practice magic. Since the Tribunal confiscates the property of those it finds guilty, abuses of power are inevitable. Tradain liMarchborg is thirteen when his family is falsely accused of sorcery; while they are executed in brutal fashion, he is consigned to prison. He escapes to wreak revenge—using magic—but his actions exact a terrible toll on him as well. A *Publishers Weekly* reviewer felt that Volsky's "treatment of the supramundane realm is generally impressive" and that the novel as a whole "is wonderfully enjoyable." Although Seidman characterized the work as "dark" and "disturbing," he concluded that *The White Tribunal* is "a captivating book that is very difficult to put down."

A long race over demanding terrain forms the crux of the action in *The Grand Ellipse.* Faced with the possibility of world domination by a violent superpower nation, an adventuresome woman named Luzelle Devaire sets out to win a race that could provide her country with a weapon that could annihilate the invaders. Pitted against her in the race is a citizen of the superpower nation—and, representing another country, her former fiancé. In a starred review, a *Publishers Weekly* critic declared that the novel provides "thrilling entertainment for readers of all genres" and "makes for unflagging reading enjoyment." *Booklist* correspondent Sally Estes likewise enjoyed the "adventure laced with humor and romance" that comes to "a literally pyromaniacal conclusion."

BIOGRAPHICAL AND CRITICAL SOURCES:

BOOKS

Reginald, Robert, *Science Fiction & Fantasy Literature,* Thomson Gale (Detroit, MI), 1992.

PERIODICALS

Analog, February, 1988, p. 185.

Booklist, May 15, 1987, p. 1412; February 1, 1992, p. 1014; November 1, 1993, p. 505; February 1, 1996, Roland Green, review of *The Gates of Twilight,* p. 920; September 1, 2000, Sally Estes, review of *The Grand Ellipse,* p. 71.

Books, November, 1991, p. 19.

Fantasy Review, May, 1986, p. 25; December, 1986, p. 38.

Kirkus Reviews, December 1, 1991, p. 1504; October 1, 1993, p. 1233; January 1, 1996, p. 32.

Kliatt, May, 1996, p. 19.

Library Journal, November 15, 1991, p. 110; November 15, 1993, p. 103; March 15, 1996, Sue Hamburger, review of *The Gates of Twilight,* p. 98; September 15, 2000, Jackie Cassada, review of *The Grand Ellipse,* p. 118.

Locus, November, 1991, p. 27; March, 1992, p. 61; January, 1994, p. 29; June, 1994, p. 60; August, 1994, p. 33.

Publishers Weekly, November 29, 1991, p. 48; December 11, 1995, review of *The Gates of Twilight,* p. 66; March 4, 1996, p. 57; July 14, 1997, review of *The White Tribunal,* p. 70; September 25, 2000, review of *The Grand Ellipse,* p. 93.

Voice of Youth Advocates, August, 1986, p. 166; June, 1994, p. 102.

ONLINE

SF Site, http://www.sfsite.com/ (November 12, 2002), James Seidman, review of *The White Tribunal.**

W-Z

WAGAMESE, Richard 1955-

PERSONAL: Born October 14, 1955, in Minaki, Ontario, Canada; son of Stanley and Marjorie Alice (Raven) Wagamese. *Education:* Studied with traditional native elders following formal education through the ninth grade, proclaimed storyteller. *Hobbies and other interests:* Sports, music, reading.

ADDRESSES: *Home*—Toronto, Canada. *Office*—c/o Author Mail, Doubleday Canada, 105 Bond St., Toronto, Ontario M5B 1Y3, Canada.

CAREER: Writer. Worked at various jobs throughout Canada during the 1970s; freelance radio writer in the 1980s; *Calgary Herald,* Calgary, Alberta, Canada, Native issues columnist, 1989-92; *Windspeaker,* columnist, 1987-91. Member of advisory committee of Grant McEwen College's Native Communications Program; member of board of governors, Old Sun Community College, and Siksika Indian Reserve, Gleichen, Alberta, Canada.

AWARDS, HONORS: Award for column writing, Native American Press Association, 1988; award for column writing, National Aboriginal Communications Society, 1988-89; nomination for National Newspaper Award for column writing, 1989; received National Newspaper Award for column writing, 1990; award for best first novel from Alberta Writer's Guild, 1995, for *Keeper'n Me.*

WRITINGS:

Keeper'n Me (novel), Doubleday Canada (Toronto, Ontario, Canada), 1994.

A Quality of Light (novel), Doubleday Canada (Toronto, Ontario, Canada), 1997.

For Joshua: An Ojibway Father Teaches His Son (memoir), Doubleday Canada (Toronto, Ontario, Canada), 2002.

Also contributor of freelance work to Canadian Broadcast Company (CBC) Radio.

SIDELIGHTS: Richard Wagamese, an award-winning newspaper columnist, won further recognition with his first novel, *Keeper'n Me,* which concerns a young man rediscovering his heritage. Garnet Raven, capable of posing as a Hawaiian, Polynesian, an African American, or a Mexican—anything but his own race—eventually becomes determined to learn of his Native American ancestry. Having spent his youth in various foster homes and wasting his early adulthood in prison, the hero finds his way to the White Dog Reserve in northern Ontario. There, he befriends the aging Keeper, a recovering alcoholic. Ultimately, Garnet Raven and Keeper serve to inspire others on the reservation. Maureen McCallum Garvie in *Books in Canada* praised the novel's "teasing, self-deprecating humour," but found its climax to be "sentimental rather than . . . emotional." Kathleen Hickey in *Quill & Quire,* however, called *Keeper'n Me* "a stunning read, and an excellent example of what real storytelling can do."

In his second book, *A Quality of Light,* Wagamese creates Joshua, an Ojibway boy raised by white foster parents, and Johnny, a white boy who has always been interested in the elements of Native American culture that his own upbringing lacks. The boys become friends, but undeniable racial tensions boil around them, eventually resulting in Joshua's hospitalization and Johnny being sent to a detention center. During their separation, Joshua discovers his heritage and Johnny becomes militant against racial injustices. When the two meet again, their friendship cannot survive the differences in their development. Years later, however, they are given another chance to examine the most important aspect of one another: the spirit.

Wagamese discloses Joshua's namesake and his own quest for spiritual enlightenment in his memoir, *For Joshua: An Ojibway Father Teaches His Son.* This work reveals the autobiographical nature of *Keeper'n Me* by presenting the author's own story, which is very similar to Garnet Raven's. Wagamese wrote *For Joshua* after a four-day vision quest during which he fasted on a mountainside and reflected on the path his life has taken. The vision quest marked the beginning of *For Joshua,* in which the author offers the story of his life, beginning with his traumatic childhood, in which he spent years hopping between white foster homes and was consumed by a need to belong. He traces his time as a teenage runaway, when he lived on the streets with only an early high school education and his rapidly developing substance-abuse problem. The author recounts his most painful struggles, such as how alcoholism led to a series of incarcerations and a general destruction of everything pure around him and how racism directed toward him bred racism within him. Wagamese unearths these painful memories with the hope that his alienated son will learn from his father's mistakes. Wagamese eventually turned to his cultural heritage, realizing that it was the missing link in his life all along. He embraces ancient Ojibway stories and ancestral spiritual rituals, such as the vision quest, and explains their importance, encouraging his son to find these cultural assets before taking a wrong turn. Wagamese uses this book to redeem himself by unburdening his spirit and to teach his son to follow the right path.

"The writer who did not know himself—and who blamed 'the white man' for his troubles—has become the man who understands how things happened and who resolves to go forward," wrote Suzanna Methot in a review of *For Joshua* for *Quill & Quire.* Methot continued, "This well-written and perceptive book shows that it is possible for aboriginal people—for any person—to go from there to here." In a review of *For Joshua* on the *Globe and Mail* Web site, contributor Drew Hayden Taylor provided a positive assessment of the book, complaining only that "if there is a flaw, it is the writer's occasional foray into New Age pseudo-psychology," but ultimately commenting that "this is a small complaint when the book offers so much. It's hard to argue with a man revealing his soul to the world, and leaving behind a testament for his absent son."

BIOGRAPHICAL AND CRITICAL SOURCES:

PERIODICALS

Books in Canada, May, 1994, p. 55.

Canadian Literature, autumn, 1998, review of *The Quality of Light,* p. 171.

Quill & Quire, February, 1994, p. 25; May, 1994, p. 24; September, 2002, Suzanne Methot, review of *For Joshua: An Ojibway Father Teaches His Son,* p. 52.

ONLINE

Eye Weekly Web site, http://www.eye.net/ (January 2, 2004), Malene Arpe, review of *Keeper'n Me.*

First Nations Drum Web site, http://www.firstnationsdrum.com/ (January 2, 2004), Chiara Snow, review of *For Joshua.*

Globe and Mail Web site, http://www.globebooks.com/ (November 25, 2002), Drew Hayden Taylor, review of *For Joshua.*

International Readings at Harbourfront Web site, http://www.readings.org/ (January 2, 2004), description of *A Quality of Light.*

Random House Web site, http://www.randomhouse.ca/ (January 2, 2004), description of *For Joshua.**

* * *

WELDON, Fay 1931-

PERSONAL: Born September 22, 1931, in Alvechurch, Worcestershire, England; daughter of Frank Thornton (a physician) and Margaret (a writer; maiden name, Jepson) Birkinshaw; married briefly and divorced in her early twenties; married Ronald Weldon (an antique

Fay Weldon

dealer), 1962 (divorced, 1994); married Nick Fox (a poet); children: (first marriage) Nicholas; (second marriage) Daniel, Thomas, Samuel. *Education:* University of St. Andrews, M.A., 1954.

ADDRESSES: *Agent*—c/o Casarotto Co., Ltd., National House, 62/66 Wardour St., London W1V 3HP, England.

CAREER: Novelist, playwright, television and radio scriptwriter. Worked as a propaganda writer for the British Foreign Office and as a market researcher for the *Daily Mirror,* London, England. Advertising copywriter for various firms in London; creator of the slogan "Go to work on an egg." Former member of the Art Council of Great Britain's literary panel and of the GLA's film and video panel; chair of the judges' panel for the Booker McConnell Prize, 1983.

AWARDS, HONORS: Society of Film and Television Arts award for best series, 1971, for "On Trial" episode of *Upstairs, Downstairs* television series; Writer's Guild award for best radio play, 1973, for *Spider;* Giles Cooper Award for best radio play, 1978, for *Polaris;* Booker McConnell Prize nomination, National Book League, 1979, for *Praxis;* Society of Authors' traveling scholarship, 1981; D.Litt., University of St. Andrew's, 1989.

WRITINGS:

NOVELS

The Fat Woman's Joke (also see below), MacGibbon & Kee (London, England), 1967, published as . . . *And the Wife Ran Away,* McKay (New York, NY), 1968.

Down among the Women, Heinemann (London, England), 1971, St. Martin's Press (New York, NY), 1972.

Female Friends, St. Martin's Press (New York, NY), 1974.

Remember Me, Random House (New York, NY), 1976.

Words of Advice, Random House (New York, NY), 1977, published as *Little Sisters,* Hodder & Stoughton (London, England), 1978.

Praxis, Summit Books (New York, NY), 1978.

Puffball, Hodder & Stoughton (London, England), 1979, Summit Books (New York, NY), 1980.

The President's Child, Hodder & Stoughton (London, England), 1982, Doubleday (New York, NY), 1983.

The Life and Loves of a She-Devil, Hodder & Stoughton (London, England), 1983, Pantheon (New York, NY), 1984.

The Shrapnel Academy, Viking (New York, NY), 1986.

The Hearts and Lives of Men, Viking (New York, NY), 1987.

The Rules of Life, HarperCollins (New York, NY), 1987.

Leader of the Band, Viking (New York, NY), 1988.

The Heart of the Country, Viking (New York, NY), 1988.

The Cloning of Joanna May, Viking (New York, NY), 1990.

Darcy's Utopia, Viking (New York, NY), 1991.

Life Force, Viking (New York, NY), 1992.

Trouble, Viking (New York, NY), published as *Affliction,* HarperCollins (London, England), 1993.

Splitting, Atlantic Monthly Press (New York, NY), 1995.

Worst Fears, Atlantic Monthly Press (New York, NY), 1996.

Big Girls Don't Cry, Atlantic Monthly Press (New York, NY), 1997.

Growing Rich, Penguin (New York, NY), 1998.

Rhode Island Blues, Atlantic Monthly Press (New York, NY), 2000.

The Bulgari Connection, Grove/Atlantic (New York, NY), 2001.

Mantrapped, Grove/Atlantic (New York, NY), 2005.

PLAYS

Permanence (produced in the West End at Comedy Theatre, 1969), published in *Mixed Blessings: An Entertainment on Marriage,* Methuen (New York, NY), 1970.

Time Hurries On, published in *Scene Scripts,* edited by Michael Marland, Longman (London, England), 1972.

Words of Advice (one-act; produced in Richmond, England, at Orange Tree Theatre, 1974), Samuel French (New York, NY), 1974.

Friends, produced in Richmond at Orange Tree Theatre, 1975.

Moving House, produced in Farnham, England, at Redgrave Theatre, 1976.

Mr. Director, produced at Orange Tree Theatre, 1978.

Action Replay (produced in Birmingham, England, at Birmingham Repertory Studio Theatre, 1979; produced as *Love among the Women* in Vancouver, British Columbia, at City Stage, 1982), Samuel French, 1980.

I Love My Love, produced in Exeter, England, at Northcott Theatre, 1981.

Woodworm, first produced as *After the Prize,* off-Broadway at Phoenix Theatre, 1981; produced in Melbourne, Australia, at Playbox Theatre, 1983.

Also author of *Watching Me, Watching You,* a stage adaptation of four of her short stories; *Jane Eyre,* a stage adaptation of the novel by Charlotte Brontë, 1986; and *The Hole in the Top of the World,* 1987.

TELEVISION PLAYS

The Fat Woman's Tale, Granada Television, 1966.

Wife in a Blond Wig, British Broadcasting Corp. (BBC-TV), 1966.

Office Party, Thames Television, 1970.

"On Trial" (episode in *Upstairs, Downstairs* series), London Weekend Television, 1971.

Hands, BBC-TV, 1972.

Poor Baby, ATV Network, 1975.

The Terrible Tale of Timothy Bagshott, BBC-TV, 1975.

Aunt Tatty (dramatization based on an Elizabeth Bowen short story), BBC-TV, 1975.

"Married Love" (part of Marie Stopes's *Six Women* series), BBC-TV, 1977.

Pride and Prejudice (five-part dramatization based on the novel by Jane Austen), BBC-TV, 1980.

"Watching Me, Watching You" (episode in *Leap in the Dark* series), BBC-TV, 1980.

Life for Christine, Granada Television, 1980.

Little Miss Perkins, London Weekend Television, 1982.

Loving Women, Granada Television, 1983.

The Wife's Revenge, BBC-TV, 1983.

Also author of *Big Women,* a four-part series, for Channel 4 television, and over twenty-five other teleplays for BBC-TV and independent television networks.

RADIO PLAYS

Housebreaker, BBC Radio 3, 1973.

Mr. Fox and Mr. First, BBC Radio 3, 1974.

The Doctor's Wife, BBC Radio 4, 1975.

"Weekend" (episode in *Just before Midnight* series), BBC Radio 4, 1979.

All the Bells of Paradise, BBC Radio 4, 1979.

Polaris, American Broadcasting Co. (ABC Radio), 1980, published in *Best Radio Plays of 1978: The Giles Cooper Award Winners,* Eyre Methuen, 1979.

The Hearts and Lives of Men, BBC Radio 4, 1996.

Also author of *Spider,* 1972, and *If Only I Could Find the Words,* BBC.

OTHER

(Editor, with Elaine Feinstein) *New Stories 4: An Arts Council Anthology,* Hutchinson, 1979.

Watching Me, Watching You (short stories; also includes the novel *The Fat Woman's Joke*), Summit Books (New York, NY), 1981.

Letters to Alice on First Reading Jane Austen (nonfiction), Michael Joseph, 1984, Carroll & Graf (New York, NY), 2000.

Polaris and Other Stories, Hodder & Stoughton (London, England), 1985.

Moon over Minneapolis; or, Why She Couldn't Stay (short stories), Viking (New York, NY), 1992.

So Very English, Serpent's Tail, 1992.

Wicked Women: A Collection of Short Stories, Flamingo (London, England), 1995, Atlantic Monthly Press (Boston, MA), 1997.

Godless in Eden: A Book of Essays, Flamingo, 1999.

Auto da Fay (memoir), Grove (New York, NY), 2003.

Also author of children's books, including *Wolf the Mechanical Dog,* 1988, *Party Puddle,* 1989, and *Nobody Likes Me,* 1997.

ADAPTATIONS: The Life and Loves of a She-Devil was adapted into the film *She-Devil* in 1989, written by Barry Strugatz and Mark R. Burns, directed by Susan Seidelman, starring Roseanne Barr and Meryl Streep.

SIDELIGHTS: After her parents divorced when she was only five, Fay Weldon grew up in New Zealand with her mother, sister, and grandmother. Returning to England to attend college, she studied psychology and economics at St. Andrews in Scotland. As a single mother in her twenties, Weldon supported herself and her son with a variety of odd jobs until she settled into a successful career as a copywriter. After marrying in the early sixties, Weldon had three more sons, underwent psychoanalysis as a result of depression, and subsequently abandoned her work in advertising for freelance creative writing. Her first novel, *The Fat Woman's Joke,* appeared in 1967 when she was thirty-six years old. Since that time she has published numerous novels, short stories, and plays for the theater, television, and radio. Throughout this work, Weldon's "major subject is the experience of women," wrote Agate Nesaule Krouse in *Critique.* "Sexual initiation, marriage, infidelity, divorce, contraception, abortion, motherhood, housework, and thwarted careers . . . all receive attention." Products of a keen mind concerned with women's issues, Weldon's novels have been labeled "feminist" by many reviewers. Yet, Weldon's views are her own and are not easily classified. In fact, feminists have at times taken exception to her portrayal of women, accusing the author of perpetuating traditional stereotypes.

Weldon's fiction fosters disparate interpretations because its author sees the complexity of the woman's experience. As Susan Hill noted in *Books and Bookmen,* Weldon has "the sharpest eyes for revealing details which, appearing like bubbles on the surface, are clues to the state of things lying far, far below." Weldon accepts feminist ideology as a liberating force, but she also understands its limitations. Thus, what emerges from Weldon's writing is more than an understanding of women's issues; she appreciates the plight of the individual woman. She told Sybil Steinberg in an interview in *Publishers Weekly,* "Women must ask themselves: What is it that will give me fulfillment? That's the serious question I'm attempting to answer."

Weldon's early novels, especially *Down among the Women, Female Friends,* and *Remember Me,* gained recognition both for their artistry and their social concerns. "Vivid imagery, a strong sense of time and place, memorable dialogue, complex events, and multiple characters that are neither confusing nor superficially observed," characterize these novels according to Krouse, making them "a rich rendering of life with brevity and wit." In her writing, John Braine added in *Books and Bookmen,* Fay Weldon "is never vague. . . . She understands what few novelists understand, that physical details are not embellishments on the story, but the bricks from which the story is made." And, like few other novelists, especially those that deal with women's issues, observed Braine, "she possesses that very rare quality, a sardonic, earthy, disenchanted, slightly bitter but never cruel sense of humour."

Although each of these books possesses elements typical of a Weldon novel, they focus on different aspects of the female experience and the forces that influence them. *Down among the Women* reflects how three generations of women, each the product of a different social climate, react to the same dilemma. Krouse found that in this book Weldon creates "a work whose very structure is feminist." She added in her *Critique* review, "The whole novel could profitably be analyzed as a definition of womanhood: passages describing how one has to live 'down among the women'contrast with anecdotes of male behavior." The image of womanhood offered here is not ideal, but as Krouse commented, Weldon's ability to blend "the terrible and the ridiculous is one of the major reasons why a novel filled with the pain endured by women . . . is neither painfully depressing nor cheerfully sentimental."

As its title suggests, *Female Friends* examines relationships among women, how the companionship of other women can be comforting to a woman wearied by the battle of the sexes. "The most radical feminist could not possibly equal the picture of injustice [Weldon] paints with wry, cool, concise words," wrote L. E. Sissman in the *New Yorker.* Sissman found that "the real triumph of *Female Friends* is the gritty replication of the gross texture of everyday life, placed in perspective and made universal; the perfectly recorded dialogue, precisely differentiated for each character; the shocking progression of events that, however rude, seem real." Weldon does not overlook the injustices committed by women in this day-to-day struggle, however. Ultimately, her characters suggest, women are responsible for their own lives. As Arthur Cooper concluded in *Newsweek,* Weldon "has penetrated the semidarkness of the semiliberated and shown that only truth and self-awareness can set them free."

Remember Me is the story of one man's impact on the lives of three women and how the resentment of one of those women becomes a disruptive force even after her death. This novel suggests that elements beyond the control of the individual often dictate her actions. "Scores of . . . coincidences . . . emphasize the theme that chance, misunderstanding, and necessarily limited knowledge play a significant part in human life," observed Krouse. Human frailties, Krouse added, body functions, pain, sickness "and death are recurrent images underscoring human mortality." Phyllis Birnbaum, writing in the *Saturday Review,* stated, "Precise satire, impassioned monologue, and a sense of limited human possibility make this novel a daring examination of twentieth-century discontent."

By the time she had written her sixth novel, *Praxis* (the fifth, *Words of Advice,* appeared in 1977), Weldon was considered, as Susan Hill put it, "an expert chronicler of the minutiae of women's lives, good at putting their case and pleading their cause." Kelley Cherry pointed out in the Chicago *Tribune Books* that *Praxis* is a novel about endurance. The central character, Praxis Duveen, must endure in a world filled with "just about every kind of manipulation and aggression that men use to get women where they want them," observed Katha Pollitt in the *New York Times Book Review,* "and just about every nuance of guilt and passivity that keeps women there." Struggling against most of the catastrophes that can befall a woman, Praxis does emerge, revealing according to Hill, that even though "Weldon's women are victims, they do have many compensatory qualities—toughness, resilience, flexibility, inventiveness, patience, nerve."

A novel in which so many misfortunes plague one character runs the risk of becoming unbelievable. Yet, Cherry wrote, "The writing throughout is brisk and ever so slightly off the wall—sufficiently askew to convey the oddness of events, sufficiently no-nonsense to make that oddness credible." And, concluded Pollitt, "As a narrative it is perhaps too ambitious, but as a collection of vignettes, polemics, epigrams, it is often dazzling, pointing up the mad underside of our sexual politics with a venomous accuracy for which wit is far too mild a word."

In her next novel, *Puffball,* "Weldon mixes gynecology and witchcraft to concoct an unusual brew," Joan Reardon noted in the *Los Angeles Times Book Review.* Here, more than before, Weldon confronts the woman's condition on a physical level, focusing on pregnancy. "Weldon has the audacity to include technical information on fertility, conception, and fetal development as an integral part of the story," commented Lorallee MacPike in *Best Sellers.* "She makes the physical process preceding and during pregnancy not only interesting but essential to the development of both story and character."

In the eyes of some reviewers such as Joan Reardon, however, the technical information weakens the novel. She wrote that in *Puffball,* "perspicacity has given way to whimsy and 'the pain in my soul, my heart, and my mind' has become a detailed analysis of the pituitary system." Moreover, some feminists faulted this book for its old-fashioned images of women; as Anita Brookner pointed out in the *Times Literary Supplement,* "superficially, it is a great leap backwards for the stereotype feminist. It argues in favour of the old myths of earth and motherhood and universal harmony: a fantasy for the tired businesswoman." Yet a reviewer for the *Atlantic* found that "the assertion of the primacy of physical destiny that lies at the center of *Puffball* gives the book a surprising seriousness and an impressive optimism."

In *The President's Child,* Weldon breaks new ground, exploring the impact of political intrigue on individual lives. Her next novel, however, is reminiscent of

Praxis. Like Praxis, the protagonist of Weldon's ninth novel, *The Life and Loves of a She-Devil,* is buffeted by the injustice of her world. Yet, whereas Praxis endures, Ruth gets revenge. Losing her husband to a beautiful romance novelist, tall, unattractive Ruth turns against husband, novelist, and anyone else who gets in her way. Unleashing the vengeance of a she-devil, she ruins them all; the novelist dies and the husband becomes a broken man. In the end, having undergone extensive surgery to make her the very image of her former competitor, she begins a new life with her former husband. "What makes this a powerfully funny and oddly powerful book is the energy that vibrates off the pages," wrote Carol E. Rinzler in the *Washington Post Book World.* Weldon has created in *She-Devil,* Sybil Steinberg noted in *Publishers Weekly,* a "biting satire of the war between the sexes, indicting not only the male establishment's standards of beauty and feminine worthiness, but also women's own willingness . . . to subscribe to these standards."

Seeing Ruth's revenge as a positive response to the injustice of the male establishment, some reviewers were disappointed by her turnaround at the novel's end. As Michiko Kakutani pointed out in the *New York Times,* "Her final act—having extensive plastic surgery that makes her irresistible to men—actually seems like a capitulation to the male values she says she despises." Weldon is aware of the contradictions suggested by her story; she discussed this issue in her interview with Sybil Steinberg: "The first half of the book is an exercise in feminist thought. . . . It's the feminist manifesto really: a woman must be free, independent and rich. But I found myself asking, what then? . . . I think women are discovering that liberation isn't enough. The companionship of women is not enough. The other side of their nature is unfulfilled."

"Central to many of [Weldon's] plots is the rise of the Nietzschean superwoman," contended Daniel Harris in prefacing his review of the author's 1993 novel *Trouble* in the *Los Angeles Times Book Review.* Paralleling Weldon's own rise to literary acceptance from her former career as a lowly advertising copywriter, Harris characterized such women as emerging "out of the seething multitudes of hungry romantic careerists just waiting for their chance to advance up a hierarchical power structure that Weldon describes as the equivalent among women of a food chain." Annette Horrocks, the pregnant protagonist of *Trouble* is just such a woman, the second wife of a chauvinistic businessman who becomes threatened when his wife publishes a novel. In a twist, the husband runs, not into the arms of yet another manipulative woman, but into the clutches of a pair of pseudo-therapists, who convince him that Annette is his enemy. The novel was faulted by some for being uncharacteristic Weldon. "The characters are thin, the plot maniacally unreal, the dialogue brisk and bleak," noted *Observer* critic Nicci Gerrard, maintaining that *Trouble* contains too large a dose of its author's personal anger.

Weldon's twentieth novel, *Splitting,* finds the author returned to form, according to Bertha Harris in the *New York Times Book Review.* Seventeen-year-old former rock star Angelica White is determined to become the perfect female companion in order to endear herself to dissolute but wealthy Sir Edwin Rice and obtain a marriage commitment. She discards her image as the rock queen Kinky Virgin, doffs the nose rings and the spectacularly colored hair, and becomes overweight, drug-abusing Edwin's helpmate. "In effect, Angelica's troubles begin when she resolves that it's 'time to give up and grow up,'" according to Harris. Soon the typical flock of avaricious females descend on Angelica, breaking up her home and causing her to fracture into four separate personalities. Ultimately banished from the Rice estate, her money having long since been usurped by her husband, Angelica ultimately avenges herself through the savvy, recklessness, and sense of fun created by her multiple selves. "The splitting device works shamelessly well," explained Kate Kellaway in the *Observer.* "Weldon uses it as a way of exploring and rejoicing in the theatricality of women, their volatility, their love of disguise, of fancy dress, of playing different parts." As the author has one of Angelica's new selves say, "Women tend to be more than one person at the best of times. Men just get to be the one."

Weldon has since continued her pace, not only with novels such as 1996's *Worst Fears,* but also with a short story collection, appropriately titled *Wicked Women,* which she published in 1995. In *Worst Fears,* a widowed woman suddenly realizes that her life has not in fact been the rosy picture she imagined it. Snubbed by her friends, and lacking sympathy in favor of her husband's mistress, Alexandra soon finds that such deception by the living is nothing compared to the deceptions practiced on her by her now dead husband. Left with nothing, she plans her revenge in true Weldon fashion in a novel in which the author "has filed down a few sharp edges," according to *New York Times Book Review* critic Karen Karbo, ". . . and that makes it one of her best novels yet." Variations on this traditional Weldon theme are also played out in the sixteen short stories in *Wicked Women.* While noting that the collection is somewhat uneven in effectiveness, *Spectator* reviewer Susan Crosland hastened to add, "When the seesaw swings up, Fay Weldon is on form: sparkling, sharply observing, insights delivered with a light touch that puts us in a good mood, however dark the comedy. And one of the great things about short stories is that you can pick and chose."

Writing for the *Knight-Ridder/Tribune News Service,* Jean Blish Siers stated: "Perhaps the funniest of all Fay Weldon's very funny novels, *Big Girls Don't Cry* tackles the feminist movement head-on with the wry, ironic comedy for which Weldon is famous." This 1997 volume is also typical of Weldon's work in that its story is presented episodically, with short paragraphs and scenes often delivered in a temporally fragmented fashion. "It is a tapestry Weldon weaves," observed a critic for the online publication *The Complete Review,* "and the story does come together very well. Weldon's succinct style, with few wasted words, her dialogue brutally honest and straightforward, her explanations always cutting to the quick make for a powerful reading experience. Not everyone likes their fiction so direct, but we approve heartily and recommend the book highly." The plot of *Big Girl's Don't Cry* moves from the early seventies to the present and concerns five women who found a feminist publishing house called Medusa. As the novel opens we meet Zoë, a young mother in a loveless marriage, the beautiful Stephanie, the sexy Layla, the intellectual Alice, and Nancy, who has just broken off an unsatisfying engagement. While the publishing house thrives over the next three decades, the women's lives evolve dramatically. Husbands and friends change; children are abandoned; internecine conflicts sometimes plague the five while at other times they must rally in support of one another. "In the end," noted Siers, "the five—older but not much wiser—must face the consequences of decisions made a quarter-century earlier." A *Complete Review* critic commented: "The characters are all very human, and while they profess idealism Weldon ruthlessly shows how difficult it is to live up to it." Siers concluded: "Weldon never paints simple pictures of right and wrong. The men might be pigs, but they simply don't know any better. The women might mean well, but they blunder ahead with little thought of ramifications."

In 1999 Weldon's collection of essays *Godless in Eden* was published. Therein she covers a wide range of topics and examines a variety of controversial issues, including sex and society, the feminization of politics, the Royal Family, therapy, her own life and loves, and the changing roles of men and women in the contemporary world.

Weldon's understanding of the individual woman, living in a world somewhere between the nightmare of male chauvinism and the feminist ideal, has allowed her to achieve a balance in her writing. "She has succeeded in uniting the negative feminism, necessarily evident in novels portraying the problems of women, with a positive feminism, evident in the belief that change or equilibrium is possible," wrote Agate Nesaule Krouse. For this reason, "[Weldon] speaks for the female experience without becoming doctrinaire," noted *New York Times Book Review* contributor Mary Cantwell, "and without the dogged humorlessness that has characterized so much feminist writing." Having found an audience for her writing—insights into the condition of woman, shaped by her intelligence and humor—Fay Weldon has risen to prominence in literary circles. Writing in the *Times Literary Supplement,* Anita Brookner called Weldon "one of the most astute and distinctive women writing fiction today."

BIOGRAPHICAL AND CRITICAL SOURCES:

BOOKS

Barreca, Regina, *Fay Weldon's Wicked Fictions,* University Press of New England (Lebanon, NH), 1994.

Contemporary Literary Criticism, Volume 122, Thomson Gale (Detroit, MI), 2000.

Dictionary of Literary Biography, Volume 194: *British Novelists since 1960, Second Series,* Thomson Gale (Detroit, MI), 1998.

Dowling, Finuala, *Fay Weldon's Fiction,* Fairleigh Dickinson University Press (Madison, NJ), 1998.

Faulks, Lana, *Fay Weldon,* Twayne (Boston, MA), 1998.

PERIODICALS

Atlantic Monthly, August, 1980.

Best Sellers, October, 1980.

Booklist, May 1, 1995, p. 1554; June 1, 1995, p. 1804; May 1, 1996, p. 1470.
Books and Bookmen, January, 1977; March, 1979; May, 1979.
Critique, December, 1978.
Entertainment Weekly, June 16, 1995, p. 57.
Knight-Ridder/Tribune New Service, January 20, 1999, Jean Blish Siers, review of *Big Girls Don't Cry.*
Library Journal, February 15, 1995, p. 198; April 15, 1995, p. 117; March 15, 1996, p. 110; May 15, 1996, p. 85.
Los Angeles Times Book Review, September 7, 1980; April 19, 1987; April 10, 1988; December 18, 1988; June 4, 1989; June 25, 1995, pp. 3, 9.
New Statesman and Society, February 11, 1994, p. 40; January 5, 1996, p. 39.
Newsweek, November, 1974; December 4, 1978.
New Yorker, March 3, 1975; November, 1978.
New York Times, November 24, 1981; December 21, 1981; August 21, 1984; October 29, 1988; May 31, 1989; March 16, 1990.
New York Times Book Review, June 11, 1995, p. 48; June 9, 1996, p. 19.
Observer (London, England), February 13, 1994; May 7, 1995.
Publishers Weekly, January 13, 1984; August 24, 1984.
Saturday Review, December, 1976.
Spectator, March 1, 1980; July 1, 1981; October 2, 1982; February 12, 1994, pp. 29-30; May 13, 1995, pp. 39-40.
Times Literary Supplement, September 10, 1971; February 22, 1980; May 22, 1981; September 24, 1982; January 20, 1984; July 6, 1984; August 9, 1985; February 13, 1987; July 15, 1988; February 18, 1994.
Tribune Books, November 12, 1978; September 28, 1980; February 14, 1982; March 13, 1988; November 20, 1988; June 18, 1989; March 18, 1990.
Washington Post Book World, November 3, 1974; September 30, 1984; July 14, 1985; May 10, 1987; April 24, 1988; November 13, 1988; April 1, 1990.

ONLINE

Complete Review, http://www.complete-review.com/, (August 8, 2000), review of *Big Girls Don't Cry and Big Women.*
Fay Weldon, http://redmood.com/ (August 8, 2000).
HomeArts: Fay Weldon, http://homearts.com/ (August 8, 2000), "Fay Weldon."*

WESLEY, Valerie Wilson 1947-

PERSONAL: Born November 22, 1947; married Richard Wesley (a screenwriter and playwright); children: two daughters. *Education:* Howard University, B.A., 1970; Bank Street College of Education, M.A.; Graduate School of Journalism, Columbia University, M.A.

ADDRESSES: *Agent*—c/o Author Mail, HarperCollins, 10 E. 53rd St., 7th Floor, New York, NY 10022. *E-mail*—Valwilwes@aol.com.

CAREER: *Scholastic News,* associate editor, 1970-72; *Essence,* New York, NY, began as travel editor, 1988, became senior editor, 1990, became executive editor, 1992-94, contributing editor, 1994—; writer. Member of board of directors, Newark Arts Council, Newark, NJ.

AWARDS, HONORS: Griot Award, New York chapter of National Association of Black Journalists; Best Book for Reluctant Readers citation, American Library Association, c. 1993, for *Where Do I Go from Here?;* Shamus Award nomination, c. 1994, for *When Death Comes Stealing;* named author of the year, Go Go, Girls book club; Award for Excellence in Adult Fiction from Black Caucus of the American Library Association, 2000, for *Ain't Nobody's Business If I Do.*

WRITINGS:

(With Wade Hudson) *Afro-Bets Book of Black Heroes from A to Z: An Introduction to Important Black Achievers for Young Readers,* Just Us Books (East Orange, NJ), 1988.
Where Do I Go from Here? (young adult novel), Scholastic (New York, NY), 1993.
Freedom's Gifts: A Juneteenth Mystery (juvenile), illustrated by Sharon Wilson, Simon & Schuster (New York, NY), 1997.
Ain't Nobody's Business If I Do (novel), Avon (New York, NY), 1999.
Willimena and the Cookie Money (juvenile), Hyperion (New York, NY), 2001.
Always True to You in My Fashion (novel), Morrow (New York, NY), 2002.

"TAMARA HAYLE" MYSTERY NOVELS:

When Death Comes Stealing, Putnam (New York, NY), 1994.

Devil's Gonna Get Him, Putnam (New York, NY), 1995.
Where Evil Sleeps, Putnam (New York, NY), 1996.
No Hiding Place, Putnam (New York, NY), 1997.
Easier to Kill, Putnam (New York, NY), 1998.
The Devil Riding, Putnam (New York, NY), 2000.

Contributor of fiction to periodicals, including *Essence, New York Times, Ms., Family Circle, Creative Classroom,* and *TV Guide.*

SIDELIGHTS: Valerie Wilson Wesley's contribution to literature includes books for children and young adults, as well as adult relationship novels and mysteries. What unifies the whole of Wesley's work is that she writes from an African American perspective for a primarily African American audience. Her detective novels feature an African American heroine who is a single mother, and her relationship novels explore the dynamics of African American families. To quote a contributor to *Contemporary Black Biography,* Wesley excels in depicting a "literary character representing the millions of smart, tough, single African American mothers who live in big cities all over America."

A former senior editor with *Essence* magazine, Wesley wrote her first book with Wade Hudson. *Afro-Bets Book of Black Heroes from A to Z: An Introduction to Important Black Heroes* was reviewed by Sylvia Meisner of *School Library Journal,* who noted that the book satisfied an increasing demand for new information on African American leaders and celebrities. Her next book was a more personal one, based upon the experiences of her own family members. *Where Do I Go from Here?* tells the story of Nia, a young black female who receives a scholarship to a prestigious white boarding school and tries to find her place there. When a racially based fight causes Nia and a wealthy white peer to be suspended from the school, Wesley creates a situation which reviewer Kim Carter, in a review for *Voice of Youth Advocates,* called a success in "portraying the human similarities that cross racial and economic distinctions."

It was with her "Tamara Hayle" series that Wesley found a niche for her creative talents. Tamara Hayle is a street-smart private detective in Newark, New Jersey, who solves crimes in the seedier sections of that city and some of its neighboring towns. The contributor to *Contemporary Black Biography* wrote: "Tamara Hayle is a character who is instantly identifiable to her admiring audience of African American women. . . . Any single parent . . . will sympathize with Hayle, an ex-cop whose resignation from the force can be laid at the door of a fellow officer guilty of harassing a car full of black teenagers, Hayle's son Jamal among them." According to an article in *American Visions,* mystery writing such as Wesley's has contributed to a rising trend that features black authors publishing mysteries with black characters. As a result, the article noted, "the American fictional detective is changing." Throughout the series, Wesley places Hayle in a number of life-threatening situations from which she must save herself by using her wits, strength, and courage.

In the first mystery of the series, *When Death Comes Stealing,* Hayle investigates the murders of several sons of her ex-husband, fearing that her own son is next. A *Publishers Weekly* critic noted that while Wesley's adult fiction debut revealed little of Hayle's character, the author had created "a broad, interesting cast." The reviewer added that the book's strength lay in "its portrayal of black family life in dangerous times." A critic for *Kirkus Reviews* commented that Hayle's "descriptions of other characters are quick and often funny, even in grim situations. . . . Her colorful personality and cultural insight spice up a serviceable plot."

Wesley's second book in the series, *Devil's Gonna Get Him,* places protagonist Hayle in a situation where she is hired to follow the boyfriend of the daughter of a wealthy and powerful African American Newark man, Lincoln Storey. Hayle is reluctant to trail the boyfriend, who is a former lover, but through a number of events and twists, ends up delving into Storey's dirty past and becoming the target of danger herself. Stuart Miller, in a review for *Booklist,* declared: "Wesley has crafted an intriguing plot showcasing the appealing Tamara." A *Publishers Weekly* critic was less enthusiastic about the plot, but commented that the author's "characterization is powerful; the down-to earth observations of single-mother Tamara . . . amply fill out the thin spots." A *Kirkus Reviews* commentator also praised Wesley's characterization of Hayle, and commented that "her unapologetically plainspoken voice . . . makes this tale as memorable as her debut."

Where Evil Sleeps features Hayle solving mysteries and putting herself in dangerous situations in Jamaica. On vacation in Kingston, Hayle is persuaded to accompany a friend and her husband to a seedy bar for drinks. While there, a power outage allows someone to steal Hayle's purse and murder her friend's husband and another man. Though an old friend surfaces to remove Hayle from the events surrounding the crime, she eventually finds herself again embroiled in sleuthing.

A fourth book in the series, *No Hiding Place,* is driven, according to a *Publishers Weekly* reviewer, more by "Wesley's compassion for the people of inner-city Newark than by her plotting." Nonetheless, the story—which features murder, suicide, old flames, and troubled teenagers—takes a look at the impact of the rise of a new African American middle class and how it relates to the poorer inner-city. A critic for *Kirkus Reviews* also commented that the novel's strength lay its "sharp, subtle portrait of two families whose tangled relationship packs a world of insight into a single painful case." The *Publishers Weekly* reviewer praised Hayle's "consistently sharp, honest voice" for its ability to drive the novel as it explores "complex social issues." *Booklist* correspondent Stuart Miller wrote that Wesley's depiction of urban ghetto life had the "ring of authenticity," adding "there is not a shred of sentimentality in this story's grim but ultimately satisfying resolution."

A fifth Tamara Hayle mystery, *Easier to Kill,* features Mandy Magic, a popular and successful radio personality. After finding herself the victim of tire slashings, graffiti, and anonymous notes, Mandy hires Hayle to investigate. As Hayle checks out these seemingly small crimes, she realizes that Mandy's past holds damaging secrets, including time she spent working as a prostitute. *The Devil Riding* also explores the dangers of prostitution as Hayle searches for a runaway teenager in Atlantic City. The determined sleuth plumbs the depths of that city's crime rings, only to discover ties between hardened criminals and the parents of the missing teen. A *Publishers Weekly* reviewer cited *The Devil Riding* for a "stellar cast of peripheral characters and a gripping plot." Stuart Miller in *Booklist* likewise praised the "solid characterizations . . . well-realized setting, and authentic depiction of teenage runaways."

Wesley has also written for young adults and children. *Freedom's Gifts: A Juneteenth Story,* illustrated by Sharon Wilson, addresses racial issues and the African American fight for freedom in a context that can be appreciated by young and older readers alike. The story, set in 1943 Texas, refers to the celebration of "Juneteenth": June 19th, the anniversary of Texas black slaves' freedom in 1865. Two young protagonists from New York visit their great-great-aunt in Texas, who moves them with her tale of slavery and subsequent freedom. Ironically, segregation is still a reality in the 1943 setting, prompting the aunt to remind the children that there is still more freedom to fight for. A *Publishers Weekly* critic called the story "sophisticated and distinctive" and praised Wesley's treatment of a "sensitive and important subject." *Willimena and the Cookie Money* begins with a dilemma: Willimena Thomas has spent the money she collected selling Girl Scout cookies and is now expected to turn it over to the scouts. In vain she and her sister try to raise the funds in other ways, but in the end she has to confess to her parents—and only then does she reveal how she used the cash. A *Publishers Weekly* reviewer deemed the work a "snappy novel . . . ideal for beginning and reluctant readers."

Although she loves to write about Tamara Hayle and plans more books in the series, Wesley has lately begun to pen relationship novels that take a realistic look at changing family dynamics over time. In *Ain't Nobody's Business If I Do,* forty-year-old Eva must adjust to life after her longtime husband leaves her. Eva begins a love affair with a younger man but must then cope with her children's response to her changing situation. Lillian Lewis in *Booklist* called the novel "a heartwarming tale" with "compelling turning points." *Always True to You in My Fashion* is set in the black artists' community in Manhattan and details the romantic dalliances of art dealer Randall Hollis who juggles lovers because he cannot commit himself to a monogamous relationship. Not only does Wesley explore the disappointments of Randall's many love interests, but she also examines the family history that has led Randall into his plight. *Black Issues Book Review* contributor Lynda Jones found the work "a page-turning delight" in which Wesley "winningly details the stupid choices that smart women continually make when it comes to trifling men."

Wesley told *Black Issues Book Review* that she enjoys creating fictional characters who are middle-aged and successful—at least in their work. "I just write characters that I can connect to, and that I can enjoy writing and learning about," she said. "The reality is, the older we get, the richer we become and often, but not always, the wiser. This is an area I'm interested in, this is what I know, this is what I'm learning."

BIOGRAPHICAL AND CRITICAL SOURCES:

BOOKS

Contemporary Black Biography, Volume 18, Thomson Gale (Detroit, MI), 1998.

Heising, Willetta L, *Detecting Women 2,* Purple Moon Press (Dearborn, MI), 1996-97.

Who's Who among African Americans, Thomson Gale (Detroit, MI), 1996.

PERIODICALS

American Visions, April-May, 1997, pp. 18-21.

Armchair Detective, fall, 1994, p. 495; fall, 1995, p. 463; fall, 1996, p. 499.

Black Enterprise, August, 1982, pp. 39-44.

Black Issues Book Review, November-December, 2002, Lynda Jones, review of *Always True to You in My Fashion* and "BIBR Talks to Valerie Wilson Wesley," p. 26.

Booklist, December 15, 1993, p. 748; March 15, 1994, p. 1361; June 1, 1994, pp. 1775, 1787; July, 1995, pp. 1862-1863, 1869; May 1, 1997, p. 1468; August, 1997, p. 1884; August, 1999, Lillian Lewis, review of *Ain't Nobody's Business If I Do,* p. 2031; May 1, 2000, Stuart Miller, review of *The Devil Riding,* p. 1625.

Book Report, January, 1994, p. 50.

Bulletin of the Center for Children's Books, June, 1997, p. 378.

Children's Book Review Service, February, 1994, p. 121; spring, 1997, p. 145.

Emerge, June, 2000, Sheree R. Thomas, review of *The Devil Riding,* p. 70.

Essence, February, 1994, p. 121; October, 1999, Martha Southgate, "No Business Like Wesley's Business," p. 76.

Horn Book Guide, spring, 1994, p. 92.

Kirkus Reviews, December 1, 1993, p. 1531; May 15, 1994, p. 670; June 1, 1995, p. 744; July 15, 1996, p. 1010; August 1, 1997, p. 1164.

Kliatt, May, 1995, p. 53; July, 1996, p. 16.

Library Journal, July, 1994, p. 132; November 1, 1999, Ann Burns and Emily J. Jones, review of *Ain't Nobody's Business If I Do,* p. 103.

Los Angeles Times Book Review, August 14, 1994, p. 7.

Ms., July, 1995, p. 75.

New York Times Book Review, June 22, 1997, pp. 102-103.

Publishers Weekly, November 8, 1993, p. 79; May 23, 1994, p. 80; May 22, 1995, p. 50; April 15, 1996, p. 63; July 15, 1996, p. 59; March 31, 1997, p. 75; July 7, 1997, p. 53; May 1, 2000, review of *The Devil Riding,* p. 53; June 18, 2001, review of *Willimena and the Cookie Money,* p. 81.

Rapport, June, 1996, p. 24.

School Library Journal, December, 1988, p. 117; November, 1993, pp. 126-127; June, 1997, pp. 102-103; August, 2001, Barbara Auerbach, review of *Willimena and the Cookie Money,* p. 166.

Voice of Youth Advocates, February, 1994, p. 375.

Washington Post Book World, August 21, 1994, p. 6; August 18, 1996, p. 8.

ONLINE

Valerie Wilson Wesley Home Page, http://www.TamaraHayle.com/ (November 24, 2002).*

* * *

WEST, Edwin
See WESTLAKE, Donald E(dwin)

* * *

WESTLAKE, Donald E(dwin) 1933-
(John B. Allan, Curt Clark, Tucker Coe, Timothy J. Culver, J. Morgan Cunningham, Allen Marshall, Richard Stark, Edwin West)

PERSONAL: Born July 12, 1933, in New York, NY; son of Albert Joseph (a salesman) and Lillian Marguerite (Bounda) Westlake; married Nedra Henderson, August 10, 1957 (divorced, 1966); married Sandra Foley, April 9, 1967 (divorced, 1975); married Abigail Adams, May 18, 1979; children: Sean Alan, Steven Albert, Tod, Paul Edwin; stepchildren: Adrienne Adams, Patrick Adams, Katharine Adams. *Education:* Attended Champlain College and State University of New York at Binghamton.

Donald E. Westlake

ADDRESSES: Agent—c/o Author Mail, Mysterious Press, 1271 Avenue of the Americas, New York, NY 10020.

CAREER: Worked at odd jobs prior to 1958 ("the same list as every other writer, except that I was never a short-order cook"); associate editor at literary agency, 1958-59; writer, 1959—. *Military service:* U.S. Air Force, 1954-56 ("no awards, by mutual agreement").

AWARDS, HONORS: Edgar Allan Poe Award from Mystery Writers of America, 1967, for *God Save the Mark;* Academy Award nomination, 1990, for screenplay adaptation of *The Grifters,* based on Jim Thompson's novel; Edgar Allan Poe Grand Master Award from Mystery Writers of America, 1992.

WRITINGS:

The Mercenaries, Random House (New York, NY), 1960.

Killing Time, Random House (New York, NY), 1961.

361, Random House (New York, NY), 1962.

Killy, Random House (New York, NY), 1963.

Pity Him Afterwards, Random House (New York, NY), 1964.

The Fugitive Pigeon, Random House (New York, NY), 1965.

The Busy Body, Random House (New York, NY), 1966.

The Spy in the Ointment, Random House (New York, NY), 1966.

God Save the Mark, Random House (New York, NY), 1967, Forge (New York, NY), 2004.

Philip, Crowell (New York, NY), 1967.

(Compiler, with Philip Klass) *Once against the Law,* Macmillan (New York, NY), 1968.

The Curious Facts preceding My Execution, and Other Fictions, Random House (New York, NY), 1968.

Who Stole Sassi Manoon?, Random House (New York, NY), 1968.

Somebody Owes Me Money, Random House (New York, NY), 1969.

Up Your Banners, Macmillan (New York, NY), 1969.

Adios, Scheherezade, Simon & Schuster (New York, NY), 1970.

I Gave at the Office, Simon & Schuster (New York, NY), 1971.

Under an English Heaven, Simon & Schuster (New York, NY), 1971.

Cops and Robbers (also see below), M. Evans (New York, NY), 1972.

(With Brian Garfield) *Gangway,* M. Evans (New York, NY), 1972.

Help, I Am Being Held Prisoner, M. Evans (New York, NY), 1974.

Two Much, M. Evans (New York, NY), 1975.

A Travesty, M. Evans (New York, NY), 1975.

Brothers Keepers, M. Evans (New York, NY), 1975.

Dancing Aztecs, M. Evans (New York, NY), 1976, published as *A New York Dance,* Hodder & Stoughton (London, England), 1979.

Enough!, M. Evans (New York, NY), 1977.

Nobody's Perfect, M. Evans (New York, NY), 1977.

Castle in the Air, M. Evans (New York, NY), 1980.

Kahawa, Viking (New York, NY), 1982, reprinted, Mysterious Press (New York, NY), 1995.

Levine, Mysterious Press (New York, NY), 1984.

A Likely Story, Penzler Books (New York, NY), 1984.

High Adventure, Mysterious Press (New York, NY), 1985.

(With wife, Abby Westlake) *High Jinx,* Macmillan (New York, NY), 1987.

(With Abby Westlake) *Transylvania Station,* Macmillan (New York, NY), 1987.

Trust Me on This, Mysterious Press (New York, NY), 1988.

Tomorrow's Crimes (includes *Anarchaos,* a novel, and other stories published between 1961-84), Mysterious Press (New York, NY), 1989.

Sacred Monster, Mysterious Press (New York, NY), 1989.

Humans, Mysterious Press (New York, NY), 1992.

Baby, Would I Lie?: A Romance of the Ozarks, Mysterious Press (New York, NY), 1994.

Smoke, Mysterious Press (New York, NY), 1995.

What's the Worst That Could Happen?, Mysterious Press (New York, NY), 1996.

The Ax, Mysterious Press (New York, NY), 1998.

The Hook, Mysterious Press (New York, NY), 2000.

Money for Nothing, Mysterious Press (New York, NY), 2003.

The Road to Ruin, Mysterious Press (New York, NY), 2004.

Thieves' Dozen, Mysterious Press (New York, NY), 2004.

"JOHN A. DORTMUNDER" CRIME SERIES:

The Hot Rock, Simon & Schuster (New York, NY), 1970.

Bank Shot, Simon & Schuster (New York, NY), 1972.

Jimmy the Kid, M. Evans (New York, NY), 1974.

Why Me? (also see below), Viking (New York, NY), 1983.

Good Behavior, Mysterious Press (New York, NY), 1986.

Drowned Hopes (also see below), Mysterious Press (New York, NY), 1990.

Don't Ask, Mysterious Press (New York, NY), 1993.

UNDER PSEUDONYM JOHN B. ALLAN:

Elizabeth Taylor: A Fascinating Story of America's Most Talented Actress and the World's Most Beautiful Woman, Monarch, 1961.

UNDER PSEUDONYM TUCKER COE:

Kinds of Love, Kinds of Death, Random House (New York, NY), 1966.

Murder among Children, Random House (New York, NY), 1968.

Wax Apple, Random House (New York, NY), 1970.

A Jade in Aries, Random House (New York, NY), 1971.

Don't Lie to Me, Random House (New York, NY), 1972.

UNDER PSEUDONYM RICHARD STARK:

The Hunter (also see below), Pocket Books (New York, NY), 1963, published as *Point Blank,* Berkley (New York, NY), 1973, reprinted under original title with a new introduction by the author, Gregg Press, 1981.

The Man with the Getaway Face (also see below), Pocket Books (New York, NY), 1963, published as *The Steel Hit,* Coronet (London, England), 1971, Berkley (New York, NY), 1975.

The Outfit (also see below), Pocket Books (New York, NY), 1963.

The Mourner (also see below), Pocket Books (New York, NY), 1963.

The Score (also see below), Pocket Books (New York, NY), 1964.

The Jugger, Pocket Books (New York, NY), 1965.

The Seventh (also see below), Pocket Books (New York, NY), 1966, also published as *The Split,* Allison & Busby (London, England), 1984.

The Handle, Pocket Books (New York, NY), 1966, published as *Run Lethal,* Berkley (New York, NY), 1966.

The Damsel, Macmillan (New York, NY), 1967.

The Dame, Macmillan (New York, NY), 1967.

The Rare Coin Score, Fawcett (New York, NY), 1967.

The Green Eagle Score, Fawcett (New York, NY), 1967.

The Black Ice Score, Fawcett (New York, NY), 1968.

The Sour Lemon Score, Fawcett (New York, NY), 1969.

The Blackbird, Macmillan (New York, NY), 1969.

Deadly Edge, Random House (New York, NY), 1971.

Slayground, Random House (New York, NY), 1971.

Lemons Never Lie, World Publishing 1971.

Plunder Squad, Random House (New York, NY), 1972.

Butcher's Moon, Random House (New York, NY), 1974.

Stark Mysteries (contains *The Hunter, The Man with the Getaway Face, The Outfit, The Mourner, The Score,* and *The Seventh*), G. K. Hall, 1981.

Comeback, Mysterious Press (New York, NY), 1997.

Backflash, Mysterious Press (New York, NY), 1999.
Flashfire, Mysterious Press (New York, NY), 2000.
Firebreak, Mysterious Press (New York, NY), 2001.
Breakout, Mysterious Press (New York, NY), 2002.
Nobody Runs Forever, Mysterious Press (New York, NY), 2004.

SCREENPLAYS:

(With Michael Kane) *Hot Stuff,* Columbia, 1979.
The Stepfather, New Century/Vista, 1986.
The Grifters, Miramax, 1990.

Also author of screenplays *Cops and Robbers,* upon which Westlake based the novel, and *Why Me?,* based on the novel.

OTHER:

(Editor) *Murderous Schemes: An Anthology of Classic Detective Stories,* Oxford University Press (New York, NY), 1996.

Contributor to anthologies. Author of science fiction, sometimes under the pseudonym Curt Clark. Author of books under the pseudonyms Timothy Culver, J. Morgan Cunningham, Alan Marshall, and Edwin West.

ADAPTATIONS: Many novels by the author, either under the name Donald E. Westlake or pseudonym Richard Stark, have been made into films, including: *The Jugger,* adaptation produced in France as *Made in the USA,* 1966; *The Busy Body,* film produced by Paramount, 1967; *The Hunter,* adaptation produced as *Point Blank,* Metro-Goldwyn-Mayer, 1967; *The Score,* adaptation produced in France as *Mise en Sac,* 1967; *The Seventh,* adaptation produced as *The Split,* Metro-Goldwyn-Mayer, 1968; *The Hot Rock,* film released by Twentieth Century-Fox, 1972; *Bank Shot,* film produced by United Artists, 1974; *The Outfit,* film produced by Metro-Goldwyn-Mayer, 1974; *Jimmy the Kid,* film produced by New World, 1982; *Slayground,* film produced by Universal, 1984; *Two Much,* adaptation produced in France as *Le Jumeau;* and *What's the Worst That Could Happen?,* Metro-Goldwyn-Mayer, 2001. *Drowned Hopes* has been recorded on audio cassette and released by Dove Audio, 1992.

SIDELIGHTS: "The Neil Simon of the crime novel" is how Donald E. Westlake was described by *New York Times Book Review* critic Newgate Callendar. It is a title Westlake earned through such popular books as *The Hot Rock, Bank Shot,* and *Two Much,* all characteristic of the author's talent for combining laughs with thrills in his fiction. In a Westlake tale, criminals and law enforcement officers are equally incompetent, and daring felonies fall prey to bad timing, bad weather, and bad luck. The author's plots revolve around the offbeat: "Who else could write a book about a man who pretends to be twins in order to marry a pair of identical heiresses?" asked Sheldon Bart in another *New York Times Book Review* article.

Westlake's first published books were more conventional crime novels; funny cops-and-robbers stories were not considered marketable. He had been working on a running character named Parker, a thief who "handles frustration very badly—he gets annoyed and kills everybody," according to Westlake in Bart's article. The "Parker" books, written under Westlake's pseudonym Richard Stark, are no less than "the best caper novels ever written," in the opinion of *Austin Chronicle* writer Jesse Sublett. These tales crackle with "lean and mean prose and chapters that flash back and forward to drive a narrative that zips along at whiplash speed despite the infinite convolutions of the heists, take-downs, betrayals and general mayhem of the plot."

The character of Parker, furthermore—"cold as an iceberg, sure as lightning"—is one that stands out, in Sublett's view, thanks to a professional demeanor that does not bend to the chaos that inevitably surrounds him. Some of Parker's rules of the trade: "Never have sex when working on a caper. (Before and after is a different story.)" And, "During a takeover job, learn and use the first names of the people you're holding at gunpoint. It boosts their ego and makes them easier to deal with."

When the author realized the comic potential in a no-win criminal, Westlake created another character, John Dortmunder, and starred him in a gem-stealing caper, *The Hot Rock.* So successful was this character, who, noted *Newsweek* writer David Lehman, "makes burglar seem synonymous with bungler," that Westlake continued Dortmunder's adventures in several subsequent novels, including *Bank Shot* and *Jimmy the Kid.*

Critics and fans of Westlake's work are quick to point out that his comic novels are as intricately plotted as any serious thriller. In a *Los Angeles Times* review of *Why Me?,* a book in which Dortmunder is once again the hapless victim of his own crime, Carolyn See found that "the characterization . . . is flawless, if unregenerately silly. And the plot is absolutely masterful, so that a dozen pleasing little details making you smile, even giggle, as they first slide by, are discovered in Chapter 29 to have been part of an elaborate literary setup, making you laugh till the tears come."

To Jerome Charyn, writing in the *New York Times Book Review,* Westlake's novels "are quite different from the classical mystery and espionage novels of Graham Greene and John le Carré. . . . [The author] shoves cartoons at us, instead of characters we might love, fear or despise. There are no murderous boy gangsters [or] pathetic drunken spies. . . . But we do have energized masks that babble at us in all sorts of crazy tongues, come alive for a minute, then return to their normal frozen position. This allows Westlake to push his narrative along at a tremendous pace, and supply his masks with the marvelous illogic of a cartoon world."

Westlake departed from the crime novel format with his works *A Likely Story* and *Trust Me on This.* A farce about the world of publishing and one writer's attempt to market his Christmas book, *A Likely Story* almost did not get published. *Washington Post* critic Alan Ryan found no small irony in the fact that "all the big-time New York publishers turned this book down. Why? Because it wasn't a crime novel, because it was different from Westlake's previous books, and—one assumes—because they didn't think it was funny and/or didn't think it would sell." But even writing out of his usual genre, "Westlake knows what he's doing," continued Ryan. "[His] comic eye is hilariously perceptive and ruthlessly unsparing. The result is likely the funniest book of the year."

In *Trust Me on This,* aspiring journalist Sara Joslyn lands a job with *The Weekly Galaxy* tabloid and is soon immersed in the world of madcap reportage. The bulk of the book involves the *Galaxy* crew invading Martha's Vineyard to cover a movie star's wedding. William A. Henry III, writing in *Time,* stated: "Rather than mock the already preposterous, Westlake explores the mentality that capable, rational people would need in order to crank out such stuff." Henry described *Trust Me* as "perhaps the most beguiling beheading of journalists since Evelyn Waugh's *Scoop,*" and called the work "a frantic, inventive story with lots of good dialogue." In *Newsweek,* reviewer Peter S. Prescott proclaimed: "Donald E. Westlake writes a comic novel so well it's a wonder he bothers with crime at all."

Westlake returned to his "Dortmunder" series with the publication of *Good Behavior.* In this novel, the clever thief crash-lands in a Manhattan convent, the sanctuary of a sisterhood of nuns vowed to silence. They persuade Dortmunder to rescue Sister Mary Grace, a tycoon's daughter who has been spirited away by her father and held prisoner in a high-security skyscraper's penthouse. Dortmunder and crew attempt to save the girl, but in typical fashion, their plans go haywire when they confront mercenaries training for the overthrow of a South American dictatorship. Writing in the *Washington Post Book World,* Jean M. White emphasized: "In the midst of these antics, Westlake never allows his comedy to slide into silly farce or buffoonery," and Callendar remarked in the *New York Times Book Review:* "He has a wonderful feeling for the absurd, revels in farce and slapstick, [and] piles complication upon complication" on the hapless burglars.

Drowned Hopes, another Dortmunder caper, pits the ill-fated crook against ex-cellmate Tom Jimson, who plans to blow up a dam, endangering thousands of lives, to retrieve his hidden loot, now buried under fifty feet of water. In the Chicago *Tribune Books,* Kevin Moore observed that "Westlake, the Mel Brooks of mayhem, has great fun making it all much more complicated than that." About the "Dortmunder" novels, Katherine Dunn commented in the *New York Times Book Review,* "These are hard-nosed but never hard-boiled romps, with a hero you could trust to babysit but wouldn't ask to polish the silver." Dunn gave high marks to *Drowned Hopes,* claiming that "Westlake's lean prose and deadpan delivery are engaging, as always. His psychology is sharp and his characters colorful."

A later work, *Sacred Monster,* unfolds as a lengthy interview with a drunken, drug-using Hollywood superstar. Charles Champlin, in the *Los Angeles Times Book Review,* deemed the book "a sparkling little set-piece," and commented that "Westlake's ingenuity in spinning out his tale and working his sleight-of-hand finale is an audacious treat." *Tomorrow's Crimes* gathers Westlake's previously unpublished 1967 novel, *Anarchaos,* and nine shorter science fiction-mystery stories. Gary Dretzka, in the Chicago *Tribune Books,* called the stories "fast, thought-provoking studies" of humankind in a universe disrupted by the inherited evils of corporate and individual greed and a deteriorating environment. Despite minor reservations, Randall Short, in the *New York Times Book Review,* determined that "devotees of either genre can look forward to a smooth, satisfying read."

In *Humans,* God orders the angel Ananayel to bring about the Apocalypse. Ananayel enlists five human agents to assist him, but the bringer of doom is drawn off course by a growing concern for humanity, as well as his battle with X, the force who wishes to perpetuate humanity's suffering for his own demonic pleasure. Garry Abrams, in the *Los Angeles Times Book Review,* suggested that "a major purpose of the book" may be "to satirize the cleverness and conventions of the typical thriller through the stereotypes of an earlier, more faithful era," but he pointed out: "In [its] final section, *Humans* becomes more and more like the standard thriller it parodies. . . . The climax also is something of a whimper, considering the buildup." The *New York Times Book Review's* Michael Upchurch felt that Westlake's "narrative building blocks include . . . a labyrinthine plot and an unnerving insight into the depths of human behavior. The writing isn't as crisp as it could be, however, and the author has a persistently hokey side to him that may seem simply sophomoric to some readers." Upchurch did note that the human agents, "with their sense of rage and helplessness . . . give *Humans* a compelling urgency that, in its best passages, outweighs its obvious gimmicks," and found that "in bringing his characters to the brink of oblivion, Donald Westlake zeroes in on what is most precious about life. The ride may be bumpy in terms of technique but the view is, in unexpected ways, divine." Howard Waldrop, writing in the *Washington Post Book World,* declared: "This is a book that in many ways hurts, when so many others don't work up emotions in the reader at all. It's about the way the world mangles (and always has) the good and bad indifferently." He concluded: "We get a few glimpses, true ones, of the Third World hells that have been created because no one gives a damn one way or the other. It does these things in a frightening, sometimes funny, and unpreachy way."

Westlake returns to the character of Sara Joslyn and the seamy world of tabloid journalism with his novel *Baby, Would I Lie?* Sara is now working for a weekly newsmagazine, *Trend: The Magazine for the Way We Live This Instant,* and is sent to Branson, Missouri, to cover the trial of Ray Hanson, a country-western star accused of murder. Ronald C. Miller, writing for *The Armchair Detective,* called *Baby, Would I Lie?* "a comedic cornucopia . . . [that] lampoons journalists, contemporary music, entrepreneurs, and the IRS, among others." Charles Champlin in the *Los Angeles Times Book Review* termed it "a deliciously nutty sequel" to *Trust Me on This,* and "the funniest mystery of the year." Michael Lewis, reviewer for the *New York Times Book Review* was less complimentary. Although praising "Mr. Westlake's usually fine work," he felt that the novel's "humor . . . seems more like an excuse for the absence of any real mystery and its mystery an apology for the fact that it isn't very funny." He concluded, "In the end, the book's real satire is of itself."

Smoke lampoons the tobacco industry and resurrects the concept of the Invisible Man, but as Don Sandstrom warned in *The Armchair Detective,* "Do not dismiss [Westlake's protagonist] Freddie Noon as another invisible man like H. G. Wells's Doctor Griffin, Thorne Smith's George Kirby, or . . . H. F. Saint's Nick Holloway. This is a Westlake production." Gary Dretzka, writing for Chicago's *Tribune Books,* called *Smoke* "the kind of novel mystery fans will pass along to the unconverted as an example of just how enjoyable genre writing can be." In the *Washington Post Book World,* Kathi Malo characterized it as "one of his best books in years." And Terry Teachout, writing for the *New York Times Book Review,* compared Westlake to P. G. Wodehouse and said of *Smoke,* "Squirrel it away for emergency use the next time you find yourself stuck in an airport lounge with a departure time of maybe. The bartender may resent the fact that you're too busy laughing to order another drink, but you'll definitely feel better in the morning."

Between 1998 and 2000, Westlake wielded *The Ax* and *The Hook,* two thrillers that take a decidedly grim view of the effects of modern society. In *The Ax,* described by D. Keith Mano in his *New York Times Book Review* article as "pretty much flawless," downsized executive Burke Devore decides—literally—to kill off the competition as he strives to reestablish himself in the paper business. While a *Kirkus Reviews* writer noted a lack of "any sense of cumulative horror or revulsion" in Devore's systematic assassinations, the review also acknowledged Westlake's expertise in the genre as he "rises effortlessly to the challenge of varying these executions [and] keeping up the tension."

With *The Hook,* Westlake again examines the lengths one will go to in order to strike it rich in a competitive society. This time, famous novelist Bryce Proctorr, facing a deadline and a severe case of writer's block, meets up with old friend Wayne Prentice, a struggling writer who happens to have a promising manuscript in his hands. The two strike a Faustian bargain—Prentice will let Proctorr submit the novel as his own, and the two will split the hefty book advance. But the deal is more complex: Wayne must also kill Bryce's wife, who would stand to devour Proctorr's profits in messy divorce proceedings. "Like *The Ax,*" remarked *Kirkus Reviews, The Hook* shows the often-genial Westlake "at his dourest." And while the novel's "opening conceits are clever," wrote *New York Times Book Review* contributor Valerie Sayers, the author "doesn't play it for the satire; [instead] he concentrates on building suspense with as many twists and bends as a plot can endure." Craig Shufelt, writing in *Library Journal,* also concluded that though *The Hook* "is not a comfortable read—there are no heroes to cheer for"—Westlake still earns plaudits for producing a book "this reader was unable [put] down."

To Sublett, "the bulk of Westlake's work [since the early 1970s] proved that he's just as good at being soft-boiled and biting and satirical as he is at being dark and suspenseful." In some of the author's most successful works, "he had already pushed the envelope just about as far as it could be pushed. Push it a little farther, the envelope turns inside out, and the payoff for a suspenseful setup isn't a sock in the jaw . . . but a tickled funny bone." In quoting the author, Sublett pointed out that "the line between noir suspense and dark comedy is a fine one. Or as Westlake says, 'It's the other side of the same street.'"

BIOGRAPHICAL AND CRITICAL SOURCES:

BOOKS

Contemporary Authors Autobiography Series, Volume 13, Thomson Gale (Detroit, MI), 1991.

Contemporary Literary Criticism, Thomson Gale (Detroit, MI), Volume 7, 1977, Volume 33, 1985.

PERIODICALS

Armchair Detective, spring, 1995, p. 206; winter, 1996, p. 106.

Austin Chronicle, December 29, 1997, "No Prozac for the Wicked."

Booklist, August, 1995, p. 1911; January 1, 2000, review of *The Hook.*

Connoisseur, December, 1989.

Entertainment Weekly, February 28, 1992; April 2, 1993; May 12, 1995, p. 59.

Film Quarterly, winter, 1987.

Harper's, September, 1988.

Kirkus Reviews, May 15, 1997, review of *The Ax;* January 15, 2000, review of *The Hook,* p. 88.

Library Journal, July, 1994, p. 130; November 1, 1994, p. 126; January, 1995, p. 158; February 1, 2000, review of *The Hook,* p. 120.

Los Angeles Times, February 28, 1983; August 7, 1985.

Los Angeles Times Book Review, April 25, 1981; July 13, 1986; May 8, 1988; June 4, 1989; April 15, 1990; March 1, 1992; September 11, 1994, p. 18.

Ms., June, 1986.

National Review, February 16, 1973.

New Republic, December 13, 1975.

New Statesman, January 10, 1986.

Newsweek, February 21, 1983; April 22, 1985; July 18, 1988; September 5, 1994.

New York, July 3 1989.

New Yorker, August 15, 1988.

New York Times, March 5, 1982; February 24, 2000, review of *The Hook,* p. B9.

New York Times Book Review, November 19, 1972; June 3, 1973; July 14, 1974; May 18, 1975; October 31, 1976; October 2, 1977; April 13, 1980; May 16, 1982; January 9, 1983; June 22, 1986; July 10, 1988; July 30, 1989; October 15, 1989; April 8, 1990; April 14, 1991; June 28, 1992; September 11, 1994, p. 20; October 8, 1995, p. 3; March 19, 2000, "Publish or Perish."

Observer (London, England), February 9, 1986.

People, November 6, 1989; October 24, 1994.

Publishers Weekly, January 17, 2000, review of *The Hook,* p. 43.

Saturday Review, May 29, 1971; September 25, 1971.

Spectator, January 29, 1977.

Time, July 22, 1974; August 8, 1988.

Times Literary Supplement, September 24, 1971; December 7, 1979.

Tribune Books (Chicago, IL), April 25, 1982; November 9, 1986; October 1, 1989; April 1, 1990; October 1, 1995, p. 4.

Wall Street Journal, September 30, 1994.
Washington Post, December 24, 1984; July 23, 1985.
Washington Post Book World, May 18, 1986; March 22, 1992; March 29, 1992; December 17, 1995, p. 11.
West Coast Review of Books, September 1986; Volume 13, number 6, 1988.

ONLINE

Donald Westlake Home Page, http://www.donaldwestlake.com/ (October 16, 2004).*

* * *

WHITCHER, Susan (Godsil) 1952-

PERSONAL: Born January 29, 1952, in Tokyo, Japan; daughter of Augustus R. (a management consultant) and Anne (an artist; maiden name, Cleveland) White; married John Lee Whitcher (an engineer), 1980; children: Ursula Anne, Susannah Mattson. *Education:* Portland State University, B.A., 1974; attended University College (London, England), 1974-75; Warburg Institute (London, England), M.Phil, 1977; Ph.D. studies at Johns Hopkins University. *Politics:* Liberal. *Religion:* "Non-aligned."

ADDRESSES: Home and office—4260 Reed St., West Linn, OR 97068. *Agent*—Emilie Jacobson, Curtis Brown, Ltd.

CAREER: Writer. Whitcher informed: "I don't think I've ever had a job that could be dignified by the term 'career.' For two or three years I taught Renaissance intellectual history/literature at Johns Hopkins, but only as a graduate student teaching assistant. Other work experience includes: teaching night school, selling tourist trinkets in London, running a small English-language school in Sicily for one year, 'exotic' dancing in nightclubs, manning a domestic violence hotline, and freelance garden design."

MEMBER: Society of Children's Book Writers and Illustrators.

WRITINGS:

Moonfall (picture book), illustrated by Barbara Lehman, Farrar, Straus (New York, NY), 1993.
Real Mummies Don't Bleed: Friendly Tales for October Nights (short stories), Farrar, Straus (New York, NY), 1993.
Something for Everyone (picture book), illustrated by Barbara Lehman, Farrar, Straus (New York, NY), 1995.
Enchanter's Glass (novel), Harcourt Brace (New York, NY), 1995.
The Key to the Cupboard (picture book), illustrated by Andrew Glass, Farrar, Straus (New York, NY), 1997.
The Fool Reversed, Farrar, Straus (New York, NY), 2000.

WORK IN PROGRESS: A novel, *Stealing.*

SIDELIGHTS: Susan Whitcher writes books for young people in which fantastical elements are employed in a straightforward, almost deadpan, manner that is often found enchanting by reviewers and commentators. In her first effort, *Moonfall,* a girl is certain that the moon is falling from the sky, despite her parents' reassuring explanations. Two weeks after the moon has disappeared from the sky, however, Sylvie's suspicions are borne out when she finds it in her neighbor's garden and "goes about saving the moon in a sensible, magical fashion," according to Janice Del Negro in a *Booklist* review. Critics singled out Whitcher's poetic text for special praise; although the author refuses to define the moon's qualities consistently, "children will not be stalled by the dreamlike vagaries of this debut author's text," noted a *Publishers Weekly* reviewer. Indeed, Whitcher's "whimsical fantasy," when combined with Barbara Lehman's effective illustrations, yields a book that is "destined to become a read-aloud favorite in many a household," Susan Scheps predicted in *School Library Journal.*

For her next book, Whitcher again paired magical elements with deliberately ordinary language in a collection of stories for young readers called *Real Mummies Don't Bleed: Friendly Tales for October Nights.* Each story is set during the time of Halloween and features contemporary American children encountering humorous and/or frightening elements from the supernatural world. A critic for *Kirkus Reviews* commended the "original sense of the bizarre" displayed by the author in these "five fresh, witty tales."

In *Something for Everyone,* Whitcher paired up with illustrator Lehman for a second picture book, this time to tell the story of great-aunt Elsie Applebaum, who abruptly decides to retire, leaving behind a motley collection of memorabilia for her unpleasant relatives to sort through. Only Elsie's young friend, Tilda, knows what to do with the odd assortment of objects and promptly fashions them into a magic traveling machine and flies off to join Elsie. "Whitcher has poetic sensibility . . . that she never overuses," noted a *Kirkus Reviews* critic. *School Library Journal* contributor Barbara Kiefer commented favorably on the way Lehman's humorous illustrations enhance the author's text, making this "an agreeable book that children should find entertaining."

Whitcher is also the author of a novel for young people titled *Enchanter's Glass,* in which an unpopular and unhappy girl finds a piece of glass that alters her perspective and leads her into a world of fantastic adventures. "Whitcher has a gift for characterization and the deft turn of phrase," maintained a *Fantasy & Science Fiction* contributor, who added: "*Enchanter's Glass* is a delight from start to finish; lyrical, with a touch of *Alice in Wonderland* absurdity and a compassionate heart."

The Fool Reversed is a novel for older teens with mature subject matter. Fifteen-year-old Anna begins a relationship with a poet almost twice her age and soon finds herself in very adult situations. A teenaged boy named Dylan helps her to maintain some stability as her older lover seeks to manipulate her. *School Library Journal* correspondent Francisca Goldsmith maintained that Whitcher's writing "is cohesive, well constructed, and compelling," adding poignancy to a "disturbing novel." A *Publishers Weekly* reviewer felt that Whitcher "has hit her stride with this probing, acutely observed novel." The same reviewer commended *The Fool Reversed* for its "memorable scenes and insights."

Explaining how she began her career as a writer, Whitcher once commented: "As a child, I yearned for magical adventures. Later, I thought time travel might be good enough, especially if as a side effect it could make me slimmer and not need glasses. When I grew up I got contact lenses and studied history.

"I'm not saying I missed out altogether on adventures. I met a man with a huge mustache and a greasy black motorcycle. Together we traveled around Europe. We had children. I looked forward to a cutthroat university career.

"At university, I asked the school's health services to refer me to a counselor for depression. One day the counselor chided me for indulging in what she called 'magical thinking.' *Magical* thinking. I carried the phrase home with me like a gift."

"That's when I began to write stories. Halfway through writing *Enchanter's Glass* I suddenly realized why magical adventures don't just happen: not because they don't exist, but because you have to make them."

BIOGRAPHICAL AND CRITICAL SOURCES:

PERIODICALS

Booklist, July, 1993, Janice Del Negro, review of *Moonfall,* p. 1978; September 1, 1997, Susan Dove Lempke, review of *The Key to the Cupboard,* p. 136.

Fantasy & Science Fiction, June, 1997, review of *Enchanter's Glass,* pp. 26-28.

Kirkus Reviews, August 15, 1993, review of *Real Mummies Don't Bleed: Friendly Stories for October Nights,* p. 1082; October 1, 1995, review of *Something for Everyone,* p. 1438.

New York Times Book Review, October 26, 1997, Lisa Shea, review of *The Key to the Cupboard,* p. 47.

Publishers Weekly, June 14, 1993, review of *Moonfall,* p. 69; September 20, 1993, review of *Real Mummies Don't Bleed,* p. 31; March 6, 2000, review of *The Fool Reversed,* p. 112.

School Library Journal, October, 1993, p. 114; November, 1995, Barbara Kiefer, review of *Something for Everyone,* pp. 84-85; March, 2000, Francisca Goldsmith, review of *The Fool Reversed,* p. 243.*

* * *

WHITNEY, Polly (Louise) 1948-
(Hialeah Jackson)

PERSONAL: Born October 22, 1948, in St. Louis, MO; daughter of Donald Van Leer (an actor) and Margaret Eden (maiden name, Head; present surname, Windsor) Seewoster; married Michael R. Whitney, October 25, 1969; children: Michael James, Elizabeth

Daisy. *Education:* State University of New York, B.A.; Yale University, M.A. *Politics:* Democrat. *Hobbies and other interests:* The internet, the tropics, cities.

ADDRESSES: Home—New York, NY, and Boca Raton, FL. *Agent*—Russ Galen, Scovil, Chichak & Galen, 381 Park Ave. S., New York, NY 10016. *E-mail*—gypsy.scholar@aya.yale.edu.

CAREER: Gulliver Preparatory School, Miami, FL, teacher of English, 1987-91; writer, 1991—. Short story writer for the internet news group DorothyL.

MEMBER: Sisters in Crime, Mystery Writers of America.

AWARDS, HONORS: Nominated for Agatha Award, best first novel category, 1994, for *Until Death.*

WRITINGS:

MYSTERY NOVELS

Until Death, St. Martin's Press (New York, NY), 1994.
Until the End of Time, St. Martin's Press (New York, NY), 1995.
Until It Hurts, St. Martin's Press (New York, NY), 1997.
(As Hialeah Jackson) *The Alligator's Farewell,* Dell (New York, NY), 1999.

OTHER

Until All the Mysteries of the Universe Are Solved, We Give You Some Quick Guesses and a Warp-Speed Whodunit (cyberbook), 1997.
This Is Graceanne's Book, St. Martin's Press (New York, NY), 1999.

SIDELIGHTS: Polly Whitney has written three mystery novels—*Until Death, Until the End of Time,* and *Until It Hurts*—featuring the amateur sleuthing team of television producer Abby Abagnarro and his ex-wife, Ike Tygart, a news director. Speaking to Elena Santangelo, in an interview posted at the Polly Whitney Web site, Whitney explained how she chose the names of her two major characters: "Their names are more or less an accident. I wasn't making any gender statements or attempting any reversals. Ike just got her nickname from the jeans she was wearing when she and Abby met the first time. . . . As for Abby himself, that's a fairly natural shortening of his somewhat difficult Italian name (Abagnarro). I never once thought of their familiar names as being gender-specific. 'Ike' and 'Abby' are simply who those people are to me."

A serial killer is on the loose in *Until the End of Time.* Nicknamed the Yellow Man because that is the color he paints his victims' faces, the serial killer has been preying on homeless vagrants. But then a local doctor, who has been fighting the time-consuming Federal Drug Administration testing process for new drugs, is found murdered. His face is painted the characteristic yellow. Then Abby is mugged by a homeless man who claims he knows a secret, and Ike and Abby uncover family feuding between the murdered doctor's relatives. A *Publishers Weekly* reviewer found that "Whitney skates deftly through the maze of deadlines, backbiting and fragile relationships at the TV station while untangling the meaning of the murders on the streets in this briskly paced, absorbing mystery."

Until It Hurts focuses on the New York Knicks basketball player Archie "The Big Chill" Thorpe. Thorpe is taking his team to the playoffs, but instead of being a hero with the city's fans, he is resented. Fans know that his business interests in South America include ranches that are destroying the rain forest. When Ike and Abby manage to get Thorpe to agree to a rare interview, there is a shootout at the basketball court during practice and most of the team's players are injured. Thorpe himself is dead, but not from any gunshot wound. He was stabbed in the heart with a knife. While the New York police work on their investigation, Ike and Abby refuse to hand over what may be important videotape of the incident, hoping to solve the murder themselves. Harriet Klausner, in a review of the novel posted at the *Under the Covers* Web site, found *Until It Hurts* to be "witty, charming, and delightful." She also believed that "the chemistry between the two protagonists, who still love each other, enhances the engaging story line."

In addition to her mystery novels, Whitney has also written a cyberbook, available on the internet, entitled *Until All the Mysteries of the Universe Are Solved, We Give You Some Quick Guesses and a Warp-Speed Whodunit.* In this book, Whitney examines the various kinds of subgenres within the mystery field. She especially criticizes the frequent assumption in mystery stories, according to Peggy Itzen of the *Austin American-Statesman,* that "females do incredibly dumb things that no one would expect a man to do." Speaking of Whitney's own work as a novelist, Itzen called her "one of my favorite mystery writers."

Whitney once told *CA:* "I am motivated to write by a love of language and by the need to perform. If I weren't writing novels, I'd probably be on the stage. I suppose the greatest influence on my work is twofold: my education in canonical literature at Yale, which may seem like an odd thing for a mystery writer to say; and the need to be funny, which is probably a product of sanity.

"I am compulsive, disciplined, and thorough during the writing process. I revise each book at least seven times before I let it out of my hands. Behind each of my mysteries lie months of intensive research. I think mystery writers are archivists of their time, and they should present the social scene accurately.

"I write mysteries because, for me, this genre is the most suited for exploring human nature and for demonstrating how well human society is coping with human nature. We are killers and that fascinates me. I wouldn't kill anyone, and I am constantly amazed that people kill each other quite frequently. Society seems unable to stop us."

BIOGRAPHICAL AND CRITICAL SOURCES:

PERIODICALS

Austin American-Statesman, March 23, 1997, Peggy Itzen, "Smart Women, Foolish Mystery Plots," p. E10.

Library Journal, July, 1995, Rex E. Klett, review of *Until the End of Time,* p. 127.

Publishers Weekly, July 24, 1995, review of *Until the End of Time,* p. 50; March 31, 1997, review of *Until It Hurts,* p. 66.

ONLINE

Polly Whitney's Home Page, http://www.thewindjammer.com/polly/ (April 8, 2003), Elena Santangelo, interview with Polly Whitney.

Under the Covers, http://www.silcom.com/~manatee/whitney_until.html/ (March 23, 1997), Harriet Klausner, review of *Until It Hurts.**

* * *

WILKINSON, Richard H(erbert) 1951-

PERSONAL: Born April 26, 1951, in Skipton, England; son of Herbert and Mary (Coates) Wilkinson; married Anna Wagner, 1975; children: Ryan Hayes, Mark Walden. *Education:* Ambassador College, B.A., 1975; California State University—Dominguez Hills, M.A., 1982; University of Minnesota—Twin Cities, M.A., 1984, Ph.D., 1986.

ADDRESSES: Office—Egyptian Expedition, P.O. Box 210105, University of Arizona, Tucson, AZ 85721-0105.

CAREER: University of California—Los Angeles, scholar in residence, 1987; University of Arizona, Tucson, began as lecturer, 1988-93, senior lecturer, 1994-97, associate professor, 1997-2000, professor, 2001, director of Egyptian Expedition, 1990—. American Research Center in Egypt, president of Arizona chapter, 1990-2000, member of national board of directors, 1994-97, 1997-2000; University of Arizona Center for Middle Eastern Studies, member of governing board, 1995-98; Amarna Foundation, member of board of trustees, 1996—.

WRITINGS:

Reading Egyptian Art: A Hieroglyphic Guide to Ancient Egyptian Painting and Sculpture, Thames & Hudson (New York, NY), 1992.

Symbol and Magic in Egyptian Art, Thames & Hudson (New York, NY), 1994.

(With Nicholas Reeves), *The Complete Valley of the Kings: Tombs and Treasures of Egypt's Greatest Pharaohs,* Thames & Hudson (New York, NY), 1996.

The Complete Temples of Ancient Egypt, Thames & Hudson (New York, NY), 2000.

The Complete Gods and Goddesses of Egypt, Thames & Hudson (New York, NY), 2003.

Editor of *Valley of the Sun Kings: New Explorations in the Valley of the Kings,* 1994. Compiler of the annual *Directory of North American Egyptologists,* American Research Center in Egypt, 1988—. *KMT: A Modern Journal of Ancient Egypt,* member of editorial board, 1994—. Contributor of numerous articles and reviews to professional journals.

Wilkinson's work has been published in other languages, including Swedish, Spanish, Japanese, Dutch, and German.

WORK IN PROGRESS: Ongoing research and excavation in the royal tombs of the Valley of the Kings, and in the area of Thebes, Egypt.

SIDELIGHTS: Richard H. Wilkinson draws upon his expertise as an archaeologist to write books about ancient Egypt's architecture, hieroglyphics, mythology, and art. Wilkinson's "Complete" books in particular are written for general readers, but they are also of value to more serious students in the field. *Library Journal* correspondent Mary Morgan Smith found *The Complete Temples of Ancient Egypt* an "indispensable work for a student of Egyptian life or architecture." In her *Journal of Near Eastern Studies* review of *The Complete Valley of the Kings: Tombs and Treasures of Egypt's Greatest Pharaohs,* Catharine Roehrig wrote: "The principal value of this book is that it brings together in one volume a wide variety of sources, providing information not easily accessible or widely known to the general reader or even to Egyptologists who do not specialize in the subject matter." *Antiquity* reviewers Timothy Taylor and Cyprian Broodbank felt that *Reading Egyptian Art: A Hieroglyphic Guide to Ancient Egyptian Painting and Sculpture* is "accessible and delightful—a book that could easily gain converts to Ancient Egypt."

BIOGRAPHICAL AND CRITICAL SOURCES:

PERIODICALS

Antiquity, March, 1993, Timothy Taylor and Cyprian Broodbank, review of *Reading Egyptian Art: A Hieroglyphic Guide to Ancient Egyptian Painting and Sculpture,* p. 157; June, 1994, Cyprian Broodbank, review of *Symbol and Magic in Egyptian Art,* p. 431; June, 2001, N. James, review of *The Complete Temples of Ancient Egypt,* p. 423.

Archaeology, March-April, 1995, Robert S. Bianchi, review of *Symbols and Magic in Egyptian Art,* p. 72.

Booklist, June 1, 2003, Patricia Monaghan, review of *The Complete Gods and Goddesses of Ancient Egypt,* p. 1713.

Journal of Near Eastern Studies, July, 2000, Catharine Roehrig, review of *The Complete Valley of the Kings: Tombs and Treasures of Egypt's Greatest Pharaohs,* p. 195.

Library Journal, September 15, 2000, Mary Morgan Smith, review of *The Complete Temples of Ancient Egypt,* p. 95; June 15, 2003, Richard K. Burns, review of *The Complete Gods and Goddesses of Ancient Egypt,* p. 64.

Science News, May 24, 2003, review of *The Complete Gods and Goddesses of Ancient Egypt,* p. 335.

* * *

WILLAN, Anne 1938-

PERSONAL: Born January 26, 1938, in Newcastle, England; naturalized U.S. citizen, 1973; daughter of William (a lawyer) and Joyce (Todd) Willan; married Mark Cherniavsky (a banker), July 9, 1966; children: Simon, Emma. *Education:* Cambridge University, M.A., 1959; attended cookery schools in London and Paris, 1960-64.

ADDRESSES: *Office*—Ecole de Cuisine La Varenne, Burgundy, France. *Agent*—Janis McLean, P.O. Box 25574, Washington, DC 20007.

CAREER: *Gourmet,* New York, NY, member of editorial staff, 1965-66; *Washington Star,* Washington, DC, food editor, 1966-68; cookery editor and consultant, 1969-74; Ecole de Cuisine La Varenne, Paris, France (currently Chateau du Fëy, Burgundy, France), founder and president, 1975—. Host of television show *Anne Willan's Look and Cook.* Also gives cooking classes at The Greenbriar resort, West Virginia, elsewhere in the United States, Europe, and Australia. Member of board, COPIA: The American Center for Wine, Food and the Arts, Napa, CA.

AWARDS, HONORS: Tastemaker Award, 1977, for *Great Cooks and Their Recipes,* and 1980, for *La Varenne's Basic French Cookery;* named to "Who's

Who of Food and Beverage," 1986; James Beard award for *In and Out of the Kitchen in Fifteen Minutes or Less;* International Association of Culinary Professionals lifetime achievement award and induction into Hall of Fame, both 1999; named "Cooking Teacher of the Year," *Bon Appétit* magazine, 2000.

WRITINGS:

Entertaining Menus, Coward (New York, NY), 1974, published as *Entertaining: Complete Menus for All Occasions,* Batsford (London, England), 1980, David & Charles (North Pomfret, VT), 1981.

Great Cooks and Their Recipes: From Taillevent to Escoffer, McGraw-Hill (New York, NY), 1977, Little, Brown (Boston, MA), 1992.

The Observer French Cookery School, Macdonald (London, England), 1980.

La Varenne's Basic French Cookery, H. P. Books (Tucson, AZ), 1980.

French Regional Cooking, Morrow (New York, NY), 1981.

La Varenne's Paris Kitchen, Morrow (New York, NY), 1981.

La Varenne French Cookery Course, Morrow (New York, NY), 1982.

Classic French Cooking, illustrated by Susan Alcantarilla, Pantheon Books (New York, NY), 1986.

La Varenne Pratique: The Complete Illustrated Cooking Course, Techniques, Ingredients, and Tools of Classic Modern Cuisine, Crown (New York, NY), 1989.

La France Gastronomique, Pavilion (London, England), 1991.

Perfect Pasta, D. Kindersley (New York, NY), 1992.

Main Dish Vegetables, D. Kindersley (New York, NY), 1992, reprinted as *Perfect Main Dish Vegetables,* 1997.

Meat Classics, D. Kindersley (New York, NY), 1992, reprinted as *Perfect Meat Classics,* 1997.

Perfect Fruit Desserts, D. Kindersley (New York, NY), 1992, revised edition, 1998.

Chateau Cuisine, photography by Christopher Baker, Maxwell Macmillan (New York, NY), 1992.

Chicken Classics, D. Kindersley (New York, NY), 1992, reprinted as *Perfect Chicken Dishes,* 1997.

Chocolate Desserts, D. Kindersley (New York, NY), 1992, reprinted as *Perfect Chocolate Desserts,* 1997.

Creative Appetizers, D. Kindersley (New York, NY), 1993, reprinted as *Perfect Appetizers,* 1997.

Superb Salads, D. Kindersley (New York, NY), 1993, reprinted as *Perfect Salads,* 1997.

Italian Country Cooking, D. Kindersley (New York, NY), 1993, reprinted as *Perfect Italian Country Cooking,* 1997.

Creative Casseroles, D. Kindersley (New York, NY), 1993.

Delicious Desserts, D. Kindersley (New York, NY), 1993, reprinted as *Perfect Desserts,* 1997.

Fish Classics, D. Kindersley (New York, NY), 1993, reprinted as *Perfect Fish Classics,* 1997.

Asian Cooking, recipe consultant, Lucy Wing, D. Kindersley (New York, NY), 1994, reprinted as *Perfect Asian Cooking,* 1997.

Perfect Pies and Tarts, D. Kindersley (New York, NY), 1994, reprinted, 1998.

Splendid Soups, D. Kindersley (New York, NY), 1994, reprinted as *Perfect Soups,* 1998.

Classic Breads, D. Kindersley (New York, NY), 1995.

French Country Cooking, D. Kindersley (New York, NY), 1995.

In and Out of the Kitchen in Fifteen Minutes or Less, photography by Sara Taylor, Rizzoli (New York, NY), 1995.

Cook It Right: Achieve Perfection with Every Dish You Cook, Reader's Digest (Pleasantville, NY), 1997, published in England as *Cooked to Perfection: A Complete Guide to Achieving Success with Every Dish You Cook,* Quadrille (London, England), 1997.

Anne Willan: From My Chateau Kitchen, photography by Langdon Clay, C. Potter (New York, NY), 2000.

Cooking with Wine, photography by Langdon Clay, Harry N. Abrams (New York, NY), 2001.

Good Food, No Fuss: 150 Ideas for Easy-to-Cook Dishes, photography by Simon Wheeler, Stewart, Tabori & Chang (New York, NY), 2003.

The Good Cook: 70 Essential Techniques: 250 Step-by-Step Photographs: 350 Easy Recipes, Stewart, Tabori & Chang (New York, NY), 2004.

Editor-in-chief of "Grand Diplome Cooking Course," Grolier, 1970-73. Contributor of monthly column to *Los Angeles Times* food syndicate. Contributor to *Washington Post.*

SIDELIGHTS: Anne Willan is an internationally known cooking teacher who is equally at home in print, on television, and in intimate classes at her chateau in Burgundy, France. Originally known for her expertise in French cookery, Willan has become a respected authority on other regional cuisine as well as an instructor in reliable cooking techniques. In *Booklist,* Mark Knoblauch cited Willan for a "candid, unassuming attitude" that marks her as "an outstanding teacher."

Willan began her La Varenne cooking school in Paris in 1975. Seven years later, she and her husband bought a seventeenth-century Burgundian estate named Chateau du Fëy and moved the school there. She also travels frequently for classes in the United States and Australia and is the host of *Anne Willan's Look and Cook* on television. Many of the recipes she tries wind up in the pages of cookbooks, and these have garnered mostly positive reviews for their straightforward approach and daring cuisine. In a *Library Journal* review of *Anne Willan: From My Chateau Kitchen,* Judith C. Sutton concluded: "Most readers should find the text engrossing and the recipes delicious." A *Publishers Weekly* critic found *Anne Willan's Cook It Right* to be a "valuable guide," and another *Publishers Weekly* piece called *Chateau Cuisine* an "exquisite book." A reporter in the *Winston-Salem Journal* noted that Willan is "esteemed as a culinary instructor," and her book *Cooking with Wine* "is recommended for anyone interested in wine, food—or both."

BIOGRAPHICAL AND CRITICAL SOURCES:

PERIODICALS

Booklist, December 15, 1993, Alice Joyce, review of *Chateau Cuisine,* p. 731; February 15, 1998, Mark Knoblauch, review of *Fruit Desserts, Pies and Tarts,* and *Soups,* p. 962; May 15, 1998, Mark Knoblauch, review of *Cook It Right: Achieve Perfection with Every Dish You Cook,* p. 1581; March 15, 2000, Mark Knoblauch, review of *Anne Willan: From My Chateau Kitchen,* p. 1309; February 15, 2002, Mark Knoblauch, review of *Cooking with Wine,* p. 982.

Library Journal, March 15, 2000, Judith C. Sutton, review of *Anne Willan: From My Chateau Kitchen,* p. 121.

Publishers Weekly, July 26, 1993, review of *Chateau Cuisine,* p. 67; March 16, 1998, review of *Cook It Right,* p. 58; March 6, 2000, review of *Anne Willan: From My Chateau Kitchen,* p. 99; October 1, 2001, review of *Cooking with Wine,* p. 54.

Winston-Salem Journal, May 1, 2002, "Vintage Fare: Author Lives Up to Her Reputation As Teacher in Her New Cookbook," p. E2.

ONLINE

La Varenne, http://www.lavarenne.com/ (December 6, 2002), author's home page.*

* * *

WILSON, Jacqueline 1945-

PERSONAL: Born December 17, 1945, in Bath, England; daughter of Harry Albert (a civil servant) and Margaret (a local government officer; maiden name, Clibbens) Aitken; married William Millar Wilson (a police superintendent), August 28, 1965 (divorced); children: Emma Fiona. *Hobbies and other interests:* Browsing in bookshops, visiting art galleries, going to movies, swimming, line dancing.

ADDRESSES: Home—1B Beaufort Rd., Kingston-on-Thames, Surrey KT1 2TH, England. *Agent*—David Higham Associates, 5-8 Lower John Street, Golden Square, London W1R 4HA, England.

CAREER: Journalist, freelance magazine writer, and author of books and radio plays. Employed by D. C. Thomsons, Dundee, Scotland, 1963-65.

AWARDS, HONORS: Young Telegraph/Fully Booked Award, 1995, for *The Bed and Breakfast Star;* Smarties Prize and Sheffield Children's Book Award, both for *Double Act;* Whitbread shortlist, 1999, and *Guardian* Children's Fiction Award, 2000, both for *The Illustrated Mum;* Children's Book of the Year, British Book Awards, 1999; Order of the British Empire, 2002, for services to literacy in schools; W. H. Smith Book Award (children's genre), 2003, for *Girls in Tears.*

WRITINGS:

FICTION

Ricky's Birthday, illustrated by Margaret Belsky, Macmillan (London, England), 1973.

Nobody's Perfect, Oxford University Press (Oxford, England), 1982.

Waiting for the Sky to Fall, Oxford University Press (New York, NY), 1983.

The Other Side, Oxford University Press (Oxford, England), 1984.

The School Trip, illustrated by Sally Holmes, Hamilton (London, England), 1984.

The Killer Tadpole, illustrated by Rebecca Campbell-Grey, Hamilton (London, England), 1984.

How to Survive Summer Camp, illustrated by Bob Dewar, Oxford University Press (Oxford, England), 1985.

Amber, Oxford University Press (Oxford, England), 1986.

The Monster in the Cupboard, illustrated by Kate Rogers, Blackie (London, England), 1986.

Glubbslyme, illustrated by Jane Cope, Oxford University Press (Oxford, England), 1987.

The Power of the Shade, Oxford University Press (Oxford, England), 1987.

This Girl, Oxford University Press (Oxford, England), 1988.

The Party in the Lift, Blackie (London, England), 1989.

The Left-Outs, Blackie (London, England), 1989.

Falling Apart, Oxford University Press (Oxford, England), 1989.

Is There Anybody There? (includes *Spirit Raising* and *Crystal Gazing*), Armada (London, England), 1990.

Take a Good Look, Blackie (London, England), 1990.

The Dream Palace, Oxford University Press (Oxford, England), 1991.

The Story of Tracy Beaker, illustrated by Nick Sharratt, Doubleday (London, England), 1991, Delacorte (New York, NY), 2001.

The Werepuppy, illustrated by Janet Robertson, Blackie (London, England), 1991.

Video Rose, illustrated by Janet Robertson, Blackie (London, England), 1992.

The Suitcase Kid, illustrated by Nick Sharratt, Doubleday (London, England), 1992, illustrated by Ying-Hwa Hu, Delacorte (New York, NY), 1997.

Mark Spark, illustrated by Bethan Matthews, Hamilton (London, England), 1992.

Mark Spark in the Dark, illustrated by Bethan Matthews, Hamilton (London, England), 1993.

Deep Blue, Oxford University Press (Oxford, England), 1993.

The Mum-Minder, illustrated by Nick Sharratt, Doubleday (London, England), 1993.

The Werepuppy on Holiday, illustrated by Janet Robertson, Blackie (London, England), 1994.

The Bed and Breakfast Star, illustrated by Nick Sharratt, Doubleday (London, England), 1994, published as *Elsa, Star of the Shelter!,* Whitman (Morton Grove, IL), 1996.

Twin Trouble, illustrated by Philipe Dupasquier, Methuen (London, England), 1994.

The Dinosaur's Packed Lunch, illustrated by Nick Sharratt, Doubleday (London, England), 1995.

Cliffhanger, illustrated by Nick Sharratt, Doubleday (London, England), 1995.

Jimmy Jelly, illustrated by Lucy Keijser, Piccadilly (London, England), 1995.

Love from Katy, illustrated by Conny Jude, Ginn (Aylesbury, England), 1995.

Sophie's Secret Diary, illustrated by Natacha Ledwidge, Ginn (Aylesbury, England), 1995.

Double Act, illustrated by Nick Sharratt and Sue Heap, Doubleday (London, England), 1995, Delacorte (New York, NY), 1998.

Beauty and the Beast, illustrated by Peter Kavanagh, A & C Black (London, England), 1996.

Mr. Cool, illustrated by Stephen Lewis, Kingfisher (New York, NY), 1996.

Bad Girls, illustrated by Nick Sharratt, Doubleday (London, England), 1996, Delacorte (New York, NY), 2001.

Connie and the Water Babies, illustrated by Georgien Overwater, Methuen (London, England), 1996.

The Monster Story-Teller, illustrated by Nick Sharratt, Doubleday (London, England), 1997.

The Lottie Project, illustrated by Nick Sharratt, Doubleday (London, England), 1997, Delacorte (New York, NY), 1999.

The Wooden Horse, illustrated by Jan Nesbitt, Ginn (Aylesbury, England), 1998.

Rapunzel, illustrated by Nick Sharratt, Scholastic (London, England), 1998.

Buried Alive!, illustrated by Nick Sharratt, Doubleday (London, England), 1998.

Monster Eyeballs, Heinemann (London, England), 1999.

The Illustrated Mum, illustrated by Nick Sharratt, Doubleday (London, England), 1999.

Lizzy Zipmouth, Young Corgi (London, England), 2000.

Vicky Angel, Doubleday (London, England), 2000, Delacorte (New York, NY), 2001.

The Dare Game, illustrated by Nick Sharratt, Doubleday (London, England), 2000.

My Brother Bernadette, illustrated by David Roberts, Heinemann (London, England), 2001, Crabtree (New York, NY), 2003.

The Cat Mummy, illustrated by Nick Sharratt, Doubleday (London, England), 2001.

Dustbin Baby, illustrated by Nick Sharratt, Doubleday (London, England), 2001.

Sleepovers, illustrated by Nick Sharratt, Doubleday (London, England), 2001.

Secrets, illustrated by Nick Sharratt, Doubleday (London, England), 2002.

The Worry Web Site, illustrated by Nick Sharratt, Doubleday (London, England), 2002, Delacorte (New York, NY), 2003.

Lola Rose, illustrated by Nick Sharratt, Doubleday (London, England), 2003.

Midnight, illustrated by Nick Sharratt, Doubleday (London, England), 2003.

"GIRLS" SERIES

Girls in Love, illustrated by Nick Sharratt, Doubleday (London, England), 1997, Delacorte (New York, NY), 2002.

Girls under Pressure, illustrated by Nick Sharratt, Doubleday (London, England), 1998, Delacorte (New York, NY), 2002.

Girls out Late, illustrated by Nick Sharratt, Doubleday (London, England), 1999, Delacorte (New York, NY), 2002.

Girls in Tears, illustrated by Nick Sharratt, Doubleday (London, England), 2002, Delacorte (New York, NY), 2003.

"STEVIE DAY" SERIES

Supersleuth, Armada (London, England), 1987.

Lonelyhearts, Armada (London, England), 1987.

Rat Race, Armada (London, England), 1988.

Vampire, Armada (London, England), 1988.

"READ-ON" SERIES

Teddy Goes Swimming, Longman (Harlow, England), 1994.

Teddy at the Fair, Longman (Harlow, England), 1994.

Teddy in the Garden, Longman (Harlow, England), 1994.

Teddy Likes the Little One, Longman (Harlow, England), 1994.

Teddy Plays Hide and Seek, Longman (Harlow, England), 1994.

Come Back, Teddy!, Longman (Harlow, England), 1994.

Freddy's Teddy, Longman (Harlow, England), 1994.

SUSPENSE NOVELS; FOR ADULTS

Hide and Seek, Macmillan (London, England), 1972, Doubleday (Garden City, NY), 1973.

Truth or Dare, Macmillan (London, England), 1973, Doubleday (Garden City, NY), 1974.

Snap, Macmillan (London, England), 1974.

Let's Pretend, Macmillan (London, England), 1976.

Making Hate, Macmillan (London, England), 1977, St. Martin's Press (New York, NY), 1978.

Author of radio plays *Are You Listening, It's Disgusting at Your Age,* and *Ask a Silly Question,* British Broadcasting Corporation (BBC; London, England), 1982-84; and contributor to *Winter's Crimes,* edited by Virginia Whitaker, Macmillan (London, England), 1973. Wilson's books have been translated into twenty-three languages.

ADAPTATIONS: Double Act was adapted for stage; *The Story of Tracy Beaker* has been adapted as a miniseries by BBC-1; three other titles have been adapted for television; *The Story of Tracy Beaker, The Bed and Breakfast Star,* and *The Dare Game* were all adapted for radio.

SIDELIGHTS: Jacqueline Wilson is considered one of England's best-known writers for young readers. "Her books have sold two million copies, been translated into eleven languages, and she receives over 200 letters from readers a week (replying to them all)," wrote Anne Karpf in an introduction of Wilson in London's *Guardian.* In 2003, she ranked fourth in the Treasure Islands Favourite Children's Author poll, and the BBC's "The Big Read" poll ranked her novel *Double Act* tenth favorite out of one hundred—the only novel in the top ten written by a contemporary writer. Her books *Girls in Love, The Story of Tracy Beaker,* and *Vicky Angel* were also among the top one hundred. Sue Blackhall of the *Evening Standard* proclaimed, "Jacqueline Wilson is the latest phenomenon in the world of storytelling."

According to Mary Leland of the *Irish Times,* Wilson's books feature "fierce funny girls who tell silly jokes and muck around and do wicked things," as Wilson herself described these heroines in *Books for Keeps.* Linda Newbery, reviewing Wilson's *The Dream Palace* in *School Librarian,* summarized the author's typical plot line as a story of "an ordinary young girl landing in a desperate situation and finding new resilience as a result." Many of the girls come from dysfunctional backgrounds, and all struggle with the reality of their world, trying to make the best of what they are given. Often told with humor as well as pain, Wilson's award-winning books include *Nobody's Perfect, The Other Side, The Story of Tracy Beaker, The Suitcase Kid, Bad Girls,* and *Double Act.* Though many of her early titles are available in the United States only as imports in British editions, she is increasingly gaining recognition on both sides of the Atlantic.

"I wrote my first novel when I was nine years old," Wilson once commented. Written in a school exercise book, this early work told the story of the Maggot family and their unruly offspring. An only child herself, Wilson happily gave the Maggots a slew of offspring. She had a richly imaginative childhood with fantasy friends, beasts lurking under the stairs, a love of magic, and a horror of joining in at school games. In an interview with the *Scotsman,* she explained, "I knew all I ever wanted to do was write and wrote throughout my schooldays." She was, as she noted in *Books for Keeps,* "a sad, shy, weedy little kid." Such an upbringing also led to an early love for books. Wilson not only read voraciously, but also continued writing throughout her school years. Though she loved to read, her family did not own a lot of books. She told London *Sunday Times* reporter Louise Johncox, "There was a bookcase but we didn't have loads of books. Money was tight, but Mum always made sure I had a new book every birthday, Christmas, and summer holiday. . . . When I was ten, Mum asked if I could join the adult library because I'd run out of books to read."

Wilson responded to an advertisement looking for first a typist, then a writer, when she was seventeen years old. "By the time I was seventeen I was earning my own living by writing stories for teenage magazines," she once commented. "I was thrilled to see my stories in print (though the magazine editors cut out my finest descriptive passages and pared each character down to a sad stereotype), but it wasn't the sort of fiction I really wanted to write. I wasn't interested in the glossy fantasy world of the magazines. I wanted to write about young people and their problems, but I didn't want to pretend there were the easy solutions offered in the magazine stories."

Married at the age of nineteen to a police superintendent, Wilson turned her hand once again to the writing of novels, but now crime was her centerpiece. "I wrote five crime novels for adults," Wilson once commented, "but each one had a child as one of the major characters, and I knew I didn't really want to write about crime at all, I wanted to write about children." Her first juvenile novel was inspired by a newspaper account about adopted children trying to trace their biological parents, and in Wilson's mind this developed into the story of a young girl, Sandra, trying to track down her real father in *Nobody's Perfect.* Sandra's home life is a mess, and her stepfather is no substitute for the real thing, so one day Sandra sets out to find her real dad who, she knows, once wanted to be a writer just like she does now. Aided in her efforts by a younger teenage boy, Michael, whom she encounters in the British Museum, Sandra succeeds in finding her birth father, only to be disappointed. But she is not disappointed in her new-found friend. Zena Sutherland of the *Bulletin of the Center for Children's Books* noted that in this sensitively written story, "the characterization, plot, and pace all have impact," while the "treatment of relationships" is both "realistic and perceptive." A *Junior Bookshelf* commentator also praised this first juvenile novel, concluding that with the help of Michael, the book was "a good and worthwhile read which ends in a realistic but satisfying way." Lucinda Fox in *School Librarian* called *Nobody's Perfect* a "perceptive story which will appeal to teenagers identifying themselves with Sandra and some of her problems."

Apparent in Wilson's first title were several elements that would recur throughout her novels for young readers: the female heroine; the outsider or quirky character; and the love of setting books partially or in whole in museums and galleries. Her next title, *The Other Side,* is the story of young Alison who thinks—as Wilson herself did as a girl—that if she stares at the ceiling hard enough, she will be able to levitate. In fact, Alison learns to fly around her bedroom and out of the window to navigate her neighborhood. Or is it all a dream induced by the difficulties Alison is having in her waking life with her parents' divorce and her mother's breakdown? "The book's called *The Other Side* because Alison learns the other side of her parents' situation, and she also has occult experiences on the 'Other Side,'" Wilson once explained. David Bennett, writing in *Books for Keeps,* noted that Wilson has shown "convincingly" how the collapse of family relationships "leaves only victims in its wake, no winners," and concluded that it was a "moving novel."

Another broken family is featured in *How to Survive Summer Camp,* when Stella is sent off to camp during her mother's honeymoon with her second husband. "I wrote [that book] to comfort all the shy subversive children who find the whole idea of summer camp sheer hell," Wilson once commented, and for her protagonist, Stella, the experience is far from delightful. She is afraid of water, the food at camp is terrible, and her favorite book is ruined—perhaps by jealous girls at the camp. A kindly camp counselor manages to save the day when he discovers Stella's love for storytelling by suggesting she start a camp magazine. Margery Fisher of *Growing Point* called the book a "pleasing and pointed look at a girl of ten or so in difficulties with her peers," while a *Junior Bookshelf* reviewer dubbed it a "shrewd and well observed story."

Wilson's love of books literally led her to her next teen novel. An inveterate reader—at last count she had well over 10,000 volumes scattered about her home—Wilson enjoys a favorite outing to a nearby village which has some twenty secondhand bookstores. Once, while visiting these shops, she also noticed the hippies who lived nearby, and the hippie children wandering about the town. She wondered what it would be like to have one of those children rebel against their unconventional life, and thus was born the eponymous heroine *Amber.* Amber has come to resent the freedom and unstructured nature of her life with her mother and longs for clean sheets and a steady home. Rescued for a time by a childhood friend, Amber finally must find her own way in the world. Dorothy Nimmo noted in *School Librarian* that the "stages in Amber's journey are small, true, and moving," and concluded that this was a story "to be enjoyed and admired." Bennett, writing in *Books for Keeps,* called *Amber* a "well-written, thought-provoking read for mid-teenagers."

Magic in various forms and guises comes to the fore in several of Wilson's titles, including *Glubbslyme, The Power of the Shade,* and *Is There Anybody There?,* which involve seances and time-travel. With *Glubbslyme,* witchcraft becomes a theme, in a book told from the perspective of a long-lived toad who is a witch's familiar. "I've tried to make him behave like a seventeenth-century character who is utterly appalled by the noisy new inventions of the modern world," Wilson once commented. In *The Power of the Shade,* May starts to believe she really *can* make magic when her friend Selina initiates her into witchcraft. May believes in these powers, even though Selina is probably only kidding, and subsequently spends hours in London's National Gallery staring at a painting of witches.

Typical problem novels from Wilson include *This Girl* and *The Dream Palace.* The former story is, according to *Books for Keeps* reviewer Adrian Jackson, a "brave exploration" of how a young girl copes with "opportunity and relationships." Coral is caught between her father's unemployment malaise and her mother's coquetry, and opts out of her home when she takes a position as a nanny. Her employers have created a Victorian fantasy in their home, yet the same old problems abide under the surface, and Coral turns to a young single mother, Deb, to help her make sense of the world. Dorothy Atkinson, writing in *School Librarian,* considered *This Girl* a "fine novel for teenagers" and "also an unusual one." In *The Dream Palace,* insecure Lolly thinks she does not measure up to her prettier friend, Lynn, and when Lynn goes on a fine vacation, Lolly is stuck taking a summer job at a nursing home. At her own home, things are not much better with her mother and stepfather, but when Lolly meets Greg, who is a member of a group of squatters, things start to change in her life. And when she finally leaves her home with Greg, she learns new truths about the world, as well. Linda Newbery noted in *School Librarian* that "teenage readers will be engrossed and challenged by this unputdownable, skillfully crafted book," a sentiment that was echoed by Stephanie Nettell in *Books for Keeps,* who wrote that Wilson's story "shocks, entertains, moves, and instructs," calling the book "teenage reading at its most skillful."

Though Wilson's books were received fairly well, it was not until 1991 with *The Story of Tracy Beaker* that Wilson finally hit her extreme level of popularity. Her novels had been around for quite awhile, but Tracy Beaker's story was the one that caught the media's eye. Wilson's first novel to be told in first person from a child's standpoint, *The Story of Tracy Beaker* was also the first of Wilson's books to be accompanied by the illustrations of Nick Sharratt. Tracy Beaker—"-gutsy, stroppy and spirited," as Wilson once described her—is an aspiring ten-year-old writer who tells the story of the children's home where she resides. "Here is the ultimate in first-person journal writing . . . flip and funny," noted Maurice Saxby in a review for *Magpies.* Tracy's dream is to be taken in by a family that measures up to her demanding standards, though as Saxby observed, "underneath the brashness and bravado is a desperately unhappy, self-deluding, insecure personality." Angela Redfern, writing in *School Librarian,* concluded that a "real bonus is that the book genuinely celebrates the act of writing—and not by preaching." In *Horn Book,* a critic wrote that the author "does a commendable job of providing . . . a surprisingly well rounded picture of the seemingly callous but lonely young girl," while a critic for *Publishers Weekly* thought Tracy's "indomitable spirit and grit leaves little doubt that she will end up on top."

Humor is at the heart of some of Wilson's prize-winning novels, including *The Suitcase Kid* and *Double Act,* and it is comedy also that in part informs such popular works as *Elsa, Star of the Shelter!* and *Girls in Love.* Yet Wilson's humorous books are not frivolous—they deal with topics ranging from divorce and homelessness to bullying and developing a positive self-image. Wilson took on the difficult subject of divorce in *The Suitcase Kid,* another story told in diary form by a ten-year-old protagonist, detailing the tug-of-war Andrea is going through as she shuttles back and forth between mom and dad. Added to the brew are step-siblings and a new half-sister to make Andrea's life totally confusing. Deborah Stevenson, writing in the *Bulletin of the Center for Children's Books,* maintained that the book "taps into the righteous indignation of a child torn between two households, and it does so deftly," while Valerie Bierman in *Books for Your Children* observed that to "portray divorce with humour and sympathy takes great skill."

In *Double Act,* Wilson explores the trials and tribulations of being a twin in the story of ten-year-olds Ruby and Garnet. Identical physically, Garnet is shy and somewhat wimpy while her sister Ruby is brash and rude, and the girls take turns narrating this story in which they reluctantly move from the city to the country with their father and his new girlfriend—their mother being long dead. Ann Sohn-Rethel declared the book "another winner" in a review for *School Librarian,* while Stevenson, writing in the *Bulletin of the Center for Children's Books,* felt the book would "intrigue youngsters who wonder what twinship would be like, and there are enough down and dirty double details here to satisfy them." Originally published as *The Bed and Breakfast Star, Elsa, Star of the Shelter!* deals with life in a children's shelter in a novel both "funny and brave," according to Roger Sutton in the *Bulletin of the Center for Children's Books.* Humorously narrated by precocious, ten-year-old Elsa, the book "is a far cry from traditional middle-grade fiction," according to a *Publishers Weekly* reviewer who also felt the book was "eye-opening." *Booklist's* Lauren Peterson called *Elsa, Star of the Shelter!* a "bittersweet account of life in [a] . . . shelter," and concluded that though long, "the story is nicely paced and tender, and it provides loads of avenues to explore through discussion."

Taking up the situation of another young girl in *Bad Girls,* Wilson spins the tale of ten-year-old Mandy, the victim of incessant teasing by three girls at school, through her first-person narrative. She is hit by a bus, leaving her with a sprained arm, while fleeing from the girls, but they refuse to stop the bullying. Mandy must also deal with her over-protective mother. Her situation improves when Tanya, a foster child four years her senior, moves into the neighborhood. Through their relationship—despite getting into a bit of trouble with Tanya—"Mandy develops a strength and maturity that enables her to relate better to her mother and to brush off the barbs of the bullies," explained a *Publishers Weekly* reviewer, concluding, "Shaping convincing characters, dialogue and plot, Wilson proves that bad girls can make for a good story."

Adding a bit of historical fiction to her work, Wilson's *Lottie Project* features Charlie, or Charlotte as her strict new teacher insists on calling her, and her changing life circumstances. Though eleven-year-old Charlie is content with her life, she is not able to prevent major changes: her single mother loses her steady job, must find multiple part-time work, and starts dating a man with a five-year-old son. In the midst of these events, Charlie develops a fictional journal of a girl living in Victorian times as part of a school project, and those entries intermix with Charlie's life to add another dimension to the story. A critic for *Kirkus*

Reviews noted, "Funny, incisive, and true to life, this book introduces a heroine who is easy to root for—she's a terrific combination of feisty and fragile." Kitty Flynn, writing for *Horn Book,* concluded that "readers will empathize with many of the situations Charlie copes with and appreciate the message that, as in life, all loose ends may not be tied up at the end, but we can take what we've learned and carry on from there."

Delving deeper into social distress with *The Illustrated Mum,* Wilson speaks through the first-person account of Dolphin, the eleven-year-old daughter of unstable mother Marigold. It is eventually revealed that Marigold suffers from manic depression, but Dolphin and her older sister, Star, have developed numerous coping strategies. Inevitably, Marigold is hospitalized for treatment of her condition. Though a serious story, Valerie Coghlan wrote in *Books for Keeps* that "Wilson's style keeps a degree of the grimness at a distance, and the love which Marigold has for her daughters and they for her is evident throughout the story."

Wilson's "Girls" series is aimed at a slightly older audience and features three girls—Ellie, Magda, and Nadine—as they struggle with the teenage years, especially with body image and self-esteem. Narrated by Ellie, who is insecure about her weight when compared to her two willowy friends, *Girls in Love* tells of Ellie's attempt to use a male friend to play the part of her gorgeous boyfriend—and because he lives far away, she can describe him however she likes. When he comes to visit her, however, she begins to realize that judging him by his appearance may have made her miss out on a great friendship. In *Girls under Pressure,* Ellie struggles with her weight, opting to stop eating and flirting with bulimia. But when she meets a girl who actually suffers from an eating disorder, she realizes that the path she is treading is a dangerous one. Ellie gets into trouble by staying out with her friends and her artistic boyfriend in *Girls out Late. Girls in Tears* follows Ellie as she learns that the relationships she had assumed would be there forever might not be as sturdy as she had thought. "The way these best friends deal with these issues creates an amusing, entertaining tale with which teenagers will identify," wrote Ginny Harrell for *School Library Journal. School Librarian* critic Pat Williams noted that Wilson "finds the right mix of humour and hard-hitting content to deliver a message without lecturing or patronising" in *Girls under Pressure.* In a review of *Girls in Love,* a contributor to *Publishers Weekly* found "Ellie's first-person narration possesses a Bridget Jones-like energy and compulsiveness." In a review of the first three books in the series, *Kliatt* contributor Paula Rohrlick wrote, "Wilson deals with the road bumps of adolescence with insight and humor."

Vicky Angel, the story of best friends Jude and Vicky, takes a tragic twist when Vicky is hit by a car and killed. In the midst of her grief, Jude revisits the site of the accident and finds, to her great surprise, Vicky's ghost. Vicky's continued presence is a comfort to her but at times interferes with the efforts of other people in Jude's life. Eventually, the friends must let go. "Wilson . . . poignantly addresses a tragic and traumatic experience," commented a *Publishers Weekly* reviewer. Ilene Cooper of *Booklist* noted, "Wilson's wonderful way with dialogue . . . makes this more incisive than depressing." A critic for *Kirkus Reviews* claimed the book worked well due to "its honest characters and dialogue, its unique coverage of grief, and its ability to unite readers with Jude's healing process."

It is not a traumatic death but a traumatic birth that plagues April, the heroine of Wilson's *Dustbin Baby.* Born on April 1st, April was discarded in an alley behind a restaurant, to be found later and raised by a caring, if not entirely understanding, foster mother. After an argument with her foster mother about April's inherent right to own a cell phone, April wanders off to learn more about her past, trying to come to terms with the mother who rejected her the moment she was born. "This is a book that will resonate with many teenage girls and encourage them to give their mums, or caring guardians, a hug this Christmas, even if there's no Nokia under the tree," wrote Helen Brown in the *Daily Telegraph.*

Secrets is one of Wilson's few books to feature a girl from an economically well-off family. India, an only child whose parents do not pay her much attention (except to help her mind her weight), deals with her frustrations about life by keeping a diary, just like her hero, Anne Frank. India becomes friends with Treasure, a girl from the poor side of town who also keeps a diary; when Treasure's life begins to fall apart, India hides her friend in her attic to protect her. But though Treasure's family has its issues, they truly love her—a feeling India misses from her own parents. "Wilson's chatty style is effortless to read," praised Julia Eccleshare in the *Guardian.* Lisa Allardice of the *Daily*

Telegraph wrote that Wilson "is not just an astute chronicler of contemporary childhood, but an imaginative storyteller."

Six short stories by Wilson and one short story by one of her fans, the winner of an online contest sponsored by Wilson, make up the content of *The Worry Web Site.* Each story features a narrator who posts his or her troubles on a Web site, and each of the stories are linked together by shared characters. In sponsoring the contest, Wilson received more than 15,000 entries, which led a *Kirkus Reviews* critic to comment that *The Worry Web Site* "shows plenty of potential for turning young readers into young writers."

Wilson, who visits schools in England regularly, tries to stay in touch with her young readers and their problems, anxieties, and sense of humor. Her appearance is not necessarily what her readers expect; according to Daphne Lockyer of the London *Times,* "She dresses only in black from head to toe, and wears a large ring on each of her fingers. Her hair is that of a spiky grey elf; her boots are those of a pixie." Wilson has told reporters that when in her "full jewelry," she sets off metal detectors in airports. But her eccentric dress does not detract from the realism of her books. As she noted in *Books for Keeps,* "I might write about girls but I want to be read by girls *and* boys." To that end, her female protagonists are not "girly girls so the boys don't feel funny reading about them." As she once commented, her inspiration over the years has not really changed: the desire to tell a story, to create a pretend life and universe. "When I was young, I used to keep quiet about my imaginary games to my friends because I knew they'd think I was crazy—some of them seemed to think that anyway—but now that I'm grown up and a writer, I can play pretend games all the time so long as I write them down on paper and turn them into novels."

BIOGRAPHICAL AND CRITICAL SOURCES:

BOOKS

St. James Guide to Children's Writers, 5th edition, St. James Press (Detroit, MI), 1999.

PERIODICALS

Booklist, January 1, 1996, Lauren Peterson, review of *Elsa, Star of the Shelter!,* p. 836; October 15, 1997, Kay Weisman, review of *The Suitcase Kid,* p. 407; January 1, 1998, Ilene Cooper, review of *Double Act,* p. 799; October 1, 1999, Ilene Cooper, review of *The Lottie Project,* p. 360; June 1, 2001, Ilene Cooper, review of *The Story of Tracy Beaker,* p. 1884; November 15, 2001, Ilene Cooper, review of *Vicky Angel,* p. 575; May 15, 2002, Gillian Engberg, review of *Girls in Love,* p. 1592; January 1, 2004, Gillian Engberg, review of *The Worry Web Site,* p. 864.

Books for Keeps, March, 1987, David Bennett, review of *The Other Side,* p. 13; September, 1988, David Bennett, review of *Amber,* p. 12; November, 1990, Adrian Jackson, review of *This Girl,* p. 12; May, 1991, p. 14; January, 1992, Stephanie Nettell, review of *The Dream Palace,* p. 24; March, 1995, p. 12; March, 1996, p. 24; September, 1996, p. 13; September, 1999, Valerie Coghlan, review of *The Illustrated Mum,* p. 28.

Books for Your Children, spring, 1993, Valerie Bierman, review of *The Suitcase Kid,* p. 23.

Bulletin of the Center for Children's Books, April, 1984, Zena Sutherland, review of *Nobody's Perfect,* p. 158; July-August, 1986, p. 219; February, 1996, Roger Sutton, review of *Elsa, Star of the Shelter!,* p. 209; July-August, 1997, Deborah Stevenson, review of *The Suitcase Kid,* pp. 416-417; February, 1998, Deborah Stevenson, review of *Double Act,* p. 224; December, 1999, Deborah Stevenson, review of *The Lottie Project,* p. 154.

Carousel, summer, 1998, p. 31.

Daily Telegraph (London, England), December 1, 2001, Helen Brown, "Of Hormones, Hair, and Handsets," review of *Dustbin Baby;* March 30, 2002, Lisa Allardice, "Modern Girls Keep It Real," review of *Secrets.*

Evening Standard (London, England), January 4, 2002, Sue Blackhall, "Another Success Story Thanks to Children's Books," p. 19.

Growing Point, March, 1985, pp. 4390-4391; March, 1986, Margery Fisher, review of *How to Survive Summer Camp,* p. 4596; March, 1988, pp. 4935-4937; July, 1989, pp. 5188-5190; November, 1989, pp. 5241-5243.

Guardian (London, England), November 6, 1999, Anne Karpf, article about Jacqueline Wilson, p. 11; March 25, 2000, Julia Eccleshare, "In Dol's House," p. 9; March 28, 2001, Dina Rabinovich, "The Original Jackie," p. 9; June 22, 2002, Julia Eccleshare, "Treasure in the Attic," review of *Secrets,* p. 32; March 1, 2003, Julia Eccleshare, "Family Fortunes," p. 33; March 26, 2003, Maggie Brown, "Drama Queen," p. 14; February 13,

2004, John Ezard, "Granny Spice Becomes Queen of Libraries," p. 12.

Horn Book, November, 1999, Kitty Flynn, review of *The Lottie Project,* p. 746; September, 2001, review of *The Story of Tracy Beaker,* p. 598.

Independent (London, England), October 20, 2001, Hilary Macaskill, interview with Jacqueline Wilson, p. 10.

Irish Times (Dublin, Ireland), May 1, 2003, review of the stage version of *Double Act,* p. 31.

Junior Bookshelf, August, 1982, review of *Nobody's Perfect,* p. 156; April, 1986, review of *How to Survive Summer Camp,* p. 83; February, 1992, pp. 24-25; December, 1992, pp. 248-249; February, 1994, pp. 37-38; April, 1994, p. 76; August, 1996, p. 152.

Kirkus Reviews, August 1, 1997, p. 1230; January 1, 1998, p. 63; October, 1999, review of *The Lottie Project,* p. 1585; September 1, 2001, review of *Vicky Angel,* p. 1304; November 1, 2001, review of *Girls in Love,* p. 1556; September 15, 2003, review of *The Worry Web Site,* p. 1185.

Kliatt, September, 2002, Paula Rohrlick, review of *Girls in Love, Girls under Pressure,* and *Girls in Tears,* p. 14; July, 2003, Paula Rohrlick, review of *Girls under Pressure* and *Girls out Late,* p. 28.

Magpies, November, 1991, Maurice Saxby, review of *The Story of Tracy Beaker,* pp. 29-30; March, 1993, pp. 29-30.

Observer (London, England), March 2, 2003, Kate Kellaway, "Dear Ms. Comfort," p. 19.

Publishers Weekly, December 18, 1995, review of *Elsa, Star of the Shelter!,* p. 55; January 12, 1998, review of *Double Act,* p. 60; November 29, 1999, review of *The Lottie Project,* p. 72; January 8, 2001, review of *Bad Girls,* p. 68; July 23, 2001, review of *The Story of Tracy Beaker,* p. 77; August 13, 2001, review of *Vicky Angel,* p. 312; December 3, 2001, review of *Girls in Love,* p. 61; July 1, 2002, "The British Invasion," p. 26; April 21, 2003, review of *Vicky Angel,* p. 65; April 28, 2003, review of *Girls under Pressure,* p. 73; June 9, 2003, "And Now, Back to Our Story," p. 54; July 7, 2003, review of *Girls out Late,* p. 74; December 1, 2003, review of *The Worry Web Site,* p. 56.

School Librarian, September, 1982, Lucinda Fox, review of *Nobody's Perfect,* p. 256; September, 1986, Dorothy Nimmo, review of *Amber,* p. 276; February, 1989, Dorothy Atkinson, review of *This Girl,* p. 32; May, 1991, Angela Redfern, review of *The Story of Tracy Beaker,* p. 62; May, 1992, Linda Newbery, review of *The Dream Palace,* p. 74; May, 1994, pp. 63, 74-75; August, 1995, Ann Sohn-Rethel, review of *Double Act,* p. 111; November, 1997, p. 216; spring, 1999, Pat Williams, review of *Girls under Pressure,* p. 49.

School Library Journal, February, 1996, Jane Gardner Connor, review of *Elsa, Star of the Shelter!,* p. 104; September, 1997, Kathy East, review of *The Suitcase Kid,* p. 227; March, 1998, Miriam Lang Budin, review of *Double Act,* p. 226; June, 2000, Ginny Harrell, review of *Girls under Pressure,* p. 86; March, 2001, Marilyn Ackerman, review of *Bad Girls,* p. 258; July, 2001, B. Allison Gray, review of *The Story of Tracy Beaker,* p. 116; October, 2001, Marlyn K. Roberts, review of *Vicky Angel,* p. 175; January, 2002, Susan Riley, review of *Girls in Love,* p. 141; December, 2002, Susan Riley, review of *Girls under Pressure,* p. 151; July, 2003, Michele Shaw, review of *Girls in Tears,* p. 135; December, 2003, Rebecca Sheridan, review of *The Worry Web Site,* p. 162.

Scotsman (Edinburgh, Scotland), November 30, 2002, "Bibliofile," p. 7; December 4, 2002, Leila Farrah, "My School Days," interview with Wilson, p. 14.

Sunday Times (London, England), March 3, 2002, Nick Rennison, review of *Secrets,* p. 44; November 2, 2003, Louise Johncox, interview with Jacqueline Wilson, p. 3.

Time International, March 12, 2001, "Watch Out, Harry Potter: Childhood Can Be Hard and Parents Weird, but Jacqueline Wilson's Best-Sellers Don't Need Fantasy," p. 57.

Times (London, England), February 23, 2002, interview with Jacqueline Wilson, p. 3; February 24, 2002, Catherine O'Brien, "Nice Smile," p. 8; March 29, 2003, Daphne Lockyer, "Are You Sitting Uncomfortably?," p. 26.

Western Mail (Cardiff, Wales), March 30, 2002, "Children's Drama to Be Filmed in Wales," p. 14; May 28, 2003, "Tracy Beaker Creator Wows Young at Hay," p. 2.

ONLINE

Kids at Random House, http://www.randomhouse.co.uk/childrens/ (February 1, 2004), profile of Jacqueline Wilson.

Young Writer, http://www.mystworld.com/youngwriter/ (February 14, 2002), "Issue 15: Jacqueline Wilson."*

WINEGARTEN, Renee 1922-

PERSONAL: Born June 23, 1922, in London, England; daughter of Sidney (a sales manager) and Debbe (Tobias) Aarons; married Asher Winegarten (deputy director general of National Farmers Union), March 24, 1946. *Education:* Girton College, Cambridge, B.A., 1943, M.A., 1945, Ph.D., 1950. *Politics:* "Liberalism with a small 'l'." *Religion:* Jewish. *Hobbies and other interests:* Theater, travel, gardening.

ADDRESSES: *Home*—12 Heather Walk, Edgware, Middlesex HA8 9TS, England. *Agent*—Georges Borchardt, Inc., 145 E. 52nd St., New York, NY 10022.

CAREER: British Foreign Office, London, England, research assistant in Latin American section of research department, 1943-45; Cambridge University, Girton College, Cambridge, England, research scholar and supervisor, 1946-47; Westminster Tutors, London, tutor in French and Spanish, 1947-54; freelance literary critic, beginning 1954.

MEMBER: Society of Authors.

WRITINGS:

French Lyric Poetry in the Age of Malherbe, Manchester University Press (Manchester, England), 1954.
Writers and Revolution: The Fatal Lure of Action, Franklin Watts (New York, NY), 1974.
The Double Life of George Sand, Woman and Writer: A Critical Biography, Basic Books (New York, NY), 1978.
Mme. de Stael, Berg (Dover, NH), 1985.
Simone de Beauvoir: A Critical View, Berg (New York, NY), 1988.
Accursed Politics: Some French Women Writers and Political Life, 1715-1850, Ivan R. Dee (Chicago, IL), 2003.

Contributor to books, including *Bernard Malamud: A Collection of Critical Essays,* edited by Leslie Field and Joyce Field, Prentice-Hall (Englewood Cliffs, NJ), 1975; and *Reappraisals of Fascism,* edited by Henry A. Turner, Jr., Franklin Watts (New York, NY), 1975. Contributor to literary and political journals. Member of editorial board, *Jewish Quarterly.*

SIDELIGHTS: Renee Winegarten once told *CA:* "My chief interests lie in the fields of French, English, and American writing, and more particularly, in the interrelation of literature and politics."

BIOGRAPHICAL AND CRITICAL SOURCES:

PERIODICALS

Library Journal, May 1, 2003, Bob T. Ivey, review of *Accursed Politics: Some French Women Writers and Political Life, 1715-1850,* p. 114.*

* * *

WISHINSKY, Frieda 1948-

PERSONAL: Surname is pronounced "wish-*in*-ski"; born July 14, 1948, in Munich, West Germany (now Germany); daughter of Herman (originally a pastry chef; became a sculptor) and Mala (a homemaker) Reches; married Solomon W. (Bill) Wishinsky (a family doctor), 1971; children: David, Suzanne. *Education:* City University of New York, B.A., 1970; Ferkauf Graduate School, Yeshiva University, M.Sc., 1971. *Politics:* "Independent (but usually Democrat)." *Religion:* Jewish.

ADDRESSES: *Home*—292 Horsham Ave., Willowdale, Ontario M2R 1G4, Canada. *Agent*—Transatlantic Literary Agency, 72 Glengowan Rd., Toronto, Ontario M4N 1G4, Canada. *E-mail*—wish@inforamp.net.

CAREER: Montcrest School, Toronto, Ontario, Canada, teacher of children with learning difficulties, beginning 1980; currently full-time writer. Participant in "Writer in the Classroom" program, Borough of North York, Ontario, Canada. Literature and young author's conference speaker and workshop leader at schools and libraries. Has appeared on television and radio, and in a documentary about Frederick Law Olmsted on the Discovery Channel.

MEMBER: Society of Children's Book Writers and Illustrators, Canadian Association for Children's Writers and Performers (CANSCAIP).

AWARDS, HONORS: "Pick of the list" citation from American Booksellers' Association, for *Oonga Boonga;* "outstanding" citation from Parents' Council of the U.S., 1999, for *The Man Who Made Parks;* "book of the week" citation from *Sunday Times* (London, England) and "Children's Choice 2001" from IRA/CBC, 2001, for *Nothing Scares Us;* Governor General nominee, for *Each One Special;* Blue Spruce and Tiny Torgi nominees, for *Give Maggie a Chance.*

WRITINGS:

Oonga Boonga, illustrated by Sucie Stevenson, Little, Brown (Boston, MA), 1990, reprinted with illustrations by Carol Thompson, Dutton (New York, NY), 1998, reprinted with illustrations by Michael Martchenko, Scholastic (Toronto, Ontario, Canada), 1998.

Why Can't You Fold Your Pants Like David Levine?, HarperCollins (New York, NY), 1992.

Crazy for Chocolate, illustrated by Jock McRae, Scholastic Canada, 1998.

Each One Special, illustrated by H. Werner Zimmermann, Orca (Victoria, British Columbia, Canada), 1998.

The Man Who Made Parks: The Story of Parkbuilder Frederick Law Olmstead, illustrated by Song Nan Zhang, Tundra Books (Plattsburgh, NY), 1999.

No Frogs for Dinner, illustrated by Linda Hendry, Fitzhenry & Whiteside (Markham, Ontario, Canada), 1999.

Give Maggie a Chance, illustrated by Ann Iosa, ITP Nelson (Toronto, Ontario, Canada), 1999, reprinted with illustrations by Dean Griffiths, Fitzhenry & Whiteside (Toronto, Ontario, Canada), 2002.

A Quest in Time, illustrated by Bill Slavin, Firefly Books (Toronto, Ontario, Canada), 2000.

Nothing Scares Us, illustrated by Neal Layton, Carolrhoda (Minneapolis, MN), 2000.

So Long Stinky Queen, illustrated by Linda Hendry, Fitzhenry & Whiteside (Toronto, Ontario, Canada), 2000.

Just Mabel, illustrated by Sue Heap, Kingfisher (New York, NY), 2001.

What's the Matter with Albert?: A Story of Albert Einstein, Maple Tree Press (Toronto, Ontario, Canada), 2002.

Manya's Dream: A Story of Marie Curie, Maple Tree Press (Toronto, Ontario, Canada), 2003.

Jennifer Jones Won't Leave Me Alone, illustrated by Neal Layton, Carolrhoda (Minneapolis, MN), 2003.

Just Call Me Joe, Orca Books (Custer, WA), 2003.

A Noodle up Your Nose, illustrated by Louise-Andrée Laliberté, Orca Books, (Custer, WA), 2004.

(With Louise-Andrée Laliberté) *A Bee in Your Ear,* Orca Books (Custer, WA), 2004.

Queen of the Toilet Bowl, Orca Books (Custer, WA), 2005.

Albert Einstein, DK Publishing (New York, NY), 2005.

EDUCATIONAL:

Airplanes, Teacher Created Materials, 1997.

Construction, Teacher Created Materials, 1997.

Farm, Teacher Created Materials, 1997.

Cars & Trucks, Teacher Created Materials, 1997.

Boats & Ships, Teacher Created Materials, 1997.

Nelson Language Arts 5, Supplementary Readings, ITP Nelson (Toronto, Ontario, Canada), 1998.

Nelson Language Arts 6: Going the Distance, Choosing Peace, Supplementary Readings, ITP Nelson (Toronto, Ontario, Canada), 1998.

Nelson Language Arts 3, Supplemental Readings, ITP Nelson (Toronto, Ontario, Canada), 1999.

Author of titles in the "Inforead" series of math and social studies books, published by Thompson Nelson Canada, 2003.

Contributor of reviews, features and profiles to "Books for Young Readers" department, *Quill & Quire.* Contributor to *Parentalk, Canadian Living,Owl Canadian Family,* and *Publishers Weekly.* Writer of author profiles for *Books in Canada.*

WORK IN PROGRESS: Picture books; nonfiction; novels; easy-to-read works.

SIDELIGHTS: "I love writing probably because I've always loved reading," Frieda Wishinsky once commented. "As an only child, books were some of my best companions. Many of my happiest memories are heading home from the library laden with six books (the maximum you could take out at one time) and opening each one like a treasure. Then would come the hard part; deciding which book to read first. The choice was all mine.

"As a child I had few choices. I had to make my bed, go to school, learn multiplication tables and do my homework. What to read, on the other hand, was up to me. My parents, immigrants from Europe, never censored my reading and so I read everything: fiction, travel books, history. I especially loved books about magic, adventure and biographies. The *Mary Poppins* series was a particular favorite and as for biographies, I loved reading about scientists who changed the world: people like Louis Pasteur or Madame Curie. In my fantasies, I dreamed about becoming a scientist and perhaps discovering a cure for cancer or a new vaccine. (That all changed when I realized I liked the romance of science a lot more than the reality.)

"Aside from the pleasure I derived from reading, I soon discovered that I liked writing too. In seventh grade I had a teacher who introduced us to some exciting literature and gave lots of creative writing assignments. Rereading some of them now, I realize they were full of flowery phrases and elaborate sentences, but my teacher saw beyond that. On one paper he wrote: 'You know how to use words effectively. Therefore you should attempt to read and write poetry, stories and essays in order to develop your writing talent.' His words have stayed with me all these years.

"I majored in International Relations in university. I loved history and political science and still do, but right before entering graduate school I realized that it wasn't what I wanted to do with my life. So I started to hunt for a job. I stumbled into an excellent M.S. program in Special Education and before I could fully think it through, I was headed in an entirely new area. I earned my degree and began teaching. Since then I've taught in three countries and with every age group. Teaching has been rewarding, and generally a pleasure. It's also led me back into writing.

"About ten years ago, when I taught in a high school for students with very low reading abilities, I began to search for books at their reading level that would also be fun. At that time, 'hi interest-low vocabulary books' had hit the market, but the kids and I found the stories boring. So I started to introduce them to picture books that I liked and felt were suited for any age. These books delighted me and my students. They were funny and touching and always universal in feeling. I began buying picture books and early novels with a school library budget that had never been used because no one thought these kids would ever read. Soon I was adopted as an honorary librarian by the head librarian of the school board and invited on buying trips. On those trips, I discovered Arnold Lobel, James Marshall, Jean Fritz, Katherine Paterson, the "Narnia" books, *The Secret Garden* and *Tom's Midnight Garden.* And then, when I was on a two-month sabbatical with my husband in Eugene, Oregon (where he was doing a family medicine rotation), I started to write. I haven't stopped since.

When asked where she receives inspiration for her stories, the author responded, "I often use my memories and experiences of childhood as a starting point for my writing. I vividly remember what I felt like when I was young. I am also inspired by other writers and how they handle a story. I learn from reading." Wishinsky also remarked that she enjoys creating her stories while out of the house, commenting, "I like writing in coffee shops. I can tune out the noise and concentrate. At home there are too many distractions, phones ringing, chores to be done, bills to be paid, etc."

Frieda Wishinksy's books deal with everyday childhood events such as school crushes and fussy babies, with emphasis on how youngsters can learn to get along with one another. In *Oonga Boonga,* for instance, baby Louise refuses to be comforted except by her older brother's special brand of baby talk. *Why Can't You Fold Your Pants Like David Levine?* explores a boy's reaction to his mother's comparisons with another youngster, and *Jennifer Jones Won't Leave Me Alone!* illustrates the ups and downs of a girl-boy crush. In every case Wishinsky leavens her serious ideas with humor. *School Library Journal* contributor Ellen Fader praised *Oonga Boonga* for the "warmth and sweetness of a family story touched by just the right sense of silliness." Gwyneth Evans in *Quill & Quire* felt that the message of friendship in *Jennifer Jones Won't Leave Me Alone!* is "implicit rather than explicit, and the book remains light and funny."

Crazy for Chocolate is an adventure novel for young readers in which Anne Banks travels back through time with the help of a magical CD-ROM given to her by a local librarian in order to research a school assignment. With the help of her computer mouse, Anne clicks in and out of fun and sometimes frightening countries and historical eras in her quest for information on the history of chocolate. "Although the text of the novel is extremely simple, readers will be engaged and intrigued by the situations and difficulties

Anne encounters," noted Sheree Haughian in *Quill & Quire. Nothing Scares Us* deals with "the sensitive topic of fears in a humorous and reassuring manner," to quote Sheila Kosco in *School Library Journal.* Lucy and Lenny claim to be fearless, but each harbors a secret anxiety: Lucy is terrified of a television monster, Lenny of spiders. When they admit this to one another, their friendship is strengthened.

Wishinsky has also written *Each One Special,* a story of a pastry chef named Harry who is suddenly laid off from his job, and a youngster named Ben who helps Harry to redirect his talents. Mary Beaty in *Quill & Quire* declared that the book succeeds "as a work portraying 'special' talents and warm relationships between generations." In *Booklist* Ilene Cooper cited the work as a "sweet trifle of a tale" notable for its "ebullience of doing a beloved activity well."

The Man Who Made Parks: The Story of Parkbuilder Frederick Law Olmstead won several awards for its melding of pictures and story of a noted landscape architect of the nineteenth century. Olmstead was famous for creating urban parks such as New York City's Central Park, and Wishinsky's book contains illustrations by Song Nan Zhang that convey the beauty and utility of these green zones. *Booklist*'s Carolyn Phelan concluded of the work: "This short, fully illustrated biography makes its statement with style."

Wishinsky once said, "Throughout these years of writing, I've learned that publishing is an iffy business but I've also learned I'm persistent and that there's nothing more satisfying to me than writing for children. It's just what I want to do."

As a writer, Wishinsky noted that she has "learned that each story has its own rhythm and 'life.' It's important to know where you are going, to surprise your reader but make sure everything is believable so that a reader feels it could have happened."

When asked what kind of an effect she hopes her books have, the author concluded, "I hope they will spark an interest and make the reader feel connected. . . . I hope my stories ring 'true,' and I hope I make someone laugh."

BIOGRAPHICAL AND CRITICAL SOURCES:

PERIODICALS

Booklist, March 1, 1990, pp. 1350-1351; January 1, 1999, Ilene Cooper, review of *each One Special,* p. 892; May 1, 1999, Shelley Townsend-Hudson, review of *Oonga Boonga,* p. 1602; August, 1999, Carolyn Phelan, review of *The Man Who Made Parks: The Story of Parkbuilder Frederick Law Olmstead,* p. 2061.

Children's Book News, summer-fall, 1999, p. 7.

Kirkus Reviews, April 15, 1990, p. 588; May 1, 1999.

New York Times Book Review, November 21, 1999, Cynthia Zarin, "A Joyful Noise," p. 54.

Publishers Weekly, February 23, 1990, p. 216; December 14, 1998, review of *Each One Special,* p. 74; December 2, 2002, review of *Jennifer Jones Won't Leave Me Alone!,* p. 51.

Quill & Quire, September, 1990, Theo Hersh, review of *Oonga Boonga,* p. 20; January, 1994, p. 37; March, 1995, Gwyneth Evans, review of *Jennifer Jones Won't Leave Me Alone!,* p. 77; May, 1998, Haughian, Sheree, review of *Crazy for Chocolate,* p. 34; September, 1998, Mary Beaty, review of *Each One Special,* p. 66.

School Arts, December 1, 1999, Ken Marantz, review of *The Man Who Made Parks,* p. 48.

School Library Journal, May, 1990, Ellen Fader, review of *Oonga Boonga,* p. 93; November, 2000, Sheilah Kosco, review of *Nothing Scares Us,* p. 138; November, 2002, Dona Ratterree, review of *What's the Matter with Albert?: A Story of Albert Einstein,* p. 151.

Toronto Star, October 17, 1999.

* * *

WOLLEN, Peter 1938-

PERSONAL: Born June 29, 1938, in London, England; married Laura Mulvey (an author and film director). *Education:* Studied English at Christchurch College, Oxford.

ADDRESSES: Agent—British Film Commission, 70 Baker St., London W1M 1DJ, England.

CAREER: Independent filmmaker, film theorist, and critic. University of California, Los Angeles, chair of film department, beginning 1993; has also taught filmmaking at universities, including Brown University, New York University, Columbia University, and Northwestern University; Distinguished Luce Professor, Vassar College. Director or codirector of films, including *Penthesilea: Queen of the Amazons,* 1974; *Riddles of the Sphinx,* 1977; *Amy!,* 1980; *Crystal Gazing,* 1982; *The Bad Sister,* 1983; *Friendship's Death,* 1987, *Frida Kahlo and Tina Modotti, Welcome Aboard Soyuz,* and *Reading the U.S. Press.* Curator of exhibitions, including "Kahlo and Modotti," "The Situationist International," "Global Conceptualism," and "100 Years of Art and Fashion."

WRITINGS:

NONFICTION

Signs and Meaning in the Cinema, Indiana University Press (Bloomington, IN), 1969, 4th edition, 1998.

Readings and Writings: Semiotic Counter-Strategies, NLB (London, England), 1982.

On the Passage of a Few People through a Rather Brief Moment in Time: The Situationist International 1957-1972, MIT Press, 1989.

Singin' in the Rain, British Film Institute (London, England), 1992.

Raiding the Icebox: Reflections on Twentieth-Century Culture, Indiana University Press (Bloomington, IN), 1993.

Paris Hollywood: Writings on Film, Verso (New York, NY), 2002.

(With Richard Dyer and Jean Fisher) *Electronic Shadows: The Art of Tina Keane,* Black Dog Publishing (London, England), 2003.

Paris/Manhattan: Writings on Art, Verso (New York, NY), 2004.

Also contributor to *Other Than Itself: Writing Photography,* Cornerhouse Publications, 1989; with Ralph Rugoff and Anthony Vidler, *Scene of the Crime,* UCLA/Armand Hammer Museum of Art (Cambridge, MA), 1997; *Addressing the Century: 100 Years of Art & Fashion,* Hayward Gallery, 1998; and *Glen Seator: Moving Still,* edited by Nina Holland, Hatje Cantz Publishers, 2002. Contributor to periodicals, including *Studio International.* Editor, *Screen* magazine.

EDITOR

Working Papers on the Cinema: Sociology and Semiology, British Film Institute (London, England), 1969.

(With Lynne Cooke) *Visual Display: Culture beyond Appearances,* Bay Press (Seattle, WA), 1996.

(With Jim Hillier, and contributor) *Howard Hawks, American Master,* BFI Publishing (London, England), 1996.

(With Colin MacCabe and Mark Francis) *Who Is Andy Warhol?,* Andy Warhol Museum (Pittsburgh, PA), 1997.

(With Lynne Cooke) *Visual Display: Culture beyond Appearances,* New Press (New York, NY), 1998.

(With Amy Cappellazoo and Adriano Pedrosa) *Making Time: Considering Time As a Material,* Art Publishers, 2000.

(With Joe Kerr) *Autopia: Cars and Culture,* Reaktion Books (London, England), 2002.

SCREENPLAYS

(And director, with Laura Mulvey) *Penthesilea: Queen of the Amazons,* 1974.

(And director, with Laura Mulvey, and producer) *Riddles of the Sphinx,* 1977.

(And director, with Laura Mulvey, and actor) *Amy!,* 1980.

(And director, with Laura Mulvey) *Crystal Gazing,* 1982.

(And director) *Friendship's Death* (science fiction), 1987.

Also coauthor of *The Passenger.*

SIDELIGHTS: Avant-garde filmmaker Peter Wollen has made independent films that reflect his interest in feminist issues, semiotics, psychoanalysis, modernism, and experimental artistic forms. In addition to making films and videos, Wollen teaches film and has written several books on film theory and criticism. His 1975 article "The Two Avant Gardes," published in *Studio International,* is considered a seminal contribution to British avant-garde film theory and practice.

In the late 1960s, Wollen was associated with the Education Department of the British Film Institute (BFI), where he worked on *Signs and Meanings in the Cinema.* The book, an analysis of film according to structuralist and linguistic theories, attracted the attention of a serious academic audience and became an influential text among film students and teachers. Though *New Statesman* reviewer John Coleman found the book incomprehensible, a reviewer for the *Times Literary Supplement* praised it as "the best exposition of [French auteur] theory, its genesis and its justifications ever to appear in English." Though the critic also commented that Wollen's analysis of American films did not sufficiently consider the "specificity of the film medium," the reviewer went on to express admiration for the author's ability to relate film theory "to wider areas of linguistic theory and theory of art." The critic further noted that Wollen's section on early Russian director Sergei Eisenstein's aesthetic theories was of particular value. *London Review of Books* critic Michael Wood, commenting on an updated edition of the book, noted that it "still reads well." In addition to his own book, Wollen also edited an anthology in 1969, *Working Papers on the Cinema: Sociology and Semiology.* Like *Signs and Meanings,* this volume was intended for a scholarly audience.

During the 1970s and 1980s, Wollen began to focus on making his own films. He attracted critical notice with *Penthesilea: Queen of the Amazons,* a film he directed with feminist filmmaker Laura Mulvey in 1974. Like their later collaboration, 1977's *Riddles of the Sphinx,* the film uses experimental forms to explore such issues as the ways in which myth and history construct sexuality, and the practical difficulties of caring for children. The team went on to make 1980's *Amy!,* a short feature based on the life of British aviator Amy Johnson, who set records in solo flights from England to Australia, to Japan via Siberia, and to Cape Town in the early 1930s. In *Crystal Gazing* and *The Bad Sister,* Wollen and Mulvey used video to explore the ways in which fantasy is structured. Wollen's later films include *Friendship's Death,* which *People*'s Peter Travers found a "punishingly claustrophobic sci-fi treatise" with an uninvolving plot about a female extraterrestrial and a journalist who discuss political and ethical dilemmas in the Middle East while the PLO wage war around them.

In 1984, Wollen's second book on theory, *Readings and Writings: Semiotic Counter-Strategies,* was published. *London Review of Books* critic Christopher Norris found it a "mixed bag of texts," including both essays and "experimental fictions." Norris observed that Wollen's essays, grounded in theory from the late 1960s, can seem somewhat dated, but added that "Wollen succeeds in reviving . . . [the] heady radical flavour [of that time] by picking up ideas where he needs them, and not attempting any large-scale unwieldy synthesis." Norris commented, "What [Wollen's essays] lack in consistency or rigour, his essays make up for in 'intellectual verve.'" Colin MacCabe, writing in the *Times Literary Supplement,* rated *Readings and Writings* even more highly. "In some ways it is difficult to praise the book highly enough," he wrote. "Wollen is never less than lucid and he is constantly aware both of the variety of the cinema's own history and the relation of that variety to developments in other arts. The book is full of illuminating cultural juxtapositions and acute historical parallels." Nevertheless, MacCabe faulted the book for its failure to address in sufficient depth the relation between popular artistic forms and the avant-garde, and its failure to consider the political climate of the 1960s and 1970s. Despite these problems, MacCabe concluded that *Readings and Writings* "remains the best collection of writings on politics and art to have emerged for a decade."

In *Singin' in the Rain,* Wollen examines that film in terms of the history of American dance, the development of the Metro-Goldwyn-Mayer (MGM) studio, and the post-World War II anti-Communist climate in the United States. Wollen, wrote J. Belton in *Choice,* "makes astute observations about the use of sound and Kelly's ecstatic descent into the pleasures of infantilism as he splashes about in puddles." Belton recommended the study for both general and academic audiences. John Fell commented in the *Film Quarterly* that the book follows the evolution "of character-inflected dance performance developed on stage," which Gene Kelly later arranged for film. Fell noted that, although Wollen's section on blacklisting might seem exaggerated, it accurately reflects the impact on Hollywood.

Raiding the Icebox, a collection of Wollen's essays that *World Literature Today* reviewer Marcel Cornis-Pope called "a lucid revisioning of modernism," was well received among critics. *Spectator* contributor Bryan Appleyard praised this "ambitious inquiry," but questioned Wollen's fragmented approach and his serious consideration of developments (such as situationism) that Appleyard maintained were unnecessary. Nevertheless, Appleyard appreciated Wollen's understanding of the ways in which mass production and Third World influences have affected artistic forms and meanings. Roger Cardinal, writing in the *Times Literary Supplement,* deemed *Raiding the Icebox* a "thoughtful, informed and absorbing book," observing that it "manages to remain erudite while being both entertaining and provocative." He enthusiastically praised the author's "talent for parallels and interpolations which pluck revelatory threads out from that all-too-even fabric we have come to identify as 'Modernism.'" Though *Sight and Sound* reviewer James Donald found that Wollen "accepts too easily the current American orthodoxy" regarding postmodernism, Donald concluded that Wollen "is best at deciphering the intricate surfaces of modern culture, and at showing how threadbare rags like 'postmodernism' have become."

A number of Wollen's projects in the 1990s were edited books, such as *Visual Display: Culture beyond Appearances,* a collection of essays about the production of spectacle that he edited with Lynne Cooke. *Afterimage* reviewer Kenneth L. Ames, who found the book generally lacking in coherence and sometimes marred by an "aggressive display of academic jargon," gave Wollen credit for his introduction, which helped place the essays in context and outlined their intent. Russell T. Clement praised the book in *Library Journal* as "lively" and readable. Among other edited works about movies, Wollen has also edited *Autopia: Cars and Culture* with Joe Kerr, a book that, while still concerning culture, steers clear of Wollen's usual works on film. "The collection," explained Ralph Harrington in the *Journal of Transport History,* "is one of the first substantial works to approach the automobile in culture not as wholly good or . . . wholly bad but as a cultural product located in and expressing the preoccupations and perceptions of the society that produces and uses it." Critics of *Autopia* appreciated the balanced perspectives of the essays. For example, *Independent* reviewer Stephen Bayley asserted that "the editors have made a real attempt to be even-handed in their treatment of the car."

More recently, Wollen completed another work of film criticism, *Paris Hollywood: Writings on Film.* The release of this collection of essays and lectures provided Jonathan Rosenbaum an opportunity to comment on Wollen's contributions as a whole to film criticism, as well as a chance to remark on his style. In a *Cineaste* article, Rosenbaum observed, "One of the more interesting paradoxes of Peter Wollen's writing career is that he was perceived as an academic well before he had a long-term teaching post whereas today, with a seemingly permanent berth in the critical studies program at UCLA's film department, he's more apt to come across as a journalist." Rosenbaum went on to express his opinion that Wollen has a tendency to generalize when he is writing about film, and this has both an advantage and a disadvantage: the disadvantage is that Wollen "falls too readily into certain easy generalizations"; but the "advantage of this approach when it works is its invitation to rethink whole clusters of films in meaningful ways." Despite having some criticism for *Paris Hollywood,* Rosenbaum concluded that this addition to Wollen's oeuvre is evidence that the film scholar "may finally matter more as a historian than as a critic."

BIOGRAPHICAL AND CRITICAL SOURCES:

PERIODICALS

Afterimage, November-December, 1996, Kenneth L. Ames, review of *Visual Display: Culture beyond Appearance,* pp. 14-16.

American Film, December, 1980, Jeanine Basinger, review of *Signs and Meaning in the Cinema,* p. 65; July-August, 1983, Seymour Chatman, review of *Readings and Writings: Semiotic Counter-Strategies,* pp. 56-57.

Choice, September, 1993, J. Belton, review of *Singin' in the Rain,* p. 132; November, 1993, W. B. Holmes, review of *Raiding the Icebox: Reflections on Twentieth-Century Culture,* p. 448; July-August, 2003, C. J. Myers, review of *Autopia: Cars and Culture,* p. 1946.

Cineaste, fall, 2003, Jonathan Rosenbaum, review of *Paris Hollywood: Writings on Film,* p. 63.

Film Comment, January-February, 1980, Richard T. Jameson, review of *Signs and Meaning in the Cinema,* p. 45.

Film Quarterly, fall, 1983, Lulu McCarroll and Fabrice Ziolkowski, review of *Readings and Writings,* pp. 49-51; summer, 1993, John Fell, review of *Singin' in the Rain,* p. 61.

Historical Journal of Film, Radio and Television, August, 1997, Graham Roberts, review of *Howard Hawks, American Master,* p. 418.

Independent (London, England), December 28, 2002, Stephen Bayley, "Books Interview: 'No Dignity without Chromium,'" p. 18.

Journal of Transport History, September, 2003, Ralph Harrington, review of *Autopia,* pp. 283-284.

Library Journal, July, 1995, Russell T. Clement, review of *Visual Display,* p. 79; February 15, 2003, Eric C. Shoaf, review of *Autopia,* p. 158.

London Review of Books, July 7, 1983, Christopher Norris, review of *Readings and Writings,* pp. 21-22, 24; July 2, 1998, Michael Wood, review of *Signs and Meaning in the Cinema,* pp. 14-16.

Los Angeles Times Book Review, April 10, 1983, Irwin R. Blacker, review of *Readings and Writings,* p. 8.

Nation, May 28, 1988, Edward W. Said, review of *Friendship's Death,* p. 766.

New Statesman, June 20, 1980, John Coleman, review of *Amy!,* p. 944; November 20, 1987, Judith Williamson, review of *Friendship's Death,* p. 26.

New York Review of Books, November 20, 1997, Michael Wood, review of *Howard Hawks,* p. 30.

New York Times, March 25, 1988, Caryn James, review of *Friendship's Death,* p. N14.

People, January 23, 1989, Peter Travers, review of *Friendship's Death,* p. 18.

Sight and Sound, June, 1993, James Donald, review of *Raiding the Icebox,* p. 42, 44.

Spectator, April 10, 1993, Bryan Appleyard, review of *Raiding the Icebox,* pp. 34-35.

Times Higher Education Supplement, September 3, 1993, Graham McCann, review of *Raiding the Icebox,* p. 17; March 26, 1999, Philip Kemp, review of *Signs and Meaning in the Cinema,* p. 26; August 1, 2003, John Higgins, "Lovers Who Look beyond Thrills," p. 26.

Times Literary Supplement, June 12, 1969, review of *Signs and Meaning in the Cinema,* p. 637; May 25, 1984, Colin MacCabe, review of *Readings and Writings,* p. 581; May 28, 1993, Roger Cardinal, review of *Reading the Icebox,* p. 14; April 4, 1997, Richard Combs, review of *Howard Hawks,* p. 31.

Virginia Quarterly Review, spring, 1998, Jeffrey Meyers, review of *Howard Hawks,* p. 362.

World Literature Today, summer, 1994, Marcel Cornis-Pope, review of *Raiding the Icebox,* p. 647.*

* * *

WOODRUFF, Joan Leslie 1953-

Joan Leslie Woodruff

PERSONAL: Born April 4, 1953, in Albuquerque, NM; daughter of Charles (a mechanic) and Lila Ray (a registered nurse; maiden name, Siler) Woodruff; married Paul Harold Ney, 1978 (divorced, 1995). *Ethnicity:* "American Indian; Cherokee, Shawnee." *Education:* Loma Linda University, B.S., 1975; attended California State University—San Diego, 1976; California State University—San Bernardino, M.Ed., 1983. *Religion:* Buddhist. *Hobbies and other interests:* "Raising happy animals, caring for my ranch, working with the Mountainair Heritage Foundation."

ADDRESSES: *Home*—P.O. Box 687, Mountainair, NM 87036. *E-mail*—seyhanjo@aol.com.

CAREER: San Bernardino Community Hospital, San Bernardino, CA, director of occupational therapy services at Hand Rehabilitation Clinic, 1975-77, director and administrator of clinic, 1976-87; Riverside American Indian Center, Riverside, CA, member of board of directors, 1987-91; forensic counselor, 1993—. Occupational Therapy Association, certified and registered occupational therapist, 1975—, specialist advisor to Hand Rehabilitation Division, 1985-98; Redlands Hospital, administrator and clinical representative, 1980; Martin Luther Memorial Hospital, administrator and clinical representative, 1982; hand surgeon in Fullerton, CA, 1983; Hemet Valley Hospital, hand surgeon, 1984; Torrance County Alcohol and Drug Abuse Planning Council, member of executive board and alcohol/drug dependency counselor, 1993-98; American Indian Relief Council, member. Volunteer substance abuse counselor; volunteer to help abused animals. National Campaign for Tolerance, Montgomery AL, founding member.

MEMBER: Occupational Therapy Association, Humane Society of the United States.

AWARDS, HONORS: Award for outstanding support, American Indian Relief Council, 2003.

WRITINGS:

Traditional Stories and Foods: An American Indian Remembers, Esoterica Press (Barstow, CA), 1990.
Neighbors (novel), Third Woman Press, (Berkeley, CA), 1993.
The Shiloh Renewal (novel), Black Heron Press (Seattle, WA), 1998.
Ghost in the Rainbow, Hats Off Books (Tucson, AZ), 2002.

Contributor to professional journals, popular magazines, and newspapers, including *America's Intercultural, Our Town, News from Native California, Indian-Artifact, Independent News* (Edgewood, NM), and *East Mountain Telegraph News.*

WORK IN PROGRESS: Witches and Windmills, a collection of previously published short stories.

SIDELIGHTS: Joan Leslie Woodruff once commented to *CA:* "I am an American Indian woman, with some Anglo ancestry. My family is a mix of odd but wonderful people. I write because of them. My life has been full of stories and crises. The sad stuff is where the books come from. I try to add humor, but I want to show my readers that suffering can lead to growth and compassion."

Recently Woodruff added: "My primary motivation for writing has always been life. Every day is a continuum of lessons where the full range of human emotions must be experienced. I grew up with the tradition of storytelling within the family as a way of communicating. Writing became a way of storytelling to larger populations.

"Compassion particularly influences my work. Those items of everyday life which push me up and down the emotional roller coaster cause me to want to find my pencils and paper.

"My writing process begins with a feeling. It might be happy or sad. The feeling forces new perspectives into my thinking. I never know why or when this will happen, but when it does, I hear ancient voices of the ancestors. They say 'Tell the story,' and I feel compelled to do so. A story always has a specific cord for me. I have changed forever because of that cord. I do not know how the story will affect a person who reads it, but I hope they change forever as well. Change is what makes us grow.

"I am inspired to write about the subjects I have chosen because I know them so well. They are parents, sisters, brother, cousins, friends, coworkers; they are places I have been; they are experiences I have struggled with; they are things that I have failed at; they are things that I did especially well. What is important for me is that the subjects made me feel something to its fullest, whether joyful or sorrowful.

"I hope everything I write exhibits changes. My life changes from moment to moment, and I become a new person every day that I am given the honor of waking up. Change is necessary. Springtime is such a time of change, and people always recognize that it is so; but then, so are summer, and autumn, and winter. I love every season of life. I have reached the half-century mark of my life, I am in 'autumn.' I hope I have done a good job with my summer and my spring. I hope I do a good job with my autumn and winter.

"My work in progress, *Witches and Windmills,* is a collection of short fiction. Most stories are mainstream, with a focus on how culture, old thinking, and perception affect the everyday life of Native Americans in the twentieth and twenty-first centuries."

* * *

ZWEIG, David 1950-

PERSONAL: Born November 30, 1950, in Toronto, Ontario, Canada; son of Robert Isaac (a manufacturer) and Belma Speigal (a manufacturer; maiden name, Jacobson) Zweig; married Joy Poretzky (a merchandiser), May 4, 1992; children: Rachel Ilana. *Education:* York University, B.A. (with honors), 1972, M.A., 1974; Beijing Language and Culture University (formerly Beijing Languages Institute), certificate in Mandarin Chinese, 1975; Beijing University, certificate in philosophy, 1976; University of Michigan, Ph.D., 1983.

ADDRESSES: Office—Division of Social Science, Hong Kong University of Science and Technology, Clear Water Bay, Kowloon, Hong Kong. *E-mail*—sozweig@ust.hk.

CAREER: Professor and author. Florida International University, Miami, FL, lecturer, 1982-83, assistant professor, 1983-84; University of Waterloo, Waterloo, Ontario, Canada, assistant professor, 1985-86; Tufts University Fletcher School of Law and Diplomacy, Medford, MA, assistant professor, 1986-90, associate professor of international politics, 1990-2000; Hong Kong University of Science and Technology, Hong Kong, China, professor of social science, 2000—. Nanjing University, visiting research scholar, 1986 and 1991-92; Harvard University Fairbank Center for East Asian Research, associate in research, 1986, member of executive committee, 1989-91; University of International Business, visiting research scholar, 1992. Conference coordinator and conductor of seminars; commentator for radio and television.

MEMBER: Canadian Institute for International Affairs, American Political Science Association, Association for Asian Studies.

AWARDS, HONORS: Sino-Canadian student exchange fellow, Association of Universities and Colleges of Canada and Department of External Affairs, 1974-76; doctoral fellow, Social Sciences and Humanities Research Council of Canada, 1981-82; postdoctoral fellow, Harvard University Fairbank Center for East Asian Research, 1984-85; research grants from Social Sciences and Humanities Research Council of Canada, 1985-86 and 1992-95; Henry Luce Foundation, 1989-91; and Ford Foundation, 1992-93; Advanced Scholars Program for Study in the People's Republic of China fellow, Committee on Scholarly Communication with the People's Republic of China, 1991-92. Also received a research grant from the United States Institute for Peace.

WRITINGS:

Agrarian Radicalism in China, 1968-1981, Harvard University Press (Cambridge, MA), 1989.

(Editor, with William A. Joseph and Christine Wong) *New Perspectives on China's Cultural Revolution,* Harvard University Press (Cambridge, MA), 1991.

(Editor, with Suzanne Ogden, Kathleen Hartford, and Lawrence Sullivan) *China's Search for Democracy: The Student and Mass Movement of 1989,* M. E. Sharpe (Armonk, NY), 1992.

(With Chen Changgui) *China's Brain Drain to the United States: View of Overseas Chinese Students and Scholars in the 1990s,* Institute of East Asian Studies, University of California (Berkeley, CA), 1995.

Freeing China's Farmers: Rural Restructuring in the Reform Era, M. E. Sharpe (Armonk, NY), 1997.

Internationalizing China: Domestic Interests and Global Linkages, Cornell University Press (Ithaca, NY), 2002.

Democratic Values, Political Structures, and Alternative Politics in Greater China, United States Institute of Peace (Washington, DC), 2002.

Contributor to books, including *Chinese Rural Development: The Great Transformation,* edited by William L. Parish, M. E. Sharpe (Armonk, NY), 1985; *Everyday Forms of Peasant Resistance,* edited by Forrest Colburn, M. E. Sharpe (Armonk, NY), 1990; *Building Sino-American Relations: An Agenda for the 1990s,* edited by William Tow, Paragon Press (New York, NY), 1991; *China Briefing, 1991,* edited by William A. Joseph, Westview Press (Boulder, CO), 1992; and *China Briefing, 1992,* edited by William A. Joseph, Westview Press (Boulder, CO), 1993. Contributor of articles and essays to periodicals, including *China Quarterly, Peasant Studies, Journal of Northeast Asian Studies, China Business Review, Harvard International Review, Boston Globe, New York Times, Asian Wall Street Journal,* and *American Political Science Review.*

SIDELIGHTS: David Zweig, a renowned professor of political and social science with a special interest in Chinese politics and political economy, teamed up with scholar Chen Changgui in 1995 to conduct a large-scale social research project involving Chinese students living in the United States and the resultant effect on China. Compiling their research, the two scholars published *China's Brain Drain to the United States: Views of Overseas Chinese Students and Scholars in the 1990s.* Writing in the *International Migration Review,* Qirong Li deemed the book "one of the best scholarly accounts of 'China's Brain Drain,'" stating that it "deserves a wide readership."

As part of their research for *China's Brain Drain to the United States,* Zweig and Changgui interviewed 277 Chinese students and scholars using a representative questionnaire, which primarily asked the subjects to divulge their intentions to return to China or remain in the United States. The results were unlike those of any previously conducted study. Eighteen percent of those surveyed said they would rather stay in the United States than return to China. These subjects cited reasons such as greater political freedom and availability of jobs. About fifty-eight percent of the subjects surveyed said they planned to return to China. These subjects mentioned motivations such as the desire for strong cultural and family connections, as well as elevated social status. Zweig and Changgui discovered that certain factors affected both groups, such as original intention of returning or not upon arrival to the United States, gender (far more men than women intended to return to China), or academic concentration (those in the humanities and arts were more likely to remain in the United States than those in the social sciences). The study was well received by its subject-educated critics. In *Pacific Affairs,* Ruth Hayhoe deemed the study "well-documented and thoughtfully researched," pointing out that *China's Brain Drain to the United States* "goes beyond numbers, trends, emphases that can be identified from consular files, the press, and the research literature, to an understanding of the subjective experience of the major actors in this drama—the Chinese students and scholars themselves." Reviewer Lawrence K. Hong, in the *Journal of Asian and African Studies,* suggested that "in spite of the fact that the book uses advanced statistical analyses, it is very readable even for the average reader not so familiar with logistic regression models."

Zweig's next publication was a sole venture titled *Freeing China's Farmers: Rural Restructuring in the Reform Era.* This work focuses on economic reform in China and how different sectors have handled it, profited from it, and lost as a result of it. The book discusses the responsibility system, privatization and changing property rights, and industrialization among other topics. Particular attention is paid to the relationship between state enterprises and township and village enterprises (TVEs), with the former at a disadvantage because of enforced limitations. In *Pacific Affairs,* contributor Keith Griffin called the book a "splendid volume" that "should be warmly welcomed."

In his next work, *Internationalizing China: Domestic Interests and Global Linkages,* Zweig defines internationalization as "the expanded flow of goods, services, and people across state boundaries, thereby increasing the share of transactional exchanges relative to domestic ones, along with a decline in regulating those flows." In this book, Zweig focuses on four components of Chinese economy: urban zones, rural areas, education and career, and foreign assistance organizations contributing to the country. Zweig provides an analysis of each sector and how each developed its own market. "This book provides excellent documentation and analysis of how China developed markets for several types of products within four main sectors. . . . This thorough analysis is especially useful for scholars in comparative politics and international relations," stated *Library Journal* reviewer Peggy Spitzer Christoff. In *Foreign Affairs,* Lucian W. Pye observed that the book is "rich both in ideas and as a statistical resource." Writing in *Business Week,* Mark Clifford reported, "This book is not for everyone: Zweig's writing is often dense and academic. But it contains much valuable information and analysis."

David Zweig told *CA:* "When I was twenty-one I had two choices in front of me: become a lawyer or go to graduate school and study China. In envisioning the first, I saw myself ten years later, married, with two kids, and living in the suburbs of Toronto. The second option seemed much more exciting. I have never regretted the choice."

BIOGRAPHICAL AND CRITICAL SOURCES:

PERIODICALS

American Political Science Review, March, 2000, David Zweig, review of *The Entrepreneurial State in China: Real Estate and Commerce Departments Reform in Era Tiankin.*

Business Week, November 11, 2002, Mark L. Clifford, "Winds of Change," review of *Internationalizing China: Domestic Interests and Global Linkages,* p. 24.

China Review International, spring, 1997, review of *China's Brain Drain to the United States: Views of Overseas Chinese Students and Scholars in the 1990s,* p. 298; spring, 1999, review of *Freeing China's Farmers: Rural Restructuring in the Reform Era,* p. 300.

Choice, January, 1998, review of *Freeing China's Farmers,* p. 900.

International Migration Review, winter, 1997, Qirong Li, review of *China's Brain Drain to the United States,* pp. 1128-1129.

Journal of Asian and African Studies, June, 1997, Lawrence K. Hong, review of *China's Brain Drain to the United States,* pp. 153-154.

Library Journal, August, 2002, Peggy Spitzer Christoff, review of *Internationalizing China,* p. 121.

National Interest, fall, 1999, Henry Rowen, response to "Undemocratic Capitalism: China and the Limits of Economism," p. 129.

Pacific Affairs, spring, 1998, Keith Griffin, review of *Freeing China's Farmers,* pp. 91-92; summer, 1998, Ruth Hayhoe, review of *China's Brain Drain to the United States,* pp. 240-241.

Reference and Research Book News, November, 1997, review of *Freeing China's Farmers,* p. 90.

ONLINE

Asia Pacific Foundation of Canada Web site, http://www.asiapacificresearch.ca/ (November 25, 2002), "Canada-Asia Pacific Research Network (CAPRN) Specialist Listing: Dr. David Zweig."

Foreign Affairs Web site, http://www.foreignaffairs.com/ (November 25, 2002), Lucian W. Pye, review of *Internationalizing China.*

Hong Kong University of Science and Technology Web site, http://www.ust.hk/ (November 25, 2002), "David Zweig."

M. E. Sharpe Web site, http://www.mesharpe.com/ (February 18, 2004), description of *Freeing China's Farmers.*

United States Institute of Peace, http://www.usip.org/ (February 18, 2004), online text of *Democratic Values, Political Structures, and Alternative Politics in Greater China.**